THE PAPERS OF

# THOMAS JEFFERSON

RETIREMENT SERIES

# THE PAPERS OF
# Thomas Jefferson

## RETIREMENT SERIES

## Volume 1
## 4 March to 15 November 1809

J. JEFFERSON LOONEY, EDITOR

SUSAN HOLBROOK PERDUE AND ROBERT F. HAGGARD,
ASSOCIATE EDITORS

JILL E. ANDERSON, L. DIANE BARNES, AND JULIE L. LAUTENSCHLAGER,
ASSISTANT EDITORS

HEIDI M. HACKFORD, MANAGING/ELECTRONIC EDITOR

LISA FRANCAVILLA, EDITORIAL ASSISTANT

JULIANA M. BOUCHER, CATHERINE COINER CRITTENDEN, KEVIN B. JONES,
AND JAYNE C. STOREY, DIGITAL TECHNICIANS

PRINCETON AND OXFORD
PRINCETON UNIVERSITY PRESS
2004

Published by Princeton University Press, 41 William Street,
Princeton, New Jersey 08540
In the United Kingdom:
Princeton University Press, 3 Market Place,
Woodstock, Oxfordshire OX20 1SY



*Library of Congress Cataloging-in-Publication Data*

Jefferson, Thomas, 1743–1826.
The papers of Thomas Jefferson. Retirement series / J. Jefferson Looney, editor . . . [et al.]. p.cm.
Includes bibliographical references and index.
Contents: v. 1. 4 March to 15 November 1809.
ISBN 0-691-12121-4 (cloth: v. 1: alk. paper)
1. Jefferson, Thomas, 1743–1826—Archives. 2. Jefferson, Thomas, 1743–1826—Correspondence. 3. Presidents—United States—Archives. 4. Presidents—United States—Correspondence. 5. United States—Politics and government—1809–1817—Sources. 6. United States—Politics and government—1817–1825—Sources. I. Looney, J. Jefferson. II. Title. III. Title: Retirement series.
E302.J442 2004b
973.4'6'092—dc22 2004048327

This book has been composed in Digital Monticello

Princeton University Press books are printed on acid-free paper and meet the guidelines for permanence and durability of the Committee on Production Guidelines for Book Longevity of the Council on Library Resources

Printed in the United States of America

DEDICATED TO THE MEMORY OF

ADOLPH S. OCHS

PUBLISHER OF THE NEW YORK TIMES

1896–1935

WHO BY THE EXAMPLE OF A RESPONSIBLE

PRESS ENLARGED AND FORTIFIED

THE JEFFERSONIAN CONCEPT

OF A FREE PRESS

# ADVISORY COMMITTEE



THIS EDITION was made possible by a founding grant from The New York Times Company to Princeton University. The Retirement Series in its turn was created with a five-year founding grant from The Pew Charitable Trusts to Princeton University and to the Thomas Jefferson Foundation, enabling the latter to take over responsibility for the volumes associated with this period. For these essential donations, and for other indispensable aid generously given by librarians, archivists, scholars, and collectors of manuscripts, the Editors record their sincere gratitude.

# INTRODUCTION

On 6 March 1809, as Thomas Jefferson eagerly prepared to depart for the last time from Washington to Monticello, he exulted to John Armstrong that he was now writing "merely as a private individual, which I am now happily become. within two or three days I retire from scenes of difficulty, anxiety & of contending passions to the elysium of domestic affections & the irresponsible direction of my own affairs." Safely ensconced at Monticello, in another of many similar variations on this theme Jefferson wrote Charles Willson Peale on 5 May that "I am totally occupied without doors, & enjoying a species of happiness I never before knew, that of doing whatever hits the humor of the moment without responsibility or injury to any one."

Jefferson lived for seventeen years after leaving the presidency. He enjoyed generally good health and many happy hours with his family and friends, but due especially to steadily worsening and ultimately catastrophic financial troubles, this long retirement was not always the elysium he had anticipated. It was also far more productive than his initial anticipation of undirected pleasure might have foretold. Early in this period Jefferson was sued by Edward Livingston for his decision as president to seize the Batture Sainte Marie in New Orleans as public property, and Jefferson devoted a great deal of time and energy to researching and writing a lengthy brief defending his actions and otherwise preparing for the case, which was dismissed in 1811. These years also saw the composition of Jefferson's memoirs and his sale to the nation of his library, among the largest owned by an individual in America at the time and certainly one of the most varied, a transfer that helped transform the Library of Congress from a legislative reference tool into a great scholarly institution. Jefferson's major preoccupation was, however, a long and difficult but ultimately successful campaign to found the University of Virginia, which he regarded as one of his three greatest accomplishments. He devoted countless hours, not just to obtaining the necessary legislation and resources but also to recruiting the faculty, designing and supervising the construction of the buildings, choosing books for the library, and drafting the school's curriculum and regulations.

Even more important than such individual achievements is the sheer breadth and depth of material represented in Jefferson's late correspondence. Freed from the direction of public affairs and able to risk somewhat less circumspection in expressing himself, Jefferson had the time, energy, and inclination to write on a dazzling variety of subjects, including agriculture, architecture, astronomy, biography, botany, education, gardening, geography, history, law, linguistics, philosophy, politics, religion, slavery, and states' rights. His retirement-era correspondence with John Adams and James Madison is rightly regarded as a priceless literary treasure, but his extensive exchanges with other writers are almost equally rich and not nearly as well known, such as his letters to and from Thomas Cooper, Pierre Samuel Du Pont de Nemours, Albert Gallatin, Louis H. Girardin, William Lambert, Robert Patterson, Charles Willson Peale, Horatio Gates Spafford, Francis Adrian Van der Kemp, and William Wirt.

Jefferson often complained about the demands unsolicited correspondence placed on him, and the quantity of paper that crossed his desk during his retirement is impressive. After he left office Congress conferred on him, as it had on his predecessors, the franking privilege on incoming as well as outgoing letters, which only increased the flow of letters from persons rich and poor, learned and unlettered, American and foreign, all seeking his views. He did not in fact reply to everyone, especially those who sought favors or charity, nor did he try to match the output of such frequent writers as Adams. Nonetheless, Jefferson maintained a vast correspondence. He was careful to retain file copies of his own epistles, using a polygraph or stylograph in most cases to make exact replicas.

Despite its subsequent dispersal, most of his own archive has survived, making Jefferson's literary legacy for his last years surprisingly complete. After six decades of collecting reproductions of texts from hundreds of public institutions and generous private owners, the Editors now have access to at least one version of some thirteen thousand retirement-period documents of which Jefferson is either the author or recipient. Due to his careful practice of recording almost all of his incoming and outgoing correspondence in an epistolary register, it can be inferred that for the same period fewer than fifteen hundred letters that he wrote or received are missing. Thus, the Retirement Series will be able to work with at least one text of almost ninety percent of the total corpus of Jefferson documents written during this period. More incoming than outgoing letters are missing, raising the percentage for documents written by Jefferson even higher.

Despite its intrinsic interest, and although the survival rate for papers from the retirement period is high, most of the material in question has never been published. Less than a third of the extant documents authored by Jefferson have appeared in print in whole or in part. No one source even comes close to this figure, since what has been published hitherto is scattered across a wide range of books and articles, transcribed by varying rules and with doubtful accuracy, and generally having little if any annotation. For letters to Jefferson, the proportion is even lower, with more than four in five never having been published.

This volume inaugurates a new series to address this great need and produce the definitive edition of papers documenting the written legacy of Thomas Jefferson between his return to private life on 4 March 1809 and his death on 4 July 1826. In the "General View of the Work" in the first volume of *The Papers of Thomas Jefferson* (pp. vii, xiv), Editor Julian P. Boyd stated in 1950 that the project's goal was the presentation of "the writings and recorded actions of Thomas Jefferson as accurately and as completely as possible." To achieve this end he proposed to print, note, or otherwise account for "everything legitimately Jeffersonian by reason of authorship or of relationship," while excluding materials with "only a technical claim to being regarded as Jefferson documents."

The project's scope and ambition remain fundamentally unchanged. Subsequent shifts in thinking by historical editors have led to some modifications in practice, especially in transcription policy, but in most important particulars Boyd's editorial method remains viable. The Editors continue to include incoming as well as outgoing letters; to collect and compare all known texts of documents and account for significant variations; to annotate so as to provide "a certain minimum basis of information essential to the understanding of each document," with the emphasis on "minimum" and "essential" (p. xxxiv); and to use the same basic textual apparatus, descriptive symbols, design, and breakdown of annotation into a descriptive note, optional explanatory note, and numbered textual notes. The reader is directed to the "Guide to Editorial Apparatus" that follows for details and to the "General View" for a discussion of the rationale behind this approach.

The appearance at this time of the *Papers of Thomas Jefferson: Retirement Series* was made possible through the creative thinking and generosity of Princeton University, the Thomas Jefferson Foundation, Inc., and The Pew Charitable Trusts. Since 1943 the *Papers of Thomas Jefferson* have been edited at Princeton under the sponsorship of Princeton University, and the original plan was for all of the chronological volumes to be edited there. However, at a 1997 retreat of the trustees of the Thomas Jefferson Foundation, which owns and operates Monticello, Rebecca W. Rimel, the head of The Pew Charitable Trusts, became inspired by the vision of splitting off the retirement-period documents and creating a new team to edit them at Charlottesville under the aegis of the Thomas Jefferson Foundation. This approach would enable work to proceed on two different periods of Jefferson's life simultaneously and thereby double the production of volumes with no compromise of the high standards so important to this work. With crucial help from Dr. W. W. Abbot, a distinguished editor of George Washington's papers who had long dreamed of bringing a Jefferson editing project to Monticello, a proposal was prepared and submitted to Princeton University, which agreed to turn over administrative and editorial responsibility for the retirement years to the Thomas Jefferson Foundation, after obtaining assurances that the new arrangement would not jeopardize its own longstanding commitment to the completion of this enterprise or diminish its quality in any way. A board composed of members from Princeton and the Foundation and headed by Professor John M. Murrin was established to coordinate the work of the two projects, a task made much easier by the appointment in 1998 of Dr. Barbara B. Oberg as general editor of the Jefferson Papers at Princeton. Dr. Oberg's unfailing cooperation, assistance, and friendly advice, especially during the initial copying and transfer from Princeton to Charlottesville of many thousands of document folders and bibliographic control files, has helped minimize the logistical problems associated with creating a new project of this magnitude.

Initially funded by a generous five-year grant from The Pew Charitable Trusts, work on the Retirement Series officially began with the appointment of the first editor and his installation at the beginning of October 1999 in rented space at Peter Jefferson Place in Charlottesville. Since then, a talented and dedicated staff has been assembled, the necessary intellectual foundations have been laid, a search for additional Jefferson documents has been completed, new digital tools have been created, and the project has moved into permanent quarters on the third floor of the Foundation's new Jefferson Library at the International Center for Jefferson Studies near Monticello. The Editors eagerly embrace the weighty responsibility of presenting fully and accurately the documentary record associated with Thomas Jefferson's retirement years and thereby contributing to a truly comprehensive understanding of his significance, both in his own time and ours.

# FOREWORD

THE 547 DOCUMENTS printed in this volume span the period from 4 March 1809 through 15 November 1809, the opening date marking Thomas Jefferson's final retirement from public life at the age of sixty-five. During the week following James Madison's inauguration, Jefferson stayed on at the President's House, consulted with the new president on foreign and internal affairs, inventoried his belongings and arranged for their shipment home to Monticello, and made his final farewells to friends and acquaintances in Washington. Even before his departure from Washington, Jefferson began to receive a steady stream of congratulatory letters from supporters of his administration. He continued to receive accolades from a variety of political organizations, large and small, north and south, long after he arrived home. Jefferson's supporters in Virginia were eager to escort him on his journey southward, and he met with enthusiastic followers long before he reached the border of his native Albemarle County, whose residents welcomed him en masse. Thankful for their attentions, he was nevertheless intent on returning swiftly to Monticello to join his family, put his affairs in order, and regain a measure of solitude and time for quieter pursuits.

Jefferson began his retirement from public life determined to fill his time with useful activities and glad that his health was as "firm" as could be expected at his age. He joyfully entered into his new life as an industrious farmer in "constant emploiment in the garden & farm." From Washington he brought as many nursery plants as he could transport, and he exchanged seeds and plant cuttings with his numerous American and European acquaintances. Like many of his contemporaries, Jefferson procured and bred merino sheep for their profitable wool. He looked to his mill complex at Shadwell as another source of revenue and was disappointed to find that it had suffered from mismanagement in his absence, requiring him to devote much of his energy in the first months of his retirement to finding a reliable tenant and overseer for its operation.

Jefferson devoted equal attention to the activity that he claimed to enjoy most, that of spending time with his extended family. In Margaret Bayard Smith's account of her visit to Monticello, Jefferson appeared to be at his most relaxed while in the company of his guests and his daughter Martha Jefferson Randolph's large family. He also monitored the education of his grandson Thomas Jefferson Randolph throughout this period, arranging for his lodgings and advising on his studies, and at Jefferson's invitation his son-in-law Charles Bankhead came to Monticello to study law. Jefferson served as mentor to local youths of limited means in search of a "useful pursuit," offering to teach them surveying and letting them use his extensive library.

During the period of his retirement, Jefferson's greatest challenge was to balance his substantial debts with an unpredictable income. His entanglement in the legal issues arising out of the estates of his father-in-law and his deceased wife Martha Wayles Skelton's first husband seemed to be unending. Furthermore, a good deal of the correspondence in this volume relates to Jefferson's efforts to pay off his own "unfortunate deficit at Washington" through the assistance of his agents, John Barnes and George Jefferson, and friends such as James Madison and Tadeusz Kosciuszko, from whom he obtained short-term loans.

Although Jefferson had much more time than heretofore to engage in such domestic pursuits, he continued to get an "extremely burthensome" amount of mail. He worried enough about applications for help from office seekers that he prepared a printed form letter to decline such requests, but he still received a never ending flow of letters from strangers, anonymous individuals, cranks, and blackmailers. Because of his well-known interest in science and technology and his continuing role as president of the American Philosophical Society, Jefferson also regularly received news of scientific discoveries and inventions; most notable in this regard are two reports of Louis Nicolas Vauquelin representing what may be the first chemical analysis of nicotine in tobacco.

Despite his claims to the contrary, Jefferson maintained a strong interest in public affairs and events in Europe. In the thirty-six letters exchanged between Jefferson and Madison during this period, they shared ideas about America's relations with Great Britain and France, information on Napoleon's military campaigns, and the illusory hope that the Erskine agreement would restore good commercial relations with Britain. Moreover, even as he pursued his personal interests, Jefferson remained a vigilant advocate of the Republican party and insistent that its members support their new president. The delicate balance of public and private concerns exhibited in Jefferson's correspondence from the early months of his retirement is a compelling theme that will recur throughout this series.

# ACKNOWLEDGMENTS

THE RETIREMENT SERIES would not be possible without the interest and generosity of a host of individuals and institutions. It is brought to fruition now primarily because of six decades of patient work by our predecessors and contemporaries at the Papers of Thomas Jefferson, and so our thanks must first go to Julian P. Boyd, Charles T. Cullen, John Catanzariti, Barbara B. Oberg, and their colleagues in the editorial offices at Princeton University, who collected, sorted, and accessioned the vast majority of the documents we will be publishing in the years ahead. The work is also built on the cooperation of hundreds of archivists and librarians at institutions large and small, as well as manuscript dealers and private owners of documents, who have responded favorably to requests for information and photoduplicates since the 1940s.

Princeton University has sponsored and sustained the Papers throughout the vicissitudes of many years. The Retirement Series is especially grateful to President Harold T. Shapiro for his essential role in approving the Retirement Series and to key members of the History Department, including Robert C. Darnton, Stanley N. Katz, John M. Murrin, Philip D. Nord, Daniel T. Rodgers, and Sean Wilentz, who helped work out the details and oversee the transition. Professors Katz and Rodgers were especially generous with their time and energy in the countless meetings devoted to hammering out the final agreement between Monticello and Princeton.

The Thomas Jefferson Foundation, Inc., sponsor of the Retirement Series, has already demonstrated its strong commitment, fully supporting our initial efforts and planning for the duration of the project. We are grateful to the Board of Trustees for its courage and vision in taking on this responsibility, and especially to Richard Gilder, Mrs. Martin S. Davis, and Thomas A. Saunders III for gifts that assure the long-term viability of the Retirement Series, and to David McCullough, both for his central role in the original vision and his ongoing and invaluable assistance in generating the financial support necessary to complete this series. While many colleagues have earned our heartfelt gratitude, those especially deserving of recognition include Henry Fairfax Ayres, Kate Bakich, James Horn, Michael B. Merriam, Paula F. Newcomb, Andrew J. O'Shaughnessy, Christine Piorkowski, Jack Robertson, Ann Taylor, Laura Terry, Douglas L. Wilson, Chad Wollerton, and, above all, Daniel P. Jordan, who from his arrival in 1985 as president of the Foundation championed the idea of bringing Jefferson's retirement papers to Monticello and has been instrumental in every subsequent advance.

The Pew Charitable Trusts provided almost all of the funds required to reproduce and transfer thousands of Jefferson documents and supporting material from Princeton to Charlottesville, furnish editorial offices, equip the project with sophisticated technological tools, engage excellent consultants, and recruit a staff. We owe a profound debt of gratitude to the Trusts, to their president, Rebecca W. Rimel, and to Linda M. Chicchi, Susan B. Harper, Luis Lugo, and Liz Williams.

Foreign-language documents present special challenges for documentary editions, and in preparing and reviewing our transcriptions and translations we have been fortunate to obtain the expert assistance of Genevieve Moene, Amy Ogden, and Roland H. Simon for French material; of Edward Courtney and John F. Miller for Latin; and of David T. Gies, Jennifer McCune, and Pedro Alvarez de Miranda for Spanish. Rick Britton created the original maps of Jefferson's Virginia and Albemarle County that appear in this volume.

Our colleagues at our sister editing projects in Charlottesville, the Papers of James Madison and the Papers of George Washington, have been welcoming from our inception and extremely generous in sharing information, insights, and sources. We are grateful to everyone in their offices at the University of Virginia's Alderman Library, but especially to Philander D. Chase and Frank E. Grizzard Jr. of the Washington Papers and Anne Mandeville Colony, Mary A. Hackett, Martha King, Angela Kreider, David B. Mattern, and John C. A. Stagg of the Madison Papers. Our counterparts at the Jefferson Papers in Princeton, who have offered guidance on issues of every kind and graciously tolerated several extended visits to borrow and copy their materials, include Shane Blackman, John E. Little, James P. McClure, F. Andrew McMichael, Barbara B. Oberg, Elaine Weber Pascu, and the invaluable Linda Monaco. Other colleagues in the documentary editing community who have helped with research questions or in other ways include Anne Decker Cecere, Ellen R. Cohn, Charles F. Hobson, John P. Kaminski, Robert Karachuk, Richard Leffler, Daniel Preston, Charles H. Schoenleber, and Holly C. Shulman. Even after leaving this field to head the Newberry Library, Charles T . Cullen has promoted the cause of scholarly editing in general and this project in particular.

The Retirement Series has and will benefit greatly from the digital images of a growing proportion of the Jefferson documents from its period supplied by important institutional owners. For help in this scanning project and for more conventional reference assistance, we stand indebted to Vincent Golden of the American Antiquarian Society; Robert S. Cox, Elaine delDucca, Roy Goodman, and Valerie-Anne Lutz of the American Philosophical Society; William Faucon of the Boston Public Library; Genie Guerard, Lilace Hatayama, Jennifer Schaffner, and Suzanne Tatian of the University of California, Los Angeles; Chris Coover, Christina Geiger, and Bendetta Roux of Christie's; Bonnie Kirschstein of the Forbes Collection; Sandra Trenholm and Inga Wilson of the Gilder Lehrman Collection; John Rhodehamel and Roy Ritchie of the Huntington Library; Fred Bauman, Jeffrey Flannery, Gerald W. Gawalt, Glenn Gardner, Laura Graham, James H. Hutson, and Mary Wolfskill of the Library of Congress; Sara B. Bearss, Brent Tarter, Patricia Watkinson, and Minor T. Weisiger of the Library of Virginia; Peter Drummey, William M. Fowler Jr., Nancy Heywood, Brenda M. Lawson, and Jennifer Smith of the Massachusetts Historical Society; Bob Buckeye of Middlebury College; Dane Hartgrove of the National Archives; James D. Folts of the New York State Library; Jesse Lankford and Jason Tomberlin of the North Carolina Office of Archives and History; Robert J. Milevski, Gretchen Oberfranc, Ben Primer, Margaret Rich, and Don C. Skemer of Princeton University; Margaret Bennett and Bill Edwards of Pro Libra Associates; Joseph Rubinfine; Bradley J. Daigle, Edward Gaynor, Michael Plunkett, and Rebecca Yokum of the University of Virginia; John D. Haskell and Susan A. Riggs of the College of William and Mary; and Diane E. Kaplan and Sandra Staton of Yale University.

For advice and information on specific questions that have arisen during the annotation of this volume, we are indebted to Gail Boswell, Janice Brockley, David A. Gerber, Greg Higsby, Andrew J. Lewis, D. Brett Mizelle, Charles L. Perdue Jr., and Elaine Stroud. The Thomas Jefferson Foundation has an immense pool of accumulated expertise on Jefferson and his times, and we have benefited especially from that of William L. Beiswanger, Elizabeth Chew, Bryan Craig, Peter Hatch, Justin Sarafin, Robert L. Self, Lucia C. Stanton, Susan R. Stein, and Carrie Taylor.

Advances in technology have greatly increased our productivity, given us access to better-quality texts and new research tools, and improved our ability to manage our work. We are indebted to Daniel E. Pitti and David M. Seaman of the University of Virginia for early conceptual advice, to Joel Smith for database customization, and to

Paul Hayslett and Stephen Perkins of Dataformat.com for a host of improvements to every aspect of our digital work. At a crucial period in our development, Mr. Perkins provided creative solutions to many of our problems, and he has been a friendly and resourceful supplier of guidance and assistance ever since.

Olga Tsapina and Lita Garcia of the Huntington Library, Yvonne Brooks of the Library of Congress, Peter Drummey and Kate Dubose of the Massachusetts Historical Society, Jennifer Robertson of the Smithsonian Institution's National Portrait Gallery, and Carrie Taylor and Lisa Williford of the Thomas Jefferson Foundation, Inc., assisted in the search for illustrations.

Princeton University Press has a long and distinguished history of publishing this edition without requiring subventions and with a spirit of helpfulness and commitment to quality. As director, Walter Lippincott has continued in that tradition. Others at the Press whose talents and keen eyes have contributed to this volume include Charles Creesy, Alison Kalett, Dimitri Karetnikov, Jan Lilly, Neil Litt, and Linny Schenck.

# EDITORIAL METHOD AND APPARATUS

## *1. RENDERING THE TEXT*

From its inception *The Papers of Thomas Jefferson* has insisted on high standards of accuracy in rendering text, but modifications in textual policy and editorial apparatus have been implemented as different approaches have become accepted in the field or as a more faithful rendering has become technically feasible. Prior discussions of textual policy appeared in Vols. 1:xxix–xxxiv, 22:vii–xi, 24:vii–viii, and 30:xiii–xiv of the First Series.

The textual method of the Retirement Series will adhere to the more literal approach adopted in Volume 30 of the parent edition. Original spelling, capitalization, and punctuation is retained as written. Such idiosyncrasies as Jefferson's failure to capitalize the beginnings of most of his sentences and abbreviations like "mr" are preserved, as are his preference of "it's" to "its" and his characteristic spellings of "knolege," "paiment," and "recieve." Modern usage is adopted in cases where intent is impossible to determine, an issue that arises most often in the context of capitalization. Some so-called slips of the pen are corrected, but the original reading is recorded in a subjoined textual note. Jefferson and others sometimes signaled a change in thought within a paragraph with extra horizontal space, and this is rendered by a three-em space. Blanks left for words and not subsequently filled by the authors are represented by a space approximating the length of the blank. Gaps, doubtful readings of illegible or damaged text, and wording supplied from other versions or by editorial conjecture are explained in the source note or in numbered textual notes. Foreign-language documents, the vast majority of which are in French during the retirement period, are transcribed in full as faithfully as possible, and followed by a full modern translation.

Two modifications from past practice bring this series still closer to the original manuscripts. Underscored text is presented as such rather than being converted to italics. Superscripts are also preserved rather than being lowered to the baseline. In most cases of superscripting, the punctuation that is below or next to the superscripted letters is dropped, since it is virtually impossible to determine what is a period or dash as opposed to a flourish under, over, or adjacent to superscripted letters.

Limits to the more literal method are still recognized, however, and readability and consistency with past volumes are prime considerations. In keeping with the basic design implemented in the first volume of the *Papers*, salutations and signatures continue to display in large and small capitals rather than upper- and lowercase letters. Expansion marks over abbreviations are silently omitted. With very rare exceptions, deleted text and information on which words were added during the process of composition is not displayed within the document transcription. Based on the Editors' judgment of their significance, such emendations are either described in numbered textual notes or ignored. Datelines for letters are consistently printed at the head of the text, with a comment in the descriptive note when they have been moved. Address information, endorsements, and dockets are quoted or described in the source note rather than reproduced in the document proper.

## 2. *TEXTUAL DEVICES*

The following devices are employed throughout the work to clarify the presentation of the text.

| | |
|---|---|
| [. . .] | Text missing and not conjecturable. The size of gaps longer than a word or two is estimated in annotation. |
| [ ] | Number or part of a number missing or illegible. |
| [roman] | Conjectural reading of missing or illegible matter. A question mark follows when the reading is doubtful. |
| [*italic*] | Editorial comment inserted in the text. |
| <*italic*> | Matter deleted in the manuscript but restored in our text. |

## 3. *DESCRIPTIVE SYMBOLS*

The following symbols are employed throughout the work to describe the various kinds of manuscript originals. When a series of versions is included, the first to be recorded is the version used for the printed text.

| | |
|---|---|
| Dft | draft (usually a composition or rough draft; multiple drafts, when identifiable as such, are designated "2d Dft," etc.) |
| Dupl | duplicate |
| MS | manuscript (arbitrarily applied to most documents other than letters) |
| PoC | polygraph copy |

PrC press copy
RC recipient's copy
SC stylograph copy

All manuscripts of the above types are assumed to be in the hand of the author of the document to which the descriptive symbol pertains. If not, that fact is stated. On the other hand, the following types of manuscripts are assumed *not* to be in the hand of the author, and exceptions will be noted:

FC file copy (applied to all contemporary copies retained by the author or his agents)
Tr transcript (applied to all contemporary and later copies except file copies; period of transcription, unless clear by implication, will be given when known)

### *4. LOCATION SYMBOLS*

The locations of documents printed in this edition from originals in private hands and from printed sources are recorded in self-explanatory form in the descriptive note following each document. The locations of documents printed from originals held by public and private institutions in the United States are recorded by means of the symbols used in the *MARC Code List for Organizations* (2000) maintained by the Library of Congress. The symbols DLC and MHi by themselves stand for the collections of Jefferson Papers proper in these repositories. When texts are drawn from other collections held by these two institutions, the names of those collections are added. Location symbols for documents held by institutions outside the United States are given in a subjoined list. The lists of symbols are limited to the institutions represented by documents printed or referred to in this volume.

A-Ar Alabama Department of Archives and History, Montgomery
CLjC Copley Newspapers Incorporated, La Jolla, California
CLU-C William Andrew Clark Library, University of California, Los Angeles
CSmH Huntington Library, San Marino, California
JF Jefferson File
JF-BA Jefferson File, Bixby Acquisition
JF-RAB Jefferson File, formerly in Robert A. Brock Collection

CtY Yale University, New Haven, Connecticut

DeGH Hagley Museum and Library, Greenville, Delaware

DLC Library of Congress, Washington, D.C.

TJ Papers Thomas Jefferson Papers (this is assumed if not stated, but also given as indicated to furnish the precise location of an undated, misdated, or otherwise problematic document, thus "DLC: TJ Papers, 4:628–9" represents volume 4, folios 628 and 629 as the collection was arranged at the time the first microfilm edition was made in 1944–45. Access to the microfilm edition of the collection as it was rearranged under the Library's Presidential Papers Program is provided by the *Index to the Thomas Jefferson Papers* [1976])

DNA National Archives, Washington, D.C., with identification of series (preceded by record group number) as follows:

- CD Consular Dispatches
- DCI Diplomatic and Consular Instructions
- DD Diplomatic Dispatches
- DL Domestic Letters
- LAR Letters of Application and Recommendation
- MLR Miscellaneous Letters Received
- NL Notes from Legations
- PPR Presidential Pardons and Remissions
- RD Resignations and Declinations

IaU University of Iowa, Iowa City

MBCo Countway Library of Medicine, Boston

MdHi Maryland Historical Society, Baltimore

MHi Massachusetts Historical Society, Boston

MiD Detroit Public Library, Michigan

MiKV-M Kalamazoo Valley Museum, Kalamazoo, Michigan

MiU-C Clements Library, University of Michigan, Ann Arbor

MNS-SS Smith College, Sophia Smith Collection, Northampton, Massachusetts

MoSHi Missouri Historical Society, Saint Louis

- TJC Thomas Jefferson Collection
- TJC-BC Thomas Jefferson Collection, text formerly in Bixby Collection

| | |
|---|---|
| MWA | American Antiquarian Society, Worcester, Massachusetts |
| MWiW-C | Chapin Library, Williams College, Williamstown, Massachusetts |
| N-Ar | State Archives, New York State Library, Albany |
| NcU | University of North Carolina, Chapel Hill |
| NHi | New-York Historical Society, New York City |
| NIC | Cornell University, Ithaca, New York |
| NjP | Princeton University, Princeton, New Jersey |
| NN | New York Public Library, New York City |
| NNGL | Gilder Lehrman Collection, New York City |
| NNPM | Pierpont Morgan Library, New York City |
| PHC | Haverford College Library, Pennsylvania |
| PPAmP | American Philosophical Society, Philadelphia, Pennsylvania |
| ScU | University of South Carolina, Columbia |
| TxU | University of Texas, Austin |
| Vi | Library of Virginia, Richmond |
| ViCMRL | Thomas Jefferson Library, Thomas Jefferson Foundation, Inc., Charlottesville, Virginia |
| ViHi | Virginia Historical Society, Richmond |
| ViU | University of Virginia, Charlottesville |
| | TJP — Thomas Jefferson Papers |
| | TJP-CC — Thomas Jefferson Papers, text formerly in Carr-Cary Papers |
| | TJP-ER — Thomas Jefferson Papers, text formerly in Edgehill-Randolph Papers |
| ViW | College of William and Mary, Williamsburg, Virginia |
| | TJP — Thomas Jefferson Papers |
| | TC — Tucker-Coleman Collection |
| | TC-JP — Jefferson Papers, Tucker-Coleman Collection |

The following symbols represent repositories located outside of the United States:

| | |
|---|---|
| GyLeU | Leipzig University Library, Germany |
| RuAVPR | Arkhiv Vneshnei Politiki Rossii, Moscow, Russia |
| UkLi | Liverpool Record Office, United Kingdom |

## 5. *OTHER ABBREVIATIONS AND SYMBOLS*

The following abbreviations and symbols are commonly employed in the annotation throughout the work.

Lb Letterbook (used to indicate texts copied into bound volumes)
RG Record Group (used in designating the location of documents in the Library of Virginia and the National Archives)
SJL Jefferson's "Summary Journal of Letters" written and received for the period 11 Nov. 1783 to 25 June 1826 (in DLC: TJ Papers). This epistolary record, kept in Jefferson's hand, has been checked against the TJ Editorial Files. It is to be assumed that all outgoing letters are recorded in SJL unless there is a note to the contrary. When the date of receipt of an incoming letter is recorded in SJL, it is incorporated in the notes. Information and discrepancies revealed in SJL but not found in the letter itself are also noted. Missing letters recorded in SJL are accounted for in the notes to documents mentioning them, in related documents, or in an appendix
TJ Thomas Jefferson
TJ Editorial Files Photoduplicates and other editorial materials in the office of the Papers of Thomas Jefferson: Retirement Series, Jefferson Library, Thomas Jefferson Foundation, Charlottesville
d Penny or denier
*f* Florin
£ Pound sterling or livre, depending upon context (in doubtful cases, a clarifying note will be given)
s Shilling or sou (also expressed as /)
tt Livre Tournois
℔ Per (occasionally used for pro, pre)

## 6. *SHORT TITLES*

The following list includes short titles of works cited frequently in this edition. Since it is impossible to anticipate all the works to be cited in abbreviated form, the list is revised from volume to volume.

*Acts of Assembly* *Acts of the General Assembly of Virginia* (cited by session and date of publication; title varies over time)
Ammon, *Monroe* Harry Ammon, *James Monroe: The Quest for National Identity*, 1971

*ANB* John A. Garraty and Mark C. Carnes, eds., *American National Biography*, 1999, 24 vols.

*Annals* *Annals of the Congress of the United States: The Debates and Proceedings in the Congress of the United States . . . Compiled from Authentic Materials*, Washington, D.C., Gales & Seaton, 1834–56, 42 vols. All editions are undependable and pagination varies from one printing to another. Citations given below are to the edition mounted on the American Memory website of the Library of Congress and give the date of the debate as well as page numbers.

APS American Philosophical Society

*ASP* *American State Papers: Documents, Legislative and Executive, of the Congress of the United States*, 1832–61, 38 vols.

Axelson, *Virginia Postmasters* Edith F. Axelson, *Virginia Postmasters and Post Offices, 1789–1832*, 1991

Bashkina, *United States and Russia* Nina N. Bashkina and others, eds., *The United States and Russia: The Beginning of Relations, 1765–1815*, 1980

*BDSCHR* Walter B. Edgar and others, eds., *Biographical Directory of the South Carolina House of Representatives*, 1974– , 5 vols.

Betts, *Farm Book* Edwin M. Betts, ed., *Thomas Jefferson's Farm Book*, 1953

Betts, *Garden Book* Edwin M. Betts, ed., *Thomas Jefferson's Garden Book, 1766–1824*, 1944

*Biog. Dir. Cong.* *Biographical Directory of the United States Congress, 1774–1989*, 1989

*Biographie universelle* *Biographie universelle, ancienne et moderne*, new ed., 1843–65, 45 vols.

Brant, *Madison* Irving Brant, *James Madison*, 1941–61, 6 vols.

Brigham, *American Newspapers* Clarence S. Brigham, *History and Bibliography of American Newspapers, 1690–1820*, 1947, 2 vols.

Bryan, *National Capital* Wilhelmus Bogart Bryan, *A History of the National Capital: From its Foundation through the Period of the Adoption of the Organic Act*, 1914, 2 vols.

Bush, *Life Portraits* Alfred L. Bush, *The Life Portraits of Thomas Jefferson*, rev. ed., 1987

Chambers, *Poplar Forest* S. Allen Chambers, *Poplar Forest & Thomas Jefferson*, 1993

Clay, *Papers* James F. Hopkins and others, eds., *The Papers of Henry Clay*, 1959–92, 11 vols.

Connelly, *Napoleonic France* Owen Connelly and others, eds., *Historical Dictionary of Napoleonic France*, 1985

*CVSP* William P. Palmer and others, eds., *Calendar of Virginia State Papers . . . Preserved in the Capitol at Richmond*, 1875–93, 11 vols.

*DAB* Allen Johnson and Dumas Malone, eds., *Dictionary of American Biography*, 1928–36, 20 vols.

*DBF* *Dictionnaire de biographie française*, 1933– , 19 vols.

Dexter, *Yale Biographies* Francis Bowditch Dexter, *Biographical Sketches of the Graduates of Yale College*, 1885–1912, 6 vols.

*DNB* Leslie Stephen and Sidney Lee, eds., *Dictionary of National Biography*, 1885–1901, 22 vols.

Dolley Madison, *Selected Letters* David B. Mattern and Holly C. Shulman, eds., *The Selected Letters of Dolley Payne Madison*, 2003

*DSB* Charles C. Gillispie, ed., *Dictionary of Scientific Biography*, 1970–80, 16 vols.

*DVB* John T. Kneebone and others, eds., *Dictionary of Virginia Biography*, 1998– , 2 vols.

*EG* Dickinson W. Adams and Ruth W. Lester, eds., *Jefferson's Extracts from the Gospels*, 1983, *The Papers of Thomas Jefferson*, Second Series

Ford Paul Leicester Ford, ed., *The Writings of Thomas Jefferson*, Letterpress Edition, 1892–99, 10 vols.

Greene, *American Science* John C. Greene, *American Science in the Age of Jefferson*, 1984

HAW Henry A. Washington, ed., *The Writings of Thomas Jefferson*, 1853–54, 9 vols.

Heitman, *Continental Army* Francis B. Heitman, comp., *Historical Register of Officers of the Continental Army during the War of the Revolution, April, 1775, to December, 1783*, rev. ed., 1914

Heitman, *U.S. Army* Francis B. Heitman, comp., *Historical Register and Dictionary of the United States Army*, 1903, 2 vols.

Hening William Waller Hening, ed., *The Statutes at Large; being a Collection of all the Laws of Virginia*, 1809–23, 13 vols.

Hoefer, *Nouv. biog. générale* J. C. F. Hoefer, *Nouvelle biographie générale depuis les temps les plus reculés jusqu'a nos jours*, 1852–83, 46 vols.

*Hortus Third* Liberty Hyde Bailey, Ethel Zoe Bailey, and the staff of the Liberty Hyde Bailey Hortorium, Cornell University, *Hortus Third: A Concise Dictionary of Plants Cultivated in the United States and Canada*, 1976

Jackson, *Letters of Lewis and Clark* Donald Jackson, ed., *Letters of the Lewis and Clark Expedition with Related Documents, 1783–1854*, 2d ed., 1978, 2 vols.

Jackson, *Papers* Sam B. Smith, Harold D. Moser, and others, eds., *The Papers of Andrew Jackson*, 1980– , 6 vols.

*Jefferson Correspondence*, Bixby Worthington C. Ford, ed., *Thomas Jefferson Correspondence Printed from the Originals in the Collections of William K. Bixby*, 1916

*JEP* *Journal of the Executive Proceedings of the Senate of the United States*

*JHD* *Journal of the House of Delegates of the Commonwealth of Virginia*

*JHR* *Journal of the House of Representatives of the United States*

*JS* *Journal of the Senate of the United States*

*JSV* *Journal of the Senate of Virginia*

Kimball, *Jefferson, Architect* Fiske Kimball, *Thomas Jefferson, Architect*, 1916

*L & B* Andrew A. Lipscomb and Albert E. Bergh, eds., *The Writings of Thomas Jefferson*, Library Edition, 1903–04, 20 vols.

Latrobe, *Papers* John C. Van Horne and others, eds., *The Correspondence and Miscellaneous Papers of Benjamin Henry Latrobe*, 1984–88, 3 vols.

Lay, *Architecture* K. Edward Lay, *The Architecture of Jefferson Country: Charlottesville and Albemarle County, Virginia*, 2000

*LCB* Douglas L. Wilson, ed., *Jefferson's Literary Commonplace Book*, 1989, *The Papers of Thomas Jefferson*, Second Series

Leavitt, *Poplar Forest* Messrs. Leavitt, *Catalogue of a Private Library . . . Also, The Remaining Portion of the Library of the Late Thomas Jefferson . . . offered by his grandson, Francis Eppes, of Poplar Forest, Va.* [1873]

Leonard, *General Assembly* Cynthia Miller Leonard, comp., *The General Assembly of Virginia, July 30, 1619–January 11, 1978: A Bicentennial Register of Members*, 1978

*List of Patents* *A List of Patents granted by the United States from April 10, 1792, to December 31, 1836*, 1872

*MACH* *Magazine of Albemarle County History*, 1940–

Madison, *Papers* William T. Hutchinson, Robert A. Rutland, J. C. A. Stagg, and others, eds., *The Papers of James Madison*, 1962– , 28 vols.

*Congress. Ser.*, 17 vols.
*Pres. Ser.*, 5 vols.
*Sec. of State Ser.*, 6 vols.

Malone, *Jefferson* Dumas Malone, *Jefferson and his Time*, 1948–81, 6 vols.

Marshall, *Papers* Herbert A. Johnson, Charles T. Cullen, Charles F. Hobson, and others, eds., *The Papers of John Marshall*, 1974– , 11 vols.

Mazzei, *Writings* Margherita Marchione and others, eds., *Philip Mazzei: Selected Writings and Correspondence*, 1983, 3 vols.

*MB* James A. Bear Jr., and Lucia C. Stanton, eds., *Jefferson's Memorandum Books: Accounts, with Legal Records and Miscellany, 1767–1826*, 1997, *The Papers of Thomas Jefferson*, Second Series

McGehee and Trout, *Jefferson's River* Minnie Lee McGehee and William E. Trout III, *Mr. Jefferson's River: The Rivanna*, 2001

Merrill, *Jefferson's Nephews* Boynton Merrill Jr., *Jefferson's Nephews: A Frontier Tragedy*, 1976

Nichols, *Architectural Drawings* Frederick Doveton Nichols, *Thomas Jefferson's Architectural Drawings, Compiled and with Commentary and a Check List*, 1978

Norfleet, *Saint-Mémin* Fillmore Norfleet, *Saint-Mémin in Virginia: Portraits and Biographies*, 1942

*Notes*, ed. Peden Thomas Jefferson, *Notes on the State of Virginia*, ed. William Peden, 1955

*OED* James A. H. Murray, J. A. Simpson, E. S. C. Weiner, and others, eds., *The Oxford English Dictionary*, 2d ed., 1989, 20 vols.

Papenfuse, *Maryland Public Officials* Edward C. Papenfuse and others, eds., *An Historical List of Public Officials of Maryland*, 1990– , 1 vol.

Peale, *Papers* Lillian B. Miller and others, eds., *The Selected Papers of Charles Willson Peale and His Family*, 1983– , 5 vols. in 6

Pierson, *Jefferson at Monticello* Hamilton W. Pierson, *Jefferson at Monticello: The Private Life of Thomas Jefferson, From Entirely New Materials*, 1862

Poor, *Jefferson's Library* Nathaniel P. Poor, *Catalogue. President Jefferson's Library* [1829]

*Princetonians* James McLachlan and others, eds., *Princetonians: A Biographical Dictionary*, 1976–90, 5 vols.

*PTJ* Julian P. Boyd, Charles T. Cullen, John Catanzariti, Barbara B. Oberg, and others, eds., *The Papers of Thomas Jefferson*, 1950– , 31 vols.

*PW* Wilbur S. Howell, ed., *Jefferson's Parliamentary Writings*, 1988, *The Papers of Thomas Jefferson*, Second Series

Randall, *Life* Henry S. Randall, *The Life of Thomas Jefferson*, 1858, 3 vols.

Randolph, *Domestic Life* Sarah N. Randolph, *The Domestic Life of Thomas Jefferson, Compiled from Family Letters and Reminiscences by His Great-Granddaughter*, 1871

Randolph, *Randolphs* Robert Isham Randolph, *The Randolphs of Virginia*, 1936

*RCHS* *Records of the Columbia Historical Society*, 1895–

Robinson, *Philadelphia Directory for 1809* James Robinson, *The Philadelphia Directory for 1809*, 1809

Shackelford, *Descendants* George Green Shackelford, ed., *Collected Papers to Commemorate Fifty Years of the Monticello Association of the Descendants of Thomas Jefferson*, 1965

*Sibley's Harvard Graduates* John L. Sibley and others, eds., *Sibley's Harvard Graduates*, 1873– , 18 vols.

Smith, *Forty Years* Gaillard Hunt, ed., *The First Forty Years of Washington Society, Portrayed by the Family Letters of Mrs. Samuel Harrison Smith* [1906]

Sowerby E. Millicent Sowerby, comp., *Catalogue of the Library of Thomas Jefferson*, 1952–59, 5 vols.

Stanton, *Free Some Day* Lucia Stanton, *Free Some Day: The African-American Families of Monticello*, 2000

Stein, *Worlds* Susan Stein, *The Worlds of Thomas Jefferson at Monticello*, 1993

*Terr. Papers* Clarence E. Carter and John Porter Bloom, eds., *The Territorial Papers of the United States*, 1934–75, 28 vols.

*TJR* Thomas Jefferson Randolph, ed., *Memoir, Correspondence, and Miscellanies, from the Papers of Thomas Jefferson*, 1829, 4 vols.

*U.S. Statutes at Large* Richard Peters, ed., *The Public Statutes at Large of the United States . . . 1789 to March 3, 1845*, 1855–56, 8 vols.

Washington, *Papers* W. W. Abbot, Dorothy Twohig, Philander D. Chase, and others, eds., *The Papers of George Washington*, 1983– , 44 vols.

*Colonial Ser.*, 6 vols.
*Confederation Ser.*, 10 vols.
*Pres. Ser.*, 11 vols.
*Retirement Ser.*, 4 vols.
*Rev. War Ser.*, 13 vols.

*WMQ* *William and Mary Quarterly*, 1892–

Woods, *Albemarle* Edgar Woods, *Albemarle County in Virginia*, 1901

# CONTENTS

INTRODUCTION vii
FOREWORD xi
ACKNOWLEDGMENTS xiii
EDITORIAL METHOD AND APPARATUS xvii
MAPS xliii
ILLUSTRATIONS xlvii
JEFFERSON CHRONOLOGY 2

## 1809

Account with Joseph Dougherty, [*4–10 March*] 3
From the Students of Jefferson College, *4 March* 4
Memoranda to James Madison, [*ca. 4–11 March*] 6
Margaret Bayard Smith's Account of Madison's Inauguration and Ball, [*4 March*] 8
From the Citizens of Washington, D.C., *4 March* 11
To the Citizens of Washington, D.C., *4 March* 13
To John Benson, *5 March* 14
From John Norvell, *5 March* 14
From James Ronaldson, *5 March* 15
To John Armstrong, *6 March* 19
From the Republicans of Georgetown, *6 March* 21
From Thomas Gimbrede, *6 March* 23
To Alexander von Humboldt, *6 March* 24
Notes on Presidential Appointments, [*ca. 6 March*] 25
From Nathaniel Rochester and William L. Brent, *6 March* 26
To Margaret Bayard Smith, *6 March* 29
To Samuel H. Smith, enclosing Circular to Office Seekers, *6 March* 30
Account with John Barnes, *7 March* 31
To Thomas Gimbrede, *7 March* 32
From William Ray, *7 March* 33
To the Republicans of Georgetown, *8 March* 34
Account with Joseph Milligan, [*8–10 March*] 35
To William Short, *8 March* 38
To John Threlkeld, *8 March* 40
From John Threlkeld, [*8 March*] 40
Notes on Expenses, *9 March* 41
From Thomas Claxton, *10 March* 42

From Richard Harrison, *10 March* 43
To George Jefferson, *10 March*, enclosing Packing List from John Barnes, *7 March* 44
To Charles Willson Peale, *10 March* 45
From the Inhabitants of Albemarle County, [*ca. 11 March*] 46
To Mary Daingerfield, *11 March* 47
To William Duane, *11 March* 48
To Levi Lincoln, *11 March* 49
To Mayer & Brantz, *11 March* 50
To George C. Shattuck, *11 March* 50
Edmund Bacon's Account of Thomas Jefferson's Reception at Culpeper Court House, [*13 March*] 51
From Isaac A. Coles, *13 March* 53
From William Lambert, *14 March* 54
From John Taggart, *15 March* 55
To Etienne Lemaire, *16 March* 55
From James W. Wallace, [*received 16 March*] 56
From James Hochie, *17 March*, enclosing Resolutions of the Antient Plymouth Society, *16 March* 58
From Etienne Lemaire, *17 March* 59
To James Madison, *17 March* 60
From the Republicans of Queen Annes County, Maryland, *18 March* 62
From the Albemarle Buckmountain Baptist Church, *19 March* 63
From Joseph Dougherty, *19 March* 64
From James Leitch, *19 March* 64
From James Madison, *19 March* 65
From John Wyche, *19 March* 66
From Ann Craig, *20 March* 67
From James Ronaldson, *20 March* 68
From Anonymous, *21 March* 69
From Charles Willson Peale, *21 March* 70
From Etienne Lemaire, *22 March* 71
From Samuel H. Smith, *22 March* 72
From Elizabeth Trist, *22 March* 73
From William D. Meriwether, [*23 March*] 74
From Samuel DeButts, *24 March* 75
To Joseph Dougherty, *24 March* 76
To Henry Foxall, *24 March* 76
To George Jefferson, *24 March* 77
To James Madison, *24 March* 77
To William D. Meriwether, *24 March* 79

From the New York State Legislature, *24 March* 79
To Elizabeth Trist, *24 March* 80
To George Jefferson, *25 March* 81
From James Maury, *25 March* 82
From John MacGowty, *26 March* 83
From Cunningham Harris, *27 March* 84
From George Jefferson, *27 March* 84
From James Madison, *27 March* 85
To the Republicans of Essex County, Massachusetts, *28 March* 85
From James Madison, *28 March* 87
From Larkin Smith, *28 March* 87
To the Convention of Bristol County, Rhode Island, *29 March* 88
To the Republican Mechanics of Leesburg, Virginia, *29 March* 89
To William McCandless, *29 March* 90
From James McKinney, *30 March* 91
To James Madison, *30 March* 92
To the Citizens of Allegany County, Maryland, *31 March* 94
From Jonathan Law, *31 March* 95
To James Madison, *31 March* 96
To John Taggart, *31 March* 97
From John Breck Treat, *31 March* 97
From Elizabeth Trist, *31 March* 98
To the Republicans of Washington County, Maryland, *31 March* 98
To the Democratic Republican Delegates of Washington County, Pennsylvania, *31 March* 99
To Caspar Wistar, *31 March* 100
From William B. W. Allone, *March* 101
To James Hochie, *2 April* 102
To the Inhabitants of Albemarle County, *3 April* 102
From Charles Willson Peale, *3 April* 103
From Horatio G. Spafford, *3 April* 105
To Robert Wright, *3 April* 106
To John B. Colvin, *4 April* 107
From Larkin Smith, *4 April* 108
To Jonathan Shoemaker, *6 April* 108
To James Jay, *7 April* 110
From Philip Tabb, *7 April* 111
From John Taggart, *7 April* 111
From Benjamin F. Whitner, *7 April* 112
From Philip Freneau, *8 April* 112
From James Madison, *9 April* 113
From George Jefferson, *10 April* 114

From William Short, *10 April* 115
From Henry Foxall, *11 April* 122
List of Goods Sent by George Jefferson, with Thomas Jefferson's Notes, *11 April* 123
From Thomas Gillet, *12 April* 123
To the New York State Legislature, *12 April* 125
To the Albemarle Buckmountain Baptist Church, *13 April* 126
To Jonathan Law, *13 April* 126
To the Republicans of Queen Annes County, Maryland, *13 April* 127
From Louis Philippe Gallot de Lormerie, enclosing Memoir on American Forest Management, *14 April* 128
To Samuel DeButts, *15 April* 134
James Dinsmore's List of Thomas Jefferson's Tools, *15 April* 135
To Larkin Smith, *15 April* 136
To Eli Alexander, *17 April* 137
From Caleb Cross, *17 April* 138
To Isaac Shoemaker, *17 April* 138
From Jonathan Shoemaker, *17 April* 139
From David Bailie Warden, *17 April*, enclosing Nicolas Louis Vauquelin's Analysis of Green Tobacco, *12 January*, and Vauquelin's Analysis of Prepared Tobacco, [*12 January–17 April*] 140
From Joseph Dougherty, *19 April* 153
To George Jefferson, *19 April* 153
To James Madison, enclosing Deed of John Freeman's Indenture to James Madison, *19 April* 154
From George Jefferson, *21 April* 157
From George Divers, *22 April* 157
From William W. Hening, *23 April* 158
From George Jefferson, *24 April* 159
From James Madison, *24 April* 160
To John Graham, *25 April* 161
To Etienne Lemaire, *25 April* 161
From John MacGowty, *25 April* 162
From William Roscoe, *25 April* 163
From Augustus B. Woodward, *25 April* 164
To John Barnes, *27 April* 165
From John Graham, *27 April* 167
From Isham Lewis, *27 April* 167
To James Madison, *27 April* 168
From William Davy and Others, *28 April* 170
To Thomas Moore, *28 April* 172

From Madame de Corny, *29 April* 173
Invoice from George Jefferson, *29 April* 176
From the Baltimore Tammany Society, *1 May* 176
From William C. C. Claiborne, *1 May* 179
To George Jefferson, *1 May* 180
To Isham Lewis, *1 May* 181
From William Lyman, *1 May* 182
From James Madison, *1 May* 183
From Daniel Lescallier, *2 May* 184
From Benjamin Rush, *3 May* 184
From John Graham, *5 May* 186
From George Jefferson, *5 May* 186
To Charles Willson Peale, *5 May* 187
From Etienne Lemaire, *6 May* 188
To Thomas Jefferson Randolph, *6 May* 189
To William Hamilton, *7 May* 191
To John M. Perry, *7 May* 192
From Robert Patterson, *10 May* 193
From Gerardus Vrolik, *10 May* 194
From Henry Hiort, *11 May* 195
To Horatio G. Spafford, *14 May* 196
From Joseph Dougherty, *15 May* 199
From Edmund Pendleton, *15 May* 200
To Pierre Samuel Du Pont de Nemours, André Thoüin, and Bartelémy Faujas de Saint-Fond, *16 May* 201
From William C. C. Claiborne, *17 May* 202
From John Minor, *17 May* 204
To George Jefferson, *18 May* 204
To John Wyche, *19 May* 205
From Tadeusz Kosciuszko, *20 May* 206
From David Bailie Warden, *20 May* 207
From James Sylvanus McLean, [*21 May*] 209
From Rufus Morgan, *21 May* 209
To William Brown, *22 May* 210
To Philip Freneau, *22 May* 211
To Cunningham Harris, *22 May* 211
To James Madison, *22 May* 212
To Thomas Ritchie, *22 May* 214
To Gideon Fitz, *23 May* 215
To Seth Pease, *23 May* 216
From William Pelham, *23 May* 216
To John Barnes, *24 May* 217

William Dawson to Samuel Greenhow, *24 May* 218
From Claude Alexandre Ruelle, *24 May* 219
To the Baltimore Tammany Society, *25 May* 221
From Etienne Lemaire, *25 May* 222
From Wilson Cary Nicholas, *25 May* 223
To Wilson Cary Nicholas, *25 May* 224
To Joseph Dougherty, *27 May* 224
From Philip Freneau, *27 May*, enclosing Poem on Thomas Jefferson's Retirement, *February* 225
From William Short, *27 May* 229
To Augustus B. Woodward, *27 May* 236
To Elijah Griffiths, *28 May* 236
To William Lambert, *28 May* 237
From Mary Ann Archbald, *29 May* 238
From Samuel Greenhow, *29 May* 240
From Thomas Jefferson Randolph, *29 May* 245
From George Jefferson, *30 May* 246
From James Madison, *30 May* 246
From Antoine François Tardieu, *30 May* 247
From Lacépède, *31 May* 248
From Bishop James Madison, *31 May* 251
To Philip Tabb, *1 June* 252
From Augustus B. Woodward, *3 June* 253
From James Fishback, *5 June* 254
From Jonathan Shoemaker, *5 June* 256
From Kimber & Conrad, *7 June* 256
To George Jefferson, *8 June* 257
From Shadrach Ricketson, *8 June* 257
From Augustin François Silvestre, *8 June* 258
From John Armstrong, *11 June* 260
From Destutt de Tracy, *12 June* 260
From Pierre Samuel Du Pont de Nemours, *12 June* 263
From Alexander von Humboldt, *12 June* 264
To George Jefferson, *12 June* 267
From George Jefferson, *12 June* 268
From George Jefferson, *12 June* 269
From Lafayette, *12 June* 269
From James Madison, *12 June* 271
From Madame de Tessé, *12 June* 271
From William Lambert, *13 June* 274
To Wilson Cary Nicholas, *13 June* 276
To Henry Dearborn, *14 June* 279

CONTENTS


To John Barnes, *15 June* 281
To David Gelston, *15 June* 281
To Jonathan Shoemaker, *15 June* 282
From Binny & Ronaldson, *16 June* 283
From George Jefferson, *16 June* 284
To James Madison, *16 June* 284
From Joseph Dougherty, *18 June* 286
From William C. C. Claiborne, *19 June* 287
From George Jefferson, *19 June* 287
From Skelton Jones, *19 June* 288
From William Nelson, *19 June* 290
From "Goodwill," *20 June* 291
From James Madison, *20 June* 292
To Thomas Jefferson Randolph, *20 June* 293
From David Gelston, *21 June* 294
To Shadrach Ricketson, *21 June* 294
From Benjamin Waterhouse, *21 June* 295
From Henry Dearborn, *23 June* 301
From Henry Dearborn, *23 June* 301
From George Jefferson, *23 June* 302
To James Leitch, *23 June* 302
From John W. Butler, *24 June* 303
To David Copeland, *25 June* 304
To Skelton Jones, *25 June* 305
To Thomas Ladd, *25 June* 306
From Charles Willson Peale, *25 June* 307
To Joseph Dougherty, *26 June* 310
From George Jefferson, *26 June* 311
From Stephen Cathalan, *27 June* 312
From James Madison, *27 June* 313
To Binny & Ronaldson, *28 June* 314
To Pierre Samuel Du Pont de Nemours, *28 June* 315
From David Bailie Warden, *28 June* 316
William Dawson to Samuel Greenhow, *1 July* 317
To George Jefferson, *1 July* 318
To William Jenkings, *1 July* 319
From Benjamin Brown, *3 July* 320
From Joseph Dougherty, *3 July* 320
From Joseph McCoy, enclosing Poem, "The Expedient," *3 July* 321
From James Madison, *4 July* 327
From André Daschkoff, *5 July* 328
From Thomas Ladd, *5 July* 329

From Robert Patterson, *6 July* 330
From Skelton Jones, *7 July* 331
From James Madison, *7 July* 331
To Joseph Milligan, *7 July* 332
To Benjamin Brown, *8 July* 333
From William W. Hening, *8 July* 333
To William Nelson, *8 July* 334
To Samuel Smith (of Pennsylvania), *9 July* 335
From John Wayles Eppes, *10 July* 336
To John Minor, *10 July* 338
From Henry Skipwith, *10 July* 339
To Robert Smith, *10* [*July*] 340
From William Wirt, *10 July* 341
From Louis Philippe Gallot de Lormerie, *11 July* 342
To James Madison, *12 July* 343
From George Jefferson, *14 July* 344
From Robert Smith, *15 July* 345
From John Martin Baker, *16 July* 345
Samuel J. Harrison to Gibson & Jefferson, *16 July* 346
From James Monroe, *18 July* 348
From Wilson Cary Nicholas, *18 July* 349
From Joseph Wheaton, *20 July* 350
To Eli Alexander, *22 July* 353
From Eli Alexander, *22 July* 353
To George Jefferson, *22 July* 353
To Louis Philippe Gallot de Lormerie, *22 July* 354
From Alexander McRae, *22 July* 355
From William Lambert, *23 July* 356
From James Madison, *23 July* 359
From Samuel Smith (of Maryland), *23 July* 360
To David Copeland, *24 July* 362
To John Wayles Eppes, *24 July* 362
To William Fleming, *24 July* 363
To Jonathan Shoemaker, *24 July* 364
To Henry Skipwith, *24 July* 364
To John Martin Baker, *25 July* 365
From William Caruthers, *25 July* 367
To Gordon, Trokes & Company, *25 July* 368
To William W. Hening, *25 July* 369
From Isaac A. Coles, *26 July* 370
To Samuel Smith (of Maryland), *26 July* 377
From William Fleming, *27 July* 378

To Levett Harris, *27 July* 379
From Leonard Jewett, *28 July* 380
To Skelton Jones, *28 July* 381
From Joseph Milligan, *28 July* 384
From John W. Campbell, *29 July* 385
To Pierre Samuel Du Pont de Nemours, *29 July* 385
Margaret Bayard Smith's Account of a Visit to Monticello, [*29 July–2 August*] 386
To Samuel Smith (of Maryland), *29 July* 402
From Jonathan Brunt, *31 July* 402
From William W. Hening, *31 July* 403
From John Monroe, *1 August* 404
From Jonathan Shoemaker, *1 August* 407
To John Barnes, *3 August* 408
From James Madison, *3 August* 408
To Samuel H. Smith, *3 August* 410
From Josef Yznardy, *3 August* 410
From C. & A. Conrad & Company, *4 August* 412
To John Armstrong, *5 August* 412
To Alexander McRae, *5 August* 413
To William Pinkney, *5 August* 414
From Craven Peyton, *6 August* 415
To William C. Rives, *6 August* 416
To Louis Marie Turreau, *6 August* 417
From William Dawson, *7 August* 417
From George Gilpin, *7 August* 418
From Daniel Davis, *8 August* 419
Agreement with William McGehee, *8 August* 419
To Jonathan Shoemaker, *8 August* 421
To Jones & Howell, *10 August* 422
From Alexander McRae, *10 August* 423
From William Smith, *10 August* 425
From Charles F. Welles, [*ca. 11 August*], enclosing Charles Miner's Poem on Thomas Jefferson, [*ca. 21 July*], and Charles F. Welles's Poem on Thomas Jefferson, [*ca. 11 August*] 428
To André Daschkoff, *12 August* 433
From John Martin Baker, *14 August* 434
From Samuel H. Smith, *15 August* 434
From Jones & Howell, *16 August* 435
To Meriwether Lewis, *16 August* 435
From James Madison, *16 August* 437
To Craven Peyton, *16 August* 439

To James Madison, *17 August* 441
From David Porter, enclosing Plan for a Voyage of Discovery to the Northwest Coast of America, *17 August* 443
From Madame Deshay, *18 August* 450
From George Jefferson, *18 August* 451
From Jonathan Shoemaker, *18 August* 451
From John Vaughan, *19 August* 452
To Craven Peyton, *20 August* 453
From Craven Peyton, [*20 August*] 454
From John Vaughan, *20 August* 455
To John Barnes, *22 August* 455
From Samuel R. Demaree, *22 August* 455
To George Jefferson, *22 August* 457
From James Leitch, *22 August* 458
To Charles Willson Peale, *22 August* 458
Craven and Jane Peyton's Conveyance of the Henderson Lands, [*22 August*] 459
Declaration to Craven Peyton, *22 August* 463
From James Madison, *23 August* 464
To Joseph Dougherty, *24 August* 464
From James Long, *24 August* 464
To William Thornton, *24 August* 465
To James W. Wallace, *24 August* 466
To John Barnes, *25 August* 467
To Joseph Dougherty, *25 August* 467
From William Dunn, *25 August* 467
To Robert Graham, *25 August* 469
From George Jefferson, *25 August* 469
To Craven Peyton, *25 August* 470
From Valentín de Foronda, *26 August* 470
To George Jefferson, *27 August* 472
To Alexander McRae, *27 August* 472
To William W. Hening, *28 August* 472
From Benjamin Henry Latrobe, *28 August* 473
To Charles Pinckney, *29 August* 475
From William Thornton, *30 August* 476
From Abraham Bradley, *31 August* 480
From Joseph Dougherty, *31 August* 480
To Robert Patterson, *31 August* 482
To John Vaughan, *31 August* 482
From George Jefferson, *1 September* 483

From William D. Meriwether, [*received 1 September*] 483
From André Daschkoff, *2 September* 484
From Robert Graham, *2 September* 486
To John W. Campbell, *3 September* 486
From Thomas Eston Randolph, *3 September* 488
From William W. Hening, *4 September* 488
From William Lambert, *4 September* 489
From James Monroe, *4 September* 498
To James Monroe, [*4 September*] 500
From Hugh Nelson, [*4 September*] 500
From James Wood, *5 September* 501
To Jones & Howell, *6 September* 503
To Joseph McCoy, *6 September* 504
From J. Philippe Reibelt, *6 September* 504
To Abraham Bradley, *7 September* 505
To William Caruthers, *7 September* 506
To George Gilpin, *7 September* 507
From John Wyche, *7 September* 508
To William Brown, *10 September* 509
To William C. C. Claiborne, *10 September* 509
To William Clark, *10 September* 510
To William Lambert, *10 September* 511
From Charles Pinckney, [*ca. 10 September*] 513
From Abraham Bradley, *11 September* 514
From Thomas A. Digges, *11 September* 515
From James Madison, *11 September* 518
From John Minor, *11 September* 519
To James Madison, *12 September* 519
To George Jefferson, *13 September* 520
From Benjamin Smith Barton, *14 September* 520
From J. B. Moussier, *14 September* 522
From Thomas Mann Randolph (1792–1848), *15 September* 524
From George Sullivan, *15 September* 524
From William Fontaine, *16 September* 525
From Lafayette, *16 September* 528
From the General Republican Committee of the City and County of New York, *16 September* 530
From William Lambert, *17 September* 534
From David Bailie Warden, *17 September* 535
To James Madison, *18 September* 536
From John Armstrong, *19 September* 536

From John W. Campbell, *19 September* 538
From William Lambert, enclosing Table for Computing the Moon's Motion, with Examples, *19 September* 539
From William Johnson, *20 September* 555
To Benjamin Smith Barton, *21 September* 555
From George Jefferson, *22 September* 557
From Dudley Richardson, *22 September* 558
To Benjamin Rush, *22 September* 558
From Robert Quarles, *24 September* 560
From William Lambert, *25 September* 560
Notes on Distances between Monticello and Montpellier, [*ca. 25 September*] 562
Jefferson's Letter to James Fishback 563
I. To James Fishback (Draft), *September* 563
II. To James Fishback (Final State), *27 September* 565
From Samuel Kercheval, *28 September* 566
From Isaac Riley, *29 September* 567
To the General Republican Committee of the City and County of New York, *30 September* 568
To John W. Campbell, *1 October* 569
To William W. Hening, *1 October* 570
To Alexander Macomb, *1 October* 571
To Robert Patterson, *1 October* 571
From John Stout, *1 October* 572
To Henry Dearborn and Elbridge Gerry, *2 October* 572
From John Koontz, *2 October* 573
To Thomas Mann Randolph (1792–1848), *2 October* 574
From William Henry Harrison, *3 October* 574
To Samuel R. Demaree, enclosing Supplemental List of Recommended Books, *4 October* 575
To Valentín de Foronda, *4 October* 577
To Robert Quarles, *4 October* 579
To John Wyche, enclosing List of Recommended Books, *4 October* 579
From Thomas Cadwalader, *6 October* 583
To William Eustis, *6 October* 583
From James Madison, *6 October* 584
To John Minor, *6 October* 585
To John Smith (1750–1836), *6 October* 585
To John Adlum, *7 October* 586
To Isaac Riley, *7 October* 587
To Joel Barlow, *8 October* 588
To George Jefferson, *8 October* 590

To George Sullivan, *8 October* 591
To William Fontaine, *9 October* 591
To James Madison, *9 October* 592
From Madame de Tessé, *9 October* 593
To George Jefferson, *10 October* 595
To Benjamin Henry Latrobe, *10 October* 595
To John Milledge, *10 October* 596
From George Williamson, *10 October* 597
To Albert Gallatin, *11 October* 597
To William Thornton, *11 October* 599
From Isaac Riley, *16 October* 600
From Clotworthy Stephenson, *16 October* 601
From Luis de Onís, *17 October* 601
From John Brahan, *18 October* 602
From Valentín de Foronda, *18 October* 604
From James Neelly, *18 October* 606
To John Austin, *20 October* 608
From Thomas T. Hewson, *20 October* 608
From the Citizens of Richmond, [*20 October*] 609
From Augustin François Silvestre, *20 October* 611
From John Tyler, *20 October* 613
From Henry Banks, *21 October* 614
From Alexander McRae, *21 October* 615
From St. George Tucker, *21 October*,
enclosing Ode to Thomas Jefferson, *20 October* 617
From William W. Hening, *22 October* 619
To the Citizens of Richmond, *22 October* 620
From Alexander Burot, *23 October* 622
From William Eustis, *25 October* 624
From Samuel Greenhow, *25 October* 625
To James Madison, *25 October* 626
From Lafayette, *26 October* 627
From David Bailie Warden, *27 October* 629
From Zadok Cramer, *30 October* 630
From Thomas Lomax, *30 October* 631
From James Madison, *30 October* 632
To Louis H. Girardin, *31 October* 633
To George Jefferson, *31 October* 634
From Gideon Fitz, *1 November* 635
From Elias Glover, *1 November* 643
To William Miller, *1 November* 644
To John Porter, *2 November* 644

To Dudley Richardson, *2 November* 645
From William Fontaine, *3 November* 645
From David K. Hopkins, *3 November* 646
To Clotworthy Stephenson, *3 November* 649
To Albert Gallatin, *4 November* 650
To Luis de Onís, *4 November* 651
From Johann Severin Vater, *4 November* 651
From David Campbell, *5 November* 652
From Thomas Eston Randolph, *5 November* 654
From William Turpin, [*received 5 November*] 654
To George Jefferson, *6 November* 655
From Jacob L. Kesteloot, *6 November* 656
To Thomas Lomax, *6 November* 657
To James Madison, *6 November* 657
From James Madison, *6 November* 658
To Samuel Greenhow, *7 November* 659
From William Fleming, *9 November* 660
From Gabriel Richard, *9 November* 660
From Nathaniel Chapman, *10 November* 663
From Albert Gallatin, *11 November* 664
From John Milledge, *11 November* 666
From Isaac A. Coles, *12 November* 667
From C. & A. Conrad & Company, *13 November* 668
From George Jefferson, *13 November* 669
Notes on Ivy Creek Lands, *14 November* 670
From the Citizens of Lynchburg, [*14 November*] 671
From Anonymous, [*15 November*] 671
From Marc Antoine Jullien, *15 November* 674

APPENDIX: Supplemental List of Documents Not Found 677

INDEX 679

# MAPS

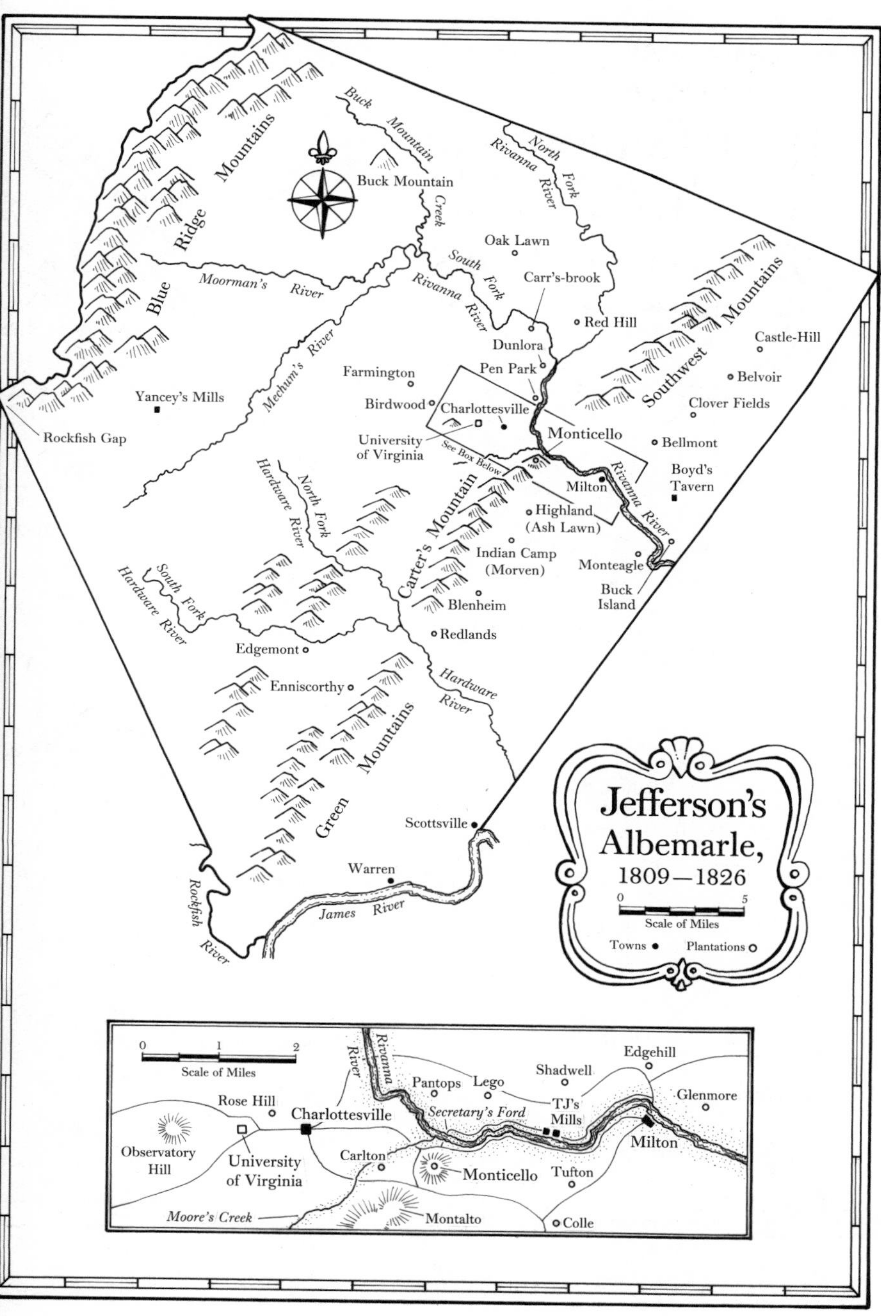

Jefferson's Albemarle, 1809–1826
0 5
Scale of Miles
Towns
Plantations
Blue Ridge Mountains
Buck Mountain Creek
Buck Mountain
North Fork Rivanna River
Oak Lawn
South Fork Rivanna River
Carr's-brook
Moorman's River
Red Hill
Southwest Mountains
Castle-Hill
Dunlora
Pen Park
Farmington
Mechum's River
Belvoir
Yancey's Mills
Birdwood
Charlottesville
Clover Fields
Rockfish Gap
University of Virginia
See Box Below
Monticello
Bellmont
Milton
Boyd's Tavern
Hardware River
North Fork
Carter's Mountain
Highland (Ash Lawn)
Rivanna River
Indian Camp (Morven)
Monteagle
South Fork Hardware River
Blenheim
Buck Island
Redlands
Edgemont
Hardware River
Enniscorthy
Green Mountains
Scottsville
Warren
Rockfish River
James River
0 1 2
Scale of Miles
Rivanna River
Edgehill
Shadwell
Pantops
Lego
Glenmore
Rose Hill
Charlottesville
Secretary's Ford
TJ's Mills
Milton
Observatory Hill
University of Virginia
Carlton
Monticello
Tufton
Moore's Creek
Montalto
Colle

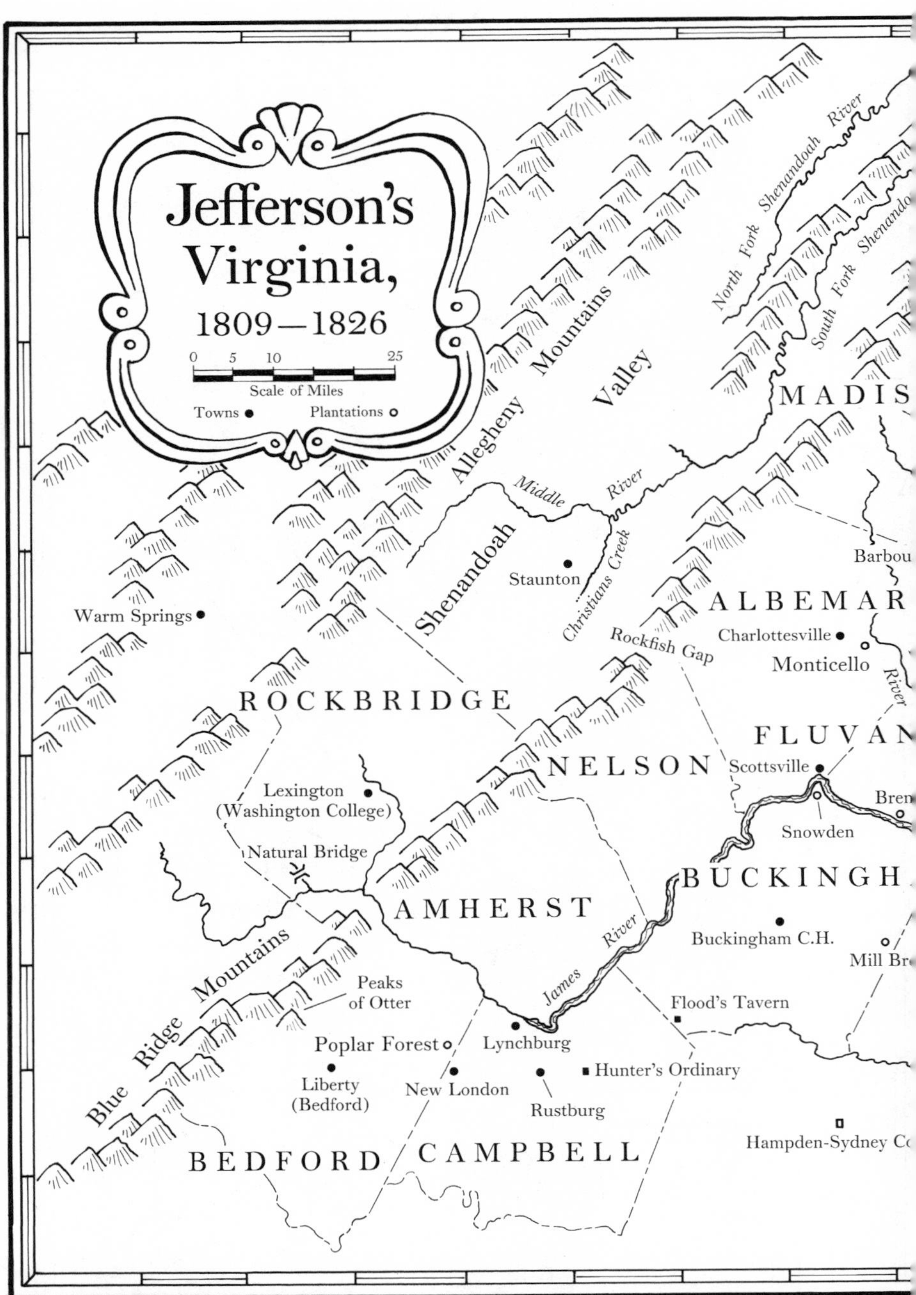
Jefferson's Virginia,
1809—1826
0 5 10 25
Scale of Miles
Towns
Plantations
Allegheny Mountains
Valley
North Fork Shenandoah River
South Fork
Middle River
Shenandoah
Staunton
Christians Creek
Warm Springs
ALBEMAR
Charlottesville
Monticello
Rockfish Gap
River
ROCKBRIDGE
NELSON
Scottsville
Lexington
(Washington College)
Natural Bridge
Snowden
BUCKINGH
AMHERST
Buckingham C.H.
James River
Blue Ridge Mountains
Peaks of Otter
Flood's Tavern
Poplar Forest
Lynchburg
Liberty
(Bedford)
New London
Rustburg
Hunter's Ordinary
BEDFORD
CAMPBELL

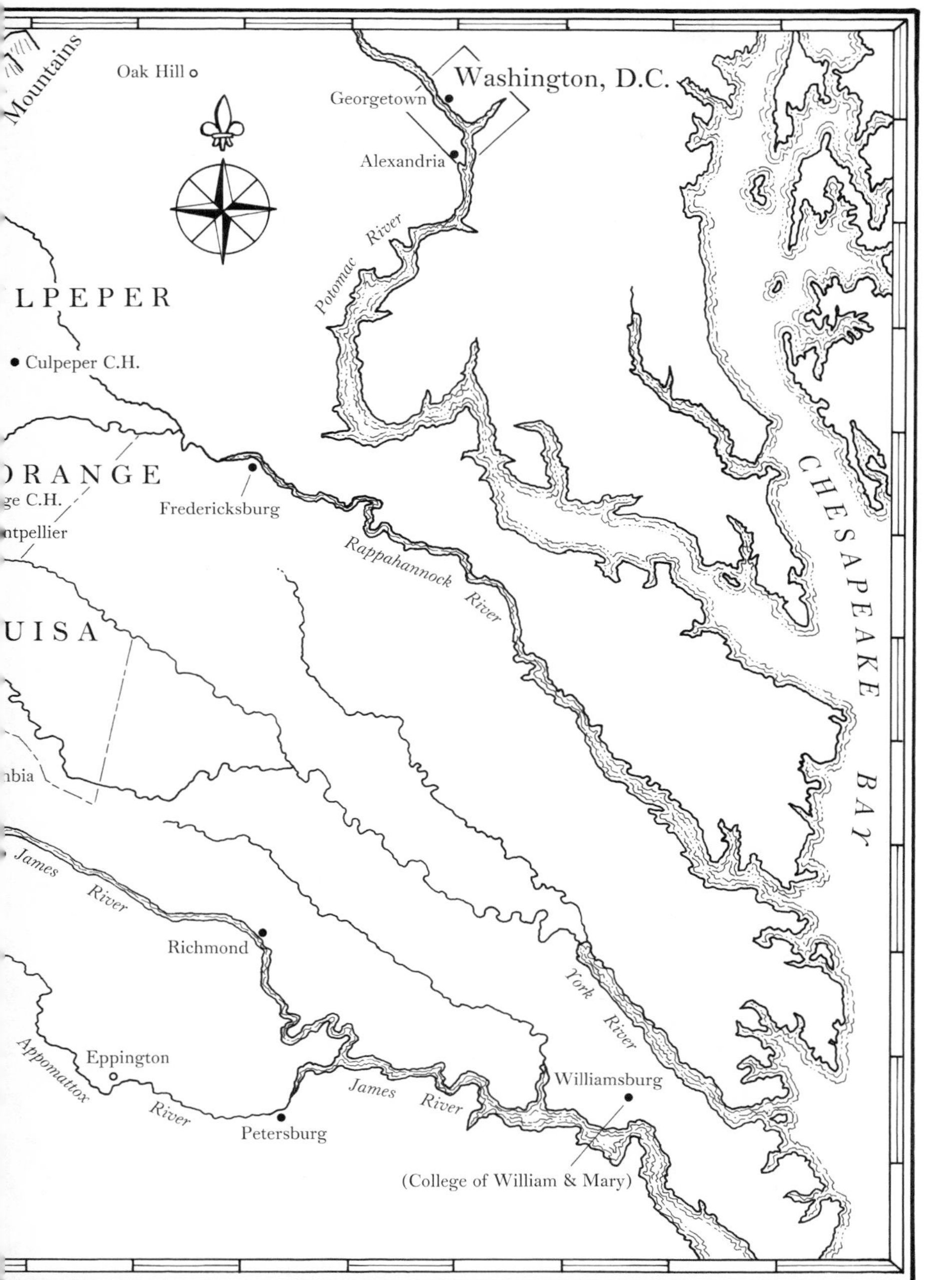
Mountains
Oak Hill
Washington, D.C.
Georgetown
Alexandria
Potomac River
LPEPER
Culpeper C.H.
ORANGE
ge C.H.
ntpellier
Fredericksburg
Rappahannock River
CHESAPEAKE BAY
UISA
nbia
James River
Richmond
York River
Appomattox River
Eppington
Petersburg
James River
Williamsburg
(College of William & Mary)

# ILLUSTRATIONS

*Following page 380*

THOMAS JEFFERSON BY THOMAS GIMBREDE

Gimbrede based his engraving entitled *Tho: Jefferson the Pride of America* (New York, 1809), issued to commemorate Jefferson's retirement from the presidency, on Charles Balthazar Julien Fevret de Saint-Mémin's copper-plate engraving of his life portrait of Jefferson in black and white chalk, which had been drawn on 27 Nov. 1804 (Bush, *Life Portraits*, 51–3).
*Courtesy of the National Portrait Gallery, Smithsonian Institution.*

EAST FRONT OF MONTICELLO

Jefferson left Washington for the last time on 11 Mar. 1809 and arrived at Monticello four days later. He never left Virginia again and, with the exception of regular visits to Poplar Forest, his estate near Lynchburg, he seldom strayed from Monticello thereafter.
*Courtesy of the Thomas Jefferson Foundation, Inc.*

JEFFERSON'S MEMORANDUM BOOK

Throughout his adult life Jefferson kept a meticulous record of his daily expenditures. He jotted them down initially in a tiny, fan-like notebook (made of leaves of ivory so that the writings could be rubbed out and the surface reused) and regularly transferred the information and other notes into a memorandum book like the one pictured here, which covers the period of his return to Monticello in March 1809. The exactitude of these records may have lulled Jefferson into a false sense of security, for although he indexed this material he seldom totaled his accounts, and each time he did so he was appalled to find that his financial situation was far worse than he had imagined (Stein, *Worlds*, 103; *MB*).
*Courtesy of the Massachusetts Historical Society.*

JEFFERSON'S SUMMARY JOURNAL OF LETTERS

Jefferson recorded nearly all of his incoming and outgoing correspondence during the final forty-three years of his life in his summary journal of letters. The first entry in this 656-page epistolary register was made on 11 Nov. 1783 and the last on 25 June 1826. Each page was separated into two columns, one on the left for "letters written by me" and one on the right for "letters received." Although he compiled four separate alphabetical indexes of his correspondence for the period prior to his final retirement from politics in March 1809, he did not maintain one during his retirement. Initially Jefferson summarized his own letters in some detail, a practice he soon abandoned as unnecessary when he acquired a letterpress and later a polygraph that enabled him to retain mechanical reproductions of his outgoing correspondence. Thereafter, for outgoing correspondence he typically noted only the date and intended recipient, while for incoming letters he recorded the author's name, the letter's date and its date of receipt, and the place from which it had been written. He occasionally also added a very short note on the contents or a single word describing the nature of the letter or its author (PTJ, 6:vii–ix).

*Courtesy of the Library of Congress.*

LETTERHEADS OF MOUSSIER AND SILVESTRE

The letters Jefferson regularly received from French intellectual and scientific luminaries occasionally were written on stationery with printed letterheads and decorative elements.

*Courtesy of the Huntington Library and the Library of Congress.*

SEED PRESS CONSTRUCTED FOR JEFFERSON AT THE MONTICELLO JOINERY

Jefferson kept his five-and-a-half foot tall seed press in his private study and used it to store seeds and beans in vials and tin canisters with, as Margaret Bayard Smith noted in August 1809, "everything labeled and in the neatest order." Apparently constructed by his slave John Hemmings during the first half of 1809 at the Monticello joinery, it was made of walnut, mahogany, yellow pine, and nails from the plantation's nailery (Stein, *Worlds*, 293; Smith, Account of a Visit to Monticello, [29 July–2 Aug. 1809]).

*Courtesy of the Thomas Jefferson Foundation, Inc.*

MASTODON JAWBONE DONATED BY JEFFERSON TO THE INSTITUT DE FRANCE

Both of these drawings of a portion of the lower jaw of *Mastodon americanus* were reproduced in Georges Cuvier's revised edition of *Recherches sur les Ossemens Fossiles des Quadrupèdes* (Paris, 1821), a memoir on paleontology. They were based on the bones that Jefferson and Caspar Wistar had organized in 1808 and presented as a gift to the Institut de France. Jefferson believed them to be from the American "incognitum" but Cuvier and the comte de Lacépède determined that they came from a new genus called mastodon. Cuvier demonstrated that the mastodon was a species distinct from the African or Asian elephant based on its teeth and concluded that it was extinct (Howard Rice, "Jefferson's Gift of Fossils to the Museum of Natural History in Paris," APS, *Proceedings* 95 [1951]: 597–627).

*Courtesy of the Howard C. Rice Archive, Jefferson Library, Thomas Jefferson Foundation, Inc.*

THOMAS JEFFERSON RANDOLPH BY CHARLES WILLSON PEALE

Peale executed this portrait of Jefferson's favorite grandson in oil on paper, 1808–09, while the youth was in Philadelphia studying at the University of Pennsylvania and boarding with the Peale family. Jefferson's old friend, who was evidently quite pleased by the opportunity to revive "an art which was long neglected by attachments to the charming Study of Natural History," sent the 26 by 22½ inch portrait to the president on 21 Feb. 1809, and Jefferson acknowledged its receipt on 10 Mar. 1809 (Peale to TJ, 30 Aug. 1807, 21 Feb. 1809, and TJ to Peale, 24 Sept. 1807 [DLC]; TJ to Peale, 10 Mar. 1809).

*Courtesy of the Thomas Jefferson Foundation, Inc.*

# Volume 1

## 4 March to 15 November 1809

# JEFFERSON CHRONOLOGY

## 1743 • 1826

| | |
|---|---|
| 1743 | Born at Shadwell, 13 April (New Style). |
| 1760–1762 | Studies at the College of William and Mary. |
| 1762–1767 | Self-education and preparation for law. |
| 1769–1774 | Albemarle delegate to House of Burgesses. |
| 1772 | Marries Martha Wayles Skelton, 1 January. |
| 1775–1776 | In Continental Congress. |
| 1776 | Drafts Declaration of Independence. |
| 1776–1779 | In Virginia House of Delegates. |
| 1779 | Submits Bill for Establishing Religious Freedom. |
| 1779–1781 | Governor of Virginia. |
| 1782 | Martha Wayles Skelton Jefferson dies, 6 September. |
| 1783–1784 | In Continental Congress. |
| 1784–1789 | In France on commission to negotiate commercial treaties and then as minister plenipotentiary at Versailles. |
| 1790–1793 | Secretary of State of the United States. |
| 1797–1801 | Vice President of the United States. |
| 1801–1809 | President of the United States. |

## RETIREMENT

| | |
|---|---|
| 1809 | Attends James Madison's inauguration, 4 March. |
| | Arrives at Monticello, 15 March. |
| 1810 | Completes legal brief on New Orleans batture case, 31 July. |
| 1811 | Batture case dismissed, 5 December. |
| 1812 | Correspondence with John Adams resumes, 1 January. |
| | Batture pamphlet preface completed, 25 February; printed by 21 March. |
| 1814 | Named a trustee of Albemarle Academy, 25 March. |
| | Resigns presidency of American Philosophical Society, 23 November. |
| 1815 | Sells personal library to Congress, 29 April. |
| 1816 | Writes introduction and revises translation of Destutt de Tracy, *A Treatise on Political Economy* [1818]. |
| | Named a visitor of Central College, 18 October. |
| 1818 | Attends Rockfish Gap conference to choose location of proposed University of Virginia, 1–4 August. |
| | Visits Warm Springs, 7–27 August. |
| 1819 | University of Virginia chartered, 25 January; named to Board of Visitors, 13 February; elected rector, 29 March. |
| | Debts greatly increased by bankruptcy of Wilson C. Nicholas. |
| 1820 | Likens debate over slavery and Missouri statehood to "a fire bell in the night," 22 April. |
| 1821 | Writes memoirs, 6 January–29 July. |
| 1823 | Visits Poplar Forest for last time, 16–25 May. |
| 1824 | Lafayette visits Monticello, 4–15 November. |
| 1825 | University of Virginia opens, 7 March. |
| 1826 | Writes will, 16–17 March. |
| | Last recorded letter, 25 June. |
| | Dies at Monticello, 4 July. |

# THE PAPERS OF
# THOMAS JEFFERSON

## Account with Joseph Dougherty

Washington Feb. 17th 1809
[4–10 Mar. 1809]

Thomas Jefferson Esqr
To Jos Dougherty Dr

| | | D–cts |
|---|---|---|
| | To 30 bushels oats a 40 cts per bushel | 12–00 |
| | To a stable broom | 00–14 |
| Mar 1st | To paid the stage office for freight of a box containing bust | 00–75 |
| | To a roap | 00–20 |
| | To 6 trunks a 4 Dollars each | 24–00 |
| | To 2 Do for the girls | 8–50 |
| 4 | To hack hire to a ball | 4–00 |
| | To paid the stage[1] office, freight of a small box | 0–25 |
| | To 2 saddle girths | 1–25 |
| | To cash paid Shorter going after horse | 2–18½ |
| | To cash paid for hawling packages | 3–62½ |
| | To cash paid for a toy | 0–25 |
| | To 3 groce screws | 2–70 |
| | To the blacksmith for horshoeing & repairs to the waggon | 1–50 |
| | | 61–35 |

Washington March 10th 1809
Received payment Jos Dougherty

MS (MHi); in Dougherty's hand; date revised based on internal evidence discussed below; endorsed by TJ with the notation: "acct pd Mar. 10. 09."

Joseph Dougherty (ca. 1774–1832) was a native of Londonderry, Ireland, who lived in Washington, D.C., and served as TJ's coachman there. He corresponded regularly with TJ on the breeding of dogs and merino sheep. A porter and ale bottling business Dougherty started in 1810 failed three years later, when TJ recommended him for a revenue post, and as late as 1823 his wife was requesting financial aid from TJ. In 1830 Margaret Bayard Smith described him as a "favorite and confidential servant of Mr. Jefferson" possessed of "a degree of elevation and refinement of feelings and views, seldom or ever found in his class" (Dougherty to TJ, 6 Dec. 1810, 8 Aug. 1813; TJ to Samuel H. Smith, 15 Aug. 1813; Mary Dougherty to TJ, 25 Oct., 7 Dec. 1823, 27 Jan. 1824; Smith, *Forty Years*, 313–4; Washington *National Intelligencer*, 25 July 1832).

Despite its inscribed date of 17 Feb. 1809, which presumably applies to the first two entries, Dougherty evidently submitted this account to TJ between 4 Mar. 1809, the date of the last entry, and 10 Mar. 1809, when Dougherty added the receipt for TJ's payment, also confirmed in *MB*, 2:1243.

[1] Manuscript: "sage."

# From the Students of Jefferson College

SIR, 4th of March 1809

As you now retire from the great theatre of political action, after having spent a number of years in the immediate service of your country—Permit us to hail your retreat from the important office you so lately filled with honor and dignity—to the calm retreats of domestic life. With hearts abounding with gratitude to you as an instrument in the hand of divine Providence, in promoting the peace and prosperity of this nation we humbly present our most sincere thanks. We are well apprised that it does not become youth who are in pursuit of knowledge, to engage in the political contests of the day; yet we trust it will not be disagreeable to you to find that the walls of this college, which bear your name, contain a number of the sons of freedom possessed with political principles congenial to your own. When the enemies of our country boast that they have sown discord among our citizens—When we behold the attempts made to dissolve our union—And alienate the affections of the people from government—And hear the calumnies heaped upon the character of the executive, we cannot be altogether silent.

We have been permited to hear the thunder of war at a distance, and peacably tread the arduous path of intellectual improvement, unmolested by the awful din of battle, or the more dreadful scenes of devastation that now desolate the nations of the world. Amid scenes of blood and carnage the youthful mind may acquire the more masculine virtues, that render man more alert in shedding the blood of his fellow-man—That steel the human heart against the tender feelings of sympathy and benevolence, and dissolve the finer sensibilities of our nature into those fierce passions that animate the bosom of the warrior. But the delicate hand of peace alone can cultivate and foster the tender plants of science. Though we cannot boast that our fleets and navies have carried dismay to the most distant regions of the world, yet we may congratulate ourselves on the rapid progress of the arts and sciences from one end of this mighty continent to the other. This might not be a valuable acquisition in a land where the iron hand of despotism crushes liberty in the germ. Where the ignorance of the people forms the principal pillars that support the temple of tyrany, at whose unhallowed shrine the unhappy nations of the world bow with the most profound reverence. But in a land of liberty, where every citizen participates in the general government—is a stone in the great national arch, is the deffusion of knowledge of little or no consequence? While the nations of Europe have been fertilizing their fields with human blood, and committing outrages upon Justice, that are degrading to human nature—that disgrace the page of history, and will sooner or later awake the deep rooted vengence of exasperated Justice—Industry has found ample reward for her labours in the cultivation of the earth—our territories have been extended, not by lawless and unmerciful conquests, but by rightful purchase—public improvements have been making that cement more firmly the grand chain of national union, which binds these confederated states in one mighty republic—The envy of Europe—The envy of the world. Though your endeavours have been directed to the good of the people, yet you are accused of cowardice in not resenting by force of arms the agressions of foreign powers. Revenge is pleasant to the haughty mind of man. The anticipation of victory is often fallacious. Happy for the nation whose[1] rulers are parsimonious of its blood and treasures—who view war as it really is, full of hazard, and only to be resorted to, when the voice of humanity is disregarded—When the ears of offenders, are deaf to the calls of justice.—When the arm of the Almighty can be expected to preside in their counsils, and direct the fury of war against their enemies. The Romans once the sovreigns of the world, extended their empire by conquests, untill it fell by its own weight. A martial spirit infused into a nation, Alexander like, seems to stop short of the conquest of the world. Let the nations already buried in the ruins of corroding time. Let England and France teach mankind that war is the bane of religion, the sink of civil liberty, and the greater evil that can befall any people. The present crisis seems to portend that the olive which has so long covered the sons of Columbia with its foliage, is now about to fall. Can even the tongue of malivolence say that you have accelerated the progress of war, or cherished the fire of dissention which now exists between the united states France and England. Even your most inveterate enemies must confess that all has been done that could have been done to preserve our peace, and awake the tyrants of Europe to a sense of their duty and injustice. If we must engage in battle with our enemies, you may justly exclaim with Cæsar, though with greater purity of intention "They would have it so." Though you now receive the applause of the greater part of this nation yet you need not expect, that ample justice will be done to your character by your cotempories. We believe you enjoy that satisfaction which arises from integrity of heart. This will afford more solid contentment, th[an] the approbation of the world, when the heart is stung with the pangs of conscious guilt.

May happiness attend you down the peaceful vale of life untill you drop into the embraces of silent death—lamented by the friends of liberty, and crowned with the applauses of a grateful people.

MS (DLC); slightly torn; between dateline and salutation: "From the Students of Jefferson College of the Borough of Canonsburg Washington County Pa To Thomas Jefferson Esq. President of the United States"; addressed: "Thomas Jefferson Esqr Washing Citty"; franked; postmarked in Canonsburg 18 Mar. and Washington, D.C., 27 Mar. before forwarding to Milton; endorsed by TJ as "Address Students of Jefferson college Canonsburg P^a^." Recorded in SJL as received 30 Mar. 1809.

Jefferson College was originally chartered as the Canonsburg Academy and Library Company in 1794 and rechartered by the Pennsylvania legislature in 1802 as Jefferson College. Students were primarily educated to be Presbyterian ministers at the college, which merged in 1865 with nearby Washington College (chartered in 1787), to form Washington and Jefferson College located at Washington, Pennsylvania (Joseph Smith, *History of Jefferson College* [1857], 51–5).

At the conclusion of the battle of Pharsalus on 9 Aug. 48 BC Julius CÆSAR said of his slain enemies: "They would have it so. Even I, Gaius Caesar, after so many great deeds, should have been found guilty, if I had not turned to my army for help" (Suetonius, *The Lives of the Caesars*, trans. J. C. Rolfe, Loeb Classical Library [1979], 1:43).

[1] Manuscript: "whse."

# Memoranda to James Madison

[ca. 4–11 Mar. 1809]

Memoranda for the President.

Information having been recieved in October last that many intruders had settled on the lands of the Cherokees & Chickasaws; the letter from Gen^l^ Dearborn to Col^o^ Meigs was written to have them ordered off, & to inform them they would be removed by military force in the spring if still on the lands. these orders remain still to be given, & they should go to the officer commanding at Highwassee. a very discreet officer should be selected. on the Cherokee lands, Wafford's settlement should not be disturbed as the Indians themselves expect to arrange that with us, & the exchange for lands beyond the Misipi will furnish a good opportunity. from the lands of[1] the Chickasaws all should be removed except those who settled on Doublehead's reserve under titles from him; & they should be notified that those lands having been claimed by the Chickasaws as well as the Cherokees, we purchased[2] the Cherokee right with an exception of Doublehead's reserve, which we did not guarantee to him, but left it as it stood under the claims of both nations; that consequently they are not under our protection. that whenever we purchase the Chickasaw right, all their titles under Doublehead will become void; as our laws do not permit individuals to purchase lands from the Indians: that they should therefore look out for themselves in time.

---

At Detroit. Gen[l] Dearborne & myself had concluded to purchase for the War-departm[t] farm, near Detroit, now held by the Treasury office in satisfaction of a delinquency, provided it could be bought at it's real value, supposed about 1000. or 1200. D. to employ the dwelling house and appurtenances for a school for the instruction of the Indian boys & girls in reading E[t]c learning English & houshold & mechanical arts under the care of Pere Richard, to place in the farm house a farmer (a labourer) of proper character to cultivate the farm with the aid of the Indian lads for the support of the institution, and to place on the same land the blacksmith & carpenter, who would have Indian apprentices under them. the advantages of assembling the whole at one place are obvious. father Richard goes to France in the Mentor to procure an aid. if, when he brings him, he could exchange him with Bishop Carroll for an American, it would be infinitely more desirable.

MS (DLC: TJ Papers, 187:33233); in TJ's hand; undated; at foot of first page: "Presid[t] US."; docketed "Mach 1809" at foot of text in an unknown hand. Tr (MHi); second paragraph only; posthumous copy.

James Madison (1751–1836), president of the United States, 1809–17, was TJ's lifelong friend and confidante. They became acquainted in 1779 when TJ was governor of Virginia and Madison sat on the Virginia Council of State. Madison served as a Virginia delegate to the Continental Congress, 1780–83 and 1787–88, played a key role in drafting the United States Constitution in 1787, enjoyed great prominence in the United States House of Representatives, 1789–97, and served as secretary of state under TJ throughout the latter's presidency. In addition to their republican ideals and belief in religious toleration, the two men shared interests in science, agriculture, natural history, and the promotion of education. Throughout their long political careers they corresponded frequently and supported each other with mutual respect and admiration (*ANB*; *DAB*; Brant, *Madison*, esp. 1:272–80; Madison, *Papers*).

WAFFORD'S SETTLEMENT was a 135-square-mile tract in Georgia ceded to the United States by the Cherokee in a 24 Oct. 1804 treaty, the first of four such transactions during TJ's administration by which the federal government gained title to over 15,000 square miles of Cherokee land (Russell Thornton, *The Cherokees: A Population History* [1990], 55).

[1] Word interlined in place of "claimed by."

[2] TJ here canceled "only."

# Margaret Bayard Smith's Account of Madison's Inauguration and Ball

[4 Mar. 1809]

On the morning of Mr Madison's inauguration, he asked Mr Jefferson to ride in his carriage with him to the Capitol, but this he declined, & in answer to one[1] who enquired of him why he had not accompanied his friend—he smiled & replied, "I wished not to divide with him the honors of the day—it pleased me better to see them all bestowed on him." A large procession of citizens, some in carriages, on horse back, & a still larger on foot, followed Mr Madison along Pensylvania avenue to the Capitol—Among those on horse-back was Mr Jefferson, unattended by even a servant, undistinguished in any way[2] from his fellow citizens—Arrived at the Capitol he dismounted & "Oh![3] shocking," as many, even democrats, as well as the british minister M. Foster,[4] might have exclaimed, he hitched his own horse to a post, & followed the multitude into the Hall of Representatives. Here a seat had been prepared for him near that of the new President—this he declined—& when urged by the Committee of arrangement, he replied, "this day I return to the people & my proper seat is among them." Surely this was carrying democracy[5] too far, but it was not done, as his opponents said, from a mere desire of popularity; he must have known human nature too well, not to know that the People delight to honor, & to see honored their chosen favorite; besides what more popularity could he now desire—his cup was already running over & could have held no more.—No, he wished by his example as well as his often expressed opinions, to establish the principle of political equality.[6]

After the ceremony of Inauguration, Mr Madison followed by the same crowd returned home[7] to his private house, Where he & Mrs Madison recieved the visits of the foreign ministers & their fellow citizens.

It was the design, as generally understood, after paying their respects to the new President, that citizens[8] should go to the President's House

& pay a farewell visit to Mr Jefferson; but to the surprise of every one, he himself, was among the visitors at Mr Madison's. A lady who was on terms of intimacy with the ex-President & could therefore take that liberty, after telling him that the present company & citizens generally, desired to improve this last opportunity of evincing their respect by waiting on him, added her hopes that he would yet be at home in time to[9] recieve them.[10] "This day should be exclusively my friend's," replied he, "& I am too happy in being here, to remain at home." "But indeed Sir you must recieve us, you would not let all these ladies—all your friends find an empty house, for at any rate we are determined to go, & to express[11] even on this glad occasion, the regret we feel on losing you."

His countenance discovered some[12] emotion—he made no reply, but bowed expressively. The lady had no positive information to give those who had requested her to enquire whether Mr Jefferson would recieve company, but watching his motions, found that after a little while he had silently slipped through the crowd & left the room. This she communicated to the company, who with one accord determined to follow him to the President's house—It was evident that he had not expected this attention from his friends & fellow citizens, as his whole house-hold had gone forth to witness the ceremonies of the day—He was alone—But not therefore the less happy, for not one of the eager crowd that followed Mr Madison, was as anxious as himself, to shew every possible mark of respect to the new President.

How mournful was this last interview!—Every one present seemed to feel it so, & as each in turn shook hands with him, their countenances expressed more forcibly than their words the regret they felt on losing one who had been the uniform friend of the city, & of the citizens, with whom [he][13] had lived on terms of hospitality & kindness—

In the evening there was an Inauguration Ball. Mr Jefferson was among the first that entered the Ballroom; he came before the President's arrival—"Am I too early?" said he to a friend—"You must tell me how to behave for it is more than forty years since I have been to a ball."

In the course of the evening, some one remarked to him, "you look so happy & satisfied Mr Jefferson, & Mr Madison looks so serious not to say, sad, that a spectator might imagine that you were the one coming in, & he the one going out of office."

"There's good reason for my happy & his serious looks," replied Mr Jefferson, "I have got the burthen off my shoulders, while he has now got it on his."

MS (DLC: Margaret Bayard Smith Papers, Commonplace Books); entirely in Smith's hand; undated, excerpted from an essay entitled "The President's House Forty years ago" filed in book dated 1826–31, but evidently composed about 1841. Printed in Smith, *Forty Years*, 410–2.

Margaret Bayard Smith (1778–1844), a shrewdly observant leader of Washington society, was also an accomplished novelist and essayist. Born in rural Pennsylvania, she was educated at a Moravian boarding school in Bethlehem, Pennsylvania, and read widely in the classics, sciences, and literature while living with a married sister in New Brunswick, New Jersey. In 1800 Smith married her second cousin Samuel Harrison Smith and resided thereafter in Washington and at a farm retreat called Sidney. Her publications included *The Diversions of Sidney* (Washington, 1805); *A Winter in Washington: or, Memoirs of the Seymour Family*, 3 vols. (New York, 1824); *What is Gentility?: A Moral Tale* (Washington, 1828); a short biography of Dolley Madison; and numerous articles for periodicals. Smith also supported such civic causes as the Washington Female Orphan Asylum (*ANB*; *DAB*; Smith, *Forty Years*; James G. Wilson, "Col. John Bayard and the Bayard Family of America," *New York Genealogical and Biographical Record* 16 [1885]: 49–72).

About the time Smith composed this memoir, Augustus John FOSTER, secretary to the British legation, 1804–08, and chargé d'affaires, 1811–12, angered her with the publication of his notes on the United States, in which he criticized TJ's democratic lifestyle as insincere posturing (*DNB*; *Quarterly Review* 68 [1841]: 12–32). TJ reportedly arrived about noon at the HALL OF REPRESENTATIVES, which was filled to "overflowing" several hours earlier. The INAUGURATION BALL, held at Long's Hotel, was attended by more than four hundred people and described as "the most brilliant and crowded ever known in Washington" (Washington *National Intelligencer*, 6 Mar. 1809).

Smith published an account of the same events in a novel, stating that TJ "stole unperceived away" from the ball, at which he "did not stay above two hours, and no one had ever before seen him in such high spirits; his countenance beamed with a benevolent joy. Certainly father never loved son more than he loves Mr. M——n; and it was observed, that every demonstration of regard or respect shewn to him, gave him more evident satisfaction than those paid to himself" (Smith, *Winter in Washington*, 3:281–7).

[1] Word interlined in place of "a friend."

[2] Preceding three words interlined.

[3] Smith here canceled "barbar."

[4] Preceding two words interlined.

[5] Reworked from "democratic equality."

[6] Reworked from "of equality in that high office."

[7] Word interlined and next two words, mistakenly canceled but present in Smith, *Forty Years*, here restored.

[8] Word interlined in place of "every one."

[9] Reworked from "would be at home to."

[10] Smith here canceled "& expressed her surprise at seeing him [']I am here too happy, in paying my respects to my friend,' replied he, 'to lose this opportunity of joining with my fellow citizens in their demonstration.'"

[11] Word interlined in place of "shew that."

[12] Preceding two words interlined in place of "expressed."

[13] Omitted word editorially supplied. Smith, *Forty Years*: "they."

# From the Citizens of Washington, D.C.

SIR.

The Citizens of Washington cannot forego the last opportunity, which may, perhaps ever occur, to bid you a respectful and affectionate farewell. As members of the great and flourishing nation, over which you have so illustriously presided, your virtues, talents, and services command their esteem, admiration and gratitude. Embarked in the fate of this solitary republic of the world, they have in common with their fellow-citizens, rejoiced in its prosperous and sympathised in its adverse fortunes as involving every thing dear to freemen. They have marked with exultation, the firm column of its glory, laid on imperishable foundations, rising as a monument of the reign of principle in this quarter of the globe. To you they have been instructed to ascribe the memorable Act, which by declaring a gallant people free and independent, in a tone that appalled tyranny, instilled those sentiments and principles, which, inspiring every virtue, and urging every sacrifice, led them to triumph and empire.

We have since beheld you, with parental solicitude, and with a vigilance that never sleeps, watching over the fairest offspring of liberty, and by your unremitted labors, in upholding, explaining and vindicating our system of government, rendering it the object of love at home, and respect abroad.

It would be a pleasing task for us, as Citizens of the U. S. to fill up and extend the outlines we have sketched. But it is as Citizens of the National metropolis that we now appear before you. In addition to every patriotic feeling that can warm our breasts, we have still further inducements to open our hearts to you on this proud yet painful occasion.

The world knows you as a philosopher and philanthropist; the American people know you as a patriot and statesman;—we know you, in addition to all this as a Man. And, however your talents have extorted our respect, there is not one among us, whose predominant feeling at this moment is not that of affection for the mild and endearing virtues, that have made everyone here your friend, and you his. We should be lost to gratitude, did we not acknowledge that it is to you we owe much, very much of that harmony of intercourse and tolerance of opinion, which characterises our State of society,—of that improvement which amidst unpropitious circumstances, has progressed with sure and steady steps, and above all, of that spirit of enterprise, which your beneficence and liberality have invariably aided, and which promises in a few years to render this place the fairest seat of wealth and science.

Deeply as we feel your retirement, we approve, nay applaud it. Personal considerations aside, it was to be expected from the friend and protector of republican institutions, that he would follow, and by his co-operation strengthen the example of the illustrious hero of the revolution.

May you in the retirement, to which you go, be happy! As Your fellow Citizens will still look towards you with interest, and pray for your felicity, so will you find it impossible to lose sight of the arduous scenes through which we have passed as well as those in store for our Country. Your heart will still beat with patriotism, and the energies of your mind continue to be engaged on national objects. In your retreat, may every anxious thought be softened by the mild and tender occupations of private life! Happy, thrice happy retreat! where patriotism and philosophy, friendship and affection will animate, direct and soften the purest feelings of the heart! With a grateful nation, we pray that you may be happy, and if the just Being, that presides over the Universe insure to you but a portion of that felicity you have conferred on others our prayers will be fulfilled.

ROBERT BRENT—Chairman.
NICH[s] KING. Sec[y]

City of Washington
March 4[th] 1809

MS (DLC); in King's hand, signed by Brent and King, dateline in Brent's hand; at head of text: "To Thomas Jefferson"; endorsed by TJ as an "Address citizens of Wash[n]" received 4 Mar. 1809 and so recorded in SJL. Printed in Washington *National Intelligencer*, 6 Mar. 1809. Enclosed in a brief covering letter of 4 Mar. 1809 from Brent, Samuel H. Smith, and James H. Blake (RC in DLC; in Smith's hand, signed by Brent, Smith, and Blake; dateline adjacent to first signature; endorsed by TJ as received 4 Mar. 1809 and so recorded in SJL).

Robert Brent (1764–1819) served as mayor of Washington from 1802 to 1812, an unpaid post that he tried to relinquish in 1809. His paid positions included justice of the peace and judge of the orphans' court for the District of Columbia's Washington County and paymaster general of the army (*JEP*, 1:388, 423, 2:110 [2 Mar. 1801, 28 Apr. 1802, 17 Feb. 1809]; Madison, *Papers, Pres. Ser.*, 1:193; Bryan, *National Capital*, 1:411; Washington *National Intelligencer*, 9 Sept. 1819).

Nicholas King (1771–1812) was an English-born surveyor who arrived in Washington in 1796. He worked on his own until TJ appointed him surveyor of the city in 1803, a postion he held until his death (Ralph E. Ehrenberg, "Nicholas King: First Surveyor of the City of Washington, 1803–1812," *RCHS* 69/70 [1969/70]: 31–65; Washington *National Intelligencer*, 23 May 1812).

MEMORABLE ACT: the Declaration of Independence. ILLUSTRIOUS HERO OF THE REVOLUTION: George Washington.

# To the Citizens of Washington, D.C.

I recieve with peculiar gratification the affectionate address of the citizens of Washington, and in the patriotic sentiments it expresses, I see the true character of the National Metropolis. the station which we occupy among the nations of the earth is honourable, but awful. trusted with the destinies of this solitary republic of the world, the only monument of human rights, & the sole depository of the sacred fire of freedom & self-government from hence it is to be lighted up in other regions, of the earth, if other regions of the earth shall ever become susceptible of it's benign influence. all mankind ought then, with us, to rejoice in it's prosperous, & sympathize in it's adverse fortunes, as involving every thing dear to man. and to what sacrifices of interest, or convenience ought not these considerations to animate us & to what compromises of opinion & inclination, to maintain harmony & union among ourselves, & to preserve from all danger this hallowed ark of human hope & happiness. that differences of opinion should arise among men, on politics, on religion, & on every other topic of human enquiry, & that these should be freely expressed in a country where all our faculties are free, is to be expected. but these valuable privileges are much perverted when permitted to disturb the harmony of social intercourse, and to lessen the tolerance of opinion. to the honour of society here, it has been characterised by a just & generous liberality, and an indulgence of those affections which, without regard to political creeds, constitute the happiness of life. That the improvement of this city must proceed with sure & steady steps, follows from it's many obvious advantages, & from the enterprizing spirit of it's inhabitants, which promises to render it the fairest seat of wealth & science.

It is very gratifying to me that the general course of my administration is approved by my fellow citizens, & particularly that the motives of my retirement are satisfactory. I part with the powers entrusted to me by my country, as with a burthen of heavy bearing: but it is with sincere regret that I part with the society in which I have lived here. it has been the source of much happiness to me during my residence at the seat of government, and I owe it much for it's kind dispositions. I shall ever feel a high interest in the prosperity of the city, and an affectionate attachment to it's inhabitants.

Th: Jefferson
March 4. 1809.

PoC (DLC); at head of text: "To the Citizens of Washington." Tr (MHi); posthumous copy. Printed in Washington *National Intelligencer*, 6 Mar. 1809. Recorded in SJL as "answer to citizens of Wash$^{n}$."

## To John Benson

SIR Washington Mar. 5. 09.

I recieved last night your favor of the 3$^{d}$ and am very sensible of the kind wishes of my friends at Fredericksbg that I should pass a day with them on my return home. at any other season I should have done this with great pleasure; but we have such terrible information of the impassable state of the roads that I dare not attempt it. the route I go is by cross roads altogether, not cut by waggons, & 20. miles nearer than by Fredericksburg. I shall have a Caravan also on the road, ahead of me, which, in case of any casualty I might overtake & relieve. I must pray you therefore to make my thanks acceptable to my friends, and to tender them and accept for yourself the assurances of my esteem & respect. TH: JEFFERSON

PoC (DLC); at foot of text: "M$^{r}$ Benson"; mistakenly endorsed by TJ as a letter to former New York congressman Egbert Benson and so recorded in SJL.

John Benson (d. ca. 1815) served as postmaster at Fredericksburg, 1802–15, and kept a tavern in that town at which TJ had stayed previously (Axelson, *Virginia Postmasters*, 177; *MB*, 2:903; Fredericksburg *Virginia Herald*, 27 Sept. 1815). In his FAVOR Benson invited TJ to spend a day with his Fredericksburg friends on his way to Monticello (Benson to TJ, 3 Mar. 1809 [MHi]).

## From John Norvell

VENERABLE SIR, Washington City, March 5. [1809]

Your liberality and goodness will pardon the liberty I take in addressing this note to you.

Believing that if you can be satisfied of my reputation and real character as a moral and honest young man, and of my competency to fill the situation of a clerk in one of the departments, you will be kind enough to interest yourself in my favor, I beg leave to solicit your patronage, in procuring a clerkship for me in the navy, war, treasury, or state department. One of a common or inferior nature would be acceptable: because I think that my conduct in a short time would insure promotion.

The honorable Mr. Boyle, from Kentucky, was so obliging last evening as to mention this subject to me, and to offer me any aid in his power to forward my interest. He will leave the city on Tuesday morning: and I should be very thankful, if you should deem it right to give an immediate answer, in order that I may be enabled to give any satisfaction as to my conduct character or qualifications, which may be desired. The honorable gentleman is well acquainted, not only with myself, but with my father and all his family.

I can give additional satisfaction as to my moral character and rectitude from some of the most respectable gentleman of this city; particularly from captain Davidson.

Be pleased to accept, venerable patriot and fellow citizen, the assurances of my profound regard. JOHN NORVELL

RC (DNA: RG 59, LAR, 1809–17); partially dated; in left-hand margin: "Thomas Jefferson, Esq."; endorsed by State Department clerk Daniel Brent: "John Norvell asks for a clerkship." Recorded in SJL as received 6 Mar. 1809 with the notation: "emplom$^{t}$."

John Norvell (1789–1850), printer, was a native of Kentucky who later edited the Baltimore *Whig* (1813–14), *Baltimore Patriot* (1815–17), Lexington *Kentucky Gazette* (1817–19), Philadelphia *Franklin Gazette* (1819–28; from 1824 as *Aurora and Franklin Gazette*), and Philadelphia *Pennsylvania Inquirer* (1829–31). Admitted to the Maryland bar in 1814, in 1831 he became the postmaster of Detroit, and he served as one of Michigan's first United States senators, 1837–41 (*Biog. Dir. Cong.*; Brigham, *American Newspapers*, 1:245, 251–2, 2:907; Washington *National Intelligencer*, 27 Sept. 1832).

# From James Ronaldson

SIR Philadelphia March 5 1809

I was favored with your's accompanying the wool, on the 21$^{st}$ ult; and have delayed answering untill I could make my-self sufficiently acquainted with the subject and communicate such facts as would enable you to form some oppinion on it yourself—

I find non of the wool you alude as sold so high in N York, has been employed by our hatters;—and M$^{r}$ Tybout says when wool is much disposed to <u>full</u> it becomes impossible to <u>bow</u> it, and is unfit for their business, he also observes when very long in the staple, it won't bow and this applies to the sample you sent, it is some times cut, but this he considers a bad practice—As it would be very difficult to express in words the peculiar properties of each particular wool, I have taken the liberty of sending a few specimens; by a comparison of them you will be able to form a judgement of their respective merits and an oppinion which of them are most deserving the attention of carefull farmers, some of the Specimens are rather small, but it was not in my power to procure such as I wished, however they will serve our purpose in the meantime

Nº 1 Full blood marino from Col Humphrey's stock
" 2 half do do "
" 3 Three forth do do "
" 4 do do from Duponts Ram that specimen is off a lamb now in D^r Logans possession
" 5 Lamb wool from N Hampshire, much used by hatters value about .50 ℔ lb—
" 6 Called by M^r Tybout /hatter/ Camils hair prefered by hatters to all wool value two dollars ℔ lb—
I am inclined to think this is from goats and not camils—
" 7 Third cross from a Spanish ram imported by D^r Mease
" 8 Wool from W^m Davy, of Penn^y production

M^r Whittle the stocking manufacturer remarks on the sample you sent—It is of long staple but not fine—and would sell at about .45 ℔ lb—it is understoood that marinos produce a light fleece and being very usefull to the clothier he can give a higher price for it than the stocking maker otherwise it would be employed in that business, as M^r W uses non of it he cannot give the price of marino[1] wool indeed there is non at this market which puts it out of my power to quot its price, he says M^r Wilson clothier at the Head of Elk Maryland is a person who is likely to give the best information being a judicious practical manufacturer and now in business.

M^r Davy has been so obliging as comit his oppinon to paper—I shall beg leave to refer to his note,—M^r D having been bred to the woolen manufacture, and spent some years in Spain as an agent for buying wool, I am inclined to respect his oppinion as equal to any that can be got in this country; he has lately erected a wool carding mill, and carries on the spinning by machinery, He has produced some very superior stockings—some handsom fancy vests &^ca and now has a stock of upwards of 10000 lbs of wool, it is likely he will soon be an extensive woolen-manufacturer—he is very much disposed to communicate any information, and desires me to mention he will with pleasure attend to any enquiries you may address to him—I have for some years imagined, I perceived a sensible improvment in the quality of our mutton, particularly as respects its flavr but as 'tis now 16 years since I tasted the Scots, it sometimes occured it might be an alteration in my pallate, I asked M^r D if he observed any alterations on the sheep of this country—his observations go much farther and, are more accurate than mine—in general he mentions, that the sheep are greatly improven, both in wool and flesh, that 14 years ago he procured specimens of the wools which are much inferior to what is now produced—This fact is very flattering, and is an earnest of the future perfection we are likely to arrive at in breeding sheep—The dealers in wool wish samples, to be sent just as it is taken from the sheep

Our proper business is Type making, but Binny & I cannot help steping out of the 5 ℔ Cent calculation now and then, and some five years ago we bought a farm,—farming we must observe even in this farming country is not so shure a way of making money as manufacturing—however we think sheep graizing will be the most profitable way of employing it, this has been our oppinion for years past, and have only been detered from going into it by the mischief sustained from Dogs, we could neither reconcile ourselves to hazard the loss or mortification we should be exposed to from this source, but the Legistlature has given the county our land is in, a law taxing dogs, the proceeds of which tax is to form a fund to indemnify those who suffer from the deperdations of these animals.—This has given us courage and we engaged with Col Humphreys for one Ram & one Ewe of full blood and a ewe of the half blood marino the first one to cost $150 each the half blood 10 or 15 now if we can rear lambs that will sell for 10 dollars this must be more profitable than graizing large cattle or cultivating grain—We have also another idea, that is, to let out the ram on shares for half the produce when the lambs are fit to wean, for various reasons this is preferable to charging money,—Cash is allways scarce with people who make few transactions on their capital, and this is generaly the case where farmers & consumers are not mixed together—on this account they part reluctantly with money, and readily pay in produce from this plan it is probable more ewes will be offered, than if the price was two dollars, and it is very evident we will be abundantly paid, the idea is borrowed from Col Humphreys. Without both ewe & ram we never could possess the pure race and not a neigh aproximation for several generations—In the variety of ewes our plan will meet, it affoards chances to produce accidental valuable results. The random or natural fruit trees of this country are certainly good in a much greater proportion, than stated I think by Forsyeth to occur in Britain, may we not infer a Similar result among the animals; the observations of M^r^ Davy gos to establish the improvment of sheep

The management of Sheep in Europe is a Special business; with us it will be only an accessary one, and that with little knowledge, you must therefore be sensible we have great difficulties to encounter, and shall be guilty of considerable blunders,—There is one point in which the cultivating of sheep may be view'd—When peice is restored in Europe and her inhabitants return to the avocations of trade and agriculture, our grain will from want of market find but an indifferent sale and little price. But the market for wool is not likely to be overstocked while society continues to improve

In a letter we received from Coll Humphreys he tells us he has about 10 Rams and as many ews for sale, and has wrote some friends here to know if the Penn$^{y}$ Legistlature are to purchase any of them; this I presume is in consequence of some conversations he had with some of our citizens when here. my own oppinion is the Legistlature will leave the business with the citizens, and M$^{r}$ Humphreys will sell his stock—to private individuals—I cannot help sugesting the getting some of them for your neighborhood, they might produce a good result in crossing with your long wool'd—which I think is not esteem'd by any of my friends—M$^{r}$ Humphreys proposes to forward ours about the middle of June—D$^{r}$ Mease observes that Duponts Ram is larger than Col Humphreys' the former will be most desirable for farmers who understand[2] the business, have good pasture and winter food & lodging—probably the latter will suit beginners best.

I beg you will make no appology for writing me on any subject it is likely I can serve you in, or promote the interests of the country. I am sorry so little is in my power the only thing I have to offer is some industry and good intentions

I had almost forgot to mention an observation of D$^{r}$ Mease—he thinks the specimen of wool sent for the oppinions of the trade here is from a race of sheep called "Churros" of which notice is taken in the Domestic encyclopedia Birch & Smalls edition but I have not been able to find the article it is a race cultivated only for the flesh—he farther observes that 14 years ago—it was not permitted to take from Spain a Marino[3] sheep

With sentiments of respect and esteem—I am your well wisher—

James Ronaldson

P.S we have not yet been able to find antimony in the United States and consequently our business is almost at a stand, Could no plan be devised in the present state of our foreign relations whereby a supply might be obtained from France or Spain?

RC (DLC); endorsed by TJ as received 7 Mar. 1809 and so recorded in SJL. Enclosures not found.

James Ronaldson (1769–1841) was born in Edinburgh and immigrated about 1794 to Philadelphia, where he opened a biscuit bakery. In 1796 he formed a printing partnership with Archibald BINNY (ca. 1762–1838) under the name Binny & Ronaldson. Binny, a fellow native of Edinburgh, brought his typefounding equipment to Philadelphia when he arrived there in 1795. During the 1790s customers for the partnership's type included firms in Baltimore, New Haven, and New York. Binny & Ronaldson was the first permanent type foundry in the United States and the first to print specimen books. Binny and Ronaldson retired in 1815 and 1823, respectively (Jennifer B. Lee, "'Our Infant Manufactures': Early Typefounding in Philadelphia," *Printing History* 11 [1989]: 31–9).

TJ's letter ACCOMPANYING THE WOOL had enclosed a sample of what he thought to be merino wool and requested an opinion on its quality and value as determined by hatters, whose judgment TJ respected. Ronaldson accordingly consulted Andrew TYBOUT, a Philadelphia hatter, and James Mease, both of whom supplied some of the wool enclosed here. Mease also responded directly to TJ that the latter's sample wool was of the CHURROS rather than merino breed and fit only for blankets and worsted stuffs, with the two breeds not to be crossed with each other (Robinson, *Philadelphia Directory for 1809*; TJ to Ronaldson, 13 Feb. 1809, and Mease to TJ, 27 Feb. 1809 [DLC]).

David Humphreys, American minister to Spain from 1796 until 1802, provided samples from his STOCK of merino sheep raised at his farm in Connecticut. DUPONTS RAM, Don Pedro, was a celebrated merino imported to America in 1801 and purchased by Éleuthère Irénée du Pont de Nemours in 1805 (*Agricultural History* 33 [1959]: 86–8).

As the editor of an American edition of Anthony F. M. Willich, *The Domestic encyclopædia: or, a dictionary of facts and useful knowledge, comprehending a concise view of the latest discoveries, inventions, improvements, chiefly applicable to rural and domestic economy*, published by BIRCH and Small in five volumes (Philadelphia, 1803–04), Mease quoted Humphreys (4:487) on the "two distinct species" of sheep found in Spain, the Merinos and Churros, with the former "famous for their short and fine wool, peculiarly fit for carding," and the latter "distinguished for their long and coarse wool, more suitable for combing."

Binny & Ronaldson frequently faced a shortage of ANTIMONY, an element used in the casting of type. It allowed the hot metal, which sometimes contained lead, tin, and copper, to expand when it cooled and thereby take the shape of a mold (Lee, "'Our Infant Manufactures,'" 39n).

[1] Manuscript: "mario."
[2] Manuscript: "undersand."
[3] Manuscript: "Mario."

# To John Armstrong

DEAR SIR Washington Mar. 6. 09.

This will be handed you by mr Coles, the bearer of public dispatches, by an Aviso. he has lived with me as Secretary, is my wealthy neighbor at Monticello, & worthy of all confidence. his intimate knolege of our situation has induced us to send him, because he will be a full supplement as to all those things which cannot be detailed in writing. he can possess you of our present situation much more intimately than you can understand it from letters. the belligerent edicts rendered our embargo necessary to call home our ships, our seamen, & property. we expected some effect too from the coercion of interest. some it has had; but much less on account of evasions & domestic opposition to it. after 15. months continuance it is now discontinued, because, losing 50 millions of D. of exports annually by it, it costs more than war, which might be carried on for a third of that, besides what might be got by reprisal. war therefore must follow if the edicts are not repealed before the meeting of Congress in May. you have thought it advisable sooner to take possession of adjacent territories. but we know that they are ours the first moment that any war is forced upon us for other causes, that we are at hand to anticipate their possession, if attempted by any other power, and, in the meantime, we are lengthening the term of our prosperity, liberating our revenues, & increasing our power. I suppose Napoleon will get possession of Spain: but her colonies will deliver themselves to any member of the Bourbon family. perhaps Mexico will chuse it's sovereign within itself. he will find them much more difficult to subdue than Austria or Prussia; because an enemy (even in peace an enemy) possesses the element over which he is to pass to get at them; & a more powerful enemy (climate) will soon mow down his armies after arrival. this will be, without any doubt, the most difficult enterprise the emperor has ever undertaken. he may subdue the small colonies; he never can the old & strong: & the former will break off from him the first war he has again with a naval power.

I thank you for having procured for me the Dynamometer which I have safely recieved, as well as the plough. mr Coles will reimburse what you were so kind as to advance for me on that account. The letters which will be written you by the new Secretary of State (mr Smith) will say to you what is meant to be official. for altho' I too have written on politics, it is merely as a private individual, which I am now happily become. within two or three days I retire from scenes of difficulty, anxiety & of contending passions to the elysium of domestic affections & the irresponsible direction of my own affairs. safe in port myself, I shall look anxiously at my friends still buffeting the storm, and wish you all safe in port also. with my prayers for your happiness & prosperity, Accept the assurances of my sincere friendship & great respect.

TH: JEFFERSON

RC (NN: Thomas Jefferson Papers); at foot of first page: "Gen[l] Armstrong"; endorsed by Armstrong. PoC (DLC). Tr (MHi); posthumous copy.

John Armstrong (1758–1843), a native of Carlisle, Pennsylvania, attended the College of New Jersey and served as a Continental army staff officer during the Revolutionary War. After representing New York in the United States Senate, 1800–02 and 1803–04, he was appointed minister to France by TJ in June 1804, replacing his brother-in-law Robert R. Livingston. Armstrong held this appointment until 1810. He was commissioned a brigadier general during the War of 1812 and became James Madison's secretary of war in February 1813, resigning in September 1814 shortly after the British capture of Washington, for which he was widely blamed (*ANB*; *DAB*; *Princetonians*, 1776–83, pp. 4–14; *JEP*, 1:471, 473 [12, 20 Nov. 1804]; C. Edward Skeen, *John Armstrong, Jr., 1758–1843: A Biography* [1981]).

An AVISO is a ship commissioned to carry dispatches (*OED*). The BELLIGERENT EDICTS were Napoleon's Berlin and Milan decrees (1806 and 1807, respectively) allowing French ships to capture neutral vessels that visited British ports, and the British Orders in Council (November 1807), which established an economic blockade of European ports. On 1 Mar. 1809, shortly before its final adjournment, the Tenth Congress repealed the EMBARGO by enacting the Non-Intercourse Act, which opened trade with other countries but prohibited it with Great Britain and France. The Embargo Act of December 1807 had prohibited all ships in United States ports from sailing abroad. An early session of the Eleventh Congress was called for 22 MAY 1809 in order to review foreign policy.

TJ had wanted a DYNAMOMETER since 1796, although he did not then know what it was called. In May of that year William Strickland attempted to get him one in London. A spring-operated instrument for measuring the amount of energy exerted by an animal or any mechanical force, the dynamometer was used in testing a plough's resistance. TJ received a Guillaume PLOUGH from the Société d'agriculture du département de la Seine sometime in the spring of 1808 (*PTJ*, 29:115–6; Betts, *Farm Book*, 58; Betts, *Garden Book*, 372, 374, 376).

# From the Republicans of Georgetown

SIR George Town March 6th 1809

The republicans and friends of the late administration, of George Town, animated by the purest sentiments of gratitude and affection, beg leave to express to you those emotions inspired by the interesting crisis of your departure from public life.

Devoted as you have been for so long a period of time, to the service of your country, endeared by your unceasing cares for our national prosperity, can we reflect on your retirement from public duty without feelings of the liveliest nature! But Sir, your country can demand no more. You have contributed your share to the public weal. At the shrine of patriotism, long have you[1] sacrificed domestic ease and quiet.

When we reflect on the various & trying scenes thro which you have passed, from the dawn of our national existence to the present period; your unremitted exertions to promote the happiness of your country, and the signal success with which your labors have been crowned, we feel a reverential gratitude to that providence, who has conferred on us such an instrument of his favor:

In reviewing your long political career, from its commencement to the concluding scene, in the many and high departments you have filled, in times of war, and in times of peace, it is a matter of triumph to your fellow citizens, that you have ever pursued one undeviating course; in no instance, have you departed from those sublime principles, proclaimed by that charter, which declared our independence as a nation. Justice, moderation, and philanthropy have been the distinguishing characteristics of your public conduct, and in your late arduous and exalted station, your talents and virtues have shone with undiminished splendor:

To preserve peace, to promote agriculture, commerce, and manufactures, to diminish public burthens, to cement the union, and to perpetuate the rights and liberties of your country, these have been the grand objects of your unwearied efforts; Nor can we forget the enlargement of our empire, by the acquisition of territory incalculable in value.

Such has been your administration; May your successors profit by the illustrious example!

While we regret that your just and liberal policy has not exempted us from the rapacity of foreign nations, actuated solely by interest and ambition, we feel assured that no American[2] will hesitate to rally round the standard of his insulted country in defence of that freedom and independence, atchieved by the wisdom of sages, and consecrated by the blood of heroes.

With proud exultation we reflect that our country has produced patriots, whose memories will be inscribed in the temple of fame, among those immortal benefactors of man, who have delighted to employ their lives in mitigating the evils, and advancing the happiness of the human race: In this number Sir, Your name will stand eminently conspicuous.

In contimplating your domestic virtues and social qualities, the picture tho less dazzling is equally pleasing. Benevolence, generosity, and charity, those amiable ornaments of the human character, have been displayed by you in their fullest lustre, and those best acquainted with your private walks, are your most ardent and sincere admirers.

The applause of a grateful people, that brightest of rewards, will follow you to the shades of retirement, while the recollection of the past, and the prospect of the future will enliven your declining days.

Before we conclude the valedictory tribute, accept the genuine effusions of our hearts; May many years of health and happiness be yet in store for you! May you long enjoy that exalted felicity resulting from conscious rectitude, and may the evening of your life be as serene and tranquil, as its meridian has been resplendent & glorious.

J: MASON Chairman

DAN^L REINTZEL Secretary

MS (DLC); in Reintzel's hand, signed by Mason and Reintzel; at foot of text: "To Thomas Jefferson Esquire"; endorsed by TJ as an "Address repub. Geo.T." received 7 Mar. 1809 and so recorded in SJL. Printed with proceedings of meeting in Washington *National Intelligencer*, 13 Mar. 1809.

This address resulted from a public meeting at Semme's Tavern in Georgetown on this date. A committee consisting of Mason, Reintzel, Joseph Nourse, Alexander Scott, and Richard Parrott drafted it, after which the meeting unanimously approved it; ordered that it be presented to TJ by Mason, Mayor Thomas Corcoran, Scott, Parrott, and Tench Ringold; and voted that the address and TJ's reply be published.

John Mason (1766–1849), son of Virginia statesman George Mason, lived on Mason's Island (also known as Analostan or Barbadoes Island), in the Potomac River. Mason was a merchant and banker who served as brigadier general of the Washington militia after 1802 and commissary general of prisoners during the War of 1812. A member of the Columbian Agricultural Society for the Promotion of Rural and Domestic Economy, he was also involved in breeding merino sheep (Robert Rutland, ed., *The Papers of George Mason, 1725–1792* [1970], 1:lxxvii; Mary E. Curry, "Theodore Roosevelt Island: A Broken Link to Early Washington D.C. History," *RCHS* 48 [1971/72]: 20–1; Washington *National Intelligencer*, 21 Mar. 1849). Daniel Reintzel (ca. 1754–1828) served as mayor of Georgetown in 1796, 1799–1804, and 1806–07. In 1812 James Madison appointed him justice of the peace for Washington County, District of Columbia (*JEP*, 2:303, 306 [12, 23 Nov. 1812]; Washington *National Intelligencer*, 22 Nov. 1828).

1 Reintzel here canceled "laboured."
2 Manuscript: "Amecan."

# From Thomas Gimbrede

Union tavern George.—March the 6th 1809.

Mr Gimbrede has the honor to offer to Mr Jefferson a Little Sketch in Cameo, which if he should deem it worthy of his acceptance, he will please to receive it, as an evidence of my Esteem & high consideration, with an unfeigned wish that in your retirement—you may experience that tranquility & happiness that your usefulness in public Life has so Eminently entitled you to.

RC (DLC); dateline at foot of text; addressed "Mr Jefferson"; endorsed by TJ as received 6 Mar. 1809 from Georgetown and so recorded in SJL.

Thomas Gimbrede (1781–1832), engraver and miniature painter, immigrated to the United States from France in 1802. He was appointed instructor of drawing at the United States Military Academy at West Point in 1819 and held the position until his death (Mantle Fielding and Glenn B. Opitz, *Mantle Fielding's Dictionary of American Painters, Sculptors & Engravers*, 2d ed. [1986], 327; Washington *National Intelligencer*, 4 Jan. 1833).

The enclosed LITTLE SKETCH IN CAMEO, Gimbrede's engraving of *Tho: Jefferson the Pride of America* (New York, 1809), is reproduced elsewhere in this volume.

## To Alexander von Humboldt

Dear Sir Washington Mar. 6. 09.

I recieved safely your letter of May 30. & with it your astronomical work & Political essay on the kingdom of New Spain, for which I return you my sincere thanks. I had before heard that this work had begun to appear, & the specimen I have recieved proves that it will not disappoint the expectations of the learned. besides making known[1] to us one of the most singular & interesting countries on the globe, one almost locked up from the knolege of man hitherto, precious addition will be made to our stock of physical science, in many of it's parts. we shall bear to you therefore the honorable testimony that you have deserved well of the republic of letters.

You mention that you had before written other letters to me. be assured I have never recieved a single one, or I should not have failed to make my acknolegements of it. indeed I have not waited for that, but for the certain information, which I had not, of the place where you might be. your letter of May 30. first gave me that information. you have wisely located yourself in the focus of the science of Europe. I am held by the cords of love to my family & country, or I should certainly join you. within a few days I shall now bury myself in the groves of Monticello, & become a mere spectator of the passing events. on politics I will say nothing, because I would not implicate you by addressing to you the republican ideas of America, deemed horrible heresies by the royalism of Europe. you will know, before this reaches you, that mr Madison is my successor. this ensures to us a wise & honest administration. I salute you with sincere friendship & respect.

Th: Jefferson

RC (GyLeU); at foot of text: "M. le Baron Humboldt" and later presentation inscription by Humboldt to Konstantin Karl Falkenstein, a Dresden librarian: "Ich Sollle mich schamen immer Lobende Briefe mitzutheilen, aber hei der bosen Gewohnheit die ich habe, alles zu zerieissen um in allen Zustanden des Lehens, alles mitfuhrer zu konnen. bleibt mir unter dem Wenigen nicht zerstohrten keine Wahl fur Herr Bibl. Falkenstein uhrig, Den Tadel schreiben einem die Menschen Selten auf directem Wege. Humboldt" ("I should be ashamed of myself for always communicating letters of praise, but the bad habit I have of tearing everything up in order to be able to carry everything with me, no matter what life's conditions are, means that among the few not destroyed there is no choice for Librarian Falkenstein. People rarely fault one directly in writing." Humboldt translation in Ingo Schwarz, "From Alexander von Humboldt's Correspondence with Thomas Jefferson and Albert Gallatin" [Berlin: Alexander von Humboldt Research Center, 1991], 7). PoC (DLC).

Baron Friedrich Wilhelm Heinrich Alexander von Humboldt (1769–1859), a Berlin-born natural scientist and explorer, studied a broad range of disciplines, including archaeology, botany, ethnography, meteorology, and mineralogy. In

1799 he and fellow botanist Aimé Goujaud Bonpland began a five-year scientific expedition through South and Central America to study plant geography and collect quantitative data using a wide variety of scientific instruments. They returned via the United States, where in May 1804 they traveled to Philadelphia and Washington, meeting with TJ, Charles Willson Peale, and other scientists (*DSB*; Humboldt, *Personal Narrative*, trans. Jason Wilson [1995]; Helmut de Terra, "Alexander von Humboldt's Correspondence with Jefferson, Madison, and Gallatin," APS, *Proceedings* 103 [1959]: 783–806). Humboldt wrote about their scientific findings in a series entitled *Voyage aux régions équinoxiales du nouveau continent, fait en 1799, 1800, 1801, 1802, 1803, et 1804*, 34 vols. (Paris, 1805–34), which was divided into six subject groups as follows: (1) travel narratives (7 vols.). (2) zoology (2 vols.). (3) Mexico (3 vols.). (4) astronomy (3 vols.). (5) plant geography (1 vol.). (6) botany (18 vols.). He sent TJ segments of this work in parts that did not always correspond to the final volume numbering.

With his letter to TJ of 30 May 1808 (NNPM), Humboldt enclosed an ASTRONOMICAL volume from group four, *Recueil d'observations astronomiques, d'opérations trigonométriques et de mesures barométriques faites pendant le cours d'un voyage aux régions équinoxiales du nouveau continent, depuis 1799 jusqu'en 1803* (Paris, 1808); and two parts from group three on NEW SPAIN, *Essai politique sur le royaume de la Nouvelle-Espagne: ouvrage qui presente des recherches sur la geographie du Mexique* (Paris, 1808–19; Sowerby, no. 4157).

[1] Manuscript: "knon."

# Notes on Presidential Appointments

[ca. 6 Mar. 1809]

| | | | | candidates |
|---|---|---|---|---|
| [Sec]retary of State | | | | |
| War | | | | |
| [Missisi]pi | Gov$^{r}$ | v.[1] | Williams | Holmes. |
| [Missisipi?] | Judge | v. | Bruin | Martin |
| | | | | Poindexter |
| Illinois | Gov$^{r}$ | | | Boyle |
| | 3. judges | | | King |
| Newbury port | Collector v. | | | Varnum. Cook. |
| | Inspector | | | |
| Richm$^{d}$ | Loan off$^{r}$ | v. | Page. | Nelson |
| | | | | Barbour |
| | | | | Smith |
| | | | | Selden |
| | | | | Hylton |
| | | | | M$^{c}$rae |
| | | | | Munford |
| | | | | Robertson |

| | | | | |
|---|---|---|---|---|
| Brazil | Consul | | | Parker<br>Hill<br>Jarvis |
| Western road | Comm$^r$ | v. | Kerr | |
| Tunis | Consul | v. | Coxe | Keteltas |
| Tripoli | Consul | v. | Davis | |
| Paris | Consul | v. | Skipwith | Warden. Russel |
| Chickasaw | Agent | v. | Wright | Timothy Meigs.<br>David Hog. |

MS (current location unknown; photostat in TJ Editorial Files); written entirely in TJ's hand on a ragged scrap, the verso of which is a reused address cover to "The President of the U. States"; undated; left margin frayed.

TJ probably compiled these notes on unfilled offices and CANDIDATES for them for use in briefing incoming president James Madison. He most likely prepared the list no earlier than 1 Mar. 1809, when he sent the Senate his final nomination letter, and no later than 6 Mar. 1809, when Madison sent nominations for a majority of these posts to the Senate (*JEP*, 2:113–4, 118–9).

[1] Here and below, the abbreviation is for "vice," meaning "in place of."

# From Nathaniel Rochester and William L. Brent

SIR Hagers Town March 6$^{th}$ 1809

In conformity to a resolution entered into by the republican Citizens of Washington County in the State of Maryland, assembled at Hagers Town, we, the Chairman and the Secretary of the meeting, have the honor of transmitting to you the following extract from their proceedings.—we remain with sentiments of the highest esteem and respect yrs,

N. ROCHESTER
W$^M$ L. BRENT

"A[1] numerous meeting of the republicans of Washington County, in the state of Maryland, was convened by public notice, at the Court-house square in Hager's Town, on the 4$^{th}$ day of March 1809, for the purpose of celebrating a day, which will ever be hailed, with joy by the friends of freedom in these United States, as a time when correct political principles, eight years ago, obtained the ascendence over a party, whose obnoxious measures whilst in power, deservedly lost them the confidence of the people, and also to celebrate the exaltation of James Maddison to the presidential chair.—

The day was ushered in, by the ringing of bells, martial music and the firing of canon.—at 12 oClk M. William L. Brent Esq[r] delivered an address to the meeting and recommended the propriety of entering into resolutions, expressive of their sentiments on the political situation of our Country and also the propriety of addressing the late President of the united States.—Col[o] Nathaniel Rochester was then appointed Chairman and W[m] L. Brent Esq[r] Secretary of the meeting.

After the meeting had passed several resolutions, expressive of their sentiments upon the situation of their Country, on motion made it was

resolved, that William L. Brent Esq[r], Maj[r] Martin Kersner, Col[o] Jacob Schnebly, Cap[t] Henry Lewis and Col[o] Nath Rochester, be a committee to prepare and report a Suitable address to Tho[s] Jefferson, late President of the united States, upon his retiring from office.

The committee, after retiring for a short time, returned and reported the following address, which was unanimously received and approved of by the meeting.

Much respected Sir:

Upon Your retiring from the first office in the gift of Your Country, permit the republican Citizens of Washington County in the State of Maryland, in full meeting assembled, to express their earliest gratitude for the Services You have rendered these united States.—When the rights and liberties of the numerous and patriotic Citizens of these extensive States, were in imminent danger: When the inveterate foreign enemies of our Liberty and Independence, were not more assiduous to forge fetters for us, than many of our disaffected, disappointed Citizens were diligent to delude the people and zealous to persuade them to oppose "the best government under Heaven": When the growing wealth of our Country, was benumbed and almost parylised by the extended hand of oppressive taxation: At this alarming period—eight years ago,—You were called upon by the voice of your Country to rule her destinies and to guard her rights and Liberty.—The voice of millions, whose interests were blended with Your administration, will testify, that you have done it faithfully: and when that time arrives, (and Soon it must in the course of nature), when the man is no more, and nothing is left but his virtues and his reputation, the unerring and impartial page of history, shall record your transcendent Services to your Country and the wisdom, virtue and patriotism by which you were actuated.—

We cannot refrain from expressing the overflowing gratitude of our hearts, for the happiness, prosperity, and peace, this our beloved Country enjoyed, at a time, when all Europe was visited,[2] by the distressing calamities of war.—It was to You, worthy Sir! and to your administration, we were indebted, for such infinite blessings. We venerate the wisdom and admire that policy of your late administration, which abrogated internal taxes,—decreased public expenditure—reduced the national debt and annexed to our national domain the immense territory of Louisiana and Secured to us forever, the wealth and incalculable sources of commerce, which flow down the Missisippi and Missouri and their tributary streams.—These are but few of the great measures of Your administration, which We approve.—We highly estimate the wisdom of your counsel, the purity of motives and the goodness of heart, which have uniformly guided Your public conduct: and permit us to express our fullest reliance on the late great leading measures of Your administration, dictated by patriotism and wisdom, as the most Salutary alternative to war—or a Submission of our rights as a free and independent republic: that they would have been productive of the most happy effects, had they not been frustrated by causes disgraceful to a certain portion of our Citizens, which we as americans deprecate, detest and Sincerely deplore.—

You have now retired to the "humble station" of a private Citizen: You will carry with you into the shades of retirement, all the tender endearing Sympathies and regrets of a people, attached to you from principle, and grateful for the services You have rendered these united States—Trophies! more honorable to the friend of Liberty and Independence, than "the blood stained steel" or the "tattered flag" of the "tented field."—The former is the trophy of republican Patriots—the latter only of Kings and Despots.—Accept this, as the strongest, last, best Testimonial of our admiration for Your wisdom; as the sincere expression of our gratitude for your distinguished Services and as the only proof we can now give, of our veneration for Your character.—

In retirement, we wish you every blessing and happiness, which this casual and illfated life can bestow and when You pass into "the valley of shades" "from which no traveller returns," may Your virtues be the theme of every american tongue, and may "unborn ages" profit by Your glorious example of wisdom, virtue and patriotism, must be the heartfelt wish of every true american.

resolved that a copy of the above adress be forwarded to the late President of the united States.

N. ROCHESTER Chairman
W^M L. BRENT. Secretary

RC (DLC); in Brent's hand, signed by Rochester and Brent; endorsed by TJ as an "Address rep. cit. Wash^n c^ty Mar^d" received 16 Mar. 1809 and so recorded in SJL. Printed in *Maryland Herald, and Hager's-Town Weekly Advertiser*, 10 Mar. 1809.

Nathaniel Rochester (1752–1831) was born in Westmoreland County and moved in 1783 to Hagerstown, Maryland. There he founded the Hagerstown Bank and served as a state legislator, postmaster, county court judge, and sheriff. Rochester represented Washington County in the House of Delegates in 1790, and in 1808 he was a presidential elector. In 1810 he moved his family to the Genesee Valley in New York, where he later founded the city of Rochester (*DAB*; Blake McKevey, "Colonel Nathaniel Rochester," *Rochester History* 24 [1962]: 1–23; Papenfuse, *Maryland Public Officials*, 1:264).

William Leigh Brent (1784–1848) was born in Charles County, Maryland, served in the Maryland legislature, practiced law in Hagerstown, and represented Washington County in the House of Delegates in 1809. He moved to Louisiana, which he represented in the United States House of Representatives, 1823–29 (*Biog. Dir. Cong.*; Papenfuse, *Maryland Public Officials*, 1:264; Washington *National Intelligencer*, 19 July 1848).

On behalf of the meeting, Rochester and Brent sent James Madison a similar message of support on the same day (Madison, *Papers, Pres. Ser.*, 1:25–6).

[1] Manuscript lacks closing quotation mark.

[2] Word interlined in place of "convulsed."

# To Margaret Bayard Smith

Washington Mar. 6. 09

Th: Jefferson presents his respectful salutations to mrs Smith, and sends her the Geranium she expressed a willingness to recieve. it is in very bad condition, having been neglected latterly as not intended to be removed. he cannot give it his parting blessing more effectually than by consigning it to the nourishing hand of mrs Smith. if plants have sensibility, as the analogy of their organisation with ours seems to indicate, it cannot but be proudly sensible of her fostering attentions. of his regrets at parting with the society of Washington, a very sensible portion attaches to mrs Smith, whose friendship he has particularly valued. her promise to visit Monticello is some consolation; and he can assure her she will be recieved with open arms & hearts by the whole family. he prays her to accept the homage of his affectionate attachment & respect.

RC (DLC: TJ Papers, ser. 9); dateline at foot of text; addressed: "Mrs S. H. Smith." PoC (CSmH: JF-BA); endorsed by TJ.

Smith wrote that TJ's personal space in the President's House had windows filled with "stands for the flowers and plants which it was his delight to attend" (Smith, *Forty Years*, 385).

## To Samuel H. Smith

Mar. 6. 09.

Th: Jefferson asks the favor of mr Smith to print for him 100. copies of the within letter each on a separate sheet of 4$^{to}$ letter paper. he would be glad to have them by Thursday evening if practicable. he salutes him with esteem & respect.

RC (DLC: Henley Smith Papers); dateline at foot of text; endorsed by Smith. Not recorded in SJL.

Samuel Harrison Smith (1772–1845) was born in Philadelphia and received an A.B. from the University of the State of Pennsylvania in 1787. He opened a printing business in Philadelphia in 1791 and published two comparatively short-lived periodicals before achieving success with the *Universal Gazette* in 1797. That same year his essay promoting free public schools, published as *Remarks on Education* (Philadelphia, 1798), won him an award from the American Philosophical Society and brought him to TJ's attention. TJ appreciated Smith's moderate Republicanism and in 1800 urged him to move the *Gazette* to Washington, D.C. Although the election was still in doubt, Smith complied and began the tri-weekly *National Intelligencer and Washington Advertiser* on 31 Oct. 1800, continuing the *Universal Gazette* as its weekly counterpart. For the duration of his presidency, the *Intelligencer* served as TJ's journalistic spokesman, and Smith also benefited from lucrative government printing contracts. In September 1810 he sold the paper to Joseph Gales Jr. Smith accepted a position as commissioner of revenue in 1813, served briefly as secretary of the treasury in 1814, and was president successively of the Bank of Washington and the Washington branch of the Second Bank of the United States. He was also active in the American Colonization Society, the Washington City Library, and the Washington National Monument Society (*ANB*; *DAB*; Brigham, *American Newspapers*, 1:103–4, 106–7, 2:927, 960; William E. Ames, *A History of the National Intelligencer* [1972]).

ENCLOSURE

### Circular to Office Seekers

THE friendship which has long subsisted between the President of the United States and myself gave me reason to expect, on my retirement from office, that I might often receive applications to interpose with him on behalf of persons desiring appointments. Such an abuse of his dispositions towards me would necessarily lead to the loss of them, and to the transforming me from the character of a friend to that of an unreasonable and troublesome solicitant. It therefore became necessary for me to lay down as a law for my future conduct never to interpose in any case, either with him or the Heads of Departments (from whom it must go to him) in any application whatever for office. To this rule I must scrupulously adhere; for were I to depart from it in a single instance, I could no longer plead it with truth to my friends in excuse for my not complying with their requests. I hope therefore that the declining it in the present, as in every other case, will be ascribed to its true cause, the obligation of this general law, and not to any disinclination existing in this particular case; and still less to an unwillingness to be useful to my friends on all occasions not forbidden by a special impropriety.

Printed form (unused specimens at DLC: Henley Smith Papers and MHi); undated. Dft (DLC: Henley Smith Papers); entirely in TJ's hand; undated; addressed: "M$^{r}$ Samuel H. Smith." PoC (DLC: TJ Papers, 187:33232). Not recorded in SJL.

TJ employed this printed form in a letter to William Tunnicliff, 23 Jan. 1810, adding a salutation, date, conclusion: "I pray you to accept this with indulgence in answer to your favor of the 13$^{th}$ inst. and with it the assurances of my esteem & respect," and his signature (FC in DLC, at foot of text: "William Tunnicliff"; recorded in SJL).

# Account with John Barnes

The President of the U States

To John Barnes,

| | | | | |
|---|---|---|---|---|
| 1809. | | | | |
| Feb$^{y}$ 8$^{th}$ | for 12$^{lb}$ dipt Candles | @ 20$^{d}$ | 1. 0 | |
| " | 2$^{lb}$ Imperial tea | 17/6. | 1.17.6 | |
| | | | | 2.17. 6 |
| 9$^{th}$ | 9½$^{lb}$ loaf Sugar | 1/10½ | 17.4½ | |
| 10 | 37½ Mus sugar | 13$^{d}$ | 2 0.7½ | |
| " | 2 gall$^{s}$ Old Tenniss | 15/ | 1.10 | |
| | | | | 4. 8. |
| 13 | 8$^{lb}$ 3. loaf sugar | 1/10½ | 15.4½ | |
| " | 2$^{lb}$ Cinnimen | d$^{o}$ | 3.9. | |
| | | | | 19. 1½ |
| 16 | 12$^{lb}$ Sperm$^{e}$ Candles | 4/6. | 2.14 | |
| " | 12$^{lb}$ Moulds d$^{o}$ | 1/10½ | 1. 2.6. | |
| " | 1$^{lb}$ Black pepper | " | . 3.9 | |
| " | 8$^{lb}$ 15. loaf sugar | 1/10½ | .16.9. | |
| | | | | 4 17– |
| 18 | 7 4 supr Fine loaf | 2/6. | | 18. 1½ |
| 20 | 2½ gall$^{s}$ Sperm Oil | 11/3 | 1. 8.1½ | |
| " | 2 Bottles salad d$^{o}$ | 7/6 | .15 | |
| | | | | 2 3. 1½ |
| 22 | 25$^{lb}$ Coffee | 2/6 | | 3 2.6. |
| 25 | ¼$^{b}$ Mus$^{o}$ sugar | \$16 | | 1 10. |
| Mar 2 | 6$^{lb}$ 8 loaf | 1/10½ | 12.2 | |
| " | ½ Imperial | 17/6 | 8.9 | |
| " | ½ Hyson skin | 7/6 | 3.9. | |
| | | | | 1 4 8 |
| | for Amo$^{t}$ car$^{d}$ on | | | £22. 0–0½ |

[*Page 2:*]

| | | | | | |
|---|---|---|---|---|---|
| " | 4 | 1 galls Cogniac | | | 18.9. |
| " | 7 | 6lb Mould Candles | 1/10½ | 11 3. | |
| | | 6lb Muso sugar | 13d | 6.6. | |
| | | | | | 17.9. |
| " | | Equal to $ 63 52/100 | EE | | £23 16.6½ |
| " | | George Town. | | | |
| " | | 7th March 1809. JOHN BARNES. | | | |

MS (ViU: TJP); in Barnes's hand; repeated intermediate sum at head of p. 2 omitted.

John Barnes (ca. 1731–1826) emigrated from England to America about 1760. He was a tea merchant and grocer in New York and Philadelphia, relocating to the latter city when the federal government moved there in 1791. Barnes remained in Philadelphia until 1800, when he moved to Washington to serve as a contractor with the Treasury Department. TJ had known him for many years and appointed him customs collector at Georgetown in 1806, a position Barnes held until his death. He was TJ's banker and commission agent, helped him manage the investments of Tadeusz Kosciuszko and William Short, and supplied him with groceries from 1795 until TJ's retirement (Cordelia Jackson, "John Barnes, A Forgotten Philanthropist of Georgetown," *RCHS* 7 [1904]: 39–48; *MB*, 2:927; *The New-York Directory, and Register, for the Year 1790* [New York, 1790], 11; Clement Biddle, *The Philadelphia Directory* [Philadelphia, 1791], 6; Washington *National Intelligencer*, 14 Nov. 1800; TJ to John Peter Muhlenberg, 10 Oct. 1802, 30 June 1803 [DLC]; *JEP*, 2:44, 45 [15, 17 Dec. 1806]; Washington *Daily National Intelligencer*, 17 Feb. 1826).

HYSON SKIN is a green tea made from the light and inferior leaves separated from hyson by a winnowing machine.

# To Thomas Gimbrede

Washington Mar. 7. 09.

Th: Jefferson presents his compliments to mr Gimbrede and his thanks for the very elegant Cameo he has been so kind as to send him. he considers it as a flattering mark of the indulgence with which mr Gimbrede has been so good as to contemplate his public conduct, and it adds to the consolation he recieves from the testimony of the worthy that the purity of his intentions, at least, has atoned for whatever of error he may have involuntarily committed. he salutes mr Gambrede with thankfulness & respect.

PoC (DLC); dateline at foot of text; endorsed by TJ.

## From William Ray

Amsterdam, Montgomery County, New York State,

SIR, March 7th 1809;

On the 28th of Decr last, I received your letter of the 14th in which you are pleased to observe—"that you should have read the book* I sent you with more satisfaction, had you found the author's position in it more equal to his talents." All men are fond of receiving satisfaction, and I trust, Sir, you will encrease yours by contributing to make some alteration in my position; which is a very disagreeable one indeed. A great part of my late publication lies in the hands of a knavish printer, and if I can not raise money to redeem it, will be sacrificed. I have an indigent family, and this has been our chief hopes for support.

I am unable to labor, and my health is too much impaired to attend to any business at present. Poverty and starvation stare me in the face—My friends who would assist me are unable to do it. To whom shall I go?—With about One hundred Dollars I could redeem my publication (4,000 books) and place myself and family above present want. I have tried in vain to raise this sum—money is scarce in this quarter, and I fear I shall lose all my dependence. I hope therefore you will deem it no imposition when I ask you to grant me the loan of the above sum. I doubt not but I might refund it in the course of at most 4 or 5 years. I have applied to you as my last resort, and I ask the favor of you with conscious honesty and full hopes of success.

Wishing you all the happiness in your retirement which Heaven can bestow, I am, Sir, with unabated Esteem, your most obt Huml Servt

WM RAY

*Horrors of Slavery

RC (DLC: Madison Papers); with author's note in left margin of first page; addressed: "Thomas Jefferson, Esquire, Late President of the United States Washington"; franked and postmarked; endorsed by TJ as received 23 Mar. 1809 and so recorded (with the notation: "P.") in SJL. Enclosed in TJ to James Madison, 24 Mar. 1809.

William Ray (1771–1827) was captured near Tripoli on board the USS *Philadelphia* in 1803. He wrote about his ensuing nineteen months in captivity in *Horrors of Slavery: or, The American Tars in Tripoli, containing an account of the loss and capture of the United States frigate Philadelphia* (Troy, N.Y., 1808; Sowerby, no. 320). Ray subsequently became a merchant and magistrate, published poetry and a novel, and edited the Elizabethtown (N.Y.) *Reveille* (1812–16) and Onondaga *Gazette* (1816) (Ray, *Poems, on Various Subjects, Religious, Moral, Sentimental and Humorous* [Auburn, N.Y., 1821], with autobiography, 199–252; Paul Baepler, ed., *White Slaves, African Masters: An Anthology of American Barbary Captivity Narratives* [1999], 187; Brigham, *American Newspapers*, 1:570, 713).

Ray quoted from TJ's brief LETTER OF THE 14TH Dec. 1808 (ViW: TC-JP) acknowledging receipt of *Horrors of Slavery*. The KNAVISH PRINTER may have been Oliver Lyon, its publisher.

# To the Republicans of Georgetown

The affectionate address of the Republicans of George Town on my retirement from public duty, is received with sincere pleasure. in the review of my political life, which they so indulgently take, if it be found that I have done my duty as other faithful Citizens have done, it is all the merit I claim. Our lot has been cast on an Awful period of human history. the contest which began with us which ushered in the dawn of our National existence and led us through various and trying Scenes, was for every thing dear to free born man. the principles on which we engaged, of which the charter of our independence is the record, were sanctioned by the laws of our being, and we but Obeyed them in pursuing undeviatingly the course they called for. it issued finally in that inestimable state of freedom which alone can ensure to man the enjoyment of his equal rights. from the moment which sealed our peace & independence our nation has wisely pursued the paths of peace & justice. during the period in which I have been charged with it's concerns no effort has been spared to exempt us from the wrongs and the rapacity of foreign Nations, and with you I feel assured that no American will hesitate to rally round the standard of his insulted country, in defence of that freedom and independence atchieved by the wisdom of Sages, and consecrated by the blood of Heroes.

The favorable testimony of those among whom I have lived, and lived happily, as a fellow citizen, as a neighbor, and in the various relations of social life, will enliven the days of my retirement and be felt and cherished with affection & gratitude.

I thank you, fellow citizens, for your kind prayers for my future happiness. I shall ever retain a lively sense of your friendly attentions, and continue to pray for your prosperity and well being—

Th: Jefferson
Mar. 8. 09.

FC (DLC); in the hand of Isaac A. Coles, signed and dated by TJ; at head of text in TJ's hand: "To the Republicans of George town." Printed in Washington *National Intelligencer*, 13 Mar. 1809. Recorded in SJL as "Answer to Republicans of Geo. T."

# Account with Joseph Milligan

[8–10 Mar. 1809]

Thomas Jefferson Esq[r]

| | | | | |
|---|---|---|---|---|
| 1807 | | To Joseph Milligan | | |
| November | 7[th] | To 1 Malthus on population—<br>2 vols Calf Gilt | | $ 8–00 |
| 1808 | | | | |
| March | 8 | To 1 Middletons Cicero 3 vols calf Gilt | | 10–50 |
| | " | To 1 M[c]Mahons gardeners calender | | 3–50 |
| " | 31 | To 1 Bells Anatomy plates 4 vols | | 20 00 |
| | " | To 1 Bartons Botany Boards | | 6 00 |
| April | 30 | | | |
| | | To Binding | | |
| | | " Columbiad calf Gilt 4[to] | $4–00 | |
| | | " Agriculture de Serres<br>2 vols 4[to] | $6 00 | |
| | | " Histoire de Pologne 4 vols 8[vo] | 4–00 | |
| | | " Ramseys washington—8[vo] | 1–00 | |
| | | " Corinne 3 vols 12mo | 1–50 | |
| | | " Ditto 2 vols 8[vo] | 2–00 | |
| | | " Ainsworths Dictionary 2 vols | 2–00 | |
| | | " Maxime de Tyr 2 vols | 2 00 | |
| | | " Pharmicopia of Boston | 0 50 | |
| | | " Societe D,Agriculture<br>4 vols ½ Bound | 2 00 | |
| | | " Poudre par Cossigne | 0 50 | |
| | | " Burrs Trial | 0 50 | |
| | | " Memoirs Agricoles 1806 | 0 50 | |
| | | " Nautical Almanack 1797 | 0 50 | |
| | | " Connaisance de Tems | 0 50 | |
| | | " Le Vin par Cossigne | 0 50 | |
| May | 2[nd] | " Preface de Ballendenies | 0 50 | 28–50 |
| | | " Life of Cumberland | | 2–00 |
| | 7 | " Coopers Surgery | | 2–75 |
| | " | " Childrens Books as ℔<br>Bill furnished | | 7–68 |
| June | 13 | " Spences pamphlet | | 0–50 |
| July | 13 | " Broughams Speech | | 0–37½ |
| | 14 | " Examination of the conduct of<br>Great[1] Britain | | 0–37½ |
| | | Amount carried over | | $90–18 |

[*Page 2:*]

| | | | | | |
|---|---|---|---|---|---|
| 1808 | | | | | |
| September | 3rd | To | Binding | | |
| | | | State papers 3 vols 8vo—75 | $2–25 | |
| | " | " | Ditto 1 vol folio | 1–50 | |
| | " | " | Dictionary of the Bible | $2–00 | $5–75 |
| October | 14th | " | Foxes Historical Work | | 2–50 |
| 1809 | | | | | |
| January | | " | Conversations[2] on chemistry 2 vols | | 5–00 |
| Feby | 17 | " | Scientific dialogues 6 vols | | 5–75 |
| | 24 | | Binding | | |
| | " | " | American Philosophical Transactions | $2 00 | |
| | | " | Vocabularie Marine de L,Escalies | $4–50 | |
| | " | " | Physics ½ Bound | 1–50 | |
| | " | " | Poems | 1–50 | |
| | " | " | Political | 1–50 | |
| | " | " | Louisiana | 1–50 | |
| | " | " | Arts | 1–00 | |
| | " | " | Commercis de Romani | 1–00 | |
| | " | " | Agriculture | 1–00 | |
| | " | " | Ship New Jersey | 1–00 | |
| | " | " | Political American 2 vols 8vo | 1–00 | |
| | " | " | Medecine | 0–75 | |
| | " | " | Local | 0–75 | |
| | " | " | Political English 1805–7 | 0–75 | |
| | " | " | Ditto 1808 | 0–75 | |
| | " | " | Ditto American 1806 | 0–75 | |
| | " | " | Historical | 0–75 | |
| | " | " | Yellow Fever | 0–75 | |
| | " | " | Arts | 0–75 | |
| | " | " | personal | 0–75 | |
| | " | " | Religious | 0–75 | |
| | " | " | Agricultural | 0–75 | |
| | " | " | Orations | 0–50 | |
| | " | " | Natural History | 0–50 | |
| | " | " | Military | 0–50 | |
| | " | " | Topographical | 0–50 | |
| | " | " | Fine Arts | 0–50 | |
| | " | " | Gregoire des Negers | 0–50 | |
| | | | | $28–75 | $109–18 |

[*Page 3:*]
1809

| | | | | |
|---|---|---|---|---|
| | | Binding | | |
| February | 24 | To Lastirie du Cottonier 8vo | $00–50 | |
| | " | " Natural Philosophy | 00–50 | |
| | " | " Canals | 00 50 | |
| | " | " Mathematical | 00 37½ | |
| | " | " Commerce | 00 37½ | |
| | " | " Manufacturies | 00 25 | |
| | " | " Societe de Agriculture vol 10th | 00 50 | |
| | " | " Ecoles Normales vol 6th | 00 50 | |
| | " | " Foxs History Calf Gilt | 1 00 | |
| | " | " Ludlows Memoirs—Do 3 vols | 3 00 | |
| | " | " Fables | 0 50 | $36–75 |
| March | 8 | Binding | | |
| | | " Conversations on Chemistry 2 vols | $1–50 | |
| | " | " Batture 1808 | 0–50 | |
| | " | " Ditto 4to 1808 | 0–75 | |
| | " | " Political 1808 | 0–50 | |
| | " | " Embargo 1808 | 0–50 | |
| | " | " Louisiana | 0–75 | |
| | " | " Voyage de Humboldt (Boards) | 0–50 | |
| | " | " Hortus Siccus—Crowninshield | 0–75 | |
| | " | " Penmanship Morocco Gilt | 1–25 | |
| | " | " Newspapers 9 vols | $22–50 | |
| | " | " Blue Morocco case | 1–50 | |
| | " | " Letter List | 2 00 | $33 00 |
| | | Cr | | 178–93 |
| | | By 2 Setts Mrs Warrens American war | $12–00 | |
| | | By 2 Maps U States—7 00 | | |
| | | | 14–00 | $26 00 |
| | | | | $152–93 |

MS (DLC: TJ Papers, 187:33189–90); in Milligan's hand; undated; repeated intermediate sums at head of pp. 2–3 omitted; on verso of last page: "Thomas Jefferson Esqr in A/C with Joseph Milligan"; endorsed by TJ.

Joseph Milligan (d. 1834), Georgetown bookseller and binder, succeeded John March's widow in 1808 as proprietor of the first bookstore in Washington, on M Street. Milligan aspired to be a magazine editor but his 1811 quarterly, the *Literary Visitor*, lasted only briefly. He operated the Union Circulating Library from his shop in 1815 (Bryan, *National Capital*, 2:336, 589; Washington *National Intelligencer*, 22 Apr. 1808, 10

Sept. 1834). TJ settled this account with Milligan on 10 Mar. 1809 (*MB*, 2:1242).

Further details on the following collections of short works bound by Milligan can be gleaned with reasonable confidence from TJ's manuscript library catalogue or the printed catalogue of books acquired by the Library of Congress in 1815: PHYSICS (Sowerby, 1:321); LOUISIANA (bill of 24 Feb. 1809) (Sowerby, nos. 3469–74); POLITICAL ENGLISH 1805–7 (Sowerby, nos. 2809–14); DITTO 1808 (Sowerby, nos. 3359–64); DITTO AMERICAN 1806 (Sowerby, nos. 3348–55); YELLOW FEVER (Sowerby, nos. 972–8); RELIGIOUS (Sowerby, nos. 1679–1706); NATURAL PHILOSOPHY (Sowerby, nos. 3770–9); CANALS (Sowerby, nos. 1233–6); BATTURE 1808 (Sowerby, no. 3484); DITTO 4TO 1808 (Sowerby, nos. 3485–92); EMBARGO 1808 (Sowerby, nos. 3448–64); LOUISIANA (bill of 8 Mar. 1809) (Sowerby, nos. 3475–83).

[1] Manuscript: "Geat."

[2] Manuscript: "Convesations."

# To William Short

DEAR SIR — Washington Mar. 8. 09.

It is with much concern I inform you that the Senate has negatived your appointment. we thought it best to keep back the nomination to the close of the session, that the mission might remain secret as long as possible, which you know was our purpose from the beginning. it was then sent in with an explanation of it's object & motives. we took for granted, if any hesitation should arise, that the Senate would take time, & that our friends in that body would make enquiries of us, & give us the opportunity of explaining & removing objections. but to our great surprize, & with an unexampled precipitancy, they rejected it at once. this reception of the last of my official communications, to them, could not be unfelt, nor were the causes of it spoken out by them. under this uncertainty, mr Madison, on his entering into office, proposed another person (John Q. Adams.) he also was negatived, & they adjourned sine die. our subsequent information was that, on your nomination, your long absence from this country, & their idea that you do not intend to return to it had very sensible weight: but that all other motives were superceded by an unwillingness to extend our diplomatic connections, & a desire even to recall the foreign ministers we already have. all were sensible of the great virtues, the high character, the powerful influence, & valuable friendship of the emperor. but riveted to the system of unentanglement with Europe, they declined the proposition. on this subject you will recieve the official explanations from mr Smith, the Secretary of state. I pray you to place me rectus in curiâ in this business, with the emperor, and to assure him that I carry into my retirement the[1] highest veneration for his virtues and[2] fondly cherish the belief that his dispositions &

power are destined by heaven to better, in some degree at least, the condition of oppressed man.

I have nothing new to inform you as to your private friends or acquaintances. our embargo has worked hard. it has in fact federalised three of the N. England states. Connecticut you know was so before. we have substituted for it a non-intercourse with France and England & their dependancies,[3] and a trade to all other places. it is probable the belligerents will take our vessels under their edicts, in which case we shall probably declare war against them.

I write this in the midst of packing & preparing for my departure, of visits of leave & interruptions of every kind. I must therefore conclude with my affectionate Adieux, to you, & assurances of my constant attachment & respect.

TH: JEFFERSON

RC (ViW: TJP); at foot of first page: "M[r] Short"; endorsed by Short. PoC (DLC).

William Short (1759–1849), diplomat, businessman, and TJ's longtime friend and frequent correspondent, graduated from the College of William and Mary in 1779. Short acted as TJ's private secretary in Paris from 1785 to 1789 and remained there as chargé d'affaires, hoping to be appointed minister plenipotentiary to France. In 1792 he was instead appointed minister resident at The Hague and served as treaty commissioner to Spain from 1793 to 1795, when Thomas Pinckney replaced him. Short then lived in Paris until 1802, when he moved to Philadelphia. During his seventeen years abroad, TJ managed some of Short's funds and loaned himself some of them to invest in his own nail manufactory and flour mill, money he did not repay until 1815. Short returned to Paris in September 1808 with an interim appointment as minister to Russia. After he failed to be confirmed in this post, he left Europe in 1810 and settled permanently in Philadelphia, amassing a large fortune through investments with Dutch bankers and land purchases in Kentucky and New York and serving as an officer of the American Colonization Society (*ANB*; *DAB*; George Green Shackelford, *Jefferson's Adoptive Son: The Life of William Short, 1759–1848* [1993]).

The SENATE rejected TJ's nomination of Short as minister plenipotentiary at Saint Petersburg on 27 Feb. 1809, due in part to his long ABSENCE from the United States, which Senator Samuel Taggart believed had rendered Short "a mere Frenchman." The Senate further concluded that Russo-American diplomatic intercourse could be handled adequately by other public agents, making any appointment "inexpedient and unnecessary" (Taggart to John Taylor, 28 Feb. 1809, in George H. Haynes, ed., "Letters of Samuel Taggart," American Antiquarian Society, *Proceedings* 33 [1923]: 335–6; *JEP*, 2:112, 113 [24, 25, 27 Feb. 1809]).

RECTUS IN CURIÂ: innocent, set right in point of law (*OED*).

[1] Manuscript: "the the."

[2] Preceding two words substituted for "character."

[3] Preceding three words interlined.

# To John Threlkeld

Mar. 8. 09.

Th: Jefferson presents his compliments to mr Threlkeld and takes the liberty of asking a few small[1] plants of the English mulberry & peach-Apricot, of which mr Threlkeld thought he could spare some. Th:J. can convey only such & so many as are very portable, & will occupy but little space. he begs leave to present to mr & mrs Threlkeld & family his friendly Adieux, and assurances of his sincere attachment & respect.

RC (Berkeley Cox Jr., Hartford, Connecticut, 1969); dateline at foot of text; addressed: "Mr Threlkeld." Not recorded in SJL.

John Threlkeld (ca. 1758–1830) was a lifelong resident of Georgetown and justice of the peace who represented Montgomery County in the Maryland House of Delegates in 1792 and 1793 and served a one-year term as mayor of Georgetown in the latter year. He helped found the Columbian Agricultural Society for the Promotion of Rural and Domestic Economy in 1809 and frequently exchanged cuttings of fruit trees and other plant specimens with TJ during the latter's presidency (Grace Dunlop Ecker, *A Portrait of Old George Town* [1933], 85–6; Papenfuse, *Maryland Public Officials*, 1:229; Betts, *Garden Book*, 344–5, 353; Washington *National Intelligencer*, 9 Sept. 1830).

[1] Word interlined.

# From John Threlkeld

Wednesday [8 Mar. 1809]

Mr Threlkeld sends Mr Jefferson three English Mulberys on American ones, & five Peach Apricots he reccommends great attention to be paid by the Waggonner to them as the Shoots are but Small in[1] some, & may co[me] off. Mr Threlkeld & Family wish Mr Jefferson all health and happiness & that respect & regard from his fellow Citizens in his retirement he is so justly Entitled to

RC (MHi); partially dated at foot of text; torn at fold and corners; addressed: "Thomas Jefferson Esqr"; with endorsement by TJ (torn) as a letter of 8 Mar. [1809]. Recorded in SJL as a letter of 8 Mar. 1809 received the same date.

Threlkeld grafted ENGLISH MULBERYS onto the AMERICAN mulberry tree.

[1] Manuscript: "is."

# Notes on Expenses

| | | | | D |
|---|---|---|---|---|
| 1809. Mar. 9. | Balance at the bank in favor of Th: Jefferson | | | $2291.77\frac{1}{2}$ |
| | a warrant from the Treasury | | | 1148. |
| | | | | $3439.77\frac{1}{2}$[1] |
| | Th:J. proposes to draw as follows | | | |
| | J. Barnes | 1000. | | |
| | Lemaire about | 768.84[2] | | |
| | I. A. Coles | 140 | | |
| | Jos. Milligan | 152.93 | | |
| | John Cox | 22.50[3] | | |
| | Peter Lenox | 16.[4] | | |
| | Levi Lincoln | 45.62[5] | | |
| | Jones & Howell | 273. | | |
| | C. W. Peale | 150.[6] | | |
| | Jos. Dougherty about | 74.27[7] | | |
| | ThJ. about | 466.29[8] | | |
| | | 3169.45 | | 3169.45 |
| | leaves balance in favr ThJ. | | | 330.32 |
| | Mr Madison will pay at his convenience for ThJ. | | 735. | |
| | and Th:J. will remain indebted on his own acct | | 2934 | 3669.68 |
| | but will give his note for the whole | | 3669. | |
| | instead of his present note for | | | 4000. |

MS (CSmH: JF); entirely in TJ's hand; on verso: "Bank US. Mar. 10. 09"; filed with a series of notes, estimates, and expenses, with a covering sheet labeled by TJ: "Bank US. loose memms, estimates, notes Etc of my dealings with it while I lived in Washington." Dft (CSmH: JF); entirely in TJ's hand; undated; with additional entries, variant order, and lacking concluding comments on agreement with Madison.

As he planned here, on 10 Mar. 1809 TJ did indeed DRAW as indicated on the Bank of the United States (*MB*, 2:1242–3).

[1] In Dft TJ here estimated additional income from items sold in Washington, including a chariot (sold to Dr. Elzey for \$500 on 10 Mar., *MB*, 2:1242) and several items sold to James Madison (see TJ to Madison, 19 Apr. 1809), for a total of \$4,674.775 in assets.

[2] Reworked from "770.," the figure in Dft.

[3] In Dft TJ here included entries for "Ingle for Pechin 7.29/Gannin [*no amount given*]/ Melvin 5." TJ paid "Gannin the barber" \$6 on 11 Mar. (*MB*, 2:1243).

[4] Reworked from what appears to be "76.50." Dft: "abt 20." In Dft TJ here included an entry for "Bacon 10."

[5] In Dft TJ here included entries for "G. Jeff. 100./Dangerfield 590" (paid on 10 and 11 Mar.; see *MB*, 2:1243).

[6] In Dft TJ indicated that this payment

was "for Th:J.R." and also included three more entries, grouped by a brace, for "Julien ab[t] 75/Shorter 20/Th:J. 212.805," for a total of $307.805 (first two debts paid 17 Mar. and 7 Apr.; see *MB*, 2:1244).

[7] Reworked from "61.35," the amount TJ owed specifically to Dougherty (*MB*, 2:1243), with the revised figure incorporating payments made for TJ by Dougherty to Ingle and Melvin (see note 3). Dft: "ab[t] 80."

[8] Reworked from what appears to be "479.21," with the revised figure repeated at right for clarity.

# From Thomas Claxton

HONORD SIR 10[th] March 1809

The Bearer, one of my Sons attends with the List of furniture to aid M[r] La Mare in the Delivery of the furniture of the Presidents House to such person as may be authorised by the President of the United States to recieve the same—My son is a smart boy and very capable of assisting in this Business, more especially as he was present at the taking of the inventory—I have told him, Sir, that the best way will be to go from room to room, as the list is made out—Such form of an acknowledgement of the receipt of these things as you may think proper ought to be signed by the person who receives, and placed after the whole list, which together with the list I shall copy fairly and forward to you shortly—Your caution Sir, on this occasion, is necessary, as in a few short hours, great depredations may take place—And should a general Sale take place, as has been reported, there will remain a document to shew what the house contained when you left it—

Very severe exertion in the line of my duty before the adjournment took place, brought on me a severe fit of sickness, of which I am now recovering, but am fearful of turning out, otherwise I should take a very great pleasure & interest in complying with your wishes

Believe me, Dear Sir, when I assure you, that, when I occasionally view my past life, one of the greatest pleasures I shall enjoy will be, that of having assurances from you that I was worthy of your particular notice and I trust that I shall, by the help of God, be able always to maintain principles which will at all times, render me worthy of the same favorable opinion—

I now beg leave, Sir, to bid you an affectionate farewell, flattering myself with a hope that the remainder of your days may be rendered happy by good health and rural pleasures

I have the honor to be Sir Your Humble and sincere friend

THO[S] CLAXTON

RC (MHi); dateline below signature; endorsed by TJ as received 10 Mar. 1809 and so recorded in SJL.

Thomas Claxton (d. 1821) originally trained as a printer but spent most of his career as doorkeeper of the House of Representatives, a position he held for thirty-two years beginning as assistant doorkeeper during its first session in 1789. He was responsible for the Furniture Fund, a Treasury account approved by Congress from which he purchased furniture for the President's House. After the burning of the United States Capitol in 1814, Claxton refurnished the House of Representatives (Linda Grant DePauw and others, eds., *Documentary History of the First Federal Congress* [1972– ], 3:8; Conover Hunt-Jones, *Dolley and the "great little Madison"* [1977], 35–6; Margaret B. Klapthor, "Furniture in the Capitol: Desks and Chairs Used in the Chamber of the House of Representatives, 1819–1857," *RCHS* 47 [1969/70]: 192–8; Washington *National Intelligencer*, 3 Dec. 1821).

The BEARER of the LIST OF FURNITURE was probably Thomas Claxton (ca. 1794–1813), Claxton's eldest son. A list of existing furnishings in the President's House was requested by Benjamin H. Latrobe, who had been appointed to furnish it in mid-February 1809 by James and Dolley Madison. Latrobe was authorized to sell any public furniture that needed replacing, using the proceeds to make new purchases for the incoming president. Etienne Lemaire added kitchen items to the inventory that TJ prepared (TJ to Claxton, 19 Feb. 1809, and enclosed inventory of furnishings [DLC]; Latrobe, *Papers,* 2:705–6; Washington *National Intelligencer*, 14 Oct. 1813).

# From Richard Harrison

March 10. 1809.

R. Harrison presents his respectful compliments to Mr Jefferson, and has the honor to inform him that a Warrant will probably be ready by 2. o'Clock for the balance due on his Account as Min. Plen: at Paris.

R. Harrison avails him self of this occasion to offer his sincere thanks to Mr Jefferson for his past friendship & civilities; and to wish him every happiness in the retirement he has sought from the burthen & cares of an exalted, but arduous Station.

RC (DLC); dateline at foot of text; endorsed by TJ. Not recorded in SJL.

Richard Harrison (ca. 1750–1841) was an Alexandria merchant who served as Virginia agent in Martinique, 1778–80, and unofficial consul to Cádiz, 1780–86. George Washington appointed him auditor of the United States Treasury in 1791, a position he held until 1836 (Washington, *Papers, Pres. Ser.*, 2:229–30; *PTJ*, 9:223; *JEP*, 1:90–1 [25, 29 Nov. 1791]; Washington *National Intelligencer*, 12 June 1841).

On 21 Oct. 1789, while TJ was in Great Britain on his return trip to the United States from Paris, he sent a letter of credit for 2,800 florins banco to the French firm of Grand & Cie. The letter was never presented for payment and was assumed to be lost by 1809. In an effort to settle TJ's accounts as minister to France, Harrison credited TJ for the amount in United States currency ($1,148), for which he issued a WARRANT on this date. In 1822 an essayist writing as "A Native Virginian" publicly asserted that TJ had thereby accepted double payment for the same sum, prompting TJ to issue a rare newspaper rebuttal (*PTJ*, 15:526–7, 24:174–5, 187; *MB*, 2:1243; Harrison to TJ, 3 June 1822, and enclosures).

# To George Jefferson

Dear Sir [Washi]ngton Mar. 10. 09.

By a vessel just departing hence for Richmond I send a number of packages as by the inclosed, in which however I believe there may be an error or two, for I have not yet got the bill of lading. I must pray you to procure for me 3. dozen stick chairs, of the kind marked in the margin, painted black with yellow rings, & forward them for me to Lynchburg. Couch's boats are, I believe, the most to be depended on. I inclose you 100.D. to cover that & other expences. being all hurry on my departure I must here close with the assurances of my constant affection

Th: Jefferson

PoC (MHi); one word faint; at foot of text: "Mr G. Jefferson"; endorsed by TJ.

George Jefferson (1766–1812) was a grandson of TJ's uncle Field Jefferson. The Richmond-based mercantile firm of George Jefferson & Company that he founded in 1797 sold flour and other produce, and in 1804 he joined Patrick Gibson to form Gibson & Jefferson. The firm acted as agent and factor for TJ in Richmond beginning in December 1797. Madison nominated George Jefferson as consul to Lisbon in March 1811, but he did not take up the post until February 1812, relinquished it due to poor health later that year, and died at sea on his return trip (Landon C. Bell, *The Old Free State* [1927], 294–6; TJ to Jefferson, 2 Dec. 1797, *PTJ*, 29:577–8; Madison, *Papers, Pres. Ser.*, 3:340n, 4:497; Richmond *Enquirer*, 4 Aug. 1812).

TJ ordered the bow-back Windsor chairs to be made at Richmond for Poplar Forest. William Couch, of Warren, Albemarle County, employed boats to transfer goods between Richmond and Lynchburg on the James River (Chambers, *Poplar Forest*, 42–3; *MB*, 2:1243).

ENCLOSURE

## Packing List from John Barnes

The following packages on Board the Sloop Rebecca for Richmond Jno Hall Master.

| | | | |
|---|---|---|---|
| △1 | One Barrel Muscovado Sugar Nt | 2 1 4 | |
| 2— | one Ditto 15 loaves Single refd loaf Sugar | lbs 219 | ozs 13 |
| 3— | one Ditto 16 loaves Do Nt Wt | | |
| 4— | one Ditto containg tea Chest | lbs | |
| | young Hyson tea | 13 – | |
| | one Bag fresh Rice | 25.– | |
| | pearl Barley 25.– | | |
| | Superfine Chocolate | 25.– | |
| | Cloves | –.4 oz | |
| | Cinnamon | –.4 oz | |
| | Nutmegs | –.4 oz | |

| | | | |
|---|---|---|---|
| | Alspice | –.8 oz | |
| | peper | 1.– | |
| | Mustard Bottles | 6– | |
| | Water Crackers | 20lb | |
| | | ——— | lbs |
| 5 | one half Cask fine cheese | | 29½ |
| | ordinary do | | 35 |
| 6 | Sqr Box Water Crackers | | 22lb— |

George Town 7t March 1809.
J. BARNES

MS (ViU: TJP); in a clerk's hand, with dateline and signature written lengthwise by Barnes in left margin; endorsed by TJ: "Barnes John groceries Mar. 09."

A statement of account from Barnes to TJ, Georgetown, 3 Mar. 1809 (ViU: TJP), charged $152.91 for these goods, a lined keg, and one bushel of clover seed. The TEA CHEST was there described as being "small Japoned."

# To Charles Willson Peale

MY DEAR SIR — Washington Mar. 10. 09

Being just on the eve of my departure for Monticello I must write you a short letter returning you a thousand thanks for the portrait of my grandson, which is indeed inimitably done. I do not know whether age impairs the faculties of your art, but I am sure it would do honor to any period of life. it will be a treasure to his parents & not less so to me. as he wished to see them & had a month to spare, he sat out two or three days ago for Monticello; and will be with you again before the commencement of the botanical lectures. I now inclose you an order of the bank of the US. here on that at Philadelphia for an hundred & fifty dollars, which I imagine will carry him through that course of lecture, when he will return home. I believe you never ramble for the purposes of looking out subjects for your Museum. were a ramble to lead you to Monticello, we should all recieve you with open arms & hearts. God bless you & give you many & happy years.

TH: JEFFERSON

RC (Anonymous, 1948); at foot of text: "Mr Peale." PoC (DLC); endorsed by TJ. Enclosure not found.

Charles Willson Peale (1741–1827), inventor, artist, and founder of the Philadelphia Museum, was a lifelong friend and frequent correspondent of TJ. Peale began his career as a saddler and sign painter but soon began painting portraits and studied in London under Benjamin West. In 1776 Peale moved his family from Annapolis to Philadelphia, where his portraits of officers and their wives included one of his seven life portraits of George Washington. Peale began the museum in 1782 as a portrait gallery in his home. Expanded to include natural history and art, the Philadelphia Museum was housed at the American Philosophical Society starting in 1794 and from 1802 at the Philadelphia State House (Independence Hall). A principal attraction was the skeleton of a prehistoric mastodon. Peale worked with John Isaac Hawkins and TJ himself to develop the polygraph, a machine using two pens writing simultaneously that TJ used to keep copies of his correspondence beginning in 1805. Peale retired in 1810 to his farm in Germantown, Pennsylvania (*ANB*; *DAB*; Peale, *Papers*, esp. autobiography in vol. 5; Silvio Bedini, *Thomas Jefferson and His Copying Machines* [1984]).

Peale had sent his PORTRAIT of TJ's grandson Thomas Jefferson Randolph on 21 Feb. 1809. Peale painted the likeness, now at Monticello and reproduced elsewhere in this volume, while the youth was attending Benjamin Smith Barton's BOTANICAL LECTURES in Philadelphia and boarding at TJ's expense with the Peale family (Peale, *Papers*, vol. 2, pt. 2, p. 1183; *MB*, 2:1243).

# From the Inhabitants of Albemarle County

SIR, [ca. 11 Mar. 1809]

The Inhabitants of Albemarle, your fellow citizens & your friends, beg leave to congratulate you on your return to themselves & to your native county. They invite you to the enjoyment of that domestic happiness from which your public services have so long abstracted you, & for which you have so just a claim on their warmest wishes, & best exertions to establish.

In the bosom of your family, surrounded by your neighbours, & followed by the affections of a grateful Country they hope to see realized those sweets of retirement for which you have often sighed, and to which they are now anxious personally to contribute. While gratulations of love and applause from every part of the Union testify the feelings of the nation towards you, We your Countymen strongly participating in the public sentiment, find we have no thing to add on the score of public gratitude: We hear with pleasure & delight the plaudits of a free & grateful people, attending their cheif Magistrate as he voluntarily descends from the highest offices of state to the tranquil walks of private life, and we dare not express our feelings when we reflect that this voluntary relinquishment of honours & power, restores to us our nieghbour & our Friend, about to contribute that part to our Social Happiness which he has already atchieved for the public good.—The Mariner who has weathered the tempest & the Storm, feels a delicious pleasure in contrasting present safty with former Peril; So the cares, the labours, the perplexities, the Pomp, the turmoil & the bustle of office will doubly endear to you the calm enjoyments of domestic life. As Individuals among whom you were raised & to whom you have at all times been dear, We again Welcome your return to your native county, to the bosom of Your Friends, & to the affections & feelings of those neighbours who have long known, & have long revered you in Private life. We assure you Sir, We are not insensible of the many sacrifices you have already made in the various stations to which your country has assigned you, We have witnessed your disinterestedness, and while we feel the benefits of your past services, it would be more than ingratitude in us did we not contribute our best efforts to make your latter days as tranquil & as Happy, as your former have been bright & glorious.

Signed on behalf of the Meeting
W[M] D. MERIWETHER Cha[n]

Attest
P. MINOR Sec[y]

MS (DLC: TJ Papers, 187:33238); in Meriwether's hand, signed by him and Peter Minor; undated; at head of text: "To Thomas Jefferson Esq[r] Late President of the United States"; endorsed by TJ as an "Address Inhabitants of Albemarle. Meriwether W[m]" received 3 Apr. 1809 and so recorded in SJL. Enclosed in Meriwether to TJ, [23 Mar. 1809]. Printed with proceedings of meeting in Richmond *Enquirer*, 14 Apr. 1809.

This address resulted from a series of public meetings held in Albemarle County to honor TJ on his retirement. At the first meeting, late in February, militia companies and citizens planned to meet TJ "in a body at the extremity of the county, and conduct him home." TJ declined to put them to this trouble, especially because he was uncertain of the date of his return. On 6 Mar. 1809, at a meeting at the county courthouse chaired by Meriwether and with Alexander Garrett as secretary, "the idea was accordingly given up." A committee consisting of Meriwether and Minor was instead appointed to draft an address that was unanimously approved at the final meeting on 11 Mar. 1809 and ordered to be presented to TJ by Meriwether, Nimrod Bramham, Charles Everette, Thomas W. Maury, and Dabney Minor (Martha Jefferson Randolph to TJ, 24 Feb. 1809 [MHi]; TJ to Thomas Mann Randolph, 28 Feb. 1809 [DLC]; Richmond *Enquirer*, 14 Apr. 1809).

# To Mary Daingerfield

MADAM Washington Mar. 11. 09.

By the post of this day I inclose to the President of the bank of Fredericksburg five hundred & ninety dollars on account of the hire of your negroes and subject to the order of yourself and miss Dangerfield, and tender you the assurances of my great respect.

TH: JEFFERSON

PoC (MHi); at foot of text: "M[rs] Dangerfield"; endorsed by TJ.

Mary Willis Daingerfield (1745–1818), widow of Continental army veteran William Daingerfield, raised ten children, including Sarah Daingerfield, on their Spotsylvania plantation, Coventry. Sarah Daingerfield married Nathaniel H. Hooe in 1807 (TJ to John Minor, 10 Aug. 1806 [MHi]; Washington, *Papers, Retirement Ser.*, 1:90; Lawrence MacRae, "Descendants of John Daingerfield and his Wife, New Kent County, Virginia, 1640" [1928 typescript at Vi]; Fredericksburg *Virginia Herald*, 25 Aug. 1807, 25 Feb. 1818).

On this day TJ wrote David C. Ker, PRESIDENT OF THE BANK OF FREDERICKSBURG, enclosing and asking him to deposit in that bank "five hundred and ninety Dollars to be paid to the order of mrs [i.e., Miss] Sarah Dangerfield & miss [i.e., Mrs.] Mary Dangerfield" (PoC in MHi; at foot of text: "M[r] David C. Kerr"; endorsed by TJ). On 16 Mar. Ker replied that he had received and deposited the money as directed (RC in MHi; endorsed by TJ as received from Fredericksburg on 23 Mar. 1809 and so recorded in SJL).

John Holmes Freeman, who served as overseer at Monticello from August 1805 to the autumn of 1806, engaged in July 1806 with Mary and Sarah Daingerfield for the annual HIRE of nine of their slaves (four for $239 from the former, five for $351 from the latter). This day's payment was for 1808 (TJ to Mary Daingerfield, 5 Apr. 1808 [MHi]; *MB*, 2:1185, 1243). A missing letter of 18 Mar. 1809 from Freeman is recorded in SJL as received from Culpeper on 3 Apr. 1809.

# To William Duane

SIR — Washington Mar. 11. 09

Such has been the hurry & bustle of the close of a session of Congress & of my departure, which now takes place in an hour that I have not been able to acknolege the reciept of your letters, but I did what was essential as to the most important one. I consulted with Gen[l] Dearborne and we concluded that the public service permitted the indulgence and the proceeding which would accomodate your own private affairs, & I presume you saw him on his passage through Philadelphia. I have also taken the necessary measures here with the proper persons, for the same purpose, and I expect you will be accomodated. you know best whether it would be adviseable for you to go into the same explanations with the new Secretary at war as he passes through your city. I sent a few days ago to mr Weightman for his account, expecting it would as usual include that for the Aurora but it did not.[1] will you be so good as to forward it to me at Monticello, and hereafter send me the country Aurora only. altho' pressed in time I cannot conclude without thanking you for the information you have usefully conveyed to me from time to time, & for the many proofs of your friendship & confidence. I carry into retirement deep seated feelings for these favors, and shall always recollect them with pleasure. wishing you every felicity & success I pray you to accept the assurances of my great esteem & respect. TH: JEFFERSON

PoC (DLC); at foot of text: "Col^o^ W^m^ Duane"; endorsed by TJ.

William Duane (1760–1835) was the outspoken and impecunious editor of the Philadelphia *Aurora,* the nation's most influential Republican newspaper, and a leader of the party's radical egalitarian wing. Born in what is now Vermont, he spent his early decades as a printer and journalist in Ireland, England, and India, from which he was expelled in 1795 for anti-British rhetoric. The following year Duane settled in Philadelphia with his family and soon attracted notice with a pseudonymous pamphlet critical of George Washington. Duane took over the editorship of the *Aurora* on the death of editor Benjamin Franklin Bache in 1798 and ran the newspaper until 1822. From 1801–07 he operated a Washington, D.C., bookstore and printed the proceedings of the United States Senate with his son William J. Duane and Roger C. Weightman, who assumed management of both in the latter year (*ANB*; *DAB*; Bryan, *National Capital*, 1:595).

Duane was appointed lieutenant colonel of riflemen on 8 July 1808 and resigned on 31 July 1810 (Heitman, *U.S. Army*, 1:385). In his MOST IMPORTANT letter to TJ of 4 Feb. 1809 (DLC), Duane cited his precarious finances and ongoing litigation in requesting that his printing business not be disrupted by military service distant from Philadelphia and expressing concern that the NEW SECRETARY AT WAR might not agree to such an arrangement.

[1] Preceding four words interlined.

# To Levi Lincoln

MY DEAR SIR Washington Mar. 11. 09.

I ought before this to have acknoleged the reciept of two or three letters from you, but the hurry of a close of Congress and bustle of my own departure which takes place in an hour, has prevented me. yours of Feb. 15. is just now recieved, & I hasten to inclose you an order of the bank of the US. here on that at Boston for 45.62 D to reimburse what you have been so kind as to pay for me for the newspapers, and I add one further request that you will be so good as notify them my desire for their discontinuance. I shall give over reading newspapers. they are so false & so intemperate that they disturb tranquility without giving information. accept this brief epistle as the pledge of a longer one from the leisure of Monticello, & be assured of my constant friendship & respect TH: JEFFERSON

RC (John Herron, Dobbs Ferry, New York, 2002, on deposit MWA); at foot of text: "the honble Levi Lincoln"; endorsed by Lincoln. PoC (DLC); endorsed by TJ. Enclosure not found.

Levi Lincoln (1749–1820), a Massachusetts lawyer and a leading New England Republican, graduated from Harvard and practiced law at Worcester. He served briefly in the United States House of Representatives, 1800–01, but gave up the office when TJ appointed him attorney general, a position he held until his resignation at the end of 1804. Lincoln subsequently won a term as lieutenant governor of Massachusetts in 1807, and served as governor, on the death of the incumbent, from December 1808 to 1 May 1809. Lincoln declined James Madison's appointment in 1810 as a justice to the Supreme Court, pleading age and poor eyesight, and retired to his Worcester farm (*ANB*; *DAB*; *Sibley's Harvard Graduates*, 18:121–8).

The TWO OR THREE LETTERS from Lincoln were probably those of 31 Jan., 15 and 23 Feb. 1809 (NNPM, MHi, and DLC, respectively). The 15 Feb. letter did not relate to TJ's newspaper subscriptions but may have enclosed a bill for the four Massachusetts NEWSPAPERS TJ had received since 1804, namely the Boston *Democrat*, Boston *Independent Chronicle*, *Salem Register*, and Worcester *National Aegis* (*MB*, 2:964, 1123).

# To Mayer & Brantz

Washington Mar. 11. 09

The non-intercourse law prohibiting the importation of any thing from France directly, I must still rely on the indirect importation from Amsterdam. making no use therefore of the letter to mr Backer which you were so kind as to send me, I now return it with a renewal of my request that you will suffer your former orders for the books to go into execution, and the tender of assurances of my great esteem & respect

TH: JEFFERSON

RC (Jim Reasoner, Casper, Wyoming, 1993); at head of text: "Messieurs Meyer & Brantz"; endorsed as received 11 Mar. 1809 and answered 13 Mar. 1809. PoC (MHi); endorsed by TJ. Enclosure not found.

The Baltimore mercantile firm of Mayer & Brantz, founded in 1802, handled tobacco and other commercial trade between Maryland and the Netherlands, Italy, Denmark, France, and India. Christian Mayer (1763–1842) arrived in Baltimore from Germany in 1784 and worked for the Netherlands firm of Valck & Company, where he met Lewis Brantz (ca. 1765–1838), a fellow German who was an explorer and surveyor before becoming supercargo of Mayer & Brantz (Brantz Mayer, *Memoir and Genealogy of the Maryland and Pennsylvanian Family of Mayer* [1968], 33–41, 44–6).

TJ requested some books from Mayer & Brantz early in 1808 and informed the company that government vessels sailing to Brest, Cádiz, and Lisbon would enable the firm to transact this business. The books not having arrived one year later, TJ wrote that the public vessel *Mentor* was going to France and could convey the books within four months, assuming that the order had not already been sent. Mayer & Brantz responded that their Amsterdam agent, T. H. BACKER, had been unable to send the books for want of a vessel, and they enclosed an open letter to Backer, directing TJ to forward it or not as he saw fit (TJ to Mayer & Brantz, 18 Jan. 1808, 7 Feb. 1809, and Mayer & Brantz to TJ, 8 Feb. 1809 [MHi]).

Mayer & Brantz's reply of 13 Mar. 1809, mentioned on the endorsement to the RC above, is not recorded in SJL and has not been found.

# To George C. Shattuck

Washington Mar. 11–09.

Th: Jefferson presents his compliments to mr Shattuck and his thanks for the copy of the Boylston prize dissertation which he was so kind as to send him. he shall read it with pleasure in the leisure of Monticello, to which place he [is] now in the moment of departure. he prays mr Shattuck to accept the assurances of his respect.

PoC (MHi); right margin faint; dateline below body of letter; at foot of text: "Geo. C. Shattuck"; endorsed by TJ.

George Cheyne Shattuck (1783–1854) graduated from Dartmouth College in 1806 and studied medicine at Harvard Medical School and the University of Pennsylvania, receiving a degree from the latter in 1807. He practiced medicine in Boston, where in 1808 he published *Three Dissertations on Boylston Prize Questions for the Years 1806 and 1807* (Sowerby, no. 986), a copy of which he sent to TJ in October 1808. Shattuck established an endowed professorship at the Harvard Medical School and was president of the Massachusetts Medical Society, 1836–40 (*DAB*; Martin Kaufman and others, *Dictionary of Medical Biography* [1984], 2:675–6; Edward Jarvis, *Memoir of the Life and Character of George Cheyne Shattuck, M.D.* [1854]).

# Edmund Bacon's Account of Thomas Jefferson's Reception at Culpeper Court House

[13 Mar. 1809]

We got loaded up ready to start home, and I left Washington on the third of March. Mr. Jefferson stayed to attend the inauguration, but overtook us before we got home. I had three wagons from Monticello—two six-mule teams loaded with boxes, and the other four sorrel Chickasaw horses, and the wagon pretty much loaded with shrubbery from Maine's nursery. The servants rode on these wagons. I had the carriage horses and carriage, and rode behind them.

On our way home we had a tremendous snowstorm. It snowed very fast, and when we reached Culpepper Court House it was half-leg deep. A large crowd of people had collected there, expecting that the President would be along. When I rode up, they thought I was the President, and shouted and hurrahed tremendously. When I got out of the carriage, they laughed very heartily at their mistake. There was a platform along the whole front of the tavern, and it was full of people. Some of them had been waiting a good while, and drinking a good deal, and they made so much noise that they scared the horses, and Diomede backed, and tread upon my foot, and lamed me so that I could hardly get into the carriage the next morning. There was one very tall old fellow that was noisier than any of the rest, who said he was bound to see the President—"Old Tom," he called him. They asked me when he would be along, and I told them I thought he would certainly be along that night, and I looked for him every moment. The tavern was kept by an old man named Shackleford. I told him to have a large fire built in a private room, as Mr. Jefferson would be very cold when he got there, and he did so. I soon heard shouting, went out, and Mr. Jefferson was in sight. He was in a one-horse vehicle—a phaeton—with a driver, and a servant on horseback. When he came up, there was great cheering again. I motioned to him to follow me; took him straight to his room, and locked the door. The tall old fellow came and knocked very often, but I would not let him in. I told Mr. Jefferson not to mind him, he was drunk. Finally the door was opened, and they rushed in and filled the room. It was as full as I ever saw a bar-room. He stood up, and made a short address to them. Afterwards some of them told him how they had mistaken me for him. He went on next day, and reached Monticello before we did, so that I did not see the large reception that the people of Albemarle gave him when he got home.

Printed in Pierson, *Jefferson at Monticello*, 114–6; undated transcription by Hamilton W. Pierson of conversations with Bacon about 1861.

Edmund Bacon (1785–1866), a native of Albemarle County, served as overseer at Monticello from 1806 until 1822, the longest tenure for one of TJ's overseers there. In 1823 Bacon moved to Trigg County, Kentucky, where he farmed successfully until his death (Pierson, *Jefferson at Monticello*; Betts, *Farm Book*, 149; Russell Martin, "Mr. Jefferson's business: The Farming Letters of Thomas Jefferson and Edmund Bacon" [Ph.D. diss., University of Virginia, 1994]; Memoranda Book of Edmund Bacon, 1802–22 [ViU]).

TJ had recommended that Bacon bring the empty wagons to Washington "by the courthouses, Ewell's mill, Songster's, Lane's & Ravensworth," the only passable route northward (TJ to Bacon, 27 Feb. 1809 [CSmH: JF]). DIOMEDE was one of two carriage horses owned by TJ that were descended from the British racehorse Diomed (*MB*, 2:1221n, 1236n). Leaving Washington on 11 Mar. 1809, TJ crossed the Potomac on John Mason's Georgetown ferry. He spent his first night ten miles west of Washington at Ravensworth, a house in Fairfax County owned by Richard Fitzhugh. TJ's second day of travel included a stop midway at Sangster's and Ewell's Mill, near Centreville, where he bought oats and corn, after which he spent the night at Barnett's Tavern in Fauquier County (about seven miles east of Warrenton in Auburn). He passed his third night at the TAVERN operated by Benjamin Shackelford at Culpeper Court House in Culpeper County. TJ paid $4.43 for "supper, lodgg. &c." at Shackelford's and fifty cents for a barber. On 14 Mar. TJ stopped for oats at Orange Court House and continued on to Gordonsville, Orange County, where he spent the night at Nathaniel Gordon's tavern at a cost of $4.50. He arrived home on 15 Mar. 1809 (*MB*, 2:903n, 1148–9n, 1243).

## From Isaac A. Coles

Dear Sir, Presidents House Mar. 13. 1809.

The inclosed letters which have come to hand since you left this, were given me yesterday by Mr Madison with a request that I would forward them to you.

Joseph has just been to tell me that the Vessel on board of which your baggage was shiped, had got aground in the eastern branch, and had received so much injury that it was deemed unsafe for her to continue her voyage—we have thought it best under these circumstances to have the things put on board of an other Vessel (the Dolphin of York) which will sail in the course of a day or two—in this way we shall avoid the delay that we had at first apprehended, without incuring any additional expense.

Mr & Mrs Madison came here on the evening of the day that you went away, and Mr & Mrs Cutts on the day following. until my departure which cannot be delayed much longer, but which[1] is not as yet fixed, I remain with them at Mr Madison's request.

At present every thing is very much upon the old establishment, but I find several changes are contemplated. they are preparing to fit up the Secretary's Office for the Presidents Cabinet, and the present Cabinet for a dining room by closing up the two windows to the West. Mr and Mrs Cutts occupy the suite of appartments in the South east corner of the building,[2] and Mr & Mrs Madison those in the South West.

I fear Mr Madison has not been fortunate in his Choice of a Maitre d'Hotel. it is apprehended that in the irregular life he has been leading for some time he has acquired a habit of insobriety. I hear he was so drunk last night as to be incapable of attending to his duty. Robert is already[3] evincing symtoms of discontent and I think it probable that he will not remain long. Joseph goes to day but will neither carry Mary nor any of his Children along with him—

I beg you to present me in the kindest manner to Mr & Mrs Randolph and their family, and to believe that towards yourself my heart will never cease to overflow with sentiments to which I have no power to give utterance I. A. Coles

RC (DLC); endorsed by TJ as received 16 Mar. 1809 and so recorded in SJL. FC (Robert Coles, Cloverfields, Albemarle County, 1970); first page only; in Coles's hand; dated Mar. 1809. Enclosures: (1) Pierre Samuel Du Pont de Nemours to TJ, 28 Nov. 1808 (MHi). (2) Jérome Pagowski to TJ, 14 Nov. 1808 (ViW: TC-JP).

Isaac A. Coles (1780–1841), planter and lawyer, was a 1798 graduate of the College of William and Mary who lived at Enniscorthy in Albemarle County. He and TJ regularly corresponded about agriculture and were both founding members of the Agricultural Society of Albemarle, with Coles as its first treasurer. He was personal secretary to TJ, who found him invaluable, during the latter's second term as president. Coles served James Madison in the same capacity even after his appointment in January 1809 as a captain in the Light Dragoons, United States Army, but he gave up both posts and returned to Virginia shortly after scuffling in November 1809 with a congressman from Maryland. Coles rejoined the United States Army as a major in 1812 and was honorably discharged as a colonel in 1815. He represented Albemarle County in the Virginia House of Delegates, 1840–41 (William Runge, "Isaac A. Coles," *MACH* 14 [1954/55]: 49–57; Madison, *Papers, Pres. Ser.*, 1:49n, 2:150–1; Heitman, *U.S. Army*, 1:316; Coles to TJ, 29 Dec. 1809; Coles to Rebecca Tucker Coles, [ca. 1 Mar. 1809] [Robert Coles, Cloverfields, Albemarle County, 1970]).

Dolley Madison's sister Anna Payne CUTTS, her husband Richard Cutts, United States representative from the Maine district of Massachusetts, 1801–13, and their three sons lived in the President's House with the Madisons (Dolley Madison to John C. Payne, 21 Sept. 1809, Dolley Madison, *Selected Letters*, 128; *Biog. Dir. Cong.*).

[1] Preceding seven words omitted in FC.
[2] Remainder of sentence omitted in FC.
[3] FC ends here.

# From William Lambert

SIR, City of Washington, March 14th 1809.

As you are now retired from the important and dignified station of Chief magistrate of the United States of America, the duties of which you have fulfilled with the deserved approbation of all well disposed and discerning citizens, permit me to congratulate you on the magninimity you have evinced, in thus voluntarily relinquishing the highest and most responsible office in the power of the American people to bestow, and which, no doubt can be entertained of their wish to have continued you in much longer. Whatever may be the united efforts of malicious, designing men in this country, or elsewhere, to traduce your character, or lessen your merits, their contemptible schemes will be frustrated and Exposed in due time. That you may continue to an advanced period of life, an ornament and pattern to and for the nation which gave you birth, is the sincere wish of Sir, Your sincere well-wisher, and obedient servant,

WILLIAM LAMBERT.

RC (MHi); at foot of text: "Thomas Jefferson, Esqr"; endorsed by TJ as received 23 Mar. 1809 and so recorded in SJL.

William Lambert (d. 1834), astronomer, was a native Virginian who became acquainted with TJ as a State Department clerk, 1790–92. He regularly informed TJ of his new calculations throughout the latter's retirement and established the longitude of Monticello. Lambert served as a clerk in the House of Representatives and in the pension section of the War Department, temporarily losing the former position late in the 1790s because of his passionate Republican views. He devoted most of his spare time to proposals for building a national astronomical observatory and establishing an American prime meridian in Washington. For years Lambert vainly sought congressional support for these plans while fruitlessly seeking better government positions and complaining that his enemies were frustrating his professional and scientific efforts. In 1818 he helped found and played a leading role in the Columbian Institute for the Promotion of Arts and Sciences (*PTJ*, 26:234–5; Lambert to TJ, 15 Dec. 1804 [DLC]; Silvio A. Bedini, *The Jefferson Stone: Demarcation of the First Meridian of the United States* [1999]; *Annals*, 11th Cong., 2d sess., 1660–1 [28 Mar. 1810]; Lambert to James Madison, 26 Apr. 1812 [DNA: RG 59, LAR, 1809–17]; Washington *National Intelligencer*, 21, 23 Oct. 1834).

# From John Taggart

SIR Philad[a] March 15th 1809

Your letter of the 15th Ulto I rec[d] and acording to Your Instructions[1] have Shiped the Oil and Lead on bord the Schooner Jane Benoni Jackson Master bound for Richmond to the Care of Mess[rs] Gibson & Jefferson of that place She is Expected to Sale on the 17th Inst. You will find a bill Enclosed I wish the artickles may be pleasing to you—

I am with the highest respect Your Obedent Servant—

JOHN TAGGART

RC (MHi); between dateline and salutation: "Thomas Jefferson Esq[r]"; endorsed by TJ as received 23 Mar. 1809 and so recorded in SJL.

John Taggart, a merchant at 7 North Water Street, Philadelphia, typically supplied TJ with paint ingredients (Robinson, *Philadelphia Directory for 1809*).

TJ's LETTER of 15 Feb. 1809 (MHi) requested sixty gallons of linseed oil and one hundred pounds of dry white lead along with Taggart's bill.

[1] Manuscript: "Instrutions."

# To Etienne Lemaire

MY DEAR M. LEMAIRE Monticello Mar. 16. 09.

When I parted with you at Washington, it was my intention to have expressed to you all the sentiments of obligation I have felt myself under to you. but my heart was so full that I could utter but the single word Adieu. indeed the enlivening idea of rejoining my family and of being once more master of my own time & actions, was lost in the moment of separation from those who had lived so long in the house with me, & served me so much to my mind. I must supply now in writing, what I then could not express, the sense of my attachment to you & satisfaction with your services. they were faithful, & skilful, and your whole conduct so marked with good humour, industry, sobriety & economy as never to have given me one moment's dissatisfaction: and indeed were I to be again in a situation to need services of the same kind, yours would be more acceptable to me than those of any person living. I have thought it my duty thus to declare what is just & true respecting you; it may give some satisfaction to you, as assuredly it does to myself to bear this testimony to your merit. I shall be glad to know where letters may find you hereafter, & to hear from you at times and at your own convenience, as I shall ever feel a deep interest in your happiness & success. I salute you with affectionate esteem

TH: JEFFERSON

PoC (DLC); at foot of text: "M. Etienne Lemaire"; mistakenly endorsed by TJ as a letter of 11 Mar. 1809 but correctly recorded in SJL.

Etienne Lemaire (d. 1817) served as maître d'hôtel during TJ's presidency beginning in the summer of 1801, having previously worked for William Bingham in Philadelphia. Lemaire managed the domestic staff and supervised dining as well as shopping (*MB*, 2:1053–4n; Honoré Julien to TJ, 7 Nov. 1817).

# From James W. Wallace

[received 16 Mar. 1809]

I send to Mr Jefferson the following Articles Viz
Jeffersonia Antivenena (the Roots) in a large wafer Box
Sun Brier in a Box
Balsam Copaiba Tree in a Box (copaiba Brasiliensis)
one Beet & one Carrot for Seed in the half Barrel. the Beet weighed $15\frac{3}{4}$ lbs in Oct. $12\frac{1}{4}$ lbs in Decr. March 10th 9.$\frac{3}{4}$ lbs an astonishing loss
2 wild Geese—tis feared they are of one sex
The Summer Ducks a wicked boy shot, to my great mortification

The leaf of the Copaiba Brasiliensis grows large, is famous for relieving head achs &c. you may ride a week with a Switch of it—& at the end of that time stick one end in the ground & you will soon have a tree, like the Lombardy Poplar it will grow quick any where.

The Jeffersonia Antivenena must be used in the following manner (tis an accommodating plant & thrives equally well on the summits of barren & stony mountains as in the fertile plain) beat well three or four of the roots tops & all and boil the mass in one pint of new milk, give the afflicted unfortunate one Tablespoonful hourly & apply the boiled pulp to the wound. a smaller quantity I presume will answer for a person under puberty. an instance of its powers occurred near this place last June. a negroe boy was bit on the foot by a snake (the name unknown—) Horehound & Plantain juice was freely given—the pain increased also the swelling untill the size of the foot leg & thye had become almost incredible, his Screams[1] were heard as far as his voice could reach, untill he became weak & faint, his Pulse trembling, his body covered with a profuse cold sweat & he delerious bordering on madness—in this situation the Jeffersonia Antivenena as before derected was used—by degrees the excrutiating pains & the swelling abated, his Pulse became better his mind composed & free from delerium—he survived—but the swelled parts were covered with Blisters which broke and discharged a Green fluid, to which were applied for a few days the boiled pulp which soon healed the Sores.

If provedence will grant you my will of happiness you will have a plenty

God bless You Sir James W. Wallace

NB N° 1 Marvel of Peru
N° 2 Wax Work Flower

JWW

RC (DLC: TJ Papers, 203:36103); undated; endorsed by TJ as received 16 Mar. 1809 and so recorded in SJL.

James Westwood Wallace (ca. 1769–1838) studied medicine at Edinburgh University and lived near Warrenton in Fauquier County. He and TJ had exchanged information on the medicinal properties of plants ("Old Kecoughtan," *WMQ*, 1st ser., 9 [1900]: 130–1; TJ to Wallace and Gustavus Horner, 15 May 1808 [DLC]; Richmond *Enquirer*, 11 Sept. 1838).

TJ asked Wallace for these ARTICLES in a letter of 28 Feb. 1809 (ViU: TJP), and in a note of the same date to Edmund Bacon (MHi) asked him to deliver the request to Wallace on his way to Washington and collect the specimens about 10 or 11 Mar. 1809 at Fauquier Court House during his return trip to Monticello.

JEFFERSONIA ANTIVENENA was probably Wallace's idiosyncratic name for *Jeffersonia diphylla*, or Twinleaf. Native to the northern and western states, it was first identified by John Clayton and then found in the Blue Ridge Mountains by André Michaux in 1791. Benjamin Smith Barton named it in honor of TJ the following year on behalf of the American Philosophical Society. TJ probably never saw it in the wild but was growing it at Monticello in 1807. Twinleaf, also known as "rheumatism root," has medicinal qualities concentrated in the root. It acts as a stimulant and when used as described by Wallace can increase capillary circulation or wash sores and ulcers.

*Prenanthes serpentaria* (Lion's foot) and *Alisma plantago-aquatica* (water PLANTAIN) had been used on snakebites in Virginia, a remedy learned from the Indians (Lucia Stanton, "A Botanical Anniversary," *Twinleaf Journal* [1992]; Betts, *Garden Book*, 172–3, 335, and plate 11; William Cook, *The Physio-medical Dispensatory: A Treatise on Therapeutics, Materia Medica, and Pharmacy* [1869], 298; Richard Harlan, "Experiments Made on the Poison of the Rattlesnake," APS, *Transactions* 3 [1830]: 301–2; Reuben Gold Thwaites, *Early Western Travels, 1748–1846* [1904–07], 22:95–6).

BALSAM COPAIBA: a tropical tree, copaiba balsam grows up to one hundred feet in height, and its oily resin is used for a wide variety of medicinal purposes both internal and external. MARVEL OF PERU: *Mirabilis jalapa*, or four-o'clock, is a tropical American species whose flower blossoms open late in the afternoon. WAX WORK FLOWER: *Celastrus scandens*, or American bittersweet, also known as Waxwork (*Hortus Third*, 239–40, 735).

[1] Manuscript: "Scrams."

# From James Hochie

SIR. NewLondon March 17th 1809

In obeidiance to a resolve, of the Antient Plymouth Society, of this City, passed on the 16h Inst, I have the honor to inclose herewith, to your Excellency, their[1] Vote of Thanks: Expressing the sentiments of the Society, towards your Person and Character.

It will not perhaps be displeasing to your Excellency, to learn, that altho, our Society Constitutes but a small part of the community, who profess sentiments, equally cordial and respectfull, yet, I may be permitted; without vanity, to assure you, that for respectabillity of Character, Talents, virtue, and Patriotism, the Antient Plymouth Society of this City, will not suffer, by a Contrast with any other voluntary Society, in the United States.

I pray your Excellency, to accept the Assurances, of my most Cordial respect And Esteem, and remain Sir, your Obeidient Servant

JAMES HOCHIE Prt

RC (DLC); in the hand of John Palm, signed by Hochie; addressed: "His Excellency Thomas Jefferson Esquire Late President United States Monticello"; endorsed by TJ as an "Address antient Plymouth Society" sent by Hochie and received 30 Mar. 1809 and so recorded in SJL.

[1] Manuscript: "thier."

ENCLOSURE

## Resolutions of the Antient Plymouth Society

At a meeting of the Members, of the "Antient[1] Plymouth Society. (Instituted in the Seventeenth Century; in commemoration of the first landing of our Fore Fathers, in New England, and preserved, thro succeeding generations to the present day:) in the City of NewLondon, State of Connecticut, on the 16th March 1809, at Otis's Hall; previous notice being given to all the Members; James Hochie Esqr President. The following Resolutions being passed, was ordred to be recorded, upon the Journals of the Society.

1st Resolved. that the thanks, of this Antient Plymouth Society, be given, to Thomas Jefferson[2] Esquire, late President of the United States of America; for his faithfull services, during the past Eight years of his Administration: And that the prayers of the Society, for His welfare and happiness, thro the remainder of his Life, will be Commesurate, with the Illustrious public services, he has rendred his Country, during the Momentous period of thirty years, Ending the Fourth Instant.

2d Resolved. That the President of this Society, be directed to transmit a coppy of the foregoing resolve to Thomas Jefferson Esquire at his seat at Monticello.

A true Coppy of Record
Test

JOHN PALM. Secretary

MS (DLC); entirely in Palm's hand.

[1] Manuscript lacks closing quotation mark.

[2] Manuscript: "Jerfferson."

# From Etienne Lemaire

MONSIEUR De Washington city 17. mars 1809

Biens des pardon de la liberty que Je prend d'avoir l'honneur de vous adreser la presente, elle est pour minformer de votre sentez, Sachant que vous avés Éprouvé Un mauvais voÿage aûcassionné, par la neige et la plui, Je Crain qu'il ne vous soy ariver quélque accident, oû Biens soufair, de Même que vous n'avié a votre suite que shorter, qu'il n'auroit peû êttre pas sufit a vous rendre les secour,[1] necessaire, mes Enfin[2] monsieur, l'honneur de vôtre repônce me sur prendra agréablement que vous Jouisez d'une parfaite senté, ainsy à votre honorable famille, Ceque Je vous desire du mellieur de mon Cœurs—Je fini Mr an vous prïant d'avoir la Bontez de saluer vôtre respectable famille, pour moy.

Vous aûbligéré Seluy qui lhonneur D'Ettre avec le plus profond respecque qui est possible de vous exprimer—

ETIENNE LEMAIRE

mon adrese sera chez, M^r^ marinot, opposite the City taverne second street,

p.s.v.

Monsieur Estant a philadelphie, si Je peu vous êttre, de quelque Utilité, Je vous pri de m'enploÿer, vous serré servie avec l'exatidude poss

M^r^ Juliens doit partir lundi, où mardi

EDITORS' TRANSLATION

SIR Washington city 17. March 1809

Many pardons for the liberty I take of having the honor of sending you the present letter, it is to inform myself of your health, knowing that you had a bad journey due to the snow and the rain, I fear you may have had an accident, or suffered a lot, as you had only Shorter with you, that he might not have been sufficient to give you the necessary help, but finally Sir, the honor of your response will agreeably surprise me that you are enjoying perfect health, as well as your honorable family, which I desire with all my heart—I end this Sir praying you to be so kind as to salute your respectable family for me.

You will oblige him who is honored to be with the most profound respect which is possible to express to you— ETIENNE LEMAIRE

My address will be at Mr. Marinot's, opposite the City Tavern Second Street,

p.s.v.

Being at Philadelphia, Sir, if I may be of any help, I pray you to employ me, you will be served with all possible attention to detail

Mr. Julien has to leave Monday, or Tuesday

RC (DLC); endorsed by TJ as received 23 Mar. 1809 and so recorded in SJL. Translation by Dr. Roland H. Simon.

Jack SHORTER was a hostler at the President's House who returned to Washington after accompanying TJ to Monticello (Stanton, *Free Some Day*, 80; *MB*, 1:1244). Michael MARINOT was a confectioner at 93 South Second Street in Philadelphia (James Robinson, *The Philadelphia Directory for 1805* [Philadelphia, 1805], 147; Robinson, *Philadelphia Directory for 1809*).

P.S.V.: "please see verso." Lemaire's concluding note was written on the verso.

[1] Manuscript: "scour."

[2] Apparent idiosyncratic accent mark over one of the first two letters in this word omitted.

# To James Madison

DEAR SIR Monticello Mar. 17. 09.

On opening my letters from France in the moment of my departure from Washington, I found from their signatures that they were all from literary characters except one from mr Short, which mentioned in the outset that it was private, & that his public communications were in the letter to the Secretary of State, which I sent you. I find however on reading his letter to me (which I did not do till I got home) a passage of some length proper to be communicated to you and which I have therefore extracted.

I had a very fatiguing journey, having found the roads excessive bad, altho' I have seen them worse. the last three days I found it better to be on horseback, and travelled 8. hours through as disagreeable a snow storm as I was ever in. feeling no inconvenience from the expedition but fatigue, I have more confidence in my vis vitae than I had before entertained. the spring is remarkably backward. no oats sown, not much tobacco seed, & little done in the gardens. wheat has suffered considerably. no vegetation visible yet but the red maple, weeping willow & Lilac. flour is said to be at 8.D. at Richmond, & all produce is hurrying down.

I feel great anxiety for the occurrences of the ensuing 4. or 5. months. if peace can be preserved, I hope & trust you will have a smooth administration. I know no government which would be so embarrassing in war as ours. this would proceed very much from the lying & licentious character of our papers; but much also from the wonderful credulity of the members of Congress in the floating lies of the day. and in this no experience seems to correct them. I have never seen a Congress during the last 8. years a great majority of which I would not implicitly rely on in any question, could their minds have been purged of all errors of fact. the evil too increases greatly with the protraction of the session, and I apprehend, in case of war their sessions would have a tendency to become permanent. it is much therefore to be desired that war may be avoided if circumstances will admit. nor in the present Maniac state of Europe should I estimate the point of honour by the ordinary scale. I believe we shall on the contrary have credit with the world for having made the avoidance of being engaged in the present unexampled war, our first object. war however may become a less losing business than unresisted depredation. with every wish that events may be propitious to your administration, I salute you with sincere affection & every sympathy of the heart.

TH: JEFFERSON

RC (DLC: Madison Papers). PoC (DLC); at foot of first page: "The President of the US." Recorded in SJL as a letter of 16 Mar. 1809. Enclosure: William Short to TJ, 25 Nov. 1808, extract by TJ of Short's expressions of concern about inadequate diplomatic expense allowances for travel and his outfit for Saint Petersburg (DNA: RG 59, DD, Russia).

For the letters from French LITERARY CHARACTERS, see TJ to Caspar Wistar, 31 Mar. 1809. LETTER TO THE SECRETARY OF STATE: Short to James Madison, 29 Nov. 1808 (DNA: RG 59, DD, Russia). VIS VITAE: vital force.

# From the Republicans of Queen Annes County, Maryland

SIR,

Among the numerous farewell Addresses presented to you by the Inhabitants of this great and flourishing Country, permit us, a part of the Republicans of Queen Ann's County convened for the purpose at the Town of Centre Ville, to add ours—

We are sure none can feel more Gratitude for your great Services and none can more appreciate the inestimable Blessings flowing from that Independence, in obtaining and securing which you bore so conspicuous a Share.

We have strictly observed the measures of your Administration, We expected much from you and have not been disappointed—We may indeed say that more has been done, than was, or could reasonably have been expected.

History does not afford an Instance of a Country having risen in so short a period to such a State of prosperity.

The public Debt without the Aid of Taxes extinguished beyond Example—

A great and fertile Country containing large Rivers flowing through it, conveying it's surplus produce to distant Shores and reconveying the various Articles of foreign Climes under your Auspices has been obtained—the Accession of which precludes incessant Causes of Hostility and is an inexhaustible Source of Wealth to the Nation—

By an economical Use of Money—there is now in our Treasury a large surplus ready to be applied, if necessary, for our Defence against the unprincipled powers of Europe—

We have seen a Catilinian conspiracy, which aimed a Death Blow at our vitals, without shedding a Drop of Blood, dispelled like a Charm—

We are confident, that with Respect to foreign powers, you have observed a strict Neutrality, and if Hostilities must succeed, we shall have this Consolation, that Justice will be on our Side—

These Sir are some of the Advantages derived from your Administration, and as Freemen we express our Opinions of them not like the fawning sycophants of despotic Counts, with Adulation Approaching, while power lasts—No, we now address you when you have returned to the Bosom of your fellow Citizens—

And may the Supreme Ruler of the Universe reward you with peace and Tranquility here, and eternal Happiness hereafter—

ROBERT EMORY Chairma[n]
THOMAS WRIGHT Sec$^{y}$
Centre Ville QA County Es Md
March 18$^{th}$ 1809

MS (DLC); edges frayed; in Wright's hand, signed by Emory and Wright; at head of text: "To Thomas Jefferson Esq$^{r}$ late President US"; endorsed by TJ as an "Address republ. of Q. Anne's c$^{ty}$ Maryl$^{d}$" received 6 Apr. 1809 and so recorded in SJL. Enclosed in a brief covering letter from Wright dated Centreville, 22 Mar. 1809 (RC in DLC; at foot of text: "Thomas Jefferson Esqr"; endorsed by TJ as received 6 Apr. 1809 and so recorded in SJL).

Robert Emory was a Republican and a supporter of TJ (Frederic Emory, *Queen Anne's County, Maryland: Its Early History and Development* [1950], 364–6, 381). Thomas Wright (of Thomas) belonged to a prominent Republican Queen Annes County family (Emory, *Queen Anne's County*, 184, 373).

The CATALINIAN CONSPIRACY probably alludes to the western expeditions of Aaron Burr, 1805–07.

# From the Albemarle Buckmountain Baptist Church

DEAR SIR, Buckmountain Church March 19. 1809.—

Albemarle Buckmountain Baptist Church, Sendeth Greeting to our much esteemed friend, M$^{r}$ Thomas Jefferson.

We Congratulate you in your Return home, from your labour and painful Servis of eight years. now to take some Sweet hours of retirment and rest.—Injoying at pleasure the Company of your loveing Friends, and neighbours. not that We were werey, or Dissattisfied with your Conduct, but were wel pleased; for which Be pleas'd to accept of these our kind Thanks.—May your Days be many and Comfortable. in a word (may we say) we wish you health, wealth, and prosperity through life, And in the world to come life everlasting

Signed by order of the Church GEORGE TWYMAN

MS (DLC); salutation below greeting; addressed: "M$^{r}$ Thomas Jefferson"; endorsed by TJ as an "Address" of 17 Mar. 1809 received 9 Apr. 1809 and so recorded (with correct date) in SJL. Printed in Richmond *Enquirer*, 26 May 1809.

George Buford Twyman (1731–1818), an Albemarle farmer and longtime acquaintance of TJ, was an original member of the Albemarle Baptist Church of Christ, serving as moderator and record keeper from its organization in 1773 until

1811. The name of the church was changed to Buckmountain Baptist Church in 1801, when the congregation took possession of the church by that name formerly occupied by Episcopalians (1811 autobiography, George Twyman Papers, and Chesnut Grove Baptist Church Records, 1773–1970, both in ViU; *MB*, 1:22, 153, 206, 874, 878; Woods, *Albemarle*, 132–3).

A letter from Twyman to TJ of 3 July 1809, not found, is recorded in SJL as received the same day.

## From Joseph Dougherty

DEAR SIR, City of Washington Mar. 19th 1809

Inclosed is the bill of leading for your goods which left this place a few days ago, Mr Coles wrote you of the accident which happned to the vessel, on which they were first shipd—I re-shiped them on board the dolphin of york. Captn John Mager—Master—a dove colour silk in the form of a bed, I think filled with down—was got in your bed room—after you left the Presidents house. no one knows which it belongs; to you or the Presidents house. I will wait your instructions about it. Mr Coles set out from here this morning for N. york. I will write you more fully in a few days

Sir your Hble Servt JOS DOUGHERTY

N.B. a trunk left with me by Mr T. J. Randolph. for Frank Carr of Charlottsville. I send in care of Mr Julian who will hand this to you

RC (MHi); endorsed by TJ as received 24 Mar. 1809 and so recorded in SJL. Enclosure not found.

## From James Leitch

SIR, Charlottesville Mar. 19th 1809

By Mr Dinsmore I take the liberty of rendering you, your account. You will see from the memorandum annexed thereto the agreement between Mr Dinsmore & myself & afterwards Acceded to by Mr Bacon—

I should not at this time made Application but have been so much disappointed lately by Mr Bacon in the delivery of nails that I expected he did not find himself Obliged to let me have them. Should you think proper I am willing to receive the Ballance in nails if delivered in any short time; Or for any future dealings you may have as far as I can dispose of them

Yours respectfully JAS LEITCH

RC (MHi); endorsed by TJ as received 21 Mar. 1809 and so recorded in SJL.

James Leitch (d. 1826), a Charlottesville merchant, dealt extensively with TJ, who died owing him $2,807.40. Leitch was an original donor for the founding of Central College (now the University of Virginia) (*MB*, 2:1253n, 1291; Malone, *Jefferson*, 6:511; Leitch, Charlottesville store daybook, 1820–23, ViU; Central College Donors and Founders, Authorization to transfer Central College holdings, [before 1 Aug. 1818],Vi: Executive Papers; Albemarle County Court Order Book, 4 Dec. 1826, 1 Jan. 1827).

On 17 Apr. 1809 TJ settled his account with James Dinsmore and acknowledged a debt to him of $618.40. At some point Dinsmore assigned the note to Leitch. The ACCOUNT and MEMORANDUM, not found, evidently related to this transaction. TJ paid the note in 1813 (*MB*, 2:1245, 1291).

# From James Madison

DEAR SIR Washington Mar. 19. 1809

Altho' I feel reluctance in trespassing for a moment on the repose to which you have just retired, I can not well avoid enclosing a letter from M[r] La Trobe which he wishes may be seen by you before it be decided on, because he thinks you have already acquiesc'd in the reasonableness of its object: and which I wish you to see, because I am so raw on the whole subject, as to need any intimations you may find it convenient to give. You will observe that his proposal includes $700 for past services.

M[r] Coles left us this morning. The mail of yesterday brought a letter from Armstrong of Dec[r] 25. & Paris papers of the 27[th]. No change had taken place in our affairs. The occurrences & prospects in Spain will appear in the Nat[l] Intelligencer. No letter from Short, nor is he named by A. I conclude he had set out for S[t] P.

Health & happiness. JAMES MADISON

RC (DLC: Madison Papers); endorsed by TJ as received 23 Mar. 1809 and so recorded in SJL. Enclosure: Benjamin Henry Latrobe to Madison, 12 Mar. 1809, noting that the pace of work on the public buildings had slackened; proposing accordingly that, instead of filling the vacant post of clerk of the works at its salary of $1,400, he would oversee its duties himself if his son were engaged to assist him as an additional clerk with a salary of $600; noting that the public would save not only the $800 difference between these two salaries but also the $150 cost of renting a separate office; and requesting payment of $700 for the preceding six months during which Latrobe had acted as clerk of the works himself (RC in DLC: Madison Papers; printed in Latrobe, *Papers*, 2:703–4).

John Lenthall, the incumbent clerk of the works, died on 19 Sept. 1808 when a vault in the north wing of the Capitol building fell on him (Latrobe, *Papers*, 2:661).

# From John Wyche

SIR, Westwardmill (Brunswic V[a]) 19[th] March 1809

Your retirement from the presidency of the United States affords (I hope) a favourable oppertunity for me (although an entire stranger) to address you on a Subject which (from your known Patriotism—& Opinion that to be happy & free we must be Informed) I am assured will be pleasing to you: And without farther preface I will proceed to state to you that some fifteen or eighteen Months ago the Gentlemen (or some of them) of this Neighbourhood agreed to procure a collection of Books—establish a Library and form ourselves into a Society the stile & Title of which should be "The Westwardmill Library Society." We have accordingly drawn & ratified a Constitution contributed each Member a mite of ten Dollars for the purchase of Books & the most of the Money has allready been expended in that way—The Terms of admission are ten Dollars and the unanimous consent of the general meeting to form which a majority (at least) of all the members must be present we have some thoughts of applying to the Assembly for an Act of incorporation and under a belief that we shall do so I have taken the liberty of addressing you on the Subject & will If agreeable to you send a Copy of our Constitution and some of our fundamental Laws for your inspection & Correction And shall think myself very happy if by this means the Society shall gain your patronage and the advantages ensuing from your superior Information & experience though I have been & still am so much affraid you will treat it with neglect not to say contempt that the secret of my writing to you does & shall rest with my self untill I know the kind of reception you give this.

Our Society is composed of Farmers, Mechanics Justicies of the Peace Ministers of the Gospel—Militia Officers Lawyers, Schoolmasters—Merchants—Postmasters one Member of Assembly & one member of Congress VIZ Tho[s] Gholson.

Our present president is W[m] E. Brodnax a substantial & respectable farmer—Our Librarian James Wyche one of M[r] Grangers many Deputies—And Hubbard Hobbs—John Harrison (both planters) Joseph Percivall (a naturalised Cytizen) Jesse Coe (an Elder in the Methodist Church) Joseph Saunders (a Deacon in the Baptist Church) and Mark Greene (a Major in the Militia of Virginia) are our Six Directors for this year. Query will such an heterogeneous body ever firmly & lastingly coalesce?

I have gone thus far in detail in order to remove every doubt that you might possibly have as to the existance[1] of the Society Pardon this attempt in an obscure Individual to procure for a society (of which he is a Member) your countenance[2] If consistent with your dignity—ease & favourite persuits save him from the mortification of thinking you contemn him & the Society And believe me to be one among the many thousands of (Sir) your great admirers & most obt humble Servts

John Wyche

RC (MoSHi: TJC-BC); endorsed by TJ as received 7 May 1809 and so recorded in SJL.

John Wyche (d. 1848) was a surveyor and justice of the peace, a lieutenant in the Brunswick County militia in 1799, county coroner in 1815, sheriff, 1819–20, and a member of the county's first school board in 1819 (Gay Neale, *Brunswick County, Virginia: 1720–1975* [1975], 150, 378, 387, 389, 396, 410; *Richmond Whig & Public Advertiser*, 25 Feb. 1848).

[1] Word interlined in place of "reality."
[2] Wyche here canceled "& support."

# From Ann Craig

Dear Sir March 20th[1]–1809

You will be surprisd, I doubt not, on receiving a Letter from a very old acquaintance, Ann Craig, formerly of Williamsburg, who takes the liberty of addressing you. When you studied law in Williamsburg, you did me the honor to lodge in my house: I was then in easy Circumstances; but from the fire in Richmond, the death of my Brother Doctor Pasture, and other misfortunes, this is far from being the case now; insomuch that I have been for several years, and now am, under the necessity of depending upon my relations for support But from the death of several of my nearest relations, and others of them being in debt, so it is, that so little is rais'd for my support, that the Lady with whom I am plac'd (Mrs Markham near Manchester) is but indifferently paid for my Board. Being thus, Dear Sir, very old infirm, and dependent, I avail myself of the privilege these give the unfortunate, to request the favor of a small annual contribution for the support of a needy relation, being Cousin german to your Father. my greatest wish is to be enabled by my Friends to return to my native place Williamsburg, and there to end my days.

The above statement, Dear Sir, is but too true; but should you have any doubts on the subject, or wish for further information, I beg leave to refer you to my Friend Mr Edm'd Randolph, or Dr Turpin: and should you think proper to grant me any assistance, I shall ever retain a most grateful sense of the obligation. I am Dear Sir with the greatest

respect and consideration your most obt hbl Ser Ann Craig

RC (MHi); endorsed by TJ as a "begging" letter received 23 Mar. 1809 and so recorded in SJL.

Ann Pasteur Craig (ca. 1739–1810) married Thomas Craig, a Williamsburg tailor and tavern keeper who ran the Market Square Tavern in the 1760s. She evidently based her claim of relationship to TJ on the marriage of her BROTHER William Pasteur to Elizabeth Stith, TJ's second cousin through their shared great-grandparents William Randolph and Mary Isham Randolph. Although her brother provided for her in his will upon his death in 1791, Craig had no other means of support and was living with Mary MARKHAM in Chesterfield County (Armistead C. Gordon, "The Stith Family," *WMQ*, 1st ser., 22 [1913]: 47; Jonathan Daniels, *The Randolphs of Virginia* [1972]; Richmond *Virginia Argus*, 21 Dec. 1810).

COUSIN GERMAN: The son or daughter of one's uncle or aunt; first cousin (*OED*).

On 5 Apr. 1809 Rachel Satterwhite sent TJ a similar request for financial aid, not found but recorded in SJL as received 14 Apr. 1809 from Alexandria with the notation: "Begging."

[1] Manuscript: "thj20."

# From James Ronaldson

SIR Philadelphia March 20 1809

I take the liberty of inclosing coppy of a bill now before the Legistlature of Penny, that may be considered as passed, wanting only the concurrence of the H R to some amendments made by the Senate I think it will confer honor on the Legistlature and[1] produce incalculable benefit to the state; It is gratifying to observe the good sense and sound policy embraced in this bill, and if we may judge by the change of sentiment that has taken place amongst the farmers on this subject, it will soon be extended to all the populous counties in the state, so strong were the prejudices against taxing dogs; that a few years ago it was with difficulty a law could be got for the county of Delaware, and was so modified it could not go into operation until it met the approbation of the Grand Jury of the County, and several juries met and rejected it, even after it was adopted litigeous persons were found, who disputed it constitutionality, Saying the "Legistlature had no right to delegate to any body the power of imposing Taxes" to remove this objection the last section has been introduced into the bill and Delaware county included in this new act

I hope the specimens of wool were safely received and will be usefull

With sentiments of Respect & esteem I am Your well wisher

JAMES RONALDSON

RC (DLC); endorsed by TJ as received 30 Mar. 1809 and so recorded in SJL.

The Pennsylvania statute TAXING DOGS as sent to TJ has not been found, but as passed on 23 Mar. 1809, it provided for an annual tax of from twenty-five cents to two dollars per dog in Philadelphia and in Bucks, Chester, Montgomery, and Delaware counties; stipulated that the resulting fund be used to reimburse farmers for sheep killed by dogs; dedicated any surplus from the dog tax to the purchase of full-blooded merino sheep and other imported sheep and cattle to improve local bloodlines; and in the LAST SECTION repealed a 10 Apr. 1807 act taxing dogs in Delaware County superseded by the new legislation (*Acts of the General Assembly of the Commonwealth of Pennsylvania* [Philadelphia, 1809], 87–90).

[1] Manuscript: "and and."

## From Anonymous

HONORED SIR, Charleston (S° Car.) 21st March 1809.

I feel a reluctance in addressing myself to you, which the knowledge of your character will always inspire. For to occupy one moment of your time so well employed in noble pursuits, will I fear be too great an intrusion. But when I behold you in the character of the Father and Protector of youth, I am inspired with a confidence which at once overcomes every obstacle. As an individual you are to me a stranger, but as a member of the American Republic, we are fellow-citizens. You have, in your public capacity, been to me a father, a protector, a preserver. For these services I will forever render you the tribute of a grateful heart. Accept then the present assurances of my respect, my esteem—my admiration. Think not however Sir, that what I have here said proceeds from a fawning adulation. Think not that I desire to gain a favor by insidious flattery. This cannot be more abhorrent to your disposition, than it is to mine. I have long viewed you as the brightest example of the effect of industry combined with talents. You have shewn to the world that in an Elective Government it is possible to be raised to the highest stations, without having deviated from the paths of virtue and honor. When exalted to the Presidency, of the only free Government on Earth, we were taught by your former conduct what to expect. Our expectations were exceeded.—But it is time to come to the subject of my Letter—When I beheld you in the exercise of your Official duties, it was impossible that I could avoid feeling an anxious[1] wish that I could have marked out, to me, the outlines of the path you trod to greatness. Not, that ever my soaring ambition could asscend to the height, which you have so lately voluntarily left. Not that even in the pleasing dreams of anticipation, this Golden prospect was ever presented to my mind. No—my views were more confined. I would pursue the same course which you have done, and strive to ascend as high as industry and virtue will exalt me. When I behold a great Man I am always induced to beleive that he has become so by pursuing an uncommon road, for how many thousands who tread the beaten path, and who add the most persevering industry, to natural vigor of mind, perish in obscurity. Fully convinced of this, I am induced to request that you would point out to me the way to Glory—You have been a successful traveller there. You then can surely direct me. In History we admire the characters of eminent Statesmen, and renouned Heroes, but we have not seen recorded the <u>private plans</u> they followed in order to become so. We are told indeed how Demosthenes, and a few others acted, but these accounts are either too romantic for beleif, or by no means satisfactory. It is from living characters therefore that we must seek this information. And Sir, if all the great Men of Antiquity could this moment rise from their Graves, and dwell in our Country, I yet would make the inquiry of you. I have now explained the motives of this application. It may not be <u>now</u> proper for me to inform you of my name. It will be sufficient to say that I am a Young Man whose character in his native State has not yet been clouded by the breath of Calumny. Perhaps Sir, my name, might be an advantage to me. But disdaining to receive any favor through the merits of my Ancestors, I am induced to rest my claim upon your Kindness alone. It is not impossible but that at some future period I may have the happiness of returning my acknowledgments in Person—Should you be disposed to gratify me in this my request you will please direct to A.U. at this place—

I am Honored Sir, with every sentiment of Esteem Your most ob$^{t}$ serv$^{t}$

RC (MHi); addressed: "Thomas Jefferson Esquire Late President of the United States—Monticello—Virginia"; franked and postmarked in Charleston, South Carolina; endorsed by TJ as a "respectful" anonymous letter received 8 Apr. 1809 and so recorded in SJL.

A.U.: Anthony Ulmo, physician and druggist, is the only entry with these initials in the 1809 Charleston city directory (Richard Hrabowski, *Directory for the District of Charleston* [Charleston, S.C., 1809], 101).

[1] Manuscript: "axious."

## From Charles Willson Peale

Dear Sir — Museum March 21$^{st}$ 09

It was my intention in this to have given you the particulars of expenditures for & to M$^{r}$ Randolph at my settlement with him on his departure, but I have a variety of bussiness that engrosses my whole attention at this moment, in my next I will do it. I write now only to acknowledge the receipt of your favor of the 10th Instant inclosing one hundred & fifty Dollars for the use of Mr Randolph on his return to the botanical lectures.

My son Rembrandt is now perpairing to return again to Paris to resume his labour of making Portraits of the eminent Characters in Europe to furnish my Gallery—I have given him the opportunity of painting to the number of 50, when that is completed, very probably I may be enabled to pay him for an encrease of Numbers. by this exertion I hope we shall possess a Gallery of Pictures equal in real Value to any in the world.

Mrs Peale desires her love to Mrs Randolph.[1] I am with much esteem your friend

C W PEALE

RC (DLC); at foot of text: "Thomas Jefferson Esqr"; endorsed by TJ as received 30 Mar. 1809 and so recorded in SJL. PoC (PPAmP: Peale Letterbook).

Armed with a special passport from TJ, Rembrandt Peale first traveled to Europe in April 1808 to paint a dozen PORTRAITS of scholars and politicians in Paris and Rome for his father's museum. TJ provided a list of French worthies as possible subjects (TJ to Charles Willson Peale, 13 Mar. 1808 [PPAmP]; Peale, *Papers,* vol. 2, pt. 2, pp. 1060–2).

[1] Manuscript: "Randolp."

## From Etienne Lemaire

MONSIEUR George town 22. Mars 1809

Recevez mes tres humble remercis mens pour la Letre tres flatteuse que vous m'avez fait lhonneur de mecrire, vous plaire pendent tout le tens que j'ai Été a votre service, a tous Gours été un de mes premiers soins, et il mest biens agréable, apres l'avoir quitté, d'apprendre que j'ai eu le bonheur de reusir. Ce seroit ingratitude de ma part de ne pas dire aussi que vous avez su Monsieur, rendre la servitude non seulement supportable, mais même agréable et je declare sincerement que de toutes les personne que j'ai eu a servir vous êtes Celle chez qui j'ai Joui du plus de bonheur et de satisfaction car vraiment vous servir Étoit pour moi,—plutôt un plaisir qu'ùne tâche;—Je suis Encore incertain ou je restera a Philadelphie mais en m'addressant Chez Mr marinot, vos lettres seront sures de me parvenir—et vous pouvez bien croire que ce sera toujours avec Grand plaisir que j'executerai[1] les ordres que vous voudrez bien me donner—

J'ai Lhonneur d'etre Monsieur bien respectueusement Votre tres humble serviteur

ETIENNE LEMAIRE

EDITORS' TRANSLATION

Sir Georgetown 22 March 1809

Accept my very humble thanks for the very flattering letter with which you have honored me, to please you all the time that I was in your service was always one of my first concerns, and it is quite a pleasure to learn, after I have left, that I had the good fortune to succeed. It would be ingratitude on my part not also to say that you Sir, knew how to make servitude not only bearable, but even pleasant and I sincerely declare that of all the persons that I have served you are the one in whose home I enjoyed the most happiness and satisfaction because to serve you was for me—truly a pleasure rather than a chore. I am still uncertain where I will stay in Philadelphia but in addressing me at Mr. Marinot's, your letters will be sure to reach me—and you can truly believe that it will always be with great pleasure that I will execute the orders that you wish to give me—

I have the honor to be Sir quite respectfully your very humble servant

Etienne Lemaire

RC (DLC); endorsed by TJ as received 30 Mar. 1809 and so recorded in SJL. Translation by Dr. Roland H. Simon.

[1] Manuscript: "j'excecuterai."

# From Samuel H. Smith

Sir Washington Mar. 22. 1809

I have received the accompanying tract from D[r] Fothergill of Phila[a] w[ch] I have the pleasure of transmitting to you in compliance with his desire.

I am very respectfully Sa. H. Smith

RC (DLC); at foot of text: "Thomas Jefferson Esq."; endorsed by TJ as received 30 Mar. 1809 and so recorded in SJL.

The accompanying tract may have been Anthony Fothergill, *Remarks on the Smut and Mildew of Wheat With Hints on the Most Probable Means of Prevention* (Philadelphia, 1808). Best known for his work on reviving drowning victims, Fothergill was a physician and foreign member of the American Philosophical Society (1792) who practiced medicine in Philadelphia between 1803 and his return to England in 1812. He sent TJ several of his tracts after he visited him in Washington in 1804 (*DNB*; Christopher Lawrence and others, eds., "'Take time by the forelock': The Letters of Anthony Fothergill to James Woodforde, 1789–1813," *Medical History*, suppl. 17 [1997]: xiii–xiv; APS, Minutes, 20 Jan. 1792 [MS in PPAmP]; Fothergill to TJ, 8 June 1804 [DLC]).

## From Elizabeth Trist

My Dear Sir Farmington 22d March 1809

In the number of gratulations on your return to private life I present mine with assurences that no one, is more sincerely gratified at the honorable termination of your Political career than I am, or derives greater happiness from the additional lustre reflected on your character, which has even impressd your enemies with sentiments of respect and admiration

May Heaven spare you long to your family and friends with health to enjoy life and the pleasing reflection of conscious rectitude and the approbation of the friends of your country

I received a letter from Wm Brown dated 29th Jany mentions that he shall send by the next weeks mail $500 for Harriot and my self which for better security he shall take the liberty of enclosing under cover to you as there is no certainty in the Mail particularly at this season I have my anxiety least it never comes to hand. I expected also a small parcel from Philad which I requested to be commited to the care of Jefferson if he did not return soon him Self to solicit the favor of him to forward to you to bring on, have you any recollection of receiving any thing directed to me you must have had little leisure to attend to any thing of the kind and I ought to have adverted to that circumstance when I made the request Please to present me affectionatly to Mrs Randolph I hope to have the pleasure of seeing all my beloved friends at Mounticello as soon as the roads get better I have been Stationary since the 16th of October and tho we have had a most unpleasant Winter I have been very tranquil and comfortable thanks to the kindness and hospitallity of Mr and Mrs Divers

I am Dear Sir with every sentiment of respect and regard your very sincere friend

E. Trist

RC (MHi); endorsed by TJ as received 23 Mar. 1809 but recorded in SJL as received a day later.

Elizabeth House Trist (ca. 1751–1828) was the daughter of Mary Stretch House, the widow of Nicholas Trist, a British army officer, and the grandmother of Nicholas P. Trist, who married TJ's granddaughter Virginia Jefferson Randolph at Monticello in 1824. Elizabeth Trist is best known for her journal detailing a trip to Natchez, 1783–84. TJ formed an enduring friendship with her when he stayed at her mother's Philadelphia boardinghouse during service in the Continental Congress, 1782–84. He advised her in recurring financial difficulties, wrote her regularly, persuaded her to move her family to Albemarle County in 1798, and appointed her only child, Hore Browse Trist, port collector for the lower Mississippi River in 1803, upon which she moved with him to New Orleans. Hore Browse Trist died in 1804 and Elizabeth Trist returned to Virginia in 1808, spending some of her remaining years as an itinerant houseguest at a variety of

Albemarle County estates, including Monticello, where she died and is buried in an unmarked grave.

William BROWN, the brother of Elizabeth Trist's daughter-in-law Mary, became port collector after Hore Browse Trist's death. Mary Brown Trist remarried Philip Livingston Jones. William Brown sold some of his plantation land to Jones to satisfy his own debts, and Brown agreed to provide for his nephews Nicholas P. Trist and Hore Browse Trist Jr. Evidently Brown also assisted Elizabeth Trist and his sister HARRIOT Brown, who accompanied Trist on her travels in Virginia (William L. Andrews, ed., *Journeys in New Worlds: Early American Women's Narratives* [1990], 183–7; Jane Flaherty Wells, "Thomas Jefferson's Neighbors: Hore Browse Trist of 'Birdwood' and Dr. William Bache of 'Franklin,'" *MACH* 47 [1989]: 1–13; Madison, *Papers, Pres. Ser.*, 2:424–6; Mary Brown Trist Jones to Harriot Brown, 6 Aug. 1809, and Virginia Jefferson Randolph Trist to Nicholas P. Trist, 10 Dec. 1828 [NcU: Nicholas P. Trist Papers]).

# From William D. Meriwether

SIR Thursday Evening [23 Mar. 1809]

The Committee appointed by a meeting of your County men to express to you their feelings & sentiments on your late return, inclose you a copy of an address which they are instructed to present—Those gentlemen who live at a distance & are now in Town, wish to be inform'd at what Time & place it will be most agreeable to you to receive them—

By order of the committee
W D. MERIWETHER
Chrm[n]

RC (DLC: TJ Papers, 187:33214); partially dated; endorsed by TJ as a letter of 23 Mar. 1809 received the same day and so recorded in SJL. Enclosure: Inhabitants of Albemarle County to TJ, [ca. 11 Mar. 1809].

William Douglas Meriwether (1761–1845) was a miller, surveyor, and land speculator who inherited Cloverfields, a large estate in Albemarle County. His milling operations on the Rivanna River in and near Charlottesville and Milton produced wool, cotton, flour, and timber, and in 1810 he was a director of the Rivanna Company, incorporated in 1806 to make improvements on the river. Meriwether represented Albemarle County in the Virginia House of Delegates, 1809–10, and served as sheriff in 1801 and 1828–30. After the death of his cousin Meriwether Lewis, he became agent for settling his affairs, having been his guardian since Lewis's father died. In the years after TJ's return to Monticello, Meriwether became a leading opponent of his development efforts at Milton (Louisa H. A. Minor, *The Meriwethers and Their Connections* [1892], 24; William D. Meriwether to Charles Meriwether, 14 July 1830 [NcU: Meriwether Family Papers]; Lay, *Architecture*, 16, 29, 72, 157, 162; Woods, *Albemarle*, 272; McGehee and Trout, *Jefferson's River*, 19).

# From Samuel DeButts

SIR, Mount Welby near Alexandria March 24 1809

It is with great diffidence that I give you at this time the trouble of a letter. Yet I have a lively hope from your general character that you will overlook my presumption when you are acquainted that with every plea of honesty on my side I approach you to ask your influence to obtain justice for me from M$^{r}$ Sam$^{l}$ Carr. You will now recollect Sir my former application. Having purchased & paid for the place near the city formerly in occupation of M$^{r}$ S. Carr. I petitioned you to use your influence in my behalf to obtain my title & to induce M$^{r}$ S. Carr to pay the balance due to M$^{r}$ Lingan to effect this. Soon after I received a letter from M$^{r}$ S. Carr assuring me that every requisite step should be immediately taken to settle the business to my satisfaction. A year ago the Chancellor's decree was issued unfavourable to M$^{r}$ S. Carr, who has not appealed & I am this day served by the sheriff with an ejectment & obliged besides to pay all M$^{r}$ S. Carr's law expences he having without permission joined my name with his own in his bill of Chancery.

I formerly (by a M$^{r}$ Brodie) sent you the papers proving my payment in full to M$^{r}$ S. Carr for the place & by the Chancellor's decree (a copy of which was immediately by direction of his attorney sent to him) it appears that M$^{r}$ S. Carr yet owes eight hundred pounds with interest from the year 1800 to M$^{r}$ Lingan.

I know well Sir that this is not a business of yours, nor do I advance any plea but justice feeling a confident assurance that you will see this done. I have the honor to be Sir

most respectfully & most humbly Y$^{r}$ obed$^{t}$ Serv$^{t}$

SAM$^{L}$ DEBUTTS

RC (DLC); endorsed by TJ as received 30 Mar. 1809 and so recorded in SJL.

Samuel DeButts (ca. 1750–1815), physician, was born in Ireland and practiced medicine in England before immigrating in 1792 to Prince Georges County, Maryland (Norfleet, *Saint-Mémin*, 158–9; DeButts family letters, 1782–1840 [ViU]).

In his FORMER APPLICATION of 28 Jan. 1806 (DLC), DeButts requested TJ's assistance in obtaining title to Gale Hill, an Albemarle County property that he wanted to sell to Francis Brodie. The business had awaited resolution for more than four years, with several letters to TJ's nephew Samuel Carr going unanswered (Richard Earle Welby to DeButts, 24 Dec. 1805 [ViU: DeButts family letters]).

## To Joseph Dougherty

Dear Joseph Monticello Mar: 24. 09.

I have recieved yours of the 19th just in time by the return of this day's post, to inform you that the dove coloured silk, with down in it, is mine. it is an Eider-down coverlet which I bought in Philadelphia in 1793. when I lived there. as it can be rolled into a compass not bigger than a man's leg, I would wish it to be packed in as small a box as it can be got into, & forwarded by the stage; but not until you can find somebody coming on, who will take it under his care, as it is a very costly article. I really thought I had sent this home last fall, and have no idea where it could have been left in the house so as to escape me. I do not suppose I can have left any thing else of mine, but should doubt arise on any article, mr Claxton can decide who knows what he bought for the house. I tender you my best wishes for your health & success Th: Jefferson

PoC (MHi); at foot of text: "Mr Jos. Dougherty"; endorsed by TJ.

## To Henry Foxall

Sir Monticello Mar. 24. 09.

The cook which I had in Washington (mr Julien) and who is now with me for a time, informs me you made for the President's kitchen some irons of casting for the stoves or stew-holes in the kitchen, in which the box-part & the grille[1] or bars were all solid together, and that you made them of three sizes. I must ask the favor of you to make 8. for me, to wit, 2. of the largest size & 3 of the middle & 3 of the smallest size, and forward them for me to Richmond to the care of Messrs Gibson & Jefferson, forwarding me the bill at the same time. I must pray you to do it without delay, if convenient, as they are indispensable in a kitchen. Accept the assurances of my esteem & respect Th: Jefferson

PoC (MHi); at foot of text: "Mr Foxhall"; endorsed by TJ.

Henry Foxall (1758–1823), British-born iron founder and entrepreneur, immigrated to Philadelphia in 1797 and in December 1800 followed the federal government to the District of Columbia, where he established the Foxall Foundry (also known as the Columbia Foundry) in Georgetown. He immediately signed lucrative contracts with the Navy and War departments, prospered, and was a key armaments producer for the United States during the War of 1812. Foxall was a prominent Methodist donor and lay minister and served as mayor of Georgetown, 1821–23. TJ purchased other Foxall products for Monticello, including cast-iron window sashes, clock weights, and fireplace linings (*DAB*; Madison Davis, "The Old Cannon Foundry above Georgetown, D.C., and its First Owner, Henry Foxall," *RCHS* 11 [1908]: 16–70; Louis F. Gorr, "The Foxall-Columbia Foundry: An Early Defense Contractor in Georgetown," *RCHS* 48 [1971/72]: 34–59; TJ to Foxall, 8 June 1806 [MHi]; *MB*).

A stew stove had an elevated fire over which iron STEW-HOLES were suspended (*OED*).

[1] Reworked from "grilles."

# To George Jefferson

DEAR SIR Monticello Mar. 24. 09.

My packages from Washington must be now near arriving with you, and I will pray you to forward them by such boats as are deemed trusty. there will also be from mr Taggert of Philadelphia a cask of linseed oil & keg of white lead. I inclose you a bill of lading for a box belonging to one of my workmen, mr Nelson, which he had addressed to me, to the care of your firm, which as you will see has been mistaken. he supposes it to have been long at Richmond, probably mislaid from the mistake of the firm. I will thank you to have it enquired after & forwarded. I must pray you to send me 2. barrels of salt herrings & a hogshead of Molasses.

I am extremely anxious to see you here, and hope some matter of business may render it convenient for you to come into this quarter. I salute you with affectionate esteem TH: JEFFERSON

PoC (MHi); at foot of text: "Mr G. Jefferson"; endorsed by TJ. Enclosure not found.

# To James Madison

DEAR SIR Monticello Mar. 24. 09.

I inclose you several letters which must have been intended for the office, & not the person named on the back. they belong therefore to your files, and I will pray you particularly as to those asking office on this & all other occasions to consider me merely as the channel of conveyance, & not as meaning to add an atom of weight to the sollicitations they convey. unless indeed I know any thing on the subject & mention it particularly. as in the case of Francis Page, being acquainted with him it is my duty to say that he is a most amiable young man, educated to the bar, perfectly correct in his conduct, and, as the son of our late friend, of good standing. I do not presume that York can present a more worthy or unexceptionable subject.

Among these letters is one from Ray author of the War of Tripoli.

he sent me one of his books, & in answering him with thanks I used the complimentary phrase he quotes. he lays hold of it to beg 100.D. of which I shall not be the dupe. I inclose it to you, as I think he has too much genius for the low station in which he was in the navy, and to place him in your recollection, if any occasion should arise wherein such a man can be useful in the navy or elsewhere. I send Mazzei's letter for your perusal. the part for your attention is in ⌈ ⌋ altho' no part of it is secret. I intended, but forgot to mention to you Gen[l] Dearborne's son for a military commission. I should have named him; but mr Smith of the W.O. told me Pickering had been collecting some stories to oppose his nomination, which might have weight if not answered. I desired him therefore to write to the General & in the mean time to hold up the nomination. God bless you & prosper you. TH: JEFFERSON

Mazzei's letter to be returned, but not the others

RC (DLC: Madison Papers); at foot of text: "Pr. US." PoC (DLC); lacks postscript; endorsed by TJ. Enclosure: William Ray to TJ, 7 Mar. 1809.

The SEVERAL LETTERS enclosed probably also included the following missing items, all of which were recorded in SJL as received on 23 Mar. 1809 and for all of which, as well as the Ray letter, TJ recorded "P" next to the SJL entry, presumably to indicate that the subject matter was presidential or that he had sent them to the president: (1) Anonymous to TJ, 2 Jan. 1809 (with the notation "land speculns"). (2) Joseph Crocket to TJ, Lexington, 14 Feb. 1809. (3) William Sampson to TJ, New York, 12 Mar. 1809. (4) St. George Tucker to TJ, Richmond, 17 Mar. 1809 (with the notation "Page"). (5) Gershom Tuttle and others to TJ, Watertown, undated (with the notation "Jereme").

Madison had already given a recess appointment to FRANCIS PAGE, son of OUR LATE FRIEND John Page, as collector and inspector of revenue at Yorktown (Madison to TJ, 28 Mar. 1809; *JEP*, 2:123, 125 [16, 21 June 1809]).

The extant text of MAZZEI'S LETTER of 28 Oct. 1808 (Archivio Filippo Mazzei, Pisa; printed in Mazzei, *Writings*, 3:494–7) lacks TJ's brackets, but the highlighted section was probably that which dealt with payment to Giuseppe Antonio Franzoni of one hundred Spanish pieces. Among other things Mazzei's wide-ranging letter also discussed his past attempts to discover from Latrobe the welfare of Franzoni and his fellow sculptor Giovanni Andrei. Mazzei had hired them in 1805 and established the terms of their payment and accommodations in the United States. Two earlier Mazzei letters forwarded to Latrobe through TJ had not elicited any news on this matter. Mazzei enclosed in the 28 Oct. letter a third copy of his letter to Latrobe, probably similar to that of 20 July 1807 (DLC) (Mazzei to TJ, 20 July 1805, 22 June 1807, 29 Mar. 1808 [Archivio Filippo Mazzei, Pisa]).

John SMITH was chief clerk of the War Department.

## To William D. Meriwether

DEAR SIR  Monticello Mar. 24. 09.

I intended to have answered your kind letter by mr Stevenson yesterday evening but he left us without my knowing it. perhaps he considered as an answer, my saying to him that I presumed it would be most convenient for the gentlemen of the committee to meet on our next court day at Charlottesville, where I will attend them. I take the liberty therefore of proposing this to them, as other business will probably call us all there on that day.

I salute yourself & them with affection & respect.

TH: JEFFERSON

PoC (MHi); at foot of text: "W. D. Meriwether esq."; endorsed by TJ.

TJ delivered his reply in Charlottesville on 3 Apr. 1809, the NEXT COURT DAY (TJ to the Inhabitants of Albemarle County, 3 Apr. 1809).

## From the New York State Legislature

SIR,

The legislature of the state of New York, on the occasion of your voluntary retirement to the shades of private life, from the office of chief magistrate of the United States, cannot, without injustice to their feelings refrain from expressing their respect for your exalted character, their gratitude for your public services, and their best wishes for your personal happiness.

Like your great predecessor the immortal Washington, you have evinced to the world by the whole tenor of your political life, and more especially by your magnanimous determination to retire from office after having faithfully served the republic, that your only ambition was to promote the welfare of the people, and to perpetuate the principles of our republican institutions. Examples of such disinterested and distinguished patriotism are rarely found in the history of nations. They add a lustre to the American name and character.

While we look back with satisfaction on your administration of the general government, we look forward with confidence to that of your successor—May he be animated by your illustrious example, and under the auspices of the Almighty dispenser of all good, direct the destinies of our country in safety amidst the agitations and convulsions of a troubled world. And may the remainder of your days be spent in the enjoyment of all those blessings which flow from an honorable and virtuous life zealously devoted to the good of mankind. Albany March 24th 1809

By Order of the Senate
JNO BROOME Presidt
By order of the Assembly,
JAS, W, WILKIN Speaker

MS (DLC); in a clerk's hand, signed by Broome and Wilkin; at head of text: "To Thomas Jefferson late president of the United States"; endorsed by TJ as an "Address legislatre N. York" received 6 Apr. 1809 and so recorded in SJL. Enclosed in a brief undated covering letter from Broome and Wilkin to TJ (RC in DLC: TJ Papers, 187:33245; in a clerk's hand, signed by Broome and Wilkin; at foot of text: "Thomas Jefferson Late President of the United States"; endorsed by TJ as received 6 Apr. 1809 and so recorded in SJL).

John Broome (ca. 1738–1810), merchant and politician, was a 1777 delegate to the New York state constitutional convention, a member of the New York state senate, 1803–04, and lieutenant governor of New York, 1804–10 (Francis S. Drake, *Dictionary of American Biography, Including Men of the Time* [1879], 128).

James Whitney Wilkin (1762–1845), speaker of the New York Assembly, was a 1785 graduate of the College of New Jersey who became an attorney in Goshen, New York. He served intermittently in both houses of the New York state legislature, 1800–14, and sat in the United States House of Representatives, 1815–19 (*Princetonians*, 1784–1790, pp. 100–3).

## To Elizabeth Trist

DEAR MADAM Monticello[1] Mar. 24. 09.

I recieve with great thankfulness your kind congratulations on my liberation from the duties & anxieties of my late situation. five & twenty years of affectionate acquaintance (perhaps it is uncivil to recall such a period to a single lady) leave me without a doubt of their sincerity. of the ground of congratulation nobody can be a more feeling judge than myself. my present freedom of pursuit is a perfect contrast to the burthen under which I have been oppressed. I intend to see you at mr Divers's as soon as my garden & other new concerns will admit. I come to him as a pauper, begging for the garden. Jefferson has recieved nothing for you; nor has any thing come to me from Wm Brown. in a letter to my daughter some time ago, I answered your enquiries relative to the Campeachy hamocks & Paccans, to wit that the vessel had never been heard of since she left N. Orleans & consequently that she must have perished with her cargo & crew.—since writing so far Jefferson tells me he brought a bundle for you which he now takes on to you.—we embrace with eagerness the hope you hold out to us of seeing you soon at Monticello, and for all the time you can give us; and I salute you with constant & affectionate respect.

TH: JEFFERSON

RC (CSmH: JF-RAB); mutilated at seal, with losses supplied from PoC; at foot of text: "Mrs Trist." PoC (MoSHi: TJC-BC); endorsed by TJ.

TJ requested two CAMPEACHY HAMOCKS and a barrel of pecans from William Brown in August 1808 and was subsequently informed of the loss with all hands of the *Sampson*, the schooner carrying the goods. Variously described as a "siesta" or "lolling" chair, the campeachy is a reclining chair made of mahogany wood from Campeachy, Mexico (TJ to Brown, 18 Aug. 1808 [MHi]; Brown to TJ, 10 Oct. 1808 [DLC]; TJ to Martha Jefferson Randolph, 27 Feb. 1809 [James H. Eddy, Charles B. Eddy Jr., and John B. Eddy, New York City, 1948]; Stein, *Worlds*, 280–1).

[1] To left of this word TJ erased "Wash."

# To George Jefferson

DEAR SIR

Monticello Mar. 25. 09.

My letter by post yesterday desired you to send my goods from Washington by trusty boatmen. I did not then know that mr Randolph's boats would go off to-day. as they are entirely trusty, I pray you to deliver to them whatever you may have for me. the molasses particularly will come safe by them. we are entirely unable to get cotton seed in this part of the country. mr Bacon at my request wrote to you for some. if you have or can procure it, it will be rendering me a great service.

Your's affectionately

TH: JEFFERSON

SC (MHi); at foot of text: "Mr George Jefferson"; endorsed by TJ.

A list of expenses incurred by Edmund BACON between December 1808 and March 1809, ending with the sale by Nicholas Giannini of two thousand pounds of fodder for $11.67 payable on 15 Mar. 1809 (MS in CSmH: JF; entirely in TJ's hand; undated; at head of text: "E. Bacon's debts from Dec. 10. 08—to Mar. 15. 09"), confirms that in his capacity as Monticello overseer, Bacon regularly purchased corn, beef, fodder, and livestock for TJ's plantation. TJ reimbursed Bacon for these purchases on 6 Dec. 1808 and 8 and 23 Jan. 1809 (*MB*, 2:1236, 1238, 1239).

## From James Maury

DEAR SIR, Liverpool 25th March 1809

I beg leave to congratulate you on your return to Monticello & hope you there enjoy that comfort in retirement which you had contemplated.

I think the laws of the United States exempt from the expence of postage those who have served the high office you so lately filled: I therefore sent you a few days ago a packet of Newspapers: since the date of which the Duke of York has resigned.

Annexed are the prices of our produce. Cotton greatly fallen, in consequence of a considerable decrease in consumpt;—aided by the arrival of more than thirty cargoes within the district of this Consulate since the commencement of last month: and this too in American vessells direct from ports of the United States. I however hope & trust that, when the late additional Embargo restrictions shall have taken place, such violations of the law will cease.

The orders of council of this countrey & blockading decrees of France statu quo &, for the present, I see no prospect of change.

The death of that good man whom you so invariably & so affectionately mentioned in the letters you have, from time to time, honored me with, has indeed afflicted me greatly. It could not be otherwise for such a brother; but he had lived long & when I consider how, well may I say "let my last end be like his." I present you my best wishes and am

dear Sir, Your's truly JAMES MAURY

| | | | | |
|---|---|---|---|---|
| Sea Island Cotton | 2/. | a | 4/. | |
| Upland | 1/9 | | 2/. | ℔ lb |
| leaf Tob° | 1/3 | | 2/2 | ℔ lb |
| stemed d° | 2/ | | 2/4 | ℔ lb |
| Rice | 55/ | | 60/ | Cwt |
| Turpintine | 78/ | | 85/. | Cwt |
| Tar | 52/ | | 56/. | Barrel |
| Wheat | 14/ | | 14/6 | 70 lb |

RC (DLC); at foot of text: "His Excellency Thomas Jefferson &C &C Monticello"; endorsed by TJ as received 18 June 1809 and so recorded in SJL.

James Maury (1746–1840), merchant and American consul at Liverpool, 1790–1829, was TJ's lifelong friend and regular correspondent, having been a classmate with TJ at the Albemarle County school of his father, the Reverend James Maury (Anne Fontaine Maury, ed., *Intimate Virginiana: A Century of Maury Travels by Land and Sea* [1941], 1–21, 319).

Frederick Augustus, DUKE OF YORK and Albany and the second son of George III, RESIGNED as commander-in-chief of the British army when it was revealed that his mistress, Mary Anne Clarke, had taken money in exchange for promises to use her influence over the duke to obtain military promotions (*DNB*). THAT GOOD MAN, Maury's recently deceased brother Matthew Maury, succeeded his father as rector of Fredericksville Parish in Louisa County, taught a school attended by TJ's nephew Dabney Carr, officiated at Monticello marriages and funerals, and received an annual contribution from TJ (Woods, *Albemarle*, 268–9; William Meade, *Old Churches, Ministers, and Families of Virginia* [1857], 2:44; *MB*).

# From John MacGowty

SIR Windham Con March 26th 1809

I take the liberty of Writing to you as a sea faring man who has been to sea for 22 years and have had the Honour of Sailing Master of vessls with the Sea Letters, with your signature to them, Sir I have been about the world considrably and have red some, but I do not recoollect to have ever read or seen the instance of a man's having Honour and riches enough, as it Seams Sir you have convenced the world that you have, which appears so by your Choice of becoming a private Citizen once more, I have seen and heard a good deal of this bad partys talk against your measures and in particular against your Person, but at the Same time I have not heard or seen any measures which you have taken to gard your self, but by returning good for Evil, and at the Same time Sir you have Said to them as the greatest being that ever was on Earth Said, Father forgive them for they know not what they do as to your being President Sir I could have wished that you would have kept that office for four years longer, but as you have prefured a private life my sincere Prays are that you may live to enjoy that Private Life with as much happiness,[1] as your public life has been usefull to your Country—

Sir I beg that you will excuse my freedom I have herein taken, but Sir as an american and Born in the Republican state of Virginia, but have lived in this state 20-years has made me here take the Liberty I have, Sir with the greatest pleasur I am your most obedant and most Humble Servant

JOHN MACGOWTY

RC (MHi); between dateline and body of letter: "Thomas Jefferson Esqr"; endorsed by TJ as received 14 Apr. 1809 and so recorded in SJL.

John MacGowty, seaman and sometime master and owner of a vessel, was a native Virginian of Scottish ancestry who settled in Windham, Connecticut, and died in North Carolina (William L. Weaver, *History of Ancient Windham, Ct. Genealogy, Containing a Genealogical Record of all the Early Families of Ancient Windham* [1864], pt. 1, 23–4; MacGowty to James Madison, 19 Mar. 1809, Madison, *Papers, Pres. Ser.*, 1:67).

[1] Manuscript: "hapness."

## From Cunningham Harris

SIR, Harrisburg. Dis[t] of Lancaster So. Car. March 27[th] 1809.

From a conviction that the cultivation of the Benni would prove a useful acquisition to both the medical and agricultural departments, and uncertain where to procure even a partial supply of the seed, I have taken the liberty to request that you will have the goodness to forward me by an early post such a supply as may not be deemed an unwarrantable requisition on that department.

I have further to request that you will accept of an assurance of my sincere congratulations on your honorable & dignified retirement from the toils of public life; with every assurance that the best wishes of the great mass of the citizens of United America will not cease to attend you through the remaining portion of a long and useful life.

I am with sentiments of the highest respect & consideration, Sir, your obedient servant CUNNINGHAM HARRIS. M.D.

RC (DLC); dateline at foot of text; at head of text: "Mr Jefferson"; endorsed by TJ as a letter of 23 Mar. 1809 received 14 Apr. 1809 and so recorded in SJL.

TJ's interest in cultivating BENNI (benne, *Sesamum indicum*) began in 1808 when he tried substituting sesame oil for olive oil in cooking. The leaves and oil from the seed were also used medicinally (Betts, *Garden Book*, 359–60, 361–2; James Thacher, *The American New Dispensatory* [Boston, 1810], 210; *Hortus Third*, 1039).

## From George Jefferson

DEAR SIR Richmond 27[th] Mar: 1809

I have made diligent search after M[r] Nelson's box, but cannot find it.—Cap[t] Hand I understand belongs to Philadelphia, or to Alexandria,—he is however frequently here: I will make a point of ascertaining what he has done with the box, on his return to this place.—I hope to have the pleasure of seeing you at Monticello in the course of the spring or summer.

I am Dear Sir Y[r] M[t] humble serv[t] GEO. JEFFERSON

RC (MHi); at foot of text: "Thomas Jefferson esq[r]"; endorsed by TJ as received 30 Mar. 1809 and so recorded in SJL.

## From James Madison

Dear Sir Washington Mar. 27. 1809

Altho' the letter from M^r Brown was probably intended for you, I could not hesitate in carrying it into effect; and finding that the Bill on the Navy Dep^t will be paid, I inclose, in order to avoid the delay of a week, the sum drawn for in Bank notes. I send them to you rather than directly to M^rs T. first because I do not know what the direct address ought to be, & 2^dly because it is possible, that you may be possessed of authority from her to give them a particular destination.

Your letter of the 17^th was safely deliverd by Shorter. I wish your exemption from ill effects from the Snow storm may be permanent.

M^r Short complains without reason on the subject of his allowances. Nothing was said as to an outfit, because it was more than possible that the Senate might reject him, and not certain that the Mission would be made permanent. And as to his expences of travelling, his running salary was as adequate at least to them, as to his stationery expences.

I forget whether the time piece in the sitting room be monthly or weekly? Will you please when you inform me, to add a memorandum of the Newspapers retained by you out of the list sent you whilst here, that I may know how to dispose of them.

Y^rs with the highest esteem & truest affection.

James Madison

RC (DLC: Madison Papers); at foot of text: "M^r Jefferson"; endorsed by TJ as received 30 Mar. 1809 and so recorded in SJL.

Madison enclosed $500 from William brown for Elizabeth Trist (TJ to Madison, 31 Mar. 1809).

## To the Republicans of Essex County, Massachusetts

The reciept of your kind address in the last moments of the session of Congress, will, I trust offer a just apology for this late acknolegement of it. I am very sensible of the indulgence with which you are so good as to review the measures of my late administration: and I feel for that indulgence the sentiments of gratitude it so justly calls for. the stand which has been made on behalf of our seamen enslaved & incarcerated in foreign ships, & against the prostration of our rights on the ocean under laws of nature acknoleged by all civilized nations, was an effort due to the protection of our commerce, & to that portion of our fellow citizens engaged in the pursuits of navigation. the opposition of the same portion to the vindication of their peculiar rights has been as wonderful, as the loyalty of their agricultural brethren in the assertion of them has been disinterested & meritorious. if the honour of the nation can be forgotten, Whether the abandonment of the right of navigating the ocean may not be compensated by exemption from the wars it would produce, may[1] be a question for our future councils, which the disclaimer of our navigating citizens, may, if continued, relieve from the embarrasment of their rights.

Sincerely & affectionately attached to our national constitution, as the ark of our safety, & grand Palladium of our peace & happiness, I learn with pleasure that the number of those in the county of Essex, who read & think for themselves, is great, & constituted of men who will never surrender, but with their lives, the invaluable liberties atchieved by their fathers. their elevated minds put all to the hazard for a three penny duty on tea, by the same nation, which now exacts a tribute equal to the value of half our exported produce.

I thank you, fellow citizens for the kind interest you take in my future happiness, and I sincerely supplicate that overruling Providence which governs the destinies of men & nations to dispense his choicest blessings on yourselves, & our beloved country.

TH: JEFFERSON
Monticello Mar. 28. 1809

PoC (DLC); at head of text: "To the Delegates from the various towns in the county of Essex & commonwealth of Massachusets, assembled on the 20th of February at Topsham"; at foot of first page: "Stephen Cross esq. Topsham." Recorded in SJL as "Answer to Address c^ty of Essex. Cross."

In their 20 Feb. 1809 ADDRESS from Topsfield, signed as president by Stephen Cross and as secretary by Joseph Sprague Jr. (DLC), the Essex County Republicans commended TJ on his presidential achievements, especially his efforts to prevent the impressment of American seamen. From a county reputedly opposed to the Jefferson administration, they promised to counteract a Massachusetts legislative memorial protesting the Embargo, which was submitted to Congress on 27 Feb. 1809 (*Annals*, 10th Cong., 2d sess., 443–50 [27 Feb. 1809]).

[1] Word interlined in place of "will."

# From James Madison

DEAR SIR Mar. 28. 1809

I have yours of the 24. The enquiry as to Franzoni will be made as soon as an opp[y] offers. F. Page had been app[d] before your letter was rec[d], & his Comission forwarded.

We have letters from Erving to Jan[y] 28. He was at Cadiz, intending it appears to adhere to the Junta Suprema, till the drama should close, and then leave Spain, by way of Gibralter, Tangier, or England, if no other course offered itself. I fear he has run from one Extreme to another, under the[1] influence of the Existing Atmosphere. His news is pretty much like that in the paper inclosed. Yrujo was at Cadiz, going on with his Mills, which involving a Monopoly, were odious & not likely to survive popular fury in the only turn of things that c[d] preserve his patent. He says he has sacrificed his fortune in promoting the patriotic cause. Adieu. Y[rs] JAMES MADISON

RC (DLC: Madison Papers); at foot of text: "M[r] Jefferson"; endorsed by TJ as received 30 Mar. 1809 and so recorded in SJL. Enclosure not found.

[1] Manuscript: "the the."

# From Larkin Smith

DEAR SIR March 28[th] 1809 Norfolk

I cannot suppress the gratification which I feel, in expressing to you my sentiments of exalted respect, and veneration, for your eminent public services and private virtues. and altho' the latter part of your Administration, was attended with circumstances, that must have been wounding to your feelings, and which I consider as eminating directly from a widely extended British influence, in the eastern and deluded part of our Country; I am nevertheless satisfied, that those very acts, will in a short time, be viewed by your present political enemies in a very different light; and that they will do you the justice, to acknowledge them to be amongst the most correct, important, and brilliant acts, which have so strongly marked, your long, and beneficial public labors. as an obscure individual, amongst the great mass of your fellow Citizens I feel the most unbounded gratitude, for the successfull efforts which you have made, in support of the true interests, and happiness of our Country. and[1] I offer my sincere prayers, that you may long live, in the perfect enjoyment of health and happiness, and that you may experience that fullness of consolation, to which your merits, give you so strong a claim. these are the effusions of my heart, and for their expression, and in trespassing on your time, I ask to be excused, as it may be the last tribute of my sincere Esteem and respect.

I am Sir with the most exalted Sentiments your Ob[t] Servant

LARKIN SMITH

RC (MoSHi: TJC-BC); at foot of text: "Thomas Jefferson Esq[r] late President of the U. States "; endorsed by TJ as received 8 Apr. 1809 and so recorded in SJL.

Larkin Smith (1745–1813) was a captain in the Fourth Regiment of Dragoons during the Revolutionary War and a member of the Virginia House of Delegates intermittently from 1784–1803. TJ appointed Smith customs collector for the district of Norfolk and Portsmouth in 1807, a position he held until his death. Smith received 4,000 acres of bounty land for his Revolutionary War service, and his heirs posthumously petitioned for additional land due him (Heitman, *Continental Army*, 505; *JEP*, 2:57, 59, 450 [9, 18 Nov. 1807, 7 Jan. 1814]; Affidavit of John H. Smith, Larkin Smith File, Revolutionary War Bounty Warrants, Vi; Richmond *Enquirer*, 8 Oct. 1813).

[1] Manuscript: "an."

# To the Convention of Bristol County, Rhode Island

The reciept of your friendly address in the last moments of the session of Congress, will, I trust, offer a just apology for it's late acknolegement.

We have certainly cause to rejoice that since the waves of affliction & peril, raised from the storm of war by the rival belligerents of Europe, have undulated on our shores, the councils of the nation have been able to preserve it from the numerous evils which have awfully menaced, & otherwise might have fallen upon us. how long we may yet retain this desirable position is difficult to be foreseen. but confident I am that as long as it can be done consistently with the honour & interest of our country, it will be maintained by those to whom you have confided the helm of government. a surer pledge for this cannot be found than in the public & private virtues of the successor to the chair of government, which you so justly recognise. your reflections are certainly correct on the importance of a good administration in a republican government, towards securing to us our dearest rights, & the practical enjoiment of all our liberties; and such an one can never fail to give consolation to the friends of free government, & mortification to it's enemies. in retiring from the duties of my late station, I have the consolation of knowing that such is the character of those into whose hands they are transferred, & of a conviction that all will be done for us which wisdom & virtue can do.

I thank you fellow citizens for the kind sentiments of your Address, & am particularly gratified by your approbation of the course I have pursued; & I pray heaven to keep you under it's holy favor.

Monticello. Mar. 29. 09. TH: JEFFERSON

MS (MWiW-C); at head of text: "To the friends of the administration of the US. in Bristol county Rhode island"; addressed: "Charles Collins esq Bristol Rhode island"; stamped and postmarked. PoC (DLC). Recorded in SJL as an "Answer to Address" from "Bristol c[ty] R.I. Collins."

Charles Collins, chairman of the Bristol County convention, signed an ADDRESS on behalf of its members in support of TJ's administration and republican government on 20 Feb. 1809 (DLC). In 1804 TJ named Collins customs collector and revenue inspector for Bristol, Rhode Island, positions he held for twenty years (*JEP*, 1:464, 465 [24, 25 Feb. 1804]).

# To the Republican Mechanics of Leesburg, Virginia

The reciept of your kind address, in the last moments of the session of Congress, will, I trust, offer a just apology for it's late acknolegement.

Your friendly salutations on the close of my public life, and approbation of the motives which dictated my retirement are recieved with great satisfaction.

That there should be a contrariety of opinions respecting the public Agents & their measures, & more especially respecting that which recently suspended our commerce, & produced temporary privations, is ever to be expected among free men: and I am happy to find you are in the number of those who are satisfied that the course pursued was marked out by our country's interest, and called for by her dearest rights. while the principles of our constitution give just latitude to enquiry, every citizen, faithful to it, will, with you, deem embodied expressions of discontent, & open outrages of law & patriotism, as dishonorable as they are injurious; and there is reason to believe that had the efforts of the government against the innovations & tyranny of the belligerent powers been unopposed among ourselves, they would have been more effectual towards the establishment of our rights.

Unconscious of partiality between the different callings of my fellow citizens, I trust that a fair review of my attentions to the interests of commerce in particular, in every station of my political life, will afford sufficient proofs of my just estimation of it's importance in the[1] social system. what has produced our present difficulties, and what will have produced the impending war, if that is to be our lot? our efforts to save the rights of commerce & navigation. from these, solely & exclusively the whole of our present dangers flow.

With just reprobations of the resistance made or menaced against the laws of our country, I applaud your patriotic resolution to meet hostility to them with the energy & dignity of freemen: and thankful for your solicitude for my health & happiness, I salute you with affectionate sentiments of respect.

TH: JEFFERSON
Monticello March 29. 09.

PoC (DLC); at head of text: "To the republican Mechanics of the town of Leesburg & it's vicini assembled on the 27th of February last"; at foot of first page: "Mr John Littlejohn. Leesburg." Recorded in SJL as an "Answer to Address" from "Mechanics Leesbg Littlejohn."

The mechanics of Leesburg formally expressed their approval of TJ's conduct as president after their meeting on 13 Feb. 1809 in a 27 Feb. ADDRESS (DLC) prepared by committee members John Littlejohn, chairman, and John Newton, secretary.

[1] TJ here canceled "political."

## To William McCandless

SIR Monticello. Mar. 29. 09.

I recieved on the evening of the 1st of March the resolutions inclosed in your letter of Feb. 20. for the purpose of being laid before both houses of Congress. usage & perhaps sound principle not permitting the President to place himself between the representatives & their constituents, who have a right to address their legislature directly, I delivered, the next day a copy of your resolutions to a member[1] of Pensylvania in each house of Congress. but as that body was to rise on the day ensuing that, the mass of indispensable business crouding on the last moments of the session scarcely admitted the opportunity of a compliance with your wishes.

I avail myself of this occasion of returning sincere thanks for the kind dispositions towards myself expressed in your letter, and for the sentiments, which it conveys, of approbation of my conduct in the administration of the public affairs. if that conduct has met the general approbation of my country, it is the highest reward I can recieve: and I shall ever feel towards them that gratitude which the confidence they have favored me with so eminently calls for. Accept for yourself the assurances of my high respect.

TH: JEFFERSON

PoC (DLC); at foot of text: "William M[c]andless esq. Pittsburg." Recorded in SJL as an "Answer" to "Resoln Pittsb[g] M[c]andless."

William McCandless (1773–1833), merchant and a director of the first bank in Pittsburgh, was sheriff of Allegheny County, 1804–07, and prothonotary of the county and district courts, 1824–32 (*Daily Pittsburgh Gazette*, 21 Oct. 1833). By order of a meeting of Pennsylvania Republicans convened in Pittsburgh, McCandless, as chairman, sent TJ a copy of resolutions to be presented to Congress, which took no action (McCandless to TJ, 20 Feb. 1809 [ViW: TC-JP]).

[1] Reworked from "the members."

# From James McKinney

SIR Short Creek Brooke County Virginia March 30[th] 1809.

For a number of years past I have wish[d] to be in your employ, (provided it would be under your immediate direction) in Any capacity that I would be found usefull, that wish is now encreas[d] Since you have declined all publick business—I am a Native of Pennsylvania (Lancaster County) & have been regularly bred to farming & Manufactering of flour on an extencive Scale—I removed with my family about 7 years ago to this place I am the flour Inspector & Post Master here, but the perquisites of both are Small—But the principal disadvantage I labour under here is the want of Schools & Suitable Mecanicks to put my sons to, to learn trades, as few of them are Masters of their Several branches they profess[1] & what is [worse],[2] are generally disapated Characters—I have Six Sons & one Daughter all promising children, the eldest is 14 years, If I could get them taught Some usefull Mechanical branch, Accompanied with a tolarable english education, that they would become usefull Citizens I would close the Scene as it respects this world, without a wish—My constitution is good 36 years of age & able to undergo the fatagues of any reasonable business—I am well Aware it is useless to Apply to you, without the most Satisfactory recommendation, as to Honesty, [Sobrie]ty, & Industry, Also being fully capable of rende[ring] full Satisfaction in whatever I would undertake, which I trust I can do—I was in Richmond & the City of Washington in November last & intended to call on you personally but Congress being then in Session I thought it was not probable you could attend to any local business at that time—If you would think of employing me a line directed to me at this place will be promptly attended to—The name of this Office is Short Creek Va

I am Sir Your Hu S[t] JAMES M[c]KINNEY

RC (MHi); mutilated at seal; addressed: "Thomas Jefferson Esqr Monticello"; franked and postmarked; endorsed by TJ as received 17 Apr. 1809 and so recorded in SJL.

James McKinney (b. ca. 1773) was a postmaster (1808–10) and miller in Brooke County, in what is now West Virginia. By 1810 he was living at Slate Mills in Culpeper (now Rappahannock) County but later that year he settled in Milton, where he began a partnership with Thomas Mann Randolph to operate TJ's manufacturing mill (Axelson, *Virginia Postmasters*, 26; Betts, *Farm Book*, 342).

[1] Preceding two words interlined.
[2] Omitted word editorially supplied.

# To James Madison

Dear Sir Monticello Mar. 30. 09.

Yours of the 19th came to hand by the last post; but that allows us so little time that I could not answer by it's return. I had not before heard of mr Latrobe's claim of Lenthall's salary in addition to his own. that some of Lenthall's duties must have fallen on him I have no doubt; but that he could have performed them all in addition to his own so as to entitle himself to his whole salary,[1] was impossible. Lenthall superintended directly the manual labors of the workmen, saw that they were in their places every working hour, that they executed their work with skill & fidelity, kept their accounts, laid off the work, measured it, laid off the centers & other moulds Etc if the leisure of mr Latrobe's own duties allowed him to give one half or one third of his time to these objects, it is more than I had supposed. the whole of them we know occupied every moment of Lenthall, as laborious, as faithful, & as able in his line as man could be. this claim is subject to another consideration. it would be a bad precedent to allow the principal to discontinue offices indefinitely and absorb all the salaries on the presumption of his fulfilling the duties. it may sometimes happen that a place cannot be immediately & properly filled, or that the arrangements for suppressing it cannot be immediately taken; and as some extra service may in the mean time fall on others, some extra allowance may be just. but this interval should be reasonably limited & accounted for. on weighing these considerations with mr Latrobe's explanations you will be able to judge what proportion of Lenthall's salary should be allowed him. I must add that tho he is a masterly agent in the line of his emploiment, you will find that the reins must be held with a firmness that never relaxes. Colo Monroe dined & passed an evening with me since I came home. he is sincerely cordial: and I learn from several that he has quite separated himself from the junto which had got possession of him, & is sensible that they had used him for purposes not respecting himself always. he & J.R. now avoid seeing one another, mutually dissatisfied. he solemnly disclaims all connection with the anomalous paper of the place & disapproves it. His only tie remaining is a natural one, & that is said to be loosened. I did not enter into any material[2] political conversation with him, & still less as to the present course of things because I shall have better opportunities on his return with his family, whom he is gone to bring permanently to his residence here, and I think the daughter is expected to make a part of his family during the summer at least. on the whole I have no doubt that his strong & candid mind will bring him to a cordial return to his old friends after he shall have been separated a while from his present circle, which separation I think is one of the objects of his removal from Richmond, with which place he expressed to me much disgust.

On the 27th 28th 29th the thermometer was at 23. 21. 32. attended by a piercing N.W. wind, which rendered it as cold to our sensations as any day in winter had been. the peach trees whose buds were so forward as to shew the colour of the blossom, have generally lost their fruit. those less forward are safe. for this fruit therefore all will depend on the forwardness or backwardness of the situation[3] this year. altho' my situation is much forwarder than others, I have lost scarcely any thing. fears of injury to the wheat are entertained. I salute you with constant affection.

TH: JEFFERSON

RC (DLC: Madison Papers, Rives Collection); at foot of text: "The President of the US." PoC (DLC).

Monroe had apparently severed his ties with a group of Virginia Republicans who were known as the Richmond JUNTO, or Old Republicans, which supported Monroe for president instead of Madison. J.R., John Randolph of Roanoke, advocated the idea in letters to Monroe in 1806–07 that also expressed opposition to the Jefferson administration. To champion his candidacy Monroe's supporters established an ANOMALOUS PAPER in Richmond, the *Spirit of 'Seventy-Six*.

Unsuccessful in his run for the presidency and clearly lacking Republican support, Monroe sought to restore his relationship with TJ and vindicate his actions as minister to Great Britain. He forwarded TJ copies of his letters to Randolph and one from William Branch Giles in order to counter criticism of his public service. With TJ's reluctant consent, Monroe published some of their own correspondence. He decided to return to Highland, his home in Albemarle County, rather than practice law in Richmond. The ONLY TIE REMAINING was probably that with his son-in-law George Hay who, despite having managed Monroe's campaign, maintained his standing in the party. Hay and Eliza Monroe Hay planned to visit Highland in the SUMMER of 1809 (Monroe to TJ, 22 Mar., 27 Sept. 1808 [DLC]; TJ to Monroe, 28 Sept. 1808 [DLC: Monroe Papers]; Richmond *Virginia Argus*, 1 Nov. 1808; Ammon, *Monroe*, 270–7).

[1] Preceding nine words interlined.

[2] Word interlined.

[3] Preceding three words interlined.

# To the Citizens of Allegany County, Maryland

The sentiments of attachment, respect & esteem expressed in your address of the 20th Ult. have been read with pleasure, and would sooner have recieved my thanks, but for the mass of business engrossing the last moments of a session of Congress. I am gratified by your approbation of our efforts for the general[1] good, and our endeavors to promote the best interests of our country, & to place them on a basis firm & lasting. the measures respecting our intercourse with foreign nations were the result, as you suppose, of a choice between two evils, either to call & keep at home our seamen & property, or suffer them to be taken under the edicts of the belligerent powers. how a difference of opinion could arise between these alternatives is still difficult to explain on any acknoleged ground: and I am persuaded, with you, that when the storm & agitation characterising the present moment shall have subsided, when passion & prejudice shall have yielded to reason it's usurped place, and especially when posterity shall pass it's sentence on the present times, justice will be rendered to the course which has been pursued. to the advantages derived from the choice which was made will be added the improvements and discoveries made & making in the arts, & the establishments in domestic manufacture, the effects whereof will be permanent & diffused through our wide extended continent. that we may live to behold the storm which seems to threaten us pass like a summer's cloud away, & that yourselves may continue to enjoy all the blessings of peace & prosperity is my fervent prayer.

TH: JEFFERSON
Monticello Mar. 31. 09.

PoC (DLC); at head of text: "To the Citizens of Alleghaney county in Maryland"; at foot of text: "Benjamin Tomlinson. Cumberland Pensva." Recorded in SJL as an "Answer" to "citizens Alleghany c^ty Maryl^d Tomlinson."

As chairman of a meeting of Allegany County citizens held on 20 Feb. 1809, Benjamin Tomlinson signed an ADDRESS and five resolutions in support of the Embargo and TJ's administration (DLC). Tomlinson (1752–1838) was elected to the Maryland House of Delegates twelve times between 1791 and 1822 (Papenfuse, *Maryland Public Officials*, 1:128–9; gravestone inscription in Tomlinson Cemetery, Ellerslie, Maryland).

[1] Word interlined in place of "public."

# From Jonathan Law

SIR, Hartford, March 31, 1809—

I have the honor, as secretary of a general meeting of the Republicans of Connecticut, holden in this City, on the 2^d day of March Inst., to enclose to you some resolves passed at said meeting, ordered to be transmitted to the then president of the U. States.

The duty of forwarding the Resolves, having by the meeting been omitted to be assigned to any particular individual, I have considered it as, ex officio, devolving upon myself, & ought perhaps to apologize for having so long postponed the discharge of it.

Directly after passing the Resolutions they were handed to the printer for publication, from whom it was my intention, with as little delay as could consist with his having put them in types, to procure them for the purpose of sending you a copy.

The alarming progress of a Disorder which has recently afflicted us, persuaded me, in the mean time, at the solicitations of my family friends in a neighboring town, to retire a little suddenly from Hartford, so that it became inconvenient, immediately to make to you the enclosure which I could have wished. I might, to be sure, since my return, have been a little more prompt in making amends for the past, but the Resolutions having gone out before the public & most probably fallen under your observation, in the papers, I was led to indulge myself in some delay which I should rather ask of you to forgive than attempt entirely to justify.

With the highest respect, Sir permit me to subscribe myself your most Obed^t Serv^t

JONATHAN LAW

RC (DLC); between dateline and salutation: "Thomas Jefferson Esq^r Late president of the U. States"; endorsed by TJ as a letter from "Low Jonathan" received 6 Apr. 1809 and so recorded (with the notation: "resolns.") in SJL.

Jonathan Law was appointed postmaster at Hartford, Connecticut, on 1 July 1809 (CtY: Bristol Family Papers; DNA: RG 28, Record of Appointment of Postmasters). The enclosed RESOLVES may have been the "Republican Protest" signed by Jabez Fitch and thirty-six other members of the Connecticut House of Representatives, Hartford, 2 Mar. 1809, consisting of five resolves supporting the Embargo and protesting against four anti-Embargo resolves passed that day by a majority of the Connecticut House as assuming "unwarranted authority" and being "directly at war with the laws of the United States" (printed in Hartford *American Mercury*, 9 Mar. 1809). The DISORDER may have been an outbreak of spotted fever (typhus) in Hartford that caused numerous deaths in February and March 1809 (*American Mercury*, 23 Feb. 1809; Hartford *Connecticut Courant*, 1, 8 Mar. 1809).

# To James Madison

Dear Sir Monticello Mar. 31. 09.

Since my letter of yesterday I have recieved yours of the 27th & 28th and in the former the 500.D. for mrs Trist. the bronze time piece mentioned will run a fortnight, but I found it better to wind it up once a week, as during the 2d week the greater expansion of the spring occasioned her to lose time. with respect to newspapers, none can now come to Washington for me. of those which, while there, I ordered & paid for, I directed a discontinuance except 3. or 4. which will come on to me here. many others were sent gratis (which I rarely opened) to me as President of the US. they probably will be continued to you on the same principle.

I inclose a letter from the Speaker of Indiana on the election of two persons for the legislative council. such an one was forwarded to me in Oct. by mr Thomas then Speaker, as he told me; but I never recieved it. he therefore wrote back for another copy which is but now recieved. you will find among the papers I left you, a letter from Govr Harrison advising as to the choice to be made. Erving seems to have erred in principle, by not taking his stand with the government of Spain de facto. it is the more unlucky as Joseph Bonaparte has been said to be well disposed towards us.

Affectionately yours Th: Jefferson

RC (DLC: Madison Papers); at foot of text: "The President of the US." Enclosure: General Washington Johnston to TJ, 17 Feb. 1809, not found but recorded in SJL as received from Vincennes on 30 Mar. 1809, with TJ's notation "P.," probably his indication that the subject matter was presidential or that the document was sent to the president.

The newspapers for which TJ was terminating his subscriptions probably included the New York *Mercantile Advertiser*. On 30 Oct. 1809 SJL records the receipt from New York of a missing 12 Oct. 1809 letter from John Crookes, publisher of the *Mercantile Advertiser*, 1799–1816. In a 3 Nov. 1809 reply (recorded in SJL but not found) TJ enclosed ten dollars to cover his subscription for the year 1808 (Brigham, *American Newspapers*, 2:661–2; *MB*, 2:1249).

By territorial ordinance the Indiana House of Representatives submitted two names to the president when a vacancy on the territory's Legislative Council was to be filled. Speaker Jesse B. Thomas wrote TJ on 12 Oct. 1808 (MoSHi: TJC-BC) enclosing the 6 Oct. nominations of Hugh McCally and Charles Beggs (*Terr. Papers*, 7:597–8). TJ notified him that this had miscarried and Thomas, now the territorial delegate to Congress, agreed to send for another copy on 10 Dec. 1808 (DLC). The letter from William Henry Harrison advising on the choice is not recorded in SJL and has not been found, but Madison soon appointed McCally (*JEP*, 2:122, 125 [16, 21 June 1809]).

## To John Taggart

SIR Monticello Mar. 31. 09

I recieved by our last post your favor of the 15th informing me you had sent on the oil & paint requested, and stating the amount 72.D. I accordingly now inclose you US. bank bills for 70.D. and for want of smaller, I have desired my grandson Th:J. Randolph to call on you and pay the additional 2.D. on his arrival in Philadelphia, and I pray you to accept my thanks with my respectful salutations.

TH: JEFFERSON

PoC (MHi); at foot of text: "Mr John Taggert"; mistakenly endorsed by TJ as a letter of 30 Mar. 1809 but correctly recorded in SJL.

The payment described here is noted in *MB*, 2:1244.

## From John Breck Treat

SIR, Arkansa in Louisiana. March 31st 1809.

Having the preceeding three and half years resided at this place, during which time I have taken the observations contained in the following pages, if, from their perusal, you can derive, either, information or amusement, respecting the Climate of this part of our Country, your acceptance will be highly gratifying to

Sir Your respectfully Obedient servant

JOHN BRECK TREAT

RC (PPAmP); dateline at foot of text; above salutation: "To Thomas Jefferson, Esquire"; notation in an unidentified hand: "Presented to the Amn Philosl Society Minutes 20. Oct. 1809 by Thomas Jefferson." Enclosure: Treat, journal of Arkansa meteorological observations, 1 Oct. 1805–31 Dec. 1808, describing Arkansa as "situated on the left bank of the Arkansa river, which is about fortyfive feet above the lowest fall of its waters," latitude 34° 21′ North, fifty miles by water and twenty miles in a direct line from the Mississippi, with generally level land "much diversified with Forests and open extensive Prairies," much of which overflowed annually "to within four or five miles of the town"; stating that the observations were formed on the plan of William Dunbar in APS, *Transactions*, vol. 6, pt. 1, and that Treat's instruments were "suspended, on the North side of a Gallery, about fifteen feet from the Ground, against the Wall of a log or Timber house, with open Grass plat in front"; and reporting thrice-daily readings of thermometer, barometer (until that instrument broke on 14 May 1807), wind direction and strength, rainfall, and state of the weather, as well as monthly general remarks and a yearly recapitulation giving monthly highs, lows, and mean values (MS in PPAmP; in Treat's hand). Letter and enclosure enclosed in TJ to Robert Patterson, 31 Aug. 1809.

John Breck Treat was appointed agent of the trading house in 1805 and agent for Indian affairs in 1807 at Arkansa, Louisiana Territory (*Terr.*

*Papers*, 13:106, 276–84, 463–6, 503–4, 511–2, 543–4, 14:129). His meteorological OBSERVATIONS were presented to the members of the American Philosophical Society at its 20 Oct. 1809 meeting (APS, Minutes [MS in PPAmP]).

# From Elizabeth Trist

D[R] SIR Farmington March 31[st] [1809]

Your note made me very happy as I began to entertain doubts of the safety of the letter in question I will take it as a favor when you write to the President to tell him I am not insensible to his very polite attention and return him many thanks any time when convenient to you will answer my purposes either sunday or any later day I am with Sincerity your ever obliged and affectionate friend E. TRIST

RC (ViU: TJP-ER); partially dated; addressed: "M[r] Jefferson Monticello"; endorsed by TJ as received 31 Mar. 1809.

TJ visited Trist and the Divers family as promised, arriving at Farmington on SUNDAY, 2 Apr. 1809. Trist observed that "M[r] Jefferson call[d] last week, and dined here yesterday I never saw him look better nor appear so happy" (Trist to Elizabeth Kortright Monroe, 3 Apr. 1809 [DLC: Nicholas P. Trist Papers]).

# To the Republicans of Washington County, Maryland

The affectionate sentiments you express on my retirement from the high office conferred on me by my country, are gratefully recieved, & acknoleged with thankfulness. your approbation of the various measures which have been pursued, cannot but be highly consolatory to myself, & encouraging to future functionaries, who will see that their honest endeavors for the public good will recieve due credit with their constituents. that the great & leading measure respecting our foreign intercourse was the most salutary alternative, & preferable to the submission of our rights as a free & independant republic, or to a war at that period, cannot be doubted by candid minds. great and good effects have certainly flowed from it, & greater would have been produced, had they not been, in some degree, frustrated by unfaithful citizens.

If in my retirement to the humble station of a private citizen, I am accompanied with the esteem & approbation of my fellow citizens, trophies obtained by the blood stained steel, or the tattered flags of the tented field, will never be envied. the care of human life & happiness, & not their destruction, is the first & only legitimate object of good government.

I salute you, fellow citizens, with every wish for your welfare, & the perpetual duration of our government, in all the purity of it's republican principles.

TH: JEFFERSON

Monticello Mar. 31. 09.

MS (CtY: Franklin Collection); at head of text: "To the republican citizens of Washington county Maryland, assembled at Hager's town on the 6th instant." PoC (DLC); at foot of text: "Col° Nathaniel Rochester, Hager's Town." Recorded in SJL as an "Answer" to "rep. cit. Washn cty Maryld Rochester." Printed in *Maryland Herald, and Hager's-Town Weekly Advertiser*, 14 Apr. 1809.

TJ's answer to his supporters in Washington County, Maryland, as with other responses in this volume, borrows some of its language from the address to which he replied.

# To the Democratic Republican Delegates of Washington County, Pennsylvania

The satisfaction you express, fellow citizens, that my endeavors have been unremitting to preserve the peace & independance of our country, & that a faithful neutrality has been observed towards all the contending powers, is highly grateful to me, and there can be no doubt that in any common times they would have saved us from the present embarrasments, thrown in the way of our national prosperity by the rival powers.

It is true that the embargo laws have not had all the effect in bringing the powers of Europe to a sense of justice, which a more faithful observance of them might have produced. yet they have had the important effects of saving our seamen & property, of giving time to prepare for defence; and they will produce the further inestimable advantage of turning the attention & enterprize of our fellow citizens, and the patronage of our state legislatures, to the establishment of useful manufactures in our country. they will have hastened the day when an equilibrium between the occupations of agriculture manufactures & commerce shall simplify our foreign concerns to the exchange only of that surplus which we cannot consume for those articles of reasonable comfort or convenience which we cannot produce.

Our lot has been cast, by the favor of heaven, in a country & under circumstances, highly auspicious to our peace & prosperity, & where no pretence can arise for the degrading & oppressive establishments of Europe. it is our happiness that honorable distinctions flow only from public approbation; & that finds no object in titled dignitaries and pageants. let us then, my fellow citizens, endeavor carefully to guard this happy state of things, by keeping a watchful eye over the disaffection of wealth & ambition to the republican principles of our constitution, & by sacrifising all our local & personal interests to the cultivation of the Union, & maintenance of the authority of the laws.

My warmest thanks are due to you, fellow citizens for the affectionate sentiments expressed in your address, & my prayers will ever be offered for your welfare & happiness.

TH: JEFFERSON
Monticello Mar. 31. 09.

PoC (DLC); at head of text: "To the Democratic republican delegates from the townships of Washington county in Pensylvania, convened on the 21[st] of February 1809"; at foot of first page: "James Kerr esq. Washington P[a]." Recorded in SJL as an "Answer to rep: del. Wash[n] c[ty] Pensva Kerr."

James Kerr chaired a meeting of sixty delegates from twenty-one townships in Washington County, Pennsylvania, that approved six resolutions and an accompanying ADDRESS praising TJ for his services as president, supporting the Embargo, and commending state legislators who voted to wear homespun rather than imported clothing to show support for republican principles and domestic manufactures (Delegates of Washington County, Pennsylvania, to TJ, 21 Feb. 1809 [DLC]). James Kerr (d. 1825) was a farmer and native of Chester County, Pennsylvania (J. H. Beers & Co., *Commemorative Biographical Record of Washington County, Pennsylvania* [1893], 579).

# To Caspar Wistar

DEAR SIR Monticello Mar. 31. 09.

My grandson being on his return to attend the botanical lectures gives me a safe opportunity of forwarding a livraison of a botanical work of M. Tussac for the Philosophical society, together with his letter, which the society will probably answer. I inclose also for your own perusal a letter to myself from Tenon, Delambre & Cuvier on the subject of the big bones sent to the institute, which I shall ask the favor of you to return, retaining a copy if you please which Jefferson proposes to make for you.

Affectionately yours TH: JEFFERSON

PoC (DLC): at foot of text: "D[r] Wistar"; endorsed by TJ. Enclosures: (1) François Richard de Tussac, *Flora Antillarum: seu, Historia Generalis Botanica, ruralis, oeconomica vegetabilium in Antilles indigenorum*, 4 vols. (Paris, 1808–27), vol. 1, pt. 1. (2) Tussac to TJ, 22 Nov. 1808 (not found but recorded in

SJL as received from Paris on 11 Mar. 1809). (3) Jean Baptiste Joseph Delambre, Jacques Tenon, and Georges Cuvier to TJ, 14 Nov. 1808, thanking him for his gift of fossil bones to the Institut de France (PPAmP: Caspar Wistar Papers).

Caspar Wistar (1761–1818), physician and educator, corresponded with TJ on scientific and other subjects from 1791 until his death. He received medical degrees from the University of the State of Pennsylvania in 1782 and Edinburgh University in 1786 and set up practice in his native Philadelphia the following year. Starting in 1789, Wistar held several professorships at the College of Philadelphia before and after it merged with his local alma mater to become the University of Pennsylvania in 1791, and he was professor of anatomy from 1808 until his death. An innovative and popular instructor, he published the first American textbook in anatomy, 1811–14. Wistar was elected to the American Philosophical Society in 1787, eventually succeeding TJ as its president in 1815. He was one of the scientists charged with preparing Meriwether Lewis for the Lewis and Clark Expedition. Wistar was active in prison reform and became president of the Pennsylvania Society for the Abolition of Slavery in 1813 (*ANB*; *DAB*; *DSB*; Wistar to TJ, [19 Mar. 1791], *PTJ*, 19:614–5; TJ to Wistar, 28 Feb. 1803 [DLC]; APS, Minutes, 20 July 1787, 6 Jan. 1815 [MS in PPAmP]).

In 1807 TJ sought Wistar's advice about educational opportunities in Philadelphia for his GRANDSON Thomas Jefferson Randolph and asked Wistar to arrange for Randolph to lodge at the home of Charles Willson Peale (TJ to Wistar, 21 June 1807 [PHC]; Peale to TJ, 30 Aug. 1807 [DLC]).

On behalf of Tussac, Wistar presented the enclosed beginning of his ambitious BOTANICAL WORK to the American Philosophical Society on 21 Apr. 1809 (APS, Minutes). Georges CUVIER, French naturalist and founder of vertebrate paleontology (*DSB*), headed a committee of the Institut de France that analyzed the BIG BONES TJ and Wistar had organized and presented as a gift in 1808. TJ thought that his donation, and similar specimens excavated by Peale in 1801, all came from the American "incognitum," or mammoth. While Cuvier and Lacépède classifed portions of TJ's donation as coming from the Siberian mammoth, they determined that other parts, as well as Peale's skeleton, came from a new genus, the extinct mastodon. Cuvier incorporated these findings in his *Recherches sur les Ossemens Fossiles*, 2d ed. (Paris, 1821), which TJ probably never owned (*Notes*, ed. Peden, 45; TJ to Lacépède, 14 July 1808 [DLC]; Howard Rice, "Jefferson's Gift of Fossils to the Museum of Natural History in Paris," APS, *Proceedings* 95 [1951]: 597–627).

# From William B. W. Allone

RESPECTED SIR Peekskill March 1809

I know no other Apology for the Liberty I have taken than that of Dire Necessity and As I know you to be a man of few words I will proceed briefly to state my case to you

I have been engaged all this Winter in writing a political pamphlet entitled Thoughts, on the Administration, of our late President, Thomas Jefferson. (Which I hope will meet with due encouragement from all true Republicans) but being in want of Money I cannot Publish it. I have therefore taken the Liberty (of writing You)[1] to beg the Loan of 25 Dollars (NY currency) which I have been informed will set it agoing. And if Possible I will pay you with the first Money I receive for the Pamphlet, and if not (as I know you are worth a great deal) you will not lose[2] it I assure you

If you should be so good as to send me any Direct to William B W Allone Peekskill State of New York WILLIAM B W ALLONE

RC (DLC); partially dated; at foot of text: "Thomas Jefferson Esquire"; endorsed by TJ as a "begging" letter from "Albone Wm" received 14 Apr. 1809 and so recorded in SJL.

[1] Closing parenthesis editorially supplied.

[2] Word interlined in place of "miss."

# To James Hochie

SIR Monticello Apr. 2. 09.

I have duly recieved your favor of Mar. 17. covering resolutions of the antient Plymouth society of New London, approving my conduct, as well during the period of my late administration, as the preceding portion of my public services. our lot has been cast in times which called for the best exertions of all our citizens to recover and preserve the rights which nature had given them; and we may say with truth that the mass of our fellow citizens have performed with zeal & effect the duties called for. if I have been fortunate enough to give satisfaction in the performance of those alloted to me, by our country, I find an ample reward in the assurances of that satisfaction. possessed of the blessing of self-government, and of such a portion of civil liberty as no other civilized nation enjoys, it now behoves us to guard & preserve them by a continuance of the sacrifices & exertions by which they were acquired, & especially to nourish that union which is their sole guarantee. I pray you to accept for yourself & your associates the assurance of my high consideration & respect.

TH: JEFFERSON

PoC (DLC); at foot of text: "James Hochie esq. President of the ancient Plymouth society of New London." Recorded in SJL as an "Answer" to "Antt Plymth co. of N. London. Hochie."

# To the Inhabitants of Albemarle County

Returning to the scenes of my birth & early life, to the society of those with whom I was raised, & who have been ever dear to me, I recieve, fellow citizens & neighbors, with inexpressible pleasure, the cordial welcome you are so good as to give me. long absent on duties which the history of a wonderful aera made incumbent on those called to them, the pomp, the turmoil, the bustle & splendour of office, have drawn but deeper sighs for the tranquil & irresponsible occupations of private life, for the enjoyment of an affectionate intercourse with you, my neighbors & friends, and the endearments of family love, which nature has given us all, as the sweetener of every hour. for these I gladly lay down the distressing burthen of power, & seek, with my fellow citizens, repose & safety under the watchful cares, the labours & perplexities of younger and abler minds. the anxieties you express to administer to my happiness, do, of themselves confer that happiness: and the measure will be compleat, if my endeavors to fulfill my duties in the several[1] public stations to which I have been called, have obtained for me the approbation of my country. the part which I have acted on the theatre of public life, has been before them; & to their sentence I submit it: but the testimony of my native county, of the individuals who have known me in private life, to my conduct in it's various duties, & relations, is the more grateful as proceeding from eye witnesses & observers, from triers of the vicinage. of you then, my neighbors, I may ask, in the face of the world, 'whose ox have I taken, or whom have I defrauded? whom have I oppressed, or of whose hand have I recieved a bribe to blind mine eyes therewith'? on your verdict I rest with conscious security. your wishes for my happiness are recieved with just sensibility, & I offer sincere prayers for your own welfare & prosperity.

TH: JEFFERSON

April 3. 1809

MS (Vi); at head of text: "To the Inhabitants of Albemarle county in Virginia." PoC (DLC). Recorded in SJL as an "Answer" to "Inhab. of Albemarle c$^{ty}$."

TJ's biblical reference, WHOSE OX HAVE I TAKEN, . . . TO BLIND MINE EYES THEREWITH?, is to 1 Samuel 12.3.

[1] Word interlined.

# From Charles Willson Peale

DEAR SIR — Museum April 3$^{d}$ 1809

In the report by M$^{r}$ Cuvier on the fossil bones which you presented to the National Institute I find the committee have given the name Mastodonte to the animal which we commonly call Mammoth. How well this name may accord with the Skelleton I have, I can better judge off after hearing the deffinition by the learned in Languages, It is pleasant however to have a name by which we may know it from the Sibirian Animal, which evidently must be a Graminivorous animal if the Grinders correspond with the flat surfaced teeth found here. I would willingly change the name of Mammoth if you think the Name which M[r] Cuvier has givin is appropriate. therefore I will be much obleged by your opinion previous to a christening. and which (the thought of a moment) may be done in stile, by giving a dinner to 13 men seated within the Thorax.

I began this letter the day before M[r] Randolph arrived here, a multiplicity of things to attend to for Rembrandt previous to his leaving Philad[a] has engaged almost[1] all my attention, and having nothing of any importance to communicate delayed writing until this time. Rembrandt is gone to Baltimore to wait for the first public Vessel going to France, employing the intermediate time in painting some portraits promised in that City, should you want any commission executed in Paris it will give my Son pleasure to serve you.

M[r] Randolph intimates his desire to attend a course of Lectures on Minerology which M[r] Godon has published his intention of delivering; the commencement will be early in May, to be followed occasionally with excursions with his Pupels to the hills in the Vicinity of Philad[a]. I have not given any opinion of the advantages in this study, doubtful of my abilities to judge on it. I was anxious for M[r] Randolph's attention to Chemistry, because I have found a substantial sourse of amusement as well as some benefits in its study.

The improvements of your farms I hope will give you[2] funds of pleasing amusements, and that the exercise you must take in a salubrious air will contribute to good health and long life with a serene mind is the wish of your obleged & sincere friend

C W PEALE

RC (DLC); at foot of text: "Thomas Jefferson Esq[r]"; endorsed by TJ as received 23 Apr. 1809 and so recorded in SJL. PoC (PPAmP: Peale Letterbook).

In 1808 Georges CUVIER had distinguished between the mastodon discovered by Peale in 1801 and the Siberian MAMMOTH (see TJ to Caspar Wistar, 31 Mar. 1809). Peale proposed but did not actually host a DINNER similar to the one held at the Philadelphia Museum in December 1801 for thirteen men seated WITHIN THE THORAX of his newly excavated mastodon skeleton (Peale, *Papers*, vol. 2, pt. 1, p. 401). Shortly after settling in Philadelphia, French mineralogist Silvain GODON began offering lectures on that subject (Philadelphia *Aurora*, 20, 26 Apr. 1809).

[1] Word interlined.

[2] Peale here canceled "inifite."

# From Horatio G. Spafford

FRIEND JEFFERSON— Hudson, N.Y., 4 Mo. 3, 1809.

It is with sentiments of very great respect, but with extreme diffidence, that I offer to obtrude upon thy retirement, & invite again thy labors in the field of science. I ask thy aid. To a mind so constituted, & so long accustomed to exertion in every mean of usefulness to mankind;—I know that, having relinquished thy public employments, the more active exertions of private research will become pleasurable. And I am anxious early to solicit the assistance of such talents, in forwarding a design announced in the enclosed printed letters.

I enclose thee also, one of my Books; & must hope thou wilt give it publicity. If, after having had sufficient time to form thy judgement of its merits, thou wouldest write me thereon, the favor would be duly appreciated.

I send also a Stalactic curiosity;—formed in a cavity, attached to a porous rock, through which the watery medium formed a passage.

If I succeed in my intentions, I may personally obtrude upon thy retirement at Monticello, during the ensuing summer. And I need, hardly, to add that, an interview with Thomas Jefferson, at his own home, would be one of the most desirable objects that engage my fancy. The World has much to expect yet, from thee—and that world is anxiously looking toward thy home, for a finish to a most interesting picture.

May I expect that a little Philosopher, will be well received by the greatest our country has yet to boast?—

Forgive my freedom—I have only thy domestic virtues to awe me—& with them I love to fancy perfect freedom & universal good will. In short, if my mind does not[1] adopt the more plausible style of official reverence, it is only because that neither myself or thee (as I imagine,) can choose it. I behold thee unburdened by the formalities of official dignity, & regard thee as a friend to private worth. As such I again solicit thy aid with assurances that no one more wishes thee the blessings of a mind usefully at ease, than, he who now address thee

In the hope to hear from thee as soon as may be convenient, I remain, thy friend, HORATIO G. SPAFFORD

P.S.—The Benni, which promises to become an important article in Husbandry, is little known here. Some bottles of the Seed, would be very acceptable, accompanied with the most interesting particulars of its Natural History.

His Honor the Mayor of New-York, will interest himself in taking charge of, & forwarding to me, any article of this kind: with a view to facilitate the means of conveyance of intelligence from the Southern States.

Please hand the inclosed Letters to some literary friends.

I wish to obtain information respecting a new invention of a Metallic pen, in some part of Virginia. I have invented one, which I deem so great an improvement that I intend applying for a patent, soon. When I can have one made to suit me, I'll forward one to thee.

Be so good as to excuse the imperfections which thou wilt perceive, as I am compelled to write in very great haste. If I have another occasion to communicate, & leave to do so, I'll endeavor to do it more leisurely. With assurances of very great respect, I remain, thy friend,

H. G. SPAFFORD

RC (DLC); addressed: "Thomas Jefferson, Esquire, Monticello, Virginia"; endorsed by TJ as received 17 Apr. 1809 and so recorded in SJL. Enclosure: Spafford, *General Geography, and Rudiments of Useful Knowledge. . . . Illustrated with an Elegant Improved Plate of the Solar System . . . A Map of the World . . . of the United States . . . and several Engravings on Wood. Digested on a New Plan, and Designed for the Use of Schools* (Hudson, N.Y., 1809; Sowerby, no. 3828).

Horatio Gates Spafford (1778–1832), geographer, editor, and inventor, corresponded frequently with TJ during the latter's retirement. The native of Vermont followed the *General Geography*, his first publication, with *A Gazetteer of the State of New-York* (Albany, N.Y., 1813; rev. ed., 1824; Sowerby, no. 4172), but his perpetual financial difficulties doomed his ambitious schemes to publish gazetteers of all the states and the lives of TJ and Counts Volney and Rumford. Spafford was the sole editor and a regular contributor to the *American Magazine* (1815–17), which produced only twelve issues and numbered TJ among its eight hundred subscribers. In 1817 Spafford moved to Pennsylvania, where he had purchased ten thousand acres, but the venture failed and he returned to New York two years later (Julian P. Boyd, *Horatio Gates Spafford: Inventor, Author, Promoter of Democracy* [1942]).

TJ did not receive the PRINTED LETTERS, copies of a 29 Mar. 1809 circular, until 1810 (TJ to Spafford, 14 May 1809; Spafford to TJ, 14 Jan. 1810). The MAYOR OF NEW YORK was DeWitt Clinton. The METALLIC PEN was not one of the five inventions Spafford patented between 1805 and 1822 (*List of Patents*, 53, 142, 242, 244).

[1] Word interlined.

# To Robert Wright

DEAR SIR Monticello Apr. 3. 09.

Your friendly note of Mar. 3. was delivered to me on that day. you know the pressure of the last moments of a session of Congress, and can judge of that of my own departure from Washington, & of my first attentions here. this must excuse my late acknolegement of your note.—the assurances of your approbation of the course I have observed are highly flattering, & the more so, as you have been sometimes an eye-witness & long of the vicinage of the public councils. the testimony of my fellow citizens, & especially of one who having been himself in the high departments, to the means of information, united the qualifications to judge, is a consolation which will sweeten the residue of my life. the fog which arose in the East, in the last moments of my service will doubtless clear away and expose under a stronger light the rocks & shoals which have threatened us with danger. it is impossible the good citizens of the East should not see the agency of England the tools she employs among them, & the criminal arts & falsehoods of which they have been the dupes. I still trust & pray that our union may be perpetual, and I beg you to accept the assurances of my high esteem & respect. TH: JEFFERSON

PoC (DLC); at foot of text: "H. E. Gov^r Wright."

Robert Wright (1752–1826), lawyer, Revolutionary War veteran, and politician, was born in Queen Annes County, Maryland. He served in both houses of the Maryland legislature and as a Republican member of the United States Senate, 1801–06, and House of Representatives, 1810–17 and 1821–23. As governor of Maryland from 1806–09, Wright supported TJ and his policies, in particular the Embargo, leading to an erosion of his support in the state and his resignation later in 1809 (*ANB*, *DAB*).

Wright's FRIENDLY NOTE expressed his APPROBATION of TJ's presidency and congratulated him on his retirement (Wright to TJ, 3 Mar. 1809 [DLC]).

# To John B. Colvin

Monticello Apr. 4. 09.

Th: Jefferson presents his compliments to mr. Colvin and having recieved but two of his Monitors since left Washington on the 11^th of Mar. he ascribes it to his having failed to give mr Colvin his address which is at Monticello near Milton. the post for Milton leaves Washington on[1] Mondays in the afternoon.

PoC (DLC); dateline at foot of text; endorsed by TJ.

John B. Colvin (ca. 1778–1826), newspaper editor and Republican supporter, edited the Baltimore *Daily Advertiser* (1800–01) before establishing the *Republican Advocate* in Frederick, Maryland (1802–06). In Washington he published *Colvin's Weekly Register* (1808), succeeded by the *Monitor*, which folded in August 1809 due to lack of subscriptions. Thereafter Colvin worked as a clerk at the State Department (Brigham, *American Newspapers*, 1:103, 265; Washington *National Intelligencer*, 4 Aug. 1809, 6 Apr. 1826).

TJ had subscribed to Colvin's Frederick and Washington newspapers (Sowerby, no. 3359; *MB*, 2:1123, 1191, 1215, 1238).

[1] TJ here deleted "Tuesdays."

## From Larkin Smith

Dear Sir Norfolk April 4th 1809

Believing that the importance of the information brought by a British sloop of war[1] which arrived yesterday in Hampton Roads will be acceptable to you, I take much pleasure in communicating it. she brings a secretary of Legation to Mr Erskine with dispatches, and an account of the arrival of the remnant of the British army from Spain. they were attacked by the French when in the act of Embarking, their commander Sir John Moore and another genl officer were killed, and their other loss no doubt very considerable. King Joseph had been crowned at Madrid, and Bonaparte had returned to Paris, leaving an Army of 250 thousand men in Spain.[2] it is also said that the orders of council are or will be repealed.

I have the honor to be Sir with sincere Esteem & high respect your Obt Servt Larkin Smith

RC (CSmH: JF-BA); at foot of text: "Thomas Jefferson Esqr Late President of the U. States"; endorsed by TJ as received 14 Apr. 1809 and so recorded in SJL.

Sir David Baird was probably the other genl officer alluded to, although he was severely wounded rather than killed during the evacuation under French bombardment of a British army from Corunna in northern Spain in January 1809 (*DNB*).

[1] Preceding two words interlined.
[2] Preceding two words interlined.

## To Jonathan Shoemaker

Dear Sir Monticello Apr. 6. 09.

It is with great regret that I write you a letter which I am sure must give you pain, but your interest as well as my own makes it my duty, & yours is still more urgent than mine. I have little doubt that your sons write you flattering accounts of their proceedings & prospects at the Shadwell mills, & it is possible they may flatter themselves with retrieving their affairs, but however I doubt it, the sooner your attention to it is warned, the more possible it may be. I shall write no fact of my own knolege, because I have not been to the mill, but such as I have from such persons as cannot be doubted, & either have no interest or such an interest as enables them to speak with the more certainty. one of these told me he went over the mill as thro' curiosity but with a view to see what quantity of wheat was in the mill & he was satisfied there was not more than 200. bushels, & he at the same time enumerated to me claims for[1] upwards of 2000. bushels which he knew to be due for wheat recieved & not ground, besides the quantities of which he was not informed. one of them being asked how they would make up their deficit, said he supposes they must buy. but this must be with ready money, for no one will trust them an hour. mr Randolph, to his great mortification was obliged to send his wheat to Richmond. mr Rogers did not bring his crop there. mr Divers sent his by the mill to Magruder's, 9. miles further, to his extreme inconvenience. mr Carter wished to have brought his there, but was afraid from the accounts he recieved. these persons make about 12,000. bushels. Craven & Alexander brought theirs, & by dint of attendance got it ground. others, who have had their wheat in the mill for months are not able to get it at all. I am assured by the neighbors that from 40. to 50,000 bushels of wheat would have been carried there this year, but that people were afraid to trust them with it; & that the ensuing year there will not be 1000. bushels carried there, except what they can pay ready money for, and you may rely on it they are considered as in a state of perfect bankruptcy. I have encouraged the expectation that you would come on & establish yourself there and then all would go right, & such is the distress of the neighborhood for want of a mill, that they fix their hope on this. but be assured, Sir, you have no time to lose to prevent an avowed bankruptcy. come and inform yourself; ask such questions as you can see whether the answers are true or not, and judge for yourself, & not from what they or any body else shall tell you. but the sooner you come & look to it, the more practicable a recovery of the affairs of the concerned may be. I shall say nothing of myself. within a month, they will have had the mill 2. years & not a cent of rent paid. I could distrain, but this would bring all their creditors on them in an instant, & I trust more to your good faith than to the law, which I abhor. you were the person to whom alone I trusted so important a portion of my interest as the mill. I knew you, but I knew nothing of your son. it was your wish to have him in partnership, to which I did not object, because I had entire confidence in you. I write you this to excite your attention to this concern, because no one else will do it. I wish it for your own reading only, because I do not wish to have any quarrel with your son. yet when you come, I will state facts to enable you to enquire. in the mean time be assured of my real friendship. TH: JEFFERSON

PoC (MHi); at foot of first page: "Mr Jonathan Shoemaker"; endorsed by TJ.

Jonathan Shoemaker (1756–1837), miller, was a native of Pennsylvania who served as a manager of the Pennyslvania Hospital, 1781–90, and sat the latter year in a state constitutional convention. In 1804 he became the first proprietor of Columbia Mills on Rock Creek in

Washington, D.C. Shoemaker leased the manufacturing mill at Shadwell from TJ for $1,250 a year beginning in 1807. Remaining at Columbia Mills, he put Isaac Shoemaker in charge of the Shadwell operation, with at least one more of his SONS also involved (Benjamin D. Shoemaker, *Genealogy of the Shoemaker Family of Cheltenham, Pennsylvania* [1903], 75; TJ to Jonathan Shoemaker, 18 Apr. 1807 [MHi]). Martha Jefferson Randolph wrote TJ on 2 Mar. 1809 (MHi) advising him of mismanagement at the Shadwell mill. The Shoemakers gave up the lease in 1810.

MAGRUDER'S mill, or Union Mills, was built by John Bowie Magruder in 1796 on the Rivanna River in Fluvanna County (McGehee and Trout, *Jefferson's River*, 21, 72). A letter from Magruder to TJ of 2 Oct. 1809, not found, is recorded in SJL as received on 4 Oct. 1809.

[1] Preceding two words interlined.

# To James Jay

DEAR SIR Monticello Apr. 7. 09.

Your favor of Feb. 27. came to hand on the 3^d of March. the occupations of the moment & of those which have followed must be my apology for this late acknolegement. the plan of civilising the Indians is undoubtedly a great improvement on the antient & totally ineffectual one of beginning with religious missionaries. our experience has shewn that this must be the last step of the process. the following is what has been succesful. 1. to raise cattle E^tc & thereby acquire a knolege of the value of property 2. arithmetic to calculate that value. 3. writing, to keep accounts and here they begin to inclose farms, & the men to labor, the women to spin & weave. 4. to read. Aesop's fables & Robinson Crusoe are their first delight. the Creeks & Cherokees are advanced thus far, & the Cherokees are now instituting a regular government.

An equilibrium of agriculture, manufactures & commerce is certainly become essential to our independance. manufactures sufficient for our own consumption of what we raise the raw material (and no more). commerce sufficient to carry the surplus produce of agriculture, beyond our own consumption, to a market for exchanging it for articles we cannot raise (and no more.) these are the true limits of manufactures & commerce. to go beyond them is to increase our dependance on foreign nations, and our liability to war. these three important branches of human industry will then grow together, & be really handmaids to each other. I salute you with great respect & esteem. TH: JEFFERSON

P.S. Lady Huntington's address & your circular are enclosed.

PoC (DLC); at foot of text: "S^r James Jay." Enclosures not found.

Sir James Jay (1732–1815), physician, was born in New York, the brother of

John Jay, the American statesman. Jay received a medical degree from the University of Edinburgh in 1753. He spent the years 1762–78 in Great Britain, where he was knighted in 1763. During the American Revolution he used an invisible ink of his own invention to pass on intelligence about British activities, but late in the war he undertook a personal peace mission that left his loyalties in dispute. Jay corresponded with TJ about his plans for manufacturing and naval warfare and his attempts to obtain reimbursement for his $20,000 loan to the United States in 1778 (*DAB*; Jay to TJ, 14 Apr. 1806 [DLC]; *New-York Evening Post*, 2 Nov. 1815).

In his FAVOR OF FEB. 27 (DLC), Jay wrote of his interest in establishing American manufactures and enclosed two papers, an ADDRESS autographed by Selina Hastings, countess of Huntingdon, the patroness of early Methodism, and a CIRCULAR that evidently detailed Jay's plan to civilize the Indians through Christianity and the development of manufacturing.

# From Philip Tabb

SIR

Toddsbury 7th April 1809

Having just learnt from Captn Decatur who delivered a moleboard I did myself the pleasure to send to you at Washington, that you had not received my letter ℔ post which left Gloster Ct House about the 20th of Jany last—& which I expect was destroyed by a villainous rider who we now know was in the habit of robing the mail about that time, I trouble you with the copy, not willing that the appearance of neglect should pertain to one who will always feel himself honored by an oppy of rendering you any services in his power—

I am Sir mo. Respectfy Yours

PHILIP TABB

RC (MoSHi: TJC-BC); endorsed by TJ as received 3 May 1809 and so recorded in SJL; with subjoined Dupl of Tabb to TJ, [21] Jan. 1809, informing TJ that although he was unable to send more hickory nuts, he was sending a Pennsylvania moldboard.

Philip Tabb (1750–1822) was a Gloucester County planter, agricultural reformer, and Revolutionary War veteran ("Tabb Family," *WMQ*, 1st ser., 13 [1905]: 169–70; Avery O. Craven, "The Agricultural Reformers of the Ante-Bellum South," *American Historical Review* 33 [1928]: 307; *Norfolk and Portsmouth Herald*, 12 Apr. 1822).

# From John Taggart

SIR

Philada April 7th 1809

Your favor of 31th Ulto I recd. Seventy Dollars inclosed is passed to your Credit which Balances your Account except two Dollars which Mr Randolph is to Call and pay which I have now Doubt of—

I am with the highest respect Your Obedient Servent

JOHN TAGGART

RC (MHi); between dateline and salutation: "Thomas Jefferson Esq$^{r}$"; endorsed by TJ as received 17 Apr. 1809 and so recorded in SJL.

## From Benjamin F. Whitner

HON$^{D}$ SIR, Columbia April 7$^{th}$ 1809.

Well knowing you to be an open and sincere friend and patron of literature, and presuming that it would [be][1] highly pleasant for you to hear and see the rapid growth and progression of Science, in all parts of our happy Union, I have taken the liberty of Sending you this catalougue of the Trustees, officers, &C. of the S$^{o}$ Ca. College. Accept this small tribute of esteem and respect for those talents and virtues which have so long & so wisely directed and governed the helm of our political vessel through troubled and stormy seas. from one unknown who takes the liberty of subscribing himself a sincere and respectful friend, B. F. WHITNER

RC (ScU); addressed: "Hon. Thomas Jefferson, Monticello"; endorsed by TJ as received 23 Apr. 1809 and so recorded in SJL; enclosure on verso. Enclosure: *Catalogue Of the Trustees, Faculty and Students of the South-Carolina College, February, 1809* (printed broadside).

Benjamin Franklin Whitner (1790–1859) was born in the Pendleton District of South Carolina, graduated from South Carolina College in 1809, and became a lawyer and merchant. He represented the Edgefield District in the South Carolina House of Representatives, 1826–28, and subsequently became a planter in Florida (*BDSCHR*, 5:282–3).

[1] Omitted word editorially supplied.

## From Philip Freneau

SIR, Philadelphia, April 8th. 1809.—

I do myself the pleasure to enclose to You a copy of Proposals for the publication of a couple of volumes of Poems shortly to be put to press in this City. Perhaps some of your particular friends in Virginia may be induced from a view of the proposals in your hands to subscribe their names. If so, please to have them forwarded to this place by Post, addressed to the Publisher at N$^{o}$ 10, North Alley, Philadelphia. Accept my congratulations on your retirement from public cares, and that you may long enjoy every happiness a private situation can afford.

I am, Sir, with the highest respect and regard, Your obedient humble servant. PHILIP FRENEAU

RC (DLC); endorsed by TJ as received 14 Apr. 1809 and so recorded in SJL. Enclosure not found.

Philip Freneau (1752–1832), journalist and poet, graduated from the College of New Jersey in 1771. During the American Revolution he published patriotic poems and satires, served in the New Jersey militia and on privateers, and spent several weeks in captivity on a British prison ship. Freneau subsequently alternated between the seafaring life and clerical and publishing positions in Philadelphia and New York. In 1791, encouraged by James Madison and others, TJ hired Freneau as a translating clerk for the State Department. In Philadelphia he also edited the fiercely pro-Republican *National Gazette* from October 1792–October 1793. Following its demise Freneau returned to New Jersey, where his attempts to establish other political newspapers met with little success. He continued to write and publish verse in newspapers until his death, but his last volume of poetry appeared in 1815 (*ANB*; *DAB*; *Princetonians*, 1769–1775, pp. 149–56; Editorial Note on Jefferson, Freneau, and the Founding of the *National Gazette*, *PTJ*, 20:718–53).

Freneau wrote Madison a similar letter on the same date (Madison, *Papers, Pres. Ser.*, 1:106). The VOLUMES appeared as Freneau's *Poems Written and Published during the American Revolutionary War, and Now Republished from the Original Manuscripts; Interspersed with Translations from the Ancients, and Other Pieces not Heretofore in Print*, 3d ed., 2 vols. (Philadelphia, 1809; Sowerby, no. 4438).

# From James Madison

DEAR SIR Ap[l] 9. 1809

I return the letter of Mazzei, without however having ascertained the fact as to the remittance by the Sculptor. Latrobe I presume, will give the information in his answer to the letter which I have forwarded to him. He is now in Philad[a].

A Secretary of Legation with a sort of Extra establishment has just arrived from England, with despatches for Erskine. I have a private letter only from Pinkney. The Ministry of G.B. are pretty certainly shaken with respect to this Country. The Catastrophe in Spain, and the new policy to which it leads, have doubtless contributed towards it. But it is unquestionable that the documents cmunicated to Cong[s] and the countenance presented by their earlier resolutions, afford the true explanation. Erskine has not yet opened much of his budget to M[r] Smith. The contents of it were not disclosed to Pinkney; perhaps from an unwillingness to risk a discovery by France, or a use of them by Armstrong. Private letters from individuals in England, leave no doubt that a great dread prevailed of our perseverence in the Embargo.

Among the faux pas of Erving,[1] he has brought about an arrangement between Iznardi, & Hackley, much to be regretted on acc[t] of the latter. It is a sort of simoniacal contract, by which H. gives Iz 600 dol[rs] a year, and receives from him the app[t] of vice Consul; Iz: retaining the title without the responsibility of Consul. The contract, with sundry details, apportioning the functions & formalities, is executed in due form, with the sanction of Erving as a witness, and transmitted hither for that of the Gov[t]. Erving (who appears to have become a little aware of the folly committed) was to have applied to the Spanish Authorities, for an exequatur to the Vice Consulate; but has suspended the application till he hears from us. In the mean time, the contract is in operation. No time was lost by the Dep[t] of State, in giving notice of the nullity & impropriety of such a transaction. I am persuaded from what appears that M[r] H. has been betrayed into it by his confidence in the judgm[t] & experience of others. Erving remarks particularly that his conduct was unexceptionably delicate. It becomes a serious question nevertheless whether the contemplated appointment of him at Cadiz, would not leave suspicions that the bargain with Iznardi, was secretly in fulfilment, and of course furnish a handle to a disapp[d] Candidate for injurious attacks on the Gov[t] as well as M[r] H. If it were certain that Jarvis w[d] not remain at Lisbon, it w[d] mitigate the difficulty by transferring H. thither. It is not probable that Jarvis w[d] be willing to remove to Cadiz, which I believe is not rated as high as Lisbon, as a Consular birth. I recollect no other vacancy that would bear a comparison with Cadiz.

Y[rs] Affect[ly] JAMES MADISON

RC (DLC: Madison Papers); at foot of text: "M[r] Jefferson"; endorsed by TJ as received 14 Apr. 1809 and so recorded in SJL.

For the enclosed LETTER OF MAZZEI and the letter from Philip Mazzei FORWARDED to Benjamin Henry Latrobe by Madison, see TJ to Madison, 24 Mar. 1809, and note.

In 1806 TJ appointed Richard S. HACKLEY, the husband of Thomas Mann Randolph's sister Harriet, consul to San Lúcar, Spain (*JEP*, 2:45 [15, 17 Dec. 1806]). George Erving described the CONTRACT between Hackley and Josef Yznardy for the vice-consulship at Cádiz in a private letter to Madison of 12 Jan. 1809 (MHi: Winthrop Family Papers). Hackley did not receive a new government appointment.

[1] Below TJ's endorsement to this letter, at a later date Madison wrote: "see if any thing further explains the faux pas of E."

# From George Jefferson

DEAR SIR Richmond 10[th] April 1809

I inclose your last quarterly account, which shews a balance in your favor of $:207.43.—

Eleven of the boxes lately received for you were forwarded by M[r]

Randolph's boats on the 30th ultimo, with a Hhd of Molasses.—There were no herrings to be had.

I am Dear Sir Yr Mt humble servt GEO. JEFFERSON

RC (MHi); at foot of text: "Thomas Jefferson esqr"; endorsed by TJ as received 17 Apr. 1809 and so recorded in SJL; notation by TJ: "No 28. 11 Dumbfish. cotton." Enclosure not found.

TJ's notation alludes to dunfish, salted New England cod that turns a dun color when cured (*OED*).

# From William Short

DEAR SIR Paris April 10–09

You will be surprize[d to see by] the date of my letter that I am still at Paris. I hope when you shall have seen how this has been gradually occasioned that you will approve it. I hope also that it will be approved by your successor to whom I wrote on the subject not long ago by an occasion which Genl Armstrong made use of, being the first he has had since the departure of the Union. It was by a vessel from Holland. I was then so much indisposed that I could only write one letter & my anxiety made me address that to the Government. I should have made a greater effort & have written to you also, if the opportunity had been a sure one, but as it was one of the vessels disembargoed in Holland, we thought it very uncertain whether it would be allowed to reach the U.S.

When I last wrote to you by the return of the Union I was about to return from the country in order to prepare & set out on my journey. I informed you in what manner my mission had been communicated to Count Romanzoff by Genl A. It was a favorable circumstance to meet here with the Minister with whom I was to treat at St Petersburgh—It was on a kind of neutral ground, from a variety of circumstances his acquaintance & confidence were much more accessible to me here than they could have been there. This will be readily concieved from observing the relative situation of a Minister of foreign affairs in his own cabinet, on his throne as it were, & in a foreign country. Immediately on my return to Paris I waited on Count Romanzoff who shewed me in the most unquestionable manner how much his Court would be gratified by the measure you had taken of sending a Minister to St Petersburgh—& let me clearly see that it was a thing which not only the Emperor but himself had particularly at heart. I suppress all the flattering expressions that he used as to me personally & his satisfaction that your choice had fallen on me &c.

&c. These could be only words of course at that time, as he certainly knew[1] less of me than he pretended—I repaid his expressions [with those of a?] [si]milar nature & by letting him suppose that my inducement to enter again into p[. . .] [w]hich I had so long abandoned, was, to have the honor of being the first to establish [. . .] [rela]tions between our two countries which I hoped would conduce to the advantage of both, & to reside near so great a Sovereign who still acknowleged the sacredness of public law, whilst it was exiled from the thrones of the other Powers of the earth.—On quitting him, he pressed me to give him as much of my time as I could, & assured me that he should have particular pleasure in laying here the foundation of an acquaintance that he flattered himself would ripen into confidence & friendship at Petersburgh. On my assuring him that nothing could give me more satisfaction, & that I should only be restrained by the fear of taking too much time from the important concerns which engrossed it, he said that he would always tell me candidly & unreservedly when it was necessary for him to withdraw, & hoped I would therefore be perfectly at my ease on that head—He added that he was then writing to the Emperor his Master, & that he should inform him how much he had been satisfied by this interview &c. &c.—Such things are always of course to be understood sub mode. I continued until his departure to cultivate assiduously his acquaintance, & I must say that I had ample reason to be satisfied & pleased with it—His principles & his dispositions towards the U.S. are such as we could wish—and wherever he can follow his own impulsion I am persuaded he will give us proofs of this—But as you know, there is now in Europe & indeed in all the civilized world, instead of the ordinary flux & reflux of human affairs, a torrent & eddy which sweep off or act with violence on every thing. You may judge from the influence & forced position in which we are placed, though separated from them by the Ocean & by our habits & dispositions, how this impetuous, unexampled state of things must operate on those bodies, even the largest, which are placed within its immediate action. Nothing is left to its natural course, & therefore it is difficult to say what we may [. . .] those whose dispositions you know to be the best.

To return to [the reason for?] my being still here; It was the month of January before I could have sat out, under the most pressing circumstances. The making preparations for such a journey & in such a season, procuring a proper carriage &c. &c. I found to take up much more time in detail, than I had expected. I was the more easily reconciled to this from the fortunate circumstance of Count Romanzoff being here, & the advantage to be derived from it, of which I availed myself to the full, as already mentioned. The season was now at its greatest rigor & the winter in the north, of which we recieved frequent intelligence, was uncommonly severe; insomuch that the Austrian Ambassador on his way to S[t] Petersburgh was frostbitten though accustomed to that climate & mode of travelling. Still I should have sat out when ready, if it had not been that Count Romanzoff was then here, his departure altogether uncertain, & more particularly that I then expected that the next Aviso, which was to succeed the Union, must be near the time of its arrival. I was satisfied that the month of January could not pass off without bringing it. Your letters, before I left America, informed me that Government would despatch these vessels during the embargo, successively from six weeks to two months—I calculated therefore that the next would sail about the first of December, & the more so as Congress had met. Indeed this circumstance had led both Gen[l] Armstrong & myself to suppose that the departure of the Aviso would be rather accelerated than retarded beyond the ordinary term. Throughout the month of January therefore we were constantly hoping for the arrival of this vessel. Every day that elapsed in the month of February made us suppose that this hope was the nearer being realized. We then calculated that the vessel had been retarded until Congress should have come to some decision as to the embargo, & that it would be immediately despatched with that decision. Vague reports coming through England, led us to believe that this had taken place in December. Thus in daily, & as I thought, certain expectation did I remain until the midd[le] [. . .] Soon after, Count Romanzoff left us. I saw his departure with real pain, notw[ithstanding I] then expected to follow him in a short time, although I had then determined to wait the [arrival o]f the Aviso at all events. As I had already staid so long I thought it most advisable not to lose the advantage I expected from being here at that arrival. The uncertain & precarious mode of recieving my despatches at S[t] Petersburgh after their being brought thus far by the messenger to Gen[l] Armstrong, & the supplement to my instructions which were promised me, made me particularly desirous to recieve them here, as I had so far postponed my departure, & as I foresaw no possibility of inconvenience to what I supposed must be a short delay unquestionably at that time; & as Count Romanzoff had been made acquainted with the cause of it, & entered perfectly into it.

Could I have known in the beginning that the Aviso would not have arrived before this time I should not have waited for it—but it was impossible for me to have the most distant idea of such a delay;

& to this moment neither Gen[l] A. or myself can conjecture the cause. Neither of us have recieved any thing from America since my arrival—We have only heard a few days ago indirectly that the embargo is raised as to neutral countries—commerce forbidden with the belligerent—Gen[l] A. appointed Minister of war—& a vessel ordered to sail from New-York at the end of February to bring him back—This vessel we therefore now expect every moment—Gen[l] A. gets this intelligence from a person here & from the Consul at Bordeaux. It comes in a newspaper brought by a French Government vessel despatched from the U.S. by Gen[l] Thureau. This vessel was still kept in the stream at Bordeaux under quarantine & no communication allowed with it. An account came by it also that a vessel was to be sent to bring back M[r] Pinckney from London. We know nothing more, & even this we know very imperfectly as you will percieve. An article has been printed in the papers here, which is taken without doubt from some American paper brought by Thureau's vessel, stating that "it is now ascertained that neither M[r] [. . .] Giles accept the place of Sec. of State—J.Q. Adams is the person most talked of for that [. . .]

From my last letters wri[tten to you] in America & that which I wrote from this country by the Union, you will have seen how anxious I was to have some uncertainties removed, & how sollicitous therefore to hear from you. I regretted very much having not had that done before I left the U.S.—But some of them did not occur until it was too late—I had supposed Monroe's appointment when he last sailed, similar to mine, & would therefore remove any uncertainty—I considered it certain that whilst he was travelling, his expences were born—I considered therefore either that w[d] be the case or an outfit allowed &c.—It is useless to repeat here when & how the uncertainty was produced in my mind as I have already mentioned it—A few days now must bring here the vessel announced & despatches which will remove all doubts of every kind.

Since I have put on the harness again my mind has naturally occupied itself on subjects of public concern. I have perused with more & pointed attention all the public documents furnished me by the Department of State, & particularly as they regard our foreign relations. I have frequently had occasion to regret having not done this before I left America, & particularly under your eye at Washington—I have wished for your ideas & explanation on some points which have presented themselves, as antecedents to the forced situation in which we now find ourselves in our foreign relations. It is too late now & I am too far removed from the scene to recieve those lights. I do not find any where in the various difficulties that presented themselves to the deliberations of Congress in their choice of evils, that the idea of leaving Commerce to calculate its own risks, was taken into consideration. In the several alternatives proposed by the Senator (Anderson I think) in his report, this idea has no place. Priestley suggests somewhere in his works, if I mistake not, a plan of this kind. If it could be ever admissible it must certainly be during the present violent & unprecedented crisis of the world, I should imagine. I have not sufficiently exam[ined] [. . .]ble the bearings of an experiment of this kind to pronounce on it with confidence. But [having po]ndered it a good deal I think it would have been worth the consideration of the legislature [if onl]y as a temporary means of weathering the storm which the belligerent world has gathered up & suspended over our heads, who may be considered as the only neutrals. It would seem to me that the most important & substantial interest of our country (the agricultural) would suffer less under this experiment than under the prolongation of the embargo. Commerce would become still more a game of hazard unfortunately, than it has been with us for some years past, but the losses would fall first on the gamesters, where it is more just & less prejudicial that it should be. They besides would be more dexterous to parry or mitigate those losses. It may be further said that this would be a game of their own seeking, since they have been the most impatient under the embargo & the most hostile to the measures adopted by Government in consequence of it.

It is possible however that there may be some consideration, of which I am not aware, that may present[2] the alternative I mention, in the choice of evils, as absolutely inadmissible & therefore not worthy of having been taken into discussion. I remember once at a dinner before I left America, where the subject of the embargo was agitated as never failed to be the case, that I incidentally threw out this idea, merely as it were, for information. The convines, as well as I recollect, were all of the same party politics with one or two exceptions—but they were divided on the subject of the embargo—The idea of Government abandoning the protection of commerce, as they called it, was repelled in such a manner by all hands without a doubtful or dissenting voice, as prevented me (who always avoid discussion over a bottle, where there is inevitably more passion than reason) from saying any thing more on it.—Every observation however made on the subject was founded on a petitio principii or some other false basis—& accompanied with such false reasoning, as tended rather to confirm the contrary doctrine: in the same manner as a pious parson once in producing arguments to prove the truths of the Christian religion, tended to prod[uce doubt in the?] mind of one of his auditors, who before had never doubted.

Having no certain[ty of the decision?] which has been adopted by Congress I shall make no observation on that which is reported as mentioned above—Indeed I had not intended to have extended this letter to subjects of that kind. I will hereafter inform you more particularly of various conversations with Count Romanzoff & the ideas they have suggested to me—The present occasion though by a vessel to be despatched by Gen[l] A is not absolutely certain. Should M[r] Daschkoff embark in it I shall confide my letter to him. M[r] Daschkoff is the Consul General & Chargè des affaires of Russia—He goes with his family—He arrived here about the time I did. He stands well with Count R. who told me that he had chosen him particularly & recommended him to the Emperor for this mission. He asked me more than once in his style "d'avoir des bontés pour lui." I have given M[r] Daschkoff a letter of introduction to you at Montecello, where he will pay you a visit.—as soon as he can after having recieved an invitation from you, if he should send on his letter of introduction; or perhaps he will go & carry it in the first instance.

I cannot end my letter without giving you the satisfaction to inform you with how much candor & impartiality, your administration[3] is discussed & judged of by a great mass of enlightened & respectable people here—some of them who know you & others who do not. It has been a curious circumstance to me, who had been so long accustomed to hear every act of your administration, I cannot say discussed, but pronounced on with passion & violence & prejudice, to be so suddenly transported to another world as it were—where distance has produced the effect of time, so that they now pass the same judgment on you here which posterity will do in America, when all the passions have subsided. To a great many philosophic minds it seems here to be a real gratification to dwell on & pass in review the acts of your administration. It is your lot here to experience th[. . .] ["datis] viris." In every company where I have been I am questioned as to your retiring [. . .]—the line that your successor will adopt &c. &c.—Some regret your retreat—others [do not o]n account of the example, & as the complement of the system & conduct they have admired in you.

You have many warm personal friends yet alive here—among them several women—they are of that age at which it is said in this country 'there is no sex'—The meaning of which is that a woman may then say & do what she pleases & be considered as an honest man—desire & the other passions of the sex being considered as extinguished—One of your old friends however who has been all her life a phenomenon, is exhibiting a most extraordinary exception to the general rule—You certainly remember your old correspondent whose writing was so difficult to decypher—When she & her husband celebrated their cinquantaine with a fête, complets &c—it was observed that in one year more she might repeat the same fête with her lover to whom she could then boast a constancy of forty nine years—Time alone put an end to that union—& at this moment with seventy eight years on her head, her heart still alive to the passion of youth, is by some special grace devoted to an object young in proportion, sensible, agreeable, wealthy, & who appears to be occupied exclusively to make her happy, with the tenderness of an affectionate son—It is a strange sight & I mention it merely on account of your knowing one of the persons, & its being a trait in the exposition of the human heart of which I know no other example. This passion gives inconcievable activity to such an age—Promenades—visites—diners en ville—theatre—soupers—all are undertaken & gone through as at eighteen—so that her friends here say that having soixante dixhuit ans, she has only laid aside the soixante.—I end my letter, my dear Sir, with assurances of what will never end, the sentiments of attachment of your friend & servant

W SHORT

P.S. I mentioned above that Gen[l] A. had not written during the winter except by the Vessel by which I wrote to your successor—He has just informed me that he wrote once at a venture by the way of England—but did not expect it w[d] arrive—If it did, it will perhaps be thought extraordinary that I had not written to explain the cause of my being here—but I did not know of the occasion.

RC (DLC); torn at seal; endorsed by TJ as received 10 July 1809 and so recorded in SJL. FC (DLC: Short Papers, 34:6184–5); abstract in Short's hand from a portion of his epistolary record containing entries from 6 June 1808 to 16 Oct. 1809, written on sheets folded to make narrow pages. Enclosed in TJ to James Madison, 12 July 1809, and Madison to TJ, 23 July 1809.

YOUR SUCCESSOR TO WHOM I WROTE: Short to James Madison, 29 Mar. 1809, in which Short reported that he was INDISPOSED with catarrh and requested Madison to inform TJ that he was too fatigued to write him (Madison, *Papers, Pres. Ser.*, 1:86–7). When Short LAST WROTE to TJ on 25 Nov. 1808 (DLC), he described his discussions with Count Nicolas de ROMANZOFF, the Russian foreign minister. Karl Philipp Schwarzenberg was AUSTRIAN AMBASSADOR to Saint Petersburg, 1806–09. William Lee was the CONSUL AT BORDEAUX.

LEAVING COMMERCE TO CALCULATE ITS OWN RISKS was proposed by Joseph PRIESTLEY in his *Letters to the Inhabitants of Northumberland and its neighbourhood* (Northumberland, Pa., 1799; Sowerby, no. 3217), pt. 2, pp. 36–8, where he suggested that the nation paid more in profits to merchants and the cost of diplomacy and warships to protect trade than it received back as benefits, and that if "any person will send his goods to sea, it should be at his own risque."

CONVINES: those who convene (*OED*). PETITIO PRINCIPII: correctly, "petito principii," or begging the question. D'AVOIR DES BONTÉS POUR LUI: "to be kind to him."

ONE OF YOUR OLD FRIENDS: Elisabeth Françoise Sophie de la Live Bellegarde, comtesse d'Houdetot, had lived with her LOVER Jean François de Saint-Lambert and her husband in the same household since 1753. Saint-Lambert died in 1803 (TJ to Abigail Adams, 21 June 1785, *PTJ*, 8:242n). CINQUANTAINE WITH A FÊTE, COMPLETS: "fiftieth anniversary with a grand celebration." DINERS EN VILLE: "dinners in town." SOIXANTE DIX-HUIT ANS: "seventy-eight years." SOIXANTE: "sixty."

[1] Manuscript: "kew."
[2] Word interlined in place of "render."
[3] Manuscript: "admistration."

# From Henry Foxall

SIR Georg Town Ap[l] 11[th] 1809

Your favor of the 24[th] Ulto came to hand in due course, The Stew holes you request me to Send You, I have Made and put them on board a vessele bound for Richmond which is to sail this day

I observe the Information you have received respecting our Method of Makeing the Stew holes is not agreeable to our practice, we cast the Cheeks, and grates, sepperate and not Solid or together, the reason is that one set of Cheeks will Last as long as Many sets of grates—

I have Sent you a duble set of grates two to Each Stew hole, be-lieveing it might be difficult for you to obtain others when the first set of Grates might become useless—

I have not given up the Intention of Executing the Stove you were so kind as to send me the Model of—when done I will inform you of its success, Should it answer the Expectation I have of it I will Send you one on agreeable to your request

I am Respectfully Sir Your Obed[t] Serv[t] HEN:[Y] FOXALL

RC (MHi); between dateline and salutation: "Thomas Jefferson Esquire"; endorsed by TJ as received 19 Apr. 1809 and so recorded in SJL.

CHEEKS: the side-pieces of a grate or stove (*OED*). TJ sent Foxall a MODEL of a Swedish stove he had received from David Steuart Erskine, eleventh earl of Buchan. Foxall did not produce one until 1811 (TJ to Foxall, 7 May 1811, and Foxall to TJ, 12 Oct. 1811).

## List of Goods Sent by George Jefferson, with Thomas Jefferson's Notes

Sent M[r] Jefferson by M[r] Randolph's boats

| | | |
|---|---|---|
| √ | 1 pipe | N[o] 16. |
| | 3 Hhds | N[o] 6. 9. & probably the cask of oil |
| | 1 quarter Cask | |
| | 10 barrels | N[o] 4. 5. 10. q. 11. 12. 18. △1 △2 △3 △4 |
| | 1 half barrel | △5 |
| | 1 keg | paint |
| | 4 trunks | N[o] 26. 27. & an empty one. |
| | 5 boxes | No 20.[1] 23. △6 △7 qu. 19. |
| √ | 1 screw bench | |
| | 27 packages | |

G.J.
11[th] Ap[l] 1809

MS (MHi); right-hand column and check marks in TJ's hand; remainder in George Jefferson's hand.

[1] Number interlined.

## From Thomas Gillet

SIR Salisbury Square London April 12[th] 1809.

As every addition to the Literature of Europe by which America may be ultimately benefited, especially where the amelioration of the condition of mankind is the object, cannot be a subject of indifference to a Legislator of your enlarged views and liberal understanding: I am desired by the Author of "An Essay on Government" to request your acceptance of two Copies of her work, just published in England.

To you who followed the immortal Washington in the administration of the Government of the most free and happy nation in the universe, and, like him, retired into private life with the approbation of your fellow citizens, a work calculated to clear the hands and strengthen the arms of all departments of civil authority, cannot fail to prove interesting. It would not become me to enlarge upon the merits of the performance, or to attempt to bias that candid judgme[nt] which the Author hopes will be pronounced upon it on this, and on your side the Atlantic. I may however be allowed to add, that it is the production of no vulgar pen, the unaided effort of a

Lady, not altogether unknown to you, Mrs R. F. A. Lee, only daughter of the late Francis Lord Le Despencer, the friend of Franklin and of Freedom.

Mrs Lee writes not for emolument, but from a patriotic desire to be thought useful to her country; she is a Lady of uncommon endowments, and joins to a brilliant fancy, the most vigorous and manly understanding, and her work throughout breathes a spirit of rational liberty, which however it may be accepted in this country, will no doubt prove highly gratifying to the people of the United States.

Previous to the French Revolution Mrs Lee passed some agreeable hours at your villa near Paris, but as she was then young, you may have forgotten the circumstance. In July 1807 she sent you a communication by a Capt Hinckley; no answer to which having been received, she concludes the messenger failed in his endeavors to forward the packet to you.

Should the present opportunity, through the kindness of General Pinckney, prove more fortunate, she hopes to be favored with a few lines in reply. Eighteen Copies are also sent for the American Universities, and the Author will esteem herself singularly happy, if you will have the goodness to cause them to be forwarded to the respective seminaries for which they are intended

With every sentiment of respect for Your character, and every wish that you may long enjoy in domestic retirement that well earned reputation to which your public services have entitled you, I have the honor to be Sir Your faithful & obedt Servant

Thomas Gillet.

Mrs Lee's address is 36, Clarges Street, Piccadilly.

RC (DLC); torn at fold; endorsed by TJ as received 2 Mar. 1811 and so recorded in SJL. Enclosure: Rachel Fanny Antonina Lee, *An Essay on Government* (London, 1809; Sowerby, no. 2339). Enclosed in William Pinkney to TJ, 25 Sept. 1810.

Thomas Gillet, the printer of the enclosed publication, was active in London between 1799 and 1810 (William B. Todd, comp., *A Directory of Printers and Others in Allied Trades: London and Vicinity, 1800–1840* [1972], 78).

The enclosure's AUTHOR was the illegitimate daughter of Sir Francis Dashwood, baron le DESPENCER. Benjamin FRANKLIN was a guest at Dashwood's house in 1773 (*DNB*; Franklin, *Papers*, 27:177, 28:243n). On 3 Oct. 1807 TJ recorded receipt in SJL of her earlier, undated COMMUNICATION, not found, from Castle Godwin Paradise in Gloucestershire.

# To the New York State Legislature

I recieve with respect & gratitude, from the legislature of New York, on my retirement from the office of Chief magistrate of the United States, the assurances of their esteem, & of their satisfaction with the services I have endeavored to render. the welfare of my fellow citizens, & the perpetuation of our republican institutions having been the governing principles of my public life, the favorable testimony borne by the legislature of a state so respectable as that of New York, gives me the highest consolation. and this is much strengthened by an intimate conviction that the same principles will govern the conduct of my successor, whose talents, whose virtues, & eminent services, are a certain pledge that the confidence in him expressed by the legislature of New York will never be disappointed.

Sole depositories of the remains of human liberty, our duty to ourselves to posterity & to mankind call on us by every motive which is sacred or honorable, to watch over the safety of our beloved country, during the troubles which agitate & convulse the residue of the world, & to sacrifice to that all personal & local considerations. while the boasted energies of monarchy have yielded to easy conquest the people they were to protect, should our fabric of freedom suffer no more[1] than the slight agitations we have experienced, it will be an useful lesson to the friends, as well as to the enemies of self-government. that it may stand the shocks of time & accident, & that your own may make a distinguished part of the mass of prosperity it may dispense, will be my latest prayer.

TH: JEFFERSON

Monticello Apr. 12. 1809.

RC (N-Ar: New York Legislature, Correspondence and Legislative Action Files); at head of text: "To the Legislature of the State of New York." PoC (DLC). Recorded in SJL as "Answer to legislature of N. York." Printed in *Raleigh Star*, 4 May 1809. Enclosed in a brief covering letter to John Broome and James W. Wilkin, 12 Apr. 1809 (RC in N-Ar: New York Legislature, Correspondence and Legislative Action Files, at foot of text: "John Broom President of the Senate James W. Wilkin Speaker of the Assembly"; PoC in DLC).

[1] Reworked from "nothing."

## To the Albemarle Buckmountain Baptist Church

I thank you, my friends & neighbors, for your kind congratulations on my return to my native home, & on the opportunities it will give me of enjoying, amidst your affections the comforts of retirement & rest. your approbation of my conduct is the more valued as you have best known me, & is an ample reward for any services I may have rendered. we have acted together from the origin to the end of a memorable revolution, and we have contributed, each in the line allotted us, our endeavors to render it's issue a permanent blessing to our country. that our social intercourse may, to the evening of our days, be cheered & cemented by witnessing the freedom & happiness for which we have laboured will be my constant prayer. Accept the offering of my affectionate esteem & respect.

Th: Jefferson
Monticello Apr. 13. 09

MS (A-Ar: J. L. M. Curry Autograph Collection); at head of text: "To the members of the Baptist church of Buckmountain in Albemarle." PoC (DLC). Recorded in SJL as an "Answer" to the "Baptist church of Buckmountain." Printed in Richmond *Enquirer*, 26 May 1809.

## To Jonathan Law

Sir — Monticello April 13. 09.

I recieved on the 6th inst. your favor covering the resolutions of the General meeting of the republicans of the state of Connecticut who had been convened at Hartford: and I see with pleasure the spirit they breathe. they express with truth the wrongs we have sustained, the forbearance we have exercised, & the duty of rallying round the constituted authorities, for the protection of our union. surrounded by such difficulties & dangers, it is really deplorable that any should be found among ourselves vindicating the conduct of the aggressors, cooperating with them in multiplying embarrasments to their own country, & encouraging disobedience to the laws provided for it's safety. but a spirit which should go further, & countenance the advocates for a dissolution of the Union, and for setting in hostile array one portion of our citizens against another, would require to be viewed under a more serious aspect. it would prove indeed that it is high time for every friend to his country, in a firm & decided manner, to express his sentiments of the measures which government has adopted to avert the impending evils, unhesitatingly to pledge himself for the support of the laws, liberties & independance of his country; and, with the General meeting of the republicans of Connecticut, to resolve, that, for the preservation of the Union, the support & enforcement of the laws, & for the resistance & repulsion of every enemy, they will hold themselves in readiness, & put at stake, if neccesary, their lives & fortunes, on the pledge of their sacred honour.

With my thanks for the mark of attention in making this communication, I pray you to accept for yourself & my respectable fellow citizens from whom it proceeds the assurance of my high consideration & my prayers for their Welfare. TH: JEFFERSON

RC (Anonymous, Cheshire, Connecticut, 1987); addressed: "Jonathan Low esquire Hartford Connecticut"; stamped and postmarked; with 1831 notation that "If memory err not Mr Law wrote the address to which this letter is in reply." PoC (DLC). Tr (ViU: TJP); posthumous copy. Recorded in SJL as letter to "Low Jonathan for the Republicans of Connecticut."

# To the Republicans of Queen Annes County, Maryland

I have recieved, fellow citizens, your farewell address with those sentiments of respect and satisfaction which it's very friendly terms are calculated to inspire. with the consciousness of having endeavored to serve my fellow citizens according to their best interests, these testimonies of their good will are the sole & highest remuneration my heart has ever desired.

I am sensible of the indulgence with which you review the measures which have been pursued: and approving our sincere endeavors to observe a strict neutrality with respect to foreign powers, it is with reason you observe that, if hostilities must succeed, we shall have the consolation that justice will be on our side. war has been avoided from a due sense of the miseries, & the demoralization it produces, and of the superior blessings of a state of peace & friendship with all mankind. but peace on our part, & war from others, would neither be for our happiness or honour; & should the lawless violences of the belligerent powers render it necessary to return their hostilities, no nation has less to fear from a foreign enemy.

I thank you, fellow citizens, for your very kind wishes for my happiness, and pray you to accept the assurances of my cordial esteem, & grateful sense of your favor. TH: JEFFERSON

Monticello Apr. 13. 1809.

PoC (DLC); at head of text: "To the Republicans of Queen Anne's county"; at foot of text: "Thomas Wright esquire Centreville, Maryland." Recorded in SJL as "Answer to the repub. Q. Anne's c[ty] Maryl[d]."

## From Louis Philippe Gallot de Lormerie

MONSIEUR Philad[a] 14 avril 1809

J'ai Eu lhonneur de vous Ecrire Lors de Votre Elevation a la Presidence des E.u. pour vous en féliciter. Jai aujourd huy celui de vous prier d'agrèer mon sincère Complimens sur la Situation tranquile alaquelle vous etes rendu par votre propre volonté, ayant desiré de n'Etre pas reèlu. Vous Emportés dans Votre retraite L'Estime et la reconnoissançe de tous les bons citoyens, et vous allés reposer a L'ombre de vos Lauriers.—

Mon Dessein de retourner en france est toujours le même aussitôt que je pourai l'Exècuter. Mais semblable à un arbre transplanté depuis pres de quinze ans sur ce sol Jy tiens par des raçines profondes. il est difficile de m'en arracher, parcequ'il m'est resté malgré moi beaucoup d'objets dont je n'ai pu rèaliser Cy devant que quelques uns, et comme ils sont articles français et de Superfluité il est impossible de les vendre si ce n'est a une perte presque totale. il vaut mieux les remporter ou ils seront de mise et de valeur.

Lacte de non intercourse n'Empêchera pas sans doute qu'il n'y ait des parlementaires, notamment pour françe. mais ils ne veulent rien prendre qu'une Malle ou deux. cependant comme ils vont en Leste ils ont de la plaçe pour loger bien plus que mes meubles, savoir Livres, malles, tableaux, tapisseries linge &[c] (mais non aucune marchandise)—Laisser ici ces Effets seroit les Exposer a être Gâtés dans les magazins et a une foule d'autres Evènemens tels que[1] je les ai Eprouvés sur des objets Envoyés icy avant moi.

Presque tous ces Effets, notamment les Livres me seront nècessaires en france.

Puis je solliciter avec confiançe de votre bonte d'obtenir pour moi une permission d'Emporter ces Effets avec moi sur le même navire, ainsi que qques[2] objets dhist. naturelle, comme m[r] michaux qui a eté, authorisé par votre Gouvernement de transporter plusieurs caisses sur le navire L'union a Lautomne passé. Je desire etre muni de cette permission d'avançe ou de la certitude de l'obtenir. le Collecteur de ce port ou de celui d'ou je partirai ètant authorisé d'avançe a remplir le nom du Navire.

Je vous prie, Monsieur, de vouloir bien être assuré de toute ma discrétion a Cet Egard, en ne communiquant a personne qu'au Collecteur, cette permission—elle m'est absolument neçessaire car a deffaut je me trouverois plongé dans de nouvelles pertes presque insurmontables car comme j'ay Eu Lhonneur de vous dire Je me trouve avoir perdu ici 25 mille dollars ou Environ tant par les malversations de swanwick auquel javois adressé des marchandises pour me servir de ressources icy, que par d'autres circonstances—

quant ames terres au contrat desquelles vous avés bien voulu Etre présent et Signer, pouriès vous avoir la Bonté de m'indiquer quelque moyen d'En tirer parti. celui qui En a acheté la majeure partie pour une Miserable somme de taxes, (par la faute de M fowler de Kent^y qui avoit promis de Lacquitter et qui les a Laisseès vendre)[3] consent Suiv^t ce que m'a Ecrit M^r Madison de frankford de me les remettre pour 200 dollars Jai oui dire qu'elles n'avoient pas Ete annonçées, ni achetées en formes Légales et que vos Tribunaux repriment sevèrement ces fraudes. mais la pénurie de ma fortune ne me permet pas d'aller faire un voyage et séjour en Kentucky et la nécessité de retourner En france au plutot ne m'en Laisse pas le tems. que faire en telle Circonstance?—votre opinion me seroit bien Essentielle. Laisser des pouvoirs, c'est tout perdre a peu pres. Jai LExpèrience que le propriètaire Eloigné peut regarder a comme nulle pour lui ce qu'il abandonne a dautres, a une telle distance! vous verrés par lExtrait cÿ aprés que jai voulu jusqu'au d^er[4] moment donner des preuves de mon attachem^t aux E.u par un memoire sur un sujet rural des plus importans.—Jay Lhonneur dEtre attendant celui de Votre reponse trés respectueusement

Votre tres humble & dévoué serviteur De Lormerie

EDITORS' TRANSLATION

Sir Philad^a 14 April 1809

I had the honor to write to you on the occasion of your elevation to the presidency of the U.S. to congratulate you on it. Today, I have the honor of asking you to accept my sincere compliments on the tranquil situation that you have achieved by your own will, having desired not to be reelected. You take with you into your retirement the regards and the gratitude of all good citizens, and you are going to rest in the shade of your laurels.—

My plan to return to France is still the same as soon as I am able to execute it. But like a tree that has been transplanted on this soil for almost fifteen years I am holding on to it through deep roots. It is difficult to pull myself out, because despite myself, I am left with a lot of objects of which I could sell only a few, and as they are French articles and superfluous it is impossible to sell them except at an almost total loss. It is better to take them back where they will be appreciated.

The Non-Intercourse Act will probably not prevent parlementaires, notably those for France, but they only want to take a trunk or two. However as they travel East they have room for much more than just my furniture, such as books, trunks, paintings, tapestries, linen &c (but no merchandise)—To leave these belongings here would be to expose them to damage in storage and by a host of other events such as I have experienced with objects sent here ahead of me.

Almost all of these possessions, especially the books, I will need in France.

May I solicit from you, with trust in your kindness, to obtain for me permission to take these possessions with me on the same ship, as well as a few objects of natural history, like Mr. Michaux who was authorized by your government to transport several boxes on the ship the Union last fall. I wish to have this permit in hand in advance or to be assured that I will obtain it. The collector of this port or of the one from which I will leave being authorized in advance to fill in the name of the ship.

Please, Sir, be assured of my complete discretion in this regard, by handing over this permit to nobody but the collector. I absolutely need this permit, as without it I would find myself drowning in almost insurmountable new losses because, as I had the honor of telling you, I find myself having lost 25 thousand dollars here or about as much through the malpractice of Swanwick to whom I had sent merchandise to be used as resources here, as well as through other circumstances.

As for my lands, the contract for which you were so good as to witness and sign, could you be kind enough to indicate to me some means of making them profitable. The person who bought most of them for a miserable amount of taxes, (through the fault of M. Fowler from Kentucky who had promised to pay them and who let them be sold) agrees according to what Mr. Madison from Frankfort wrote me to return them to me for 200 dollars. I have heard that they had not been advertised, nor bought according to law and that your tribunals severely repress these frauds. But the scarcity of my financial resources does not allow me to make a trip to Kentucky and stay there awhile and the necessity of returning to France as soon as possible does not allow me time for this. What to do in such circumstances? Your opinion would be essential to me. To leave someone else in charge is to lose just about everything. My experience is that an absentee landlord may regard as worthless what he abandons to others, at such a distance! You will see from the following extract that I wanted until the last moment to prove my attachment to the U.S. with a memoir on a most important rural topic. I have the honor, while very respectfully awaiting the honor of your response, to be

Your very humble and devoted servant De Lormerie

RC (DLC); dateline below signature; at foot of first page: "M[r] Th[s] Jefferson la president des E.U. Monticello"; endorsed as received 19 Apr. 1809 and so recorded in SJL. Translation by Dr. Genevieve Moene.

Louis Philippe Gallot de Lormerie (b. ca. 1746), a French scientist who identified himself as a member of the agricultural societies of London and Paris and claimed to be an associate of Lafayette's, began his correspondence with TJ during the latter's service as minister to France. Their correspondence lasted well into TJ's retirement, with Lormerie writing on a wide variety of aesthetic, scientific, and political subjects. Lormerie occasionally sent TJ pamphlets and frequently sought assistance with travel and transportation of items between the United States and France (Lormerie to TJ, 30 Nov. 1806 [DLC], and 9 Apr. 1816; Lormerie to James Madison, 24 Feb. 1802, Madison, *Papers, Sec. of State Ser.*, 2:486–7).

In 1808 Lormerie claimed to have been invited by the French government to return EN FRANCE, but he had been notified by the State Department that he needed official permission to travel there (Lormerie to TJ, 6 June 1808 [DLC]). PARLEMENTAIRES were French ships bearing a flag of truce (*OED*). François André MICHAUX had been granted governmental permission to travel to France (Lormerie to TJ, 15 Aug. 1808 [DLC]). The bankruptcy late in the 1790s of Philadelphia merchant John SWANWICK cost Lormerie heavily (*ANB*; Lormerie to TJ, 15 Aug. 1808 [DLC]). TJ witnessed the CONTRAT signed by Lormerie in February 1787 for his purchase of 5,277 acres of Kentucky land from Samuel Blackden (TJ to Richard Claiborne, 25 Sept. 1789, Lormerie to TJ, 1 July 1787, Memorandum on Deed of Lormerie, 7 Mar. 1792, *PTJ*, 11:518–9, 15:478, 23:230–1). MADISON DE FRANKFORD: possibly George Madison, an 1810 resident of Franklin County, Kentucky (Ronald Vern Jackson and others, *Kentucky 1810 Census* [1978], 484).

[1] Manuscript: "que que."

[2] Abbreviation for "quelques" here and in enclosure.

[3] Lormerie here placed a comma rather than a closing parenthesis.

[4] Abbreviation for "dernier."

ENCLOSURE

## Memoir on American Forest Management

Extraits d'un Mémoire sur l'Aménagement des forêts dans les E:u de L'Am$^{que}$ Septent$^{le}$

Les forêts (dit L'auteur dans son Début) sont un des premiers prèsens de la nature Elles fournissent a Lhomme sauvâge presque toute sa subsistance, et un abri contre les attaques des betes féroces, a Lhomme civilisé les matèriaux les plus prècieux pour les constructions civiles et militaires pour les usages ordinaires de la vie, et pour le Combustible d'un besoin Journalier.

Lasie majeure autrefois si peuplée n'est devenue stèrile et dèserte que par la destruction des forêts. ne seroit-il pas douloureux a tout citoyen Americain de penser que sa patrie peut Eprouver le même sort par l'Effet de la meme imprévoÿance. . . . &$^{c}$ &$^{c}$

Lauteur pense que sans porter atteinte a La Liberté des personnes et des proprietés il est possible de faire qques reglemens pour la Conservation et la réproduction des bois a Construire (timber) dont la réproduction Est bien loin dEtre proportionnée a la Consommation très rapide, surtout dans un paÿs qui sEtablit.—il indique la nécessite des plantations et le produit considerable qu'en pouroient retirer les compagnies des routes publiques a Barrieres—(turnpike roads.)

il Expose le dommâge qu'occasionnent a la societé non seulement par la destruction des Bois, mais par le deffaut de fertilité qu'Eprouve toujours une terre depouîllee darbres, les Défricheurs ignorans qui coupent impitoyablement et indiscretement tous les Bois. il conseille de Laisser en cas de defrichemens Des Ceintures dArbres de 10. en 10 acres, plus ou moins afin de subvenir aux besoins de bois qui sont nècessaires a chaque ferme et quant aux terrains dèpouilles il conseille de les planter ainsi En ceintures de bois a Bâtir. il Est convaincu par Experience comme agronome que ces arbres rassemblent sur le sol Lhumidite de L'atmosphère et le defendant de la rigueur des vents accroissent de beaucoup les récoltes En Grains et en foin—

il cite plusieurs anecdotes qui prouvent que le produit darbres plantés pour futaÿe, bois a Bâtir, En 20 ou 25 ans a quelque fois surpassé la valeur intrinseque de toute La propriète du sol quoiqu'ils n'en aient occupé qu'une foible partie et la moins productive—

il demontre que la négligence et le deffaut d'Elagâge (trimming) des Gros arbres prive les propriètaires de trés beaux bois a bâtir parceque les Branches laterales Epuisent la seve de ces arbres Et en Empechent le Corps de Grossir. ainsi tous les 3 ou 4 ans il faudroit couper les branches laterales afin de laisser le Corps de Larbre profiter de toute la seve—le vaste ombrâge de ces arbres abandonnés a la nature prive aussi les animaux qu'on Eleve, de beaucoup de pâture parceque Lherbe qui croit sous leur ombre n'est pas bonne. c'est donc une double perte sans compter le produit que donneroit L'Elagâge.

Enfin il invite les societés savantes a Eclairer les legislatures diverses sur cette importante matiére et a les Engager sinon a faire des règlements du moins a avertir solemnellement les proprietaires de forêts que L interest general de la societé et le leur en particulier Exige un meilleur aménagement des Bois et leur reproduction par des Plantations darbres pour les besoins delavenir—

P:s Dans vos Proprietes au sud des E:u ne seroit ce pas une speculation sage de faire planter des futaÿes de bois de Construction, car en supposant que par des circonstances imprevues vos recoltes En cotton, en tabac, en Riz n'ayent plus les mêmes Demandes, ou[1] diminuent par pertes de nègres &c on retrouveroit toujours par[2] les bois a bâtir des Capitaux assurès—et ce Capital croitroit sans culture et dans des terreins souvent steriles d'ailleurs, que les Couches de feuilles chaque annee Enrichiroient—La nature fait seule tous les frais.

Si un pere dans des circonstances aïsees plantoit pour chaque Enfant a sa naissance qques milliers d'arbres il prepareroit a Cet Enfant des moyens dEntrer dans le monde avec un Capital a lage de 20, ou 25 ans, car le produit d'arbres a Batir plantés regulierement en futaye est bien plus Considerable que celui des arbres plantes des mains de la nature—ceux ci fournissant rarement de Beau bois de Construction—les autres en donnent tous de superbe etant bien dirigés—

Si cet Enfant a la naissance duquel on auroit planté qques milliers d'arbres en recouvrant le produit a Lâge de 25 ans prelevoit une petite somme pour la replantation d'une quantité a peu près semblable il se trouveroit a Lage de 50—ou 60 ans un nouveau Capital pour les besoins de sa Vieillesse

ce seroit une Caisse de prevoÿance pour la societé et pour L'individu—

N.B. J'ai Envoyé mon mémoire au President de la societé dAgriculture de Philad[a] depuis peu de jours, il pouroit le faire passer a La societe Philosoph que vous presidés, Monsieur, si vous en témoignes le Desir.
La societé dAgric[re] des E:u Etablie a Washington voudrait Elle s'occuper de cette matière importante?—

EDITORS' TRANSLATION

Excerpts from a memoir on forest management in the United States of North America

Forests (says the author at the beginning) are one of the first gifts of nature. They provide the primitive man with almost all of his subsistence needs and a shelter against the attacks of ferocious animals, to civilized man, forests provide the most precious materials for civilian and military construction, for general use, and fuel for daily fires.

Asia, which was a long time ago densely populated, became sterile and desert-like because of the destruction of its forests. Would it not be painful for any American citizen to think that his fatherland might undergo the same fate as a result of a similar lack of foresight. . . . &c &c

The author thinks that, without infringing on the freedom of persons and their property, it is possible to pass some regulations for the conservation and replenishment of timber, whose replenishment is far from being proportionate to its rapid consumption, especially in a country that is establishing itself.—He indicates the need for planting and the considerable benefit that public turnpike companies could derive from it.

He points out the harm done to society, not only through the destruction of forests but also the weakening of the soil resulting from a land stripped of its trees, by ignorant loggers who cut down the forests without pity or discrimination. When clearing land, he advises us to let stand barriers of trees every 10 acres or so, in order to provide the wood needed on any given farm. As for the land already cleared, he advises us to plant tracts of trees for timber. He is convinced from his experience as an agronomist that the trees, by redistributing to the soil the humidity from the atmosphere and shielding the crops from the harshness of the wind, increase the production of cereals and hay.

He recounts several anecdotes proving that the harvest of trees planted for timber, (wood for building) has in 20 or 25 years sometimes surpassed the intrinsic value of the entire property, although the woods have occupied only a small portion of it and the least productive—

He demonstrates that the neglect and lack of trimming of big trees deprive owners of beautiful construction wood, because the lateral branches use up the sap of these trees and prevent the trunks from growing. Thus every 3 or 4 years, lateral branches should be cut off so as to let the trunks take advantage of all the sap. The vast shade of these trees left in their natural state also deprives farm animals of a lot of pasture, because the grass that grows under them is not good. Therefore it is a double loss, not counting the product which arises from the act of tree trimming.

Finally he invites learned societies to enlighten the different legislatures about this important matter and to encourage them, if not to pass regulations at least solemnly to warn forest owners that society's common interest and theirs, in particular, mandate a better management of woods and their replenishment through the planting of trees to meet the needs of the future—

P.S. On your properties in the southern U.S. would it not be a wise speculation to plant tracts of trees for timber? Supposing that through unforeseen circumstances your cotton, tobacco, and rice crops are not in the same demand as they are now or decline through loss of negroes &c one would always be assured of capital thanks to timber, and that capital would grow without cultivation and even in frequently poor soil that would be enriched year after year by layers of leaves. Nature foots the whole bill.

If a father with means were to plant a few thousand trees for each child at birth, he would set aside for that child the means to make his entry into the world with capital at age 20 or 25, because the value of timber regularly planted in tree farms is far greater than that of trees planted by the hands of nature. The latter rarely provide beautiful construction wood—all the others give superb wood when well managed—

If that child, at whose birth a few thousand trees had been planted, took out of the sale, at 25 years of age, a small sum for reforestation of a somewhat similar quantity, he would find himself at age 50 or 60 with a new capital to provide for the needs of his old age.

It would be a reserve fund for society and for the individual—

N.B. I sent my memoir to the president of the agricultural society of Philadelphia only a few days ago. He could pass it along to the philosophical society over which you preside, Sir, if you so desire.
Would the U.S. agricultural society, founded in Washington, wish to take care of this important matter?—

MS (DLC: TJ Papers, 187:33262); in Lormerie's hand; undated; ellipsis in original; on same sheet as covering letter. Translation by Dr. Roland H. Simon.

Richard Peters was a founder and PRESIDENT DE LA SOCIETÉ DAGRICULTURE DE PHILAD[A], 1805–28 (Simon Baatz, *"Venerate the Plough": A History of the Philadelphia Society for Promoting Agriculture, 1785–1985* [1985], 12, 16). The SOCIETÉ DAGRIC[RE] DES E:U ETABLIE A WASHINGTON was probably the Columbian Agricultural Society for the Promotion of Rural and Domestic Economy.

[1] Manuscript: "on."
[2] Manuscript: "pas."

# To Samuel DeButts

SIR Monticello Apr. 15. 09.

Your letter of Mar. 24. has been duly recieved, and finds me disposed to render you any service within the line of propriety or right. my connection by blood gives me a certain claim on the affections of mr S. Carr, but none at all over his actions or proceedings with others: and no one, more unwillingly than myself, intermeddles with the affairs of others. mr Carr's known integrity will secure you in every thing which he believes to be right, & where there is any difference of opinion, it will be properly controuled by the course in which the matter now is. I must pray you therefore to excuse me from the interference you request, & to indulge my love of quiet & good will with all men, accepting at the same time the assurances of my respect.

TH: JEFFERSON

PoC (MHi); at foot of text: "Sam[l] DeButts esq."; endorsed by TJ.

# James Dinsmore's List of Thomas Jefferson's Tools

Mem[dm] of Carpenters tools belonging to mr Jefferson—

15 pair hollows & rounds,. & 1 plane for making spouts
1 pair[1] quarter rounds, 1 Do Snipe Bills
1 Do Side rabbitt planes—4 rabbitt planes & astragal
3 philasters. & one Spring plane—
4 pair Groveing planes & 1 Cut & thrust—
2 Plow planes & 9 plow bits
5 bead planes 9, ogees. & 2 quarter rounds—
2 Sash ovolos, 2 astragal Do—
1 Scotia & ovola & 1 ogee & ovola.
1 raising plane. 2 pair Base & surbase planes—
1 architrave Do.—11 Cornice planes of different kinds
3 Straight & 3 Circular Smoothing planes—1 toothing Do
4 Sets of Bench planes 5 in each Set[2]—& 1 double Iron jointer—
3 try planes for Circular work, 3 Steel blade Squares—
1 bench vice 2 plated gages, 1 mortise Do[3]—1 brace & 15 bits—
2 pair pincers & 1 pair cutting plyers—
2 Drawing knives 2 pair Compasses—
4 Sockett Chishels 4 mortise Do. & 13 former Do—
19 Gouges, 2 rasps 4 files,—15 Gimblets
3 pair hand screws, 3 iron Screws for pining up work
6 augres: 3 hand Saws 1 pannel Do 1 table Do 1 tenon Do—
1 Sash Do. 1 dove tail Do 1 frame[4] Do & 2 lock Saws; 9 new plane irons
3 Saw files 1 axe 1 adz 1 bevel 1 miter Do 1 turkey Whet[5] Stone &c &c

JAS DINSMORE

April 15th 1809

[*verso:*]
planes borrowed by Ja[s] Dinsmore
1 Tuscan Cornice plane—
1 Sash astragal—
1 ogee & quarter round—

Bo[t]—

| | | | |
|---|---|---|---|
| 1. Screw. do worth.[6] | 9/. | by J Dinsmore | £0–9 |
| 2 Flooring. Do–worth | 4/6 each | by J Nelsen | 0 9 |

MS (MHi); in Dinsmore's hand; written on two sides of single sheet; at foot of text: "Mem[dm] of Carpenters tools"; endorsed by TJ.

James Dinsmore (ca. 1772–1830), house joiner, was a native of Ulster living in Philadelphia in 1798 when he began a decade of service with TJ at Monticello. In anticipation of his 17 Apr. 1809 settlement of accounts with TJ, Dinsmore compiled this tool list, distinguishing between those borrowed or purchased from TJ and those presumably left at Monticello. With carpenter John Neilson, who had worked with him at Monticello since 1804, Dinsmore then worked for three years on renovations to Montpellier, James Madison's house. Dinsmore co-owned a mill at Pen Park near Charlottesville with John H. Craven from 1811 to 1815, settled in Charlottesville after 1818, and worked as the principal master carpenter at the University of Virginia and on renovations to Bremo, John Hartwell Cocke's house, before drowning in the Rivanna River (*PTJ*, 30:249; *MB*, 2:985, 991, 1245; TJ to Madison, 23 Sept. 1808 [DLC]; Lay, *Architecture*, 96–8; Charlottesville *Virginia Advocate*, 14 May 1830).

Planes, chisels, gouges, gimlets, and drawknives are used for fine woodwork such as window trim, wainscoting, and pilasters. HOLLOWS & ROUNDS are planes used for shaping, the former concave and the latter convex. A RABBITT (rabbet) is a long groove cut at right angles (Carl Lounsbury, *An Illustrated Glossary of Early Southern Architecture & Landscape* [1994], 159, 303).

[1] Dinsmore here canceled "hollows &."
[2] Preceding four words interlined.
[3] Preceding three words interlined.
[4] Manuscript: "frane."
[5] Manuscript: "Set."
[6] Manuscript: "wdorth."

# To Larkin Smith

DEAR SIR Monticello Apr. 15. 09.

I have duly recieved your very friendly letter of Mar. 28. and am extremely sensible to the kind spirit it breathes. to be praised by those who themselves deserve all praise, is a gratification of high order. their approbation, who, having been high in the office themselves, have information & talents to guide their judgment, is a consolation deeply felt. a conscientious devotion to republican government, like charity in religion, has obtained for me much indulgence from my fellow citizens, and the aid of able counsellors has guided me through many difficulties which have occurred. the troubles in the East have been produced by English agitators, operating on the selfish spirit of commerce, which knows no country, and feels no passion or principle but that of gain. the inordinate extent given it among us, by our becoming the factors of the whole world, has enabled it to controul the agricultural & manufacturing interests. when a change of circumstances shall reduce it to an equilibrium with these, to the carrying our produce only, to be exchanged for our wants, it will return to a wholesome condition for the body politic, & that beyond which it should never more be encouraged to go. the repeal of the drawback system will either effect this, or bring sufficient sums into the treasury to meet the wars we shall bring on by our covering every sea with our vessels. but this must be the work of peace. the correction will be after my day, as the error originated before it.     I thank you sincerely for your kind good wishes, & offer my prayers for your health & welfare with every assurance of my great esteem & respect.

TH: JEFFERSON

P.S. I thank you for the information of your letter of the 4th this moment recieved. I sincerely wish the British orders may be repealed. if they are, it will be because the nation will not otherwise let the ministers keep their places. their object has unquestionably been fixed to establish the Algerine system, & to maintain their possession of the ocean by a system of piracy against all nations.

PoC (DLC); postscript written lengthwise in left margin; at foot of text: "Col° Larkin Smith."

# To Eli Alexander

SIR Monticello Apr. 17. 09.

Being much pressed by mr Higginbotham for a debt I owe him, and towards the discharge of which I promised him my rents, I paid over to him immediately the 200. D. you paid me the other day, & must sollicit the paiment of the balance of rent due since the 1st day of December last. this I trust the sale of your crop of wheat will have enabled you to do, and that the request will be deemed justified, not only by my own necessities, but by the consideration that rent is the first money which ought to be paid out of the proceeds of the land. I salute you with esteem.

TH: JEFFERSON

PoC (MHi); at foot of text: "Mr Eli Alexander"; endorsed by TJ.

Eli Alexander was a farmer who worked from 1794–95 as overseer at TJ's

Shadwell and Lego properties, brought there by TJ to implement some of the agricultural practices of Alexander's native Cecil County, Maryland. He remained in Albemarle County and leased a 320-acre tract consisting of Shadwell and part of Lego from TJ, 1805–12. Alexander's turbulent tenancy included disputes over the terms of the lease that had to be settled by arbitrators in 1810 (Henry C. Peden Jr., *Revolutionary Patriots of Cecil County, Maryland* [2000], 1; *PTJ*, 28:235; *MB*, 2:897, 1244).

# From Caleb Cross

VENERABLE SIR, Post Office Newburyport, April 17. 1809

That you may see by means the passions of the People of this town are worked up to such a mad pitch I now enclose you two sermons of Sam[l] Spring DD last fast

I am with due respect Your hum[ble] Servant CALEB CROSS

RC (DLC); addressed (torn): "[Thom]as Jefferson Esq <*Washington City*> Monticello Milton, Virg[a]"; franked; endorsed by TJ as received 26 Apr. 1809 and so recorded in SJL. Enclosure: Samuel Spring, *Two Sermons, Addressed to the Second Congregational Society in Newburyport, Fast Day, April 6, 1809* (Newburyport, Mass., 1809).

Caleb Cross (ca. 1777–1813), Republican postmaster and newspaper editor of Newburyport, Massachusetts, published its *Merrimack Gazette*, 1803–04, and *Political Calendar*, 1804–05 (Brigham, *American Newspapers*, 1:381, 382–3; Benjamin W. Labaree, *Patriots and Partisans: The Merchants of Newburyport, 1764–1815* [1962], 140–2, 143–4; Newburyport *Herald and Country Gazette*, 23 July 1813).

The first of the two SERMONS by Samuel SPRING criticized TJ's administration and the "adverse consequences" of the Embargo on shipping and commerce, lamented the moral decline of New England and the rise of poverty, and bemoaned the inadequate state of the army and navy. The second sermon, on "The Division of Service," claimed Federalist administrations under George Washington and John Adams had prospered, that the Jefferson administration had lost millions of dollars, and that the nation shared some responsibility for the actions of its rulers and must repent its sins. In 1803 Spring, an evangelical Calvinist, had preached a Fast Day sermon condemning TJ as a deist (*Princetonians*, 1769–1775, pp. 166–71).

# To Isaac Shoemaker

SIR Monticello Apr. 17. 09.

A little before I went to Washington in September last, you promised to accept & pay my order in favor of mr Higginbotham for 500. D. on account of rent of the mill for the year 1807–8. he has lately returned me the order on which he sais nothing has been paid. I must therefore request the paiment of that sum to him or myself without further delay, and express a hope that the rent for the $2^d$ year, which will be due within three or four weeks will be provided in time. I offer my salutations.

TH: JEFFERSON

PoC (MHi); at foot of text: "M$^r$ Isaac Shoemaker"; endorsed by TJ.

Isaac Shoemaker (1781–1843) contracted in partnership with his father, Jonathan Shoemaker, to operate TJ's manufacturing mill at Shadwell from the beginning of 1807. He did not occupy it until a drought ended in May 1807, and he relinquished the lease in 1810 amid charges of gross mismanagement. With TJ's support Shoemaker obtained a contract for a postal route in 1808 between Milton and Fredericksburg, with partner Hazlewood Farish. By March 1809 residents of Milton were complaining that packages intended for them were not removed from the mail portmanteau by Shoemaker "much to their injury." Shoemaker was advised to divide the mail into smaller bags "and send them by a white (and sworn man) two and from Milton." In August 1808 he unsuccessfully asked to manage TJ's toll mill at Shadwell. Martha Jefferson Randolph described Shoemaker as a dishonest and poor businessman and an enemy of TJ's who had reportedly declared that he would not pay his rent until he both found it convenient and had a settlement with TJ (Benjamin H. Shoemaker, *Genealogy of the Shoemaker Family of Cheltenham, Pennsylvania* [1903], 75; Abraham Bradley to TJ, 11 May 1808 [DLC]; Shoemaker to TJ, 26 Aug. 1808, and Martha Jefferson Randolph to TJ, 2 Mar. 1809 [MHi]; Gideon Granger to Shoemaker, 7 Mar. 1809 [DNA: RG 28, Letters Sent by the Postmaster General]; Baltimore *Sun*, 11 Jan. 1843).

David Higginbotham probably RETURNED TJ's ORDER on Shoemaker and requested a different arrangement for payment of TJ's debt in a letter he wrote him on 11 Apr. 1809, not found but recorded in SJL as received from Milton on 13 Apr. 1809. SJL also records a missing letter from TJ to Higginbotham, 22 May 1809.

# From Jonathan Shoemaker

MY FRIEND Columbia Mills $17^{th}$ $ap^l$ 1809

Thine of the $6^{th}$ Instant duly came to hand & is now before & feel somewhat alarmed at the[1] Contents of it but having some General knowledge of their Affairs, & as thee does not State facts from thy own knowledge Except as to the Rent not being Paid, & that circumstance I believe has arose in this way, they took a large contract from the General Post Office Commencing the $1^t$ of april 1808 the Arangment they had to make to fullfil that Contract Cost them more than \$3000 in horses Stages &$^c$ which kept them hard run for money the Expences to keep it up being great at the End of the year however the General Post office was in their debt & all their horses &$^c$ paid for, they have now got a new Contract for 2 Years their Line is Extended so that their Esstablishment now[2] on the line must be at Least worth 3500\$ they are to recive upwards of Six Thousand Dollars of the General Post office Per year & their Account Stands well in the Office so that at the End of the first Quarter they can Draw in thy favour for One Moiety that is due & at the End of the Second for the Ballance, & this is what I Intend Shall be done & hope thee will be so Obliging as to let things lay as they are untill I come down wich will be I think in all May I Should come Sooner but I have business that I must attend too to the northward & Expect to Start tomorrow for Phila[a]

how it is Possible they can be so deficient in their flour Account with their Customers I can not tell but can not believe they have spent it by Profligacy I hope it is not true to the full Extent as has been Stated to thee, however when I Come down Shall Examine fully into the Matter, in the Mean Wile I am

Sincerely thy Friend &[c] JONATHAN SHOEMAKER

RC (MHi); at foot of text: "Thomas Jefferson Esq"; endorsed by TJ as received 23 Apr. 1809 and so recorded in SJL.

[1] Manuscript: "the the."
[2] Word interlined.

## From David Bailie Warden

SIR, Paris 17 april, 1809.

I had the honor of writing to you, by M[r] Purviance, the bearer of dispatches. I now beg leave to inclose, for your perusal,[1] an analysis of tobacco, which you will please to[2] present to the Philosophical Society of Philadelphia. As it is curious and interesting, it[3] may be deemed worthy of a place in the next volume of their memoirs. The essence of tobacco, prepared in America, if allowed to enter France and other Countries, free of duty, might bring an immense fortune, to him who would have an exclusive right to its sale. It would seem, however, almost impossible, to succeed in this speculation, as a duty would be imposed as soon as the qualities of the liquor were ascertained—

I hear that General Armstrong is appointed Minister at War. I hope to be able to send you some pamphlets by the vessel which is daily expected, and by which he will return. He seems to believe, that all intercourse, between our Country and this, will cease—at this awful moment, when the laws of nations are despised, and expediency substituted in place of morals, it will be exceedingly difficult to preserve a commercial connection with Europe. Much depends on the fate of Austria. It is believed here that she has numbers and courage. Her enemy, by the events of Spain, has lost much of moral, and of physical influence—He cannot, with safety,[4] withdraw his forces from that Country—However, his hitherto matchless troops, aided by eighty thousand men, furnished by[5] the Confederation of the Rhine, may still be victorious.[6]

I send, for your acceptance, a small packet of garden seeds. Messrs Humboldt, Lasteyrie, Thouin, Lacepede &[7] bid me present you their affectionate Compliments—

I am, Sir, with great esteem, Your very obed^t and very humb^l Serv^t

David Bailie Warden

RC (DLC); at foot of text: "The Hon^ble Thomas Jefferson"; endorsed by TJ as received 10 July 1809 and so recorded in SJL. FC (MdHi: Warden Letterbook). Enclosed in TJ to James Madison, 12 July 1809, and Madison to TJ, 23 July 1809.

David Bailie Warden (1772–1845), diplomat and scholar, was born in Ireland, studied medicine, and trained for the Presbyterian ministry. Arrested in 1798 for his association with the United Irishmen, he was banished from Ireland the next year and immigrated to the United States, where he became an educator in New York. Warden came to Paris about the end of 1805 as tutor to the family of John Armstrong, American minister to France. Armstrong made Warden acting consul and agent for prizes in 1808, but they soon quarreled when Armstrong failed to recommend him to TJ as permanent consul at Paris. After a subsequent lobbying trip to America, Warden did receive the appointment on 3 Mar. 1811, but his efforts to become minister to France and his diplomatic career ended with his removal as consul in June 1814 over controversies involving prize cases. He remained in France and made his greatest contribution as an informal cultural agent, author, and translator of French and American scientific works. In addition to his frequent correspondence with TJ on topics ranging from science to literature, Warden was the official agent of the American Philosophical Society in France and a major collector of Americana (*ANB*; *DAB*; Francis C. Haber, *David Bailie Warden, A Bibliographical Sketch of America's Cultural Ambassador in France, 1804–1845* [1954]; Armstrong to TJ, 28 July 1808 [DLC]; *JEP*, 2:173, 174–5 [1, 3 Mar. 1811]).

Taking advantage of Napoleon's weakness elsewhere while he sought to pacify the Iberian Peninsula, on 10 Apr. 1809 Austrian forces entered Bavaria, one of the French-dominated German states included in the CONFEDERATION OF THE RHINE (David G. Chandler, *The Campaigns of Napoleon* [1966], 677).

[1] Preceding three words omitted in FC.
[2] FC here adds: "read and."
[3] FC here adds: "perhaps."
[4] Preceding two words omitted in FC.
[5] FC substitutes "the armies of" for preceding five words.
[6] FC ends here.
[7] Thus in manuscript.

ENCLOSURES

# I

# Nicolas Louis Vauquelin's Analysis of Green Tobacco

## Analysis of the Nicotiana latifolia.

By M. Vauquelin.

translated by D. B. Warden.

Though we cannot doubt that the different methods in the preparation of tobacco modify the principles contained in this plant, it is nevertheless certain that the changes which these principles undergo do not entirely destroy their particular properties; for if this were not so, it is evident that we could also make tobacco of all the herbaceous plants; which is not the case.

We are therefore led to believe that there exists in the Nicotiana a substance, which is not found in the other plants with which it has been attempted in vain to fabricate tobacco.

These considerations induced us to undertake a careful chemical analysis of different kinds of Nicotiana, employed to prepare tobacco, as well as of the tobacco of the different manufactures of France and foreign countries.

In undertaking this research, we thought that some advantage might result from it to the manufactury in the preparation of tobacco; or at least that chemical philosophy might draw from it some principle, with the aid of which it may be possible to give a satisfactory explanation of the changes which have taken place in the materials which enter into the composition of tobacco.

I must here mention that M. Robiquet, a young Apothecary of Paris, who is well informed; and M. Warden, Consul of the United States at Paris, who consecrates, with uncommon zeal, the hours not occupied by the functions of his employment, to the exercise of practical chemistry, have assisted me in this long and laborious analysis.

### First Operation.

After having pounded the leaves in a mortar of marble, of the Nicotiana latifolia, they were compressed in a towel to seperate all that was soluble. This operation was repeated three times, adding a small quantity of water.

Altho the vegetable was sufficiently squeezed in the towel, the juice contained a great quantity of green matter in suspension, which was seperated by filtration, by means of Joseph paper. The green matter which remained on the filtre was washed and put aside. We shall speak of it afterwards.

### Examination of the filtered juice by reactives.

1° This juice reddened deeply the paper of turnsole: a proof that it contains a free acid.

2° The abundant precipitate formed by the oxalat of ammoniac demonstrates the presence of lime, and consequently of lime calcareous salt.

3° The infusion of gall nuts and mineral acids announce, by their brown and voluminous precipitates, the existence of an animal matter, and particularly of albumine.

4° The temperature increased to 30° of Reaumur in determining an abundant coagulation, confirms what the acids and gall nuts announced.
5° The acetate of lead forms a greyish brown depôt, and very abundant, of which the greatest part[1] dissolves in distilled vinegar.

### Second Operation.

This last precipitate leading us to suspect, in the juice of tobacco, the presence of the malic acid, we precipitated, by means of the acetate of lead, a considerable quantity of this liquor coagulated by the heat: thro this precipitate washed and diluted with water, we passed a current of sulphurate hydrogen gas until there was a small excess.

The object of this operation was to reduce the lead to a sulphure, and by this means, to seperate it from the matter to which it was united. To facilitate the precipitation of the sulphurated lead, and to drive away the superabundance of sulphurated hydrogen, we heated and filtered the liquor.

This liquor thus filtered was carefully evaporated to the consistence of a syrop. In this state it had a very acid taste, reddened deeply the infusion of turnsole, formed with ammoniac and alkohol abundant deposits, which, by announcing the presence of an animal matter, prove that a portion of this substance had been taken off by the lead in its precipitation.

Hoping that the acid contained in this thickened liquor would be soluble in the spirit of wine, and that by this method we might seperate it from the animal matter that held it in dissolution, we treated it warm by this agent at 40°; and as soon as the mixture of these two matters took place, an abundant coagulation was produced: the color of the alkohol was yellow, and it became acid.

This acid alkohol having been gently evaporated, left a yellowish residue, very acid, very soluble in water, not crystallizing, giving with the acetate of lead a whitish precipitate, soluble in distilled vinegar, swelling by heat, and emitting vapors which had the odor of caramel; in short converting itself quickly into an oxalic acid by the action of the nitric acid.

From these properties it is not doubtful that the acid, extracted from the leaves of tobacco by the above mentioned method, is the malic. We shall afterwards make known the matter to which it is united in this plant. As to the animal matter which accompanies it, and which was seperated by alkohol, we shall return to it also in a particular article.

### Third Operation.

As we had put in the juice of the tobacco an excess of the acetate of lead, for the purpose of seperating all the malic acid, we passed thro this liquor sulpherate hydrogen gas until no more precipitate was formed; then we heated, filtered, and evaporated this liquor to the consistence of a thick syrup

Presuming that it still contained animal matter, we treated it by alkohol, which seperated from it a brownish flocconous matter, whose properties left no doubt of its animal nature.

Having evaporated the alkoholic dissolution with precaution, it left a reddish substance of a very bitter taste, which created in the mouth and throat[2] absolutely similar to that which prepared tobacco produces.

After some days there was formed in this substance still liquid small crystals, of a needle form, which seperated by means of a very dephlegmated alkohol, presented all the properties of the nitrat of potash.

The bitter matter divested of the alkohol by its evaporation continued a concentrated acid, which appeared to us to be acetic. This acid having been saturated by potash, and the mixture submitted to distillation, gave a clear liquor, and colorless, of which the bitter taste was the same as that of the entire substance before saturation and distillation. The matter remaining in the retort had almost none of this bitter taste, which proves that what it possessed was entirely volatilized. It appears that this singular substance was combined with the acid that accompanied it, because the latter, before it was saturated with an alkali, was not volatilized.

The principle of which we speak has no smell when dissolved in water, which announces that it is not very volatile. It appears difficult to destroy it; for when mixed with a sufficient quantity of oxygenated muriatic acid it still preserved its acrity after a spontaneous evaporation.

The bitter taste and volatility altogether peculiar to this body seem to evince that it is a principle which belongs exclusively to the genus Nicotiana, and which for this reason is new, since the chemists who have given an analysis of this plant, have not, to our knowledge, spoken of it.

Hence we may conclude that this principle which we find in prepared tobacco, of which we shall treat in another memoir experienced any[3] change by the different operations which it has undergone; and consequently that it is not the product of any change which has taken place in the constitution of the materials of the plant.

Second method of obtaining the bitter principle contained in the leaves of tobacco.

Instead of precipitating, by the acetate of lead, the juice of tobacco coagulated by the heat as we have described above, the juice may be evaporated by a gentle heat. When reduced to about $\frac{1}{4}$ of its volume, it is allowed to cool, leaving it to repose: then it deposits a considerable quantity of the malate of lime under the form of small gritty crystals, which, by exposure to air, become opaque. In concentring the liquor by evaporation, it furnishes new quantities of the same salt: at last when it has acquired such a consistence as no longer permits its saline molecules to reunite, it is treated by alkohol to dissolve the malic and acetic acids which are free, as well as the bitter matter, and an ammonical salt, of which we shall afterwards speak, to obtain apart a portion of the animal matter which the heat could not coagulate, on account of the malic and acetic acids which retained it in dissolution.

This animal matter is really combined with the acids, and owes to them its solubility, seeing that saturating those last by an alkali, it precipitates almost entirely.

The action of the above vegetables is so strong for this animal matter, that if the combination be not sufficiently intimate, and that there remains a little water, the alkohol dissolves a portion of it. But when the mixture of these different substances has been sufficiently concentered, the alkali dissolves only the free acids, the bitter matter, the coloring substance, and the muriat of ammoniac, whilst the animal matter, the malat of neutral lime, the nitrate of potash, and the gum form a residue insoluble in alkohol.

To ascertain whether their bitter principle be volatile, we submitted the alkoholic dissolution to distillation, but the liquid product obtained had none of the products which characterise this principle. Hoping to be more fortunate with the aqueous dissolution, we replaced the alkohol by distilled water, and the result was absolutely the same. The water passed off without taste, the substance remaining in the retort was still as bitter as before.

Having put in this liquor a quantity of potash sufficient to saturate the acids it contains, and having recommenced the distillation, we obtained a liquid product without color, which had then all the acrity of the liquor before distillation, whilst the portion that remained in the retort was almost entirely deprived of it.

This experiment seems to prove that this acrid principle contracts an intimate union with the acids, and that the latter retains it sufficiently to prevent it from being influenced by the expansive force of heat.

If, at the moment when the greatest part of this acrid principle has passed, (which takes place when the matter contained in the retort begins to take the consistence of honey,) we change the recepient, in continuing the distillation, we obtain ammoniac oil, and at the close of the operation muriat of ammoniac, which attaches itself to the upper part of the neck of the retort in the form of sublimate: but if we have put more potash than is necessary to saturate the acids, the acid principle we obtain is mixed with ammoniac, and no ammonical salt is sublimed.

The matter which the alkohol does not dissolve is for the most part formed of an animal substance, which appears very analagous to albumine. This matter divested, by alkohol, of the acids which rendered it soluble in water, ceased entirely to be so. Nevertheless there is so great an abhorrence between this substance and the acids, that it always retains a small portion, if not often washed with boiling alkohol.

Having washed this animal matter with alkohol, it was treated with cold water, to which it communicated a light brown color; and the liquor gives by evaporation crystals of nitrat and muriat of potash in small quantity. The coloring matter which accompanies these salts appears to be of a gummous matter.

The animal substance submitted to distillation gives much carbonat of ammoniac partly crystalised and partly dissolved in water, a thick and jetted oil, charcoal which leaves after combustion a substance of which the greatest part is carbonat of lime, doubtless proceeding from some portions of the malate of lime decompozed.

It follows from the above experiments that the juice of the Nicotiana latifolia contains 1° a great quantity of animal matter of the nature of albumine. 2° A gummous matter in very small quantity. 3° Malat and acetate of lime, with an excess of acid. 4° Nitrat and muriat of potash. 5° Muriat of ammoniac. 6° and lastly, a volatile acid principle without color, and which appears to be of a nature altogether different from all those known in the vegetable kingdom.

It nevertheless appears to us nothing else than a very fine oil, which has a certain degree of volatility,[4] the property of dissolving in water, and also in vegetable acids, like the usual volatile. For in treating directly by alkohol dry prepared tobacco in leaves, we obtained independently of the acid principle, a brown and thick oil, which has a similar taste.

It is probable that this oil existed originally in the plant in a state of volatile oil, and by the progress of vegetation and desication of the vegetable, it has been in some sort resinated by the accumulation of carbon. It is nevertheless possible that it owes its acrity to a portion of the volatile principle which is there combined.

At least it cannot be doubted that it is to this acrid principle, and to an oil which we have found in the green and dried leaves of Nicotiana that the prepared tobaccoes owe the greatest part of the properties which distinguish them; for these two substances produce in the mouth, and throat, and nose, the same sensations as prepared tobacco.

In the tobacco which is smoked these sensations are modified by an empyrumatic oil, by a pyroligneous acid, and ammoniac formed during the combustion; but we distinguish besides, in a very sensible manner, those which belong to the substances of which we have spoken. In passing the smoke of tobacco thro' water, as practised in certain countries in smoking, the odor and taste of these particular substances are more pure and agreeable.

We shall not speak of the insoluble residue, nor of the ligneous part of the leaves of tobacco, because we have found nothing therein which does not exist in other plants. It contains much green resin, a small portion of animal matter, of oxalat and phosphat of lime, of iron, silex, ligneous matter, &c.

In a second memoir we shall present an analysis of the tobacco in leaves, and in powder prepared in different countries, to ascertain the effects of art on this vegetable.

January 12, 1809.

MS (PPAmP: APS Archives, Manuscript Communications); in David Bailie Warden's hand. Enclosed in TJ to Robert Patterson, 31 Aug. 1809.

Nicolas Louis Vauquelin (1763–1829), experimental chemist, was founding director of the École de Pharmacie de Paris in 1803, served as professor of applied chemistry at the Muséum d'Histoire Naturelle from 1804 until his death, and was longtime professor of chemistry at the Faculté de Medecine. He published over three hundred papers on his experiments, discovered the element chromium, and contributed to the discovery of beryllium. Vauquelin was made a foreign member of the American Philosophical Society in 1811 (*DSB*; APS, Minutes, 18 Jan. 1811 [MS in PPAmP]).

Pierre Jean ROBIQUET was a chemist and professor at the École de Pharmacie (Hoefer, *Nouv. biog. générale*, 42:414–5). JOSEPH PAPER was used to clean microscope lenses. The violet-blue TURNSOLE plant (*Crozophora tinctoria*) was used to dye paper or linen that acted as a litmus by turning red when exposed to acids. ACRITY is sharpness in taste, tartness. EMPYRUMATIC (empyreumatic) tastes or smells of burnt organic matter (*OED*).

[1] Manuscript: "parts."

[2] Thus in manuscript.

[3] Thus in manuscript, but "no" was probably intended.

[4] Manuscript: "volalitility."

# II
# Nicolas Louis Vauquelin's Analysis of Prepared Tobacco

[12 Jan.–17 Apr. 1809]

Analysis of Snuff
of the Hôtel Longueville—By Mr Vauquelin.

In occupying myself in this research, my object was to know whether the principles discovered in the green Nicotiana also exist in the prepared tobacco; and if not, to find out what kind of change it undergoes. I also hoped to discover the substances employed in the preparation of snuff.

240 grammes of tobacco in powder washed five different times, with a litre of warm water each time, after dessication, weighed 105 grammes. It therefore lost in this operation $56\frac{1}{4}$ per cent, as well in humidity as in soluble matter—a quantity which is very considerable. The tobacco thus washed, had neither smell nor taste. Hence we may conclude, that it is in the soluble principles the properties of this substance are contained. It produced no effervescence with acids, which proves that it contained no insoluble carbonate.

When thrown on live coals, it emits a sharp smoke like that of wood, and which has no resemblance to that of unwashed tobacco.

We shall leave, for a moment, this residue, to occupy myself with the infusion of tobacco.

The first waters of the tobacco had an odor and smell like those of tobacco itself. They were alkaline, for they instantly re-established the color of turnsole reddened by an acid. We ought not[1] to be surprised at this, when we recollect that in presenting to snuff a glass rod dipped in weak muriatic acid, white thick vapors are formed, doubtless occasioned by the combination of ammoniac with the acid.

The infusion of prepared tobacco differs then from that of the green plant in this respect, that the first is alkaline, and the other acid. This infusion precipitated abundantly a dissolution of silver in a substance which does not dissolve in the nitric acid, indicating that it contains a muriate.

Gall nuts occasion there a colored flocconous precipitate, which announces the presence of animal matter.

Lastly, potash developes a very sensible odor of ammoniac, and the oxalic acid proved that it contained lime.

The different infusions united were distilled in a retort until they were reduced to about $\frac{1}{20}$. The liquor which passed over had at first no color, but in the course of some days it became slightly yellowish. Its taste was extremely acrid.

I had divided the products of this distillation to ascertain whether they presented some difference in their properties, but I perceived none that merit attention; except that the first contained carbonat of ammoniac, and were more colored than the last, of which the taste was stronger.

This taste was absolutely the same as that produced by tobacco when it falls into the throat.

The color of the infusion, thus concentrated, was singularly heightened, and the taste was thus insupportable by its acridness. Potash still developed from it the odor of ammoniac. During the distillation, the liquor had deposited a small quantity of brown dust, which appears to have proceeded from a portion of carbonated oil.

Having filtered the liquor, I continued to evaporate it by a gentle heat to the consistence of honey, and I treated the residue several times with alkohol, until it was no longer colored. There remained a brown matter viscous like thick mucilage. I leave this, for a moment, to continue the examination of the alkoholic dissolution.

The latter had a red brown color, and a taste extremely acrid: during the time of cooling, it deposited many needle-shaped crystals, which were found to be nitrat of potash.

The alkoholic liquor decanted from the crystals, was distilled to the consistence of syrop: the alkohol which passed over had not carried off an atom of the acrid matter; which proves that it is not volatile at the same temperature as the spirit of wine. The liquor remaining in the retort had preserved its acridness in all its force. This matter, thus concentrated, contained some portions of a thick oil, which was seperated by the addition of a little water and filtration. This oil well washed, had none of the acrid taste of the liquor from which it was seperated. In this state of concentration, caustic potash disengaged a strong odor of ammoniac, and produced in the same a flocconous precipitate. The nitrat of silver formed a precipitate which was the true muriat of silver. Lastly, the oxolat of amonniac occasioned therein a very abundant precipitate. It therefore contains muriat of ammoniac and muriat of lime.

Desirous to know whether the red brown color which this liquor had, was owing to a portion of the animal matter which had not been seperated by the alkohol, I poured into a portion gallic alkohol, and I obtained a yellowish precipitate. I filtered the liquor, which had then lost a great part of its color; and added a new quantity of gallic alkohol, which still formed a precipitate, but less abundant and less colored than the first. After a second filtration, the infusion of gall nuts always formed a precipitate, but was now white, and dissolved in an excess of gallic alkohol, and also in pure alkohol.

Having remarked that the last precipitate dissolved in alkohol, I wished to know if the first also dissolved therein, which I found to be the case.

The first precipitate formed by gall nuts in the dissolution of the acrid matter, had a yellow brownish color, as above mentioned. it dissolved for the most part in alkohol, which it colored with the same tint. There remained only an atom of a brownish substance in flacons. This precipitate dried was pulverulent. When kept for some time in the mouth, and moistened with saliva, it produced a strong acridness like that which the liquor[2] itself occasioned. Exposed to heat in a crucible of platina, it exhaled as soon as warmed, vapors whose acridness was insupportable, which affected the eyes, and glided into the mouth, producing the same sensation as the liquor. When the matter began to decompose, it swelled in a singular manner, and left a very small portion of ashes.

This portion convinced me that the matter which communicated the color to the liquor in question, is not of an animal nature, which would have been extraordinary being dissolved in alkohol.

It appeared that in proportion as I added gallic alkohol to the liquor, its acrity diminished, and I suspected that the principle was itself precipitated and neutralized by the           ; in consequence of which, I tried, by the same reactive, the distilled water of tobacco of which we have spoken above, and there was formed a white milky precipitate.

Fearing that the small quantity of the carbonat of ammoniac contained in this distilled water, was the cause of this effect, I saturated the alkali with some atoms of acid, and there was also a precipitate. I put, on the other hand, some drops of the carbonat of ammoniac in a glass of water, and I added thereto of the infusion of galls, but I obtained no precipitate. The mixture was not even troubled.

I saw that the presence of an acid, of carbonat of ammoniac, and of alkohol in this distilled water, prevented the gall nuts from there forming a precipitate.

Suspecting that the effect here produced by gall nuts was owing to a volatile oil, I put of[3] this reactive in distilled rose water, and no effect was produced. On the other hand, I shook olive oil with this water, hoping that it would charge itself with the acrid principle, and that the water would become insipid, which did not take place; whilst it is known that the distilled water of plants yields to the fat oils their aromatic principle when produced by an essential oil.

This might lead us to suspect that the acrid matter contained in tobacco, is not of an oily nature.

The dissolutions of the nitrat of silver, of mercury, and of the acetate of lead particularly, are precipitated by the distilled water of tobacco; but fearing that the small quantity of carbonat of ammoniac contained in this, was not the sole cause of these effects, by means of a gentle heat I reduced a certain quantity of this water to about the twentieth part of its bulk, and although it was no longer alkaline, it always precipitated the metallic dissolutions in the same manner, the lead in large white floccules, the mercury of a yellowish color, which soon passed to gray; silver in a white matter which did[4] not deposit, which only gave a milky half-transparent appearance to the liquor.

A portion of the infusion of tobacco thickened by distillation, and seperated by means of alkohol, exposed to the heat of a crucible of platina, also exhaled before boiling a gas of extreme acridity, which attacked the eyes, irritated the tracheal artery so as to excite a violent cough, and left for some time in the mouth the taste and odor of the smoke of tobacco: in proportion as the liquor concentered,[5] the vapors became more abundant and stronger; and when the greatest part of the humidity was dissipated, the substance swelled, blackened, and inflamed: it left a coaly matter very divided, of which the washing gave alkali and muriat of potash. The charcoal thus washed and put in nitric acid produced a lively effervescence, and[6] we obtained, by the evaporation, nitrat of lime in a considerable quantity. This matter then contained a salt with potash for its base, and another with lime. I suspect that it was the acetate of potash and muriat of lime, or perhaps the contrary.

All these experiments, which I multiplied and varied, appear to me to prove, that the matter which produced all the effects above-related, is a new vegetable principle of which the chemists have never spoken, which constitutes the essential and distinctive character of tobacco; and which does not perhaps exist except in this genus of plants; a principle very difficult to be destroyed, seeing it preserves itself notwithstanding the numerous operations to which the plant is submitted to bring it to a state of snuff—Operations which[7] modify several other principles also found in this plant, as we shall soon see.

It will be recollected that I treated by alkohol the extract of the infusion, and that this reactive did not dissolve the totality of this extract; that, on the contrary, it left a considerable quantity of a brownish matter, and viscous like gum.

Of this matter we shall now examine the nature.

I dissolved it in water, and passed thereon acetate of lead, which occasioned an abundant brownish yellow precipitate, which, washed and diluted with water, was submitted to a current of sulphurated hydrogen gas. By this means the lead was converted to a state of sulphure. The liquor, filtered and concentered, was treated by alkohol to seperate the animal matter, and to obtain the malic acid. When we precipitate the malic acid, from any vegetable infusion whatever which contains an animal matter, by the acetate of lead, the malat of lead constantly carries with it a portion of this animal matter which colors it, and this matter is partly redissolved in the malic acid seperated by the sulphurated hydrogen. This acid, freed from alkohol, was considerably pure. The precipitate which it formed in the acetate of lead, redissolved entirely in the acetous acid, and the nitric acid converted it into oxalic acid. There exists then, in the prepared tobacco, malic acid as in the green plant. It has therefore not undergone any change by the preparation of tobacco.

Having ascertained, by experiments made on the infusion, that it contained a calcareous salt, I naturally supposed that the malic acid was combined with lime, and that consequently I ought again to find this earth combined with the acetous acid in the liquor precipitated by the acetate of lead.

To demonstrate the presence of the acetate of lime in this liquor, I began to precipitate of it a portion of the salt of lead which had been in excess by means of hydrogen sulphur. It was afterwards filtered and evaporated; but a fact which surprised me was, that a considerable quantity of malat of lime escaped the decomposing action of the acetate of lead, altho' the latter was in excess. This salt, during evaporation, presented itself under the form of terrous crusts. The matter being dried, the residue was washed with small quantities of cold water; and I seperated by this means the acetate of lime from the malate of the same base.

I know not how to explain this effect. Is it owing to a portion of the malate of lime which, by some new combination, has eluded the action of the acetate of lead? Or is it produced by a portion of the malate of lead remaining in dissolution in the liquor, and of which the acid, made free by sulphurated hydrogen, shall have decomposed a portion of the acetate of lime, and have formed anew a malate of the same base? I am more disposed to believe in this latter manner of action; for after the lead is seperated by the sulphurated hydrogen, the acetate of lead precipitates a new quantity of malic acid. This proves at least, that the acetate of lead is not a very rigorous means of determining the quantity of malic acid contained in plants.

I found, as we see, in the infusion of tobacco in powder, the same substances as those which I had found in the juice of the green tobacco—to wit.—1° An acid principle. 2° An animal matter. 3° Malate of lime. 4° Muriat of ammoniac and of potash. 5° Nitrat of potash. 6° Acetate of potash. I moreover found carbonat of ammoniac and muriat of lime, which do not exist in the green tobacco: these two substances are probably formed there by the substances usually added to tobacco to make it stronger or sharper.

It is however possible that a part of the ammoniac, which is continually disengaged from the tobacco when it is in air, was produced during the fermentation of a portion of the animal matter of the plant, for I found this last singularly changed in snuff: it does not give a sufficient quantity of ammoniac by distillation.

Having several times washed the snuff with water, as mentioned above, I treated it warm by alkohol; but the latter gave, by evaporation, a sort of yellowish green resin, which had no bitter taste, and which was nothing else, as I believe, than the green resin of the plant changed in its color; for it had almost the same taste, and burned like it, and with the same odor. This experiment proves that water alone is sufficient to carry off from the tobacco all its acrid matter, and that this principle is very soluble in water.

The tobacco freed from every thing it contained Soluble in water and alkohol, had neither taste nor smell. A new proof that these properties reside in the soluble parts. Treated by a gentle heat with weak nitric acid, it communicated to the latter a deep brownish color. After 48 hours, the liquor was well expressed and filtered.

This liquor precipitated abundantly by the oxolat of ammoniac in a whitish gritty substance, which was oxolat of lime; the alkalis produced therein colored and flocconous precipitates. Nevertheless when the quantity of these acids was not sufficient to saturate completely the nitric acid, we obtained a gritty precipitate, which had the same appearance as that formed by the oxalat of ammoniac.

To know the nature of this precipitate, I operated, as I have said above, on a sufficient quantity of liquor, and I was convinced that the matter was calcareous oxalat. First, I boiled it with the carbonat of potash, and this first changed to a carbonat of lime: the potash saturated by the nitric acid gave the acidulous oxalat of potash.

Thus, there is no doubt that the prepared tobacco does not contain, like the green plant, oxalat of lime. Having also obtained from the liquor this oxolat of lime, I saturated it by ammoniac, and then there was formed a new precipitate, but more abundant than the first, colored and flocconous.

This precipitate distilled in a retort, furnished carbonat of ammoniac, fetid oil, and charcoal, which gave yellow ashes entirely soluble in nitric acid.

Ammoniac mixed with the dissolution occasioned an abundant precipitate, which was composed of phosphat of lime mixed with a little oxyd of iron.

Carbonated potash still determined a precipitate in the filtered liquor, and this precipitate was carbonat of lime, which proves that the nitric acid had retained a small quantity of the oxolat of lime, which was decomposed by heat.

It is even probable that the whole of the calcareous oxalat was not precipitated in the two above mentioned operations; for I am not sure that the oxalat of lime dissolved directly in the nitric acid, is not entirely precipitated by ammoniac, seeing that having added an excess of this alkali, if we pour in the oxalic acid, a precipitate is formed anew.

This then is not a good method to determine the quantity of oxalat of lime contained in vegetables, when extracted by the nitric acid.—The residue of tobacco washed successively by water, spirits of wine, and nitric acid, being burned, gave ashes consisting chiefly of silex: there were, however, traces of the phosphat and carbonat of lime, and of iron which escaped the action of the nitric acid.

I have then found in snuff the same substances above mentioned, which exist in the green tobacco, and this proves that they are not decomposed by the different operations they have undergone during the examination of the plant. I think, however, that the animal matter has experienced some small changes from which may result Carbonat of ammoniac: but I also found in the snuff muriat of lime, and carbonat of ammoniac doubtless proceeding from the addition of lime, or of the carbonat of lime and salt ammoniac, which are mixed with the wines to give them sharpness.

This tobacco, as well as the green vegetable that furnishes it, have presented nothing particular except the acrid principle above mentioned, and which I have not found in any plant that I have hitherto examined.
It is this principle that distinguishes tobacco from every other vegetable preparation with which it can be compared. According to the properties we have mentioned, we easily conceive how it so readily acts on the membrane of the nose, which it so irritates as to occasion violent sneezings, and dangerous sometimes for the persons not accustomed to it—How it occasions in the throat an insupportable acridity, and creates nausea and vomiting when it descends into the stomach—how introduced, by glyster, into the large intestines, it brings back [to][8] life by the irritation it produces, persons asphyxed by submersion, &c. In fine, this principle, which is soluble in alkohol, and in water, which is volatile, but not so much so as to prevent it from being centered in water, and especially in spirit of wine by a slow evaporation of its dissolutions, may be preserved, and employed to form an artificial tobacco with other vegetable powders, or to improve adulterated tobacco, or to give more force to that which is weak. To this principle concentered in water, we may give the name of essence of tobacco.—

MS (PPAmP: APS Archives, Manuscript Communications); in David Bailie Warden's hand; undated; endorsed at the American Philosophical Society as "read 15 Sept. 1809." Enclosed in TJ to Robert Patterson, 31 Aug. 1809.

Vauquelin's two memoirs were presented to the members of the American Philosophical Society at its 15 Sept. 1809 meeting (APS, Minutes [MS in PPAmP]). On 16 Mar. 1810 a committee presented to the society its "Report relative to the Memoire of M. Vauquelin," signed by Silvain Godon (PPAmP: APS Archives, Manuscript Communications). The committee observed that because "several periodical publications gave an account of the work," it was uncertain whether Vauquelin still wanted his work published in the society's transactions. It therefore directed Warden or Robert Patterson to ask Vauquelin if he would "present them again, with some new additions, which will restore to this piece a Character of originalness." The society published neither memoir.

FLACONS: flagons. GLYSTER or clyster is an enema or suppository (*OED*).

[1] Manuscript: "not not."
[2] Manuscript: "liqor."
[3] Thus in manuscript.
[4] Manuscript: "dit."
[5] Manuscript: "contentered."
[6] Manuscript: "and and."
[7] Warden here canceled "multiply."
[8] Omitted word editorially supplied.

# From Joseph Dougherty

Sir Washington Ap[l] 19. 1809

I beg you will pardon me for not returning you thanks for the noble recommendation you were so good as to send me by Short[er]. I do not see that there is any thing wanting in it.

M[r] T:J. Randolph left this place on the 4[th] of this month on his way to Philad[a]—he spent the preceeding evening with me, he was in good health, I recieved your letter respecting the eider down coverlet, which I will take good care of, and send it by the first cary person I find going that way, your wild geese will be here in two or three weeks from this time,—this day I got the last of the documents from the printing office, I will take care to send you all in due time,—tomorrow I set out to Wilmington for the sheep M[r] Dupon promised to me, if you have any commands[1] that way, a letter will find me at Wilmington untill the third or fourth of may, I shall wach the post office I have many things to wright to you of the proceed[ings] at the Presidents house, but I have no time now

Sir your Hbl[e] Serv[t] Jo[s] Dougherty

RC (DLC); right margin frayed; addressed: "Thomas Jefferson Esq[r] Monticello"; franked and postmarked; endorsed by TJ as received 23 Apr. 1809 and so recorded in SJL.

The noble recommendation has not been identified. dupon: probably Éleuthère Irénée du Pont de Nemours.

[1] Manuscript: "commnds."

# To George Jefferson

Dear Sir Monticello Apr. 19. 09.

The articles sent by mr Randolph's boats are arrived safe, except a trunk N° 28. your note by the boatmen mentions 4. trunks. they brought only 3. & suppose they recieved no more, which I presume is the fact as the contents could not be useful to them or easily disposed of. the contents were almost entirely stationary, with a mathematical machine & some odd things intermixed. it has probably been left by mistake. I really rejoice that this is the last great parcel of packages[1] with which I shall have occasion to trouble you. smaller matters will always be dropping in; but they will not occupy so much of your warehouse. of this kind I expect daily an address to you of 2. kentals of Dumb fish & some tongues & sounds[2] for me from Gen[l] Dearborne at Boston, which will come safest by mr Randolph's boats if they should be passing. I must ask the favor of you to procure &

send me, by the return of his boats, a bag of cotton of about 50 ℔. do we stand any chance of getting cotton seed with you. not a seed is to be had here. I salute you affectionately.

Th: Jefferson

PoC (MHi); at foot of text: "Mr G. Jefferson"; endorsed by TJ.

your note: List of Goods Sent by George Jefferson, with Thomas Jefferson's Notes, 11 Apr. 1809. kentals: quintals, or hundredweight. The tongues and sounds (air bladders) of codfish were considered delicacies. They were usually soaked, boiled, and then fricasseed, or the sounds were served with sauce (Mary Randolph, *The Virginia House-Wife* [1825], 75–6, 234).

[1] Preceding two words interlined.
[2] Preceding five words interlined.

# To James Madison

Dear Sir Monticello Apr. 19. 09.

I have to acknolege your favor of the 9th and to thank you for the political information it contained. reading the newspapers but little & that little but as the romance of the day, a word of truth now & then comes like the drop of water on the tongue of Dives. if the British ministry are changing their policy towards us, it is because their nation, or rather the city of London which is the nation to them, is[1] shaken, as usual, by the late reverses in Spain. I have for some time been persuaded that the government of England was systematically decided to claim a dominion of the sea by conquest, & to levy contributions on all nations, by their licenses to navigate, in order to maintain that dominion to which their own resources are inadequate. the mobs of their cities are unprincipled enough to[2] support this policy in prosperous times, but change with the tide of fortune, & the ministers, to keep their places, change with them. I wish mr Oakley may not embarras you with his conditions of revoking the orders of council. enough of the non importation law should be reserved 1. to pinch them into a relinquishment of impressments, & 2. to support those manufacturing establishments which their orders, & our interests, forced us to make.

I suppose the conquest of Spain will soon force a delicate question on you as to the Floridas & Cuba which will offer themselves to you. Napoleon will certainly give his consent without difficulty to our recieving the Floridas, & with some difficulty possibly Cuba. and tho' he will disregard the obligation whenever he thinks he can break it with success, yet it has a great effect on the opinion of our people &

the world to have the[3] moral right on our side of his agreement as well as that of the people of those countries.

M^r Hackley's affair is really unfortunate. he has been driven into this arrangement by his distresses which are great. he is a perfectly honest man, as is well known here where he was born; but unaccustomed to political subjects he has not seen it in that view. but a respect for the innocence of his views cannot authorize the sanction of government to such an example. if Jarvis continues to wish to go to Rio Janeiro, Lisbon would become vacant, & would suit Hackley. ought the lying, malicious, & impudent conduct of Meade to force him on the government for Cadiz? I know that the present Secretary of State has not seen his conduct in that light, or he would have removed him as Navy agent: but such has been his conduct in truth; and I have no doubt he will bring forward the transaction between Hackley & Yznardi, in new appeals to the public through the newspapers. rather than he should obtain what he has so little merited, I would suggest mr Jefferson as a competitor, altho' I do not know that he has ever thought of a Consulship, nor would I suggest him, if Yznardi remains in the way. but as to all this do what circumstances will best permit; I shall be satisfied that whatever you do will be right.

I now inclose you the statement which I promised, with Le Maire's note of the articles within his department. if they were not found to be what he has stated, be so good as to make the necessary corrections, & whatever the amount is may be paid, entirely at your own convenience into the bank of the US. in diminution of my note.

Dinsmore & Neilson set out yesterday[4] for Montpelier. if mrs Madison has any thing there which interests her in the gardening way, she cannot confide it better than to Nielson. he is a gardener by nature, & extremely attached to it. be so good as to assure her of my most friendly respects, and to accept the same for yourself.

TH: JEFFERSON

| | cents | D |
|---|---|---|
| 392. bushels of coal @ .25 | | 98. |
| 100. bottles of Madeira | | 100. |
| 36. d^o Noyau | | 36. |
| expences filling the ice-house | | 77.205 |
| a horse | | 200. |
| months months | | D |
| John Freeman. 76½ out of 132 @ 400. | | 231.81 |
| | | 743.015 |

the deed for John is inclosed.

RC (DLC: Madison Papers); at foot of first page: "The President of the US." PoC (DLC: TJ Papers, 187:33266, 33268); endorsed by TJ.

TJ's biblical reference to the thirst of DIVES in hell is in Luke 16.19–31. Charles OAKLEY, the newly appointed secretary to the British legation, arrived in Washington on 7 Apr. 1809 bearing the conditions under which the British would revoke the Orders in Council (Brant, *Madison*, 5:43–5, 87). TJ had suggested earlier that Richard S. Hackley might become consul at Cádiz after Josef Yznardy but that Richard Worsam MEADE would not be seriously considered for the post (TJ to Martha Jefferson Randolph, 2 Feb. 1808 [MHi]). George JEFFERSON did not receive a CONSULSHIP at this time. Etienne Lemaire's inventory of the ARTICLES WITHIN HIS DEPARTMENT at the President's House is described in Thomas Claxton to TJ, 10 Mar. 1809, and note. NOYAU is brandy flavored with the kernels of certain fruits (*OED*).

[1] Word interlined in place of "was."
[2] TJ here canceled "join."
[3] Word interlined.
[4] Word interlined.

ENCLOSURE

## Deed of John Freeman's Indenture to James Madison

I hereby assign & convey to James Madison President [of the Uni]ted States the within named servant, John, otherwise called John Freeman during the remaining term of his service from the 11th day of March last past when he was delivered to the said James[1] for the consideration of two hundred and thirty one Dollars 81. cents. Witness m[y hand] this 19th day of April 1809. at Monticello in Virginia. TH: JEFFERSON

MS (DLC: Carter G. Woodson Collection); in TJ's hand; mutilated; written on verso of original deed of sale, 23 July 1804.

Having leased his time by the month since May 1801, TJ purchased the indenture of John Freeman for $400 in 1804. Freeman was a dining room SERVANT during TJ's presidency and was married to Melinda Colbert, a slave given by TJ to Maria and John Wayles Eppes in 1797. At Freeman's request, the deeds outlining his eleven-year indenture were recorded on 8 Mar. 1809, confirming that he was the property of TJ and ensuring that he would obtain his freedom on 22 July 1815 (Deeds of Freeman's Indenture from William Baker, 10, 23 July 1804 [DNA: RG 351, District of Columbia Deed Book, V21:30–2]; *MB*, 2:1043; Freeman to TJ, 2 Mar. 1809 [DLC]; Stanton, *Free Some Day*, 80, 129, 185n; Marriage Settlement for Mary Jefferson, [12 Oct. 1797], *PTJ*, 29:549–51).

[1] Remainder of sentence interlined.

## From George Jefferson

DEAR SIR Richmond 21st Apl 1809

I have received eleven Hhds of your Tobo, which the person who sent it informs me is all there is.

It is inspected, and is said by those who saw your crop last year, to be greatly inferior to it.

I do not suppose it would at this time command more than 5 $, if even that; there being scarcely any demand at this time for Tobacco, except for that of a very superior quality, which would suit the British markets.

I am Dear Sir Your Very humble servt GEO. JEFFERSON

RC (MHi); at foot of text: "Thomas Jefferson esqr"; endorsed by TJ as received 24 Apr. 1809 and so recorded in SJL.

The ELEVEN hogsheads of tobacco, grown at Poplar Forest and probably SENT by Burgess Griffin, eventually fetched $6.50 per hundredweight (*MB*, 2:1255).

## From George Divers

DR SIR Farmington 22. Apr 1809

I send you some parsnep seed which I think had better be sow'd pretty thick. they do not look very well and can easily be thin'd if they come up better than I expect—I sow 200 feet each of parsnep and beet. 320 feet each salsafy and carrots and 400 feet cellery, all running measure in the rows, which is a very ample provision for my table and indeed more than sufficient, The small seed should be sown in drills 18 inches wide, I put my cellery in rows 6 feet wide and 10 inchs apart in the row, I send you a few of the early black eyed pea which you brought from France, and can furnish you with some of the Cow pea and a large grey pea of the Crouder kind, which think a very good one for the table, but fear I shall not be able to supply you with seed potatoes they having been feed away to my sheep nearer than I intended—I thank you for your attention to my memo for the mill Irons. The amt of cost shall be sent by first oppy—

Yrs affectionately GEORGE DIVERS

RC (MHi); endorsed by TJ as received 22 Apr. 1809 and so recorded in SJL.

George Divers (ca. 1748–1830), farmer, miller, and longtime friend of TJ's, married Martha Walker, daughter of Dr. Thomas Walker. Their one child, Thomas Jefferson Divers, died young. In 1785 Divers purchased Farmington, a 3,421-acre Albemarle County plantation, where in 1802 TJ designed an addition to his house. Divers served on a committee to rebuild the Albemarle County courthouse in 1803 and was a director of the Rivanna Company in 1810. He and TJ often exchanged seeds and corresponded about gardening and farming (Albemarle County Deed Book, 9:82; TJ's Plan and Elevation Drawing for Farmington [MHi]; Divers to TJ, 14 July 1803 [MHi]; McGehee and Trout, *Jefferson's River*, 19; Charlottesville *Virginia Advocate*, 11 Apr. 1829, 14 May 1830).

MILL IRONS: TJ paid in advance when he ordered iron castings for himself and Divers from Henry Foxall in February 1809 (*MB*, 2:1240).

# From William W. Hening

DEAR SIR, Richmond 23rd April 1809.

I have not sooner acknowledged the receipt of the MSS which you were so obliging as to send me, because I was unwilling to trespass for a moment on your time, which was incessantly occupied with the cares of government, and in an honest endeavour to avert those evils with which the injustice of the two great belligerent powers of Europe seemed to threaten us.—Permit me to congratulate you on the prospect of a favourable termination of all our differences;—produced by that wise, firm and just policy which characterized the late administration, and which, I am confident, will be pursued by the present.

The first volume of MS. which was in such a decayed state, has been transcribed by myself, and is in print, with the omission of a few words, which were entirely obliterated—I expect to publish the first volume in about three months.

Mr Clements, who will present this to you, is a gentleman of Philadelphia, engaged in furnishing the profession with law-books.—Having often heard you express a wish to exchange your old law books, for new editions, I would recommend Mr Clements in the strongest terms, as a person well-qualified to assist in the arrangement. His knowledge in this branch of trade, and the reputation for integrity which he has so justly acquired, has ensured him the confidence of the bar of Richmond, as well as the parts of the United States, whose orders to a large amount, he annually executes.

I am respectfy Yrs. WM: W: HENING

RC (DLC); endorsed by TJ as received 29 Apr. 1809 and so recorded in SJL.

William Waller Hening (1767–1828), attorney and legal scholar, represented Albemarle County in the House of Delegates, 1804–05, served on the Virginia Council of State, 1805–10, and was deputy adjutant general, 1808–14. He became clerk of the Superior Court of Chancery for the Richmond District in 1810 and served until his death. Hening was best known for his extensive legal writings, beginning with his *New Virginia Justice* (Richmond, 1795; Sowerby, no. 1971), to which TJ subscribed, and culminating with his edition of *The Statutes at Large; being a Collection of all the Laws of Virginia*, 13 vols. (Richmond, 1809–23; Sowerby, no. 1863), a landmark of legal scholarship that printed the commonwealth's laws from 1619–1792, along with many other public documents. His correspondence with TJ during the retirement period focused primarily on his preparation of this work, which drew extensively on TJ's collections of legal records (*ANB*; *DAB*; *PTJ*, 28:105–6; Samuel M. Walker Jr., "William Waller Hening," in W. Hamilton Bryson, ed., *The Virginia Law Reporters Before 1880* [1977], 19–24; Richmond *Enquirer*, 4 Apr. 1828).

A year earlier TJ had sent Hening eight volumes of manuscript laws for the years 1623–1711, the FIRST VOLUME of which contained the laws for 1623–24 given to TJ by Peyton Randolph (Hening to TJ, 17 May 1808, and TJ to Hening, 7 June 1808 [DLC]; Sowerby, no. 1822). CLEMENTS may have been one of two merchants in Philadelphia named James Clement (Robinson, *Philadelphia Directory for 1809*).

# From George Jefferson

DEAR SIR Richmond 24th Apl 1809

I hope that you will have received the trunk No 28, as it certainly is not here.

I thought I had been particular in counting the last packages sent you, but suppose I may have made a mistake, & that perhaps has caused you to make one.—I find from referring to the bill of lading, that there were only 3 trunks, Nos 26, 27, & 28.—I have no recollection of having received one at any other time—& suspect that on your seeing there was one short of the number I mentioned, you[1] concluded without examination there was one missing, & perhaps did not examine the Nos so particularly as you would otherwise have done.

I fear there will be no chance of getting cotton seed here.—I doubt if there ever was a bushel sold in the place.—this information I would have given you sooner, but was out of Town when Mr B's letter was received, & it escaped my notice on my return.

I am Dear Sir Your Very humble servt GEO: JEFFERSON

RC (MHi); at foot of text: "Thomas Jefferson esqr"; endorsed by TJ as received 30 Apr. 1809 and so recorded in SJL.

In December 1808 TJ instructed Edmund Bacon to plant at least two acres of cotton for making cloth and suggested that he procure seed from those possessing cotton gins. When Bacon replied that he could not get seed locally, TJ recommended that he write Gibson & Jefferson (TJ to Bacon, 26 Dec. 1808 [CSmH: JF], 30 Jan. 1809 [Foreman M. Lebold, Chicago, 1947]; Bacon to TJ, 26 Jan. 1809 [MHi]).

[1] George Jefferson here canceled "took it for."

## From James Madison

Dear Sir Washington Ap[l] 24. 1809

I have rec[d] your favor of the 19[th]. You will see in the newspapers the result of the Advances made by G.B. Attempts were made to give shapes to the arrangement implying inconsistency and blame on our part. They were however met in a proper manner & readily abandoned; leaving these charges in their full force, as they now bear on the other side. The B. Cabinet must have changed its course under a full conviction that an adjustment with this Country, had become essential; & it is not improbable that this policy may direct the ensuing negociation; mingling with it, at the same time, the hope that it may embroil us with France. To this use it may be expected the Federalists will endeavor to turn what is already done, at the coming Session of Cong[s]. The steps deemed proper to give the proceeding a contrary turn will not be omitted. And if France be not bereft of common sense, or be not predetermined on war with us, she will certainly not[1] play into the hand of her Enemy. Besides the general motive to follow the example of G.B. she cannot be insensible of the dangerous tendency of prolonging the commercial sufferings of her Allies, particularly Russia, all of them already weary of such a state of things, after the pretext for enforcing it shall have ceased. She must be equally aware of the importance of our relations to Spanish America, which must now become the great object of Napoleon's pride & Ambition. Should he repeal his decrees with a view to this object, the most probable source of conflict will be in his extending the principle on which he required a prohibition of the Trade with S[t] Domingo, to the case of the Spanish Colonies. Nor is it improbable that he may couple such a requisition with an offer to cede the Floridas, which would present a dilemma not very pleasant.

Accept my sincerest affection & highest esteem

James Madison

RC (DLC: Madison Papers); endorsed by TJ as received 26 Apr. 1809 and so recorded in SJL.

[1] Madison here canceled: "be the dupe of."

# To John Graham

Dear Sir Monticello Apr. 25. 09

A gentleman of Dumfries of your name, & I think he was your brother, was so kind as to promise me a pair of wild geese, & to say he would take some occasion of sending them to Washington by water. I would now prefer their remaining where they are, as being so much nearer than Washington, & I will send for them as soon as the roads are good. not knowing the Christian name of mr Graham nor exactly his address, I have ventured to trespass on your friendship by this letter, presuming you will know the person I describe, & that you will be so good as to convey to him my request to retain the geese until I can send for them. with my excuses for this liberty I tender you the assurances of my great esteem & respect.

Th: Jefferson

PoC (DLC); at foot of text: "M^r^ Graham"; endorsed by TJ.

John Graham (1774–1820) was born in Dumfries, graduated from Columbia College in 1790, and moved to Kentucky, serving in the state legislature in 1800. TJ appointed him secretary of legation at Madrid in 1801 and secretary of Orleans Territory in 1804. Late in 1806 Graham went to Ohio as TJ's confidential agent to gather information on the suspected conspiracy of Aaron Burr, testifying the following year at Burr's treason trial. James Madison appointed Graham chief clerk of the State Department in 1807, a position he held until James Monroe placed him on a three-member fact-finding mission to study the Spanish provinces in South America in 1817. Named minister plenipotentiary to Portugal at Brazil in 1819, Graham found the climate too severe and returned to the United States, dying shortly thereafter (*ANB*; *DAB*; *JEP*, 1:401, 405, 476, 477 [6, 26 Jan. 1802, 11, 12 Dec. 1804]).

# To Etienne Lemaire

Monticello Apr. 25. 09.

You were so kind, my good friend, as to offer to execute any little commissions for me in Philadelphia; and it is certain there will at times be some small articles which I can only get good from there, and so well chosen by nobody as yourself. I trouble you at present to send me a box of good sallad oil, and some Vanilla. the Vanilla may come by post, but the oil must be addressed to Mess[rs] Gibson & Jefferson by some vessel bound to Richmond. you mentioned to me once the Syrop of Vinegar as a substitute for the Syrop of punch. if you could send a small parcel of this with the oil, that I may try it, I should be obliged to you. perhaps you could inform me how to make it. my grandson, Jefferson, whom you will find at Peale's Museum, will pay you for these things on your shewing him this letter. my birds arrived here in safety & are the delight of every hour. mr Julien staid with us between 2. & 3. weeks. his pupils are going on very well & much to our comfort & satisfaction. I am constantly in my garden or farm, as exclusively employed out of doors as I was within doors when at Washington, and I find myself infinitely happier in my new mode of life.

I salute you with great affection & esteem.

TH: JEFFERSON

PoC (MHi); at foot of text: "M. LeMaire"; endorsed by TJ.

French chef Honoré Julien taught his art to HIS PUPILS, TJ's slaves Edith (Edy) Hern Fossett and her sister-in-law Fanny Gillette Hern, for several years in Washington, and he returned with them to Monticello to complete their training after TJ retired. They continued the tradition of French cooking there, with Fossett taking over the position of head cook from Peter Hemmings (Stanton, *Free Some Day*, 129–31; *MB*, 2:1091, 1189, 1244; Pierson, *Jefferson at Monticello*, 113).

## From John MacGowty

HONORED SIR— Windham, Connecticut April 25th 1809

here is a number of high Federal Characters that wish to misrepresent the causes of our difficulties, with the other Nations and say that the french Nation was the first that did take our shipping and Property, Both in their Ports and at sea, therefore Sir I have said to a number of these Characters that the french did not take any of our vessles and Cargoes, that was true american property until after Jays Treaty, and said Characters declare that the french did take Millins of dollars long before Jays treaty, and have wanted to lay me a suite of Cloths and a New Hat, if that is not the Case, therefore Sir We have agreed to leave the Business to your Honour, to say, and if Sir you will be so good as to state the fact I shall ever be much obliged to you and Remain with great Pleasure Sir—your very obedant Servant

JOHN McGOWTY

P.S—from a sea faring man

RC (MoSHi: TJC-BC); between dateline and body of letter: "Thomas Jefferson Esquire"; endorsed by TJ as received 3 May 1809 and so recorded in SJL.

# From William Roscoe

SIR, Allerton near Liverpool 25th Ap. 1809

I presume upon your well known partiality to liberal & scientific pursuits, to introduce to your notice Mr Jno Bradbury, a Fellow of the Linnean Society[1] who has undertaken a tour thro' the province of Louisiana, for the purpose of collecting the various specimens of Natural History which it may be found to furnish. Among those who have encouraged his[2] undertaking, in which he will be accompanied by his two Sons, are[3] the Proprietors of the Botanic Garden in Liverpool, by whom he is requested to offer to your Acceptance a Copy of their regulations & a Catalogue of their collection. Shou'd he have the honour of delivering these in person, I trust you will find him well informed in the different branches of his favourite science, and capable of informing you of the progress which is here making in it. Any information, assistance, or advice, which you may have the goodness to afford him, will be gratefully acknowledged, as an obligation conferred—both on him, & on those who patronize his undertaking.—

It was with great concern that I found from the Letter with which you some time since honour'd me, that the volumes of the Life of Leo X. had been so long in arriving at their destination. If however they shou'd have the good fortune to afford you any amusement, and particularly if the sentiments on political & moral subjects, which unavoidably obtruded themselves in its composition, should meet with your assent, it will much more than compensate me for the[4] bigotted censures & illiberal remarks of those who[5] assume to themselves the same intolerance as they condemn in the Church of Rome. But it is much more probable that the discord which has arisen in Europe, the effect of which has been but too powerfully felt in the United States, has called your attention from the transactions of former ages,[6] to more important & immediate objects.—Would to Heaven that your efforts for maintaining the[7] honour and interests of your Country, and preserving it from those wars which still continue to desolate Europe, may be attended with a result equal to your own wishes; and that in retiring from your high station, you may carry with you into private life, in addition to the consciousness of having devoted yourself to the service of your Country, the satisfaction of finding that your efforts have been crown'd with success!—

I am, with the highest esteem & respect, Sir Your very faithful & obedt Servant, W: ROSCOE

RC (DLC); dateline below signature; at foot of text: "Thomas Jefferson Esq$^{r}$"; endorsed by TJ as received 6 Aug. 1809 and so recorded in SJL. Dft (UkLi: Roscoe Manuscripts); dated 26 Apr. 1809.

William Roscoe (1753–1831), historian, poet, and botanist, was a prominent supporter of the arts in Liverpool. TJ owned both of his major works, biographies of Lorenzo de Medici and Pope Leo X. After his retirement from the law in 1796, Roscoe became acquainted with James Edward Smith, the botanist and president of London's Linnean Society. In 1802 Roscoe helped found and was first president of the Botanic Garden at Liverpool, and three years later he became a fellow of the Linnean Society (*DNB*; Donald A. Macnaughton, *Roscoe of Liverpool: His Life, Writings and Treasures, 1753–1831* [1996]; Sowerby, no. 170).

John Bradbury, an English botanist and naturalist, proposed to explore Kentucky and the Louisiana Territory to study plant life. Although neither of his SONS actually traveled with him, he hoped to establish John Leigh Bradbury as a gardener in New Orleans. Bradbury had financial backing from the PROPRIETORS of the Liverpool Botanic Garden. Prior to his departure from Great Britain on 25 Apr. 1809, he obtained this letter and a COPY both of Roscoe's *Address at the Opening of the Botanic Garden of Liverpool* (Liverpool, 1802; Sowerby, no. 1085), to which the institution's REGULATIONS were appended, and of *A Catalogue of Plants in the Botanic Garden, at Liverpool* (Liverpool, 1808; Sowerby, no. 1086), all of which he delivered personally to TJ at Monticello when he arrived on or about 6 Aug. 1809 (H. Stansfield, "Plant Collecting in Missouri: A Liverpool Expedition, 1809–11," *Liverpool Libraries Museums & Arts Committee Bulletin* 1 [1951]: 17–31; H. W. Rickett, "John Bradbury's Explorations in Missouri Territory," APS, *Proceedings* 94 [1950]: 59–62; TJ to Meriwether Lewis, 16 Aug. 1809).

In his LETTER of 1 July 1806 (UkLi: Roscoe Manuscripts), TJ informed Roscoe that it took him a year to receive his gift of a copy of *The Life and Pontificate of Leo the Tenth,* 4 vols. (London, 1805; Sowerby, no. 171).

[1] Preceding six words canceled in Dft and interlined in RC.

[2] Preceding two words interlined in Dft in place of "patronized this."

[3] Remainder of sentence interlined in Dft in place of "Lord Stanley, Mr. I Leigh Philips & the Prop$^{rs}$ of the Bot gardens in Liverp$^{l}$ & Dublin."

[4] Preceding nine words interlined in Dft in place of "I shall think myself fortunate & shall have an additional motive for disregarding the."

[5] In Dft Roscoe here canceled "can see nothing right but in the."

[6] Preceding five words interlined in Dft in place of "past events."

[7] In Dft Roscoe here canceled "dignity &."

# From Augustus B. Woodward

Philadelphia, April 25. 1809.

I have the honor to transmit to you, Sir, a work on the Executive of the United States. In every constitution formed in America, during the æra of the revolution, a council was attached to the executive. It is even a part of the British constitution. The federal constitution is the first without it. It is certainly of less importance in the State governments, than in that of the Union. You are yourself aware, Sir, of the extreme severity of the executive duties. To lessen that severity, without abandoning the advantages of a single executive magistrate, would be desirable. The difficulty of constituting a republican executive, of energy and vigor, without a resort to the monarchical principle of a[1] supremacy in one individual, qualified however[2] by the elective right, limitation of period, and a veto in one branch of the legislative body, has deterred from the attempt. I do not flatter myself that I have been so happy as to have attained the correct medium in the propositions I have made; but I am certain, Sir, that the clearest refutation of all the principles I have advanced is to be found in your example. My thoughts often follow you to your retirement. It is one which monarchs may envy, and when the most distinguished of them are consigned to oblivion, your name Sir will be grateful to the American ear; and your steady fame reach distant times, and extend to remote countries. A. B. WOODWARD.

RC (DLC); addressed: "Thomas Jefferson esq. Monticello. Virginia"; franked and postmarked; endorsed by TJ as received 30 Apr. 1809 and so recorded in SJL. Enclosure: *Considerations on the Executive Government of the United States of America* (Flatbush, N.Y., 1809).

Augustus Elias Brevoort Woodward (1774–1827), jurist and political writer, first met TJ in 1795 at Monticello, where he was disappointed by the lack of warmth exhibited by TJ, who treated him as "an entire stranger." TJ did eventually appoint Woodward judge of the Michigan Territory, a position he held until 1824, and he subsequently became a territorial judge in Florida. Woodward compiled the first publication of Michigan laws in 1806, but his tenure was marked by his opposition to Governor William Hull and a lack of popular support. He wrote on a variety of political and scientific topics, was a civic planner, and helped to found the University of Michigan (*ANB*; *DAB*; Frank B. Woodford, *Mr. Jefferson's Disciple: A Life of Justice Woodward* [1953]; Augustus B. Woodward, "Notes on my Visit to Mr. Jefferson," 29 July 1796 [typescript in MiD: Augustus B. Woodward Papers]; *JEP*, 1:483–4 [26 Feb., 1 Mar. 1805]).

Woodward sent a second copy of the enclosed WORK to TJ with a brief covering letter on 15 May 1809 (RC in DLC; endorsed by TJ as received 24 May 1809 from New York and so recorded in SJL).

[1] Word interlined in place of "an absolute."

[2] Word interlined.

# To John Barnes

DEAR SIR Monticello April 27. 09.

Your letters of the 17th & 18th were recieved only the last night, having loitered some where a week, altho' there are 3. days of departure from Washington of the post for Milton every week. that of the 24th of March covering your account was recieved in due time, but being occupied constantly out of doors from an early breakfast to a late dinner every day, writing, as with other country farmers is put off to a rainy day. hence it is that I have not taken time to collate your accounts with my own, which indeed is only necessary that I may send you the statement & acknolegement in proper form. it shall be done soon. with respect to Kosciusko's 8. percent stock, I have not the certificates. I have carefully & over & over again examined every paper of his in my possession. I have the certificates of his 20. Pensva bank shares, but of the 8. per cents I find only a memm in my own hand that I had transferred 10. bank shares to you to be invested in 8. p^r cents, & that you had done it at 23. p^r cent. I am satisfied therefore you will find that you have the certificates in your possession. I think they should be converted immediately into some other profitable stock. that of the banks allied to the Government of the US. or to that of Pensylvania, I should think the surest. as the certificates were made out in your name, my agency will not be necessary.

I am sorry to learn that your arm is not yet restored. I thought the case so exactly like that which happened to me that I expected it would be an affair of some months. but it will be perfectly restored in time. the total change of occupation from the house & writing table to constant emploiment in the garden & farm has added wonderfully to my happiness. it is seldom & with great reluctance I ever take up a pen. I read some, but not much. All my packages have arrived here safe, except a trunk of Stationary, which I am in hopes has been left at Richmond by mistake. I shall know this in a few days. should I write to you but rarely, you must ascribe it to my course of life, into which writing enters so little as to become a serious undertaking. it will never be owing to any diminution of affection for you or of my sense of your multiplied favors. these are deeply impressed, & will ever inspire the sincerest wishes for your health & happiness as they now do the assurances of my constant & affectionate esteem.

TH: JEFFERSON

PoC (DLC); at foot of first page: "M^r Barnes."

Barnes's missing LETTERS to TJ of 17 and 18 Apr. 1809 are recorded in SJL as received from Georgetown on 26 Apr. 1809. His letter of the 24TH OF MARCH, also not found, is recorded in SJL as received from Georgetown on 30 Mar. 1809. The enclosed ACCOUNT may have been that printed at 7 Mar. 1809. THAT WHICH HAPPENED TO ME: TJ dislocated his right wrist in 1786 and was unable to use it for three MONTHS (*PTJ*, 10:600).

# From John Graham

SIR City of washington 27th april 1809

I was this day honored by your Letter of the 25th Inst and shall immediately write to Mr Robert Graham that you wish him to keep the wild Geese which he promised you, until you can send to him for them.

Mr Graham lives about a mile below Dumfries on the South side of the Creek, on which the Town stands.

Permit me, Sir, to offer my Congratulations on the success of the measures dictated by your wisdom, and the assurances of the profound Respect & Esteem with which

I have the Honor to be Your Mo: Obt Sert

JOHN GRAHAM

RC (DLC); at foot of text: "Thos Jefferson Esqr"; endorsed by TJ as received 7 May 1809 and so recorded in SJL. Enclosed in Graham to TJ, 5 May 1809.

# From Isham Lewis

DEAR SIR. Snowden 27th April 1809

The great desire which I feel to be placed in some employ whereby, I may secure to myself the happiness derivable from the idea of enjoying the fruits of well spent industry and the difficulty I find in attaining this object unassisted by any influentiel friend has induced me to beg the favour of your endeavours in my behalf, I am in hopes you will be less disposed to think hard of this request when I assure you it is produced from necessity, brought on not from my own imprudences but those of an unfortunate father whose promises of wealth and neglect to bring me up in any useful pursuit has brought on me the want of the former and occasions me to deplore his inattention to the latter. It is too commonly the case that after we are sensible of having err'd to excuse ourselves we endeavour, to throw the blame on the innocent, whether or not this is the case with me you and all those who are acquainted with the cause of my situation are left to determin, I can only say that if I am chargable in this respect it proceeds from an error in judgment, and not from a wish to charge a father wrongfully whose foibles I would with the greatest freedom alleviate, was it in my power. But I fear I am dweling too long on a subject which however it effects me, may appear to you unimportant, and shall therefore conclude with the firmest belief of your readiness to do the best for me in your power

I am with affectionate respect Yrs &C IHM: LEWIS

N.B. I will thank you to inform me whether you suppose the Louisiana country will be laid off into Townships &C within any short time, and provid'd it should be, whether you suppose it will be in my power to get a part of the undertaking I:L

RC (MHi); endorsed by TJ as received 29 Apr. 1809 and so recorded in SJL.

Isham Lewis (b. ca. 1788) was the son of Charles Lilburne Lewis and TJ's sister Lucy Jefferson Lewis, and the grandson of Charles Lewis Jr., Peter Jefferson's brother-in-law. Although he had prospered a decade previously, by 1803 Charles L. Lewis, the UNFORTUNATE FATHER, was dependent on his children. Isham Lewis left home in 1804, receiving 230 acres of poor land on Three Chopt Road that he soon sold. He remained in Virginia with TJ's brother Randolph Jefferson at Snowden after his parents and his brothers Randolph and Lilburne Lewis moved to Kentucky in 1807. In 1811, while visiting Lilburne Lewis and his family at Rocky Hill, Livingston County, Kentucky, Isham Lewis assisted his brother in the grisly murder of a slave named George. Facing disgrace and intending to commit suicide by shooting each other, the pact failed when Lilburne Lewis accidentally shot himself dead and Isham lost his nerve. Imprisoned and facing a capital trial, Lewis escaped from jail and disappeared from the record, possibly having fled to New Orleans under an assumed name. The indictment against him was dismissed (Merrill, *Jefferson's Nephews*).

# To James Madison

DEAR SIR Monticello Apr. 27. 09.

Yours of the 24th came to hand last night. the correspondence between mr Smith & mr Erskine had been recieved three days before. I sincerely congratulate you on the change it has produced in our situation. it is the source of very general joy here, & could it have arrived one month sooner would have had important effects not only on the elections of other states, but of this also, from which it would seem that wherever there was any considerable portion of federalism it has been so much reinforced by those of whose politics the price of wheat is the sole principle, that federalists will be returned from many districts of this state. the British ministry has been driven from it's Algerine system, not by any remaining morality in the people but by their unsteadiness under severe trial. but whencesoever it comes, I rejoice in it as the triumph of our forbearing & yet persevering system. it will lighten your anxieties, take from cabal it's most fertile ground of war, will give us peace during your time, & by the compleat extinguishment of our public debt, open upon us the noblest application of revenue that has ever been exhibited by any nation. I am sorry they are sending a minister to attempt a treaty. they never made an equal commercial treaty with any nation, & we have no right to expect to be the first. it will place you between the injunctions of true patriotism & the clamors of a faction devoted to a foreign interest in preference to that of their own country.[1] it will confirm the English too in their practice of whipping us into a treaty. they did it in Jay's case; were near it in Monroe's, & on failure of that, have applied the scourge with tenfold vigour, & now come on to try it's effect. but it is the moment when we should prove our consistence, by recurring to the principles we dictated to Monroe, the departure from which occasioned our rejection of his treaty, and by protesting against Jay's treaty being ever quoted, or looked at, or even mentioned. that form will for ever be a millstone round our necks unless we now rid ourselves of it, once for all. the occasion is highly favorable, as we never can have them more in our power. As to Bonaparte, I should not doubt the revocation of his edicts, were he governed by reason. but his policy is so crooked that it eludes conjecture. I fear his first object now is to dry up the sources of British prosperity by excluding her manufactures from the continent. he may fear that opening the ports of Europe to our vessels will open them to an inundation of British wares. he ought to be satisfied with having forced her to revoke the orders on which he pretended to retaliate, & to be particularly satisfied with us by whose unyielding adherence to principle she has been forced into the revocation. he ought the more to conciliate our good will, as we can be such an obstacle to the new career opening on him in the Spanish colonies. that he would give us the Floridas to withold intercourse with the residue of those colonies cannot be doubted. but that is no price; because they are ours in the first moment of the first war, & until a war they are of no particular necessity to us. but, altho' with difficulty, he will consent to our recieving Cuba into our union to prevent our aid to Mexico & the other provinces. that would be a price, & I would immediately erect a column on the Southernmost limit of Cuba & inscribe on it a Ne plus ultra as to us in that direction. we should then have only to include the North in our confederacy, which would be of course in the first war, and we should have such an empire for liberty as she has never surveyed since the creation: & I am persuaded no constitution was ever before so well calculated as ours for extensive empire & self government. as the Mentor went away before this change, & will leave France probably while it is still a secret in that hemisphere, I presume the expediency of pursuing her by a swift sailing dispatch was considered. it will be objected to our recieving Cuba, that no limit can then be drawn for our future acquisitions. Cuba can be defended by us without a navy, & this developes the principle which ought to limit our views. nothing should ever be accepted which would require a navy to defend it.

Our spring continues cold & backward, rarely one growing day without two or three cold ones following. wheat is of very various complexions from very good to very bad. fruit has not suffered as much as was expected except in peculiar situations. gardens are nearly a month behind their usual state. I thank you for the Squashes from Maine. they shall be planted to day. I salute you with sincere & constant affection. TH: JEFFERSON

RC (DLC: Madison Papers, Rives Collection); at foot of first page: "the Pr. US." PoC (DLC).

British minister David Erskine began negotiations with Secretary of State Robert Smith after receiving instructions from his government early in April 1809. Largely because Erskine did not reveal three stipulations to which George Canning, the British foreign minister, expected the United States to concede, Erskine concluded an agreement with the Madison administration that trade with Great Britain would be resumed and the British Orders in Council of January and November 1807 would be withdrawn. Madison accordingly issued a proclamation on 19 Apr. 1809 formally suspending the Non-Intercourse Act of 1 Mar. 1809 effective 10 June 1809 and announcing the imminent withdrawal of the Orders in Council. The proclamation was printed along with related CORRESPONDENCE BETWEEN Smith and Erskine (Madison, *Papers, Pres. Ser.*, 1:117–9, 125–6; Washington *National Intelligencer*, 21 Apr. 1809; Bradford Perkins, *Prologue to War: England and the United States, 1805–1812* [1961], 211–3).

THEY ARE SENDING A MINISTER: Francis James Jackson was officially appointed the British minister to the United States on 6 July 1809 but apparently had no power to make treaties. Madison's government demanded his recall in November 1809 (Madison, *Papers, Pres. Ser.*, 1:275; Washington *National Intelligencer*, 13 Nov. 1809). TJ and Madison rejected the treaty negotiated with Great Britain by William Pinkney and James MONROE in 1806 because it did not ban impressment and it prohibited the United States from using economic sanctions for ten years (Ammon, *Monroe*, 257–64). MAINE: Thomas Main, a Georgetown nurseryman.

[1] Reworked from "to their own."

# From William Davy and Others

SIR, *PHILADELPHIA, April* 28, 1809.

FROM a variety of causes, and more particularly the late embargo, a spirit of enterprize in the establishment of useful manufactures in almost every part of the United States has been exhibited—great exertions have been made, and large capitals have been embarked in this line, and the *manufacturing* interest is forming a new link in the Chain of Society, and if properly united, its strength will, in an individual and national point of view, become powerful, beneficially influential, and permanent.—To promote these effects, a communication between distant manufacturers and a co-operation in plans for the general good, may be of the first importance. In this city a society is established under the protection of an Act of Incorporation of the State Legislature, for the support and encouragement of Domestic Manufactures, and much good has emanated from it. The manufacturers and artists have been encouraged to hold meetings and appoint various committees to attend to their concerns. The late arrangements of our government with England have produced general satisfaction, and the manufacturers have participated therein, as preventing the evils of war, which all were apprehensive of; yet they feel that these events are likely to produce a powerful effect on the manufacturing interest of the United States, and will require extraordinary exertion and powerful support to counteract it. Thus impressed, the manufacturers and artists in this city have appointed a committee to correspond with their brethren in every part of the union.—This committee now address you as a respectable manufacturer, or as a friend to that interest, requesting your assistance, and that of such of your neighbouring manufacturers as can be consulted, in an application to Congress at their meeting in May next, for such protection and support as the state of the manufactories of the United States shall appear to them to be entitled to—to this end it will be of importance to furnish this committee, with all the information possible on the *nature and extent* of the manufactures in your neighbourhood, and they will arrange and combine it, so as to bring the whole into one point, and prepare it for the view of Congress.—It is also particularly recommended to form societies of manufacturers and artists in convenient districts, and to encourage every individual to give the best information on the state of manufactures to such members of Congress as can be immediately communicated with, and in order to produce the most permanent advantages to the manufacturing interest, it is proposed to hold a meeting of Deputies from such societies as may be formed in different districts, on Wednesday the 25th of October next, at the Mechanic Hall, New York: when by a full exhibition of facts, and a free communication of opinion, such plans may be devised and carried into effect, as may tend to cement and strengthen this interest, and produce extensive advantage to individuals and to the nation at large.

Your communications addressed to William Davy, C. C. M. A. Philadelphia, will receive a respectful attention from

Sir, your most humble Servants,

William Davy,<br>John Harrison,<br>James Ronaldson,<br>Adam Seybert,<br>Abraham Small.

} *Committee of Correspondence.*

RC (DLC); printed broadside; endorsed by TJ as a "circular" from "Davy, Ronaldson & others" received 11 May 1809 and so recorded in SJL. Printed in Richmond *Enquirer,* 26 May 1809.

William Davy and John Harrison were merchants and Abraham Small was a printer and stationer with the firm of W. Y. Birch & A. Small (Robinson, *Philadelphia Directory for 1809*). Adam Seybert (1773–1825), physician and chemical manufacturer, represented Pennsylvania in the United States House of Representatives, 1809–15 and 1817–19. He was elected to the American Philosophical Society in 1797 and served as a secretary, 1799–1809, and a councillor, 1810–14 (*DAB*; Robinson, *Philadelphia Directory for 1809*; APS, Minutes, 20 Jan. 1797, 4 Jan. 1799, 5 Jan. 1810 [MS in PPAmP]).

## To Thomas Moore

SIR Monticello Apr. 28. 09.

Your letter of the 20th was recieved two days ago. I distinctly recollect that on your satisfying me that the law for locating & opening the Western road could not be executed by barely the agents named in it, I authorised you to employ others, particularly a packhorseman, with a packhorse & tent, and one or more assistants in the surveying (I do not recollect the number exactly) and that I did it on this ground that it is the intention of every law that itself shall be executed; that so far as it directs by what agents & means, it's directions are to be obeyed, & so far as it does not specify these, the Executive, on whom the constitution makes it incumbent to see that the laws are executed, must supply them according to a sound & responsible discretion. I remember too the authorising you to have 22. feet of the width felled and so opened as that horsemen might pass, for the sake of preserving the trace of a location made at such an expence. and I cannot help believing such an authority is given or plainly implied to have been given, in some of my letters to you. I think I never failed to consult with the Secretary of the treasury on such of these subjects as were of some importance, & to mention the others to him, and I believe the result was generally, perhaps always agreeable to our joint opinion or acquiescence. I return your letter for the sake of making a general reference to it as being I think correct in the facts it states, and I salute you with esteem & respect. TH: JEFFERSON

P.S. I think Gen[l] Mason could testify some of these facts.

PoC (CtY: Franklin Collection); at foot of text: "M[r] Thomas Moore"; endorsed by TJ. Enclosure: Moore to TJ, 20 Apr. 1809, not found but recorded in SJL as received from Washington on 26 Apr. 1809.

Thomas Moore (ca. 1759–1822), civil engineer and inventor, kept a farm in Montgomery County, Maryland. He corresponded regularly with TJ about his refrigerator. Moore patented the invention on 27 Jan. 1803 and TJ bought one the following year. Moore's mercantile business had failed by January 1804, when he sought a western appointment. From 1818 until his death he was principal engineer of Virginia's Board of Public Works (Thomas H. S. Boyd, *The History of Montgomery County, Maryland, from its Earliest Settlement in 1650 to 1879* [1879, repr. 1968], 90–2; Henry Moore to TJ, 30 Jan. 1804 [DNA: RG 59, LAR, 1801–09]; *List of Patents*, 31; *MB*, 2:1132; Richmond *Enquirer*, 8, 29 Oct. 1822).

On 14 Apr. 1806 TJ appointed John MASON, Moore, and Joseph Kerr commissioners for laying out the Cumberland Road from Maryland to the Ohio River. Mason resigned several months later (*JEP*, 2:33 [14, 16 Apr. 1806]; *ASP, Misc.*, 1:474; Mason to TJ, 7 July 1806 [DNA: RG 59, RD]).

# From Madame de Corny

le 29 avril 1809.

en effet, mon cher monsieur, il y a bien longtems que je nay recu de vous aucune preuve de souvenir, je naurois pas été arrêtée par ce manque de mémoire de votre coeur, si je navois craint de me rendre importune des affaires publiques, de grands interêt nuisent nécessairement aux affections particulieres, sur tout quand une grande distance ajoute encore par la difficulté des communications, p[r1] moi qui nay dautres occupations que de Songer a ceux que jay aimes, de regretter ceux que jay perdu chaque jour je repasse dans mon esprit le passé si doux, et ce passé a dèja 20 ans, le present est denué d'interêt p[r] moi c'est une vrai grisaîlle point de Couleur—eh! quel avenir bon dieu! jay fatigué M[r] Short de questions sur votre Compte, jay Souffert de ce qu'il ne maportoit aucune lettre, il se prête avec Complaisance a Satisfaire ma Curieuce amitié p[r] vous, la nouvelle qui le fixe dans ce pays cy luy est fort agréable je le vois souvent,—je luy crois des remords, davoir été 3 ou quatre ans peut être plus Sans vouloir approcher de mes chagrins, C'est ou de legoisme ou de la bonté jaime mieux croire au dernier motif

jecris le lendemain du jour que jay recu votre lettre je nay point encore la visitte de M[r] Cols je verrai avec interêt votre éleve et la personne qui vien de vous je vous felicitte dêtre rendu a vos gouts, de ne plus vous separer de votre famille, et de pouvoir fixer votre sejour a montechillo C'est une idée importune p^r moi de songer que jamais jamais je ne verrai Ce beau lieu, jay toujours conservé ma passion p^r les arbres mais elle est malheureuse, je nay ni jardin ni même un balcon, les fleurs que je place dans mon interieur Sont autant de victimes que je vois perir faute d'air. jay toujours dit que je voulois un petit arbuste sur ma tombe mais ni parent ni amy pour me rendre le dernier soin et ma tombe Sera Seul Comme ma vie M^de church est a Angelica et le depart du Mentor ne ma rien apporter delle, mais un mot dattention de sa fille pour mexpliquer cette infortune—eh mon dieu je me mêle beaucoup trop de politique elle est triste à suivre celle daujourdhuy, la guerre me fatigue de corp et desprit enfin croyez voir en moi M^de Western de tome jhones—et que cela ne vous paroisse pas trop ridicule, désinteressée de toute chose je maccroche a tout—je ne suis pas femme a negliger une occasion de maffliger. pauvre humanite que na telle pas a souffrir— votre bonne amitie vous fait desirer p^r moi une longue vie, je ne men soucie gueres—une forte sante et la mienne est tres foible quoique la maniere dont jexiste soit un modele de regime continu; je me couche a 9 heures depuis 15 ans, il y en a juste 20 que je nay été a aucun spectacle, encore 15 annèe que je nay diner en ville, tout cela n'est point par amour p^r ma sante mais bien par eloignement du monde que jay vraiment quitte quant[2] a larticle bonheur qui forme le 3^eme article de vos souhaits vous voyez quil ny a pas lieu

ecrivez moi mon cher Monsieur vous me ferez le plus grand plaisir et recevez lassurance dun attachement bien veritable

de Corny

EDITORS' TRANSLATION

29 April 1809.

Indeed, my dear sir, for a very long time I have not received from you any proof of remembrance, I would not have been held back by your heart's forgetfulness, if I had not feared making myself importunate in public affairs, great concerns necessarily harm personal affections, above all when great distances add even more to the difficulty of communication, for me, who has no other pastimes than to dream of those whom I have loved, to regret those whom I have lost, each day I replay in my mind a past that is so very sweet, and this past is already 20 years old, the present is barren of interest for me, it is a true grisaille without color—Oh! good god what a future! I fatigued Mr. Short with questions on your account, I suffered because he brought me no letter, he obligingly gives himself over to satisfying my curious friendship for you, the news that keeps him in this very country is very agreeable to him I see him frequently—I believe him to have regrets for having spent 3 or four years perhaps more not wanting to draw near to my sorrows, it is either egoism or kindness I prefer to believe the latter motive

I am writing the day after I received your letter I have indeed not yet received a visit from Mr. Coles I am eager to see your student and the person who comes from you I congratulate you on having yielded to your preferences, on no longer separating yourself from your family, and on being able to settle yourself at Monticello it vexes me to imagine that never never will I see that beautiful place, I have yet preserved my passion for trees but it is an unhappy one, I have neither a garden nor even a balcony, the flowers that I place inside are just so many victims that I see perish from want of air. I have always said that I wanted a little bush on my tomb but I have neither relative nor friend to give me this last kindness and my tomb will be as lonely as my life Madame Church that is Angelica and the departure of the Mentor did not bring me anything from her but a note from her daughter to explain this misfortune to me—oh good god I meddle too much in politics it is sad to follow those of today, the war tires me both in body and in spirit, in a word believe that you see in me Madame Western of Tom Jones—and if that does not seem too ridiculous to you, disinterested in all things, I cling to everything—I am not the kind of woman to pass by an opportunity to be distressed. poor humanity what does it not have to suffer— your good friendship makes you wish me a long life, I hardly worry about this—good health and mine is very weak although the manner in which I exist is a model of continuous regimen; I have gone to bed at 9 o'clock for 15 years, it has been just 20 since I was at a play, and again 15 years since I dined in town, all this is not out of love for my health but indeed due to my retirement from the world that I have truly left as to the article regarding happiness that forms the 3rd article of your wishes you see there is no place for it

write to me my dear Sir you will give me the greatest pleasure and accept this assurance of true and real attachment DE CORNY

RC (MHi); endorsed by TJ as received 3 Aug. 1809 and so recorded in SJL. Translation by Dr. Amy Ogden. Enclosed in James Madison to TJ, 3 Aug. 1809.

Marguérite Victoire de Palerne de Corny (1747–ca. 1829) was a widow when she became the second wife of Louis Dominique Ethis de Corny in 1782. During TJ's residence in Paris she became part of his circle of women friends and acted as a surrogate mother to his daughter Maria. In 1790 Madame de Corny's husband died, his finances ruined by the onset of the French Revolution. Sometime thereafter she took up permanent residence in Rouen (*PTJ*, 26:215, 723, 30:23; Gilbert Chinard, *Trois Amitiés Françaises de Jefferson: d'apres sa correspondance inédite avec Madame de Bréhan, Madame de Tessé et Madame de Corny* [1927], 152; "Memorandum on conversation with Monsieur Louis de Corny," 18 Nov. 1947, ViCMRL: Howard C. Rice Jr. Collection).

VOTRE LETTRE: TJ's letter to Madame de Corny, 2 Mar. 1809 [DLC], was carried by Isaac A. Coles and concluded with TJ's wishes for her life, health, and happiness. Catherine "Kitty" Church Cruger, the daughter of TJ's friend ANGELICA Schuyler Church, was a close friend of his daughter Maria when they lived in Paris. The fictional Mrs. WESTERN read widely, "had attained a very competent skill in politics, and could discourse very learnedly on the affairs of Europe" (Henry Fielding, *A History of Tom Jones, a Foundling* [1749], bk. 6, ch. 2).

[1] Abbreviation for "pour."

[2] Manuscript: "quand."

## Invoice from George Jefferson

Sent by M^r Randolph's boat—29^th Ap^l 1809
A box lately received from George Town,
2 barrels of cut herrings, &
a bag of Cotton (50^lbs)

G.J.

The dumb fish not arrived

| | | |
|---|---|---|
| Herrings | @ $5\frac{1}{2}$ | \$:11— |
| Cotton | 20 Cents | 10— |

MS (MHi); addressed: "Thomas Jefferson esq^r Monticello"; endorsed by TJ as received 6 May 1809.

On 13 May 1809 Jefferson wrote TJ that he had sent two boxes of DUMB fish by Randolph's boat (RC in MHi; addressed: "Thomas Jefferson esq^r Monticello"; endorsed by TJ as received 21 May 1809 and so recorded in SJL).

## From the Baltimore Tammany Society

SIR,

The retirement of a citizen from Public life, who has possessed as long as you have, the voluntary & unlimited confidence of a free & enlightened people, excites reflections the most gratifying to the friends of humanity & the advocates of Republican Government.

In beholding the cheerful and spontaneous, abdication of the first office of State, by one neither iritated by disappointment, satiated with power nor wearied with duties beyond his ability—we are taught, that principle is not so impracticable as its enemies woul'd represent & that in a nation able to appreciate virtue, such an example will never be without its imitators. The impossibility of popular approbation being converted to popular prejudice & the Liberties of the nation falling a sacrifice to its confidence, is thus secured, by an impartial & stated review of men & measures, periodically invited, free from any bias arising from the glare of office, or the seducements of authority—where the action of Interest fails, the imputation of flattery will not be made, & even personal enmity can not deny the sincerity of commendations, when the only reward which can flow from them, is the consciousness of Gratitude or of truth—

Induced by these[1] considerations The Tammany Society or Columbian order[2] of the City of Baltimore, composed of American Citizens, united by the bands of paitriotic friendship, & pledged to maintain the liberties of their Country, Beg leave to approach your Retirement—& tender you, their free & cordial salutations—You have ceased to occupy the first Station in our Republic—but this very circumstance has rendered you more worthy [the homage][3] of freemen. You have set the Seal of principle on your public life; & your fellow Citizens hail with exultation, the splendid example you have given, of usefulness without Interest[4] & greatness without ambition: when the mad freaks of power, the dark intricacies of Diplomacy, & the artful machinations of competition for popular favor will be remembered only to be dispised, the example of your disinterestedness & forbearance will live in the memory of a greatful people.

As Citizens deeply involved in the fate of their Country, the members of this Society have regarded your political course with an interest & admiration, encreasing with successive proof[5] of your attachment to her welfare, & your zeal in her cause—we mean not to recapitulate the leading features of that policy which has for the last eight years, with parintal tenderness conducted us in the ways of prosperity & Peace, & unfolded to us the true blessings of a free Constitution. The diminution of public burdens, the reduction of the Public debt, the economical administration of Finance & the repeal of obnoxious & injurious Laws, are monuments to your honer—which will stand as beacons to succeeding navigators, against which the storms & waves of faction will exhaust themselves in vain—The opposition which you invariably encountered in your wise & benevolent exertions for the common good—the revilings and denunciations, accrimoniously poured upon you by a prostitute Press, which were as destitute of truth as of decency—have all served but to confirm your mission & sanctify your services.[6] It has ever been the lot of the benefactors of mankind to excite a rancor in proportion to their own mildness and forbearance, & when we look to the foundations of our Religion we behold them deep laid in persecution—

The most minute as well as most important rights of the individual & the nation, were observed & held sacred by you. We are bold to assert & do confidently beleive, that every measure of consequence, which was adopted by the General Government & approved of by you, was done with the most unmingled purity of motive, & with the soundest policy, that circumstances would admit of—If the Nation have made large pecuniary sacrifices, it was to avoid an odious & deadly alliance with transatlantic despots, & to spare the lives of Thousands of our Citizens.—You Sir, without the horrours of war have extended the Physical limits of our Republic & gathered

together under the wings of the American Eagle, a various people, heretofore subject to bigotry & tyranny, But now enjoying the blessings of our Constitution & the Rights of Freemen.
Domestic arts & Sciences have flourished beneath your guardianship. Agriculture & manufactures, the grand sourses of wealth & independance in a Democracy, have been patronised & fostered by your example and recommendation—& if Commerce have for a short time retired from her legitimate Elements, it is only again to return in safety when, the unalienable rights of a sovereign & neutral nation shall be acknowledged & respected, & the Law of Nations shall again regulate & protect maritime rights. But we even now see that the clouds which have so long hovered over & envelloped the Deep are at last about to be rolled away, dissipated & dissolved. This prosperous & momentous change is produced by an undeviating adherence, to those principles of action, which your wisdom & honesty & love of Country pointed out & approved, which the Republican Representatives of the Nation adopted & pursued & which the large Patriotic majority of the People acknowledged to be right, acquiesced in and enforced—
That your successor will continue in the same system of measures, is fondly & confidently hoped for. Then the Belligerents of Europe will feel the necessity of doing complete justice to the violated rights & insulted dignity of our Country—

Great & good friend of our Nation & the whole human family, farewel—The great Spirit looks down with complacency and approbation on your virteus[7] & most peculiarly difficult Labours in the cause of Freedom and Humanity—May the days of thy age be pleasant in the Halls of thy Youth May no cloud[8] pass between thee and thy setting sun. Thy memory shall live for ever, and future Statesmen emulate Thy fame—And when it shall please the Great Spirit to call you to himself, may the consciousness that you have fulfilled the great purposes of your creation console & support you in the last moment of this life—

In behalf of the Society
Jn^o Bankson
Grand Sachem
H Niles Secretary

Baltimore, May 1. 1809

MS (DLC); in a clerk's hand except for attestation and signature by Bankson and dateline and signature by Niles; at head of text: "To Thomas Jefferson, late president of the United States"; endorsed by TJ as an "Address Tamany society of Baltimore" received 14 May 1809 and so recorded in SJL. Printed in Baltimore *American, and Commercial Daily Advertiser*, 3 June 1809 (suppl.).

John Bankson (ca. 1757–1814) rose from lieutenant to major during service with Pennsylvania troops in the Continental army. Later he became a lumber merchant in Baltimore (Washington, *Papers, Pres. Ser.*, 7:189–90; *Baltimore Directory and Citizens' Register for 1808* [Baltimore, 1808], 15; Baltimore *American & Commercial Daily Advertiser*, 7 June 1814). Hezekiah Niles was the editor of the *Baltimore Evening Post* (Brigham, *American Newspapers*, 2:230–1).

Named for a seventeenth-century Delaware Indian named Tammany (*ANB*) to whom many virtues were posthumously assigned, Tammany societies emerged in American cities in the 1770s as patriotic clubs. By late in the 1790s organizations with this name had become associated with the emerging Republican party. Their customary feast day was 1 May.

[1] Manuscript: "the these." Baltimore *American*: "these."
[2] Word interlined.
[3] Omitted words supplied from Baltimore *American*.
[4] Manuscript: "Inerest." Baltimore *American*: "interest."
[5] Baltimore *American*: "proofs."
[6] Baltimore *American*: "service."
[7] Baltimore *American*: "virtuous."
[8] Manuscript: "clould." Baltimore *American*: "cloud."

# From William C. C. Claiborne

D^R^ Sir, New-Orleans May 1st 1809

Permit me the honor to introduce to your acquaintance, Mr Poidrass, the Delegate from Orleans to the Congress of the United States.

Mr Poidrass possesses a great share of the esteem and confidence of his fellow Citizens, and has uniformly used his influence in support of the measures of the General Government.

As relates to this Territory, there is no one more interested in its welfare than Mr Poidrass, nor is there an Individual who enjoys a fairer private character, or whose public Conduct could be directed by purer motives of honest patriotism

I have the honor to be Sir, With great Respect Your faithful friend

William C. C. Claiborne

RC (DLC); at foot of text: "Mr Thomas Jefferson Monticello Virginia"; endorsed by TJ as received 14 Sept. 1809 and so recorded in SJL.

William Charles Coles Claiborne (1775–1817), territorial governor, was born in Sussex County and briefly attended the College of William and Mary. In 1791, while in Philadelphia as an assistant congressional clerk, he first met TJ, who offered to lend him books. Claiborne moved to Tennessee in 1794, began the practice of law, and served in the United States House of Representatives, 1797–1801. He helped to secure the state's electoral votes for TJ in the election of 1800, and in 1801 TJ appointed him governor of Mississippi Territory. In 1803 TJ sent Claiborne and General James Wilkinson as commissioners to New Orleans to ease the transfer from French to American authority, and he appointed Claiborne governor of Orleans Territory the same year. Claiborne was elected the first governor of the new state of Louisiana, serving from 1812–16, and he won a term in the United States Senate in 1817 but died before taking his seat (*ANB*; *DAB*; Joseph T. Hatfield, *William Claiborne: Jeffersonian Centurion in the American Southwest* [1976]; TJ to Claiborne, 13 July 1801 [DLC]).

Julien Lalande Poydras (POIDRASS), a French-born resident of Pointe Coupee, was one of the wealthiest planters in Orleans Territory. He served as president of the territory's legislative council from 1804 until his election as territorial delegate to the United States House of Representatives in 1809 (Jared William Bradley, *Interim Appointment: W. C. C. Claiborne Letter Book, 1804–1805* [2002], 69; George Dargo, *Jefferson's Louisiana: Politics and the Clash of Legal Traditions* [1975], 71).

## To George Jefferson

Dear Sir Monticello May. 1. 09.

Yours of the 21st & 24th are recieved. the amount of my crop of tob° is much less than I expected. Griffin is a good overseer, but has the fault of never writing to me; so that I never learn the amount of my crop of tob° till it gets to your hands. he had informed me that the frost had been very fatal to his tob° & as I supposed from his expression, had killed about one third. I now find it falls short two thirds. it will therefore make a much less impression on my note to mrs Tabb than I had hoped. however it must do what it can. I would not have you hesitate should the late pacification have enabled you to get 7.D. and in consideration of it's bad quality I leave to your judgment to take 6.D. the accomodation with England only opens her market, & unless the French decrees are revoked (which may be doubted) we shall still be excluded from the continent. I must pray you to remit to David Gelston of N. York 18. D 25 C the freight & duty of some boxes of wine he will forward to you for me, & after paying yourself your commission & any balance which may be due you, to apply the proceeds of my tob° to mrs Tabb's demand, always doing first with Griffin's proportion, what he shall direct, as I do not wish ever to have that enter into my accounts.

I am sorry to find there is danger that my trunk N° 28. may have miscarried. among my packages from Washington were only 3. trunks, N° 26. 27. containing books & N° 28. containing chiefly stationary, but other things also of value. you sent me 3. trunks N° 26. & 27. & a small empty trunk of a dollar or two value, having no mark, & not being mine. (I forgot to return it by the last boats) N° 28. is a hair trunk, square, of about 6. or 7. feet cubic contents, & very heavy.[1] besides the large stock of stationary which it contained and which was of considerable value it contained a pocket telescope of 5. guineas sterling cost, a Dynamometer just recieved from France of 4. guineas, and other things which I do not recollect. for in the hurry of our packing I noted only the principal article in each package & therefore shall not know every thing in this trunk, but as I recollect them & find they are not here; as every other package is arrived safe. I am still in hopes that a conference between mr Randolph's boatmen & the draymen may trace it to it's deposit—perhaps it may have been mis-delivered to a boat of some other destination. perhaps sent in lieu of the little empty trunk which came to me by mistake. it's contents could be no object of plunder to draymen or boatmen. I salute you with affectionate attachment TH: JEFFERSON

PoC (MHi); at foot of first page: "M^r George Jefferson"; endorsed by TJ.

Despite TJ's complaints of his NEVER WRITING TO ME, Burgess Griffin wrote TJ on 15 Apr., 26 June, and 26 Sept. 1809 (letters not found but recorded in SJL as received from Poplar Forest on 23 Apr., 5 July, and 29 Sept. 1809). SJL also records a missing letter of 6 May 1809 from TJ to Griffin, the overseer at Poplar Forest from 1801 to 1811 (Betts, *Farm Book*, 517).

MY NOTE TO MRS TABB: Frances Peyton Tabb was a wealthy Amelia County landowner who made a private loan to TJ of $8,000 through Abraham Venable for six months beginning in January 1809 (Gibson & Jefferson to TJ, 20 Jan. 1809 [MHi]; Venable to TJ, 28 Jan. 1809 [DLC]; *MB*, 2:1238, 1246, 1252; Williamsburg *Virginia Gazette* [Purdie & Dixon], 22 Mar. 1770).

[1] Preceding three words interlined.

# To Isham Lewis

DEAR SIR Monticello May 1. 09

It is with real concern that I learn the disagreeable situation in which you are for want of emploiment, & the more so as I do not see any way in which I can propose to you any certain relief. as to offices under the government, they are few, are always full, & twenty applicants for one vacancy when it happens. they are miserable also, giving a bare subsistence without the least chance of doing any thing for the future. the army is full and, in consequence of the late pacification, will probably be reduced. so that from the government nothing seems attainable, & besides in that way I could not be useful to you, as I stand solemnly engaged never to sollicit it for any person. The public lands in the Orleans & Missisipi territories are now under a course of survey, & offer, I think the best chance of emploiment. I am acquainted with the Surveyor general, mr Pease, and could give you a letter to him which might probably induce him to employ you as a surveyor, if there be any room: and this would give chances of doing something for yourself. mr Gideon Fitch, whom you know, is in that department. if you have never learnt to survey, and will come & stay here some time, I will teach it to you. it is not the affair of more than a week or a fortnight, if you already understand common arithmetic, say multiplication & division. if you will do us the favor to come and see us, perhaps in this or some other way, something may, on consultation, be thought of. I salute you with affectionate esteem.

TH: JEFFERSON

PoC (MoSHi: TJC-BC); at foot of text: "Mr Isham Lewis"; endorsed by TJ.

TJ mistakenly gave FITCH as Gideon Fitz's surname. On 23 May 1809 TJ gave Lewis $50 "as a gift to bear his expences back to Tennissee" (*MB*, 2:1245).

# From William Lyman

SIR, American Consulate, London, May 1. 1809.

I had the honour to address you on the 21st of December last by Lieut. Gibbon in the Union, which I doubt not you will have duly received as we have information of the safe arrival of that vessel in the United States. At this time, urgency of business and the opportunity allow me only to add that I have taken the liberty to send you a Report of the Examination before the House of Commons into the Conduct of the Duke of York late Commander in Chief, and hope the same will prove both acceptable and interesting.

I beg you to be assured of the consideration and regard with which I am, Your obedient Servant

WM LYMAN

RC (MoSHi: TJC-BC); at foot of text: "Thomas Jefferson"; endorsed by TJ as received 14 June 1809 and so recorded in SJL. Enclosure: *History of the Proceedings of the House of Commons, in the Inquiry into the Conduct of His Royal Highness the Duke of York* (London, 1809).

William Lyman (1755–1811), a Yale graduate and Revolutionary War veteran, was elected to the Massachusetts state house of representatives in 1787 and the state senate in 1789. He was twice elected to the United States House of Representatives, first as a Federalist and then as a Republican, serving from 1793 to 1797. Lyman's shift of political parties hurt him financially and he sought assistance from TJ, who appointed him United States consul to London in 1804. Lyman, who sent TJ a stylograph in 1807, held the consulship until his death (Dexter, *Yale Biographies*, 3:619–20; *Biog. Dir. Cong.*; Samuel Fowler to Levi Lincoln, 15 Jan. 1804 [DNA: RG 59, LAR, 1801–09]; *JEP*, 1:476, 477 [11, 12 Dec. 1804]; Lyman to TJ, 11 July 1807 [DLC]).

Lyman's letter of 21 DECEMBER 1808 (DLC) congratulated TJ on his retirement and discussed British policies.

# From James Madison

DEAR SIR Washington May 1. 1809

I am just favored with yours of the 27th. Young Gelston is here preparing to take his passage for France as bearer and expositor of dispatches, in the Syren sloop of war which is waiting for him at Baltimore. He leaves this tomorrow morning. Mr Gallatin has had a conversation with Turreau at his residence near Baltimore. He professes to be confident that his Govt will consider England as broken down by the example she has given in repealing her orders, and that the F. Decrees will be repealed as a matter of course. His communications by the Syren will, if he be sincere, press the policy of an immediate repeal. No official accts have been recd from the French letter of Marque arrived at Boston. The difficulty most likely to threaten our relations with France, lies in the effort she may make to render us in some way subservient to the reduction of Span: America; particularly by witholding our commerce. This apprehension is corroborated by the language of Turreau. He alluded to his conversations with you relating to Cuba on which he builds jealousies which he did not conceal. Cuba will without doubt be a cardinal object with Napoleon.

The Spirit which England will bring into the ulterior negociations must differ much from that which influenced former Treaties, if it can be moulded to our just views; and we must be prepared to meet it with a prudent adherence to our essential interests. It is possible however that the school of adversity may have taught her the policy of substituting for her arrogant pretensions, somewhat of a conciliating moderation towards the US. Judging from the tone lately used, a change of that sort[1] would be the less wonderful. If she can be brought to a fair estimate of her real interest, it seems very practicable to surmount the obstacles which have hitherto kept us at variance, and untill surmounted must continue to do so. The case of impressments, hitherto the greatest obstacle, seems to admit most easily of adjustment, on grounds mutually advantageous.

Yrs with affectionate respects JAMES MADISON

It is understood that the Election in the State of N. York has issued very favorably.

RC (DLC: Madison Papers); endorsed by TJ as received 5 May 1809 and so recorded in SJL.

Maltby GELSTON, son of New York customs collector David Gelston, was hired to deliver dispatches to John Armstrong (Robert Smith to Maltby Gelston, 1 May 1809 [DNA: RG 59, DL]). In his CONVERSATIONS with French minister

Louis Marie Turreau RELATING TO CUBA, TJ was rumored to have said that the United States needed the Floridas and Cuba, a suspicion that was repeated anonymously to Turreau and that he in turn described as American efforts to incite revolt in Mexico, Cuba, and the Floridas (Turreau to Robert Smith, 15 Apr. 1809 [DNA: RG 59, NL]).

[1] Madison here canceled "may."

# From Daniel Lescallier

SIR Au havre 2 May 1809

Your favour of feb$^{y}$ 25$^{th}$ has been lately forwarded to me by Gen$^{l}$ Armstrong. I return my thanks for your kind remembrance of me, sincerely wishing matters may settle to mutual satisfaction, and the true interest of both nations to preserve peace, and a profitable intercourse.

I ardently wish for opportunities of being agreable to you, or any of your countrymen.

I beg you will please to accept of a small notice on the geology of the Island Guadeloupe, here inclosed, and remain with great respect,

Sir Your most obed$^{t}$ hble Serv$^{t}$ LESCALLIER

RC (MoSHi: TJC-BC); at foot of text: "Tho$^{s}$ Jefferson Esq$^{r}$"; endorsed by TJ as received 3 Aug. 1809 and so recorded in SJL. Enclosure not found. Enclosed in James Madison to TJ, 3 Aug. 1809.

Daniel Lescallier (1743–1822), French diplomat and writer on maritime topics, produced maps of the West Indies and studied marine life during a two-year visit to Saint Domingue starting in 1764. He was named colonial prefect to Guadeloupe in 1800 and met TJ when he returned to France via the United States in 1804. Napoleon named Lescallier consul general to the United States in 1810, and he held that position until 1815. He initially remained in New York after the French emperor's fall from power but died in Paris (*Biographie universelle*, 24:287–90; Lescallier to TJ, 12 May 1817).

In his FAVOUR of 25 Feb. 1809 (CSmH: JF-BA), TJ had acknowledged Lescallier's letter of 11 Sept. 1808 (MoSHi: TJC-BC) enclosing a copy of his *Vocabulaire des Termes de Marine Anglais et Français* (Paris, 1798; Sowerby, no. 1232).

# From Benjamin Rush

DEAR SIR, Philadelphia May 3$^{rd}$ 1809.

Though late, I hope I am not among the last of your friends in congratulating you upon your escape from the high and dangerous appointment which your Country (to use the words of Lord Chesterfield) inflicted upon you during the last eight years of your life.—Methinks I see [you][1] renewing your Acquaintance with your philosophical instruments, and with the friends of your Youth in your library—a place in which Voltaire has happily said "every mans humor is subject to us," and of Course, the reverse of a public Situation in the world, "in which we are subject to every man's humor."—

Accept further of my Congratulations upon the auspicious issue of your firm, and protracted negociations with Great Britain.

My 3[rd] Son who has lately graduated as Doctor of medicine requests Your Acceptance of a Copy of his inaugural dissertation.

I was much pleased to hear that your Grandson had returned to Philadelphia to prosecute the Study of medicine. After nearly 50 years spent in this study, and in all the laborious duties connected with its practice, I can truly say, they are both more agreeable to me than any other pursuits, and when it shall please God to cut the last of the few threads which remain of my life, I shall suffer nearly as much pain in being torn from my profession, as from the common Attachments of blood & friendship. I was about to conclude my letter by expressing a wish that we could in a long evening, review the early and late political events of our Country together, and trace the influence of the same principles under different names, upon each of them,—but—no—we would not waste a moment in conversing Upon such little Subjects. We would dismiss them to unite with the Speculations upon Alchemy and perpetual motion, and dwell only upon those topics of Science and literature which are calculated to encrease the agricultural, domestic & moral happiness of our fellow Citizens.

ADieu! my dear Sir and be assured of the respect & Affection of your Old and sincere friend of 1775.

BENJ[N]: RUSH

RC (DLC); at foot of text: "M[r] Jefferson"; endorsed by TJ as received 11 May 1809 and so recorded in SJL. Enclosure: James Rush, *An Inquiry into the Use of the Omentum* (Philadelphia, 1809; Sowerby, no. 992).

Benjamin Rush (1746–1813), physician, was born near Philadelphia, graduated from the College of New Jersey in 1760, attended medical lectures at the College of Philadelphia, and received an M.D. from the University of Edinburgh in 1768. He established a successful practice in Philadelphia and taught medicine both privately, and in succession at the College of Philadelphia, the University of the State of Pennsylvania, and the University of Pennsylvania. Rush was active in the Revolutionary movement, signing the Declaration of Independence and serving from 1777–78 as surgeon-general of the armies of the Middle Department. He participated in a wide range of reform activities including temperance, the abolition of slavery, health care for the poor and the mentally ill, prison reform, and education for women. Medically Rush was perhaps best known for his personal bravery and controversial advocacy and application of strong purgatives and bleeding during Philadelphia's 1793 yellow fever epidemic. He was appointed treasurer of the United States Mint in 1797, a post he held until his death. Rush's friendship and broadly ranging correspondence with TJ continued without interruption from Revolutionary times until Rush's death. In 1811, after several abortive attempts, Rush brought about the reconciliation of TJ and John Adams (*ANB*; *DAB*; *Princetonians*, 1748–68, pp. 318–25; Whitfield J. Bell Jr., ed., *Patriot-Improvers: Biographical Sketches of Members of the American Philosophical Society* [1997– ], 1:452–64; George W. Corner, ed., *Autobiography of Benjamin Rush* [1948]; Lyman H. Butterfield, ed., *The Letters of Benjamin Rush*, 2 vols. [1951]).

[1] Omitted word editorially supplied.

# From John Graham

DEAR SIR City of Washington 5th May 1809.

The inclosed was written on the day I received the Letter you did me the Honor to write me—accident prevented its going by the last Mail; but I hope it will yet be in time to inform you of the Residence, and to give you the name of the Gentleman who promised you the wild Geese. I have written to him as you requested, and I beg you to beleive, Sir, that I shall always be proud to receive and execute your commands—

With Sentiments of the most profound Respect I have the Honor to be—Your Most Obt Sert JOHN GRAHAM

RC (DLC); at foot of text: "Thos Jefferson Esqr"; endorsed by TJ as received 7 May 1809 and so recorded in SJL. Enclosure: Graham to TJ, 27 Apr. 1809.

# From George Jefferson

DEAR SIR Richmond 5th May 1809

Your favor of the 1st leaves me no hope of recovering the trunk No 28.—it confirms me in the opinion that I sent four trunks, than which I never had been more confident of any thing in my life, until by referring to the bill of lading, I found that you had only three: but since the receipt of your letter, it occurs to us that Wm A. Burwell had an empty trunk here, which we find is gone.

It appears to me that I recollect the trunk which you describe, & a remark of the drayman of its being very heavy.—As to a mistake in delivering it to a wrong boat, it could not well have happened, as one dray carried all the articles, having a full load each time. I was very particular too, in directing Harry to go with every load.—he went off, and returned, each time with the dray.—It must have been stolen from him on his way up.—There is no hope of the trunk having been wrong delivered by the Captain, as Mr Gibson tells me that he was more than commonly particular in examining the packages, (I was absent) the Capt having made such an enormous charge of freight, as to induce him to measure each, and compare them particularly with the bill of lading. Had I sent the things by a white Man, I should have thought my self remiss in not taking a receipt—but with a negro, I should have[1] considered my memorandum as good evidence, as a receipt written & read by myself, even had he not belonged to Mr Randolph.

Shall I advertize the trunk?

I am Dear Sir Your Very humble servt GEO. JEFFERSON

RC (MHi); addressed: "Thomas Jefferson esqr"; endorsed by TJ as received 11 May 1809 and so recorded in SJL.

[1] Preceding two words interlined.

# To Charles Willson Peale

DEAR SIR Monticello May 5. 09.

Your favor of Apr. 3. came to hand on the 23d of April. I have no doubt that the marked differences between the elephant & our colossal animal entitle him to a distinct appellation. one of those differences, & a striking one, is in the protuberances on the grinding surface of the teeth, somewhat in the shape of the mamma, mastos, or breast of a woman, which has induced Cuvier to call it the Mastodonte, or bubby-toothed; which name perhaps may be as good as any other, & worthy of adoption, as it is more important that all should agree in giving the same name to the same thing, than that it should be the very best which might be given. I am afraid we shall lose mr Rembrandt Peale as we have lost all our great painters because we are not rich enough to bid against other nations for their services. I have communicated to my grandson our consent to his attending mr Godon's lectures in Mineralogy till the botanical course ends, after which he is to return home. I am totally occupied without doors, & enjoying a species of happiness I never before knew, that of doing whatever hits the humor of the moment without responsibility or injury to any one. letter writing having ceased to be a business, is very much neglected, and the exercises of the farm & garden engross nearly my whole time. I salute you with constant affection & respect. TH: JEFFERSON

RC (TxU: Hanley Collection); at foot of text: "Mr Peale." PoC (MHi); endorsed by TJ. Enclosed in TJ to Thomas Jefferson Randolph, 6 May 1809.

# From Etienne Lemaire

philadelphie may 6–1809

Monsieur j'ai Reçû l'honneur de la votre En date du 25 avril par la qu'elle vous desirré avoire quelque petitte article, aûsitot Je mensuy aucûpé, j'ai áchêtté deux douzainne de boutteille D'huil exellante, une idem de siróp de vinaigre de mail et une demi livre de vanilla; jespairre que vous sérré satisfait Des trois article, idé doit ce rapeller de la manier que j'employait la vanilla avec Économis, un baton E-demi, peû faire pour deux fois, la promier, elle ne doit que Casser la vanilla, En[1] trois aux quatre morceaux, et la second de les fendre avec le Couteaut En petit morceaux mince, la Crême aûra la même Odeur.

Monsieur Je ne pas Encor[2] eut lhonneur de voire M$^{r}$ Jefferson Ramdolp, deux fois j'ai Été Chez M$^{r}$ peale aû museum, Je ne les pas trouvé mais monsieur Comme Cela nest pas biens praicé, j'espair le voire aû promié Jours, Je sui biens Comtent, idé et fanné son[3] biens tous deuse, ce son deuse bonne[4] fille et je sui persuadé—quel, vous donneron Beaucoup de satisfactions,—

Cy monsieur a besoin de quelque aûtres Chosse Je le prie dans eûsere librement avec moi les ordre seront executtez avec toujour baucoup de plaisir. j'ai inclus le reconnoissement! Monsieur Je fini avec toute lhonneur et respecque possible votre tres humble tres óbeisant servi-teur,

E. Lemaire

| Conte des article: ½ de vanilla | $5 |
|---|---|
| 12 Boutteille de sirop de vinaigre mail | 10 |
| 24 idem d'huille d'olive | 20 |
| 1 Boitte, et transpor | 00–75 |
| Costume hous, &.&.&. | 38 |
| | $36–13 |

Monsieur recevra la vanilla avec la presente reçû

EDITORS' TRANSLATION

Philadelphia May 6–1809

Sir I have the honor of receiving yours of 25 April in which you express your desire to have some small articles, I took care of it right away, I bought two dozen bottles of excellent oil, the same of Maille vinegar syrup—and half a pound of vanilla; I hope that you will be satisfied with these three articles, Edy ought to remember the way I used vanilla sparingly, one-and-a-half sticks can do for two times, the first, she only has to break the vanilla in three or four pieces, and the second to split them into small pieces with the knife, the cream will have the same smell.

Sir I have not yet had the honor of seeing Mr. Jefferson Randolph, twice I went to Mr. Peale's at the museum, I did not find them but Sir since it is not pressing, I hope to see him soon, I am quite happy, Edy and Fanny are both good workers, they are two good girls and I am convinced that they will give you much satisfaction,—
If your honor needs some other things I pray him to make use of me freely with orders which will always be carried out with much pleasure. I have included the list of goods! Sir I end with all possible honor and respect your very humble very obedient servant, E. LEMAIRE

| List of articles: | | |
|---|---|---|
| | $\frac{1}{2}$ of vanilla | $5 |
| 12 | Bottles of Maille vinegar syrup | 10 |
| 24 | same of olive oil | 20 |
| 1 | Crate, and shipping | 00–75 |
| | Customhouse, &.&.&. | 38 |
| | | $36–13 |

Your honor will receive the vanilla with the present receipt

RC (MHi); endorsed by TJ as received 14 May 1809 and so recorded in SJL. Translation by Dr. Roland H. Simon.

IDÉ ET FANNÉ: Edith Fossett and Fanny Hern. SIRÓP DE VINAIGRE DE MAIL: a condensed syrup made by boiling vinegar with sugar, probably that popularized by Parisian vinegar distiller Antoine Maille (*PTJ*, 14:xxxv).

[1] Apparent idiosyncratic accent mark over one of the letters in this word omitted, here and later in sentence.

[2] Apparent idiosyncratic accent mark over one of the first two letters in this word omitted.

[3] Manuscript: "fon."

[4] Word interlined.

# To Thomas Jefferson Randolph

DEAR JEFFERSON Monticello May 6.[1] 09.

Your's of the 28th ult. came to hand by our last post. I have consulted your father on the subject of your attending mr Godon's lectures in mineralogy, and we consent to it so long as the Botanical lectures continue. we neither of us consider that branch of science as sufficiently useful to protract your stay in Philadelphia beyond the termination of the Botanical lectures. in what you say respecting the preservation of plants, I suppose you allude to mr Crownenshield's specimens which I shewed you. but I could not have promised to give you his method because I did not know it my self. all I know was from Genl Dearborne, who told me that mr Crownenshield's method was, by extreme pressure (with a screw or weight) on the substance of the plants but that he could never make it adhere to the paper until he used garlick juice either alone, or in composition with something else. I communicated to mr Randolph your wish respecting the specimens of antimony. but how shall we convey them. by an unintended omission in the act of Congress allowing my letters to be free, they omitted those from me, mentioning those to me only. it will be corrected at their ensuing session as the letters of my predecessors were privileged both to & from. and in truth the office of president commits the incumbent, even after he quits office, to a correspondence of such extent as to be extremely burthensome. to avoid the expence of postage to mr Peale, I inclose his letter in yours, that it may be paid out of your funds. I send you one also for mr Hamilton, open for your perusal. when read, stick a wafer in it before delivery. attend particularly to the assurances of using his indulgence with discretion and to the study of his pleasure grounds as the finest model of pleasure gardening you will ever see. I wrote to Lemaire to send me some Vanilla & vinegar syrop, & that you would pay him for it on presenting my letter. I must desire you to send me 9 feet of brass chain to hang the Alabaster lamp you got for me. I inclose you 4. links as a specimen of the kind & size. this was furnished me by Mess[rs] Caldcleugh & Thomas, stationers N[o] 66. & 68. Chesnut street at 67. cents per yard, who probably can furnish the same now. I must also pray you to get for me a gross of vial-corks of different sizes, & 4. dozen phials of 1. 2. 3. & 4. ounces, one dozen of each size—the largest mouthed would be the best as they are for holding garden seeds. I have not yet seen D[r] Watson the family here are all well, and I recollect no small news of the neighborhood worth mentioning. we wish to hear from you oftener. God bless you.

TH: JEFFERSON

P.S. the above articles to be packed in a box addressed to Gibson & Jefferson & sent by water. it would be well if Lemaire's articles were packed in the same box, as they would all come safer in one than two boxes. but for this purpose you must see him immediately, or he will have sent away his alone. I must pray you to put half a dozen pounds of scented hair powder into the same box. none is to be had here, & it is almost a necessary of life with me. to spare your funds I shall have the postage of this package paid here.

PoC (MHi); at foot of first page: "T. J. Randolph"; endorsed by TJ. Enclosures: (1) TJ to Charles Willson Peale, 5 May 1809. (2) TJ to William Hamilton, 7 May 1809.

Thomas Jefferson Randolph (1792–1875) was born at Monticello, the eldest son of Martha Jefferson Randolph and Thomas Mann Randolph. TJ supervised his grandson's education at home and in Philadelphia and Richmond. Randolph studied botany, natural history, and anatomy before becoming a farmer. Soon after his marriage in 1815 to Jane Hollins Nicholas, the daughter of Governor Wilson Cary Nicholas, Randolph took over the management of his grandfather's affairs and displayed an aptitude for finance. In 1817 the young couple moved from Monticello to nearby Tufton, where they raised twelve children. As chief executor of TJ's estate, Randolph fought a long and ultimately successful battle to settle his grandfather's debts, although it meant the sale of Monticello and the family's removal to Edgehill. He published the first collection of TJ's writings in four volumes in 1829. Randolph served the University of Virginia as a visitor, 1829–57, and rector, 1857–64. Six times between 1831 and 1843 he represented Albemarle County in the Virginia House of Delegates, where he supported the gradual emancipation and deportation of slaves. Randolph also sat in the state constitutional convention of 1850–51 and voted for secession at the Virginia convention of 1861 (*DAB*; Shackelford, *Descendants*, 76–88).

Randolph's letter OF THE 28TH ULT., not found, is recorded in SJL as received from Peale's Philadelphia Museum on 3 May 1809. Late in 1808 William Bentley sent botanical SPECIMENS assembled by TJ's recently deceased friend Jacob Crowninshield (TJ to Bentley, 29 Dec. 1808 [NNGL]; Sowerby, no. 1074). During its first SESSION the Eleventh Congress passed a bill granting TJ the franking privilege on outgoing LETTERS despite objections from Nathaniel Macon (*Annals*, 11th Cong., 1st sess., 448 [27 June 1809]). TJ had purchased lamps and chains from CALDCLEUGH & THOMAS in 1804 and 1807 (*MB*, 2:1140, 1209). He probably wanted the VIAL-CORKS and PHIALS to equip his new seed press (Stein, *Worlds*, 293).

[1] Number interlined in place of "8."

# To William Hamilton

DEAR SIR Monticello May 7.[1] 09

I have a grandson, Thos J. Randolph, now at Philadelphia, attending the Botanical lectures of Doctr Barton, and who will continue there only until the end of the present course. altho' I know that your goodness has indulged Dr Barton with permission to avail himself of your collection of plants for the purpose of instructing his pupils, yet as my grandson has a peculiar fondness for that branch of the knolege of nature, & would wish, in vacant hours to pursue it alone, I am led to ask for him a permission of occasional entrance into your gardens, under such restrictions as you may think proper. I have so much experience of his entire discretion as to be able with confidence to assure you that nothing will recieve injury from his hands. I have desired him to deliver this to you himself, as well for the honor of personally presenting his respects to you, as of giving you assurances of the discreet use he will make of your indulgence. I have pressed upon him also to study well the style of your pleasure grounds, as the chastest model of gardening which I have ever seen out of England. in presenting him to my friends at Philadelphia I take the liberty of requesting them not to consider it as an introduction to such civilities as might abstract him from the studies which are his sole object there. the allurements of society are better deferred, & will always present themselves early enough.

I have heard with much concern of your increased afflictions from the gout. have you never thought of trying the warm springs of Augusta for it? altho' much of an infidel in what is called the healing art, I have seen such radical cures of rheumatism, and relief of the Gout, effected by those waters, that I would certainly resort to them myself, & with much confidence were I to suffer from either of those disorders. I am the more tempted to recommend them to you, as it would lead you near this place where I should be very happy to see you, & to take from you some of those lessons for the improvement of my grounds which you have so happily practised on your own. with every wish for your better health & happiness, I beg leave to assure you of my high respect and esteem. TH: JEFFERSON

PoC (MHi); at foot of first page: "W^m Hamilton esq."; endorsed by TJ. Enclosed in TJ to Thomas Jefferson Randolph, 6 May 1809.

William Hamilton (ca. 1746–1813), avid horticulturist and patron of the arts, owned the Woodlands, a large estate on the Schuylkill River outside of Philadelphia famous for its extensive gardens inspired by English landscape design. He maintained almost ten thousand plants in a 140-foot greenhouse flanked by hothouses. TJ greatly admired the Woodlands and its gardens and hoped to incorporate some of the same principles at Monticello. The two men shared an interest in exotic and native plants and exchanged seeds and specimens. Hamilton reportedly introduced the Lombardy poplar, gingko, and witch elm to America. TJ selected him and Bernard McMahon to receive and attempt to propagate the seeds collected on the Lewis and Clark Expedition (TJ to Hamilton, 6 Nov. 1805 and July 1806, TJ to McMahon, 6 Jan. 1807, and Hamilton to TJ, 5 Feb. 1808 [DLC]; Betts, *Garden Book*; William Howard Adams, ed., *Jefferson and the Arts: An Extended View* [1976], 137–57; Richard J. Betts, "The Woodlands," *Winterthur Portfolio* 14 [1979]: 213–34; "The Woodlands," *Port Folio* 2 [1809]: 505–7; Philadelphia *Pennsylvania Gazette*, 26 May 1813).

[1] Number interlined in place of "9."

# To John M. Perry

SIR Monticello May 7.[1] 09.

When I bespoke of you the other day the thousand feet of heart pine plank, cut crosswise in the stock into bars of a full inch or rather inch & eighth,[2] I forgot to desire that the planks might not after sawing, be separated by splitting them asunder at the butt end [but] that the stock may come entire. perhaps the end should be bound round with a hiccory withe. if the planks are separated, the planks will be very apt to break.

Yours E^tc TH: JEFFERSON

PoC (MHi); faint; at foot of text: "M^r John Perry"; endorsed by TJ.

John M. Perry, master brickmason and carpenter, was involved with building projects at Monticello, Poplar Forest, and TJ's mill between 1800 and 1811. His work on residential buildings and churches in Albemarle and surrounding counties enabled him to purchase large amounts of land, part of which he sold in 1817 to Central College (later the University of Virginia). A condition of the sale was that he would have carpentry and joinery contracts during construction of the university. Perry served as a local magistrate, and as a justice of the peace in 1826, he helped to appraise TJ's estate. He began selling off his real estate holdings in 1829 and moved from his Albemarle County home, Montebello, to Missouri about 1835. At the time of his death Perry lived in Mississippi (Woods, *Albemarle*, 294–5; Lay, *Architecture*, 99–101, 160–1; Richard Charles Cote, "The Architectural Workmen of Thomas Jefferson in Virginia," 2 vols. [Ph.D. diss., Boston University, 1986], 1:62–3, 148–55; Perry to TJ, 3 May 1817; *MB*, esp. 2:1023).

Letters Perry wrote TJ on 13 June and 26 Sept., not found, are recorded as received 13 June and 29 Sept. 1809 in SJL, which also records a missing, undated letter from Perry received 8 Oct. 1809.

[1] Number interlined in place of "9."
[2] Manuscript: "eigthth."

# From Robert Patterson

SIR Philad[a] May 10[th] 1809.

My younger son, Robert Maskill, having gone thro the usual course of collegiate studies in our Seminary, and of medical studies under D[r] Barton, and obtained degrees both in the Arts & in medicine; has devoted the last twelve months chiefly to the study of mineralogy under M[r] Godon; in which, it is said, he has made considerable proficiency. He has a strong desire of visiting some parts of Europe, particularly Paris, with a view to his further improvement from the opportunities which he would then enjoy—I have yielded to his inclination; and he is about to embark in a vessel which will sail from this port for Amsterdam, probably in the course of about two or three weeks from this time.

He is extremely solicitous, as well as myself, to obtain a letter from you, Sir, to some of your correspondents in Paris. It is true, he has not the happiness of being personally known to you. Sometime last spring he had indeed the pleasure of being introduced by his uncle M[r] Findly, which you will probably recollect. How far a compliance with this request may be consistant with propriety, under the present circumstances, you will judge & determine; and will have the goodness to excuse this freedom in—Sir, your most respectful servant

R[T] PATTERSON

RC (MHi); endorsed by TJ as received 14 May 1809 and so recorded in SJL.

Robert Patterson (1743–1824), mathematician and educator, emigrated from Ireland to Philadelphia in 1768. In 1779, following service in the American Revolution, Patterson became professor of mathematics at the newly organized University of the State of Pennsylvania (from 1791 the University of Pennsylvania). He held the position until 1814, with service as the university's vice-provost, 1810–13. Patterson was elected to the American Philosophical Society in 1783 and was a secretary, 1784–97, a curator, 1797–99, a vice president, 1799–1819, and president from 1819 until his death. Patterson was one of five society members TJ selected to give Meriwether Lewis scientific instruction prior to his expedition to the Pacific Ocean. TJ also appointed Patterson director of the United States Mint, and he served in that capacity from 1805–24 (*ANB*; *DAB*; Carolyn Myatt Green, "The Robert Patterson Family—Eminent Philadelphians, Scholars, and Directors of the United States Mint: 1743–1854" [Ph.D. diss., University of Georgia, 1974]; APS, Minutes, 18 Jan. 1783, 2 Jan. 1784, 6 Jan. 1797, 4 Jan. 1799, 1 Jan. 1819 [MS in PPAmP]; *JEP*, 2:7, 10 [20, 23 Dec. 1805]).

Robert Maskell Patterson's UNCLE William Findley was a United States congressman from Pennsylvania, 1803–17.

# From Gerardus Vrolik

MONSIEUR! Amsterdam ce 10 de Mai 1809

Sa Majesté, le Roi d'Hollande, aÿant bien voulu honorer de Son approbation le Voeu de la Première Classe de l'Institut Roÿal des Sciences, de Littérature et des beaux Arts, de Vous associer à Ses Membres, j'ai l'honneur, de Vous en informer.

La Classe ne doute pas, que Vous ne contribuiez par vos talens distingués, au grand but, que Sa Majesté s'est proposée par cette Institution et que Vous ne fassiez part à la Classe de tout ce qui pourroit l'intéresser dans les Sciences physiques, que Vous cultivez avec tant de Succès.

J'ai l'honneur, d'être avec la plus haute estime, Monsieur! Votre Obéissant Serviteur. G: VROLIK

EDITORS' TRANSLATION

SIR! Amsterdam 10 May 1809

His Majesty, the King of Holland, having agreed to honor with his approbation the wish of the first class of the Royal Institute of Sciences, Literature and the Fine Arts to make you one of its members, I have the honor to inform you of it.

The class has no doubt that, with your distinguished talents, you will contribute to the great goal that His Majesty proposes to achieve through this institution and that you will inform the class of anything that might be of interest to it in the realm of the physical sciences, which you study with so much success.

I have the honor to be, with the highest esteem, Sir! your obedient servant.

G: VROLIK

RC (CSmH: JF-BA); between dateline and salutation: "Le Secretaire perpétuel de la Première Classe de l'Institut Roÿal des Sciences, de Littérature et des beaux Arts à Monsieur T. Jefferson Associé étranger de la Première Classe de l'Institut Roÿal des Sciences, de Littérature et des beaux Arts"; endorsed by TJ as received 4 Mar. 1810 and so recorded in SJL. Translation by Dr. Genevieve Moene.

Gerardus Vrolik (1775–1859) was a Dutch scientist who taught botany, anatomy, physiology, and obstetrics at the Amsterdam Athenaeum Illustre, later the University of Amsterdam. During his extensive research and publication on human, plant, and animal anatomy, he assembled a large collection of specimens that became known as the Museum Vrolikianum. On the founding of the Royal Netherlands Academy of Arts and Sciences in 1808, Vrolik was appointed secretary of the first section (Frank Spencer, ed., *History of Physical Anthropology* [1997], 2:1095–7).

# From Henry Hiort

SIR! City of Washington 11th May 1809.

Knowing that you are a Patron of every useful invention, I take the liberty to enclose to you, a statement of Mr Morneveck's very valuable Patent impenetrable Stucco, as a substitute for Slate, Shingles and Tiles.

The Certificate of The Justices of the Supreme Court of The United states, who were witnesses to the experiments on a shingle covered with the same Stucco, would be a sufficient apology for obtruding it on your Attention; but a greater inducement bears with me, which is, your well known Zeal to promote works of Public Utility. To enlarge upon its merits, would be an Offence to your discernment and judgment; suffer me therefore merely to urge your consideration of it, satisfied that your sanction & influence exerted in its support, will raise it in the public estimation, to the Acme of the Wishes of The Inventor,—which is the safety and happiness of The United states.

I have the honor to be with sincere wishes for an uninterrupted enjoyment of your health & with the greatest respect

Your most obdt servt HENRY HIORT

RC (DLC); at foot of text: "Thos Jefferson Esqr"; endorsed by TJ as received 14 May 1809 and so recorded in SJL. Enclosure: Description of Morneveck's impenetrable stucco, reporting that James Madison had awarded a patent to the stucco; that Morneveck had succeeded where all ancient and modern efforts had failed; that his stucco was far superior to slates, tiles, and shingles, being far lighter and harder, "and not in the least fragile being elastic, and will not crack by a blow from a hammer, nor the strongest frost, and also resists a brand of fire"; that the inventor is too modest to say much more, and therefore adding a 28 Feb. 1809 testimonial by United States Supreme Court justices John Marshall, Bushrod Washington, William Livingston Jr., and Brockholst Livingston that they had witnessed a demonstration in which the stucco withstood intense flame, that the inventor asserted that it was "equally secure against the heaviest rains," and that he therefore deserved "the patronage of the public for so useful a discovery"; with a fuller description on verso indicating that the stucco's color was "a dark and brilliant slate, which is the prevailing taste"; that roofs covered with it would be safe from firebrands from nearby blazes; that the stucco can be used to treat wood from trees not otherwise useful for building, such as Lombardy poplar, gum, and willow; that it can be prepared throughout the year in towns and on farms and plantations at a cost of only one cent per square foot; that it is best applied in "serene weather, from the spring to the fall," but that the trial on a shingle before the Supreme Court succeeded even in a stormy season; that those wanting to make and use the stucco were encouraged to apply to the patentee in Baltimore or to his agent Hiort in Washington; and that American printers were urged to insert this notice in their publications as a public service (printed broadside in DLC: Rare Book and Special Collections, addressed by Hiort: "Thos Jefferson Esqr"; partially printed in Philadelphia *Aurora General Advertiser*, 19 May 1809).

Henry Hiort practiced law in Norfolk, 1790–1802, and then moved to Washington, D.C. He unsuccessfully sought a position as federal marshal during TJ's administration and later returned to his native Great Britain ("The Willis Family," *WMQ*, 1st ser., 6 [1897]: 27–8; Hiort to TJ, 9 Nov. 1807 [DNA: RG 59, LAR, 1801–09]).

Charles Morneveck of Baltimore received a PATENT on "cement intended as a substitute for slates, tiles, &c. for covering houses" on 13 Mar. 1809 (*List of Patents*, 71).

# To Horatio G. Spafford

SIR Monticello May 14. 09.

I have duly recieved your favor of Apr. 3. with the copy of your General Geography, for which I pray you to accept my thanks. my occupations here have not permitted me to read it through, which alone could justify any judgment expressed on the work. indeed as it appears to be an abridgment of several branches of science, the scale of abridgment must enter into that judgment. different readers require different scales according to the time they can spare, & their views in reading; and no doubt that the view of the sciences which you have brought into the compass of a 12mo volume will be accomodated to the time & object of many who may wish for but a very general view of them.

In passing my eye rapidly over parts of the book, I was struck with two passages, on which I will make observations, not doubting your wish; in any future edition, to render the work as correct as you can. in page 186. you say the potatoe is a native of the US. I presume you speak of the Irish potatoe. I have enquired much into this question, & think I can assure you that plant is not a native of N. America. Zimmerman, in his Geographical Zoology, says it is a native of Guiana; & Clavigero, that the Mexicans got it from S. America, it's native country. the most probable account I have been able to collect is that a vessel of S^r Walter Raleigh's, returning from Guiana, put into the West of Ireland in distress, having on board some potatoes which they called earth apples. that the season of the year, & circumstance of their being already sprouted induced them to give them all out there, and they were no more heard or thought of, till they had been spread considerably into that island, whence they were carried over into England, & therefore called the Irish potatoe. from England they came to the US. bringing their name with them.

the other passage respects the description of the passage of the Potomac through the Blue ridge in the Notes on Virginia. you quote from Volney's account of the US. what[1] his words do not justify. his words are 'on coming from Frederick town one does not see the rich perspective mentioned in the notes of Mr Jefferson. on observing this to him a few days after he informed me he had his information from a French engineer who, during the war of Independance ascended the height of the hills & I concieve that at that elevation the perspective must be as imposing as a wild[2] country, whose horizon has no obstacles, may present.' that the scene described in the Notes is not visible from any part of the road from Frederick town to Harper's ferry is most certain. that road passes along the valley. nor can it be seen from the tavern after crossing the ferry; & we may fairly infer that mr Volney did not ascend the height back of the tavern from which alone it can be seen, but that he pursued his journey from the tavern along the high road. yet he admits that at the elevation of that height the perspective may be as rich as a wild country can present. but you make him 'surprised to find by a view of the spot, that the description was amazingly exaggerated.' but it is evident that mr Volney did not ascend the hill to get a view of the spot, and that he supposes that that height may present as imposing a view as such a country admits. but mr Volney was mistaken in saying I told him I had recieved the description from a French engineer. by an error of memory he has misapplied to this scene what I mentioned to him as to the Natural bridge, I told him I recieved a drawing of that from a French engineer sent there by the Marquis de Chastellux, & who has published that drawing in his travels. I could not tell him I had the description of the passage of the Potomak from a French engineer, because I never heard any French man say a word about it, much less did I ever recieve a description of it from any mortal whatever. I visited the place myself in Oct. 1783. wrote the description some time after, & printed the work in Paris in 1784. & 1785. I wrote the description from my own view of the spot, stated no fact but what I saw, & can now affirm that no fact is exaggerated. it is true that the same scene may excite very different sensations in different spectators according to their different sensibilities. the sensations of some may be much stronger than those of others. and with respect to the Natural bridge, it was not a description, but a drawing only which I recieved from the French engineer. the description was written before I ever saw him. it is not from any merit which I suppose in either of these descriptions, that I have gone into these observations, but to correct the imputation of having given to the world as my own, ideas, & false ones too, which I had recieved from another. nor do I mention the subject to you with a desire that it should be any otherwise noticed before the public than by a more correct statement in any future edition of your work.

You mention having inclosed to me some printed letters announcing a design in which you ask my aid. but no such letters came to me. any facts which I possess & which may be useful to your views shall be freely communicated, & I shall be happy to see you at Monticello, should you come this way as you propose. you will find me engaged entirely in rural occupations, looking into the field of science but occasionally & at vacant moments.

I sowed some of the Benni seed the last year, & distributed some among my neighbors; but the whole was killed by the September frost. I got a little again the last winter, but it was sowed before I recieved your letter. Col[o] Few of New York recieves quantities of it from Georgia, from whom you may probably get some through the Mayor of N. York. but I little expect it can succeed with you. it is about as hardy as the Cotton plant, from which you may judge of the probability of raising it at Hudson.

I salute you with great respect. TH: JEFFERSON

PoC (DLC); at foot of first page: "M[r] Spafford." Mistakenly recorded in SJL as a letter of 7 May 1809.

ZIMMERMAN and CLAVIGERO comment on the potato's origins in Eberhard August Wilhelm von Zimmermann, *Zoologie Géographique. Premier Article L'Homme* (Kassel, 1784; Sowerby, no. 1031), 26, and Francesco Saverio Clavigero, *Storia Antica del Messico* (Cesena, 1780–81; Sowerby, no. 4121), 1:58.

VOLNEY'S ACCOUNT of Harper's Ferry (*Tableau du Climat et du Sol des États-Unis d'Amérique* [Paris, 1803; Sowerby, no. 4032], 140) and Spafford's paraphrase (*General Geography, and Rudiments of Useful Knowledge* [Hudson, N.Y., 1809; Sowerby, no. 3828]) were at odds with the SCENE DESCRIBED in TJ's *Notes on the State of Virginia*: "The passage of the Patowmac through the Blue ridge is perhaps one of the most stupendous scenes in nature. You stand on a very high point of land. On your right comes up the Shenandoah, having ranged along the foot of the mountain an hundred miles to seek a vent. On your left approaches the Patowmac, in quest of a passage also. In the moment of their junction they rush together against the mountain, rend it asunder, and pass off to the sea" (*Notes*, ed. Peden, 19).

Baron de Turpin, the FRENCH ENGI-

NEER, executed a drawing of the Natural Bridge in 1782 for the Marquis de CHASTELLUX but did not describe Harper's Ferry (Chastellux, *Travels in North America in the Years 1780, 1781 and 1782* [Paris, 1786; English trans. London, 1787, repr. 1963; Sowerby, nos. 4021, 4023], 2:44; *PTJ*, 6:193).

[1] TJ here canceled: "was an error of fact in him, but in terms which."

[2] Word interlined in place of "savage."

# From Joseph Dougherty

DEAR SIR City of Washington May 15th. 1809

Since my arival at this place, from Wilmington[1] I had the happiness to hear from you. by the Honble Mr Burwell on his way to Baltimore two weeks yesterday: and from the Honble Mr Howard of K: whom I saw yesterday. he says your well, and I am happy to hear it. I asked him if he saw your flock of sheep, he said no, but you were that day sending to some place for a broad tail ram, Doctr Thornton has asked me to go to his farm, to chuse one of his best rams of the full bread broad tail for you, we are to go this week, I will wait your instructions to send him to you: the wild geese I expected to have received last week, they are not arived yet. your documents will be finished in two or three weeks.—I have here two verry fine rams of the marino sheep—of the three quarter breed. I will inclose here a sample of the wool for your & my good friend, Mr Randolphs inspection Mr Dupont would not set a price on them, nor will he ask any pay for them until I make it out of their produce, he sells the same breed at forty dollars. viz. ram lambs.

I brought with me from Mr Bauduys place at Willmington four breeding mares to Doctr Thornton. for my trouble besides paying the expence of my journey home,—Mr Bauduy has promised to send me in the fall of 1810 two full bread ewes; Mr Dupont says he will let me have a full bread ram at the same time this will enable me to have the full breed in two years I will give you the first of the full breed if youl be so good as to accept them. I am in no way of earning any thing since you left this place I was not deceived in my opinion of Mr Latrobe respecting his promises to find me employ, when you were gone from here. there was no vacant place for me. although he said, whilst you were here, that he would creat an office for me if none was vacant Sir if you were now at the Presidents house you would scarcely know it, The north front is become a wilderness of shrubry and trees, there's wonderfull changes in the house, the president, or rather Mrs Madison, has changed the office to Mr Coals room This reminds me of a class of people in Ireland called fortune-tellers, who makes their bread by going among the most ignorant class of the community, telling them to change their fire places to the other end of the house and they would be rich verry soon, this may not be M[rs] Madison[s] intention for changing M[r] Barry is painting in the Presidents house, but M[rs] Madison cannot abide the smell of the paint: that may be on account of her pregnancy, but I think she will bring forth nothing more than dignity

I will be glad to know the state of your flock of sheep and if any of the second cross has four horns

Sir your Humbl[e] Serv[t] Jo[s] DOUGHERTY

RC (DLC); endorsed by TJ as received 19 May 1809 and so recorded in SJL.

Benjamin HOWARD was a member of the United States House of Representatives from Kentucky. Peter BAUDUY was a business partner of Wilmington gunpowder manufacturer Éleuthère Irénée DUPONT de Nemours (*ANB*, 7:116).

[1] Preceding two words interlined.

# From Edmund Pendleton

SIR, Caroline May 15. 1809

The money due from the late William Tompkins for a tract of Land purchased by him of the Trustees of Col[o] Bernard Moore deceased has all been paid to me as Agent for the Administrators of the Estate of John Robinson Esq[r] deceased; the particular quantity of Land will be ascertained and described in a Deed to be prepared by Gen[l] Jn[o] Minor for your signature as surviving Trustee.

I am, with great respect, Sir Your most Obed[t]

EDM: PENDLETON

RC (MHi); endorsed by TJ as received 7 July 1809 and so recorded in SJL. Enclosed in John Minor to TJ, 17 May 1809.

Edmund Pendleton (1745–1827) completed his studies at the College of William and Mary in 1764, two years after TJ, became an attorney, and served as a militia officer in the Revolutionary War (David John Mays, ed., *The Letters and Papers of Edmund Pendleton, 1734–1803* [1967], esp. 2:402, 596, 670–1; Hamilton J. Eckenrode, *Virginia Soldiers of the American Revolution* [1912, repr. 1989], 1:346; Richmond *Enquirer*, 10 July 1827).

In 1770–71 TJ served as one of five TRUSTEES when Bernard Moore sold his property for the benefit of his creditors (*PTJ*, 1:59–60, 64–5). Pendleton's uncle Edmund Pendleton (1721–1803), an eminent Virginia jurist who helped raise his nephew, had administered the complicated estate of JOHN ROBINSON, the former speaker and treasurer of the colony of Virginia, and spent many years attempting to repair the damage caused by Robinson's financial irregularities. Pendleton aided his uncle and later served as an agent to the administrators who oversaw the Robinson estate after the elder Pendleton's death (Mays, ed., *Pendleton Letters* [1967], esp. 2:587, 589, 627).

# To Pierre Samuel Du Pont de Nemours, André Thoüin, and Bartelémy Faujas de Saint-Fond

MY DEAR SIR & FRIEND[1] Monticello May 16.[2] 09.

The bearer hereof, mr Robert M. Patterson, is son of mr Robert Patterson, professor of Mathematics in the college of Philadelphia, Director of the mint of the US. & a Vicepresident of the Philosophical society. having gone through his course of studies[3] here he goes to Paris to advance his stock of knolege by the superior aids which that place affords. I have not the pleasure of being[4] personally acquainted with him, but learn from sources worthy of all confidence, that he is correct in his morals, & conduct, & earnest[5] in the worthy pursuits which carry him to Europe. a friendship of long standing with[6] his father, & the desire of being useful to himself induce me to take the liberty of making him known to you, of solliciting your friendly attentions & counsel to him in the objects of his journey & of expressing my entire belief that he will prove[7] himself worthy of any good offices you may be so kind as to render him. I avail myself with pleasure of this & every occasion of renewing to you the assurances of my great esteem & respect. TH: JEFFERSON

RC (DeGH: Pierre Samuel Du Pont de Nemours Papers, Winterthur Manuscripts). PoC (DLC); at foot of text: "M. Dupont de Nemours Membre de l'Institut"; endorsed by TJ. RC (IaU: Presidential Letters); dated 18 May 1809; wording nearly identical to text to Du Pont de Nemours; endorsed by Thoüin as received 30 Sept. 1809. PoC (MHi); dated 16 May 1809; at foot of text: "M. Thouin Membre de l'institut et de plusieurs societés Professeur d'agriculture au Museum d'histoire naturel"; endorsed by TJ. PoC (DLC); dated 16 May 1809; at foot of text: "M. Faujas de S[t] Fond Membre de l'institut <*national de France*> et de plusieurs societés, Professeur de geologie au Museum d'Histoire naturelle"; endorsed by TJ. Recorded separately in SJL under 16 May 1809 as three texts "Introductory of Robert M. Patterson." Enclosed in a brief covering letter from TJ to Robert Patterson, Monticello, 16 May 1809, stating that his "desire of answering your request by the return of the same post which brought it, & which is now in the moment of it's departure induces me to hurry the present inclosure" and adding only his regards (RC in possession of Major R. M. Patterson, Chicago, 1945, addressed: "M[r] Robert Patterson Philadelphia," stamped and postmarked, endorsed by Patterson; PoC in MHi, endorsed by TJ).

Pierre Samuel Du Pont de Nemours (1739–1817), a native of Paris who became one of the chief propagandists of the Physiocratic school of thought during the 1760s, was appointed inspector of French manufactures in 1774. By the time he met TJ in the fall of 1787, he had already made a name for himself as a writer, political economist, and public servant. Du Pont was elected to the Estates General as a member of the Third Estate from Nemours in 1789, and he held a seat in the Constituent Assembly until 1791. He fled from Paris during the Reign of Terror, returned to join the Conseil d'Anciens in

1795, and relocated in 1799 to New York City, where he established an import-export business with his sons. One year later, at TJ's request, Du Pont composed a treatise on the reform of American education. France's refusal to honor drafts drawn on his company for provisions sent to the French troops stationed on the island of Saint Domingue caused him to return to France in 1802. During his prolonged stay in Paris, Du Pont edited a multivolume edition of the writings of Anne Robert Jacques Turgot, served as a high-ranking member of the local chamber of commerce, helped to administer the distribution of aid to needy Parisians, and continued to write on a multitude of subjects. Upon hearing of Napoleon's escape from Elba early in 1815, he returned to the United States and there spent the remainder of his life (*DBF*; Ambrose Saricks, *Pierre Samuel Du Pont de Nemours* [1965]; James McLain, *The Economic Writings of Du Pont de Nemours* [1977]; Dumas Malone, ed., and Linwood Lehman, trans., *Correspondence between Thomas Jefferson and Pierre Samuel du Pont de Nemours 1798–1817* [1930]; Washington *National Intelligencer*, 15 Aug. 1817).

André Thoüin (1747–1824), botanist, served as chief gardener of the extensive Jardin des Plantes in Paris from 1764 until his death. He met TJ during the latter's years as American minister to France and subsequently sent him seeds and corresponded with him about agricultural topics, including plant cultivation and the plow moldboard. Under Thoüin, the Jardin became the Muséum d'Histoire Naturelle in 1793 and more than doubled in size. He published frequently, received seventy-two diplomas from academies and learned societies, and was active in the Société Royale d'Agriculture and Académie Royale des Sciences (*DSB*; Yvonne Letouzey, *Le Jardin des Plantes à la Croisée des chemins avec André Thouin, 1747–1824* [1989]; TJ to Thoüin, 29 Apr. 1808 [CSmH: JF-BA]).

Bartelémy Faujas de Saint-Fond (1741–1819) wrote extensively on the geology of Europe as well as on his travels to England in 1782–84. Appointed French royal commissioner for mines in 1788, he established the volcanic origin of basalt. Faujas was professor of geology at the Muséum d'Histoire Naturelle, 1793–1818 (*DBF*; *DSB*; Sowerby, no. 640).

[1] Preceding two words omitted in PoC to Faujas.
[2] RC to Thoüin: "18."
[3] PoC to Faujas: "education."
[4] PoC to Faujas: "I am not."
[5] PoC to Faujas: "assiduous."
[6] PoC to Faujas: "my friendship for."
[7] PoC to Faujas: "shew."

# From William C. C. Claiborne

DEAR SIR, New-Orleans May 17th 1809.

At the request of Colo: Liblong late an Officer in the Spanish service, and one of the most respectable and Antient Inhabitants of this City, I have the honor to enclose for your acceptance, a Tragedy in manuscript, of which the Colonel is himself the Author.—I do not know, that this production as relates to the stile & manner, possesses any peculiar merit; But when we bear in mind, that the tragical Scene which it is designed to perpetuate, was really exibited, (and of which several aged citizens can testify) I trust, the perusal will be found interesting.—

Assured, that altho' retired to the calm walks of private Life, the Interest of your beloved Country, will remain the dearest object of your heart, I take pleasure in informing you; that this Territory continues to prosper, and that the attachment of the People (particularly of the Natives of Louisiana) to the Government is becoming every Day the more sincere.—I fear however, that the misfortunes of Spain & her Colonies will give to this Territory an encrease of population, which may retard the growth of the true American Principles;—Of the French banished from Cuba, sixty have reached this City;—near 600 are supposed to have arrived at the Belize, and from 12 to 1500 more from St Yago, are daily expected. The French Consul (Mr Deforge) has also advised me, that in addition to those coming from St Yago, many families residing in & near the Havannah including several thousand Souls propose to take refuge in this Territory, and will probably arrive in the course of three or four weeks.—These unfortunate People, are for the most part destitute of pecuniary Resources, and for the means of present support must depend upon the Bounty of this Society.—It is reported to day, that the few french families who resided at Pensacola have been obliged to remove, and that the French or their descendants who are attached to the Army of Spain in the Florida's, will probably find it safe to retire from the service. In these evil Days—When the Revolutionary Spirit has approached so near, and a War of such Bitterness is raging, the issue of which must affect more or less, the whole civilized World, I greatly rejoice, that the Government should have made seasonable provision for the protection of this remote and exposed Section of the Union.—The Ordering on this Station so strong a Detachment of Troops & of Gun Boats were indeed wise measures of precaution.

Receive I pray you my best wishes—and believe me to be Dear Sir, Your grateful fellow Citizen and faithful friend

William C. C. Claiborne

RC (DLC); at foot of text: "Mr Thomas Jefferson Monticello Virginia"; endorsed by TJ as received 30 June 1809 and so recorded in SJL. Enclosure: manuscript text, not found, of Paul Louis le Blanc de Villeneufve, *La Fête du Petit Blé; ou, L'Heroisme de Poucha-Houmma, tragedie en cinq actes* (New Orleans, 1814), a play about a Houma chief who sacrificed his life for that of his son.

Claiborne wrote the next month that nearly one thousand French refugees had been BANISHED FROM CUBA (Claiborne to Julien Lalande Poydras, 4 June 1809, *Terr. Papers*, 9:843). In June 1809 New Orleans had twenty-four GUN BOATS in service, more than any other American city (*ASP, Naval Affairs*, 1:195).

## From John Minor

DEAR SIR Fredericksburg May 17th 1809

You being the only surviving Trustee, or one of the only two surviving Trustees of Bernard Moore; the Title of the purchaser of certain Lands in the County of Caroline, cannot be perfected without your signature; it is therefore that I now trouble you with a request to Execute the Deed which accompanies this Letter; my friend Mr Peter Carr will take charge of it & have it proven and certified in Albemarle Court in order to a regular Recordation in Caroline

Will you permit me my dear Sir to tender you my grateful thankes for the able and faithful manner in which you have administered the Government of Our common Country during the last Eight Years: May you long live in Health to enjoy that Peace which is the result of your own measures and prudence; is the prayer of your Affectionate Servt JOHN MINOR

RC (MHi); endorsed by TJ as received 7 July 1809 and so recorded in SJL. Enclosure: Edmund Pendleton to TJ, 15 May 1809. Other enclosure not found.

John Minor (1761–1816), a native of Caroline County, served in the Revolutionary War, studied law with George Wythe, and became a prominent attorney, residing at an estate called Hazel Hill in Fredericksburg. An occasional correspondent with TJ on legal and personal matters, Minor declined a federal appointment from him in 1803. He served as a general in the Virginia militia during the War of 1812 (Norfleet, *Saint-Mémin*, 191–2; Minor to TJ, 15 July 1803 [DLC]; Richmond *Enquirer*, 12 June 1816).

## To George Jefferson

DEAR SIR Monticello May. 18. 09.

On the subject of the trunk No 28. I am not without a hope that an interview by yourself with the drayman and Harry, the first time he goes down, may yet discover it's fate. I am anxious, not so much for the value, tho that was considerable and the assortment of paper particular, as for the instrument (Dynamometer) which it contained, the only one in America, & imported for a particular object which had not yet been fulfilled. it is well ascertained by the concurrent information of the other three boatmen who remained with the boats that but 3. trunks came to them, which were the 3. I recieved including mr Burwell's empty one. and as you saw 4. delivered the missing one must have miscarried between your warehouse & the boats. this fixes it absolutely on the drayman & Harry jointly, and an examination of them may bring the matter to light. I think it would be well to advertize the trunk, because if they disposed of the contents, their description will betray them. it may be described as 'a hair trunk of about 7. or 8. feet cubic contents, labelled on a card on the top TI. N° 28. containing principally writing paper of various qualities, but also some other articles of stationary, a pocket telescope with a brass case, a Dynamometer in steel and brass[1] or instrument for measuring the exertions of draught animals, a collection of vocabularies of the Indian languages, & some other articles not particularly noted in the memorandum taken.' make the reward what you think proper under 20. or 30. Dollars. the value was probably about 150. Dollars exclusive of the Vocabularies, which had been the labour of 30 years in collection for publication. I salute you affectionately

TH: JEFFERSON

PoC (MHi); at foot of text: "Mr Jefferson"; endorsed by TJ.

In an advertisement that ran from 30 May until 30 June 1809 in the Richmond *Enquirer*, Gibson & Jefferson offered a twenty dollar REWARD for the missing trunk, said to have been "put in charge of a negro waterman, on the 11th ult. to be carried to Milton," with the contents described just as TJ requested. The same language was used almost verbatim to describe the trunk's contents in a deposition taken after the alleged thief was apprehended (Deposition of Samuel J. Harrison, 13 July 1809, *Commonwealth v. Couch's Ned*, cause ended 25 July 1809, Richmond Hustings Court Suit Papers, Vi).

[1] Preceding four words interlined.

# To John Wyche

SIR

Monticello May 19. 09.

Your favor of March 19. came to hand but a few days ago and informs me of the establishment of the Westward mill library society, of it's general views & progress. I always hear with pleasure of institutions for the promotion of knolege among my countrymen. the people of every country are the only safe guardians of their own rights, and are the only instruments which can be used for their destruction. and certainly they would never consent to be so used were they not decieved. to avoid this they should be instructed to a certain degree. I have often thought that nothing would do more extensive good at small expence than the establishment of a small circulating library in every county to consist of a few well chosen books, to be lent to the people of the county under such regulations as would secure their safe return in due time. these should be such as would give them a general view of other history & particular view of that of their own country, a tolerable knolege of geography, the elements of Natural philosophy, of agriculture & mechanics. should your example lead to this, it will do great good.[1] having had more favorable opportunities than fall to every man's lot of becoming acquainted with the best books on such subjects as might be selected, I do not know that I can be otherwise useful to your society than by offering them any information respecting these which they might wish. my services in this way are freely at their command, & I beg leave to tender to yourself my salutations & assurances of respect. TH: JEFFERSON

PoC (DLC); at foot of text: "Mr John Wyche."

[1] TJ here canceled "perhaps."

# From Tadeusz Kosciuszko

Mai 20 [1809]

Je suis faché d'apprendre par vottre lettre la mauvaise santé d'un homme si éstimable que Mr Barnes; mais si L'ange du ciel lui apporte l'ordre de quitter Le service du monde Je ne doute pas que vous ne trouviez en Amerique ou les moeurs ne sont pas si corrompues qu'en Europe—quelqu'un qui approche de son méritte de son bon Coeur et de son honnetté.—

Je ne vois pas comment vous pouriez étre en guerre avec la France si ce n'est par lettres, manifestes ou Journeaux.—a l'egard de L'Angleterre c'est toute autre chose car vous pouriez être maitre de l'Amerique du Nord et ce qui doit arriver avec le tems.—

Ne perdez pas de vue l'Ecole Militaire pour les Jeunes gens de chaque province, afin qu'ils soyent un jour capable de guider votre Milice; quoique vous ne soyez plus en place votre motion Sera adoptée sans contre dit, car vous étes cheri de tout Le monde.—

Que le ciel vous protege pour le bienfait de L'humanité, La justice, L'exemple et Le bonheur de vos Amis aussi Sincere que moi—

T KOSCIUSZKO

EDITORS' TRANSLATION

20 May [1809]

I am sorry to learn through your letter that a man as estimable as Mr. Barnes is in poor health; but if the angel of heaven brings him orders to quit the service of this world I do not doubt that you will find in America where customs are not as corrupt as they are in Europe someone who will come close to him in merit, kindness and honesty.—

I do not see how you could be at war with France, except through letters, manifestos or newspapers.—Regarding England that is a different matter as you could be master of North America and that must happen in time.—
Do not lose sight of the Military School for young men from each province, so that they may be able some day to lead your militia; even though you are no longer in office, your proposal will be adopted without opposition, as you are beloved by everybody.—
May heaven protect you for the benefit of humanity, justice, as an example to and for the happiness of your friends who are as sincere as I am—

T Kosciuszko

RC (MHi); partially dated at foot of text; endorsed by TJ as received from Paris 3 Aug. 1809 and so recorded in SJL. Translation by Dr. Genevieve Moene. Enclosed in James Madison to TJ, 3 Aug. 1809.

Tadeusz (Thaddeus) Andrzej Bonawentura Kosciuszko (1746–1817) studied military engineering in Poland and France and traveled to America in 1776 to offer his services to the Continental army. As colonel of engineers he designed fortifications at Philadelphia, Fort Ticonderoga, Saratoga, and West Point and was promoted a brevet brigadier general as the war ended. After returning to Poland, Kosciuszko commanded an army that in 1792 unsuccessfully opposed the second partition of his country, and two years later he led the failed uprising against the Russians that bears his name. He visited the United States briefly, 1797–98, and settled into a life of exile, first in France and from 1815 in Switzerland. Kosciuszko became acquainted with TJ in Philadelphia in 1798, when he gave TJ power of attorney to manage his American assets. Their financial relationship continued in TJ's retirement, when TJ first loaned himself this money in 1809 and then repaid it in 1815 with part of the proceeds of the sale of his library (*ANB*; *DAB*; Miecislaus Haiman, *Kosciuszko in the American Revolution* [1943] and *Kosciuszko, Leader and Exile* [1946]; *PTJ*, 30:195–6, 313–5; TJ to John Barnes, 15 June 1809; *MB*, 2:1264–5, 1307).

In 1805 Kosciuszko proposed an ECOLE MILITAIRE for the young men of each state to be supervised by members of Congress (Kosciuszko to TJ, [15 Nov. 1805] [MHi]).

# From David Bailie Warden

Sir, Paris, 20 May, 1809.

I had the honor of receiving your letter, of the 25th of February, from Mr. Coles. I forwarded the packet and letter for Mr Mazzei, to Mr. Cathalan, by a safe and private conveyance. The one for Professor Blumenbach shall be transmitted to him by the first opportunity.[1]

The information you are pleased to communicate, concerning a candidate for the place I occupy, gives me much uneasiness. I have been informed that a Mr. Joseph Russel, a native of Boston has made application for it, but he, in no wise, resembles the person to whom you allude. Besides, he is a federalist, which induces me to believe that he has no chance of success. May I again pray you, Sir, to recommend me to the President. I have heard that the circumstance of my not being a native American operates against my appointment. I am bound to the united States by my principles, my feelings, and the solemnity of the oath which made me a Citizen; and I can say, with truth, that no Individual is more American than myself. I still cherish the hope, that I shall be allowed to remain in my present situation. I have now become, in some measure, acquainted with the duties of my employment, and flatter myself that my knowledge of some of the most useful living languages, my acquirements, and industry, will enable me to merit some degree of approbation.

I have the pleasure of sending, for your acceptance, twelve kinds of rice, of different countries, all cultivated at the isle of France, where these seeds were, last year, gathered—Mr. Thouin, who gave them to me, observes in his note accompanying them, that they are different in their forms, and in their qualities, which renders them susceptible of different economical uses, and especially in the greater, or less abundance of their products. This rare collection merits a careful cultivation in those countries, where rice forms an essential portion of the food of the Inhabitants.

The names, written on the different specimens of rice, are those by which they are known in the Isle of France. They ought to be sown like the common rice. They continue in preservation, for several Years, in a state of germination.[2]

I took the liberty of addressing to you, by the last Bearer of dispatches, a MS. memoir on the analysis of tobacco—I feel much flattered by your invitation to write to you, mo[re] particularly as I have long admired your character and talents, and long wished to be known to you—

I am, Sir, with the highest esteem, Your very oblig[d] Serv[t]

David Bailie Warden

RC (DLC); torn at fold; at head of text: "To the Hon[le] Thomas Jefferson"; endorsed by TJ as received 3 Aug. 1809 and so recorded in SJL. FC (MdHi: David Bailie Warden Letterbook). Enclosure: André Thoüin to Warden, 29 Apr. 1809, enclosing rice grains from Île-de-France that might be used for augmenting the agricultural resources of the United States, especially those of the South, and requesting Warden to send them to whomever will use them best (RC in DLC; in French). Enclosed in James Madison to TJ, 3 Aug. 1809.

TJ's letter of 25 Feb. 1809 to Warden (MdHi: David Bailie Warden Papers) did not mention an enclosed letter to Johann Friedrich blumenbach (not found and not recorded in SJL). TJ did inform Warden that the threat of war made it unlikely that the Senate would appoint new consuls to France or Great Britain, and that an unnamed candidate competing for the Parisian consulate was well qualified and could command a majority of the votes. Jonathan Russell, who was actually a native of Rhode Island and a Republican, was appointed secretary to the American legation at Paris in 1810 and succeeded John Armstrong as chargé d'affaires (Warden to Madison, 18 Aug. 1810, Madison, *Papers, Pres. Ser.*, 2:493–4).

[1] Sentence omitted from FC.
[2] FC ends here.

# From James Sylvanus McLean

SIR [21 May 1809]

The result of calm reflection this morning is a conviction of the impropriety of intruding myself further on your attention, & indeed of having at all attempted it; & also of the propriety of apologizing for the intrusion—Apology will be in part suggested by the inclosed, to which I propose the honour of adding personal acknowledgement at my departure—Accept my sentiments of due respect

JAMES SYLVANUS M^c^LEAN

RC (MHi); undated; at head of text: "Thomas Jefferson Esq^r^"; endorsed by TJ as received 21 May 1809 and so recorded in SJL; notation by TJ: "(written at Mont^o^)." Enclosure not found.

James Sylvanus McLean, a native of York, Pennsylvania, received a patent for an improvement in pianofortes on 27 May 1796 and wrote TJ about his ideas for using steam engines to power agricultural machinery. He apparently spent the night of 20 May 1809 at Monticello. In 1812 McLean was acquitted due to insanity in a trial for conspiracy to extort money from Stephen Girard, a wealthy merchant and philanthropist in Philadelphia. Witnesses then described McLean as educated, well read, and a talented musician, but also as a paranoiac man who claimed that he had "been educated in the family of General Washington, been ill treated by Mr. Jefferson, and had lost his fortune by col. Burr." They also reported that he was once "prevented from murdering his wife and children in a fit of madness" (*List of Patents*, 11; McLean to TJ, 30 Sept. 1802 [DLC]; *A Report of the Trial, of James Sylvanus M'Clean, alias J. Melville, and William L. Graham before the Supreme Court of Pennsylvania* [Philadelphia, 1812]; quotations on pp. 8, 18).

# From Rufus Morgan

Speedwell Iron Works Wythe County Virginia

DEAR SIR May 21^t^ 1809

Your retiring from public[1] life will I hope enable you to attend to matters of small importance, which still may leed to public utility.

I have it in contemplation to establish a Nail Manufactory, and knowing that you once carried on that business, I have taken the liberty of requesting your Idea of it. Whether it is proffitable, and if you are disposed to sell your tools and Machinery, if so, your price.

I remain Dear Sir yours with Esteem RUFUS MORGAN

RC (MHi); between dateline and salutation: "Mr Thomas Jefferson"; endorsed by TJ as received 4 June 1809 and so recorded in SJL.

Rufus Morgan (1781–1826) was born in Connecticut but settled in Virginia before moving to Roane County, Tennessee. In December 1808 he began a brief involvement with the Speedwell Iron Works as foreman under the firm of King, Trigg, & Morgan (John A. Whitman, *The Iron Industry of Wythe County from 1792* [1935], 5–7; Mary B. Kegley, *Glimpses of Wythe County, Virginia* [1986], 126; Walter H. Cunyus, "Morgan and allied families records" [1969 typescript at Vi]).

[1] Manuscript: "bublic," here and later in sentence.

# To William Brown

Dear Sir Monticello May 22. 09.

My new situation & the active occupations to which it has given occasion, must be my apology for this late acknolegement of the reciept of your favor of Oct. 10. informing me you had been so kind as to send me some articles by the schooner Sampson Capt Smith. the answer was deferred long in expectation of her arrival, and that becoming at length desperate, my removal from Washington, & the preparations for it suspended for a considerable time all correspondence which could bear delay. the concern for the loss of the articles shipped is obliterated by the deeper regret for the loss of the unfortunate persons who were in the vessel. but my sense of obligation to you for the intended kindness is the same as if it's issue had been different from what it was. I embrace this occasion too of returning you my thanks for the many attentions you have been so good as to shew on the several occasions of shipments for me[1] which have passed through your hands. mrs Trist is with us at present & well, as is Miss Harriet also. they talk of a visit to Philadelphia some time hence.

Accept the assurances of my great esteem & respect.

Th: Jefferson

PoC (DLC); at foot of text: "Mr William Brown"; endorsed by TJ.

William Brown came to New Orleans with the commission that took possession of the Louisiana Purchase. He served first as deputy collector and became collector of New Orleans in 1804 after the death of his brother-in-law Hore Browse Trist. TJ appointed him partly to help Brown support his extended family. An expensive lifestyle, disreputable friends, and his purchase of a plantation led him to financial ruin. Brown eloped with a woman and absconded from his post on 14 Nov. 1809 with approximately $90,000 of federal money. He was arrested in London in August 1810, gave up what remained of his public funds, and returned to the United States (*JEP*, 2:473, 474 [19, 20 Nov. 1804]; John M. Gelston to TJ, 1

Sept. 1804 [DNA: RG 59, LAR, 1801–09]; TJ to William C. C. Claiborne, 28 Oct. 1804 [DLC]; Joseph Saul to Albert Gallatin, 20 Nov. 1809, *ASP, Finance*, 2:395; Washington *National Intelligencer*, 22 Aug., 12 Oct. 1810; Elizabeth Trist to Catharine Wistar Bache, 24 Oct. [1810] [PPAmP: Catharine Wistar Bache Papers]).

In his FAVOR Brown informed TJ that he had placed his shipment of campeachy chairs and pecans on a vessel bound for Georgetown (Brown to TJ, 10 Oct. 1808 [DLC]). HARRIET: Harriot Brown.

[1] Preceding two words interlined.

# To Philip Freneau

DEAR SIR Monticello May 22. 09.

I subscribe with pleasure to the publication of your volumes of poems. I anticipate the same pleasure from them which the perusal of those heretofore published has given me. I have not been able to circulate the paper because I have not been from home above once or twice since my return, and because in a country situation like mine, little can be done in that way. the inhabitants of the country are mostly industrious farmers employed in active life & reading little. they rarely buy a book of whose merit they can not[1] judge by having it in their hand, & are less disposed to engage for those yet unknown to them. I am becoming like them myself in a preference of the healthy & chearful[2] emploiments without doors, to the being immured within four brick walls. but under the shade of a tree one of[3] your volumes will be a pleasant pocket companion. wishing you all possible success & happiness, I salute you with constant esteem & respect.

TH: JEFFERSON

PoC (DLC); at foot of text: "Mr Freneau"; endorsed by TJ. Tr (NjP: General Manuscripts); posthumous copy.

[1] Word interlined.
[2] Preceding two words interlined.
[3] Preceding two words interlined.

# To Cunningham Harris

SIR Monticello May 22. 09.

Your favor of March 23. requesting some Benni seed, was near a month getting to my hands. the last year I had recieved & distributed portions of the seed to many persons, but the September frost had killed the whole. this year I had got a very small supply of fresh seed, which however was all sown before I recieved your letter. Judge Johnson of your state proposes to cultivate it largely this year, as does also Gov[r] Milledge of Georgia from whom therefore it is probable you may get a supply for a beginning. I think it well worthy the attention of the gentlemen of the South. here it's success is doubtful. from a full trial of the oil I think it as good as that of the olive, and the quantity yielded at even half the price of that would render it a very profitable cultivation.

I thank you for the kind expressions of your letter respecting myself, and pray you to accept assurances of my great respect.

Th: Jefferson

PoC (DLC); at foot of text: "M[r] Harris. Harrisburg S. C."; endorsed by TJ.

Harris's favor was actually dated 27 Mar. 1809.

## To James Madison

Dear Sir Monticello May 22. 09.

It is my duty to write to you on the subject of the Note you were so kind as to endorse for me at the bank of the US. and I do it willingly altho' painfully. notwithstanding a fixed determination to take care that at the termination of my duties at Washington my pecuniary matters should at least be square, & my confidence that they would be so, I found, by an estimate made in December last, that there would be a deficit in them of several thousand dollars. I took immediate measures for transferring that debt to Virginia, and did it the more easily as I was enabled to pledge certain resources which I had in possession, or not very distant. however after this liquidation effected, other demands, which had not come under my view, came upon me, one after another, and required to answer them the amount of the Note you indorsed for me. the forms of the bank requiring two Indorsers, for an absentee, I asked of mr Barnes to be the second, which he very readily assented to, the cashier previously assuring me that it would have no effect on their transactions with mr Barnes on his private account, & so I assured him. but by a letter I have recieved from the old gentleman, I find that he is made uneasy by some circumstance in the execution of the note, which makes him liable in the first instance, were the bank, contrary to expectation, to make a sudden demand of the money. it would add much to my affliction to give him uneasy nights at his age, which obliges me to ask you to satisfy him by interposing yourself between him & the first liability to the bank, which I believe is done by your subscribing the words 'credit the drawer' instead of his doing it. he however can best say how this may be done. I might, without much delay, have relieved you from this unpleasant responsibility had I not engaged my earliest resources on my first estimate, which I then thought would discharge all demands. it is this circumstance which renders me unable to fix any time with confidence. I limit my expences here to my income here, leaving that of my Bedford estate free, which is about 2500.D. clear one year with another. but as this would take an improper course of time I am endeavoring to sell several detached parcels of land, unconnected with my possessions either here or in Bedford, & which I can spare without diminution of revenue or other inconvenience. they amount to between two & three thousand acres, & at the market prices would bring the double of these deficits. I trust that the bank, will find no interest in calling for a reimbursement before I shall have been able to avail myself of all my resources.

I had seen with much pleasure that the dispute with Pensylvania was likely to go off so smoothly; but am much mortified to see the spirit manifested by the prisoners themselves as well as by those who participated in the parade of their liberation. one circumstance in it struck my attention disagreeably, but it admitted a different explanation. I trust that[1] no section of republicans will countenance the suggestions of the Federalists that there has ever been any difference at all[2] in our political principles, or any sensible one in our views of the public interests.

After a most distressing drought of 5. or 6. weeks we had on the 18th instant a very fine rain, followed by calm & tolerably warm weather, and yesterday & last night a plentiful rain has fallen again. the coldness & backwardness of the spring however had not advanced plants sufficiently to enable the planters to avail themselves of them as seasons. I tender always to mrs Madison my affectionate respects & to your self the assurances of my constant & cordial attachment.

TH: JEFFERSON

RC (DLC: Madison Papers); addressed: "The President of the United States." PoC (DLC); endorsed by TJ.

For the LETTER received from John Barnes, see TJ to Barnes, 24 May 1809. Madison and Barnes cosigned a NOTE loaning $3,746.68 to TJ when he left Washington. An earlier or duplicate version promising to make a payment in sixty days to "James Madison and John Barnes, or order (without offset)" was left blank and canceled (MS in MHi; entirely in TJ's hand; dated 1809; see also Barnes to Madison, 21 Mar. 1809, Madison, *Papers, Pres. Ser.*, 1:70–1). The original note was replaced by another to the BANK of the United States on 24 May 1809 for sixty days (MS in MHi; in TJ's hand; signed by Barnes at foot of text with the notation: "paid by JB—23d July"; endorsed by Madison and Barnes on verso and canceled).

The DISPUTE WITH PENSYLVANIA came in the case of *Olmstead v. the Executrices of the Late David Rittenhouse*, a longstanding dispute that originated in 1778 as a prize case. The final action was Madison's 6 May 1809 pardon of eight Pennsylvania militiamen headed by General Michael Bright, who had been convicted of federal charges after obeying the order of Governor Simon Snyder to protect the daughters of David Rittenhouse against enforcement of a writ by a United States marshal (Washington *National Intelligencer*, 12 May 1809; Madison, *Papers, Pres. Ser.*, 1:102–4, 173–4; J. Thomas Scharf and Thompson Westcott, *History of Philadelphia, 1609–1884* [1884], 1:540–1).

Patrick Byrne, a printer and bookseller in Philadelphia, sent TJ an advertisement for his edition of *A Report of the Whole Trial of Gen. Michael Bright and Others; before Washington & Peters, in the Circuit Court, of the United States, in and for the district of Pennsylvania, in the Third Circuit* (Philadelphia, 1809), consisting of trial proceedings taken down by Thomas Lloyd and corrected by the judges, available for $1.50 (Byrne to TJ, 12 June 1809 [printed circular in DLC: Rare Book and Special Collections]; signed by Byrne and addressed by him to "Thomas Jefferson Monticello. V[a]"; franked and postmarked; endorsed by TJ as received 13 July 1809 and so recorded in SJL).

[1] TJ here canceled "the republic."
[2] Preceding two words interlined.

# To Thomas Ritchie

Monticello May 22. 09.

Th: Jefferson presents his friendly salutations & compliments to mr Ritchie, and observes to him that he has not recieved a single Enquirer since he came home the 15[th] of March, which makes him apprehend that some circumstance consequent on his change of residence may have occasioned the failure. he has taken for granted that mr Ritchie would call on his correspondent mr G. Jefferson annually for his subscription, which mr Jefferson has been desired annually to pay. the proper direction is to Th:J. Monticello near Milton.

PoC (MHi); dateline at foot of text: endorsed by TJ.

Thomas Ritchie (1778–1854), newspaper editor, studied law and medicine before he purchased the Richmond *Examiner* in 1804. He renamed the paper the *Enquirer* and was immediately awarded the local contract to publish federal laws by TJ. The paper flourished and Ritchie achieved a national reputation as an independent spokesman, first for the moderate Republican viewpoint of TJ, and eventually for the Democratic administrations of Andrew Jackson, Martin Van Buren, and James K. Polk. Ritchie was also a leader of the state Republican party and corresponded regularly with TJ about anonymous pieces TJ wrote and other materials he contributed to the newspaper. In 1845 Ritchie turned the paper over to one of his sons, moved to Washington, and published the *Union* there until his retirement in 1851 (*ANB*; *DAB*; Brigham, *American Newspapers*, 2:1138; Sowerby, no. 575; Richmond *Enquirer*, 4 July 1854).

## To Gideon Fitz

Dear Sir Monticello May 23. 09.

The bearer hereof is mr Isham Lewis, son of Col$^{o}$ Charles L. Lewis of Buckisland, whom you must have known while you resided in this part of the country. he is my nephew, & a young man of excellent dispositions, correct conduct, & good understanding, little aided by education. the shipwreck of the fortunes of his family leaves him without resource but in his own industry, & the defects in his education narrow his means of exertion. he has learned the common principles of surveying & therefore proposes to try himself in that line, and carries from me a letter to mr Pease, recommending him to his patronage. his capacity will enable him, with time, opportunity & practice, to attain any eminence in the higher branches of surveying which may be useful. arriving among you a stranger, I recommend him to your attentions, & pray you to take him by the hand & befriend him in the getting into emploiment. his entire want of resources will render early emploiment very important to him. any insight too which you can give him into the functions of his new vocation will be worthily bestowed on him. having his success & welfare much at heart, any service in his promotion which you can render[1] him will be considered an obligation to Dear Sir

Your friend & servt. Th: Jefferson

PoC (MHi); at foot of text: "M$^{r}$ Gideon Fitch"; endorsed by TJ.

Gideon Fitz, a native Virginian, worked as a carpenter at Monticello, 1802–03. TJ assisted with his education and in 1803 recommended him as a surveyor to Isaac Briggs, whom TJ had appointed surveyor of federal lands south of Tennessee. In 1806 Briggs appointed Fitz his deputy for the western district of Orleans Territory and sent him to manage surveying in Washington County, Mississippi Territory. Fitz's descriptions of irregularities in territorial land policy led Treasury secretary Albert Gallatin to put him on the board of land commissioners for the western district of Orleans Territory in 1810. Fitz filled similar posts thereafter and was ultimately appointed surveyor of public lands in 1831. His correspondence with TJ during the latter's retirement focused primarily on land policy and mutual engineering interests (*MB*, 2:1082; TJ to James Dinsmore, 1 Dec. 1802 [ViU: TJP]; Fitz to TJ, 31 Mar. 1803 [MHi]; Briggs to TJ, 2 May 1803 [DLC]; Fitz to TJ, 1 Nov. 1809; TJ to Gallatin, 4 Nov. 1809; *Terr. Papers*, 9:882–3; *JEP*, 4:158 [19 Feb. 1831]).

[1] Manuscript: "rendere."

## To Seth Pease

SIR                                                            Monticello May 23. 09.

I beg leave to present to your notice the bearer hereof mr Isham Lewis, a nephew of mine who proposes to become a resident of the Missisipi or Orleans territory. you will find him to be of excellent dispositions, correct in his conduct, and of a sound understanding,[1] aided only by a common education. he wishes to find employment in the business of surveying; and it is to request you to aid him in effecting this desire that I take the liberty of recommending him to your patronage. I would not do it, were he not worthy of your entire confidence, and possessing qualities which might render him useful & of value to you. he is without resources, but in his own industry; and has learnt only the common principles of surveying, having had as yet but little opportunity of practising it. but he has the capacity and the desire of advancing himself in it's higher branches, and if favored by proper opportunities, will make himself eminent. having his welfare & success much at heart, I sollicit your good offices for him, and will consider any service[2] you may be so good as to render him in the way of emploiment as done to myself; and I take this opportunity of assuring you of my great esteem & respect.

TH: JEFFERSON

PoC (MHi); at foot of text: "Seth Pease esq."; endorsed by TJ.

Seth Pease (ca. 1764–1819), surveyor and mathematician, was a native of Suffield, Connecticut, who surveyed the Western Reserve of Ohio, including the site of present-day Cleveland, the Holland Purchase in western New York, and the district of Maine during the mid-to-late 1790s. In 1806, as word spread of Aaron Burr's supposed conspiracy, Pease's brother-in-law Gideon Granger, the postmaster general, dispatched him along the route to New Orleans with the authority to replace any postal official whose loyalty could not be relied on. Perhaps partially to reward Pease for this service, TJ appointed him surveyor of public lands south of Tennessee early in 1807. He resigned this post in July 1810 to become second assistant postmaster general under Granger (Charles Whittlesey, *Early History of Cleveland, Ohio* [1867], 169, 329–30; *JEP*, 2:50, 54 [23 Feb., 2 Mar. 1807]; Madison, *Papers, Pres. Ser.*, 2:433; TJ to Granger, 9 Mar. 1814; Washington *National Intelligencer*, 6 Sept. 1819).

[1] TJ here canceled "little."

[2] Word interlined in place of "assiss."

## From William Pelham

SIR                                                            Boston May 23. 1809

On the publication of my System of Notation I took the liberty of presenting you a copy and was much gratified by your favourable acceptance of it. A Periodical work published in this town has lately presented an analysis of the work and I have had it reprinted. I beg your acceptance of a copy.

I am Sir with great respect Your very hble Serv$^{t}$

W$^{M}$ PELHAM.

RC (MHi); at foot of text: "M$^{r}$ Jefferson"; endorsed by TJ as received 1 June 1809 and so recorded in SJL. Enclosure not found.

William Pelham (1759–1827) was a native of Williamsburg who served as a surgeon during the Revolutionary War. He moved to Boston about 1800 and owned a bookstore and publishing house, ran a circulating library, and sent TJ books, including his work, *A System of Notation: Representing the Sounds of Alphabetical Characters by a New Application of the Accentual Marks in Present Use* (Boston, 1808; Sowerby, no. 1129). Pelham sold his business in 1811 and moved in succession to Newark, New Jersey; to Philadelphia, where he operated a circulating library; to Zanesville, Ohio, where he edited the *Ohio Republic*; and finally, in 1825, to New Harmony, Indiana, where he published the *New-Harmony Gazette* (Caroline Creese Pelham, "William Pelham," *WMQ*, 2d ser., 8 [1928]: 42–5; TJ to Pelham, 12 July 1808 [ViU: TJP]; Sowerby, no. 1505).

# To John Barnes

DEAR SIR Monticello May 24. 09.

On reciept of your favor of the 8$^{th}$ I determined to take the first hour of leisure to make a more scrupulous search through Genl. Kosciuzko's papers, for his 8. p$^{r}$ cent certificates; the belief that you had them, had rendered the first search less particular, which belief your last letter put an end to. entering on it a day or two ago, and unfolding every paper in his bundle, I had at length the happy sight of the certificates in a paper whose endorsement had before decieved me. in the mass of papers I had been in the habit of recieving, these had been put into an improper one, & had entirely escaped my memory. I now inclose them to you; to wit, N$^{o}$ 2. for 4000.D. N$^{o}$ 12. for 400. N$^{o}$ 13. for 100 = 4500. D to be invested in such other stock as you think best.

I also inclose your last statement of our account with an acknolegement subscribed of the balance of 866.$\frac{81}{100}$ D due & payable with interest from the date.

The principal uneasiness which my unfortunate deficit at Washington occasioned me was on account of the unpleasant responsibility under which I was obliged to lay my friends. the President was the effectual person whom I named to mr Davidson, & on his saying their forms required two endorsers for an absentee, I told him I would propose it to you on condition it should have no influence on any business you might wish to transact for yourself with that bank. he assured me it would not, & was merely to preserve their forms. if therefore the signing the words 'credit the drawer' has the effect of making you liable in the first instance, it is not understood by the President, to whom I now write on the subject, & who I am sure will conform to any form which shall be requisite to interpose himself between you and any call which might be made, so that nothing but an accident both to him & myself & a failure in both our representatives could subject you to the call. I sincerely wish it were in my power to discharge the note at once; but I had been obliged to employ all the resources in possession to reduce the deficit to what it was & those of a farmer are slow in the renewal. to aid these, I am now offering several tracts of land for sale in order to hasten the moment when I may relieve my friends as well as myself from this unpleasant situation, which will certainly be a moment of great joy to me.

I am glad to learn that your arm has got strong enough for writing & other ordinary offices. the similarity of your accident to my own, assures me you will perfectly recover it in time. wishing you as many days & years as you may wish yourself, & that they may all be enjoyed in health & happiness, I salute you with constant affection & respect. TH: JEFFERSON

PoC (DLC); at foot of text: "M[r] Barnes." Enclosures not found.

Barnes's FAVOR of 8 May 1809, not found, is recorded in SJL as received from Georgetown on 14 May 1809. While he sent Barnes the CERTIFICATES of Tadeusz Kosciuszko, TJ retained a memorandum consisting of an enumeration of the three stocks in Barnes's hand and a subjoined notation in TJ's hand that "these were delivered to me by mr Barnes for safe keeping & on the 24[th] May 1809. I returned them to him by post, to recieve the reimbursement & invest it in other stock for Gen[l] Kosciuzko" (MS in MHi; undated; endorsed by TJ). TJ wrote James Madison ON THE SUBJECT of Barnes's potential liability on 22 May 1809.

## William Dawson to Samuel Greenhow

DEAR SIR Albermarle now at Cap[t] John Harriss. May 24[th] 1809

I have had a very fatuaging Jurney, and my horse is lame, I moove on Slowly I have takun four new declarations and Seven Revaluations.

M[r] Jefferson has declared two Mills with the Miller houses. he has posponed his Monticelli Buildings until he hears from you. he wishes you to write him what you think of the Chance of being paid provided he Should be burnt out. I had a great deal of Conversation with him on the Subject which is too long to Communicate by pen Ink &c. The declarations of his, is to be held up until he hears from you, at which time Should he like your a/c he will emediatly ans[r] you, and direct them to be recorded and also advise M[r] George Jefferson (of Richmond) to pay the premiom &c you will please to advise him how he Stands with his present Buildings Insured I conceive he is in arrears for the ⅔ Quota and So I told him for he Could find nothing to Convince me that it was paid (however I may be mistaken) you know better what to Say & do therefore I Stop my pen only Saying Should there be ainy work for me in Richmond I hope my friends will wait for me, who will return as Soon as possable.

I am with due respect Your Obed[t] Ser[vt] W DAWSON

RC (Vi: Mutual Assurance Society, Incoming Correspondence); addressed: "Samuel Greenhow Esq[r] Principle Agent of the Mutual Assurence Sot[y] against fire of Virg[a] in Richmond"; endorsed by Greenhow.

William Dawson was an agent for the Mutual Assurance Society, which was incorporated by the Virginia General Assembly in 1794. Founder and first principal agent William Frederick Ast modeled it on a corporation begun by Frederick the Great in Prussia, formed to insure property against fire damage. Ast corresponded with TJ in 1793 while unsuccessfully seeking federal sponsorship of the plan, and a policy was first drawn up for TJ in 1796, but he did not pay for coverage until 1800, when some of his concerns about the policy were addressed (*PTJ*, 27:306–9, 359–60, 591–2, 29:190–1, 239–44; *DVB*, 1:233–4). REVALUATIONS of property were required every seven years or when an addition was made. Annual premiums were first introduced in 1809.

# From Claude Alexandre Ruelle

MONSIEUR, Paris le 24 Mai 1809

J'ai reçû avec la plus vive reconnaissance la lettre que vous m'avés fait l'honneur de m'écrire le 25 février dernier. Il était sans doute naturel qu'un homme qui a doublé la prospérité de son Pays, et qui est lui même un modèle de gouvernement, accüeillît un ouvrage dans lequel se trouvent ses propres principes, et je m'y étais attendu; mais le soin que vous avés bien voulû prendre de le déposer, le choix du Dépôt et la recommandation que par là vous en avés faite sont le Suffrage le plus marquant et le plus glorieux que je pûsse jamais désirer.

j'espere à présent que quelqu'un des Membres de votre Législature aura l'heureuse inspiration de faire traduire et imprimer cet ouvrage dans votre langue. sa publicité est en effet le seul moyen d'amener les changemens que l'humanité réclame et sur-tout de mettre fin à la férocité des gouvernemens Royaux.

Agréés, je vous prie, Monsieur, que je joigne mes voeux aux bénédictions de votre Pays; Rien ne m'intéressera jamais autant que de savoir que vous joüissiés dans votre Retraite de toutes les Satisfactions humainement possibles.

Je Suis avec la plus haute considération et le plus profond respect, Monsieur, Votre très humble et très obéissant serviteur

RUELLE
Rue d'Argenteüil, N° 38.

EDITORS' TRANSLATION

SIR, Paris 24 May 1809

I received with deepest appreciation the letter that you honored me by writing last February 25. It was no doubt natural that a man who has doubled the prosperity of his country, and who is himself a model of government, should welcome a work in which his own principles are to be found, and I had expected it; but the care that you so kindly took in having it recorded, the choice of the depository, and the recommendation which you thus gave it are the most distinct and most glorious endorsement I could ever have desired.

I am hoping that a member of your legislature will be so happily inspired as to have the work translated and printed in your language. Making it known to the public is in fact the only means of bringing about the changes that humanity calls for and especially of putting an end to the ferocity of royal governments.

Please, Sir, allow me to add my prayers to your country's blessings; nothing will ever interest me more than to know that you enjoy in your retirement all satisfactions humanly possible.

I am with the highest consideration and the most profound respect, Sir, your very humble and very obedient servant

RUELLE
Rue d'Argenteüil, No. 38.

RC (ViW: TC-JP); between dateline and salutation: "Ruelle, ancien Agent diplomatique; A Monsieur Jefferson, ex Président des Etats-Unis de l'Amérique"; endorsed by TJ as received 3 Aug. 1809 and so recorded in SJL. Translation by Dr. Roland H. Simon. Enclosed in James Madison to TJ, 3 Aug. 1809.

Claude Alexandre Ruelle (1781–1846), diplomat and political writer, was the French chargé d'affaires in the Netherlands in the 1790s. With his letter of 11 July 1808 (ViW: TC-JP), he sent TJ a copy of his OUVRAGE, *Constitution de la république Beninienne, ou, Modèle d'une constitution républicaine*, which TJ deposited in the Library of Congress. When the work was formally published in 1815, Ruelle sent additional copies to TJ and Madison and offered to replace copies lost during the War of 1812 (Felix Allemand, *Dictionnaire Biographique des Hautes-Alpes* [1911, repr. 1973], 411; Abraham P.

Nasatir and Gary E. Monell, *French Consuls in the United States* [1967], 351, appendix G; TJ to Ruelle, 25 Feb. 1809 [DLC]; Ruelle to James Monroe, 21 July 1817 [DNA: RG 59, MLR]).

# To the Baltimore Tammany Society

Your free & cordial salutations in my retirement, are recieved fellow citizens, with great pleasure, & the happiness of that retirement is much heightened by assurances of satisfaction with the course I have pursued in the transaction of the public affairs, & that the confidence my fellow citizens were pleased to repose in me has not been disappointed.

Great sacrifices of interest have certainly been made by our nation under the difficulties latterly forced upon us by transatlantic powers. but every candid & reflecting mind must agree with you, that while these were temporary & bloodless, they were calculated to avoid permanent subjection to foreign law & tribute, relinquishment of independant rights, & the burthens, the havoc, & desolations of war. that these will be ultimately avoided, we have now some reason to hope; & the succesful example of recalling nations to the practice of justice by peaceable appeals to their interests, will doubtless have salutary effects on our future course. as a countervail too to our short lived sacrifices, when these shall no longer be felt, we shall permanently retain the benefit they have prompted, of fabricating for our own use the materials of our own growth, heretofore carried to the workhouses of Europe, to be wrought & returned to us.

The hope you express that my successor will continue in the same system of measures, is guaranteed, as far as future circumstances will permit,[1] by his enlightened & zealous participation in them heretofore, & by the happy pacification he is now effecting for us. Your wishes for my future happiness are very thankfully felt, & returned by the sincerest desires that yourselves may experience the favors of the great dispenser of all good.

Th: Jefferson

Monticello May 25. 1809.

PoC (DLC); at head of text: "To the Tammany society of the city of Baltimore." Printed in Baltimore *American, and Commercial Daily Advertiser*, 3 June 1809 (suppl.). Recorded in SJL as "Answer to Tammany society of Baltimore."

[1] Reworked from "admit."

## From Etienne Lemaire

MONSIEUR de philadelphia le 25 may 1809

Je prend la liberty de vous adresser la presente pour vous informer la facon de faire le sirôp de vinaigre, ille feau qu'il soy fait aû vinaigre de vin rouge, où blanc, le rouge est le mellieur, ille feau que le sirop soÿ Clarifié a la Comsistance du miel, sur 12 Boutteille de sirôp, de sûcre En[1] pain—ÿ A'Joutter deux Boutteille vinaigre; ci vous avez des franboisse roûge Je comseille dont fair mesurer deux quat et les faire Écrasser et les meller dant le vinaigre le passer aû tamis fin, le l'aisez repôssez—Six heur, le tirré a Cler, et le meller dans le sirôp Chaux, aûsitôt que la decôqtions est froide la faire mêttre En boutteille

Cy monsieur a bisoint d'eautres Chôsse Je le prie dans user librement avec moÿ. Monsieur j'espaire que le presente vous trouve biens portent ainsy votre Respectable famille, J'ai Biens l'honneur dêttre votre tres humble et tres O'beisente Serviteur

STEPHEN LEMAIRE

Mon adrese francis payerne N° 96 North third Street

EDITORS' TRANSLATION

SIR Philadelphia 25 May 1809

I take the liberty in this letter to inform you how to make vinegar syrup, it can be made from red, or white wine vinegar, red is the best, the syrup must be clarified to the consistency of honey, for 12 bottles of syrup, a loaf of sugar—add two bottles of vinegar; if you have red raspberries I advise you to measure out two quarts have them crushed and mixed with the vinegar and strained through a fine sieve, let it rest six hours, decant it, and mix in the hot syrup, as soon as the decoction is cold, have it put into bottles.

Sir, if you need other things, please feel free to use me. Sir I hope this will find you and your respectable family in good health, I have the honor to be your very humble and very obedient servant

STEPHEN LEMAIRE

My address Francis Payerne No. 96 North Third Street

RC (DLC); endorsed by TJ as received 1 June 1809 and so recorded in SJL; notation by TJ: "Recipe. Syrop of Vinegar." Translation by Dr. Genevieve Moene.

SÛCRE EN PAIN (loaf-sugar) is hardened refined sugar molded in a conical shape of varying weights *(OED)*.

[1] In this word and second to last word in paragraph, apparent idiosyncratic accent mark over one of the letters is omitted.

## From Wilson Cary Nichols

My Dear Sir — Warren May 25. 1809

I have had a severe attack of the rheumatism, which has prevented my going to Washington, I am now better and I hope in four or five days to be able to set out if there is a necessity for my going. Will you do me the favour to give me your opinion as to the probability of the duration of the present session? It does not seem to me that any legislative measure wou'd now be necessary or proper as to G. B. as to France I do not know what can be done. Non intercourse or war appear to be the only measures in our power, and I presume some time will be given before war wou'd be resorted to. I sincerely congratulate you upon the prospect of an adjustment with G. B. Your enemmies seem to sicken at it, as the merit of it must be ascribed to the measures taken by you. If you have a spare copy of the Presidents speech you wou'd oblige me very much if you wou'd let me have it. It will not reach this for a week by the mail.

I am with the greatest respect & esteem your friend & hum. Serv.

W. C. Nicholas

RC (DLC); endorsed by TJ as received 25 May 1809 and so recorded in SJL.

Wilson Cary Nicholas (1761–1820), a native of Williamsburg, attended the College of William and Mary and briefly served with a Virginia volunteer unit prior to relocating to Albemarle County at the close of the Revolutionary War. He represented his adopted county in the Virginia House of Delegates for several terms during the 1780s and from 1794 to 1799. In the latter year Nicholas was elected to a seat in the United States Senate, from which he resigned in 1804 to become collector of the port of Norfolk. He served in the United States House of Representatives from March 1807 until November 1809 and as governor of Virginia from 1814 to 1816. Nicholas incurred mounting debt through land speculation and an extensive complex consisting of flour mills, warehouses, a tavern, and a distillery that he built in the town of Warren on the bank of the James River near his home estate of Mount Warren. In 1818, as president of the Richmond branch of the Second Bank of the United States, Nicholas convinced TJ, his longtime friend and political ally, to act as his security for notes totaling $20,000. The collapse of the Richmond bank and Nicholas's subsequent default on these debts caused TJ irreparable financial harm. Having lost all of his property, Nicholas moved to Tufton, the home of his daughter Jane and her husband, TJ's grandson Thomas Jefferson Randolph. Nicholas was buried at Monticello (*ANB*; *DAB*; V. Dennis Golladay, "The Nicholas Family and Albemarle County Political Leadership, 1782–1790," *MACH* 35/36 [1977/78]: 123–56; *JEP*, 1:471, 473 [12, 20 Nov. 1804]; *MB*, 2:1344, 1350, 1355, 1356).

## To Wilson Cary Nicholas

Dear Sir Monticello May 25. 09.

I am sorry to hear of your attack of rheumatism both on your own account & that of the public, as[1] I think you will have to go on as soon as you are able. I believe that immediately on the pacification with England, a vessel was dispatched to France for the Ultimatum of that government as I presume. Turreau was earnest in giving assurances that Napoleon would revoke his decrees, considering Great Britain as having retraced her steps. but as a contrary answer is possible, I suppose Congress will await the return of the vessel. if she brings a determination to continue taking our vessels on the high seas, the question of War on our part cannot but be brought on, because on his part it is all the war he can wage, and we may as well recieve the offers of[2] the Floridas & Cuba, which will probably be made to us by their inhabitants. should the republican party think we might as well make war on our part also, they will for once probably have the concurrence of the federalists. this question is too important to admit of your absence, & the importance of giving good support to the new admn is an additional reason for your going. as to the merit of the result of our measures against England, mr Madison is justly entitled to his full share of it, as he is of all the measures of my administration. our principles were the same, & we never differed sensibly in the application of them. I am glad therefore that my enemies, & hope that my friends will do him justice as to this & all our other measures. we shall be happy to see you here on your passage, being affectionately & respectfully yours Th: Jefferson

RC (ViU: TJP, photostat); at foot of text: "Mr Nicholas"; endorsed by Nicholas. PoC (DLC). Tr (ViW: TC-JP); fragment ending in second sentence.

[1] Reworked from "&."

[2] Preceding three words interlined.

## To Joseph Dougherty

Dear Joseph Monticello May 27. 09.

Your's of the 15th I have recieved, and am thankful to you for the information as to the broadtailed ram, & shall be particularly so to Dr Thornton if he can spare me one, as I have no chance of getting one in this state. mr Howard was mistaken in supposing I was sending for one. there is no such animal nearer than Washington. will you be so good as to inform me whether the one Dr Thornton is so kind as to give me is a lamb of this year or of the last. if of this year, I had better not send for him till he is weaned. if older I would send soon: & at the same time the cart might return by Dumfries, which is in the way for the geese.[1] I had desired mr Graham to retain them there till I should send for them, because it is so much nigher.

I am very much pleased indeed that you are likely to get so cleverly into the way of raising the Merino sheep. I am sure it will be a very easy business & of great profit. the fine commons of Washington will be of the same value to you as if they were all your own. the members of Congress will be a valuable market to you, & at good prices. as soon as you get the full breed, I shall be glad to get a pair of you at the prices others pay, the privilege of being the first served being a sufficient favor, & thankfully accepted as such. the sample of wool you sent was very fine. my many horned lambs of this year do not yet shew how many horns they will have. the 4. horned one of the last year is equal to his sire. I shall send him on to Gov[r] Milledge after he shall have returned home from Congress. will you enquire of mr Milligan if he returned me the Nautical almanacs he had to bind for me. if he did not he can send the one of this year by post. I do not find them here. I salute you with affection TH: JEFFERSON

PoC (DLC); at foot of text: "M[r] Joseph Dougherty"; endorsed by TJ.

[1] Preceding three words interlined.

# From Philip Freneau

SIR, Philadelphia, May 27[th] 1809.

Yesterday Your Letter, dated May 22[d] came to hand.—Perhaps You a little misunderstood me, when I wrote to You from this place in April last, inclosing the Proposal Paper, respecting the Poems.—I only wished Your name to be placed at the head of the list, and did not wish You to be at the pains of collecting subscriptions, further than as any of Your neighbours might choose to put down their names.—Indeed, the whole subscription plan was set a going without my knowledge or approbation, last winter. But, as I found the matter had gone too far to be recalled, I thought it best to submit, in the present Edition, to the course and order of things as they are and must be——Sir, if there be any thing like happiness in this our state of existence, it will be such to me, when these two little Volumes reach You in August ensuing, if the sentiments in them, under[1] the poetical Veil, amuse You but for a single hour.—This is the first Edition that I have in reality attended to, the other two having been published, in a strange way, from manuscripts left to the destiny of the winds, while I was wandering over gloomy seas, until embargoed by the necessity of the times, and now again, I fear, I am reverting to the folly of scribbling Verses.—

That Your shades of Monticello may afford You complete happiness is the wish and hope of all the worthy part of Mankind, and my own in particular. In such the philosophers of antiquity preferred to pass life, or if that was not allowed, their declining days.—

Will You be so good as to read the inclosed Verses? They were published early[2] in March last in the Trenton True American Newspaper, and in the Public Advertiser, of New York.—

I am, Sir, with all esteem, Your obedient humble servant

PHILIP FRENEAU

RC (DLC); addressed: "Hon[ble] Thomas Jefferson Monticello, Virginia"; endorsed by TJ as received 4 June 1809 and so recorded in SJL.

[1] Word interlined in place of "in."
[2] Word interlined.

ENCLOSURE

## Philip Freneau's Poem on Thomas Jefferson's Retirement

LINES

ADDRESSED TO MR. JEFFERSON,

*On his approaching Retirement from the Presidency of the United States.*

TRENTON, *N.J. February*, 1809.
FROM THE TRUE AMERICAN.

Præsenti tibi maturos largimur honores—HOR.

*To you, great Sir, our heart-felt praise we give,*
*And your ripe honours yield you—while you live.*

AT length the year, which marks his course, expires,
And JEFFERSON from public life retires;
That year, the close of years, which own his claim,
And give him all his honours,[1] all his fame.
Far in the heaven of fame I see him fly,
Safe in the realms of immortality:
On EQUAL WORTH his honoured mantle falls,
HIM, whom Columbia her true[2] patriot calls;
Him, whom we saw her codes of freedom plan,[3]
To none inferior in the ranks of man.

When to the helm of state your country called
No danger awed you and no fear appalled;
Each bosom, faithful to its country's claim,[4]

Hailed JEFFERSON, that long applauded name:
All, then, was dark, and wrongs on wrongs accrued,
Our treasures wasted,[5] and our strength subdued;
What seven[6] long years of war and blood had gained,
Was lost, abandoned, squandered, or restrained;
Britannia's tools had schemed their *easier* way,
To conquer, ruin, pillage, or betray;
Domestic traitors, with exotic, joined,
To shackle this *last refuge* of mankind;
Wars were provoked, and FRANCE was made our foe,
That George's race might govern all below,
O'er this wide world, unchecked, unbounded, reign,
Seize every clime, and subjugate the main.
All this was seen—and rising in your might,
By genius aided, you reclaimed our Right,
That RIGHT, which conquest, arms, and valour gave
To this young nation[7]—not to live a slave.
And what but toil has your long service seen?
Dark tempests gathering o'er a sky serene—
For wearied years no mines of wealth[8] can pay,
No fame, nor all the plaudits of that day,
Which now returns you to your rural shade,
The sage's heaven, for contemplation[9] made,
Who, like the ROMAN, in their country's cause
Exert their valour, or enforce its laws,
And late retiring, every wrong redressed,
Give their last days to solitude and rest.
This great reward a[10] generous nation yields—
REGRET attends you to your native fields;
Their grateful thanks for every service done,
And hope, your thorny race of care is run.
From your sage counsels what effects arise!
The vengeful[11] Briton from our waters flies;
His thundering ships no more our coasts assail,
But seize the advantage of the western gale.
Though bold and bloody, warlike, proud, and fierce,
They shun your vengeance for a MURDERED PEARCE,
And starved, dejected, on some meagre[12] shore,
Sigh for the country they shall rule no more.
Long in the councils[13] of your native land,
We saw you cool,[14] unchanged, intrepid, stand;
When the firm CONGRESS, still too firm to yield,
Stay'd masters of the long contested field,
Your wisdom aided, what their councils framed—
By you the murdering savages are[15] tamed—[16]
That INDEPENDENCE we had sworn to gain,
By you asserted (nor DECLARED in vain)
We seized, triumphant,[17] from a tyrant's throne,
And Britain tottered when the work was done.

You, when an angry *faction* vexed the age,
Rose to your place at once, and checked their rage;
The envenomed shafts of malice you defied,
And turned all projects of revolt aside:—
We saw you libelled by the *worst of men*,
While hell's red lamp hung quivering o'er his pen,
And fiends congenial, every effort try
To blast that merit which shall never die—
These had their hour, and traitors winged their flight,
To aid the screechings of distracted night.
Vain were their hopes—the poisoned darts of hell,
Glanced from your flinty shield, and harmless fell.
All this you bore—beyond it all you rose,
*Nor asked despotic laws to crush your foes.*—
Mild was your language, temperate though severe;
And not less potent than ITHURIEL'S spear
To touch the infernals in their loathsome guise,
Confound their slanders and detect their lies.
All this you braved—and now, what task remains,
But silent walks on solitary plains:
To bid the vast luxuriant harvest grow,
*The slave be happy and secured from woe*—[18]
To illume the statesmen of the times to come
With the bold[19] spirit of primeval Rome,
To taste the joys your long tried service brings,
And look, with pity, on the cares of kings:—
Whether, with NEWTON, you the heavens[20] explore,
And trace through Nature the creating power,
Or, if with morals you reform the age,
(Alike in all the patriot and the sage)
May peace, and soft repose attend you, still,
In the lone vale or on the cloud-capp'd hill,
While smiling plenty decks the abundant[21] plain,
And hails ASTREA[22] to the world again.

Printed broadside (DLC: Rare Book and Special Collections). Printed in New York *Public Advertiser*, 3 Mar. 1809, Trenton *True American*, 6 Mar. 1809, and Freneau, *A Collection of Poems on American Affairs* (New York, 1815), 2:24–7.

PRÆSENTI TIBI MATUROS LARGIMUR HONORES: "Upon you, however, while still among us, we bestow honours betimes," from Horace, *Epistles*, 2.1.15 (Horace, *Satires, Epistles and Ars Poetica*, trans. H. Rushton Fairclough, Loeb Classical Library [1970], 396–7). MURDERED PEARCE: while forcing an American merchant ship to stop and submit to search on 25 Apr. 1806, a cannon shot from the British ship *Leander* killed American seaman John Pierce just off Sandy Hook. The incident led to rioting in New York, and in the absence of a strong navy TJ issued a proclamation calling for the arrest of the *Leander's* captain, Henry Whitby, and ordering it and two other British ships out of United States territorial waters. Whitby evaded an American trial and was acquitted by a British court-martial (TJ: Proclamation regarding Henry Whitby, 3 May 1806 [DLC]; Malone, *Jefferson*, 5:114–7; Bradford Perkins, *Prologue to War: England and the United States, 1805–1812* [1961], 106–8). The touching of Satan by the Archangel ITHURIEL'S SPEAR exposed his falsehood and revealed his true form in Milton's *Paradise Lost*, 4.800–23 (Frank Allen Patterson, ed., *The Works of John Milton* [1931], 2:135).

[1] *Public Advertiser*: "merit."
[2] *Public Advertiser*: "joint."
[3] Footnote keyed to this line with asterisk in *Public Advertiser* and *True American*: "It is generally understood, that the constitution of the United States, now in force, in most of the important particulars, was the draft of Mr. Madison's pen."
[4] *Public Advertiser*: "fame."
[5] *Public Advertiser*: "lavish'd."
[6] *Public Advertiser*: "eight."
[7] *Public Advertiser*: "country."
[8] *Public Advertiser* substitutes "treasured gold" and *True American* substitutes "hoarded gold" for preceding three words.
[9] *Public Advertiser* substitutes "chiefs and patriots" for this word.
[10] *Public Advertiser*: "our."
[11] *Public Advertiser*: "angry."
[12] *Public Advertiser*: "hungry."
[13] *Public Advertiser*: "assemblies."
[14] *Public Advertiser* and *True American*: "firm."
[15] Freneau, *Collection*: "were."
[16] Preceding four lines omitted in *True American*.
[17] *Public Advertiser*: "indignant."
[18] Preceding two lines placed four lines farther down in *Public Advertiser*.
[19] *Public Advertiser* and *True American*: "firm."
[20] *True American*: "all heaven."
[21] *Public Advertiser*: "abounding."
[22] Footnote keyed to this word with dagger in *Public Advertiser*: "The goddess of justice, among the Romans."

# From William Short

DEAR SIR Paris May 27.–09

Your letter of the 8th of March was delivered to me by Mr Coles. I write this answer by precaution, as it is not certain that I shall not return with him. It will depend on the answer which Genl Armstrong will recieve from this Govt on the subject of his communications to them in consequence of the despatches by Mr Coles. Should the answer be such as to shew that it would be unadvisable for an American & improper for me[1] to remain in this country under the present circumstances, I shall make use of the Mentor as the best season & best conveyance I can expect—Genl A. expected his answer (from Germany) some days ago & is now expecting it every day—I have been writing my letters by way of precaution as he purposes sending off Mr Coles without more than one day's delay—so that I should not have time to write if I should not go—It is therefore yet uncertain whether you will learn from this letter—or from myself in person how I came to recieve at Paris your last letter.

After the proceeding of the Senate it must be considered as a fortunate circumstance that I had not arrived at St Petersburgh, under every point of view, whether it respects the two Governments or my poor individual self. But as my delay was produced by no expectation of that sort, I hope that the letters which I have written on the subject as well to yourself as to your successor, will have arrived before this & given the necessary explanations. The first occasion of writing (of which I was informed) was in March last—I then addressed M[r] Madison on the subject, considering it as certain that he was then in the chair of estate & being too much incommoded to write more than one letter This was sent via Holland.[2] On the 10[th] of April I wrote to you & on the 12[th] to him—These letters were left with Gen[l] Armstrong & sent with his despatches to Dunkirk to go by a vessel which sailed from thence—They were full both to yourself & your successor & I hope will have been satisfactory to both. Indeed the delay coming from day to day, admitted of no question at the time as to its being advisable & even necessary—& what has occurred in the Senate proves it to have been fortunate—

Count Romanzoff, the premier & the Minister with whom I was to treat at Petersburgh, being then at Paris gave me an advantage which I could have no where else of cultivating his confidence so as to lay the foundation of the work for the protection of our neutral rights—He invited this unreserved communication & indeed from all that passed—& from peculiar & unexpected marks of confidence which he shewed me in the most undisguised manner—I may say, in the most flattering manner as to me personally, & on points particularly delicate & interesting to him, I did hope that I had employed the time most advantageously for the advancement of the interests of the U.S.—I early saw that I should have need of the additional instructions (alluded to in those of Sep[r] 8[th] furnished me on my departure) as to conventional stipulations, & I feel I was not too sanguine in my belief that I should procure some points useful to my Country—honorable to the administration & to myself—& by thus attaching my name to an instrument of the kind designed to avert the evils of war from the U.S.—& to secure to them the rights of peace whilst others are warring—terminate a short residence in the manner I wished & desired, at S[t] Petersburgh—Before my preparations[3] for the journey were made & which as you know must have required expence both of time & money[4] & before I could have sat out independently of the considerations abovementioned, we had a right to expect the arrival of the succeeding[5] Aviso, as you informed me that it was the intention of Government to despatch them from six weeks to two months. The Union had sailed in the beginning of October—The next I did not doubt would sail in the beginning of Dec[r] & particularly as Cong[ress] had met in November—Not knowing how I should receive from hence the instructions expected, if I sat out before their arrival—knowing I should want them immediately on my arrival at S[t] Petersburgh—expecting the aviso to arrive every day, there could be no doubt of the propriety of waiting for them here—Day after day passed in this manner & every day that passed seemed to make it the more impossible that many more could pass without the arrival—After a certain time we heard that an armed vessel was appointed at Norfolk to come for Gen^l Armstrong—I could have no hesitation (though it gave me pain to see the time thus pass off) in waiting to see what the true state of things was in America—& what would be the additional instructions of the Government under them.   It was particularly desirable for me also to know all the circumstances relative to the embargo, so as to be able to speak fully & clearly with Count Romanzoff on it—He took a deep interest in it—had meditated a great deal on that subject—& wished for a free communication on it—I was aware that by being here on the arrival of the messenger, by conversing with him, & by seeing the newspapers (which I had no chance of getting at S^t Pet^h) I should be much better instructed as to the details—& the details which I should want, than I could be by the despatches even when they should reach[6] me in Russia, & the time & manner of which were altogether uncertain.

You at first wished me to arrive at S^t P. before the mission could be known to x—— & x——. but you will recollect the idea was renounced as impracticable so far as related[7] to both. And as to one of them the situation in which I found the negociation satisfied me there was nothing to be apprehended from that one to make me hurry—As I passed through France I was directed to make a general communication. This involved my being presented & necessarily gave then publicity to my mission. Hav[ing] a public character, & that character being of course known, it would have been without example & improper in every point of view to have gone through the country & not have been presented at Court—It would have been a marked neglect—& would have produced a peculiarly bad effect at S^t P.—As you mention that the nomination was postponed till the end of the session with a view to secrecy, I hope it will be seen that I did not unnecessarily make it public, nor sooner than was unavoidable—Indeed Gen^l A. had communicated it to C^t Romanzoff before I did, & before I had removed from him the injunction of secrecy, as was explained to M^r Madison in my letter of Nov. 29. & I believe to you in mine of Nov. 25—both by the Union.—If the present administration should have forgotten that I was to let my appointment be known on arriving here (which of course involved presentation & publicity)—I hope you will have the goodness to recall this—& in all things see that I be rectus in curia, with them & with the public in this business—I see that my turn for being gridironed also by the terrorist editors is come—The papers brought by Mr Coles are irregular—not a single regular file—I have only found one article against me—& that by Major Jackson, who says[8] the appointment was to reward a "gossipping resident"—I really know not what he means—but I see that he means to be bitter—I suppose the same disposition will exist with his compeers. From being of no party I have been & probably shall be abused by the violent of all parties—Some will consider me a monarchist—& others a jacobin. All that I wish for is the approbation of good men—& I am sure I have done nothing to forfiet that. Mr Secy Smith is civil in his letter & expresses his regrets for which I thank him—but I do not believe he is friendly to me—I have heard, & I suppose it true that his b[ro]ther the Senator, & Mr Giles were particularly active against me—I had no right to expect any[th]ing from that body, except they adopted de confiance, as I concieved they would, the person proposed by you & particularly being so long & so particularly known to you & not at all to them.

There is one circumstance in which I must ask your aid if necessary—Mr Sec. Smith in his letter on the subject of my salary or account says not a word except that he is directed to inform me that a mission like mine was not entitled to an outfit—& as to this I am perfectly[9] satisfied—But as to the quarter for return, if I should return, it would seem that would belong to every mission—for the expence of getting back must be the same—I had intended to have been most particular before my departure as to every item that was to enter into account—& if you will recollect I wrote to know. You were so good as to say Mr Madison would lay down the rule—This was not done by him until the last moment & when it was too late to ask for further explanation—In the instructions he said only that I was to recieve the ordinary allowance of a Min. Plenipo. from the time of my departure from Philadelphia—This was the 1st of Octob.—I received notice of my rejection on the 26th of April. It would certainly be very unjust that my salary were to cease before—However on reflecting that the office is supposed to expire on the 4th of March I have not chosen to make up my account beyond it, lest Mr Sec. Smith may take advantage of the claim if he should be disposed to make a merit of rejecting it—I was waiting public orders until that epoch—I was subjected to the same expenses as before, carrige here—appartments & servants &c.—I was furnished by the Dept of State with a credit of 10000. dolls on the Bankers in Holland—for some time I made use of my own funds, & did not begin to draw on this until Jany or Feby—I have not therefore been obl[iged] to draw more than 20271. fcs—not equal to 4000. dolls—& of course within the salary due to th[e] 4th of March—

I took up this money here as Gen[l] Armstrong & shall send M[r] Smith simply a note of the sums from the banker certified by him in the way he does for Gen[l] Armstrong—I shall not make out an account of U.S. D[s] to so much salary for the reasons abovementioned—& C[r] for what has been recieved—I should be very glad if you would speak to M[r] Madison when you have an opportunity—that he may give directions for having this affair settled—They must know what I am entitled to receive—I send them a certified list of what I have recieved—They can therefore want nothing more to settle the account—Pardon this trouble if you please—but I have really a great aversion to have any thing of the kind to arrange with M[r] Smith.—I wrote to him via Amsterdam to acknowlege his letter by M[r] Coles—& mentioned that I would send my acc[t] by M[r] Coles—& that the credit which had been furnished me by the department of State on Holland would remain there untouched except as had been already used for salary—Is it possible that it could have been that I should have been entitled only to salary to 4[th] of March, & no outfit nor any thing more than five month's salary, if I had gone to Petersburgh, remained until I should have heard of this decision of the Senate which might have been about this time or might have been a month later, & then had to have got back to America as I could—It is impossible that I can suppose such can be the intention of the administration notwithstanding the change—It would be absurd to suppose a Minister in the service of Government & living at his own expence—By pushing the argument thus I think it will appear that the allowance under all circumstances must be until the notification of the change.

I have taken great pains in my letter to Count Romanzoff to explain to him for the Emperor, the state of this affair—It is somewhat like talking of colors to the blind as to such people in general—but C[t] Romanzoff is much more capable & enlightened on the subject of different constitutions than the Ministers of European courts generally—& his disposition towards the U.S. & towards you particularly is all that could be asked.

The Russian Ambassador here told me when I went to explain this business to him verbally, that the Emperor had not then appointed a Minister to the U.S. on account of the difficulty of finding a person[10] of his choice & who was at the same time willing to cross the sea—I have just heard that an appointment is now made of Count Pahlen, whom I knew two years ago in America. He appeared to be a worthy & a well disposed young man.

I will say nothing to you of an improved plough which our countryman Parker has had made, & of which he intends to send you one—

M^r Coles saw it work & will be able to give you the details which really shew a great improvement in this useful instrument.

I will say nothing either of Indian camp—I know not what to say except what I said before my departure—I beg you now that you are near to take it under your care—I regret much that your system as to it was changed—Pray direct Price, so as to preserve it & that its preservation may be attended to & not revenue—I can say nothing more—Should any accident happen to Price—I beg you to let your steward direct it—or any other you may chuse—It will be lost & ruined if left to chance & common cultivation—I am willing that Lively should remain—But I had rather have no tenant than that the land should not be nursed as much as possible—And the rents will probably be less recovered now, that I am absent, than they were before—I directed Price to rent hereafter only for money—But I leave this as every thing else to you & shall be satisfied if you would now & then take the trouble wit[hin?] dictatorial powers to[11] exercise the ne quid detrimenti.

I will end this letter with asking one favor, suggested by the distance we are, the uncertainty of our meeting—& the years that have already passed since my unlimited confidence in you & your friendship for me begun—I cannot ask or expect of you to read over our voluminous correspondence—& yet there are a great many things in a great number of them particularly whilst you were Sec. of State, which being intended only for your eye, would not bear the inspection of any other—And yet that inspection must come if not prevented—There is no other certain means than destroying them now—It is impossible to separate them—& therefore the surest & best mode would be to burn all, including what I wrote during my late residence in America—Several that passed between us at different periods of my last residence there[12] were burnt at the time by us both—but there were others probably that were not burnt of mine which it would not be agreeable for me to know would be one day submitted to the inspection of any other—I ask the favor of you therefore to destroy or take measures for having them all destroyed without risk of other inspection—As to those of yours which were not burnt at the time there is not one which you could object to being seen by any of those who are to come after me—You will recollect[13] in what the difference consisted—If you have no objection I wish them all destroyed in order to secure those to which I allude, as it would be impossible to read them over & separate; & not worth the trouble—After all I suggest this wish of universal destruction leaving the decision of course to you.  I hope now that you are retired you will sometimes let me hear from you—If there is any thing in which I can serve you you know your right to command & my real gratification to obey—Should a messenger come let[14] your letter be confided to him—In all other cases to the care of the American Minister or Consul for time being—or my bankers Messr Delessert & Cie à Paris.[15] Adieu, my dear Sir,—May Heaven long[16] preserve you for your country—your friends—your family & yourself—Believe in the affectionate & invariable sentiments of

Your friend & servant Wm Short

RC (DLC); mutilated at seal; at foot of first page: "Mr Jefferson &c. &c."; endorsed by TJ as received 3 Aug. 1809 and so recorded in SJL. FC (DLC: Short Papers, 34:6184–5); abstract in Short's hand from a portion of his epistolary record containing entries from 6 June 1808 to 16 Oct. 1809, written on sheets folded to make narrow pages. Enclosed in James Madison to TJ, 3 Aug. 1809.

Short refers to letters to James Madison of 29 MARCH and 12 APRIL 1809 (Madison, *Papers, Pres. Ser.*, 1:86–7, 110–1). His instructions and letter of credence FURNISHED ME ON MY DEPARTURE were covered in Madison to Short, 8 Sept. 1808 (DNA: RG 59, DCI). John Armstrong, the American minister to France, COMMUNICATED the nature of Short's mission to Nicolas de Romanzoff soon after Short's arrival in Paris and before Short sent his two letters BY THE UNION (Armstrong to Madison, 24 Nov. 1808 [DNA: RG 59, DD, France]; Short to TJ, 25 Nov. 1808 [DLC]; Short to Madison, 29 Nov. 1808 [DNA: RG 59, DD, Russia]). TJ used the expression RECTUS IN CURIA to describe his own role in Short's mission in his 8 Mar. 1809 letter. John G. JACKSON represented Virginia in the United States House of Representatives. Secretary of State Robert SMITH wrote Short on 17 Mar. 1809 (DLC: William Short Papers) informing him of the failed appointment and explaining the administration's policy for reimbursement of expenses. Short replied from AMSTERDAM on 24 May 1809 (abstract in DLC: William Short Papers). DE CONFIANCE: "with confidence."

Short's LETTER TO COUNT ROMANZOFF was dated 1 May 1809 (RuAVPR [microfilm at DLC]). A wealthy American who had lived in France since 1787, Daniel PARKER owned more than one thousand acres and conducted agricultural experiments at Draveil, his estate on the Seine River north of Paris (C. Edward Skeen, *John Armstrong, Jr., 1758–1843* [1981], 61–2). INDIAN CAMP was Short's 1,334-acre Albemarle County estate, for which TJ collected rents from Joseph PRICE and Charles LIVELY before its purchase in 1813 by David Higginbotham, who renamed it Morven (Lay, *Architecture*, 40; *MB*, 2:944, 953, 989). NE QUID DETRIMENTI: a play on the phrase "ne quid detrimenti respublica capiat" ("that the republic is not harmed").

[1] Preceding four words interlined.
[2] Preceding five words interlined.
[3] Manuscript: "prepartions."
[4] Preceding fourteen words interlined.
[5] Word interlined in place of "second."
[6] Word interlined in place of "arrive."
[7] Reworked from "impracticable. The situation."
[8] Word interlined in place of "calls."
[9] Word interlined in place of "particularly."
[10] Word interlined in place of "proper."
[11] Preceding three words interlined in place of "vested powers to see the."
[12] Previous five words interlined.
[13] Word interlined in place of "see."
[14] Word interlined in place of "give."
[15] Preceding two words interlined.
[16] Remainder of letter written lengthwise in right margin.

## To Augustus B. Woodward

Sir Monticello May 27. 09.

I have recieved very thankfully the two copies of your pamphlet on the constitution of the US. and shall certainly read them with pleasure. I had formerly looked with great interest to the experiment which was going on in France of an executive Directory, while that of a single elective executive was under trial here. I thought the issue of them might fairly decide the question between the two modes. but the untimely fate of that establishment cut short the experiment. I have not however been satisfied whether the dissensions of that Directory (and which I fear are incident to a plurality) were not the most effective cause of the succesful usurpations which overthrew them. it is certainly one of the most interesting questions to a republican, and worthy of great consideration. I thank you for the friendly expressions of your letter towards myself personally, & the sincere happiness I enjoy here, satisfies me that nothing personal or self interested entered into my motives for continuing in the public service. the actual experiment proves to me that these were all in favor of returning to my present situation. I salute you with great esteem & respect. Th: Jefferson

PoC (DLC); at foot of text: "The honble Judge Woodward."

## To Elijah Griffiths

Dear Sir Monticello May 28. 09.

Your favor of Nov. 14. came to me in due time, but much oppressed with business then & to the end of my political term, I put it by as I did the civilities of my other[1] friends till the leisure I expected here should permit me to acknolege them without the neglect of any public duty. I am very sensible of the kindness of the sentiments expressed in your letter, & of the general indulgence with which my republican friends generally, and those of Pensylvania particularly have viewed my public proceedings. I hope I may be allowed to say that they were always directed by a single view to the best interests of our country. in the electoral election, Pensylvania really spoke in a voice of thunder to the Monarchists of our country, and while that state continues so firm, with the solid mass of republicanism to the South & West, such efforts as we have lately seen in the antirepublican portion of our country cannot ultimately affect our security. our enemies may try their cajoleries with my successor. they will find him as immoveable in his republican principles as him whom they have honored with their peculiar enmity. the late pacification with England gives us a hope of 8. years of peaceable & wise administration within which time our revenue will be liberated from debt and be free to commence that splendid course of public improvement & wise application of the public contributions of which it remains for us to set the first example. I salute you with real esteem & respect.

TH: JEFFERSON

PoC (DLC); at foot of text: "Doct^r Elijah Griffith. Phila."

Elijah Griffiths (1769–1847), a physician in Philadelphia, graduated from the University of Pennsylvania in 1804 and sent TJ a copy of his dissertation, *An Essay on Ophthalmia, or Inflammation of the Eyes* (Philadelphia, 1804; Sowerby, no. 982). He worked at the Pennsylvania Hospital and with the Board of Health, 1809–16, and in 1821 he was elected a fellow of the College of Physicians of Philadelphia. Griffiths and TJ occasionally corresponded on political matters (Robinson, *Philadelphia Directory for 1809*; Lisabeth M. Holloway, *Medical Obituaries: American Physicians' Biographical Notices in Selected Medical Journals before 1907* [1981], 186).

Griffiths's FAVOR of 14 Nov. 1808 (DLC) assured TJ that the Republican party in Pennsylvania supported the new administration.

[1] Word added in margin.

# To William Lambert

SIR Monticello May 28. 09.

Your favor of March 14. was recieved in due time. the apology for so late an acknolegement of it must be the multiplied occupations of my new situation after so long an absence from it. truth requires me to add also that after being so long chained to the writing table, I go to it with reluctance, and listen with partiality to every call from any other quarter. I have not however been the less sensible of the kind sentiments expressed in your letter nor the less thankful for them. indeed I owe infinite acknolegements to the republican portion of my fellow citizens for the indulgence with which they have viewed my proceedings generally. in the transaction of their affairs I never felt an interested motive. the large share I have enjoyed, & still enjoy, of anti-republican hatred & calumny, gives me the satisfaction of supposing that I have been some obstacle to antirepublican designs; and if truth should find it's way into history the object of their falsehoods & calumnies will render them honorable to me. with sincere wishes for your welfare & happiness I tender you the assurances of my esteem & respect. TH: JEFFERSON

PoC (DLC); at foot of text: "Mr W. Lambert."

# From Mary Ann Archbald

SIR Creekvale 29[1] May 1809

I anxiously waited for the Period of your retirement in hopes of being able to summon up courage sufficient to address you, a conciderable time has elapsed since that event & still[2] when I would make the attempt this hoped for courage seems not [to][3] arrive, Contrasting my own situation with yours the pen appears about to drop from my hand—

You have long been at the head of a great, Peacefull & prosperous[4] Nation—have been surrounded by men of talents—Your transactions have been with Princes & the great ones of the earth—how different the station & circomstances of her who now presumes to address you; bred upon one of the smallest of the British Islands where nought was visible to the eye of a stranger but the lofty Rock & dashing wave to me however the sound of waves had always been familiar & was not disagreeable many a calm evening too they were hushed in peace & the music of the birds alone was heard, many a flower also adorned the cliffs, which tho' for the most part "born to blush unseen" yet were never suffured to bloom unheaded or unenjoyed[5] in my path, in this solitary spot I would most willingly have ended my days but my husband's Lease being out & an extravagant rent demanded by the propriator we determined to cross the Atlantic with our young family & seek an asylum on the hospitable[6] shores of America, it is now two years since we landed at N. York & by the advice of an acquaintance my husband consented to settle here &[7] purchased a farm of 120 acres[8] for which he payed 3000 Dols[9] we had seen no other part of the country & were rather too hasty in making the purchase. Our sole motive for crossing the ocian[10] was to earn by honest industry a comfortable subsistance for our family, if at the same time we could in any degree Promote the wellfare of society it would be a most agreeable reflection, the only regrete I felt at my former solitude was from the idea of leaving the world without having done any good in it my sphere of usefulness being confined to the little family circle

my husband has from infancy been acustomed to the raising &

improving of Sheep in which he took pleasere & was very successfull—now what I would presume to ask is[11]

might not his talents in this way be rendered beneficial to the country—is the increase & improvement of so useful an animal not beneath the nottice of the Statesman & philosopher, if Mr Gefferson[12] should think it is not will he be so kind as favour us with his countinance & advice as to what part of the United States would be most proper for the above purpose &c. the mild regions of Kentucky (the dream of my youth) might perhaps be preferable to any other but the great distance from markets &c is against it—we would at any rate require to be a few degrees farther to the south[13] where we might expect 8 or 9 months of mild weather in the year, on the bleak mountains of Scotland where thousands[14] of sheep are reared the climate seems much less favourable than in most parts of this country & some hardy winter shrubs & plants[15] which supply the Place of grass might perhaps be introduced here with advantage such as the Broom (Scoparium) Furze &c &c but I traspas sadly on your patience[16]—if I have taken too much liberty it proceeds from my having long represented Mr Gefferson to my mind as one who wishes to increase the sum of human happiness & would regard nothing beneath his nottice which had a tendancy to Promote this great end. Already I have indulged the idea of his encouraging by his countenance & advice a family of humble Strangers & have contrasted this Picture with the aristocratic haughtiness & averice which drove from their native spot the improvers of the soil, Would you Sir but condecend to honour us with a few lines it would answere at least one good end that of banishing[17] from my husbands mind the thoughts of returning to his native country by inspiring him with the hope of employing himself more usefully & profitably here than he has hitherto been able to do. this part of the country has for me many charms notwithstanding the cold climate & colder countinances of our Dutch nieghbours, yet I confess I shoul[d] Prefer a more southerly situation & one where the ax has been rather more sparingly used where I could cultivate in my little garden some of the plants & flowers that delighted my youth with the addition of a few american natives not less attractive

After writing this I hardly know how to get it forwarded—our presuming to address you would by one Party be deemed sacrelage & by another we would be suspected of Ploting against the wellfare of the country Posterity will judge more impartially nor will it feel less respect for the memory of Mr Gefferson for his having cheered the cottage of humble industry & attended to the rural as well as

Political improvement of his country in the anxious hope of hearing from you I am honoured Sir with due Respect Your most Obed[t] Humble Serv[t] &c— MARY ANN ARCHBALD

Our letters are adressed to M[rs] James Archbald Creekvale moungomery County State of New York care of M[r] John Ried Merch[t] Albany

RC (MHi); second sheet torn at fold; endorsed by TJ as a letter of 22 May 1809 received 16 June 1809 and so recorded in SJL. FC (MNS-SS: Lb in Mary Ann Wodrow Archbald Papers); entirely in Archbald's hand; undated; at head of text: "M G——."

Mary Ann Wodrow Archbald (1762–1840) immigrated to Montgomery County, New York, from Little Cumbrae Island, Scotland, with her husband James Archbald and a FAMILY of four children in 1807. Archbald's half-brother Andrew Wodrow Romney had settled in Hampshire County (now West Virginia), perhaps influencing her to consider moving to Virginia and continue raising sheep and cattle there. For this purpose she claimed to "have opened a correspondance with some of the great men about the rearing & improvement of sheep a thing greatly wanted in this country." Although TJ did not respond to her inquiries, Archbald received a response from George Washington Parke Custis that she summarized as "diswading us from settling in any of the southern states." The Archbalds remained in New York (Archbald to Margaret Wodrow, 20 June 1809, and Archbald to Custis, [1809] [MNS-SS, Lb in Archbald Papers]; David A. Gerber, "Ethnic Identification and the Project of Individual Identity: The Life of Mary Ann Wodrow Archbald [1768–1840] of Little Cumbrae Island Scotland and Auriesville, New York," *Immigrants & Minorities* 17 [1998]: 1–22).

BORN TO BLUSH UNSEEN is quoted from Thomas Gray, "Elegy Written in a Country Churchyard," line 55 (Roger Lonsdale, ed., *The Poems of Thomas Gray, William Collins, Oliver Goldsmith* [1969], 127).

[1] Reworked from "22."

[2] FC substitutes "but now" for preceding ten words.

[3] Omitted word supplied from FC.

[4] RC: "properous." FC: "prosperous."

[5] Preceding two words omitted in FC.

[6] RC: "hospitab." FC: "hospitable."

[7] From "it is now" to this point is replaced in FC by "by the advice of an acquaintance we came up here & my husband."

[8] FC: "a small farm."

[9] Remainder of sentence omitted in FC.

[10] FC: "motive in coming to this country."

[11] FC substitutes "Pray sir" for preceding eight words.

[12] Here and on two later occasions, FC reads "G—."

[13] FC: "farther south in a climate."

[14] RC: "thousans." FC: "thousands."

[15] Preceding two words interlined.

[16] FC: "some hard winter plants might be introduced with advantage."

[17] FC: "lines it might banish."

# From Samuel Greenhow

SIR Richmond 29[th] May 1809.

I received this evening a letter from M[r] W[m] Dawson, who has long acted as a Special Agent of the M. A. Society; in that Character, he has obtained[1] two declarations for Assurance from you, which, he tells me, you have directed him to with-hold, until I shall inform you, what is the probability of payment, in case of Loss by fire, and You, having received & reflected on that Information, shall direct their disposition.—

I therefore now address this Letter to you, containing such Information as I presume to be of the description required.

The present State of the Institution furnishes no very Strong Inducements to the house owners of Virginia to become Members.—The sum insured in the Country amounts to about two & a half millions of Dollars—The funds in hand are nothing; there is due to the Country part of the Association about $44,000.—It owes about $12,000.—It's annual Expences are about $2,500—The averaged Losses & Expences of The Country, from the 1st March 1804 until 1st March 1809 appear to have been about $9          per Annum—But, in this year, the Losses alone have already amounted to $9,000.—

A late General Meeting, satisfied that the Original plan of raising a fund from original præmiums, which would either by its Interest, or Its Interest united with the principal, produce a safe and permanent Assurance could not succeed, resolved, that, the Members of the Country Association, should annualy, after the lapse of the year in which they shall have paid their originial præmiums, pay One Seventh part of the Original præmium—This Seventh will produce, on the sum assured at this time, about $10,500, and after deducting the expence of collection would amount to about $9,700, allowing 7½ PrCt for collection, this somewhat exceeds the average of Losses & Expences for the five years mentioned above—But, the excess is not sufficiently large, I ventured to suggest a sixth in lieu of the seventh, but it was instantly rejected.—

If however it should be admitted, that, the Annual contribution is probably adequate to defraying the expences & payment of Losses.—I do not think that the Institution can flourish, except some other mode of collecting what is due to it, than that, at present in Use, should be adopted.—It is prudent to distribute our risks as much as possible—in doing so, we take in a number of small buildings owned by the poor, their præmiums are very small, and their annual contributions will not[2] in many Instances exceed $2.—Altho' these people might not be able always to pay such a sum immediately, yet, if there was a Collector in each County they would find it easy to pay in the Course of a few months, and the Receiver being at hand, the money would be paid—But, we can not get Collectors who will undertake the business, as the Commissions would not remunerate them; The course pursued has therefore been, to place the claims in the hands of a Lawyer, he gives notice of an intended motion, and before the poor man can raise the money to pay, he finds his debt of $2. increased to $7. by Costs of Suit—

There are other Objections to this mode of Collection.—The time of the Principal agent is greatly engrossed by correspondence with Lawyers at a distance—It was a heavy burden on him when the District Courts were in Operation, but it is greatly increased since the new Organization of the Superior Courts of Law—The Society is subjected to Costs in some Instances, from informality, or other causes—The quibbles of Lawyers can not be anticipated by the P. Agent, hence the Counsel for the Society is not always provided with proper documents.—Lawyers neglect to act upon Judgements, & they run out of date—Sheriffs receive the money & fail to pay it over—These are some of the Evils resulting from the present mode of Collection—But, the Greatest is, that the money is not collected—The Institution can not prosper without Credit—It can not aquire Credit, without punctuallity—It can not be punctual—If it has not the means of enforcing its claims instantly.—

To remedy this evil, an expedient was proposed and adopted at the last General Meeting—It was this—That, the claims of the Institution should annually be placed in the hands of the Sheriffs who should collect in the same manner, receive the same commissions, account at the same time—, and be liable in the same way, as they are for public tax.—The consent of the Legislative body was necessary to the effectual Operation of this Resolution, which would have been obtained, if a single Vote had been given for it, which was given against it. It was lost by one vote only.

If this mode of collection had been given to us, I should have entertained strong & I think well grounded hopes of the final Success of the Institution—I hope that it will yet be permitted—the refusal however in the last Session, will subject us to very considerable Inconvenience, inasmuch as it will delay our Collections considerably.—

Without this, or some other mode of obtaining our money speedily & certainly, I confess I do not perceive how we are to pay losses—A mere nominal Capital dispersed through the State, in a thousand hands will not answer.—

But, I would not yet abandon the Institution, I think it a valuable one—It is certainly calculated to procure much benefit, by a very small tax on the house-owners of Virginia—It has proved to be a very cheap Insurance—The whole sum paid and due for Losses & expences both in Towns and Country, was equal to an averaged annual rate of præmium not exceeding 50 Cents on the hundred dollars Insured, down to Jan^y^ last.—I think that $\frac{4}{5}$ths of the buildings are built of Wood—This is less than a third of the rate of Insurance paid in the London Phœnix Office on buildings in Virginia, taking the same proportion of Wooden houses.—

If the Institution should now be abandoned, It would not be possible to restore it; or to create one founded[3] on similar principles.—If the Institution is in itself a good, It's misfortunes heretofore, & its consequent present depressed State, are not sufficient reasons for relinquishing it.—If they are so, there certainly was a period, when there were very sufficient reasons for ceasing to struggle in the Revolutionary cause of the United States—when submission to a foreign despot, would have been more correct, than a firm adherence to the cause of Liberty:—There is also propriety in abandoning a Virtuous man in Adversity;—But, there never was a time when Virginia was disposed to abandon her claim to Independence however gloomy the prospect of immediate Success.—neither can there be a time in which, it would be proper to abandon the Institution of Mutual Assurance, if it be really good—if its effects may be useful.—Is it then useful?—Is that Institution likely to be useful, which proposes the creation of a Joint Stock, to be used in providing a Shelter for the unfortunate?—which proposes to restore the house of an Unfortunate Sufferer, by a trivial contribution of many?—Which unites two opposite & conflicting Sentiments, Benevolence & Self interest, and causes them to co-operate for the attainment of the same Object?—Does it tend to increase the happiness of Man, that, his Selfish passions should be enlisted in the cause of philanthropy—And, that, the great principles of Christian Charity should be carried into actual practise—Can it contribute to the well being of Man in Society, that an Institution should exist, which induces the Sordid money-lover to contribute his mite toward the relief of the wretched houseless Widow or old man?—

These are the effects to flow from the Success of this Institution—They doubtless tend to the happiness of Man—It is[4] then Useful—But, if each individual, fearful, that, others may not follow this Example, Shrinks from the undertaking—holds back until some more bold adventurers shall have made the thing certain—how is it possible to attain Success.—The path however is not untrodden—fifteen hundred persons have already entered on it—Some have turned back, but they are only a few—of that Number of those who have continued to be Members of the Society. You Sir are one—I think it merits the patronage of every good Citizen—I believe it will be benefited by your patronage—And as its Official Advocate, I solicit that patronage What, I might say or have said unofficially, the principles & Object of the Institution will urge more forceably, than I can.—

As something has lately been said, in the Style of complaint, of the Salary of the principal Agent, It may not be unnecessary to mention the amount of Salary paid to this Officer—It is $1500 P^r^ Annum—I think it also proper to mention to you, that, one Stephen C. Rozell, a delegate from Loudoun to the Virginia Assembly, has excited great discontent in that County, by Misrepresentations relative to the M.A. Society, which in truth, he knows nothing of; and I doubt whether he has Capacity to comprehend it's Utility &c &c—Yet, such has been the Effect of his Statements as to lead a large number of the Insurers in his County, to speak of an Attempt to Abolish the Institution—When called on for Information, I think it right to communicate this.—I trust however, that, the Explanations which I have given to two or three respectable Men, will tend to place the Institution on a better footing in that County, than heretofore. My reports to these Gentlemen will be presented to a Meeting of the Insurers to be held on next Monday.—And I shall be supplied with information of the result—A Serious attempt at Abolition, made even by a minority, will succeed, I think; because the friends of the Institution are not Zealous—and because, at present, it has not that commanding Attitude which is derived from full Coffers, and consequent popularity with the Rich.—

I have endeavored Sir to give you a true state of the Institution as it relates to the Country part of the Association.—I have mixed with it, many, perhaps impertinent remarks—And the whole has of necessity been given in great haste—If you should require farther Information, Your Application shall be promptly attended to, by

Yrs with great respect. SAMUEL GREENHOW.

RC (DLC); at head of text: "Albemarle. Mr Thomas Jefferson Monticello"; endorsed by TJ as received 5 June 1809 and so recorded in SJL.

Samuel Greenhow (1771–1815), a merchant in Richmond, sat on the Richmond City Council and later served in the War of 1812. He succeeded founder William F. Ast as principal agent of the Mutual Assurance Society and held the position from 1808 until his death (Valentine Museum, *Richmond Portraits . . . 1737–1860* [1949], 83; Richard Love, *Founded upon Benevolence: A Bicentennial History of the Mutual Assurance Society of Virginia* [1994], 11; Richmond *Enquirer*, 18 Feb. 1815).

The LETTER from William DAWSON to Greenhow, 26 May 1809 (Vi: Mutual Assurance Society, Incoming Correspondence), repeated much of the information on TJ's position given in an earlier letter (see Dawson to Greenhow, 24 May 1809).

The Mutual Assurance Society required an initial capitalization of three million dollars from its members, delaying its full operation for a year after its incorporation in 1794. In 1805 the society divided its business between a town branch and properties INSURED IN THE COUNTRY because fewer rural than urban buildings were damaged by fire. The two divisions operated separately with their own agents, policies, and accounts, posing a challenge to the society's collectors in the country, where homes were far apart and farmers short of cash. The society stopped issuing country policies in 1818 and eliminated the country branch altogether in 1821 (Love, *Founded upon Benevolence*, 10–1, 30).

A bill about the Mutual Assurance Society introduced in the General Assembly on 11 Feb. 1809 included a section allowing SHERIFFS to collect premiums in the same manner as auditors of public accounts. The bill passed only after the removal of this section (*JHD*, 1808–09 sess., 119–20, 121 [11, 13 Feb. 1809]).

[1] Manuscript: "obtoained."
[2] Word interlined.
[3] Word interlined.
[4] Preceding two words interlined in place of "They are."

# From Thomas Jefferson Randolph

DEAR GRANDFATHER May 29 1809 Museum Philedelphia[1]

I recieved your letter of the 5th about the 20th. Mr Lemaire had sent the Articles which you wrought for before; I have got phials & hair powder; chain I have sent to New york for, there being none here;[2] corks, I have not been able to get, as yet of that size; I paid Mr Lemaire, as you will see by his receipt, which, however,[3] he sent before I could find him out.

You desire to hear from me oftener; I have written three times, this making the fourth, & have received one letter 50 days after I left you. My mother Father & yourself who are so much occupied, I could hardly expect to hear from; Mr Bankhead I suppose is so studious; he can think of nothing else but Blackstone; Sister Ann, & Ellen, particularly are so fond darning stockings, that I could not expect to hear from them

Yours affectionately THOS J, RANDOLPH

P S I shall leave this place in four weeks

N B Dr Barton has informed me the Lectures end the 12th of June

RC (ViU: TJP-ER); endorsed by TJ as received 25 June 1809.

TJ's LETTER OF THE 5TH was actually dated 6 May 1809. Charles L. BANKHEAD read law under TJ, his father-in-law, for several years (TJ to Ann C. Bankhead, 8 Nov. 1808 [MHi]; TJ to Thomas Jefferson Randolph, 24 Nov. 1808 [DLC]).

[1] Manuscript: "Phledelphia."
[2] Manuscript: "her."
[3] Randolph here canceled "I paid him."

## From George Jefferson

Dear Sir Richmond 30th May 1809

I send you by Mr Randolph's boat two boxes which we have lately received.—There is some nail rod & bar iron which I had reserved, but Ben cannot carry it.—If you find you will require it before Mr R's boats will be down again, be pleased to inform me, that I may forward it by others.

I am Dear Sir Yr Very humble servt Geo. Jefferson

RC (MHi); endorsed by TJ as received 4 June 1809 and so recorded in SJL.

George Jefferson oversaw delivery of the NAIL ROD & BAR IRON early in July, when eighty bundles of nail rod and sixteen bars of iron—one bar more than was on the bill of lading received from Philadelphia—were consigned to John Priddy for delivery to TJ at Milton (Receipt from Priddy to Gibson & Jefferson, Richmond, 3 July 1809 [Dupl in MHi; in George Jefferson's hand, signed by Priddy; above signature: "(duplicate)"; with subjoined clarification initialed by George Jefferson; addressed: "Thomas Jefferson esqr Monticello"; endorsed by TJ as from George Jefferson]; this document or a missing covering letter of this date from George Jefferson is recorded in SJL as received from Richmond on 13 July 1809).

## From James Madison

Dear Sir Washington May 30. 1809

Your favor of the 22d did not come to hand till the day before yesterday. It will give me pleasure to take the place of Mr Barnes in the note to the Bank; the more so as it will, it seems, be a relief to the Old Gentleman's pecuniary anxieties. I will have an early communication with him on the subject. I wish the original arrangement had taken the shape now proposed, and hope that you will make free use of my services if they can at any time or in any way be made convenient to your arrangements of money or other matters.

The newfangled policy of the federal party, you will have noticed, has made a considerable figure in the Newspapers. Some of the Editors are resuming the Old cant, and the others will doubtless soon follow the example. Nothing could exceed the folly of supposing that the principles & opinions manifested in our foreign discussions, were not, in the main at least, common to us; unless it be the folly of supposing that such shallow hypocrisy could deceive any one. The truth is, the sudden & unlooked for turn of the B. Cabinet, has thrown the party entirely off the Center. They have at present no settled plan. There is reason to believe that the leaders are soured[1] towards England, and much less disposed than heretofore to render our interests subservient to hers. Expressions have been used by one at least of the Essex Cabinet, whether sincerely or insidiously may not be absolutely certain, from which it is inferred that a disposition exists in that quarter not even to continue the non-intercourse Act ag$^{st}$ France. Certain it is, that the desire of war with her is no longer manifested; that the deficiency of the English markets, excites a keen appetite for a trade with the Continent; and that a real uneasiness is felt lest the negociations with G.B. should end in sacrifices on our part, which they have been reproaching the Administration for not being ready to make. As one proof of their present feelings, the federal leaders shew a marked alienation from Erskine. The Elections in Mass$^{ts}$ as well as in N.H. & N.Y. have issued unfavorably. But the smallness of the majority, and the overstrained exertions it has required, seem to depress rather than flatter the successful party. No confidence is felt in the permanency of the triumph.

Not a line has been rec$^{d}$ of late from any of our foreign Agents. All that is known is therefore to be gathered from the ordinary and fallacious channels.

Accept my sincerest respects & attachment

James Madison

RC (DLC: Madison Papers); endorsed by TJ as received 1 June 1809 and so recorded in SJL.

The essex cabinet, or Essex Junto, was a predominantly Federalist group of merchants and lawyers, many of whom came from Essex County, Massachusetts.

[1] Manuscript: "souered."

## From Antoine François Tardieu

Monsieur 30 Mai 1809.

Je vous remercie beaucoup de la carte du Haut Mississipi que vous m'avez fait remettre par Monsieur Coles, ainsi que de celle de la Louisiane du capitaine Louis dont vous voulez bien me promettre un exemplaire. Je ferai ces changemens Sur ma carte avant que d'en faire imprimer de nouveau et cela y ajoutera un interet de plus encore. Je joints à cette lettre une Carte Marine de la Mediterrannée en quatre feuilles, que je viens de graver d'après les dessins de Messieurs Rizzi-Zannoni et Lapie; elle est grande et fort exacte. Les planches de cette carte ne m'appartiennent point, mais comme il me revient toujours une douzaine d'épreuves de mes ouvrages par droit de graveur, Je vous prie de vouloir bien accepter cet exemplaire comme un témoignage de la haute estime et Considération avec lesquelles j'ai l'honneur d'être, Monsieur,

Votre dévoué Serviteur TARDIEU

EDITORS' TRANSLATION

SIR 30 May 1809.

I thank you very much for the map of the Upper Mississippi that you had Mr. Coles deliver to me, as well as for Captain Louis's Louisiana, a copy of which you are kind enough to promise me. I will make these changes on my map before printing it anew and this will make it more interesting yet. I enclose with this letter a maritime map of the Mediterranean in four sheets, that I have just engraved from the drawings of Messieurs Rizzi Zannoni and Lapie; it is large and quite exact. The plates of this map do not belong to me, but since by engraver's rights a dozen proofs of my work are mine to keep, I pray that you will accept this copy as a testimony of the high esteem and consideration with which I have the honor to be, Sir,

Your devoted servant TARDIEU

RC (DLC); at head of text: "P. F. Tardieu, graveur géographe, place de l'Estrapade N° 1 à Paris, à monsieur T. Jefferson Ex Président des Etats Unis"; endorsed by TJ as received 3 Aug. 1809 and so recorded in SJL. Translation by Dr. Roland H. Simon. Enclosure: Giovanni Antonio Rizzi Zannoni and Pierre Lapie, *Carte réduite de la Mer Méditerranée et de la mer Noire. Incisione su rame di Pierre Antoine Francois Tardieu* (Paris, 1808). Enclosed in James Madison to TJ, 3 Aug. 1809.

Antoine François Tardieu (1757–1822), geographer and map engraver, belonged to a family of eminent French engravers. He exchanged maps with TJ on this and a previous occasion. TJ sent a copy of Meriwether Lewis's map of LOUISIANE from which Tardieu revised his *Carte des États Unis* of 1802 (Tardieu to TJ, 26 Aug. 1808 [MoSHi: TJP]; Sowerby, no. 3845; Roger Portalis and Henri Béralid, *Les Graveurs du Dix-Huitième Siècle* [1880–82, repr. 1970], 3:581, 587).

# From Lacépède

MONSIEUR le 31 mai, 1809

je saisis avec bien de l'empressement, une nouvelle occasion de vous remercier de la lettre honorable que vous avez bien voulu m'adresser le 14. juillet dernier. l'un des secrétaires perpétuels de la première classe de l'institut, a du vous exprimer, Monsieur, combien tous mes confrères ont été flattés de recevoir de leur illustre associé, une marque de souvenir, et une collection précieuse pour le progrès des sciences naturelles. il a du avoir l'honneur de vous adresser a même temps, le rapport que la première classe de l'institut a cru devoir adopter, au sujet des objets qui composoient cette belle collection, et qui déposé maintenant dans les galeries du muséum d'histoire naturelle, y seront un monument durable de votre bienfait, et de notre reconnoissance. je recevrai avec bien de la gratitude, et je lirai avec bien de l'intéret, l'important ouvrage que M. le gouverneur lewis faisoit imprimer pour donner l'histoire du grand et curieux voyage exécuté par lui et par M. le g[al] clarke, d'après vos vues et sous votre direction. j'attendrai de l'avoir étudié, avant de terminer l'histoire de l'espèce humaine, à laquelle je travaille depuis trente ans, et dont je m'empresserai de vous faire hommage d'un exemplaire, si vous voulez bien le permettre. Mon sommeil n'étant ordinairement que d'une heure et demie, ou environ, je puis malgré le grand nombre d'heures que je suis obligé de donner aux affaires publiques, m'occuper tous les jours, de mes études favorites, depuis une heure après minuit, jusques à nœuf heures.

Vous, Monsieur, qui vous êtes recommandé à la postérité, d'une manière si distinguée, non seulement comme homme d'état, mais encore comme savant, vous allez jouir dans votre honorable retraite, de votre gloire, de l'affection de vos concitoyens, de tout le bien que vous avez fait à votre patrie, d'un loisir que les sciences réclameront. puissiez vous, lorsque vous serez amené par le cours de vos travaux, à vous occuper de vos confrères de france, penser que personne n'a pour vous plus d'attachement, dévouement, de haute considération et de respect que moi! B. G. E[T] L C[TE] DE LACEPÈDE

P.S. aurez vous la bonté de faire remettre à l'ambassadeur de france, le paquet que je prends la liberté de mettre sous votre paquet, à fin qu'il lui parvienne plus surement? Ce paquet contient des papiers de famille très intéressants pour une des dames de première classe de la maison impériale napoléon établie à écouen, pour l'éducation des filles des membres de la légion d'honneur.

EDITORS' TRANSLATION

SIR 31 May, 1809

I seize with great eagerness, a new chance to thank you for the honorable letter that you were kind enough to send me last 14 July. One of the perpetual secretaries of the first class of the Institut must have expressed to you, Sir, how flattered all my fellow members were to receive from their illustrious honorary member, a mark of remembrance, and a collection valuable to the progress of the natural sciences. He must have had the honor to send to you at the same time the report that the first class of the Institut believed it should adopt, regarding the objects which compose this fine collection, and now deposited in the galleries of the natural history museum, which will constitute there a lasting monument of your kindness, and our recognition of it. I will receive with much gratitude, and read with much interest the important work that Governor Lewis had printed to relate the story of the long and curious trip taken by him and by General Clark, according to your views and under your guidance. I will wait until I have studied it, before finishing the history of the human species, on which I have been working for thirty years, and of which I will eagerly offer you a copy, if you are kind enough to allow it. My sleep ordinarily lasting only about an hour and a half, I am able despite the great number of hours that I am obliged to give to public affairs, to devote time every day to my favorite studies, from one in the morning until nine.

You, Sir, who have recommended yourself to posterity in such a distinguished manner, not only as a statesman, but also as a scholar, will enjoy in your honorable retirement, your glory, the affection of your fellow citizens, all the good that you have bestowed on your fatherland, a leisure that the sciences will reclaim from you. Please remember, when your work leads you to deal with your fellow members in France, that no one has for you more attachment, devotion, high consideration and respect than I do!

B. G. E[T] L C[TE] DE LACEPÈDE

P.S. would you be kind enough to have delivered to the ambassador of France, the parcel that I am taking the liberty to put under cover of your parcel, so that it will be delivered to him more surely? This parcel contains family papers of great interest to one of the highest-ranking ladies in Napoleon's imperial household in residence at Écouen, for the education of the daughters of members of the légion d'honneur.

RC (NNPM); dateline between signature and postscript; endorsed by TJ as received 3 Aug. 1809 and so recorded in SJL. Translation by Dr. Genevieve Moene. Enclosure not found. Enclosed in James Madison to TJ, 3 Aug. 1809.

Bernard Germain Étienne de La Ville-Sur-Illon, comte de Lacépède (1756–1825), French zoologist and writer, was a protégé and associate of Georges Louis Leclerc, comte de Buffon. He sent copies of some of his extensive writings on quadrupeds, reptiles, and fish to TJ, with whom he had been acquainted since the 1780s. Lacépède served in both the Constituent and National Assemblies during the French Revolution. In 1794 he accepted the chair of zoology at the Muséum d'Histoire Naturelle, and two years later he joined the Institut de France. Under Napoleon, Lacépède was named a senator and in 1803 a grand chancellor of the légion d'honneur. He wrote about political subjects later in life (*DBF*; *DSB*; *PTJ*, 12:287–8; Sowerby, nos. 1029, 1044, 1050; David Bailie Warden to TJ, 2 Sept. 1808 [DLC]).

TJ to Lacépède, 14 July 1808 [DLC], inventoried the mastodon bones that TJ sent to the Institut de France (see TJ to Caspar Wistar, 31 Mar. 1809). Lacépède's work on L'ESPÈCE HUMAINE, *Histoire naturelle de l'homme* (Paris, 1827), grew out of his collaboration with Georges Cuvier. The lady DE LA MAISON IMPÉRIALE NAPOLÉON was probably Jeanne Louise Henriette Campan, a confidante of Marie Antoinette and teacher of Napoleon's stepdaughter Hortense and his sister Caroline, whom she taught at her imperial academy at ÉCOUEN (Louis Bonneville de Marsangy, *Mme Campan à Écouen* [1879]).

## From Bishop James Madison

My dear Sir, Williamsburg May 31. 1809.

Mr Wm Rives, the Son of Mr Rives of Nelson County, will present this to you. He has lately been obliged to[1] leave College, on Acct of his yielding to that false notion of Honour, which is, unfortunately, so prevalent. The Sentence of the College was unavoidable, tho pass'd with sincere Regret; & I take a particular Pleasure in giving you the full assurances, that I believe him to be not only,[2] a Youth of the best Disposition, & of Manners always polite & engaging; but also, that he has been richly gifted by nature with a fine Genius, & with that mental Energy, which merits the highest Cultivation. His Father, as well as himself, is anxious that the Expulsion should not operate against him, in your Decision with Respect to a Proposition, which will be submitted[3] to you; &, therefore, it is; that I have made this Representation. I feel, also, a warm Interest in his future Welfare; & am persuaded, that under your Auspices, we may expect that he will become one of the Ornaments of his Country.

I congratulate you, most heartily, on the full, unanswerable Demonstration, which late Events have given of the Wisdom & sound Policy of the Measures of your Administration, with Respect to our foreign Relations. One Triumph only is wanting; & that, I think, is even now at our very Doors. The French Emperor, if consistent, must also abrogate his injurious decrees. We shall then[4] hear what those will say, who are so emphatically styled—"their Friends"—by British Orators. But really, we appear to have intermingled with our social Connections such a mass of Corruption, that it may be doubted whether a sufficient Anteseptic can be found to counteract its putrid Tendency.

With the sincerest Sentiments of Respect & Esteem, I am, Dr Sir
Yr Friend & St J Madison

RC (DLC); endorsed by TJ as received 28 June 1809 and so recorded in SJL.

James Madison (1749–1812), president of the College of William and Mary, 1777–1812, and first bishop of the Protestant Episcopal Church in Virginia, 1790–1812, was a cousin of the United States president of that name. In 1772 Madison received one of the first A.B. degrees awarded by William and Mary, and the following year he joined its faculty, where he taught natural philosophy and mathematics and took an active interest in the welfare of his students. He corresponded regularly with TJ on scientific topics and geography and did the survey work for *A Map of Virginia Formed from Actual Surveys* (Richmond, 1807) (*ANB*; *DAB*; Richard W. Stephenson and Marianne M. McKee, eds., *Virginia in Maps: Four Centuries of Settlement, Growth, and Development* [2000], 120–1, 139–45).

[1] Madison here canceled "quit."

[2] Preceding two words interlined, with editorial correction of caret misplaced one word to the right.

[3] Word interlined in place of "made."

[4] Word interlined.

# To Philip Tabb

DEAR SIR Monticello June 1. 09

Your favor of Apr. 7. has been duly recieved, with the copy of that of January. on reading the first paragraph of it respecting the nuts, I was confident I had recieved it, as I had forwarded the nuts on to a friend in Philadelphia. on searching my letter bundles, I accordingly found that of January recieved on the 27th of that month. yet when Capt Decatur sent me the Mould board, the part of your letter respecting that had as entirely escaped me as if I had never seen it. indeed I had found on other occasions that for[1] the immense mass of matter which I was in the way of recieving, the memory was quite an insufficient storehouse. I thank you for the mould board. it's form promises well, & I have no doubt of it's good performance. it resembles extremely one which I made about 20. years ago, which has been much approved by the agricultural societies of England and France, the latter of which sent me a gold medal as a premium. the form as I observed is very much that of yours, with the advantage of being made by so easy a rule, that the coarsest negro workman can do it, & cannot possibly make it a hair's breadth different from the true form. if I can find a conveyance, I will send you a small model, with it's block which will shew you at once how to make it. a description of it may be found in Mease's[2] edition of Reese's domestic encyclopedia. in agriculture I am only an amateur, having only that knolege which may be got from books. in the field I am entirely ignorant, & am now too old to learn. still it amuses my hours of exercise, & tempts to the taking due exercise. I salute you with great esteem & respect.

TH: JEFFERSON

PoC (MoSHi: TJC-BC); at foot of text: "Philip Tabb esquire"; endorsed by TJ.

TJ designed his first plow moldboard in 1790 and later sent models to the British Board of Agriculture. In 1807 his moldboard was awarded a GOLD MEDAL by the Société d'agriculture du département de la Seine (Betts, *Farm Book*, 47–64; TJ to Sir John Sinclair, 23 Mar. 1798, *PTJ*, 30:197–209; TJ to Augustin François Silvestre, 29 May 1807 [DLC]). TJ confused James Mease's EDITION of Anthony F. M. Willich's *Domestic encyclopædia* with that of Rees's *New Cyclopædia* (see notes to James Ronaldson to TJ, 5 Mar. 1809, and Samuel R. Demaree to TJ, 22 Aug. 1809).

[1] Word interlined in place of "amidst."

[2] Manuscript: "Maese's."

## From Augustus B. Woodward

New-York, june 3. 1809.

Your letter of may 27. awakens, sir, anew, my sense of your undeviating kindness and condescension.—

The system, of which the work I have transmitted is a partial developement, was formed in 1795, in rockbridge; and just before I had the happiness of a first interview at monticello. The result of the presidential elections of 1796, and 1800, prevented me from presenting it to the public. In the latter instance, and during the ensuing eight years, it would have appeared to me particularly unseasonable; a truly republican administration requiring every kind of honorable support.

I found the situation of the public concerns more propitious to an introductory investigation of this subject, at the present æra, than it was ever likely to be, during my life; or that short period, in which it is permitted to an individual to be useful. In this long interval I had full opportunity to consider the subject, deliberately; and, if my mind had not cordially approved a change, at some period, these propositions would have been forever suppressed.

I transmit you, sir, a prospective view of the whole subject, so far as relates to the executive department. The discussion of the legislative part, and the establishment of a national system of jurisprudence, are too remote in prospect to permit me the pleasure of a communication of them.

In the course of time, europe, and the events in it, will cease to be so interesting to us, as they have been. Our power, already firm, is sensibly advancing; and the foundation is laid for every production and manufacture desirable to a nation. France has failed in the republican experiment, less from the particular modifications of either her legislature, or executive; than from the want of republican habits in the people. I doubt not that under any[1] arrangement of the executive authority the event would have been equally unfavorable to liberty.

Asia, and particularly China, ought not to be pretermitted in our comparisons. We shall attain a permanent, or asiatic population, at a period more early than we are aware of; and in proportion as we approach it, the present construction of our executive will prove incommodious.

I apprehend not the establishment of a monarchy in the United States; but I greatly fear a separation of them, if our political institutions, and particularly the construction of the executive, cannot be rendered more appropriate to our national circumstances.—

That the wing of time may not cease to fan with a sweet felicity the retirement of monticello; and him, who enjoys in its elevated shades, the grateful veneration of a free and magnanimous nation; is the constant wish of one, who bears for you, Sir, a respect, alike cordial, and unlimited. A. B. WOODWARD.

RC (DLC); addressed: "The honorable Thomas Jefferson. Monticello. Virginia"; endorsed by TJ as received 11 June 1809 and so recorded in SJL.

In outline form Woodward enclosed a PROSPECTIVE VIEW (MS in DLC: TJ Papers, 187:33327–9; in Woodward's hand; undated) for a three-part study of the government. The first part had already appeared as his *Considerations on the Executive Government of the United States of America* (Flatbush, N.Y., 1809). The other sections, evidently never published, were a proposed "review of the constructions of executive governments in different ages and countries," focusing on Greece, Rome, France, Great Britain, and the United States, followed by chapters on the opinions of Thomas More, James Harrington, John Locke, David Hume, William Godwin, and TJ; and a third part on "the construction of the ministerial departments of the American government."

[1] Woodward here canceled "other."

# From James Fishback

D^R^ SIR Lexington (K^y^) June 5^th^ 1809

Your name has become so familiar to the people of these United States, & been so long associated with whatever is of interest to society I have ventured to send you a Pamphlet of my production—.

The question which it professes to investigate may appear at first sight to be too stale, & hackneyed to merit serious regard.

The plan of the enquiry as far as I know is new, & may suggest some thoughts not before excited—Although imperfect in the composition I have taken the liberty of sending you one with a hope of avoiding the imputation of impertenance or unmeaning obtrusion— Be assured Sir that the high veneration I feel for your Character can never permit me knowingly to be justly chargeable with a want of respectfulness in my conduct towards you—It was by your patriotic efforts that religious freedom was atchieved some of the fruits of which I now present you with—

In your dignified retirement from the theatre of public life, followed by the sentimental voice of millions of your Fellow Citizens in greatful acknowledgments for a life employed in rendering to your Country the most important services, & breathing aspirations for the happiness of the remnant of your days; I have thought it not incompatible with your philosophic & philanthropic mind to solicit a reading of my little piece, & a communication of your judgment upon the conclusiveness of the reasoning—

Be assured that no partiality for the view taken of the subject will render me incapable of seeing or unwilling to receive any strictures discovering either an error in my premises or a fallacy of deduction—Truth has been my object, & I have endeavoured to make right reason my guid— Whether approbatory or not any suggestions will be received[1] as an act of Friendship ever to be acknowledged—

After appologising for this liberty of adress I bid you an affectionate adieu as a greatful son would a beneficient Father, though unknown to him, with the unfeigned wish that the sun of your life which has shown with so much lustre in the great volumes of Science may continue without a cloud to darken his desk until about to leave the horizon of time, & then to set full orbed—Could I by any devout wish of my soul cause him to run back upon the dial of your life with what chearfulness & rapture would I not secure his immediate beams to future ages—but man is borne once to die, & may your death be a sweet transition to a bless[ed immor]tality— Bound togather by the common ties of humanity, & united in the same destiny I am respectfully your

very Ob[t] H Servt

JAMES FISHBACK

RC (MHi); mutilated at seal; addressed: "Thos Jefferson Esq[r] Charlotte ville Albemarle Ct[y] Virginia"; franked and postmarked; endorsed by TJ as received 29 June 1809 and so recorded in SJL. Enclosure: Fishback, *A new and candid investigation of the question, is revelation true?* (Lexington, Ky., 1809).

James Fishback (1776–1845) was a native of Culpeper County who lived near Lexington, Kentucky. His varied careers included service as a physician, lawyer, and newspaper editor. Fishback wrote TJ as an outspoken Presbyterian layman, but in 1816 he became a Baptist minister. He opposed natural religion in favor of revelation and believed that Christian principles and the ultimate success of the American republic were inextricably linked. Fishback's published orations and sermons often embroiled him in religious controversy, later resulting in his resignation from the board of trustees of Transylvania University (Willis Miller Kemper, *Genealogy of the Fishback Family in America* [1914], 113–8; Niels Henry Sonne, *Liberal Kentucky: 1780–1828* [1968], 109–17, 233–4; Brigham, *American Newspapers*, 1:168–9).

[1] Fishback here canceled "with."

## From Jonathan Shoemaker

MY FRIEND Washington City 5th June 1809

I sometime back wrote thee I Should be at Shadwell in all May but Owing to a Variety of Untoward Sircumstances have been Prevented from coming on, I a few days ago have Sold my Mills neer this place & Shall give Possession on or about the 20th Instant & Shortly after that time I Shall come on to Shadwell

Thy Friend &c JONATHAN SHOEMAKER

RC (MHi); at foot of text: "Thomas Jefferson Esq"; endorsed by TJ as received 11 June 1809 and so recorded in SJL.

## From Kimber & Conrad

ESTEEMED FRIEND Philadel. 6 mo 7th 1809

We are engaged in the Publication of a work of the first Character and importance, which has recently appeared in London, edited by John Pinkerton, Author of Modern Geography &c. The prospectus, which developes the Plan the Author has pursued, we have directed to be handed to thee with this note, by John Hellings who is engaged in obtaining subscribers; and as the undertaking is a very arduous one and far more extensive than any thing of the kind, hitherto undertaken in the United States, we take the Liberty of requesting thee, if thou should approve the work, to favor us with thy subscription[1]— KIMBER & CONRAD

RC (MWA); at foot of text: "To Thomas Jefferson"; endorsed by TJ as received 7 Aug. 1809 and so recorded in SJL.

Kimber & Conrad was a book-publishing firm at 93 High Street, Philadelphia. Emmor Kimber and Solomon White Conrad started their partnership about 1806 and continued together for a decade. About 1816 Kimber joined with Blakey Sharpless as Kimber & Sharpless, booksellers, while Conrad began his own business and later became professor of botany at the University of Pennsylvania and librarian of the Academy of Natural Sciences in Philadelphia (James Robinson, *The Philadelphia Directory for 1806* [Philadelphia, 1806] and *The Philadelphia Directory for 1816* [Philadelphia, 1816]; *DSB*, 391).

Scottish historian John PINKERTON was the author of a *Modern Geography*, 2 vols. (Philadelphia, 1804; Sowerby, no. 3827). The PROSPECTUS, not found, described the forthcoming American edition of his new work, *A General Collection of the Best and Most Interesting Voyages and Travels, in all Parts of the World*, 6 vols. (Philadelphia, 1810–12).

[1] Manuscript: "subscrption."

## To George Jefferson

DEAR SIR Monticello June 8. 08. [1809]

Yours of May 30. was duly recieved[1] informing me you had sent by mr Randolph's boat 2 boxes lately recieved. these have since come to hand. the one was from Lemaire at Philadelphia, containing oil & syrops. the other was from mr Gelston of N. York and contained 3. doz. bottles of Burgundy wine. I inclose you his letter stating that he had recieved & should forward for me to you two boxes containing 8. dozen bottles of Burgundy. I do this merely for enquiry as to the box not come, whether it came to Richmond, or has been left at N. York. on your information that it did not come to Richmond, I will write to mr Gelston. had you a bill of lading?

I suppose the trunk N° 28. is desperate. Harry has been committed to jail, but confessed nothing. his companions protest so solemnly & sincerely to appearance that but 3. trunks ever came to the boats that I have no doubt that Harry & the drayman made way with it jointly. if the drayman cannot be punished, he should at least be stigmatised & thrown out of business. Adieu affectionately TH: JEFFERSON

PoC (MHi); misdated; at foot of text: "Mr G. Jefferson"; endorsed by TJ with correct date and so recorded in SJL. Enclosure: David Gelston to TJ, 22 Apr. 1809, not found, but recorded in SJL as received from New York on 30 Apr. 1809.

[1] Manuscript: "recived."

## From Shadrach Ricketson

New York, 6 Mo. 8th 1809.

Shadrach Ricketson presents his respectful Esteem to his Friend, Thomas Jefferson; & herewith sends him his Treatise on Health, which he desires he will accept as a Testimony of the same: also his pamphlet on the Influenza, & two other small ones.

RC (MHi); endorsed by TJ as received 14 June 1809 and so recorded in SJL. Enclosures: (1) Ricketson, *Means of Preserving Health, and Preventing Diseases: Founded principally on an attention to Air and Climate, Drink, Food, Sleep, Exercise, Clothing, Passions of the Mind, and Retentions and Excretions* (New York, 1806; Sowerby, no. 913). (2) Ricketson, *A Brief History of the Influenza, Which prevailed in New-York in 1807* (New York, 1808). Other enclosures not found.

Shadrach Ricketson (1768–1839), physician, studied medicine under Benjamin Anthony and practiced in Dutchess County, New York, where he served as the president of the county's medical society, 1823–24. He advocated wellness and hygiene (Fred B. Rogers, "Shadrach Ricketson (1768–1839): Quaker Hygienist," *Journal of the History of Medicine* 20 [1965]: 140–50).

## From Augustin François Silvestre

Monsieur, Paris, le *8 juin* 1809

J'ai reçu et communiqué à la Société d'agriculture de Paris la lettre que vous m'avez fait l'honneur de m'écrire en date du 11 fevrier dernier. La Société a vu, dans l'empressement avec lequel vous avez daigné vous occuper de la demande, que j'avais pris la liberté de vous faire en Son nom, d'une certaine quantité de graine de coton, un nouveau témoignage de l'intérêt[1] que vous voulez bien prendre à ses travaux; et elle m'a chargé de vous en exprimer Sa vive reconnaissance. Comme il parait que[2] les deux barils de graines, que vos Soins lui avaient destinés, n'ont pu étre envoyés assez-tôt à Newyork, pour pouvoir partir par l'aviso qui a été expédié de ce port (ce qui du reste ne doit point laisser de regrets, puisque ces graines seraient arrivées encore trop tard en france pour les semis de cette année), la Société accepte l'offre que vous voulez bien lui faire de renouveller vos Soins à cet égard pour l'année prochaine.[3] Elle vous prie, lorsque vous aurez la bonté de vous occuper de ce Second envoi, de le composer, ainsi que vous aviez fait le premier, au moins pour moitié de graine verte, qu'elle se propose, non Sans quelque espérance de Succès, de faire essayer le long des côtes de la Méditerranée et dans quelques parties des départemens maritimes du Sud-Ouest. Les renseignemens, qui lui ont été donnés par un voyageur distingué, Monsieur Michaux, qui vient de parcourir une grande partie des Etats-Unis, Sur la nature et la Situation des terreins dans lesquels on y cultive cette espèce de coton, font présumer à la Société, malgré la juste confiance que mérite votre opinion, qu'elle pourra réussir également dans les contrées maritimes de la france méridionale; du reste c'est à l'expérience Seule qu'il appartient de confirmer ou de détruire cette conjecture.

J'avais espéré pouvoir vous envoyer, par le retour de l'aviso qui m'a porté votre lettre, le 11[e] Volume de nos mémoires; mais quoique l'impression en Soit terminée, il ne Sera prêt à paraître que dans quelques jours; je ne manquerai pas de profiter de la première occasion qui se présentera pour vous le faire parvenir.[4]

Je vous prie, Monsieur, de vouloir bien agréer l'assurance de ma trez haute considération. Silvestre

EDITORS' TRANSLATION

SIR, Paris, *8 June* 1809

I have received and communicated to the Agricultural Society of Paris the letter you did me the honor to write me last 11 February. The Society saw, in the attentiveness with which you deigned to take care of the request that I had taken the liberty to make to you on its behalf of a certain quantity of cotton seeds, a renewed evidence of the interest that you are willing to take in its works; and for this the Society has asked me to express to you its warmest gratitude. As it seems that the two barrels of seeds you sent to the Society could not be sent soon enough to New York to be shipped on the sloop that was sent from this port (which should not be regretted, since these grains would still have arrived in France too late to be sown this year), the Society accepts your kind offer to renew your kindness regarding this matter next year. The Society respectfully asks you, when you will be kind enough to take care of this second shipment, to include in it, as you had done with the first one, at least half in green seeds, that the Society plans, not without some hope of success, to try to grow along the Mediterranean coast and in some parts of the maritime regions in the Southwest. The information given to the Society by a distinguished traveler, Mr. Michaux, who just traveled through a great part of the United States, on the nature and situation of the lands in which this kind of cotton is cultivated, induces the Society to assume, despite the justifiable confidence your opinion deserves, that it will be equally successful in maritime regions of southern France; in any case, it is only through experience that we will be able to confirm or destroy this hypothesis.

I had hoped to be able to send you, on the return trip of the sloop that brought me your letter, the 11th volume of our memoirs; but even though it is printed it will not be ready to come out for a few days; I will not fail to take advantage of the first opportunity that presents itself to have it sent to you.

Please accept, Sir, the assurance of my highest consideration.

SILVESTRE

RC (DLC); on printed letterhead of "Société d'agriculture du département de la Seine," with its insignia, partial dateline (with Silvestre's handwritten completion indicated in italics), and handwritten identification of himself as "membre de l'Institut de France" and secretary of the society; above salutation: "A Monsieur Jefferson, associé-étranger de l'Institut et de la Société d'agriculture"; endorsed by TJ as received 3 Aug. 1809 and so recorded in SJL; notation by TJ: "write to Gov[r] Milledge for Cotton seed." Dft (Boston Public Library); at head of text: "N° 1225." Translation by Dr. Genevieve Moene. Enclosed in James Madison to TJ, 3 Aug. 1809.

Augustin François Silvestre (1762–1851), scientist, public administrator, and teacher, studied painting and antiquities in Rome before he was appointed librarian to the future Louis XVIII in 1782. He became a member of the Société d'agriculture du département de la Seine in 1792 and served as its secretary for more than thirty years, publishing numerous reports in its name. In 1806 Silvestre was named a member of the Institut de France. He sent TJ all of the society's memoirs over several years, the most recent being the tenth, sent in September 1808 (Hoefer, *Nouv. biog. générale*, 43:1011–2; TJ to Silvestre, 15 July 1808 [DLC]; Sowerby, nos. 693, 776).

TJ's letter of 11 FEVRIER 1809 (DLC) explained that the freezing of the river at Baltimore postponed delivery to New York of two casks containing VERTE (green or Sea Island) cottonseed, grown on the seacoast of Georgia, and black cottonseed grown in Georgia and the Carolinas.

[1] In Dft Silvestre here canceled "philantropique."

[2] Preceding three words added in margin of Dft.

[3] Remainder of paragraph added to Dft.

[4] In Dft Silvestre here canceled "j'ai l'honneur de vous addressez par celleci le Programme de la Séance publique tenue cette année par la Société, avec le tableau, que j'ai esquisié, de ses travaux pendant l'année 1808. je desire que vous y reconnaissez la constance de ses efforts pour le perfectionnement de l'art agricole et pour l'encouragement de ceux qui contribuent à Ses progrès" ("I have the honor to send you by this means the program of the public session held this year by the Society, with the table, that I have sketched, of its works during 1808. I hope that you will recognize the persistence of its efforts towards the perfection of the agricultural arts and the encouragement of those things that contribute to its progress").

# From John Armstrong

DEAR SIR, Paris 11th of June 1809.

I received the letter you did me the honor to write to me by M. Coles, whom I found to be everything that you had said of him,—well informed & confidential & therefore an excellent supplement to[1] letters both public and private. In discharge of this new obligation, I employed myself in writing to you a long letter, filled with facts, conjectures and forebodings. On looking over it, I found it's color much too somber for my own taste, and I recollected, that you were not prone to despair of the Republic. I therefore committed it to the fire, and am now obliged to substitute for it these few & hurried lines, which have no Object but to assure You, of the high respect and constant attachment of, Dear Sir,

Your most Obedient & faithful friend & servant

JOHN ARMSTRONG

RC (DLC); at foot of text: "M. Jefferson, Monticello"; endorsed by TJ as received 3 Aug. 1809 and so recorded in SJL. Enclosed in James Madison to TJ, 3 Aug. 1809.

[1] Armstrong here canceled "my."

# From Destutt de Tracy

MONSIEUR a auteuil ce 12 juin 1809.

je Suis Saisi de la plus timide inquietude quand je pense qu'un ouvrage de moi Sur les objets les plus importants au bonheur des hommes, va etre mis Sous les yeux de l'homme de l'univers que je respecte le plus et dont j'ambitionne le plus le Suffrage. cependant je ressens une joye vive de penser qu'aprés avoir fait le bonheur de votre pays, aprés lui avoir donné le plus grand et le plus utile exemple dont l'histoire fasse mention, aprés avoir rempli, autant que possible, par cet exemple, une dangereuse lacune de Sa constitution, vous avez du loisir pour vous occuper de Spéculation, et que vous daignera peut-etre examiner les idées que je vous Sousmets. Si je Suis assez heureux pour qu'elles vous plaisent je remets entre vos mains le livre et l'auteur. je Serois charmé qu'on leur fit l'honneur de transporter ces idées dans votre langue maternelle, et qu'elles pussent etre publiées Sous vos auspices. mais il est de la plus grande importance pour moi qu'on ne Sache jamais, ou du moins qu'aprés ma mort, que cet ouvrage vient de moi. Si meme le nom de Condorcet pouvoit conduire a le Soupçonner, il Seroit peut-etre a propos de le Suprimer. disposez, je vous Suplie, du tout comme il vous plaira, pour le corriger et l'ameliorer, Si vous voulez bien en prendre la peine.

je Suis avec les Sentiments de la plus vive reconnoissance et du plus profond respect que vous doivent tous les amis de l'humanité dans toutes les nations.

Votre trés humble et trés obeissant Serviteur.

Destutt-Tracy

P.S. Depuis que je n'ai eu l'honneur de vous ecrire, j'ai perdu mon excellent et illustre ami M[r] Cabanis qui etoit penetré pour vous de la plus tendre veneration. Sa mort a achevé d'empoisonner le reste de ma vie. ma plus douce consolation est dans les Sentiments que m'accorde le Genereux ami qui me procure l'avantage de vous presenter mes hommages. il est bien malheureux, lui meme, et je partage bien douloureusement Ses chagrins.

permettez moi de vous offrir le discours que j'ai prononcé a l'institut quand j'ai eu le malheur d'y prendre la place de mon ami, et quelques vers de lui qui ont été lus dans cette Séance, et d'y joindre les hommages de Sa digne veuve qui est la fidelle dépositaire de tous Ses Sentiments, et qui me charge d'etre Son interprete auprés de vous.

### EDITORS' TRANSLATION

Sir Auteuil 12 June 1809.

I am seized with the most apprehensive anxiety at the thought that a work of mine about the objects most important to the happiness of man is going to be placed under the eyes of the man I respect the most in the universe and from whom I crave approval the most. However I am delighted to think that after having made your country prosperous, after having given it the greatest and the most useful example known in history, after having filled, as much as possible, by this example, a dangerous gap in its constitution, you find enough leisure to be engaged in speculation, and you will perhaps deign to examine the ideas that I am submitting to you. If I am fortunate enough that they please you, I put into your hands the book and the author. I would be delighted if they had the honor of being translated into your native tongue and if they were published under your auspices. But it is of the greatest importance to me that it never be known, at least not until after my death, that this work is mine. If even only the name of Condorcet could cause suspicion, it would perhaps be appropriate to suppress it. I beg you to do as you please with all of this, to correct it and to improve it, if you would be kind enough to take the trouble to do it.

I am, with the warmest feelings of gratitude and the most profound respect which is owed to you by all friends of humanity in all nations,

Your very humble and obedient servant.

DESTUTT-TRACY

P.S. Since the last time I had the honor to write you, I have lost my excellent and illustrious friend Mr. Cabanis, who was filled with the most tender veneration for you. His death finished poisoning the rest of my life. My sweetest consolation is in the sentiments accorded to me by the generous friend who gives me the means of presenting my regards to you. He himself is quite unhappy, and I very painfully share his grief.

Allow me to offer you the speech I gave at the Institut when I had the misfortune to take the place of my friend, and a few of his verses that were read during that session, and to join to them the regards of his worthy widow who is the faithful trustee of all his sentiments, and who charges me to be his interpreter with you.

RC (DLC); endorsed by TJ as received 28 Sept. 1809 and so recorded in SJL. Translation by Dr. Genevieve Moene. Enclosures: (1) French-language Dft, not found, of Destutt de Tracy, *A Commentary and Review of Montesquieu's Spirit of the Laws* (Philadelphia, 1811; Sowerby, no. 2327). (2) *Discours prononcés dans la séance publique tenue par la classe de la langue et de la littérature françaises de l'Institut de France* (Paris, 1808), which included Destutt de Tracy's eulogy of Pierre Jean Georges Cabanis.

Antoine Louis Claude Destutt de Tracy (1754–1836), a French writer and philosopher, was an influential voice for reform during the French Revolution. He renounced his title of nobility in 1789 and joined ranks with the Third Estate. A member of the liberal group known as the Idéologues, Destutt de Tracy was a member of the Institut de France and a vocal opponent of Napoleon. He corresponded frequently with TJ after 1804, when he sent him the first two installments of his *Élémens d'Ideologie* (Sowerby, no. 1239). TJ thought so highly of Destutt de Tracy and his work that he arranged for the translation and publication of the manuscript on Montesquieu enclosed here, and he spent a great deal of time in 1816 preparing his own translation of another of Destutt de Tracy's works, *A Treatise on Political Economy* (Georgetown, 1817 [1818]), for which TJ found a publisher and supplied a preface under his own name (*DBF*; *Biographie universelle*, 42:77–9; Gilbert Chinard, *Jefferson et les Idéologues d'après sa correspondance inédite avec Destutt de Tracy, Cabanis, J.-B. Say et Auguste Comte* [1925], 97–188; Malone, *Jefferson*, 6:208–11, 305–7; *MB*, 2:1320).

Destutt de Tracy's commentary on Montesquieu's *Esprit des Lois* also included a discussion of that work by CONDORCET. Destutt de Tracy succeeded philosopher and physiologist Pierre Jean Georges CABANIS as president of the Académie Française. TJ had known Cabanis when he was in France and had received his publication on the physical and moral faculties of man in 1803 (Chinard, *Jefferson et les Idéologues*, 44; TJ to Cabanis, 13 July 1803 [DLC]; Sowerby, no. 1246).

# From Pierre Samuel Du Pont de Nemours

MONSIEUR Paris 12 juin 1809.

J'apprends que M[r] Coles, dont je croyais le départ retardé pour longtems encore, montera en voiture dans une heure.

Je n'ai donc qu'un moment pour vous exprimer toute ma reconnaissance de la Lettre qu'il m'a remise de votre part.

Quoique je sois convaincu que M[r] Madison, votre Ami et votre Elève, gouvernera dans les mêmes Principes que vous, je ne puis m'empêcher de regretter que vous n'ayiez pas voulu conserver la Présidence quatre ans de plus. Vos raisons pour la quitter, ont êté belles. L'Etat politique du Monde en donnait de bonnes pour ne la point abandonner.

La chose est faite.

J'ai l'honneur de vous envoyer Sept volumes des oeuvres de M[r] Turgot, que je prie Monsieur Votre Successeur de vous faire parvenir, et j'en adresse un aussi à la Societé philosophique.

Je n'ai pu obtenir la permission de vous faire passer des merinos.

J'aurai je l'espere le tems de vous écrire plus au long par l'officier qui releve M[r] Coles, et je tiendrai ma lettre prête d'avance.

agréez, Grand Homme, mon profond respect, et mon inviolable attachement DUPONT (DE NEMOURS)

EDITORS' TRANSLATION

SIR Paris 12 June 1809.

I understand that Mr. Coles, whose departure I thought would be delayed for a long time still, will board the coach in an hour.

I have therefore only a moment to express to you all my gratitude for the letter he gave me from you.

Though I am convinced that Mr. Madison, your friend and your student, will govern according to the same principles as you have, I cannot help regretting that you did not want to retain the presidency for four more years. Your reasons for leaving it were fine. The political shape of the world gave good reasons for not abandoning it.

The deed is done.

I have the honor of sending you seven volumes of Mr. Turgot's works, that I ask your successor to forward to you, and I am also sending one to the philosophical society.

I was unable to obtain permission to send you the merinos.

I hope to have time to write you at greater length through the officer who replaces Mr. Coles, and I will have my letter ready ahead of time.

Please accept, Great Man, my profound respect, and my inviolable attachment

DuPont (de Nemours)

RC (DLC); at head of text: "a Monsieur Jefferson Ancien President des Etats unis"; endorsed by TJ as received 3 Aug. 1809 and so recorded in SJL. Translation by Dr. Genevieve Moene. Enclosed in James Madison to TJ, 3 Aug. 1809.

la lettre: TJ to Du Pont, 2 Mar. 1809 (DLC). Du Pont sent the promised sept volumes (vols. 2–8) of his edition of Anne Robert Jacques Turgot, *Oeuvres*, 9 vols. (Paris, 1808–11; Sowerby, no. 2436) via Madison on 11 July 1809 (Madison, *Papers, Pres. Ser.*, 1:285–6).

# From Alexander von Humboldt

à Paris à l'Ecole polytechnique Montagne Ste Genevieve ce 12 Juin 1809.

Monsieur,

Vous connaissez assez les sentimens respectueux d'attachement et d'amitié que je Vous porte, pour sentir Vous même la satisfaction que j'ai eu en recevant Votre lettre en date du 6 Mars. Je n'ai pas eté heureux depuis que j'ai quitté Votre beau pays. Battu par la tempête, on est plus sensible aux vrayes jouissances morales. Quelle carriere que la Votre! Quel exemple ravissant, Vous avez donné, d'energie de caractere, de douceur et de profondeur dans les affections les plus tendres de l'ame, de moderation et de justice comme premier magistrat d'un Etat puissant! Ce qui a eté creé par Vous, Vous le voyez prosperer. Votre retraite à Monticello est un événement, dont la memoire ne s'éteindra jamais dans les fastes de l'humanité. Il est difficile de Vous parler de Vous même sans avoir l'air de flatter. Que mon ame franche et emue est éloignée de cet artifice!

Je Vous offre l'hommage de mes travaux. J'ai l'honneur de Vous présenter la seconde et la troisieme partie de mon ouvrage sur le Mexique le 2[d] 3[me] et 4[me] cahier de mon Recueil astronomique y compris le Nivellement des Andes. J'ajoute la traduction que l'on a faite de mes Tableaux de la Nature, traduction qui auroit bien mieux rempli en anglais. Si l'ouvrage parait jusqu'a demain jé Vous envoie aussi le volume de notre petite Societé d'Arcueil dans lequel Vous trouverez mon travail sur la respiration des poissons et qui Vous présente les beaux memoires de mes deux amis les plus intimes, Gay Lussac et Thenard.

Veuillez recevoir toutes ces bagatelles avec cette indulgence qui Vous distingue et dont Vous m'honorez particulierement. Pourrais-je me flatter que Vous serez un peu content de mon morceau sur l'état moral du peuple mexicain. Je me repends beaucoup de ce que j'ai dit sur les esclaves p. 10. J'ai seu depuis que lorsque ces lignes furent imprimées le Congrès avait dejà pris des mesures trés énergiques pour l'abolition totale. J'ai eté egaré par un zele pour la cause des noirs dont je ne rougis pas. Je saurai reparer l'injustice que j'ai commise vis a vis les Etats du Sud dans une note et des additions qui seront placés à la fin de l'ouvrage. Mon livre a eté dedié au Roi Charles IV pour calmer par là l'humeur que le Gouvernement de Madrid auroit pu montrer contre quelques individus à Mexico qui m'ont fourni plus de renseignement que peutetre la Cour aurait voulu.

Je suis bien en peine de voir que ma lettre du 30 mai est la première qui Vous soit parvenue. Vous n'auriez donc pas non plus recu mon ouvrage sur la Geographie des plantes?

J'ai une priere à Vous faire. J'y tiens beaucoup. Nous sommes deja éloigné l'un de l'autre de 1200 lieues. Si je m'enfonce à Kaschemir ou à Lassa, l'année prochaine, je serai plus loin encore.

Je possede Votre excellent[1] ouvrage sur la Virginie mais je voudrois le posseder de Vos mains avec une ligne de Votre écriture. Ce seroit pour moi un souvenir bien precieux. Vous m'avez fait cadeau de Votre exemplaire de Playfair, mais Votre nom n'y est pas et j'ai peur de cette misere publique qui monte en lignes rouges et bleues. Ne me refusez pas ma priere. Madame de Tessé, qui Vous est dévouée comme moi, dit que ma priere est très raisonnable.

Je n'est pas écris à Mr Madison, j'aurois du le faire plûtôt. Je félicite l'Etat du choix qu'ont fait les citoyens de l'Amerique. Il m'a laissé une impression très belle. J'aime Votre expression "it now permits us a wise and honest administration." Ce mot d'honnéte renferme tout ce qui est juste, liberal, vertueux. Veuillez si Vous écrivez aù President lui offrir l'expression de mes sentimens respectueux.

Agreéz, Monsieur, l'hommage de mon admiration et de ma reconnaissance.

Alexander Humboldt

Il a paru en allemand le second Volume du Mithridates d'Adelung et de Vater sur les langues. Il contient des recherchés qui se tient à Vos ideés.

EDITORS' TRANSLATION

Paris Ecole polytechnique Montagne Ste Genevieve 12 June 1809.

SIR,

You know well enough the respectful feelings of attachment and friendship that I have for you to be aware of the satisfaction I felt when I received your letter dated 6 March. I have not been happy since I left your beautiful country. Beaten by storms, one is more sensitive to true moral pleasures. What a career yours has been! What a magnificent example you have given of strong character, of sweetness in the most tender affections of the soul, of moderation and justice as head magistrate of a powerful state! What has been created by you, you have seen prosper. Your retirement to Monticello is an event the memory of which will never fade from the splendors of humanity. It is difficult to talk to you about yourself without seeming to flatter. How far from this artifice my truthful and emotional soul is!

I respectfully offer you my works. I have the honor to present to you the second and third parts of my work on Mexico, the 2d, 3d and 4th notebooks of my astronomical work, including the leveling of the Andes. I have added the translation that was done of my Tableaux of Nature, a translation which could have been done much better in English. If the work appears by tomorrow, I will also send you the volume by our small society in Arcueil in which you will find my work on the respiration of fish, and which gives you the beautiful memoirs of my two closest friends, Gay-Lussac and Thénard. Please receive all these trifles with the indulgence for which you are known and with which you particularly honor me. May I flatter myself that you will be somewhat satisfied with my piece on the moral state of the Mexican people? I am sorry for much of what I said about slaves p. 10. Since then, I have learned that when these lines were printed, Congress had already taken very strong measures toward complete abolition. I was misled by a zeal for the cause of the blacks, for which I do not blush. I know how I will repair the injustice that I committed toward the southern states, with a note and additions placed at the end of the book. My book was dedicated to King Charles IV in order to calm the displeasure the government in Madrid could have shown toward some people in Mexico, who provided me with more information than perhaps the court would have liked.

I am sorry to see that my letter dated May 30 was the first one to reach you. Have you not also received my work on the geography of plants?

I have another request for you. It means a lot to me. We are already 1,200 leagues apart. If I find myself deep in Kashmir or in Lhasa, next year, I will be farther away still.

I own a copy of your excellent work on Virginia but I would like to receive it from your hands with a line written by you. It would be a very precious memento for me. You gave me as a gift your copy of Playfair, but your name is not on it, and I am afraid of this public misery that goes up in red and blue lines. Do not refuse me this request. Madame de Tessé, who is as devoted to you as I am, tells me that my request is very reasonable.

I have not written Mr. Madison, I should have done it earlier. I congratulate the nation on the choice made by the citizens of America. He made a very fine impression on me. I like your expression "it now permits us a wise and honest administration." This word "honest" contains all that is just, liberal, and virtuous. When you write the president please be kind enough to send him my respectful regards.

Please accept, Sir, this token of my admiration and gratitude.

ALEXANDER HUMBOLDT

The second volume of Mithridates, a study of languages by Adelung and Vater, has been published in German. It contains research that adheres to your ideas.

RC (DLC); dateline at foot of text; endorsed by TJ as received 3 Aug. 1809 and so recorded in SJL. Translation by Dr. Genevieve Moene. Enclosures: (1) parts 2–3 of Humboldt, *Essai politique sur le royaume de la Nouvelle-Espagne: ouvrage qui presente des recherches sur la geographie du Mexique*, 2 vols. (Paris, 1808–19; Sowerby, no. 4157). (2) parts 2–4 of Humboldt, *Recueil d'observations astronomiques, d'operations trigonométriques et de mesures barométriques faites pendant le cours d'un voyage aux régions équinoxiales du nouveau continent, depuis 1799 jusqu'en 1803*, 3 vols. (Paris, 1808–09). (3) Humboldt, *Tableaux de la Nature, ou Considerations sur les Deserts, sur la Physionomie de Vegetaux, et sur les Cataractes de l'Orenoque* (Paris, 1808; Sowerby, no. 646), originally published in German and translated the same year into French. Enclosed in James Madison to TJ, 3 Aug. 1809.

The SOCIÉTÉ D'ARCUEIL was a small circle of naturalists and scientists that met in Arcueil at the home of its leader, Claude Louis Berthollet, and included his assistant, chemist Joseph Louis Gay-Lussac, Jean Baptiste Biot, Humboldt, and Louis Jacques Thénard. The group published its findings as memoirs from 1807–17 (David Bailie Warden to TJ, 28 June 1809; Helmut de Terra, "Alexander von Humboldt's Correspondence with Jefferson, Madison, and Gallatin," APS, *Proceedings* 103 [1959]: 785–6).

Humboldt was correcting his statement SUR LES ESCLAVES in the first enclosure, in which he observed that since the acquisition of Louisiana the annual importation of slaves to the southern part of the United States had greatly increased and that Congress and the president still lacked the power "to oppose this augmentation, and to spare by that means much distress to the generations to come" (Humboldt, *Political Essay on the Kingdom of New Spain*, trans. John Black [London, 1811], 1:15). TJ had in fact signed an act barring such imports effective 1 Jan. 1808 (Malone, *Jefferson*, 5:541–7).

LA GEOGRAPHIE DU PLANTES: Humboldt's *Essai sur la géographie des plantes, accompagné d'un tableau physique des régions équinoxiales* (Paris, 1807) was the only volume published in group five of his series, *Voyage aux régions équinoxiales du nouveau continent* (note to TJ to Humboldt, 6 Mar. 1809).

Humboldt was probably intimidated by the colored charts in one of the works of William PLAYFAIR on political economy (*DNB*; Sowerby, nos. 2940–2). MITHRIDATES: Johann Christoph Adelung, *Mithridates: Oder Allgemeine Sprachenkunde* (Berlin, 1806–17). See note to Johann Severin Vater to TJ, 4 Nov. 1809.

[1] Word interlined in place of illegible word.

# To George Jefferson

DEAR SIR Monticello June 12. 09

It becomes necessary for me to establish a correspondence somewhere for the supply of my groceries, that is to say, of sugar, coffee tea and salted fish[1] and I believe Richmond will be more convenient than Baltimore, Philadelphia, & New York, if to be had there on nearly equal terms. but as I know nobody there I must ask the favor of you to select the most eligible correspondent there for me—to whom I may apply directly, without troubling you with being the intermediate of the correspondence. our wants through the year would be about 900. or 1000 ℔ of sugar, brown & white, from 100 to 200 ℔ of coffee, about 25. ℔ of tea, 15 to 20. barrels of fish, besides the smaller articles of French brandy, syrop of punch, rice, barley E^t^c a periodical settlement & paiment of accounts must be understood between us & the periods made known. great attention must be paid to the strength & security of the packages, & to the reciepts for the delivery, to guard against the extraordinary dishonesty of the boatmen. I begin with asking a supply of 50. ℔ of coffee. Bourbon or E. India would always be preferred, but good West India will give satisfaction, always excepting against what is called Green coffee which we cannot use. not knowing whether mr Randolph's boats will go down soon (which are always to be preferred) I must get you to recommend some safe boatman. When shall we see you here? I wish to know lest I should be gone to Bedford, to which place I think of going towards the end of this month: but am not bound to any fixed time

Affectionately yours TH: JEFFERSON

PoC (MHi); at foot of text: "M^r^ G. Jefferson"; endorsed by TJ.

[1] Preceding three words interlined, with "&" canceled before "tea."

# From George Jefferson

DEAR SIR Richmond 12^th^ June 1809

The two boxes mentioned in M^r^ Gelston's letter were received, but Major Gibbon called soon after, with a letter from Cap^t^ Tingey of Washington, saying that one of them belonged to him, and had been forwarded to us by mistake.—it is still here, waiting for a good opportunity by which to send it to Washington.—There is no direction on the box, a card appearing to have been rubbed off.—

I am sorry that we cannot even have the satisfaction of punishing the drayman who took the lost[1] trunk, as, if I knew him, I have forgotten who he was.

Harry, as one of M^r^ R's men informed me, says he does not know him.

I am Dear Sir Your Very humble serv^t^ GEO. JEFFERSON

RC (MHi); at foot of text: "Thomas Jefferson esq[r]"; endorsed by TJ as received 14 June 1809 and so recorded in SJL. Enclosed in TJ to David Gelston, 15 June 1809.

[1] Word interlined.

# From George Jefferson

DEAR SIR Richmond 12[th] June 1809

Since writing you by this mail, a M[r] James Scott has called on me, with a few of the papers which must have come out of the lost trunk. M[r] S. lives within about five miles of Charlottesville, and, having been waiting for some Tobacco which he expected down the river, he concluded to go some miles up it, in the expectation of meeting the boat. He found the papers about a mile above the locks on the South side, on the margin of the river, some hanging to bushes, and shewing evidently as he says, that they had been thrown into the river. As from the vocabularies, he knew them to be those advertized by us, he says he looked up and down the river for about a mile, but found none except within the space of about 150 yards.

I will myself however go up tomorrow, and see if I can make any further discovery.

The papers found are a very small portion of the vocabularies lost as I suppose, (about a fourth of a quire) and some short lists of books, with names of persons against a part,[1] as if they had been lent out.—One of the papers, I inclose you. Most of them are much defaced.

I am Dear Sir Your Very humble serv[t] GEO. JEFFERSON

RC (MHi); at foot of text: "Thomas Jefferson esq[r]"; endorsed by TJ as received 14 June 1809 and so recorded in SJL. Enclosure not found.

[1] Preceding two words interlined in place of "some."

# From Lafayette

MY DEAR FRIEND Paris 12[th] June 1809

While I was indulging the Hope to See M[r] Coles at La Grange, to possess Him Some days in our family, to go with Him to Aulnay where M[r] et M[de] de tessé, expected the pleasure to Receive Him, I Have Been Yesterday informed of His Sudden departure—I immediately Came to town, But am much Vexed at My disappointment—The impression M[r] Coles Has made Upon me Makes me Heartily Regret Not to Have improved the time of His Stay in france—So

Many things also I Had to tell Him of You, of me of public and private Concerns which Had Been Ajourned to the Uninterrupted Hours of a Country Life: But it Cannot Be Helped.

How Happy I would Be, My dear friend, to Accompany Him to Monticello, in those days of Retirement when Your Heart Cannot fail to be Blessed with the Remembrances which the Lovers of freedom and Your personal friends So fully Enjoy! Among those who Have Not the Advantage of personal intimacy there is none More Attached to You than M. de tracy—He Has intrusted me with a Secret, and a wish, Both of Which I Have Encouraged Him to Communicate to You.

He Has Made Some observations on Montesquieu's Esprit des Loix—will not Be known to be the Author of them—and thinks that, if You Approve them, which I am Sure will be the Case, they Had Better Be translated in English, and published from An American press as Being the Work of a Citizen of the U.S.—Then Copies Might Be Sent to Europe and translated in french, for public Use, as Coming from the other, and Now the only Republican shore—the propriety of keeping the Secret is obvious—that of translating and publishing the Work is Left to Your Judgement.

M[r] Coles Will Give You the present State of public Affairs—What Has Been Attempted, and the only Way in Which it Can Be done, Respecting My pecuniary Business Will also By Him Be laid Before You, and More fully Expatiated Upon in My Next Letter.

Receive the Best Thanks, Wishes, Regard, and Love of Your Affectionate friend LAFAYETTE

RC (DLC); endorsed by TJ as received 3 Aug. 1809 and so recorded in SJL. Enclosed in James Madison to TJ, 3 Aug. 1809.

Marie Joseph Paul Yves Roch Gilbert du Motier, marquis de Lafayette (1757–1834), soldier and statesman, was a lifelong supporter of liberty in America, beginning in 1777 when he was a volunteer in the Continental army under George Washington. He led an assault by American light infantry during the seige of Yorktown in 1781 and continued to support American interests in France while TJ was minister there. Lafayette was head of the Paris National Guard, 1789–91, and imprisoned from 1792–97 in Austria for his support of a constitutional monarchy in France. He spent most of the remainder of his life at Château La Grange forty miles east of Paris, where he provided a haven for European revolutionaries. Having lost his fortune during the Revolution, Lafayette declined TJ's offer of the governorship of the Louisiana Territory but did solicit his aid in securing 11,520 acres of Louisiana land promised him by the United States Congress as recompense for his service during the American Revolution. His correspondence with TJ after 1804 frequently related to his desire to sell this land to repay his debts. At the invitation of President James Monroe, Lafayette toured widely in America in 1824–25. During this trip he was hailed as a hero, visited Monticello and, partly at TJ's urging, received a gift of $200,000 and an additional land grant from Congress

(*ANB*; *DAB*; Gilbert Chinard, *The Letters of Lafayette and Jefferson* [1929]; Stanley J. Idzerda and others, eds., *Lafayette in the Age of the American Revolution: Selected Letters and Papers*, 5 vols. [1977–83]; *U.S. Statutes at Large*, 2:236–7, 306, 4:320 [3 Mar. 1803, 27 Mar. 1804, 28 Dec. 1824]; Paul V. Lutz, "Lafayette's Louisiana Estate: The Unusual Dealings between the Marquis and Three Wealthy Englishmen," *Louisiana Studies* 6 [1967]: 333–60).

# From James Madison

D[R] SIR Washington June 12. 1809

The Pacific has just returned from G.B. bringing the acc[ts] to be seen in the Newspapers. The communications from Pinkney add little to them. The new orders, considering the time, and that the act was known on the passage of which the instructions lately executed by Erskine, were predicated, present a curious feature in the conduct of the B Cabinet. It is explained by some at the expence of its sincerity. It is more probably ascribed, I think to an awkwardness in getting out of an awkward situation, and to the policy of witholding as long as possible from France, the motive of its example, to advances on her part towards adjustment with us. The crooked proceeding seems to be operating as a check to the extravagance of credit given to G.B. for her late arrangement with us; and so far may be salutary.

Be assured of my constant affection JAMES MADISON

RC (DLC: Madison Papers); endorsed by TJ as received 14 June 1809 and so recorded in SJL.

Accounts from London stated that, far from implementing the Erskine agreement and repealing the Orders in Council, NEW ORDERS issued by the British government on 26 Apr. 1809 strengthened the British blockade of European ports controlled by Napoleon (Washington *National Intelligencer*, 12 June 1809).

# From Madame de Tessé

Aulnay 12 juin 1809

je demande sans cesse depuis un mois, Monsieur, d'etre prevenue du depart de M[r] Coles et j'ai L'ambition de le Recevoir, non dans La maison, mais dans le jardin ou je dois terminer mes jours, pour que vous connoîssiés au moins mon tombeau. il n'a Rien d'attristant et pourroit exciter en moi trop d'orgueil, si je prenois un peu serieusement à lá plaisanterie de M[r] Short qui ne Rougit point de dire—je serois aussi fier d'avoir planté ce jardin que d'avoir gâgné une bataille—mais voila que M[r] de la Fayette m'aprend a 3 heures après midi que M[r] Coles part demain. un miracle pourroit Ranimer mes esperances, mais il ne s'en fait plus gueres, et j'y compte si peu que je vais envoier en ville pour vous faire parvenir surement un temoignage de ma Reconnoissance, de mon attachement, et permettés moi de le dire de mon Respect. je ne vois pas pourquoi une femme n'emploieroit pas le terme qui exprime ce quelle sent Lorsque ce quelle sent est juste et honnorable.

il ne me convient d'applaudir a votre administration que dans La foule, par des battemens de main, Lorsque je vous suis dans La visite Respectueuse que vous allés Rendre au nouveau President, mais il me semble qu'une femme a le droit d'exprimer La satisfaction quelle a Ressentie à La Lecture des plus nobles discours qui aient jamais ete inspirés par les plus nobles penseés. il me paroit même quelle devroit Remercier toutes les fois quon autorise en elle le sentiment de L'enthousiasme qui lui est si naturel, et si souvent Reproché. je puis donc vous temoigner ma Reconnoissance pour un plaisir que je ne devois plus gouter depuis que L'approbation la plus commune a fui Loin de moi.

vos derniers et trés magnifiques dons ont eté visités et pillés en differens ports comme jai eu L'honneur de vous le mander. le quart de ma superbe caisse m'est arrivé en trop mauvais etat pour que beaucoup de semences aient pu germer. mais je ne Laisse pas d'avoir á moi seule plus de cornus Florida de vos graines quil n'en existe dans toutes les pepinieres des environs de Paris. nos ports ont eté entierement fermés depuis que vous m'avés demandé des marons et des chênes verds. ces deux semences ne peuvent se garder impunement quatre mois ce qui ne me permet pas de vous en envoier par M^r Coles. mais je desire passionnement planter un arbre a monticello et il me paroit assés piquant quil soit le produit de ceux que jai plantés depuis cinq ans. je joins donc ici quelques graines d'un arbre qui paroit venir du nord de La chine. on L'a d'abord apelle Paulinia aurea je lui ai conservé son nom quoiquil en ait pris depuis peu un autre. il croit tres promptement, s'eleve peu, son feuillage est beau, sa fleur agreable. je me suis persuadée quil vous manquoit parceque je desirois que vous eussiés la bonte de le distinguer avec interêt comme une offrande du culte que je vous Rends.

je suis facheé qu'on ne Rende pas chès vous a M^r Short autant de justice quil en merite. mais jai trop vecu dans une Revolution pour ne pas savoir que de Legeres preventions suffisent pour L'egarer. je desire passionnement que les affaires de M^r de La Fayette se terminent en amerique. on ne cesse de desirer et de se plaindre qu'en cessant de vivre. j'ai vu le moment ou je me serois autorisée du danger d'etre jettée dans La Baltique pour decider mes compagnons d'infortune a passer en amerique. votre idée soutenoit mon courage. je m'en trouve bien peu pour La certitude de ne jamais vous offrir personnellement Monsieur, Lhommage d'un attachement dont je m'honnore et qui Restera gravé dans mon coeur jusqu'a mon dernier soupir.

NOAILLES TESSÉ

M[r] de Tessé vous supplie d'agreer des sentimens qui ne le cedent pas aux miens.

### EDITORS' TRANSLATION

Aulnay 12 June 1809

I have been asking ceaselessly for a month, Sir, to be informed of Mr. Coles's departure, and I intend to receive him, not in the house, but in the garden where I must end my days, so that you know at least where my tomb will be. There is nothing sad about it, and it could excite too much pride in me, if I took at all seriously the joke of Mr. Short who does not blush in saying—I would be just as proud to have planted this garden as I would be to have won a battle—but here is Mr. de Lafayette who tells me at 3 in the afternoon that Mr. Coles leaves tomorrow. A miracle could reanimate my hopes, but miracles rarely happen nowadays, and I count on it so little that I am going to send someone to town to make sure that this expression of my gratitude, attachment, and permit me to say, my respect, will reach you. I do not see why a woman should not use the word that expresses her feelings when what she feels is just and honorable.

It behooves me to applaud your administration only from the crowd, by clapping my hands, when I follow you in the respectful visit that you are going to pay the new president, but it seems to me that a woman has a right to express the satisfaction she has felt when reading the most noble speeches that were ever inspired by the noblest thoughts. It even seems to me that she should give thanks every time that she is allowed to feel enthusiasm, a feeling so natural to her, and so often reproached in her. I am therefore able to express to you my gratitude for a pleasure that I have not enjoyed since the most common approbation has fled from me.

Your latest and most magnificent gifts were paid a visit and pillaged in various ports, as I had the honor to tell you. One fourth of my superb box reached me in too bad a shape for a lot of the seeds to germinate. However, it remains that I alone have more Cornus florida from your seeds than there are in all the nurseries around Paris. Our ports have been completely closed since you asked me for chestnuts and green oaks. These two seeds cannot be kept for four months without being damaged, which prevents me from sending you any through Mr. Coles. But I passionately desire to plant a tree at Monticello and I find it rather piquant that it will be the product of the ones I have been planting for the past five years. So, I am enclosing a few seeds of a tree that seems to come from northern China. It was first called Paulinia aurea. I have kept this name though it has been given a new one lately. It grows very quickly, does not grow tall, its foliage is beautiful, its blossom pleasant. I persuaded myself that you were lacking it because I wanted you to be kind enough to single it out with interest as a token of the cult in which I venerate you.

I am upset that Mr. Short does not receive in your country the justice he deserves. But I have lived too long in the midst of a revolution not to know that slight reservations are enough to lead it astray. I passionately desire that Mr. de Lafayette's affairs be brought to closure in America. One stops desiring and complaining only when one ceases to live. I have had moments when I would have risked being thrown into the Baltic in order to convince my comrades in misfortune to go to America. Your idea sustained my courage. I find little of it in myself knowing with certainty that I will never have the honor to express to you in person, Sir, the respectful attachment that will remain engraved in my heart until my last breath.

NOAILLES TESSÉ

Mr. de Tessé begs you to accept his regards which do not yield to mine.

RC (MoSHi: TJC-BC); endorsed by TJ as received 3 Aug. 1809 and so recorded in SJL. Translation by Dr. Genevieve Moene. Enclosed in James Madison to TJ, 3 Aug. 1809.

Adrienne Catherine de Noailles de Tessé (1741–1814) and her husband, René Mans Froulay, comte de Tessé, became acquainted with TJ during his years in Paris, when the comtesse held gatherings in her salon at the Château de Chaville. She and TJ shared interests in architecture, botany, liberal politics, and literature. Tessé's niece Adrienne de Noailles was the wife of Lafayette, who referred to Tessé as his aunt. The comtesse and her husband went to Aulnay in Switzerland after fleeing the Hôtel de Tessé in 1790 during the French Revolution. Many of the plants she had cultivated at Chaville were taken for the Jardin du Roi in Paris (Gilbert Chinard, *Trois Amitiés Françaises de Jefferson: d'apres sa correspondance inédite avec Madame de Bréhan, Madame de Tessé et Madame de Corny* [1927]; Lafayette to TJ, 14 Aug. 1814; Beatrix Cary Davenport, ed., *A Diary of the French Revolution by Gouverneur Morris, 1752–1816* [1939], 1:6, 233; William Howard Adams, *The Paris Years of Thomas Jefferson* [1997], 227–33).

Every autumn since 1790 TJ had sent Madame de Tessé a box of seeds that she was to plant the following spring. The TRÉS MAGNIFIQUES DONS referred to here was probably his February 1807 shipment, which included seeds of the CORNUS FLORIDA, or dogwood. On 5 Oct. 1809 TJ planted the enclosed seeds of the PAULINIA AUREA (*Koelreuteria paniculata*), or goldenrain tree, probably the first grown in North America (TJ to Tessé, 21 Feb. 1807 [DLC]; TJ to Lafayette, 28 Apr. 1808 [NIC: Fabius Collection]; Betts, *Garden Book*, 339, 387).

# From William Lambert

SIR, City of Washington, June 13th 1809.

I received yesterday your friendly letter of the 28th ult^o^ in answer to a communication of mine, dated the 14th of March;—and with great pleasure accept the apology you have been pleased to make for a delay in its' acknowledgment;—for as well as I now recollect its' contents, (having kept no copy) it might have remained in the hands of one of our self important would-be great men, an age, without any reply at all. So far as my feeble efforts can extend, I shall, from principle, vindicate your character from the base aspersions hatched and brought forth in the hearts and on the tongues of jealous, malignant reptiles, unworthy the appellation of men.—When you were set up by your friends as a candidate for the presidency, in opposition to M^r^ Adams, I was in Bedford during the summer and fall of 1800, and thought my time could not be better employed than by preparing manuscript ballots, containing the names of 21 Electors, that were known to be in your favor; and without any assistance, I wrote 1200 of those ballots, which were distributed not only in Bedford, but some of the other counties composing the district: there is[1] reason to believe, that my exertions had an effect, which was not expected at that time, (particularly in Bedford.) It is probable I never should have informed you of this, during your continuance in office; but since you have retired, I think it not improper to state, that I acted from <u>principle</u>, without any prospect of <u>interest</u> to myself. You may, perhaps, have heard that I was again a candidate for the appointment of Clerk to the House of Representatives at the commencement of the present session of Congress, and have again been disappointed. A combination of envious calumniators have, in an assassin-like manner, endeavored to destroy me for some years past, and the minds of the members of Congress have, it seems, been poisoned by their malicious exertions.—You have hitherto (or in an essential degree, at least) been attacked in vain, for you were exalted above their impotent attempts to injure your fame:—it is far otherwise with me:—and after having devoted upwards of twenty years of the prime of my life (most part of which was spent in laborious, and (I may add) <u>useful</u> endeavors to promote a proper arrangement of business in the office of the House of Representatives) the members have listened to, and it appears, implicitly believed reports against me, without reflecting from what quarters and motives they have been propagated, and without any consideration of the length of time I have been employed, and the superior knowledge I must have attained of their forms of proceeding. I can no longer submit to be a <u>convenient drudge</u> in a subordinate situation under them, doing, in fact, the principal duties of Clerk to their House in the back ground; for the ease and credit of a person whom they delight to honor, but will never, perhaps, be sufficiently competent to understand or execute the part they have assigned him. Having long been desirous of fixing a first meridian for the United States at the permanent seat of their government, I am now engaged in a revision of former astronomical calculations for that purpose:—the result will be ascertained by different methods from the data observed or given, and a mean taken of the whole.—The computation will be founded on a supposition,—

1. That the Earth is a perfect sphere or globe.
2. That it's form is that of an oblate spheroid, whose equatorial axis is to it's polar, in a ratio of 334 to 333.
3. Admitting the ratio to be as 230 to 229.

The parallaxes in longitude and latitude will be computed[2] from rules given in some of the cases of oblique angled spherical trigonometry, by finding the ⋆'s true altitude, angle of position and the angle between the vertical circle and a parallel to the Ecliptic,—and by the altitude and longitude of the nonagesimal (or highest point of the ecliptic), at the respective times of immersion and emersion of the Star at Washington and Greenwich.—

Your sentiments on this undertaking, and any support you may be pleased to give, will be gratefully remembered by

Sir, Your most obedient servant, WILLIAM LAMBERT.

☞ An apology is due from me for not using "esquire" or some other style or title of distinction; but as I consider you above it, I hope the omission will be duly appre[ciated]

RC (DLC); torn; addressed: "Thomas Jefferson late President of the U.S. Monticello, Virginia"; postmarked; endorsed by TJ as received 13 July 1809 and so recorded in SJL.

Patrick Magruder was chief CLERK of the United States House of Representatives, 1807–15. With intermissions, Lambert had worked as principal clerk under the chief clerk since 1789.

[1] Lambert here canceled "some."

[2] Preceding three words interlined.

## To Wilson Cary Nicholas

DEAR SIR Monticello June 13. 09.

I did not know, till mr Patterson called on us, a few days ago, that you had passed on to Washington. I had recently observed in the debates of Congress, a matter introduced, on which I wished to give explanations more fully in conversation which I will now do by abridgment in writing. mr Randolph has proposed an enquiry into certain prosecutions at Common law in Connecticut, for libels on the government; and not only himself but others have stated them with such affected caution & such hints at the same time as to leave on every mind the impression that they had been instituted either by my direction or with my acquiescence at least. this has not been denied by my friends, because probably the fact is unknown to them. I shall state it for their satisfaction, & leave it to be disposed of as they think best. I had observed in a newspaper (some years ago, I do not recollect the time exactly) some dark hints of a prosecution in Connecticut, but so obscurely hinted that I paid little attention to it. some considerable time after, it was again mentioned so that I understood that some prosecution was going on in the federal court there[1] for calumnies uttered from the pulpit against me by a clergyman. I immediately wrote to mr Granger, who, I think, was in Connecticut at the time, stating that I had laid it down as a law to myself to take no notice of the thousand calumnies issued against me, but to trust my character to my own conduct & the good sense & candor of my fellow-citizens; that I had found no reason to be dissatisfied with that course, & I was unwilling it should be broke through by others as to any matter concerning me, & therefore requested him to desire the district attorney to dismiss the prosecution. some time after this I heard of subpoenas being served on Genl Lee, David M. Randolph & others as witnesses to attend the trial. I then for the first time conjectured the subject of the libel. I immediately wrote to mr Granger to require an immediate dismission of the prosecution. the answer of mr Huntington, the district attorney was that these spas[2] had been issued by the defendant without his knolege, that it had been his intention to dismiss all the prosecutions at the first meeting of the court & to accompany it with an avowal of his opinion that they could not be maintained because the federal court had no jurisdiction over libels. this was accordingly done. I did not till then know that there were other prosecutions of the same nature, nor do I now know what were their subjects. but all went off together, & I afterwards saw in the hands of mr Granger a letter written by the Clergyman disavowing any personal ill will towards me, & solemnly declaring he had never uttered the words charged. I think mr Granger either shewed me, or said there were affidavits of at least half a dozen respectable men who were present at the sermon & swore no such expressions were uttered, & as many equally respectable who swore the contrary. but the clergyman expressed his gratification at the dismission of the prosecution. I write all this from memory & after too long an interval of time to be certain of the exactness of all the details, but I am sure there is no variation material, and mr Granger, correcting small lapses of memory, can confirm every thing substantial. certain it is that the prosecutions had been instituted & had made considerable progress without my knolege, that they were disapproved by me as soon as known, and directed to be discontinued. the attorney did it on the same ground on which I had acted myself in the cases of Duane, Callender & others, to wit that the sedition law was unconstitutional and null, & that my obligation to execute what was law, involved that of not suffering rights secured by valid laws, to be prostrated by what was no law. I always understood that these prosecutions had been invited, if not instituted, by judge Edwards, & the Marshal, being republican, had summoned a grand jury partly, or wholly republican: but that mr Huntington declared from the beginning against the jurisdiction of the court & had determined to enter Nolle prosequis before he recieved my directions to do it.[3]

I trouble you with another subject. the law making my letters post free, goes to those <u>to me</u> only, not those <u>from me</u>. the bill had got to it's passage[4] before this was observed (and first I believe by mr Dana) & the house under too much pressure of business near the close of the session to bring in another bill. as the privilege of freedom was given to the letters <u>from</u> as well as <u>to</u> both my predecessors, I suppose no reason exists for making a distinction, and in so extensive a correspondence as I am subject to, & still considerably on public matters, it would be a sensible convenience to myself as well as those who have occasion to recieve letters from me. it happens too, as I was told at the time (for I have never looked into it myself) that it was done by two distinct acts on both the former occasions. mr Eppes I think mentioned this to me. I know from the Postmaster general that mr Adams franks all his letters. I state this matter to you as being my representative which must apologise for the trouble of it. we have been seasonable since you left us. yesterday evening & this morning we have had refreshing showers which will close & confirm the business of planting. Affectionately Yours

TH: JEFFERSON

RC (DLC: Wilson Cary Nicholas Papers); endorsed by Nicholas. PoC (DLC); at foot of first page: "W. C. Nicholas."

On 25 May 1809 John RANDOLPH of Roanoke moved in the United States House of Representatives that a committee be appointed to "inquire whether any, and what, prosecutions have been instituted before courts of the United States for libel at common law, and by what authority." Debate on the motion centered on the role of the district attorney in a series of libel cases in Connecticut begun by a predominantly Republican court appointed during TJ's administration, and especially on whether the district attorney had initiated criminal prosecutions at TJ's DIRECTION. If such an order had been issued, Representative George Troup claimed it was not only "highly censurable" but merited impeachment (*Annals*, 11th Cong., 1st sess., 75–89 [25 May 1809]). In the second of two letters to Gideon Granger (24, 26 Aug. 1807, letters not found; see Granger to TJ, 8 Sept. 1807 [DLC]) attempting to quash the PROSECUTION, TJ sought to dismiss the charges against CLERGYMAN Azel Backus, who purportedly lambasted TJ in an 1804 sermon. TJ presumably inferred from the intended calling as defense witnesses of Henry LEE and David Meade RANDOLPH that one SUBJECT OF THE LIBEL was his attempted seduction as a young man of the wife of his friend John Walker. Lee and Randolph were both known by their Federalist counterparts in New England to be aware of this controversy (Malone, *Jefferson*, 4:216–23). For an argument that TJ actually knew more about these prosecutions earlier and acted to stop them only when he became aware that the Walker scandal would be aired, see Leonard W. Levy, *Jefferson and Civil Liberties: The Darker Side* (1963), 61–6; by contrast Malone, *Jefferson*, 5:370–91, basically accepts TJ's version above; Granger's account, in Nicholas to TJ, 18 July 1809, lends some credence to Levy. The federal MARSHAL was Joseph Willcox.

[1] Word interlined.

[2] Abbreviation for "subpoenas."

[3] Preceding three words omitted in PoC.

[4] Preceding three words interlined in place of "nearly through."

# To Henry Dearborn

DEAR GENERAL Monticello June 14. 09.

So entirely are my habits changed from constant labour at my writing table, to constant & active occupation without doors, that it is with difficulty I can resolve to take up my pen. I must do it however as a matter of duty to thank you for the dumb fish you have been so kind as to have forwarded, & which are recieved safely & are found to be excellent. but I do it with pleasure also as it gives me an opportunity of renewing to you the assurances of my esteem and of the friendship I shall ever bear you as a faithful fellow labourer in the duties of the cabinet the value of whose aid there has been always[1] justly felt & highly estimated by me.[2] I sincerely congratulate you on the late pacification with England, which while it gives facility & remuneration to your labours in your new functions, restores calm in a great degree to the troubles of our country: our successors have deserved well of their country in meeting so readily the first friendly advance ever made to us by England. I hope it is the harbinger of a return to the exercise of common sense & common good humour, with a country with which mutual interests would urge a mutual & affectionate intercourse. but her conduct hitherto has been towards us so insulting, so tyrannical & so malicious as to indicate a contempt for our opinions or dispositions respecting her. I hope she is now coming over to a wiser conduct, & becoming sensible how much better it is to cultivate the good will of the government itself, than of a faction hostile to it; to obtain it's friendship gratis than to purchase it's enmity by nourishing at great expence a faction to embarras it, to recieve the reward of an honest policy rather than of a corrupt & vexatious one. I trust she has at length opened her eyes to federal falsehood & misinformation and learnt, in the issue of the presidential election, the folly of believing them. such a reconciliation to the government if real & permanent will secure the tranquility of our country and render the management of our affairs easy & delightful to our successors for whom I feel as much interest as if I were still[3] in their place. certainly all the troubles & difficulties in the government during our time proceeded from England: at least all others were trifling in comparison with them.

Some time before[4] I retired from office I proposed to mr Smith of the War office to[5] place your son in the list of some nominations for the new army. he called on me & stated that Pickering had prepared materials for an opposition to his appointment which he was satisfied could be easily met with proper information, but without it, might embarrass & endanger the appointment. we concluded therefore that it was best to put it off to the ensuing session of Congress & in the mean time give you notice of it. he promised to write & explain the delay to you, & I stated the matter to mr Madison who would attend to the nomination at the proper time. perhaps late events may supercede all further proceeding, as to that army.

Be so good as to present my affectionate respects to mrs Dearborne. I hope that her health as well as your own may be improved by a return to native climate, and that you may both enjoy as many years as you desire of health & prosperity is the prayer of yours sincerely & affectionately.

TH: JEFFERSON

PoC (DLC); at foot of first page: "Gen[l] Dearborne."

Henry Dearborn (1751–1829), the recently appointed customs collector for the port of Boston, was TJ's secretary of war from 1801 to 1809. A native of Hampton, New Hampshire, and a physician by training, he joined the Continental army at the outbreak of the Revolutionary War and eventually attained the rank of lieutenant colonel. From 1781–82 Dearborn was deputy quartermaster general of the Continental army. He represented the District of Maine in the United States House of Representatives, 1793–97, served as a notably incompetent United States Army major general during the War of 1812, and was minister plenipotentiary to Portugal, 1822–24 (*ANB*; *DAB*; Richard A. Erney, *The Public Life of Henry Dearborn* [1979]; *JEP*, 1:395–6, 2:97, 109 [5 Mar. 1801, 25 Jan., 11 Feb. 1809]).

[1] Word added in margin.

[2] Preceding two words interlined.

[3] Word interlined.

[4] TJ here canceled "I retired from office I gave a note to mr Smi."

[5] TJ here canceled "make out a commission for your son."

## To John Barnes

DEAR SIR Monticello June 15. 09.

Yours of the 9th came to hand last night, and the course it suggested was like a ray of light beaming on my uneasy mind. indeed I know that had I time to consult Genl Kosciuzko he would be delighted with the opportunity of accomodating me. and I accede to it with the more readiness, because before his departure he made me the depository & sole executor of his will, by which it appears his intention only to use the interest of his money here, & never to draw the principal from this country: and the uses to which it is to be applied after his death will occupy time in their execution. the making use of it as you propose will enable me to offer my lands on the credits usual in this country, & much facilitate their sale, and I will charge the debt on my whole estate which is of 50 times that amount in the event of any accident to myself before the sale of the lands destined to it's repaiment. I will therefore pray you to place his 4500.D. now undisposed of to my account, & to apply them immediately to taking up my whole note in the bank of the US. and the balance to the discharge of what I am in your debt: leaving the matter in the President's hands to his own entire convenience according to my agreement with him. in this way we shall all sleep sound and I shall have time to discharge the debt without sacrificing my lands by sales for cash, which might not yield half value. the punctual paiment of the interest shall be sacredly attended to, and will be the more certain as it will be at the period when the produce of the year is usually sold. I salute you with assurances of great esteem & respect. TH: JEFFERSON

PoC (DLC); at foot of text: "Mr J. Barnes."

Barnes's letter of THE 9TH of June, not found, is recorded in SJL as received 14 June 1809 from Georgetown. Letters from Barnes of 25 and 30 May and 4 June 1809, also missing, are recorded in SJL as received from Georgetown on 28 May, 4 and 11 June 1809. Taduesz Kosciuszko's 5 May 1798 WILL (*PTJ*, 30:332–3), contested and ultimately disallowed long after his and TJ's deaths, dedicated his American property to the manumission of slaves.

## To David Gelston

SIR Monticello June 15. 09.

Immediately on the reciept of your favor of Apr. 22. I desired messrs Gibson & Jefferson, my correspondents at Richmond to remit you the 18. D 25 c amount of duties of the two boxes of wine which you informed me you had recieved for me. this I trust they have done. in the mean time I have recieved one of the boxes containing 3. doz. bottles of wine (considerable breakage excepted) as you had mentioned that there were 2. boxes, I wrote to Gibson & Jefferson on the subject, and now inclose you their answer. having as yet recieved no advice respecting this wine but your letter I am unable to throw any light on the subject, or to state any claim respecting it. perhaps the information which accompanied the boxes to your hands may do it. Accept the assurances of my esteem & respect. TH: JEFFERSON

PoC (MHi); at foot of text: "Mr Gelston"; endorsed by TJ. Enclosure: George Jefferson to TJ, 12 June 1809 (first letter).

David Gelston (1744–1828), a native of Suffolk County, New York, was a merchant who served in the state provincial congress from 1775 to 1777 and the state assembly from 1777 to 1785. In 1786 he moved to New York City. Three years later he represented New York in the last Confederation Congress, and he served in the state senate, 1791–94 and in 1798 and 1802. Gelston was a zealous Republican and a close associate of Aaron Burr. TJ appointed him collector of the district of New York early in July 1801, and he held that post until 1820 (Frederic Gregory Mather, *The Refugees of 1776 from Long Island to Connecticut* [1913], 355–6; *JEP*, 1:403, 405, 3:218 [6, 26 Jan. 1802, 27 Nov. 1820]; Mary-Jo Kline and others, eds., *Political Correspondence and Public Papers of Aaron Burr* [1983], 1:225–6, 535–6, 570; Washington *National Intelligencer*, 25 Aug. 1828).

TJ's 1 May 1809 letter TO GIBSON & JEFFERSON was actually addressed to George Jefferson.

# To Jonathan Shoemaker

DEAR SIR Monticello June 15. 09.

Your favor of the 5th was recieved on the 11th & recieved with great joy. I had begun to despair of your coming, & in that case I must have proposed the rescinding the lease, for that it is a concern compleatly bankrupt everybody in the neighborhood seems convinced, and some (I am told, for I do not know the fact) have brought suits for their wheat, & others propose to do it. that there are many demands for wheat delivered which cannot be obtained I have assured[1] evidence. I wrote myself to your son two months ago for a paiment of rent, & altho' two years are due & not a copper paid he has never condescended to give me a word of answer. in the mean time I am in real distress, insomuch that in buying bread for my family I have been obliged to give 15/ a barrel on a little credit, when it was offered me at 12/ cash. my nailery too will shortly be stopped for want of rod, which cannot be obtained but on short paiments. I take patience however under the expectation of your coming and I have given such assurances in the neighborhood that you will put all to rights, that I think they will await your coming. the total discredit into which the mill is brought will lay you under disadvantages, but a good disposition towards yourself prevails. you must take the concern however into your own hands entirely, and the entire separation of your son from it can alone give confidence in it. indeed the mail contracts are quite as much as he can manage & engross all his attention. it is painful to me to say these things to you. but others who have not the same interest in the mill as I have, will not give you the information. it's importance to me is too great to let you be ignorant of the true state of things.[2] resting therefore in the hope of seeing you soon, & that all will be well on your arrival I conclude with assurances of my sincere esteem

TH: JEFFERSON

PoC (MHi); at foot of text: "Mr Jonathan Shoemaker"; endorsed by TJ.

[1] Manuscript: "asssured."
[2] Preceding six words interlined.

## From Binny & Ronaldson

SIR

Philadelphia June 16. 1809

Our efforts to procure antimony from some source within the United States have failed, and the want of it having obliged us to part with upwards of thirty Journeymen & boys, we are under the necessity of making an extraordinary effort to procure this material so necessary in making printing types, indeed without a supply we will be obliged soon to reduce the number of our workmen still more—We have concluded our James Ronaldson must go to the continent of Europe to procure a supply and make arrangements for being regularly furnished with it in future for this purpose he is to go to Hamburgh and thence to France where it is abundent; but it being the policy of France to embarrass the manufactures[1] of Britain as much as possible, and as this article with the latter is scarce and dear, we are much affraid the French will not be much disposed to permit its shipment to the United States, fearing it will through this channel reach England. We solicit your assistance, and request an introduction to some persons in Hamburg, Paris &ca to whose representations the French would attach credit in order that we might be permitted to export enough for our own consumption in the United States

We are With Respect & esteem

BINNY & RONALDSON

RC (DLC); in James Ronaldson's hand; endorsed by TJ as received 22 June 1809 and so recorded in SJL.

[1] Manuscript: "manufatures."

## From George Jefferson

DEAR SIR Richmond 16th June 1809

I have duly received your favor of the 12th, and have selected the house of Gordon Trokes & Co, as being the most eligible in my opinion for the supply of your groceries.—They consent to receive payment half annually, which is more I expect than any other house here would do for such articles.

I doubt however if you will be supplied even on nearly as advantageous terms, as you might be from the Northern Towns, for the reason which I think I have before assigned.—You can however, if you think proper, try it for awhile, and then, if you find it will not answer, make some other arrangement.

I made the promised excursion up the river, but to no purpose, having only found a few fragments of papers which I suppose[1] escaped the notice of Mr Scott, by being mostly covered in mud.

It will not I expect be in my to[2] make you a visit until toward the last of August: at any rate it will not be until you will have returned from Bedford, even although you should defer going for several weeks.

I am Dear Sir Your Very humble servt GEO. JEFFERSON

RC (MHi); at foot of text: "Thomas Jefferson esqr"; endorsed by TJ as received 29 June 1809 and so recorded in SJL.

[1] Preceding two words interlined.
[2] Thus in manuscript.

## To James Madison

DEAR SIR Monticello June 16. 09.

I inclose you three letters from detained seamen which came to hand by the last post. your favor of the 12th was recieved at the same time. the intelligence by the Pacific gives me great anxiety. when I consider the tenor of the new order of council & the official exposition of it by the Lords of trade to the London American merchants (in the inclosed paper) and compare it with the engagement of Erskine under instructions given two months before, I am at a loss from which we have most to fear, the folly or the faithlesness of the Cannings & Castlereaghs of the British ministry. is it possible that to get themselves out of a former hobble they should have involved themselves in another so much more difficult? and yet if they mean to adhere to the new order, their instructions to Erskine to enter into engagements in direct opposition to it, would be such a wanton abandonment of all pretensions to common honesty as one would suppose no men could deliberately intend. et cui bono? merely to catch a partial supply by a temporary relaxation of our measures? it seems impossible to believe either alternative, & yet the one or the other must be true. I presume it will produce some caution & hesitation in the proceedings of Congress. my joy on our supposed settlement is extremely damped by the occurrence of a trick, so strange, whatever solution may be given of it, and I fear a return of our difficulties, & it will be with increased force if they do recur. I sincerely wish a happy issue from them, for your own sake as well as for that of us all.

I am very happy in being enabled to relieve you from the disagreeable situation into which my improvidence had drawn your kind friendship. I felt severely the impropriety of dragging your name into the bank, as I had often been mortified with my own being there. but a too late attention to the state of my affairs at Washington had rendered it unavoidable. mr Barnes is now[1] enabled to discharge my note at the bank, as well as a balance due to himself, and the separate account between you & myself may await your own entire convenience without in the least incommoding me, and I pray you to be assured of the sensibility with which I have experienced your kind accomodation to my difficulties.

For the last three days we have had fine & plentiful showers of rain, & were willing they should cease as appearances[2] promised last night. but it commenced raining in the night & now continues with the wind at North East. this may become dangerous to the wheat which at best can only be a midling crop. that of tobacco cannot become great if the observation of the planters is correct that there never was a great crop of tobacco which was not pitched before the last of May. this year not a plant was in the ground till June: but the rains have been so favorable since that the whole crop is now standing & growing. I salute you with sincere affection & respect

TH: JEFFERSON

RC (DLC: Madison Papers); at foot of first page: "The President of the US." PoC (DLC); endorsed by TJ. Enclosures not found.

TJ was reacting to Madison's FAVOR of 12 June and related news reports of Britain's failure to revoke the Orders in Council, including an official statement late in April by Spencer Perceval, the chancellor of the exchequer, that the orders "had not been rescinded; but that certain alterations had been made," which was conveyed by the president of the Board of Trade to AMERICAN MERCHANTS in London (Washington *National Intelligencer*, 14 June 1809). ET CUI BONO: and for what advantage. PITCHED: planted in a fixed or definite place so as to remain firm (*OED*).

[1] Word interlined.

[2] Word interlined in place of "it."

# From Joseph Dougherty

Dear Sir City of Washington June 18th. 1809

your letter of the 27 May I received; I went the other day to Doct[r] Thorntons farm to select a ram lamb of this year for you: you may take him from the Ewe the 15 or 20 of Aug[t] which is about the time that the lambs quits the Ewes; and it will be as soon as necessary to put him to your broad tail ewe. I remember of you saying that Gen[l] Washington[s] rule was to put his ewes to the ram about Michaelmas day: which is the 29 of Sept[r]. your lambs would then come about the 29 of Feb. but the ewe lambs that comes at that time should not be put to the ram until the year following: because if they do go to the ram in the same year they are droped; it stunts their growth and your flock degenerate:

The Eider down coverlet I sent by M[r] P: Carr, your books were not finished when he went from here. I will put them in a box and send them by the stage: M[r] Milegan says he had no nautical almanacs from you he & I looked over the List of books and papers he had to bind for you; but could find none; I took the liberty of requesting him to procure one for you of this years; as soon as he get[s] it I will send it to you:

I have sir two modes of proceeding in view with respect to my merino rams; nither of which I intend to fix upon until I receive your opinion and advise: Several people wishes me to take ewes at so much for the season. this way in my opinion would destroy the sale of my own lambs. would it not be beter to purchas ewes; and sell the lambs Otherways charge more for the season of the rams, than I would for the ram lambs. one thing is my purse is not heavy enough to purchas a sufficient quantity of ewes: will you be so good sir to advise me as soon as you can make it convenient

I am still ready to serve you; any thing you want done here

Sir your Hbl[e] Serv[t] Jo[s] Dougherty.

Gov[r] Millege is not here this session; nor I believe do not intend to com

RC (DLC); addressed: "Thomas Jefferson Esq[r] Late President of the U: States. Monticello Virginnia"; franked and postmarked; endorsed by TJ as received 24 June 1809 and so recorded in SJL.

## From William C. C. Claiborne

DEAR SIR, New-Orleans June 19h 1809.

Believing that the discussion which the question as to the right of property in the Batture in front of the Suburb St Mary, has given rise to, will not be uninteresting to you, I have the pleasure to enclose Mr Thierry's Answer to Mr Duponceau's last Pamphlet.

With the best wishes for your Health & happiness—

I am Dr Sir, Your faithful friend

WILLIAM C. C. CLAIBORNE

RC (MHi); at foot of text: "Mr Thomas Jefferson Monticello Virginia"; endorsed by TJ as received 13 July 1809 and so recorded in SJL. Enclosure: Jean Baptiste Simon Thierry, *Reply to Mr. Duponceau* (New Orleans, 1809; Sowerby, no. 3491).

After his arrival in New Orleans in 1804, Edward Livingston acquired and began working to perfect a claim to the BATTURE IN FRONT OF THE SUBURB ST MARY. This riverfront property had traditionally been used by the public, and Livingston's claim was met with consternation and the possibility of violent resistance. TJ became convinced that the batture belonged to the United States and ordered Livingston's eviction in November 1807. An extraordinarily complicated series of lawsuits and appeals to various government authorities followed, including an unsuccessful lawsuit filed in 1810 by Livingston against TJ in the federal circuit court for the district of Virginia and the publication by both men of pamphlets supporting their positions. Livingston eventually did obtain undisputed possession of a share of this extremely valuable property, but he was still litigating related issues in the 1830s (Malone, *Jefferson*, 6:55–73; William B. Hatcher, *Edward Livingston: Jeffersonian Republican and Jacksonian Democrat* [1940], 139–89; George Dargo, *Jefferson's Louisiana: Politics and the Clash of Legal Traditions* [1975], 74–101, 208–18; John Wickham to TJ, 16 May 1810, and note).

## From George Jefferson

DEAR SIR Richmond 19th June 1809

If you go to Bedford as soon as you contemplate, you will be surprised I expect at not finding the 3 dozen chairs there, which you ordered several months ago.—The first person who engaged to make them disappointed us altogether, & the next one has been a long time about them.—They are however at last ready, and shall be forwarded by the first safe boat, to the care of Saml J. Harrison

I am Dear Sir Your Very humble servt GEO. JEFFERSON

RC (MHi); at foot of text: "Thomas Jefferson esqr"; endorsed by TJ as received 29 June 1809 and so recorded in SJL.

# From Skelton Jones

SIR, Richmond, June, 19. 1809.

I find in a letter from you to the late John D. Burke, dated Washington June 1. 1805, the following passage—"After my return to live at Monticello, I am persuaded it will be in my power, as it is certainly in my wish, to furnish you with some useful matter, not perhaps to be found elsewhere." Knowing this to be the case, and that your inclination and ability, to throw every possible light on Virginian History, are both great, I have taken the liberty to address you. From April 22. '75, to the 4th of March last, is the period of which it was my intention to have written the history; though for reasons, which in justice to myself I cannot conceal, I am certain that I shall be obliged, in my present undertaking, to depart widely from my original design, as expressed in my prospectus. When I was hurried into this business, I was made to believe that materials were collected and chronologically arranged, and that nothing remained but the finishing touches of composition. On the contrary I find myself compromitted on this subject, under more embarrassing circumstances than can well be imagined.—The collection of materials, and compiling the narrative have commenced and progressed together: I have to deal with sordid merchants, (with whom Burk had entangled himself,) whose knowledge extends not beyond the counter & the yard stick. It is prescribed to me when the first chapter is to go to press; when the volume is to be finished; and, I am limited as to the number of pages it is to contain:—You will readily perceive, under these circumstances, that it surpasses human exertion to bring out the work as it should be. I foresee therefore that my literary reputation must suffer for a time; but I am resolved, if life and health is spared me, to redeem it, when the galling fetters of commercial cupidity shall have fallen from my limbs.

But now sir to the principal object of this letter. I have files of newspapers, or access to them, for '75, '76 and '77. I have examined three several files in this town, viz: master commissioner Hay's, Doctr Benjn Duval's, and Chs Copeland's, and find that the file for '78 is missing in them all. It has been suggested to me that in consequence of the difficulty of obtaining paper, there were no news papers issued in that year; but this I think extremely improbable: you can certainly inform me. I wish not only information from you but advice also: After Dunmore left the coast of Virginia, in the summer of '76, and joined the British to the southward, Virginia was not the theatre of hostilities, until Matthews burnt Suffolk, in '79, which was followed up by the invasion of Philips and Arnold, from which time it continud to be the scene of active warfare, until the surrender of Cornwallis and the conclusion of peace. Now, I wish your advice what the historian is to do with the latter part of '76, the whole of '77 & '78, and a part of '79? As our state was happily exempt during nearly three years, from the calamities of war, and its history during that therefore barren of battles and bloodshed, what else can be done than search into the laws, religion, manners, & customs of those times? A philosophical historian had he time and materials, might usefully employ his pen upon these subjects during the recess from actual war. Upon this subject, sir you will greatly oblige me by your advice as to the plan; as you will also by information where materials for its execution can be obtained.

My motive, I trust, will be my apology for making this application. May you, sir, enjoy in old age and retirement that happiness, which a devotion of the best years of your life to public service so amply merits.

Very respectfully Y[r] obedt. servt. SKELTON JONES

RC (DLC); addressed: "Thomas Jefferson, Esquire. Late President of the U.S. Monticello"; franked and postmarked; endorsed by TJ as received 29 June 1809 and so recorded in SJL; notation by TJ: "from 1741–60 lent to Burke." Enclosures: (1) Jones's Prospectus for volume four of John Daly Burk, *The History of Virginia*, Richmond, 2 Aug. 1808, stating that the volume would start with the American Revolution and conclude with the end of TJ's administration; that it would include biographies of "heroes, statesmen and patriots" as well as an appendix on "police, literature, arts, manners, manufactures, commerce, government, naval and military strength, population, productions, mode of living. &c. &c. &c." and charters and other public papers "interesting to the politician and antiquary"; that it would be a large octavo volume costing three dollars in sheepskin and two-and-a-half dollars in boards; and concluding with a blank for subscribers' names. (2) Circular letter from Jones, August 1808, requesting information from the addressee for the period outlined in the prospectus on twenty topics including parents, early life and education, public life, physical description, family life, personal anecdotes, temperament, and a request for a miniature; asking for even "the most trifling circumstances"; and promising that no political use was intended, that responses would be used only for research, and that they would be returned if requested (printed broadsides in DLC, with No. 2 endorsed by TJ as a "circular" received 29 June 1809 and so recorded in SJL).

Skelton Jones (d. 1812), an attorney in Richmond, published the Richmond *Examiner*, 1803–04. He contracted with the estate administrator of Burk, who was killed in a duel in 1808, to write the concluding volume of Burk's *The History of Virginia: from its First Settlement to the Present Day* (Petersburg, 1804–05; Sowerby, no. 464; Poor, *Jefferson's Library*, 4 [no. 127]). Jones was delayed by ill health and did not finish the fourth volume before his own death in a duel, but his work was incorporated in 1816 in the last published volume, completed by Louis Hue Girardin and only taking the history through 1781 (Norfleet, *Saint-Mémin*, 179; Brigham, *American Newspapers*, 2:1139; Jones to TJ, 17 Apr. 1811; Lewis H. Jones, *Captain Roger Jones, of London and Virginia* [1891], 55; Richmond *Enquirer*, 30 Oct. 1812).

TJ loaned Burk his file of Virginia newspapers in JUNE 1805 for use in preparing his history (TJ to Burk, 1, 12 June 1805 [DLC]).

# From William Nelson

DEAR SIR Westover June 19$^{th}$ 1809

Your power and disposition to give information and assistance to others in various ways must be my apology for obtruding this address upon you in your retirement—If this were not sufficient, your former acquaintance with Col$^{o}$ Byrd, and the kindness you have shewn on other occasions in informing M$^{rs}$ Byrd of the situation of some property to which the estate was entitled, would justify my troubling you on this occasion—

M$^{rs}$ Byrd lately observed in the "Argus" published in Richmond, an advertizement signed "James Irwin," directed "to all Officers and Soldiers, or their legal representatives, who served in the regiment called "Virg$^{a}$ Blues" commanded by the late Gen$^{l}$ (then Col$^{o}$) Geo. Washington, from the year 1754 to 1764, and all those who served in the corps called the 60$^{th}$ regiment Royal Americans commanded by Col$^{o}$ Henry Bouquet; and also all those who served in the Pennsylvania-Provincials" (which are enumerated). Notice is thereby given that they are entitled to a valuable bounty of Crown-land, by virtue of the King of England's proclamation, dated the 7$^{th}$ October, 1793. (This probably ought to be 1763)—Applications are to be made before the 15$^{th}$ of July next.

Col$^{o}$ Byrd, (as M$^{rs}$ Byrd informs me) went into the Army in 1756, and had the Command of the 2$^{d}$ Virginia Regiment untill it was disbanded, she thinks, in the year 1758. Col$^{o}$ Washington had the command of the first Virginia-Regiment—He married and retired, M$^{rs}$ B says—She adds that the Virginia-Assembly, she believes, at the requisition of the King, and the Commander in Chief (Sir Jeff$^{y}$ Amherst I think) raised another Regiment called the Virginia-Regiment, chiefly composed of the Officers and Soldiers, who had served in the first Regiments. Col$^{o}$ Byrd was appointed to the command of this Regiment & served[1] untill it was disbanded.

Can you inform us, my dear Sir, why[2] Col$^{o}$ B's Regiment is omitted from those to whom the Notice is directed?

Is the Bounty now to be paid in Land confined to inferior-Officers? And

Do you suppose that Col$^{o}$ B's representatives have a right to any part of this Bounty?

It is well known to you that they have rec$^{d}$ a Bounty in Land under the King of England's Proclamation. It is probable that Gen$^{l}$ Washington had also, & others mentioned in the advertizement—

If therefore this be an additional Bounty, and the Colonels are included in it, Col° B's representatives may probably be entitled.
As soon as your leisure from more important concerns will permit, I beg the favor of you to let me hear from you by a letter directed to me at Wmsburg—

I am, with all possible Respect, & esteem, Dr Sir, Yr obedt St

Wm NELSON

RC (DLC); addressed: "Thomas Jefferson Monticello near Charlottesville"; franked and postmarked; endorsed by TJ as received 29 June 1809 and so recorded in SJL.

William Nelson (ca. 1760–1813), attorney and law professor at the College of William and Mary, rose to lieutenant colonel in the Continental army, represented James City County in 1783 and York County from 1788 to 1791 in the House of Delegates, served on the Council of State, 1784–86, and sat on the Virginia General Court from 1791 until his death. His second wife, Abby Byrd, was the daughter of William Byrd (1728–77), and his second wife, Mary Willing Byrd (*PTJ*, 28:63–4; Heitman, *Continental Army*, 411; Marion Tinling, ed., *The Correspondence of the Three William Byrds of Westover, Virginia, 1684–1776* [1977], 2:829; Richmond *Enquirer*, 16 Mar. 1813).

The advertisement was dated 15 Apr. 1809 and PUBLISHED in the Richmond *Virginia Argus* on 9 June 1809. During the French and Indian War, William Byrd enlisted under Lord Loudoun in 1756, became colonel of the 2d Virginia Regiment in 1758, and in 1759 WAS APPOINTED commander of the 1st Virginia REGIMENT (*DVB*).

1 Preceding two words interlined.
2 Reworked from "what."

# From "Goodwill"

HONORED SIR, June 20, 1809

After a long silence your unknown friend begs leave once more to address you, on a subject of the greatest importance. And can there be any subject, that is diserving of this name, but that one, which equally deserves & demands the attention of each & all the human family, viz. the care of the immortal part, to secure for it an inheritance in that blessed world, "where the moth nor rust cannot corrupt nor thieves break thro & steal"

Dear Sir, as you are now retired from the busy scenes in which you have long been occupied let me invite you, Sir, to take religion into your social circle, that she may animate your spirits & cheer you in the evening of your days. Respected friend, you must be sensible, that your continuance on earth will not be long, even at the longest period which is alotted to man. And doubtless, Sir, you have a something within, that tells you, that your better part will exist beyond the reach of death. The immortal mind of man can be satisfied with nothing short of God & the joys of heaven. All other contemplations are too low & groveling to occupy the attention of the soul.

The holy volume of revelation contains the most excellent and glorious promises. O that we may take hold of Christ by faith & rest entirely on him for our salvation. Then we shall not fear death but when we drop this body we shall enter with triumph into the joys of our Lord.

That this may be our happy case, is the earnest desire & sincere prayer of your friend, and humble servant GOODWILL

RC (MHi); at foot of text: "Hon. Thomas Jefferson"; endorsed by TJ as an anonymous "religious" letter received 29 June 1809 and so recorded in SJL.

"Goodwill" wrote a series of letters to TJ during his retirement as an unsigned correspondent, "Goodwill," or "A Friend to the Christian Religion." He did not reveal his identity but acknowledged having spent some time at Monticello ("A Friend to the Christian Religion" to TJ, 28 Apr. 1811; Anonymous to TJ, 1 June 1812). His biblical reference WHERE THE MOTH . . . & STEAL is to Matthew 6.19–34.

On the same day as he got this letter, TJ received, possibly from "Goodwill," a PRAYER "*To be used after the declaration of our independence is read, on the fourth of July*," that "We, thy human beings, desire to implore thee for thy mercy's sake, to keep the United States of America free from the stupidity, power and tyranny of kings" and keep the nation's rulers "free from the temptations of designing men" (printed broadside in DLC: TJ Papers, 229:41065; undated; endorsed by TJ as an anonymous item "postmark Brunswick. June. religious" received 29 June 1809 and so recorded in SJL).

# From James Madison

DEAR SIR Washington June 20. 1809

Yours of the 16th came to hand yesterday. I hope you have not made any sacrifice of any sort to the scruple which has superseded my arrangemt with Mr Barnes. The execution of it would have equally accorded with my disposition & my conveniency.

The Gazette of yesterday contains the mode pursued for reanimating confidence in the pledge of the B. Govt given by Mr Erskine in his arrangemt with this Govt. The puzzle created by the order of April struck every one. E. assures us that his Govt was under such impressions as to the views of this, that not the slightest expectation existed, of our fairly meeting its overtures, & that the last[1] order was considered as a seasonable mitigation of the tendency of a failure of the experiment. This explanation seems as extraordinary as the alternatives it shuns. The fresh declarations of Mr E. seem to have quieted the distrust which was becoming pretty strong; but has not destroyed the effect of the ill grace stamped on the British retreat,[2] and of the commercial rigor evinced by the new & insidious duties stated in the newspapers. It may be expected, I think that the B. Gov[t] will fulfil what its Minister has Stipulated; and that if it means to be trickish, it will frustrate the proposed negociation, and then say, their orders were not permanently repealed, but only withdrawn, in the mean time.

The only question likely now to agitate Cong[s] will be on the Bill which opens our ports to French, as well as B. ships of war. The Senate have passed it unanimously. Whether the Feds were sincere, or wished the debate &c to take place in the H. of R. remains to be seen.

Y[rs] truly. JAMES MADISON

RC (DLC: Madison Papers); at foot of first page: "M[r] Jefferson"; endorsed by TJ as received 24 June 1809 and so recorded in SJL.

[1] Word interlined.

[2] Preceding two words interlined in place of "proceedings."

# To Thomas Jefferson Randolph

DEAR JEFFERSON Monticello June 20. 09.

In the even current of a country life few occurrences arise of sufficient note to become the subject of a letter to a person at a distance. it would be little interesting to such an one to be told of the distressing drought of the months of April & May, that wheat & corn scarcely vegetated and no seeds in the garden came up; that since that we have had good rains but very cold weather, so that prospects are disheartening for the farmer & little better to the gardener E[t]c E[t]c yet these circumstances excite a lively interest on the spot, & in their variations from bad to good, & the reverse fill up our lives with those sensations which attach us to existence, altho' they could not be the subject of a letter to a distant friend. hence we write to you seldom, & now after telling you we are all well, I have given you all our news which would be interesting to you. but tho' we do not write, we think of you, & have been for some time counting the days before you will be with us. the death of D[r] Woodhouse & loss of his lectures leave no inducement to protract your stay after the Botanical lectures are ended, for I do not think the mineralogical course important enough for that. we shall expect you therefore when the botanical course is finished. in the mean time it is necessary I should know the state of your funds. before I left Washington I remitted to mr Peale what I supposed would suffice during your stay: but having made some draughts on you, & the one for Lemaire more considerable than I had expected, there will probably be a deficiency. your Mama desires you will get for Mary a little book she has seen advertised, called the Adventures of Mary & her cat. anticipating the pleasure of your return, & assuring you of the happiness it will give us to have you again among us, to the salutations of the family I add only my own affectionate Adieux.

TH: JEFFERSON

PoC (MHi); at foot of text: "Th: J. Randolph"; endorsed by TJ. Enclosed in Charles Willson Peale to TJ, 25 June 1809.

University of Pennsylvania chemistry professor James WOODHOUSE died on 4 June 1809 (*DAB*). MARY: Mary Jefferson Randolph. The LITTLE BOOK was Eliza Fenwick, *Mary and Her Cat: In Words Not Exceeding Two Syllables* (London, 1804).

# From David Gelston

SIR, New York June 21st 1809

I have this day receivd your letter of the 15th instant. and I have no doubt by what I have learned, that one of the boxes of wine mentioned, belongs to Capt Tingey—

When Capt Webster of the Ship Pilgrim entered here in March last, on his manifest were noted "six boxes sundries," which he had taken on board from another Ship in Salem—I understood they were all for you, soon after it appeared, two of the boxes contained minerals &ca for another person—one box contained a large Turkish fowling piece for Colo Williams of the military academy, and one box of toys for Capt Tingey—The boxes being in such bad order, the marks so defaced and the Captain knowing so little about the business, it was difficult to ascertain the real owners—I should have explained this business earlier, but presumed it would have been done by Mr Tingey—

very truly your's

DAVID GELSTON

RC (MHi); at foot of text: "Mr Jefferson"; endorsed by TJ as received 29 June 1809 and so recorded in SJL.

# To Shadrach Ricketson

Monticello June 21. 09.

Th: Jefferson presents his compliments & his thanks to Doctr Ricketson for his treatise on the means of preserving health & the pamphlets he has been so kind as to send him. he shall read the former especially with particular pleasure, having much more confidence in the means of preserving than of restoring health. he salutes D^r Ricketson with assurances of his respect.

PoC (MHi); dateline at foot of text; endorsed by TJ.

# From Benjamin Waterhouse

SIR, Cambridge June 21. 1809

I ought perhaps[1] to apologize for breaking in upon the tranquility of your retirement with this Letter—I have tried to avoid it, but find that I cannot, because it relates to a Stab at my Character, which,[2] from the poison of the Weapon, would, without some Exertion on my part, have left behind it an "immedicabile vulnus."—

Among several charges transmitted to me by the Secretary of the Treasury respecting my Conduct in the Marine Hospital there is one which reads thus

"5^t Entertaining parties at the Hospital from the public Stores, and before some of them ridiculing the president of the United States."—

Although General Dearborn detected, at once, the falsehood of the first part of this charge, it was apparent, so much was he a Stranger to me, and my Character, that he was inclined to believe the latter.[3]—so entirely predjudiced was the General on this subject, that when I denied it, he seemed desirous to stop me, lest I should sink my self still deeper in infamy—The Anecdote as related by Gen^l D, was this—the Scene of it one of the Hospital rooms, where were a Number of prints—I was represented as saying "there" pointing to the picture of your Excellency—"is our philosophical president"—"and there"—pointing through the Window—"is the Effects of his Wisdom"—Viz the Embargo breakers, lying at the Navy Yard-Wharf—I cannot perhaps do better, than transcribe from my defence (which I addressed to the Collector) my Sentiments on this Anecdote[4] "I cannot even guess who related this of me—but I hesitate not a moment in pronouncing it a falsehood in all its parts—No man ever heard me say any thing of M^r Jefferson in any way resembling it. It is a wonder to me what could have been the concurrence of circumstances, and of Arts, that could have induced the late president to have inclined his Ear, for a moment, to such an Anecdote of me as this! I shall write to him e're long on this subject; and shall only remark now, that were this a Case of Life and Death, the Jury would acquit me, from the physical impossibility of the thing, as related. It is impossible to see the Vessells at the Navy

Yard from that Room or any other Room in the Hospital, owing to the intervention of a Hill. Should it be said, that it meant the Ships lying at the Wharves in Charlestown, or Boston, I Answer that they are equally out of sight, from the same Cause—A falsehood is therefore imprinted on the very face of this Anecdote. There is another remarkable Circumstance of it. The picture never was hung up in any room of the Hospital, but lay with its face downwards in a large Desk, until I carried it to Cambridge to place it in my parlour—Having proved the physical impossibility of this Anecdote, let me leave to my friends to prove the moral impossibility of it"—I would here remark that distrusting my own feelings, I endeavoured to clarify my own Ideas of this unpleasant Subject, by passing them thro the judgement of such men, as are not easily duped or deceived: I therefore put a Copy of my defence, and of the documents tending to illustrate it, into the hands of some of the first Characters among us in the political, Clerical, Literary, and[5] Mercantile Departments;—among others Mr John Quincy Adams gave his View of the whole Affair, which he concluded thus—"I have said that some of the facts alledged against Dr Waterhouse shame inquiry. I allude particularly to that of entertaining Company at the Hospital, and ridiculing the president of the United States—the very allegation of such an Offence indicates the Source, in the Accusers heart, from which it Sprung—I have Known Dr Waterhouse many Years—I have been during the last three Years in particular habits of intimacy with him—I have heard his Sentiments open and confidential; expressed at all times, with perfect freedom;—I know it is impossible he should have ridiculed the president of the United States"—

"But what could have been the Motive for such an Accusation? Why—Dr Waterhouse holds his Office at the pleasure of the president. And if a Number of petty Official Malversations, should, as it must have been expected they would turn out, upon explanation, to be meer inaccuracies of form, unluckily liable to glosses of an odious Nature, this last Article was reserved, as an Appeal to the personal resentments, or at least suspicions of the person who was to be the Ultimate Judge—the Accuser must have thought the Heart of the president Constituted like his own. I am well assured, that this hopeful Artifice will not only fail of its intended Effect; but that it will give a Key to, and furnish a Guard against the temper, and purpose upon which the whole Structure of Malignity has been raised" Thus far Mr Adams—

When Mr Gerry had perused the same papers he wrote me as follows—"I have read your Defence and the Documents which relate to it, and am exceedingly gratified, and satisfied by the perusal—I will, with great pleasure, address a Letter to the president (Maddison) on the subject; And if you are not justified in your Conduct, shall conclude, that intrigue, infamous intrigue, and injustice, have triumphantly superceded great Abilities, patriotic Zeal, indefatigable exertion, and compleat success in the Administration of the concerns of the Marine Hospital"

As M[r] Gerry allowed me to Copy his Letter to M[r] Madison I make the following Extract for your Satisfaction for I presume you must feel a little interested in the question whether I have honored, or discredited your Appointment.

"I have been intimately accquainted with D[r] Waterhouse for thirty Years—so far at least as to have been able to form for my self a correct Opinion, which has ever been a respectable one, of his Moral, political, and professional Character. I have Seen his defence, & a number of Certificates to support it; all of which have been productive of no change in that Opinion.—His Lady, who is respected, beloved, and Admired, for her amiable disposition, correct Conduct, and excellent qualifications, Social and domestic, had I perceive, been induced, from her Attachment to her Husband, and family, to submit to become for sometime Directress of the Hospital; a Measure which appears to me to demand the Approbation, and Eulogium of every Lady, and Gentleman of the United States.—a Measure which has eminently contributed to place the reputation of the Hospital on an Eminence not before attained by any in this Quarter—In the Year 1774 I was concerned with Genl Glover and others in Erecting an Innoculating Hospital, at the request of the Town of Marblehead, then in Danger of being ruined by the Small pox; and it was allowed by foreigners to have been as complete as any Institution of the Kind in Europe—but the System of the Marine Hospital, at Charlestown, was, under the direction of D[r] Waterhouse, as much Superior to that, in point of Oeconomy, Cleanliness, Comfort to the Sick, and regularity of every Kind, as that was to a common Hospital Ship—beside the internal regulations D[r] Waterhouse has improved and cultivated the Grounds, and rendered it more Valuable, by planting a great number of fruit Trees, and Ornamental Trees—the Aspect of the Buildings, and Grounds, strike the Eye as the Effect of valuable improvements and the internal parts of Excellent Management. and I have been informed all this has been done by the Doctor, either with no Additional or very trifling annual Expence to the funds—The professional Skill of the Doctor is placed on very high Grounds by the Certificates mentioned, which are from some of the oldest, and most Eminent physicians of the State—They have Visited the Hospital, and think it not to be surpassed. It is painful to remark, that from the time D[r] W took the lead of Vaccination, a number of reputable Medical Gentlemen became his Enemies."

"When the Doctor's Appointment was announced it was generally remarked, that no Appointment of M[r] Jefferson excited more general Approbation from all parties—The D[r] is surrounded, by, not only Competitors for his Office, but by the highest Federalists who influence the Affairs of the University; and have been long labouring, in vain, to remove him from his Medical professorship therein; which he has filled these 30 Years. (27 Years) The D[r] is obnoxious to these Men (the Essex Junto) because he is friendly to the Administration of our republican Government."

"Lest all other Charges should fail of removing the D[r] one is added that explains, in my mind, the whole matter I mean that of having ridiculed & spoken sarcastically of president Jefferson. all who are most intimately accquainted with the D[r] pronounce that charge to be impossible. D[r] W. has uniformly, in public, and so far as I can testify, in private & in print spoken respectfully of M[r] Jefferson" More need not be added to convince you that in this also have I been basely Calumniated—

Cunning and Malice had so dressed up some of these Charges, that I do not wonder that they made an Unfavorable impression on the Minds of some of the highest Officers of the Government at Washington. Not that I would insinuate that my Conduct has been entirely free from Errors—I am however impressed with the Opinion that my Conduct had been misrepresented at Washington, prior to Gen[l] Dearborn's coming to Boston. If a Man's Correct Deeds may be Misrepresented, may not his Errors be distorted into Crimes, and imprudence bear the stamp of fraud?

Although Complaints have been made to the Secretary of the Treasury, at different times, and apparently, from different quarters, I find no difficulty in tracing them all to the same Source: The thing is well understood in Boston—We know here that they are all ramifications of the same Root—Nor is it too much for me to say, that there are those who are now striving to effect my ruin, by the most exaggerated reports and the vilest calumnies, which, were my removal from the Hospital to take place at this time, would never be wholly effaced; as each person would believe according to his disposition—

I never was so anxiously Situated; because I fear an Avenue may possibly be opened, through which my most powerful Enemies (I mean the Essex Junto) may effect the ruin of me & my family—Not as it regards the Hospital merely, but through that, as it regards my professorship in the University.—My Situation in this respect, is peculiar and clouded with Anxiety; more so than any one out of this Vicinity can well imagine—I therefore wait the decision of the president, respecting my Conduct of the Hospital, with feelings of anxious sollicitude; natural to the head of a large family, who knows that his all hangs upon his determination. Others, besides M^r Gerry, know that my professional Enemies are waiting, in joyful expectation of an unfavorable issue, that they may use it to my destruction—previous steps have been already taken by the Government, or rather individuals of the Government of this University, who are still ignorant of the true Situation of things, as explained in my defence, but I hope the Young, & envious may be overruled by the wise and prudent.

I have done all the good I could in the Hospital you gave me, with the least expence. I have given the Sick better beds, cleaner Cloths, & neater rooms, than they ever had before. I have encreased the Value of the Hospital property. I have had fewer deaths, in a given number of men; and can produce the most ample documents of general good management. besides moralizing the House, and transfusing Order and Neatness throughout every part of it, I succeeded in establishing the sober drink of Beer Tea & Coffee to rum and wine— Before I took the Hospital the Expence of the two last Articles amounted to upwards of $1200 per Annum—In no one Act have I been more censured at Washington, than in the Appointment of a Directress, and yet there is nothing we are so much applauded for here—So far has this been from trenching on the funds of the Hospital, that it has been a clear saving to it of more than 300. Dollars a Year—Every person, who has attentively examined the State of this Hospital, acknowledges the great improvements made in it; and yet I have not encreased, or but very little, if any, the annual Expence—Nay to speak correctly, I have lessened the Expence—And yet how am I represented at Washington

I have never addressed a single Line to president Madison—Excepting M^r Gerrys Letter, he knows me only perhaps by the representations of my Accusers.

I hope they will never induce him to believe that I am ungrateful, or that I ever, at any Moment, expressed a Sentiment, or tone other than that of high respect for his Venerable predecessor.

Allow me therefore to Subscribe my self (in the plain Language of that religious Society in which I was Educated)

Your ever grateful, respectful, and steady friend

BENJ^N WATERHOUSE

RC (DLC); in a clerk's hand, signed by Waterhouse; at head of text: "His Excellency Thomas Jefferson Esq"; endorsed by TJ as received 2 July 1809 and so recorded in SJL. Dft (MBCo: Waterhouse Letterbook); dated June 1809; incomplete, omitting quotations, and with substantial variations.

Benjamin Waterhouse (1754–1846), physician, was born in Rhode Island of Quaker parents, educated in London, Edinburgh, and Leiden, and served as the first professor of theory and practice of physic at Harvard University, 1783–1812. Starting with his first exposure to the work of Edward Jenner in 1799 and his own clinical trials the following year, Waterhouse is credited with introducing smallpox vaccination to the United States. Hearing that TJ was greatly interested in the new procedure, he sent him a supply of the vaccine in 1801, and TJ eventually succeeded in inoculating two hundred people in Virginia. In 1807 he appointed Waterhouse head physician of the United States Marine Hospital in Charlestown, Massachusetts. Waterhouse had a contentious relationship with his Boston medical colleagues, but TJ admired his work and they corresponded regularly on medical and scientific matters (*ANB*; *DAB*; I. Bernard Cohen, ed., *The Life and Scientific and Medical Career of Benjamin Waterhouse*, 2 vols. [1980]; Waterhouse, *A Prospect of Exterminating the Small-pox: Being the History of the Variolæ Vaccinæ, or Kine-Pox* [Cambridge, Mass., 1800], 22–9).

IMMEDICABILE VULNUS: "incurable wound." Waterhouse quoted extensively from Elbridge Gerry's LETTER TO THE PRESIDENT of 20 May 1809, parenthetically inserting THE ESSEX JUNTO (Madison, *Papers, Pres. Ser.*, 1:194–5). Madison did not reply to that letter and in July 1809 relieved Waterhouse of his position as physician to the Marine Hospital amid charges of nepotism and corruption, but he appointed him a military hospital surgeon in 1813. Waterhouse commented in 1810 that "I have received nothing but abuse; nay, more, I have been intrigued out of my place, as Physician to the United States Marine Hospital, worth £500 sterling a-year, and given me, by Mr. Jefferson, as a reward for my labours in Vaccination; and this merely in consequence of his going out of office and others coming in" (Thomas Joseph Pettigrew, *Memoirs of the Life and Writings of the late John Coakley Lettsom* [London, 1817], 2:484–5). As he predicted, his SITUATION at Harvard was affected when in October 1809 he was relieved of his duties as caretaker of Harvard's mineralogical cabinet (John Blake, "Benjamin Waterhouse, Harvard's First Professor of Physic," in Cohen, *Life of Waterhouse*, 2:776–7).

[1] Word omitted in Dft.

[2] Remainder of paragraph in Dft reads "may leave the vulnus immedicabile unless I can heal it by an explanation with you excellency."

[3] Dft: "I should have been less affected by this groundless charge had I not perceived that Genl Dearborn believed it."

[4] Dft: "I cannot perhaps express my feelings on better on <*this ungrateful subject*> than by transcribing that passage in my defense which relates to this ungrateful subject."

[5] Dft ends here, as follows: "mercantile line. From most of them I receivd only a verbal opinion, while others have given it in writing: of these I shall select only two, because having acted conspicuous parts in public stations these characters are known to you, & to the whole American nation."

# From Henry Dearborn

Dear Sir, Boston June 23d 1809

I had this day the pleasure of receiving your very freindly and highly esteem'd letter of the 16th I am very glad that the fish arrived safe and was satisfactory in quality.—

The Tories in this quarter have been making great exartions to induce their subordinate, deceived, adherents, to believe that Mr Madison is intitled to their confidence, and they effect to believe that he will abandon the policy of his predecessor, and shape his course so as to meet their views and wishes, but it is a mere subterfuge for the relief of their mortified pride, the overtures of England were so unexpected and so directly opposite to their predictions & wishes as to require some speedy and strong exartion on their part to prevent a general insurrection in their followers, and having frequently succeeded by the most barefaced falshoods they determined on the groce subterfuge above alluded to, and boldly ascerted that Mr Madison had in a very honorable manner accepted the offers from England that had been constantly[1] held out to you in vain, and by adding impudence to Insult & falshood, they held up their Insurgent resolutions as the principle agent in procureing relief from past imbarrasments—Mrs Dearborn & myself have found a snug retreat about three miles from Town where we endeavor to make ourselves as happy as possible, we unite in the most sincere and respectfull and gratefull salutations to your self, and best wishes for the happiness of Mr & Mrs Randolph & children. H. Dearborn

RC (DLC); endorsed by TJ as received 2 July 1809 and so recorded in SJL.

TJ's letter of the 16th was actually dated 14 June 1809.

[1] Manuscript: "constanly."

# From Henry Dearborn

Dear Sir, Boston June 23d 1809

In your letter of the 16th you were good enough to mention my Son,—I was inform'd by Mr Smith my former principle Clerk that an attempt would probably be made by Pickering to injure the character of my Son as an agent for fortifications, and Mr Smith observed that he had mentioned the subject to you & that a postponement was thought advisable of his nomination as an officer in the Army, I was highly pleased with the measure, I have since prevailed on my Son to give up all ideas of going into the Army at present, and I have the satisfaction of assuring you that on a full investigation of the circumstances of the transactions on which Pickering proposed founding his complaint, I found my Son had conducted himself with strict honesty and integrity.

Please to accept Sir my gratefull acknowledgements of the many[1] favors receivd and my most sincere prayers that the evening of your life may be tranquil & happy. H. DEARBORN

RC (DLC); at foot of text: "Hon$^{bl}$ Thomas Jefferson esq$^{r}$"; endorsed by TJ as received 2 July 1809 and so recorded in SJL.

[1] Manuscript: "may."

# From George Jefferson

DEAR SIR Richmond 23$^{d}$ June 1809

M$^{r}$ Venable has received notice from M$^{rs}$ Tabb that she will require her money at the expiration of the six months for which it was borrowed.—This will render it necessary for it to be procured from the bank.—As the sum is larger than M$^{r}$ V. wishes to ask for in one day, I inclose you at his request two notes, which you will be pleased to sign & return, leaving the day of the month blank.—There will be no hope I fear of shortly obtaining any thing like the price you mention for your Tobacco.

I am Dear Sir Your Very humble serv$^{t}$ GEO. JEFFERSON.

RC (MHi); at foot of text: "Thomas Jefferson esq$^{r}$"; endorsed by TJ as received 29 June 1809 and so recorded in SJL. Enclosures not found.

# To James Leitch

SIR Monticello June 23. 09.

On more maturely considering the different objects for which the padlocks are wanting, I find I must entirely change the assortment of yesterday; that I shall want 12.[1] locks assorted as follows.

| | |
|---|---|
| 8 coachrooms | 4.[2] single locks to open with the same key. (1. returned. 3 remain) |
| garden. | 3. single d$^{o}$ to open with the same key, but different from the former all returned |

| | |
|---|---|
| my stable<br>strangers d°<br>saddle room } | 3. double locks, opening with the same key. these may be the same laid by yesterday |
| mr B's stable & coachroom. | 2. single d° opening with the same key, but different from all the others 1. returned |
| & other stable coachroom | 1.[3] single lock opening with a key different from[4] all the former. |

To these be pleased to add the underwritten articles. the bearer brings you 50.℔ ten penny & 50.℔ sixpenny nails as I presume, having desired mr Bacon to make up those quantities. Accept my respects

Th: Jefferson

6. yds oznabrigs
2. tin lantherns
6. milkpans, the largest size you have
one of those looking glasses I was examining yesterday, [cov]ered with red leather & folding down on a dr[esser?]

PoC (MHi); faint; with notes on return of locks presumably added by TJ at a later date; at foot of text: "Mr Leitch"; endorsed by TJ.

oznabrigs: Oznaburg was a coarse linen originally made in Osnabrück, Saxony (*OED*).

[1] Number reworked from "10."
[2] Number reworked from "2."
[3] Number reworked from "2."
[4] TJ here canceled "one another and from."

## From John W. Butler

[S]ir

Baltimore, 24th June, 1809.

Having commenced the publication of the enclosed Paper, and being solicitous to grace my list with a name so deservedly dear to the Republican cause, I take the liberty of forwarding you the first number of the Maryland Republican, accompanied by a Proposal, to which, if it should meet your approbation, you will please to signify your patronage by returning it (with your Signature) to your obliged Humble Servt

John W. Butler.

P.S. Please direct to J. W. Butler, Annapolis.

RC (DLC); corner torn; addressed: "Thomas Jefferson, Esq. Monticello, Va."; franked and postmarked; endorsement by TJ torn. Recorded in SJL as received 29 June 1809. Enclosures: (1) Annapolis *Maryland Republican*, 17 June 1809. (2) *Proposals By John West Butler, for Publishing a Paper in the City of Annapolis, To Be Called The Maryland Republican* (Annapolis, 18 May 1809), with

Butler as editor declaring himself "unreservedly a disciple of the Jefferson school, and that his whole efforts shall be directed to support those great principles of political truth which has rendered the late President's name so deservedly dear to his countrymen, and extended his fame as a statesman throughout the world" (printed broadside in DLC; corner torn).

John West Butler was an Annapolis bookseller, printer, and publisher. He described himself as a young Federalist when he obtained a book subscription from TJ in 1801, at which time he was active professionally in Baltimore as well as Annapolis. He published the weekly and semiweekly Annapolis *Maryland Republican* from 17 June 1809 to 1 July 1811, when he sold it to Jehu Chandler (Brigham, *American Newspapers*, 1:223, 251; Butler to TJ, 13 Apr. 1801, and TJ to Butler, 8 May 1801 [DLC]).

# To David Copeland

DEAR SIR Monticello June 25. 09.

I recieved yesterday by your son a copy of a summons in the suit of Gilliam v. Fleming E$^{t}$ al. and have given him a proper acknolegement of it. altho' not interested one cent in the issue of this suit (because whichever party is debtor to the other I pay a third & recieve a third) yet no one living is more anxious to have a final settlement of it than myself. having been the depository of the papers for 30. odd years, more intimate with the transactions probably than any other person living, I wish to settle it myself, & not leave it to my family who are utterly ignorant of it. for the reason that I wish a real meeting & am too old to take useless journies I shall this day write to mr Ladd & mr Jones on the appointment of the 1$^{st}$ of Aug. at which I fear no sufficient meeting can be expected. indeed I know that at that time one if not more of the persons who must be present, will be absent for his health at the springs; and it is a season when every one who can, leaves the tidewater country. I shall request them therefore to appoint some other day as early as the return of the healthy season will permit, in October for instance[1] at which I will attend myself, and strongly urge mr Skipwith & mr Eppes (the only defendants having any interest in the result,) & judge Fleming also to attend, who like myself has no interest in it but is intimate with the transactions, & was present at the settlement with Meriwether Skelton about 34. or 35. years ago, when the whole of the charges against B. Skelton's estate were examined & passed except a few inconsiderable ones which laid over for vouchers. his presence will be necessary. I learn with great pleasure that you enjoy good health, & with my compliments to mrs Copeland I pray you to be assured of my constant esteem & respect TH: JEFFERSON

PoC (DLC); at foot of text: "D. Copeland Esq."; endorsed by TJ.

Copeland's letter of 23 June 1809, not found but recorded in SJL as received from Springfield on 24 June 1809, probably enclosed a COPY OF A SUMMONS in the case of GILLIAM V. FLEMING, the suit that arose over the settlement of Bathurst Skelton's estate. Martha Wayles married Skelton in 1766 and TJ in 1772, four years after Skelton died. Martha's dower right to her first husband's estate transferred to TJ upon the death of her son John Skelton in 1771 and her own death in 1782. In addition to TJ, Bathurst Skelton's estate was distributed among his siblings and their heirs, including Meriwether Skelton; Reuben Skelton, who married Elizabeth Lomax (her second marriage was to Martha's father John Wayles); Sally Skelton, who married Thomas Jones and was the mother of Skelton Jones; and Lucy Skelton, who married Robert Gilliam. Gilliam, representing the estate of Bathurst Skelton, initiated this chancery suit against the executors of John Wayles's estate. William Fleming was named as defendant because his father John Fleming had been executor of the estate of James Skelton, Bathurst's father, to which the Fleming estate still owed money. As an executor of his father-in-law John Wayles's estate, TJ was involved on both sides of this suit, which primarily involved land in Goochland and Fluvanna counties named Elk Hill and Elk Island on the James River. The suit was not settled until at least 1813 (Richard D. Gilliam, "Skelton and Shelton: Two Distinct Virginia Families," *WMQ*, 2d ser., 9 [1929]: 209–16; "Woodhouse-Meriwether-Bathurst-Skelton-Gilliam," *WMQ*, 1st ser., 12 [1903]: 60–4; TJ to Farrell & Jones, 9 July 1773, *PTJ*, 15:657–71; *MB*, 1:349, 2:1051, 1248).

[1] Preceding four words interlined.

# To Skelton Jones

SIR Monticello June 25. 09.

I recieved yesterday from the Master Commissioner Ladd a notification in the suit of Gilliam v. Fleming to attend at his office on the 1st of Aug. a settlement of the accounts in that case. altho' not a cent interested in the result, no one can be more anxious than I am to have the settlement compleated. having for upwards of 30. years been the depository of the papers, & better acquainted with the transactions perhaps than any other person living, I think it a happiness that I have been spared to settle it, rather than that it should have devolved on my representatives who are quite uninformed on the subject. hence my anxiety that our meeting whenever it takes place should be rendered[1] effectual & final, by the attendance of all material persons, & particularly by mr Skipwith & mr Eppes the only[2] defendants interested, & judge Fleming who, like myself, tho having no interest, has much acquaintance with the transactions. but the day appointed is in a season when considerations of health draw from the tide-water country all who can leave it, & forbid others to visit it. altho my health is as good as at my age could be expected, I had rather not risk it when I am certain the nonattendance of others at the meeting would render it useless; as I know that one of the gentlemen before named considers the rheumatic state of his health as obliging him to pass that season at the springs. I have therefore proposed to mr Ladd to change the day to one in the healthy season, say in October after the frosts will have set in, & long enough before the next meeting of Congress to admit mr Eppes's attendance. I shall be happy if this meets your approbation, & as soon as I can be informed of the day appointed, I will write to the gentlemen before named to ensure their attendance. I shall, at the meeting, with perfect impartiality be ready to communicate to the pl^s^ as well as def^s^ every paper & fact within my knolege. with a wish to learn that the proposition respecting time is agreeable to you, I tender you the assurances of my esteem & respect.

TH: JEFFERSON

PoC (DLC); at foot of text: "Skelton Jones esq."; endorsed by TJ.

[1] Word interlined.

[2] TJ here canceled "persons in."

# To Thomas Ladd

SIR Monticello June 25. 09

I recieved yesterday your notification in the suit of Gilliam v. Fleming that you should proceed to a settlement of the accounts on the 1st of Aug. at your office. no person can be more anxious for a settlement than myself. for altho' my interests being balanced on both sides, I have none at all in the result, yet having been for 30. odd years the depository of the papers, & more intimate with the transactions probably than any other person living, I wish not to leave it to be settled by my family who are utterly unacquainted with the case. it is my anxiety for an effectual meeting which induces me to trouble you, because I have no expectation that in the month of August the necessary attendance can be obtained. it is a season when considerations of health draw every one from the tidewater country who can leave it, & forbid every one to go to it. mr Skipwith & mr Eppes, the only defendants having any interest in the issue, & judge Fleming well acquainted with the case must be present. but one of them I know, if not more, will then be at the springs for his health. altho' my own health is as firm as I could expect at my age, yet having for 30. years avoided being in the tidewater country during the months of Aug. & Sep. I would rather avoid exposing myself to a risk which the nonattendance of others would render useless. I therefore refer to your consideration a change of the day to the return of the healthy season, so long before the next meeting of Congress as to admit the attendance of mr Eppes some day in October for instance.[1] as soon as you will be so good as to favor me with a line on your determination I will write to the gentlemen abovenamed to engage their attendance & to ensure the meeting being effectual & final. I write now[2] to mr Skelton Jones on this subject, who I presume will approve the delay for such an object. and I tender you the assurances of my great respect

TH: JEFFERSON

PoC (DLC); at foot of text: "M^r Thomas Ladd, Master Com^r in Chancery"; endorsed by TJ.

Thomas Ladd (1769–1834), surveyor and merchant, moved from Charles City County to Richmond about 1795 and began a flour milling firm, Ladd, Anthony & Company. He supplied iron for the construction of the state penitentiary, served on its board of inspectors, and was master commissioner, an officer of the Superior Court of Chancery for the Richmond District (Thomas Mifflin Ladd III, *The Ladd Family: A Genealogy* [1964], 3–5).

[1] Preceding six words interlined.
[2] Word interlined.

# From Charles Willson Peale

DEAR SIR Museum June 25th 1809.

Mr Randolph took his passage in the New Castle line of Land and water Stages on Wednesday last, since which we have received the inclosed letter to him. And the enclosed bill of lading will shew that I have sent by the Schooner Liberty, Captn Lewis two Boxes & one Trunk, directed to the care of Messrs Gibson & Jefferson at Richmond, belonging to Mr Randolph.

Although I sent you part of the acct of the Mr Randolph's expences &c in my letter of Decr 23d 1808. yet for the better view of his whole expences, I shall transcribe the various interies from my book. as follows. Vizt

| | | |
|---|---|---|
| | Octr 6. 1808. | c |
| | Lens to a seal for yr self | 25 |
| | Umberella for Mr Randolph | 5,50 |
| Novr 19. | Cash for the carriage of a Polygraph to Baltre | 25 |
| 25. | Washing womans Bill 5 Dozn & 5 pieces | 3.62½ |
| | Bells Anatomy | 22.00 |
| | Chaptals Chemistry neatly bound | 5.75 |
| | Doctr Phisicks Ticket to surgical Lectures[1] | 15.— |
| | Doctr Woodhouse Do to Chemical do | 20.— |

| | | |
|---|---|---|
| 31$^{st}$ | Case of dissecting[2] Instruments | 9.— |
| | 2$\frac{1}{4}$ Y$^{ds}$ of Drab cloath for a surtout | 11.25 |
| | Ticket of Matriculation (University) | 4.— |
| | Hospital Ticket | 10.— |
| | Pocket money to M$^{r}$ Randolph | 4.— |
| | Taylors Bill for triming, & making Surtout | 6.50 |
| Dec$^{r}$ 23$^{d}$ | Cash to M$^{r}$ Randolph to purchase a Skeleton &c | 10.— |
| | 2$\frac{1}{2}$ y$^{ds}$ of Cotton Cassimer @ 1,50 | 3.75 |
| | 3$\frac{1}{2}$ Doz$^{n}$ Buttons (home manufacture) | 1.18 |
| 25$^{h}$ | 10 Weeks board of M$^{r}$ Randolph @ 4$ ℔ Week | 40.— |
| | Carried over—— | $172,05$\frac{1}{2}$[3] |
| 1808 | | |
| Dec$^{r}$ 27. | Cash to M$^{r}$ Randolph | 5.— |
| | Cost of repairing his Watch | 1,50 |
| | Doct$^{r}$ Bartons Ticket[4] of Lectures on N. history | 7.— |
| Jan$^{y}$ 9. 1809 | Cash to M$^{r}$ Randolph for stockings & a Book on Anatomy[5] | 10.— |
| | Boots foxed & a P$^{r}$ of New boots | 9.87$\frac{1}{2}$ |
| | Washing bill paid Jan$^{y}$ 6. | 3.44 |
| 19. | Cash | 10.— |
| 20. | Ditto | 5.— |
| 31. | Ditto | 10.— |
| Feb$^{y}$ 8 | Cash to pay M$^{r}$ Dobson | 6.— |
| | Cash for M$^{r}$ Randolph to purchase Wax for Injections | 10.— |
| 16. | Cash | 5.— |
| 20. | Ditto | 3.— |
| | Cash for silk. 18$^{c}$ Hat 6$ Leather Trunk 9. | 15.18. |
| | Washing Womans bill. 8 Doz & 5. piecs @ 5/ ℔ Doz. | 5.56 |
| 28. | Cash—20$ Six pieces 2/6 | 23.33 |
| | Cash—on his Visit home | 26.25 |
| | Board 9$\frac{1}{2}$ Weeks @ 4$ P$^{r}$ Week | 38.00. |
| April 11. | Cash to M$^{r}$ Randolph | 5.— |
| 25 | Bartons Elements of Botany | 6.— |
| May 2. | Jean & Muslin for Vests | 4.62$\frac{1}{2}$ |
| 8. | Cash to M$^{r}$ Randolph | 12.— |
| 13. | Ditto | 5.— |
| 15. | Doct$^{r}$ Bartons botanical Lectures | 12.— |
| 23. | Cash for a P$^{r}$ of Boots | 10. |
| 25. | Cash | 36.— |
| | Voils & Powder | 3.36 |

| | | | |
|---|---|---|---|
| | Lamp Chain for M[r] Jefferson | | 1.50 |
| June 20. | Cash | | 5.— |
| | Board from the 2[d] April to June 22. | | 44.— |
| | Washer womans Bill for 13 Doz[n] & 11 piecs | | 9.27 |
| | Cash had on the 10[th] of Rubens Peale | | 5.— |
| | Cash to bear M[r] Randolph expenses home | | 41.11. |
| | | $ | $565,05½ |
| 1808. Oct[r] 15 | Rec[d] of M[r] Jefferson | 100. | |
| Nov. 9 | Ditto | 50 | |
| Dec. | Ditto | 60 | |
| 1809 Jan[y] 8. | Ditto | 50 | 516.[6] |
| Feb. 8. | Ditto | 56 | |
| 13. | Ditto | 50 | |
| March 13. | Ditto | 150 | |
| | | $516 | |
| | Ballance | | $ 49,05½ |
| | Errors Excepted | | |

C W PEALE

DR SIR I have endeavored to be correct in the forgoing acc[t] and particular as conveniently as I could for the better government of M[r] Randolphs expences, as he knew I would give you the particulars. taking into view his age he may be considered an Œconomist. Doct[r] Wistar told me that he wished him to have staid a few days longer that he might have had the pleasure of some rides with into[7] the neighbouring country. Please to tell him for me, that I think M[rs] Wistar will be pleased if he can send her some of the Chrystals, from Wires Cave, to ornament her mantle piece.

My Son Rembrandt is now with me waiting with much anxiety to get a passage to some part of the Continant of Europe with his family, to persue what he calls his glorious plan of Portraits. I hope he will shortly find a public Vessel going—in such case I have said as much as ought to be said to enduce the Executive to appoint him Messenger, because I really beleive his talents intitle him to such favors.

I am with much esteem Dear Sir your friend C W PEALE

RC (MHi); at foot of text: "Tho[s] Jefferson Esq[r] Monticello"; endorsed by TJ as received 2 July 1809 and so recorded in SJL. PoC (PPAmP: Peale Letterbook). Enclosure: TJ to Thomas Jefferson Randolph, 20 June 1809. Other enclosure not found.

Peale sent an account for Thomas Jefferson Randolph through 25 Dec. 1808 in his LETTER of 23 Dec. 1808 (DLC). Boots are FOXED by renewing the upper leather (*OED*). VOILS: probably vials (phials) that TJ ordered on 6 May 1809. WIRES CAVE: Weyers Cave, Augusta County.

[1] Manuscript: "Letures."
[2] Manuscript: "discecting."
[3] Repeated intermediate sum at head of page two omitted.
[4] Manuscript: "Tcket."
[5] Manuscript: "Antomy."
[6] In PoC Peale here noted: "Rec$^{d}$ of M$^{r}$ Jefferson."
[7] Thus in manuscript.

# To Joseph Dougherty

DEAR JOSEPH Monticello June 26. 09.

Your's of the 18$^{th}$ came to hand on the 24$^{th}$. altho' three posts a week leave Washington for[1] Milton, & perform the rout in 2. or 3. days, yet from a negligence somewhere our letters are often a week coming to hand. with respect to the best mode of proceeding with your Merinos, I have no doubt, if you were able that it would be best for you to purchase as many ewes as the rams would suffice for. and I wish I were able to assist you in doing it, as I should do it with great pleasure. but the heavy debt, which on winding up my affairs at Washington, I found I had contracted there, has placed me under great difficulties, & will keep me long in a crippled state, as I have to pay it out of the profits of my estate, & the sale of a part of it, which I am endeavoring to effect. your next best method would be, I think, to recieve ewes to your ram, and be paid for it in ewes. I think it not improbable the farmers would give you one ewe for the season of the ram to another. in this way you would get for yourself the first year half as many as they could cover, & the 2$^{d}$ year would furnish as many more, after which you would have the whole to yourself. if one ewe for the season of another is too much, you might certainly have one for the season of two. in this way you would be three years getting the whole number of ewes you would want.

I recieved my Eiderdown quilt safely by mr Carr. I am very thankful for the bigtailed ram, & will send for him the last week in August and put him for this year only to the ewe which I have of the same kind. I think the beginning of Sep. is the best time to put them together, because the lamb then comes in February. January is generally the severest winter month we have. I salute you with great attachment. TH: JEFFERSON

RC (NNGL, on deposit NHi); addressed: "M$^{r}$ Joseph Dougherty Washington"; stamped and postmarked; endorsed by Dougherty as received 29 June 1809. PoC (DLC); ink stained; endorsed by TJ.

[1] TJ here canceled "this place."

# From George Jefferson

Dear Sir Richmond 26th June 1809

I have received information from a boatman of the name of Calloway, who lives near Lynchburg, that our lost trunk is in the possession of one Danl Northcut, residing about 5 or 6 miles from that place, in Amherst. C. has not heard particularly what the trunk contains, but was told there were some blank books, and some blank paper in it—he has not heard of the instruments.—he understands there is some writing, which is not understood, so that I hope the vocabularies of the indian languages are not all distroyed.—The story given out is, that N. purchased the trunk with its contents of his negro waterman for 3$!—the waterman says he found it, broken open, about two miles above the locks.—I have written to Mr Saml J. Harrison of Lynchburg, to aid C. in the recovery of the articles, and have requested him to have N. prosecuted for dealing with a negro for things which he must have known were stolen.

I have likewise desired him to have the negro prosecuted, both because he deserves punishment, & because it will be important to Mr R. to ascertain whether his boatmen sold the trunk, or whether they were robbed of it.

Their having averred so positively that they did not receive it, certainly operates against them; and I think rather more (if there is a difference) against the three who remained at the landing, than against Harry who received the articles of me: for he might have made a mistake by miscounting—whereas I have all along thought it very improbable, that the three in receiving 27 packages from their head man, should have counted them, and that too with such exactness, as to recollect positively that there was one, and that of a particular kind, short of the number said to have been delivered.—Some allowance however should be made for the poor devils being frightened, & I suppose that we ought not to be surprised at their endeavoring to acquit themselves of blame, by imputing it to another.

I most sincerely hope it may turn out, that they were only negligent, & suffered the trunk to be stolen.

I am Dear Sir Yr Very humble servt Geo. Jefferson

RC (MHi); at foot of text: "Thomas Jefferson esqr"; endorsed by TJ as received 5 July 1809 and so recorded in SJL.

# From Stephen Cathalan

Sir— Marseilles the 27th June 1809

I hope my Letter of the 14th october 1807 with the Provisions by the Ship Fabius,[1] reached you Safe, and in good order; & that Mr Wam hazard bearer of my Bill on you ℔ D. 87–10 ct for their amount, whom I took the Liberty of Introducing you, had the honor of Paying you his Personal Respects, with those of my Family & my Self with our best wishes!

after the Long & Emminent Services you rendered to your Country, having fullfilled the Last Eight years the Presidency of the United states, you are at Last, according to your wishes, Returned in the Bosom of your Dear Family & Retired to your Books and Farms! enjoying of the Gratitude & Blessings of the People of the United States, to whom you had Sacrifice'd the best part of your Life for their Well fair & future Prosperity! Leaving them for Successor your Collaborator & Good Friend James Madison,

but in your Letter to me of the 29th June 1807. you had in Contemplation to Visit again a Part of Europe and this Country; I hope the state of your health is so Good as not to be an obstacle to put this Project in Execution, nor the actual State of Political affairs;—I am only apprehensive that, tho' wishing to travel as a Private Gentleman, your Modesty could not avoid to be yourself witness of the Tribute of admiration that would be paid everywhere, to your Past Public Caracter, Private virtues, Patriotism, Philanthropick Philosophy & Proffound Knowledge in Sciences & your Constant Study for the benefit of mankind;

on the Contrary, I think your Travel & short Stay in Some Capital Places of Europe,[2] might be usefull and advantageous to Respective[3] Countries, tho' in a Private & not in a Public Capacity;

For my Part, you will not Doubt of the Great Pleasure it would afford me, if I should once more have the honor of Seeing you here or in Paris &c as I apprehend I will not be able to pay you a Long desired visit at Monticelo!

my old Mother Says She hopes Still of not Leaving this world before that happy Day; my Daughter & Mr J. Oliver present their Best Respects to you

I have the honor to be always at your Commands & with Great Respect Sir

Your admirer & most Devoted Servant!

Stephen Cathalan Jr

RC (MHi); dateline below signature; at foot of text: "Thos Jefferson Esqr Monticelo Virginia"; endorsed by TJ as received 13 Aug. 1809 and so recorded in SJL. Dupl (MHi); in a clerk's hand, signed by Cathalan; postscript in Cathalan's hand: "I am to the 21st october this Goes with 13 araan Seamen in Distress, whom I am directed to Send to Bord F. by Genl J. armstrong to be Shipped there, for the U.S. Your's &c St. Can"; on stationery with seal of "Comal & Navy Agency of the United States of America at Marseilles"; at head of text: "Copy"; endorsed by TJ as received 15 Mar. 1810 and so recorded in SJL. Enclosed in a brief covering letter from State Department clerk Richard Forrest to TJ, 8 Aug. 1809 (RC in DLC; endorsed by TJ as received 13 Aug. 1809 and so recorded in SJL).

The French merchant Stephen (Etienne) Cathalan (d. 1819), the namesake son of an American commercial agent, had corresponded with TJ since the summer of 1786. George Washington appointed him United States vice-consul at Marseilles in June 1790, and he remained in the American consular service (as commercial agent from 1801) until his death. For decades Cathalan regularly shipped TJ food and wine, as well as olive trees and other items (*PTJ*, 10:173–4; *MB*, esp. 1:675, 2:1361; *JEP*, 1:47–8, 51–2, 403, 405 [4, 17 June 1790, 6, 26 June 1802]; TJ to Martha Jefferson Randolph, 28 July 1819).

Cathalan sent French wine and olives in OCTOBER 1807. Julius OLIVER was a close family friend of Cathalan's and owner of the brig *Jefferson* (Cathalan to TJ, 2 Nov. 1805 [MHi] and 14 Oct. 1807 [DLC]).

[1] Dupl here adds "Captn Cole."

[2] Preceding two words omitted in Dupl.

[3] Dupl substitutes "both" for this word.

# From James Madison

DR SIR Washington June 27. 1809

I have recd a private letter of Mar. 30. from Genl Armstrong, in which he desires me "to present him most respectfully and cordially to you, and inform you that by the next public ship that goes to America, he shall have the pleasure to send you, an alteration of Mr Guillaumes' plough, which in light soils, is a great improvement upon the old one."[1]

To me he adds, "By the same vessel I propose consigning &c.[2] a machine of prodigious consequence under present circumstances, combining great usefulness & little expence, and meant to take the place of the common small spining Wheel in the manufacture of flax tow & hemp. It occupies little more room than the old spinning wheel, is put & kept in motion by any old or young negro wench,[3] gives you twelve threads instead of one, & those of better texture & (if you chuse it) of greater fineness than can be given by fingers. The maker, who is an American, will probably accompany it"

On public affairs, he says, that the French Govt had made several favorable regulations, among them, one for restoring the Cargoes sequestered under the municipal operation of the Berlin Decree; all of which had been arrested by a belief founded on language used in the British Parl[t] that the U.S. were about to make war on France. The Mentor which is said to have arrived the latter end of Ap[l] will have given more correct, tho' possibly not satisfactory information of the policy prevailing here. Nothing more is known of the late Battle in Germany than you will see in the newspapers. The Senate passed, unanimously the Bill of non-intercourse with France, with a paragraph admitting French Ships of war, in common with British into our waters. The House of Rep[s] rejected yesterday by a large Majority, a motion to discriminate in favor of the British Ships.

Be always assured of my affectionate & high respects

James Madison

RC (DLC: Madison Papers); endorsed by TJ as received 29 June 1809 and so recorded in SJL.

The private letter was John Armstrong to Madison, 30 Mar. 1809 (Madison, *Papers, Pres. Ser.*, 1:89–90).

1 Closing quotation mark editorially supplied.

2 Madison here substituted "&c." for "to your patronage."

3 Madison here omitted "on your farm."

# To Binny & Ronaldson

Mess[rs] Binney & Ronaldson — Monticello June 28. 09

Your letter of June 16. by some accident of the post, was longer than it should have been on the way, which has occasioned the delay of the answer. having no acquaintance in Hamburg or Amsterdam, I can only send you a letter for Paris. in doing this, I have selected the person who of all others in France will serve you with the most zeal, & understanding of the subject, who will best know the springs to be put in motion & whose intimacy with Taleyrand and other members of the government will be most able to be useful to you. you will probably have thought of getting a letter from the Secretary of State to our minister at Paris. in that case I must apprise you that there is a misunderstanding of a strong character between Gen[l] Armstrong & M[r] Dupont, and that if the aid of both is to be used in any case, it must be separately & without any intercommunication. you will percieve that the letter is calculated for the meridian of France, where the antipathy to England is such that considerations of injury to her are those most likely to advance your object. wishing you every success I salute you with esteem & respect. Th: Jefferson

PoC (DLC); endorsed by TJ. Enclosure: TJ to Pierre Samuel Du Pont de Nemours, 28 June 1809.

# To Pierre Samuel Du Pont de Nemours

DEAR SIR Monticello. June 28. 09.

The interruption of our commerce with England, produced by our embargo & non-intercourse law, & the general indignation excited by her bare-faced attempts to make us accessories & tributories to her usurpations on the high seas, have generated in this country an universal spirit of manufacturing for ourselves, & of reducing to a minimum the number of articles for which we are dependant on her. the advantages too of lessening the occasions of risking our peace on the ocean, & of planting the consumer in our own soil by the side of the grower of produce, are so palpable, that no temporary suspension of injuries on her part, or agreements founded on that, will now prevent our continuing in what we have begun. the spirit of manufacture has taken deep root among us, and it's foundations are laid in too great expence to be abandoned. the bearer of this, mr Ronaldson, will be able to inform you of the extent & perfection of the works produced here by the late state of things; and to his information, which is greatest as to what is doing in the cities, I can add my own as to the country, where the principal articles wanted in every family are now fabricated within itself. this mass of houshold manufacture, unseen by the public eye, and so much greater than what is seen, is such at present, that, let our intercourse with England be opened when it may, not one half the amount of what we have heretofore taken from her, will ever again be demanded. the great call from the country has hitherto been of coarse goods. these are now made in our families, & the advantage is too sensible ever to be relinquished. it is one of those obvious improvements in our condition, which needed only to be once forced on our attentions, never again to be abandoned.

Among the arts which have made great progress among us is that of printing. heretofore we imported our books, & with them much political principle, from England. we now print a great deal, & shall soon supply ourselves with most of the books of considerable demand. but the foundation of printing you know, is the type-foundery, and a material essential to that is Antimony. unfortunately that mineral is not among those as yet found in the United States, and the difficulty & dearness of getting it from England, will force us to discontinue our type-founderies, & resort to her again for our books, unless some new source of supply can be found. the bearer, mr Ronaldson, is of the concern of Binney & Ronaldson, type-founders of Philadelphia. he goes to France for the purpose of opening some new source of supply, where we learn that this article is abundant. the enhancement of the price in England has taught us the fact, that it's exportation thither from France must be interrupted either by the war, or express prohibition. our relations however with France, are too unlike hers with England, to place us under the same interdiction. regulations for preventing the transportation of the article to England, under the cover of supplies to America may be thought requisite. the bearer, I am persuaded, will readily give any assurances which may be required for this object, & the wants of his own type-foundery here are a sufficient pledge that what he gets is bonâ fide to supply them. I do not know that there will be any obstacle to his bringing from France any quantity of Antimony he may have occasion for: but lest there should be, I have taken the liberty of recommending him to your patronage. I know your enlightened & liberal views on subjects of this kind, & the friendly interest you take in whatever concerns our welfare. I place mr Ronaldson therefore in your hands, and pray you to advise him, & patronize the object which carries him to Europe, & is so interesting to him & to our country. his knoledge of what is passing among us, will be a rich source of information for you, and especially as to the state & progress of our manufactures. your kindness to him will confer an obligation on me, & will be an additional title to the high & affectionate esteem & respect of an antient & sincere friend. TH: JEFFERSON

RC (DeGH: Pierre Samuel Du Pont de Nemours Papers, Winterthur Manuscripts); at foot of first page: "M. Dupont de Nemours." PoC (DLC). Enclosed in TJ to Binny & Ronaldson, 28 June 1809.

## From David Bailie Warden

SIR, Paris, June 28th–1809.

I had the honor of writing to you, by Mr Coles, and of sending you several parts of Humboldts work on South America. a volume, of the society of Arcueil, mentioned in his letter, was not then received. I now send it, accompanied with a copy of Callets' Logarithms, which Mr Didot bids me offer you. the tables are more correct than any others that have yet appeared. Indeed they are said to be free from error.

The price is not yet fixed, but it will be less than that of any other Collection of a similar kind. It is a work which will be extremely[1] useful to navigators, and those employed in Mathematical Calculations.[2] Mr Didot would wish that you would take the trouble of making it known in the united States. I was obliged, in the Introduction, for the sake of clearness, to confine myself to a very literal translation—[3]

If no serious dispute should take place between France and the United States, I would fain hope, Sir, that you will be pleased to recommend me as Consul for Paris. If the person who has applied for my place, should be successful, I could wish to be established as Consul elsewhere, or employed, in some way or other, by the Government, but I flatter myself that Mr. Madison will have no objection to my remaining here.

I am, Sir, with the greatest respect and esteem, Your very obedt and humb Servt

DAVID BAILIE WARDEN

RC (DLC); at foot of text: "Thos Jefferson Esquire"; endorsed by TJ as received 13 Aug. 1809 and so recorded in SJL. FC (MdHi: Warden Letterbook). Enclosures: (1) *Mémoires de Physique et de Chimie de la Société d'Arcueil*, vol. 2 (Arcueil, 1809), including memoirs by Joseph Louis Gay-Lussac and Louis Jacques Thénard, and Alexander von Humboldt's essay, "Recherches sur la respiration des poissons." (2) Jean François Callet, *Tables of Logarithms, Containing the Logarithms of all Numbers, from 1 to 108000 . . . translated from the French by D. B. Warden . . . A stereotype Edition, Engraved, Cast and printed, by Firmin Didot*, dedicated by Didot to TJ on 25 Oct. 1807 (Paris, 1809; Sowerby, no. 3696). Enclosed in Richard Forrest to TJ, 8 Aug. 1809 (see note to Stephen Cathalan to TJ, 27 June 1809).

[1] FC substitutes "highly" for this word.
[2] FC substitutes "investigation" for this word.
[3] FC ends here.

# William Dawson to Samuel Greenhow

DEAR SIR, 1809 July 1st Charlitsville

I wrote you from Milton yesterday. I Breakfasted at Mr Jeffersons this morning, took some Memos of his curioscittes, was treated exstreamly Polite by him, &c. he informs me that he receved your letter and[1] that he means to have the declarations of his Mills &c[2] recorded, and Shall write, and make remittences to Mr Geo. Jefferson for that purpose.

I hinted to him (as he thought his house fire proof) had he not better revalue his other houses. he did not Say, but observed that, he had made a good deal of alteration in his Stable by enlarging of it &c[3] and Supposed it of Course was loped off from insurrences, I told him not, as the Size was taken when declared for, and that I Should take the dementions again if he would please to Suffer me &c.

I Saw Col° John Nicholas a few Munites this day[4] and at him about his Buildings around this Town which he tells me has Several houses near, but he Said he wished to See how we paid up before he came in. I rang Jeffersons Mills in his ears, and told him likewise that perhaps a North Wind might blow fire on Some of his Building while he was waiting his ans[r] was to be sure, the way to bring the Institution into repute was by giting Subscribers, and Said he would wish to See me again I told him I would wait on him with pleasure. I am Still in good health, I thank the Lord—

Adue. Farewell your friend W DAWSON

Please to excuse Interlineations Blots &c. you know I allways Seem to be in a hury yours. WD.

RC (Vi: Mutual Assurance Society, Incoming Correspondence); addressed: "Samuel Greenhow Esquire Principl Agent to the Mutuel Assurrence Cociety Against fire &c in the State of Virginia Richmond—Fav[d] by M[r] Raphal"; also addressed: "William Taylor Charlottesville July 1[st] 1809"; endorsed by Greenhow.

[1] Preceding six words interlined.
[2] Word interlined.
[3] Preceding five words interlined.
[4] Preceding two words interlined.

## To George Jefferson

DEAR SIR Monticello July 1. 09.

Your three letters of June 16. 19. & 23. came to hand by our last post, and I now inclose you the two notes signed as desired. I am sincerely sorry for the transfer of this debt into the bank, & to have subjected mr Venable to a responsibility there which I know must be painful to him, & on that account doubles my uneasiness. a person near the Natural bridge had made me an offer for my lands there, which for want of information I could not then accept. he promised to call on me this spring, but not having done it, I have written to him my readiness to conclude with him. Griffin writes me from Bedford that he has a hope of selling the lands which I offer there, soon after I shall have gone there. the prospect of selling several detached tracts here is as yet unpromising, & all these operations you know are slow. they shall be pressed however in aid of my Bedford crops.

I accede to your choice of Gordon & co. for my correspondents in groceries, & will take care to have paiments duly made at the epochs proposed. I mentioned in my letter my request that they would send on 50.℔ of coffee by the first boats, as we shall be in want by that time. I am much in want of the bar iron which is with you. I will pray you to send that & 20. bundles of rod by the first boat. the remaining 60. bundles of rod may wait for mr Randolph's boats, which will be down after harvest. if the chairs are gone up they will probably be in Bedford [in?] time for me, as I have not yet fixed a day for my departure.

Your's affectionately TH: JEFFERSON

PoC (MHi); one word faint; at foot of text: "M^r G. Jefferson"; endorsed by TJ.

The TWO NOTES were enclosed in Jefferson to TJ, 23 June 1809. The PERSON was William Jenkings (TJ to Jenkings, 1 July 1809).

On this date Jefferson wrote a brief note to TJ: "Sent by Harry for M^r Jefferson one small box—M^r Gordon is to send by him 50^lbs of Coffee" (RC in MHi; addressed: "Thomas Jefferson esq^r Monticello"; endorsed by TJ as received 5 July 1809 and so recorded in SJL).

# To William Jenkings

SIR Monticello July 1. 09.

When you spoke with me at Washington, on the sale of my lands at the Natural bridge, the proposition was new, & I wished to consider of it. on reflection I find that it is a dead capital in my hands, that in other hands it may be useful to the owner & the public. I am therefore willing to sell it. with respect to price, you said you supposed it worth as much as the adjacent tract which had sold two or three times at 10.D. & some of it at £4. the acre. within these limits therefore we may probably agree, altho in considering it merely as land we omit what gives it distinguished value, it's including the Natural bridge, undoubtedly one of the sublimest curiosities in nature. I had always believed that if there were accomodations there, the healthy part of the company which frequents the various springs, would pass the same season at the bridge of preference, as their object is merely to be absent from the lower country at that season & the climate & curiosity of the bridge would render a stay there much more eligible. I shall be glad to hear from you on this subject and tender you the assurances of my respect. TH: JEFFERSON

P.S. I inclose the courses E^tc taken from the patent.

PoC (ViCMRL, on deposit ViU); at foot of text: "M^r W^m Jenkings. Rockbridge"; endorsed by TJ. Enclosures not found.

William Jenkings lived four or five miles from the Natural Bridge. In a visit to TJ in Washington he had proposed to purchase this property and build a public house there. Jenkings regarded the land as poor agriculturally, but TJ thought that it had potential both as a tourist attraction and for production of metal shot using the site's vertical drop (TJ's notes on Jenkings's visit and on possible rental terms, both 20 Oct. 1808 [MHi]). TJ retained ownership of the Natural Bridge until his death.

# From Benjamin Brown

SIR July 3. 1809

I have lately rec[d] a list of Debts due to the M[l] Assurance Society against Fire in which I find you charged thus 1806 Decem[r]: 10[th] two thirds Quota $55.20 If it be right I should be glad to receive it so soon as it may suit your Convenience. With the greatest respect I am Sir Y Mo Ob[t] Serv[t] BENJ[N] BROWN

RC (MHi); endorsed by TJ as received 3 July 1809 and so recorded in SJL; with Brown's subjoined 5 Sept. 1809 receipt for payment of $63.55, consisting (with an addition error) of $55.20 principal and $8.55 interest calculated from 10 Dec. 1806 to 3 July 1809.

Benjamin Brown, attorney for the Mutual Assurance Society, owned Mooresbrook in the Carter's Mountain area of Albemarle County and a share in the Eagle Tavern in Charlottesville. In 1802 TJ bought a bordering parcel of sixty-one acres on Montalto from Brown (*MB*, 2:1082–3; Lay, *Architecture*, 12–3, 57; Deed from Brown to TJ, 9 Sept. 1802, Albemarle County Deed Book, 1:166–7).

# From Joseph Dougherty

DEAR SIR City of Washington July 3[rd]–09

yours of the 26[th] of last month I rec[d] the 29 your kind wish and always ready and willing to aid me, is a thing nither strange[1] nor unknown to me; and had I any reason to suppose that you were able to assist me I should solicit you, on such an occasion, with more confidence than any person I know. you may[2] have thought sir, that I hinted at somthing of that in my last letter. but I can assure you, that nothing of that entered my mind

I went the other day to a M[r] scotts plantation in Virg. 6 miles above the little falls, to look at his flock of sheep and a spanish ram. a sample of the wool of the spanish ram is here inclosed. whilst I was there, we weighed 3 of his best ram lambs from an iceland ram and spanish ewes, one of the lambs was droped the 15[th] of January, and on saturday last, the 1[st] July: his weight was 122 lbs. that is, 12¼ ounces he has[3] growed each day

sir, you say in a letter, that the privilege of being first supplyd with the merinoe[s] is a sufficient favor, that is not my wish. When your cart comes for the broad tail ram if you have nothing to send by it, if you would think proper to send me some of M[r] T. M. Randolphs ewes such as the one we had here with one ear cut short, ther[s] another ewe in your flock, which I bought here, with verry short fine wool and her tail cut short, she is the finest ewe of the short tailed ones that was here. sir if you should think of sending any, either yourself or M[r] Randolph let them be of the finest wool, and I will supply yourself and M[r] Randolph from your own ewes, which will make verry fine wool the first cross of them and my merino rams this together with one of your many horn breed when they become pure; will satisfy me. it would [be][4] necessary to keep them from the ram

sir it may be that you have some old negro[s] that is of little or no use to you. if such you should have, and would think it right to send one to me to take care of my sheep; I will agree to give you any reasonable compensation you would ask, for such a man I canot find in this place

I sent your books in care of M[r] Eppes[s] Betsy as far as Fredericksburgh wher M[r] T.J. Randolph was to take charge of them

Sir, your Humble Servt JOS. DOUGHERTY

RC (DLC); at foot of text: "Thos Jefferson Esq[r]"; endorsed by TJ as received 10 July 1809 and so recorded in SJL.

The PLANTATION was probably Strawberry Hill, from which John Scott had recently won a "prize cup for tups . . . for his lamb Palafox" (Washington *National Intelligencer*, 10 May 1809). BETSY: probably Betsy Hemmings, a slave given by TJ to John Wayles Eppes when Eppes married Maria Jefferson in October 1797 (*PTJ*, 29:550; Stanton, *Free Some Day*, 106, 132; Hemmings's gravestone inscription at John Wayles Eppes's Millbrook Estate, Buckingham County).

[1] Manuscript: "srange."
[2] Word interlined.
[3] Manuscript: "heas."
[4] Omitted word editorially supplied.

# From Joseph McCoy

SIR Philadelphia, July 3, 1809.

A Youth, who is fond of making Verses, takes the liberty of sending you one of his little Poems, to which he has ventured to affix your name. Perhaps, if adopted, the Expedient would prove a very silly one. Little qualified to decide on this point, I have pleased myself with the thought of some good effects it might produce, without knowing what bad ones they would bring along with them, or whether consistently with its dignity & duties, legislative authority might descend to the subject. Superlative wisdom, however is not always expected in a fanciful trifle; & though my little effusion may contain some truths, as a spontaneous offering of respect, I must beg it may be estimated, rather by the motives with which it is tendered, than by its own value.

With the greatest veneration, Sir, Your ob[t] Serv[t]

JOSEPH M[c]COY
N[o] 3, Lombard S[T]

RC (CSmH: JF-BA); at foot of text: "M[r] Jefferson"; endorsed by TJ as received 13 July 1809 and so recorded in SJL.

Joseph McCoy subsequently published *The Frontier Maid; or, A Tale of Wyoming: A Poem in five cantos* (Wilkes-Barre, Pa., 1819), and was residing in Luzerne County, Pennsylvania in 1820 (Ronald Vern Jackson and others, *Pennsylvania 1820 Census Index* [1977], 232; Stewart Pearce, *Annals of Luzerne County* [1860], 401–6).

ENCLOSURE

## Joseph McCoy's Poem: "The Expedient"

The Expedient;
Addressed to M[r] Jefferson

Let the slave, with treacherous zeal,
Skill'd to weave the flattering wile,
Win, without a heart to feel,
Folly's friendship, greatness' smile;

Sage, not such addrisses thee—
No, to freedom early won,
Proud he boasts a spirit free,
Friend of all as slave of none.

Calm, thro thy eventful time,
Wedded to thy country's fame,
Thou hast led thy march sublime,
Honor'd still, for still the same.

Peace thy lov'd retirement guard!
Happy be thy rural reign!
Were desert its own reward
Not my warmest wish were vain.

But not mine 'tis here to seek
Praise's language, Sage revered;
Let a glorious nation speak!
Let the great & good be heard!

Thou thy fondest wish dost gain,
Ease domestic, rural peace;
Hast thou done? does nought remain?
Do thy public wishes cease?

No, while lives a vital spark,
Glowing in that patriot breast,
As its genius shalt thou mark
Every movement of the West:

As its genius, fondly true,
Watch to ward impending ill;
As its genius cherish too
Taste & Wisdom, Toil & skill.

Hence, the undistinguish'd Muse
Fond thy bow'rs among would steal;
Haply fanciful her views—
Haply all his merit Zeal—

Nations have their infant time;
Slow the steps, progressive traced,
Which have led them to the prime
Mark'd by knowledge, Wealth, & Taste

As political advance,
So is literary made,
Harmonizing, not by chance[1]
This by that has still been sway'd.

So the Nations *have* come forth,
But the western world is new;
Not alone by recent birth,
But by modes of thinking too.

Empires have been born, have grown,
Shook the world, & passed away;
Yet, as this peculiar, none
Ever issued into day.

Young in an enlighten'd time,
Well Columbia truth explored;
Wisdom's radience on her clime
Rich as morning sunshine pour'd

Hence the mild & stable form
Of her plan of ruling pow'r;
Not th'expedient in a storm
Rashly seazed to serve the hour.

Balancing & balanced all,
'Tis a system self secure;
On, as the terrestrial ball,
Rolling regular & sure.

Yet this cause, that misery check'd,
And advanced this glorious end,
Visits us with an effect
Which should wake his country's friend.

Britain's[2] rude barbaric rage
Gradual, feelings mild replaced;
Gradual mounting, stage by stage,
Rose her learning, arts, & taste.

How were those, in early time,
To the pen their lives who gave?
Fed by Vanity or Crime
Or dependents of a slave.

Public taste the Muse should guard;
Public taste gave not support;
Great the toil for small reward,
Hence the piteous poor resort.

Yet 'twas thus the british muse
Up the heights of glory drew
But the course which she could choose
Will the western Muse persue?

No: the cause her steps that press'd
Here exerts to urge astray;
But strong causes of the West
Work with counteracting sway.

Britain, tho up reason's hill
Marching 'fore the neighbouring climes,
Lugg'd with her, as lugs she still,
Relic's of her feudal times

Mark'd distinctions, severing wide
These from those, the gentle mind,
Chill repress'd its native pride,
Oft to this poor shift inclined.

No such here; or if there were
Where's the man of regal wealth
Animating stately glare
With thy eye-beam labouring Health?

Or suppose that selfish care
Here might feed a minion crew;
Yet what oft was kindness there
Were flat insult in our view.

Thus, th'intelligence that gave
Western liberty to live,
Then secured, to bless the brave,
All equality can give

That, with ordering hand sublime,
Framed our mighty league profound,
Fill'd with works of peace our [time?][3]
Breathing life & joy around

Habits settles, thoughts inspires,
Blackening the dependent's views;
For the West, while freedom fires,
Claims an independent Muse.

Or if public scorn, that great,
Pow'rful scourge of graceless deed,
By some spell had lost its weight,
Nor could make a heart to bleed;

Genius ever had its pride,
Nought can combat here its force;
Nor by birth nor wealth outvied
Merit mounts its lofty course—

Here this pride, then, ne'er can fail
Ever, hence, must Genius' soul
Spurn, tho wrechedness assail,
Ostentation's chilling dole.

There's the point: methinks tis plain
What oft guarded Britain bard,
Individual bounty vain,
Ne'er the western muse can guard.

Shall she perish then unknown?
Shall her pride her lyre destroy?
Or, if not, shall she alone
Weep amidst a world of Joy?

Time will come, a glorious time!
Rising fast, nor far away,
When her warble, round our clime,
Welcome as delight, shall stray.

Nought to cheer her, then, indeed,
Need peculiar hand extend,
No defender will she need,
For a world will be her friend.

Everywhere her steps shall rove,
All the continent her home,
Open arms & looks of love
Waiting her where'er she roam

Duty, then, shall, martyring Will,
Wake no more th'enthusiast's sigh
Wild her airy harp shall thrill
Vivid roll her radient eye.

In the South, as breaks the morn,
Oft shall she, while all is still,
Listening to the farm house horn,
Pause upon the distant hill

Then from high too widely see
Driving Teams, & Youths who come
O'er gray heights, with shouts of glee,
Hurrying to the harvest home.

But when flames the sun on high,
Languid, hush'd the world beneath,
Then, when scarce the South's warm sigh
Stirs the thistle on the heath

Wrapt into the mighty grove,
Cool while play the rustling leaves,
She shall find the maid of love
Whose full bosom anxious heaves;

And with wildest mellowest lay
Soothe her thought of fondness pure,
Where the waters dash, that stray
Sounding down the dell obscure.

Then the lover shall she mark
Gliding thro the path unknown
Tracing swift the winding dark
Hid now in th'Elysium lone.

In the North she fond shall stray
Where, to neighbouring shoreland height,
Hums the lively City gay,
All its bustling ports in sight.

Proud moves out th'Adventurer new,
Looking forth to unknown skies;
Hark! she sounds the long adieu,
Wide the shouting port replies!

Rising o'er the white sea foam
Mounts the dim sail, far away
Lofty, now, rejoicing home,
Comes the great ship, thundering gay.

Where near woody headland rude
Busy fishers haunt the shore
Oft shall she, across the flood,
Sit to mark the clanking oar.

And while in th'inclement night
Whistling whirls the drifting snow,
From thy fairy watch-tow'r, White!
Hear the stormy sea below.

Then, how will she shrinking gaze,
When, thro squally[4] gloom so dark,
Lone the lanthern'd ship-light's blaze
Dances with the bounding bark.

Or when, thro the night unblest,
Awful from the roaring main
Signal guns of Ship distress'd
Flash, & pause, & flash again.

Yes, her glorious day shall come,
Bright to rise, & long to last;
But shall she unheeded roam
Till her day of gloom be past?

Let us not th'unjudging join
Pleased to blame the mind:
Gold is moulded 'ere 'tis coin
Form'd a nation 'ere refined.

Flying crualty, & shame,
Persecuted, lorn, distress'd
When the fathers of our name
Sought the solatery West

Scatter'd round the mighty coast
Where treed Bear oft growl'd from high
Was it their's of song to boast?
Or in letter'd love to vie?

No: while Safety might have bred
Genius to each art of grace;
Danger that same Genius led
Proud to toil, to fight, & chace.

When the rising Country's hum,
Shrieks & war-whoops swell'd afar
When the rolling frontier drum
Roused them to the midnight war

Bold would they, with flaming eye,
Fortress seek array'd for fight;
Or to marshalling bugle fly
Sounding from the ridgy height

Then rush forth: The foes give way,
Dogg'd thro dell & woodland thick,
Round the hills the bugles play,
Rattling rifles flashing quick.

Toiling, battling, mastering game,
All their pow'rs & thoughts required
Excellence in these gave fame
These Ambition roused & fir'd

Thus were form'd the men to ills
Who in time we well may boast
Bursting from their hundred hills
Hurl'd the ruthless from our coast.

Revolution's tumults o'er,
Purchased liberty divine,
Might they Taste's fair worlds explore
Anxious but to please, refine?

Happier toil the race endears:
Freedom, as its nature pure,
Hardly won, with blood & tears,
Twas their glory to secure.

Struggling from their dangerous state
Careful they, new born to fame,
As some tuneful Organ great,
Built their government's fair frame

Faintly yet Taste's glimmer shone;
Yet the grand machine was new,
Genuine to preserve its tone
Fir'd each thought, & fix'd each view.

Thus, if languish Poesy
Without favour or applause,
Ill distressful! yet may we
Trace it to a glorious cause.

Murmers, then, were vile & vain,
Selfish spleen's resort unwise,
Yet, forbearing to complain,
Let us not the theme despise.

Poesy, in Rudeness' spite,
Wins to gentleness the mind;
And, tho wild, it wakes delight,
Leaves no latent thorn behind.

Here, where broadest views expand
Of a world of peace & joy,
Skillful be the Muse, & bland,
Nor let drivelling thrift destroy.

How has wakeful Wisdom watch'd
O'er the western counsels blest;
Battle's Genius, how unmatch'd,
Hast thou thunder'd in the West!

Thou, Philosophey, hast mild
Bid the dancing lightnings play
Round thy brow, & roving wild,
Off thy pointed finger stray!

Fond Health's guardian genius cheers
Beauty sinking on his breast;
Sage, yet kind as youth in tears,
Goes he forth in blessing blest.

Nor depress'd the maid who still
Spends in silent walk her hours,
Thro the vale & round the hill
Placed gathering plants & flow'rs.

Moral ethics, Politics
Clime more favouring never knew;
Idle, hence, the Juggler's tricks,
But, alas! deplored by few,

Poesy the fields alone,
All her feet with brambles torne,
Loose in air her tresses blown,
Strays, neglected girl! forlorn.

On the lonely rock reclined,
Listening to the sounding fall,
World! what art thou to her mind,
With thy cares & follies all!

But such scene not still employs,
She is but of human mould,
Human cares still human Joys,
Twining viper like, enfold.

Till the bard unpunish'd may
Make his life a life of song,
How shall she, till that proud day,
Struggle thro the listless throng?

Shall she, as in Europe oft,
Be the minion of the Great
While her gentle spirit soft
Sinks beneath dependence' weight?

Shall e'er, amidst th'alarms
Of mischance & poverty,
Fly into a villain's[5] arms,
Or embrace an idiot's knee?

O, forbid it, Sire of Time!
Rather let the Maid unblest
Never with a gleam sublime
Hence emblaze to shame the West—

For the West is freedom's home,
And, while seasons take their round,
Never there, whate'er her doom,
Be a shackled spirit found.

Yet to cheer her early hours
Can no glorious patron be?
Sure not worthless that whose pow'rs
Soothe the gentle, fire the free.

Let Columbia then be heard,
And, to bid her genius rise,
From her senate house revered,
Shew on high the annual prize

But not song alone should claim
Honours from the nation's hand;
Every studious son of fame
Scatters riches round the land.

Nay, the theme must soon be scan'd;
Else some institution blest,
National & bountious plan'd
Shall enliven Genius' breast.

Thus might grecian days revive
Maros, Newtons come again
Talents would with Talents strive,
Never could such strife be vain.

Yet the nation's finger free
Annual pointing out th'elect,
Tho it genius roused, would be
Still more glorious in effect.

For the frequent test to ply
Must o'er genius' toils refined
Throw an air of import high
That would catch the public mind.

Not all Homer's blaze of soul
With all Newton's world of mind
Could so much effect the Whole
If to that one end combined.

Silent as the mellowing dew
Show'rs refreshing thro night veil
Would th'impression, soft as true,
On th'unconscious nation steal

So enquiry, curious still,
Wide would knowledge rich difuse;
And with touch of joy & skill
O'er her loved harp live the Muse

O, whence was it, melting oft,
Long, that spelling pow'r you stole,
That sweet witchery that so soft
Weaves itself thro feeling's soul?

Not rude genius e'er alone
Could the fairy charm impart;
For, tho but to genius known,
Yet is, Poesy an art.

One in which not taste refined
Genius pow'rful, subtile, warm,
Till long practice mould his mind,
Can the graceful master form.

Wandering rays, dispersed in air,
To a focus, must be lured
'Ere, concentring, glowing there,
Sense be of their force assured.

At a point the mental beams
Thus converged, we bright behold;
But if lost in scatter'd gleams
Faint each fitful glimmer cold.

Where the mind's full force to bind
Sweet seductive song to thee,
Were fond boyhood's dreams to end
E'en in want & misery.

Shall the drivelling dolt complain
That his country's genius sleeps?
Nay, while, hapley, waked in vain,
Haughty in disgust, it[6] weeps—

Be the people roused to guard
Those who form the mind & heart;
Let their toils command reward,
Else what bard dare court his art?

For still be it full in mind,
The Republican with scorn,
Child of feeling, proud as kind!
Private Patronage will spurn.

Taste for fancy's toils of fame
Rapidly gains ground, tis true,
Nature, every where the same,
Renders sure its triumph too;

Yet to it the touch of pow'r
May a hastening impulse give—
So may Bards, at no far hour,
Live to write & write to live.

In his vale, then, blest to prove
Thought & feeling's full controul,
Shall the son of song & love
Form his little world of soul

Take sweet Eve's relaxing walk
With his fond one, who, the while,
Asks & tells, in playful talk
Twenty nothings, for a smile

Elegance & tasteful care
Shall that home of love pervade
Books & hearts each thought to share
Make it all home can be made.

There shall fond, oer human strife,
Breathe the philanthropic pray'r;
Pow'rful as the pulse of life,
Thrill the patriot feeling there.

Thence shall, o'er our country wide,
Th'informing light of Genius play;
Thence, in glow of patriot pride,
Come his Glory's lofty lay.

Honour'd be the Poet's name!
Ever honour'd they who dare
Glorious raise their country's fame,
Tho denied that country's care.—

As for me, my pow'r is nought;
Fond the patriot thought I tell,
Tho without t'endear that thought
E'en a friend to say "tis well"—

Yet oft flying city noise
As thy banks that court delay
Schuylkill, dear for pensive joys
In sequester'd walk I stray

Pleased can I the strain unknown,
Hanging oft the blue wave o'er,
Mingle with the gale that lone
Breathes along the silent shore.

Nature's both, they both shall die,
As, while no one listening heeds,
Falls the Evening's latest sigh,
Waving slow the distant reeds

MS (CSmH: JF-BA); undated; entirely in McCoy's hand.

MAROS: the reference is to the Roman poet Virgil (Publius Vergilius Maro).

[1] Manuscript: "chace."
[2] Manuscript: "Britian's."
[3] Omitted word editorially supplied.
[4] Manuscript: "sqully."
[5] Manuscript: "villian's."
[6] Manuscript: "in."

# From James Madison

DEAR SIR July 4. 1809

The inclosed letter accompanied y^e^ skin of an Animal, not named by the writer, which belongs to the Region of the Rocky Mountains. The bundle being too large for the Mail, I shall forward it by some other opp$^{y}$; perhaps as far as Orange, by a waggon I shall soon have on the return thither.

You will have seen that a re-nomination of J. Q. A. for Russia, has succeeded with the Senate. In framing his Credence, it will be proper to adapt it to that given to M$^{r}$ Short,[1] which deviated from the beaten form; and it appears that the original in that case passed on to M$^{r}$ Short, without being opened at the Office of State. No copy therefore exists but the one retained by yourself. Will you be so good as to lend me that, sending it to Orange C$^{t}$ House to await my arrival there; which will probably be at an early day next week. We continue without news from Europe later than the rumour from Holland of a defeat of the Austrians.

Y$^{rs}$ truly & respectfully JAMES MADISON

RC (DLC: Madison Papers); dateline repeated at foot of text; endorsed by TJ as received 10 July 1809 and so recorded in SJL. Enclosure: William Clark to TJ, 2 June 1808 (MHi).

The SKIN came from a Rocky Mountain (bighorn) sheep (TJ to Clark, 10 Sept. 1809). J. Q. A.: on 27 June 1809 the Senate reversed its earlier rejection of Madison's nomination of John Quincy Adams as minister plenipotentiary to Russia (*JEP*, 2:127). Napoleon's armies had defeated the AUSTRIANS at Landshut, Eckmühl, and Ratisbon in April 1809 (Washington *National Intelligencer*, 7 July 1809).

[1] TJ here wrote in the left margin "Aug. 29. 09.," a misdated reference to his 29 Aug. 1808 letter of credence to Alexander I for William Short (RuAVPR [microfilm at DLC]).

## From André Daschkoff

MONSIEUR! Philadelphie ce 5 Juillet. 1809

Arrivé dans le pays par ordre de Sa Majesté l'Empereur de toutes les Russies en Conséquence de ma nomination de chargé d'Affaires près les Etats Unis et de Consul Général à Philadelphie, j'ai l'honneur de vous envoyer Monsieur deux lettres ci jointes à votre adresse Confiées à mes Soins. Je Saisis avec empressement cette occasion de vous présenter mes hommages réspéctueux du moment de mon arrivée, de vous faire part de la haute considération dont vous jouisser à tant de titres, chez une Grande puissance du Nord, amie de vôtre pays, et de vous assurer des Sentimens distingués et du respect profond avec lequel j'ai l'honneur d'être

Monsieur! Votre très humble et très obeissant Serviteur

ANDRÉ DASCHKOFF.

EDITORS' TRANSLATION

Sir! Philadelphia 5 July. 1809

Having arrived in the country by order of His Majesty the Emperor of all the Russias in consequence of my nomination as chargé d'affaires to the United States and consul general at Philadelphia, I have the honor to send you, Sir, two enclosed letters addressed to you and entrusted to me. I eagerly seize on this occasion to pay my respects at the moment of my arrival, and to let you know the high esteem you enjoy for your numerous accomplishments, in a great power of the North, friend of your country, and to assure you of the profound respect with which I have the honor to be

Sir! Your very humble and very obedient servant

André Daschkoff.

RC (DLC); at foot of text: "Monsieur Jefferson"; endorsed by TJ as received 10 July 1809 and so recorded in SJL. Translation by Dr. Genevieve Moene. Enclosures: (1) William Short to TJ, 9 Apr. 1809 (FC in DLC: Short Papers, 34:6184–5; consisting only of brief description: "letter of introduc[t] for Daschkoff"; entirely in Short's hand; from a portion of Short's epistolary record containing entries from 6 June 1808 to 16 Oct. 1809, written on sheets folded to make narrow pages; recorded in SJL as received from Paris on 10 July 1809). (2) Short to TJ, 10 Apr. 1809.

André Daschkoff (1777–1830) attended Moscow University, served in the Russian army, and joined that nation's consular service in 1805. His connections with Count Nicolas de Romanzoff helped him win the dual appointment of chargé d'affaires to the United States and consul general at Philadelphia in 1808. Daschkoff also served simultaneously as correspondent of the Russian-American Company, which regulated trading activities between Russians, Americans, and Native Americans in the Pacific Northwest. He was the first Russian diplomat sent to the United States. Temporarily outranked by Count Théodore Pahlen, who served as Russian minister to the United States from June 1810 to July 1811, on his departure Daschkoff replaced him as minister. Daschkoff was recalled in 1816 when the successful assertion of diplomatic immunity following the arrest for rape of his successor as consul general made both men political liabilities. After his return home in 1819, with the exception of a mission in Istanbul from 1820–21, Daschkoff's remaining postings were inside Russia (Daniel L. Schlafly Jr., "The First Russian Diplomat in America: Andrei Dashkov on the New Republic," *Historian* 60 [1997]: 39–57; Alexander I to TJ, 12 Sept. 1808 [DNA: RG 59, NL, Russia]; Bashkina, *United States and Russia*, 774, 1131).

# From Thomas Ladd

Esteemed Friend Richmond 7[th] M[o] 5[th] 1809

Thy favor of the 25[th] Ult[o] requesting a postponement of the time fixed on by me for the settlement of the Accounts between the Parties, in the case of Gilliam v Fleming, I received in due course of Mail, and would have replied to it sooner, had I not have expected Skelton Jones, (to whom thou hadst written on the same subject) to have called on me and signified his assent to the postponement: I have not yet seen him. I however can have no hesitation in complying with thy reasonable request, provided thou will be good enough to give the parties interested the necessary information of the time being changed to 10th Month (October) 20th next, at 9 OClock A.M. David Copland brought the Order for an Account to me, it is necessary that he be particularly informed of the change; and as early as may be; Skelton Jones I will inform myself—

I am with Assurances of great respect thy Friend

THOMAS LADD

RC (DLC); endorsed by TJ as received 13 July 1809 and so recorded in SJL.

## From Robert Patterson

SIR, Philadelphia July 6th 1809

I have the pleasure to inform you, that the people of Passamaquoddy are now furnished with a new object of pursuit—gold finding. There was yesterday brought to the Mint, as a deposit, part of a grain or lump of native gold, weighing 14 oz 7¼ grs which was lately found, by a little boy, on Sewards neck beach, in the town(ship) of Eastport, near the mouth of the bay. This piece of gold, when assayed, was found to be 22. c 0½ gr fine, or a little better than the U.S. or British standard—the alloy was nearly or altogether silver. It contained about 1½ per cent. of white quartz with which mineral native gold is frequently found united.

The piece when found, we are informed in a letter from a Mr Stephen Jones of that place, weighed 2. ℔ 3½ oz. It is observed by Mr Jones that the bank adjoining that part of the beach on which the piece of gold was found, is washed away several feet every year, and thus, no doubt, was the piece left bare on the surface of the beach.

These gifts of Providence have, indeed, been frequently the occasions of evil rather than of good to man, thro the eagerness which too many manifest to obtain gold at first hand, without the intermediate steps of honest labour in the ordinary pursuits of life. But still the discovery of this precious metal, in different and distant parts of the U. States, must be considered as important, especially as it regards the natural history of our country.

I have the honour to be with sentiments of the greatest respect & esteem Your obedient servant RT PATTERSON

I take this opportunity of returning you my most grateful thanks for your kind letters of introduction in favour of my son Robert—He left the capes of Delaware, in the ship Pekin, on the 18th of last month—

RC (MHi); endorsement by TJ torn. Recorded in SJL as received 13 July 1809.

The discovery of the PIECE OF GOLD and the confirmation of its purity by the United States Mint were subsequently reported in very similar language by at least one newspaper (Wilkes-Barre *Luzerne Federalist*, 11 Aug. 1809).

# From Skelton Jones

SIR, Richmond July 7. 1809.

Your letter dated June the 25th came duly to hand. I have seen the master commissioner Ladd and informed him that any arrangement which should be made between you and himself would be satisfactory to me. He has appointed the 20th of Octr as the day of meeting, of which I expect he will inform you. He will also give notice of the postponement to David Copeland one of the parties concerned. You will, as you suggest in your letter, be good enough to endeavour to procure the punctual attendance of Messrs Skipwith Eppes &c—.

I address'd to you some weeks past two letters on the subject of the History of Virginia:—I should be glad to hear from you, shortly, on that subject.—

With great respect Yr obedt. servt. SKELTON JONES

RC (DLC); endorsed by TJ as received 13 July 1809 and so recorded in SJL.

TWO LETTERS: see Jones to TJ, 19 June 1809, and enclosure.

# From James Madison

DEAR SIR Washington July 7. 1809

The inclosed letter from Mr S.[1] came under cover to me. It was brought by the vessel lately arrived at Phila from Dunkirk. It appears that he had not left Paris, for Petersbg: nor meant to do so, untill he shd hear further from the U.S; as he has probably explained to you. Mr Coles had reached[2] Paris; but in the absence of the French Court, nothing could be said very interesting on the subject of his errand. From a Paragraph in a letter from Genl Armstrong to Mr Gallatin, it would seem that the French Ministers were disposed to patronize a relaxation of the commercial policy of the Emperor, and that he was disposed to listen to any expedient that would save him from the appearance of inconsistency and retreat from his stand ag$^{st}$ G. B. There is some ground therefore to hope that the previous retreat of the latter may have a good effect; unless his new[3] successes should inspire a pertinacity in his old projects. It is certain that great inconveniencies are felt in France, from the want of external commerce; and that the opening presented by the repeal of the B. orders, not only for a reasonable trade with the U.S. but thro' that between the different parts of the Continent itself, must render a continuance of the blockading system, peculiarly grating every where. The arrival of Dashkoff, makes it proper that I should not leave Washington before he reaches it; which I fear will not be for some days. My purpose was to have set out tomorrow, or on Monday at farthest.

Y$^{rs}$ Affect$^{ly}$ JAMES MADISON

RC (DLC: Madison Papers); at foot of text: "M$^{r}$ Jefferson"; endorsed by TJ as received 10 July 1809 and so recorded in SJL. Enclosure: William Short to TJ, 10 Apr. 1809.

[1] Late in life Madison here interlined "Short."

[2] Manuscript: "reahed."

[3] Word interlined.

# To Joseph Milligan

SIR Monticello July 7. 09.

By a note in the 5$^{th}$ vol. of Joyce's Scientific dialogues I see that the 7$^{th}$ & 8$^{th}$ vol$^{s}$ were published in Mar. 1807. I presume therefore they must have come to the US. and will pray you to get them for me to compleat the set you procured me, which consisted of the first 6. vols only. the two volumes wanting are on the subject of chemistry. it is a book of inestimable value, & renders all the branches of science on which it treats easily intelligible to very young minds. remember it is in petit format, or in 18$^{o}$. these two volumes are so small they may come in the mail.

I will also thank you for a ream of hot pressed 4$^{to}$ letter paper. if you can lodge this safely at the stage office of Alexandria, directed to me at Monticello near Milton, paying the portage to Fredericksburg, it will come safely to Milton where the residue of the portage can be paid. the undertakers from Alexa to Fredsbg, & from Fredsbg to Milton are different which renders it necessary to pay the former at Alexandria, as I have no correspondent at Fredericksbg. this may serve as a general rule for things to be sent me hereafter too bulky for the mail. I salute you with esteem. TH: JEFFERSON

PoC (DLC); at foot of text: "Mr Milligan"; endorsed by TJ.

The seventh and last-known volume of Jeremiah JOYCE's *Scientific dialogues, intended for the instruction and entertainment of young people*, 1st ed. (London, 1803–05), was *A Companion to the Scientific Dialogues: or, The Tutor's Assistant and Pupil's Manual in Natural and Experimental Philosophy*. Joyce's work was not among those that TJ sold to the nation in 1815, but he owned four volumes, not further identified, at his death (Poor, *Jefferson's Library*, 7 [no. 298]).

# To Benjamin Brown

SIR Monticello July 8. 09.

Mr Dawson, an agent for the Fire insurance co. lately told me there had been a call, two years ago, of $\frac{2}{3}$ of their original quota, on the members of that company. I did not recollect nor do my papers inform me that such a call came to me, or was paid by me. I suppose however that the information of the society to you that there is such a charge against me must of course be right, and therefore I have no hesitation at assuming it. I expect shortly to recieve a sum of money, out of which I will take care to make this paiment to you. I salute you with esteem & respect TH: JEFFERSON

PoC (MHi); at foot of text: "Mr Benj. Brown"; endorsed by TJ in part: "additional assessmt of 1806."

# From William W. Hening

DEAR SIR, Richmond, 8th July 1809

I have lately received a letter from Judge Tucker, inclosing an extract from a gentleman in Salem (Mass.) who is collecting materials for a history of printing in America, from its first introduction.—The writer suggests, that at one period, the publication of News-papers, in Virginia, was either discouraged or totally prohibited; and the object of Judge Tucker's enquiry of me is, to know, whether any of the old statutes in my possession will throw any light on the subject.

I have progressed, in printing the Statutes at Large, as far as the March session 1657–8, and have discovered nothing on that subject.—I have also examined the MSS. in my possession to the year 1699, with as little success. Not having time to enter into a minute examination of this subject, and having nothing to guide me to any particular period, I must request the favour of you to answer the enquiry.—Your superior knowledge of our early history, and your devotion to the cause of literature, induce me to ask this favour.

The publication of the statutes at large, will unfold a volume of history, hitherto unexplored.—I have already discovered that many of the most important incidents are totally misunderstood by all our historians—They have, indeed, from a want of access to original documents, servilely copied from English historians; and such was their disposition to disguise the injuries and oppressions of the mother country towards the colonies, that the truth was seldom told.

In one of the old statutes for regulating the coins of the colony, I discovered two species mentioned, the value and quality of which I could not ascertain; nor could I derive any information from any source, respecting them.—They were called "Roanoake" and "Wompompeeke."—If you could favour me with any information on this head, I might take a fit opportunity, in a note to some of the subsequent acts, to introduce it.

The Second volume of Hening & Munford's Reports, has been just published.—You have been furnished with the 1st & 2nd Nos only of the first Volume.—On returning them, I would send you the two volumes complete, executed in a very handsome style.—

As soon as the gentlemen appointed for that purpose shall have compared the printed laws with the MS., I will return at least three of your volumes; which have been transcribed, and the matter printed.—They contain some valuable State papers, which may be useful to some future historian.—After the year 1699, (to which date my collection is complete,) I shall have to trouble you for a further supply of Sessions Acts.

I am respectfy Yrs Wm: W: Hening

RC (DLC); addressed: "To Thomas Jefferson Esqr late President of the United States Monticello"; franked and postmarked; endorsed by TJ as received 20 July 1809 and so recorded in SJL.

Isaiah Thomas, the GENTLEMAN IN SALEM, subsequently published *The History of Printing in America* (Worcester, Mass., 1810). ROANOAKE and WOMPOMPEEKE are Algonquian terms for shell money. Roanoke was worth less than wampumpeag, which is a variant of wampum (*OED*; Hening, 1:397).

## To William Nelson

Dear Sir Monticello July 8. 09.

Your favor of June 19. was recieved a few days ago and I regret that it is not in my power to give any information in answer to your enquiries which may be useful to mrs Byrd. during the war of 1755. I was at school, and paid no attention to public transactions; nor, after I came into public life, had I ever occasion to make myself acquainted with the rights or claims of the several regiments employed in that war. the proclamation of 1763. to be sure was known to every one; but it is equally known to yourself. had I known who James Irwin was, or where he lived, I would have inclosed him your letter, in order to save time, as the 15th of July is near at hand, and to manifest my willingness to render service to mrs Byrd. but the advertisement as extracted in your letter, does not state his residence. I pray you to present my friendly respects to mrs Byrd, & to accept yourself assurances of my great esteem & respect. TH: JEFFERSON

PoC (DLC); at foot of text: "The honble William Nelson"; endorsed by TJ.

# To Samuel Smith
## (of Pennsylvania)

SIR Monticello July 9. 09.

I recieved, a few days since your favor of June 28. covering a letter from Morrow & Andrew Lowry requesting information whether the pardon to them was not a remission of the costs of prosecution also. as it is official, & not personal opinion which can alone answer their purposes, I now, to save time, transmit their & your letter to the Secretary of state, whose opinion, or that of the Attorney General will doubtless be transmitted to you on the subject. accept the assurances of my respect. TH: JEFFERSON

PoC (DLC); at foot of text: "The honble Samuel Smith of Erie"; endorsed by TJ.

Samuel Smith, of Mill Creek, Erie County, Pennsylvania, served as associate judge of that county, 1803–05, and sat in the United States House of Representatives, 1805–11. In 1812 he was appointed receiver of public moneys for the district east of the Pearl River in Mississippi Territory. Smith was removed from this post and ruined financially in 1817 when he could not account for all of the public funds (*History of Erie County, Pennsylvania* [1884], 1:342, 415; *Biog. Dir. Cong.*; *Terr. Papers*, 6:287, 782, 784; *JEP*, 2:281, 284 [1, 2 July 1812]; Philip S. Klein, ed., "Memoirs of a Senator from Pennsylvania: Jonathan Roberts, 1771–1854," *Pennsylvania Magazine of History and Biography* 62 [1938]: 241–2).

Smith's FAVOR OF JUNE 28, not found, is recorded in SJL as received from Washington on 2 July 1809. MORROW & ANDREW LOWRY and their brother John Lowry, of Erie County, were charged with obstructing a deputy marshal executing a writ and threatening violent resistance to their eviction. In April 1808 they were convicted in the United States circuit court for the Pennsylvania district, sentenced to three months in prison, and ordered to pay fines and court costs. On 16 Sept. 1808, after the Lowrys served their sentences, TJ accepted their plea of poverty and issued a PARDON remitting the fines and court costs of all three men

(*The Federal Cases: Comprising Cases Argued and Determined in the Circuit and District Courts of the United States* [1894–97], 26:1008–10; DNA: RG 59, PPR, 1:157; Thomas Lloyd to TJ, 16 Aug. 1808, and Albert Gallatin to TJ, 17 Aug. 1808 [DLC]).

# From John Wayles Eppes

DEAR SIR, Eppington July 10th 1809.

I had written to you by Jefferson who travelled on with us as far as Dumfries, but his going off in the stage before I was up, in the morning prevented my giving him the letter—I should long before receiving your letter have written to you had I followed only the impulse of my feelings—I had however postponed from time to time announcing to you the change in my situation, until your friendly congratulation taught me to feel, that I have been guilty of apparent neglect towards one for whom I have & ever shall cherish a sincere and affectionate attatchment—The assurances of continued attatchment on your part are grateful to my heart—No event could inflict on that heart a severer wound than a withdrawal of that affectionate regard, which it ever has been and ever will be the first object of my life to deserve—Equally ignorant with yourself of the cause of feelings which may render me a stranger to your family & deprive my child of the society and protection of his nearest connections it is impossible for me to say how long this state of things may remain—To my child I look forward as the prop of my declining years—His happiness or misery must be mine—The idea of his forming attatchments, intimately connected with his future happiness in a circle from which I am excluded excites in me serious apprehensions—It can I fear ultimately end only in a total alienation of my child, or in what would be to me the greatest misfortune, to find all the feelings of his heart & even his happiness dependent on society from which his Father is banished—The God of nature never intended that Parent & child should move in different circles—In a former letter I expressed to you my sentiments on this subject & although it is impossible for me to refuse to allow Francis to return with you if such is your wish, in the existing circumstances I feel that I risque for your comfort, the destruction of all that future happiness which I have looked forward to in old age from the society of my child—I feel too most powerfully on the other hand all the evils & inconveniences my child must experience from being brought up a stranger to his nearest connections—It renders him indeed completely an Orphan—He will grow up deprived of many of those attatchments which are sanctioned by family ties & which you so justly observe are the most durable and useful through life—Too young at present to feel this deprivation, all that a tender & affectionate father can do to compensate his loss shall be performed by me—

In every thing which relates to his education he can have although absent the complete benefit of your instructions to which I shall consider it a sacred duty to conform—If deprived by absence of the strongest ties of affection his claims on your justice will be sufficient to insure a scrupulous attention to his rights—In ordinary minds the feelings of affection may be too powerful—In those of the first order the principles of rigid Justice will rise superior even to those powerful feelings, which a daily intercourse with natures fairest work "an innocent child never fails to inspire"—

If in my feelings or opinions on this subject I am wrong I shall with candour surrender them to your better Judgement—you may act the part of an impartial Judge—Next to my own your claim to Francis on the ground of affection & connection is nearest—My visiting you produces in a part of your family feelings calculated to destroy its harmony as we have found from past experience—To prevent a repetition of these evils I have suspended my visits—I have given up the society of one for whom I have the affectionate feelings of a son—I have given up also one who holds in my affections the same place with the dearest of[1] my sisters—These are sacrifices the weight of which I can never cease to feel—For your comfort & happiness and for that of my sister I would willingly make any sacrifice—point out to me the course best calculated to promote your comfort & the interest of my child & I will pursue it whatever p[ain?] it may ultimately inflict on my heart—

We shall expect you at Eppington [. . .] not declare to you with what pleasure we all look forward to this visit—My mother has recovered her health but her spirits are gone I fear for ever—Present me affectionately to my sister & accept for your joint welfare & happiness every wish of affection—

Yours sincerely JNO: W: EPPES

RC (MHi); mutilated at seal; addressed: "Thomas Jefferson Esq[r] near Milton albemarle"; stamped and postmarked 23 July at "Springhill V[a]"; endorsed by TJ as received 26 July 1809 and so recorded in SJL.

John Wayles Eppes (1773–1823), attorney and planter, represented Virginia in the United States House of Representatives, 1803–11 and 1813–15, and in the Senate, 1817–19. In 1797 he married his cousin, TJ's daughter Maria Jefferson. Their only surviving child, Francis Wayles Eppes, was born in 1801 at Monticello and returned there frequently to visit his grandfather, who oversaw his education as he had that of his father. Eppes was a staunch political supporter and regular correspondent of TJ even after Maria Jefferson Eppes's death in 1804 and Eppes's second marriage, to Martha Burke Jones on 15 Apr. 1809 (*ANB*; *DAB*; Washington *National Intelligencer*, 26 Apr. 1809).

YOUR LETTER: probably TJ to Eppes, 19 June 1809, recorded in SJL but not found. A missing letter from Eppes to TJ, 8 Sept. 1809, is recorded in SJL as received from Eppington on 14 Sept. 1809. Eppes had most likely SUSPENDED his VISITS because of his strained relationship with Thomas Mann Randolph, whose wife, TJ's daughter Martha, Eppes evidently ranked with THE DEAREST OF MY SISTERS. Eppes's MOTHER Elizabeth Wayles Eppes was the half-sister of Martha Wayles Skelton Jefferson, TJ's wife.

[1] Preceding three words interlined.

# To John Minor

DEAR SIR                                        Monticello July 10. 09

I recieved, three days ago only, your favor of May 17. I was intimately acquainted with Col$^{o}$ Bernard Moore & much attached to him, & would certainly have done any thing I could for him then, or his family now. but I do not recollect that I was one of his trustees, & still less that I ever acted in the trust. my distance from him & my other occupations were such as to prevent it; & I certainly do not possess a scrip of pen in evidence that I ever intermeddled in a single act concerning the trust. still it is possible. after a lapse of forty odd years, and a total abstraction from matters of this kind, I can affirm nothing on my memory alone. I know that mr Lyons was an admr of the Speaker Robinson, & that Col$^{o}$ Moore was a considerable debtor. if mr Lyons knows that I acted as a trustee I shall be ready to act again, where right. but the case must be made very plain, & I must incur no risk by what I do. in the present case for instance, I must undertake to convey only whatsoever title, interest or authority may still exist in me as a trustee. I could not even covenant against any former act of my own, because I have no means of knowing that I may not have joined in a conveyance of this very land, for instance, to another. if the purchaser errs in stating a right to be in me, he must be contented to obtain no more than such right as may be in me.

I thank you for the kind indulgence with which you have viewed the acts of my administration. of it's wisdom the world must judge. of it's integrity my conscience is to me the witness. I rejoice in the prospect of a pacification with England. in what degree it is owing to the past or present administration is not worth a thought. whatever claims the former might have, mr Madison had the principal agency, and the latter acts are entirely his. I always considered it as among the happiest circumstances of my administration that the harmony & cordiality which subsisted among all it's members amalgamated us into one mind. we had never a question who had a right to the merit or demerit of any particular measure; for in truth all measures of importance were the measures of all. the prospect of peace with England is delightful, & the preservation of it with all the world most desirable. on that depends our liberation from debt and the example & the benefit of applying the public contributions towards making our country a paradise instead of a slaughter house.

Will you be so good as to communicate to mr Pendleton what may be requisite as an answer to the letter from him inclosed in yours? I salute you with the highest esteem & respect.

Th: Jefferson

PoC (CSmH: JF-BA); at foot of first page: "Minor Gen[l] John"; endorsed by TJ.

## From Henry Skipwith

My dear Sir. Williamsburg. July 10. 1809

After congratulating you on your happy return to the shades of retirement, and wishing you from my soul every sublunary happiness.—I beg leave to mention a suit in Richmond chancery court in which you, M[r] Eppes & myself are comprehended, among others; and which I am totally unacquainted with,—It is the old claim of Gilliam revived, and a Notice served on me some five days since,—As my total ignorance of this matter renders me unfit for defence,—I pray you Sir! to write me a few lines, and inform me whether there is any thing for me to do in this matter, and whether any services of mine can render good to the common cause.—Your compliance will ever oblige

Dear Sir! Yours truly & sincerely Henry Skipwith

RC (MHi); at foot of text: "Thomas Jefferson Esq[r]"; endorsed by TJ as received 20 July 1809 and so recorded in SJL.

Henry Skipwith (1751–1815) became TJ's brother-in-law when he married Anne Wayles on 7 July 1773. Skipwith served as a lieutenant colonel in the Virginia forces during the American Revolution and represented Cumberland County in the House of Delegates in 1782. Skipwith, TJ, and (until his death in 1808) Francis Eppes were the executors of their father-in-law John Wayles's estate following his death in May 1773. Skipwith and his wife lived on lands inherited from Wayles until her death in 1798, after which he married Elizabeth Byrd and moved with her to Williamsburg (*PTJ*, 1:100; John C. Biller, "Henry Skipwith of Hors du Monde, Cumberland County, Virginia" [master's thesis, University of Virginia, 1963]).

# To Robert Smith

DEAR SIR Monticello. June [July] 10. 09.

I inclose you a letter from mr Smith of Erie, one of the members of Pensylvania, which you will readily percieve ought to have been addressed to you by himself; as it is official, & not personal opinion which can answer his views. I am however gratified by his mistake in sending it to me, inasmuch as it gives me an opportunity of abstracting myself from my rural occupations, & of saluting one with whom I have been connected in service & in society so many years, & to whose aid & relief on an important portion of the public cares, I have been so much indebted. I do it with sincere affection & gratitude, and look back with peculiar satisfaction on the harmony & cordial good will which, to ourselves & our brethren of the Cabinet so much sweetened our toils. from the characters now associated in the administration, I have no doubt of the continuance of the same cordiality so interesting to themselves & to the public; & great as are the difficulties & dangers environing our camp, I sleep with perfect composure knowing who are watching for us. I pray you to present me respectfully to mrs Smith, & to accept my prayers that you may long continue in the enjoiment of health & the public esteem in return for your useful services past & to come. TH: JEFFERSON

PoC (DLC: TJ Papers, 187:33333); at foot of text (faint): "The hon[ble] Robert Smith Sec[y] of State"; misdated, but recorded in SJL under 10 July 1809. Printed, dated 10 June 1809 and with minor alterations, in Smith's *Address to the People of the United States* (Baltimore, 1811), 39.

Robert Smith (1757–1842), James Madison's first secretary of state, was a lawyer in Baltimore who served as TJ's secretary of the navy, 1801–09, and as his attorney general for a few months in 1805. After an extended feud with Albert Gallatin, the treasury secretary, Smith resigned on 1 Apr. 1811 at the request of Madison, who cited inefficiency and Smith's public criticism of the administration. Shortly thereafter Smith publicly accused Madison of financial improprieties while secretary of state, effectively ending his own political career and his correspondence with TJ, which after 1809 was principally concerned with the controversy over the Batture Sainte Marie in New Orleans (*ANB*; *DAB*; *Princetonians*, 1776–83, pp. 342–52).

TJ neglected to enclose the LETTER from Samuel SMITH (note to TJ to Samuel Smith [of Pennsylvania], 9 July 1809; Robert Smith to TJ, 15 July 1809).

## From William Wirt

DEAR SIR Richmond. July 10. 1809.

Alexander M[c]Rae esq[r] & Maj[r] John Clarke, two gentlemen, justly reputed for integrity and talents, and well known I believe, Sir, to you, are just about to embark for Europe, with views which I am authorized to state to you. In conjunction with several other gentlemen, they have formed a project of introducing m[anu]factures into Virginia on a grand scale and permane[nt] basis and with that view to enlist into their association the skill and capital of European artists and owners. It is believed that in this season of agitation and dismay in the old world, their proposal, combining the highest profit with a safe & peaceful asylum, will be embraced with alacrity: and they are pleased with the hope of promoting, by the same act, their own independence and that of their country.

The object of this is to enquire, at their request, whether it may be convenient and agreable to you to give them such letters of introduction to your acquaintances abroad as may either promote their views or render their excursion the more pleasant. They will sail for England in about a fortnight; and after some time spent there will proceed to France, unless their object shall be accomplished in the first country.

You will easily percieve that in order to ensure success & safety to their views, it is necessary that their object should be known to as few as possible: hence, I hope, you will excuse me for begging that this communication may be recievd in confidence.—And that you [w]ill believe me as I truly am with the highest consideration

Yo. obt. Servt, W[M] WIRT

RC (DLC); mutilated at seal; at foot of text: "Thomas Jefferson esq[r]"; endorsed by TJ as received 31 July 1809 and so recorded in SJL. Enclosed in Alexander McRae to TJ, 22 July 1809.

William Wirt (1772–1834), lawyer and author, frequently corresponded with TJ, who chose him as one of his counsel when he was sued in 1810 by Edward Livingston in the controversy concerning the Batture Sainte Marie and who unsuccessfully recruited him for the presidency of the University of Virginia in 1826. Born in Maryland, Wirt lived in Albemarle County, 1795–99, served with TJ's recommendation as clerk of the Virginia House of Delegates, 1799–1802, and after stints in Williamsburg and Norfolk, became a prominent member of the Richmond bar in 1806, appearing a year later for the prosecution at the treason trial of Aaron Burr. Wirt's best-known publications were *Sketches of the Life and Character of Patrick Henry* (Richmond, 1817), and two volumes of essays, *The Letters of the British Spy* (Richmond, 1803) and *The Old Bachelor* (Richmond, 1814). He served as United States attorney general from 1817–29 and remained in Washington thereafter. In 1832 Wirt was the presidential candidate of the Anti-Masonic party (*ANB*; *DAB*; John P. Kennedy, *Memoirs of the Life of William Wirt, Attorney-General of the United States*, 2 vols. [1849]; Anya Jabour, *Marriage in the Early Republic: Elizabeth and William Wirt and the Companionate Ideal* [1998]).

McRae and Clarke were traveling to Europe to pursue a secret and ultimately unsuccessful silk-manufacturing PROJECT. McRae departed in December 1809 without Clarke, who by then had dropped out of the scheme (Wirt to James Madison, 10 July 1809, and McRae to Madison, 22 July, 11 Aug., 8 Dec. 1809, Madison, *Papers, Pres. Ser.*, 1:283–4, 296–7, 323–4, 2:118–9).

## From Louis Philippe Gallot de Lormerie

MONSIEUR, Philad[e] 11 Juillet 1809

Votre silençe Constant que j ai attribué d'abord a vos Occupations m'inquiète, enfin, autant qu'il m'afflige. Je ne puis que me rèferer aux Lettres que j'ai Eu Lhonneur de vous Écrire les 13 avril et 6 Juin dernier.

J'ignore absolument ce qui me prive de Lhonneur de votre réponse il est Egalement contre mes intérest et contre mon intention de vous dèplaire en aucune chose. or vous savés que sans intention il n'y a point de faute, il ne peut y avoir qu'une Erreur; et vous avés sans doute trop d'Elévation dans LEsprit et dans L'ame pour ne pas oublier une Erreur si elle a eu Lieu.

Si vous ne jugés pas a propos de me donner votre Opinion sur mes Terres de Kentucky veuillés avoir la Bonté de me procurer par Votre intercession, la faculté de remporter ma Bibliothèque et qques objets d'art, dhist: naturelle, &[c] ainsi que L'a obtenu le naturaliste Michaux, vous ayant prouvé que j'appartiens aux memes societés savantes avec le titre de correspond[t] du gouvernem[t] francais pour L'Agriculture dans les E:u.

J'Espére aussi et desire votre sentiment a LEgard de mon "memoire[1] sur L'amènagement des forêts dans les E:u: et sur la nècessité des plantations d'arbres, notamment sur les routes publiques en ces Etats," duquel J ay Eu Lhonneur de V[s] remettre un Extrait par ma Lettre du 6 Juin d[er].—

L'Avantâge que j'ai de vous avoir eté recommandé par Le respectable Marquis de la Fayette, les sacrifices que jai faits pour des terres et pour mon azile dans les E.u. Enfin L'interest que j'ai toujours témoigné pour votre Bonheur personnel, et pour la prosperité de ces Etats me permettent dEsperer une Réponse favorable

Je vous prie dEtre persuadé de toute ma Discrétion et de celle dont Juserai pour ne pas vous importuner par aucune Correspondance superflue. Daignes agrèer L'assurance de mes sentimens trés respectueux DE LORMERIE

EDITORS' TRANSLATION

SIR, Philadelphia 11 July 1809

Your constant silence, which I first attributed to your occupations, at last worries me as much as it pains me. I can but refer to the letters which I had the honor to write you on 13 April and 6 June of this year.

I do not know in the least what deprives me of the honor of your response. It is equally contrary to my interests and my intention to displease you in anything. Now, you know that without intention there is no fault at all—there can only be an error—and you doubtless have too elevated a mind and soul not to forget an error if one happened.

If you do not judge it appropriate to give me your opinion on my properties in Kentucky, would you kindly have the goodness to procure for me by your intercession the same right to take away my library and several art objects, natural histories, etc. as was granted the naturalist Michaux, having proved to you that I belong to the same scholarly societies with the title of correspondent for the French government for agriculture in the U.S.

I also hope for and desire your opinion with regard to my "memoir on forest management in the U.S. and on the necessity of planting trees, notably alongside public roads in these states," of which I had the honor to send you an extract with my letter of 6 June of this year.

The advantage that I have of having been recommended to you by the honorable Marquis de Lafayette, the sacrifices that I have made for my properties and for my asylum in the U.S., and finally, the interest that I have always manifested in your personal happiness, and in the prosperity of these states permit me to hope for a favorable response.

I beg you to be persuaded of my full discretion and that I will not trouble you with any superfluous correspondence. Please accept this assurance of my very respectful feelings DE LORMERIE

RC (DLC); dateline below signature; at foot of first page: "Thomas Jefferson Esq[r] late President of the u:S:"; endorsed by TJ as received 20 July 1809 and so recorded in SJL. Translation by Dr. Amy Ogden.

Lormerie's letter of 13 AVRIL was actually dated a day later. His letter of 6 JUIN, not found, is recorded in SJL as received from Philadelphia on 14 June 1809. The EXTRAIT on forest management was enclosed in the former letter.

[1] Opening quotation mark editorially supplied.

# To James Madison

DEAR SIR Monticello July 12. 09.

Your two letters of the 4[th] & 7[th] were recieved by the last mail. I now inclose you the rough draught of the letter to the emperor of Russia. I think there must be an exact facsimile of it in the office, from which mr. Short's must have been copied; because that the one now inclosed has never been out of my hands appears by there being no fold in the paper till now, and it is evidently a polygraphical copy. I send for your perusal letters[1] of W. Short & of Warden; because, tho private, they contain some things & views perhaps not in the public letters. Bonaparte's successes have been what we expected, altho' Warden appears to have supposed the contrary possible. it is fortunate for Bonaparte that he has not caught his brother emperor; that he has left an ostensible head to the government who may sell it to him to secure a mess of pottage for himself. had the government devolved on the people, as it did in Spain, they would resist his conquest as those of Spain do. I expect, within a week or 10. days to visit Bedford. my absence will be of about a fortnight. I know too well the pressure of business which will be on you at Montpelier to count with certainty on the pleasure of seeing mrs. Madison & yourself here; yet my wishes do not permit me to omit the expression of them. in any event I shall certainly intrude a flying visit on you during your stay in Orange. with my respectful devoirs to mrs. Madison, I salute you with constant friendship & respect.

TH: JEFFERSON

RC (DLC: Madison Papers); at foot of text: "The President of the US." PoC (DLC). Enclosures: (1) TJ to Alexander I, emperor of Russia, letter of credence for William Short, 29 Aug. 1808 (DLC). (2) Short to TJ, 10 Apr. 1809. (3) David Bailie Warden to TJ, 17 Apr. 1809.

The BROTHER EMPEROR was Francis I of Austria. In the Bible, Esau sold his birthright to Jacob for a MESS OF POTTAGE (Genesis 25.29–34).

[1] Reworked from "send you letters."

## From George Jefferson

DEAR SIR Richmond 14th July 1809

Mr Venable is now of opinion that Mrs Tabb will not require her money when due, but that she will let you have it for another 6 months.—Of this however he is not certain, but requests me to forward you the inclosed note, in case it should be wanted—and which shall be returned, if it is not.

I am Dear Sir Your Very humble servt GEO: JEFFERSON

RC (MHi); at foot of text: "Thomas Jefferson esqr"; endorsed by TJ as received 20 July 1809 and so recorded in SJL. Enclosure not found.

## From Robert Smith

MY DEAR SIR, Washington July 15. 1809.

Your very friendly letter of the 10h I have had the pleasure to receive. A[nd] most sincerely do I thank you for this additional instance of your goodness and for the interest you so kindly take in whatever concerns me personally.

I am happy in learning that your rural occupations afford you so much gratification. After having so usefully devoted to your Country so many years, you are enjoying, in my estimation, the highest degree of happiness, [to] which a rational man ought to aspire,—living amidst your family, for a few real friends, for the muses and for the comforts of retirement.

'Deus vobis hæc otia fecit.'

Accept, I entreat you, the best wishes of your sincere friend.

R SMITH

PS. Mr Smiths letter, as intended, was [no]t enclosed in yours of the 10h July

RC (DLC); frayed at edges; at foot of text: "[Honb]le Thomas Je[ffe]rs[on]"; endorsed by TJ as received 20 July 1809 and so recorded in SJL.

DEUS . . . FECIT: "It is a god who gave you this peace," reworked from "Deus nobis hæc otia fecit" ("it is a god who gave us this peace"), in Virgil, *Eclogues*, 1.6 (Virgil, *Eclogues, Georgics, Aeneid I–VI*, trans. H. Rushton Fairclough, Loeb Classical Library [1999], 24–5). Virgil's phrase was initially proposed for the reverse of the great seal of Virginia during the American Revolution (Edmund Randolph, *History of Virginia*, ed. Arthur H. Shaffer [1970], 276).

## From John Martin Baker

SIR, Washington City July 16th 1809

I have the Honor to make known to You, that in all the present month, I shall embark with my family for the Balearick Islands; (via Algiers) immediately on my arrival at Majorca, I shall have the satisfaction Sir, to select, and Ship per the very first opportunity, the Two Pipes Albaflor wine, and address them, as you were pleased to direct me, and now take the liberty Sir, to inclose a list of the other articles the production of the Island of Majorca, any of which, that you may please to have sent; I pray you to oblige me with your order, I will have the gratification to select them, see them packed, and Shipped. Mrs. Baker prays you Sir, to accept her most Respectful

Compliments, and joins me with our Children in prayers for your Preservation, Health and Happiness.

I have the Honor to be With the Highest Respect and Gratitude Sir, Your Most obedient humble Servant.

JOHN MARTIN BAKER.

M^rs Baker desires me to say Sir, that she would be highly gratified with the view of Monticello, to have it inlayd in Landscape, at Majorca

RC (MHi); below signature: "To The Most Honorable Thomas Jefferson. Monticello"; postscript on separate page; endorsed by TJ as received 20 July 1809 and so recorded in SJL. Enclosure not found.

John Martin Baker (d. 1841), a naturalized American citizen born in British-controlled Majorca, was appointed United States consul for the islands of Minorca, MAJORCA, and Ibiza by TJ in February 1803. In 1807 he received an additional appointment as consul at Tarragona, and in May 1808 TJ selected him to carry dispatches to France. In January 1809 Baker became a State Department clerk, but in October of that year he embarked for the Mediterranean and served in his consulships until his return to the United States in 1816. During his service in the Balearic Islands he regularly shipped groceries and wine to TJ, who subscribed to Baker's book, *A View of the Commerce of the Mediterranean* (Washington, 1819; Poor, *Jefferson's Library*, 11 [no. 705]). In 1831 he was appointed consul at Rio de Janeiro, and in 1840 he became consul for the port of Nuevitas in Cuba (James Madison to TJ, 20 Aug. 1802 [DLC]; Madison, *Papers, Sec. of State Ser.*, 4:397; *JEP*, 1:441–2, 2:60, 4:178, 193, 5:298, 301 [4, 8 Feb. 1803, 2 Dec. 1807, 7, 30 Dec. 1831, 8–11 July 1840]; Baker to TJ, 28 Aug. 1805 [DLC]; *MB*, 2:1352n; Baker to TJ, 1 June 1813, 29 Aug. 1817; TJ to Baker, 8 Mar. 1819; Washington *Daily National Intelligencer*, 21, 23 July 1841).

# Samuel J. Harrison to Gibson & Jefferson

SIRS Lynchburg July 16. 1809

Agreeable to your request I have been in Search of the Trunk lost last Spring: Which I presume I have found with a part of its contents, as ℘ List annexed—I believe I have also got the Thief; by name Ned, the property of James B. Couch Dec^d late of Buckingham County—He is found guilty by the Examining magistrate here, & is now in Irons, & will be sent on, in a Day or Two, to take his Trial in Rich^d where the offence was Commited, on the 24. Ins^t—Ned is a Noted Villain, & from the Testimony here, I have no doubt of his Guilt—the Two hands that run in the same Boat with him; as well as Several others prove, that he Brocke the Trunk open in thier presence, Took Such of the Articles as he thought would be of any Service to him; & as the Head, & Sterne hand, objected to the Trunk remaining in the Boat, (for fear of their being Implicated) he Threw it, with the Balance of the articles overboard, just below Britains Landing, nearly opposite westham—where it will be proven, it was found, & brought up to this Place, some time after—It Seems Ned came to his Boat in the Basin about 2. Hours before Day, & Insisted to Start, but the Headman not being present the other hand objected, & refused to get up: but Such was Neds anxiety, that he Shoved the Boat to the Locks himself—It seems the Trunk was not Known to be in the Boat, by the other Two Hands untill they Stoped to get Breakfast—& that the other Hands Immediately protested against it; as Being Stolen, which he acknowledged; & from a north River Boat; near Pickets Lumber House—One of the Articles proven here, was a Small Bag of wheat, which Ned retaind—The Bag with M^r^ Jeffersons, Name, in part, is found now in Neds possession by the witness Billy: w^ch^ of itself, is quite Convincing—

It seems the Trunk was found by a parcell of white Boat Men, who Declare there was nothing, but paper, & papers; that they were Chiefly wet; & many of them out of the Trunk, & perhaps 100 yards Distant; the paper was all Taken to [pieices?], & Spread in the Boat for Several Days to Dry—that when they arrivd here Geniral Enquiry was made for an owner for 10 Days, without Effect; when they sold it to a M^r^ Northcut of Amherst, for $3.—Northcut said He would not Deliver the things without having his $3 paid back to him: this he has no right to demand; but as I was obliged to have the things, to Send down to Establish the guilt of the Thief; I have promised to pay him provided he has a right to Claim it—I have paid $1. for bringing the things from Northcuts here.—perhaps you had better send up to M^r^ Jeffersons, for some Evidence, if any you think there can be had? as I should be glad this Villain Could meet his Desert—The witnesses prove that a case, with a parcell of Brass, Instruments, were Thrown over with the Trunk; & may be found, I suspect, if Searched for—

I am told, since the Trunk has come, that there is not more than Half the paper sent: this I shall see about. though it is worth nothing—

Yr M^o^ Obt S J Harrison

a Trunk, with about 8. to 10 Quire Large paper, 1 p^s^ home made Linen, used perhaps for an inside Wrapper; 1 p^s^ Hempen Linen, said to Contain wheat. 2. Rules, 1 Small [Draw^r^?] Sundree little Gilt Books, some Scraps, with writing thereon &c &c &c

SJH.

Couches Billy, & Peter, are the hands, that run in the Same Boat with Ned, & are the most material Witnesses—Michael Smuthers, is one of the men that found the Trunk—William Creasy was present when the Trunk was found, but is not hear, or he would have been bound to attend as a witness. he Perhaps may be down, at the time of the Trial in Chief. when you Can have him Summon'd—The other witnesses, that are recognized, were present when the Trunk was broke.—

SJH.

RC (MHi); two words illegible; addressed: "Mess[rs] Gibson & Jefferson Richmond"; endorsed by TJ. Enclosed in George Jefferson to TJ, 21 July 1809, a brief note transmitting "some further information with respect to the lost trunk" (RC in MHi; at foot of text: "Thomas Jefferson esq[r]"; endorsed by TJ as received 25 July 1809 and so recorded in SJL).

Samuel J. Harrison (1771–1846), a prominent tobacco merchant, had been a Lynchburg alderman since the town was incorporated in 1805. In 1810 TJ sold him two tracts of land along Ivy Creek for £1,200 (Ruth H. Early, *Campbell Chronicles and Family Sketches, Embracing the History of Campbell County, Virginia, 1782–1926* [1927], 63–4; *MB*, 2:1254–6).

On 14 July 1809 the slave NED, property of the recently deceased James Bartlett COUCH, was arrested for the theft of TJ's property from a boat that had been docked in the James River Canal basin in Richmond. His trial began on 24 July 1809. Ned was found guilty of a felony and sentenced to "be burnt in his left hand and receive thirty-nine lashes on his bare back at the public whipping post," an unusually severe punishment for such an offense (*Commonwealth v. Couch's Ned*, cause ended 25 July 1809, Richmond Hustings Court Suit Papers, Vi; Richmond Hustings Court Order Book, 8:326, Vi; George Jefferson to TJ, 1 Sept. 1809; James Sidbury, "Thomas Jefferson in Gabriel's Virginia," in *The Revolution of 1800: Democracy, Race, and the New Republic*, ed. James Horn, Jan Ellen Lewis, and Peter S. Onuf [2002], 213–4).

# From James Monroe

18. July 09.

Ja[s] Monroe's best respects to M[r] Jefferson. He has the pleasure to send him the Edinburg review which M[r] Jefferson expressd a desire to peruse. J M. has also the pleasure to send to M[r] Jefferson a copy of La Place's systeme du Mondes, which he brought for him in 97. from France. it being a work then recently published which he presumed had not found a place in his library. J M begs M[r] Jefferson's acceptance of this work. He would have sent it to him long since had it not been packed with other books which the want of room prevented his opening.

RC (DLC); dateline at foot of text; endorsed by TJ as received 18 July 1809 and so recorded in SJL. Enclosure: Pierre Simon, marquis de Laplace, *Exposition du Système du Monde*, 2 vols. (Paris, 1796).

James Monroe (1758–1831), president of the United States, 1817–25, was a longtime friend, political ally, and frequent correspondent of TJ. He attended the College of William and Mary, attained the rank of major in the Continental army during the Revolutionary War, and studied law under TJ before his admission to the Virginia bar in 1782. Monroe represented Virginia in the Confederation Congress, 1783–86, and opposed the new federal constitution at the state ratification convention two years later. He played a key role in the emergence of the Republican party during service in the United States Senate, 1790–94, and as minister plenipotentiary to France, 1794–97. Monroe then returned to Virginia and with TJ's encouragement began work on Highland, his new home in Albemarle County near Monticello. He was governor of Virginia, 1799–1802, and starting in 1803 TJ successively appointed him minister to France, Spain, and Great Britain. While in Paris, Monroe helped to negotiate the Louisiana Purchase. He returned from Europe in 1807, ran unsuccessfully for president the following year, was governor of Virginia again in 1811, and served as James Madison's secretary of state, 1811–17, with some concurrent stints as acting secretary of war (*ANB*; *DAB*; Ammon, *Monroe*; Daniel Preston, *A Comprehensive Catalogue of the Correspondence and Papers of James Monroe*, 2 vols. [2001]; note to TJ to Madison, 30 Mar. 1809).

TJ later subscribed to the New York reissue of the quarterly *Edinburgh Review* (Sowerby, no. 4733). The issue sent by Monroe has not been identified. TJ had already ordered a COPY of Laplace's work in 1802 (Sowerby, no. 3801).

# From Wilson Cary Nicholas

MY DEAR SIR Warren July 18. 1809

But for Macon, who thinks no man honest or independent, who does not abuse his friends, the law to permit letters from you to be franked wou'd have had an unnanimous vote, notwithstanding his opposition the vote was nearly so.

There was no opportunity to mention the prosecutions while I stayed in Washington, I had several conversations with Granger, his recollection of the circumstances did not correspond with yours precisely, particularly as to the time of your interference to stop the prosecutions in Connecticut; and from what he did say, I found he was under an impression, that it was believed by some of those who had some agency in directing them, that altho' you did not direct the commencement of them, you had no objection to their being carried on. This was rather an inference from what he did say than a positive declaration—this imposed upon me great caution & reserve, he promised to put upon paper what he thought wou'd be satisfactory every where, I called upon him the day before I left Washington to see what he had written, when he said he had been so much occupied (in attending Monroe's suit) that he had not been able to do it, but that he wou'd make a publication in Smiths paper, without his name, but one that wou'd have equal authority, that wou'd satisfy the public and wou'd be acceptable in Connecticut. I thought this cou'd do no harm and might do good, but avoided every thing that might in any degree make you responsible for it, or that cou'd in any manner justify a belief that it was done at your instance. The papers mention that J. R. made a report the last moment of the Session according to his custom, what it was I do not understand. I beg you to be assured I felt upon this occasion, as I do upon all others interesting to you[1] the utmost anxiety to render you service; but from its delicacy I feared to stir in it, my caution was the greater because I have not full confidence in Granger.

I am Dear Sir Yours most sincerely W. C. NICHOLAS

RC (DLC); addressed: "Thomas Jefferson Esq$^{r}$ Monticello"; endorsed by TJ as received 20 July 1809 and so recorded in SJL.

Writing as "Veritas" in his newspaper PUBLICATION, Gideon Granger asserted that TJ had not instigated the Connecticut libel prosecutions and had in fact called for their dismissal, upon which the district attorney entered a nolle prosequi, and claimed that Azel Backus had denied using the expressions with which he was charged and could produce many witnesses to prove it, with Backus reportedly adding that "if he had used it he ought to be punished, by being sent to a madhouse, not a prison," and admitting that while he disliked TJ as a politician, Backus "held his character in high respect as a person who had rendered many important services to his country, as the friend of science and as a man" (Washington *National Intelligencer*, 21 July 1809). J. R.: John Randolph of Roanoke.

[1] Preceding three words interlined.

# From Joseph Wheaton

SIR Washington City July 20. 1809—

I cannot refrain again to make communication to you, and which I will thank you to take into consideration—you will please to recollect the various Statements I made to you respecting the road from Athen in Georgia to Fort Stoddert, I believed, I knew you wanted correct information, I therefore took proper means to obtain, & communicate it and set up truth against design, and Interest, which was so evident in David Meriwether & Col Hawkins—M$^{r}$ Bloomfield who carried the mail from Coweta to Fort Stoddert During Burrs Conspiracy, & for which I was so highly charged in M$^{r}$ Grangers report for its lying 9 days at coweta is now here, & M$^{r}$ Granger has contracted with him to cut out the road, & make Bridges over all the Creeks, waggon <u>width</u> for which he is to receive $4500—Now Sir this proves that no fault could attach to him about the Mail, would you believe that, that mail carried a letter from M$^{r}$ Granger ordering the P master to send it by express & not by the mail carriers, this is a fact & he detained it 5 days to procure one again the very Graham of Whom Mr Granger speaks of as the bearer of dispatches in the report agst me to you, was [. . .] by Mr Bloomfield from Fort Stoddert to Coweta in Jany and they Swam 17 Creeks at the risk of their lives to meet this mail, the other Messenger spoken of was the man who by letter informed Mr Bloomfield of his rider being frozen and Carried by Indians to Mr whites 20 miles South of Tuckababby—all which it is believed Mr Granger knew when he made his report to you—Such things to my mind Levelled against a man labouring to Serve the public, and Serve the views of his executive as I was doing deserves a name which I cannot find Language to express—and what has been the result of these things to me My reputation Stabbd by the assassins dagger, My wife & Children beggared—and am now told Sir that you put me out of my little office in the H of R. Sir I Leave it to you, to use your influence to do me Justice I have a right to refute it, I am an Injured insulted man. My family beggard for exertions the most faithful in my Countrys Service—I am free to declare the whole report which Mr Granger made to you Sir respecting my conducting that mail the last 9 months a misrepresentation—there was every exertion possible made, every expence incured by me to have made it answer your wish but the thing proved impossible—120 miles Pr day in Such a winter as has not been known in 20 years was found impossible—when it is now well known also that Col Hawkins never left his house notwithstanding your friendly letter to him, & the order of the Secretary of war to give me all his aid to fix the Stations—the report of the referees which I inclosed for your examination is proof of my fidility and exertion—you also know Sir that I reconciled the indians to the path, and it has now become the great travelling road—and as Soon as Mr Bloomfield will have made the Bridges—Such a number of Settlers will immediately pass with their waggons & effects to Tombegby & Allabama rivers, as will make that fine rich country a perfect Cotton garden, and[1] place Such a Strength of inhabitants in the centre of that Indian Country as will induce the Indians to dispose of the whole on very easy terms and return to the west all which I fore saw must have this effect and for which object Sir, knowing the Indian character as I do it increased my Zeal, and determined that perseverance Should not be wanted—but Sir I lament, I mourn to have found men, that have obtained first your confidence, & then turned it to the purpose of peculation, and to their private advantage, and Such is the case with too many of the new and noisy pretended patriots, I regret[2] I do not See more of the pure, patient, persevering, patriotism, of the revolution—Mr Granger now indeavors to force me to pay M[r] Bloomfield in full [. . .] for carrying the mail altho his heavy complaint is against him from Coweta to Fort Stoddert, at the Same time Cuts me off 44 days pay for thirty two Horses & Seven men from this to appalachy River a thing to my Sense of Justice, unheard of in the annals of any Country, I have the Sense of M[r] Duval on this Subject and which is directly adverse of his, yet I have been vexd with 7 Suits, and all the effects of vingence, persecution & malignancy of a Demon. I cannot Submit to persecution like this—give me truth, give me Justice, let me have the reward of fidility, not measured to me by the hand of eniquity—with Sincere wishes for your every comfort, and a long injoyment of the Prosperity of our Common Country— I am Dear Sir faithfully & affectionately your most Obedient & very Humble Servant

JOSEPH WHEATON—

RC (DLC); two words illegible; at foot of text: "His Excellency Thomas Jefferson Esq[r]"; endorsed by TJ as received 31 July 1809 and so recorded in SJL.

Joseph Wheaton (1755–1828), postal contractor and perennial office-seeker, was a native of New York who served as a junior officer in a Rhode Island regiment of the Continental army. He was sergeant at arms of the United States House of Representatives from 1789–1807, losing a bid for reelection in the latter year and unsuccessfully seeking reinstatement in May 1809. Wheaton served in the office of the quartermaster general during the War of 1812 and had a long-standing reputation as a political supporter of Aaron Burr (Heitman, *Continental Army*, 583; *Annals*, 11th Cong., 1st sess., 57 [22 May 1809]; Washington *National Intelligencer*, 20 July, 4 Aug. 1809; Madison, *Papers, Pres. Ser.*, 3:502–4, 4:167–8; Washington *United States' Telegraph*, 26 Nov. 1828).

On 15 Aug. 1806 Wheaton contracted with Postmaster General Gideon Granger to cut a post road and carry mail from Athens, Georgia, to Fort Stoddert in present-day Alabama. That autumn he fell ill and was unable to complete the contract, although he engaged others, including Samuel F. Bloomfield, to carry the mail. Service was slow, and Wheaton, who had received advance payment for his services, was charged with misuse of federal funds. Despite repeated petitions to Congress, he appears to have received no satisfaction in this particular case (Henry deLeon Southerland Jr. and Jerry Elijah Brown, *The Federal Road through Georgia, the Creek Nation, and Alabama, 1806–1836* [1989], 22–32, 147–8; *JHR*, 8:38, 158–9 [26 Nov. 1811, 4 Feb. 1812]).

For his initial STATEMENTS, see Wheaton to TJ, 21 June 1805, 20 Sept., 9 Oct. 1806 (DLC). Wheaton's appeals to TJ for assistance with regard to the charges against him began in the autumn of 1807, but TJ refused to intervene (Wheaton to TJ, 17 Oct. 1807, 29 July, 23 Aug. 1808, and TJ to Wheaton, 11 Sept. 1808 [DLC]). Although BLOOMFIELD had also been implicated in the investigation of mail abuse by Lieutenant Henry R. GRAHAM, Granger contracted with him in July 1809 to clear and improve the post road "from Chatahouchee to Alabama" (Southerland and Brown, *Federal Road*, 27–8; Madison, *Papers, Pres. Ser.*, 1:295–6).

[1] Manuscript: "an"

[2] Manuscript: "regreet."

## To Eli Alexander

Sir Monticello July 22. 09

Being extremely pressed by mr Higginbotham I must again urge you on the subject of the arrearages of your rent. this has been rendered the more necessary by a total disappointment of mr Shoemaker to pay the order on him in favor of mr Higginbotham who had a right to expect a large sum from these two resources. your answering your balance to him therefore will oblige Sir

Your humble serv[t] Th: Jefferson

PoC (MHi); at foot of text: "M[r] Eli Alexander"; endorsed by TJ.

Missing letters of 18 July and 1 Aug. 1809 from David HIGGINBOTHAM are recorded in SJL as received from Milton on 20 July and 2 Aug. 1809. A letter from TJ to Higginbotham of 22 Oct. 1809, not found, is also recorded in SJL.

## From Eli Alexander

Dear Sir Shadwell July 22–1809

your note of today is before me. I have notised the contents & am sorry its not in my power to discharge the ballence of the Rent due at this time. but hope it will be in my power in a few days as I have sold and deliverid to M[r] Shoemaker all the old wheat I had on hand for the express purpose of paying of that claim—as soon tharefore as M[r] Shoemaker returns who is now gone to Fredricksburg. I will urge the payment for the wheat and will se you amediately in order to have a settlement—

Im Dr Sir Respectly yor Ob St Eli Alexander

RC (MHi); at foot of text: "M[r] Thomas Jefferson"; endorsed by TJ as received 22 July 1809 and so recorded in SJL.

## To George Jefferson

Dear Sir Monticello July 22. 09

I now inclose you the renewal of my note of January for 8000.D. and sincerely wish it may be used instead of the two prepared for the bank, as I am anxious to keep out of that at least until a good impression is made on the debt. your letter of the 14[th] did not get to me till the 20[th] and as I observe these delays frequently I suspect carelessness in the post-office somewhere. a dysentery prevailing in the neighborhood generally, and with which several of my labouring people are ill, has prevented my setting out for Bedford as yet.

Yours affectionately TH: JEFFERSON

PoC (MHi); at foot of text: "Mr G. Jefferson"; endorsed by TJ. Enclosure not found.

# To Louis Philippe Gallot de Lormerie

SIR Monticello July 22. 09.

Your letters of Apr. 14. June 6. & July 11. have been all duly recieved & you have done me but justice in ascribing the want of answers to my occupations. these have not been less, nor less imperious since my retirement from public life. an abstraction from my private affairs, almost entire, for 25. years, calls for great efforts for putting them again into train; they employ me without doors during all the active hours of the day, and the rare occasions in which they permit me to sit down to my writing table are given of necessity to the most indispensible objects. under these circumstances I have found it necessary to withdraw myself in a great degree from the extensive correspondences in which I have heretofore been engaged. with respect to the subjects of your letters, I was not able to give any answer of the least importance to you. as to the renewal of our forests by replanting I am not sufficiently acquainted with their state in the several parts of our union, to judge whether they are beginning to be deficient or not, so as to need the interposition of the laws. in this part of the country it is not the case. with respect to the transportation of your books & articles of Natural history to Europe[1] I am no longer the person authorised to give or refuse permission. the application to the existing government is open to every one: they will refuse no proper indulgence on your personal application, nor grant an improper one, on my sollicitation were I to ask what is improper. and indeed I am uninformed of the state of the laws on this subject since the last session of congress. thus unable to fulfill the wishes of your letters I had devoted the few moments I had to spare for correspondence, to cases where I could be of more effect, and I trust that your liberality will accept this apology with the assurances of my great respect & consideration TH: JEFFERSON

PoC (DLC); at foot of text: "M. de Lormerie"; endorsed by TJ.

[1] Preceding two words interlined.

# From Alexander McRae

DEAR SIR, Richmond 22nd July 1809.

Mr Wirt was so obliging before his departure from the City, as to leave with me the letter I have now the honor of forwarding to you, by which you will perceive, that my friend & I intended to have commenced our voyage about this period; but the previous arrangements necessary to the success of our plan, required more time than we had anticipated: It is now probable, that we shall not be detained here beyond the 3rd of August.

I am aware that the plan may be difficult of execution, and that it is liable to some degree of hazard, which can only be obviated by great caution; our hopes however of success, embolden us to risque the consequences of engaging in such an enterprize.

Satisfied that you would regard our project as unexceptionable, because the successful result of it, while it can injure no one, will combine public with private advantage; I had intended so far to have intruded, as to ask for our guidance, the benefit of such advice as it might have been agreeable to you to afford; but my engagements have been such, as to deny me the pleasure of waiting on you for that purpose.

If it shall suit your convenience to honor us with letters to Europe, I must beg that they may be enclosed to one of us, as Mr Wirt will not return to Richmond for many days, and in his absence, letters addressed to him will be opened by his friend here, to whom, (tho a gentleman of honor) we would not willingly at this time disclose our views.

It is probable that during our absence, we may be not only in England and in France, but also in Ireland, Germany, Portugal, Spain,[1] and Holland, and permit me to assure you, that wherever we may be, it will give me great pleasure to render you any service in my power.

Sincerely wishing you health & happiness I am with the highest respect

Dear Sir, Yr. mo. ob. Servt AL: McRAE.

RC (DLC); at foot of text: "Thomas Jefferson esq."; endorsed by TJ as received 31 July 1809 and so recorded in SJL. Enclosure: William Wirt to TJ, 10 July 1809.

Alexander McRae (ca. 1765–ca. 1840) was an attorney in Richmond who represented Dinwiddie County in the House of Delegates, 1794–96, during an earlier residence in Petersburg. He sat on the Virginia Council of State from 1796 to 1809, ending as its senior member. McRae was one of the lawyers for the prosecution in Aaron Burr's 1807 treason trial. Late in 1809 he traveled to England

and France to promote a private and ultimately unsuccessful silk-manufacturing venture. McRae served as acting American consul at Paris, 1810–11, returned to Richmond in 1812, and sat in the state senate, 1814–15. After suffering financial reverses, he served as consul at Amsterdam, 1818–20, and lived thereafter in Paris and London, dying in the latter city (Valentine Museum, *Richmond Portraits . . . 1737–1860* [1949], 113–5; Leonard, *General Assembly*, 195, 199, 203, 278; *JEP*, 3:138, 140, 203 [18, 20 Apr. 1818, 21 Mar. 1820]; *Gentlemen's Magazine*, new ser., 15 [1841]: 217; *Richmond Compiler*, 11 Feb. 1841).

On this date McRae wrote a similar letter to James Madison (Madison, *Papers, Pres. Ser.*, 1:296–7). MY FRIEND: John Clarke.

[1] Preceding two words interlined.

# From William Lambert

SIR, City of Washington, July, 23[d] 1809.

In my last communication to you, I stated my intention of entering into astronomical calculations for the purpose of fixing a first meridian for the United States at the permanent seat of their government. It is, perhaps, to be regretted, that a dependence on Great Britain, for a spot of ground from which American navigators and geographers have been hitherto in the habit of estimating their longitud[e] has existed so long as it has done; and it is my wish that this kind of dependence, at least, on that nation, should cease as soon as possible. I have already made my design, known to the public, thro' the medium of the newspapers, and there appears at this place some degree of anxiety to see a publication of the work: The calculations are now finished, according to the following principles:—

1. The longitude between the Capitol in this City and Greenwic[h] Observatory, has been ascertained on the Spheroid.—
2. The same, reducing the form of the Earth to a sphere, as referred to it's center, admitting the equatorial to the polar axis, to be as 334. to 333.
3. Supposing the ratio to be as 230 to 229.

The computation has been made from the data afforded by an occultation of x. Pleiadum (Alcyone) by the Moon on the 20[th] of October, 180[4] which is known to be among the best methods hitherto devised for an accurate determination of the longitude,—and is, in fact, a revision of former calculations for the same object, made in the year 1805, in which the requisite elements have been found with greater precision.—The parallaxes in longitude and latitude have been ascertained by different rules, viz: from the Star's true altitude, angle of position, and the angle formed between the vertical circle and a parallel to the Ecliptic; also from the altitude and longitude of the nonagesima; (or highest point of the ecliptic) and the Star's distance therefrom;—and [the] results have been compared with those obtained by the difference of time between the ecliptical conjunction of the Moon and Star at Was[h] and Greenwich: the greatest variance is not more than $\frac{1}{3}$ of an Americ[an] mile, and this has been lessened considerably by taking a mean of three quantities, so that as far as small errors which may then [have?] existed in the lunar tables, will admit, we have a result, if not strictly correct, yet very nearly approximated t[o the] truth.

With respect to the different ratios that have been assumed, it will be recollected, that the proportion of the equatorial to the polar diameter of the Earth, adopted by the celebrated Sir Isaac Newton, is as 692 to 689; that of 230 to 229, (which is nearly the same) has been used by Mr Vince, and several other eminent European mathematicians; but from discoveries of new lunar equations by M. de la Place and M. de Lambre, in France, about the beginning of the present century, the ratio of 334 to 333, seems now to be allowed as more correct. I am disposed to take an arithmetical mean of the two, which will be as 282 to 281; for if the former might have made the figure of the Earth less spherical than it really is, it is possible that the latter may make it more so,—and for this reason, a mean of the two will not be considered improper.

| | | |
|---|---|---|
| The latitude of the Capitol, in Washington, is stated by Mr Ellicott, in the plan of the City, to be | | ° ′ ″<br>38.53. 0.N. |
| Mr Richard Freeman, a clerk in the Treasury department, by a mean of several observations taken with a good sextant, at Rhode's hotel, N.70° W. $1\frac{3}{8}$ of our miles from the Capitol, has found the latitude of that place to be | ° ′ ″<br>38.53.18. | |
| difference of lat. N. to the nearest second., | —24. | |
| | | 38.52.54. |
| Mean Latitude of the Capitol on the Spheroid | | 38.52.57. |
| This latitude I have assumed in the calculations, and it's reduction to a sphere, admitting the ratio to be as 334 to 333, is | | ° ′ ″ dec.<br>38.42.52.939. |
| allowing the ratio of 230 to 229, | | 38.38.19.465. |
| The latitude of Greenwich Observatory is known to be | | 51.28.40. N. |
| reduced, (334 to 333) | | 51.18.36.869. |
| d° (230 to 229) | | 51.14. 3.279. |

The longitude of the Capitol from Greenwich, by a mean of the several methods that have been used, taking the Moon's motion in the relative orbit, instead of the motion reduced to the ecliptic, to ascertain the different intervals of time, is as follows:—

| | h.m. s. dec. | | ° ′ ″ dec. |
|---|---|---|---|
| Spheroid | 5.7.53.201 | = | 76.58.18.015.W. |
| reduced (334 to 333.) | 5.7.42.249 | = | 76.55.33.735. |
| " (230 to 229) | 5.7.36.739 | = | 76.54.11.085. |

From which, if other ratios of the equatorial to the polar diameter of the Earth, be [occult]ated, the result will be—

| | h.m. s. dec. | | ° ′ ″ dec. | |
|---|---|---|---|---|
| 334 to 333. | 5.7.42. 249. | = | 76.55.33.735. | very nearly. |
| 308 to 307. | 5.7.40.8715. | = | 76.55.13.072. | |
| 282 to 281, | 5.7.39. 494. | = | 76.54.52.410. | |
| 256 to 255. | 5.7.38.1165. | = | 76.54.31.747. | |
| 230 to 229. | 5.7.36. 739. | = | 76.54.11.085. | |

The[1] care taken to find all the elements correctly to three decimal places of a second, and the small variance discovered in the result by different methods, will, it is presumed, be sufficient to fix our first meridian with as much, if not greater accuracy, than some in Europe have been settled. I have seen no computation of the kind, in which such strict attention has been paid to ascertain the necessary elements with due precision, as I have used throughout the work.—I have also annexed the most useful cases in oblique angled spherical trigonometry, with rules for their solution in full, unclog'd with algebraical process or formulæ, which have been too often adopted by mathematical writers, and serve only to render the subject more abstruse to the student, without the smallest advantage to be derived therefrom.—As the Moon's place in longitude, latitude, &c. and the hourly velocity, at intermediate times between noon and midnight, and midnight and noon, are often required in astronomical calculations to great exactness, I have given new[2] series and formulæ, by which those elements may be obtained with due precision, extending the equations of differences to the fourth order.

I inclose a newspaper, containing the toasts and proceedings of the Tammany society of Washington, at their anniversary meeting on the 12th of May last. Having been a short time before, appointed secretary of that society, I was the first named of three persons to prepare toasts for the occasion; and, in fact, drafted the whole number of 17, which were agreed to with slight alterations in a few of them—I was happy to avail myself of the opportunity to shew that respect for your character, talents and services, to which I have always considered you entitled; and surely, it ought not to be termed adulation, when you were in your retirement at the time, and divested of presidential powers.

Permit me to hope, that you will be good enough to answer such parts of my former and this letter, as relate to the object herein mentioned.

I am, Sir, with great respect, Your mo[st o]bed$^{t}$ servant,

WILLIAM LAMBERT.

RC (DLC); on two folio sheets; chipped at foot and edges of each page; at foot of text: "Thomas Jefferson, late President of the U.S."; endorsed by TJ as received 26 July 1809 and so recorded in SJL.

Lambert announced in THE NEWSPAPERS that he had given up his clerkship in the United States House of Representatives, that he would instead be making calculations (described at length) intended to fix an American first meridian in Washington, and suggesting that his efforts should receive the support of every citizen "who has any regard for the prosperity and independence of this country" (Washington *National Intelligencer*, 24 May 1809).

The enclosed NEWSPAPER reported on the 12 May 1809 meeting and banquet of the TAMMANY SOCIETY OF WASHINGTON at Lindsey's Hotel, at which the fifth of seventeen toasts honored TJ: "Amidst the din of war and the wreck of nations his wisdom has hitherto secured our peace; his eminent public services are engraved on the hearts of his children" (*National Intelligencer*, 18 May 1809).

[1] Lambert here canceled "great."

[2] Word interlined.

# From James Madison

DEAR SIR Montpellier July 23. 1809

On my arrival at O. C. House on thursday I found your favor of the 12$^{th}$ inst: with the document expected, & the letters from Short & Warden enclosed. The whole[1] are now returned. No copy of the document was in the Office of State, as you suppose must have been the case. This was owing to the letter being written by your own hand at Monticello,[2] and being sent on to M$^{r}$ S. without being opened at Washington. M$^{r}$ Shorts idea of leaving commerce to shift for itself, is not as new as he seems to think; and is liable to greater objections; in the case stated at least. A decisive objection w$^{d}$ have been that the expedient[3] would have given all the trade wanted to the power commanding the sea, whilst this would have cut off the commerce with its enemy; & thus have found an adequate motive to keep in force its obnoxious orders, as answering all its purposes. It was to be considered also as a further objection, that such an expedient[4] would have involved our ignorant & credulous mariners, in the penalties incurred by the mercantile adventurers, without the indemnifying advantages which the latter would secure to themselves. It may be added that so formal an[5] abandonment of the national rights, would not have borne an honorable appearance; tho' the discredit would have been mitigated by examples of powerful nations, & still more by the peculiarities of the actual state of the world.

I have not rec[d] a line from any quarter, nor even a Newspaper since I left Washington. I can say nothing therefore on the score of news. I was detained at Washington some days, by an unwillingness to leave it at the Moment Daschkoff was to be expected. Altho' not more than titularly even a Chargè, he brought a letter of Credence from the Emperor himself. His conversation was in the spirit of this evidence of the respect & good will of his Sovereign towards the U.S. Adams has accepted his app[t] and will embark as soon as practicable. Daschkoff was extremely anxious for an interview with him before his departure; and had proposed one at N.Y. if consistent with M[r] A's arrangements.

It is a part of our plan to pay our respects to Monticello; but we can say nothing as yet of the time. It will afford us much gratification to welcome you here, & with all of your family, that can accompany you.

Be assured of my most Affectionate respects

James Madison

RC (DLC: Madison Papers); endorsed by TJ as received 26 July 1809 and so recorded in SJL. Enclosures listed at TJ to Madison, 12 July 1809.

Madison left Washington for Montpellier on 17 July 1809, several days after the arrival in Washington of André daschkoff (Washington *National Intelligencer*, 17 July 1809).

[1] Word interlined in place of "two last."
[2] Preceding two words interlined.
[3] Reworked from "that it."
[4] Manuscript: "expdient."
[5] Reworked from "that the formal."

## From Samuel Smith
### (of Maryland)

D[r] Sir. Baltimore 23[d] July 1809

M[r] Adams has been So polite as to invite my Son, John Spear Smith to accompany him to Russia as a Member of the legation to Petersburg. the opp[y] was favorable and I hope may be a mean of rendering him capable of serving his Country at Some future day, in the diplomatic line—He goes at his own Expense—It is a great Object that he should be properly introduced. Will it be too great a liberty for me to ask of you letters of introduction to Petersburg, and Paris? if not, I pray you to send those for Russia by the return of Mail, those for Paris, if inconvenient to you now, may be sent after him—I doubt whether his health will permit him to join M$^{r}$ Adams at Boston, if not he will proceed by way of Hamburg to S$^{t}$ Petersburg—

A Report was put in Circulation in this City by Whispers prior to the last session against my Character of the most malicious kind, which I believe was put to M$^{r}$ Randolph & induced him[1] to bring forward his Committee of investigation a Report from the Treasury Dep$^{t}$ was made which was calculated to confirm such report, no application was made to the Navy Dep$^{t}$ where correct information might have been obtained—fortunately M$^{r}$ Smiley One of the Committee called on my Brother & informed him of what was doing—in Consequence all was set right & a new report was made, which was with difficulty received by the house—who originated the tale & by whom propagated I will not[2] pain you by telling, but it has had an influence in Maryland that may lose us the October Elections—I pray you to Accept assurances of the sincere friendship of D$^{r}$ sir, Your Obed serv$^{t}$

S. SMITH

RC (DLC); endorsed by TJ as received 26 July 1809 and so recorded in SJL.

Samuel Smith (1752–1839), soldier, merchant, and politician, was born in Pennsylvania but spent most of his life in Baltimore. During the American Revolution he rose to lieutenant colonel in the Continental army, sustained a wound, and received the thanks of Congress before resigning his army commission in 1779 and beginning to amass a fortune through privateering, commerce, and land speculation. Smith represented Maryland in the United States House of Representatives, 1793–1803 and 1816–22, and in the Senate, 1803–15 and 1822–33. Originally a Federalist, he came to be a strong Republican and played an important role in TJ's election to the presidency. Smith served briefly as acting secretary of the navy in 1801 and was generally supportive of TJ's policies, but he led a faction that thwarted President James Madison's desire to appoint Albert Gallatin secretary of state and opposed Gallatin's fiscal policies. Smith communicated amicably with TJ throughout the retirement years, but his relationship with Madison was always strained. He led the successful defense of Baltimore against British forces in 1814 and served as the city's mayor, 1835–38 (*ANB*; *DAB*; Frank A. Cassell, *Merchant Congressman in the Young Republic: Samuel Smith of Maryland, 1752–1839* [1971]; Malone, *Jefferson*, 4:487–93).

Smith's SON John Spear Smith was one of three secretaries appointed by John Quincy Adams to his Russian LEGATION early in July 1809 (Worthington C. Ford, ed., *Writings of John Quincy Adams* [1913–17], 3:330–1).

Smith's term in the Senate expired at the end of the Tenth Congress, and his reelection became uncertain when Republican control of the Maryland Senate and Federalist control of the House of Delegates resulted in a deadlock. Governor Robert Wright gave Smith an interim appointment, with the issue to be decided after the October elections changed the state legislature. The long-standing dispute between Gallatin and Smith received new fuel when Gallatin became convinced that the Smith family firm, S. Smith & Buchanan, had used public funds for private investment by withholding government funds exchanged with the firm of Degen & Purviance in Leghorn, Italy. Gallatin published his findings in Baltimore and Republican representative John RANDOLPH of Roanoke convened a COMMITTEE OF INVESTIGATION to examine the pertinent transactions. Nothing untoward was found, and Gallatin's official report was preempted when Smith's BROTHER Robert, the secretary of state and formerly the secretary of the navy, called for a reexamination of records in the Navy Department, which concluded that the Degen & Purviance transactions were legitimate in a report announced in the House on 27 June 1809 (Baltimore *Federal Republican and Commercial Gazette*, 19, 20, 22, 26 June 1809; *Annals*, 11th Cong., 1st Sess., 61–73, 448 [24 May, 27 June 1809]; Cassell, *Merchant Congressman*, 146–51; Raymond Walters Jr., *Albert Gallatin: Jeffersonian Financier and Diplomat* [1957], 224–6; Brant, *Madison*, 5:22–5, 52–4).

[1] Reworked from "which induced M[r] Randolph."

[2] Word interlined.

# To David Copeland

DEAR SIR Monticello July 24. 09.

In my letter of June 25. I mentioned the request I should make to Comm[r] Ladd to postpone the meeting of the parties in the suit of Gilliam v. Fleming to October, when we might hope a full & effectual meeting, & a final settlement of matters which are every day vanishing from memory & knolege. he has fixed on the 20[th] of Oct. at 9. A.M. at his office, of which he desired me to write you notice. I have written to mess[rs] Skipwith, Eppes & Fleming urgently to attend, as I shall certainly do myself, and hope we shall have the pleasure of seeing you there. I think your knolege of most of the transactions will be of essential service towards the rendering justice to all parties. I salute you with assurances of great esteem & respect.

TH: JEFFERSON

PoC (DLC); at foot of text: "D. Copeland esq."; endorsed by TJ.

# To John Wayles Eppes

DEAR SIR Monticello July 24. 09.

I recieved some time ago a summons from Commissioner Ladd to attend a settlement in the case of m[r] Wayles & mr Skelton's accounts on the 1[st] of Aug. I expressed to him, in answer, my extreme anxiety to have that settlement made, & that I would attend any meeting which promised to be effectual; that I doubted whether in the sickly season an effectual meeting could be had at Richmond, & prayed a postponement to October. he has accordingly appointed the 20th of October. I write to Col° Skipwith & judge Fleming earnestly pressing their attendance, & I hope you will attend also. I have no interest in the issue, as the proportion I should have to recieve & pay would be the same. this renders the attendance of mr Skipwith & yourself indispensable. the demand is formidable, but, if attended to, is perfectly safe. I have all the papers in perfect order. one only paper is not under our command. it is the account of John Fleming, in possession of judge Fleming, on which we depend for vouching several articles. I press him to bring it to the meeting. I shall probably go by his house to the meeting. this circumstance must fix the time of my visit to Eppington. I will be there some days before the meeting, as it is possible some information may be had from your father's papers. probably mr Skipwith will meet me there, which will give an opportunity to yourself & him to go over the papers with me and understand them before the meeting at Richmond. I pray you to present me affectionately to mrs Eppes the elder & to accept for yourself the assurances of my constant attachment & respect.

TH: JEFFERSON

PoC (MHi); at foot of text: "The honble J. W. Eppes"; endorsed by TJ.

# To William Fleming

DEAR SIR Monticello July 24. 09

The settlement of the accounts in Gilliam's suit, to which we were summoned on the 1st of Aug. has, on my request, been postponed to the 20th of Oct. I was induced to ask it by the improbability of getting an effectual meeting at Richmond during the sickly season, & my extreme anxiety to have an effectual meeting & final settlement of those accounts. it is on this ground I earnestly pray you to be so good as to attend then. your intimacy with the transactions preceding B. Skelton's death, & mine with the subsequent part of them, makes our presence indispensably necessary to a fair settlement, to which our families would be entirely incompetent, & might thereby be extremely injured, were the case to lie over till we are dead. you too[1] were present also at the preceding meeting where Jerman Baker acting for M. Skelton & in his presence, went over the vouchers, & passed most of the articles by marking them thus ✓ with his pen; which account with these marks I have to produce. I hope therefore you will meet us, & I think a single day will suffice to go through the accounts. I propose to be at Eppington some days before the meeting, & if I can, with any convenience, I will have the pleasure of seeing you at your own house on my way. this however must depend on my being able to get from home in time. Accept the assurances of my great esteem & respect. TH: JEFFERSON

PoC (MHi); at foot of text: "The honble Wm Fleming"; endorsed by TJ.

William Fleming (ca. 1735–1824), attorney and judge, was a classmate of TJ's at the College of William and Mary. He represented Cumberland County in the House of Burgesses, 1772–76, in all five Virginia Revolutionary Conventions, 1775–76, and in the House of Delegates, 1776–78. Fleming served briefly in the Continental Congress in 1779, and he sat on the Virginia Court of Appeals, the state's highest court, from its creation in 1789 until his death, presiding as senior member from 1809 (*Biog. Dir. Cong.*; Richmond *Enquirer*, 19, 20 Feb. 1824; Fredericksburg *Virginia Herald*, 25 Feb. 1824).

[1] Word interlined.

# To Jonathan Shoemaker

SIR Monticello July 24. 09.

Mr Higginbotham informs me he did not recieve from you the order for the 500.D. on the Postmaster General as had been arranged between us, owing perhaps something to the day of paiment proposed. I must therefore pray you to inclose to me the order paiable on the earliest day on which it will be entitled to paiment. our post leaves Washington 3. times a week, on Sundays, Tuesdays, & Thursdays, & I shall hope to recieve it by the first return of post, as I stand peculiarly pledged to him for that paiment. I must at the same time intreat a prompt remittance of the further sum of 500.D. according to what you gave me reason to expect, as I have no other source of compliance with demands which afflict me extremely. I salute you with esteem & respect. TH: JEFFERSON

PoC (MHi); at foot of text: "Mr Jonathan Shoemaker"; endorsed by TJ.

# To Henry Skipwith

DEAR SIR Monticello July 24. 09.

Your favor of the 10th has been duly recieved. I had also been summoned by Commissioner Ladd to attend at his office on the 1st of August to have a settlement with the representatives of the Skeltons.

I immediately informed mr Ladd that nothing was so much desired by the representatives of mr Wayles as a settlement of those accounts; & that I would attend any meeting for that purpose which promised to be effectual. but that an appointment for August could scarcely be so, as that season would call or keep many in the upper country for considerations of health, & I proposed to him to postpone the meeting to October, & promised myself to urge the punctual attendance of the defendants. he has accordingly appointed the meeting to be at his office on the 20th of Oct. at 9. A.M. I will certainly attend punctually, & I earnestly pray you to do the same, as I shall also mr Eppes & judge Fleming. we ought to thank heaven that we live to make that settlement ourselves. the demand is a formidable one, but if attention be observed on our part, and justice by our judges, it is a safe one. much will depend on the principles of settlement, but if just ones are established, they must be indebted considerably to mr Wayles's representatives. being myself a creditor with the creditors plaintiffs, in the same proportion in which I should be a debtor with the defendants, I have no pecuniary interest in the issue, & therefore would not proceed unless those interested were present. the draught of an answer which I sent mr Eppes for yourself & him, will have given you an accurate view of the case. I thank you for your congratulns on my retirement. it had become necessary as my mind began to be sensibly oppressed by the load of labor & anxiety. I am equally relieved & delighted by my new occupations. Accept the assurances of my constant esteem & respect.

TH: JEFFERSON

P.S. I shall be at Eppington a few days before the meeting. could you not meet me there, so as to see & understand the true state of this business, before the meeting in Richmond.

PoC (MHi); at head of text: "Col° H. Skipwith"; endorsed by TJ.

TJ's DRAUGHT OF AN ANSWER to Eppes is not recorded in SJL and has not been found.

# To John Martin Baker

DEAR SIR Monticello July 25. 09.

Your favor of the 16th has been duly recieved, and your kind offers of service, on your return to the Balearian islands is recieved with the thankfulness to which it is so justly entitled. the prices of the productions of Majorca are really so favorable as to tempt me to trespass on your goodness by adding to the two pipes of Albaflor wine, some other small articles as noted below. your draught on me for the amount shall be punctually honored. perhaps it had better be at some days sight (say 30.) because there being no commerce in the interior country in which[1] I live, some time will be necessary to procure elsewhere a bill on the place where the draught is payable. I mention this by way of precaution, & to prevent disappointment. should the intercourse with Majorca be found practicable, even for once a year it is possible I may avail myself of your friendly agency there, to obtain my annual supplies of the productions of the place, that is to say of wine, oil, raisins,[2] capers, anchovies. I should, with great pleasure have communicated to mrs Baker the view of Monticello desired; but that none such has ever been taken, & I am not painter enough to do it. mr Latrobe has promised me a visit, when it will probably be well done, & in that case I shall take great pleasure in sending it to mrs Baker. I pray her to accept the homage of my respect & attachment, & that you will both be assured that among the characters with which my late duties gave me the pleasure of becoming[3] acquainted, I distinguished the worth[4] of yours & hers with particular satisfaction & interest in your welfare. retired as I am, it is not probable I can become useful to either of[5] you: but should the case occur I pray you to command my services. with my best wishes for your success & happiness, I tender you the assurances of my esteem & respect.

TH: JEFFERSON

2. pipes of Albaflor wine
a quarter cask of Banalbufar, as a sample.
a box of Muscatel raisins
4. doz. bottles of olive oil of best quality.
a Keg of Anchovies. some Dates

RC (Vi: Personal Papers Collection); addressed: "John Martin Baker esq. Washington Col."; franked. Dft (MHi); endorsed by TJ.

[1] Reworked in Dft from "commerce where."

[2] In Dft TJ here canceled "dates."

[3] Preceding six words interlined in Dft in place of "brought me."

[4] Reworked in Dft from "observed the merit."

[5] Preceding two words interlined in Dft.

## From William Caruthers

SIR Lexington 25th July 1809

The friends of litterature in and[1] Near this plaice, encouraged by their Success in establisheing An Accademy for the education of Youth, which now bears the Name of its Liberal patron the friend of Mankind by Whom it was so liberally endowed—have also undertaken to establish an Accademy for education of Young ladies; in Order to which Trustees have incorporated by the legislature and by the liberal and Gratutitous attention of Miss Ann Smith formerly of Baltimore who Taught also in George Town the Scool has been in Operation Near Two Years with from fifty to Sixty pupils, and we flatter ourselves Meets the entire Aprobation of all employers & Visitors—we have also by the aid of Subscriptions already rec^d embarked in Building and Got up the Walls of a large & Commodious house to finish which Will exceed our funds On hand, and as aid from the Treasury of our state is seldome Obtained we feel Ourselves under the Necessity of Asking farther Donations from individuals—this institution has a Stronger claim than almost any other on the public as there is no Other in Our State on a Simelar plan for the education of young Ladies Or None that promises so fair to be usefull

Being perfectly persuaded of Your disposition to aid as far as You can undertakings of this Kind I now Take the liberty of mentioning to You a Small fund of Yours which has lain so long in my hands I suppose You have forgotten it about $90—Arrising from the sale of Salt petre Got for rent of a little Cave on the N Bridge Tract of land it ought to have been More But Two of the fellows run off and I have never been able to collect from them What they Owed You if You think proper to Appropriate this or any part of it to the use of the Ann Smith Accademy You may Direct me By letter to Do with it as You Wish

With Sentiments of profound Respect I am Your Ob^t Sev^t

W^M CARUTHERS

RC (DLC); between dateline and salutation: "Honb^l Thomas Jefferson"; endorsed by TJ as a letter of 21 July 1809 received 2 Aug. 1809 and so recorded in SJL.

William Caruthers (d. 1817), a Lexington merchant, was TJ's agent in Rockbridge County (Rockbridge County Will Book, 5:150–4, Vi microfilm; *MB*, 2:1262n). He and TJ subsequently corresponded about their mutual interest in sheep breeding and various proposals for leasing the lands around the Natural Bridge, including Caruthers's own proposal for establishing a shot manufactory there in partnership with William Thornton.

George Washington was the LIBERAL PATRON whose gift of one hundred shares in the James River Company in 1796 led to the renaming in 1798 of Lexington's

Liberty Hall Academy, first incorporated in 1782, as the Washington Academy (now Washington and Lee University) (Washington, *Papers, Retirement Ser.*, 2:236–7, 3:207–9). Caruthers was a founding trustee of the Ann Smith Academy, established in 1807 to educate YOUNG LADIES and chartered by the legislature on 7 Jan. 1808 (Samuel Shepherd, *The Statutes at Large of Virginia, from October Session 1792 to December Session 1806* [1835–36], 3:403–4). Its headmistress and namesake left the school in 1812, but it survived past the Civil War (William W. Pusey, *Elusive Aspirations: The History of the Female Academy in Lexington, Virginia* [1983]; Ollinger Crenshaw, *General Lee's College: The Rise and Growth of Washington and Lee University* [1969], 72–4). Caruthers had had the SMALL FUND from the sale of SALT PETRE at the Natural Bridge in his hands for eight years (Caruthers to TJ, 29 July 1801 [MHi]).

[1] Manuscript: "and and."

# To Gordon, Trokes & Company

MESSRS GORDON TROKES & CO. Monticello July 25. 09

Having desired my relation mr George Jefferson to establish a correspondence for me at Richmond for the supply of my groceries & the terms of paiment to be observed, he informs me he has arranged with you for my supplies, and that paiment shall be made semi-annually. with this I shall accordingly take care to comply. I now, in consequence subjoin a list of articles which I must pray you to send by some trusty boat; mr Jefferson's knolege of them will enable him to advise you as to their selection—in general I wish mr Randolph's boat to be preferred when there. this list amounts to about an ordinary quarter's consumption of 3. months.[1] every thing should be packed in the strongest & securest manner to guard against depredation, the expence of which is small in comparison of the ordinary plunder. be so good as to forward an account of the articles sent & their prices. I have to acknolege a preceding reciept of 50.℔ of coffee from you.

I am gentlemen Your most obedt servt TH: JEFFERSON

8.℔. best tea. young Hyson usually preferred.
50.℔ coffee (not green) E. India is preferred.
single refined sugar. 12. loaves.
best brown sugar 200.℔.
raisins 10.℔
rice 20.℔
pearl barley 10.℔ crackers. a keg of 20. or 25.℔
spices. 1. oz. cinnamon. 1. oz. mace. 2. oz. nutmeg. 2.℔ black pepper
Syrop of punch. 3. doz. bottles.
best French brandy. a keg of 10. or 15 gallons.
1. best cheese for the table.

1. poorer d° for cookery. the rich cheeses do not answer for this
Cod's tongues & sounds. 1. keg
herrings. 5. barrels of best quality.
salted white shads. 1. barrel of best quality

PoC (MHi); endorsed by TJ.

Gordon, Trokes & Company, a mercantile firm in Richmond, may have been a partnership between Richmond merchant Robert Gordon (ca. 1773–1847) and New York-based merchant Maxwell Trokes, who married Sarah H. Goode of Manchester, Virginia, in August 1809. TJ ended his relationship with the firm in 1811, concerned about his inability to make timely payments. By 1819 Gordon was listed without a partner in a Richmond city directory, and that same year saw the bankruptcy of Trokes, then identified as a Liverpool merchant in partnership with James Frisney Leitch of London and Robert Graham of Manchester, Virginia, in the firm of Maxwell Trokes & Company (*MB*, 2:1264; TJ to Gordon, Trokes & Co., 4 Apr. 1811; *Richmond Directory, Register and Almanac, for the Year 1819* [Richmond, 1819], 48; *Liverpool Mercury*, 13 Sept. 1819; Richmond *Enquirer*, 20 Aug. 1809, 24 Aug. 1847).

Missing letters of 31 July and 29 Aug. 1809 from Gordon, Trokes & Co. are recorded in SJL as received from Richmond on 8 Aug. and 5 Sept. 1809.

[1] Sentence interlined.

# To William W. Hening

DEAR SIR Monticello July 25. 09

Your favor of the 8th was recieved only on the 20th. I do not know that the publication of Newspapers was ever prohibited in Virginia. my collection of newspapers begins in 1741. but I have seen one newspaper of about 3. years earlier date, as well as I can recollect. The first laws printed in Virginia, was I believe the collection of 1733. till the beginning of our revolutionary dispute we had but one press, & that having the whole business of the government & no competitor for public favor, nothing disagreeable to the governor could be got into it. we procured Rind to come from Maryland to publish a free paper. I do not suppose there ever was a legal obstacle. It is now so long since I was conversant in our early history, and my mind has during that time been so entirely engrossed by affairs foreign to it, that it has become almost a blank as to what it ever possessed in that line. it retains indeed the terms Roanoake & Wampompeke, but not their import. I am not able therefore to inform you respecting them. on observing that you would want sessions acts (printed) I examined the state of my collection, & found that precisely the volume containing my printed laws from 1734. to 1772. is not in the library. having recieved often applications from courts & individuals for copies from that volume, I imagine it has been trusted to some one in the neighborhood to copy some act, & not returned. I shall immediately enquire for it & hold it at your service. I inclose you the part of Hening & Munford's reports you were so kind as to send to me formerly, according to the request in your letter & salute you with esteem & respect.

TH: JEFFERSON

PoC (DLC); at foot of text: "W$^{m}$ W. Hening esq."; endorsed by TJ. Enclosure: Hening and William Munford, *Reports of Cases argued and determined in the Supreme Court of Appeals of Virginia* (Philadelphia and Flatbush, N.Y., 1808–09; Sowerby, no. 2093), vol. 1, nos. 1–2.

William Parks began the PUBLICATION OF NEWSPAPERS in Virginia with the Williamsburg *Virginia Gazette* in 1736 (Sowerby, no. 535). Parks also published the first laws printed: *A Collection of all the Acts of Assembly, now in force, in the colony of Virginia* (Williamsburg, 1733; Sowerby, no. 1833). In 1766 William RIND established an opposition press in Williamsburg and challenged the official *Virginia Gazette* with his own newspaper of the same name (Brigham, *American Newspapers*, 2:1161; Sowerby, no. 537). In response to a request from John Daly Burk, in 1805 TJ gave him access to his copy of PRINTED LAWS FROM 1734. TO 1772. via George Jefferson, who still had it in 1809 (TJ to Burk, 1, 12 June 1805 [DLC]; George Jefferson to TJ, 25 Aug. 1809; Sowerby, no. 1841).

# From Isaac A. Coles

DEAR SIR, At Sea, off New York. July 26$^{th}$ 1809.

I am sorry to inform you that my return brings nothing to satisfy the expectations of the American people—On landing at L'Orient on the 24$^{th}$ of April I lost not a moment in hastening on to Paris where I arrived after a journey of fifty eight hours—the Emperor had left it some time before, and Champagny was on the eve of his departure to follow him—I saw him for a few moments & delivered Gen$^{l}$ Turreau's despatches. From Augsburg he wrote to acknowledge the receipt of Gen$^{l}$ Armstrongs first note, and afterwards from Munich[1] to say that he would hasten to put under the eyes of his Majesty the representations that he had made by the direction of his Government. On the 13$^{th}$ of June when I left Paris no answer had been received, tho' I am induced to believe that this has proceeded not so much from an indisposition in the French Governm$^{t}$ to take up this subject, as from the peculiar circumstances under whch the Emperor has found himself placed—with these circumstances you cannot be wholly unacquainted.

It was not 'till the night of the 12$^{th}$ of April, that he learnt by a Telegraphic despatch that the Austrians had crossed the Inn—in a few hours he was in his carriage, and the Parisians learnt it first by hearing that their Emperor had passed the Rhine. On the fifth day he was with his Army, directing it's movements, and every where beating back the enemy. On my Arrival in Paris they were thanking God for the Victory of Ratisbon—like a torrent he passed on, and we were told that there no longer remained any thing that could present an obstacle in the way of his Victorious course. the scattered fragments of the Austrian Army had fled beyond the Danube and the Parisians again thanked God on hearing that their Emperor had entered Vienna on the 12th of May and was giving law to Germany. it was said, that the war was finished, and that the Sun of the Austrian Monarchy had set to rise no more—subsequent events however have proven that these views were not entirely correct—the Austrians had fled but they were not conquered: they yielded for a moment only to be able to present a more effectual resistance—Prince Charles had wisely resolved not to hazard every thing on the fate of a battle, but to nurse his strength, and only to fight when he could have an advantage. he abandoned his capitol to the enemy, and calculating on his impetuosity determined to dispute with him the passage of the Danube should he attempt to pass it—in this he was not deceived—the Emperor believing he had done nothing while there yet remained any thing to do, ordered bridges to be thrown over the River a little below Vienna, where it is divided into three channels by some Islands, and in Opposition to the advise of every Genl in his army prepared to pass it—On the 20th a part of the army crossed over & on the 21st the Emperor himself—at 4. in the evening the enemy commenced an Attack on the Duke of Rivoli, & afterwards on the whole extent of the french line which lasted 'till eight at night—on the next morning (the 22d) the battle was renewed, and continued with unexampled obstinacy thro' the day—Prince Charles having at one time extended his wings, apparently with a design to take the french Army in flank, the Emperor according to his usual system of warfare, ordered Lannes to put himself at the head of the invincibles of the army & to break thro' their centre, which was supposed to have been too much weakened, and after dividing the enemy's army into two parts, to beat them in detail—but it seems that if the Austrian General had weakened his centre he had time to correct the error, or possibly the movement was only a feint, and intended to deceive; for Lannes with the divisions of Oudinot, St Hilaire & Boudet, the very best troops of the french Armies, and men who had never marched but to Victory, was repulsed with the most horrible carnage. two hundred pieces of cannon showering upon them an incessant discharge of round and Grape shot, cut down whole ranks and for a time threatened the total destruction of the french army.—the brave Duke of Montebello was killed—eight out of ten of his Aids de camp fell in the charge. Mouton, S[t] Hilaire, Boudet, Claparède, Foulers, Despagne Darosnel, S[t] Sulpice, Cervone, Lallemande Molitor, Davenay, Jervaux & Debue—34 Colonels and 1500. Officers were left dead on the field of battle. Massena, Oudinot, Clement, Peray, Dorsenna, & Lagrange were wounded. During the night the remains of the french army regained their position on the large Island in the Danube, leaving the Austrians Masters of the left bank—what has been the loss of the french in this action it is impossible to say with any accuracy—in the Official bullatin they Acknowledge only 1100. private letters, state it at 36,000. and the Austrians in their Account make it 48,000. it has unquestionably been very great and the Bullatin of the emperor while it claims a victory, bears on the face of it evidence of his defeat—he attributes his want of success to the breaking of the Bridges behind him, which cut him off from his supplies: which deprived him of his Ammunition and his corps of reserve—but all this is probably only intended to take from the mortification which he must feel, and is more specious than true. it is denied that he wanted Ammunition, & the corps of reserve of which he speaks under the Duke of Auerstaedt, is said to have been at Vienna, and not to have been more than was necessary to guard that place—that he had at length sustained a great defeat was acknowledged on all hands, and the only question seemed to be as to the effects which were likely to flow from it—whether he would still be able to maintain his ground, and advance in the career of Victory, or whether he would not be obliged to retreat thro' the Tyrol into Italy! and whether if he should be obliged to turn his back on the enemy, the whole of Germany would not be found in array against him? these and a thousand such questions were beginning to be agitated—but without giving credit to speculations of this sort, I can assure you that the battle of Esling is viewed with much seriousness by the most intelligent men at Paris, and that much apprehension & uneasiness existed in the minds of those connected with the Government at the situation in which they saw their Chief placed.—It is true that he has since been powerfully reinforced by the junction of the army of Italy, but this has not increased his relative force, as the army of the Archduke John, which has lately been retreating thro' the Tyrol for fear of being cut off by the march of the french Armies down the Danube, is also united to that of Prince Charles, and is probably more numerous and as well disciplined.

If the Emperor should be able to meet his Enemy in the field, and give him a signal defeat, it would no doubt at once retrieve his affairs; but as the Danube is between them, there seems to be no immediate prospect of this—at the time I left Paris it was said that his army was beginning to suffer much for the want of provisions, & there was even some indication of such a state of things to be found in one of the last Bullatins—great efforts were making to collect magazines—supplies were to be sent off even from Augsburg, and other places high up, on the Danube and the Rivers which run into it, while the austrians being Masters of the Country on the left Bank, would have it in their power perpetually to intercept them—Thus situated it will not be a subject of wonder if he has not been able to find time to attend to us—Champagny was with him only for a single day at Vienna, and it was said at Paris that every one was prohibited to speak to him of Politics—for once he has found enough in the duties of a General alone, to occupy him—perhaps too his policy towards us, and towards other Nations will be not a little influenced by the success or failure of the plans in which he is now engaged—'tis said he is beginning to be weary of his system of Commercial restriction, and of late he has even connived at exportations direct to England—th[ro'] every part of his Empire the stagnation of commerce is felt, and immediately by himself in the difficulty of collecting his revenue. even in the neighborhood of Paris wheat will not command more than 2. Shillings per bushel, a price too low to pay for the labor of rearing it; and the people in the wine countries actually rejoiced at the loss of their Grapes which have been destroyed this Spring by frost, as they would not raise on the wine after it was made the tax which it was necessary to pay to the Government.

But altho' the general idea seemed to be that this system was breaking down of itself, and that it would soon be changed or in some way modified, yet there has been no act of the Government indicating such a disposition—on the contrary all the American Vessels that have arrived since the Embargo was removed in Holland, in the Ports of Spain and Italy have been seized, and are still in the hands of the Officers of the Government—and altho' the Mentor was received and treated well, yet the Siren was subjected to the most rigorous quarantine, and had custom-House officers put on board of her, who remained 'till the moment of her leaving Port—we were made to pay duty for every little article laid in for our sea stores—but all this must have been done in consequence not of any new Orders, but under those previously issued—indeed on the subject of our Affairs I have not been able to learn any one fact which ought to be relied on as indicating the disposition or feelings of the french Government, or which can enable one to form any Opinion as to the Course which will be ultimately pursued.

Before the Siren arrived, Gen$^{l}$ Armstrong had come to a determination to Send off the Mentor, and to detain me to carry home the answer of the french Government when he should receive it. when he heard that she had come with another messenger, & that she would be too small for the Accommodation of his family, should he be obliged to return, his first intention was immediately to have sent her back, & to keep me and the Ship—but the quarantine producing a considerable delay in the arrival of the Messenger, and it being somewhat uncertain whether it might not still be extended, he resolved to wait no longer, and gave me an order to depart & to take the Brig if I found her at liberty to go to sea—I had only a few hours to make my preparations—I left Paris on the 13$^{th}$ of June, & sailed on the 18$^{th}$ being detained at L'orient two days by the indolence of the Consul in providing the necessary stores—M$^{r}$ Gelston reached Paris the night before I left it

Gen$^{l}$ Armstrong will still continue to press the french Government in compliance with his instructions, and will probably succeed at last in getting an answer of some sort, if it be possible at this time to succeed in such an application—The french think him a little <u>too dry</u> for the present times, but I believe they respect his integrity, and the honest frankness of his character—I was sorry to percieve that there was not a good understanding between him and M$^{r}$ Pinkney, and I fear the public interests may suffer from this unfortunate state of feeling—M$^{r}$ Pinkney has never written him a single line on the important political events which have taken place in England, and which have changed so materially the state of our relations with that country; he was left to grope his way in the dark, and when I came away was beginning to complain in terms of great bitterness—I fear the breach between them is not in a way to be healed—Gen$^{l}$ Armstrong most unfortunately has about him a man who, in my Opinion, is one of the greatest Scoundrels in the world; a wretch whose hands have been soiled with bribes, and who greatly abuses the unbounded confidence which he reposes in him,—it is this wretch who has involved him in so many quarrels, and who for some time has made a traffic of his countenance—during my stay in Paris he was absent on a confidential mission to London.

The General I believe is not desirous of remaining longer in Europe, & he talks of returning as soon as he has got rid of the business with which he is at present Occupied—It was reported before I reached Paris that he was made Secretary at War; the report came in such a way as to gain credit, and I was told by those most in his confidence that it was a situation which he would have been much gratified to fill. Mr Short whom these reports had reached, seemed almost as much disappointed in finding them untrue as he was mortified at the rejection of his own nomination. on learning what had been done by the Senate, he at one time seemed very firmly to have made up his mind to return with me to America in the Mentor, and actually employed me to engage a place for him—his friends he said were in the country and he could go without being exposed to the painful ceremony of taking leave—it was not long however before he relapsed into irresolution, and on quitting Paris for the Chateau de Reuil he abandoned the idea, I believe, altogether—he proposed to spend a part only of the summer at the Chateau, after which he would go to some of the watering Places—About a week before he left Paris I spent some days with him at Draveil, the country seat of Mr Parker, a very rich and intelligent American, who has resided for many years in France—he devotes himself very much to Agriculture, and has lately invented a plough which is calculated I think to produce immense benefit—He carried us to witness an experiment which he had made with it, the result of which I send you—The plough was drawn by three horses at the rate of 2. miles per hour—the mean force was five hundred pounds—the ground ploughed in an hour, was 860 feet long, & 24 feet wide, containing 20412 Square feet = to 21870 feet English, or equal to the half of a British Statute Acre—the earth was most perfectly turned, the furrow about 6. inches deep, and 24. inches wide—it is rather two ploughs than one, each fixed to the same beam, which is crooked to receive them. it works with so much ease and steadiness as hardly to require to be touched by the hand of the Ploughman, and is drawn with less force than the common plough of the Country—it would answer best on our flat lands in the lower part of Virginia, and would save there one half of the labour employed in preparing land for a crop. Mr Parker has had a fine model made which will be sent out to you by the Mentor, and I think on trying it you will find it one of the finest machines of the kind that has ever yet been Known—

Mr Parker has also on his estate of Draveil one of the best flocks of Marinos in all France—from his Rams he took this Spring as much as 16. pounds of wool. he would have let me have half a dozen of them, if I could have got permission to bring them out—but this was impossible—I had desired very much to get a pair for you—it had occurred to me that I could bring you, nothing that you would have been so well pleased to receive, and for a long time I would listen to no objections—Gen[l] Fayette also interested himself very much to gratify my wishes, but all our plans proved Abortive—there were too many others who had the same views—suspicion was wide awake,—I could obtain nothing in my own name, and I would not consent to use any other.

with the Shepherd's Dogs there would have been less difficulty, but here too a misfortune awaited me. Gen[l] Fayette in whose neighborhood[2] the breed was said to be most pure, and who had promised to obtain them for me was prevented from coming to Paris by the indisposition of one of his family so that the Dogs did not arrive until the very day that I was leaving it. the Cabriole which was to carry me to L'Orient was already nearly filled with my baggage, when Gen[l] Armstrong sent to let me know, that the Purser of the Syren was in Paris, and that I must if possible give him a seat, as the vessel could not well sail without him—the Dogs therefore were on the point of being sent back to Gen[l] Fayette, when my fellow traveller from America, M[r] Waddell of Philadelphia, relieved me by promising to take charge of them, and they will now come out in the Mentor—they are fine Animals and it is probable that better could not have been obtained in France—

Gen[l] Fayette was in Paris when I arrived there—I saw him very often and he spoke to me freely of his Affairs—I was sorry to find him so much embarrassed by Debts which are every day pressing more and more upon him, and must subject him to the most painful feelings—M[r] Parker had suggested a plan which he flattered himself would retrieve his affairs, but it's success was still doubtful—It was to borrow for ten years, on the Security of his American lands, a sum of money large enough to meet all his wants. this sum was to be divided into shares of so many hundred francs each, to be advanced by different persons at a fixed interest, they being also entitled at the end of this period, to receive in addition to their interest, a certain proportion of the increase in the value of the lands—Shares to a pretty considerable amount had been taken by different capatalists in Paris, and M[r] Parker was not without a hope that the whole might be subscribed for.

It was to this Gentleman (M[r] Parker) that you were indebted for your Dynamometer—I paid him for it as you directed, and purchased for you a Briquet Pneumatique, and also a Briquet Phosphorique which appeared to me to be much more convenient than the

Other, tho' probably less durable. M[rs] Randolph's letter for Mad[slle] Botideau, I left with M[de] de Corny who was not without some hope of being able, with the assistance of M[r] Short, to hear something of her. the person from whom they expected information died unfortunately just as they sent off a letter to make the enquiry, but there was still some one else, down in Normandy perhaps, from whom they had some expectations—at any rate the letter is in good hands, and I hope, notwithstanding my failure, that I shall not be subjected to the denunciations with which M[rs] Randolph threatened me.

I fear Sir, I have fatigued you with too long a letter—having arrived now on the American Coast, and knowing that I should have no time after I got on shore to write to any one, I sat down this morning to give you some details which I supposed might not be unacceptable, but without any intention, I assure you, of trespassing so unreasonably—we have just got soundings, and I flatter myself I shall get on shore either this evening or early tomorrow—I have only to add my good wishes, and the assurances, which I pray you to accept, of my constant and devoted attachment—

I. A. COLES

RC (DLC); ink stained; endorsed by TJ as received 6 Aug. 1809 and so recorded in SJL.

Jean Baptiste de Nompère de CHAMPAGNY, soon to become duc de Cadore, was French minister of foreign affairs, 1807–11 (Connelly, *Napoleonic France*, 104–5). ESLING: undeterred by his check at the Battle of Aspern-Essling, 21–22 May 1809, Napoleon defeated the Austrians at Wagram in July and forced them to sue for peace (David G. Chandler, *The Campaigns of Napoleon* [1966], 707–32). BRIQUET PNEUMATIQUE and BRIQUET PHOSPHORIQUE were glass tubes that started fires by creating a vacuum in the former and a chemical reaction using phosphorus in the latter. Coles had undertaken to forward a LETTER from Martha Jefferson Randolph to her schoolmate and friend Marie Jacinthe de Botidoux (TJ to Randolph, 27 Feb. 1809 [James H. Eddy, Charles B. Eddy Jr., and John B. Eddy, New York City, 1948]; Randolph to TJ, 2 Mar. 1809 [MHi]).

[1] Manuscript: "Minich."
[2] Manuscript: "neghborhood."

# To Samuel Smith
## (of Maryland)

DEAR SIR Monticello July 26. 09.

Your favor of the 23[d] was recieved yesterday. my acquaintance at S[t] Petersburg is very limited. those who were elderly are dead; of the young, there are two persons with whom I was acquainted at Paris, who were in the early administration of the present emperor, but who have been out for some time, & on what ground, I know not. having never renewed my acquaintance with them by letter, I have, on consideration of all circumstances, thought the inclosed letter the best means in my power of giving your son the benefit of any thing I can do for him at S$^{t}$ Petersburg. by another post I will write to Paris, altho' your own means there must render that a work of supererogation.

Happily withdrawn from the knolege of all the slanders which beset men in public life, I am totally uninformed of the tale respecting yourself alluded to in your letter, & equally unable to conjecture the author of it. should it have the effect you suppose on the election of October, he will certainly not have merited the thanks of his country. but I presume it impossible that in a state where you are known by character to every individual, their representatives can be led away by tales of slander, a weapon so worn as to be incapable of wounding the worthy. that the views of the person who procured the appointment of a committee of investigation were merely malignant, I never doubted, but his passions are too well known to injure any one. I pray you to be assured of the constant friendship & respect of Dear Sir

Your obed$^{t}$ serv$^{t}$ TH: JEFFERSON

RC (Mrs. Leonard A. Hewett, Louisville, Kentucky, 1944); at foot of text: "The honble Gen$^{l}$ Sam$^{l}$ Smith." PoC (DLC); endorsed by TJ. Enclosure: TJ to Levett Harris, 27 July 1809.

## From William Fleming

DEAR SIR, Richmond, July 27$^{th}$ 1809.

I have just received your favor of the 24$^{th}$ instant, and was preparing to meet the parties concerned in Gilliam's suit at the commissioner's office on the 1$^{st}$ of august: the postponement of the business, however, to the 20$^{th}$ of October, will occasion no inconvenience to me, as the court of appeals will then be in session; and I can devote three or four hours in the day to that subject.—I have the original account, mostly in my own hand writing, that was submitted to the meeting at my house, with Jerman Baker's notes thereto; which shall be laid before the commissioner.

Should I be at home, shall be happy to see you at my house, on your way to Eppington; but as the next term of our court commences on the 1$^{st}$ of October, and continues nine weeks, I shall be in Richmond the whole of the term, except perhaps once or twice, on a sunday.

I shall set out in about ten days, to the springs, and shall have the pleasure of paying you my respects, at Monticello, on my way.

Accept the assurance of my high respect and regard.

W[M] FLEMING.

RC (MHi); endorsed by TJ as received 31 July 1809 and so recorded in SJL.

# To Levett Harris

DEAR SIR Monticello July 27. 1809.

The bearer hereof, mr Smith, is the son of the honble Gen[l] Samuel Smith of Baltimore, of whose revolutionary services you cannot be uninformed, & who has been a distinguished member of our public councils during the present government, first in the H. of Representatives, & latterly of the Senate of the US. the son goes in connection with the American legation to S[t] Petersburg, but on his own foundation, and with a view to his own improvement, & the acquiring a knolege of public affairs on an extended scale. anxious to promote views so laudable and useful in the young men of our country, whose fortune and station of life will procure them a participation in the public administration of our affairs, I take the liberty of recommending him to your particular attentions & civilities, as one who will prove himself entirely worthy of them. and I will further request you to present him, in my name, to such characters at your residence as, either from the personal acquaintance I may have had the advantage of forming with them, or from other considerations, would find, in my recommendation, a motive for favoring mr Smith with their attentions. to the acknolegement of the obligations you will confer on me by the good offices you may render mr Smith, I add the assurances of my great esteem & consideration for yourself.

TH: JEFFERSON

PoC (DLC); at foot of text: "Levitt Harris esq. S[t] Petersburg"; endorsed by TJ. Enclosed in TJ to Samuel Smith (of Maryland), 26 July 1809.

Levett Harris (ca. 1780–1839), a merchant and diplomat from Philadelphia, had been appointed American consul at Saint Petersburg by TJ in 1803 after evidently declining the consulship for Rotterdam earlier that year. In 1813 President James Madison appointed Harris secretary to the peace commission, in which role he traveled to Amsterdam and London before being recalled in 1814 to Saint Petersburg, where he acted as chargé d'affaires in the absence of John Quincy Adams. Harris's alleged willingness as consul to turn a profit by clearing questionable ships through Russia's neutrality commission led to a charge of corruption in 1819, followed by an epic libel suit by Harris against his accuser, in which the Supreme Court of Pennsylvania ultimately awarded Harris only nominal damages. The dispute thwarted

Harris's efforts to become minister to Russia, but in 1833 Andrew Jackson appointed him chargé d'affaires in France. Harris corresponded with TJ during his presidency and retirement, occasionally forwarded books, and visited TJ at Monticello several times (Bashkina, *United States and Russia*, 361–2, 593–4; *JEP*, 1:447, 453, 456, 2:353, 390–1, 4:314, 321 [1, 3 Mar., 11, 18 Nov. 1803; 11, 14 June, 19 July 1813, 22, 28 Feb. 1833]; Harris to TJ, 22 June 1814, 2 July 1818, 15 June 1820; Samuel Flagg Bemis, *John Quincy Adams and the Foundations of American Foreign Policy* [1949], 159n, 169, 188).

# From Leonard Jewett

D^R^ SIR Athens State of Ohio July 28th 1809

You will probably think it very extraordinary in an individual unknown to you, to take the Liberty of addressing a Letter to you—Nothing but the importance of the enquiry, & the Confidence I have in your Judgement, to answr it would ever have induced me to take the Liberty—The Subject on which I crave your Opinion is simply this—

Have the Judges of our high Judicial Courts the right of declaring a Law unconstitutional Null & Void, whenever the Law is manifestly at Variance with the Constitution?—[1]

This question Sir, has agitated our State for two or three years, & still threatens us with unpleasant forebodings—It has divided the Republicans into two Contending parties a thing much to be deprecated, at the present Moment,—We have hitherto had a very remarkable and uprecedented unanimity of Sentement prevailing on the subject of Politics, & I very much fear that a division will take place, unless some salutary antidote can be found—Having been several years a member of the Ohio Legislature, I felt very anxious to have your Opinion, which Sir if you will be so good as to give me, I shall ever consider it as a distinguished mark of your favor—

I am Sir your Obdt humble Servant LEONARD JEWETT

RC (CSmH: JF-BA); at foot of text: "Thomas Jefferson Esqr"; endorsed by TJ as received 10 Aug. 1809 and so recorded in SJL.

Leonard Jewett (1770–1816), a native of Littleton County, Massachusetts, received medical training in Boston, worked in a New York hospital, moved to Ohio in 1802, and settled in the town of Athens by 1805. Jewett served in the Ohio state senate, 1806–11, and was a military surgeon during the War of 1812 (Charles M. Walker, *History of Athens County, Ohio* [1869], 272–4).

[1] For emphasis Jewett or someone else rendered this sentence in a distinctive style.

Thomas Jefferson by Thomas Gimbrede

East Front of Monticello

75.

Mar. 14. Culpeper C.H. barber. 50 supper, lodg. &c. 4.43
Orange C.H. oats. .35
15. Gordon's dinner, lodging &c. 4.50 whole expences = 17.14
arrived at Monticello
17. rec^d back from E. Bacon 5.D. of the 10.D. ante Mar. 9.
pd Shorter wages & expences back to Wash^n. 25.D
rec^d of Eli Alexander 200.D. on acc^t of rent
18. paid the same to Higginbotham viz. 200.D.
gave E. Bacon 10.D. to pay 60 gall^s. cyder from mr Terril
paid for small expences 20.D.
28. rec^d of John H. Craven on acc^t of rent 700.D
balance remaining due to me p^r settlem^t £78-6
pd Garner repairing clocks 2.D.
30. rec^d of W^m. Brown thro' Presid. Madison 500.D. to be delivered to mr Inst. sen^r & deliv^d it accordingly.
gave mr Divers's hostler 1.D.
31. inclosed to John Taggert of Philad^a 70.D. for oil and paint.
gave to Tho^s. J. Randolph 50.D. for his expences to Philadelphia, out of which he is to pay 2.D. to J. Taggert whose bill is 72.D. and 6.50 to M^c. Mahon for seeds.
pd Robert Burruss for 52. barr^ls. corn @ 9/9 84.5
paid David Higginbotham 600.D. & gave him an order on J.H. Craven for £78-6 = 261. ante Mar. 28
April 3. hostler at Charlottesville .25
7. pd mr Julien for his trip here 75.D.
pd d^o. a small acc^t. of Lamaire's 3.75
sent Catlett for butter 1.D.
9. paid for a plough 2.D.
12. houshold exp. Patsy. 2.D.
15. purchased a beef of the 4. quarters weighed 637.lb & allowing the average for the 5^th. to wit 159¼ makes the whole 796¼ lb @ 5^d. comes 55.28 of which E. Bacon paid 27.D. out of the monies formerly sent him, & I paid 10.D. so there remains 18.28
16. settled with John Nielson, and the balance of 435.75 D agreed to be due him, & to bear interest from this date.
Patsy for small exp. 3.D.
17. settled with James Dinsmore & the balance of 618.40 D agreed to be due him & to bear interest from this date.
pd Critta on his order 1.25
19. inclosed to Pres^t. Madison a note of the articles he bought on my leaving Washington, amounting to 743.015 to be pd into the bank U.S. in Washington to the credit of my note there, which was for 3706.72
23. pd Bowles for fish 2.D. ~~Patsy~~ small exp. 2.
24. rec^d of Geo. Divers the 69.18 paid for him ante Feb. 6.
~~29. E. Bacon to pay for cotton ... 2.D~~ returned
30. Patsy for sm. exp. 4.D.

Jefferson's Memorandum Book

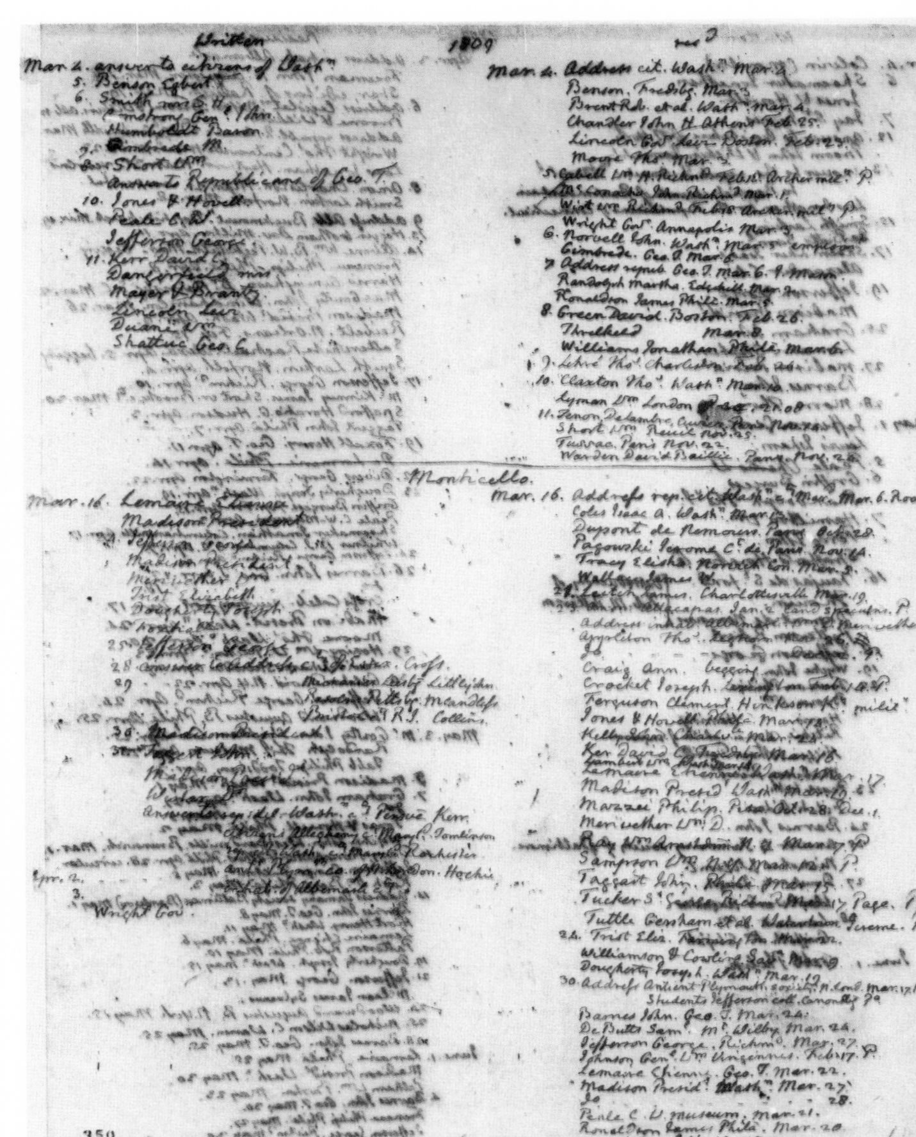

Jefferson's Summary Journal of Letters

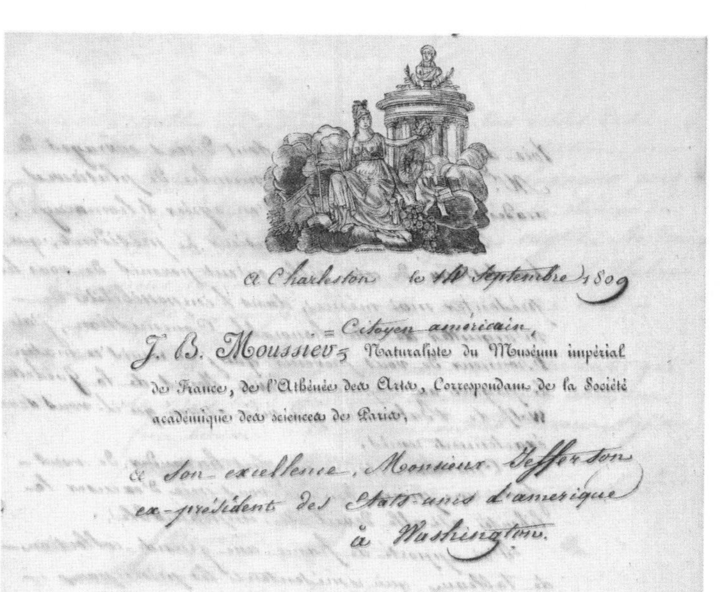
a Charleston le 14 Septembre 1809

Citoyen americain,
J. B. Moussier, Naturaliste du Muséum impérial de France, de l'Athénée des Arts, Correspondant de la Société académique des sciences de Paris,

a Son excellence, Monsieur Jefferson
ex-président des Etats-unis d'amerique
à Washington.

Paris, le [illegible] Juin 1809

Silvestre membre de l'Institut de France
Secrétaire de la
SOCIÉTÉ D'AGRICULTURE
DU DÉPARTEMENT DE LA SEINE.

A Monsieur Jefferson, associé étranger
de l'Institut, et de la Société d'agriculture

Letterheads of Moussier and Silvestre

Seed Press Constructed for Jefferson at the Monticello Joinery

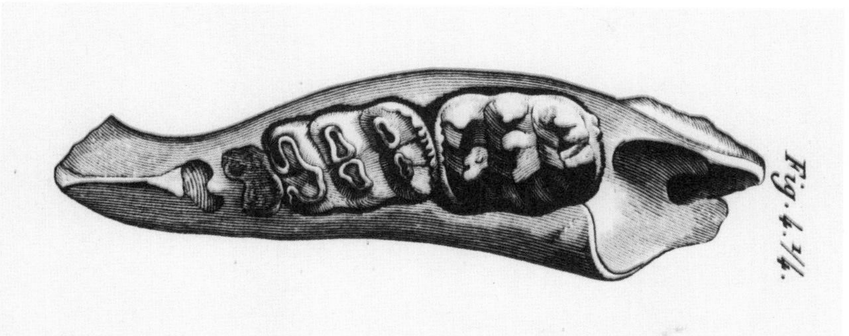


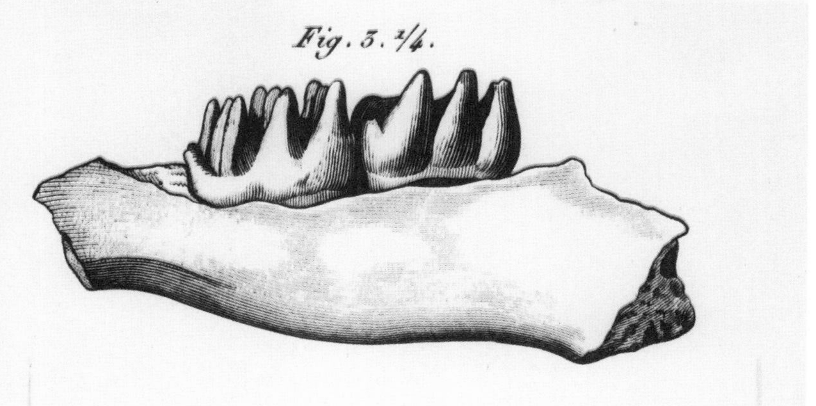


Mastodon Jawbone Donated by Jefferson to the Institut de France

Thomas Jefferson Randolph by Charles Willson Peale

# To Skelton Jones

[DEAR SIR?] Monticello July 28. 09

Your favor of June 19. did not come to hand till the 29th & I have not been able to take it up till now. I lent to mr Burke my collection of newspapers from 1741. to 1760. and the further matter which I suggested I might be able to furnish him after my return to Monticello, was the collection of M.S. laws of Virginia, which I expected would furnish some proper & authentic materials for history, not extant any where else. these I lent the last year to mr Hening, who is now in possession of them, & is printing them. but tho' this was within mr Burke's period, it is entirely anterior to yours. the collection of newspapers which I lent to mr Burke I have never been able to recover, nor to learn where they are. they were all well bound, & of course have not probably been destroyed. if you can aid me in the recovery you will oblige me. I consider their preservation as a duty, because I believe certainly there does not exist another collection of the same period. I have examined the sequel of my collection of newspapers, and find that it has but one paper of 1778. that is one of Purdie's of the month of May. but my not having them is no evidence they were not printed; because I was so continually itinerant during the revolution that I was rarely in a situation to preserve the papers I recieved. and altho' there were probably occasional suspensions for want of paper yet I do not believe there was a total one at any time. I think however you might procure a file for that, or any other year in Philadelphia or Boston. these would furnish all the material occurrences of Virginia. you ask what is the historian to do with the latter part of 1776. the whole of 77. & 78. & a part of 79? this is precisely the period which was occupied in the reformation of the laws to the new organisation & principles of our government. the committee was appointed in the latter part of 76. & reported in the spring or summer 79. at the first and only meeting of the whole committee (of 5. persons) the question was discussed whether we would attempt to reduce the whole body of the law into a code, the text of which should become the law of the land? we decided against that, because every word & phrase in that text would become a new[1] subject of criticism & litigation until it's sense should have been settled by numerous decisions, & that in the mean time the rights of property would be in the air. we concluded not to meddle with the common law, i.e. the law preceding the existence of the statutes, farther than to accomodate it to our new principles & circumstances, but to take up the whole body of statutes, and Virginia laws[2] to leave out every thing obsolete or improper, insert what was wanting, and reduce the whole within as moderate a compas as it would bear, and to the plain language of common sense, divested of the verbiage, the barbarous tautologies & redundancies which render the British statutes unintelligible. from this however were excepted the antient statutes, particularly those commented on by Lord Coke, the language of which is simple, & the meaning of every word so well settled by decisions as to make it safest not to change the words where the sense was to be retained. after settling our plan, Col° Mason declined undertaking the execution of any part of it, as not being sufficiently read in the law. mr Lee very soon afterwards died, & the work was distributed between Mr Wythe, mr Pendleton & myself. to me was assigned the Common law (so far as we thought of altering it),[3] & the statutes down to the Reformation, or end of the reign of Elizabeth; to mr Wythe the subsequent body of the statutes, & to mr Pendleton the Virginia laws. this distribution threw into my part the laws concerning crimes & punishments, the law of descents, & the laws concerning religion. after completing our work separately, we met (mr W. mr P. & myself) in Williamsburg, and held a very long session, in which we went over the 1st & 2d parts in the order of time, weighing & correcting every word, & reducing them to the form in which they were afterwards reported. when we proceeded to the 3d part, we found that mr Pendleton had not exactly seised the intentions of the committee, which were to reform the language of the Virginia laws, and reduce the matter to a simple style & form. he had copied the acts verbatim, only omitting what was disapproved; and some family occurrence calling him indispensably home, he desired mr Wythe & myself to make it what we thought it ought to be, and authorised us to report[4] him as concurring in the work. we accordingly divided the work, & reexecuted it entirely so as to assimilate it's plan & execution to the other parts, as well as the shortness of the time would admit, and we brought the whole body of British statutes, & laws of Virginia into 127. acts, most of them short. this is the history of that work as to it's execution. it's matter & the nature of the changes made will be a proper subject for the consideration of the historian. experience has convinced me that the change in the style of the laws was for the better, & it has sensibly reformed the style of our laws from that time downwards, insomuch that they have obtained in that respect the approbation of men of consideration on both sides of the Atlantick. whether the change in the stile & form of the criminal law, as introduced by mr Taylor, was for the better is not for me to judge. the digest of that act employed me longer than I believe all the rest of the work; for it rendered it necessary for me to go with great care over Bracton, Britton the Saxon statutes, & the works of authority on criminal law: & it gave me great satisfaction to find that in general I had only to reduce the law to it's antient Saxon condition, stripping it of all the innovations & rigorisms of subsequent times, to make it what it should be. the substitution of the Penitentiary instead of labor on the high road, & of some other punishments truly objectionable, is a just merit to be ascribed to mr Taylor's law. when our report was made, the idea of a Penitentiary had never been suggested: the happy experiment of Pensylvania we had not then[5] the benefit of.

To assist in filling up those years of exemption from military invasion, an enquiry into the exertions of Virginia in the common cause during that period, would be proper for the patriotic historian because her character has been very unjustly impeached by the writers of other states, as having used no equal exertions at that time. I know it to be false; because having all that time been a member of the legislature, I know that our whole occupation was in straining the resources of the state to their utmost, to furnish, men, money, provisions & other necessaries to the common cause. the proofs of this will be found in the journals & acts of the legislature, in the Executive proceedings, & papers, & in the Auditor's accounts. not that Virginia furnished her quota of <u>requisitions</u> of either men or money, but that she was always above par, in what was <u>actually</u> furnished by the other states. a letter of mine, written in 1779, or 80, if still among the executive papers, will furnish full evidence of these facts. it was addressed to our delegates in answer to a formal complaint on the subject, and was founded in unquestionable vouchers.

The enquiries in your printed letter of Aug. 1808. would lead to the writing the history of my whole life, than which nothing could be more repugnant to my feelings. I have been connected, as many fellow labourers were, with the great events which happened to mark the epoch of our lives. but these belong to no one in particular. all of us did our parts, & no one can claim the transactions to himself.[6] the most I could do would be to revise, correct, or supply any statements which should be made respecting public transactions in which I had a part, or which may have otherwise come within my knolege.

I have to apologize for the delay of this answer. the active hours of the day are all devoted to employments without doors, so that I have rarely an interval, & more rarely the inclination, to set down to my writing table, the divorce from which is among the greatest reliefs in my late change of life. still I will always answer with pleasure any particular enquiries you may wish to address to me, sincerely desiring for the public good as well as your own personal concern to contribute to the perfection of a work from which I hope much to both; & I beg leave to tender you the assurances of my great esteem & respect.

TH: JEFFERSON

PoC (DLC); salutation faint; at foot of first page: "Skelton Jones."

Based on similarities between this letter and his autobiography, TJ most likely employed the former when composing the passage relating to the COMMITTEE that revised the Virginia laws, 1777–79. After a delay of six years due to a piecemeal approach that led to the passage of certain laws and the removal of others, the remaining body of laws was considered in October 1785. Included in them were TJ's "Bill for Establishing Religious Freedom" (*PTJ*, 2:545–53), adopted in January 1786, and his review of CRIMES & PUNISHMENTS, the "Bill for Proportioning Crimes and Punishments in Cases Heretofore Capital" (*PTJ*, 2:492–507), which was never adopted because of its controversial reliance on the lex talionis ("law of retaliation," *OED*) to punish maiming with comparable mutilations and rape with castration (Bill for the Revision of the Laws, [15 Oct. 1776], and Editorial Note on the Revisal of the Laws, 1776–1786, *PTJ*, 1:562–4, 2:305–24; TJ's autobiography, Ford, 1:57–66; Malone, *Jefferson*, 1:261–3, 269–73).

George Keith TAYLOR's bill amending the penal statutes of Virginia became law in 1796. By HAPPY EXPERIMENT TJ meant the authorization in 1790 of the construction of solitary cells in Philadelphia's Walnut Street prison (*PTJ*, 29:310n, 335–6n). The LETTER OF MINE was probably TJ to Samuel Huntington, 27 July 1780 (*PTJ*, 3:508–13).

[1] Word interlined.

[2] Preceding three words interlined.

[3] Closing parenthesis editorially supplied.

[4] Word interlined in place of "state."

[5] Word interlined.

[6] Preceding two words added in margin.

# From Joseph Milligan

DEAR SIR George town July 28th 1809

On the 13th instant I forwarded you ℘ stage done up in a little box one ream best american hot prest paper Which I hope has ere this reached you in safety

| | |
|---|---|
| 1 Ream American hot prest paper | \$7 50 |
| Box to pack in | 25 |
| Expences to Fredericksburg | 37½ |
| | \$8–12½ |

I have not yet been Able to procure the 7th & 8 vols Scientific dialogues but I hope to be able to get them shortly and as soon as I get them They Shall be forwarded ℘ Mail without delay

yours With Esteem & respect JOSEPH MILLIGAN

RC (DLC); at foot of text: "Thomas Jefferson Esqr"; endorsed by TJ as received 31 July 1809 and so recorded in SJL.

## From John W. Campbell

RESPECTED SIR, Petersburg V^a July 29^th 1809

I avail myself of this method of making a proposition to you, respecting the publication of a complete Edition of your different writings, as far as they may be designed for the public; including the, "Notes on Virginia."

The work should be executed in Philadelphia, by the best publisher in the city, & in a stile, not inferiour to any prose work yet published in our country.

Should the proposal meet your approbation, I will have it in my power to confer with you on the subject previous to undertaking the work. It was my design to have made this proposal, viva voce, & for this purpose I had received several letters from Your friends; but I have been induced first to know your mind respecting this undertaking & afterwards I would repair to your place of residence, should my solicitation be likely to prove successful

I beg you to receive my warmest wishes for your welfare

JOHN W CAMPBELL

RC (DLC); dateline at foot of text; endorsed by TJ as received 31 July 1809 and so recorded in SJL.

John Wilson Campbell (1779–1842), a printer and bookseller in Petersburg, ultimately decided against publishing TJ's writings. He was the author of a *History of Virginia, from Its Discovery Till the Year 1781* (Philadelphia, 1813) and compiler of *The Columbian reader* (Philadelphia, 1814) (Margaret Campbell Pilcher, *Historical Sketches of the Campbell, Pilcher, and kindred Families* [1911], 206; Richmond *Enquirer*, 5 Jan. 1843).

## To Pierre Samuel Du Pont de Nemours

DEAR SIR Monticello July 29. 09

The bearer hereof, mr Smith, is the son of Gen^l Smith of Baltimore, whose revolutionary services, as well as his civil station among us, that of a Senator, & a distinguished one of the United States, cannot be unknown to you who have taken so long, & so friendly an interest in whatever regards, or is done in the US. his son, who wishes to qualify himself to be useful to his country hereafter, will visit Paris, and will wish to derive from the visit, all the useful information he can acquire. urged by my own desire to aid the laudable views of our young men whose station & circumstances in life may bring them into our councils or commands, & knowing your particular sense of the importance of a right direction in youth to those on whom are to devolve the care of the liberties & interests of their country, I take the liberty of presenting him to you, & of praying you to befriend his views while in your Metropolis. you will do it with the greater satisfaction on being assured he will prove himself not unworthy of your attentions. mihi, tu, tui, tua omnia maximae curae sunt, et, dum vivam, erunt. cura ut valeas, et me, ut amaris, ama. Vale.

TH: JEFFERSON

RC (DLC: Samuel Smith Papers); addressed: "M. Dupont de Nemours à Paris favored by mr Smith." PoC (DLC); endorsed by TJ. Tr (DeGH: H. A. Du Pont Papers, Winterthur Manuscripts). Enclosed in TJ to Samuel Smith (of Maryland), 29 July 1809.

MIHI . . . ERUNT and VALE: "You and your family and your possessions are all the objects of my closest care, and shall be while I live. Good-bye" (Cicero to A. Torquatus, in Cicero, *Letters to Friends*, ed. and trans. E. R. Shackleton Bailey, Loeb Classical Library [2001], 2:387). TJ added the phrase "cura ut valeas, et me, ut amaris, ama" ("take care that you fare well, and love me as you are loved").

# Margaret Bayard Smith's Account of a Visit to Monticello

Montecello—August 1st [29 July–2 Aug.] 1809.

After a very delightful journey of three days, we reached Monticello on the morning of the fourth. When I crossed the Ravanna, a wild & romantic little river, which flows at the foot of the mountain, my heart beat, for I thought I had now entered as it were the threshhold of his dwelling, & I looked around every where expecting to meet with some trace of his superintending care.—In this I was disappointed, for no vestige of the labour of man appeared; nature seemed to hold an undisturbed dominion; We began to ascend this mountain, still as we rose I cast my eyes around, but could discern nothing but untamed woodland,—after a miles winding upwards, we saw a field of corn, but the road was still wild & uncultivated.—I every moment expected to reach the summit, & felt as if it was an endless road; my impatience lengthen'd it, for it [is][1] not two miles from the outer gate on the river to the house.—At last we reached the summit, & I shall never forget the emotion the first view of this sublime scenery excited.—Below me extended for above 60 miles round, a country cover'd with woods, plantations & houses; beyond arose the blue mountains, in all their grandeur! Montecello rising 500 feet above the river, of a conical form & standing by itself commands on all sides an unobstructed, & I suppose one of the most extensive views any spot of the globe affords.— The sides of the mountain covered with wood, with scarcely a speck of cultivation, presents a fine contrast to its summit, crowned with a noble pile of building, surrounded by an immence lawn, & shaded here & there with some fine trees.—Before we reached the house, we met Mr J. on horseback, he had just returned from his morning ride, & when on approaching, he recognized us, he recieved us with one of those benignant smiles, & cordial tones of voice that convey an undoubted welcome to the heart.—He dismounted & assisted me from the carriage, led us thro' a noble portico[2] to the hall; where he again bade us welcome—I was so struck with the appearance of this Hall, that I lingered to look around, but he led me forward, smiling as he said, "you shall look bye & bye, but you must rest now,"[3] leading me to a sopha in a drawing room as singular & beautiful as the Hall. He rung & sent word to Mrs Randolph that we were there, & then ordered some refreshments.—"We have quite a sick family" said he; "My daughter has been confined to the sick bed of her little son; my Grand-daughter has lost her's &[4] still keeps her room & several of the younger children are indisposed.—for a fortnight Mr & Mrs Randolph have sat up every night, untill they are almost worn out." This information clouded my satisfaction & cast a gloom over our visit.—But Mrs R soon entered, & with a smiling face, most affectionately welcomed us; her kind & cheerful manners soon dispersed my gloom & after a little chat, I begged her not to let me detain her from her nursery, but to allow me to follow her to it; she assented & I sat with her untill dinner time.—Anne, (Mrs. Bankhead)[5] also had been confined 3 weeks before & had lost her child looked delicate & interesting; Ellen my old favorite I found improved as well as grown[6]—At five oclock the bell summoned us to dinner—Mr Randolph, Mr Bankhead, & Jefferson R—were there, They are 12 in family, And as Mr J. sat in the midst of his children & grand children, I looked on him with emotions of tenderness & respect. The table was plainly, but genteely & plentifully spread & his immence & costly variety of french & Italian wines, gave place to Madeira & a sweet ladies wine.[7]—We sat till near sun down at the table, where the desert was succeeded by agreeable & instructive conversation, in which every one seemed to wish & expect Mr J. to take the chief part.[8]—As it is his custom after breakfast to withdraw to his own apartments & pursuits & not to join the family again untill dinner, he prolongs that meal, or rather the time after that meal & seems to relish his wine the better, for being accompanied with conversation.—& during the 4 days I spent there these were the most social hours.—When we rose from table, a walk was proposed & he accompanied us. He took us first to the garden he has commenced since his retirement—It is on the south side of the mountain & commands a most noble view.—Little is as yet done—A terrace of[9] 700 or 8[10] feet long & about 40 wide, is already made & in cultivation[11]—a broad grass walk leads along the outer edge, the inner part is laid off in beds for vegetables.—This terrace is to be extended[12] in length & another to be made below it.[13]—The view it commands, is at present its greatest beauty. We afterwards walked round the first circuit.—There are 4 roads about 15 or 20 feet wide, cut round the mountain, from 100 to 200 feet apart.[14]—These circuits are connected by a great many roads & paths & when compleated will afford a beautiful shady ride or walk of seven miles.—The first circuit is not quite a mile round, as it is very near the top—It is in general shady, with openings through the trees for distant views. We passed the out houses for the slaves & work men; they are all much better, than I have seen on any other plantation, but to an eye unaccustomed to such sights, they appear poor &[15] these cabins form a most unpleasant[16] contrast with the palace that rises so near them.—Mr J. has carpenters, cabinet-makers, painters, blacksmiths & several other trades all within himself, & finds these slaves excellent work men.[17]

As we walked, he explained his future designs.[18] "My long absence from this place, has left a wilderness around me;" "but you have returned" said I, "& the wildness shall blossom like the rose & you I hope will long sit beneath your own vine & your own fig-tree"—It was near dark when we reached the house, he led us into a little tea room which opened on the terrace[19] & as Mrs R— was still in her nursery he sat with us & conversed till tea time—We never drank tea untill near nine, afterwards there was fruit, which he seldom staid to partake of, as he allways retired immediately after tea.—I never sat above an hour afterwards, as I supposed Mrs R— must wish to be in her nursery.[20]—I rose the morning after my arrival very early & went out on the terrace, to contemplate scenery, which to me was so novel.—The space between Montecello and the Allegany, from sixty to eighty miles, was covered with a thick fog, which had the appearance of the ocean & was unbroken except where wood cover'd hills rose above the plain & looked like islands.—As the sun rose, the fog was broken & exhibited the most various & fantastic forms, lakes, rivers, bays, & as it ascended, it hung in white fleecy clouds on the sides of the mountains; An hour afterwards you would scarcely believe it was the same scene you looked on.—In spite of the cold air from the mountains, I staid here untill the first breakfast bell rung. Our breakfast table was as large as our dinner table; instead of a cloth, a folded napkin lay under each plate; we had tea, coffee, excellent muffins, hot wheat and corn bread, cold ham & butter.—It was not exactly the virginian breakfast I expected.—here[21] indeed was the mode of living in general that of a virginia planter—At breakfast the family all assembled, all Mrs R's children eat at the family table, but are in such excellent order, that you would not know if you did not see them that a child was present.[22] After breakfast, I soon learned that it was the habit of the family each seperately to pursue their occupations. Mr J. went to his apartments, the door of which is never opened but by himself & his retirement seems so sacred that I told him it was his sanctum sanctorum.[23] Mr Randolph rides over to his farm & seldom returns untill night; Mr Bankhead who is reading law to his study; a small building at the end of the east terrace, opposite to Mr Randolphs which terminates the west terrace; these buildings are called pavilions. Jefferson R— went to survey a tract of woodland afterwards make his report to his grandfather.[24] Mrs Randolph withdrew to her nursery & excepting the hours house-keeping requires she devotes the rest to her children whom she instructs.—As for them, they seem never to leave her for an instant, but are always beside her or on her lap.—[25]

Visitors generaly retire to their own rooms, or walk about the place; those who are fond of reading can never be at a loss, those who are not, will sometimes feel wearied in the long interval between breakfast & dinner.[26] The dinner bell rings twice, the first collects the family, in time to enter the room[27] by the time the second announces dinner to be on table, which while I was there was between 4 &[28] 5 oclock. In summer the interval between rising from table & tea (9 oclock) may be agreeably passed in walking.—but to return to my journal—After breakfast on sunday morning, I asked Ellen to go with me on the top of the house;[29] Mr J. heard me &[30] went along with us & pointed out those spots in the landscape most remarkable—The morning was show'ry, the clouds had a fine effect, throwing large masses of shade on the mountain sides, which finely contrasted with the sunshine of other spots.[31]—He afterwards took us to the drawing room, in the dome 26 or 7 feet diameter[32]—It is a noble & beautiful apartment—perfectly round with 8 circular windows & a sky-light—It was not furnished, & being in the attic story, is not used.—which I thought a great pity, as it might be made the most beautiful room in the house.[33]—The attic chambers are comfortable & neatly finished but no elegances[34] When we descended to the Hall, he asked us to pass into the library, or as I called it his sanctum sanctorrum, where any other foot than his own seldom intrudes. This suite[35] of apartments opens from the Hall to the south. It consists of[36] 3 rooms for the library, one for his cabinet one for his chamber, & a green house, divided from the other by glass compartments & doors; so that the view of the plants it contains, is unobstructed.—He has not yet made his collection, having but just finished the room, which opens on one of the terraces. He shewed us every thing he thought would please or interest us—His most valuable & curious books—those which contained fine prints &ca—Among these I thought the most curious were the original letters of Cortez to the king of Spain, a vol, of fine views of Antient villa's round Rome, with maps of the grounds, & minute descriptions of the buildings & grounds. An old poem written by Pierce Plowman & printed 250 years ago; he read near a page, which was almost as unintelligible as if it was hebrew; & some Greek romances. He took pains to find one that was translated into french, as most of them were translated in latin & italian.—More than two hours passed most charmingly away.—The library consists of books in all languages, & contains about twenty thousand vols.—But so disposed that they do not give the idea of a great library.—I own I was much disappointed in its appearance, & I do not think with its numerous divisions & arches it is as impressive as one large room would have been. His cabinet & chamber contained every convenience & comfort, but were plain. His bed is built in the wall which divides his chamber & cabinet.[37] He opened a little closset which contains all his garden seeds. they are all in phials, labe[led] & hung on little hooks.—Seeds such as peas, beans, &ca were in tin cannisters—but every thing labeled and in the neatest order.[38] He bade us take whatever books we wished, which we did & then retired to our own room.—Here we amused ourselves untill dinner time excepting an hour I sat with Mrs R. by her sick baby.—but as she was reading I did not sit long.—After dinner Ellen & Mr Bankhead accompanied us in a long ramble in the mountain walks.—At dark when we returned, the tea room was still vacant; I called Virginia & Mary (the age of my Julia & Susan) amused myself with them untill their Grand papa entered, with whom I had a long & interesting conversation; in which he described with enthusiasm his retirement from public life & the pleasures he found in domestic.—[39]

Monday morning—I again rose early, in order to observe the scenes around me, & was again repaid for the loss of sleep, by the various appearances the landscape assumed, as the fog was rising.—But the blue & misty mountains, now light up with sun shine, now thrown into deep shadow, presented objects on which I gaze each morning with new pleasure.[40] After breakfast, Mr J. sent E. to ask me if I would take a ride with him round the mountain; I willingly assented & in a little while I was summoned; the carriage was a kind of chair, which his own workmen had made under his direction, & it was with difficulty that he, Ellen & I found room in it, & might well be called the sociable.—The first circuit, the road was good, & I enjoyed the views it afforded & the familiar & easy conversation, which our sociable gave rise to; but when we descended to the second & third circuit, fear took from me the power of listening to him, or observing the scene; nor could I forbear expressing my alarm, as we went along a rough road which had only been laid out, & on driving[41] over fallen trees & great rocks, which threaten'd an over set to our sociable & a roll down the mountain to us—

"My dear madam," said Mr J— "you are not to be affraid, or if you are you are not to show it; trust yourself implicitly to me, I will answer for your safety; I came every foot of this road yesterday, on purpose to see if a carriage could come safely, I know every step I take, so banish all fear."—This I tried to do but in vain, till coming to a rock over which one wheel must pass I jumped out, while the servant who attended on horseback rode forward &[42] held up the carriage as Mr J— passed.[43]—Poor Ellen did not dare to get out.—Notwithstanding the terror I suffered I would not have lost this ride; as Mr J— explained to me all his plans for improvement, where the roads, the walks, the seats, the little temples were to be placed—There are two springs gushing from the mountain side, he took me to one, which might be made very picturesque. As we passed the grave yard, which is about half way down the mountain, in a sequestered spot, he told me he there meant to place a small gothic building.—higher up, where a beautiful little mound was covered with a grove of trees, he meant to place a monument to his friend <u>Wythe</u>.[44] We returned home by a road which did not wind round the mountain but carried us to the summit by a gentle ascent. It was a good road, & my terror vanished and I enjoyed conversation.

I found Mrs R. deeply engaged in the Wild Irish boy, sitting by the side of her little patient;[45] I did not stay long to interrupt her, but finding[46] Mrs Bankhead likewise engaged with a book, I withdrew to my own room to read my Grecian romance. At dinner, Mrs Randolph sent an apology, she hurt her eye so badly, that it produced excessive inflamation & pain, which obliged her to go to bed.—After dinner I went up to sit by her, Mr J. came up soon after & I was delighted by his tender attentions to this dear daughter.—

As he sat by her & held her hand, for above an hour, we had a long & social conversation in which Mrs R. joined occasionaly.[47]—After he had gone, finding her disposed to sleep, I went down—It was now quite dark & too late to walk, so I took my seat in the tea-room with my little girls & told them stories till the tea bell, again collected the family.—

Tuesday—After breakfast, I went up & sat all the morning by Mrs Randolph; she was too unwell to rise; part of the time I read, but when we were alone conversed.—Our conversation turned chiefly on her father, & on her mentioning their correspondence, I begged her to shew me some of his letters—This she willingly assented to, & it was a rich repast to mind & heart.—Some of them were written when he was minister in France & she in a convent; these are filled with the best advice in the best language; his letters come down to the last days of his political life; in every one he expresses his longings after retirement.—She was so good as to give me one of these precious letters.[48] When I went down stairs I found Mr J— in the hall & Mr S— & we had a long conversation on a variety of topics.—He took us [on][49] a charming walk round the edge of the lawn & showed us the spots from which the house appeared to most advantage.

I looked upon him, as he walked, the top of this mountain, as a being elevated above the[50] mass of mankind, as much in[51] character as he was in local situation.—I reflected on the long career[52] of public duties & stations through which he had passed, & that after forty years spent on the tempestuous sea of political [life,][53] he had now reached the secure[54] haven of domestic life. Here while the storm roar'd at distance, he could hear its roaring & be at peace. He had been a faithful labourer in the harvest field[55] of life, his labours were crowned with success, & he had reaped a rich harvest of fame & wealth[56] & honor. Oh that in this, his winter of life he may enjoy the harvest he has reaped.—

In him; I percieve no decay of mind or debility of frame,[57] and to all the wisdom & experience of age, he adds the enthusiasm & ardour of youth.—I looked on him with wonder as I heard him describe the improvements he designed in his grounds[58]—they seemed to require a whole life to carry into effect, & a young man might doubt of ever completing or enjoying them.—But he seems to have transposed his hopes & anticipations into the existence of his children, it is in them he lives, & I believe he finds as much delight in the idea that they will enjoy the fruit of his present labours; as much as if he hoped it for himself.—If full occupation of mind, heart & hands, is happiness, surely he is happy! The sun never sees him in bed, & his mind designs, more than[59] the day can fulfil, even his long day.—The conversation of the morning, the letters I had read, & the idea that this was the last day I was to spend in his society, the last time I was ever to see him, filled my heart with sadness—I could scarcely look at or speak to him without tears.—After dinner he went to the carpenters shop, to give directions for a walking seat, he had order'd made for us, & I did not see him again until after sun-set—I spent the interval in walking with Mr Smith round the lawn & grove, & had just parted from him to join the children to whom I had promised another story, when as I passed the terrace, Mr J: came out & joined us—The children ran to him[60] & immediately proposed a race—we seated ourselves on the steps of the Portico, & he after placing the children according to their size one before the other, gave the word for starting & away they flew; the course round this back lawn was a qr of a mile, the little girls were well tired by the time they returnd to the spot from which they started & came panting & out of breath to throw themselves into their grandfather's arms, which were opened to recieve them; he pressed them to his bosom & rewarded them with a kiss—he was sitting on the grass and they sat down by him, untill were rested; then they again wished to set off; he thought it too long a course for little Mary & proposed running on the terrace—Thither we went, & seating ourselves at one end, they ran from us to the pavillion & back again;[61] "what an amusement," said I, "do these little creatures afford us;" "yes" replied he, "it is only with them that a grave man can play the fool." They now called on him to run with them,[62] he did not long resist,[63] & seemed delighted in delighting them.—Oh ye whose envenomed calumny has painted him as the slave of the vilest passions, come here, & contemplate this scene! The simplicity, the gaiety, the modesty & gentleness[64] of a child, united to all that is great & venerable in the human character.—His life is the best refutation of the calumnies that have been heaped upon him & it seems to me impossible, for any one personaly to know him & remain his enemy—It was dark by the time we entered the tea-room I was glad to close the windows & shut out the keen air from the mountains.—The mornings & evenings are here always cool & indeed Mrs Randolph says it is never hot.—As it was the last evening we were to pass here, Mr J— sat longer than usual after tea. All the family except Mrs Randolph[65] were[66] at tea, I gazed upon Mr J. in the midst of this interesting circle & thought of the following lines, which I copied from one of his letters.

"When I look to the ineffable pleasures of my family society, I become more & more disgusted with the jealousies, the hatred, the rancourous & malignant passions of this scene, & lament my having ever again been drawn into public view.—Tranquility is now my object; I have seen enough of political honors, to know they are but splendid torments; & however one might be disposed to render services on which many of their fellow citizens might set a value, yet when as many would deprecate them as a public calamity, one may well entertain a modest doubt of their real importance & feel the impulse of duty to be very weak. 1797."

And again, in another of a later date, he says,

"Worn down here with pursuits in which I take no delight, surrounded by enemies & spies, catching & perverting every word which falls from my lips, or flows from my pen, & inventing, where facts fail them, I pant for that society, where all is peace & harmony, where we love & are beloved by every object we see—And to have that intercourse of soft affections, hushed & suppressed by the eternal presence of strangers, goes very hard indeed, & the harder when we see that the candle of life is burning out & the pleasures we lose are lost forever!—I long to see the time approach when I can be returning to you, tho' it be for a short time only—these are the only times existence is of any value to me, continue then to love me my ever dear daughter, & to be assured, that to yourself, your sister & those dear to you every thing in my life is devoted, ambition has no hold upon me but through you—my personal affections would fix me forever with you.—Kiss the dear little objects of our mutual love," &a &a

By these dear objects, I saw him now surrounded.—I saw him in the scenes for which his heart had panted, at the time when others looked upon his elevated station with envy, & did not know that these honors which his country lavished on him & which they envied, were splendid torments, to his unambitious spirit & affectionate heart.—But why then it will be asked did he not with draw from public life, a satisfactory answer is often found in his letters; in one he says (it was while secretary) that he had made up his mind to retire, that he had arranged his affairs for it, but contrary to all his wishes he was persuaded by his friends[67] of the necessity of remaining, that a retreat at that time would be attributed to timidity or fear of the attacks made by the papers &[68] might ruin the party of which he was the head,—In one of his letters he says—"The real difficulty is that being once delivered[69] into the hands of others, whose feelings are friendly to the individual & warm to the public cause, how to withdraw from them, without leaving a dissatisfaction in their minds & impressions of pusylanimity with the public:"—From many other passages of his letters, it is evident that his own wishes were sacrificed to the remonstrances of his friends & to the wish of supporting the republican cause,—On which he sincerely & honestly believed the happiness of his country to depend.—[70]

After tea, fruit as usual was brought, of which he staid to partake; the figs were very fine, & I eat them with greater pleasure from their having been planted rear'd & attended by him with peculiar care.—Which this year was rewarded with an abundant crop, & of which we every day enjoyed the produce.[71]

Wednesday Morning. Mrs Randolph was not able to come down to breakfast, & I felt too sad to join in the conversation.—I looked on every object around me, all was examined with that attention a last look inspires; the breakfast ended, our carriage was at the door, & I rose to bid farewell to this interesting family.—Mrs. R— came down to spend the last minutes with us, As I stood for a moment in the Hall, Mr J. approached & in the most cordial manner urged me to make another visit the ensuing summer, I told him, with a voice almost choked with tears, "That I had no hope of such a pleasure—this," said I, raising my eyes to him, "is the last time I fear, in this world at least, that I shall ever again see you—But there is another world."—I felt so affected by the idea of this last sight of this good & great man, that I turned away & hastily repeating my farewell to the family,[72] gave him my hand, he pressed it affectionately as he put me in the carriage saying,[73] "God bless you dear Madam, God bless you."—"And God bless you," said I from the very bottom of my heart.—

Mr. Smith got in, the door shut & we drove from this habitation of Philosophy & virtue.—How rapidly did we seem to descend that mountain which had seemed so tedious in its ascent—And the quick pulsations I then felt were now changed to a heavy oppression.

Yes—he is truely a Philosopher, & truely a good man.—And eminently a great one.—

There is a tranquility about him, which an inward peace could alone bestow,—Like a ship long tossed by the storms of the ocean, casts anchor & lies at rest in a peaceful harbour, He is retired from an active & restless scene to this tranquil spot.—Voluntarily & gladly has he resigned honors which he never sought, & unwittingly[74] accepted.—His actions, not his words, preach the emptiness[75] & dissatisfaction attendant on a great office.—His tall & slender figure is not impaired by age, tho' bent by care—& labour.—His white locks, announce an age his activity, strength, health, enthusiasm,[76] ardour & gaiety contradict.—His face owes all its charm, to its expression & intelligence; His features are not good & his complexion bad, but his countenance is so full of soul & beams with such benignity, that when the eye rests on his face, it is too busy in perusing its[77] expressions, to think of its features or complexion.— His low & mild voice, harmonizes with his countenance rather than his figure.—But his manners,—How gentle, how humble, how kind.—His meanest slave must feel; as if it were a father instead of a master who addressed him, when he speaks.[78]—To a disposition ardent, affectionate & communicative, he joins manners timid, even to bashfulness[79] & reserved even to coldness.—If his life had not proved to the contrary I should have pronounced him rather a man of imagination & taste, than a man of judgment, a literary rather than scientific man, & least of all a Politician A character for which nature never seemed to have intended him, & for which the natural turn of mind, & his disposition, taste, & feeling equaly unfited him.—I should have been sure that this was the case, even had he not told me so.—In an interesting conversation I had one evening—Speaking of his past public & present domestic life—" The whole of my life" said he, "has been a war with my Natural taste, feelings & wishes.—Domestic life & literary pursuits, were my first & my latest inclination, Circumstances, & not my desires lead me to the path I have trod.—And like a bow tho long bent, when unstrung flies back to its natural state,[80] I, resume with delight the character & pursuits for which nature designed me."— "The circumstances of our country" continued he, "at my entrance into life, were such that every honest man felt himself compelled to take a part,[81] & to act up to the best of his abilities;"—

MS (DLC: Margaret Bayard Smith Papers: Diary 1809–28); entirely in Smith's hand; minor tears at corners; excerpted from an entry dated 1 Aug. 1809 but redated based on internal evidence. Printed from this text in Smith, *Forty Years*, 65–81, and expanded and revised in Smith's "Recollections of a Visit to Monticello," Richmond *Enquirer*, 18 Jan. 1823, with only the most important variations noted below.

TJ's granddaughter Ann C. Randolph married Charles L. Bankhead in September 1808. The child she LOST was not named. Elizabeth Trist, who left Monticello on 9 July, reported that "M[rs] Bankhead some days ago was deliver[d] of a Son it was not expected till next month tis a very small child for a day or two after its birth they had little hope of its living but it begins to thrive and she is quite hearty" (Trist to Catharine Wistar Bache, 10 July 1809 [PPAmP: Catharine Wistar Bache Papers]). The Bankheads subsequently had four children who reached adulthood.

After years of effort, late in 1795 TJ acquired a new edition of the LETTERS OF CORTEZ (Hernán Cortés, *Historia de Nueva-España*, ed. Francisco Antonio Lorenzena y Butron [Mexico City, 1790;

Sowerby, no. 4120]). His book with fine views of ANTIENT VILLA's near Rome might have been Robert Castell, *The Villas of the Ancients Illustrated* (London, 1728; Sowerby, no. 4191). William Langland's allegorical POEM, *The Vision of Pierce Plowman* (London, 1550; Sowerby, no. 4502), was written in Middle English during the fourteenth century and might well have sounded UNINTELLIGIBLE to TJ's visitors.

The LITTLE CLOSSET was the seed press probably built by John Hemmings, an illustration of which is reproduced elsewhere in this volume. TJ's granddaughters VIRGINIA & MARY Randolph were then seven and five years old, similar in age to Smith's daughters Julia and Susan. An open four-wheeled carriage, a SOCIABLE had two seats facing each other and a box-seat for the driver (*OED*). Martha Jefferson Randolph was DEEPLY ENGAGED by Charles Robert Maturin's gothic novel, *The Wild Irish Boy* (New York, 1808).

Smith quoted several LETTERS from TJ to Martha Jefferson Randolph beginning with two passages from 8 June 1797 (*PTJ*, 29:424–5). ANOTHER OF A LATER DATE as quoted by Smith has not been found, and the letter written WHILE SECRETARY was probably that of 26 Jan. 1793 (*PTJ*, 25:97–8).

A year after the newspaper version appeared, Smith included some of the same information in a fictionalized account which described entrance to "the hall through wide folding doors, which we never saw closed"; detailed its contents as including "a perfect model of the great pyramid of Egypt; the upper and lower jaw-bones and tusks of the mammoth, whose magnitude is advantageously exhibited by contrast with those of an elephant alongside of them; several maps, particularly one of the Missouri country, painted on buffalo hides by the American Indians; rough hewn stone images, or statues, likewise of their workmanship, which are supposed to be the idols they worshipped, and many other of the curiosities of our country"; and reported that TJ's suite of rooms included "a carpenter's work-bench, with a vast assortment of tools of every kind and description. This, as being characteristic, is worthy of notice; the fabrication with his own hands of curious implements and models, being a favourite amusement" (Smith, *Winter in Washington: or, Memoirs of the Seymour Family*, 3 vols. [New York, 1824], 3:218–30).

[1] Word supplied from Smith, *Forty Years*.

[2] Preceding four words interlined.

[3] Here and elsewhere a number of omitted opening and closing quotation marks have been editorially supplied.

[4] *Enquirer*: "my grand-daughter, who has been confined."

[5] Preceding two words interlined.

[6] Sentence omitted in *Enquirer*.

[7] *Enquirer*: "plentifully spread. It was the respectable board of a private gentleman, from which was discarded the French cookery and foreign luxuries, which used to distinguish his table when President; the rich and costly variety of wines, for which he used to be remarkable, were now discarded for Claret and Madeira; thus, in his public and private situation, discovering equal taste and propriety."

[8] *Enquirer* here adds "This is the part of the day, in which he gives most time to his guests, and seems himself most to enjoy society; and I found during the few days we passed at Monticello, these were the most social hours. The dessert is not removed; the wine freely, but not rapidly circulated round the table, and the ladies do not withdraw, until the hospitable master leads the way. Every one who has known, has acknowledged the colloquial powers of this excellent man. He is frank and communicative in his manner, various and delightful in his conversation. With a mind stored by much reading, long experience, accurate observation, deep research, an intimate acquaintance with the great and good men of Europe and America; with the events, and scenes and customs of both countries; he possesses a store of intellectual wealth, which falls to the lot of few; and of those, how many, who possess the treasure, have not the faculty of imparting it to others. But,

Mr. J—, has not only the sterling gold, but has the lesser coins, which afford an easy currency to thought, and are so important in social intercourse. No subject could be started, which he did not illustrate by luminous observations, or enliven by sprightly anecdotes. One quality he has, which I never knew equalled in any other man: a quick and intuitive perception of the character, taste and feelings of his guests, and with a benevolence, equalling in warmth, the greatness of his perception; he always turned the conversation, so as to draw forth the powers and talents of each guest, bestowing on all, the same gracious attention: he, above all men, has the art of pleasing, by making each pleased with himself. Why can I not recollect every word which fell from his lips, during these charming conversations, for every word deserved to be remembered! But, so many recollections are crowded in these short and interesting days, that I should fill a volume, should I record them all."

[9] Smith here canceled "250."

[10] Preceding two words interlined in manuscript and lacking in *Enquirer.*

[11] *Enquirer* here adds "Against the wall which supports it, are raised fine figs."

[12] *Enquirer*: "doubled."

[13] *Enquirer* here adds "It is still in a rough unfinished state, and I rather think Mr. Jefferson will find, in chusing a southern aspect, and in laying out his garden so as to expose it to the greatest degree of heat, that in our climate, he will have not only more than sufficient, but a degree, which will prove destructive to vegetation. He has, all his life, been so exclusively engaged in public affairs, that he has little practical knowledge of rural or domestic management. With the same inattention to the effects of the climate, he has levelled the top of his mountain, and formed on its surface, a lawn of at least ten acres, shaded only by a few trees of foreign growth; foreign I mean to the mountain soil, such as *willows*, *Italian poplars*, &c. &c. Lawns may be beautiful in the northern states, or in a humid atmosphere like England, but they do not answer in the southern states, where in the heats of mid summer, when the eye must require the reviving sight of verdure, the grass is so withered and dry, that it often crumbles to dust under the feet. And I much fear, the same fate will attend his summer vegetables, exposed as they are to the full blaze of the southern sun. The same want of practical utility, convenience and comfort, is obvious in the site of his mansion, and the arrangement of its offices. Placed on the very pinnacle of the mountain, it is exposed to all the ardours of summer, and all the bleak storms of winter. Had it been placed on the declivity of the mountain, it might have been sheltered from both, nor would he have been obliged, as he now is, to have all the water used in the family brought from the foot of the mountain. The kitchen is at a hundred, perhaps, near two hundred feet from the dining room, to which it is joined by a long cold vaulted passage. But his plans, are those of a man of taste, a statesman, a philosopher; that is, an intellectual being, wholly unacquainted with the every day wants and comforts of common life. He is a great agriculturist and horticulturist in theory, but practically, I imagine, he knows little of any cultivation, but that of flowers, of which he is extremely fond.—Here again, I have wandered from my party and the new garden, and if I can find the way, must return to where I left him explaining his plans, and gathering his figs, which were really fine. Leaving the garden, he led us through, or rather by the side of an almost impervious grove of aspins, whose straight and aspiring branches, and ever quivering leaves, formed a fine contrast with the majestic and wide spreading ashes, and other forest trees, which shade this part of the grounds."

[14] *Enquirer*: "There are three of these roads encompassing the mountain, at equal distances, about two hundred feet apart."

[15] Smith here canceled "uncomfortable."

[16] *Enquirer*: "unaccustomed to the abodes of slavery, seem poor and uncomfortable, and to *northern* feelings form an unpleasant."

[17] *Enquirer*: "Mr. J. has carpenters, cabinet-makers, blacksmiths, weavers,

tailors, shoemakers, and other tradesmen in his establishment, and finds his slaves ingenious and good workmen."

[18] *Enquirer* here adds "of cultivation and improvement."

[19] *Enquirer* here adds "Its form was a half circle, divided from the dining room by a glass, or sashed *partition*. There was a feeling of social comfort in this small apartment, which was lost in the largeness and loftiness of the other rooms."

[20] *Enquirer*: "after tea: even while President, he always retired early at night; and rose early in the morning. We generally sat an hour, and sometimes longer, with Mr. and Mrs. R. and their lovely children."

[21] Manuscript: "her."

[22] *Enquirer*: "The long table was again surrounded by the numerous family, for this affectionate parent gathered round him at his meals, even his youngest grandchildren, who at their age are generally confined to nurseries. Instead of the assistance and attendance of slaves, which is the usual custom in the southern states, these sweet little creatures were attended to by their elder brothers and sisters, between whom they were placed. There was an affectionate and patriarchal simplicity in this, with which I was delighted—and this mutual aid and dependance methought, drew closer the bands of affinity. Our breakfast was not the substantial and Virginia breakfast I expected, nor indeed was the general mode of living at MONTICELLO, that of a Virginian planter, but accorded rather with my ideas of European elegance."

[23] Manuscript: "santorum." *Enquirer*: "apartments, which occupy the south wing, where not even his children enter without permission, and so sacred seemed his retirement, that when speaking of it to him, I always called it his *sanctum sanctorum*."

[24] Preceding two sentences omitted from *Enquirer*.

[25] *Enquirer*: "Mrs. R. withdrew to the apartment of her children, whom she instructs, and to whom she devotes the greater portion of her time. As for them, they seem to be the inseparable companions of this fond and indulgent mother, this intelligent and highly informed woman—With what delight could I dilate on her excellencies; but since I have consented to the publication of this journal, I have expunged from my manuscript, all that relates to her wise management, her private virtues, her peculiar opinions, which I sought after with eager avidity, knowing that to her modest and retiring excellence, even praise would be painful—otherwise the picture I could draw of this lovely and interesting woman, would charm every heart, and kindle a noble emulation in the bosom of every mother!—Happy mother, of the best of children—worthy daughter of the best of fathers!"

[26] *Enquirer* here adds "as no amusements are provided, and the descent and ascent of the mountain is so rough and difficult, that the fatigue of riding into the adjacent country, would not be compensated by any pleasure such a ride could afford."

[27] *Enquirer*: "drawing-room."

[28] Preceding three words interlined.

[29] *Enquirer*: "after breakfast, instead of withdrawing, Mr. Jefferson proposed our taking a view from the balcony on the roof of the house."

[30] Preceding three words added.

[31] *Enquirer*: "The morning was favorable to the study of landscape: The dark and heavy clouds which announced the coming storm, threw large masses of shade athwart the mountain side, which finely contrasted with the bright sun shine which gleamed on other spots. It was a prospect so rich and so varied, so vast and so sublime, that I could have gazed whole hours and days, without weariness. The view was too wide and grand for a painter's pencil, but it was calculated to rouse and fill a poet's soul. On the top of the house was a *ghan* [gong], instead of a bell—why he preferred the Chinese invention, to our mode of calling people together, I cannot tell, except it is on account of its newness and originality. Another was placed in a tree on the lawn, to summon the workmen to their meals."

[32] Preceding five words interlined.

[33] *Enquirer*: "It was designed for a lady's drawing-room when built, but soon found, on account of its situation in the

dome, to be too inconvenient for that use, and was abandoned to miscellaneous purposes."

[34] Preceding three words interlined.

[35] Manuscript: "suit."

[36] Smith here canceled "two."

[37] *Enquirer*: "three rooms, formerly filled by his valuable and extensive library, which I cannot but regret he ever parted with: Another opening from these for his cabinet, which is furnished with every convenience for a man of letters—communicating with his chamber in which he sleeps. The bed is built into the wall, in a sort of alcove, which in winter must be very comfortable, as it excludes every draught of air—but in summer, must for the same reason be very uncomfortable. I observed the same arrangement in all the chambers I saw. On the wall, at the foot of the bed was hung his pistols and sword, which I imagine has not been moved for many a year: against the wall, at the head of his bed, was a lamp, which enabled him, when he wished to read, to do it with great safety and convenience."

[38] For preceding nine words *Enquirer* substitutes "When in his garden this stand could be carried about and placed near him, and if I remember, there must have been near a hundred kinds. It is well worthy the adoption of all gentlemen and lady gardeners. Mr. J. appears extremely fond of this delightful occupation, and has for the purpose the nicest and most convenient utensils. His *cabinet*, where most of his hours were passed, was to me the most interesting spot in the house. I noticed every chair and table, and desk, and cabinet—examined many of the books, which were chiefly the old classical authors, generally in the original, and all the best English, Italian and French poets. A coarse looking volume attracted my notice: on opening, I found it to consist of pieces cut out of newspapers, and pasted on the blank-leaves of the book. The vol. was entitled *Libels*, and contained all that has so lavishly, during the *war* of political parties, been written against him. This indeed, will one day afford curious materials for the examination of the moralist and philosopher. When all the petty jealousies of contending parties, when their violence and their rancour, when all the misrepresentations and calumnies shall be cleared away by the bright rays of truth, then shall the character of the great and good man, rise in all the beauty and majesty of virtue, like his own native mountain, when the rays of the sun has dispersed the fogs and mists which conceal its beauties in the early morning. Even now, many of the prejudices, much of the violence, and I believe all of the bitterness of party spirit, have yielded to the influence of his proved wisdom as a statesman, and his virtue as a man, and when that *wisdom* and that *virtue*, are hallowed by the lapse of ages, should this volume survive, what a fable would it seem!"

[39] *Enquirer*: "at twilight on entering the tea-room, found no one but Mr. J. with whom we had a long and interesting conversation, in which he described with enthusiasm, the tranquillity he had enjoyed since his retirement from public life, and dilated on the heart-felt pleasures domestic scenes afforded him."

[40] *Enquirer* here adds "As I walked this mountain top, and inhaled these mountain breezes, I felt as if I breathed a purer atmosphere, and as if my soul with more elastic wing, could rise from '*nature, up to nature's God*.' There was too in the sighings of the breeze among the trees—'round me, & in the louder roar of distant winds sweeping through distant forests, a soothing power, which seemed to lift me through the little cares, and little pleasures of the world below! I was awakened from the sweet trance, into which these sights and sounds had lulled me, by the distant sound of the breakfast bell, and hastened back to enjoy in the society that encircled the hospitable board, the contemplation of *moral* beauty and *moral* grandeur."

[41] Manuscript: "drving."

[42] Preceding seven words added.

[43] *Enquirer* here adds "otherwise, I really think, we must have all been rolled down the mountain" and omits following sentence.

[44] *Enquirer* here adds "These, and a variety of other similar plans, he had designed, if executed, will greatly add to the interest and beauty, of scenery which

though grand and picturesque, is now too wild and uncultivated."

[45] *Enquirer*: "Indisposition and anxiety confined Mrs. R— to the nursery of her little invalid."

[46] Manuscript: "find."

[47] *Enquirer* here adds "our conversation was characterized by that tone of intimacy, which no circumstances less affecting, could have imparted. There was something indescribably interesting in the contemplation of this illustrious citizen, this enlightened philosopher, this successful statesman, whose name was familiar to the world—to see him who had guided the helm of empire, thus cheering the sick-room of his children, and fondly supporting the head of his daughter, had in it something so touching, that it was impossible for me to repress the tears which would rise from my swelling breast."

[48] Preceding description of early Tuesday activities omitted from *Enquirer*.

[49] Omitted word editorially added.

[50] Smith here canceled "common."

[51] Smith here canceled "nature &."

[52] Manuscript: "carrier." *Enquirer*: "career."

[53] Omitted word supplied from *Enquirer*.

[54] Word interlined.

[55] Manuscript: "flied." *Enquirer*: "field."

[56] *Enquirer*: "fame & happiness."

[57] Smith here canceled "time has ripen'd the early premium &."

[58] *Enquirer* here adds "both here, and at a fine estate he has in Bedford."

[59] *Enquirer*: "active mind designs more than many hands can execute, or."

[60] *Enquirer* here adds "pulling him down on the steps, climbing on his knees, and loading him with caresses."

[61] *Enquirer*: "and gave the promised kiss, as the reward to the victor. He was setting on the steps of the portico; the last rays of the setting sun, gleamed on his mild countenance; his white locks, waved in the evening breeze, and his arms encircled his lively little ones, glowing with health and beauty. What a picture! O! how I wished for a painter's skill, to have preserved it for the view of others—for myself, it would have been unnecessary; it is imprinted too deeply on my heart, for time or distance to efface."

[62] *Enquirer* here adds "to catch them if he could."

[63] Smith here canceled "but with the grater."

[64] Word interlined in place of an illegible word.

[65] Manuscript: "Randolp."

[66] Smith here canceled "expected."

[67] Preceding two words interlined in place of "general washington."

[68] Preceding eleven words interlined in place of "pusylanimity."

[69] Manuscript: "delieverd."

[70] *Enquirer* drastically condenses preceding three paragraphs and omits quotes from TJ's letters.

[71] Paragraph omitted from *Enquirer*.

[72] Preceding three words interlined.

[73] Manuscript: "say."

[74] Thus in manuscript. Smith probably intended "unwillingly."

[75] Smith here canceled "& vanity."

[76] Smith here canceled "animation."

[77] Smith here canceled "ever easy."

[78] *Enquirer* substitutes "In his mild accents, his meanest slave must recognize a friend. What then must be the feelings of a friend?" for remainder of this sentence and omits following sentence.

[79] Preceding three words interlined in place of "reserved."

[80] Word interlined in place of "form."

[81] *Enquirer* article concludes "and when once engaged, new circumstances were continually arising; new duties devolved, which has never since allowed me to leave the course, into which I had been impelled by the force of events."

# To Samuel Smith
## (of Maryland)

DEAR GENERAL Monticello July 29. 09.

By the last post I inclosed you a letter for S[t] Petersbg and promised by this something for Paris. The Secretary of State's letters will ensure every thing with Gen[l] Armstrong. the people of the world with whom I was formerly acquainted are all swept off the stage. my correspondents there are literary characters chiefly, few of whom I personally know. I have selected Dupont for his friendly & fatherly dispositions for his knolege of every thing, & the good footing he stands on with every body, & accordingly inclose you a letter for him. I am sure he will be useful towards all useful pursuits. accept renewed assurances of my esteem & respect. TH: JEFFERSON

PoC (DLC); at foot of text: "Gen[l] Smith"; endorsed by TJ. Enclosure: TJ to Pierre Samuel Du Pont de Nemours, 29 July 1809.

# From Jonathan Brunt

HON[BLE] MR. JEFFERSON, SIR, Nashville, (Ten[e]) July 31[st] 1809.—

I was at your house at Monticello the latter end of September, 1807, where I was treated by your Excellency with Christian hospitality—in order that you may, sir, recollect my person the better, I had on a blue coat & old white wool hat, and was on my way to Lynchburg, to get employment in the printing-office there, where I worked 1½ day, the owner of which paid me liberally: I then started off for Raleigh in North Carolina, but could not get regular employment there, only I had the priviledge of printing a pamphlet there—from thence I went to Augusta, in Georgia, where I arrived the latter end of November, 1807; if my memory serves me right, I directed a letter to your Excellency, dated the latter end of said month, requesting your interference for me, to Congress, to obtain restitution for the personal injuries I have received in America from evil-disposed persons. These personal domestic injuries, sir, are of an alarming nature: advancing age creeps on and I have not a proper home in said America: where, thro' the domestic[1] mania of wicked and idle speculations, not only my father's property, but the property of all his relations, has been sacrificed, to gratify the said intriguing corruption's cause, and I am left nearly[2] destitute.—In the spring, I wrote three different letters to mr. Madison on the same subject; but I have little hopes of their being noticed in an equal & proper way in my favour.—If mr. Jefferson please, you can see, possibly, the contents of them. If my father's property is sent to America, it would be very improper for me to attempt to return to England, especially while the political war is carrying on bet[ween] the two neighbouring nations.—The principa[l inten]tion of this letter is to request your Excellency to let me come to Monticello, to have a private room there, for I must die ere long, except Deity work another miracle for me.—The sooner I get out of this knavish world, the better.—I hope sir, your religious principles are the same you had in your youth.—Tho' I have wrote to a printer at New Orleans, about the printing business there, yet I do not want to go there:—The warmness of the climate is not the only reason.—I am now printing a small pamphlet, one of which I will send by post to Monticello—next month.— Permit me, sir, to subscribe myself your obed[t] ser[t]— Jonathan Brunt, printer.—

RC (MHi); torn at seal; addressed: "Thomas Jefferson, esq[r] Monticello, Virginia"; franked and postmarked; endorsed by TJ as received 11 Aug. 1809 and so recorded in SJL.

Jonathan Brunt (b. 1760), itinerant and apparently delusional printer, was a native of Derbyshire, England, who immigrated to the United States about 1794. Later, in 1809, 1811, and 1815, TJ gave him small sums in charity (Brunt, *Few Particulars in the Life of Jonathan Brunt, Junior, Printer & Bookseller*, 3d ed. [1797]; Brunt to TJ, 25 Oct. 1802, 30 Nov. 1807 [DLC]; Sowerby, no. 3320; *MB*, 2:1250, 1270, 1306).

Two extant letters to mr. madison dwelt on past and future efforts to poison Brunt (Brunt to James Madison, 29 Apr., 1 June 1809, DLC: Madison Papers). The pamphlet was probably *The Little Medly: containing short remarks on the genuine principles and exalted spirit of the glorious gospel of the New Testament . . .* (Knoxville, Tenn., 1809).

[1] Word interlined in place of "mea[n]."
[2] Word interlined.

# From William W. Hening

Dear Sir, Richmond 31[st] July 1809

Your letter of the 25[th] Inst. has just come to hand; and, for your attention to my request, be pleased to accept my thanks.

Of the MSS. received from you, those containing the laws from 1639 to 1660 inclusive, were deficient, except the acts of a few Sessions: contained in the MS. procured from the ex[rs] of M[r] Bland—I had no difficulty, however, in supplying the defect, having procured from M[r] E. Randolph a very correct M.S. embracing the laws of that period; which, on comparison, was even more correct than those in the M.S. received from you.—But on examining the acts of October 1660, I discover that they are merely a collection of "Orders," or resolutions, on private or local subjects; and none are given in the form of Acts.—Perhaps this may be the case, with all the MSS.; but I should be very glad to know the fact. If you have the acts of October 1660, will you be so obliging as to give me some idea of their contents; at least a few lines of the first act; which will enable me to ascertain whether they agree with mine.—I am now in the acts of 1658–9, and could conclude the volume before I enter upon those of Oct^r[1] 1660; which I would do, if any delay were necessary in getting a complete copy of the last mentioned acts. It was my wish, however, to have comprised in the first volume, all the laws prior to the commencement of Purvis;—and should the acts of October 1660, be found to differ from my collection, I shall be compelled to trouble you either for the volume in which[2] they are contained, or to have them transcribed immediately; for which I will pay an amanuensis, any price.

I am respectfl^y Yrs W^M: W: HENING

P.S. I have left with your friend George Jefferson, the 1^st Vol. of Hening & Munford's reports. The second shall be forwarded as soon as we can procure one in uniform binders WWH

RC (DLC); between signature and postscript: "M^r Jefferson"; endorsed by TJ as received 8 Aug. 1809 and so recorded in SJL.

John PURVIS published *A Complete Collection of all the Lavvs of Virginia now in force* (London, 1684; Sowerby, nos. 1832, 1837), which contained laws enacted between March 1661 and November 1682. TJ owned two copies of this first printing of Virginia statutes, one with a manuscript continuation.

[1] Word interlined.
[2] Manuscript: "wich."

# From John Monroe

SIR, Lexington Kent^y Aug^st 1^st 1809.

Permit me, an individual to approach you Sir, in your retreat from those toils and labours in which you have been for some time past so arduously engaged: and which have promoted the happiness, secured the freedom, and increased the prosperity of your country. Difficult and dangerous were the times of your Administration; but your mind perceived and your wisdom avoided the dangers. It was for you, Sir, to crush the head of treason, to disappoint the views and hopes of an Ambitious and wicked faction, and to defeat the intreagues and machinations of those foreign nations, whose jealousy and hatred caused them to plot our distruction. A firm reliance on your virtue procured from the people the approbation of your measures; and events have happened, since your retirement from Office, which have manifested the wisdom of your administration. You, sir, have smoothed the road of politics, for that inlightened Statesman, and honest man who has succeeded you in Office. And the nation feels security and confidence in his patriotism and Wisdom.

Do not suppose, Sir, that I offer you the incense of flattery. If you have made observations on my character, you must acknowledge I have too much pride to flatter any man on earth. And I hope I may be permitted to add (without the imputation of vanity) that I possess too much sincerity and justice to disguise the truth, where praise has been deserved.

You once honored me with an office, from which I was removed by the repeal of the law which created it. And I ceased Sir, from pressing you with solicitation for an other, during your Administration, least the solicitation of a friend who has always been known to promote your fame and honor, might possably imbarress you in your appointment. The cause of my silence has ceased, and I now, Sir, solicit your patronage & attention.

From public report, and from the relation of many circumstances, it has been supposed in this state, that there must be a change in the Executive of the Indiana territory. Should this event happen, I shall be much pleased with the appointment. But, Sir, my object is not to confine your[1] friendship for me, to that office alone. You have some personal acquaintance with me; you can therefore form a correct estimate of my capacity to discharge the duties of any office, either in the civil or Judiciary department.

It is true I now hold an important and highly responsable office in the judiciary of this State. And I have been much gratified by being told, that I have been usefull, and that my conduct has procured me the confidence of the people. But, Sir, the salary of that office, to a man, whose whole fortune consists in his industry his integrity and his talents, cannot be otherwise than oppressive. 750. dollars P an.: cannot maintain and educate a family. I am now becoming an old man; I have passed the Ordeal of poverty and misfortune, without reproach to my morals; I have risen out of my own ashes; I feel conscious I possess powers and courage to discharge the duties of any office which may be confided to me; and I trust that experience has taught me prudence.

In the frenzy of my misery, when my reason and discreation were for a time dethroned by the anguish of malignant oppression, and the dispair of unmeritted captivity, I wrote to you from Staunton

Virginia: I do assure you, Sir, I have never reviewed that act without lively sensibility of self reproach. But, Sir, I have hoped, that your discernment would trace my imprudence, to its true cause, the disorder of my mind; and that your benevolence would bury my misconduct in the misfortunes and miseries which I have suffered.

You, Sir, have the command of my fate. You Sir, can procure comfort to the ensuing of my life, and render my remaining years more happy to myself and family, and more usefull to my country. You, Sir, can select such office in, either, the Civil, or Judiciary department as will render me most service, and be most serviceable. On you then I trust my hopes: And whatever may be my fate, I do assure you, with truth and sincerity, I shall never cease to honor & revere that man who has secured the liberties, and promoted the happiness of my country.

Accept Sir my ardent wishes for your health & happiness and believe me to be

with respectfull regard y^r Obd^t Ser^t Jn^o Monroe

RC (DLC); addressed: "Thomas Jefferson Esquire Monticello Virginia"; franked and postmarked; endorsed by TJ as received 7 Sept. 1809 and so recorded in SJL.

John Monroe (d. 1814), attorney and judge, was a cousin of James Monroe and a dedicated Republican. In 1801 TJ appointed him United States attorney for the western district of Virginia, but he lost that office the following year when the Judiciary Act was repealed. Monroe represented Monroe County in the Virginia House of Delegates, 1802–03. By 1806 he had spent twelve months imprisoned for debt. Monroe was resident in Lexington as presiding judge of Kentucky's Fayette Circuit Court, 1807–11. He resigned to practice law in Cincinnati but soon returned to Lexington. Monroe unsuccessfully sought several territorial offices (TJ to John Monroe, 25 Apr. 1801 [DLC]; *JEP*, 1:402, 405 [6, 26 Jan. 1802]; Leonard, *General Assembly*, 228; John Monroe to James Monroe, 28 Apr. 1805 [ViW: Monroe Family Papers]; Henry Clay to Caesar Rodney, 15 Sept. 1810, and Richard Mentor Johnson to James Madison, 24 Oct. 1810 [DNA: RG 59, LAR, 1809–17]; Lexington Ky. *Reporter*, 9 Apr. 1814).

Late in 1809 William Henry Harrison was reappointed governor of INDIANA TERRITORY despite local opposition grounded on his support for the introduction of slaves into the territory and the perception that he had unduly sought to influence its legislature (John D. Barnhart and Dorothy L. Riker, *Indiana to 1816: The Colonial Period* [1971], 355–6n; *Terr. Papers*, 7:703–4, 705–7, 710–1; *JEP*, 2:130, 131 [19, 20 Dec. 1809]). Monroe had requested a loan from TJ in his 14 Sept. 1804 letter from STAUNTON VIRGINIA (DLC).

[1] Monroe here canceled "good offices."

## From Jonathan Shoemaker

My Friend Aug[t] 1[t] 1809 Washington City

Supposing from what the said when I Saw the at Monticelo it would be an accomadation I Send inclosed a Check on the Bank of Pensylvanie for 350$ and in bank notes 140$[1] with respect to higenbotoms draught on me I can't[2] Conveniently pay before the 1[t] Octo as the funds of the General Post Office are so low they Can't pay a Dollar in advance, & with dificulty their bills when due, the PMG Says they will be obliged to apply to Congress for an Appropriation to keep up the Esstablishment, and the late news of the disagreament of the British Government to the propositions of their Minester with our Government for the Settlement of our differances, alarms Every body in such away as makes it very dificult to Collect Money, & the general Opinion I find is that Produce of Every kind will be Low, & perhaps we shall have an nonintercourse with France & England. taking this state of things in view, discourages me very much from Coming to Shadwell as it must in that Case be a very Loosing business to us & would rather give up the Lease at once, Except thou would think it right to make some abatement in the rent, & I Should think right to fix it in Such away that Each of us Should partake of the Loss or gain in the rise or fall of the Market, that is that the rent Should be in Proportion to the Price of Flour in this way if the Averge price of Flour through the Season at Richmond Should be but 4$ per barrel than the rent to be 800$ per year if 5$ then 1000$ and if 6$ then 1200$ and so on Either more or Less and I would m[uch] rather Flour would be at 10$ if this Arangment, or Somthing like it should meet thy approbation & thou will please to Signify it by the nex[t] Mail, I Shall be ready to come on Emediately, thou will Please to ackno[w]ledge the Receipt of the Money Sent

Thy Friend truly Jonathan Shoemaker[3]

N.B. I hope we Shall not loose sight of Clearing the falls if I am there I Shall be very Willing to Contribute my Mite towards its Completion

RC (MHi); corner torn; above postscript: "Thomas Jefferson Esq"; endorsement by TJ torn. Recorded in SJL as received 6 Aug. 1809. Enclosed money noted as received 6 Aug. 1809 "on account of rent for the mill" (*MB*, 2:1246).

[1] Dollar amount interlined.

[2] Shoemaker here canceled "at Present."

[3] Manuscript: "Shoemker."

## To John Barnes

DEAR SIR Monticello Aug. 3. 09.

Your favor of the 26th ult. came to hand by the last post. that of June 23. had been recieved in due time, & I had not adverted to the copy of the order it inclosed respecting Genl K's Pensylvania bank stock. I now inclose you an order to recieve it. I am very happy at being released from the bank in a way to incommode nobody. I am distressed by old mr Shoemaker your neighbor, who has rented a mill of me two years without paying as yet a cent. he promises fair but never performs. can you give me any information of his circumstances. he has the mill for 3. years to come at 1250.D. a year.

I was so unfortunate as to lose one of my trunks of valuable effects & papers which came by water from Washington. it was stolen from the boat on James river, plundered & destroyed, and the culprit is under trial & will doubtless be hung for it. some such example is much wanting to render property waterborne secure. wishing you many years of health & happiness I salute you affectionately

TH: JEFFERSON

P.S. I inclose my bank book according to request, & a letter concerning some things addressed to you for me from N. Orleans, but of which I fear you have heard nothing since, as I have not.

PoC (DLC); below signature: "Mr Barnes." Enclosure: TJ to Jonathan Smith, 3 Aug. 1809, directing him "to pay to the order of John Barnes the amount of the half year's dividend, due & payable on General Kosciuszko's twenty shares of Pensylvania bank stock" (RC from Roy G. Fitzgerald, Dayton, Ohio, 1950, below signature: "To Jonathan Smith esq. Cashier of the bank of Pensylva Philadelphia," notation, probably by Smith, at foot of text: "Charge Tho Jefferson 320$"; Dft in ViU: TJP-ER, in Barnes's hand, dated July 1809). Enclosed bank book not found.

Barnes's two preceding letters, of 23 JUNE and 26 July, both not found, are recorded in SJL as received from Georgetown on 29 June and 31 July 1809. The letter about SOME THINGS ADDRESSED TO YOU FOR ME may have been a duplicate of TJ to William Brown, 22 May 1809.

## From James Madison

DEAR SIR Montpellier Aug 3. 1809

Herewith you will receive a packet, which being wrapt up in a large one for me, from the Dept of State, was taken out of the mail of yesterday, and not observed before the rider had set out.

I find myself under the mortifying necessity of setting out tomorrow morning for Washington. The intricate state of our affairs with England produced by the mixture of fraud & folly in her late conduct, and the important questions to be decided as to the legal effect of the failure of the arrangement of Ap[l] on our commercial relations with her, are thought by the Heads of Dep[t] to require that I should join them. The main question is whether the non-intercourse act as continued at the last Session comes into force ag[st] England, thereby putting her on the same footing with France.

You will see by the instructions to Erskine as published by Canning, that the latter was as much determined that there should be no adjustment, as the former was that there should be one. There must however have been other instructions comprehending the case of the Chesapeak, and other communications from Canning accompanying the B. Orders of Ap[l] 26. as referred to in Erskines Quieting declaration last made to M[r] Smith. I believe also that Erskine's letter to Canning not disclosed by the latter, will not warrant his ascribing to Erskine, the statement of conversations with M[r] G. M[r] S. & myself. Pinkney will also disavow what Canning has put into his mouth.

I presume, from letters which reached me yesterday, that M[r] Smith has communications from Paris as late as the 10 or 12 of June; whether by the return of M[r] Coles or another conveyance is uncertain. The disavowal in England reached Paris the day after the arrival of the arrangemt[1] transmitted by M[r] Gelston. Our affairs with France had taken no decided turn; owing as alledged, to the absence & occupation of the Emperor. The return of Gelston will probably put us in possession of a final estimate.

Accept my sincerest respect & Attach[t] JAMES MADISON

RC (DLC: Madison Papers); endorsed by TJ as received 3 Aug. 1809 and so recorded in SJL. Enclosures: (1) John Armstrong to TJ, 11 June 1809. (2) Jacques Besse to TJ, 5 Aug. 1808 (DLC). (3) Madame de Corny to TJ, 29 Apr. 1809. (4) Pierre Samuel Du Pont de Nemours to TJ, 12 June 1809. (5) Alexander von Humboldt to TJ, 12 June 1809. (6) Tadeusz Kosciuszko to TJ, 20 May 1809. (7) Lacépède to TJ, 31 May 1809. (8) Lafayette to TJ, 12 June 1809. (9) Daniel Lescallier to TJ, 2 May 1809. (10) Claude Alexandre Ruelle to TJ, 24 May 1809. (11) William Short to TJ, 27 May 1809. (12) Augustin François Silvestre to TJ, 8 June 1809. (13) Antoine François Tardieu to TJ, 30 May 1809. (14) Madame de Tessé to TJ, 12 June 1809. (15) David Bailie Warden to TJ, 20 May 1809.

The publication in American newspapers of George Canning's INSTRUCTIONS to David Erskine revealed that in exchange for withdrawing the Orders in Council, the British foreign minister had expected the United States to agree to withdraw the embargo against Great Britain but leave it in force against France, renounce all trade with colonies of Great Britain's enemies, and agree to the capture of American vessels attempting to trade with France. Along with a copy of the king's 24 May 1809 order in council reversing the new and somewhat less stringent orders of 26 Apr. 1809, British envoy Erskine also sent the secretary of state a QUIETING DECLARATION intended to appease the United States government and express his regret that their provisional agreement had not been confirmed by the king. Erskine's violation of his instructions led to his recall and replacement by Francis James Jackson (Washington *National Intelligencer*, 24, 26 July 1809; Erskine to Robert Smith, 31 July 1809, *ASP, Foreign Relations*, 3:301–2; Brant, *Madison*, 5:66–7; TJ to Madison, 27 Apr. 1809).

[1] Madison here canceled "here."

# To Samuel H. Smith

DEAR SIR Monticello Aug. 3. 09.

The inclosed letter came to hand yesterday by mail after your departure. presuming it could not find you at the President's, I have thought it best to return it to you at Washington where you will probably find it on your return. I hope mrs Smith & yourself will have performed your journey in good health & without accident, and shall be very happy if you shall have found the same pleasure in the excursion, which we have recieved from your agreeable visit. believing such changes of scene equally advantageous to the mind as to the body, we cannot give up the hope of a repetition of it, and that I may be able to shew mrs Smith who is fond of gardening, the progress I shall have made the next year in the improvement of the grounds around me, as well those of pleasure as utility. my daughter is well enough to come downstairs to-day, & with the other members of the family join me in affectionate salutations to mrs Smith & yourself, & in the hope that you found your little family well on your return.

TH: JEFFERSON

RC (DLC: Henley Smith Papers); addressed: "Mr Samuel Harrison Smith Washington Col."; franked. PoC (DLC); endorsed by TJ. Enclosure not found.

# From Josef Yznardy

HONORABLE THOMAS JEFFERSON. Cadiz 3 de Agosto de 1809.

Muy Sor mio, y de todo mi Respecto; Aunque V.E. ha sesado de ser Presidente de los Estados Unidos, no lo han mis obligaciones de tener presente las distinciones de amistad que siempre usò conmigo, y menos las obligaciones en que me considero de haserlas vinculos perpetuos para que le suplique lo entìenda asi para mandarme en quanto guste.

El dador de la presente serà el Cavallero secretario de la Orden de

Cartos Tercero, primer Oficial que fue dela Secretaria de Estado de S.M.C. y aora Ministro Plenipotenciario, y Embiado Extraordinario serca del Presidente de los Estados Unidos, queme tomo la libertad de recomendar â V. E. como â Madama su Esposa, personas ambas las mas amables, y de trato sensillo, y genuino.

Qualesquiera atenciones que V.E. haga â estos Señores las estimarè como una prueba de la amistad que siempre le he merecido, y creo firmemente que asi lo experimentàran, mientras tengo el honor de asegurar â V.E. le deceo la mejor salud, y que Nuestro Señor guarde su vida m[s] a[s].

Ex[mo] Señor BLMa VE su mas ob[te] Seno[r] JOSEF YZNARDY

EDITORS' TRANSLATION

HONORABLE THOMAS JEFFERSON. Cadiz 3 August 1809.

Dear Sir, and with all due respect; although your excellency is no longer president of the United States, bearing in mind the marks of friendship that you have always shown me, and to a lesser extent the obligations under which I consider myself to be perpetually bound, I beg you to understand that you may command me to do whatever you wish.

The bearer of the present letter is the secretary of the Order of Cartos Tercero, an official who was first secretary of state to His Most Catholic Majesty and is now minister plenipotentiary, and sent so extraordinarily to the president of the United States, that I take the liberty to recommend him and his wife to your excellency, both of whom are most friendly, unpretentious and genuine.

Whatever attention your excellency gives to these noble people, I will regard as proof that I have always deserved you as a friend, and I firmly believe that they will feel befriended, while I have the honor to assure your excellency that I wish you the best of health and that Our Lord guards your life for many years.

Excellent Sir, I kiss your hand, your most obedient servant

JOSEF YZNARDY

RC (CSmH: JF); in a clerk's hand, with closing and signature by Yznardy; dateline above closing; endorsed by TJ as received 30 Oct. 1809 and so recorded in SJL. Enclosed in Luis de Onís to TJ, 17 Oct. 1809. Translation by Dr. Jennifer McCune.

Josef Yznardy was appointed United States consul at Cádiz by TJ in 1801. Previously he had often acted as deputy to his son Joseph Yznardi Jr., who held this consulship from 1793 until John Adams tried to replace him late in his presidency. TJ sometimes purchased sherry through the Yznardys. In 1797 the elder Yznardy began a conflict with Joseph Israel, an American sea captain, that led to litigation on both sides of the Atlantic. Earlier in 1809 the Department of State overruled an effort by Yznardy to lease the duties of his office to Richard S. Hackley (*JEP*, 1:381, 403, 405 [18 Feb. 1801, 6, 26 Jan. 1802]; *PTJ*, 25:202–4, 27:60; Madison, *Papers, Sec. of State Ser.*, 1:32n, 2:50, 53n; Sowerby, no. 3267; James Madison to TJ, 9 Apr. 1809).

## From C. & A. Conrad & Company

SIR Washington[1] August 4th 1809

As we have just finished an edition of Shakspeares Plays for which your name appears on our list as a Subscriber we have used the freedom to address You requesting that when convenient you would send to the store of Daniel Rapine Esqr of this place for your copy, or point out the manner in which it may be sent to you.

We have also taken the liberty to hand you a bill for the Artillerists Companion which as the sum cannot conveniently be remitted we request you[2] to pay to Mr Rapine.

Respectfully Your Obt Svts

for C & A CONRAD & Co<br>of Philadelphia<br>SAML CONRAD

RC (MHi); dateline adjacent to signature; endorsed by TJ as received 6 Aug. 1809 and so recorded in SJL.

C. & A. Conrad & Company was a bookselling and publishing concern at 30 Chestnut Street, Philadelphia. It adopted that name in 1807 when Cornelius and Andrew Conrad joined a firm established in 1800 by their brother John Conrad. In 1807 Conrad & Co. contracted with Meriwether Lewis to publish the journals of the Lewis and Clark Expedition, but the firm failed in 1812 before the project could be completed (Jackson, *Letters of Lewis and Clark*, 2:392-7).

TJ is not known to have acquired the Conrad EDITION of *The plays of William Shakespeare* (Philadelphia, 1809–10), which reprinted a version edited by Samuel Johnson, George Steevens, and Isaac Reed that TJ did own (Sowerby, no. 4539). TJ had subscribed in 1807 to Anne Louis de Tousard, *American Artillerist's Companion, or Elements of Artillery*, 3 vols. (Philadelphia, 1809–13; Sowerby, no. 1160). The work was issued serially, and this letter is subjoined to a BILL to TJ for $12 for six numbers sent individually between 27 Nov. 1807 and 25 May 1809, with a subjoined penciled notation that another $2 had been billed for a seventh number of this work on 20 Oct. 1809. After a reminder from Conrad & Co. and some initial confusion about whether this bill had already been paid, TJ remitted $12 in 1811 (Conrad & Co. to TJ, [received 15 Apr. 1810]; TJ to Conrad & Co., 24 Apr. 1811; *MB*, 2:1265). In 1800 Michael and John Conrad and Daniel RAPINE had opened Washington's first bookstore (Bryan, *National Capital*, 1:383, 435, 516).

[1] Conrad here canceled "July."

[2] Preceding three words interlined.

## To John Armstrong

SIR Monticello Aug. 5. 09.

The bearers hereof, mr Alexander McRae & Major John Clarke proposing to visit France on their private concerns, I take the liberty of presenting them to your notice & patronage. mr McRae has been a member of the council of state of Virginia, & Lieut Governor, highly esteemed for his talents & correctness of principle, moral & political.

Maj[r] Clarke has long also been in public employ, as Director of the armoury of this state, recommended as such by his great mechanical ingenuity, & personal worth. any good offices you may be so kind as to render them will be deservedly bestowed; & their knolege of the present state of our affairs may enable them to add acceptably to your information.

I take this occasion of thanking you for the many kind attentions I recieved from you while our public duties connected us, & for the valuable services rendered in your station, & which aided me so materially in the discharge of my functions. be assured of my constant & great attachment & respect. TH: JEFFERSON

PoC (DLC); at foot of text: "His Excellency Gen[l] Armstrong"; endorsed by TJ. Enclosed in TJ to Alexander McRae, 5 Aug. 1809.

## To Alexander McRae

DEAR SIR Monticello Aug. 5. 09.

I sincerely wish you success in the object of the visit which yourself & Maj[r] Clarke propose to make to Europe. to your country it promises advantage, & I hope it will yield it to yourselves also. as you seem sensible of the danger to which it will expose you, under the laws of those countries, I need say nothing on that head but that the secrecy enjoined on me shall be observed. the letters which I now inclose you for our ministers at Paris and London are merely of general introduction. I have said nothing of your object, because, feeling that I ought not, either on public or personal considerations to make myself an actor in any undertaking within another country which, however innocent & even laudable, it's laws think proper to deem criminal, I think it would be improper to implicate our ministers in it. their station & habits would render them awkward & ineffectual aids in attempts of that kind. it is in the obscurer walks of life you will find the characters best qualified to cooperate in your object. praying you to stick a wafer in the letters before delivery, & wishing you a pleasant voyage & happy issue from your undertaking, I salute you with esteem & respect. TH: JEFFERSON

PoC (DLC); at foot of text: "Alex[r] M[c]Rae esq."; endorsed by TJ. Enclosures: (1) TJ to John Armstrong, 5 Aug. 1809. (2) TJ to William Pinkney, 5 Aug. 1809.

## To William Pinkney

DEAR SIR Monticello. Aug. 5. 09.

The bearers hereof, mr Alexander M[c]Rae, & Major John Clarke proposing to go to Great Britain on their private concerns, I take the liberty of presenting them to your notice & patronage. mr M[c]Rae, a lawyer of distinction, has been a member of the council of state of Virginia & Lieut[t] Governor, highly esteemed for his talents & correctness of principle moral & political. Maj[r] Clarke was long also in public employ as Director of the Armoury of this state, recommended as such by his great mechanical ingenuity & personal worth. any good offices you may be so kind as to render them will be deservedly bestowed; & their knolege of the present state of our affairs may enable them to add acceptably to your information.

I am happy in an occasion of expressing to you my great esteem for you personally, and the satisfaction with which I noted the correctness, both as to matter & manner, with which you discharged the public duties you were so kind as to undertake at my request. I witnessed too with pleasure the esteem with which you inspired my successor, then more immediately engaged in correspondence with you. Accept the just tribute of mine also, & of my great respect & consideration. TH: JEFFERSON

RC (MdHi: photostat in Vertical Files); addressed: "His Excellency William Pinckney esq Minister Plenipotentiary of the US. of America at London." PoC (DLC); endorsed by TJ. Enclosed in TJ to Alexander McRae, 5 Aug. 1809.

William Pinkney (1764–1822) was American minister plenipotentiary to Great Britain, 1807–11. During a long public career he opposed the new federal constitution at the 1788 Maryland ratification convention; sat in that state's legislature and on its executive council; served in London as a claims commissioner under the Jay Treaty, 1796–1804; and returned to England in 1806 as joint commissioner with James Monroe, with whom he negotiated a commercial treaty that TJ immediately rejected. One of America's preeminent lawyers, Pinkney frequently argued cases before the Supreme Court and was United States attorney general, 1811–14. With a stint in between as minister plenipoteniary to Russia and to Naples, 1816–18, he represented Maryland in the United States House of Representatives, 1815–16, and in the Senate from 1819 until his death (*ANB*; *DAB*; Robert M. Ireland, *The Legal Career of William Pinkney, 1764–1822* [1986]; *JEP*, 2:35 [19, 21 Apr. 1806]).

# From Craven Peyton

DEAR SIR Monteagle Augt 6th 09.

I have waited this length of time under An expectation of Mr John Akers comeing to purchase a part of my Land togethar with yours, you wished me to sell. If he did not come by the last of July I was not to expect him, himself & Lons had fifty Thousand Dollars to lay Out in land, If it is entirely agreeable to you, & it can be done without throwing Any obsticle in the way of Obtaining those rights now under age. I shall be glad for you to recave the proparty, for several reasons,[1] several persons have been pushing me for the warehouse Money togethar for Othar rents, when they become due, my refusial makes them beleave I am unwilling to pay my debts, howevar I am quite willing to encountar Any thing in Any way whatevar to rendar You the least service in my power, & am in hopes no inconvenience can arise from the transfer being made. Any day that will suite your convenience I will come up.

with great esteem C PEYTON

RC (ViU: TJP); endorsed by TJ as received 6 Aug. 1809 and so recorded in SJL.

Craven Peyton (1775–1837), an Albemarle County merchant and landowner, leased TJ's farm at Shadwell from 1799 to 1801. His wife, Jane Jefferson Lewis Peyton, was the daughter of Charles Lilburne Lewis and TJ's sister Lucy Jefferson Lewis. About 1802 Peyton moved to Monteagle, the Lewis family estate southeast of Monticello, and by 1805 he had acquired it from his impecunious in-laws (Merrow Egerton Sorley, *Lewis of Warner Hall: The History of a Family* [1935, repr. 1991], 352; Merrill, *Jefferson's Nephews*, 50–4, 381–3; *MB*, 2:968n; Woods, *Albemarle*, 295).

At the time of his death in 1793, Bennett Henderson owned much of the town of Milton and adjacent property crucial to TJ's ambitious plans for a complex of mills and warehouses. Henderson's property was subsequently divided into four sections, with a portion of each reserved for his widow, Elizabeth Lewis Henderson. Each of the ten surviving children received four plots, one in each section, in a division by lottery in the autumn of 1801. TJ convinced Peyton to act as his agent by buying the numerous subdivisions thus created with funds provided by TJ and holding the purchases in his own name until TJ left office. Between 1801 and 1804 Peyton acquired most of the Henderson estate as requested, and during August 1809 he formally deeded the properties in question to TJ, although the deed was not recorded for two more years.

TJ ultimately derived little benefit and much frustration from the Henderson land purchase. In April 1803 Peyton was drawn into a legal action with Bennett Henderson's eldest son, John Henderson, who had begun constructing a canal to bring the waters of the Rivanna to the family mill seat. Peyton had previously purchased the lands affected, but John Henderson claimed that when his mother had sold them she had reserved to him the right to run a canal through them. In December 1803 Peyton secured an injunction against Henderson, but three months later the Albemarle County Court dissolved it and dismissed the case. Peyton next laid a bill of complaint composed by TJ before the Superior Court of Chancery for the Richmond District in May 1804. He obtained a second injunction against Henderson, but in March 1805 that court also decided against him, and in January 1812 the Virginia Court of Appeals upheld the lower court's ruling. TJ ultimately bought out John Henderson, only to face a similar claim from David Michie. Furthermore, three of the Hendersons later contended that their rights as minors had been violated in the original purchases, and in 1817 TJ had to pay them back-rent and repurchase their lands (Malone, *Jefferson*, 6:505–7; Merrill, *Jefferson's Nephews*, 58–70, 383–6; *MB*, 2:1125–6, 1129, 1131, 1330; TJ to Peyton, 15 Jan. 1801, 30 Apr. 1804, Peyton to TJ, 29 Apr. 1803, Declaration of Elizabeth Henderson, 7 Aug. 1803 [all ViU: TJP]; Craven and Jane Peyton's Conveyance of the Henderson Lands, [22 Aug. 1809]).

LONS may refer to Gabriel Long, owner of Long's Ordinary in Spotsylvania County (*MB*, 2:987).

[1] Repeated comma omitted.

# To William C. Rives

DEAR SIR Monticello Aug. 6. 09.

Under the constant hope of an early departure for Bedford, I have been hitherto detained by the prevalence of a disease in our neighborhood, and particularly among my own people. altho' abated, it still has not left us, and the importance of attention to it, still detains me here and for a time which cannot be ascertained. the expectation that every case might be the last, has prevented my sooner informing you of the delay, and proposing that my intended absence, which will be short, should no longer postpone the commencement of the course of study which you propose to undertake with us. should the situation of my people permit me to set out on my journey, before you come, I will leave with mr Bankhead the books which I would first recommend for your reading. with every desire to be useful to you I pray you to accept the assurances of my great esteem & respect.

TH: JEFFERSON

RC (DLC: Rives Papers); addressed: "M^r William Reeves near Warminster"; franked; endorsed by Rives. PoC (MHi); endorsed by TJ.

William Cabell Rives (1793–1868), a native of Amherst County, began legal studies with TJ in 1809 after being removed from the College of William and Mary, apparently for dueling. He was admitted to the Charlottesville bar in 1814. Rives represented Nelson County in the Virginia House of Delegates, 1817–20, and after moving to an estate called Castle-Hill, was delegate for Albemarle County, 1822–23. During a political career in which he was successively a Jeffersonian Republican, a Jacksonian Democrat, and a Whig, Rives's subsequent offices included service in the United States House of Representatives, 1823–29, two appointments as minister to France, 1829–32 and 1849–53, three discontinuous intervals in the United States Senate between 1834 and 1845, and a year in the Confederate Congress. Between 1859 and 1868 he also published an important but uncompleted early biography of James Madison (*ANB*; *DAB*; Bishop James Madison to TJ, 31 May 1809; Raymond C. Dingledine, "The Early Life of William Cabell Rives, 1793–1832" [master's thesis, University of Virginia, 1941]).

# To Louis Marie Turreau

Monticello Aug. 6. 09.

Th: Jefferson presents his friendly salutations to General Turreau, and incloses a letter which came to him under cover from M. de. la Cepede. he is happy in the occasion it furnishes him of assuring General Turreau of his great esteem & respect, and his regret that the distance and infrequency of the posts from this place, will have produced several days delay in the reciept of this.

PoC (MHi); dateline at foot of text; endorsed by TJ. Not recorded in SJL. Enclosure not found.

Louis Marie Turreau de Garambouville (1756–1816) was the French minister plenipotentiary to the United States, 1804–11. A native of Evreux, France, he fought in both the American and French revolutions. During the latter Turreau rose to the rank of lieutenant general and distinguished himself by brutally but successfully quelling revolts in the Vendée and Switzerland. Rumored to be a wife-beating profligate, after his return to France he separated from his wife and unsuccessfully pursued the late empress Josephine Bonaparte, whose own marriage to Napoleon had been annulled in December 1809 (*Biographie universelle*, 42:300–3; Brant, *Madison*, 4:266–79; Dolley Madison, *Selected Letters*, 62; Turreau, *Mémoires pour servir à l'Histoire de la Guerre de la Vendée* [Paris, 1824]).

# From William Dawson

DEAR SIR, Richmond August. 7th 1809

I have a suit at Law now depending in the Superiour Court of Loudoun County which Commences on the first monday in September next and my Attorneys informs me it will be tryed at that term, I will thank you to please to advise Mr George Jefferson to pay me my fee for the declarations for the Insureing your Mills, and Millers Houses, I left my account with you

I am Sir with Sentiments of due respects[1] your Obedient Servant

W DAWSON

RC (MHi); endorsed by TJ as received 23 Aug. 1809 and so recorded in SJL.

On 23 May 1809 William Dawson presented TJ his ACCOUNT for an $11.40 balance due for supplying a valuation of the Shadwell Mills (MS in MHi; in Dawson's hand and signed by him; at head of text: "Thomas Jefferson Esquire to Wm Dawson"; notation by TJ at foot of text: "Aug. 27. 09. gave order for it on G. Jefferson").

[1] Manuscript: "respets."

## From George Gilpin

Dear Sir, Alexandria August 7th 1809

A Sense of duty and respect has for a long time urged me to write to & to thank you for a favor which you conferred on me as an individual and also for that Obligation which I lay under with the rest of my fellow Citizens for the great and eminent Services rendered to our country as President of the United States for during the whole time it did appear to me that your desire and constant Aim was to establish compleat civil & Religious liberty and by your example precept and authority endeavoured to order things that our Country if no more might be made happy on this Globe and remain an Assileum for the persecuted and opressed, you have as far as possible given the United States a fair trial how long her Citizens will preserve the blessing time must Shew the rapid prosperity of this Country has excited in a part of the inhabitants a thirst for gain that has produced bad Symptoms, and England with whoes intrest our carreing trade interferes will use all her art and by every means in her power draw a part of the people of these States to her intrest and by their means endeavour to distract our counsels and divide us if She can and there are disappointed men who will undertake any thing, England has assumed a consequence in the Scale of nations which She cannot Support without the whole of the carreing trade the profits of which is to enable her Merchants to lend the goverment money & to rear Seamen to man her fleets when[1] they ar wanted to monopolise all the profitable part of the Carreing trade has been her Aim for many years, any nation or Set of men who think that[2] England will give up any part that She can hold will find them Selves mistaken and I believe the proposial Sent by Oakley to Mr Erskine a trick, the Embargo and non intercourse had distressed her the Baltick was shut and Supplies of navel Stores and provisions must be had for, Europe and the West Indies and that immediately and to encurge her fleet by prizes for that will come to pass, Mr Jackson has not Arived yet. I hope that you will pardon me for troubling you by writing on[3] a Subject you understand much better than I do,

I wish you health and happiness. I am with high considerations of respect your very Humble Servt,

George Gilpin

RC (DLC); at foot of text: "To the Honl Thomas Jefferson"; endorsed by TJ as received 23 Aug. 1809 and so recorded in SJL.

George Gilpin (ca. 1741–1813), a merchant, surveyor, and postmaster in Alexandria, was a native of Cecil County, Maryland. During the American Revolution he had been a colonel of the Fairfax

County militia and served on the Fairfax County Committee. Gilpin was a director of the Bank of Alexandria and the Potomac River Company and a justice of the peace and judge of the orphans' court by TJ's appointment (T. Michael Miller, *Artisans and Merchants of Alexandria, Virginia 1780–1820* [1991–92], 1:161–2; *JEP*, 1:388, 404, 423, 520, 545, 2:56, 59 [2 Mar. 1801, 6 Jan., 27 Apr. 1802, 7, 20 Jan. 1804, 9, 18 Nov. 1807]; *Alexandria Gazette, Commercial and Political*, 28 Dec. 1813).

[1] Manuscript: "when when."
[2] Manuscript: "that that."
[3] Manuscript: "on on."

# From Daniel Davis

Dear Sir, Aug^t 8. 1809.

If you have any Lackir Varnish. will you be so good as to lend or give me a few Drops, I am at a great loss to know how to Stain Gun Barrels. and I wish to make some experiment with this Kind of Varnish, M^r W^m Stewart who formerly lived with you informed me that this was used in the Compound of Staining, please excuse this liberty,

& accept my Sencire respects Daniel Davis

RC (MHi); dateline adjacent to signature; addressed: "Tho^s Jefferson Esquire Monticello"; endorsed by TJ as received 9 Aug. 1809.

Daniel Davis was a resident of Albemarle County (Bond between Tarleton Goolsby and Davis, 19 Jan. 1804, ViHi: Barbour Family Papers). William STEWART worked as a blacksmith at Monticello from 1801 to 1807, when he was dismissed for drunkenness (*MB*, 2:1052n; Pierson, *Jefferson at Monticello*, 69).

# Agreement with William McGehee

William MacGehe agrees with Thomas Mann Randolph, acting for Thomas Jefferson, that he will serve the said T.J. as Overseer, over not more than twenty hands, upon his plantation where John H. Craven now lives, during the year 1800 and ten, for the sum of fifty pounds in money, six hundred lbs of net pork, seventy lbs of Beef, twelve Barrels of Corn, one Barrel of flour and the priviledge of keeping one negroe of his own to be maintained out of the said provisions.[1]

Tho^s M. Randolph engages and agrees for the said Tho^s Jefferson as follows viz. that the money and provisions and the advantage above mentioned shall be paid, furnished, and allowed: that the s^d W^m MacGehe shall moreover be entitled to expect an additional compensation, at the discretion of the said Tho^s Jefferson, if his conduct shall be such as to give entire satisfaction to the s[d] T.J. at the end of the year, and the crop made should prove good enough to justify such gratuity: farther that the s[d] W.M. shall have the priviledge of keeping geese and Turkeys, in a reasonable number, upon condition of his giving up one half in number and value of all increase of the same to the s[d] T.J., and of his allways confining the geese within the pastures: lastly that the said W.M. may raise flax, hemp, and cotton, sufficient to cloath his own family, upon condition that he shall give equal attention to raising such crops for his employer, and shall diligently superintend and enforce the manufacturing requisite to cloath the negroes on the plantation; which shall constitute his right to the said priviledge, as it shall be his compensation for the said care. Witness our hands this 8[th] August 1809.

W[M] M[C] GEHEE
THO: M. RANDOLPH

teste JOHN FAGG

MS (MHi); in Randolph's hand, signed by McGehee, Randolph, and Fagg; endorsed by TJ as an "Agreement" with McGehee of this date.

William McGehee served as overseer at TJ's Tufton property from 25 Dec. 1809 to 15 Nov. 1811. Before that he had been an overseer for no more than a year apiece at three other plantations nearby. TJ described McGehee as industrious and skilled in old agricultural practices but resistent to innovation, insubordinate, discontented, and so harsh a disciplinarian that in an earlier position he had routinely carried a gun for fear of attack from the slaves he supervised. His father may have been the William McGehee who in 1774 sold TJ the Colle tract adjoining Monticello (*MB*, 1:344n, 2:1250, 1271; TJ to James Madison, 16 Aug. 1810; Woods, *Albemarle*, 259–60).

Thomas Mann Randolph (1768–1828) had close ties to the Jefferson family from the time of his birth. TJ's mother was Randolph's second cousin and his father, Peter Jefferson, had served as guardian to Randolph's namesake father. These ties were strengthened when Randolph married TJ's eldest daughter Martha in 1790 and built a home at Edgehill near Monticello (1798–1800). Randolph often looked after TJ's concerns when his father-in-law was absent. He shared many intellectual interests with TJ, including classics and science, which he pursued during his education at home, the College of William and Mary, and Edinburgh University. Though he did not graduate, Randolph applied his studies to scientific agriculture and became a respected botanist. He generally supported TJ's policies during a public career that included service as a United States congressman (1803–07), colonel in the regular army and lieutenant colonel of militia in the War of 1812, Virginia governor (1819–22), and delegate (1823–25). Late in life Randolph lost control of most of his property and became estranged from TJ and his own family. He eventually reconciled with his wife and children, who had moved permanently to Monticello on TJ's retirement in 1809, and he died and was buried at Monticello (*ANB*; *DAB*; William H. Gaines Jr., *Thomas Mann Randolph: Jefferson's Son-in-Law* [1966]; Lay, *Architecture*, 118–9).

John H. CRAVEN leased five hundred acres of land at Tufton and Monticello from TJ, 1800–09 (Betts, *Farm Book*, 168–71). When Craven's lease expired, TJ made Randolph responsible for the supervision of Tufton.

[1] In the right margin at this point Randolph added the following notation:

| "money | £50 | |
|---|---|---|
| pork | 9–18 | @ $5\frac{1}{2}$$ |
| beef | 17–6 | 3d |
| corn | 7– 4 | 2$ |
| flour | 1–10 | 5$ |
| | £68– 9–6" | |

# To Jonathan Shoemaker

Sir Monticello Aug. 8. 09.

I have to acknolege the reciept by the last post of your letter of the 1st inst. & in it of 490.D. that is to say a draught on the Philadelphia bank for 350.D. & 140.D. in bank bills. as mr Higginbotham's order had been drawn on the rent due the first year, he was, in all justice entitled to the first money recieved and the rather as he had waited with indulgence a twelvemonth. I therefore paid it immediately to him, & am still where I was as to my engagements at Philadelphia. these I explained to you, and the degree to which I should be injured by a disappointment. and I have still no other resource to look to but from you, which I hope therefore you will take into consideration. as to the difficulties of the post office they may be proper in answer to the demands of the creditors for the mail stage, but not to me whose claim is on the profits of my mill which you have been so long recieving. trusting to the effect of the motives which I am persuaded regulate your conduct, I hope that the pressure & the justice of my case will urge you to relieve me. you know that the rent of the 1st quarter of the 3d year is now become due.

You propose giving up the Lease unless I will consent to lower the rent of the mill according to a scale which you state. this I can by no means do. on the contrary I should insist on considerably enlarging it at the termination of the present lease. we now know the quantity of wheat which might be counted on were the mill well managed and in hands which possessed the confidence of the customers, & that this would justify the requiring double the rent I now have, & this would be but indifferent interest on the money the mill has cost me. I am aware that the present times are critical & dubious for the sale of produce. I suppose indeed that a non intercourse must take place. but this measure will be temporary, and cannot be a ground for a permanent abatement of my rent. but desiring to take no advantage of the times which you apprehend will make this lease ruinous to you, & which induce you to propose the alternative of surrendering it, if that of abating the rent be declined, I prefer the surrender & therefore accede to that proposition. fix therefore any day for the termination of the lease, not earlier than 15. days after I shall have recieved your letter or other act surrendering it, and not later than 30. days from the date of this letter, & I agree to it. I hope you will come yourself to redeliver the possession in the condition in which our articles require the redelivery. I much rather do this than continue in a course of disappointment and misunderstanding with my tenant. in the mean time I wish you every happiness.

TH: JEFFERSON

PoC (MHi); at foot of first page: "Jonathan Shoemaker"; endorsed by TJ.

## To Jones & Howell

MESSRS JONES & HOWELL Monticello Aug. 10. 09

It is with real mortification that, instead of a remittance for the last supply of rod & iron, now due, I am obliged to send you this letter. yet my feelings on the failure will not permit me to be merely silent. I have now been for 13. or 14. years a customer of your house & of it's predecessors, and have never failed beyond a few days over the term of remittance, except on one occasion, I believe, where it had escaped attention. my income is mainly from the produce or the rents of tobacco & wheat farms. knowing that this came in but once a year, and owning a mill rented at 1200.D. a year, I reserved, when I leased it, quarterly paiments of the rent with the single view of meeting therewith your quarterly supplies of rod. I had not pressed my tenant for two year's past, not then wanting the money; but did so when I desired your last supply. he made me fair promises, which I did not expect he would fail in, till within these few days. he still renews his promises, but I cannot be certain that they are better than those he has broken. we have no banks here to relieve disappointments, & little money circulation. all is barter. my nails have never commanded money. even the merchants, if cash were demanded, would prefer importing them, because they would then make paiment by remittances of produce. under these circumstances I am obliged to throw myself on your indulgence, with the assurance it shall never be wilfully abused. I am endeavoring to get rid of my present mill-tenant, in order to place that under arrangements which may ensure my paiments to you. I have no other resource but agriculture, & that can supply deficiencies but once a year. you must be so good as to indemnify yourselves by charging interest whenever I fail, for this may not be the only instance under present circumstances. formerly while I had this business under my own direction, it was very profitable, inasmuch as it employed boys, not otherwise useful. during my absence it has not been so, but has been continued merely to preserve the custom. I think to try it for a year or two, in my own hands, & if I find it is become unprofitable from causes which cannot be remedied I shall abandon it. in the mean time I see the possibility that I may be obliged to do what I have not done heretofore ask a new supply when a preceding one is unpaid for. on this however your convenience must give the law, & shorten, if necessary, the experiment I had proposed to try. I have trespassed on you with these details, that you may perfectly understand my situation, & ascribe a failure, not to a want of faith, but of those accomodations which do not exist here. in every case be assured of my esteem & respect.

TH: JEFFERSON

PoC (MHi); endorsed by TJ.

Jones & Howell, a partnership of iron merchants at 18 South Wharves, Philadelphia, was established about 1803. The firm allowed TJ to purchase iron on credit until the War of 1812 led TJ to end his nailmaking enterprise (*MB*, 2:964n; Robinson, *Philadelphia Directory for 1809*; Malone, *Jefferson*, 6:38).

TJ presumably received the LAST SUPPLY OF ROD & IRON after his payment of $273 to Jones & Howell on 10 Mar. 1809 (*MB*, 2:1242). SJL records missing letters from TJ to Jones & Howell, 10 Mar. and 6 Apr. 1809, and from Jones & Howell to TJ, 14 Mar. and 2 May 1809, received from Philadelphia on 23 Mar. and 7 May 1809.

# From Alexander McRae

DEAR SIR, Richmond 10. Aug. 1809

I had the honor this morning to receive your favor of the 5th Inst, and for the Letters it contained, introducing Majr Clarke and myself to our Ministers in France & in England, I beg your acceptance of my grateful acknowledgments.

I am particularly gratified, in perceiving that you concur with us in opinion, that the object which carries us abroad may be of great advantage to our Country, but one expression in your letter, gave me I confess no small degree of concern: the expression alluded to renders it obvious, that want of precision, or of detail, in the communications made to you on this subject, has betrayed you into a misconception of the means, by which we propose to accomplish our object;—the expression here meant, is, that which seems to suppose, that our undertaking however innocent and laudable in itself, is, or will be, deemed criminal, by the laws of the Country in which it may be prosecuted.

You were informed by our Friend Mr Wirt, that the object of the Association of which we are members, is, to conduct manufactories on a great scale, & that for that purpose our voyage to Europe is undertaken. That such is our object, is unquestionably true. In my letter covering Mr Wirt's, it was stated also, that we would incur all the difficulty and hazard, to which the enterprize might expose us. That letter was written in great haste, as I was about that time busily engaged, in preparing for a journey to Hampton. Those communications, no doubt led you to beleive, that we might endeavor to engage manufacturers workmen and Artificers, to migrate (in our service) from Europe to America, and thus it might appear, that (in England for instance) our undertaking might by law be deemed criminal. It would indeed grieve me much to depart my native State, leaving this impression on your mind. Beleive me Sir however the unmerited[1] diminution of popular good will[2] towards me may have affected my humble station in Society or injured my slender fortune; I am yet, proud and independent and I trust virtuous enough, to resist every influence even that which might plead necessity as an apology, leading to a[3] violation of the laws of any Government. Such means are never justifiable and are rarely excusable; even when the sole motive may be, to advance the public good; besides, I beg leave most solemnly to assure you, that I have the honor to be associated with gentlemen, who would feel as much awkwardness in participating even through me, the odium of such misconduct, as could be experienced by any citizen of our Country, committing in person, a like offence.

I regret, that having asked and received a favor, I should be obliged to give you this additional trouble; as it results however from the haste in which I wrote on the 22nd Ult., I hope to be excused for now making the necessary explanation. While our object is that, which has before been mentioned, we shall not attempt it's accomplishment by enticing, or persuading, or attempting to persuade, or by any kind of contract whatever, endeavor to induce any workman, artificer, or manufacturer, or any owner of any manufactory, especially in England, to migrate to this Country. We have read the Statutes of 5. Geo. 1. Cap. 27. and 23. Geo. 2. Cap. 13. and will not violate either the Letter or Spirit of those Laws. The truth is, that we are the owners of situations in the vicinity of Richmond, as valuable as any perhaps on Earth, for the establishment of all kinds of manufactories. We are uninformed of the existence of any law in any Country, which forbids us to dispose of an interest in those situations: we mean to do nothing more than to sell an interest in them, and in making such sales, we shall avoid negotiating any contract for that purpose that may be improper, with any manufacturer or the owner of any manufactory. The sales being made we shall beleive it extremely probable, that in a reasonable time, the property may be converted and we hope lawfully, to the use of which it is capable. In making these sales there will be difficulty, and the description of the property to be sold being considered, it is probable we may incur imputations we shall not deserve: That difficulty, and this hazard, we are willing to encounter. Persons who commit no intentional error tho' they may suffer, certainly ought not to dread an injury. With such views, lawful we beleive in every Country, and highly honorable according to our best information, it is our hope that we may succeed, in advancing the wellfare & independence of our native State, & in bettering our own fortunes.

Permit me to repeat, that while abroad, I shall have much pleasure in rendering to you any service that may be acceptable, and to add, that I shall be under additional obligations, in being favored by the return of the mail (if your leisure shall permit) with an acknowledgment, that you have received this letter. With the highest respect & esteem I am

Dear Sir Yr. mo. ob. Serv[t] AL: M[c]RAE

RC (DLC); at foot of text: "Thomas Jefferson esq[r]—"; endorsed by TJ as received 23 Aug. 1809 and so recorded in SJL.

The British STATUTES, enacted in 1718 and 1750, were 5. GEO. 1. CAP. 27., "An Act to prevent the Inconveniencies arising from seducing Artificers in the Manufactures of Great Britain into foreign Parts," and 23. GEO. 2. CAP. 13., "An Act for the effectual punishing of Persons convicted of seducing Artificers in the Manufactures of Great Britain or Ireland, out of the Dominions of the Crown of Great Britain; and to prevent the Exportation of Utensils made use of in the Woollen and Silk Manufactures from Great Britain or Ireland, into foreign Parts" (*The Statutes at Large, from Magna Charta to End of Last Parliament, 1761* [London, 1763], 5:236–7, 7:223–5).

McRae wrote a similar letter to James Madison a day later (Madison, *Papers, Pres. Ser.*, 1:323–4).

[1] Word interlined.
[2] Word interlined.
[3] Word interlined in place of "the."

## From William Smith

HON. SIR Washington (Pen.) Aug[t] 10[th] 1809

Having made contracts for lands on Miami upwards of five thousand dollars of which I am bound to pay upon or before the last day of this instant. I set out from my residence in the state of New York, without having collected as much money as would fulfil my contracts. I expected to borrow of some friends living near Harrisburg: I succeeded and borrowed five hundred and ninety dollars of four different men. This will enable me to comply with my agreements, and leave large allowance for contingencies. A friend of mine, the most intimate and confidential I ever had, whom I had not seen for more than ten years, came several hundred miles to see me. He arrived next day after my departure, and being informed of my expected detention near Harrisburg, he pursued and overtook me there: His business with me is the cause of this letter. He knew that in the early part of my life I had engaged and succeeded in some enterprizes that seemed too dangerous for a man in his senses to undertake. This was the cause of his visit; it was to engage me in an enterprize the most wicked and dishonorable. To assist in killing you, and destroying your buildings at Monticello. The reward which he offered me in the name of the combined assassins to join them in it, is enormous. I have not, and will not flee from danger. but I shrink from crime and disgrace. When they sent this man to me with such an errand, they did not consider (perhaps they did not know) that my success has rendered dangerous enterprise for the sake of gain to me unnecessary.

They have written an history of your life, it is the work of sundry men: the intention of it is that the evil of your conduct shall so far out-weigh the good, as to leave you in the esteem of posterity amongst the most infamous of men. I will mention two or three things which were to me as new as they were astonishing. That you had directed and protected sundry highway roberies, two of which they have detailed very minutely.—that you were chief of the smugglers during the late embargo.—That the trial of G. . . . Wilkinson, was nothing but fraud—that he was saved by false witness procured at great expense with money drawn from the treasury by your authority; and many other such acts, all of which, he asured me, was established by incontestible witnesses—any man would be convinced at reading—

The oath of secrecy is like that of masonry; but such was his confidence in me, that he did not require it—Their plans are quite new, and so subtle that nothing but compleat detection, or the death of some of their chiefs, can prevent their ultimate success. They also contemplate other objects of much grater magnitude. I have thought of these things, (as much as my business would permit) all the way from Harrisburg to this place, when a confidence that a letter directed to you will not be miscarried, determined me to write this. I have some business with doctor Joel T. Gustine, of Winchester Virginia upon my return: where I will be some time in September—I have sometimes thought of going from thence to consult with you; but when I consider how short the time I have to collect and pay the five hundred and ninety dollars, it will not admit of delay. This circumstance suggested the idea that you might probably without any embarrassment to yourself, send the 590 dollars to Doc. Gustine for me: which would enable me to visit you at leasure about three weeks after I receive it. If I go to New York to settle my business I cannot probably visit you before next spring, which I believe will be soon enough; yet I believe it would be safer for me on account of health, to travel through the southern States in winter. If you send the money, it will be more convenient for me in sundry bills, than in one or two, and you can best judge whether you should send it enclosed in a letter to me without his knowledge of the enclosure, or you would inform him of it, or you would send it seperate and take his receipt before witness, or any way you shall think best. I am not personally acquainted with the doctor, nor does he know any thing of my intended visit, or my business. I think it barely possible, that this letter may fall into the hands of your enemies, that they will comply with the proposition it contains, and send one or two men to entrap and destroy me; I am aware of this, and no stranger sent on such errand can see me. I am confident I can see all the manuscripts or perhaps get full possession of them. this might subject them to hevy damage and some of them are very rich. I cannot write the tenth part of what I wish you to know. I will tell you all when I come—

After writing the foregoing, I considered the consequence well: when my danger in pursuing the matter struck me more forcibly than before. I had almost determined to destroy this, and remain a silent spectator—in the difficulty of making choice I determined to leave it to fate when the tossing of a cent, determined in favor of sending it: and so I send it—Do what seems best unto you—

I am in sincere friendship Your very Hum[le] Ser[t]

William Smith

RC (MoSHi: TJC-BC); ellipsis in manuscript; addressed: "Hon. Thomas Jefferson Late president of the united states Monticello"; stamped and postmarked; endorsed by TJ as received 4 Sept. 1809 and so recorded in SJL.

During service on the American frontier, General James WILKINSON became involved in the schemes of Aaron Burr and was also correctly suspected of receiving bribes from foreign agents. Fearing discovery, he betrayed what he described as Burr's disunionist plans to TJ and served as chief prosecution witness at Burr's treason trial in 1807. Wilkinson himself narrowly escaped indictment then, and a military court of inquiry subsequently took six months to acquit him (*DAB*). Smith had BUSINESS with Joel Trumbull GUSTINE (1759–1839), a native of Connecticut and Revolutionary War veteran then resident in Winchester, or his namesake son and fellow physician (Gustine Courson Weaver, *The Gustine Compendium* [1929], 99–104).

# From Charles F. Welles

RESPECTED SIR Athens Feb. 29th [ca. 11 Aug.] 1809

Of the two pieces of Poetry which I have ventured to enclose No 1. is an invective against yourself & No 2 is a Reply, written by the youth who intrudes on your leisure—I should have taken no notice of a Slander so weakly & miserably written on any other account than the credit & station of its Author whose name is Chas Miner (formerly Editor of the paper in which both pieces originally appeared) for the two last years the leading Federal member in our State Legislature & now an aspirant to a higher delegation. The Inhabitants of Luzerne & Lycoming were well pleased to see "a boy in his teens," (seldom before an obtruder) step forth & rebuke a vain, presumtuous & overbearing pretender to Poetry Eloquence & a Seat in Congress.

It is not solely from vanity that I present such a performance to such a judge as Thomas Jefferson must be; but with the view of obtaining some acknowledgment, if it be no more than a mere Receipt from the pen of him who was selected from the congregated wisdom of America

"to rear
A nation's standard in its awful sphere"

The Address of this is entirely private & the honor your letter will confer will be equally so—

With veneration Your Son CHAS F. WELLES

RC (MiU-C: Jefferson Papers); misdated, with corrected date inferred from second enclosure printed below; at foot of text: "Thomas Jefferson Esquire" and "Athens Lycoming Co Penn:"; endorsed by TJ as received 22 Nov. 1809 and so recorded in SJL.

Charles Fisher Welles (1789–1866), attorney, was a native of Glastonbury, Connecticut, who moved with his family in 1798 to Athens Township, Luzerne County, Pennsylvania. From its creation in 1812 out of parts of Luzerne and Lycoming counties until 1818, he served as prothonotary, register, recorder, and clerk of the various courts of Bradford County, residing in Towanda. From 1822 Welles lived in Wyalusing in the same county, where he engaged in farming and dealt in real estate (Clement F. Heverly, *Pioneer and Patriot Families of Bradford County Pennsylvania 1800–1825* [1913–15], 2:23–4; Heverly, *History and Geography of Bradford County Pennsylvania 1615–1924* [1926], 68, 153, 175, 205, 242).

ENCLOSURES

# I

# Charles Miner's Poem on Thomas Jefferson

[ca. 21 July 1809]

*The People's Idol got a name,*
*Which prov'd much to his country's cost.*
BUT
*If we may believe the voice of fame,*
*It afterwards was some how lost.*

---

TALENTS he had: but for what use design'd?
Big bones, perhaps, or horned frogs, to scan;
But not t'illuminate a ruler's mind,
Nor meliorate the rugged state of man.

For government what pow'rs has he display'd?
Were not his patriotic virtues slim,
Whose wild caprice the nation oft betray'd,
To rove, implicitly, from whim to whim?

Then what avails the vivid flash of tho't,
When on unworthy plans and objects lost?
What wonders has his boasted genius wrought,
But th'injur'd nation's treasures to exhaust?

And what avails *fine* sense, with all its vaunting?
(Whether seen in the coward or the brave,)
If common sense and honesty be wanting,
For still the man's the more a fool or knave.

A despot's will may be a nation's law;
But where the rights of man are understood,
The people thence, the wisest maxims draw,
And rulers must, to gain respect, be good.

Wherever Liberty erects her throne,
The ill-concerted project she despises,
'Tis common sense gives government its tone;
And reprobates Quixotic enterprises.

The chieftain's wiles, true patriots descry;
And, weak or wicked systems to efface,
Inspect his conduct with an eagle's eye;
And to their origin his motives trace.

How then dar'd he, (frail monarch of a day,)
To treat our constitution with disdain;
And snatch the people's sacred rights away.
To rivet on the curs'd embargo chain?

Is that chief magistrate or just or wise,
Who, as a stubborn partisan confest,
To cringing minions, every gift applies;
And tyrant like, from office, spurns the rest?

Who gives to honest merit no reward,
But still, by bribes of place, spurs party rage,
And more to sect, than virtue, pays regard;
But marks with infamy the present age.

What tho' his predecessor miss'd the mark,
'Twas a loud call, which caution'd him to hit:
It argu'd weakness then to bilge his bark,
On the same rock, where he'd seen Adams split.

He trade and navigation, scorn'd to know
And labour'd their extinction to effect,
And to our navy gave a deadly blow,
But paid, to paltry gun-boats, all respect.

He hating Britain, met in proud disdain
The amicable treaty she propos'd;
With which (and the conditions all the same.)
Administration since, in wisdom, clos'd.

Was not he Frenchified thro' all his soul,
With predilections obstinately strong?
Did he not crouch to Bonaparte's controul,
And do the States incalculable wrong?

Domestic war already breathed disgust;
And foreign realms to hostile acts inclin'd:
And, while French pride, in dread volcanos burst,
He lockt up truth; and juggled congress blind

'Twas thro' his arts, fierce feuds began to glow;
Our states he led to ruin's awful brink;
Who (startled at the dreadful gulf below)
Turn'd from the whirlpool, where whole nations sink.

But what avail'd him all this dark disguise?
And what—all foreign love, or foreign spite,
We've seen the nation's injur'd spirit rise;
And smother'd truth, burst forth in light.

Could shrewd chicanery make a nation bless'd,
Could sly intrigue our gratitude command?
Could joy or wealth result from truth suppress'd,
This would, long since, have been a happy land.

May we forever bless the happy day,
His ill apply'd authority expir'd;
When Madison, of right, assum'd the sway;
Whose prudence cannot be too much admir'd.

Now government resumes its proper course;
Faction dissolves: its adverse parts unite;
Oppression has exhausted all its force:
Tranquility prevails, and all goes right.

Our navy's now repair'd to guard the coast;
We meet respect abroad, and peace at[1] home.
Of trade unchain'd, and rights restor'd, we boast;
And still anticipate more joys to come.

Printed in Wilkes-Barre *Luzerne Federalist*, 21 July 1809; at head of text: "FOR THE FEDERALIST."

Charles Miner (1780–1865) was a native of Connecticut who moved to Pennsylvania in 1799 and achieved some prominence as proprietor of a series of newspapers in Wilkes-Barre and West Chester, including the Wilkes-Barre *Luzerne Federalist: and Susquehannah Intelligencer*, 1802–09, the Wilkes-Barre *Gleaner*, 1811–16, and the West Chester *Village Record, or Chester and Delaware Federalist*, 1818–32. He served as a Federalist in the Pennsylvania House of Representatives, 1807–09 and 1812, and in the United States House of Representatives, 1825–29. Miner published a *History of Wyoming* (1845), opposed slavery, and sought to develop the silkworm and anthracite coal industries (*DAB*; Charles Francis Richardson and Elizabeth Miner Thomas Richardson, *Charles Miner: A Pennsylvania Pioneer* [1916]; Miner, *Essays from the Desk of Poor Robert the Scribe* [Doylestown, Pa., 1815; repr., ed. Julian P. Boyd, 1930]).

[1] *Luzerne Federalist*: "at at."

## II
## Charles F. Welles's Poem on Thomas Jefferson

[ca. 11 Aug. 1809]

TALENTS he had, exquisitely[1] design'd
To rule the worlds of action and of mind;
Talents the subtle line of right[2] to draw,
And pond'ring Senates found his judgment law.
In vain fell envy gathers all her bands,
In vain delusion lifts a thousand hands,
Beyond their reach[3] his measures rise sublime,
Their proof experience, and their champion time.

His was the fortune, in a dangerous day,
To lead a youthful nation on its way;
A pamper'd nation, proud, disdaining[4] rule,
As yet untutor'd in misfortune's school,
Mad with division—while[5] ambition's eye
Fiery and restless, watch'd its moment nigh.
His was the GLORY, *slander'd and reviled.*
*Jeer'd as he spoke, and thwarted as he toil'd,*
*While war assumed its last and mightiest forms,*
*UPRIGHT AND FIRM TO WALK BETWEEN THE STORMS.*

Stand forth, reviler! and assert thy[6] claim
To weigh his wisdom, and denounce his fame.
Art thou superior? Is it thine to rear
A nation's standard in its[7] awful sphere?
Hast thou a mind all adequate and vast,
To pierce the future, comprehend the past,
View every motive, give each[8] cause its weight,
And trace effect abroad from state to state?
Art thou the sage to guard thro' every hour
The bounds of right from fraudulence and pow'r?
To rise serene, while thunders round are hurl'd,
And stand among the mighty of the world?

He to no science, to no art confin'd
Prolong'd his journey thro'[9] the realms of mind,
Thro' all their scenery eager still to rove
And pluck a laurel forth from every grove.
Fame with a voice of exultation sweet
Salutes pale learning in his cool retreat.
On the good[10] statesman show'rs her honors down,
Clad in a glory brighter than renown.
But he, the sage whose intellectual reach
Pervades both regions and excels in each,
The son of science, and the sire of state
Reviler! say is not that mortal great?
MILLIONS pronounce him worthy of their praise,
Child! is it THINE to rob him of his bays.

By slander shadow'd, and assail'd by hate,
O sacred virtue! this must be thy fate,
Till human merit has on earth reward,
And God's right arm of thunder for its guard.
But shall the muse, the noble muse, combine,
Warm every thought, and polish every line,
To force bright truth for kinder realms to fly,
And bid young genius bow him down and die?

Is there no glory for the living great?
No ray to cheer the gathering gloom of fate?
Alone on[11] churchyards must the laurel bloom,
Grow but on graves, and darken round the tomb?

There IS a glory for the living great,
A ray to cheer the gathering gloom of fate,[12]
There IS a wreath with hoary age shall grow,
Defy the storm, and thicken round his brow!

There is a triumph, prouder still than fame;
The great man's triumph—human nature's shame.
*The foes, the slanders, that assail his seat,*
THE HOSTS OF ENVY STORMING ROUND HIS FEET.

Printed in Wilkes-Barre *Luzerne Federalist*, 11 Aug. 1809; at head of text: "FOR THE FEDERALIST. *Vide this paper of July 21.*" Variant version in unidentified printed source (undated clipping in DLC: TJ Papers, ser. 7; poem entitled "Thomas Jefferson"; with heading of "No 2" and two corrections in Welles's hand). Reprinted, generally following DLC clipping, in Washington *National Intelligencer*, 24 Nov. 1809.

Charles Miner responded with a poetic rebuttal that interspersed portions of Welles's piece with his own sarcastic rejoinder (*Luzerne Federalist*, 18 Aug. 1809).

[1] DLC clipping: "had, in nature's skill."

[2] *Luzerne Federalist*: "aught." DLC clipping: "right."

[3] DLC clipping: "Far beyond reach."

[4] *Luzerne Federalist*: "disdaiding."

[5] DLC clipping: "and."

[6] *National Intelligencer*: "the."

[7] DLC clipping: "the," corrected to "its" by Welles and thus elsewhere.

[8] DLC clipping: "its," corrected to "each" by Welles and thus elsewhere.

[9] DLC clipping: "o'er."

[10] *National Intelligencer*: "great."

[11] DLC clipping: "in."

[12] DLC clipping: "There is a ray to gild the eve of fate."

# To André Daschkoff

SIR Monticello. Aug. 12. 09.

Your favor of July 5. has been duly recieved, and, in it, that of my friend mr Short. I congratulate you on your safe arrival in the American hemisphere, after a voyage which must have been lengthy in time, as it is in space. I hope you may experience no unfavorable change in your health on so great a change of climate, and that our fervid sun may be found as innocent as our cloudless skies must be agreeable. I hail you with particular pleasure, as the first harbinger of those friendly relations with your country so desireable to ours. both nations being, in character & practice, essentially pacific, a common interest in the rights of peaceable nations, gives us a common cause in their maintenance: & however your excellent emperor may have been led from the ordinary policy of his government, I trust that the establishment of just principles will be the result, as I am sure it is the object of his efforts.

When you shall have had time to accomodate yourself somewhat to our climate, our manners, & mode of living, you will probably have a curiosity to see something of the country you have visited, something beyond the confines of our cities. these exhibit specimens of London only. our country is a different nation. should your journeyings lead you into this quarter of it, I shall be happy to recieve you at Monticello, and to renew to you in person the assurances I now tender, of my great respect and consideration. TH: JEFFERSON

RC (CtY: Franklin Collection); at foot of text: "M. Dashkoff." PoC (DLC).

## From John Martin Baker

SIR, Washington City, August 14th 1809.

I am honored with your most Respected letter of the 25th ultimo: its contents Sir, afford to myself and to Mrs Baker, a pleasing satisfaction, which ever will remain imprinted on our minds, and must endure with us while we live.

Your Note Sir, for sundries, I shall have the satisfaction to duly attend to, and forward the Articles per first eligible opportunity.

Mrs Baker Sir, is thankful for your estimable mention of her, and desires me to say, that she will be much gratified when it may be possible that she may possess the view of Monticello. We Sir, with our children join in prayers for Your Preservation, Health and Happiness. I have the Honor to be with the Highest Respect and Gratitude Sir, Your Most Obedient Humble Servant

JOHN MARTIN BAKER.

RC (MHi); at foot of text: "To The Most Honorable Thomas Jefferson Monticello"; endorsed by TJ as received 20 Aug. 1809 and so recorded in SJL.

## From Samuel H. Smith

SIR Washington, Aug. 15. 1809

I have the satisfaction of advising you of our having reached home in perfect health and safety after one of the most charming excursions we have ever taken. To crown the whole with pleasure we found our little girls as hearty and happy as we left them, and can, therefore, with full fellow feeling congratulate you and your family on the complete disappearance of[1] indisposition of which Mr Cutts has informed us. I shall not attempt to describe the gratification we experienced at Montecello, which more than equalled our expectations. We shall ever retain a lively remembrance of the affectionate welcome and kind attentions we received, mingled with a thousand associations calculated to excite the highest interest, and the precious assurance that your heart has at length found an asylum in which it may securely indulge its feelings. I have never beheld a more lovely flock of children better educated. May their felicity be equal to your wishes and their deserts! We thank you for your kind invitation to revisit you at a future period, when your improvements shall be more extended. We shall certainly cherish the hope of again seeing Montecello, tho' such are generally the obstacles to the gratification of our wishes, that we must not too confidently entertain what may end only in disappointment

In the mean time M[rs] Smith unites with me in the most affectionate remembrance to yourself and your amiable family, with an ardent desire that you may long continue to enjoy every earthly blessing.

I am with high and sincere respect SA. H. SMITH

RC (DLC); addressed: "Thomas Jefferson Esquire Monticello Virg[a]"; franked and postmarked; endorsed by TJ as received 20 Aug. 1809 and so recorded in SJL.

[1] Manuscript: "of of."

# From Jones & Howell

RESPECTED FRIEND Phil[a] 16[th] Aug[t] 1809

We have your favor of 10[th] Ins[t] Contents of which we have noted. And in reply we have to assure you that any supply of Iron you are in want of shall be sent you without any delay or hesitation at all times and you will pay us in such times and manner as will best suit your circumstances. You have been A regular & punctual customer to our house for A series of Years and we should consider ourselves ungrateful to refuse you any accomodation within our reach and the present is completely so as through the medium of the Banks we can obtain what money we want and the Interest we charge to the a/c of our Friend whenever the customary credit expires. You will therefore just mention what quantity of Iron you wish and what kind and it shall be forwarded

we are respectfully yours JONES & HOWELL

RC (MHi); idiosyncratic periods omitted; at head of text: "Thomas Jefferson Esq[r]"; endorsed by TJ as received 20 Aug. 1809 and so recorded in SJL.

# To Meriwether Lewis

DEAR SIR Monticello Aug. 16. 09.

This will be handed you [by] mr Bradbury, an English botanist, who proposes to take S[t] Louis in his botanising tour. he came recommended to me by mr Roscoe of Liverpool, so well known by his histories of Lorenzo of Medicis & Leo X. & who is president of the Botanical society of Liverpool. mr Bradbury comes out in their employ, & having kept him here about ten days, I have had an opportunity of knowing that besides being a botanist of the first order, he is a man of entire worth & correct conduct. as such I recommend him to your notice, advice & patronage, while within your government or it's confines. perhaps you can consult no abler hand on your Western botanical observations. I am very often applied to to know when your work will begin to appear; and I have so long promised copies to my literary correspondents in France, that I am almost bankrupt in their eyes. I shall be very happy to recieve from yourself information of your expectations on this subject. every body is impatient for it.

You have seen by the papers how dirty a trick has been played us by England. I consider all amicable arrangement with that nation as desperate during the life of the present king. there is some ground to expect more justice from Napoleon: & this is perhaps favored by the signal defeat he has suffered in the battle of the[1] Danube, which has obliged him to retreat & remain stationary at Vienna, till his army, literally cut up, can be reinforced. in the mean time, the spell of his invincibility being broken, he is in danger of an universal insurrection against him in Europe. your friends here are well, & have been long in expectation of seeing you. I shall hope in that case to possess a due portion of you at Monticello, where I am at length enjoying the never before known luxury of employing my self for my own gratification only. present my friendly salutations to Gen[l] Clarke, and be assured yourself of my constant & unalterable affections.

TH: JEFFERSON

PoC (DLC); torn at crease; at foot of text: "Gov[r] Lewis"; endorsed by TJ.

Meriwether Lewis (1774–1809) was born at Locust Hill, near Ivy Creek in Albemarle County, into a locally prominent family enjoying cordial relations with the neighboring Jeffersons and Randolphs. In 1795 he joined the United States Army as an ensign, rising to lieutenant in 1799 and captain in 1800. TJ made Lewis his personal secretary in 1801. Two years later TJ put him in charge of the successful 1803–06 transcontinental exploration that has become known as the Lewis and Clark Expedition. TJ appointed Lewis governor of Louisiana Territory in 1807, and he took up residence at Saint Louis. In September 1809 Lewis began a journey to Washington, D.C., in order to investigate the repudiation of several bills he had issued on the government. He died en route, in a central Tennessee inn, probably by his own hand (*ANB*; *DAB*; Richard Dillon, *Meriwether Lewis: A Biography* [1965]; Heitman, *U.S. Army*, 1:631; TJ to Lewis, 23 Feb. 1801 [DLC]; *JEP*, 2:53, 54 [28 Feb., 2 Mar. 1807]; John Brahan to TJ, 18 Sept. 1809; James Neelly to TJ, 18 Sept. 1809; TJ to Paul Allen, 18 Aug. 1813).

In SJL under this date TJ records both this letter and an undated letter by Lewis received from Mississippi; the latter is otherwise unknown and may simply be an inadvertent and incorrect reference to the former.

On 12 Aug. 1809 John BRADBURY wrote to William ROSCOE from Monticello: "I have been here about 10 Days which time I have spent in examining the neighbourhd assisted often by Coln[l] Randolph who is Son in Law to M[r] Jefferson & one of the best if not the best Naturalist I ever met with—I have made out two new Cypripedia, two new Orchidea of a Genus established by Persoon which he has separated from Serapias & calls Heleborine, two new Cacaliæ a new & most Odorous Coreopsis a new Talinum a beautiful Rock Plant and many others of which I am doubtful—Some of these are removed into M[r] Jefferson's Garden & others are Marked in the Woods & known to Col[l] R. who has this morning promised to take care of them for me, or Your use should I never return to reclaim them." TJ had informed him that Lewis was now stationed at Saint Louis as governor of Louisiana, and that the territory had not yet been explored by any botanist. Bradbury accordingly decided to travel to Saint Louis instead of New Orleans "and put myself under the direction of Cap[n] Lewis, to whom M[r] Jeff[n] & M[r] Randolph will give me Letters. . . . As I am assured by M[r] Jefferson that even War with Britain shall not obstruct my researches I purpose to establish a Garden at F[t] S[t] Louis as a place of Immediate deposit and place one of my sons at New Orleans to receive & transmit. . . . M[r] Jefferson will I suppose write to you, he has some intention of sending you seeds of a new variety of Zea Maize which was brought by Cap[n] Lewis from a Vast distance beyond the Mouth of the Missouri he found it with a Tribe of Cultivating Indians in Latitude 49° and a Country so much elevated as to render it almost a Greenland Climate. M[r] J. thinks it will be an Immense acquisition to Britain as it will grow even in the Highlands [. . .] and Yields most abundantly: At all events [I shall] not return to Europe without it—Col[l] Randolph has obtained 2 Years ago some seeds of Holcus Sorghum (Sorghum Vulgare of Persoon) and of Sesamum Indicum both of which he is cultivating the former as an article of food the Latter for Oil. The Seeds of the Holcus are much better than the Maize & it yields in greater abundance I measured some of it 14 feet high. The culture of both will become general & highly beneficial here." In a postscript Bradbury added that "Since I finished this L[r] M[r] Jefferson requested me to present his respectful compliments to you and informs me that he will forward all my Letters to M[r] Pinckney which will afford me the opportunity of making inclosures," and he enclosed "seeds of S Cypripedia . . . all inhabitants of shady Woods" (Bradbury to Roscoe, 12 Aug. 1809, RC in UkLi: Roscoe Manuscripts; torn at margin; printed in H. W. Rickett, "John Bradbury's Explorations in Missouri Territory," APS, *Proceedings* 94 [1950]: 62–4). There is no record of TJ writing to Roscoe at this time. In a similar letter of 12 Aug. 1809 to James Edward Smith, Bradbury spoke of the "Very good Botanic Library" at Monticello and remarked that "M[r] Jeffersons House stands on a Hill, on that Hill I have in a few days found 3 Cypripedia 2 of which are evidently neither discribed in Michaux's Flora Americana Boreali or by Persoon or indeed in any work that we have. Also two species belonging to the genus Heleborine as established by Persoon but not discribed by him or any Author so far as we can find Other Orchidea also not in flower or possessing marks sufficient to determine them We reckon also 2 new Cacaliæ a new Talinum & some others of dubious Genera" (RC in Linnean Society, London: James Edward Smith Manuscripts).

[1] TJ here canceled "Rhine."

## From James Madison

DEAR SIR Montpellier Aug. 16. 1809

I got home from my trip to Washington on Saturday last; having remained there three days only. You will have seen in the Procl[n] issued, the result of our consultations on the effect of what has passed on our commercial relations with G.B. The enforcement of the non-intercourse act ag$^{st}$ her, will probably be criticized by some friends and generally assailed by our adversaries, on the ground that the power given to the Ex. being special, was exhausted by the first exercise of it; and that the power having put out of force the laws to which it related, could under no possible construction restore their operation. In opposition to this reasoning, it was considered that the Act of the last Session continuing the non-intercourse, no otherwise excepted G.B. than by a proviso that it should not affect any trade which had been, or might be permitted, in conformity with the section of the original act authorizing a proclamation in favor of the nation revoking its Edicts; and that the proclamation in favor of G.B. was not conformable to that Section. It was not so in substance, because the indispensable pre-requisite, a repeal of the Orders in Council, did not take place. It was not so even in form; the law requiring a past and not a future fact to be proclaimed, and the proclamation on its face[1] pointing to a future, not to a past fact. This difficulty was felt at the time[2] of issuing the first proclamation; but it yielded to the impossibility of otherwise obtaining without great delay the coveted trade with G.B. and an example that might be followed by France; to the idea that the mode in which the repeal tho' future,[3] of the orders & of the law was coupled by the proclamn, might on the occurrence of the former, give a constructive validity to the latter; and to the opportunity afforded by an intervening Session of Cong$^{s}$ for curing any defect in the proceeding. In one respect, it would have been clearly[4] proper for Congress to have interposed its Authority, as was frequently intimated to members; that is, to provide for the contingency, not so much of a disavowal by G.B. which was never suspected, as of her not receiving the Act of her Minister, till after the 10$^{th}$ of June. Congress however never could be brought to attend to the subject, altho' it was pressed by several members I believe, certainly by Gardenier, on the general ground, that the Procl$^{n}$ however acceptable, was not in a form or under the circumstances, contemplated by law. In some of the instructions given by M$^{r}$ Gallatins circular a liberty has been taken having no plea but manifest necessity, and as such will be before Congress.

Erskine is in a ticklish situation with his Gov$^{t}$. I suspect he will not be able to defend himself ag$^{st}$ the charge of exceeding his instructions, notwithstanding the appeal he makes to sundry others not published. But he will make out a strong case ag$^{st}$ Canning, and be able to avail himself much of the absurdity & evident inadmissibility of the articles disregarded by him. He can plead also that the difference between his arrangem$^{t}$ & the spontaneous orders of Ap$^{l}$ 26. is too slight to justify the disavowal of him. This difference, seems indeed to limit its importance to the case of Holland, & to consist in the direct trade admitted by the arrangement, and an indirect one, thro' the adjoining ports, required by the orders. To give importance to this distinction, the Ministry must avow, what if they were not shameless they never w$^{d}$ avow, that their ob. is not to retaliate injury on an Enemy; but to prevent the legitimate trade of the U.S. from interfering with the London smugglers of Sugar & Coffee.

We are looking out for M$^{r}$ & M$^{rs}$ Gallatin every day. Untill they arrive, and we learn also the periods of your being at & absent from Home, we do not venture to fix a time for our proposed visit to Monticello.

Accept my most affectionate respects JAMES MADISON

Capt: Coles has been with us since sunday. I refer to him for the state of our foreign affairs with which he is sufficiently acquainted, to say more than I cou'd well put on paper.

RC (DLC: Madison Papers); at foot of text: "M$^{r}$ Jefferson"; endorsed by TJ as received 16 Aug. 1809 and so recorded in SJL.

Madison's 9 Aug. 1809 presidential PROCL$^{N}$ reimposed the Non-Intercourse Act on Great Britain in response to its unexpected failure to repeal the Orders in Council by 10 June 1809 (Madison, *Papers, Pres. Ser.*, 1:320–1). On 1 June 1809 Barent GARDENIER, a Federalist representative from New York, had unsuccessfully called for legislation to confirm Madison's 19 Apr. 1809 proclamation reopening trade with Great Britain (*Annals*, 11th Cong., 1st sess., 217). The 9 Aug. 1809 CIRCULAR issued by Albert Gallatin informed customs collectors how to reimplement trade restrictions with Great Britain (Washington *National Intelligencer*, 11 Aug. 1809).

[1] Madison here canceled "doing that."

[2] Preceding five words interlined in place of "did not escape atten."

[3] Preceding two words interlined.

[4] Word interlined.

# To Craven Peyton

SIR Monticello Aug. 16. 09.

The title to the lands of Bennet Henderson having passed to yourself thro many hands & by many deeds, I wish in the preamble to the deed to state, for each part, the conveyances by which it came to you, as a matter of information in case any of his descendants should hereafter raise a question on it. I have begun it in the following way, which I know to be imperfect.

'they (that is, the widow & children of B. Henderson) did by various deeds convey their whole right, estate & possession to the sd Craven, that is to say the sd Sarah & John B. Kerr her husband by deed to the sd Craven bearing date the 7th of June[1] 1803. recorded in the court of for the consideration of to them paid by the sd Craven & recorded in

the sd James L. H. by a deed of Dec. 28. 1799 to a certain T. Woodson & the sd Tucker by another deed of Apr. 25. 1801. to the sd Craven & the sd James L. by a subsequent deed to the sd Craven of Nov. 29. 1801. in considn of the sum of to them paid & recorded in

the sd Charles by a deed of Mar. 18. 1801. to the sd James L. who conveyed the same to the sd Craven by a deed of Mar. 19. 1801 & the sd Charles by a subsequent deed to the sd Craven of[2] Jan. 31. 1804 in considn of the sum of __ to them paid & recorded in

the sd. Isham by a deed of Mar. 17. 1801. to the same James L. & the sd James L. to the sd Craven by a deed of the same date in considn of to them paid & recorded in

The sd John by deeds of Apr. 3. 1803. to the sd Craven & of to a certain James Lewis & the sd Henderson, & the sd James Lewis & Henderson by a deed of 1808 to the sd Craven (with the exception of the 5. acre lot of the sd John in the upper field which he had before conveyed to the sd Thomas) recorded in & for the consideration of to them paid

the sd James L. Henderson by deeds of the 18th & 23d of Sep. 1802. for the rights of the sd Bennet, Eliza, Frances, Lucy & Nancy L. & as their guardian

and the sd Bennet Etc by deeds Etc recorded in in consideration of the sum of to them & for their necessary use paid.

and the sd Elizabeth, as to her right of dower, by deed of Sep. 18. 1802. to the sd Craven recorded in & in consideration of to her paid.'

---

the above statement of conveyances I suppose defective in the following particulars & probably in others.

as to John's part. was there not some conveyance to Seabrook & Anderson, & a conveyance from them to you?

Sarah's. did not this pass thro E. Moore, & Mat. Henderson & then to you?

Charles's. did it not pass to Bramham, Seabrook, Anderson?

Isham's. did it not pass to John, to Seabrook, to Anderson?

Bennet H. did not this go to John, to Seabrook, to Anderson?

Bennet H. Eliza, Frances, Lucy & Nancy L. which of them have executed deeds of confirmation, & which are still under age?

I must ask the favor of you, under each share to state the conveyances exactly, where recorded, and the consideration allowed or paid. after doing this, by the aid of your papers, perhaps it may be necessary for you to take the trouble of riding up, and explaining it to me where I may not understand it. when this is done, I will prepare the deed and ride down to your house to get it executed by mrs Peyton & yourself; which I should wish to have done before I set out to Bedford. I am Dear Sir

your friend & serv[t] TH: JEFFERSON

PoC (MHi); at foot of first page: "M[r] Craven Peyton"; endorsed by TJ.

[1] Word interlined.

[2] Manuscript: "of of."

# To James Madison

DEAR SIR Monticello Aug. 17. 09.

I recieved your's of yesterday by mr Coles. my journey to Bedford has been delayed by sickness among my laboring people. no new case having arisen for some time, I am in hopes it is at an end. still no particular object fixing my departure to any precise time, it lies over for convenience, and should I fix a time before we have the pleasure of seeing yourself & mrs Madison here I shall certainly inform you of it for my own sake, that I may not, by absence, lose what will be a great gratification to me. an antient promise from mr & mrs Gallatin entitles me to hope they will extend their journey thus far, and give us a portion of the time they have to spare.

I never doubted the chicanery of the Anglomen on whatsoever measures you should take in consequence of the disavowal of Erskine. yet I am satisfied that both the proclamations have been sound. the first has been sanctioned by universal approbation. altho' it was not literally the case foreseen by the legislature, yet it was a proper extension of their provision to a case similar tho' not the same. it proved to the whole world our desire of accomodation, & must have satisfied[1] every candid federalist on that head. it was not only proper on the well grounded confidence that the arrangement would be honestly executed, but ought to have taken place even had the perfidy of England been foreseen. their dirty gain is richly remunerated to us, by our placing them so shamefully in the wrong, & by the union it must produce among ourselves. The last proclamation admits of quibbles of which advantage will doubtless be endeavored to be taken by those to whom gain is their god, & their country nothing. but it is soundly defensible. the British minister assured that the orders of council would be revoked before the 10th of June. the Executive, trusting in that assurance, declared by proclamation that the revocation was to take place, & that on that event the law was to be suspended. but the event did not take place & the consequence, of course, could not follow. this view is derived from the former non-intercourse law only, having never read the latter one. I had doubted whether Congress must not be called; but that arose from another doubt whether their 2d law had not changed the ground so as to require their agency to give operation to the law. should Bonaparte have the wisdom to correct his injustice towards us, I consider war with England as inevitable. our ships will go to France & it's dependancies, and they will take them. this will be war on their part, & leaves no alternative but reprisal. I have no doubt you will think it safe to act on this hypothesis, & with energy. the moment that open war shall be apprehended from them, we should take possession of Baton rouge. if we do not, they will, and New Orleans becomes irrecoverable & the Western country blockaded during the war. it would be justifiable towards Spain on this ground, & equally so on that of title to W. Florida & reprisal extended to E. Florida. whatever turn our present difficulty may take, I look upon all cordial conciliation with England as desperate during the life of the present king. I hope & doubt not that Erskine will justify himself. my confidence is founded in a belief of his integrity, & in the unprincipled rascality of Canning. I consider the present as the most shameless ministry which ever disgraced England. Copenhagen will immortalize their infamy. in general their administrations are so changeable, & they are obliged to descend to such tricks to keep themselves in place, that nothing like honor or morality can ever be counted on in transactions with them. I salute you with all possible affection.

TH: JEFFERSON

RC (DLC: Madison Papers); at foot of first page: "The President of the US." PoC (DLC).

TJ regarded as infamous the British ultimatum of 1807 to neutral Denmark, followed shortly by the bombardment of COPENHAGEN and the seizure of the Danish fleet (Washington *National Intelligencer*, 5 Oct. 1807).

[1] Word interlined in place of "involved."

# From David Porter

SIR — Bay S Louis West Florida August 17. 1809

Alone supported and allmost a stranger to you, I with the utmost diffidence and respect take the liberty to present you the enclosed plan and prospects of a Voyage of discovery to the N.W. Coast of America—I should not have been emboldened to take this step, notwithstanding the repeated entreaties of Gentlemen whom I esteem as my Friends and who pass for men of science, had I not thought I discovered from the tenor of a conversation I had with you sometime since that such a Voyage would be a desirable object to the United States—The knowledge you possess of that Country derived from the Travels of Mess^rs^ Lewis and Clark as well as from other sourses, will perhaps cause you to consider as chemerical the hopes of discovering a Northern or North Western Communication between the Atlantic and Pacific and indeed I cannot for a moment seriously harbour such a hope—yet, notwithstanding all I have heard and seen on the Subject from Mess^rs^ M^c^Kinsey and Hearne, and others, I am strongly induced to believe that a more easy and direct mode of communication between the Atlantic States and the shores of the Pacific may be made than has yet been discovered—I have to apologise for having offered this plan prior to having any knowledge whatever of the discoveries of Lewis and Clark; their observations may in a measure overthrow my Theory—This sketch was drawn up prior to their return; it stands in its original form, for I have waited, with the utmost impatience, for the publication of their Journal to enable me to correct, and perhaps induce me to suppress the whole—I cannot however help thinking that they have left some valuable gleanings on that field for discovery—

You will please to observe that I have presented my plan in a rude, unpolished, unembellished state;—I have attempted no ornament, I have trusted solely to the strength of facts there stated to bear me up in my feeble efforts to be of Service to my Country.

I have stated the facts in nearly the words of the Navigators and I beg the whole to be considered a compilation, serving to point out the objects already perceived and remain yet to be examined—An enterprise of this nature offers to us prospects far superior to those of any other, we proceed on a certainty of making valuable discoveries and all must (from their local situation) tend to the exclusive interest, as well as the fame of our Country—

I have already laid a copy of my plan before the Honorable Secretary of the Navy and I know not its success—I have presumed to depend greatly on your patronage, should you consider an undertaking of this nature beneficial to our Country: and with the same pleasure I engaged in it, I shall relinquish the further prosecution when I am informed by you that circumstances do not render it necessary; or, that it would not be beneficial to the United States—

To effect a Voyage of the nature proposed, not less than two Vessels would be necessary; they should be small Frigates, large Brigs, or Bomb Ketches;—very little equipment would be requisite beyond their Ordinary equipment for Service, and I am under an impression that full Crews would not be requisite, consequently no additional expence of importance would be required—

Should you Honor this plan with your attention and deem it worthy your notice, I consider it unnecessary to request you to give it your patronage, I merely solicit you to Honor me with one Line expressive of your opinion, by which alone my conduct shall be governed and whatever may be the fate of my prospects I shall feel highly gratified and honored if any feeble effort of mine should be deemed an object worthy of your notice—

I have requested leave of absence from my present Command which has been granted me and I calculate on arriving in the Atlantic States in the latter part of October, must therefore request, if you will, that you will do me the favor to direct your Letter to the care of the Honb^le^ William Anderson Member of Congress at Chester Pennsylvania—

I have the Honor to be With Great Consideration and Respect Your Ob serv^t^ D Porter

RC (DLC); in a clerk's hand, signed by Porter; at foot of text: "Thomas Jefferson Esq^r^ Late President of the United States"; endorsed by TJ as received 8 Oct. 1809 and so recorded in SJL.

David Porter (1780–1843), then in command of the naval station at New Orleans, entered the United States Navy as a midshipman in 1798 and rose to lieutenant in 1799, master commandant in 1806, and captain in 1812. He saw combat in the Quasi-War with France and in the Tripolitan War, when he spent time as a prisoner in Tripoli. As captain of the frigate *Essex*, Porter made the first capture of a British warship (HMS *Alert*) during the War of 1812, disrupted British whaling in a daring voyage to the South Pacific, and made an ultimately unsuccessful effort to claim one of the Marquesas Islands for the United States. He served on the new Board of Navy Commissioners, 1815–22. Porter resigned his commission following his court-martial and conviction for insubordination in 1825 and then spent three years in command of the naval forces of Mexico. Following Andrew Jackson's election, Porter served briefly as American consul general at Algiers and from 1831 until his death as chargé d'affaires and (from 1839) minister resident to the Ottoman Empire at Constantinople (*ANB*; *DAB*; David F. Long, *Nothing Too Daring: A Biography of Commodore David Porter, 1780–1843* [1970]).

MCKINSEY AND HEARNE: Alexander Mackenzie, *Voyages from Montreal, on the river St. Laurence, through the Conti-*

*nent of North America, to the Frozen and Pacific* Oceans (London, 1802; Sowerby, no. 4087) and Samuel Hearne, *Journey from Fort Prince Wales in Hudson's Bay to the Northern Ocean* (London, 1795; abridged ed. Philadelphia, 1802).

On 20 Sept. 1809 Charles Goldsborough, chief clerk of the Department of the NAVY, sent Madison a copy of Porter's proposal, noting: "Altho' you may not, at this time, approve the project, yet it will I hope afford you pleasure to find that we have in our navy men of columbian ambition" (Madison, *Papers, Pres. Ser.*, 1:388). Porter himself optimistically commented that "M[r] Jeffersons patronage I do not hesitate to pronounce as secured—M[r] Smiths is to be hoped for and I do not despair of M[r] Madisons." Neither TJ nor Madison responded to Porter, however, and despite his continuing requests, this particular voyage never took place (Porter to Samuel Hambleton, 20 Aug. 1809 [DLC: David D. Porter Family Papers]). WILLIAM ANDERSON was Porter's father-in-law.

ENCLOSURE

## David Porter's Plan for a Voyage of Discovery to the Northwest Coast of America

Since the loss of that unfortunate though eminent Navigator La Perouse and the expedition fitted out in search of him, no discoveries have been made excepting some accidental ones by Persons whose qualifications and means were illy suited to afford much correct information, whose object was trade and not discovery and whose interest perhaps induced them to suppress much of their knowledge, or to represent matters wide from the truth; among the Navigators of this class we may rank those who have been concerned in the Fur Trade in that great field for discovery the South Seas and on the N.W. Coast of America. The discoveries of Cook, La Perouse and Dixon with some few made by the Spaniards may be said to be the only ones on the N.W. Coast which afford us any clear information of that part of the World.

The limits of Cooks observations in that Quarter were in a space of very small extent, and time not admitting that celebrated Navigator to explore with precision any part of the Coast that he visited, the only information of any importance we can obtain from his Journal is confined to but few places—

La Perouse, being in a similar predicament with Cook, could make but few observations in passing that Coast, and those generally in foggy weather when he was unable to approach it, so that the only information which results from his observations is a clear account of the Port des Francais (where he made a considerable stay) and an imperfect one of the rest of the Coast as far South as Montery, as in that space he had no communication with the shore—

Cook, after leaving the Sandwich Islands, proceeded for the N.W. Coast of America, made the Land in the Lat of 44.° N. and had no communication with the Shore until he arrived as far North as Nootka; of course could give no information of the more Southern parts—

Dixon (being concerned in the Fur Trade) confined himself to the Northern Latitudes where Peltry was to be procured of the best quality, in greatest quantities, and at the most reasonable rates, consequently is silent on the Southern parts.

Three small Vessels were employed by Don Antonio Maria Buccarella Vice Roy of Mexico in the year 1775 for the purpose of examining[1] the N.W. Coast of America; the only information of which Voyage we obtain from the Journal of Mourella, Pilot of the Vessel second in Command.

They sailed from S Blais the 17th March 1775. and by obstinate winds were prevented from making any observations until the 9th of June when they entered a Port which was situated in the Latitude of 41.° N. and was called by them the Port of Trinity; the Spaniards praise highly the Country and its Inhabitants—those Americans paint their Bodies black and blue, and have the same customs and arms as those described by Cook in his third Voyage when he visited the N.W. Coast.—

They quitted Trinity June 9th and anchored on the Coast June 19th in Latitude 47½ made some few exchanges with the natives who opposed their Landing; from thence they proceeded North as far as 58.°, made but few observations while running along the Coast and on their return touched at Port S Francais in Lat. 38.° 13.′—they entered a Bay well sheltered from the North and S.W. from whence they saw the mouth of a large River—they give the following description of the Indians—

"Those Indians are large and strong: their Colour is the same as all the People of this Coast; the principal trait of their character is generosity, for they appeared to expect no return for the presents they offered us, a circumstance we never had observed among any of the Savages we had before visited"

They left this place October 4th and returned to St Blais on the 20th without making further discoveries—

Mourella sailed again from St Blais in 1799; it seems he scarcely saw the Land until he arrived at Buccarella, from whence (after making a Survey of the place and proceeding as far North as 60° without making any discoveries of note) he returned to S Blais.

From Montery in the Latitude of 36½ to Nootka in the Latitude of 49½ we have only vague surmises; the Port of Saint Franscisco in that interval has been partly explored and a plan taken which appears to afford every advantage that could be expected from a good Port.

Every navigator has neglected the space occupied by that part of the Coast laying on the West side of Louisiana and between the Latitudes of 38 and 48° N, not because it was indifferent to them but because some unfortunate circumstances prevented them from approaching it, and to this day we remain in ignorance.

The principal object of Cook was to discover a N.W. passage, consequently he would not look for it in that Quarter, and La Perouse having spent so much time at the Port des Francais, he could devote none to the examination of that Coast and makes the following observations

Vol. 2. page 153.—

"This part of America as far North as Mount St Elie with the exception of the Port of Nootka (where he stopped) was only seen by Captain Cook; but from Mount St Elie to the frozen Cape this celebrated Navigator followed the Coast with a perseverance and Courage that all Europe knew he was capable of"

"The examination of that part of America comprised between Mount S[t] Elie and the Port of Montery is a work interesting for navigation and commerce; but it requires many years and I do not pretend to conceal that having but two or three months to spare in consequence of the Season, and more so as the plan of our Voyage is so vast, we shall leave many important discoveries to be made by such Navigators as may come after us; many ages will pass perhaps before all the Ports and all the Bays of this part of America will be perfectly known; but the true direction of the Coast, the determination of the Latitude and Longitude of the principal head Lands will give our exertions a degree of utility that no Seaman can contemn—"[2]

He also makes the following apology for not examining minutely that extent of Coast which in reality constituted one of the principal objects of his expedition—

"The stay I was forced to make in the Port des Francais compelled me to change the plan of my navigation on the Coast of America—I had still time to Sail along the Coast and ascertain its direction but it was impossible for me to make any calculation of remaining at any other place and still more impossible for me to examine each Bay—every calculation and arrangement must yield to the absolute necessity of arriving at Manilla by the last of January and at China in the course of February in order that I might devote the following Summer to the examination of the Coasts of Tartary, Japan, Kamtschatka and as far as the Aleutine Islands—I discovered with sorrow that so vast a plan only afforded time to perceive objects and not the means of clearing doubts; but oblidged, as we were, to navigate Seas subject to Monsoons, we were liable to lose one year unless we arrived at Montery by the 10[th] or 15[th] of September, there to spend only 6 or 7 days to compleat our water and wood, and afterwards cross the Pacific with the utmost expedition over a space of more than 120 degrees of Longitude."

He also says. "From cross Sound as far as Cape Engano in an extent of Coast of about 25 leagues I am convinced that Twenty different Ports might be found and that three months would scarcely suffice to explore this Labyrinth. I confined myself (agreeable to the plan I had formed on leaving the Port des Francais) to determine precisely the beginning and the end of the Islands as well as their direction along the Coast with the entrance of the principal Bays—"

Why Dixon and the rest of the dealers in Fur have not examined that Coast is evident, and why the Spaniards have not we are uninformed; but we are convinced the enterprise is of sufficient importance to merit a particular mission to effect it; One Season perhaps would be insufficient owing to unavoidable delays and the precautions necessary to be taken in this kind of navigation, and this object should be unconnected with any other that could present any obstacles to its execution; those who have visited that Coast on discoveries were compelled to carry their views some thousand leagues ahead of their Ships as it was necessary for them to arrive at certain places in certain Seasons to have the benefit of periodical winds to enable him to effect other objects connected with the great plan of their Voyage.

To the North and South of Cape Engano in a space of ten Leagues there are a multitude of Isles that lay along the Coast and even what appeared as a Coast may be an Archipelago as Bays appear'd of a depth and extent that La Perouse was unable to ascertain—This part of America from 51.° to 56.° may be composed of a Cluster of Islands which serve to shelter the mouth of a Gulf that may possibly have some communication with Hudsons Bay, or at all events extend to a considerable distance in the interior of America as in this neighbourhood our navigator experienced rapid Currents which were evidently counteracted by others whose influence were strongly felt by him although at the distance of three Leagues from the nearest Island. What in a measure serves to prove that this part of the supposed Coast is an archipelago, is, that the Land here has an aspect altogether different from the Northern; and Mount Crillon in the Latitude of 58½ is seen gradually to decline to the East where it loses itself—appearance of Islands continue with large openings between them until he arrives at a projection which he calls Cape Hector in the Lat. of 51.° 57.′ which he doubles but loses sight of the continuation of the Coast—in the morning he discovers he has entered a large Gulf which to him has the appearance of the Gulf of California, but from the great violence of the current I am induced to believe it to be of much greater extent; he estimates the mouth of the channel or Gulf to be about thirty leagues across—a Group of Isles lay on the East side of the Gulf to the back of which he discovered high peak'd Mountains covered with Snow which lay more than thirty leagues in the interior; he conjectures that this Gulf may extend 6. or 7 degrees to the north the Season not permitting him to clear his doubts—Should the object be the discovery of a N.W. passage into the South Sea, or to find the nearest communication between the South and Atlantic oceans, I should suppose the most likely place to find it would be between the Latitudes of 50 and 58° N. this space being entirely unknown and the external appearance serving to favor this opinion—

The Port of Buccarella, of which a plan was taken by the Spaniards, is a Gulf or Bay formed by a number of Islands and is not connected to the continent as was supposed by them; their chart of the Coast which La Perouse made use of, was found to be extremely incorrect by his account and the place is stated by him to lay at least forty leagues from Terre Firma—

The advantages that may result to the Government of the United States will no doubt compensate for the expence of fitting out some of their small Vessels and employing some of their Officers for the purpose of examining that Coast; the Spanish possessions do not extend further north than Montery; no nation whatever appears to have taken formal possession of any part between California and Nootka, consequently we have it in our power to acquire that part if we do not already possess it, perhaps prevent a dangerous[3] neighbour from settling at our backs, and at all events ascertain if any and what advantages would accrue to the United States by making establishments there

It is not to be supposed that the only object a nation can have in view by extending her Territory is to obtain more Land for cultivation; it is to be presumed that some local advantages are to be gained; should that not be the case why should we already have done it when we had so much waste Land in the interior of our Country?

We have purchased Louisiana and are no doubt desirous of reaping all its advantage, what their extent are is not yet ascertained; perhaps some of the Rivers which discharge themselves into the South Sea may be navigable so far inland as to make the land carriage to some of the great branches of the Mississipi short; Should that be the case, by means of a Commercial establishment there, the intercourse between India and the Atlantic States could be rendered easy and we should probably by means of regular Caravans (such as are established in Egypt, Persia, Barbary &c) reap all the advantages that could result to Europe from the discovery of a N.W. passage and should a northern means of communication, between the two Seas, exist, the distance of between 4 and 5000 miles of a dangerous navigation in a passage to India would be saved, and instead of America being beholden to Europe for most of the productions of the East, perhaps they may come to us to seek their supplies—

Perhaps one object in making a purchase of Louisiana was that of having a Port on the Pacific ocean; should that be the case can we too soon ascertain its advantages?

Were some of our Vessels sent on such an expedition, inteligent Persons could be sent up the different branches of the Mississipi and cross over the Continent to rendezvous established in certain Latitudes to meet the Ships, with the Commanders of which they could leave a Copy of their Journals and return by different routes bringing with them an account of the discoveries made by our Vessels, by which means we should be certain of procuring the most correct information of that newly acquired and unknown Territory—

after performing this part of their duty, which should be considered a primary object, our Vessels could return to the United States of America by a western route endeavouring to pursue a Course that has never been taken by any Navigator, touching at such places as may be considered necessary for refreshments, and at all such places endeavour to procure the best information of their Commerce, Policy, manners and Customs; Men of Science chosen by the different Philosophical societies might be embarked whose discoveries may tend very much to the advancement of useful knowledge—

America has long been a debtor to the World for Science; a fair oppertunity offers for her to acquit herself of the debt and at the same time to reap all its advantages; a peace favors the plan; her Ships are good and mostly unemployed, and her Officers young, enterprising and panting for an oppertunity to distinguish themselves in the different branches of their professions.

Bay S Louis West Florida Aug[t] 17. 1809 D PORTER

MS (DLC); in a clerk's hand, signed by Porter.

Porter drew on works describing the voyages of LA PEROUSE (Jean François de Galaup, comte de La Pérouse, *Voyage de La Pérouse autour du Monde, publié conformément au décret du 22 avril 1797 et rédige*, 4 vols. [Paris, 1797]); COOK (James Cook, *A Voyage to the Pacific Ocean . . . In the Years 1776, 1777, 1778, 1779, and 1780*, 3 vols. [London, 1784]); DIXON (William Beresford, *A Voyage Round The World; but more Particularly To The North-West Coast Of America: Performed in 1785, 1786, 1787, and 1788*, ed. George Dixon [London, 1789]); and MOURELLA (Francisco Antonio Mourelle de la Rúa, *Journal of a Voyage in 1775. To explore the coast of America, northward of California* [London, 1781]; abstracted in La Pérouse's *Voyage*).

TJ owned two editions of Cook's *Voyage* and four accounts by other members of his expedition (Sowerby, nos. 3937–41, 3943).

1 Manuscript: "examing."

2 Closing quotation mark editorially supplied.

3 Here is canceled "nation."

## From Madame Deshay

MONSIEUR de Baltimore le 18 aout. 1809

Forcée d'abandonner mes proprietes de St domaingue, obligée de sortir de l'isle de cuba ou je m'ettais réfugiée et ou je pouvois sufir a mon existence, me voici maintenent ici dans un pays etrangé pour moi; Dénué de tout, tres agée sans parents sans amis. Mon mari mon unique soutient ayant ete sacrifier par les neigres je me trouve seule au monde. Monsieur Lemerre qui étoit ùn de vos colonel[1] du temps de la guere D'amérique étoit un de mes proche parent. C'est á ce titre et au nom de l'humanité Monsieur que j'ose reclamer vos bontes et pour me fair [passer] quelques secours, pour me donner du moins les premiers besoins de la vie. Croyez que ma reconnoissance sera sans borne. j'ai l'honeur d'etre

Monsieur votre tres humble et tres obéissante Servante

V^E^ DESHAY

Si vous avez la bonté de m'envoyer quelquechose, veuillez l'adresser à M^me^ Amiot au Collège de S^te^ Marie de Baltimore.

EDITORS' TRANSLATION

SIR Baltimore 18 August. 1809

Forced to abandon my properties in Saint Domingue, obliged to leave the island of Cuba where I had taken refuge and where I could provide for my existence, I am now here in a country that is foreign to me; stripped of everything, very elderly, without relatives, without friends. My husband my sole support having been sacrificed by the negroes, I find myself alone in the world. Mr. Lemerre, who was one of your colonels during the American war, was one of my close relatives. It is on this account and in the name of humanity, Sir, that I dare to appeal to your goodness in order to obtain some assistance for myself, to procure at least the basic necessities of life. Believe that my gratitude will be without limit. I have the honor of being

Sir your very humble and very obedient Servant. WIDOW DESHAY

If you have the goodness to send me something, please address it to Mme Amiot at St. Mary's College in Baltimore.

RC (DLC); endorsed by TJ as received 11 Sept. 1809 and so recorded in SJL. Translation by Dr. Amy Ogden.

LEMERRE was probably Jacques Le Maire, a Frenchman who acted as an agent to procure arms for Virginia during the American Revolution. He was well known to TJ, who as governor signed his commission as a brevet lieutenant COLONEL in the Virginia Dragoons, later assisted him with land claims, and considered having him bring Maria Jefferson to France (Madison, *Papers, Congress. Ser.*, 1:233n; *PTJ*, 3:124, 7:430, 505, 9:212, 15:624).

COLLÈGE DE S^TE^ MARIE: many Saint Domingue refugees who settled in Baltimore were affiliated with the Church of St. Mary, a largely French-speaking church established by the Sulpicians. St. Mary's Academy, founded in 1791 as a school for West Indian boys, later became St. Mary's College and was chartered as a university in 1805 by the Maryland legislature (Winston C. Babb, "French Refugees from Saint Domingue to the Southern United States, 1791–1810" [Ph.D. diss., University of Virginia, 1954], 253, 266–7).

[1] Manuscript: "conlonel."

## From George Jefferson

DEAR SIR Richmond 18th Augt 1809

It really almost appears as if I shall never more have the pleasure of seeing you at Monticello. Mr Gibson when I last wrote you, had not the most distant thought of going to the Springs this season—not having experienced as he supposed; any benefit from his visit the last.—He has <u>suddenly</u> however, by the advice of some of his friends, determined on making one more trial, and is gone.

I now return[1] you the two notes of 4000$ each, which were intended to be used in the bank—the other arrangement having been made: but of which I do not observe that Mr G. has informed you.

I have for some weeks past been absent, & did not return until some hours after his departure.

I am Dear Sir Your Very humble servt GEO. JEFFERSON

RC (MHi); at foot of text: "Thomas Jefferson esqr"; endorsed by TJ as received 23 Aug. 1809 and so recorded in SJL. Enclosures not found.

[1] Word interlined in place of "inclose."

## From Jonathan Shoemaker

MY DEAR FRIEND Washington City 18th Augt 1809

Inclosed thee will find 300$ it will not be Neccessary to Acknowledge the receipt of the money by Letter as I Expect to Leave the City some time next weak for Shadwell, when I wrote the last we were all in a Pannick at the Prospect of trade Supposing that our produce would be worth very little, but the alarm has now very much Subsided, Flour is now worth 5.75$ at Alexa and it is thought by the Merchants hear generally it will not be much lower through the Season, & upon reconsidering the subject of the Lease I find it would be a great disadvantage to us to Surrender it at this Season as one Quarter has Expired in wich little or no business has or could be done & in addition to that we have 40.000 Staves on hand & hogs Enough to make 10,000 ℔ Pork we have also a fine garden & truck Patch wich must be lost to us in case of removing we have also the Richmond line of Stages on hand worth 1800$ upon this View of the subject thou will percieve the Loss we Should be subjected too by giving up the Mills at Present, I have therefore determined to come on next weak, I have laid in a Small Asortment of Groceries & Dry goods mostly of the coarse kind Such as I thought would best suit the Cuntry

I Salute with Esteem &c JONATHAN SHOEMAKER

RC (MHi); at foot of text: "Thomas Jefferson"; endorsed by TJ (torn) as received 20 Aug. 1809 and so recorded in SJL.

## From John Vaughan

DEAR SIR Philad. 19 Aug 1809

I enclose a letter received at the society & read last evening—with its envellope—The Rouleau mention'd on the Envellope has not made its appearance & may have [been][1] taken on by M Cole or may have come by the Syren, by which Vessel the letter possibly came—But all our packets came by the Mentor—Should you have recieved it, it will after you have Examin'd it be peculiarly acceptable to us—By a letter I have rec$^{d}$ from M$^{r}$ Humboldt, I find that the 1$^{st}$ Vol. of his Travels in S$^{o}$[2] America will appear in Nov. 1809 & that he would be pleased to find an Am$^{n}$ Bookseller who would purchase the right of the English (In that Language)[3] Ed$^{n}$ which has been edited by an Englishman of Science under his Eye & with the Notes of Pictet of Geneva—his adress is at the Polytecnique School at Paris—Michaux has been very attentive, in completing our Journals & sending us out some works on Mineralogy, which were essential to us, as we are by means of M Godon a French mineralogist now amongst us, arranging our minerals What they have already done has been of material Use & made our Collection more Valuable—D Woodhouse left us his Minerals some few are of Value but not many for the want of Localities & Circumstancies—I enclose a prospectus relative to ancient vases formerly called Etruscan now Said to be Grecian M Warden has sent us 12 Engravings—also a Report of the Institut which request Bonaparte to assist the Engravers & publishers—as we have two Copies of this prospectus, you will retain this—The National Institute has Sent us the 5; 6; & 7 Vol. Physique & Mathematique of the Institut—If I can be made serviceable to You here command me freely—I hope your retirem$^{t}$ from public life will enable you to indulge more freely in your Scientific Pursuits

Myself Individually & all our Society will be happy to hear frequently from you

I remain with respect Your ob Serv & friend JN VAUGHAN

RC (MHi); addressed: "Thomas Jefferson Esqr late Pres[t] of U States Monticello"; franked and postmarked; endorsed by TJ as received 27 Aug. 1809 and so recorded in SJL. Enclosure: Alexander von Humboldt to TJ as president of the American Philosophical Society, Paris, 12 June 1809, enclosing his barometrical observations; requesting that TJ forward them to the society "comme un faible marque de mon devouement et de ma reconnaissance" ("as a feeble mark of my devotion and gratitude"); and asking that his regards be given to Caspar Wistar, Benjamin Rush, Robert Patterson, William Thornton, Adam Seybert, Charles Willson Peale, James Woodhouse, Nicholas Collin, Robert Hare, John Vaughan, James Mease, Andrew Ellicott, and Benjamin Smith Barton (RC in PPAmP: APS Archives; at head of text: "Monsieur le President"; endorsed by the society as "read 18 Aug[t] Donation—of his acc[t] of the Barometrical obs[n] on the Andes").

John Vaughan (1756–1841), an English wine merchant who settled in Philadelphia in 1782, was elected to the American Philosophical Society in 1784 and served as its treasurer from 1791 and as librarian from 1803, holding both positions until his death. He conducted the society's routine business for many years, gathered volumes assiduously, and brought together many American and European scientists through correspondence and personal contact. In 1824 Vaughan catalogued the collection in the hope that it would become a national library (*ANB*; APS, Minutes, 16 Jan. 1784, 7 Jan. 1791, 18 Mar. 1803 [MS in PPAmP]).

Humboldt's barometrical observations in the Andes, described as enclosed in his covering letter to TJ enclosed here, evidently became separated from that letter but soon reached the American Philosophical Society (Vaughan to TJ, 20 Aug. 1809). French scientist François André MICHAUX had been elected a foreign member of the society on 21 Apr. 1809 (APS, Minutes).

The enclosed PROSPECTUS was one of two versions of a four-page printed promotional circular (both at PPAmP) for *Peintures de Vases Antiques, vulgairement appelés Vases Étrusques, tirés de différentes collections* (Paris, 1808–10), an ambitious project in which the editor Dubois Maisonneuve and the renowned Didot printing firm issued a total of 150 plates of Greek VASES engraved by Ange Clener, with accompanying text by Aubin Louis Millin de Grandmaison. Subscribers received one livraison consisting of six engravings each month, at an initial cost of fifteen francs per livraison. In its 3 Dec. 1808 REPORT the Classe des Beaux Arts of the Institut de France emphasized the significance and value of the proposed edition, praised the work involved in assembling images, and urged Napoleon to support its publication (PPAmP: APS Archives).

[1] Omitted word editorially supplied.
[2] Word interlined.
[3] Parenthetical phrase interlined.

# To Craven Peyton

DEAR SIR Monticello Aug. 20. 09.

The title purchased from Henderson's representatives is so extremely complicated as to render it indispensable to state in the deed all the several conveyances of all the parties; otherwise in case of question at any future time it might be lost for want of knowing it. I have endeavored to do this in the inclosed deed, and in order that you may have time, I send it to you To-day, & pray you to examine well the statement of title & be ready to enable me to correct it if there be any error; as also to fill up all the blanks.

1. There are still wanting the widow's deed for her dower as well in the other property as the warehouse.

2. Charles's deeds.

3. John's deeds here to Seabrook for the warehouse &
to Lewis for the 2. lots & his rights on the dower

4. Lewis's deed to you for John's rights

[. . .] [co]nveyances of John, Charles, Isham & Bennet H to Seabrook

[. . .] [Se]abrook's deed to you for their shares in the warehouse.

[. . .][1] you on Tuesday as promised. friendly salutations

TH: JEFFERSON

PoC (MHi); corner torn; at foot of text: "[Cr]aven Peyton"; endorsed by TJ. Enclosure: draft, not found, of Craven and Jane Peyton's Conveyance of the Henderson Lands, [22 Aug. 1809].

TJ promised to meet Peyton on TUESDAY, 22 Aug. 1809.

[1] Estimated three words missing.

## From Craven Peyton

DEAR SIR. August 2[0 1809]

the Deed^s not given you the othar day are in the office at Charlotesville except M^r Hendersons that being in the care of Mr. Hay at Richm^d the parts baught of R. Anderson as attorney for Seabrook is not deeded ewing to the circumstance of my objecting to pay for Hills right untill he was of age the othar parts Anderson will give deeds for at Any instant this I before named to you, I am in hopes to have every thing by Tuesday.

with great esteem [. . .]

RC (MHi); torn at bottom, with loss of signature and part of dateline below it; addressed (torn): "Thomas [Jefferson esq^r] Montice[llo]"; endorsement by TJ torn. Recorded in SJL as a letter of 20 Aug. 1809 received the same day.

HILLS: Bennett Hillsborough Henderson.

## From John Vaughan

D Sir: Philad. Aug[t] 20. 1809

The Nivellem[t] Barometrique of Humboldt has this moment come to hand—Having found two Prospectus of the publications made or proposed by Humboldt & Bonplan—I enclose one for you—I remain D sir Your friend & ser[t]

Jn Vaughan

RC (MHi); at foot of text: "Thomas Jefferson Esq[r]"; dateline below signature; endorsed by TJ as received 27 Aug. 1809 and so recorded in SJL. Enclosure not found.

nivellem[t] barometrique: Alexander von Humboldt, *Nivellement barométrique fait dans les régions équinoxiales du nouveau continent, en 1799–1804* (Paris, 1809); part of his *Recueils d'observations astronomiques*. For that and other publications by Humboldt and Aimé Goujaud Bonpland, see note to TJ to Humboldt, 6 Mar. 1809.

## To John Barnes

Dear Sir Monticello Aug. 22. 09

Yours of the 9[th] was duly recieved. having occasion to remit to mr Peale of the Museum Philadelphia a sum of 49 D–5½ C and not being able to get any Philadelphia bills here, I have taken the liberty which your goodness has rendered habitual of inclosing you George town, Alexandria, & Virginia bills (50. D.) the only kinds to be had here, & of praying you to exchange them for a draught of the B. bank US. at Washington on that at Philadelphia in favor of Charles W. Peale, & to put it under cover to him, for which purpose I inclose you a cover. I write by this post to mr Peale to save you the trouble of a letter of explanation. ever affectionately yours

Th: Jefferson

PoC (DLC); at foot of text: "M[r] John Barnes." Enclosures not found.

Barnes's letter of the 9[th], not found, is recorded in SJL as received from Georgetown on 13 Aug. 1809.

## From Samuel R. Demaree

Respected Sir, Near Danville, Ky. Aug. 22, 1809

You have doubtless been congratulated by many who have better claims to your notice than I have, on your release from the burdens of public life. . . . Altho I agree with those who believe that your country has no longer a right to claim your service; I rejoice that congress, by authorizing your letters to be franked, has offered to all the privelege of requesting that information & advice which your talents, age & experience eminently qualify you to give. . . . As an individual, I should not perhaps avail myself of a privilege which may possibly give you unwelcome trouble—tho I fondly hope it will not—but for the sake of my pupils I cheerfully hazard an application which interests me considerably, but which if disagreeable to you I hope you will at least excuse. The current of Education, every where too feeble, is much retarded in this state for want of proper books. Many are not to be got without sending to philadelphia or N. York; and few on easy terms. . . . Some students are unable, and others unwilling to procure any but the cheapest works on science; which certainly are not generally the best: and I regret extremely that neither my opportunity nor my circumstances enable me to compare the merits of different works, and thence to recommend the most valuable.

Inform me, if you please, what works are intrinsically the most excellent on the following sciences; & also what books chiefly combine perspicuity, brevity & cheapness—Annex the known or supposed philadelphia prices. . . . Geography, Geometry, Algebra, Fluxions, the several branches of Physics, Metaphysics or philosophy of Mind, Morals, Rhetoric, Logic & History.

It is schoolbooks I have enquired after: if however you deem any other on any subject peculiarly valuable, pray add it to the list.

As soon as I can afford it, I must get me a library: will you be so good as to advise me whether it would be more eligible to procure an Encyclopedia only, or separate works on the differents subjects necessary to be read? How many volumes will there be of Rees's Cyclopedia?[1] Is it the best entire work? May I ask who is author of the "Memoirs of the Hon. Thomas Jefferson," lately advertised in the Richmond papers?

You are probably apprized of the great change the soil of Kentucky has undergone since its settlement. It is in many places quite stony now, where 30 years ago no stone was to be found. . . . Since last Christmas more rain has fallen, much more, than was ever before witnessed here. I have thot a good deal on the subject, & conclude that the clearing of the ground, by facilitating the motion of winds and the evaporation of moisture, will supply us with more rain than formerly, & still leave us more subject to drouth. But very probably you are infinitely better acquainted with such matters than I am. I will not trouble you with my speculations unless I knew they would be acceptable. Accept my sincere regard, and my best wishes.

SAM[L] R. DEMAREE.

RC (DLC); ellipses in manuscript; addressed: "Hon. Thomas Jefferson Monticello Virginia"; franked and postmarked; endorsed by TJ as received 20 Sept. 1809 and so recorded in SJL; with 1st Dft of Supplemental List of Recommended Books, enclosed in TJ's 4 Oct. 1809 reply, on verso.

Samuel R. Demaree, the son of a farmer, became a schoolmaster after an injury left him unable to farm. He corresponded occasionally about literary and political subjects with TJ during his presidency and retirement (Demaree to TJ, 6 Jan. 1802, 30 May 1803, 28 Aug. 1805, and TJ to Demaree, 6 May 1805 [DLC]; Frank S. Baker, *Glimpses of Hanover's Past, 1827–1977* [1978], 23).

Abraham Rees published forty-five VOLUMES of *The New Cyclopædia* (London, 1802–20), while the American edition concluded with forty-seven volumes (*DNB*). The anonymous AUTHOR of the intensely anti-Jefferson *Memoirs of the Hon. Thomas Jefferson*, 2 vols. (New York, 1809), may have been its publisher, the political journalist and Federalist sympathizer Stephen Cullen Carpenter (*ANB*; Richmond *Enquirer*, 1 Sept. 1809).

[1] Manuscript: "cycopedia."

# To George Jefferson

DEAR SIR Monticello Aug. 22. 09.

Our last account left me some thirty odd Dollars in your debt. I now inclose you one hundred Dollars to cover it.

I wrote some little time ago to Mess[rs] Gordon & Trokes for a supply of groceries & took the liberty of referring them to you as to the most trust-worthy boatmen, mr Randolph's boats not being likely to go down soon. a number of others having gone down with the late swell of the river, will allow some choice among them. we shall be in want by their return. The Marquis Fayette has sent me a pair of Shepherd's dogs by a mr Waddell in the Mentor. mr Waddell was to send them on to you. I will thank you for your usual particular attention to them, & to send them up by a careful boatman. can you give me any account of the volumes of Newspapers I lent the late mr Burke while writing his history of Virginia. mr Eppes was to enquire for them & forward them to you.

Affectionately your's TH: JEFFERSON

PoC (MHi); at foot of text: "M[r] G. Jefferson"; endorsed by TJ. Enclosure not found.

## From James Leitch

SIR, Charlottesville Aug. 22nd 1809

The Amount of your account I cannot at present exactly ascertain; I believe the Ballance will be about Thirty pounds—six, Eight, Ten, sixteen, & Twenty penny nails of nearly equal quantities would be preferred

Yours respectfully JAS LEITCH

RC (MHi); addressed: "Thos Jefferson Esqr Monticello"; endorsed by TJ as received 22 Aug. 1809.

## To Charles Willson Peale

DEAR SIR Monticello Aug. 22. 09

I have been for some time endeavoring to procure bills of some bank in Philadelphia to enable me to remit you the balance of 49. D $5\frac{1}{2}$ C due you on account of my grandson. finding there is little hope of this, I have this day inclosed to my friend mr Barnes of George-town, bills of that place, & prayed him to exchange them for a draught of the Washington bank on that of the US. at Philadelphia in your favor, which you will probably recieve a day or two after the reciept of this. I have now to thank you for all your kindnesses & those of your family to my grandson; and at the same time to convey to you the expressions of his gratitude & affectionate remembrence. he speaks of yourself, mrs Peale & the family always as of his own parents & family. he waits till the frosts set in to go into our lower country to commence his course of Mathematics & Natural philosophy. I cannot describe to you the hope & comfort I derive from his good dispositions & understanding.

ever Affectionately Yours TH: JEFFERSON

RC (NNGL, on deposit NHi); at foot of text: "Mr Peale." PoC (MHi); endorsed by TJ.

# Craven and Jane Peyton's Conveyance of the Henderson Lands

[22 Aug. 1809]

This Indenture made on the third day of August one Thousand eight hundred and nine between Craven Peyton and Jane his wife on the one part and Thomas Jefferson on the other, all of the County of Albemarle in Virginia witnesseth that whereas Bennet Henderson dec$^{d}$ of the same county was in his lifetime Seised[1] and possessed in feesimple of a certain tract of land on the rivanna River in the same county Surrounding and adjacent to the town of Milton in its whole limit containing by Estimation Eleven Hundred and Sixty two and a quarter acres more or less, and being so Seised died without will leaving Elizabeth his widow, & Eleven Children to wit John, William Sarah, James L. Charles, Isham, Bennett Hilsborough Eliza, Frances, Lucy, & Nancy C. of whom the said William died Soon after, without will also & without issue whereupon the said widow in Right of Dower and the said Surviving Children as heirs and Coparceners became entitled to the whole feesimple estate in the said Lands which were accordingly duly allotted to them in Several purparties to wit; the lands by metes and bounds and the warehouse in common and being so Seised and entitled the said Doweress and parceners did by Several Deeds and for the Several valuable considerations therein expressed convey their whole right, estate and possession to the said Craven (with the exception of the five acre lot N$^{o}$ 10. of the said John in the upper field conveyed by him to the said Thomas Jefferson the right of the said Sarah in the warehouse on the premises and her tenth part of the said Williams eleventh part of the whole premises conveyed to Joseph Brand and the right of the said Bennett H. in the said warehouse) that is to say the said John as to his purparties or lots N$^{o}$ 1. of 102. acres in the back Lands and N$^{o}$ 9. of Six and a quarter acres in the Lower field conveyed the same by Deed of April 30. 1803 to the said Craven; as to his right in the warehouse by a deed of July 17$^{th}$ 1802. to Richard Seabrook, who by Richard Anderson his Attorney conveyed the same by Deed of June 5$^{th}$ 1805 to the said Craven and as to all his other rights in the premises by a Deed of October 9. 1806[2] to a certain James Lewis who conveyed the same to the said Craven by a deed bearing date the eighth day of November 1808.

The said Sarah with John R. Kerr her husband as to the eleventh part in the whole of the premises descended on her immediately from the said Bennet her father (except the warehouse) by deed to the said Craven bearing date the 7th day of June 1803.
The said James L. Henderson as to all his right in the premises by a Deed of December 28th 1799. to a certain Tucker Woodson, who conveyed the same to the said Craven by a Deed of April 25th 1801. which was confirmed to him by the said James L by a Subsequent Deed of November 29. 1801.

The said Charles as to all his other rights by deed to the said James L. Henderson of March 18. 1801. who conveyed the same to the said Craven by Deed of March 19. 1801. which was confirmed to the said Craven by the said Charles by a Deed of January 31. 1804 and as to his right in a mill Seat[3] on the lot N° 8 between the town and River by a Deed of           to the said John who conveyed the said Mill seat by the same Deed of October 9. 1806[4] to the said James Lewis, who conveyed the same to the said craven by his Deed of November 8. 1808 beforementioned, and the right of the said Charles in the warehouse by a Deed of October 19. 1802 to the said James W. Bramham who by Richard Anderson his attorney conveyed the same to the said Craven by his Deed of June 5th 1805 aforesaid.

The said Isham as to all his other rights in the premises by a Deed of March 17. 1801. to the said James L. Henderson who conveyed the same to the said Craven by a Deed of the same date and as to his right in the warehouse by a deed of July 17. 1802.[5] to the said John who by the same deed of July 17. 1802.[6] conveyed the same to the said Richard Seabrooks who by Richard Anderson his attorney, by the same deed of June 5. 1805. aforesaid conveyed the same to the said Craven. the said Bennett H. as to all his right in the premises, except the warehouse by a deed of September 18. 1802. executed to the said Craven by the said James L. Henderson his guardian for Valuable consideration received from him the said Craven and applied to the necessary use of the said Bennett H. which conveyance was confirmed to the said Craven by the said Bennett H. by Deed of June 28. 1804.

The Said Eliza, Frances, Lucy & Nancy C. as to all their other Rights in the premises, by the same Deed of September 18. 1802. executed to the said Craven by the said James L. Henderson one of their guardians for valuable considerations received from him the said Craven and applied to the necessary uses of the said Eliza. Frances, Lucy and Nancy C. and as to the warehouse by a deed of

February 26. 1805 from the said Eliza and John H. Bullock her husband to the said Craven and by Deeds of February 25. 1805 from the said frances Lucy, & Nancy C. and of November 17th 1807. from the said John their other guardian; which last mentioned deeds confirmed also that of September 18. 1802. by the said James L. Henderson for the other property

And the said Elizabeth as to her right of Dower in all the other of the premises by a deed of September 18. 1802. to the said Craven and as to the warehouse by another Deed to him of July 19. 1804. All of which Several Deeds and Conveyances before mentioned were duly proved and recorded in the several Courts required by Law.

By Virtue of which Several deeds and conveyances the said Craven now stands Seised in feesimple of all the right and title which was held by the said Bennet Henderson deceased in the said tract of Land and in all the parts thereof lying around the town of Milton excepting the said five acre lot N° 10 of the said John the right of the said Sarah in the warehouse and her tenth part of the said Williams eleventh part of the whole property and the right of the said Bennet H. in the warehouse.

Now therefore this Indenture witnesseth that the said Craven and Jane his wife in Consideration of the sum of Two thousand three hundred and three pounds Seven Shillings to them in hand paid by the said Thomas at divers times preceeding the present date, and the receipt whereof fully they do hereby acknowledge, have given granted bargained and Sold and by these presents do give grant bargain and Sell unto the said Thomas all the said tract or parcel of land before Described as having been the property of the said Bennet Henderson, containing by estimation after deducting the said five acre lot N° 10. of the said John, eleven hundred and fifty Seven and One quarter acres and excepting out of the said 1157.$\frac{1}{4}$[7] acres also the right of the said Sarah in the warehouse and in Williams eleventh part of the whole inheritance and the right of the said Bennet H. in the said Warehouse with all their appurtenances as fully and entirely as the same were held by the said Bennett to have and to hold the said parcel of land and its appurtenances to him the said Thomas and his heirs and the said Craven and Jane his wife for themselves their joint and Several heirs executors and administrators do covenant with the said Thomas and his heirs that they the said Craven and Jane his wife their heirs executors and administrators jointly and Severally the said parcel of land with its appurtenances to him the said Thomas and his heirs will forever warrant and defend. In Witness whereof they have hereunto set their hands on the day and year first above written.

CRAVEN PEYTON
JANE J. PEYTON

Signed Sealed & Delivered in presence of
H. PEYTON
ISAIAH STOUT
EDWARD PACE

The Preceeding Deed not having yet been committed to Record the said Craven Peyton and Jane his wife hereby renew the execution thereof, and again confirm the same by Schedule thereto annexed to take effect as from its original date; and they further declare that the exception in the said deed of the rights of Bennet H. Henderson therein named, in the warehouse was made through mistake the said rights having before that been regularly conveyed from the said Bennet H. to the said Craven Peyton in feesimple by the same deeds therein described by which the rights of Isham Henderson therein named were conveyed to him and that it was the Intention of the said Craven and Jane his wife to convey to the said Thomas Jefferson in feesimple all their rights in all the lands around the town of Milton which had been the property of the said Bennet Henderson the father, and for the same consideration and they do hereby and for the same consideration, and for the further Sum of one dollar to them in hand paid, now give grant bargain and sell to the said Thomas Jefferson the said part and purparty of the said Bennet H. Henderson in the said warehouse in possession and reversion to have and to hold the same to the said Thomas Jefferson and his heirs.

In Witness whereof the said Craven and Jane his wife have to these presents set their hands and Seals meaning that the same shall be taken as set anew to the aforesaid Deed this        day of July One thousand eight hundred and twelve,

C. PEYTON
JANE J. PEYTON

Signed Sealed and delivered in Presence of
H. PEYTON
JOHN B. STOUT
ISHAM R. JEFFERSON

Tr (Albemarle County Deed Book, 18:74–7); redated based on Declaration to Craven Peyton, 22 Aug. 1809; at foot of text: "At a Court held for Albemarle County the 6th of July 1812. This Indenture &c of bargain and sale was produced into Court and acknowledged by Craven Peyton party thereto and ordered to be recorded. Teste John Nicholas." 2d Tr (same, 17:405–10); dated 4 Aug. 1811; lacking 1812 addendum; witnessed by H. Peyton, Thomas Jefferson (son of TJ's brother Randolph Jefferson), and John B. Stout; at foot of text: "At a Court held for Albemarle County the 5th of August 1811. This Indenture of bargain and sale was produced into Court and acknowledged by C Peyton Party thereto and ordered to be recorded. Teste John Nicholas." 3d Tr (ViU: TJP); in Alexander Garrett's hand; dated 4 Aug. 1811; with same witnesses and 5 Aug. 1811 court acknowledgment as 2d Tr; lacking 1812 addendum; at foot of text: "A Copy Teste Alex Garrett C:A:C"; endorsed by Garrett and TJ.

Jane Jefferson Lewis (1777–1822), a daughter of TJ's sister Lucy and Charles Lilburne Lewis, married Craven Peyton in 1792 (Merrow Egerton Sorley, *Lewis of Warner Hall: The History of a Family* [1935, repr. 1991], 352; John Vogt and T. William Kethley Jr., *Albemarle County Marriages, 1780–1853* [1991], 1:252).

PURPARTIES: proportions or shares of an inheritance (*OED*).

[1] Tr: "Seized." 2d Tr: "seised."

[2] 2d and 3d Trs have blank space instead of date.

[3] 2d and 3d Trs: "millsite."

[4] 2d and 3d Trs have blank space instead of date.

[5] 2d and 3d Trs have blank space instead of date.

[6] 2d and 3d Trs have blank space instead of date.

[7] 3d Tr: "1157½."

# Declaration to Craven Peyton

Whereas Craven Peyton has this day executed a deed of conveyance to me for the lands of the late Bennet Henderson surrounding & adjacent to the town of Milton, which deed bears on it's face a warranty for the parts thereof which were the property of Frances, Lucy & Nancy C. three of the daughters of the sd Bennet, whose shares have been purchased & paid for, but the sd Frances, Lucy & Nancy C. being still infants, have not validly confirmed the same, now therefore I hereby declare that the said clause of warranty is not to hold the sd Craven responsible, if the sd Frances, Lucy, or Nancy C. or either of them should refuse or fail to ratify the said sales of their parts, when they come of age; but that I the sd Thomas take that risk on myself, reserving however the right of recovering whatsoever the sd Peyton might have been entitled to recover from those responsible to him for the title. Witness my hand this 22d day of August 1809.

TH: JEFFERSON

FC (ViU: TJP); entirely in TJ's hand; at foot of text: "Copy of the original delivered to Craven Peyton"; endorsed by TJ as a "Declaration" to Peyton of this date. Not recorded in SJL.

## From James Madison

Dear Sir Montpellier Aug. 23. 1809

M[r] & M[rs] Gallatin reached us on saturday last; and in fulfilment of their promise to you propose to set out for Monticello, tomorrow morning. We are preparing to accompany them. I see by the papers that M[r] Smith has probably rec[d] dispatches from M[r] Pinkney, by a late arrival; but being in Baltimore, I have not yet heard from him on the subject. The newspaper dates from London were not later than the 3[d] July; of course give nothing from the Continent. It appears only, in confirmation of late acc[ts] that Russia as well as Holland adhere with rigor to the means of excluding B. Trade. Colonial produce, even Dutch in neutral vessels, is to be warehoused in Holland.

Y[rs] with truest affection James Madison

RC (DLC: Madison Papers); endorsed by TJ as received 23 Aug. 1809 and so recorded in SJL.

## To Joseph Dougherty

Dear Joseph Monticello Aug. 24. 09.

Davy sets off tomorrow with a cart for the bigtailed ram D[r] Thornton was so kind as to promise me. as the post will be with you a day or two earlier I drop you this line to give you earlier notice. I write you more fully by Davy

Your's affectionately Th: Jefferson

PoC (DLC); at foot of text: "M[r] Joseph Dougherty"; endorsed by TJ.

davy: David Hern (1784–after 1829), the son of David Hern and Isabel Hern, was a wagoner, nailer, blacksmith, and charcoal burner at Monticello. During TJ's presidency Hern brought his cart from Monticello to Washington twice a year, and he was part of the March 1809 wagon train that brought TJ's baggage home. His wife, Fanny Gillette Hern, was one of TJ's cooks (Stanton, *Free Some Day*, 62–4).

## From James Long

Sir Philadelphia August the 24[th] 1809

I Take the Liberty of Writing to you if it is posable in your Power to Befriend me I Hope you Will as I am in a Disalut setiation at present I Was Born in the North of Ireland in the year 1770 My Father Having a larg farem after I Got My scooling I was Set to Hard Work I

Continued at that to about twenty six years of age then the uniting Buisness Began I was apointed a Capten of a Compney of the united men in 1798 I was Taken into Costady and three More tryed By a Cort Marchel and Centsed to Death But[1] by the Cleamency of the Commanding offecer We Wear sent a Bout 60 Miles to Head quarters and Deteaned six Weeks then got off to america I stead onely a quarter of a year Hear to I started Back thinkeng to Get it setled But it Was out of My power I Had to Conceal My self four Months to I Got off again I Contined Hear about six years then Got Liberty to Go Back and settle What Little was acoming to Me I Got them settled and Left Ireland the tenth of May Was a year With about three Hundred Guines With Me I thought as I was Bred to no kind of Buisness I would Join farming and started to settel on the ohio River I tryed in Different pleasis to settel But Could not Content My self I went Rown By Neworlans and Landed Hear the 26th of February Last Holland Gin Was so High that I thought I woud Make Good Gin out of Wry Whiskey so I Bought a still and I Had about fifteen Gallans off When the Candle Catched the steem of the Licker aflshed Round Me Liek Gun pouder and set my Clothes a Fire and Borned My Legs and armes the skin of My Hands is so tender that I Cant Doe aney Work as yet I am very oneasy How I will Come thrugh the World the Little Money I have It me soon Go from Me and God He onely knows What I me Do If you Would Get Me a small Commison in the standing Armey I never Would forget your kindness to Me

Your Cincer friend JAMES LONG

Sir pleas to send Me a few lines and Direct Shiping It By six—

RC (MHi); endorsed by TJ as received 27 Aug. 1809 and so recorded (misdated 26 Aug. 1809) in SJL.

The 1798 British defeat of an uprising led by the Society of the UNITED Irishmen, secretly founded in Belfast in 1791 to promote Irish independence, inspired a flood of Irish immigration to the United States (David A. Wilson, *United Irishmen, United States: Immigrant Radicals in the Early Republic* [1998], 2).

[1] Manuscript: "But But."

# To William Thornton

DEAR DOCTOR Monticello Aug. 24. 09.

Having accidentally mentioned to my former servant Joseph Dougherty my misfortune in losing both my big-tailed rams, he, in his zeal for whatever concerns me, took the liberty of mentioning it to you & informed me you were so kind as to offer to supply my loss with one from your farm. by the cart which now goes to bring it, I take the occasion of returning you my best thanks for your kindness, which alone enables me to pursue a favorite object, that of raising this breed pure.

I have the pleasure of expecting the President & his lady, mr & mrs Gallatin at Monticello this day. I sincerely wish you were of the party. with my respectful compliments to mrs Brodeau & mrs Thornton I salute you with esteem & respect. TH: JEFFERSON

RC (DLC: Thornton Papers); addressed: "Doct[r] William Thornton Washington"; endorsed by Thornton: "From M[r] Jefferson sheep—." PoC (MHi); endorsed by TJ.

William Thornton (1759–1828), first superintendent of the United States Patent Office, 1802–28, corresponded frequently with TJ on their many shared interests. A native of the British West Indies who received an M.D. from the University of Aberdeen in 1784, he came to the United States in 1786 and became a citizen two years later. Thornton was an early proponent of steamboat development and an accomplished amateur architect. TJ greatly admired his winning design for the Capitol building in Washington, D.C., and later solicited his ideas for the design of the University of Virginia. Thornton was also interested in science and mathematics, farming, animal husbandry, and the arts, and he wrote passionately in support of colonial independence movements (*ANB*; *DNB*; *PTJ*, 26:236–7; C. M. Harris and Daniel Preston, eds., *Papers of William Thornton* [1995– ]; TJ to Thornton, 9 May 1817; Thornton to TJ, 27 May 1817).

# To James W. Wallace

DEAR DOCT[R] Monticello Aug. 24. 09

Having recieved a box of fine Havanna segars & knowing your fondness for them, I cannot make any use of them so gratifying to myself as by sending them to you. having occasion to send a cart to Washington, it will go by Fauq[r] C.H. to deposit this charge with you. it will return by Dumfries for a pair of Wild geese promised me there, as I have had the misfortune to lose the goose of the pair you were so kind as to give me. ever affectionately yours

TH: JEFFERSON

PoC (DLC); at foot of text: "Doct[r] Wallace"; endorsed by TJ.

# To John Barnes

Sir Monticello Aug. 25. 09.

By the last post I acknoleged the receipt of your last letter, & at the same time took the liberty of making a remittance through you[1] to mr Peale. having occasion to send a light cart to Washington, & being in want of half a pound of Sal-Ammoniac, an article necessary for tinning our copper utensils, & not to be had here, I ask the favor of you to procure it at an Apothecary's & send it to me by the bearer Davy who will call for it. the cost shall be answered with my remaining balance ere long. I salute you with affectionate esteem.

Th: Jefferson

PoC (CSmH: JF); at foot of text: "Mr Barnes"; endorsed by TJ.

[1] Preceding two words interlined.

# To Joseph Dougherty

Dear Joseph Monticello Aug. 25. 09.

Davy now brings a cart for the big-tailed ram which Doctr Thornton has been so kind as to offer me. you will be so good as to apply for it, and to instruct Davy how to bring him & take care of him so that he may be in no danger of being hurt. with respect to the Merinos, I had rather put off beginning with them a year or two longer. my farms, which have been leased out during my absence, will return into my own hands the next winter, & will after another year, furnish me convenient separate places for my big-tailed, many horned, & Merinos. I write to mr Barnes to send me half a pound of Sel Ammoniac for which Davy must call on him. he is then to come by Dumfries for a pair of wild geese. I salute you with my best wishes.

Th: Jefferson

PoC (DLC); at foot of text: "Mr Joseph Dougherty"; endorsed by TJ.

# From William Dunn

Dear Sir Liberty Bedford County VA August 25th 1809

Necesity dier necesity has campel'd me to the following lines it is probely that you may recollect the Signature to this letter I have writen Severel letters to you while you enjoyed the Highest Seat of Honor in America on the Same Subject but unfortunately for me I received no answer and the opportunity I then had of prospering in this World I am afraid are for ever gone but as the Poet says

While the lamp holds[1] out to burn
The vilest Sinner may return

So it may be with me if I could be so fortunate as to meet some kind Benefactor that would take compassion on me and assist me to some money indeed I am not yet discourage if I could find a friend but on this character Friend rest my futer destiny if you fail I no not to whome I Shall apply this is a very gloomy time all Nature appears to be arrested in her course and every avanue of trade stoped up nothing now appears to remain to the unfortunate debtor but the utter destruction of all he posseses in this world yes Dear Sir even the Gloomy Jails presents it self to his view on the Ignominious oth of insolvency yes this the unfortunate Situation of hundreds at this day alas alas I am one of that unfortunate class

M^r^ Jefferson you are able to extricate me and I hope to God willing too from this dilemma yes Sir the small Sum of five hundred dollers would settle all my debts and then have some left to assist me to carry on my business this Sum with the assistance of God I hope to be able to refund in two or three years indeed Sir a part of the above mention Sum would greatly assist me

I hope that you will take a simpathetic view of my deplorable Situation and think[2] with what ease and pleasure you can release me from my bonds and place me independant of every man in this world except your Honor to you Sir I shall ever consider my self bound and Shall do it with pleasure to acknowledge you my Benefactor and deliverer as long as I live in this world oh how glad I would be could I have the honor to call you my friend and deliverer M^r^ Jefferson take a view of both of our Situations you Sir are basking in the Sun Shine of Fortune and roling in all the pleasures this World can afford and I in the lowest depth of humility Sighing under the yoke of Malignant Creditors and groaning under the oppession of poverty I hope that you will not expose me to the world Send me an answer if you please as soon as posible if you be So kind as to let me know when you are at your Bedford Seat and give me an opportunity to have an Interview with you. I have not the least doubt in my mind but what can explain to you to your Satisfaction the reasons why I petition to you for assistance I hope you will [be][3] So kind as to give me an opportunity of Seeing you from your humble petitioner WILLIAM DUNN

Oh how I Shall long for a pleasing answer from you never did the travaler pant for a cooling Stream more

RC (MHi); endorsed by TJ as received 11 Sept. 1809 and so recorded in SJL.

Dunn's earlier LETTERS to TJ, also addressed from Liberty (now Bedford), are dated 30 Mar., 27 May, and 9 Oct. 1807 (DLC). On 8 June 1810 in Richmond Dunn made a similar request to James Madison for "three or four hundred dollers you would Scarcely miss out of your coffers" (Madison, *Papers, Pres. Ser.*, 2:373).

Dunn was quoting the POET Isaac Watts ("Life the Day of Grace and Hope," Hymn 88, Watts, *Hymns and Spiritual Songs*, 2d ed. [London, 1709], 71).

[1] Corrected from Watts. Manuscript: "wholes."

[2] Manuscript: "thing."

[3] Omitted word editorially supplied.

# To Robert Graham

SIR Monticello Aug. 25. 09.

you were so kind, while I was at Washington as to offer me a pair of domesticated wild geese. having now occasion to send a cart to Washington, I direct the driver to return by the way of Dumfries & to recieve & bring them if you can now spare them. I should have saved you this importunity had I succeeded with a pair I recieved from another quarter. but the goose of that pair unfortunately died. Accept my thanks for your proffered kindness & the assurances of my esteem & respect. TH: JEFFERSON

PoC (MHi); at foot of text: "Robert Graham esq."; endorsed by TJ.

Robert Graham (1751–1821) served as clerk of Prince William County, 1778–97 (Horace Edwin Hayden, *Virginia Genealogies* [1891, repr. 1931], 163; Frederick Johnston, *Memorials of Old Virginia Clerks* [1888], 320; Richmond *Enquirer*, 6 July 1821).

# From George Jefferson

DEAR SIR Richmond 25th Augt 1809

Your favor of the 22d inclosing 100$ is received. I have heard nothing from Mr Eppes respecting the volume of news papers.—You sent me with that, a volume of "fugitive sheets" of laws, which you directed should not go out of my possession, and which of course has not.—I recollect soon after Mr Burke's death, to have spoken to Mr Thweatt of Petersburg respecting the volume of papers, & I think he informed me that the late Governor Page had gotten it, with a book of his own.

The Shepherd dogs have not yet arrived—will you do me the favor, after supplying those who may already have applied, & likewise those of your friends who may sooner require them, to let me have a puppy? I have some small hope, that at some time or other, it may be useful to me.

I am Dear Sir Your Very humble serv[t] GEO. JEFFERSON

RC (MHi); at foot of text: "Thomas Jefferson esq[r]"; endorsed by TJ as received 27 Aug. 1809 and so recorded in SJL.

# To Craven Peyton

DEAR SIR Monticello Aug. 25. 09

Will you be so good as to send me the account of mr T. E. Randolph, & the list of balances due from all persons for rent, firewood E[t]c of Henderson's lands, which were left with you the other day. they shall be returned immediately as I only wish their aid a little while in enabling me to state the whole accounts clearly. I see in your account but one charge for the taxes of the land. but I imagine there ought to be more. will you be so good as to look up that article, & the tickets E[t]c paid, so as to enable me to place them to your credit. after recieving these papers, I would ask the favor of you the first time you shall be passing to Charlottesville or any where near us, to call on me. I salute you with esteem TH: JEFFERSON

RC (Plummer Ltd., New York City, 1946). PoC (MHi); corner torn; at foot of text: "[Crav]en Peyton"; endorsed by TJ.

# From Valentín de Foronda

MUY SEÑOR MIO: Philadelphia Agosto 26 de 1809.

antes de que yo llegara á estos Estados conocia el nombre del sabio del Philantropo Jefferson y desde que llegue no he tenido, sino motivos de confirmarme en mi Juicio. En las dos ocasiones que tuve la honra de visitar à Vm. siendo Presidente admiré sus talentos, y su extremada amabilidad, y quedé muy agradecido del modo lisonjero con que me trato; asi para dar à Vm una pequeña prueba de mi consideracion de que no me olvido de sus honras, y de que no soy un hombre que solo me recuerdo delos que estan en mando, me tomo la libertad de remitirle dos exemplares de un folleto sobre la constitucion Española, que acabo de imprimir.

Mis ocupaciones son grandes: asi solo he empleado dos ratos en escribir mi desaliñado bosquejo, lo que basta para hacer ver, que me intereso en la felicidad Española.

Nadie sabe mejor que Vm. lo dificil que es el hacer el bien: los hombres son muy malos; sus cabezas estan rellenas de disparates, y esta materia es tan pegajosa, tan tenaz, que ni toda la quimica Philosofica del Gran Jefferson es capaz de reducirla à Gas para que se evapore de los Caletres humanos.

Deseo à Vm. tranquilidad, salud, y deseo que tenga la bondad de disponer de la inutilidad de su admirador y atento Servidor Q.S.M.B. VALENTÍN DE FORONDA

EDITORS' TRANSLATION

DEAR SIR: Philadelphia August 26, 1809.

Before I arrived in these states I was aware of the name of the wise philanthropist Jefferson and since my arrival I have only had reason to confirm my judgment. On the two occasions that I had the honor to visit you while you were president I admired your talents, and your extreme kindness, and I was very appreciative of the complimentary manner in which you treated me; thus, to give you a little proof of my consideration, and to show that I do not forget your kindnesses and that I am not a man who remembers only those who are in power, I take the liberty of sending you two copies of a pamphlet on the Spanish constitution that I just finished printing.

My occupations are many: thus I have only taken a moment to write my hasty outline, which is enough to show that I am interested in the happiness of the Spanish people.

No one knows better than you how difficult it is to do good: men are very evil; their heads are filled with nonsense, and it is so contagious, so tenacious, that not even the great, philosophical chemist Jefferson is able to reduce it to gas so that it evaporates from human judgment.

I wish you peace, health, and I hope that you have the goodness to make use of the uselessness of your admirer and attentive servant who kisses your hand VALENTÍN DE FORONDA

RC (DLC); at head of text: "Sr Dn Thomas Jefferson"; endorsed by TJ as received 4 Sept. 1809 and so recorded in SJL. Translation by Dr. Jennifer McCune. Enclosure: Foronda, *Apuntes ligeros sobre la nueva constitución, proyectada por la Magestad de la Junta Suprema Española, y reformas que intenta hacer en las leyes* (Philadelphia, 1809).

Valentín de Foronda (1751–1821) was consul general for Spain at Philadelphia, 1802–07, and chargé d'affaires, 1807–09. He published regularly on political economy, was admitted to the American Philosophical Society in 1802, and found TJ sympathetic to his liberal views. Foronda was jailed for dissent in Spain in 1814, brought to trial, and banished to Pamplona (Gonzalo Diaz Diaz, *Hombres y Documentos de la Filosofia Española* [1988], 3:270–3; Robert S. Smith, "A Proposal for the Barter and Sale of Spanish America in 1800," *Hispanic American Historical Review* 41 [1961]: 275–86; Madison, *Papers, Sec. of State Ser.*, 2:416; TJ to John Wayles Eppes, 12 July 1807 [DLC]; APS, Minutes, 16 July 1802 [MS in PPAmP]; Sowerby).

On this day Foronda also sent James Madison the enclosure (Madison, *Papers, Pres. Ser.*, 4:604).

## To George Jefferson

DEAR SIR Monticello Aug. 27. 09.

M^r W. Dawson, agent for the fire insurance company, has a claim on me for 11. D 40 c, fee on the valuation of certain property which I propose to have insured, which I will pray you to pay to him. as he informs me he is in want of it, will you be so good as to give him notice that he may call for it

Yours affectionately TH: JEFFERSON

PoC (MHi); at foot of text: "George Jefferson"; endorsed by TJ.

## To Alexander McRae

SIR Monticello Aug. 27. 09.

Your favor of the 10th is recieved. I had certainly inferred, & too hastily as I percieve by a recurrence to your former letter, that your object would be to bring artists from Europe to this country. the expressions that your plan exposed you to hazard & combined public with private advantage led me into the error. I am afraid however I have been misconstrued in my turn. I did not mean to suggest that I thought the object, even as I supposed it, to be in any degree immoral, that it could be criminal to counteract an immoral law. if ever there was a case where a law could impose no other obligation than the risque of the arbitrary penalty it is that which makes the country in which a man happens to be born his perpetual prison, obliging him to starve in that rather than seek another where he can find the means of subsistence. I wished to avoid agency in it lest the relation in which I have stood with the public might give occasion for observations injurious to them. I take the occasion of renewing to you the assurances of my esteem & respect TH: JEFFERSON

PoC (DLC); at foot of text: "Alex^r M^cRae esq."; endorsed by TJ.

## To William W. Hening

SIR Monticello Aug. 28. 09

By a letter just recieved from mr George Jefferson I learn that I had deposited with him my volume of 'Fugitive sheets' or Session acts from 1734. to 1772. with an injunction not to deliver it out of his own possession, while the volumes of newspapers were delivered to mr Burke, & are consequently lost I fear. knowing your care of such things you are freely welcome to recieve from mr Jefferson the volume above mentioned, for the delivery of which this letter, if shewn to him, will be his authority. I salute you with esteem & respect.

TH: JEFFERSON

PoC (DLC); at foot of text: "M[r] Hening"; endorsed by TJ.

## From Benjamin Henry Latrobe

DEAR SIR, Washington Aug[t] 28[th] 1809

I have packed up & sent to Richmond to be forwarded to Monticello a box containing the Model of the Capital of the Columns of the lower Vestibule of the Senatorial apartments of the North Wing of the Capitol; which is composed of Ears of Maize. On a short frustum raising it about 4 feet from the Ground it may serve for a Dial stand, and should you appropriate it to that use I will forward to you an horizontal dial cut in Pennsylvanian Marble of a proper size. This Capital, during the Summer Session obtained me more applause from the Members of Congress than all the Works of Magnitude, of difficulty & of splendor that surround them.—They christened it, the Corn Cob Capital,—whether for the sake of the allitteration I cannot tell, but certainly not very appropriately. A few days ago I struck the center of the great Arch of the Senate Chamber. It is as you know a half dome of 60 feet diam. No accident whatever attended the operation. The new Arch of the Supreme court room was compleated some time in June, & the Plaisterers have already finished it in a very superior style.—There is in fact no doubt whatever of the Senate's occupying their permanent chamber this Session. I dread however the effect of an arrangement made by a committee of the Senate appointed on the last day of the Summer Session for the purpose of examining into the accomodations proposed for the Senate on the floor of the Chamber, & directing what should be done.—This committee composed of Mess[rs] Anderson, Thruston & Lloyd, annulled the arrangement I had made to accomodate the house of Rep. with permanent seats along the Wall, &, in fact, by that means rendered their attendance on the floor very inconvenient to themselves & to the Senators. I should not wonder if the ill blood occasioned hereby, were to prevent any further appropriation for the Capitol from passing the house of Representatives.—

I have still here belonging to You a Stone from the Missouri which has now been for near two Years in the hands of our Italians. It is not yet entirely finished. Franzoni has cut on one side an Indian Warrior smoking his pipe with his Tomahawk bow & arrows besides him. The face & figure are copied from an Indian who was here & are highly characteristic. Andrei has added a venerable Oak under which the Indian reposes. An Eagle occupies a branch of the tree, & a Rattlesnake is also introduced, as well as a deer in the back ground, Andrei's part of the work is most laboriously wrought but stiff, and he in fact has delayed the compleation of the piece, which is not yet quite ready. They have worked at it, at spare hours:—The piece is about 7 inches square.—

My attention to the public work is so unremittingly required, that I despair of being able to visit you at Monticello this autumn. In fact neither my time nor my spirits permit me to look to any thing as likely to happen, which is to give me as much pleasure, as such a visit would afford. After laboring for 6 Years here for the public, I find myself an object of suspicion & hatred, & persecuted by the most unmanly abuse in the public papers. To have injured my private fortune, and wasted the best Years of my life in successful labors for the public avails me nothing. Were I a politician & could I reap the advantages of political eminence,—and enjoy the indemnity against the slander of one[1] party which is given by the praise of the other which politicians possess,—I should not complain, but for the last 10 Years of my life I have never been mentioned in the papers but to be slandered, nor has one solitary paragraph ever hinted that I might possibly possess honesty, taste or skill.—

But I beg your pardon for intruding upon you[2] these complaints. Accept the assurances of my warmest attachment & respect.

Yours most truly B H Latrobe

RC (DLC); at head of text: "Thos Jefferson Esqr"; endorsed by TJ as received 4 Sept. 1809 and so recorded in SJL.

Benjamin Henry Latrobe (1764–1820), architect and civil engineer, was born in Yorkshire, attended Moravian schools in Germany, and trained in British engineering and architectural firms. He began practicing architecture on his own in 1792 and immigrated to Virginia in 1796, where his successful design for Richmond's Virginia State Penitentiary (1797–1806) won him national recognition. Latrobe moved to Philadelphia in 1798 and Washington in 1807. TJ appointed him surveyor of public buildings on 6 Mar. 1803, and he held that post until 1812, working closely with TJ on the redesign of the United States Capitol and the President's House. After the Capitol was burned by British forces in 1814, Latrobe began the work on its reconstruction, 1815–17. In his frequent correspondence with TJ, he often defended his work on the Capitol building and its expense. Latrobe advised TJ on the building program for the University of Virginia in 1817. Other highlights of his extremely productive career included the Philadelphia Waterworks (1798), a dry dock for the Washington Navy Yard

(1802), the Baltimore Cathedral (1805–10, 1817–21), the Washington Canal (1810–15), and the New Orleans Waterworks (1809–20), on which he was working when he died (*ANB*; *DNB*; *PTJ*, 30:225n; Talbot Hamlin, *Benjamin Henry Latrobe* [1955]; Latrobe, *Papers*; TJ to Latrobe, 6 Mar. 1803 [DLC]).

TJ eventually placed a circular sun DIAL of his own design on Latrobe's CORN COB CAPITAL (TJ to Latrobe, 27 Aug. 1816). The construction supports for the GREAT ARCH were removed on 25 Aug. 1809 without a repeat of the fatal ACCIDENT that occurred when a vault of the Capitol collapsed in September 1808 (Latrobe to James Madison, 8 Sept. 1809, Latrobe, *Papers*, 2:764). The red stone block FROM THE MISSOURI was acquired during the Lewis and Clark Expedition, possibly sent by Meriwether Lewis to TJ with a collection of other specimens from Fort Mandan (Lewis to TJ, 7 Apr. 1805 [DLC]). The carving took two more years to complete (Latrobe to TJ, 1 Aug. 1811).

[1] Reworked from "our."
[2] Preceding three words interlined.

# To Charles Pinckney

DEAR SIR Monticello Aug. 29. 09.

M[rs] Trist, daughter of the late mrs House of Philadelphia, both of them probably known to you, is now with us on a visit, and has been rendered extremely miserable by a paragraph in a Charleston paper, called the Strength of the people, mentioning the death of Samuel House 'an old and respectable inhabitant of that city.' she had a brother of that name, who has been living in Charleston about 20. years & was probably something under 50 years of age. he married a miss Corse since dead, by whom he had children. he was for some time in the office of mr Hamilton, now Secretary of the Navy. she is anxious to know whether this was the person whose death is announced in the inclosed paragraph? of what disease & in what situation or circumstances he died? what children he left, & how they are disposed of? the mother of his wife is understood to be in a situation to take care of them. desirous that these her enquiries should be satisfied, & having no acquaintance herself at Charleston, I have assured her I could so far count on the indulgence of your friendship as to ask an answer to them through your agency which I now take the liberty of doing. the motive of humanity is I know sufficient to engage you in this kind office, and a sympathy with her feelings will prevent unnecessary delay.—now a word as to myself. I am here enjoying the ineffable luxury of being owner of my own time: and never was I busier, or more constantly hurried by the objects of my emploiment. but these are always pursuits of either fancy or interest, & their consummation a source of gratification to myself. satisfied as I am that the public vessel is in the hands of as able a pilot as could be found, I sleep soundly as a mere passenger without troubling myself[1] with the courses pursued. I have now leisure to think of my friends & to rejoice in their welfare. I offer my prayers for your's with the assurances of my esteem & respect.

TH: JEFFERSON

PoC (MHi); at foot of text: "Charles Pinckney esq."; endorsed by TJ.

Charles Pinckney (1757–1824), longtime governor of South Carolina (1789–92, 1796–98, 1806–08), was born in Charleston, fought in the American Revolution, and served in the Confederation Congress, 1784–87. He was prominent in the Federal Convention at Philadelphia in 1787, where he introduced a plan to strengthen the national government, and he presided over South Carolina's constitutional convention in 1790. Pinckney transferred his loyalties from the Federalists to the Republican party during the 1790s, serving as a Republican in the United States Senate, 1798–1801. During his first weeks in office, TJ appointed Pinckney minister plenipotentiary to Spain, where he served until October 1805. He often sat in the South Carolina House of Representatives, ending with service from 1808–13. Pinckney came out of political retirement for a term in the United States House of Representatives, 1819–21, and there defended slavery during the crisis over statehood for Missouri (*ANB*; *DAB*; *BDSCHR*, 3:555–60; Frances Leigh Williams, *A Founding Family: The Pinckneys of South Carolina* [1978]; Mark D. Kaplanoff, "Charles Pinckney and the American Republican Tradition," in Michael O'Brien and David Moltke-Hansen, eds., *Intellectual Life in Antebellum Charleston* [1986], 85–122, 397–408).

TJ quoted in full a brief obituary giving the death date of SAMUEL HOUSE as 12 Aug. 1809 (Charleston *Strength of the People*, 15 Aug. 1809).

[1] Word interlined.

# From William Thornton

DEAR SIR City of Washington 30th Augst 1809

I had last Night the honor of your Letter of the 24th Instt and am much gratified by any opportunity of testifying in the smallest degree my high esteem & respect.

I am exceedingly obliged by your kind wish to have seen me with the President & his Lady, and Mr & Mrs Gallatin. To see you, and your amiable & excellent Family would at all times be sufficient Inducement, but if any attraction could be added you have mentioned those I most highly admire and esteem.—My public Duties however press so much upon me that Atlas-like I imagine a world upon my Shoulders—You will say a world of notions.—

I preserved four of the best ram Lambs of my Flock—one of them was unfortunately killed by my neighbour's Dogs, but I desired Mr Dougherty to pick out for you one of the remainder, & I send you his choice, being a handsome young ram, and with the finest wool. As he informed me that he suspected your Ewe would not breed I desired him to take the Cart to my Farm, and select the best Ewe in my possession, as I could depend more on his Judgment than my own. I will also send four of my best broad tail'd Ewes to Mr Peter's Cape ram if you should incline to have that Breed; but I am not so partial to those as to the short-legged Sheep which I possess. When my old ram died this Spring my manager informed me he measured the Tail & it was sixteen Inches across independent of the wool.—I am pleased with the Account given by our Friend Judge Peters in the "memoirs of the Philadelphia Society for promoting Agriculture"—Vol: 1st P. 163. note.—Lest you should not have yet obtained the work I will insert it.—

—"I presented, several years ago, to my late most worthy & lamented Friend General Hand, as a trustee for its introduction into the County, a valuable imported Ram of the Broad-taild Breed of Sheep obtained off the mountains of Tunis, by the present General Eaton when Consul in that regency. This Ram has improved the Breed of Sheep in Lancaster County, and the Country adjacent, to a great extent. I know not any Breed of Sheep superior, and few equal to it. Its fleece is of the first quality, and the valuable Points singularly good. I regret that by accident, the old ram has been lately killed; but I have the full blood in his Descendants. No other african Sheep is to be compared to this Species; either for fleece, fattening, or hardihood.—It bears our severest winters without shelter. Some of the best Lamb & mutton sold in our market, are of this Breed; which is now spread through many parts of this State & Jersey."[1] I observe also some very good remarks on this breed of Sheep in the Preface P. vi.—finishing by observing—"Perhaps a cross with the merino would benefit both."—

I have engaged a merino ram $\frac{3}{4}$ blood, which I mean to cross with my broad-taild breed; and though a ram possessing only one cross of the same blood, I have heard, finds no difficulty in gliding under their enormous Cushions, yet a merino I suppose would be alarmed at such an unnatural mass, therefore I had the tails of my young Ewes cut off; and only lost one, which I am confident was by inattention after the operation. I directed them to be laid on their Backs, and the Skin of the tail being slipped toward the root, the tail resting on a Block a broad & sharp axe was applied near the root of the Tail (the loose Skin still intermediate) and by the stroke of a mallet the tail severed at a blow; the Skin was then drawn up over the Stump & sewed to the other on the upper sides, so as to protect the Stump, & leave the parts exposed, and thus they are prepared for any cross.—This being done in cool weather subjects the animals to very little if any risk.—

I have no doubt that the Spaniards, whose Blood is much tainted by the moors, are under obligation to their ancient Conquerors, for their fine Horses derived from the Barbs, and they from Arabia by the Caravans of religious Pilgrims; and the Sheep I have no doubt also originated from those imported by the moors into Spain, where their extensive uncultivated Hills have afforded fine pasturage for many ages, and the lazy Spaniards were well calculated for Shepherds. They had little to attend to but to give Salt, & finding the fine wool commanded a very high price they from time to time selected the finest for stock sheep.—I am confident also, that peculiar Situations are, by being adapted to Sheep, capable of producing great changes in, not only the quantity but also the quality of the wool, and I observed in the Counties of Maryland, washed by the Chesapeake, which not only tempers the Air, but encrusts the Grass overflowed by the Tide with Salt, that the Sheep thrive in a surprising manner. Many attributed the fineness of the Sheep to a peculiar breed, obtained, by a Major Chew, of Calvert County, from England, and I think it probably aided much; but I saw common Sheep, purchased from those who were supposed not to have benefitted by that breed, placed in the pastures I before mentioned, and in one Season their wool was thought by the Proprietors to have nearly doubled in quantity & to be also benefitted in quality.—These Grounds were remarkably hilly, the sides cleared to the South, the bottoms laved with Salt water, the tops shaded by Pines, by Cedars, & common woods; wild onions were also very prevalent in some places, white clover common. Thus all that could tend to feed with their choicest food, to protect them in winter, and keep them cool in Summer, were found there: but musketos were very numerous & troublesome, & Seed Ticks (unknown in most countries but very abundant in many parts of Maryland & Virg[a]) were very troublesome there. Knowing that the Hair of the Indians, who are constantly exposed, is exceedingly harsh & thick, and compared to the Hair of those who are neither exposed to great heats nor colds, as hemp is to Flax, or flax to silk, may we not suppose that if Sheep be kept where they will enjoy a temperate Climate, where sunny Banks in winter and Shady Hills in Summer will afford them the proper choice of Situation, and added to these their favourite food, sweet short grass and white Clover with wild Herbs which are very abundant on our Hills, and by plenty of Salt in sheltered troughs; where allso they are neither exposed to the continual torments of Musketos nor Seed Ticks &c, that the best & purest Stocks will in a few Years be highly improved?—

Capt. Coles says the merinos at Rambouillet are three times as large as our common Sheep, and sometimes yield sixteen ℔, of fine wool.—This shews what may be done by care.—

A Work has been published by Robt Bakewell of England wch shews that limestone Land is unfavourable to fine Wool but that Clay soil is excellent. This work is improved by the Observations of Lord Somerville.—

If our Government could obtain from France or Spain but particularly from France, permission to import thence a hundred merinos, and keep them in the public Grounds in this City fixing a value on the Lambs, and let them be sold to those who are desirous of improving the Breed, or selling them at public sale what benefit would be rendered! it is incalculable, and why not do it? Mr Parker would supply us.[2]—If the Vicuna were also to be imported it might prove valuable.—The Camel will be brought by the Turk O'Brien, and I think I was in some degree instrumental in forming his Determination.—If the Ostrich could be let loose in the sandy wilds of Louisiana or in East or West Florida it would I doubt not increase rapidly—The Hare & red legged Patridge I imagine would also succeed in this Country[3]—and while we promote valuable Animals we ought also to set a price on the Heads of wolves Foxes &c &c—

Nothing has yet been done towards the Establishment of a Botanic Garden. Mr Hamilton has a thousand valuable Exotics to dispose of at this time at the woodlands.—

I have sent a few more roots of my Fig-trees—and also a Root of the Terragon, which you were so good as to give me to propagate. I have distributed several.—

If the Fig trees be planted in very rich light wood soil, or a very light compost fit for Asparagus Beds you will find they will produce very large fruit. We had a few a third of a pound in weight, many a quarter of a pound.—

My Wife & her Mother join me in most respectful Compliments to your excellent Family and self—also to the President his Lady, Mr & Mrs Gallatin & Capt Coles. I am dear Sir with the highest respect & esteem very sincerely Yr &c William Thornton

RC (DLC); at foot of text: "Honble Thomas Jefferson"; endorsed by TJ as received 4 Sept. 1809 and so recorded in SJL; notation by TJ: "cape sheep—docking.—Vicunña—camel—partridge—lark Nightingale.—fig trees—tarragon—."

The VERY GOOD REMARKS on the broad-tailed Barbary mountain sheep praised its health and vigor, its hardihood and disposition to fatten speedily, and the fineness of its wool, described as suitable for hats, stockings, and gloves (*Memoirs of the Philadelphia Society for Promoting*

*Agriculture* 1 [1808]: vi–vii [Sowerby, no. 769]). Robert BAKEWELL, *Observations on the influence of soil and climate upon wool* (London, 1808; Sowerby, no. 797), contained notes by John Southey Somerville, LORD SOMERVILLE.

CAMEL: earlier this year a Virginia newspaper announced that "A Philadelphia gentleman, who spent many years of his life in Africa, has formed the design of carrying a number of Camels into the Southern states by way of introducing the breed," and called on planters to support the scheme (*Alexandria Daily Gazette*, 19 May 1809). The man in question was probably Richard O'BRIEN, who had been in the custody of Algerine pirates from 1785–95, served as consul general at Algiers from 1797–1803 and settled in Philadelphia after his return to the United States (*DAB*).

[1] Closing quotation mark editorially supplied.

[2] Preceding five words interlined.

[3] Preceding three words interlined.

# From Abraham Bradley

SIR General Post Office August 31. 1809

A vacancy having occurred in the post office at Milton V[a] and it being the office through which your correspondence chiefly passes, I have taken the liberty of inclosing a blank appointment, and to request your favour in addressing it to such person as may be agreeable to you. The Postmaster general is now on a tour to the eastward.

I have the honor to be very respectfully your obedient servant

ABRAHAM BRADLEY JUN[R]

RC (DLC); at foot of text: "Hon[ble] Thomas Jefferson"; endorsed by TJ as received 4 Sept. 1809 and so recorded in SJL. Enclosure not found.

Abraham Bradley (1767–1838), a native of Litchfield, Connecticut, studied law there at Tapping Reeve's law school, and then became a protégé of Postmaster General Timothy Pickering, who made Bradley a clerk in his department in 1791. As first assistant postmaster general from 1799, Bradley oversaw the general post office's relocation the following year to Washington, D.C. He created an important map of the United States in 1796, with a second edition in 1804 that incorporated the Louisiana Purchase. Bradley was dismissed from his position in 1829 as part of the Jackson administration's assertion of control over postal patronage (*ANB*; Charles S. Bradley, "The Bradley Family and the Times in which They Lived," *RCHS* 6 [1903]: 130–6).

# From Joseph Dougherty

DEAR SIR. Washington Augt. 31[st] 1809

I rec[d] yours of the 24[th] the 28[th] Ins[t]. Davy arived here on the evening of the 29[th] In my conversation with Doct[r] Thornton, I mentioned to him the improbability of your broad tailed ewe[s] breeding. he in his usual way, and, always ready to oblige you, readily mentioned that it would be proper to send you a broad tail ewe to be certain which you will receive (I hope safe) together with one of his best rams; he was so good as to give me the choice of his flock for a ram and ewe for you; this for my part I esteem as a great favour for the reason as follows; M^r R: Brent has a young ram which appears to be as full bread as Doct^r T^s imported ram which he received as a present[1] from Doct^r T: in Aug^t 1808. he weighed on the hoof 168 lbs. when one year old.[2]—When shoren his fleece weighed 8¾ lbs.

four of his lambs of this year after the best were taken out[3] was sold to the butcher for 16 Dollars, soon in the summer. The butcher (who is an englishman) that bought them, says he never saw as fine mutton, either in england or this country I am convinced that the broad tail breed may be much Impruved by proper attention being paid to them This never has been the case with Doct^r T's. flock

they are always poor

I have increased my flock of ewes to fifty and those of the best kind. Doct^r Thornton sends you some slips of the fig tree, also some of the tarragon plant, which I put up as well as I knew how;

I have been for some time back engaged in painting and will probably continue at it, if I do not succeed in procureing a berth in the new bank which is about to be established in this city

Davy will set out from here to morrow [morn?]

Sir, your humble Servant Jo^s Dougherty

N.B. If you should want me to do any thing for you here: I am as willing as usual If not more so.
And I beg you not to think that It gives me any trouble to serve you now, more than it ever did.

RC (DLC); one word damaged; addressed: "Thomas Jefferson Esq^r late President of the U. States Monticello by Davy"; endorsed by TJ as received 4 Sept. 1809 and so recorded in SJL.

The BANK of Washington was organized between June and September 1809 and chartered by Congress in February 1811 (Washington *National Intelligencer*, 30 June, 8, 15 Sept. 1809; *Annals*, 11th Cong., 3d sess., 959–60 [11 Feb. 1811]; Charles E. Howe, "The Financial Institutions of Washington City in its Early Days," *RCHS* 8 [1905]: 17–22).

[1] Preceding three words interlined.
[2] Preceding four words interlined.
[3] Preceding six words interlined.

## To Robert Patterson

Dear Sir Monticello Aug. 31. 09.

At the request of mr Warden I transmit to the A. Philosophical society an Analysis of tobacco by M. Vauquelin, translated by mr Warden.

Having lately recieved from mr Treat, an officer stationed at our post on the Arkansa, a meteorological diary of two years & three months continuance, I take the liberty of presenting it to the society. I am sure they will recieve with pleasure every essay contributing to our knolege of the different parts of that interesting country. Accept the assurances of my great esteem & respect.

Th: Jefferson

PoC (MHi); at foot of text: "M^r^ Patterson one of the V.P. of the A.P.S."; endorsed by TJ. Enclosures: (1) John Breck Treat to TJ, 31 Mar. 1809, and enclosure. (2) Enclosures to David Bailie Warden to TJ, 17 Apr. 1809.

## To John Vaughan

Dear Sir Monticello Aug. 31. 09.

Your favors of the 19th & 20th instant are both recieved and I thank you for the Prospectus of mr Humboldt's work, which I had not seen before. I now return you his letter and the Prospectus de vases antiques which promises a splendid addition to the arts. Baron Humboldt's work is voluminous & expensive, but it will add much new & valuable information to several branches of science. I have recieved one part of it and have some others on their way. one part has unfortunately miscarried, & is that which I should have valued most, on the geography of plants. I thank you for your kind offers of service. I have had too many proofs of your friendly attentions to doubt of them, & have used them heretofore too freely not to give you apprehensions of similar trouble hereafter whenever occasion shall arise. I salute you with great esteem & respect.

Th: Jefferson

P.S. can you inform me whether the instrument called the Distiller's syphon is to be had in Philadelphia, and what one sufficient to work in a cistern of 8. feet cube would cost? I believe they are usually made of tin. the machine I mean is described in the 3d. vol. of the Scientific dialogues pa. 195. Pl. IV. 29.

PoC (MHi); above postscript: "J. Vaughan esq."; endorsed by TJ. Enclosures: see Vaughan to TJ, 19 Aug. 1809.

GEOGRAPHY OF PLANTS: Alexander von Humboldt, *Tableaux de la Nature* (Paris, 1808; Sowerby, no. 646). Jeremiah Joyce was the author of the SCIENTIFIC dialogues (note to TJ to Joseph Milligan, 7 July 1809).

# From George Jefferson

DEAR SIR Richmond 1st Septr 1809

I some days since sent on your two dogs by Thomas Becks, having paid him 2$ for their feed, & for his trouble in carrying them up—as he said he was short of provisions, & had nothing to spare them. he promised to feed them well, & to take great care of them. I likewise forwarded by Becks the stolen trunk. I have not heard the particulars of the trial, but am told that the thief was sentenced to be whipt & to be burnt in the hand.—

Becks likewise took charge of your groceries from Gordon's.

I am Dear Sir Your Very humble servt GEO. JEFFERSON

RC (MHi); at foot of text: "Thomas Jefferson esqr"; endorsed by TJ as received 4 Sept. 1809 and so recorded in SJL.

In Richmond on 29 Aug. 1809 Gibson & Jefferson paid THOMAS BECKS two dollars to deliver "one Trunk & Two shepherds Dogs" to TJ (Tr of receipt in MHi; unsigned; at foot of text: "Duplicate"; addressed: "Thomas Jefferson Esqr Monticello Mr Becks"; endorsed by TJ as a letter from George Jefferson; with unrelated calculations by TJ on verso). On 11 Sept. 1809 TJ paid Becks $8.43 for delivery of "groceries &c." (*MB*, 2:1247). He compensated Becks for similar services sporadically between 1798 and 1816 (*MB*).

# From William D. Meriwether

DEAR SIR [received 1 Sept. 1809]

Our youngest son is extreamly ill with a desentery and I think a little port-wine will be of service to him will you be so good as to spare me a bottle and I will return it as soon as any can be got

Yours Respectfully W D. MERIWETHER

ps our black peaches are now ripe and I hope you will send wenever you choose for them WDM

RC (MHi); undated; at head of text: "Mr Thomas Jefferson"; endorsed by TJ as received 1 Sept. 1809 and so recorded in SJL.

Meriwether's son Thomas was still described as "extremely ill" although "out of danger" two weeks later (William D. Meriwether to Charles Meriwether, 17 Sept. 1809 [NcU: Southern Historical Collection, Meriwether Family Papers]).

# From André Daschkoff

MONSIEUR Philadelphie. le 2e Septembre 1809

La lettre que vous m'avez fait l'honneur de m'écrire en date du 14 du mois passé m'est parvenue au milieu d'une maladie Sérieuse dont je ne Suis pas encore rétabli. Je saisis le premier moment de ma convalescence pour vous présenter Monsieur mes très humbles remercimens du désir obligeant que vous daignés me marquer, de me voir à Monticello. Ayant appris à mon arrivée que c'étoit le lieu de vôtre résidence, j'ai fixé d'abord le projet que mon premier voyage dans l'interieur du pays Seroit de ce côté, et Si je ne l'ai pas fait après avoir été présenté à Mr. le President à Washington, ce fut par raison que je devois retourner incessamment à Philadelphie, où j'ai laissé ma famille, a fin de l'établir, et de mettre mon office Sur pied. Cependant mon désir de faire un tour à Monticello a été d'autant plus vif et mes dispositions de le remplir Sont d'autant mieux arrêtées, que c'étoit à vous, Monsieur, que j'ai été adressé du tems de mon départ de St. Petersbourg, qu'il m'est parfaitement connu que les assurances que j'avais à[1] vous faire de la part de mon Auguste Souveraîn, comme au President des Etats Unis, regardoient également vôtre personne et que j'avais le bonheur de porter une lettre Autographe de Sa Majesté l'Empereur pour Mr. le Président, qui devoit me Servir de lettre de créance. Si vôtre rétraite volontaire du poste important que vous occupiez ou les obstacles qui ont retardé mon arrivée dans ce pays eussent été prévus en Russie, il est très probable Monsieur, qu'avec les mêmes instructions à Suivre à l'égard de Mr. le Président, j'aurai été chargé d'un Méssage particulier de la part de Sa Majesté Impériale pour vôtre personne. Je ne pourrai Monsieur me dédommager de ce changement de circonstances, qui en a occasionné un dans mes démarches quant à la forme, que lorsque je Serai à même de vous réiterer de vive voix les Sentimens d'éstime particulière que je Suis réquis de vous temoigner de la part de mon gouvernement; et d'avoir l'honneur de vous assurer combien il m'est flatteur d'avoir été dèputé d'un grand Monarque vers un grand Homme.

Daignés agréer Monsieur les Sentimens de la Considération parfaite

et du respect profond avec lesquels j'ai l'honneur d'être
Monsieur Votre très humble et très obéissant Serviteur
ANDRÉ DE DASCHKOFF.

EDITORS' TRANSLATION

SIR Philadelphia. 2 September 1809

The letter you did me the honor of writing me on the 14th of last month reached me in the midst of a serious illness from which I have not yet recovered. I am seizing the first moment of my convalescence to present to you, Sir, my very humble thanks for the obliging wish that you were pleased to express to me, to have me visit Monticello. Having learned on my arrival that it was the site of your residence, I initially planned that my first trip into the interior of the country would be to that region, and if I did not follow my plan after having been presented to the president in Washington, it was owing to the fact that I had to return immediately to Philadelphia, where I had left my family, in order to settle them and put my affairs in order. However, my desire to make a trip to Monticello has been all the keener and my inclination to fulfill that desire all the firmer because it was to you, Sir, that I was dispatched at the time of my departure from Saint Petersburg, because I am perfectly well aware that the assurances which I was to make to you, as the president of the United States, on behalf of my August Sovereign also concerned you personally, and because I had the good fortune to carry a letter in His Majesty the emperor's hand for the president, which was to serve as my letter of credence. If your voluntary retirement from the important position that you occupied or the obstacles that postponed my arrival in this country had been foreseen in Russia, it is very probable, Sir, that along with the same instructions with regard to the president, I would have been entrusted with a particular message from His Imperial Majesty to you personally. I will only be able to compensate for this change in circumstances, which has brought about one in my procedures with regard to form, when I am in a position to reiterate to you in person the sentiments of particular esteem which I am required to express to you on behalf of my government and to have the honor of assuring you how flattering it is for me to have been the deputy of a great monarch to a great man.

Please accept, Sir, the sentiments of perfect esteem and profound respect with which I have the honor to be
Sir your very humble and very obedient servant
ANDRÉ DE DASCHKOFF.

RC (DLC); at foot of first page: "Mr. Thomas Jefferson. Monticello"; endorsed by TJ as received 11 Sept. 1809 and so recorded in SJL. Translation by Dr. Amy Ogden.

TJ's letter of 14 DU MOIS PASSÉ was actually dated 12 Aug. 1809. LETTRE AUTOGRAPHE: Daschkoff's letter of credence from Alexander I to the President of the United States, 12 Sept. 1808 (DNA: RG 59, NL, Russia), presented to James Madison on 14 July 1809 (Bashkina, *United States and Russia*, 538–9n).

[1] Manuscript: "à à."

## From Robert Graham

SIR 2d September 1809.

Your Servant arrived at my house this morning and handed Me your letter of the 25th August.—I send a pair of domesticated wild Geese & would send you two pair but there does not appear to be room enough in the Cart for another pair as he has two Lambs in the Cart and the box for the Geese is not big enough for two pair.

I hope he will bring the Lambs & Geese safe to you and I am with the greatest respect & esteem

Sir Yr very hble Servt ROB: GRAHAM

RC (MHi); endorsed by TJ as received 4 Sept. 1809 and so recorded in SJL.

## To John W. Campbell

SIR Monticello Sep. 3. 09

Your letter of July 29 came to hand some time since, but I have not sooner been able to acknolege it. In answer to your proposition for publishing a compleat edition of my different writings, I must observe that no writings of mine, other than those merely official have been published, except the Notes on Virginia, & a small pamphlet under the title of a Summary view of the rights of British America. the Notes on Virginia I have always intended to revise & enlarge, & have from time to time laid by materials for that purpose. it will be long yet before other occupations will permit me to digest them; & observations & enquiries are still to be made which will be more correct in proportion to the length of time they are continued. it is not unlikely that this may be through my life. I could not therefore at present offer any thing new for that work.

The Summary view was not written for publication. it was a draught I had prepared of a petition to the King, which I meant to propose in my place as a member of the Convention of 1774. being stopped on the road by sickness, I sent it on to the Speaker, who laid it on the table for the perusal of the members. it was thought too strong for the times & to become the act of the convention, but was printed by subscription of the members with a short preface written by one of them. if it had any merit it was that of first taking our true ground, & that which was afterwards assumed & maintained.

I do not mention the Parliamentary manual published for the use of the Senate of the US. because it was a mere compilation, into which nothing entered of my own, but the arrangement, & a few observations necessary to explain that & some of the cases.

I do not know whether your view extends to official papers of mine which have been published. many of these would be like old news papers, materials for future historians, but no longer interesting to the readers of the day. they would consist of Reports, correspondencies, messages, answers to addresses a few of my Reports while Secretary of State might perhaps be read by some as Essays on abstract subjects, such as the Report on Measures, weights & coins, on the mint, on the fisheries, on commerce, on the use of distilled sea-water E^t^c. the correspondencies with the British & French ministers, Hammond and Genet, were published by Congress. the Messages to Congress, which might have been interesting at the moment, would scarcely be read a second time, and answers to addresses are hardly read a first time.

So that on a review of these various materials, I see nothing encouraging a printer to a republication of them. they would probably be bought by those only who are in the habit of preserving state-papers, & who are not many.

I say nothing of numerous draughts of reports, resolutions, declarations E^t^c drawn as a member of Congress or of the legislature of Virginia, such as the Declaration of Independance, Report on the money Unit of the US. the Act for religious freedom E^t^c E^t^c these having become the acts of public bodies, there can be no personal claim to them, and they would no more find readers now than the Journals & Statute books in which they are deposited.

I have presented this general view of the subjects which might have been within the scope of your contemplation, that they might be correctly estimated before any final decision. they belong mostly to a class of papers not calculated for popular reading, & not likely therefore to offer profit, or even indemnification to the republisher. submitting it to your consideration I tender you my salutations & respects.

TH: JEFFERSON

PoC (DLC); at foot of first page: "M^r^ John W. Campbell."

SUMMARY VIEW: see *PTJ*, 1:127–37. PARLIAMENTARY MANUAL: see *PW*, 353–433. Among his significant reports as secretary of state on ABSTRACT SUBJECTS, TJ included those on weights and MEASURES (*PTJ*, 16:650–75), the MINT (*PTJ*, 16:345–9), FISHERIES (*PTJ*, 19:206–36), COMMERCE (*PTJ*, 27:567–79), and DISTILLED SEA-WATER (*PTJ*, 22:318–22). His official correspondence with George HAMMOND and Edmond Charles GENET WAS PUBLISHED BY CONGRESS as *A Message of the President of the*

*United States to Congress Relative to France and Great-Britain. Delivered December 5, 1793. With the Papers therein Referred to* (Philadelphia, 1793; Sowerby, no. 3167). DECLARATION OF INDEPENDANCE: see *PTJ*, 1:413–33. REPORT ON THE MONEY UNIT: see *PTJ*, 1:515–8, 7:194–203. ACT FOR RELIGIOUS FREEDOM: see *PTJ*, 2:545–53.

# From Thomas Eston Randolph

DEAR SIR Sunday 3d Sep.r 1809

I had depended on getting a Gig in Milton (which I have been in the habit of hiring) to take my Son to School. it is at present out—and very uncertain when it will return—If you can without any inconvenience accomodate me with the loan of yours—you will very much oblige me—I propose to set off on Tuesday and expect to return in a week—

with very friendly regards I am Your most Obd.t

THO.s ESTON RANDOLPH

RC (MHi); dateline below signature; addressed: "Thomas Jefferson Esq.r"; endorsed by TJ as received 4 Sept. 1809 and so recorded in SJL; with unrelated calculations by TJ on verso.

Thomas Eston Randolph (1767–1842) was the son of TJ's uncle William Randolph and the husband of Jane Cary Randolph, the sister of TJ's son-in-law Thomas Mann Randolph. In 1805 Thomas Eston Randolph purchased Glenmore, across the Rivanna from Milton, and some eight years later he disposed of this property and moved to Ashton, adjoining TJ's Pouncey's tract about five miles east of Monticello. TJ sometimes used Randolph's boats for shipments from Richmond, and in 1808 and 1809 Randolph leased Lego and some lands at Milton from TJ. From 1814 Randolph leased TJ's flour mill, first in conjunction with Thomas Mann Randolph and then by himself. In 1822 his daughter Mary Elizabeth Cleland Randolph married TJ's grandson Francis Eppes. Randolph moved his family to Florida after TJ's death and became a federal marshal there in 1831 (Woods, *Albemarle*, 303; *MB*, 2:1156, 1263, 1310; *JEP*, 4:178, 193 [7, 30 Dec. 1831]; Randolph Whitfield, "The Florida Randolphs, 1829–1978" [1978 typescript in ViU, 18]).

Randolph's SON was probably William Eston Randolph, who was thirteen years old at the time (*Monticello Association Papers*, 13; Randolph, *Randolphs*, 107; Whitfield, "Florida Randolphs," 59).

# From William W. Hening

DEAR SIR, Richmond 4th Sept.r 1809

I have received from M.r George Jefferson your volume of sessions acts from 1734 to 1772, inclusive.—The acts of 1773, which are stated to have been lost from your collection, I have in my possession.

The first volume of the statutes at large will be published in a few days. It comes down to the termination of the commonwealth of England; and gives an entirely different view of our history, especially during the four years immediately preceding the restoration of Charles II. from any thing represented by the English historians. Indeed every important public transaction during the existence of the commonwealth, has been most grossly misrepresented.

I shall commence the second volume with the acts of October 1660; but, as I have before mentioned, I am apprehensive they are incomplete in my MS. If it would not be too much trouble, I should be very thankful, if you would transcribe a line or two of the first act in your copy, of that session, so as to enable me to determine whether mine can be confided in.

I am respectf[ly] y[rs] Wm: W: Hening

P.S. The paper on which I now write was manufactured at the Petersburg mills, in this state;—the first of the quality, ever made in Virginia, at an extensive manufactory. W.W.H.

RC (DLC); endorsed by TJ as received 30 Sept. 1809 and so recorded in SJL.

## From William Lambert

Sir, City of Washington; September 4th 1809.

Some time since, I addressed a letter to you on the subject of a first meridian for the United States at the permanent seat of their government, to be effected by ascertaining the longitude of the Capitol in this city from Greenwich observatory, in England, being the spot from which many, if not the whole of our mariners are in the habit of reckoning their departure. It is proper that the result of this undertaking should be communicated to such scientific characters in this country as are supposed to feel any desire that we should shake off that kind of dependence which we have too long had on a foreign country; and as you are to be considered among the most distinguished of those characters, permit me to send you an abstract of the calculations for the purpose, founded on the occultation of η. Pleiadum, (Alcyone) by the Moon, observed near the President's house, on the evening of the 20th of October, 1804.

| | ° ′ ″ |
|---|---|
| Latitude of the Capitol, in Washington, by observation, | 38.52.57.N. |
| | dec |
| " reduced, (334 to 333) ☞ | 38.42.52.939. |
| Right ascension of η. Pleiadum, allowing aberration and nutation, | 53.59. 6.273. |
| Declination d° allowing d° d° | 23.29.45.143.N. |
| Obliquity of the Ecliptic, October 20. 1804, | 23.27.54.250. |
| Longitude of the star, by computation, | 57.16.35.925. |
| Latitude d° | 4. 1.59.809.N. |

Estimated longitude from Greenwich, in time, 5. h. 7. m. 36. sec. = 76.° 54.′ 0.″ West.

---

| | h. m. sec. dec |
|---|---|
| Time, by watch, of the immersion, reduced to the Capitol, | 9.30. 9.32. |
| Error of the watch, | – 7.32.75. |
| Apparent time of immersion at the Capitol, | 9.22.36.57. |
| Sun's right ascension, then, | 13.42. 5.28626. |
| Right ascension of <u>medium cœli</u>, in time, | 23. 4.41.85626. |

| | | ° ′ ″ |
|---|---|---|
| Equal to | ♓. | 16.10.27.8439. |

or 76.°10.′27.″8439. dec. from the beginning of ♑, the nearest solstitial point.

| | | ° |
|---|---|---|
| Altitude of the nonagesimal, | | 49.36.41.464. |
| Longitude of the nonagesimal, | ♈. | 5.52.41.926. |
| ☽'s <u>true</u> longitude, | ♉. | 26.26.10.399. |
| ☽'s <u>true</u> distance from the nonagesimal, (East) | | 50.33.28.473. |
| " horizontal parallax, reduced, | | 1.[. . .].59.0134. |
| Parallax in longitude, | | 36.17.580. |
| ☽'s <u>apparent</u> or <u>visible</u> longitude, | | 57. 2.27.979. |
| " true latitude, North, | | 4.30.25.399. |
| Parallax in latitude, | | 37.31.516. |
| ☽'s apparent latitude at immersion, North, | | 3.52.53.883. |

☞ This is the ratio of the equatorial to the polar axis of the Earth, adopted at Greenwich, in consequence of new lunar equations discovered in the year 1800, by M. de la Place, in France. The ratio of 230 to 229, was formerly used by British mathematicians.

For the Emersion.

| | | h. m. sec.dec. |
|---|---|---|
| Time by watch, of the emersion, reduced to the Capitol, | | 10.24.47.32. |
| Error of the watch, | | – 7.32.75. |
| Apparent time of emersion at the Capitol, | | 10.17.14.57. |
| Sun's right ascension, then, | | 13.42.13.82697. |
| Right ascension of medium cœli, in time, | | 23.59.28.39697. |
| equal to, | ♓. | 29°.52. 5.9545. |

or 89.°52.′5.″9545. dec. from the beginning of ♑.

| | | ° ′ ″ dec. |
|---|---|---|
| Altitude of the nonagesimal, | | 54.56.23.787. |
| Longitude of the nonagesimal, | ♈. | 17.35.28.761. |
| ☽'s true longitude, | ♉. | 27. 0.26.933. |
| " true distance from the nonagesimal, (East) | | 39.24.58.172. |
| " horizontal parallax, reduced, | | 1. 0.58.4066. |
| Parallax in longitude, | | 32. 8.867. |
| ☽'s apparent longitude, | | 57.32.35.800. |
| " true latitude, North | | 4.29. 6.143. |
| Parallax in latitude, | | 32.22.518. |
| ☽'s apparent latitude at emersion, | | 3.56.43.625. |
| " motion in apparent longitude, during the transit, | | 30. 7.821. |
| " motion in apparent latitude d° | | 3.49.742. |
| " center south of the ⋆, at immersion, | | 9. 5.926. |
| " , at emersion, | | 5.16.184. |

The difference of apparent latitude of the ⋆ and ☽'s center, was therefore greater at the immersion than at the emersion.

In occultations, the Moon's motion in apparent longitude should be multiplied by the co-sine of the star's latitude, or of the Moon's apparent latitude at the middle time between the immersion and emersion, to reduce the motion in apparent longitude to a parallel to the Ecliptic: the former is to be preferred, when the Star's latitude has been obtained with due precision.

The remaining part of the process, to find the difference of apparent longitude of the ☽'s center and the points of occultation, (or those parts of the Eastern and Western limbs of the Moon at which the Star immerged and emerged) will be explained by the following figure, and the annexed remarks.

**FSG**, represents a parallel to the Ecliptic, passing through the star **S**.

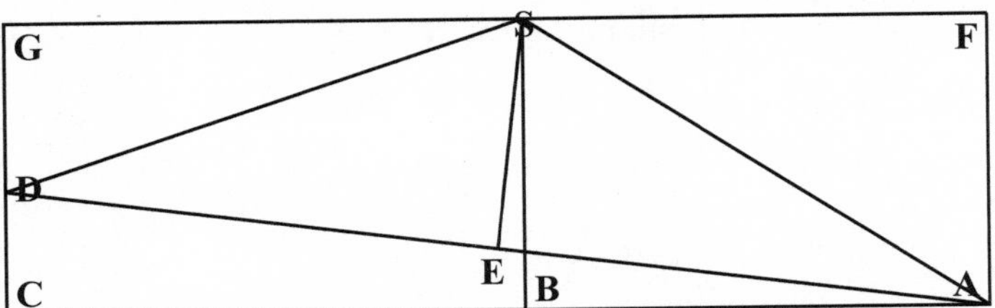


**A**, the apparent place of the ☽'s center at the immersion. **D**, at the emersion.

**ABC**, the Moon's motion in apparent longitude, × co-sine of ★'s latitude.

**CD**, the Moon's motion in apparent latitude. **AF**, **DG**, the difference of apparent latitude between the ★ and ☽'s center. **AS**, **DS**, the Moon's semidiameter at immersion and emersion, (corrected) **SE**, the nearest approach of the centers of ★ and ☽. **CAD**, the angle of inclination of the Moon's apparent orbit. **AD**, the chord of transit, or ☽'s apparent path. **AE** and **ED**, segments of the base, or Moon's apparent path. **EAS**, **EDS**, angles of conjunction, and **ASF**, **DSG**, the central angles at the immersion and emersion, whence **FS**, **GS**, the differences of apparent longitude of the ★ and ☽'s center are to be found, from which, by applying the parallaxes with a contrary sign, the true differences of longitude, as they would be seen by a spectator placed at the center of the Earth under the meridian of the Capitol, in Washington, will be obtained. The intervals of time between the beginning and end of the transit and the ecliptical conjunction, may then be determined from the Moon's motion in longitude reduced to the ecliptic.

It is customary in occultations to apply the inflexion of the Moon's light to the augmented semidiameter, both at the immersion and emersion: the quantity of that element having been variously estimated by astronomical writers, it is thought advisable to use a mean of the following—

| | | ″ |
|---|---|---|
| | Dr Mackay, | –3.5 |
| | " Vince, | 3.– |
| | Mr Garnett, (American req: tables) | 2.977. |
| | " Ferrer, ditto, | 2.18. |
| Mean | Inflexion of the Moon's light, | –2.914. |

The Moon's augmented semidiameter arising from a change of altitude, may be thus found—

ar: comp: log. cosine true altitude, + log. cosine apparent altitude, + log. sine horizontal semidiameter, – radius, = log. sine ☽'s augmented semidiam[r] from which the inflexion of light is always to be subtracted.

| | ° ′ ″ dec. | | |
|---|---|---|---|
| Log. cosine true altitude, at imm: | 32.13.45.342. | arith: comp: | 0.0726702.54 |
| " co-sine apparent altitude, | 31.23.14.461 | | 9.9312879.18. |
| " sine ☽'s horiz: semidiameter, | 16.38.375 | | 7.6848668.59 |
| " sine ☽'s augmented semidiam: | 16.47.511. | | 7.6888250.31 |
| Inflexion of light, | – 2.914 | | |
| ☽'s corrected semidiameter, **AS**, | 16.44.597. | | |

For the ☽'s corrected semidiameter at the emersion.

| | ° ′ ″ dec. | | |
|---|---|---|---|
| Log. cosine true altitude, | 42.25.22.181 | arith: comp: | 0.1318338.61. |
| " cosine apparent alt: | 41.40.52.804 | | 9.8732361.93. |
| " sine ☽'s horiz: semid: | 16.38.147 | | 7.6847679.09. |
| " sine ☽'s augm: semida | 16.49.868 | | 7.6898379.63. |
| Inflexion of light, | –2.914. | | |
| ☽'s corrected semidiameter, **DS**, | 16.46.954. | | |

| | | |
|---|---|---|
| Log. ☽'s motion in apparent longitude, | 1807.″821 dec. | 3.2571554.40 |
| " cosine ⋆'s latitude, | 4.°1.′59.″809 | 9.9989230.28. |
| ☽'s motion in a parallel to the ecliptic, **ABC**, | 1803.″3434 | 3.2560784.68. |
| ☽'s motion in apparent latitude, **CD**, | 229.″742 dec. log | 2.3612403.80. |
| Ar: comp: log. **ABC**, | 1803.3434 | 6.7439215.32. |
| Log. tangent angle of inclination, **CAD**, | 7.°15.′36.″890 dec. | 9.1051619.12. |
| Log. **ABC**, | 1803.″3434 dec. | 3.2560784.68. |
| Ar: comp: log. cosine angle of inclination, | 7.°15.′36.″890 dec. | 0.0034960.98 |
| Chord of transit, **AD**, | 1817.″9191 dec. | 3.2595745.66 |

In the oblique plane triangle, **ASD**, we have now the three sides, **AD**, 1817.″ 9191 dec., **AS**, 1004.″ 597 dec., and **DS**, 1006.″ 954 dec., to find the segments of the base, **AE** and **ED**.

| | ″ dec. | |
|---|---|---|
| Arith: comp: log. **AD**, | 1817.9191. | 6.7404254.34. |
| Sum of **AS** and **DS**, | 2011.551. log. | 3.3035310.16. |
| Difference, | 2.357. log. | 0.3723596. |
| | (x) 2.6080 | 0.4163160.50. |

| | | ″ dec. | ″ dec. |
|---|---|---|---|
| **AD**, ∓ (x) = | 2 **AE**, | 1815.3111.½ | 907.65555. = **AE**. |
| | 2 **ED**, | 1820.5271.½ | 910.26355. = **ED**. |

| | ″ dec. | |
|---|---|---|
| Log. of Segment **AE**, | 907.65555 | 2.9579210.66 |
| arith. comp: log. **AS**, | 1004.597 | 6.9980080.99 |
| Log. cosine: angle of conjunction, **EAS**, 25.°22.′39.″735 dec | | 9.9559291.65 |

When the difference of apparent latitude of the ⋆ and ☽'s center is greater a the immersion than at the emersion, the sum of the angle of inclinatio and angle of conjunction is equal to the central angle. The contrary at th emersion.

| | | ° ′ ″ dec. |
|---|---|---|
| Angle of conjunction, | **EAS**, | 25.22.39.735. |
| Angle of inclination, | **CAD**, | +7.15.36.890. |
| Central angle, | **ASF**, | 32.38.16.625. |

| | | |
|---|---|---|
| arith: comp: log. cosine ⋆'s latitude, | ° ′ ″ dec. 4.1.59.809. | 0.0010769.72 |
| Log. ☽'s semidiameter, **AS**, | ″ dec. 1004.597. | 3.0019919.01 |
| " co sine central angle **ASF**, | ° ′ ″ dec. 32.38.16.625. | 9.9253646.17 |
| " diff. of apparent long. **FS**. | ′ ″ 14.8.073.=848.073 ″ | 2.9284334.90 |

| | |
|---|---|
| ☽'s apparent long. at immersion, | 57. 2.27.979 |
| app: longitude point of occultation, | 57.16.36.052. |
| ⋆'s longitude, | 57.16.35.925. |
| point occultation East of ⋆, | 0. 0. 0.127. |

| | ′ ″ dec. |
|---|---|
| Parallax in longitude at the emersion, corrected, | 32. 8.881 |
| diff: of apparent longitude, | −15.59.777 |
| True diff: of longitude of ⋆ and ☽'s center at the emersion, | +16. 9.104 |

---

The Moon's true motion in longitude for 12 hours, reduced to the ecliptic at the middle time between the immersion and ecliptical conjunction at Washington, was ° ′ ″ 7.31.58.554.

At a middle time between the emers: and ecl: conj: 7.31.55.875.

---

For the intervals of time.

As 7.° 31.′ 58.″ 554. dec is to 12 hours, so is 50.′ 25.″ 670. dec to 1. h 20. m. 19. Sec. 909 dec., which added to 9. h. 22. m. 36. sec 339 dec., th corrected time of immersion, gives 10. h. 42. m. 56. sec. 248. dec. the tim f ecliptical conjunction of ☽ and ★, at the Capitol in Washington, by the nmersion.

.s 7.° 31.′ 55.″ 875. dec. to 12 hours, so is 16.′ 9.″ 104. dec to 25. m. 43. sec. 40 dec., which added to the time of emersion corrected, = 10. h. 17. m. 14. ec. 392. dec gives 10. h. 42. m. 58. sec. 332 dec., the time of ecliptical conınction, by the emersion.

| | | h. m. sec. dec. |
|---|---|---|
| .pparent time of ecliptical conjunction, by the immersion, | | 10.42.56.248. |
| , by the emersion, | | 10.42.58.332 |
| Iean. | Time of true conj: ☽ and ★, at the capitol, | 10.42.57.290. |

---

| pparent time t Greenwich. | ☽'s longitude. | | | |
|---|---|---|---|---|
| h. m. | ° ′ ″ dec. | | | |
| 15.30 | 57. 3.41.018 **A.** | 1st diff: | | |
| | | ′ ″ dec. | 2d diff. | |
| | | + 6.16.319. a1. | | |
| 15.40 | 57. 9.57.337. **B.** | | – 029. a2. | |
| | | + 6.16.290. b1. | | |
| 15.50 | 57.16.13.627. **C.** | | – 029. b2. | |
| | > | + 6.16.261. c1. | | |
| 16.00 | 57.22.29.888. **D.** | | – 029. c2. | |
| | | + 6.16.232. d1. | | |
| 16.10 | 57.28.46.120. **E.** | | | |

| | ° ′ ″ dec |
|---|---|
| tar's longitude, | 57.16.35.925. |
| Ioon's longitude at 15. h. 50 m (C) | 57.16.13.627. |
| difference, | 22.298. |

s c1 6.′ 16.″ 261 dec, to 10 minutes, so is 22.″ 298. dec to 35 Sec. 557 dec. e time, nearly approximated.

The equation arising from 35. Sec. 557 dec., and the second difference 029. amounts to ,0035, which added to 6.′ 16.″ 261 dec, gives 6.′ 16.″ 2645 ec., the Moon's motion in ten minutes at the approximate time; then,

As 6.′ 16.″ 2645. dec to 10 minutes, so is 22.″ 298 dec, to 35. sec. 556 dec, hich added to 15. h. 50 m., gives 15. h. 50. m. 35. Sec. 556 dec., the apparıt [time][1] of true conjunction of ☽ and ★ at Greenwich.

| pparent time of true conjunction | | h. m. Sec. dec. |
|---|---|---|
| | at Greenwich, | 15.50.35.556 |
| d° | at Washington | 10.42.57.290. |
| ongitude in time, West, | | 5. 7.38.266 = 76.°54.′33.″990 dec. |

By the emersion.

| | ″ dec. | | |
|---|---|---|---|
| Log. of segment **ED**, | 910.26355. | | 2.9591821.85. |
| " ☽'s semid: **DS**, | 1006.954 | ar. comp | 6.9969903.72. |
| | ° ′ ″ dec. | | |
| " co-sine angle conjunct: **EDS** | 25.18.35.662 | | 9.9561725.57. |
| Angle of inclination, **CAD**, | –7.15.36.890. | | |
| Central angle, **DSG**, | 18. 2.58.772. | | |

| | | | |
|---|---|---|---|
| Log. co-sine ★'s latitude, 4.° 1.′ 59.″ 809. dec. arith. comp. | | | 0.0010769.7 |
| " ☽'s Semidiam: **DS**, | 1006.″ 954 dec | lo | 3.0030096.2 |
| " co-sine central angle, **DSG**, | 18.° 2.′ 58.″ 772 dec. | | 9.9780838.3 |
| | ′ ″ dec. | | |
| diff. apparent long. **GS**, | –15.59.777. = 959.″777 dec. | | 2.9821704.3 |

| | |
|---|---|
| ☽'s apparent long. at emers: | 57.32.35.800. |
| app: long. point of occult. | 57.16.36.023. |
| ★'s longitude; | 57.16.35.925. |
| point occult: east of ★, | 0. 0. 0.098. |

The apparent longitude of the points of occultation not agreeing exact with the Star's longitude, a correction is necessary, which is thus made.—

The interval of apparent time between the immersion and emersion, is 54. m. 38 sec, or 3278 sec, and the ☽'s motion in apparent longitude reduc to a parallel to the ecliptic, **ABC**, 1803.″ 3434 dec.,—the excess at the imme sion, 3.″ 127 dec, and at the emersion, 0.″ 098. dec.—then,

As 1803.″ 3434 dec : 3278 Sec. :: {″ dec. 0.127 / 0.098.} {″ dec. 0.231. / 0.178.}

which subtracted respectively, from the apparent times of immersion a emersion, gives 9. h. 22. m. 36. sec. 339. dec. for the apparent time of i mersion, and 10. h. 17. m. 14. sec 392 dec, for the time of emersion, correcte

| | ° ′ ″ de |
|---|---|
| At the corrected time of immersion, the Moon's true longitude was | 56.26.10.25 |
| Parallax in longitude, then, | + 36.17.59 |
| Moon's apparent longitude, | 57. 2.27.85 |
| diff: of apparent longitude, | + 14. 8.07 |
| apparent longitude of the point of occultation, agreeing with the ★'s longitude, | 57.16.35.92 |

| | ° ′ ″ dec |
|---|---|
| At the corrected time of emersion, the Moon's true long: was | 57. 0.26.821. |
| Parallax in longitude, then, | + 32. 8.881. |
| Moon's apparent longitude, | 57.32.35.702. |
| diff: of apparent longitude, as above, | −15.59.777. |
| Apparent longitude of the point of occultation, agreeing with the Star's longitude, | 57.16.35.925. |

| | ′ ″ dec. |
|---|---|
| Parallax in longitude at the immersion, corrected, | 36.17.597. |
| apparent difference of longitude, | + 14. 8.073. |
| True difference of long. of the ★ and ☽'s center, at immersion, | 50.25.670. |

In recomputing the angles of conjunction and central angles, (which has been done in a similar communication to bishop Madison,) a small error has been discovered, which makes the excess of the difference of apparent longitude between the star and point of occultation to be the same at the emersion as at the immersion, viz: 0.″ 121. dec.—The mean of times of ecliptical conjunction of the Moon and Star at the Capitol, in Washington, is found to be 10. h. 42. m. 57. sec. 562 dec., and the time at Greenwich, which has also been recomputed, = 15. h. 50. m. 35. sec. 557 dec., differing only $\frac{1}{1000}$ part of a second from the former;—from which the difference of longitude, in time, between the meridians, is = 5. h. 7. m. 37. sec. 995. dec. or 76.° 54.′ 29.″ 975 dec.; hence, without a sensible error, the longitude [of] the Capitol, in Washington, admitting the ratio of the equatorial to the polar axis of the Earth to be as 334 to 333, may be estimated at 5. h. 7. m. 38 sec., or 76.° 54.′ 30.″ west of Greenwich.—

As some of the essential elements used in the operation have been calculated again, and brought to minute exactness, and great care taken to have all of them correct, the accuracy of the result will not, it is presumed, be questioned by those who are capable of understanding the process; and if I were not myself satisfied in this respect, I should not have ventured to submit with the confidence I shall do, to yourself and other scientific gentlemen, particularly those who are natives of the United States, an undertaking which has for its object an entire abolition of <u>one</u> of the sources of dependence on a foreign nation, of whose conduct to us for a series of years, let every American attached to the constitution, laws and soil of his own country, be an impartial judge.

It will be remembered, that a variance must necessarily exist between the longitude of any two places on the Earth, considered as a <u>spheroid</u>, and when reduced by any assumed ratio of the equatorial to the polar diameter, to a sphere, as referred to it's center; this difference in the distance between this place and Greenwich, will probably amount to 2 or 3 minutes of longitude: but it has always been customary in a determination of the longitude from solar eclipses or occultations (the best methods hitherto discovered) to make an allowance for the spheroidical form of the Earth: the ratio used in this computation makes the figure approach more towards a sphere than the proportion of 230 to 229.

If you can find leisure amidst the large mass of letters which no doubt, you are daily in the habit of receiving from all quarters, and the more pleasing avocations of domestic life in your retirement at Monticello, to favor me with your opinion on the subject of this communication, it will be gratefully acknowledged.

I have the honor to be, with great respect, Sir, Your most obedient servant, WILLIAM LAMBERT.

☞ I shall defer my intention of adopting the latitudes and longitudes of places on the Earth to a fi[rs]t meridian of our own, until I am favored with the sentiments of competent judges relating to the accuracy of the result affecting the distance between ours and Greenwich.

RC (DLC); on four folio sheets; mutilated; at foot of text: "Thomas Jefferson, late President of the United States." Recorded in SJL as received 11 Sept. 1809.

Andrew MACKAY, a Scottish mathematician, wrote *The Theory and practice of finding the Longitude at Sea or Land*, 2d ed., 2 vols. (Aberdeen, 1801; Sowerby, no. 3815). John GARNETT, an astronomer in New Brunswick, New Jersey, wrote the annual *Nautical Almanac and Astronomical Ephemeris* (New Brunswick, 1803–13; Sowerby, no. 3810) and the accompanying *Tables Requisite to be used with the Nautical Ephemeris* (New Brunswick, 1806; Sowerby, no. 3809), probably the text Lambert refers to as AMERICAN REQ: TABLES. The observations of the 1806 solar eclipse made by José J. de FERRER, a Spanish astronomer, were published by the astronomer William Dunbar, of Natchez, Mississippi (APS, *Transactions* 6 [1809]: 264–75, 293–9, 351, 362; Greene, *American Science*, 140–3).

[1] Omitted word editorially supplied.

# From James Monroe

DEAR SIR Albemarle Sep^r 4. 09.

It has been intimated to me by unquestionable authority, that a visit by you to Col: Walker would at this time be consider'd by him, an act of great kindness, & be received with much sensibility. You know the wretched condition in which he is, tortur'd by[1] an incurable disease, which must soon take him from this scene. The idea was suggested to me before I went to Richmond, but it did not appear then to rest on such ground as to justify the communication of it to you.[2] The friend who imparted it to me, has since led the conversation with the utmost delicacy & caution to that topick, & ascertain'd with certainty that such are Col: Walkers sentiments. I have thought that it would be agreable to you to receive this information & hasten to give it. It is proper that you should also know that Col: W. proposes to make a visit to Phil[a] in the hope of deriving some aid from the faculty there, & that the day after tomorrow is spoken of, as fix'd, for his departure. The necessity I am under of going immediately to Loudoun & the preparation incident to the journey, will excuse my not communicating this to you in person.

I am dear Sir with great respect & esteem your friend & servant

JA[S] MONROE

It may be satisfactory to you to know that I rec[d] the above from D[r] Everett. I mention this in confidence.

RC (DLC); endorsed by TJ as received 4 Sept. 1809 and so recorded in SJL. Dft (DLC: Monroe Papers); with numerous emendations; at head of text: "To M[r] Jefferson"; endorsed by Monroe in part: "presumed not sent to Mr Jefferson."

Colonel John WALKER, of Belvoir plantation in Albemarle County, died shortly hereafter, with his death occurring at Orange Court House on his way to Philadelphia to be treated for an "ulcerated face." His wife died on 10 Sept. 1809 (William D. Meriwether to Charles Meriwether, 17 Sept. 1809 [NcU: Southern Historical Collection, Meriwether Family Papers]; Lay, *Architecture*, 45, 304n; Richmond *Enquirer*, 2 Jan. 1810). Walker and TJ had been boyhood friends, attended the College of William and Mary together, and served concurrently in the House of Burgesses. TJ was an attendant at Walker's 1764 wedding to Elizabeth (Betsey) Moore. Their friendship became strained in 1790 when Walker lost a bid for reelection to the United States Senate to TJ's friend Monroe. Early in the 1800s tensions ran high when James Thomson Callender published allegations of TJ's much earlier advances toward Mrs. Walker, with the story subsequently appearing in the Boston *New-England Palladium* on 18 Jan. 1805 and attracting discussion in the Massachusetts House of Representatives. Walker believed that the advances had begun in 1768, during his temporary absence, and had continued until 1779, well into TJ's own marriage. In the spring of 1805 he demanded satisfaction from TJ. Although TJ denied that his efforts at seduction continued after his own marriage, he resolved the matter by admitting to Walker the incorrectness of his conduct and exonerating Walker's wife of any guilt (Malone, *Jefferson*, 1:153–5, 447–51).

Monroe was traveling to Oak Hill, his estate in LOUDOUN County (*ANB*). Charlottesville physician Charles EVERETT was a close friend of the Walkers (Mary Rawlings and W. Edwin Hemphill, eds., "Dr. Charles Brown's Reminiscences of Early Albemarle," *MACH* 8 [1947/48]: 60; Woods, *Albemarle*, 189–90).

[1] Preceding two words interlined in Dft in place of "languishing under."

[2] In Dft Monroe here canceled "Without any compromittment of you."

# To James Monroe

DEAR SIR [4 Sept. 1809]

Had I known before that the visit you mention was desired, I would have made it. it cannot now be done, as he sat out on his journey this morning. some opportunities of friendly attention had before occurred, during his illness, and I availed myself of them; & learning last night that ripe figs would be acceptable to him, & that he was to set out on his journey this morning, I sent a servant with a basket of figs this morning. they were putting the horses to the carriage for his journey when the servant came away. I will give you explanations on this subject too long for an extempore letter, when we meet again.

Affectionately Yours TH: JEFFERSON

RC (ViU: TJP); undated; addressed: "Col° Monroe"; endorsed by Monroe: "Mr Jefferson respecting Mr Walker." Not recorded in SJL.

# From Hugh Nelson

DEAR SIR, Belvoir Monday Morng [4 Sept. 1809]

Your present of Figs was very acceptable to Mr Walker, who begs that his grateful acknowlegements may be receiv'd for your friendly and polite Attention. We have hoped that Mr Walker has gained some strength within the last six days, and that his general Health is somewhat improved. Mrs Walker had within the last two days somewhat improved in Health, but this morning is again not so well as on Yesterday. They are both still very feeble & low. With best wishes for the Health & happiness of yourself and family, I remain with sentiments of Esteem and respect Yr hble St HUGH NELSON

RC (DLC: TJ Papers, 188:33465); partially dated; endorsed by TJ as a letter of 4 Sept. 1809 received the same day and so recorded in SJL.

Hugh Nelson (1768–1836), attorney and public official, was the son of Virginia governor Thomas Nelson, of Yorktown. He graduated from the College of William and Mary in 1790, moved to Albemarle County, married John Walker's daughter, and thereby acquired Belvoir after Walker's death. Nelson represented Albemarle County in the House of Delegates, 1805–09, the last two sessions as speaker, and he sat on Virginia's General Court, 1809–11. He exchanged political views and local news regularly with TJ while representing his congressional district in the United States House of Representatives, 1811–23. Nelson resigned that seat to become minister plenipotentiary to Spain, 1823–25, and concluded his public service with a final term in the House of Delegates, 1828–29 (*ANB*, *DAB*; Norfleet, *Saint-Mémin*, 193–4; Lay, *Architecture*, 304n; *JEP*, 3:320, 324 [13, 15 Jan. 1823]; *Lynchburg Virginian*, 28 Mar. 1836).

## From James Wood

SIR Georgia. Columbia County 5[h] September 1809—

I have received accounts from various hands, that you are in a more than common degree affected by the general calamities of our county. This is by no means a matter of surprise to me, as it in some measure corresponds with what passes in my own bosom Nevertheless, I cannot but regret that a man of your superior understanding should not rather enjoy his own good fortune, than vainly disquiet himself with the mesery of others, which it is not in his power to prevent. No flow of genius no force of eloquence, have ever bin able to advert you, from dischargeing your duty to your country with fidelity. As for myself, there is none who has more bitterly lamented the general misfortunes of the commonwealth. Yet there are many reflections from which I now derive great relief, particularly from a consciousness of the integrity of my own good intentions. I long foresaw, as from some advantageous eminence, the storm that was gathering around us, and I foresaw it, not only by the force of my own discernment, but much clearer by the assistance of your prophetic admonitions. For though I was not present during your administration, yet I was not unapprised how often you foretold these fatal misfortunes, and what measures you recommended for its prevention. In the commencement of your administration, I was not present, when you prudently endeavoured to awaken our fears, by enumerating those wars that had happened within our own memories. And if the authors of these, you told the house, unsupported by a single example of the same kind to give a colour to their conduct, had exercised such dreadful cruelties, whoever in future times should successfully turn his arms against the republic would most assuredly prove a much more intolerable tyrant. For they that act by precedent, you observed, generally think they act by right, and in cases of this nature seldom fail of improving upon their model. You should remember, therefore, that those who refused to follow your judicious advice, owe their destruction entirely to their own imprudence. But you will ask, perhaps, what relief can this consideration afford to your mind, amidst the universal distresses of the republic. It must be acknowledged, that our misfortunes will scarce admit of consolation; so total and so irrecoverable is the ruin we deplore. However, your fellow citizen looks upon you as shining forth amidst this general extinction of the great lights of the republic, in all the lustre and dignity of wisdom and virtue you[1] formerly possessed, and cant think of giving[2] you up, like a star that falls to rise no more. These considerations therefore ought greatly to alleviate the generous disquietude of your heart. Tis true you are at present with your friends and family, and this you have great reason to be thankful, as you are removed, at the same time from many very disagreeable circumstances.

I would particularly point them out to you, but that I am unwilling you should have the pain of hearing what you are so happy as not to see, an advantage which renders your situation, I think, so much the more eligible than ours. I have thus far laid before you, in the warmest friendship of my heart, those reasons which may[3] justly contribute to lighten and compose your uneasiness. The rest are to be found within yourself, and they are consolations which I know, by daily experience, to be of the best and most efficacious kind. I well remember that you passionately cultivated the whole circle of science from your earliest youth, and carefully treasured up in your mind whatever the wisest philosophers[4] have delivered concerning the best and happiest regulation of human life. Now these are contemplations both useful and entertaining even in seasons of the greatest calm and prosperity, but in the present calamitous situation of public affairs, there is nothing else that can sooth and compose our minds. I would not be so arrogant as to take upon myself to exhort a man of your superior sence and knowledge, to have recourse to those studies to which I know you have your whole life been devoted. I will only say with respect to myself (and I hope I shall be justified by your approbation) that I consecrated all my time and attention to philosophy, when I perceived there was no farther employment either in the house or the bar for my favourite art. Scarce more room is there for the exercise of that excellent science, in which you, my friend are so eminently[5] distinguished. I am persuaded, therefore, that I have no occasion to admonish you to apply your thoughts to the same philosophical contemplations, which if they were attended with no other advantage, would have this at least to recommend them, that they divert the mind from dwelling on its anxieties.

While round the british cabinet, the fraudful ivy twines,  
Robb'd of its strength the feable house declines,  
Thus envious age advanced with stealing pace,  
Clipps their chill'd limbs, and kills with cold embrace,  
Like empty monuments to heroic fame,  
Of all they were retaining but the name

I presume you begin at this time to wonder who I am, I am the little officer who presented himself to you in the year seventeen hundred and seventy nine, in your brick house in Richmond, with a draft on the treasurer for five thousand five hundred pounds (all drafts of similar nature had been paid off except mine) the treasurer Mr Brook's informed me he could not pay it, without a special order from your excellency, which I endeavoured to obtain with all my rhetoric, but to no purpose, I found you inflexible to the plan you had contemplated and laid down, which though hard upon me, yet I esteemd you the more, that you could not be adverted from the plan you had pursued, which appears to have bin your guide through life. I live in Columbia County State of Georgia near the court house—Accept of these few salutations as from a friend. JAMES WOOD

RC (MoSHi: TJC-BC); addressed: "Thomas Jefferson Esquire Late President of the united States Virginia. Mountesello ℘ Mail"; franked and postmarked; endorsed by TJ as received 1 Oct. 1809 and so recorded in SJL.

James Wood (1755–1836), a native of King and Queen County, was living in Prince Edward County when he enlisted as a volunteer in the 2d Virginia Regiment of the Continental army in 1776. He was a lieutenant in the Georgia militia, 1777–78, sustaining a wound while serving in the Carolinas, Georgia, and Florida. After the American Revolution, Wood became an attorney and lived successively in Liberty, Columbia, and Heard counties, Georgia (DNA: RG 15, Revolutionary War Pension and Bounty-Land Warrant Application Files; Alex M. Hitz, comp., *Authentic List of All Land Lottery Grants Made to Veterans of the Revolutionary War by the State of Georgia*, 2d ed. [1966], 76).

[1] Manuscript: "your."
[2] Manuscript: "given."
[3] Manuscript: "my."
[4] Manuscript: "philophers."
[5] Manuscript: "emimently."

# To Jones & Howell

MESS JONES & HOWELL Monticello Sep. 6. 09

Your favor of Aug. 16. was duly recieved, and I thank you for the indulgence of making my remittances from time to time as I can. this shall be as diligently done as the difficult circulation of money in this part of the country will permit. in the mean time I avail myself of your permission to ask a new supply of 2. tons of rod, assorted as usual, and a quarter ton of the best tough bar iron, in bars from the size of an axle tree down to the smallest, and tender you the assurances of my esteem & respect. TH: JEFFERSON

PoC (MHi); endorsed by TJ.

A letter from Jones & Howell to TJ of 21 Sept. 1809, not found, is recorded in SJL as received from Philadelphia six days later.

# To Joseph McCoy

Monticello Sep. 6. 09.

Th: Jefferson presents his compliments to mr M^c^Coy & his thanks for the poem he was so kind as to send him some time past the reciept of which he has not been able sooner to acknolege. too old now to catch the glow of poetry, he is illy qualified to become a judge of it's merits, other than that of sentiment. in this respect there is much to commend in mr M^c^Coy's little poem. the independance of genius so properly noticed in the poem, the superior course it holds, and certainty with which it attains the station in society which it's powers claim, when contrasted with the desperate prospect of unprotected genius in older countries, is as encouraging to rising merit here, as honorable to those among whom it is displayed & cherished, & ultimately rewarded with justice.

PoC (CSmH: JF-BA); dateline at foot of text; endorsed by TJ.

McCoy sent TJ his POEM, "The Expedient," on 3 July 1809. TJ soon received a 1 Sept. 1809 circular in which Philadelphia printer John Washington Scott unsuccessfully sought enough subscriptions to publish a volume featuring another of McCoy's poems, *The Moment*, which was described as having been "written in March last, when the feelings of the Nation were in high agitation, and some steps were taken preparatory to issuing it, when the *Erskine arrangement* was announced, which, in a great measure, tranquilized the public mind, and the author became indifferent about its publication. Great Britain, however, by her refusal to ratify that arrangement, entered into with such apparent frankness and good nature by both parties, having revivived [revived] the former state of things, and farther confirmed every idea of her character, it appears now appropriate, and is offered for public patronage without a variation in sentiment or opinion" (broadside in CSmH: JF-BA; with handwritten corrections by McCoy; addressed: "Thomas Jefferson Monticello Virg"; postmarked and franked; endorsed by TJ as received from Philadelphia on 25 Sept. 1809 and so recorded in SJL, with the notation: "circular").

# From J. Philippe Reibelt

Havanna,
Sept. 6–1809.

MOST HIGHLY & SINCERELY RESPECTED SIR!

You have—I hope—received the Letters, I wrote to You in the Month of febr, when Sailing from N. Orleans, & in the Month of May, when arriving here.

Also M^r^ Randolph.

I will come—for Some bussiness of a friend—back to the so happy U.S.—as Soon as my eldest Son, who is very Sick, will have recovered his health; & I will give me the Consolation, to go to see You once more in my fatefull Life.

In the mean Time, I take the Liberty, to inform You, that I will send by the first Vessel bound to Norfolk a box with Havanna Confitures under the direction of Mr Ford at Norfolk & then Mr Jefferson at Richmond—for Monticello.

By an other Vessel which sailed Yesterday I wrote a Letter to Mr Randolph.

Please to accept as favourably as You did formerly, the expression of the Sentiment of my deepest Veneration,

Always the Same. P. REIBELT

P.S. Permit me to beg You, to present my respectfull Salutatios to the houses of Mr Randolph & Carr.

RC (MHi); endorsed by TJ as received 10 Sept. 1810 and so recorded in SJL. Enclosed in Madame Reibelt to TJ, 16 May 1810.

J. Philippe Reibelt (d. 1809), a native of France who had been an archivist in Switzerland, immigrated to Baltimore in 1804 and began supplying TJ with imported books. He visited TJ at Monticello in 1805, and the following year TJ secured him an appointment as United States factor at Natchitoches in Orleans Territory. Instead of taking up his duties there, Reibelt lingered at New Orleans until Governor William C. C. Claiborne appointed him judge of Avoyelles Parish in 1807. In the spring of 1809 Reibelt moved with his family to Havana, where he died that October (Reibelt to TJ, 31 Jan. 1805 and enclosures, 2 Jan., 15 Feb. 1809, TJ to Reibelt, 11 Oct. 1805, 10 Jan. 1806, Claiborne to TJ, 4 June 1806, 3 May 1807, and TJ to Claiborne, 10 July 1806 [DLC]; *Terr. Papers*, 9:563n; Widow Reibelt to TJ, 16 May 1810).

Reibelt's letter of the MONTH OF MAY 1809 is not recorded in SJL and has not been found. Peter FORD was a merchant in Norfolk (*The Norfolk Directory* [Norfolk, 1806], 15).

# To Abraham Bradley

SIR Monticello Sep. 7. 09.

I recieved duly your favor of Aug. 31. 09. and have executed your commission according to the best information I could get, by directing your letter to Minor M. Cosby at Milton. he is a man of excellent education, a teacher of languages in that place, of irreproachable character, & diligence, & always in place. Burnley, who had acted as deputy, would have been a good appointment, but was not equal in his qualifications nor standing. he is a very honest young man, just setting up for himself as a sadler, &[1] declined the office as I was assured, & understood a person of the name of Vest would have accepted it. his character was sound, he had kept a grocer's shop there, had broken up that & become a writer in a merchant's counting house. Burnley is the only one of the three I have ever seen; tho' Cosby's character & particular qualifications I had learnt long since from others; and I trust he will do his duties with fidelity & punctuality. might I ask the favor of you to send me a bill of the present establishment of our posts at Milton, & Charlottesville, noting the days & hours of arrival & departure at & from those places & Washington. one of your latest Lists of the post offices of the US. (in a pamphlet) would be also acceptable. accept the assurances of my esteem & respect. TH: JEFFERSON

PoC (DLC); at foot of text: "M[r] Bradley"; endorsed by TJ.

MINOR M. COSBY was appointed postmaster at Milton in January 1810. Acting on behalf of John Peyton, who had been postmaster at Milton since January 1806, Nathaniel BURNLEY wrote TJ a letter from that place on 17 July 1809, not found, recorded in SJL as a letter from Peyton received 20 July 1809 with the notation: "Na. Burnley for him." The letter evidently contained TJ's Milton post office bill, which TJ satisfied by paying ten dollars to Burnley for Peyton on 22 July 1809. Charles VEST became the postmaster at Milton in December 1811, while Burnley was appointed the first postmaster at Stony Point in April 1813 (Axelson, *Virginia Postmasters*, 5, 6; *MB*, 2:1246).

[1] TJ here canceled "moreover."

# To William Caruthers

SIR Monticello Sep. 7. 09

I recieved in due time your favor of July 21. informing me you had in your hands a sum of about 90.D. recieved for me as rent for the salt-petre cave at the Natural bridge, and asking it as a donation for the female academy of that neighborhood. I have ever believed that the duty of contribution to charitable institutions would produce the greatest sum of good by every one's devoting what they can spare to the institutions of their neighborhood, or in the vicinity of their property; because under the eye of their patrons they would be more faithfully conducted than at a distance from them: and I have been led to adhere to this rule in practice as well as theory by necessity, the applications to me from every part of the union being more than any income but that of the union, could supply. on this principle I am persuaded you will think twenty five Dollars a donation fully proportioned to my property in that quarter, giving this sum therefore to the institution there, I will thank you to remit the balance either to myself, or mess[rs] Gibson & Jefferson in Richmond, retaining such commission as you think reasonable. I was applied to some time ago to sell that tract of land to a person who proposed to establish a store & tavern there, and who seemed to consider it as worth ten dollars an acre, the adjoining lands of equal quality having sold for that & more. I would now take that sum for it, payable in a twelvemonth or with a deduction of interest if paid sooner. if you can find a purchaser at that price, I would thank you to negotiate it on which I would allow you a reasonable commission. the security should be unquestionable, and the agreement on the condition that I should not have sold it to any other person before notice of that agreement. I tender you the assurances of my great respect. TH: JEFFERSON

PoC (DLC); at foot of first page: "M[r] William Caruthers. Lexington"; endorsed by TJ.

Caruthers's letter of JULY 21 was actually dated 25 July 1809. The donation of TWENTY FIVE DOLLARS took more than a year to complete (TJ to Caruthers, 9 Oct. 1810; Caruthers to TJ, 4 Nov. 1810; *MB*, 2:1262). The PERSON was William Jenkings.

# To George Gilpin

SIR Monticello. Sep. 7. 09.

I have duly recieved your letter of Aug. 7. and am much gratified by the favorable sentiments you are pleased to express towards myself. so to discharge my duties as to give satisfaction to that portion of my fellow citizens who had no views but to the good of their own country, is the only reward I ever wished. for what you are pleased to term a favor to yourself you are indebted to your own merit. in me it was an act of mere duty to look out for those most worthy of public trusts. your sentiments with respect to England are perfectly correct. since the younger Pitt came to the administration of that country, it's government has abandoned all public morality, and it's administrators (with the momentary exceptions of Addington & Fox) have had no other object but to keep themselves in place, and enrich themselves & their families. to this last war is most favorable & therefore they have been at war thro' nearly the whole of the present reign. and I fear that from the corrupt form of their government, this must continue it's permanent character. having now annihilated all other powers on the ocean, they are manifestly acting on the principle that power is right, and mean that no flag shall be seen on the high seas which does not pay tribute to them, & contribute the means of continuing their usurpations. in any other times the sacrifices & efforts of the US. would have ensured their peace & prosperity, but it has been our lot to live in times when all the bulwarks of morality & right have been broken up & Hobbes's principle of the 'bellum omnium in omnia' is become the real principle of the conduct of nations. I hope the last instance of the perfidy of the British government will at length rally all honest[1] men to their own. Accept the assurances of my entire esteem & respect TH: JEFFERSON

PoC (DLC); at foot of text: "Col^o George Gilpin"; endorsed by TJ.

BELLUM OMNIUM IN OMNIA: in 1642 Thomas Hobbes articulated the concept of "bellum omnium in omnes" ("war of all against all") (Hobbes, *De Cive: The Latin Version* [Oxford, 1983], ed. Howard Warrender, 96). See Sowerby, no. 2388.

[1] Word interlined.

# From John Wyche

SIR, Westwardmill 7th September 1809

In complyance with the wishes of the Members of the Library Society established at this place—I now have the honour to inform you that a general meeting is to be convened on friday the 6th day of October next for the purpose of designating books to be purchased, and to claim from you a fulfilment of the promise you were so condescending as to make of pointing out to us the best books on History—Natural—Philosophy—Agriculture &C

As some guide to you it may not perhaps be improper for me to observe that our present & probable fund may be estimated at from three to five hundred Dollars—that as we do not expect to be able to purchase the whole at this time your Favor will be considerably enhanced if you will add to the catalogue the probable cost of each Work—the best Edition and some notes of descrimination by which we may know which you consider the most eminently & immediately usefull & necessary.

Your having expressed an opinion favorable to our institution induces me to observe that as yet its affairs go on prosperously, and that their are several candidates for Membership to be accepted or rejected at our next general Meeting—

With sentiments of gratitude & the highest respect I am (Sir) your most Obt humble Servant JOHN WYCHE

RC (CSmH: JF-BA); endorsed by TJ as received 14 Sept. 1809 and so recorded in SJL; with Dft of List of Recommended Books, enclosed in TJ's 4 Oct. 1809 reply, on verso.

## To William Brown

Dear Sir Monticello Sep. 10. 09.

You were so kind as to forward to mr Barnes Collector of George town, for me the reciept of Cap[t] Sanford of the brig President for 3. boxes of Mammoth bones sent down the river for me by Gen[l] William Clarke. the reciept was dated January 16. it appears from documents in mr Barnes's office, from which that vessel had sailed the 21[st] of Oct. 1808. for N. Orleans, that on her return she put into Havanna, was there condemned as not sea-worthy & her enrollment was surrendered at S[t] Mary's in Georgia the 1[st] of May last. the probability seems to be that she left my boxes at the Havanna. supposing you may have some acquaintance there, or at least more frequent opportunities for enquiry than I can find here, the object of the present is to ask the favor of your having some enquiry made after these boxes if an occasion should occur, & to order their reshipment to any port of the Chesapeak Delaware, or to N. York. pardon this trouble on the consideration of my interior situation, remote from all seaports. mrs Trist is with us & is well, as is also miss Brown. mrs Jones was well by a late letter, but mr Jones's situation was still doubtful. accept the assurances of my esteem & respect.

Th: Jefferson

PoC (DLC); at foot of text: "M[r] W[m] Brown"; endorsed by TJ.

A letter from John barnes of 1 Sept. 1809, not found, is recorded in SJL as received from Georgetown on 4 Sept. 1809. Brown fled New Orleans under suspicion of embezzlement later this year (note to Brown to TJ, 22 May 1809). TJ probably never located these mammoth bones.

## To William C. C. Claiborne

Dear Sir Monticello Sep. 10. 09.

Your favor of May 17. came to hand the last day of June. it covered a Tragedy in Manuscript from Col[o] Siblong commemorative of a scene which had past on the Missisipi within the memory of persons still living. I am too old to catch the enthusiasm of poetry, and therefore unqualified to judge of it's merits other than that of the sentiment. in this respect the piece in question merits much praise, and I can say with truth I have read it with much pleasure. I must pray you to make my acknolegements, for this mark of his attention, acceptable to Col[o] Siblong & to assure him of my respect for a person who can think in the stile of Poucha-houmma.

I lament the misfortunes of the persons who have been driven from Cuba to seek Asylum with you. this it is impossible to refuse them, or to withold any relief they can need. we should be monsters to shut the door against such sufferers. true, it is not a population we can desire, at that place, because it retards the desired epoch of it's becoming entirely American in spirit. no people on earth retain their national adherence longer or more warmly than the French. but such considerations are not to prevent us from taking up human beings from a wreck at sea. gratitude will doubtless secure their fidelity to the country which has recieved them into it's bosom.

I trust that the whole system meditated for the defence of N. Orleans will be carried into effect. I consider the canal from the Misipi to the lake as an essential part of it: should war with England take place, this should be ready before hand. I salute you with great esteem & respect. TH: JEFFERSON

PoC (DLC); at foot of text: "Gov[r] Claiborne"; endorsed by TJ.

# To William Clark

DEAR GENERAL Monticello Sep. 10. 09.

Your favor of June 2. came duly to hand in July, and brought me a repetition of the proofs of your kindness to me. mr Fitzhugh delivered the skin of the sheep of the Rocky mountain to the President, from whom I expect to recieve it in a few days at his own house. for this as well as the blanket of Indian manufacture of the same material which you are so kind as to offer me accept my friendly thanks. your donations & Governor Lewis's have given to my collection of Indian curiosities an importance much beyond what I had ever counted on. the three boxes of bones which you had been so kind as to send to N.O. for[1] me, as mentioned in your letter of June 2. arrived there safely & were carefully shipped by the collector, & the bill of lading sent to me. but the vessel put into the Havanna, under embargo distress, was there condemned as un-seaworthy, and her enrollment surrendered at S[t] Mary's. what was done with my 3. boxes I have not learned, but have written to mr Brown the Collector to have enquiry made after them. the bones of this animal are now in such a state of evanescence as to render it important to save what we can of them. of those you had formerly sent me I reserved a very few for myself, got Doct[r] Wistar to select from the rest every peice which could be interesting to the Philosophical society, & sent the residue to the National institute of France. these have enabled them to decide that the animal was neither a Mammoth nor an elephant, but of a distinct kind, to which they have given the name of Mastodont, from the protuberances of it's teeth. these from their form & the immense mass of their jaws, satisfy me this animal must have been arboriverous. nature seems not to have provided other food sufficient for him; & the limb of a tree would be no more to him than a bough of Cotton tree to a horse. You mention in your letter that you are proceeding with your family to Fort Massac. this informs me that you have a family, & I sincerely congratulate you on it. while some may think it will render you less active in the service of the world, those who take a sincere interest in your personal happiness, and who know that by a law of our nature we cannot be happy without the endearing connections of a family, will rejoice for your sake as I do. the world has, of right, no further claims on yourself & Gov^r Lewis, but such as you may voluntarily render according to your convenience or as they may make it your interest. I wrote lately to the Governor, but be so good as to repeat my affectionate attachments to him & to be assured of the same to yourself with every sentiment of esteem & respect. TH: JEFFERSON

RC (MoSHi: William Clark Papers); endorsed by Clark. PoC (DLC); at foot of first page: "Gen^l W^m Clarke."

William Clark (1770–1838), soldier and explorer, was a Virginia native who served as mapmaker and effectively as joint commander of the Lewis and Clark Expedition, 1803–06. He settled in Saint Louis in 1807, serving as superintendent of Indian affairs from that year until his death, with concurrent stints as governor of Missouri Territory, 1813–21, and brigadier general of militia (*ANB*; *DAB*).

In his FAVOR of 2 June 1808 (MHi), carried most of the way by his brother-in-law Denis FITZHUGH and not delivered until 10 July 1809, Clark wrote that during his impending move from Louisville to Saint Louis he would drop off THREE BOXES OF BONES at Fort Massac for shipment to New Orleans. In December 1807 TJ had requested that Clark send him these duplicate fossils, which Clark had originally left in Kentucky with his brother George Rogers Clark (TJ to William Clark, 19 Dec. 1807 [MoSHi: William Clark Papers]). Clark's BILL OF LADING (MHi) is also dated 2 June 1808. YOUR FAMILY: Clark had married Julia Hancock early in January 1808, and their son Meriwether Lewis Clark was born on 10 Jan. 1809 (James J. Holmberg, ed., *Dear Brother: Letters of William Clark to Jonathan Clark* [2002], 133–4n, 193).

[1] Preceding abbreviation and word added in margin.

# To William Lambert

SIR Monticello Sep. 10. 09.

Your favors of June 13. & July 23. have both been duly recieved, & I am happy to find that you have been so well & successfully occupied in fixing a first meridian for our country. you will be requited by merited fame, even should no emolument more solid result from it. I have attended with interest to the methods you have adopted for obtaining correctness in the result; & concieving them to have been well chosen, I, nevertheless, do not venture on any suggestions in detail. forty two years of entire absorption by political duties, scarcely permitting me as much attention to the more beloved studies of the natural sciences as would keep me where I once was, disqualify me from instructing those daily versed in their exercise or practice. your pamphlet, when published, will be valued by that class of readers, whose esteem you will most highly prize. whether it may open to you the door for the exercise of other qualifications of which you have been so long in the acquisition, is another question. I believe there are not many astronomers in the H. of R. their duties & qualifications call for talents more immediately connected with the science of government. The newspaper you inclosed me contained proofs of your devotion to the republican principles of our inestimable government which I have ever known you to possess. for the sentiments respecting myself I am truly thankful. the favorable regards of my fellow citizens render the happiness of my retirement all I can desire, or deserve.

I had hoped for a moment that, from the other side of the Atlantic, a brighter horison was at length rising[1] to our political view. but it is suddenly clouded again by that total want of morality which seems inherent in the British constitution: and in nothing will it ever be to be trusted while that constitution remains unchanged. let it's history be examined whenever it may, & this 'stupendous fabric of human wisdom' will be found to have been, at least from the epoch of Walpole, the most corrupted & corrupting mass of rottenness which ever usurped the name of government. she went to war to force France to adopt some constitution which would qualify her to maintain relations of good faith with other nations. on this principle she ought to be put under the ban of the world; for where is the nation whose internal peace she has not attempted to destroy by the poison of her own corruption? I turn from this disgusting monument of human depravity to the pleasanter duty of saluting you with esteem and respect.

TH: JEFFERSON

RC (NjP: Andre deCoppet Collection); with notation in unidentified hand on separate sheet: "Inclosed in an Evelope [Envelope], addressed to William Lambert, city of Washington Accompanying William Lambert's letter, received 4th March 1811." PoC (DLC); at foot of first page: "Wm Lambert"; endorsed by TJ.

Thomas Paine alluded to the STUPENDOUS FABRIC OF HUMAN WISDOM in his 14 Aug. 1807 essay "On the Question, Will There Be War?" (*The Complete Writings of Thomas Paine*, ed. Philip Foner [1945], 2:1016).

[1] Word interlined in place of "presenting itself."

# From Charles Pinckney

DEAR SIR, [ca. 10 Sept. 1809]

I have just received your friendly letter, of the 28th ultimo, & hasten to answer it by the Post which goes tomorrow from Charleston, which place I left yesterday to Spend three, or four days, at this place, four miles distant from thence, for the benefit Of the Sea air, & expect to return on Saturday, when it will be in my Power to write you more fully on the Subject.—

It is with concern, I inform You, that it is Mr Samuel House, Mrs Trist's, Brother who died here, & is mentioned in the Paper you inclosed—He caught a Cold in the Spring, which hurried him rapidly into a Consumption; having when in Congress, & in the Convention & indeed Previously, when a very young man been Accustomed to lodge, at his Mother's, who was one of the kindest Ladies in the World, I contracted a very great esteem, & friendship for her, & her very Worthy, & respectable Daughter, Mrs Trist, which descended as it were, by inheritance, to their Son, & Brother, Mr House, when he came to Settle in this City—When in Town, I frequently Saw him, & hearing he was ill, went, to visit him, where I found him past recovery; he was Attended by Doctor Ramsay, & had every thing done, that Art, or Care Could do for him, but in vain.

Mr House, had been many Years, in the first Situation, under the Comptroller General, in that department, he was also, a Notary Public, & One, of the Justices of the Quorum for the City—

What Circumstances he died in, or where his Children are, I do not know, but as Soon, as I return to Town, I will enquire, & write to You,—this will, be in a day, or two—

I am Pleased to find you, So happy, I am Sure, it must be So; for if Mr Adams, Says, the last eight Years, were the happiest of his life, What must Yours be?

We are all here looking with Anxiety, to what Mr Jackson will do, but as we have the Same Opinion of our "Pilot" you have, We have no fears—

A few of us, the Other day, determined to Call a general Meeting of the Citizens of Charleston, & having done So, the federalists, attended it in great Numbers, &, endeavoured to Prevent Our Saying, any thing by moving to Adjourn,—I Opposed it with all my might, taking as my text that this was Of all, the Most Proper time, to approve the President's Conduct, & Pledge him Our Support, & We Carried it hollow.

I Sent it to Mr Madison by the Post, when You See him, Please present Me, affectionately to him, it is now 22 Years Since I Saw him, & Nothing but my Daughter's illness, has Prevented it,—I will thank you also, to present me respectfully, to M[rs] Trists, the last time I saw her, was at Our Worthy friends, Colonel Monroe, in 1801, when Govenor of Virginia—he is also in your Neighbourhood, & You will Oblige me, by tendering my respects, & best wishes to him.—

When You write be So good, as to direct for me in Charleston, & whenever any Political, literary, or Other Subject, Should tempt You, to favour, me with a line, I shall receive it with great pleasure, & pay the utmost Attention to it—

I am with the most Affectionate respect, & regard, dear Sir, always, Yours Truly,

Dupl (DLC: TJ Papers, 188:33503); undated; idiosyncratic line-ending commas omitted; in a clerk's hand; at head of text in Pinckney's hand: "(Duplicate by the last post dated from Haddrell's opposite Charleston)"; endorsed by TJ as a letter from Pinckney received 30 Sept. 1809 and so recorded in SJL. On 30 Sept. 1809 SJL also records receipt of a missing RC dated 10 Sept. 1809, a Sunday, which suggests that the undated Dupl was composed on 5 or 6 Sept. 1809, after which Pinckney returned to Charleston and completed the RC on 10 Sept. 1809.

TJ's letter of the 28TH ULTIMO was actually dated 29 Aug. 1809. Pinckney also wrote James Madison on 5 Sept. 1809 describing the 29 Aug. 1809 GENERAL MEETING in Charleston, which pledged to support the administration in the commercial crisis with Great Britain (Madison, *Papers, Pres. Ser.*, 1:353–6). The daughter with an ILLNESS was either Frances Henrietta Pinckney or Mary Eleanor Pinckney (Frances Leigh Williams, *A Founding Family: The Pinckneys of South Carolina* [1978], 338).

# From Abraham Bradley

SIR General Post Office Septem[r] 11. 1809

I have received your favour of the 7[th] and am obliged by your attention to my former letter. Inclosed you will receive a memorandum of the times of arrival & departure of the mails at and from Milton & our latest list of Post Offices agreeable to your request.

I have the honor to be very respectfully your obedient serv[t]

ABRAHAM BRADLEY JUN[R]

RC (DLC); at foot of text: "Hon[ble] Thomas Jefferson"; endorsed by TJ as a letter of 18 Sept. 1809 received 14 Sept. 1809 and so recorded in SJL. Enclosure: *List of Post Offices in the United States, including all established before December 31st*, 1807 (Washington, 1808). Other enclosure not found.

# From Thomas A. Digges

D[R] Sir Warburton, n[r] Piscat[y] Mary[d], Sep[r] 11[th] 1809

I have lamented extremely the not having it as yet in my power to pay You an intended visit at Monticello, as well as to have been with You nearly at the point of Your departure from[1] the Presidoliad: And I trust You will not take my seeming neglect to any want of regard or my sincere wishes for Your health & preservation, (for there is none I regard more) but to my mind & avocations having demanded more of home than I have ever before experiencd. I have nearly brought "an old House over my head" by attempting to repair a tottering, aged, and Eighty years old family mansion & but to day only began the shingling. I have yet however hopes to get through with it, so as to spare a ride of eight or ten days, after our Elections, and thereby make another pleasurable visit to Monticello. Altho I have never yet made winds or weather an obstacle to journeying either on business or of pleasure, the late summer of remarkable coolness (altho too dry for Farming purposes in this vicinity) would have added to my incitiments. The cause above stated, and that of looking a little after County Interests, for the Torey-Anglo Feds are assiduously at work, have wholly occupied my time—Their dark policy as to present motives, are easier fathomd than what is their actual or future intentions, for as yet they seem not to have got the text or cue upon which they are to blazen forth at our annual Elections the first mond[y] in Octo[r].

The old Currs, as well as the training Whelps, have got on the scent and yelp forth a strong cry ag[t] Gen[l] Smith—They shamelessly propogate falsehoods, & even deny Him a military valor & intrepidity during our Revolutionary struggle:—But Toreys of 1776 are Toreys in 1809. They continue to abuse Him by Barbeque tub speakers & handbills &c[a] &c[a]—Several news papers, & what we are distributing, already contain Answers to both the Charges against Him—That concerning the Bills of Exchange sold to The United States has been completely refuted by M[r] Purviances Statement, & by an extract of a letter from Washington to Annapolis. The charge ag[t] Him about the Contract with Barney (of S[t] Domingo memory) has also been refuted. The letter of M[r] Wilson fully disproves that Gen[l] Smith was privy to the partnership between Santhonax & Barney; And it is admitted that Smith stipulated that in case of a War with France the contract was to be void & at end: When it was made it was perfectly Lawful: But why should I intrude upon You what You already know. The motives of His Torey opponents is manifestly to keep Him from a seat in the Senate, & to get in one who as yet never did good to the party he espouses M^r^ Harper! They think too by getting a Federal House of maryland Representatives to finally undoe our Republican System; But I hope & fully believe their manoevres & assiduity will be abortive, altho our County is yet at risque from not getting a strong nomination—We want only honest, firm & upright Men. We have sustaind a loss by the move of The Covingtons out of it, and a particular one in the Death of Judge Ducket who was a host of service about where he lived. I hear that Alex[r] Scott of Geo town—M[r] Montgomery of Harford—M[r] Trueman Tyler (our Register at Marlbro who holds an equally beneficial Employment)[2] and M[r] Frank Digges one of our late State Councellors, are competitors for y[e] vacancy, & that some intrigues are going on to get it for M[r] Edmund Lee of Alex[a]! I am well informd that M[r] Montgomery withdraws; in which case, in my humble opinion Fr: Digges would be decidedly the fittest Man.—Those appointments, should and doubtless will emenate from The President himself, who having been with You may perhaps have mentiond something of the appointment. I have not had it in my power to be with Him but one day since His Election, & missd of him by half an hour when he departed last with M[r] Oaklys communications.

Expectation & surmise is now all agog as to how He will recieve the mighty Copenhagan Jackson (whom I formerly knew slightly in The foreign Department Office under the Duke of Leeds & his aid du Camp M[r] Hammond).[3] M[r] Jackson arrived a few days ago at Annapolis & is by this in the City. I know too well the faithless manoeuvres of His Court & present trickey Employer to augre well of this his mission—England is not yet beaten enough in Her Continental intrigues (tho she has contrived to ruin every one of Her Allys) to make a fair & proper adjustment with Us, she never will forgive our prosperity and rivalship in Maratime Commerce.

I have varied from the purpose on which I sat down to write. It was, after appologizing for seeming neglects, to solicit Your aid in obtaining information how & thro whom I can get the famous, or rather infamous Treaty of Tilsit. I never had an oppertunity to obtain it, & want to insert its substance in a paper meant to be read by the Toreys about S[t] James's palace & their amiable friends hereabouts.

I am Y[rs] with affectionate regard & Esteem Tho[s] Digges

PS Lieu[t] Cherry is at my Elbow & begs to offer You His respectful Compliments & best wishes for your health: Begs to return You his grateful acknowlegem[ts] & thanks for Your attentions & 2 different appointments in the Army, & Volunteer Corps of The City Dragoons The Fort is very nearly completed & at present in nice order. Its compliment of men is but yet 25 privates & the Guns ready to the needful either ag[t] John Bull or any other Enemy.

RC (DLC); at foot of text: "Tho[s] Jefferson Esq[r] Monticello"; endorsed by TJ as received 17 Sept. 1809 and so recorded in SJL.

Thomas Attwood Digges (1742–1821), unofficial diplomat, was a native of Maryland who wrote one of the first novels by an American, *Adventures of Alonso* (London, 1775). During a long residence in London, he actively supported the American cause during the Revolutionary War, sending supplies to the colonists via Spain, passing along political gossip to John Adams and Benjamin Franklin, and serving as an informal conduit for secret peace negotiations. Digges was discredited for embezzling funds meant for American prisoners of war in 1781, imprisoned for debt four years later, and suspected of being an unprincipled schemer at all times by virtually everyone who knew him best, although George Washington, his neighbor across the Potomac, remained convinced of his loyalty. Digges first wrote TJ in the context of Digges's attempts to smuggle skilled British artisans and textile machinery to America starting late in the 1780s. In 1798 he returned to Maryland and his ancestral home, Warburton Manor, which he had inherited in 1792 (*ANB*; *PTJ*, 20:316–8n; Robert H. Elias and Eugene D. Finch, eds., *Letters of Thomas Attwood Digges, 1742–1821* [1982]).

Samuel Smith and his supporters waged a vigorous campaign in Maryland for his reelection to the United States Senate. They held a large BARBEQUE outside Baltimore and issued handbills to counteract those published by his detractors (Frank A. Cassell, *Merchant Congressman in the Young Republic: Samuel Smith of Maryland, 1752–1839* [1971], 151–2). For the charges related to BILLS OF EXCHANGE, see note to Smith to TJ, 23 July 1809. Smith had also been accused of being aware of contracts between Joshua BARNEY and French officials when he made his own contract with Barney in 1797 to supply flour to Saint Domingue. Barney gave Smith passports obtained through Léger Félicité Sonthonax (SANTHONAX), one of the French commissioners there, to protect his ships from French interference. Smith's ships were thus enabled to sail with much lower insurance costs than his competitors lacking these protections. Statements by Smith, Barney, and Henry Wilson, who had been Barney's agent in Cap Français, circulated in the 1809 campaign (*Hagers-Town Gazette*, 15, 22 Aug. 1809; Hulbert Footner, *Sailor of Fortune: The Life and Adventures of Commodore Barney, USN* [1940], 192, 213, 219, 237, 241).

Francis James JACKSON, the new British minister plenipotentiary to the United States, had acquired the nickname "Copenhagen" for his presentation of an ultimatum to the neutral Danish government immediately prior to the British bombardment of that city in 1807 (Brant, *Madison*, 4:389). In April 1808 Digges had sold the federal government part of his estate for the construction at Digges Point of FORT Warburton, later Fort Washington, completed in December 1809 (Elias and Finch, *Digges Letters*, 499n; David L. Salay, "'very picturesque, but regarded as nearly useless': Fort Washington, Maryland, 1816–1872," *Maryland Historical Magazine* 81 [1986]: 67). Digges presumably regarded the July 1807 treaties of Tilsit between France and Russia as INFAMOUS because by one of the terms Russia, hitherto a supporter of neutral rights, joined Napoleon's Continental System (Connelly, *Napoleonic France*, 473).

[1] Digges here canceled "Monticello."

[2] Closing parenthesis editorially added.

[3] Closing parenthesis editorially added.

## From James Madison

Dear Sir Montpellier Sep[r] 11. 1809

I send herewith a few papers which have come to my hands along with those addressed to myself.

Jackson according to a note sent from Annapolis to M[r] Smith was to be in Washington on friday evening last. The letters from M[r] Pinkney brought by him, were dated June 23. and merely rehearsed a conversation with Canning; from which it would seem, that C. readily admitted that his second condition (colonial trade) had no connection with the subject, & that it was not to be expected the U.S. would accede to the 3[d] (G.B. to execute our laws). Why then make them Ultimata; or if not Ultimata, why reject the arrangem[t] of E. for not including them; For as to the 1[st] art: if he does not fly from his language to P. the continuance of the non-intercourse vs France, cannot be denied to be a substantial fulfilment of it. From this view of the matter, it might be inferred that Jackson comes with a real olive in his hand. But besides the general slipperiness of his superior, some ideas fell from him in his conversation with P. justifying distrust of his views.

The bearer of this is M[r] Palmer, a young man, respectable I believe, of New York. He is very remarkable as a linguist, and for the most part self-taught. He is perhaps the only American, never out of his own Country, who has dipt as much into the Chinese.

The letter[1] herewith for Cap[t] Coles, was to have gone by the last mail. If no earlier conveyance sh[d] offer I beg the favor of its being sent to the post office in time for the next. Be assured always of my affectionate respects James Madison

As we wish not to be from home, in case any of our friends from Monticello should indulge us with a visit, be so good as to drop us notice of the time.

I have mustered up the Weather Journals, & w[d] send them by the present opp[y] but that they w[d] encumber too much. The fall of water I find has been noted, for not more than 7 or 8 years. The other items much longer

RC (DLC: Madison Papers); endorsed by TJ as received 11 Sept. 1809 and so recorded in SJL. Enclosures not found.

Robert Smith had enclosed the letter from William pinkney in an 8 Sept. 1809 letter to Madison (*ASP, Foreign Relations*, 3:303; Madison, *Papers, Pres. Ser.*, 1:365). e.: David M. Erksine. Aaron H. palmer, a merchant in New York, sent Madison his treatise on the Chinese language earlier in 1809 (Madison, *Papers, Pres. Ser.*, 1:208). Madison and other family members kept a series of

WEATHER JOURNALS for Montpellier from 1784 until at least 1802 (Madison, Meteorological Journals, 1784–93, 1798–1802 [PPAmP]; Madison, *Papers, Congress. Ser.*, 8:514–5).

[1] Manuscript: "leter."

# From John Minor

DEAR SIR Milton Sept 11th 1809

I forgot, when at Montecello, to ask you for the Deed to Tompkins; will you be so good as to forward it to me, when you shall have acknowledged it in Court and had it certified, for probate, in Caroline Court.

I am, with high respect and Esteem Dear Sir yr. he. ob. serv

J. MINOR

RC (MHi); dateline below signature; endorsed by TJ as received 12 Sept. 1809 and so recorded in SJL.

# To James Madison

DEAR SIR Monticello Sep. 12. 09.

I had intended to have been with you before this, but my daughter, who wishes to pay her respects to mrs Madison & yourself at the same time, has been confined by the illness of her youngest child. he has been mending for some days, but slowly, & from the nature of his complaint (visceral) it will be some days yet before she can leave him. I think therefore, on the departure of our present company to take my journey to Bedford, from which I shall be returned in time to see you. I certainly shall not fail to be with you before your departure. I have another letter from Daschkoff. he is just recovering from a serious illness. I judge from his letter that he means to visit our quarter as soon as he is well enough to travel. Canning's equivocations degrade his government as well as himself. I despair of accomodation with them, because I believe they are weak enough to intend seriously to claim the ocean as their conquest, and think to amuse us with embassies & negociations until the claim shall have been strengthened by time & exercise, and the moment arrive when they may boldly avow what hitherto they have only squinted at. Always Your's with sincere affection

TH: JEFFERSON

RC (MiKV-M); at foot of text: "The President of the US." PoC (DLC).

Martha Jefferson Randolph's YOUNGEST CHILD at this time was Benjamin Franklin Randolph.

# To George Jefferson

DEAR SIR Monticello Sep. 13. 09.

We propose that my grandson, Jefferson Randolph shall attend the Mathematical department of the academy of Mess[rs] Girardin, Wood E[t]c in Richmond, and that he should go as soon as the frosts set in, say the 1[st] week in October, which is as early as an upland constitution ought to approach the tide water. can you be so good as to engage a birth for him in some good family where he can pursue his studies free from interruptions of company. indeed if there were a good French family, in which nothing but French is spoken, it would be preferable, as it would give him an opportunity of learning to speak that language which he already reads tolerably well. as to the character of his diet, the plain fare usual at schools is all that is desired. I must ask the favor of you to let me hear from you, as soon as you can ascertain where he can be placed, & particularly to inform me of the terms as well of the school as of the boarding, & what advances are to be made. I salute you with constant affection.

TH: JEFFERSON

PoC (MHi); at foot of text: "M[r] George Jefferson"; endorsed by TJ.

# From Benjamin Smith Barton

SIR, Philadelphia, Septembre 14[th], 1809.

I have, at this time, in the press a new edition of my work on the Dialects of the American Indians. This edition will be, in many respects, much more correct and satisfactory, as well as more ample, than the former, which you have seen. I am extremely anxious to possess specimens,—no matter how small,—of the languages which M[r] Lewis met with beyond the Missisippi. I will think myself much gratified, and honoured, if you will transmit to me, as early as your convenience may suit, such specimens. I do not ask, or wish for, copies of the <u>entire</u> vocabularies: but only a good selection of about ten or twelve words, from each of them. I need not tell you what words those should be—I am less anxious about the language of the Osages, as I have a tolerable specimen of this. Of the Mandan, I have only 4 or 5 words. of the Pawnees, not one, upon which I would wish to depend.[1]—I shall not fail to make a public acknowledgement of the source from which I receive the words.

You will, I think,[2] be pleased to hear, that I have received from Mexico, a very important pamphlet on the Astronomy of the ancient Mexicans. It is not a fanciful work, such as an ingenious man might write in his closet, from the traditions of Indians, or the vague facts and reports[3] of others. It is truly historical, and is principally founded upon the discovery of the "Mexican Century," a vast stone monument, which was discovered in Mexico, in the year 1790. The work is written by one Gama, a man of real[4] learning; and will serve to overturn many an ingenious theory, the work of such historians and writers as Robetson, De Pauw &c. The pamphlet is now in the hands of a friend of mine, who is translating it, with great care. I intend to publish it in English;[5] but where, or in what shape, I know not.[6] Whenever the translation shall be finished, I shall, if you wish it, send you the original Spanish, for your perusal.

I am, Sir, with very great respect, Your obedient & humble servant, &c.,

B. S. Barton.

RC (DLC); dateline below signature; endorsed by TJ as received 20 Sept. 1809 and so recorded in SJL. Dft (PPAmP: Benjamin Smith Barton Papers); at foot of text: "'To Mr Jefferson, at Monticello, Virginia.' exact copy."

Benjamin Smith Barton (1766–1815), physician and naturalist, regularly corresponded with TJ on scientific subjects. Born in Lancaster, Pennsylvania, he studied medicine in Philadelphia, Edinburgh, and London before becoming a professor at the University of Pennsylvania, where he taught botany, materia medica, natural history, and the practice of physic. Barton became a member of the American Philosophical Society in 1789 and served as a vice president, 1802–15. He was also active in the Philadelphia Medical Society, the Linnean Society of London, and the American Academy of Arts and Sciences. In 1803 TJ asked him to train Meriwether Lewis for his transcontinental expedition, for which Barton later failed in his commitment to write the natural history reports (*ANB*; *DAB*; APS, Minutes, 16 Jan. 1789, 1 Jan. 1802 [Ms in PPAmP]).

The work was Barton's *New Views of the Origin of the Tribes and Nations of America* (Philadelphia, 1797; 2d ed., 1798; Sowerby, no. 3998), which he had dedicated to TJ (*PTJ*, 29:445–7). The pamphlet was *Descripción histórica y cronológica de los piedras* (Mexico City, 1792), by Antonio de León y gama, a Mexican antiquarian whose interpretation of the "Solar Stone" discovered in Mexico City in 1790 drew on a number of indigenous Mesoamerican sources (Jorge Cañizares-Esguerra, *How to Write the History of the New World: Histories, Epistemologies, and Identities in the Eighteenth-Century Atlantic World* [2001], 127, 268–80). robetson: William Robertson, *History of America* (London, 1777; Sowerby, nos. 468–9). de pauw: Cornelius de Pauw, *Recherches philosophiques sur les américains* (Berlin, 1768–69). The friend of mine was probably William E. Hũlings, who in 1818 gave the American Philosophical Society an unpublished English translation of León y Gama's pamphlet (MS in PPAmP).

[1] Remainder of paragraph added in Dft.

[2] Preceding two words interlined in Dft.

[3] Reworked in Dft from "closet, upon the reports of Indians, or the vague facts."

[4] Word interlined in Dft.

[5] Preceding three words interlined in Dft in place of "it."

[6] In Dft Barton here canceled "Such inquiries and pursuits are very different from those which occupy the great [persons?] in Europe at this time who at the [rate?] they [prove?]."

# From J. B. Moussier

MONSIEUR LE PRÉSIDENT a Charleston le 14 Septembre 1809

J'ai L'honneur d'informer, Votre excéllence, que je viens de recevoir ici, un paquet à votre adresse, qui m'est parvenu de france par la Voie du Ship mentor, ce Sont divers ouvrages de M^r henry de Gazzera membre de plusieurs académies, qui vous prie d'en agréer L'hommage.

J'aurois desiré, Monsieur Le président, que la distance de cette ville m'eut permis de vous les présenter moi même, dans L'impossibilité de m'acquitter de cette honorable Commission, j'ai L'honneur de vous prévenir que j'ai remis ce matin Le paquet au Capitaine Levin Jones de la Goélette Wolf de Baltimore, qui m'a assuré qu'il vous Sera éxactement remis.

Cette circonstance me fait hazarder de vous faire une priere, dont je vous prie d'excuser la liberté Si elle devait être impraticable.

J'ai apporté de france une grande collection de tableaux qui représentent les principaux monumens de L'antiquité, une Caisse d'environ cinquante tableaux n'a pu-être disposée au moment de mon départ et est restée à Bordeaux; les Capitaines des batimens parlementaires envoyés en france n'ont pas voulu S'en charger, pour ne pas déroger à la loi de non-intercourse.

Cette circonstance qui retarde mes projets d'établir un muséum dans une des villes des états unis, me fait reclamer votre protection, pour donner L'ordre au Cap^e du premier batiment qui irait en france en parlementaire, de demander cette Caisse à M^r Louis ferrier Nég^t à Bordeaux, pour la remettre ensuite à M^r Joseph Thebaud Nég^t à New-york, qui la tiendrait à ma disposition.

J'ose espérer, Monsieur Le président, que La protection que vous accordez aux arts, me fera trouver mon excuse auprès de vous, Si j'ai pu me rendre importun.

J'ai L'honneur d'être avec un profond respect Monsieur Le president. Votre Tres humble & Très obéissant Serviteur

J. B. MOUSSIER

EDITORS' TRANSLATION

Mister president Charleston 14 September 1809
I have the honor of informing Your Excellency that I recently received here a package addressed to you, that came to me from France by way of the ship Mentor. It consists of various works by Mr. Henri Gazzera, a member of several academies, who wishes you to accept them with his compliments.

Mister President, I wish that the distance from this city to you would have allowed me to present them myself. Given the impossibility of fulfilling this honorable commission, I have the honor of letting you know that this morning I gave the package to Captain Levin Jones, of the schooner Wolf, who assured me that it would be delivered to you without fail. This opportunity leads me to venture a request, whose liberty I hope you will forgive, should it not be practicable.

I brought from France a large collection of paintings representing the principal monuments of antiquity. A crate of about fifty paintings was not ready at the time of my departure and remained in Bordeaux. Captains of parlementaires did not want to take it into their care, so as not to run afoul of the Non-Intercourse Act.

This situation, which sets back my plans to establish a museum in a city in the United States, induces me to ask for your assistance, so that orders may be given to the captain of the first parlementaire going to France to ask Mr. Louis Ferrier, a merchant in Bordeaux, to deliver the crate to Mr. Joseph Thebaud, a merchant in New York, who will hold it for me.

I dare hope, Mister President, that the protection you grant to the arts will excuse me in your eyes, should I have made myself tiresome.

I have the honor to be with profound respect Mister President your very humble and very obedient servant

J. B. Moussier

RC (CSmH: JF-BA); on Moussier's printed letterhead, headed by his insignia, handwritten dateline, and internal address (with handwritten sections indicated in italics): "J. B. Moussier, *Citoyen américain,* [preceding two words interlined] Naturaliste du Muséum impérial de France, de l'Athénée des Arts, Correspondant de la Société académique des sciences de Paris, *a Son excellence, Monsieur Jefferson ex-président des Etats-unis d'amerique à Washington*"; endorsed by TJ as received 27 Sept. 1809 and so recorded in SJL; on verso is Albert Gallatin's proposed language for a negative response to Moussier, signed and dated 11 Nov. 1809 and quoted verbatim in TJ to Moussier, 28 Nov. 1809. Translation by Dr. Roland Simon. Enclosures: (1) Henri Gazzera, *Importance, et Avantages d'une Morale Publique et Privée, Ou Nécessité d'une Religion dans toute sorte de Gouvernemens et de Climats* (Avignon, 1801; Sowerby, no. 1521). (2) Gazzera, *Les Veilles de Saint-Augustin, Évêque d'Hippone* (Avignon, 1803; Sowerby, no. 1553). (3) [Gazzera], *Les Nuits de Ste Marie-Magdelaine pénitente* (Paris, 1807; Sowerby, no. 1554). Enclosed in TJ to Gallatin, 11 Oct. 1809, and Gallatin to TJ, 11 Nov. 1809.

Moussier may be the Jean Baptiste Moussier (d. ca. 1831) who, as a merchant at New Orleans in the 1820s, successfully promoted a new type of bank, the capital of which was secured by stockholders' property mortgages (Irene D. Neu, "J. B. Moussier and the Property Banks of Louisiana," *Business History Review* 35 [1961]: 550–7).

Gazzera had written TJ on 25 Oct. 1808 (DLC) that he was sending him a packet of books by way of Moussier, adding that Moussier left Europe with a large collection encompassing European, Asian, and African antiquities spanning four millennia as well as recent scientific discoveries, which he hoped to open to the American public under legislative protection.

# From Thomas Mann Randolph (1792–1848)

Dear Sir! Richmond Sep[r] 15[th] 1809

Being about to leave this for the purpose of entering Harvard College I take the liberty of soliciting from you a line of introduction to some gentleman connected with that seminary

The friendly sentiments you honored me with, when I had the pleasure of being at Monticello must be my apology for this intrusion

With the highest respect I am T M. Randolph

RC (on deposit ViW); endorsed by TJ as received 1 Oct. 1809 and so recorded in SJL.

Thomas Mann Randolph (1792–1848) was the son of TJ's lifelong friend Thomas Mann Randolph and the younger half-brother of TJ's son-in-law of the same name (Randolph, *Randolphs*, 73).

# From George Sullivan

Sir, Boston 15 Sept[r] 1809.

Perhaps in the lapse of time and among the multiplicity of the favors you have variously conferred, it may not immediately occur to you how my Brother and self obtained the honor of being ranked among those, who have shared the fruits of your beneficence. In the month of last January you obligingly gave us permission to import by the Mentor an improved spinning machine, constructed on principles altogether new, and as yet unknown in America. In your letter communicating compliance with our request, you intimated a wish to be informed of the merits of this, in comparison with other machines of the kind.

The machine itself was not shipped on the Mentor; but an eminent Mechanician has come out fully competent to the fabrication of this and other scarcely less valuable machines; which, when in Europe with Mr Bowdoin, I resolved[1] to introduce[2] into our country. He is now established here in an extensive laboratory, and actually labors at the construction of a machine for spinning wool. The same mechanism, with a slight adaptation, may be adjusted for the spinning of cotton, flax or hemp. 'Tis now, Sir, two years since I saw the operation of this machine, and, though I have by me a memorandum of its comparative product, Yet such improvements of it have been made, that it would rather discredit its maturer years to detail alone the productions of its infancy; and I should therefore prefer to communicate it's great[3] comparative advantages over Arkwrights Jenny, when I shall have the honor of informing you of the completion of a machine & at the same time shall transmit a sample of its execution. In the meantime Sir, if you could favor me with your sentiments on the best mode of rendering it most extensively useful; at the same time that I[4] might obtain indemnity for the great expence and hazard of procuring the fabrication here[5] of such machines, you would add much indeed to the obligation we have already the honor to acknowledge at your hands.

With sentiments of the highest respect in which my Brother asks the honor to be associated in your remembrance, I remain

Your very obliged, and very obed[t] Serv[t] GEO SULLIVAN.

RC (CSmH: JF-BA); addressed: "Thomas Jefferson Esq[r] Montecello Virginia"; franked and postmarked; endorsed by TJ as received 25 Sept. 1809 and so recorded in SJL.

George Sullivan, an attorney in Boston with an office at 79 State Street and a house on Chesnut Street, was associated with his BROTHER in a mercantile concern, John L. Sullivan & Company, at 7 India Wharf (*Edward Cotton's Boston Directory* [Boston, 1809], 131).

George Sullivan and John L. Sullivan wrote TJ on 2 Feb. 1809 (MHi), and TJ responded on 8 Feb. 1809 (MHi), not in JANUARY. The EMINENT MECHANICIAN was Charles Artzt, of Saxony (George Sullivan to TJ, 25 May 1811; Charles Artzt to TJ, 22 June 1812).

1 Word interlined in place of "had engaged."
2 Reworked from "bring."
3 Word interlined.
4 Reworked from "we."
5 Word interlined.

# From William Fontaine

SIR Hanover 16[th] Sept[r] 1809

I fear it is to be numbered among the unfortunate incidents of my life that I accepted the invitation of M[r] Randolph to call at Montecello—My mind is tortured with the apprehension that there was something in my Demeanor, something in the heedless freedom of my conversation, that was calculated to give offence, to inflict a wound upon the feelings of persons of the first rank in Society—a trespass upon Decorum, in certain circles, excites as much disgust, if it does not as much abhorrence as a breach of morality—when I unguardedly offend in this respect, very severe is the pennance which I suffer—It is a general impression only which I have, from my own reflection, upon an imperfect recollection of paiticulars—for tis like a dream—not a whisper has reached me—nor do I suppose it possible that such characters will ever condescend to speak of my weakness—So far as I may have trespassed upon the Rules of Decorum, & have forgotten the Distinctions of Character, I must be viewed as a rude & insinseble Clown by those who have had no previous knowledge of me—This I must be content to suffer—but that which paiticularly distresses me, is the apprehension, that you, who I trust have seen me in another & a better form, you with whose acquaintance, & at one period, with whose friendship, I have been honoured, may possibly asscribe any trespasses upon propriety to personal disrespect—It is this consideration that brings the determination to make this address to you—I am incapable of addressing base adulation to any man upon Earth—not even to him who has enjoyed the highest honours which an enlightened, free & grateful People could confer—to him who has bestowed a long life of eminent & faithful services upon his Country—But when injured feelings have their just claims, & my wounded spirit seeks relief, I can & may with propriety speak the Truth—Then, tis a solemn truth that you have enjoyed, and still possess the best affections of my heart, & my most profound personal respect

To reconcile this with any appearances that may unfortunately have been recently exhibited, permit me to speak another Truth—Nature has given me the most[1] inflammatory constitution—My Family have gone off with appoplexies, & other inflammatory diseases—I am the solitary member of a House of thirteen (my Fathers) that lives—slight excitement, under paiticular circumstances, brings to me that rapid flow of the blood & Spirits, which destroys the guard of discretion, levels distinctions, & hurries me into blunders; and this predisposition has exposed me to a thousand scrapes, some ridiculous, some most serious—The extream heat of the Sun beating upon my feeble body, was a good preparation, for the powerful operation of a glass or two of wine—the excessive heat & the fatigue of the evenings duration, were quite sufficient for an equal effect from a single glass of Spirit & water—

I do not plead excess—the apology would leave me worse implicated, perhaps, than the supposed offence—No man need be more regularly temperate—knowing my weakness, I am (ordinarily) studiously & habitually guarded—

Such an address as this, I am aware, would to any man be, but is especially so to him who possesses the first distinction in our Country, paiticularly delicate—but delicate as the subject is, so well do I know the goodness of your heart, that I hesitate not one moment in making it—It is necessary for the quiet of my mind, and, what with me is equally impressive, making as an evidence of the respect I bear you—I know it will be received as a whisper in the ear—

To sin & repent, & sin again, if it be not our common Nature, is my unhappy Lot—It is the Attribute of superiour Natures, of generous & magnanimous Spirits, to be prepared with benevolence & charity to meet the first approaches of Contrition—However heedless then I may have been, this honest, simple & candid exposition, I have no doubt will take me on such ground as I have any claim to have stood at any time—It is only your indulgent consideration of any errorr committed that I ask—It is not likely that I shall ever have the pleasure to see you again—& most improbable that I shall fall in the way of those other eminent personages, before whom I may have exposed myself in my old Age[2] as nothing but business of moment takes me from that retirement which affliction has made me seek—Be that as it may, I shall remain with unabated esteem & respect,

y^r most obed^t Serv^t W. FONTAINE

P.S. I wished & expected to have met with M^r Randolph, through whom it would have better comported with my humiliation to have approached with my apology verbal—but missing the sight of him, I am forced upon this more painful & mortifying course—I do not know whether, as he left no Note in answer, I may not have committed some faux pas in the hasty Note addressed to him, the morning I left Montecello—a Note written in the very mood in which the preceding day placed me—So was I overpowered with the Heat of that & the preceding day, that I was constrained to lye by till morning—There being no post office in Hanover, I send this via Richmond—that being the single office through which my correspondence is conducted—

W.F.

it calls for the consumption of the flames as soon as read—

RC (MHi); addressed: "Thomas Jefferson Esq^r Montecello by Richmond Post"; franked; postmarked 6 Oct. at Richmond; endorsed by TJ as received 8 Oct. 1809 and so recorded in SJL.

William Fontaine (1754–1810), a farmer in Hanover County who shared TJ's interest in breeding merino sheep, attended the College of William and Mary and served as a lieutenant colonel in the Continental army contingent that guarded British and Hessian prisoners at a barracks in Albemarle County toward the end of the American Revolution (*WMQ*, 1st ser. [1921]: 121; Heitman, *Continental Army*, 231; John H. Cocke to TJ, 29 Sept. 1810; Madison, *Papers,*

*Pres. Ser.*, 2:600–1; Richmond *Virginia Patriot*, 12 Oct. 1810).

[1] Word interlined.

[2] Remainder of sentence interlined, with last word illegible.

## From Lafayette

My dear friend Paris 16h Septembre 1809

I fortunately Happened to Be at Aulnay, mde de tessé's Seat near paris, when a Messenger from America is Arrived—He is Sent Back immediately—I Hasten to write a few lines But do Not Lament this Sudden departure as I did that of mr Coles—He Had promised to Spend Some time at La Grange—I Had of Course Ajourned Every thing I wanted to Say and to Hear Respecting You, myself, public, and private Affairs—it is impossible to Express the Vexation I felt when I Heard He was Unexpectedly Going, and Had Only a few minutes to See Him—there was no fault of His, But to me it Has Been a Bitter disappointment—the more So as Your Young friend Has Left on me a very particular impression of Esteem and Attachment—mr et mde de tessé Had also depended on my Going with Him to Aulnay—they Lamented His departure which I assurd them Had Been not Less Unforeseen By Him than By myself—Such an Opportunity of intimate Communication with You who knows when I may obtain!

The public news You will find in the Journals, and What Relates to American Affairs will be Contained in gal Armstrong's Correspondance—while the British Ministry are doing, to injure and irritate the people of the U.S., Every thing that is Unfriendly and Uncandid, Bonaparte misled by His Anti Anglican passion, is palliating the faults of those He Hates at the Expence of those whom He wants to fix on His Side—those politics are So absurd that one Cannot Help to Hope for a Change whatever Be the Bad tenor of Mr Champagny's Last Letter—I Had the other day a Conversation on the Subject with the Minister fouché who Has the interim of the interior departement—He promised to Make an Effort to Enforce a truth of which Every man of Sense, about the Emperor, Except Himself, Seems to Be Convinced—But Never was a man So despiser[1] of Advice, nor So feared By those who may Give it, as the one who now Governs Europe.

I Beg You, my dear friend, to let me know Every particular Respecting You and family in Your Quiete Retirements of Monticelo—present my Affectionate Respects to the Amiable daughter whose

Happy Lot it is to Enjoy them with You—My Children Have Been dispersed for a few weeks[2]—we are to Be Reunited By the 1er October at La Grange.

Nothing on my Louïsiana Affairs Has Reached me Since the Letters Brought By mr Coles—I See that mr duplantier Had Some Expectations that the Neglect of the City who Had not Accepted within Six months the Gift of Congress would prove Beneficial to me—But I am not Sanguine about it—it were only to Be wished that the Munificent Grant I owe to Your friendship and to the Goodness of Congress may now meet the liquidation wants which By Some[3] Late Expences owing to charge[s] by Our family. But much more So By Accumulated interest at a High Rate, Have increas[ed] to an Enormous Sum, and must absolutely Be Cleared out—I See from Your kind Hopes and Computat[ions] that in the future increase of Value there would Be Ample provision for my family—But How to Remedy the present without Ruining the prospect is a Matter the More difficult as I Have no titles, Plans, Estimations, and Locations, So that Every Body to whom I Apply objects to a Negociation So pressingly Necessary on Account of my Having Nothing positive and Legal to Show—I am Sure, my dear friend, that You will do Every thing in Your power to Hasten the Arrival of those documents and titles.

it is Said that a New Convention with Russia Has Lately taken place—that all the Right Side of the danube, with[4] a part of Austria and Hungaria, Carniole, Carinthia, &c. are demanded of the Austrian Emperor—He will Refuse and fight one or two Battles Before He Yields[5] them—Anwerpe was Oppened to a Bold push of the British—they afterwards Had their chance to fight Raw militia Just from their Village or town—it Has Appeared to them more prudent to Be Satisfied with the taking of flushing—the Emperor, Napoleon,[6] Has Been Sick But Now Recovered. Adieu, my dear friend, Most Affectionately and Gratefully

Yours LAFAYETTE

I Am not without Some Hopes to push over By the Next opportunity five or Six Merinos that might Be got at Nantz as Belonging to mr Livingston who Has five to claim; Of this I will Confer With Gal armstrong—I am Sure that the idea of a division of them with you would more than any thing influence the Minister to let a dozen go. So He Said at the first word Spoken to Him on the difficulty I Had to manage it Under His predecessor.

RC (DLC); edge frayed; addressed: "Thomas Jefferson esq Monticelo State of Virginia"; endorsed by TJ as received 24 Nov. 1809 and so recorded in SJL. Tr

(DLC). Enclosed in James Madison to TJ, 6 Nov. 1809.

In his LAST LETTER of 22 Aug. 1809, Champagny, the French foreign minister, advised American minister to France John Armstrong of France's position on neutral rights and indicated that French restrictions on neutral trade with Britain would continue until the British Orders in Council were revoked (*ASP, Foreign Relations*, 3:325–6). Joseph FOUCHÉ, duc d'Otrante, the minister of police, served as interim head of the French interior department in 1809 (Connelly, *Napoleonic France*, 188–9).

Isaac A. COLES carried TJ's 24 Feb. 1809 letter to Lafayette (DLC), enclosing a letter from Armand DUPLANTIER to Lafayette, and a copy of Duplantier to TJ, 23 Nov. 1808 (DLC). Duplantier, a Frenchman who had served in the American Revolution under Lafayette, moved after the war to Louisiana, where he managed the survey of Lafayette's lands and otherwise acted as his agent in Orleans Territory (*Terr. Papers*, 9:255, 452, 566, 605).

The large-scale British invasion of Walcheren temporarily captured FLUSHING but was otherwise a failure (Connelly, *Napoleonic France*, 496).

[1] Thus in manuscript. Lafayette probably meant "such a despiser."
[2] Manuscript: "weeeks."
[3] Word interlined.
[4] Manuscript: "wit."
[5] Manuscript: "Yelds."
[6] Manuscript: "Napoleo."

# From the General Republican Committee of the City and County of New York

RESPECTED AND ESTEEMED SIR,

The Republican citizens of the City and County of New York, by their resolution unanimously passed, at a general meeting, determined to signify to you the high sense which they entertain of your virtues, talents and valuable services to our beloved country, together with their full approbation of the measures pursued during your administration. By the same resolution they have rendered us the organ to communicate their sentiments to you.

In complying with this pleasing request, we also think it our duty to state, that we speak our own opinions and feelings, as well as those of our fellow Republicans at large. You Sir, live in our affections, and in retirement attract the same, and if possible, even superior emotions of gratitude to those which were cherished while you presided over the affairs of the Union.

Your early and eminent exertions, in support of American Independence, and your unvarying attachment to the civil liberties of your fellow citizens entitle you to their affections and esteem, and, though we cannot but deplore that the errors and the prejudices of party have too frequently excited unmerited attacks; we are sensible, that a consciousness of rectitude, together with the approbation and support of Republicans must have afforded an estimable consolatio[n]

We reluctantly parted with you as President. In the difficult situation of our Country, it was honestly wished to continue the aid of your wisdom, experience and tried integrity. We felt towards you the affection of a child to a parent, and, the moment of political separation was painful in the extreme. Your reasons never-theless convinced us of the propriety of your retirement, and the election of your friend as a successor, produces at this moment our greatest consolation.

In the infancy of our government, we perceive it to have been proper that worthy and disinterested examples should be presented, and that, to prevent hereditary establishments our best men should avoid a perpetuity of power.

The more we reflect upon the measures of your administration, especially those which have been adopted towards the principal belligerent powers, the more fully we discover and understand the purity of motive and sound policy which produced them; and we principally regret, that any domestic opposition should have been made to the just regulations of a lawful government, not only intended but judiciously adapted to preserve a state of peace and to maintain the most inestimable rights of our nation.

Divine Providence has destined our existence to an extraordinary and interesting state of human affairs. The most superficial observer must perceive himself surrounded by vast and astonishing spectacles. Ambition is no longer sated with the conquest of a Kingdom or a province, but regardless of the means it aspires to the dominion of universal empire. In such a situation it was not to be expected that we should entirely escape those agitations which convulsed the nations with whom we had established continual habits of intercourse. Our relations towards the great Belligerents were too important to each, to be beheld by the others without an eye of jealousy. To this consideration we must in a great measure attribute those repeated acts of aggression which have been perpetrated with different degrees of violence but without intermission. To keep aloof from these prodigious contests, to cultivate our own resources, and, to enable our Country to profit by its favoured situation, until its natural and progressive growth should render it invulnerable to foreign attack, appears to have been the great design of your wise and salutary administration. Many of our Countrymen who have opposed the measures of government, or withheld from them a firm support, may live to regret <u>that</u> infatuation, which prompted them to violate our laws, and by presenting an appearance of domestic weakness encourage a continuance of those injuries which might otherwise have been restrained.

We believe, Sir, that the Embargo and non intercourse acts were impartial in their character, devised from the purest of intentions and wise in their operation. They furnished an opportunity to collect our floating property from abroad, they prevented inconsiderate men from placing their merchandize within the reach of inevitable capture; they recalled our Mariners from scenes of insult and imprisonment to the bosom of their native Country; they evinced to the warring world that the United States, however pacific in disposition were incapable of submitting to every extremity of injustice; they afforded our own government time to consult the opinions and wishes of the Nation before it consented to engage in more rigorous and decisive measures; they were calculated to withhold, and had they not been evaded would have effectually withheld from foreign aggressors those supplies which were necessary to the perpetuance of their own power: appealing to their own interests to restore the free exercise of those rights which their pride and passions and injustice had violated.

With deference to the better judgment of those whose experience and superior means of information have enabled them to form a more correct opinion; we believe that the truly independent situation of the United States and the power which we possess to withhold from hostile foreigners, supplies of many articles of the first necessity, is a valuable weapon in our hands; and, although a suspension of intercourse must produce its inconveniences they are incomparably less than those which result from incessant insult and capture. Patriotism should endure these temporary privations with fortitude, and we have abundant reason to be thankful to beneficent Providence, for having placed our lot in an extensive and fertile territory so abundant in the production of every essential comfort as to preclude the possibility of real distress. We exceedingly regret that untoward circumstances and an improvident opposition have prevented the effects of this rational and obvious system from being fully ascertained.

The desolating calamities inseparable from war, its innumerable distresses, its pernicious effects upon the manners and morals of Society and the dangers with which it assails the duration of free governments are powerful dissuasives against the entering into such a state without the utmost provocation and most direful necessity. With regard to ourselves a warlike disposition would entail upon us the most permanently injurious consequences; we should be enlisted in all the intricacies of European connections and alliances; we should be alternately menaced and intreated, coerced and courted, driven or seduced, to destroy our general safety and forfeit our national character of justice, and become habitually enlisted as a standing party in the distant contests of the old world.

And we farther Sir believe that when the injurious system of warfare is once adopted that it is beyond the limits of human sagacity to foretell its ultimate consequences.

But attached as we are to the continuance of peace, and adverse to any European connection, a pacific disposition, or an apprehension of danger would neither occasion timidity or produce the most distant consent to abandon the natural and national rights of our beloved country. The spirit of the revolution is unextinguished. We shall emulate the virtue and vigour of our forefathers and maintain at every hazard the liberties, Union, and Constitution of the United States together with the government of their general choice.

That you Sir, in your chosen retirement, in the bosom of your family connections and in the midst of affectionate friends may enjoy many years of happiness, and that the sweets of domestic tranquility may be united to the pleasu[re] of beholding the prosperity of your Country and the triumph of those principl[es] of Civil liberty in the defence of which your active days have been so beneficially employed, are the sincere and fervent wishes of your friends and fellow citizens

Signed by order of the General Republican Committee, of the City and County of New York.

September 16.[1] 1809

Ab$^{m}$ Bloodgood Chairman
Judah Hammond Secretary

MS (DLC); in a clerk's hand, signed by Bloodgood and Hammond; margins frayed; at head of text: "To Thomas Jefferson late President of the United States"; endorsed by TJ as an "Address of Repub. citizens of city & county of N. York" received 20 Sept. 1809 and so recorded in SJL. Printed in *Boston Patriot*, 18 Oct. 1809. Enclosed in a brief transmittal letter of Bloodgood and Hammond to TJ, 16 Sept. 1809 (RC in DLC; in a clerk's hand, signed by Bloodgood and Hammond; at foot of text: "Thomas Jefferson late President of the United States"; endorsed by TJ as received 20 Sept. 1809 and so recorded in SJL; with notation by TJ summarizing the address as follows:

"exert$^{ns}$ tow$^{ds}$ ndpdce & attamt to lib.
unmerited attacks
reluct$^{ly}$ parted with—but convince$^{d}$ of propriety
friend sucessor
disinterest$^{d}$ examples to prev$^{nt}$ hered$^{y}$ stablmt
purity of motive & sound policy of meas$^{res}$ tow$^{ds}$ belliger$^{ts}$
regret domestic opposn. they will regret
extraord$^{y}$ period of hum$^{n}$ aff$^{rs}$ & astonish$^{g}$ spectes
aspire at universal empire
to keep aloof E$^{t}$c till progressive growth E$^{t}$c
non intercourse an useful weapon
encourages our manuf.

disadvges of war & European conn[ns] spirit of revoln unexting[d]”).

Two Abraham Bloodgoods, one a shipwright and one a currier, were active in New York City in 1809. Judah Hammond was an attorney (*Longworth's New-York Directory* [New York, 1809], 108, 199).

[1] Reworked from “15.”

# From William Lambert

SIR, City of Washington, September, 17[th] 1809.

I have received your esteemed favor of the 10[th] inst[t] in answer to former letters of mine, and am much gratified by the approbation you have shewn of my undertaking to ascertain the difference of longitude of the Capitol in this city from Greenwich Observatory, with due precision, for on that circumstance will depend the establishment of a first meridian of our own, and also, the adapting to that meridian, the geographical positions of such places on the Earth as have been determined from actual observations or admeasurement. A communication in which an abstract of the computation to find our distance from Greenwich, is contained, has, no doubt, reached you before this: it is not sufficient that I am satisfied myself with the accuracy of the result; others of much higher standing in society, ought also to see & be convinced of it, before a proper effect can be produced. I do not expect emolument from the undertaking: I wished the object accomplished by a native citizen, in preference to an adopted one, and found no one that seemed to take so much interest in the measure as to venture on it's commencement. I have thought fit, therefore, to engage in a task which others as much, if not more competent, have either declined or neglected:—numerous are the opinions of some of my good friends in relation to it: some suppose, that I have been about a chimerical pursuit not to be realized, or if it is, that I have not capacity to effect it: others think that I have got upon a favorite hobby horse, and that I shall ride him to death before I get off: others have a strong desire to see the thing in print, and seem to wonder at my delay,—while others appear to be jealous that some fame will be attached to me, if I happen to succeed, &c. I agree with you in believing, that there [are][1] not many astronomers in the H. of R.—my dependence upon them, after the injustice and neglect I have experienced from them on more than one occasion, is now at an end: instead of taking into consideratio[n] the arduous labors for their service which I have endured for a series of years, they have listened with seeming avidity, to malicious tales hatched against me by unprincipled assassins of character who have been secretly combined to injure, and remove me out of their own way The station of principal clerk in the office of the Secretary of the Senate U.S. is now vacant by the appointment of Mr Samuel Elliot to be cashier of a new bank instituted in this city; and I have written to Mr Otis, declaring myself a candidate to fill the vacancy: the attachment I once had to the business of the other branch, is considerably diminished, from the treatment I have received; and whatever may be their motive, I think it oppressive and unnecessary.

With respect to the science of astronomy, as well as the subordinate branches of the mathematics, I do not suppose they ought to be acquired or pursued merely as a speculative employment of time: they ought to be directed for the attainment of some valuable purpose to the community. I can answer for myself, that I should never ride this favorite hobby horse of mine so much, if I did not imagine that the country which gave me birth might in some degree be benefited by it. If the object I had in view has not before been explained, I will candidly own it to you now, that I have for some years past, seen with regret, the advantage Great Britain has had over us, by our borrowing a first meridian from them: and that in whatever light this may be viewed by others, I consider it as one of the prominent links in the chain of dependence that ought to be broken as soon as possible.

I am preparing an astronomical table, which I shall take the liberty to transmit to you in a few days, with it's construction and application.

I have the honor to be, with perfect respect, Sir, Your most obedient servant,

WILLIAM LAMBERT.

RC (DLC); margin frayed; at foot of text: "Thomas Jefferson, late President U.S."; endorsed by TJ as received 20 Sept. 1809 and so recorded in SJL.

[1] Omitted word editorially supplied.

# From David Bailie Warden

SIR, Paris, 17 Sept^r 1809.

I have the honor of sending you, to the care of Mr. Bullus, a history of Poland, and a brochure, which are presented to you, by the author—a Polish General. I lately sent a copy of the same, via Holland: if you receive both, please to give one to the Philosophical Society of Philadelphia. I long to hear from you in your retreat. If you publish any work, I beg you to send a copy for the use of your friends in Paris. it appears, that there is little hope of an arrangement between France and the United States. If the Subject of the Consulate, at Paris, is brought before the Senate, I fondly hope that you will be pleased to recommend me[1] for this place.

I am, Sir, with great esteem, your ever oblg Servant

D. B. WARDEN.

RC (DLC); at foot of text: "Thomas Jefferson—Esquire"; endorsed by TJ as received 22 Nov. 1809 and so recorded in SJL. FC (MdHi: Warden Letterbook); in Warden's hand. Enclosures: (1) Jan Chrzciciel Komarzewski, *Coup-d'Oeil rapide sur les causes réelles de la Décadence de la Pologne* (Paris, 1807; Sowerby, no. 256). (2) Komarzewski, *Memoir on a subterranean graphometer, invented to supersede the compass in the operations of mining* (Paris, 1803; Sowerby, no. 1221).

[1] In FC remainder of sentence reads: "if you can do it with propriety."

# To James Madison

DEAR SIR Monticello Sep. 18. 09

Mr Coles, whom I saw yesterday, informs me you propose to set out for Washington this day week. I have been waiting in the hope that little Benjamin would so far recover as that his mother might leave him. but his recovery, tho' steady, is very slow. we barely discover every day some little additional proof of his getting better. I shall wait till the day after tomorrow in the hope of mrs Randolph's accompanying me: but should the little boy be still too unwell to be left I will be with you on Thursday or Friday. Affectionately Yours

TH: JEFFERSON

RC (ViU: TJP); addressed: "The President of the US. Montpelier"; franked and postmarked.

A letter of 17 Sept. 1809 from Isaac A. COLES to TJ, not found, was noted in SJL as received on that date.

# From John Armstrong

DEAR SIR, Paris 19 Sept. 1809

The glimpse of Sun-shine that we had when the Mentor Sailed, has passed away already, and without producing anything Useful—On the north side of the channel also, our prospects are becoming more clouded. M. Auriol, who left London a few days ago, tells me, that he counted in the Downs, upwards of twenty of our ships which had been brought in by British cruisers, because destined to ports blockaded by proclamation. If any thing will cure Our passion for the Ocean, this must. But in what does this differ from a state of war, except in the patient submission with which we bear it? It has been much doubted, whether there was in the World, anything of practical Christianity: or in other words, whether it was in the nature of man, when slapped on one cheek, to turn the other to the blow? If we submit much longer, we shall settle this controversy, but we shall certainly not be gainers by doing so. Nothing can be more agreeable, than to beleive in the dominion of truth, reason and justice among men—but I fear, that this is only reserved for the Milenium. Before you left the presidency, I anticipated this state of things, and offered it as my humble opinion, that you should declare war against both France & England. Every hour assures me of it's correctness. Shew them that you can feel, and that you will resent, and, (I'll pledge my life for it) their conduct will begin to change. With this Country, you will have reconcileation and redress, the moment you take this step. I feel as certain of it, as I do of my existance—And if England will go to the Devil, why should we prevent it? She has no claims on our benevolence. But why should I disturb your repose with these things? Short, who writes to you by this conveyance, will speak of your old friends and acquaintances—of himself and of his projects. Had I returned, this fall, as I seriously intended, he would have gone with me—He has now deferred it till the spring, when he ought to go, as well on your account as on his own. It would be the best possible[1] answer to the cavils, which his nomination produced. We have had here for a month past Count Pahlen, a young Russian whom Alexandre has selected as his minister at Washington. He is a mild, modest, well bred man—and as far as temper and manners go, well calculated for our meridian. I hope M.A. may be as well adapted to that of Petersburg. Were we to infer B.'s opinion of that court, from the man he has chosen to represent him at it, we would conclude, that a whiskered grenadier, who could put a great deal of fierceness into his manner and much parade into his movements, was, in his opinion, the agent who could do most with it. His first choice was Laforest, but recollecting that whatever talent he might have in speaking to the understanding of his auditor, he had none in addressing his fears—he suddenly altered his choice, & sent Laforest to Madrid & Caulancourt to Petersburg. I regret much that it was necessary for you to make a second choice, & Short, tho not more of a Hero than M^r^ A, would have won his way by the amenity of his manners. Romanzoff was much[2] pleased with him, and had secured for him, the best possible reception from his master. But these regrets are now useless. As Lafayette has written to you by this conveyance, he has perhaps told you, that he and I have put our heads together, and are endeavoring to avail ourselves of Fouche's per interim ministry of the interior, to get out a few merinos for you. this minister, who by the way is now Duke of Feltry, is not only a man of the best talents in the Empire, but of the best temper also—that is, his temper is always regulated by his understanding & he accordingly does many agreeable things, not to promote the wishes of the individual, but to promote the interests of the State. He is truly an able Man. If we suceed with regard to the Sheep, You will have them by a Ship that will reach your Coast about the last of November, and By this Ship also, you will get one of Parkers double ploughs, of which M. Cole has no doubt spoken to you. No man is without mortifications in this world, & poor Parker has met with One on the subject of his plough, which he takes much to heart. While he thought "he had found the daisy all alone" and was counting both the honors & the profits of the discovery, a little frenchman ran away with both. I really believe, that calculator as he is, he would have given half his Merinos, & he has a thousand of them, had this been otherwise. As it is, he has nothing left but the consolation of complaining with Virgil's farmer, Sic vos non Vobis &c. With the truest wishes for your happiness I am dear Sir, your faithful and most Obedient humble Servant John Armstrong

RC (DLC); at foot of text: "Mr Jefferson Monticello"; endorsed by TJ as received 24 Nov. 1809 and so recorded in SJL. Enclosed in James Madison to TJ, 6 Nov. 1809, TJ to Madison, 26 Nov. 1809, and Madison to TJ, 11 Dec. 1809.

M.A.: John Quincy Adams. B: Napoleon Bonaparte. Henri Jacques Guillaume Clarke, French minister of war, 1807–14, was the duc de Feltre (Connelly, *Napoleonic France*, 114), not Joseph Fouché, interim INTERIOR minister. FOUND THE DAISY: Armstrong paraphrased the poem "A Simile," by "Peter Pindar" [John Wolcot], about a child who cultivated a daisy with assistance from others and claimed to have done everything himself: "boast away, too happy elf, How that it found the daisy all itself." SIC VOS NON VOBIS ("Thus do ye, but not for yourselves"): customarily but not securely attributed to Virgil, the phrase was often used as shorthand to describe work for which others get credit.

[1] Word interlined.

[2] Manuscript: "muh."

# From John W. Campbell

Respected Sir Petersburg Sep 19th 1809

I feel sensibly my obligations for your attention to my letter. From looking over the list of your official Papers & other Writings I am induced to believe that I could Select what would amount to an Octavo Volume which I would be happy to have the honour of publishing.

The "Reports," While Secretary of State
Messages to Congress &
Summary View,

These or such of them as you might select, I would publish without the fear of being unrewarded for my trouble.

I have lately published in conjunction with Hopkins & Earle, of Philadelphia, "Gillies's History of the World, from the Riegn of Alexander, to that of Augustus," which I would be willing to offer as a sample of the accuracy of my publications.

I submit the proposal to your goodness & Wisdom, and solicit with diffidence & respect an Answer by mail.

I am with Sincerity & esteem Your Humb. Servt.

J. W. CAMPBELL

RC (DLC); dateline adjacent to signature; endorsed by TJ as received 30 Sept. 1809 and so recorded in SJL.

An American edition of John Gillies, *The History of the World, from the reign of Alexander to that of Augustus*, 2 vols. (London, 1807), had been LATELY PUBLISHED by HOPKINS & EARLE, the Boston firm of Farrand, Mallory, & Company, and Campbell.

# From William Lambert

SIR, City of Washington, September 19th 1809.

I inclose a table which has been constructed with great care to every 3 minutes of intermediate time between 0 and 12 hours, for computing the Moon's motion for 12 hours in longitude, latitude, &c. from which the true place may be easily obtained: it was intended to be as fair, as it is accurate, but some parts of it have been stained by accident, before it was finished. The second series for the construction, is entirely my own, having never seen it in any book or treatise on Astronomy: the principle on which it is formed, is strictly correct, and its' extension to differences of the fourth order, and to seven places of figures in the decimal fractions, may warrant a belief that it is more full and perfect than any one of the kind hitherto made: it may not be necessary to take out more than four or five places of decimals to obtain the equations arising from the successive differences. To facilitate the operation, the first differences of the respective numbers have been annexed. I have endeavored to shew the method of using it by a few examples; and nothing more is required than a knowledge of algebraical addition, subtraction and multiplication to apply the table for ascertaining the Moon's positions correctly at any time required. As you have been for many years president of the American Philosophical Society, there is a propriety in transmitting it to you, independent of other considerations, which would incline me to pay you such a mark of my respect. There is not a case for a determination of the longitude of places on the Earth in which the Moon's motions or any of them are employed, but this table will be found useful, because, if the positions at noon and midnight are correct, it will never fail to give them at intermediate times with great precision.

I have the honor to be, with perfect respect, Sir, Your most obedt servant,

WILLIAM LAMBERT.

RC (PPAmP: APS Archives, Manuscript Communications); at foot of text: "Thomas Jefferson, late President U.S."; endorsed by TJ as received 25 Sept. 1809 and so recorded in SJL. Enclosed in TJ to Robert Patterson, 1 Oct. 1809.

ENCLOSURE

## William Lambert's Table for Computing the Moon's Motion, with Examples

Table for computing the Moon's motion for 12 hours at any intermediate time.

| h. m. | (x.) | 1st diff. | (y.) | 1st diff. | (z.) | 1st diff. |
|---|---|---|---|---|---|---|
| 0. 0. | –,5000000. | +. | +,3333333. | –. | +,0833333. | –. |
| | | 20833. | | 20805. | | 1750. |
| 3. | –,4979167. | | +,3312528. | | +,0831583. | |
| | | 20834. | | 20746. | | 1779. |
| 6. | –,4958333. | | +,3291782. | | +,0829804. | |
| | | 20833. | | 20688. | | 1808. |
| 9. | –,4937500. | | +,3271094. | | +,0827996. | |
| | | 20833. | | 20631. | | 1837. |
| 12. | –,4916667. | | +,3250463. | | +,0826159. | |
| | | 20834. | | 20573. | | 1864. |
| 15 | –,4895833. | | +,3229890. | | +,0824295 | |
| | | 20833. | | 20515. | | 1893. |
| 18. | –,4875000. | | +,3209375. | | +,0822402. | |
| | | 20833. | | 20457. | | 1920. |
| 21. | –,4854167. | | +,3188918. | | +,0820482. | |
| | | 20834. | | 20399. | | 1948. |
| 24 | –,4833333. | | +,3168519. | | +,0818534. | |
| | | 20833. | | 20342. | | 1976. |
| 27. | –,4812500. | | +,3148177. | | +,0816558. | |
| | | 20833. | | 20284. | | 2003. |
| 30. | –,4791667. | | +,3127893. | | +,0814555. | |
| | | 20834. | | 20225. | | 2030. |

| h. m. | (x.) | 1st diff. | (y.) | 1st diff. | (z.) | 1st diff. |
|---|---|---|---|---|---|---|
| 33. | –,4770833. | | +,3107668. | | +,0812525. | |
| | | 20833. | | 20168. | | 2056. |
| 36. | –,4750000. | | +,3087500. | | +,0810469. | |
| | | 20833. | | 20110. | | 2084. |
| 39. | –,4729167. | | +,3067390. | | +,0808385. | |
| | | 20834. | | 20052. | | 2110. |
| 42 | –,4708333. | | +,3047338 | | +,0806275. | |
| | | 20833. | | 19994. | | 2137. |
| 45 | –,4687500. | | +,3027344 | | +,0804138. | |
| | | 20833. | | 19937. | | 2163. |
| 48. | –,4666667. | | +,3007407. | | +,0801975. | |
| | | 20834. | | 19878. | | 2189. |
| 51. | –,4645833. | | +,2987529. | | +,0799786. | |
| | | 20833. | | 19821. | | 2215 |
| 54. | –,4625000. | | +,2967708. | | +,0797571. | |
| | | 20833. | | 19763. | | 2240. |
| 57. | –,4604167. | | +,2947945. | | +,0795331. | |
| | | 20834. | | 19704. | | 2266. |
| 1. 0. | –,4583333. | | +,2928241. | | +,0793065. | |
| | | 20833. | | 19647. | | 2291. |
| 3. | –,4562500. | | +,2908594. | | +,0790774. | |
| | | 20833. | | 19589. | | 2317. |
| 6. | –,4541667. | | +,2889005. | | +,0788457. | |
| | | 20834. | | 19532. | | 2341. |
| 9. | –,4520833. | | +,2869473. | | +,0786116. | |
| | | 20833. | | 19473. | | 2366. |
| 12. | –,4500000. | | +,2850000. | | +,0783750. | |
| | | 20833. | | 19416. | | 2391 |
| 15. | –,4479167. | | +,2830584. | | +,0781359. | |
| | | 20834. | | 19357. | | 2415 |
| 18. | –,4458333. | | +,2811227. | | +,0778944. | |
| | | 20833. | | 19300. | | 2439. |
| 21. | –,4437500. | | +,2791927. | | +,0776505. | |
| | | 20833. | | 19242. | | 2464. |
| 24. | –,4416667. | | +,2772685. | | +,0774041. | |
| | | 20834. | | 19184. | | 2487. |
| 27. | –,4395833. | | +,2753501. | | +,0771554. | |
| | | 20833. | | 19126. | | 2511. |
| 30. | –,4375000. | | +,2734375. | | +,0769043. | |
| | | 20833. | | 19069. | | 2535. |
| 33. | –,4354167. | | +,2715306. | | +,0766508. | |
| | | 20834. | | 19010. | | 2558. |
| 36. | –,4333333. | | +,2696296. | | +,0763950. | |
| | | 20833. | | 18952. | | 2581. |
| 39. | –,4312500. | | +,2677344. | | +,0761369. | |
| | | 20833. | | 18895. | | 2603. |
| 42. | –,4291667. | | +,2658449. | | +,0758766. | |
| | | 20834. | | 18837. | | 2627. |

| h. m. | (x.) | 1st diff. | (y.) | 1st diff. | (z.) | 1st diff. |
|---|---|---|---|---|---|---|
| 45. | –,4270833. | | +,2639612. | | +,0756139. | |
| | | 20833. | | 18779. | | 2650. |
| 48. | –,4250000. | | +,2620833. | | +,0753489. | |
| | | 20833. | | 18721. | | 2672. |
| 51. | –,4229167. | | +,2602112. | | +,0750817. | |
| | | 20834. | | 18663. | | 2693. |
| 54. | –,4208333. | | +,2583449. | | +,0748124. | |
| | | 20833. | | 18605. | | 2717. |
| 57. | –,4187500. | | +,2564844. | | +,0745407. | |
| | | 20833. | | 18548. | | 2738. |
| 2. 0. | –,4166667. | | +,2546296. | | +,0742669. | |
| | | 20834. | | 18490. | | 2759. |
| 3. | –,4145833. | | +,2527806. | | +,0739910. | |
| | | 20833. | | 18431. | | 2781. |
| 6. | –,4125000. | | +,2509375 | | +,0737129. | |
| | | 20833. | | 18374. | | 2803. |
| 9. | –,4104167. | | +,2491001. | | +,0734326. | |
| | | 20834. | | 18316. | | 2823. |
| 12. | –,4083333. | | +,2472685 | | +,0731503. | |
| | | 20833. | | 18258. | | 2845. |
| 15 | –,4062500. | | +,2454427. | | +,0728658. | |
| | | 20833. | | 18200. | | 2866. |
| 18 | –,4041667. | | +,2436227. | | +,0725792. | |
| | | 20834. | | 18143. | | 2886. |
| 21. | –,4020833. | | +,2418084. | | +,0722906. | |
| | | 20833. | | 18084. | | 2906 |
| 24. | –,4000000. | | +,2400000. | | +,0720000. | |
| | | 20833. | | 18027. | | 2927. |
| 27. | –,3979167. | | +,2381973. | | +,0717073. | |
| | | 20834. | | 17969. | | 2947. |
| 30. | –,3958333. | | +,2364004. | | +,0714126. | |
| | | 20833. | | 17910. | | 2966. |
| 33. | –,3937500. | | +,2346094. | | +,0711160. | |
| | | 20833. | | 17853. | | 2987. |
| 36. | –,3916667. | | +,2328241. | | +,0708173. | |
| | | 20834. | | 17796. | | 3006. |
| 39. | –,3895833. | | +,2310445. | | +,0705167. | |
| | | 20833. | | 17737. | | 3025. |
| 42. | –,3875000. | | +,2292708. | | +,0702142. | |
| | | 20833. | | 17679. | | 3045. |
| 45. | –,3854167. | | +,2275029. | | +,0699097. | |
| | | 20834. | | 17622. | | 3063. |
| 48. | –,3833333. | | +,2257407. | | +,0696034. | |
| | | 20833. | | 17563. | | 3082. |
| 51. | –,3812500. | | +,2239844. | | +,0692952 | |
| | | 20833. | | 17506. | | 3101. |
| 54. | –,3791667. | | +,2222338. | | +,0689851. | |
| | | 20834. | | 17448. | | 3120. |

| h. m. | (x.) | 1st diff. | (y.) | 1st diff. | (z.) | 1st diff. |
|---|---|---|---|---|---|---|
| 57. | –,3770833. | | +,2204890. | | +,0686731. | |
| | | 20833. | | 17390. | | 3137. |
| 3. 0. | –,3750000. | | +,2187500. | | +,0683594. | |
| | | 20833. | | 17332. | | 3156. |
| 3. | –,3729167. | | +,2170168. | | +,0680438. | |
| | | 20834. | | 17275. | | 3174. |
| 6. | –,3708333. | | +,2152893. | | +,0677264. | |
| | | 20833. | | 17216. | | 3191. |
| 9. | –,3687500. | | +,2135677. | | +,0674073. | |
| | | 20833. | | 17159. | | 3209. |
| 12. | –,3666667. | | +,2118518. | | +,0670864. | |
| | | 20834. | | 17100. | | 3226. |
| 15. | –,3645833. | | +,2101418. | | +,0667638. | |
| | | 20833. | | 17043. | | 3244. |
| 18. | –,3625000. | | +,2084375. | | +,0664394. | |
| | | 20833. | | 16985. | | 3260. |
| 21. | –,3604167. | | +,2067390. | | +,0661134. | |
| | | 20834. | | 16927. | | 3277. |
| 24. | –,3583333. | | +,2050463. | | +,0657857. | |
| | | 20833. | | 16869. | | 3294. |
| 27. | –,3562500. | | +,2033594. | | +,0654563. | |
| | | 20833. | | 16812. | | 3311. |
| 30. | –,3541667. | | +,2016782. | | +,0651252 | |
| | | 20834. | | 16753 | | 3326. |
| 33 | –,3520833. | | +,2000029. | | +,0647926. | |
| | | 20833. | | 16696. | | 3343. |
| 36. | –,3500000. | | +,1983333. | | +,0644583. | |
| | | 20833. | | 16638. | | 3358. |
| 39. | –,3479167. | | +,1966695. | | +,0641225 | |
| | | 20834. | | 16579. | | 3375. |
| 42. | –,3458333. | | +,1950116. | | +,0637850. | |
| | | 20833. | | 16522 | | 3390 |
| 45. | –,3437500. | | +,1933594. | | +,0634460. | |
| | | 20833. | | 16465. | | 3405. |
| 48. | –,3416667. | | +,1917129. | | +,0631055. | |
| | | 20834. | | 16406. | | 3421. |
| 51. | –,3395833 | | +,1900723. | | +,0627634. | |
| | | 20833. | | 16348 | | 3435. |
| 54. | –,3375000. | | +,1884375. | | +,0624199. | |
| | | 20833. | | 16291 | | 3450. |
| 57. | –,3354167. | | +,1868084. | | +,0620749. | |
| | | 20834. | | 16232. | | 3465. |
| 4. 0. | –,3333333. | | +,1851852. | | +,0617284. | |
| | | 20833. | | 16175. | | 3480. |
| 3. | –,3312500. | | +,1835677. | | +,0613804. | |
| | | 20833. | | 16117. | | 3493. |
| 6. | –,3291667. | | +,1819560. | | +,0610311. | |
| | | 20834. | | 16059. | | 3508. |

| h. m. | (x.) | 1st diff. | (y.) | 1st diff. | (z.) | 1st diff. |
|---|---|---|---|---|---|---|
| 9. | –,3270833. | | +,1803501. | | +,0606803. | |
| | | 20833. | | 16001. | | 3522. |
| 12. | –,3250000. | | +,1787500. | | +,0603281. | |
| | | 20833. | | 15943. | | 3536. |
| 15. | –,3229167. | | +,1771557. | | +,0599745. | |
| | | 20834. | | 15886. | | 3549. |
| 18. | –,3208333. | | +,1755671. | | +,0596196. | |
| | | 20833. | | 15827. | | 3562. |
| 21. | –,3187500. | | +,1739844 | | +,0592634. | |
| | | 20833. | | 15770. | | 3576. |
| 24. | –,3166667. | | +,1724074. | | +,0589058. | |
| | | 20834. | | 15712. | | 3589. |
| 27: | –,3145833. | | +,1708362. | | +,0585469. | |
| | | 20833. | | 15654. | | 3601. |
| 30 | –,3125000. | | +,1692708. | | +,0581868. | |
| | | 20833. | | 15596. | | 3614. |
| 33. | –,3104167. | | +,1677112. | | +,0578254. | |
| | | 20834. | | 15538 | | 3627. |
| 36. | –,3083333. | | +,1661574. | | +,0574627. | |
| | | 20833. | | 15480. | | 3638. |
| 39. | –,3062500 | | +,1646094. | | +,0570989. | |
| | | 20833. | | 15423. | | 3651. |
| 42 | –,3041667. | | +,1630671. | | +,0567338. | |
| | | 20834. | | 15365. | | 3663. |
| 45. | –,3020833. | | +,1615306. | | +,0563675. | |
| | | 20833. | | 15306. | | 3675. |
| 48. | –,3000000. | | +,1600000. | | +,0560000. | |
| | | 20833. | | 15249. | | 3686. |
| 51. | –,2979167. | | +,1584751. | | +,0556314. | |
| | | 20834. | | 15191. | | 3698. |
| 54. | –,2958333. | | +,1569560. | | +,0552616. | |
| | | 20833. | | 15133. | | 3709. |
| 57. | –,2937500. | | +,1554427. | | +,0548907. | |
| | | 20833. | | 15075 | | 3720. |
| 5. 0. | –,2916667. | | +,1539352. | | +,0545187. | |
| | | 20834. | | 15018. | | 3731. |
| 3 | –,2895833 | | +,1524334. | | +,0541456. | |
| | | 20833. | | 14959. | | 3741. |
| 6. | –,2875000. | | +,1509375 | | +,0537715. | |
| | | 20833. | | 14902. | | 3752. |
| 9. | –,2854167. | | +,1494473. | | +,0533963. | |
| | | 20834. | | 14844. | | 3762. |
| 12. | –,2833333. | | +,1479629. | | +,0530201. | |
| | | 20833. | | 14785. | | 3773. |
| 15. | –,2812500. | | +,1464344. | | +,0526428. | |
| | | 20833. | | 14728. | | 3782. |
| 18. | –,2791667. | | +,1450116. | | +,0522646. | |
| | | 20834. | | 14671. | | 3792. |

| h. m. | (x.) | 1st diff. | (y.) | 1st diff. | (z.) | 1st diff. |
|---|---|---|---|---|---|---|
| 21. | –,2770833. | | +,1435445. | | +,0518854. | |
| | | 20833. | | 14612. | | 3802. |
| 24. | –,2750000. | | +,1420833. | | +,0515052. | |
| | | 20833. | | 14554. | | 3811. |
| 27. | –,2729167. | | +,1406279. | | +,0511241. | |
| | | 20834. | | 14497. | | 3820. |
| 30. | –,2708333. | | +,1391782. | | +,0507421. | |
| | | 20833. | | 14438. | | 3830. |
| 33 | –,2687500. | | +,1377344. | | +,0503591. | |
| | | 20833. | | 14381. | | 3838. |
| 36 | –,2666667. | | +,1362963. | | +,0499753. | |
| | | 20834. | | 14323. | | 3847. |
| 39. | –,2645833. | | +,1348640. | | +,0495906. | |
| | | 20833. | | 14265. | | 3855. |
| 42. | –,2625000. | | +,1334375. | | +,0492051. | |
| | | 20833. | | 14208. | | 3864. |
| 45. | –,2604167. | | +,1320167. | | +,0488187. | |
| | | 20834. | | 14149. | | 3872. |
| 48. | –,2583333. | | +,1306018. | | +,0484315. | |
| | | 20833. | | 14091. | | 3880. |
| 51. | –,2562500. | | +,1291927. | | +,0480435. | |
| | | 20833. | | 14034. | | 3887. |
| 54 | –,2541667 | | +,1277893. | | +,0476548. | |
| | | 20834 | | 13975. | | 3896. |
| 57. | –,2520833 | | +,1263918. | | +,0472652. | |
| | | 20833. | | 13918. | | 3902. |
| 6. 0. | –,2500000. | | +,1250000. | | +,0468750. | |
| | | 20833. | | 13860. | | 3910. |
| 3. | –,2479167. | | +,1236140. | | +,0464840. | |
| | | 20834. | | 13802. | | 3917. |
| 6. | –,2458333. | | +,1222338. | | +,0460923. | |
| | | 20833. | | 13745. | | 3924. |
| 9. | –,2437500. | | +,1208593. | | +,0456999. | |
| | | 20833. | | 13686. | | 3930. |
| 12. | –,2416667. | | +,1194907. | | +,0453069. | |
| | | 20834. | | 13628. | | 3937. |
| 15. | –,2395833. | | +,1181279. | | +,0449132. | |
| | | 20833. | | 13571. | | 3943. |
| 18. | –,2375000. | | +,1167708. | | +,0445189. | |
| | | 20833. | | 13513. | | 3950. |
| 21. | –,2354167. | | +,1154195. | | +,0441239. | |
| | | 20834. | | 13454. | | 3955. |
| 24. | –,2333333. | | +,1140741. | | +,0437284. | |
| | | 20833. | | 13397. | | 3961. |
| 27. | –,2312500. | | +,1127344. | | +,0433323. | |
| | | 20833. | | 13340. | | 3968. |
| 30. | –,2291667. | | +,1114004. | | +,0429355. | |
| | | 20834. | | 13281. | | 3972. |

| h. m. | (x.) | 1st diff. | (y.) | 1st diff. | (z.) | 1st diff. |
|---|---|---|---|---|---|---|
| 33. | –,2270833. | | +,1100723. | | +,0425383. | |
| | | 20833. | | 13223. | | 3977. |
| 36. | –,2250000. | | +,1087500. | | +,0421406. | |
| | | 20833. | | 13166. | | 3982. |
| 39. | –,2229167. | | +,1074334. | | +,0417424. | |
| | | 20834. | | 13107. | | 3988. |
| 42. | –,2208333. | | +,1061227. | | +,0413436. | |
| | | 20833. | | 13050. | | 3992. |
| 45 | –,2187500. | | +,1048177. | | +,0409444. | |
| | | 20833. | | 12992. | | 3997. |
| 48 | –,2166667. | | +,1035185 | | +,0405447. | |
| | | 20834. | | 12934. | | 4001. |
| 51. | –,2145833. | | +,1022251. | | +,0401446. | |
| | | 20833. | | 12876. | | 4005. |
| 54. | –,2125000. | | +,1009375. | | +,0397441. | |
| | | 20833. | | 12819. | | 4009. |
| 57. | –,2104167. | | +,0996556 | | +,0393432 | |
| | | 20834. | | 12760. | | 4012. |
| 7. 0. | –,2083333. | | +,0983796 | | +,0389419. | |
| | | 20833. | | 12702. | | 4016. |
| 3. | –,2062500. | | +,0971094. | | +,0385403. | |
| | | 20833. | | 12645. | | 4020. |
| 6. | –,2041667. | | +,0958449. | | +,0381383. | |
| | | 20834. | | 12587. | | 4024. |
| 9. | –,2020833. | | +,0945862. | | +,0377359. | |
| | | 20833. | | 12529. | | 4026. |
| 12. | –,2000000. | | +,0933333. | | +,0373333. | |
| | | 20833. | | 12471. | | 4032. |
| 15. | –,1979167. | | +,0920862. | | +,0369304. | |
| | | 20834. | | 12413. | | 4032. |
| 18. | –,1958333. | | +,0908449. | | +,0365272. | |
| | | 20833. | | 12355. | | 4034. |
| 21. | –,1937500. | | +,0896094. | | +,0361238. | |
| | | 20833. | | 12298. | | 4037. |
| 24. | –,1916667. | | +,0883796. | | +,0357201. | |
| | | 20834. | | 12240. | | 4039. |
| 27. | –,1895833. | | +,0871556. | | +,0353162. | |
| | | 20833. | | 12181. | | 4041. |
| 30. | –,1875000. | | +,0859375. | | +,0349121. | |
| | | 20833. | | 12124. | | 4043. |
| 33. | –,1854167. | | +,0847251. | | +,0345078. | |
| | | 20834. | | 12066. | | 4044. |
| 36. | –,1833333. | | +,0835185. | | +,0341034. | |
| | | 20833. | | 12008. | | 4046. |
| 39. | –,1812500. | | +,0823177. | | +,0336988. | |
| | | 20833. | | 11950. | | 4047. |
| 42. | –,1791667. | | +,0811227. | | +,0332941. | |
| | | 20834. | | 11893. | | 4048. |

| h. m. | (x.) | 1st diff. | (y.) | 1st diff. | (z.) | 1st diff. |
|---|---|---|---|---|---|---|
| 45. | –,1770833. | | +,0799334. | | +,0328893. | |
| | | 20833. | | 11834. | | 4049. |
| 48. | –,1750000. | | +,0787500. | | +,0324844. | |
| | | 20833. | | 11777. | | 4050. |
| 51. | –,1729167. | | +,0775723. | | +,0320794. | |
| | | 20834. | | 11719. | | 4050. |
| 54. | –,1708333. | | +,0764004. | | +,0316744. | |
| | | 20833. | | 11660. | | 4051. |
| 57. | –,1687500. | | +,0752344. | | +,0312693. | |
| | | 20833. | | 11603. | | 4051. |
| 8. 0. | –,1666667. | | +,0740741. | | +,0308642. | |
| | | 20834. | | 11546. | | 4051. |
| 3. | –,1645833. | | +,0729195. | | +,0304591. | |
| | | 20833. | | 11487. | | 4051. |
| 6. | –,1625000. | | +,0717708. | | +,0300540. | |
| | | 20833. | | 11429. | | 4051. |
| 9. | –,1604167. | | +,0706279. | | +,0296489. | |
| | | 20834. | | 11372. | | 4049. |
| 12. | –,1583333. | | +,0694907. | | +,0292440. | |
| | | 20833. | | 11313. | | 4048. |
| 15. | –,1562500. | | +,0683594. | | +,0288391. | |
| | | 20833. | | 11256. | | 4048. |
| 18. | –,1541667. | | +,0672338. | | +,0284343. | |
| | | 20834. | | 11198. | | 4047. |
| 21. | –,1520833. | | +,0661140. | | +,0280296. | |
| | | 20833. | | 11140. | | 4046 |
| 24. | –,1500000. | | +,0650000. | | +,0276250. | |
| | | 20833. | | 11082. | | 4045 |
| 27. | –,1479167. | | +,0638918. | | +,0272205. | |
| | | 20834. | | 11025. | | 4042 |
| 30. | –,1458333. | | +,0627893. | | +,0268163. | |
| | | 20833. | | 10966. | | 4041. |
| 33. | –,1437500. | | +,0616927. | | +,0264122. | |
| | | 20833. | | 10909. | | 4039. |
| 36. | –,1416667. | | +,0606012. | | +,0260083. | |
| | | 20834. | | 10850. | | 4037. |
| 39. | –,1395833. | | +,0595168. | | +,0256046. | |
| | | 20833. | | 10793. | | 4034. |
| 42. | –,1375000. | | +,0584375. | | +,0252012. | |
| | | 20833. | | 10735. | | 4032. |
| 45. | –,1354167. | | +,0573640. | | +,0247980. | |
| | | 20834. | | 10677. | | 4030. |
| 48. | –,1333333. | | +,0562963. | | +,0243950. | |
| | | 20833. | | 10619. | | 4026. |
| 51. | –,1312500. | | +,0552344. | | +,0239924. | |
| | | 20833. | | 10562. | | 4023. |
| 54. | –,1291667. | | +,0541782 | | +,0235901. | |
| | | 20834. | | 10503. | | 4020. |

| h. m. | (x.) | 1st diff. | (y.) | 1st diff. | (z.) | 1st diff. |
|---|---|---|---|---|---|---|
| 57. | –,1270833. | | +,0531279. | | +,0231881. | |
| | | 20833. | | 10446. | | 4017. |
| 9. 0. | –,1250000. | | +,0520833. | | +,0227864 | |
| | | 20833. | | 10388. | | 4013. |
| 3. | –,1229167. | | +,0510445. | | +,0223851. | |
| | | 20834. | | 10330. | | 4009. |
| 6. | –,1208333. | | +,0500115. | | +,0219842. | |
| | | 20833. | | 10271. | | 4005. |
| 9. | –,1187500. | | +,0489844. | | +,0215837. | |
| | | 20833. | | 10214. | | 4001. |
| 12. | –,1166667. | | +,0479630. | | +,0211836. | |
| | | 20834. | | 10157. | | 3997. |
| 15. | –,1145833. | | +,0469473. | | +,0207839. | |
| | | 20833. | | 10098. | | 3992. |
| 18. | –,1125000. | | +,0459375. | | +,0203847. | |
| | | 20833. | | 10041. | | 3987. |
| 21. | –,1104167. | | +,0449334. | | +,0199860. | |
| | | 20834. | | 9982. | | 3982. |
| 24. | –,1083333. | | +,0439352. | | +,0195878. | |
| | | 20833. | | 9925. | | 3977. |
| 27. | –,1062500. | | +,0429427. | | +,0191901. | |
| | | 20833. | | 9867. | | 3973. |
| 30. | –,1041667. | | +,0419560. | | +,0187928. | |
| | | 20834. | | 9809. | | 3967. |
| 33. | –,1020833. | | +,0409751. | | +,0183961. | |
| | | 20833. | | 9751. | | 3961. |
| 36. | –,1000000. | | +,0400000. | | +,0180000. | |
| | | 20833. | | 9693. | | 3956. |
| 39. | –,0979167. | | +,0390307. | | +,0176044. | |
| | | 20834. | | 9636. | | 3949. |
| 42. | –,0958333. | | +,0380671. | | +,0172095. | |
| | | 20833. | | 9577. | | 3943. |
| 45. | –,0937500. | | +,0371094. | | +,0168152. | |
| | | 20833. | | 9520. | | 3937. |
| 48. | –,0916667 | | +,0361574. | | +,0164215. | |
| | | 20834. | | 9462. | | 3931. |
| 51. | –,0895833. | | +,0352112. | | +,0160284. | |
| | | 20833. | | 9404. | | 3923. |
| 54. | –,0875000. | | +,0342708. | | +,0156361. | |
| | | 20833. | | 9346. | | 3917. |
| 57. | –,0854167. | | +,0333362. | | +,0152444. | |
| | | 20834. | | 9288. | | 3910. |
| 10. 0. | –,0833333. | | +,0324074. | | +,0148534. | |
| | | 20833. | | 9230. | | 3903. |
| 3. | –,0812500. | | +,0314844. | | +,0144631. | |
| | | 20833. | | 9173. | | 3895. |
| 6. | –,0791667. | | +,0305671. | | +,0140736. | |
| | | 20834. | | 9114. | | 3888. |

| h. m. | (x.) | 1st diff. | (y.) | 1st diff. | (z.) | 1st diff. |
|---|---|---|---|---|---|---|
| 9. | –,0770833. | | +,0296557. | | +,0136848. | |
| | | 20833. | | 9057. | | 3879. |
| 12. | –,0750000. | | +,0287500. | | +,0132969. | |
| | | 20833. | | 8999. | | 3872. |
| 15. | –,0729167. | | +,0278501. | | +,0129097. | |
| | | 20834. | | 8941. | | 3864 |
| 18. | –,0708333. | | +,0269560. | | +,0125233. | |
| | | 20833. | | 8883. | | 3855. |
| 21. | –,0687500. | | +,0260677. | | +,0121378. | |
| | | 20833. | | 8825. | | 3847. |
| 24. | –,0666667. | | +,0251852. | | +,0117531. | |
| | | 20834. | | 8768. | | 3839. |
| 27. | –,0645833. | | +,0243084. | | +,0113692. | |
| | | 20833. | | 8709. | | 3829. |
| 30. | –,0625000. | | +,0234375. | | +,0109863. | |
| | | 20833. | | 8652. | | 3820. |
| 33. | –,0604167. | | +,0225723. | | +,0106043. | |
| | | 20834. | | 8594. | | 3811. |
| 36. | –,0583333. | | +,0217129. | | +,0102232. | |
| | | 20833. | | 8536. | | 3801. |
| 39. | –,0562500. | | +,0208593. | | +,0098431. | |
| | | 20833. | | 8478. | | 3793. |
| 42. | –,0541667. | | +,0200115. | | +,0094638. | |
| | | 20834. | | 8420. | | 3783. |
| 45. | –,0520833. | | +,0191695. | | +,0090855. | |
| | | 20833. | | 8362. | | 3772. |
| 48. | –,0500000. | | +,0183333. | | +,0087083. | |
| | | 20833. | | 8304. | | 3762. |
| 51. | –,0479167. | | +,0175029. | | +,0083321. | |
| | | 20834. | | 8247. | | 3752. |
| 54. | –,0458333 | | +,0166782. | | +,0079569. | |
| | | 20833. | | 8189. | | 3741. |
| 57. | –,0437500. | | +,0158593. | | +,0075828. | |
| | | 20833. | | 8130. | | 3731. |
| 11. 0. | –,0416667. | | +,0150463. | | +,0072097. | |
| | | 20834. | | 8073. | | 3720. |
| 3. | –,0395833. | | +,0142390. | | +,0068377. | |
| | | 20833. | | 8015. | | 3709. |
| 6. | –,0375000 | | +,0134375. | | +,0064668. | |
| | | 20833. | | 7957. | | 3698. |
| 9. | –,0354167. | | +,0126418. | | +,0060970. | |
| | | 20834. | | 7900. | | 3686. |
| 12. | –,0333333. | | +,0118518. | | +,0057284. | |
| | | 20833. | | 7841. | | 3675. |
| 15. | –,0312500. | | +,0110677. | | +,0053609. | |
| | | 20833. | | 7783. | | 3663. |
| 18. | –,0291667. | | +,0102894. | | +,0049946. | |
| | | 20834. | | 7726. | | 3651. |

| h. m. | (x.) | 1st diff. | (y.) | 1st diff. | (z.) | 1st diff. |
|---|---|---|---|---|---|---|
| 21. | –,0270833. | | +,0095168. | | +,0046295. | |
| | | 20833. | | 7668. | | 3639. |
| 24. | –,0250000. | | +,0087500. | | +,0042656. | |
| | | 20833. | | 7610. | | 3627. |
| 27. | –,0229167. | | +,0079890. | | +,0039029. | |
| | | 20834. | | 7552. | | 3614. |
| 30. | –,0208333. | | +,0072338. | | +,0035415. | |
| | | 20833. | | 7494. | | 3601. |
| 33. | –,0187500. | | +,0064844. | | +,0031814. | |
| | | 20833. | | 7437. | | 3589. |
| 36. | –,0166667. | | +,0057407. | | +,0028225. | |
| | | 20834. | | 7378. | | 3576. |
| 39. | –,0145833 | | +,0050029. | | +,0024649. | |
| | | 20833. | | 7321. | | 3562. |
| 42. | –,0125000. | | +,0042708. | | +,0021087. | |
| | | 20833. | | 7263. | | 3549. |
| 45 | –,0104167. | | +,0035445. | | +,0017538. | |
| | | 20834. | | 7204. | | 3535. |
| 48. | –,0083333. | | +,0028241. | | +,0014003. | |
| | | 20833. | | 7147. | | 3522. |
| 51. | –,0062500. | | +,0021094. | | +,0010481. | |
| | | 20833. | | 7089. | | 3508. |
| 54. | –,0041667. | | +,0014005. | | +,0006973. | |
| | | 20834. | | 7032. | | 3494. |
| 57. | –,0020833. | | +,0006973. | | +,0003479. | |
| | | 20833. | | 6973. | | 3479. |
| 12. 0. | –,0000000. | | +,0000000. | | +,0000000. | |

Construction of the Table.

When three positions of the Moon at noon and midnight are taken from the Nautical Almanac immediately preceding, and two following the intermediate[1] time required, the series for the formation of the decimal fractions (x)(y)(z) will be as follows:—

Let r, represent the intermediate time equal to or less than 12 hours:
t, 12 hours, or 720 minutes.
C, the Moon's third position at noon or midnight.

Then, $C, + \frac{r.}{t.} + r. \times \frac{r-1.}{2t.} + r \times \frac{r-2.}{3t.} + r. \times \frac{r+1.}{4t.}$ .

The three last terms of the series reduced, will give the respective numerators and denominators of (x)(y)(z) which have been brought into their corresponding decimals throughout the table: or,

Let r, represent the intermediate time equal to, or less than 12 hours as before.
t, 1 hour, or 60 minutes: then

$\frac{-12.+r.}{24}$ , = (x.)

$\frac{+288,-36r.+rr}{864.}$ = (y)

$\frac{+3456,-144r.-4rr.+rrr.}{41472.}$ = (z.)

The numbers or decimal fractions on the table, answering to one hour, are required by the first series.

$\frac{1}{12}\Big|\frac{11}{24}\ \frac{23}{36}\ \frac{13}{48}.$

$\frac{11}{24}$, the value of (x), reduced, is = ,4583333.

$\frac{11}{24} \times \frac{23}{36} = \frac{253}{864}$, the value of (y) = ,2928241.

$\frac{11}{24} \times \frac{23}{36} \times \frac{13}{48} = \frac{3289}{41472}$, the value of (z) = ,0793065.

By the 2d series.

$\frac{-12+1}{24.} = -\frac{11}{24}$ (x)

$\frac{+288-36+1\times 1}{864.} = \frac{253.}{864.}$ (y)

$\frac{+3456-144-24\times 1\times 1.+1\times 1\times 1}{41472.}\ \frac{3289}{41472.}$, (z)

Equal to the fractions found by the first series,—and so of any other intermediate time from 0 to 12 hours.

Application.

to find the Moon's motion for 12 hours; also, the correct place in longitude latitude,

right ascension or declination, at any intermediate time between 0 and 12 hours.

Required the motion for 12 hours, and the Moon's correct place in longitude, September 20th 1809, at 4 h. 48 m. apparent time for the meridian of Greenwich.

Take <u>three</u> positions next before, and <u>two</u> following the given time, out of the Nautical Almanac, and set them down, with their successive differences, as follow:—

| 1809. | | s. ° ′ ″ | | ° ′ ″ | ′ ″ | ′ ″ | |
|---|---|---|---|---|---|---|---|
| Sep. 19 | Noon, | 10. 1. 50. 23. | A. | | | | |
| | | | | + 7. 0. 44 a1. | | | |
| " | Midn: | 10. 8. 51. 7. | B. | | – 2. 3. a2. | | |
| | | | | + 6. 58. 41. b1. | | – 0.23 a3. | |
| 20. | Noon, | 10. 15. 49. 48. | C. | | – 2.26 b2. | | 0. a4. |
| | > | | | + 6. 56. 15. c1. | | – 0.23 b3 | |
| " | Midn: | 10. 22. 46. 3. | D. | | – 2.49. c2. | | |
| | | | | + 6. 53. 26. d1 | | | |
| 21. | Noon, | 10. 29. 39. 29. | E. | | | | |

The third differences being uniform, the fourth difference vanishes, or becomes nothing in this example.

In all cases, c1, c2. b3, and a4. are the differences to be used in the application of the foregoing table.

| | c1 | ″ | ° ′ ″ dec. |
|---|---|---|---|
| | | | 6.56.15.000. |
| (x) – ,3000000. | × c2. | – 169 | + 50.700. |
| (y) + ,1600000. | × b3. | – 23 | – 3.680. |
| (z) + ,0560000 | × a4. | 0 | 0.000. |
| Moon's motion for 12 hours, at 4 h. 48 m | | | 6.57. 2.020. |

As 12 h. to 6.° 57.′ 2.″ 020. dec. so is 4 h. 48 m. to 2.° 46.′ 48.″ 808 dec., which added to C, gives 10. s. 18.° 36.′ 36.″ 808. dec. the Moon's true place at the required time, admitting the positions at noon and midnight stated in the Nautical Almanac to be <u>strictly correct.</u>

The reverse of the proposition, viz. what time at Greenwich on the 20th September, 1809, will the Moon's longitude be 10. s 18.° 36.′ 36.″ 808 dec., may be thus found.

| | s. ° ′ ″ |
|---|---|
| Given longitude | 10.18.36.36.808. |
| September 20th Noon, (C) | 10.15.49.48 – |
| difference, | – 2.46.48.808. |

As c1. 6.° 56.′ 15.″ to 12 h. so 2.° 46.′ 48.″ 808 dec., to 4 h. 48 m. 32 sec. 53 dec. the approximated time

The numbers in the table at the approximated time, are (x) –,2996238. (y) +,1597200, and (z) +,0559336.

| | | | ° ′ ″ |
|---|---|---|---|
| | | c1. | 6.56.15.000. |
| (x) – ,2996238. | × c2. – | 169. | + 50.636. |
| (y) + ,1597200. | × b3. – | 23 | – 3.673. |
| (z) + ,0559336 | × a4 | 0 | 0.000 |
| Moon's motion for 12 hours, at the approx: time | | | 6.57. 1.963. |

To find, by interpolation, the numbers or decimal fractions (y) and (z) at any other time not expressed in the table.

Take two numbers immediately preceding, and two next following the time required, find their first and second differences, to which the proper signs + or –, are to be prefixed. Multiply, by algebraical process, a mean of the second differences—

| | m. | sec. | | |
|---|---|---|---|---|
| For | 0. | 10 | by | $-\frac{17}{648}$ |
| | | 20 | | $-\frac{4}{81}$. |
| | | 30 | | $-\frac{5}{72}$ |
| | | 40 | | $-\frac{7}{81}$ |
| | | 50 | | $-\frac{65}{648}$ |
| | 1. | 0 | | $-\frac{1}{9}$ |
| | | 10 | | $-\frac{77}{648}$ |
| | | 20 | | $-\frac{10}{81}$. |
| | | 30 | | $-\frac{1}{8}$ |
| | | 40 | | $-\frac{10}{81}$ |
| | | 50 | | $-\frac{77}{648}$. |
| | 2. | 0 | | $-\frac{1}{9}$ |
| | | 10 | | $-\frac{65}{648}$ |
| | | 20 | | $-\frac{7}{81}$ |
| | | 30 | | $-\frac{5}{72}$. |
| | | 40 | | $-\frac{4}{81}$ |
| | | 50 | | $-\frac{17}{648}$, |

the product added to, or subtracted from the proportional part of the first difference, as the signs direct, will give the correction to be applied to the decimal fraction next preceding the required time.

☞. The first differences of (x) being uniform or as nearly so as possible, simple proportion is only necessary.

Let the decimal fractions (y) and (z) answering to 4 h. 25 m. 40 sec. be required.

| h. m. | (y) | 1st diff. | 2nd diff. | (z) | 1st diff. | 2nd diff. | |
|---|---|---|---|---|---|---|---|
| 4.21 | +,1739844. | | | +,0592634. | | | |
| | | –15770 | | | –3576 | | |
| 24. | ,1724074. | | +58. | ,0589058. | | –13 | |
| | | –15712. | | | –3589. | | –12½ mean. |
| 27. | ,1708362 | | +58. | ,0585469. | | –12 | |
| | | –15654 | | | –3601. | | |
| 30 | ,1692708. | | | ,0581868. | | | |

As 3 m: to 15712. so 1. m. 40. sec. to –8729, nearly, the proportional part of the first difference.

The second difference, +58, multiplied by $-\frac{10}{81}$, is –,7, added to 8729, makes 8736, the correction, which subtracted from ,1724074, leaves +,1715338, the decimal fraction (y.)

As 3. m to 3589. so 1. m. 40. sec to 1994, nearly. The second diff: –12.5, multiplied by $-\frac{10}{81}$, gives +1, taken from 1994, gives –1993, the correction, which subtracted from ,0589058, leaves +,0587065, the decimal fraction (z)

If (x) be sought for the above time, the first difference for 3 minutes is 20834, and the proportion for 1 m. 40 sec. = 11574, which subtracted from –,3166667, leaves –,3155093, at the time required.

---

As 6.° 57.′ 1.″ 963 dec. to 12 h. so 2.° 46.′ 48.″ 808. dec to 4 h. 48 m. 0 sec. the true time at Greenwich, when the Moon had that longitude, without a necessity of repeating the operation.

---

But if the Moon's motion for 12 hours between A and B, be required, the series so far as it respects the fourth difference (z) will be different, and of course, the value of the equation arising from that difference will not be the same:—the first series, according to that arrangement, will be—

$$A. + \frac{r.}{t} + r. \times \frac{r-1.}{2t.} + r. \times \frac{r-2}{3t.} + r. \times \frac{r-3.}{4t.}$$

The three last terms to be applied in the manner before directed.

The second series will be—

$\frac{-12 + r.}{24.}, = (x)$

$\frac{+288 - 36r. + rr.}{864.} = (y.)$

$\frac{-10368 + 1584r. - 72rr. + rrr.}{41472.} = (z.)$

(x.) and (y.) are the same as before; but (z) will at 1 h. intermediate time, be

By Series 1st

$\frac{1}{12} \Big| \frac{11}{24}\ \frac{23}{36}\ \frac{35}{48}$

$-\frac{11}{24} \times \frac{23.}{36.} \times \frac{35}{48.}, = \frac{8855}{41472}$, reduced, – ,2135175, the sign being negative. in this case, and affirmative in the other.

By the second series.

$\frac{-10368 + 1584 \times 1 - 72 \times 1 \times 1. + 1 \times 1 \times 1 \times 1.}{41472} = \frac{8855}{41472}$, the same as above.

The differences a1, a2, a3. and a4. are to be used, when one position before, and four following the intermediate time are taken, but this being a different principle of construction from that on which the table was formed, no example need be given.

---

Example II.

Required the time of full Moon at the Capitol, in the city of Washington, in the month of November, 1809.

Subtract the Sun's longitude from that of the Moon, and set down three positions next preceding, and two following the opposition, as follow:—

☽'s long. – ☉'s long.

| 1809. | | s. ° ′ ″ | 1st diff: | | | |
|---|---|---|---|---|---|---|
| Novem: 20th | Midnight | 5.17.35.30½. | ° ′ ″ | 2d diff. | | |
| | | | + 5.32.31½ a1 | | 3d diff: | |
| 21. | Noon, | 5.23. 8. 2. | | −1.34½ a2. ″ | | 4th dif |
| | | | + 5.30.57. b1 | | + 9½ a3 ″ | dec |
| ″ | Midnight, | 5.28.38.59. | | −1.25. b2 | | −0. 5 a4 |
| | | | + 5.29.32. c1. | | + 9. b3. | |
| 22. | Noon, | 6. 4. 8.31. | | −1.16 c2 | | |
| | | | + 5.28.16. d1. | | | |
| ″ | Midn: | 6. 9.36.47. | | | | |

| | s. ° ′ ″ dec. |
|---|---|
| From | 6. 0. 0. 0.000. |
| Subtract position midnight of 21st | 5.28.38.59 |
| diff. | 1.21. 1.000. |

As c1. 5.° 29.′ 32.″ to 12 h. so 1.° 21.′ 1.″ to 2 h. 57 m. 0 sec. the approximated time at Greenwich past midnight.

The numbers in the table at 2. h. 57. m. are (x) −,3770833. (y) +,2204890. (z) +,0686731.

| | ° ′ ″ dec. |
|---|---|
| C1, | 5.29.32.000 |
| (x) − ,3770833. × c2. − 760 | + 0.28.658. |
| (y) + ,2204890. × b3 + 9 | + 0. 1.984. |
| (z) + ,0686731. × a4. − 0.5 | − 0. 0.034. |
| diff: ☉ and ☽'s Long. for 12 h. at the approx. time | 5.30. 2.608. |

As 5.° 30.′ 2.″ 608. dec to 12 h. so is 1.° 21.′ 1.″ to 2. h. 56. m. 32. sec nearly, or 14. h. 56. m. 32. Sec. according to the astronomical method of reckoning.

| | D. H. M. S. |
|---|---|
| Time of opposition at Greenwich, | 21.14.56.32. |
| Longitude in time (West) | − 5. 7.38. |
| Full Moon in Novemr at Washn | 21. 9.48.54. |

Many other examples relating to the Moon's latitude, right ascension and declination, might be given; but the preceding are supposed to be sufficient to shew the usefulness of the table; great care has been taken to compute the numbers or decimal fractions correctly, which may be verified by taking the second differences: those differences are nearly uniform in (y); and in z, they gradually decrease to about the 8th hour, after which, the sign changes from − to +, and they increase for the remaining hours contained in the table.

MS (PPAmP: APS Archives, Manuscript Communications); entirely in Lambert's hand; undated; on five folio sheets; repeated column headings and hour numbers at head of pp. 2–5 omitted. Enclosed in TJ to Robert Patterson, 1 Oct. 1809.

[1] Manuscript: "intermemediate."

## From William Johnson

Charleston 20 Septem^r 1809.

Judge Johnson having heard M^r Jefferson express his Admiration of the Popinaque, avails himself of the Opportunity of M^r Mitchells Visit to Montecello to transmit one of the Pods of that delicate little Acacia. The Seeds may be put in the Ground immediately about an Inch deep but possibly they may not sprout until the Spring. The Tree blossoms so late and is so wholly incapable of withstanding the Frost that it is very seldom we are able to procure the Seed.—In the same Packet M^r Jefferson will find a few Seeds of the Grass wh^ch in Georgia is called Egyptian, & of the Bennè. The latter J J has made some Observations and Experiments upon in the Course of this Summer & is convinced from the time requisite to bring it to Maturity, that it may be cultivated in the upper Parts of Virginia. The best Mode of obtaining the Pit is to break it between Rollers working horizontally & to express it from Bags of fine Hair Cloth. J. J requests M^r Jefferson to accept his warmest Assurance of Respect & Esteem.—

RC (DLC); endorsed by TJ as received 5 Nov. 1809 and so recorded in SJL.

William Johnson (1771–1834) was TJ's first appointment to the United States Supreme Court, serving from 1804 until his death. The native South Carolinian graduated from the College of New Jersey in 1790, was admitted to the bar three years later, and served in the South Carolina House of Representatives, 1794–99, ending as speaker. Johnson sat on the state bench from 1799–1804, and he was also president of the College of South Carolina at the time of TJ's appointment. On the Supreme Court he was a nationalist Republican, often dissenting from the Marshall majority but eventually making himself unpopular in South Carolina by opposing nullification. Johnson exchanged agricultural information and seeds with TJ in addition to political commentary and discussions of Johnson's writing projects. His *Sketches of the Life and Correspondence of Nathanael Greene* (1822) prompted TJ to encourage him, unsuccessfully, to write a political history of the early republic, and Johnson published a *Eulogy on Thomas Jefferson* in 1826 (*ANB*; *DAB*; *Princetonians*, 1784–1790, pp. 494–507; *BDSCHR*, 4:322–5; Donald G. Morgan, *Justice William Johnson: The First Dissenter* [1954]; *JEP*, 1:466, 467 [22, 26 Mar. 1804]).

## To Benjamin Smith Barton

Dear Sir — Monticello Sep. 21. 09.

I recieved last night your favor of the 14^th and would with all possible pleasure have communicated to you any part or the whole of the Indian vocabularies which I had collected, but an irreparable misfortune has deprived me of them. I have now been thirty years availing myself of every possible opportunity of procuring Indian vocabularies to the same set of words: my opportunities were probably better than will ever occur again to any person having the same desire. I had collected about 50. and had digested most of them in collateral columns and meant to have printed them the last year of my stay in Washington. but not having yet digested Cap^t Lewis's collection, nor having leisure then to do it, I put it off till I should return home. the whole, as well digest as originals were packed in a trunk of stationary & sent round by water with about 30. other packages of my effects from Washington, and while ascending James river, this package, on account of it's weight & presumed precious contents, was singled out & stolen. the thief being disappointed on opening it, threw into the river all it's contents of which he thought he could make no use. among these were the whole of the vocabularies. some leaves floated ashore & were found in the mud; but these were very few, & so defaced by the mud & water that no general use can ever be made of them. on the reciept of your letter I turned to them, & was very happy to find that the only morsel of an original vocabulary among them was Cap^t Lewis's of the Pani language of which you say you have not one word. I therefore inclose it to you, as it is, & a little fragment of some other, which I see is in his handwriting, but no indication remains on it of what language it is. it is a specimen of the condition of the little which was recovered. I am the more concerned at this accident as of the 250 words of my vocabularies and the 130. words of the great Russian vocabularies of the languages of the other quarters of the globe, 73. were common to both, and would have furnished materials for a comparison from which something might have resulted. altho I believe no general use can ever be made of the wrecks of my loss, yet I will ask the return of the Pani vocabulary when you are done with it. perhaps I may make another attempt to collect, altho' I am too old to expect to make much progress in it.

I learn with pleasure your acquisition of the pamphlet on the astronomy of the antient Mexicans. if it be antient & genuine, or modern & rational it will be of real value. it is one of the most interesting countries of our hemisphere, and merits every attention.

I am thankful for your kind offer of sending the original Spanish for my perusal. but I think it a pity to trust it to the accidents of the post, & whenever you publish the translation, I shall be satisfied to read that which shall be given by your translator, who is, I am sure, a greater adept in the language than I am. Accept the assurances of my great esteem & respect. TH: JEFFERSON

PoC (DLC); at foot of first page: "D[r] Barton." Enclosures not found.

TJ hereafter published none of his research on INDIAN VOCABULARIES, but in 1817 he donated the materials that survived the JAMES RIVER to the American Philosophical Society (TJ to Peter Stephen DuPonceau, 7 Nov. 1817). PANI: Pawnee.

# From George Jefferson

DEAR SIR Richmond 22[d] Sept[r] 1809

I inclose you the terms of tuition at M[r] Girardin's Academy, which you will find to be 50 $ ℔ annum, for a student who is even taught mathematics only: and which, (not that I know any thing about it) appears to me to be very high.

I am sorry that I have not been able to procure such a situation in a private family for T.J.R. as you wish.—There are but few French families here in which it would be desirable for him to be placed, and those few decline to receive him as a boarder. indeed it is unusual in this place, for families of any respectability, to take in boarders: except indeed where they open regular boarding houses, and then I suppose they commonly[1] become places of such general[2] resort, as would be apt to divert the studies of almost any youth whatever.—The most eligible situation of which I have heard is M[rs] Pages.—she has occasionally taken in a few boarders, & will take Jefferson, but she asks 200$ for his board, fuel, & candles—he paying for his own washing, which I suppose would be 20$ more.—he would likewise have to find his own bed, unless he would partake of one with a relation of hers, who is one of M[r] G's students, and who appears to be a very decent young man.

There is a very respectable French family, who speak very good french as I am told, where there will be a chance of getting Jefferson in, (a M[r] Le Bourdais) but the Lady is at present with her daughter down the Country, where she may probably remain for a month or two and until her return, the Gentleman cannot decide positively, whether he will take him, or what the board will be

Suppose you let Jefferson enter for one quarter with M[rs] P—, by the expiration of which time, you may be able to form a better judgment of the school, from the progress he will have made in his studies, and if you should be satisfied with it, we may then perhaps get him in with M[r] B.

I am Dear Sir Your Very humble serv[t]

GEO. JEFFERSON

RC (MHi); at foot of text: "Thomas Jefferson esq$^{r}$"; endorsed by TJ as received 27 Sept. 1809 and so recorded in SJL. Enclosure not found.

[1] Word interlined in place of "generally."

[2] Word interlined.

# From Dudley Richardson

Kentucky September the 22$^{d}$ 1809 Barren County
Glasgow Post office

SIR

I have taken a Liberty to Rite to you hopeing you will Pardon me it Proseeds from A Desire of Hearing from my son Richard Richardson it appears to me that from your kindness to him while he was Living under your Direction that Perhaps he has made known to you his Place of Resedence and my Not Hearing from him since he was with me in the Ear 1804 and we Conditionially Agreed that I should moove to the Western Cuntrey Agreable to his request I movd to Kentucky in the Ear 1805 and have not heard from him sinc and am Convinst from your Goodness to Man and the Publick that if you have any knowledge of him and of his Resedence and ocaponcy you will Acquaint me of him and if he is a Living he must be Ungrateful if he has not mad you Acquanted Whear he Livs as you have been More kinder[1] to him than was Ever in my Powr to be I Flatter my self you will Condesend to Rite me and Oblige yr Obedient & Verrey Humble Srt

DUDLEY RICHARDSON

RC (MHi); endorsed by TJ as received 31 Oct. 1809 and so recorded in SJL.

Dudley Richardson was the father of RICHARD RICHARDSON, a Virginia-born bricklayer who worked at Monticello between 1796 and 1800, serving as an overseer during his last year there. In 1801 TJ informed the younger Richardson that his uncle Joseph Richardson had left him an estate in Jamaica, upon which Richardson settled in Kingston, raising a family and occasionally corresponding with TJ (*PTJ*, 29:585).

[1] Word interlined.

# To Benjamin Rush

DEAR DOCTOR

Monticello Sep. 22. 09

I have long owed you a letter in answer to yours of May 3. an acknolegement of the reciept of the pamphlet on the use of the Omentum, & congratulations on the satisfaction you must derive from having a son, entering, under auspices so promising, the career you have run before him. I am not learned enough in these branches of science to decide on the soundness of the hypothesis maintained in this pamphlet, but I have read it with pleasure as a logical investigation of a curious question, and adding usefully to our knolege of the animal economy.

I am become sensible of a great advantage your profession has over most others, that, to the close of your life, you can be always doing good to mankind: whereas a retired politician is like a broken down courser, unfit for the turf, and good for little else. I am endeavoring to recover the little I once knew of farming, gardening E[t]c. and would gladly now exchange any branch of science I possess for the knolege of a common farmer. too old to learn, I must be contented with the occupation & amusement of the art. already it keeps me so much without doors that I have little time to read, & still less to write. this must be my apology for the tardiness of the present letter.

I find I am losing sight of the progress of the world of letters. here we talk but of rains & droughts, of blights & frosts, of our ploughs & cattle; & if the topic changes to politics I meddle little with them. in truth I never had a cordial relish for them, & abhor the contentions and strife they generate. you know what were the times which forced us both from our first loves, the natural sciences. the interest I have taken in the success of the experiment, whether a government can be contrived which shall secure man in his rightful liberties & acquirements, has engaged a longer portion of my life than I had ever proposed: & certainly the experiment could never have fallen into more inauspicious times, when nations have openly renounced all the obligations of morality, and shamelessly assume the character of robbers & pyrates. in any other time our experiment would have been more easy: and if it can pass safely through the ordeal of the present trial, we may hope we have set an example which will not be without consequences favorable to human happiness. may we not hope that when the robbers of Copenhagen, and the ravagers of Spain shall be arrested in their course by those means which providence has always in reserve for the restoration of order among his works, the pendulum will vibrate the more strongly in the opposite direction, & that nations will return to the reestablishment of moral law with an enthusiasm which shall more solidly confirm it's future empire. so be it, & god bless you. TH: JEFFERSON

RC (DLC: Benjamin Rush Collection); at foot of first page: "Doct[r] Rush." SC (DLC: TJ Papers, 188:33495, 232:41515); damaged.

## From Robert Quarles

Dear Sir, Fluvanna Sep[r] 24[th] 1809.

M[r] John Ashlin a neighbour of mine, wishes to erect a mill on the Rivanna River a few miles above Columbia, & he finds much difficulty in getting information respecting the mode of proceedure to obtain permission to build. Has the County Court the power of granting leave? or must the application be made to the Legislature in consequence of their Charter to the James River Comp[y]? or must the Application be made to the company itself?

I trust you will pardon me the liberty I have taken of resorting to you for information on this Subject—Your peculear situation, in having a mill on the same water course, combined with other circumstances, induce me to believe that I could apply to no better source for correct information—I have the honor to be y[r] sincere friend & Ob[t]

Ro[T] Quarles

address to the Columbia post office

RC (MHi); endorsed by TJ as received 27 Sept. 1809 and so recorded in SJL.

Robert Quarles (1763–1827), of Columbia, Fluvanna County, served as an ensign and regimental quartermaster in the Continental army from May 1782 until the close of the Revolutionary War and was an original member of the Society of the Cincinnati. He was a major in the Albemarle County militia during the latter part of the 1780s and superintendent of the state arsenal at Point of Fork in Fluvanna County from 1793 until it closed in 1801. Quarles served on the Virginia Council of State, 1812–15, and subsequently was state quartermaster general. He relocated to Missouri shortly before his death (*PTJ*, 26:64; National Society of Daughters of the American Revolution, *DAR Patriot Index* [1990], 2389; Heitman, *Continental Army*, 456; *CVSP*, 4:546, 6:515–17, 575, 9:183–4, 202, 10:148, 445–7, 474).

## From William Lambert

Sir, City of Washington, September 25[th] 1809.

The last paragraph of your letter of the 10[th] instant, respecting the conduct of a certain European nation to us, as well as to others with whom it has any commercial intercourse, plainly evinces Your strong, unbiassed attachment to the true interests of the country which gave you birth. It is much to be regretted, that too many natives of this favored land are pusillanimous and unprincipled Enough not only to palliate, but to justify the wanton aggressions of our enemies, and meanly to submit their necks to the yoke of a monarch. There are so many charms in the words "king, crown, throne, duke," &c. that they seem to operate as powerfully on the depraved minds of those grovelling spaniels, as Merlin's enchanted wand is fabled to have done. Among the methods which may be employed to extricate us from the miserable shackles of dependence is this:[1] let men of high standing and weight in society, recommend it to our citizens to manufacture their own cloathing, and deprive the haughty nation above alluded to, of our raw materials. If this line of conduct were generally and steadily pursued for a few years by the inhabitants of the United States, the arrogance which they have assumed for a long time, would effectually be humbled; and that government and people, instead of treating us with contempt, would be taught to respect and fear their quondam colonists. Let it be impressed on the minds of the female classes, that they will appear to much greater advantage in articles of domestic manufacture, than in British fripperies. Let men take a laudable pride in assembling at churches, meeting-houses, musters, Elections, &c. in a home spun dress, instead of foreign cloathing. Let the people of Virginia, and particularly of Albemarle country, remember the tragical condition and end of their once respected and confidential fellow citizen, M^r^ Edward Moore. Honest, unsuspecting and credulous, he was a victim to cunning, avarice and intrigue: hooked in by degrees and by plausible arts, he lost his home,[2] his reason and his life, by listening to the temptations, and trusting to the integrity[3] of others who thirsted after his land and other property. "Let not such men be trusted." I do firmly believe at this moment, and have for some time past, that plots have been formed and are now forming, to dispossess and ruin the native citizens of this country, particularly in the southern states, by such detestable artifices: it must be effected gradually to avoid too much suspicion, and great address must be employed; but the consequences will be destructive to us, and confirm the malignant triumph of our inveterate foes. Let me follow your example, and turn with disgust from the scene, to better prospects; permit me, at the same time, to propose a remedy.—Such characters as yourself, (if others there be) might do much, by impressing on the minds of your neighbors and countrymen, to avoid going to stores, and obtaining foreign goods on credit, any longer; to manufacture within themselves all they can; to manure and improve their lands, instead of wearing them out as fast as can be done, by the culture of that impoverishing weed "tobacco";—to save their timber, instead of lavishing and destroying it:—to guard themselves against the persuasive, but insidious arts of foreign store-keepers and factors:—It is a source of much gratification to them, to see our natives toil like galley slaves, year after year, and the produce of their hard-earned labor, brought to them, for which they will give a few useless fripperies of female dress, that will not last a month. Credit and anticipation have produced this; and it is high time to put an effectual stop to it. It requires men of strong minds, beloved and respected by their fellow-citizens, to reason with them on this subject, and to prevail on [them] to break through long habits. It is not my intention to flatter, when I say, that you are among the number that will be heard with attention, and whose advice will have great weight. I trust, that not only you but others will exert themselves to produce so desirable an effect. These thoughts are hastily thrown together for your consideration;—and I am not, by any means, so anxious about the dress in which they are exhibited, as I am to see or hear that the native citizens of my own state, at least, should appear more neatly and properly clothed in their own manufacture.

I am, Sir, with great respect, Your most obedient servant,

WILLIAM LAMBERT.

RC (DLC); torn at seal; addressed: "Thomas Jefferson, late President of the U.S. Monticello, Virginia"; franked and postmarked; endorsed by TJ as received 27 Sept. 1809 and so recorded in SJL.

EDWARD MOORE represented Albemarle County in the House of Delegates, 1792–95, became overwhelmed by debt, and lost his plantation near Keswick in a trustees' sale in 1805. He was declared insane in 1807 and died in an asylum the following year. Moore's wife, Mildred Lewis Moore, was the sister of TJ's brother-in-law Charles Lilburne Lewis (Woods, *Albemarle*, 284; *MB*, 2:1097n; Leonard, *General Assembly*, 187, 191, 195, 199).

[1] Preceding two words interlined.

[2] Word interlined in place of "property."

[3] Manuscript: "intregity."

# Notes on Distances between Monticello and Montpellier

[ca. 25 Sept. 1809]

| 1809. Sep. 22.[1] | m |
|---|---|
| Montic° to Gordon's | 20. |
| Montpelier road | 5. |
| Montpelier | 3.75 |
| Sep. 24. | |
| Gordon's to Lindsay's | 3.17 |
| Sep. 25. | |
| Lindsay's to pub. road | 2.38 |
| to the store | 2.02 |

MS (DLC: TJ Papers, 233:41691); entirely in TJ's hand; undated; written on a small scrap.

On his way to or from Montpellier, TJ often stayed at his friend Reuben LINDSAY's home in northeastern Albemarle County (Woods, *Albemarle*, 257; *MB*).

[1] TJ here canceled "23. 24. 25."

# Jefferson's Letter to James Fishback

I. TO JAMES FISHBACK (DRAFT), SEPTEMBER 1809

II. TO JAMES FISHBACK (FINAL STATE), 27 SEPTEMBER 1809

## EDITORIAL NOTE

In crafting his response to James Fishback's letter of 5 June 1809, Jefferson completed a draft that argued passionately and at length against intolerance and forced conformity in religion. Possibly reflecting that his letter was outspoken enough to create controversy and that he knew very little about Fishback or his discretion, Jefferson then substituted a briefer and less revealing version, but took the comparatively unusual step of retaining both texts in his own records. Their intrinsic interest is so great that the draft and the final state are printed in full below.

## I. To James Fishback (Draft)

SIR Monticello Sep. 09.

Your favor of June 5. came to hand in due time, & I have to acknolege my gratification at the friendly sentiments it expresses towards myself. we have been thrown into times of a peculiar character, & to work our way through them has required services & sacrifices from our countrymen generally; &, to their great honor, these have been generally exhibited by every one in his sphere, & according to the opportunities afforded. with them I have been a fellow-labourer, endeavoring to do faithfully the part allotted to me, as they did theirs. it is a subject of mutual congratulation that, in a state of things such as the world had never before seen, we have gotten on so far well: and my confidence in our present high functionaries,[1] & in my countrymen generally, leaves me without much fear for the future.

I thank you for the pamphlet you were so kind as to send me.

at an earlier period of life I pursued enquiries of that kind with industry & care. reading, reflection & time have convinced me it is better to be quiet myself, & let others be quiet on these speculations. every religion consists of moral precepts, & of dogmas. in the first they all agree. all forbid us to murder, steal, plunder, bear false witness E$^{t}$c. and these are the articles necessary for the preservation of order, justice, & happiness in society. in their particular dogmas all differ; no two professing the same. these respect vestments, ceremonies, physical opinions, & metaphysical speculations, totally unconnected with morality, & unimportant to the legitimate objects of society. yet these are the questions on which have hung the bitter schisms of Nazarenes, Socinians, Arians, Athanasians in former times, & now of Trinitarians, Unitarians, Catholics, Lutherans, Calvinists, Methodists, Baptists, Quakers E$^{t}$c. among the Mahometans we are told that thousands fell victims to the dispute whether the first or second toe of Mahomet was longest; & what blood, how many human lives have the words 'this do in remembrance of me' cost the Christian world! we all agree in the obligation of the moral precepts of Jesus: but we schismatize & lose ourselves in subtleties about his nature, his conception maculate or immaculate, whether he was a god or not a god, whether his votaries are to be initiated by simple aspersion, by immersion, or without water; whether his priests must be robed in white, in black, or not robed at all; whether we are to use our own reason, or the reason of others, in the opinions we form, or as to the evidence we are to believe. it is on questions of this, & still less importance, that such oceans of human blood have been spilt, & whole regions of the earth have been desolated by wars & persecutions, in which human ingenuity has been exhausted in inventing new tortures for their brethren. it is time then to become sensible how insoluble these questions are by minds like ours, how unimportant, & how mischievous; & to consign them to the sleep of death, never to be awakened from it. the varieties in the structure & action of the human mind, as in those of the body, are the work of our creator, against which it cannot be a religious duty to erect the standard of uniformity. the practice of morality being necessary for the well being of society, he has taken care to impress it's precepts so indelibly on our hearts, that they shall not be effaced by the whimsies of our brain. hence we see good men in all religions, and as many in one as another.[2] it is then a matter of principle with me to avoid disturbing the tranquility of others by the expression of any opinion on the innocent questions[3] on which we schismatize, & think it enough to hold fast to those moral precepts which are of the essence of Christianity, & of all other religions. no where are these to be found in greater purity than in the discourses of the great reformer of religion whom we follow.

I have been led into these reflections by your invitation to make observations on the subject of your pamphlet, as you have treated it. the only one I permit myself is on the candor, the moderation & the ingenuity with which you appear to have sought truth. this is of good example, & worthy of[4] much commendation. if all the writers & preachers on religious questions had been of the same temper, the history of the world would have been of much more pleasing aspect.

I thank you for the kindness towards myself which breathes through your letter. the first of all our consolations is that of having faithfully fulfilled our duties. the next, the approbation & good will of those who have witnessed it: and I pray you to accept my best wishes for your happiness & the assurances of my respect.

TH: JEFFERSON

Dft (DLC: TJ Papers, 188:33502); partially dated.

THIS DO IN REMEMBRANCE OF ME: Luke 22.19.

[1] Preceding two words interlined in place of "helmsman."

[2] TJ here canceled "I decline."

[3] Preceding two words interlined in place of "unimportant points."

[4] TJ here canceled "imitation."

## II. To James Fishback (Final State)

SIR Monticello Sep. 27. 09.

Your favor of June 5. came to hand in due time, and I have to acknolege my gratification at the friendly sentiments it breathes towards myself. we have been thrown into times of a peculiar character, and to work our way through them has required services & sacrifices from our countrymen generally, and, to their great honor, these have been generally exhibited, by every one in his sphere, & according to the opportunities afforded. with them I have been a fellow laborer, endeavoring to do faithfully the part allotted to me, as they did theirs; & it is a subject of mutual congratulation that, in a state of things, such as the world had never before seen, we have gotten on so far well: and my confidence in our present high functionaries, as well as in my countrymen generally leaves me without much fear for the future.

I thank you for the pamphlet you were so kind as to send me. at an earlier period of life I pursued enquiries of that kind with industry & care. reading, reflection & time have convinced me that the interests of society require the observation of those moral precepts only in which all religions agree, (for all forbid us to murder, steal, plunder, or bear false witness.) and that we should not intermeddle with the particular dogmas in which all religions differ, and which are totally unconnected with morality. in all of them we see good men, & as many in one as another. the varieties in the structure & action of the human mind as in those of the body, are the work of our creator, against which it cannot be a religious duty to erect the standard of uniformity. the practice of morality being necessary for the well-being of society, he has taken care to impress it's precepts so indelibly on our hearts that they shall not be effaced by the subtleties of our brain. we all agree in the obligation of the moral precepts of Jesus, & no where will they be found delivered in greater purity than in his discourses. it is then a matter of principle with me to avoid disturbing the tranquility of others by the expression of any opinion on the innocent questions on which we schismatise. On the subject of your pamphlet, & the mode of treating it, I permit myself only to observe the candor, moderation & ingenuity with which you appear to have sought truth. this is of good example, & worthy of[1] commendation. if all the writers & preachers on religious questions had been of the same temper, the history of the world would have been of much more pleasing aspect.

I thank you for the kindness towards myself which breathes through your letter. the first of all our consolations is that of having faithfully fulfilled our duties: the next, the approbation & good will of those who have witnessed it: and I pray you to accept my best wishes for your happiness, & the assurances of my respect.

Th: Jefferson

RC (NjP: Andre deCoppet Collection); at foot of first page: "Mr James Fishback." PoC (DLC); at head of text: "this, & not the preceding was sent."

[1] TJ here canceled "imitation."

## From Samuel Kercheval

Sir Stephensburg. Frederick Cy Sepr 28th 1809.

I have taken the liberty of inclosing to you, a subscription paper, for the purpose of raising money towards defraying the charges, of building an Academy at this place. I need not hint to you Sir the importance of the institution; you are far better qualified to judge of its utility than I am. It may not however, be improper to remark, that the situation is both beautifull & healthy, and is capable of being improved to great advantage.

If you should think proper to patronize the undertaking, and contribute any thing for that purpose; any contributions, either from your self or any of your friends will be gratefully received. Pardon the liberty I have taken, and beleive me, (altho a stranger to your person) your Most ob[t] Ser[t]

SAM[L] KERCHEVAL
Sec[y] for the Trustees

RC (DLC); endorsed by TJ as received 31 Oct. 1809 and so recorded in SJL. Enclosure not found.

Samuel Kercheval (1767–1845), an innkeeper at Stephensburg, near Winchester, is best known for his *History of the Valley of Virginia* (1833). In 1816 he supported unsuccessful calls for a state constitutional convention by the underrepresented western half of Virginia. Writing under the pseudonym of "H. Tompkinson," in that year Kercheval elicited a memorable letter from TJ both approving of a convention and endorsing democratic reforms. However, when TJ learned that the letter was circulating widely, he demanded that Kercheval retrieve any copies, and he denied him permission to publish the letter both then and in 1824 (John Walter Wayland, *Twenty-Five Chapters on the Shenandoah Valley* [1957], 283–6; Malone, *Jefferson*, 6:348–50, 442).

# From Isaac Riley

SIR New York Sept. 29[th] 1809

Experiencing daily, in the course of my business, the constant and increasing demand there is in the Country for your Work, the Notes on Virginia, and of which the copies are becoming exceeding scarce, I am satisfied that a new Edition is wanting.

Deeming it very probable that in the period which has elapsed since the Original publication of the work, you have collected some manuscript additions, with which you would not be unwilling to favour the public, and presuming upon the supposition that you have no other arrangement in view, I take the liberty of submitting, that should you condescend to intrust me with Said additions, it would be a subject of pride with me, to print an enlarged Edition of the Notes, with an accuracy and elegance creditable to the American Press—

In this application I have proceeded upon the belief that there is no copy right already possessed by any other Bookseller, and if I am in Error on this head, I trust to your excuse—

I have also to depend much upon your goodness in pardoning the freedom which I have used in addressing you on this occasion—

I have the honour to be Your very Obedient Servant

I. RILEY.

RC (DLC); between dateline and salutation: "Hon. Thomas Jefferson"; endorsed by TJ as received 4 Oct. 1809 and so recorded in SJL.

In 1809 Isaac Riley operated a bookstore and printing office at the intersection of Wall and William streets in New York City. After several bankruptcies, he relocated his business to Philadelphia but encountered similar financial difficulties there (*Longworth's New-York Almanac* [1808], 276; [1809], 310; [1810], 314; Rosalind Remer, *Printers and Men of Capital: Philadelphia Book Publishers in the New Republic* [1996], 120).

# To the General Republican Committee of the City and County of New York

GENTLEMEN Monticello Sep. 30. 09.

The very friendly sentiments which my republican fellow-citizens of the city & county of New York have been pleased to express, through yourselves as their organ, are highly grateful to me, and command my sincere thanks; and their approbation of the measures pursued, while I was entrusted with the administration of their affairs, strengthens my hope that they were favorable to the public prosperity. for any errors which may have been committed the indulgent will find some apology in the difficulties resulting from the extraordinary state of human affairs, & the astonishing spectacles these have presented. a world in arms, & trampling on all those moral principles which have heretofore been deemed sacred in the intercourse between nations, could not suffer us to remain insensible of all agitation. during such a course of lawless violence, it was certainly wise to withdraw ourselves from all intercourse with the belligerent nations, to avoid the desolating [cal]amities inseparable from war, it's pernicious effects on manners & morals, & the dangers it threatens to free governments; and to cultivate our own resources until our natural & progressive growth should leave us nothing to fear from foreign enterprize. that the benefits derived from these measures were lessened by an opposition of the most ominous character, & that a continuance of injury was encouraged by the appearance of domestic weakness which that presented, will doubtless be a subject of deep & durable regret to such of our well intentioned citizens as participated in it, under mistaken confidence in men who had other views than the good of their own country. should foreign nations however, decieved by this appearance of division & weakness [ren]der it necessary to vindicate by arms the injuries to our country, I believe with you that the spirit of the revolution is unextinguished, & that the cultivators of peace will again, as on that occasion, be transformed at once into a nation of warriors, who will leave us nothing to fear for the natural & national rights of our country.

Your approbation of the reasons which induced me to retire from the honorable station in which my fellow citizens had placed me, is a proof of your devotion to the true principles of our constitution. these are wisely opposed to all perpetuations of power, & to every practice which may lead to hereditary establishments: and certain I am that any services which I could have rendered will be more than supplied by the wisdom & virtues of my successor.

I am very thankful for the kind wishes you express for my personal happiness. it will always be intimately connected with the prosperity of our country, of which I sincerely pray that my fellow citizens of the city & county of New York may have their full participation.

TH: JEFFERSON

PoC (DLC); mutilated; at foot of text: "mess[rs] Bloodgood & Hammond." Recorded in SJL as "Address of N.Y. answer to." Printed in *Boston Patriot* and Washington *National Intelligencer*, both 18 Oct. 1809.

## To John W. Campbell

SIR Monticello Oct 1. 09.

I recieved last night your favor of Sep. 19. and being about commencing a journey which will keep me from home some time, I answer it immediately. I think you have done well to restrict your intentions to the Summary view,

Reports as Secretary of state &
Messages to Congress.

as I do not know that a copy of the Summary view can now be found any where else, I send you a volume of the pamphlets of that day (1774) containing it. I had written it hastily at home, & hazarded some things not certain, because I expected to ascertain them on arriving at the convention. but as I was stopped on the way & the piece was published by others, before I knew of it, it went forth with it's errors uncorrected. on recieving the copy in this volume I made the M.S. corrections which you will see in it, & which, in the republication, should be made in the text.

2. Reports as Secretary of State. having had all these bound into a volume for my own use, & supposing it would be difficult for you to collect them, I send the volume. you will doubtless omit the Report of

the Census, & the French originals of the correspondence with Genet. these two volumes making part of a collection of value & constant recurrence to myself, I need not recommend them to your particular care, & to be returned as soon as you can make the necessary use of them. I never before suffered them to go out of my own hands.

3. Messages to Congress. these can be obtained correctly only from the Journals of Congress from Dec. 1801. to Mar. 1809, a copy of which I presume you can procure from some of the gentlemen who are or have been members of Congress. the copies published in the newspapers were generally very incorrect.

Hoping that these volumes will get safely to hand by post I present you my salutations & respects. TH: JEFFERSON

PoC (DLC); at foot of first page: "Mr Campbell"; endorsed by TJ.

The enclosed VOLUME OF THE PAMPHLETS of 1774, including TJ's revised copy of *A Summary View of the Rights of British America* (1774; Sowerby, no. 3085), survives at DLC (Sowerby, nos. 3084–94). His reports as secretary of state as bound FOR MY OWN USE (Sowerby, no. 3164) is lost or dispersed, but evidently included *A Message of the President of the United States to Congress Relative to France and Great-Britain* (Philadelphia, 1793; Sowerby, no. 3167), which included correspondence with Edmond Charles Genet. Campbell returned the volumes to TJ more than two years later (Campbell to TJ, 20 Dec. 1811). REPORT OF THE CENSUS: *PTJ*, 22:227–8.

# To William W. Hening

SIR Monticello Oct. 1. 09.

In answer to the request expressed in your's of Sep. 4. (which came to hand only this morning) that I would transcribe a line or two of the first act in my copy of the laws of 1660. I have to observe that the only copy of those laws I possessed was one made by myself from that in the office of the general assembly, and that it was among those I sent you & described under No 4. in the list I sent you. if you turn to this you may rely on it's correctness. I salute you with esteem & respect. TH: JEFFERSON

PoC (DLC); at foot of text: "Mr Hening"; endorsed by TJ.

TJ's COPY OF THE LAWS OF 1660 (Sowerby, no. 1826) was on his 8 June 1808 LIST of manuscripts of laws sent to Hening (DLC).

## To Alexander Macomb

Monticello. Oct. 1. 09.

Th: Jefferson presents his compliments to Maj[r] Macomb and returns his thanks for the copy of his treatise on Martial law which he was so kind as to send him, & which he was pleased to see made public in so well digested a form. he has too long delayed this acknolegement from a desire to learn to what place it should be directed; but has at length thought it best to send it through the medium of the War-office. he salutes Maj[r] Macomb with esteem & respect.

PoC (MHi); dateline at foot of text; endorsed by TJ.

Alexander Macomb (1782–1841) was a major in the United States Army Corps of Engineers serving as chief engineer of coastal fortifications in Georgia and the Carolinas. With one brief hiatus, 1800–01, the native of Detroit served in the regular army from 1798 until his death, starting as a cornet and ending with thirteen years as major general and army commander in chief. Macomb toured the southeastern frontier as secretary to General James Wilkinson, 1801–02, was one of the first two students selected for instruction at the new United States Military Academy at West Point in the latter year, and served with distinction in the War of 1812. He wrote *A Treatise on Martial Law, and Courts-Martial; as practised in the United States of America* (Charleston, S.C., 1809; Sowerby, no. 2021), the first such American study (*ANB*; *DAB*; Heitman, *U.S. Army*, 1:680; Allan Seymour Everest, *The Military Career of Alexander Macomb and Macomb at Plattsburgh, 1814* [1989]).

On 6 Oct. 1809 John Smith, chief clerk of the War Department, wrote TJ from Washington that the day before he had received TJ's note enclosing this letter and had immediately forwarded the latter to Macomb at Charleston, South Carolina, "where he is at present engaged in the duties of his profession" (RC in MHi; at foot of text: "Thomas Jefferson Esq[r]"; endorsed by TJ as received 11 Oct. 1809 and so recorded in SJL). TJ's covering note to Smith is not recorded in SJL and has not been found.

## To Robert Patterson

Dear Sir Monticello Octob. 1. 09.

M[r] Lambert does not, in the inclosed letter, say precisely that he meant it as a communication to the Philosophical society, yet from a particular expression in it, I think it was his idea. I send it to you therefore to be made such use of as you think proper, and of which you are the best judge. I salute you with constant esteem & respect.

Th: Jefferson

RC (PPAmP: APS Archives, Manuscript Communications); addressed (torn): "M[r] Robert P[atterson]"; franked. PoC (MHi); endorsed by TJ. Enclosures: William Lambert to TJ, 19 Sept. 1809, and enclosure.

On 6 Oct. 1809 the American Philosophical Society considered this letter and referred Lambert's table on lunar movements to a committee consisting of John Garnett, Patterson, and John Rhea Smith (APS, Minutes [MS in PPAmP]).

## From John Stout

SIR Buck Island Oct° 1st 1809

I have[1] for several Days thought of returning[2] your Book but not having the Opportunity for some time to Bring being afraid to intrust it to the Care of any other Person I delay^d Sending it untill M^r Rieves wrote to me for the use of by your approbation I return you my gratefull Thanks with the Book also knowing that you delight in instructing youth I am Persuaded that you'l do me the favour of Lending me another Book the work of Defoe^s entitle^d an Essay on Projects M^r Rieves will be kind Enough to Bring it to Milton & Sir you may depend upon it you shall not be kept out of it longer than I can read it through

I am Sir Y^r S^t Respectfully. JOHN STOUT

RC (MHi); at foot of text: "M^r T. Jefferson"; endorsed by TJ as received 3 Oct. 1809 and so recorded in SJL. Enclosure not found.

John Stout may have been related to Isaiah Stout, from whom TJ purchased a horse, oats, and fodder between 1806 and 1822 (*MB*).

[1] Manuscript: "I have I have."
[2] Manuscript: "returning returning."

## To Henry Dearborn and Elbridge Gerry

DEAR GENERAL[1] Monticello Oct. 2. 09.

The bearer of this is mr Thomas M. Randolph half brother of my son in law of that name whom you know.[2] he is proceeding to Harvard college to enter there as a student. having lived at a distance from me, I can say little of him from my personal knolege, but I am authorised by those in whom I have confidence to say that he is a youth of good dispositions & correct conduct. his father was my most intimate friend, having been brought up together almost from the cradle. from these different considerations I feel a just interest in his welfare, & take the liberty of presenting him to you, as he will be in a land of strangers. any countenance you shall be so good as to shew him, or counsel you shall give him, will be considered as a favor done to[3] Dear General

Your's affectionately TH: JEFFERSON

RC (ViU: TJP, photostat); at foot of text: "Gen[l] Dearborne." RC (NNPM); addressed: "Elbridge Gerry esquire Cambridge"; endorsed by Gerry. FC (MHi); note in TJ's hand describing the Gerry letter, of which he retained no other copy, as "verbatim the same" as that to Dearborn; endorsed by TJ. Enclosed in TJ to Thomas Mann Randolph (1792–1848), 2 Oct. 1809.

Elbridge Gerry (1744–1814), merchant and political leader, was born in Marblehead, Massachusetts. After graduating from Harvard in 1762, his public service began with his election to the Massachusetts General Court in 1772. A signer of the Declaration of Independence and a delegate to the 1787 Philadelphia Convention who opposed the federal constitution drafted there, Gerry served in the Continental Congress, 1776–80 and 1783–85, and the United States House of Representatives, 1789–93. A strong political supporter of TJ, Gerry won a term as governor of Massachusetts, 1810–11, but was defeated for reelection. He served as vice president of the United States from 1813 until his death (*ANB*; *DAB*; *Sibley's Harvard Graduates*, 15:239–59; George Athan Billias, *Elbridge Gerry: Founding Father and Republican Statesman* [1976]).

[1] Gerry RC: "Dear Sir."

[2] Preceding three words omitted in Gerry RC.

[3] Gerry RC concludes: "Dear Sir Your antient & constant friend."

# From John Koontz

Harrisonsburgh Rockingham County
Octr 2[nd] 1809

SIR,

I was Informed yeasterday that you had some of the morino sheep a Stock I have for some time wished to be posses[d] off—but did not until then know they where so near me

Should my information be correct and you Should think proper to sell any of them please to Drop me a line Pr mail—and Insert your price for two Ewe[s] and a ram

I have been a long time keeping Store and continue the Business but of late—owing to the Illiberal treatment the american nation has received from the british government I Can not be Satisfyed to ware british manufactured good[s] myself, and all the clothing I wore since last spring (Except Shirts) Where manufactured in my family—and have them Ingaged at pressent in making cloth of common wool for my next winter Clothing—but it is Imposible to make fine Cloath out of course wool—and is in my opinion proper for Every Citizen possesing Land[s] to Incourage the raising the morino sheep as we theirby in a little time mite[1] superceed the british superfine Cloaths and

Exonerate ourselves in a grate measure from the necessity of Importing this Costley article

with High considerations of Respect I am sir your Humble servent

JOHN KOONTZ

RC (MHi); endorsed by TJ as a letter from John Roontz received 31 Oct. 1809 and so recorded in SJL.

John Koontz (d. 1830) kept a store in Harrisonburg, owned a number of properties in Rockingham County, and operated mills, a tanyard, and a tavern. He represented Rockingham County in the General Assembly, 1797–98 and 1821–24 (J. Houston Harrison, *Settlers by the Long Grey Trail* [1935, repr. 1975], 363–6; Leonard, *General Assembly*, 209, 310, 315, 320).

[1] Word interlined.

# To Thomas Mann Randolph (1792–1848)

DEAR SIR Monticello Oct. 2. 09.

Your favor of Sep. 15. came to hand only yesterday. I hasten therefore to inclose you letters to my two most particular friends Gen[l] Dearborne & mr Gerry. the latter lives at Cambridge. Gen[l] Dearborne lives, I believe, three miles from Boston, but comes to his office in town probably every day or two. wishing you a pleasant journey & profitable residence there, I salute you with esteem & respect.

TH: JEFFERSON

PoC (MHi); at foot of text: "M[r] Tho[s] M. Randolph"; endorsed by TJ. Enclosure: TJ to Henry Dearborn and Elbridge Gerry, 2 Oct. 1809.

# From William Henry Harrison

DEAR SIR Fort Wayne 3[rd] Oct. 1809.

M[r] John Johnston the U.S. Factor & Indian Agent at this place designing to pass through your neighbourhood on his way to the Seat of Government & having expressed a wish to pay his respects to you—I take great pleasure in the opportunity it gives me of making him personally known to you as a Gentleman of Amiable private Character & a highly zealous & usefull public Officer—Knowing the interest you take in the affairs of this Country particularly in those that relate to the Aborigines I refer you to M[r] Johnston as a person well able to Satisfy your enquiries wishing that you may long enjoy in private that happiness to which your eminent public Services so justly intitle you—

I remain my dear Sir with the cincerest respect your ever faithful friend & Serv[t] WILLIAM HENRY HARRISON

FC (MiU-C: Letterbook of Indian Agency at Fort Wayne); in John Johnston's hand; at foot of text: "Thomas Jefferson Monticello." Probably never received by TJ.

William Henry Harrison (1773–1841), later the ninth president of the United States, was born in Charles City County and educated at Hampden-Sydney College. He rose from ensign to captain in the United States Army, 1791–98, served successively as secretary of and congressional delegate for the Northwest Territory, 1798–1800, and was governor of Indiana Territory, 1800–13 (with concurrent service as its Indian commissioner from 1803). Harrison won engagements with the Indians at Tippecanoe Creek in 1811 and, as a major general during the War of 1812, at the Thames River in 1813. He represented Ohio in the United States House of Representatives, 1816–19, and the Senate, 1825–28, and he held the post of envoy extraordinary and minister plenipotentiary to Colombia from 1828–29 (*ANB*; *DAB*; Dorothy Goebel, *William Henry Harrison: A Political Biography* [1926]; Logan Esarey, ed., *The Messages and Letters of William Henry Harrison*, 2 vols. [1922]).

## To Samuel R. Demaree

SIR Monticello Oct. 4. 09.

Your favor of Aug. 22. was not recieved till the 20[th] of Sep. and I undertake with chearfulness to send you a catalogue of the best books I am acquainted with on the subjects stated in your letter. having lately made out one for some gentlemen who have associated themselves to join contributions & to purchase a library for their common use, I cannot do better than send you a copy of what was prepared for them. as they however restrained themselves to history, natural philosophy, & agriculture, I add on the same paper some on the subjects of geometry, Algebra, fluxions, the philosophy of mind, morals, & rhetoric as desired in your letter. you did not say whether your views comprehended any but English books, to which therefore I have confined myself. but many subjects are much better treated in French than English.

I am not acquainted with Rees's Encyclopedia; but I suppose it inferior to the British published by Dobson. but Owen's is a very good supplement to any collection of particular treatises, & costs in England but 8. Dollars. I know nothing of the memoirs of Thomas Jefferson. the newspapers say it is a libel written by one Carpenter alias Cullen,[1] sent over in British pay to edit newspapers here. he has done it in several states for some years, from which he has been successively driven. he knows just as much of me as of the man in the moon, except that he never saw me.

I tender you my salutations & assurances of respect.

Th Jeff[erson]

PoC (DLC); signature incomplete; at foot of text: "M^r Samuel R. Demaree"; endorsed by TJ; with 2d Dft of enclosed supplemental book list, printed below, on verso. Enclosure: TJ's List of Recommended Books, [ca. 4 Oct. 1809], printed as enclosure to TJ to John Wyche, 4 Oct. 1809.

[1] Preceding two words interlined.

ENCLOSURE

## Supplemental List of Recommended Books

Pike's arithmetic. 8^vo[1]
Simpson's Algebra. 8^vo
Emerson's[2] fluxions 8^vo
Simpson's Euclid 4^to
Gibson's surveying. 8^vo
Hutton's Mathematical tables 8^vo[3]
Locke on the human understanding 2. v. 8^vo[4]
Stewart's philosophy of the human mind. 4^to[5]
L^d Kaim's Natural religion. 8^vo
mrs Carter's Epictetus 2. v. 12^mo[6]
Collins's Marcus Antoninus. 8^vo[7]
Fielding's Memorabilia of Xenophon 2. v. 12^mo
Cicero's offices.
his philosophical works generally.
Seneca's morals by Bennett.
Enfield's history of philosophy. 2. v. 8^vo
Blair's Rhetoric. 3. v. 8^vo
Sheridan on elocution. 8^vo
Mason on poetical & prosaic numbers 8^vo
Kaim's elements of criticism. 2. v. 8^vo[8]

2d Dft (DLC: TJ Papers, 188:33507); in TJ's hand; undated; on verso of PoC of covering letter. 1st Dft (DLC: TJ Papers, 188:33441); in TJ's hand; undated; on verso of RC of Demaree to TJ, 22 Aug. 1809.

TJ omitted three titles between preparation of his 1st and 2d Dfts (see notes 1 and 8 below), including them instead on the book list he prepared jointly for Demaree and John Wyche.

[1] In 1st Dft this title, lacking volume size and preceded by a line reading "Geography. Pinkerton," appears to the right of three lines reading "Geometry. Arithmetic Astronomy" and linked by a brace.

[2] Word interlined in 1st Dft in place of "Saunderson's."

[3] 2d Dft: "9^vo." 1st Dft: "8^vo." Below this title in 1st Dft TJ canceled "Ferguson's" followed by a line reading "Metaphysics."

[4] Number and size of volumes omitted in 1st Dft.

[5] Volume size omitted in 1st Dft.

[6] Number and size of volumes omitted in 1st Dft.

[7] Volume size omitted in 1st Dft.

[8] 1st Dft concludes with two additional entries: "Dobson's Encyclopedia. 18. vo. 4$^{to}$" and "Owen's dict. of arts & sciences. 4. v. 8$^{vo}$."

## To Valentín de Foronda

DEAR SIR Monticello Oct. 4. 09.

Your favor of Aug. 26. came to hand in the succeeding month and I have now to thank you for the pamphlet it contained. I have read it with pleasure, and find the constitution proposed would probably be as free as is consistent with hereditary institutions. it has one feature which I like much; that which provides that when the three co-ordinate branches differ in their construction of the constitution, the opinion of two branches shall over-rule the third.[1] our constitution has not sufficiently solved this difficulty.

Among the multitude of characters with which public office leads us to official intercourse, we cannot fail to observe many whose personal[2] worth marks them as objects of particular esteem, whom we would wish to select for our society in private life. I avail myself gladly of the present occasion of assuring you that I was peculiarly impressed with your merit & talents, and that I have ever entertained for them a particular respect. to those whose views are single & direct, it is a great comfort to have to do business with frank & honorable minds. and here give me leave to make an avowal for which, in my present retirement, there can be no motive but a regard for truth. your predecessor, soured on a question of etiquette against the administration of this country, wished to impute wrong to them in all their actions, even where he did not believe it himself. in this spirit he wished it to be believed that we were in unjustifiable cooperation in Miranda's expedition. I solemnly, & on my personal truth and honor declare to you that this was entirely without foundation, & that there was neither cooperation nor connivance on our part. he informed us he was about to attempt the liberation of his native country from bondage, & intimated a hope of our aid or connivance at least. he was at once informed that altho we had great cause of complaint against Spain, & even of war, yet whenever we should think proper to act as her enemy, it should be openly & above board, & that our hostility should never be exercised by such petty means. we had no suspicion that he expected to engage men here, but merely to purchase military stores. against this there was no law, nor consequently any authority for us to interpose obstacles. on the other hand we deemed it improper to betray his voluntary communication to the agents of Spain. Altho' his measures were many days in preparation at New York, we never had the least intimation or suspicion of his engaging men in his enterprize until he was gone: and I presume the secrecy of his proceedings kept them equally unknown to the Marquis Yrujo, at Philadelphia[3] & the Spanish Consul at New York, since neither of them gave us any information of the enlistment of men until it was too late for any measures taken at Washington to prevent their departure. the officer in the customs who participated in this transaction with Miranda, we immediately removed, and should have had him and others further punished had it not been for the protection given them by private citizens at N. York in opposition to the government, who by their impudent falsehoods & calumnies were able to overbear the minds of the jurors. be assured, Sir, that no motive could induce me at this time to make this declaration so[4] gratuitously, were it not founded in sacred truth, and I will add further that I never did, or countenanced, in public life, a single act inconsistent with the strictest good faith, having never believed there was one code of morality for a public, & another for a private man.

I recieve with great pleasure the testimonies of personal esteem which breathe through your letter, & I pray you to accept those equally sincere with which I now salute you. TH: JEFFERSON

PoC (DLC); at foot of first page: "Don Valentin de Foronda."

The EXPEDITION of Francisco de Miranda, the renowned Latin American revolutionary, sailed from New York on 2 Feb. 1806 in the *Leander*, an American ship fitted out in New York and manned with a largely American crew. His attempt to liberate Venezuela was an abject failure. TJ and James Madison acted quickly against this palpable violation of American neutrality, unsuccessfully prosecuting Samuel G. Ogden, the *Leander*'s owner, and the complicit William Stephens Smith, and removing the latter from his office of surveyor of the port of New York. Because Miranda had dined with TJ and Madison in Washington in December 1805 and given them a disputed but probably incomplete indication of his intentions, the extent of the administration's prior knowledge became a matter of public discussion and congressional investigation (Miranda to Smith, 14 Dec. 1805, translation printed in [James Biggs], *The History of Don Francisco de Miranda's attempt to effect a Revolution in South America, in a series of letters* [Boston, 1810], 272–3; Malone, *Jefferson*, 5:80–8; Brant, *Madison*, 4:323–39).

Carlos Fernando Martínez, marquis de YRUJO, was Foronda's predecessor as Spanish minister to the United States. Thomas Stoughton was the SPANISH CONSUL AT NEW YORK.

[1] TJ here began a new paragraph with "Among the" and then overwrote it with the following sentence.

[2] Word interlined in place of "private."

[3] Preceding two words interlined.

[4] Word interlined.

## To Robert Quarles

SIR Monticello Oct. 4. 09.

I am sorry it is not in my power to give you any information how far the making a dam across the Rivanna might interfere with the rights of the James river company. having been absent from the state almost continually for 25. years, I am become quite uninformed of it's laws, not having even a copy of them. my dam affords no precedent, it's rights being prior to those of the company. my mill & dam have been established 52. years, and altho carried away in the mean time, & very long in the rebuilding, yet the right was always kept up by constant renewals of the order of court. I tender you my salutations & respects.

TH: JEFFERSON

PoC (MHi); at foot of text: "Mr Robert Quarles"; endorsed by TJ.

## To John Wyche

SIR Monticello Oct. 4. 09.

Your letter of Sep. 7. came to hand about a fortnight ago, & I have taken the first sufficient portion of time I have had at my command to make a catalogue of such select books as you desired on the subjects of history, natural philosophy & agriculture, which I now inclose you. I have added a general estimate of their amount. this goes beyond the sum mentioned as the amount of your funds; but I thought it better, as you expressed an expectation that they might be enlarged, and can in the mean time strike out such as are least within your immediate[1] views. supposing you meant to confine yourselves to English books principally, I have noted two only in the French language because they have never been translated & are valuable. not always knowing the best translations, I have in such cases stated the name of the author only that yourselves, or your agent might enquire for the best. wishing this safe to hand; I tender you my salutations & assurances of respect.

TH: JEFFERSON

PoC (CLU-C); at foot of text: "Mr John Wyche"; endorsed by TJ.

[1] Word interlined in place of "own."

E N C L O S U R E

## List of Recommended Books

History
Diodorus Siculus.
Justin
Herodotus by Littlebury 2. v. $8^{vo}$
Thucydides by Smith. 2. v. $4^{to}$
[perhaps there may be an $8^{vo}$ edition]
Xenophon's Hellenics.
Xenophon's Anabasis[1] by Spelman. 2. v. $8^{vo}$
Quintus Curtius by Digby. 2. v. $12^{mo}$
Stanley's lives of the Philosophers. $4^{to}$
Anacharsis 5. v. $8^{vo}$
Dionysius Halicarnasseus. by Spelman. fol.[2]
Polybius by Hampton. 2. v. $12^{mo}$
Livy by several hands 6. v. $8^{vo}$
Sallust by Gordon. $12^{mo}$
Caesar by Bladen $8^{vo}$
Plutarch's lives by Langhorne. 6. v. $8^{vo}$
Cornelius Nepos.
Middleton's life of Cicero. 3. v. $8^{vo}$
Middleton's miscellaneous[3] works. 5. v. $8^{vo}$
Tacitus by Gordon. 5. v. $12^{mo}$
Suetonius by Thompson. $8^{vo}$
Gibbons's Roman empire.[4] 12. v. $8^{vo}$
Millot's Antient history[5]
Kennet's antiquities of Rome. $8^{vo}$
Volney's Lessons on history. $8^{vo}$
Dictionnaire historique par l'Avocat. 4. v. $12^{mo}$
Millot's Modern history.[6]
Russel's history of Modern Europe 5. v. $8^{vo}$
Millot's history of France.[7]
Voltaire's Louis XIV. $12^{mo}$
Robertson's Charles V.[8] 4. v. $8^{vo}$
King of Prussia's works. 17. v. $8^{vo}$
Voltaire's life of Peter the great. $8^{vo}$
Tooke's life of Catharine II. 2. v. $8^{vo}$
Voltaire's Charles XII. $12^{mo}$
Kennet's history of England. 3. v. fol.[9]
Rapin's history of England. 12. v. $8^{vo}$
$M^{rs}$ MacCaulay's history.[10] 5. v. $8^{vo}$
Ludlow's Memoirs. 3. v. $8^{vo}$
Fox's history of James II. $8^{vo}$
Belsham's histories. 7. v. $8^{vo}$
Baxter's history of England.[11] 2. v. $12^{mo}$
Plowden's hist. of Ireland[12]
Buchanan's history of Scotland. 2. v. $8^{vo}$[13]
Robertson's history of Scotland. 2. v. $8^{vo}$

Robertson's hist. of America. 3. v. 8vo
Gordon's hist. of the Independce of America. 4. v. 8vo
A Ramsay's hist. of the American revolution 2. v. 8vo
A Mrs Warren's hist. of the American revolution. 3. v. 8vo[14]
A Belknap's hist. of N. Hampshire. 3. v. 8vo
A Hutchinson's hist. of Massachusets. 2. v. 8vo
A Minot's hist. of the[15] insurrection of Mass. in 1786. 8vo
A Williams's history of Vermont. 8vo
Smith's hist. of New York. 8vo
Smith's hist. of New Jersey. 8vo
A Proud's hist. of Pensylvania. 2. v. 8vo
A Findlay's hist. of the Western insurrection. 1794.[16]
A Burke's hist. of Virginia. 3. v. 8vo
Hewitt's hist. of S. Carolina. 2. v. 8vo
Mosheim's Ecclesiastical history 6. v. 8vo
A Priestley's Ecclesiastical history.
Priestley's hist. of the corruptions of Christianity 2. v. 8vo

---

Natural Philosophy.[17]

Scientific Dialogues. 8. vols. in 16s by Joyce[18]
Conversations in chemistry. 2. v. 12mo
Nature displayed. 7. v. 12mo
Franklin's Philosophical works. 4to
Martin's Philosophical grammar. 8vo
Martin's Philosophia Britannica. 3. v. 8vo
Nicholson's Introduction to Natural Philosophy 2. v. 8vo
Adams's lectures in Natl & experimentl philosophy 5. v. 8vo
Adams's Geometrical & Graphical essays. 2. v. 8vo
Ferguson's lectures on Mechanics 8vo[19]
Helsham's lectures on Mechanics. 8vo
Fontenelle's Plurality of worlds. 12mo[20]
Ferguson's astronomy. 8vo[21]
Pinkerton's[22] geography. 2. v. 8vo
A Scott's Universal gazetteer. 4. v. 8vo
Baker on the microscope. 8vo[23]
Buffon's Natural history.
Turton's Linnaeus. 7. v. 8vo
A Barton's elements of Botany. 2. v. 8vo

---

Agriculture.[24]

Dixon's husbandry of the Antients. 2. v. 8vo
Theatre d'Agriculture de De Serres. 2. v. 4to
Tull's horse hoeing husbandry. 8vo
Hale's body of Husbandry. 4. v. 8vo
Home's Gentleman farmer 8vo
Young's Rural oeconomy. 8vo
Young's Farmer's guide. 8vo
Young's course of Experimentl agriculture 3. v. 8vo
Young's Travels. 2. v. 8vo
A Boardley's essays on agriculture. 8vo[25]

A The New England Dictionary of agriculture $8^{vo}$
A M$^{c}$Mahon's American gardener's calendar $8^{vo}$
Knight on Apple & Pear trees, cyder and perry. $12^{mo}$
Combrun's theory & practice of brewing. $8^{vo}$
[*page 2:*]

General.[26]

Owen's Dictionary of arts & sciences. 4. v. $8^{vo}$
A Dobson's American Encyclopedia. 18. v. $4^{to}$
The Handmaid to the arts. 2. v. $8^{vo}$[27]

A very general estimate of those not marked A. which may be bought in England.

| | | | £ s d |
|---|---|---|---|
| 5. folios | @ 31/6 | sterl. = | 7–17–6 |
| 7. $4^{tos}$ | @ 20/ | | 7– 0–0 |
| 179. $8^{vos}$ | @ 8/ | | 71–12–0 |
| 91. $12^{mos}$ | @ 4/ | | 18 –4–0 |
| 8. $16^{s}$ | @ 3/ | | 1 –4–0 |

Cost in the shop there 105–17–6 = 476. D 40 c
charges of importation to be added.
They will cost from 50. to 100. p$^{r}$ cent more if bought in an American bookshop.
Those marked A. which are American publications, & can only be bought here are
18. $4^{tos}$ Dobson's } the prices of these are not known: but they will be
31. $8^{vos}$ } dearer probably than books of the same size in Europe.

PoC (CLU–C); entirely in TJ's hand; undated; brackets in original. Dft (CSmH: JF-BA); undated; lacking marginal notations indicating American publication and most of concluding section; on verso of RC of John Wyche to TJ, 7 Sept. 1809. Also enclosed in TJ to Samuel R. Demaree, 4 Oct. 1809.

ANACHARSIS: Jean Jacques Barthélemy, *Voyage du Jeune Anacharsis en Grèce, dans le Milieu du Quatrième Siècle avant l'Ère Vulgaire*, 5 vols. (Paris, 1789; Sowerby, no. 41).

1 Dft substitutes "Cyri exp." for preceding two words.
2 Dft here adds "£3–12."
3 Word interlined in Dft.
4 Dft: "Gibbons's Decline & fall of the Rom. emp."
5 Dft here adds (brackets in original here and in next two notes) "[4. v. $12^{mo}$ Fr]."
6 Dft here adds "[5. v. $12^{mo}$ Fr]."
7 Dft here adds "[3. v. $12^{mo}$]."
8 In Dft TJ here canceled "$12^{mo}$."
9 Dft here adds "£4–4."
10 Dft: "hist. of the Stewarts."
11 In Dft this entry ends "$4^{to}$."
12 Title omitted in Dft, which here has "L$^{d}$ Orrery's hist. of Engl$^{d}$ 2. v. $12^{mo}$."
13 Title interlined in Dft.
14 Title interlined in Dft.
15 In Dft TJ here canceled "rebellion."
16 Title inserted at right in Dft.
17 Subject heading omitted in Dft.
18 Preceding two words omitted in Dft.
19 In Dft TJ here adds "7/6."
20 In Dft TJ here adds "2/6."
21 In Dft TJ here adds "9/."
22 TJ here canceled "geometry."
23 Title interlined in Dft.
24 Subject heading omitted in Dft.
25 Title interlined in Dft.
26 Subject heading omitted in Dft.
27 Dft ends here.

## From Thomas Cadwalader

Sir, Philadelphia 6. October 1809.

Having been apprized that an Application was made to you in December last, to procure my nomination to a field-Officer's Commission in the Regiment of U.S. Cavalry, I beg leave to inform you that such application was made without my knowledge, or authority.

I have the Honor to be, Sir, your most obedient, humble Servant,

Thos Cadwalader

RC (MHi); at foot of text: "Thomas Jefferson Esqre"; endorsed by TJ as received 11 Oct. 1809 and so recorded in SJL.

Thomas Cadwalader (1779–1841) graduated from the University of Pennsylvania in 1795 and was admitted to the bar in 1801. He had joined the Second Troop Philadelphia City Cavalry by 1799 and was elected captain of the unit in 1810. Cadwalader was a lieutenant colonel in the Pennsylvania militia during the War of 1812, rising to brigadier general in 1814 and major general in 1824. He was a trustee of his alma mater, 1816–36, and became a member of the American Philosophical Society in 1825 (*University of Pennsylvania: Biographical Catalogue of the Matriculates of the College, 1749–1893* [1894], 38; W. A. Newman Dorland, "The Second Troop Philadelphia City Cavalry," *Pennsylvania Magazine of History and Biography* 53 [1929]: 283–6; APS, Minutes, 15 Apr. 1825 [MS in PPAmP]).

The application of december last has not been found.

## To William Eustis

Dear Sir Monticello Oct. 6. 09

Sollicited by a poor man in an adjoining county who states his case in the inclosed letter, & truly, as far as I can learn, I take the liberty of putting it under cover to you, in the hope you will be so good as to put it into the hands of the proper clerk, that whatever is right may be done, &, if nothing can be done, that the clerk may certify the grounds, so as to inform the applicant & put him at rest. the paper, if inclosed to me, shall be safely conveyed to him.

I am glad of an occasion of congratulating you as well as my country on your accession to a share in the direction of our Executive councils. besides the general advantages we may promise ourselves from the employment of your talents & integrity in so important a station, we may hope peculiar effect from it towards restoring deeply wounded amity between your native state & her sisters. the design of the leadin[g] federalists, then having direction of the state, to take advantage of the first war with England to separate the N.E. states from the union has distressingly impaired our future confidence in them. in this, as in all other cases, we must do them full justice, and make the fault all their own, should the last hope of human liberty be destined to recieve it's final stab from them. I salute you with great esteem & respect. TH: JEFFERSON

PoC (DLC); left margin faint; at foot of text: "The honble D[r] Eustis"; endorsed by TJ. Enclosure: John Porter to TJ, 17 Sept. 1809 (not found, but recorded in SJL as received from Louisa on 25 Sept. 1809).

William Eustis (1753–1825), physician and political leader, was a native of Cambridge, Massachusetts. Following his graduation from Harvard in 1772 and subsequent medical training, he served as an army surgeon during the American Revolution. He later helped found the Society of the Cincinnati and was vice president of its Massachusetts chapter. Eustis represented Boston in the lower house of the Massachusetts legislature, 1788–94, and sat in the United States House of Representatives, 1801–05, during which he established himself as a moderate Republican. James Madison appointed Eustis secretary of war in March 1809. During his tenure Eustis reorganized his department and the army, with mixed results that led to his resignation in December 1812. He served as envoy extraordinary and minister plenipotentiary to the Netherlands, 1814–18, returned to the House of Representatives, 1820–23, and was governor of Massachusetts from 1823 until his death (*ANB*; *DAB*; *Sibley's Harvard Graduates*, 18:70–84; *JEP*, 2:118–20, 595, 596 [6, 7 Mar. 1809, 16, 17 Dec. 1814]).

# From James Madison

DEAR SIR Washington Oc[r] 6. 1809

I inclose for perusal a letter from M[r] Dupont D. N. What does he mean by his desire "to contribute" to the Execution of his project of Education? You will observe that he has sent for you a copy of the Works of Turgot, as far as Edited. Be so good as to point out the mode in which you wish them to be transmitted. I expect a Waggon here next month which can take them to Orange, if you prefer that arrangement to a water one to Richmond.

The late news from Europe will be found in the Newspapers. Jackson has been presented, and is on the threshold of business. He is not deficient in the diplomatic professions, but nothing appears, to contradict the presumption that he is so in the requisite instructions.

We left Montpellier on friday last and reached Washington on monday about 3 OC. The heat was very oppressive on the road & has so continued since our arrival; notwithstanding a fine shower of rain the evening before the last. Be assured always of my affectionate & high respects JAMES MADISON

RC (DLC: Madison Papers); endorsed by TJ as received 8 Oct. 1809 and so recorded in SJL. Enclosure: Pierre Samuel Du Pont de Nemours to Madison, Paris, 11 July 1809, congratulating the new president; avowing his attachment to

America and his eventual intention to join his sons there; expressing his desire to contribute to the implementation of his plan for national education in the United States, if Madison thinks it feasible; sending seven volumes of his edition of Turgot's works; seeking permission to come to America on a public vessel; reporting that he has sent to his family commentaries on improving American tanneries and on breeding merino sheep; complaining that he has been unable to obtain permission to export his sheep to America and hinting that Madison's intervention may be needed; and asking in a postscript for Madison's assistance in forwarding sets of Turgot to TJ, the American Philosophical Society, and his children (RC in DLC: Madison Papers; printed with condensed translation in Madison, *Papers, Pres. Ser.*, 1:285–6).

# To John Minor

Dear Sir Monticello Oct. 6. 09.

I have executed a deed to Richard Tompkins as you desired, and acknoleged it at our last court, of which I inclose you a certificate. the substance of the deed was a conveyance to him of all the right & title vested in me and which I might convey lawfully & without injury to the rights of others. it is without warranty even against my own acts done heretofore, for I had totally forgotten that I was a trustee for Bernard Moore, and much more what acts I might have performed under the trust. I believe none; for neither my situation nor occupations could have permitted it. I salute you with constant esteem & respect. Th: Jefferson

PoC (MHi); at foot of text: "Col° John Minor"; endorsed by TJ. Enclosure not found.

# To John Smith (1750–1836)

Dear Sir Monticello Oct. 6. 09.

I am desirous of sowing largely the next spring a kind of grass called Tall meadow oat, or Oat-grass, and sometimes, erroneously Peruvian grass, which I am told is much cultivated about Winchester, but cannot be had here. I have flattered myself I could so far make free with your friendship as to ask you to procure for me about a couple of bushels to be put into a tight barrel & forwarded to Staunton to the care of judge Stewart. I understand that waggons pass very frequently from Winchester to Staunton. I wish it to be of this year's seed, as I found it would not come up the second year, on a trial of some procured for me by mr Nourse which arrived too late in the first spring to be sowed. whatever the cost is, it shall be remitted to you at Washington as soon as you will be so kind as to make it known to me, including if you please the price of transportation to Staunton, that all may be settled in a single remittance. if you have cultivated it, I should thank you for any instructions your experience may enable you to give, as to the soils it will delight in, or do in, the sowing & the care of it, the produce E[t]c for I am much a stranger to it. wishing you a quiet & successful campaign at Washington, & reposing myself confidently under the care & superintendance of yourself & fellow-labourers I salute you with all possible esteem & respect. TH: JEFFERSON

PoC (MoSHi: TJC-BC); at foot of text: "Gen. John Smith"; endorsed by TJ.

John Smith (1750–1836), of Hackwood Park in Frederick County, represented that county in the House of Delegates, 1777–79 and 1786–87, sat in the state senate, 1791–94, and served as a Republican in the United States House of Representatives, 1801–15. As county lieutenant during the American Revolution, he guarded Hessian prisoners, and he was commissioned a brigadier general in the militia in 1801 and major general in 1811 (Thomas K. Cartmell, *Shenandoah Valley Pioneers and Their Descendants: A History of Frederick County, Virginia* [1909], 296; *Biog. Dir. Cong.*; Leonard, *General Assembly*; *Richmond Whig & Public Advertiser*, 12 Mar. 1836).

# To John Adlum

SIR Monticello Oct. 7. 09

While I lived in Washington, a member of Congress from your state (I do not recollect which) presented me with two bottles of wine made by you, one of which, of Madeira colour, he said was entirely factitious, the other, a dark red wine was made from a wild or native grape, called in Maryland the Fox grape, but very different from what is called by that name in Virginia. this was a very fine wine, & so exactly resembling the red Burgundy of Chambertin (one of the best crops) that on fair comparison with that, of which I had very good on the same table imported by myself from the place where made, the company could not distinguish the one from the other. I think it would be well to push the culture of that grape, without losing our time & efforts in search of foreign vines, which it will take centuries to adapt to our soil & climate. the object of the present letter is so far to trespass on your kindness, & your disposition to promote a culture so useful, as to request you, at the proper season to send me some cuttings of that vine. they should be taken off in February, with 5. buds to each cutting, and if done up first in strong linen & then covered with paper & addressed to me at Monticello near Mil-

ton, and committed to the post, they will come safely & so speedily as to render their success probable. praying your pardon to a brother-amateur in these things, I beg leave to tender you my salutations & assurances of respect.
Th: Jefferson

RC (CLjC); at foot of text: "Maj[r] Adlam." PoC (DLC); endorsed by TJ. Enclosed in Adlum to TJ, 5 June 1822, and TJ to Adlum, 13 June 1822. Printed (dated 11 Nov. 1809) in *American Farmer* 4 (1823): 343.

John Adlum (1758–1836), surveyor and viticulturist, was a native of York, Pennsylvania, a Revolutionary War veteran, an associate judge in Lycoming County, Pennsylvania, 1795–98, and a major in the United States Army, 1799–1800. In 1805 he settled at Wilton, a farm near Havre de Grace, Maryland, and developed a reputation as an authority on grapes and wine making. Adlum eventually established a farm and nursery in Georgetown. Best known for his propagation of the Catawba grape, he also actively sought government patronage for his vineyard and for experimental agriculture, and he published *A Memoir on the Cultivation of the Vine in America, and the Best Mode of Making Wine* (Washington, 1823; Poor, *Jefferson's Library*, 6 [no. 260]) and *Adlum on Making Wine* (Georgetown, 1826). Adlum's correspondence with TJ began with this letter and touched primarily on wine and grape cultivation (*DAB*; Howard H. Peckham, ed., *Memoirs of the Life of John Adlum in the Revolutionary War* [1968]; Heitman, *U.S. Army*, 1:154).

Gabriel Christie was the MEMBER OF CONGRESS from Maryland who introduced TJ to wine from the WILD OR NATIVE Alexander grape which, due to Adlum's efforts, by 1816 became the first American grape grown commercially (Adlum to TJ, 15 Feb. 1810; *MB*, 2:1323n).

# To Isaac Riley

Sir
Monticello Oct. 7. 09.

I have duly recieved your favor of Sep. 29. proposing to publish a new edition of the Notes on Virginia, and asking for such additions as I might wish to make. I have long intended to prepare an enlarged edition of that work; with such additions & corrections as information & experience might enable me to make: and I have been laying by materials from time to time, as they occurred, for that purpose. but it will be long yet before other occupations will permit me to digest them; & observations & enquiries are still to be made, which will be more correct in proportion to the length of time they are continued, and this may probably be through my life. it is most likely therefore that it may be left to be posthumously published. in the mean time I should not be willing to propose any partial execution of the design.

Such of the American editions as I have seen have been very incorrect, & some of them so much so as to be really libels on the understanding of the author. the private edition printed at Paris under my own inspection is the most correct. there were I think but one or two typographical errors in it. but this edition was never sold. there were but 200. copies printed, which I gave as presents to my friends. the London edition printed by Stockdale in 1787. is tolerably correct. should you execute your purpose of reprinting the work I have two copies of the Paris edition remaining, of which I will send you one, supposing you might not be able otherwise to procure either a copy of that or of the London edition, which is also correct enough. I tender you my salutations & respects. TH: JEFFERSON

PoC (DLC); at foot of text: "M[r] J. Riley"; mistakenly endorsed by TJ as a letter to John Riley and so recorded in SJL.

# To Joel Barlow

DEAR SIR Monticello Oct. 8. 09.

It is long since I ought to have acknoleged the reciept of your most excellent oration on the 4[th] of July. I was doubting what you could say, equal to your own reputation, on so hackneyed a subject. but you have really risen out of it with lustre, and pointed to others a field of great expansion. a day or two after I recieved your letter to Bishop Gregoire a copy of his diatribe to you came to hand from France. I had not before heard of it. he must have been eagle eyed in quest of offence to have discovered ground for it among the rubbish massed together in the print he animadverts on. you have done right in giving him a sugary answer. but he did not deserve it. for notwithstanding a compliment to you now & then he constantly returns to the identification of your sentiments with the extravagancies of the Revolutionary zealots. I believe him a very good man, with imagination enough to declaim eloquently, but without judgment to decide. he wrote to me also on the doubts I had expressed five or six & twenty years ago, in the Notes on Virginia, as to the grade of understanding of the negroes, & he sent me his book on the literature of the negroes. his credulity has made him gather up every story he could find of men of colour (without distinguishing whether black, or of what degree of mixture) however slight the mention, or light the authority on which they are quoted. the whole do not amount in point of evidence, to what we know ourselves of Banneker. we know he had spherical trigonometry enough to make almanacs, but not without the suspicion of aid from Ellicot, who was his neighbor & friend, & never missed an opportunity of puffing him. I have a long letter from Banneker which shews him to have had a mind of very common stature indeed. as to Bishop Gregoire, I wrote him, as you have done, a very soft answer. it was impossible for doubt to have been more tenderly or hesitatingly expressed than that was in the Notes of Virginia, and nothing was or is farther from my intentions than to enlist myself as the champion of a fixed opinion, where I have only expressed a doubt. St Domingo will, in time, throw light on the question.

I intended, ere this, to have sent you the papers I had promised you. but I have taken up Marshal's 5th volume & mean to read it carefully, to correct what is wrong in it, and commit to writing such facts and annotations as the reading that work will bring into my recollection and which have not yet been put on paper. in this I shall be much aided by my memorandums & letters, and will send you both the old & the new. but I go on very slowly. in truth during the pleasant season I am always out of doors employed, not passing more time at my writing table than will dispatch my current business. but when the weather becomes cold I shall go out but little. I hope therefore to get through this volume during the ensuing winter; but should you want the papers sooner, they shall be sent at a moment's warning. the ride from Washington to Monticello in the stage, or in a gigg is so easy that I had hoped you would have taken a flight here during the season of good roads. whenever mrs Barlow is well enough to join you in such a visit, it must be taken more at ease. it will give us real pleasure whenever it may take place. I pray you to present me to her respectfully, and I salute you affectionately. TH: JEFFERSON

RC (NjP: Straus Autograph Collection); endorsed by Barlow. PoC (DLC); at foot of first page: "Mr Barlow."

Joel Barlow (1754–1812), poet and diplomat, was born in Connecticut, graduated from Yale College in 1778, and served as a chaplain during the American Revolution. In 1788 he sailed for Europe as representative for the Scioto Associates. Barlow remained abroad for seventeen years following the collapse of that real-estate venture, dividing his time between France, where he was named a French citizen; Hamburg, where he established a successful mercantile business; and Algiers, where as American minister in 1797 he negotiated the release of 119 American prisoners. A liberal thinker who collaborated with William Blake and rescued the manuscript of Thomas Paine's *Age of Reason* when Paine was arrested in 1793, Barlow's own publications included *The Vision of Columbus* (Hartford, 1787; Sowerby, no. 4302), *A Letter to the National Convention of France . . . To which is added The Conspiracy of Kings* (London, 1792; Sowerby, no. 2825), *The Hasty-Pudding* (New York, 1796), *Prospectus of a national institution, to be established in the United States* (Washington, 1806), and *The Columbiad* (Philadelphia, 1807; Sowerby, no. 4301). He returned to the United States in 1804 and took up residence at Kalorama, his estate in Washington, D.C. In 1811 James Madison appointed Barlow minister plenipotentiary to France, in which capacity he died of pneumonia in Poland while seeking Napoleon's signature to a treaty. Barlow's correspondence with TJ included wide-ranging discussions of the arts and sciences in addition to political topics (*ANB*; *DAB*; Dexter,

*Yale Biographies*, 4:2–16; Barlow obituary enclosed in Pierre Samuel Du Pont de Nemours to TJ, 10 Feb. 1813; Charles Burr Todd, *Life and Letters of Joel Barlow* [1886]; James Leslie Woodress, *Yankee's Odyssey: The Life of Joel Barlow* [1958]).

ORATION: Joel Barlow, *Oration delivered at Washington, July Fourth, 1809* (Washington, 1809; Sowerby, no. 4686).

Barlow's friend Henri GREGOIRE, the constitutional bishop of Blois, was a former French revolutionist whose recently published *Critical Observations on the poem of Mr. Joel Barlow, The Columbiad* (Washington, 1809) criticized Barlow's poem as anti-Catholic and generally irreligious. Barlow's SUGARY ANSWER, dated 13 Sept. 1809, was published as the pamphlet *Letter to Henry Gregoire . . . in reply to his letter on The Columbiad* (Washington, 1809).

Grégoire's BOOK was *De la Littérature des Nègres* (Paris, 1808; Sowerby, no. 1398). TJ, who also owned Grégoire's *Lettre aux Philanthropes, sur les malheurs, les droits, et les réclamations des Gens de couleur de Saint-Domingue* (Paris, 1790; Sowerby, no. 1388), was clearly unconvinced by Grégoire's favorable assessment of the intellectual capacity of blacks (Paul Finkelman, *Slavery and the Founders: Race and Liberty in the Age of Jefferson* [2001], 164–6). Benjamin BANNEKER was a free African American who taught himself astronomy and, with the encouragement of George Ellicott and Elias Ellicott, members of the Maryland Society for the Abolition of Slavery, prepared an ephemeris for 1791. The Ellicotts' cousin Andrew Ellicott, a prominent surveyor, brought Banneker's mathematical accomplishments to TJ's notice. Banneker's long letter to TJ of 1791 enclosed a second ephemeris (Banneker to TJ, 19 Aug. 1791, and TJ to Banneker, 30 Aug. 1791, *PTJ*, 22:49–54, 97–8; Silvio A. Bedini, *The Life of Benjamin Banneker* [1972], 72–102, 152–9, 280–3). TJ sent Grégoire his VERY SOFT ANSWER on 25 Feb. 1809 (DLC).

TJ had TAKEN UP the fifth volume of John Marshall's *Life of George Washington* (1804–07; Sowerby, no. 496). He believed this biography to be overly partisan and unsuccessfully sought to persuade Barlow to counter Marshall's Federalist interpretation by writing a competing Republican history of the United States during the early national period (Malone, *Jefferson*, 5:356–9; TJ to Barlow, 3 May 1802 [DLC]).

# To George Jefferson

DEAR SIR Monticello Oct. 8. 09.

Tomorrow being the last[1] day fixed by our sheriff's for the reciept of the taxes of the year, I shall draw on you in their favor for the amount of mine, being somewhere about 70.D. this will be in one or two draughts at their convenience & paiable at sight. I know there cannot remain as much of my last remittance as will meet this sum, but I am in daily expectation of recieving a sum which will enable me to cover the excess, & to furnish also the advances necessary for my grandson. he will be with you after the first frost. a person of the name of Jones has written to mr Randolph that he takes boarders at 120.D. but we learn that his house is crouded, & a separate room is indispensable to enable a student to derive all the benefit he should from his instructions. Jefferson would be pleased to be wherever John Bankhead boards. but both might lose time by mutual intru-

sions on each other. we shall leave him therefore to your friendly discretion. I am to meet the representatives of B.[2] Skelton and J. Fleming in Richmond at mr Ladd's office on the 20th instant, and shall lodge at the Swan by recommendation of Judge Fleming who promised to engage me a room there, as our mutual concern in the business we meet on will render it convenient that we should be together. my stay will not be over one or two days. I shall then have the pleasure of seeing you as I have long wished.
in the mean time Adieu affectionately TH: JEFFERSON

PoC (MHi); at foot of text: "Mr George Jefferson"; endorsed by TJ.

[1] Word interlined.
[2] Initial added in margin.

# To George Sullivan

SIR Monticello Oct. 8. 09.

I have to acknolege the reciept of your favor of Sep. 15. the most interesting enquiries for us respecting the French spinning machine are 1. whether, when adjusted for spinning wool, cotton, & flax, it is as simple as the former spinning machines? 2. whether it requires, as they do any & what preparatory machines, such as for carding, roving Etc 3. whether they can be made on a small scale of from 6. to 20. spindles for the use of a single family. & 4. the price comparatively with the former machines. in answer to your enquiry how they may best be introduced for sale in this state, I must inform you we have no large manufactories in Virginia. this state, tho' without any comparison, manufacturing more clothing[1] than any other in the union, does it all in private families, each for it's own use, & no more. no homespun is ever to be bought scarcely in our stores. hence you see the importance to us of the above enquiries. whenever you shall be able to answer them, I shall recieve the information with thanks. I salute you with esteem & respect. TH: JEFFERSON

PoC (NjP, 1947); at foot of text: "George Sullivan esq."; endorsed by TJ.

[1] Word interlined.

# To William Fontaine

DEAR SIR Monticello Oct. 9. 09.

I recieved last night only your favor of Sep. 16. by that I percieve you are uneasy at something which you suppose to have passed from yourself here and which you now review with dissatisfaction. to what you allude I have no conception. certainly I did not remark a word or an act but of the strictest propriety. the same easy conduct & pleasant frank conversation which has ever made a part of your character with your friends, gave equal pleasure to us all here, as well the family as our guests: and the family as well as myself saw you here with great pleasure after so long an intermission of time: and we all regretted, when we met at breakfast, that you were no longer with us. I hope nothing occurred here to make you apprehend any neglect on our part. this would indeed be a subject of deep regret to me, as no such thing could have been intended. I hope therefore you will be perfectly at peace with yourself on this subject, and that under the assurance that my esteem for you has never been diminished, you will accept my sincere declaration that no one's visit can ever be more welcome here: and should any circumstance call you in future into our neighborhood, I hope you will not deny me the pleasure of recieving you here. in the mean time be assured of my constant friendship & respect.

TH: JEFFERSON

PoC (MHi); at foot of text: "Col. W. Fontaine"; endorsed by TJ.

## To James Madison

DEAR SIR Monticello Oct. 9. 09.

I recieved last night yours of the 6th & now return mr Dupont's letter. at a time when I had a hope that Virginia would establish an University I asked of mr Dupont & Dr Priestly to give me their ideas on the best division of the useful sciences into Professorships: the latter did it concisely; but Dupont wrote an elaborate treatise on education which I still possess. after I saw that establishment to be desperate, & with it, gave up the view of making it the legatory of my library, I conceived the hope, & so mentioned to Dupont, that Congress might establish one at Washington. I think it possible that the willingness he expresses to contribute to the execution of his plan, may be by becoming President, or a professor. but this is conjecture only. the copy of Turgot's works he has sent me will come best by the mailstage, if put into the care of any passenger of your acquaintance who may be coming as far as Fredericksburg, and will there get Benson to transfer the packet to the Milton stage. Jackson's mountain will, I think produce but a mouse. the affairs of Walcheren & Spain may perhaps give him a little courage. the crop of corn turns out worse than was expected. there certainly will not be half a common crop. it's scarcity and price will produce infinite distress. I set out in three days for Richmond, where I am summoned to be on the 20th.[1] with my best respects to mrs Madison I am ever affectionately yours

TH: JEFFERSON

RC (DLC: Madison Papers); closing and signature clipped. PoC (DLC); at foot of text: "The President of the US."; endorsed by TJ. Enclosure: Pierre Samuel Du Pont de Nemours to Madison, 11 July 1809 (see note to Madison to TJ, 6 Oct. 1809).

In 1800 TJ asked Du Pont and Joseph Priestley to GIVE ME THEIR IDEAS on the scientific courses to be taught at a university. Priestley responded with several pages of "Hints concerning Public Education" on 8 May 1800 [DLC]. Later that year Du Pont sent TJ his extended TREATISE *Sur l'éducation nationale dans les États-Unis d'Amérique*, which he published in Paris in 1812 (TJ to Priestley, 18 Jan. 1800, TJ to Du Pont, 12 Apr. 1800, and Du Pont to TJ, 24 Sept. 1800 [DLC]; Gilbert Chinard, ed., *The Correspondence of Jefferson and Du Pont de Nemours* [1930], xc–xcvii, 26–7; Malone, *Jefferson*, 3:448–51).

Recent newspaper accounts described the British occupation in July 1809 of the island of WALCHEREN in preparation for an attack on Flushing and Antwerp and Sir Arthur Wellesley's defeat of the French at the Battle of Talavera in SPAIN (Washington *National Intelligencer*, 4, 6 Oct. 1809).

[1] RC clipped; remainder supplied from PoC.

## From Madame de Tessé

Aulnay 9 8bre 1809

je profite, Monsieur, d'une occasion bien favorable pour vous envoier les marons d'inde que vous m'avés demander dans un juste intervale entre leur maturité et leur germination.

Mr de la Fayette m'accusera de ceder a mon Gout seulement, Lorsque je crois Remplir un devoir d'équité en vous priant de placer dans votre bibliotheque La gravure d'un illustre voyageur, passionné de votre Gouvernement, et grand admirateur de votre personne. je ne doute point que Mr humbold ne soit tres flatté de se trouver á monticello quand il en aura connoissance, mais jai pourtant quoiqu'en puisse dire mon neveu; moins d'envie de lui plaire par cet envoi, que de plaisir a le Recompenser.

S'il venoit a Apostasier, jettés la gravure au feu. que d'apostats! je ne me console point de n'avoir pas eu deux heures de Mr Coles a ma petite campagne. vous ne me verrés plus que decrepite parceque vous me verrés comme il m'a vue a Paris. s'il vous eut rendu compte de mon jardin, entierement mon ouvrage, vous sauriés que j'ai encore de Lâme, de L'imagination et L'aspect attristant de la vieillesse s'effaceroit de votre souvenir. si josois vous rendre compte d une conversation que jai eue il y a deux jours avec M[r] de La fayette je vous paroitrois peutêtre d'une jeunesse inquietante pour votre bonté. car je bâtissois un systême de choses qui vous conduira a faire un voyage en france et je me suis vue peu a peu a La descente de votre voiture ou vous aviés choisi votre Logement.

agreés je vous supplie avec votre indulgence et votre bonté ordinaire, Monsieur, tout ce que je vous ai consacré de Reconnoissance, d admiration et d'attachement, etc NOAILLES-TESSÉ

les glands du chêsne verd n'ont point muris cette anneé.

EDITORS' TRANSLATION

Aulnay 9 October 1809

I take advantage, Sir, of a very favorable opportunity to send you the horse chestnuts that you asked me to send when they were halfway between their maturation and their germination.

Mr. de Lafayette will accuse me of yielding only to my tastes, while I believe I am fulfilling a debt of equity by begging you to place in your library the engraving of an illustrious traveler, a devotee of your government, and a great admirer of your person. I do not doubt in the least that Mr. Humboldt will be very flattered to find himself at Monticello when he learns of it, but I have, however, whatever my nephew might say about it, less a desire to please him by sending it than pleasure in repaying him.

If he should come to renounce his principles, throw the engraving in the fire. So many apostates! I cannot console myself for not having had two hours with Mr. Coles at my little country house. You will always imagine me henceforth as decrepit because you will imagine me as he saw me in Paris. If he had given you an account of my garden, which is entirely my own creation, you would know that I still have soul and imagination, and the saddening aspect of old age would be erased from your memory. If I dared to give you an account of a conversation that I had two days ago with Mr. de Lafayette, I would perhaps appear to you to be too youthful for your compassion. For I was constructing a plan that would lead you to make a trip to France and little by little I imagined myself at the moment when you descended from your carriage at the place you had chosen for your lodging.

Accept I beg you with your customary indulgence and compassion, Sir, all the gratitude, admiration and affection, etc. which I have devoted to you.

NOAILLES-TESSÉ.

The acorns of the holm oak did not mature at all this year.

RC (MoSHi: TJC-BC); endorsed by TJ as received 27 Dec. 1809 and so recorded in SJL; notation by TJ (probably written in connection with his 27 Mar. 1811 reply to this and two other letters): "09. June 12 Oct. 9. 10. Mar. 24 Maron[s] d'Inde. Assculus hippocastanea Castanea sativa Humboldt by C[t] Pahlen Short's disappint Paulinia aurea. Kaelventaria my visit." Translation by Dr. Amy Ogden. Enclosure not found. Enclosed in Lafayette to TJ, 26 Oct. 1809.

## To George Jefferson

Dear Sir Monticello Oct. 10. 09

According to my letter of the 8th I had yesterday given to mr Woods our sheriff an order on you for the amount of my taxes 69. D 67 C something less than I had expected. last night I recieved my quarterly account & found that in the estimate I had made of my funds in your hands I had lost sight of the 240.D. interest on my note. not immediately prepared to make a new provision for my taxes I must pray you to honor the draught & I will take the speediest measures in my power to cover the deficiency. I expect to be at Eppington on the 15th & in Richmond the 20th.

Your's affectionately Th: Jefferson

PoC (MHi); at foot of text: "Mr George Jefferson"; endorsed by TJ.

Micajah Woods was deputy SHERIFF of Albemarle County (*MB*, 2:1231, 1248).

SJL confirms that on 9 Oct. 1809 TJ RECIEVED an undated letter from George Jefferson enclosing his QUARTERLY ACCOUNT, July–September 1809, neither of which has been found.

## To Benjamin Henry Latrobe

Dear Sir Monticello Oct. 10. 09.

Your favor of Aug. 28. came duly to hand, and I congratulate you on the succesful completion of your great arch of the Senate chamber as well as that of the Hall of Justice. I have no doubt you will finish those rooms so as to be worthy counterparts of that of the Representatives. it would give me pleasure to learn that Congress will consent to proceed on the Middle building. I think that the work when finished will be a durable and honorable monument of our infant republic, and will bear favorable comparison with the remains of the same kind of the antient republics of Greece & Rome. I have no doubt that your Cerealian capital will be handsome: and shall be happy to recieve the Model of it. the stone which Andrei and Franzoni are preparing for me, need only be sculptured on one side. I propose to set it into the middle of the frize of a Chimney piece.

Your promised visit to Monticello, whenever it can be effected, will give me real pleasure, and I think could not fail of giving some to you. my essay in Architecture has been so much subordinated to the law of convenience, & affected also by the circumstance of change in the original design, that it is liable to some unfavorable & just criticisms. but what nature has done for us is sublime & beautiful and unique.

you could not fail to take out your pencil & to add another specimen of it's excellence in landscape to your drawing of the Capitol & Capitol hill. the difficulty would be in the choice between the different scenes,[1] where a panorama alone could fully satisfy. I salute you with great esteem & respect. TH: JEFFERSON

PoC (DLC); at foot of text: "M[r] Latrobe"; endorsed by TJ.

The DRAWING may have been Latrobe's 1806 perspective of the east and north front of the United States CAPITOL (Latrobe, *Papers*, 2:410).

[1] Reworked from "between different portions."

# To John Milledge

DEAR SIR Monticello Oct. 10. 09.

I have recieved from M. Thouin, Director of the National garden of France a collection of many different species of rice. whether any of them possess any properties which might render them preferable to those we possess, either generally, or under particular circumstances of soil or climate I know not. but the scripture precept of 'prove all things & hold fast that which is good' is peculiarly wise in objects of agriculture. as ours is not a climate for experiments on that plant, I think I cannot better dispose of the packet than by putting it into your hands, who have so much the power, as well as the disposition to essay whatever promises an useful result. I have for you a very fine Iceland ram with 4. horns, who will be sent down the river, as soon as the season restores it's navigation, to Messieurs Gibson & Jefferson of Richmond to be forwarded to mr Newton at Norfolk for you. should the laws permit I must make another effort, through your kind instrumentality, to send some of your two kinds of Cotton seed to the Agricultural society of Paris. we shall probably know ere long whether our intercourse with that country will be re-opened soon. with my respectful compliments to mrs Milledge I salute you with great esteem & respect. TH: JEFFERSON

PoC (DLC); at foot of text: "Gov[r] Milledge"; endorsed by TJ.

John Milledge (1757–1818), Revolutionary War veteran and lawyer, was a member of the colonial and state assemblies, United States representative (1792–93, 1795–98, 1801–02), governor of Georgia (1802–06), and United States senator (1806–09). He strongly backed TJ politically and served as president pro tempore of the Senate from 30 Jan. 1809 until he resigned and retired from public service that November. Milledge grew wealthy as a planter and was active in experimental agriculture and husbandry, developing a method for extracting sesame oil and working on improvements in cotton and wool production. He also made a key land donation to and was otherwise instrumental in the founding of the University of Georgia (*ANB*; *DAB*; Barbara Buckley Brown, "John Milledge: Patriot, Politician, Philanthropist, 1757–1818" [master's thesis, Georgia State University, 1980]; *JS*, 4:333 [30 Jan. 1809]).

The SCRIPTURE PRECEPT is from 1 Thessalonians 5.21.

# From George Williamson

SIR, Baltimore Oct 10th 1809

No ordinary occasion should induce me to intrude on your leisure hours. you will perceive that the work, the prospectus of which I send you, has more than ordinary claims on the literati of this Country. I regreat that I have not an acquaintance in your State whom I can interest, and through whom this might have been presented to you. had my honorable friend Doctor Mitchill still continued in the U.S. I Should not have been under the necessity of thus intruding on you. however, I could hardly with justice to myself, and my country,[1] withhold a prospectus, of this nature, from one who is universally known to be the friend and patronizer of every laudable persuit; and of every literary work, which promisses, as this does, to be extensively usefull.

With respect I am &c G WILLIAMSON

RC (MHi); endorsed by TJ as received 30 Oct. 1809 and so recorded in SJL.

George Williamson, a physician residing at 61 Pratt Street, Baltimore, began his professional studies in Richmond under James Currie and completed them in Philadelphia, where he met TJ in 1792 (*PTJ*, 24:582; William Fry, *The Baltimore Directory for 1810* [Baltimore, 1810], 190).

The enclosed PROSPECTUS, not found, may have been an early promotion for Williamson's translation of the second edition of Étienne Tourtelle's *Elemens d'hygiène* (Paris, 1802), which Williamson eventually published as *The Principles of Health: Elements of hygiene, or, A treatise on the influence of physical and moral causes on man, and on the means of preserving health* (Baltimore, 1819; Poor, *Jefferson's Library*, 5 [no. 185]). See also Williamson to TJ, 5 July 1819, and TJ to Williamson, 11 July 1819. TJ knew Samuel Latham MITCHILL, a prominent New York City physician and scientist then touring Canada, from his service in Congress during TJ's presidency and their shared intellectual interests (*Some of the Memorable Events and Occurrences in the Life of Samuel L. Mitchill of New-York from the year 1786–1828* [ca. 1828], 3).

[1] Manuscript: "county."

# To Albert Gallatin

DEAR SIR Monticello Oct. 11. 09

I do not know whether the request of M. Moussier, explained in the inclosed letter, is grantable or not. but my partialities in favor of whatever may promote either the useful or liberal arts, induce me to place it under your consideration, to do in it whatever is right, neither more nor less. I would then ask you to favor me with three lines in such form as I may forward him by way of answer.

I have reflected much & painfully on the change of dispositions which has taken place among the members of the cabinet since the new arrangement, as you stated to me in the moment of our separation. it would be indeed a great public calamity were it to fix you in the purpose which you seemed to think possible. I consider the fortunes of our republic as depending, in an eminent degree, on the extinguishment of the public debt, before we engage in any war. because, that done, we shall have revenue enough to improve our country in peace, & defend it in war, without recurring either to new[1] taxes or loans, but if the debt shall[2] once more be swelled to a formidable size, it's entire discharge will be despaired of, and we shall be committed to the English career of debt, corruption & rottenness, closing with revolution. the discharge of the debt therefore is vital to the destinies of our government, and it hangs on mr Madison & yourself alone. we shall never see another president & Secretary of the Treasury making all other objects subordinate to this. were either of you to be lost to the public, that great hope is lost. I had always cherished the idea that you would fix on that object the measure of your fame, and of the gratitude which our country will owe to you. nor can I yield up this prospect to the secondary considerations which assail your tranquility. for sure I am, they never can produce any other serious effect. your value is too justly estimated by our fellow citizens at large as well as their functionaries to admit any remissness in their support of you. my opinion always was that none of us ever occupied stronger ground in the esteem of Congress than yourself, and I am satisfied there is no one who does not feel your aid to be still as important for the future as it has been for the past. you have nothing therefore to apprehend in the dispositions of Congress, & still less of the President, who, above all men, is the most interested, & affectionately disposed to support you. I hope then you will abandon entirely the idea you expressed to me, & that you will consider the eight years to come as essential to your political career. I should certainly consider any earlier day of your retirement as the most inauspicious day our new government has ever seen.       in addition to the common interest in this question, I feel particularly for myself the considerations of gratitude which I personally owe you for your valuable aid during my administration of the public affairs, a just sense of the large portion of the public approbation which was earned by your

labors & belongs to you, & the sincere friendship and attachment which grew out of our joint exertions to promote the common good, & of which I pray you now to accept the most cordial & respectful assurances.
TH: JEFFERSON

RC (NHi: Gallatin Papers); at foot of first page: "M$^r$ Gallatin"; endorsed by Gallatin, with comment: "Refers to the intrigues of R$^t$ Smith & Giles against me." PoC (DLC). Enclosure: J. B. Moussier to TJ, 14 Sept. 1809.

Albert Gallatin (1761–1849), a native of Geneva, Switzerland, immigrated to the United States in 1780 and settled in 1784 in Pennsylvania, which he represented briefly in the United States Senate in 1793 before losing his seat for not meeting the residency requirement, and again in the House of Representatives, 1795–1801, where he quickly established himself as an outspoken and effective critic of Federalist financial policies. In 1801 TJ appointed him secretary of the treasury, a post he retained until 1814. Gallatin was in Europe helping to negotiate the Treaty of Ghent with Great Britain, 1813–15, and he served as minister plenipotentiary to France from 1816–23 and to Britain from 1826–27. He corresponded regularly with TJ, with whom he shared an interest in Native American languages and culture that later culminated with service in 1842 as founder and first president of the American Ethnological Society (*ANB*; *DAB*; Raymond Walters Jr., *Albert Gallatin: Jeffersonian Financier and Diplomat* [1957]).

TJ sought to dissuade Gallatin from the GREAT PUBLIC CALAMITY of his resignation as secretary of the treasury. During his August 1809 visit to Monticello with the Madisons, Gallatin had confided to TJ that his disgust with the machinations of a faction headed by his fellow cabinet member Robert Smith and Republican senators Samuel Smith, William Branch Giles, and Michael Leib had led him to consider this option (Walters, *Gallatin*, 223–5).

[1] Word interlined.
[2] PoC: "should."

# To William Thornton

DEAR DOCTOR Monticello Oct. 11. 09

I return you a thousand thanks for the fine pair of sheep you have sent me. they arrived in perfect health & so continue and will I trust enable me to get into that breed entirely. I am also well pleased to learn both the manner & success with which you have commenced the removing the tail, for I really believe it must be practised, however heterodox to the sex it may appear to consider that part as an incumbrance. I think less of the Cape sheep on account of their long legs, & therefore shall not attempt to raise them, however thankful I am to you for the offer of procuring them. I think it possible the Vicuña might be raised in the mountains from which the rivers of the Floridas run, for I believe they are Monticolas. if the Camel can succeed at all in our continent it must be in the sands of the same country. the red legged partridge, the skylark & nightengale ought certainly to be colonized to this country, even at the public expence:

but that being hopeless, I would join in any rational plan of introducing them by private efforts. the tarragon you were so kind as to send me is now growing with the former bunch; but so extraordinary has been our drought that no efforts could save the figs. I think, in the spring, I must ask a few very small plants or cuttings to be done up in strong paper & addressed to me by post. I will take some occasion of sending you some cuttings of the Marseilles fig, which I brought from France with me, & is incomparably superior to any fig I have ever seen. since the 14th of July we have had but 2. Inches of rain. the usual quantity falling in that time is 14.I. present me respectfully to the ladies of your family & accept yourself my friendly salutations & assurances of respect T[H: JEFFERSON]

PoC (DLC); signature largely cut off; at foot of text: "Dr Thornton"; endorsed by TJ.

MONTICOLAS: classical Latin for mountain-dwellers (*OED*).

## From Isaac Riley

SIR New York October 16, 1809

I was duly honoured with your polite favour of the 7th Instant respecting the Notes on Virginia—

It is a source of regret that a work so much sought for as the Notes on Virginia, and so much valued for its accurate and various information, should have been so often given to the public in an imperfect state of typographical execution.—It is my wish to have it published in a superior style, and with the most perfect correctness. But I fear that without any thing of new matter introduced, it would not command an immediate sale, so as to reimburse me shortly for its expences. As it is one of the standing Stock Books among Booksellers, it would not fail to meet orders, but the mere copy of the Volume as it now stands, would not sell in Quantities so as to make its republication an object with any one printer—

A few pages of illustrative, additional and corrective matter, would secure the run of an edition, and would by no means interfere with the larger and more perfect Edition contemplated to be published hereafter.—If therefore it can be at all Consistent with your studies and affairs to give me these little additions, noted on blank leaves in the Paris Copy, I trust the work would then more than vindicate all that the reputation of the author has suffered from the garbled Copies already extant.—Excuse Sir my importunity, the public I concieve would be benefitted by such an Edition of the Notes on Virginia, and it would be my pride to publish the first correct and perfect Copy of the work in the United States.—

I am respectfully Your very Humble Servant I. RILEY.

RC (DLC); between dateline and salutation: "Hon. Thomas Jefferson"; endorsed by TJ as received 30 Oct. 1809 and so recorded in SJL.

# From Clotworthy Stephenson

SIR Washington City Oct^r 16^th 1809

You will particularly obliege by informing where you left my papers deposited with you respecting my Claim againts the U.S. for sevices rendred at the Mariene Barracks in this city. I have made enquiry of M^r Goldsborough he informs that he has not seen them[1] your goodness will Excuse

I am respectfully Sir your Hble Ser^t

CLOTWORTHY STEPHENSON

RC (MoSHi: TJC-BC); endorsed by TJ as received 30 Oct. 1809 and so recorded in SJL.

Clotworthy Stephenson (d. 1819), an Irish joiner, arrived in Virginia about 1787 and, with fellow joiner John Hart, constructed much of the new Virginia State Capitol's interior woodwork. In 1793 he moved to Washington, D.C., where he was heavily involved in the building of the United States Capitol and superintended work from May–July 1801 on the commandant's house at the Marine Barracks (Stephenson's fidelity oath, 8 Aug. 1787, Richmond Hustings Court Order Book, 2:190, Vi; Sumpter T. Priddy III and Martha C. Vick, "The Work of Clotworthy Stephenson, William Hodgson, and Henry Ingle in Richmond, Virginia, 1787–1806," *American Furniture* [1994]: 206–33; Benjamin Henry Latrobe to Paul Hamilton, [27?] Nov. 1811, and Latrobe to Stephenson, 30 Nov. 1811, in MdHi: Latrobe Letterbook; Jeffrey A. Cohen and Charles E. Brownell, eds., *The Architectural Drawings of Benjamin Henry Latrobe* [1994], 2:331; Washington *National Intelligencer*, 27 Nov. 1819). Stephenson had written a similar letter to TJ on 24 Feb. 1809 (MoSHi: TJC-BC).

[1] Manuscript: "th."

# From Luis de Onís

Georgetown 17th October 1809.

The Chevalier de Onis, has the honor of presenting his respects to His Excellency M^r Jefferson, and encloses to him a letter of introduction from his friend M^r Isnardy of Cadiz. The Chevalier would have wished to have delivered the letter in person, but the distance to Monticelo does not permit him, at present, to have that pleasure.

The Chevalier de Onis avails himself of this opportunity of assuring His Excellency M^r^ Jefferson of the high respect and consideration he entertains of his distinguished public & private virtues, and is extremely anxious to have the honor of forming his acquaintance.

RC (DLC); dateline at foot of text; endorsed by TJ as received 30 Oct. 1809 and so recorded in SJL, with endorsement adding that TJ replied on 4 Nov. 1809. Enclosure: Josef Yznardy to TJ, 3 Aug. 1809.

Luis de Onís y González, Vara, López y Gómez (1762–1827) was minister plenipotentiary of the Supreme Junta of Spain to the United States. He joined the Spanish Ministry of State in 1798 and helped negotiate the short-lived peace treaty of Amiens with France in 1802. Onís reached New York on 4 Oct. 1809 and had recently arrived in Washington, but due to doubts whether his British-backed government or its Napoleonic rival was actually in control in Spain, compounded by indiscretions of his own serious enough that James Madison later complained of them in a confidential message to Congress, Onís was not officially recognized as minister until 1815. His American tour of duty culminated in the Adams-Onís Treaty of 1819, under which the United States acquired Florida and the boundaries between the remaining Spanish possessions in North America and the United States were established. Onís subsequently represented Spain as ambassador to Great Britain (Angel del Rió, *La Misión de Don Luis de Onís en los Estados Unidos [1809–1819]* [1981], 193–208; Madison, *Papers, Pres. Ser.*, 3:108; Onís, *Memoria Sobre las Negociaciones entre España y los Estados Unidos de América* [1820; repr. ed. Jack D. L. Holmes, 1969], xv–xxix).

# From John Brahan

SIR, Nashville Tennessee 18^th^ October 1809

It is with painful Sensations that I Announce to You the death of His Excellency Meriwether Lewis Governor of Upper Louisiana which took place on the morning of the 11^th^ Instant; The following Circumstances attending this unhappy affair I have obtained from Major James Neelly Agent to the Chickasaw nation—he informs me that he left the Chickasaw Bluffs in Company with the Governor the last of Sep^r^ on their way to this place—that the Governor appeared some days thereafter while on their Journey, to be Some what deranged in mind; after crossing Tennessee River and traveling one day one of the Governors & one of Maj^r^ Neellys horses got away from the place where they had encamped. the Governor proposed to the Maj^r^ to remain behind and find the horses, & that he would proceed on his Journey and wait for him at the first house from there inhabited by White people. to which the Major agreed & the Governor proceeded on with his Servant[1] & Maj^r^ Neellys—to the house of a M^r^ Grinder where he arrived about sun set—no person being at home but the wife of M[r] Grinder—the woman discovering the governor to be deranged gave him up the house, and Slept herself in another house near it—the two Servants Slept in a Stable loft Some distance off: about three oClock the woman heard two pistols fire off. being alarmed She went & waked the servants when they came in they found him weltering in his blood. he had shot himself first it was thought in the head. the ball did not take effect. the other Shot was a little below his breast, which proved Mortal: he lived until Sun rise & expired—the Maj[r] had him decently buried.[2] Maj[r] Neelly informs me that he has got his two trunks with his Valuable papers, Amongst which is his Journal to the pacific Ocean, & perhaps Some Vouchers for Public Money expended in the Territorial Government of Upper Louisiana—he has also got his Silver watch—his Brace of pistols, his Rifle & Dirk—one of his horses was lost in the Wilderness which may probably be got again, the other horse John Purney the Governors Servant will ride on, who will leave here early in the Morning for Monticello: Maj[r] Neelly has Given him fifteen Dollars to take him on; and I was fearful that he might be Short of money & have furnished him with five dollars more which will be sufficient—I would have given him more but was fearful it might cause him to drink as I discover he has a propensity at present. but perhaps it may be from distress of mind at the death of the Governor—I shall remain in this place Some time and will with great pleasure attend to any instruction you may think necessary. either in Sending on the trunks of papers or the other articles of his property whereever directed—which will probably be to Monticello—I feel great distress at the premature death of the Governor he was a very particular friend of mine, being intimately acquainted, and one for whom I had the Greatest respect & Esteem—

I have the honor to be With Great respect, Your M[o] Ob Ser[t]

John Brahan Cap[t]
2[D] Regt U:S. Infy

PS. I am told that Governor Lewis left two trunks & some other articles with Capt Gilbert C Russell Commanding Officer at the Chickasaw Bluffs JB

RC (DLC); addressed: "Thomas Jefferson Esquire late President U States Monticello, near Charlottsville Virg[a] Mail"; franked and postmarked; endorsed by TJ as received 24 Nov. 1809 and so recorded in SJL.

John Brahan (1774–1834), a United States Army officer from Virginia, served as a first lieutenant in the 7th Infantry Regiment from January 1799 until the unit disbanded in June 1800, reentered the service as a second lieutenant in the 2d Infantry Regiment in February 1801, and was promoted by TJ to first lieutenant in June 1801 and captain in July

1806. He resigned his commission on 1 Jan. 1810, six months after President James Madison appointed him a receiver of public monies for Madison County, Mississippi Territory. Brahan held this post until his dismissal in 1820 for various financial improprieties. He also served as a contractor for General Andrew Jackson's forces during both the Creek War and the War of 1812, attempted to raise troops from Madison County during the latter conflict and, after hostilities had ended, was appointed a major general in the Alabama militia (Jackson, *Papers*, 2:50, 3:405, 430; Heitman, *U.S. Army*, 1:240; *JEP*, 2:122, 125 [16, 21 June 1809]; *ASP, Public Lands*, 3:485–92).

[1] Manuscript: "Sevant."
[2] Preceding six words interlined.

# From Valentín de Foronda

Muy Señor mio: Philadelphia 18 de Oct$^{e}$ de 1809.

Vm me ha escrito una carta deliciosa. La aprobacion de mi papelito por un Sabio, por un Philantropo, por un verdadero Philosofo como el Gran Jefferson hace empabonar mi sensibilidad, de modo que parece un Pabo Real.

Vuelvo à remitir à Vm el mismo folleto bastante mejorado aunque trabaxado en pocas horas: Vm. conocerà que no digo todo lo que podria decir: Confieso à un philosofo, que no me atrevo á explicarme como me explicaria, si escribiera en el Globo de la libertad que aun no se conoce. Sí—no se conoce ni en las Americas: pues muchos sabios callan por que muchos de los Gazeteros y muchisìmos de sus lectores tienen las cabezas boca à bajo. Yo estaba tentado à hacer una disertacion; pero no puedo perder un minuto para desmantelar mi casa, ordenar mis papeles, arreglar mis asuntos porque debo partir dentro de 10 dias en la Fragata que ha conducido al Ministro Plenipotenciario el Caballero Onis.

Si Vm me honra con dos lìneas de respuesta sirvase enviar la carta à D$^{n}$ Thomas Stoughton Consul de España en New York, que cuidara de remitirmela.

Espero hacer uso con mi Gobierno de quanto Vm. me dice del asunto de Miranda, y aunque es injuria al Gran Jefferson decir que creo su relacion, esperanzado en su tolerancia digo que la tengo por veridica, por cierta porque lo dice Jefferson.

He procurado traducir los pensamientòs de la carta de Vm. para que no perdierà su belleza pasando à la lengua Castellana.

He escrito algunas veces con vigor á este Gobierno, pero siempre le he respetado, jamas he hecho poner nada en los papeles publicos: nunca he intrigado, nunca he hablado à ningun Miembro del Congreso para que alborote: nunca he sembrado la cizaña, y siempre he elogiado à Vm. y al S[r] Madisson. No todo ha sido virtud: pues sabia que mi Corte deseaba la harmonia, y amistad con estos Estados.

Quito el gas à mi pluma para suplicarle me mande con toda libertad en todos los destinos con la confianza de que tendrè una particular complacencia en emplearme en cosas agradables al Gran Jefferson por cuya vida pido à Dios gue[1] su vida m[s] a[s].

B. L. M. de Vm su mas atento Servidor

VALENTÍN DE FORONDA

EDITORS' TRANSLATION

DEAR SIR: Philadelphia 18 October 1809.

You have written me a delightful letter. The approval of my little paper by a sage, a philanthropist, and a true philosopher like the great Jefferson strokes my sensibility, so that it seems like that of a peacock.

I send the same pamphlet to you again significantly improved although worked on for only a few hours. You knew that I did not say all that I could: I confess to a philosopher that I do not dare to explain myself as I would have if I had written in the world of liberty that is as yet unknown. Yes, it is not even known in the Americas: so many wise men are quiet because many journalists and a lot of their readers have their heads face down. I was tempted to give a lecture; but I cannot waste a minute from dismantling my household, putting my papers in order, and organizing my affairs because I leave in 10 days on the frigate that brought the minister plenipotentiary, Caballero Onis.

If you honor me with two lines in response, send the letter to Don Thomas Stoughton, the Spanish consul in New York, who will make sure I get it.

I hope to make useful to my government what you tell me about the Miranda matter, and even though it is an insult to the great Jefferson to say that I believe his story, hoping for his tolerance I say that I believe it to be truthful, certainly because Jefferson says so.

I have endeavored to translate the thoughts contained in your letter so that they will not lose their beauty when they are translated into Spanish.

I have written with vigor a few times to this government, but I have always respected you, I have never put anything into the public papers: never have I schemed, spoken to any member of Congress to incite a riot, nor sown discord, and I have always praised you and Mr. Madison. Not all have been so virtuous: but I knew that my Court wanted harmony and friendship with these states.

I am running out of ink for my pen as I beg you to direct me, with total freedom under all circumstances, with the confidence that I take particular pleasure in employing myself in activities agreeable to the great Jefferson for whom I ask God to preserve your life for many years.

I kiss your hand your most attentive servant

VALENTÍN DE FORONDA

RC (DLC); endorsed by TJ as received 30 Oct. 1809 and so recorded in SJL. Translation by Dr. Jennifer McCune.

EL MISMO FOLLETO: no second edition has been found of Foronda's pamphlet proposing a new Spanish constitution, for which see Foronda to TJ, 26 Aug. 1809. Possibly the copy Foronda enclosed here contained handwritten revisions.

[1] Abbreviation for "guarde."

# From James Neelly

SIR, Nashville Tennessee 18th Octr 1809

It is with extreme pain that I have to inform you of the death of His Excellency Meriwether Lewis, Governor of upper Louisiana who died on the Morning of the 11th Instant and I am Sorry to Say by Suicide;

I arrived at the Chickasaw Bluffs on or about the 18th of September, where I found the Governor (who had reached there two days before me from St Louis) in Very bad health—It appears that his first intention was to go around by Water to the City of Washington; but his thinking a War with England probable, & that his Valuable papers might be in dainger of falling into the hands of the British, he was thereby induced to Change his route, and to come through the Chickasaw nation by land; I furnished him with a horse to pack his trunks &c[1] on, and a man to attend to them; having recovered his health in Some digree at the Chickasaw Bluffs, we Set out together. And on our arrival at the Chickasaw nation I discovered that he appeared at times deranged in mind, we rested there two days & came on. one days Journey after crossing Tennessee River & where we encamped we lost two of our horses, I remained behind to hunt them & the Governor proceeded on, with a promise to wait for me at the first houses[2] he Came to that was inhabited by White people; he reached the house of a Mr Grinder about Sun Set, the man of the house being from home, and no person there but a woman who discovering the governor to be deranged gave him up the house & slept herself in one near it, his Servant and mine Slept in the Stable loft some distance from the other houses,[3] the woman reports that about three OClock She heard two pistols fire off in the Governors Room: the Servants being awakined by her, came in but too late to save him. he had shot himself in the head with one pistol & a little below the Breast with the other—when his[4] Servant came in he Says; I have done the business my good Servant give me Some water. he gave him water, he Survived but a short time, I came up Some time after, & had him as decently Buried as I could in that place—if there is any thing wished by his friends to be done to his grave I will attend to their Instructions,

I have got in my possession his two trunks of papers (amongst which is said to be his travels to the pacific Ocean) and probably some Vouchers for expenditures of Public Money for a Bill which he Said had been protested by the Sec^y of war; and of which act to his death, he repeatedly complained. I have also in my Care his Rifle, Silver watch, Brace of Pistols, dirk & tomahawk: one of the Governors horses was lost in the wilderness which I will endeavour to regain, the other I have Sent on by his Servant who expressed[5] a desire to go to the governors mothers & to Monticello:[6] I have furnished him with fifteen Dollars to Defray his expences to Charlottsville; Some days preveous to the Governors death he requested of me in Case any[7] Accident happened to him, to Send his trunks with the papers therein to the President, but I think it Very probable he meant to You—I wish to be informed what arrangements may be considered best in Sending on his trunks &c—I have the honor to be

With Great respect Y^r Ob Ser^t

James Neelly
U.S. agent to the Chickasaw nation

the governor left two of his trunks at the Chickasaw Bluffs in the Care of Capt Gilbert C. Russell. Commanding officer, & was to write to him from Nashville what to do with them.

RC (DLC); in John Brahan's hand, signed by Neelly; at foot of text: "The Honble Thomas Jefferson late President of United States Monticello near Charlottsville V^a"; endorsed by TJ as received 23 Nov. 1809 and so recorded in SJL. Dupl (ViW: TC-JP); entirely in a clerk's hand; endorsed by TJ as a "Duplicate." Enclosed in TJ to James Madison, 26 Nov. 1809, and Madison to TJ, 11 Dec. 1809.

James Neelly served as United States agent to the Chickasaw Nation from 8 July 1809 until 4 June 1812. He apparently served in the military during the War of 1812, and in 1817 Chickasaw leader Tishomingo recommended that he be reinstalled as agent (Madison, *Papers, Pres. Ser.*, 4:592n; Jackson, *Papers*, 4:476).

This and John Brahan's letter of the same date are evidently the earliest extant accounts of Meriwether Lewis's death and burial at Grinder's Inn, on the Natchez Trace in Tennessee. TJ subsequently received other accounts (Gilbert C. Russell to TJ, 4, 31 Jan. 1810) and was involved with and kept apprised of the recovery of Lewis's effects (TJ to C. & A. Conrad & Co., 23 Nov., 11 Dec. 1809; TJ to Madison, 26 Nov. 1809; Isaac A. Coles to TJ, 5 Jan. 1810; William Dickson to TJ, 20 Feb. 1810; TJ to Dickson, 20 Apr. 1810; TJ to Benjamin Smith Barton, 6 Oct. 1810; Barton to TJ, 16 Oct. 1810).

Lewis's term as territorial governor had been difficult and contentious. He was coming to WASHINGTON to defend protested official financial instruments. Even if they were honored, unsuccessful land investments had put him on the brink of financial ruin. With him he carried the journals of the Lewis and Clark Expedition, which TJ counted on him to prepare for publication but on which Lewis had in fact done no significant work. Given this background and these accounts, those who knew Lewis best, including TJ and William Clark, seem to have accepted the death as a suicide without hesitation or subsequent doubt. The counterhypothesis that Lewis was murdered did not emerge in TJ's lifetime but has since attracted its share of supporters (Nashville *Democratic Clarion*, 20 Oct. 1809; Saint Louis *Missouri Gazette*, 4 Oct. 1809, 2 Nov. 1809; TJ to Paul Allen, 18 Aug. 1813; James J. Holmberg, ed., *Dear Brother: Letters of William Clark to Jonathan Clark* [2002], 206–9, 216–23; Jackson, *Letters of Lewis and Clark*, 2:470–4, 487–8, 573–5n; Peale, *Papers*, vol. 2, pt. 2, p. 1238).

Lewis's SERVANT was John Pernier.

[1] Abbreviation omitted in Dupl.
[2] Dupl: "house."
[3] Dupl: "house."
[4] Dupl: "my."
[5] RC: "expessed." Dupl: "expressed."
[6] RC: "Monticllo." Dupl: "Monticello."
[7] In Dupl "thing" is canceled here.

# To John Austin

DEAR SIR Richmond Oct. 20. 09.

After congratulating you, which I do sincerely, on your continuance in life & good health, I have to add that I am at this place, engaged in the settlement of the accounts between mr Wayles & Bathurst Skelton's estates. a considerable article of debet in the accounts of mr Wayles is for the rebuilding the Tob$^{o}$ house & quarters on the island after the great fresh. I think there is nobody now living but yourself who can prove that fact, and the Attorney for Skelton's representatives has consented that your deposition shall be taken at m$^{r}$ Ladd's office at any time tomorro[w] before the meeting of the court, say at 10. aclock. will you, my good Sir, be so kind as to come to town by that hour, and depose whatever you can recollect on that subject. now that I am here, I am very anxious to get this business finished, which can only be done by your doing us this favor. I salute you with great esteem & respect. TH: JEFFERSON

SC (MHi); margin torn; endorsed by TJ as a letter to "Austin John."

John Austin was probably one of the men of that name living in Hanover County in 1810 (Elizabeth Petty Bentley, *Index to the 1810 Census of Virginia* [1980], 13).

# From Thomas T. Hewson

SIR, Philad$^{a}$ Oct 20$^{th}$ 1809.

The American Philosophical Society having received thro' you communications from M$^{r}$ Warden, M$^{r}$ Lambert & M$^{r}$ Treat, I am directed by the Society to express their thanks for your assistance in advancing the design of their institution, and to request that you will have the goodness to take upon yourself the trouble to transmit the enclosed to those gentlemen respectively.

I have the honour to be, Your obedient Servant,

THOS T HEWSON secretary of the A.P.S.

RC (DLC); at foot of text: "To Thos Jefferson Esqr"; endorsed by TJ as received 29 Nov. 1809 and so recorded in SJL.

Thomas Tickell Hewson (1773–1848), physician, was born in London, where Benjamin Franklin was a family friend. He immigrated to America in 1786, graduated from the University of the State of Pennsylvania in 1789, and went on to study medicine in Philadelphia, London, and Edinburgh. Hewson became prominent in Philadelphia's medical and scientific community, serving as secretary of the Philadelphia College of Physicians, 1802–35, and as its president from 1835 until his death. He took a leading role in the compilation of *The Pharmacopœia of the United States of America* (Philadelphia, 1820), the first such American work, and subsequent revisions. Elected to the American Philosophical Society in 1801, Hewson served as a secretary, 1803–17 and 1821–23, and a curator, 1817–21, and corresponded with TJ primarily concerning the society (Franklin Bache, *An Obituary Notice of Thomas T. Hewson, M.D.* [1850]; APS, Minutes, 17 Apr. 1801, [Jan. 1803], 3 Jan. 1817, 4 Jan. 1822 [MS in PPAmP]).

TJ had transmitted scientific COMMUNICATIONS from David Bailie WARDEN, William LAMBERT, and John Breck TREAT to the American Philosophical Society (TJ to Robert Patterson, 31 Aug., 1 Oct. 1809). The ENCLOSED items, not found, were probably printed acknowledgments of thanks "for your assistance, in thus advancing the design of their institution," with blanks in which a society secretary filled in the particulars of each donation. For an example, see Corresponding Secretary of American Philosophical Society to Alexander von Humboldt: Acknowledgment of Donation, 18 Aug. 1809 (PPAmP: APS Archives).

# From the Citizens of Richmond

SIR, [20 Oct. 1809]

A number of the citizens of Richmond, being informed of your arrival in this City, have assembled to testify their respect, and to welcome you to the metropolis of your native State.

Deeply impressed with a conviction of the important and distinguished services which you have rendered to your country, this meeting would deem itself as deficient in principle as in gratitude, were it not to avail itself of this occasion to give expression to its sentiments. In reviewing the incidents of your political life, this meeting sees its whole course marked with wisdom, with patriotism, and an ardent zeal in defence of the liberties of the people. At the dawn of the revolution we behold you in the public[1] councils one of the earliest and ablest asserters of the rights of your country, and one of the firmest and most undaunted opposers of the tyranny by which she was assailed. From your pen proceeded that masterly and incomparable exposition and declaration of the rights of independant America, which is justly regarded as the magna charta of the United States, which every good citizen must revere as sacred, and which he will hazard his life to preserve inviolate. From the congress of the United States, you were translated to a foreign court, where you laboured successfully to interest foreign nations in the welfare of your then infant country, which contributed to give confidence to her efforts and permanence to that independence which you had assisted to establish—Amidst the splendors of a court, you never ceased to cherish that ardent attachment to human rights, by which you have ever been distinguished, and you brought back that same republican purity of character, which was worthy of the struggle for liberty in which you were so important an actor. On your return to your native country you filled several high offices under the federal constitution, with no less honor to yourself than utility to the public; untill you were called on to preside over the affairs of the American people. The events of your administration, have passed recently before our eyes; we approv'd of your measures at the moment when they were adopted, and time and reflection have but served to confirm our original opinions. History will record that administration as characterised by œconomy in the management of the public resources, the diminution of patronage, the abolition of useless offices, steady and succesful efforts to discharge the public debt, an impartial and wise conduct to foreign nations, a solicitude to maintain peace with all the world on honorable terms, and above all by a scrupulous observance of the provisions of the constitution of the United States, and an ardent attachment and respect for the rights of the people.

The well earned glory, which you acquired, by managing the public concerns, on the principles which have been stated, could only receive additional lustre, from your voluntary and disinterested relinquishment of the highest office in the union, that you might thus illustrate by your practice, the sacred principles, for which you have always been the advocate.

But sir, we enjoy a heartfelt consolation for the loss of your services, in the acquisition of a successor, the friend and the associate of your labors, whose principles and whose views are concurrent with your own, and who will not fail to exhibit the same impartiality towards foreign nations, the same disposition to meet them on terms of reciprocity and friendship, and the same firmness in resenting their oppressions, which have uniformly marked your own administration. With such a man at the head of our executive, we will breast the storm which seems to hover over us, we view without dismay the spectacle of injustice, of open assault, of chicanery and secret intrigue, which is presented by foreign nations. We will make any sacrifices to preserve the rights & honor of our country, and for these in every exigency, we trust to the spirit and virtue of the people.

May you Sir, in the bosom of your family, surrounded by affectionate friends, and hailed by the plaudits of a grateful country, long, very long, continue to enjoy that tranquility and happiness, which are the unceasing fruits of an approving conscience, and the just and appropriate reward of a life devoted to the promotion of the public prosperity.

By Order of the Meeting. W: FOUSHEE chairman

Attest,

W^m MUNFORD Secretary—

MS (DLC: TJ Papers, 188:33543–5); undated; in a clerk's hand, signed by Foushee and Munford; at head of text: "To Thomas Jefferson Esq^r, late President of the United States"; endorsed by TJ as an "Address. citizens of Richm^d" received 21 Oct. 1809 and so recorded in SJL. Enclosed in a brief covering letter of 20 Oct. 1809 from Foushee, adding his own "most perfect accordance with the unanimous expression of the meeting" (RC in MHi; endorsed by TJ as received 21 Oct. 1809 and so recorded in SJL). Address and covering letter printed in Richmond *Enquirer*, 24 Oct. 1809.

William Foushee was a prominent Richmond physician, longtime postmaster, and the city's first mayor (Wyndham B. Blanton, *Medicine in Virginia in the Eighteenth Century* [1931], 326–8). William Munford was a court reporter and a member of the Virginia Council of State (*ANB*).

The day after TJ's 19 Oct. 1809 arrival in Richmond, a public meeting was held at the Virginia State Capitol, at which the participants resolved that they were "penetrated with the highest respect and admiration for the exalted character" of TJ and with "sincerest gratitude for the distinguished services" he had rendered; appointed a committee consisting of Philip Norborne Nicholas, William Wirt, Andrew Stevenson, Thomas Ritchie, William Robertson, Peyton Randolph, and William B. Hare to draft a suitable address; unanimously approved the result; instructed Foushee to deliver it; and appointed a committee of arrangements to hold a public dinner in TJ's honor at the Eagle Tavern on 21 Oct. 1809 (Richmond *Enquirer*, 24 Oct. 1809).

James Madison was TJ's SUCCESSOR as president.

[1] Word interlined.

# From Augustin François Silvestre

MONSIEUR, Paris, *20 octobre.* 1809

Je profite de l'occasion que m'offre le retour en amérique de l'aviso The happy Return, pour vous envoyer le 11^e volume des mémoires de la Société d'agriculture, que j'avais eu l'honneur de vous annoncer par ma dernière lettre du 8 juin. je desire qu'il vous offre quelque intérêt et que vous y reconnaissiez la persévérance des efforts de la Société pour le perfectionnement de l'art agricole.

Je joins à cet envoi le compte que j'ai rendu à la Société de Ses travaux pendant l'année 1808, et[1] quelques exemplaires d'une circulaire qu'elle a adressée à[2] ses correspondans, à l'effet d'obtenir des renseignemens Sur les différens procédés employés pour la conservation des diverses Substances alimentaires,[3] qui Servent à la nourriture soit de l'homme, soit des animaux domestiques. Son intention est de réunir dans un même ouvrage et Suivant un ordre méthodique, tous ceux de ces procédés, dont les avantages seront constatés par la pratique ou par des expériences faites en grand. La Société pense qu'un Semblable ouvrage ne Sera pas Sans un certain degré d'utilité; mais elle a besoin, pour son exécution, du concours de beaucoup[4] de coopérateurs et de la réunion d'une grande quantité de matériaux. Elle recevrait donc avec reconnaissance tous les renseignemens de ce genre qui lui Seraient adressés de vos contrées, où il doit exister Sans doute[5] des procédés économiques inconnus en Europe; elle accueillerait Surtout avec un intérêt particulier ceux que vous voudriez bien lui faire connaître vous même, et elle verrait dans cette communication un nouveau temoignage de celui que vous prenez à ses travaux.

S'il se trouvait quelque occasion où je pusse vous être utile à quelquechose dans ce païs-ci, je vous prie, Monsieur, de disposer de moi avec toute confiance, et de compter Sur mon zèle empressé à me conformer à vos desirs. Veuillez en attendant, agréer la nouvelle assurance de ma trez haute considération SILVESTRE

P.S. Oserais-je vous prier de faire-passer, par une voie sûre, la lettre ci-incluse à la personne pour laquelle elle est destinée? C'est l'un de mes plus intimes amis.

EDITORS' TRANSLATION

SIR Paris, *20 October* 1809

I take the opportunity provided by the return to America of the aviso The happy Return to send you the 11th volume of the proceedings of the Agricultural Society, which I had the honor to announce to you in my last letter of 8 June. I hope that you find it of some interest and that you recognize in it the society's persevering efforts toward perfecting the art of agriculture.

I enclose the account that I gave to the society of its work during the year 1808 and some copies of a circular that it sent to its correspondents, in an attempt to obtain information on different ways of storing the diverse foodstuffs used to feed both mankind and domestic animals. Its goal is to gather in a single volume, in methodical order, all of those modes of storage whose advantages have been noted through practice or through experiments on a large scale. The society thinks that such a book will not be without some degree of usefulness; but to bring it to fruition, we need the help of many collaborators and to gather a great quantity of material. It would therefore be grateful for all the information of this kind that it would receive from your country, where there must exist economical methods unknown in Europe. It would especially welcome with particular interest information concerning those methods about which you could personally inform us, and it would see in your contribution a renewed testimony of the interest you take in its work.

If any occasion arises for me to be of some use to you in this country, I pray, Sir, that you make use of me with full confidence, and that you rest assured of my zeal to conform to your wishes. Meanwhile, please receive renewed assurance of my very high consideration SILVESTRE

P.S. Dare I request that you have the enclosed letter sent on, through safe means, to the person to whom it is addressed? He is one of my most intimate friends.

RC (DLC); on printed letterhead of "Société d'agriculture du département de la Seine," with its insignia, partial dateline (with Silvestre's handwritten completion indicated in italics), and handwritten identification of himself as "membre de l'Institut" de France and secretary of the society; above salutation: "A Monsieur Jefferson, Associé-étranger de l'Institut et de la Société d'agriculture"; endorsed by TJ as received 7 Jan. 1810 and so recorded in SJL. Dft (Boston Public Library); at head of text: "N° 1267." Translation by Dr. Roland H. Simon. Enclosure: Silvestre, *Rapport sur les Travaux de la Société d'Agriculture du Département de la Seine Pendant l'année 1808* (Paris, 1808; Sowerby, no. 730; extracted from vol. 11 of the society's *Mémoires*). Other enclosures not found.

At Silvestre's request, on 27 Oct. 1809 David Bailie Warden forwarded TJ the MÉMOIRES DE LA SOCIÉTÉ D'AGRICULTURE, vol. 11. Peter Provenchere was UN DE MES PLUS INTIMES AMIS (TJ to Provenchere, 8 Jan. 1810).

[1] Passage from "le compte" to this point added in margin of Dft.

[2] In Dft Silvestre here canceled "tous" ("all").

[3] Word not in Dft.

[4] Preceding two words interlined in Dft in place of "d'un grand nombre" ("of a large number").

[5] In Dft Silvestre here canceled "beaucoup" ("many").

# From John Tyler

Oc$^{r}$ 20$^{th}$ 1809

The Governor's respects to M$^{r}$ Jefferson and begs leave to inform him that the Council of State and many Gentlemen wish his Company at the Eagle Tavern to morrow 4' OClock. If this be agreeable to him he will please to signify his inclination, and in that Case he will be good enough to dine with the Gov$^{r}$ the next day with his Companions

RC (DLC); dateline at foot of text; addressed: "M[r] Jefferson"; endorsed by TJ as received 20 Oct. 1809 and so recorded in SJL.

John Tyler (1747–1813), governor of Virginia, 1808–11, became acquainted with TJ in the 1760s at Williamsburg, where Tyler studied at the College of William and Mary and read law. He represented Charles City County in the Virginia House of Delegates, 1778–86 (as speaker, 1781–85), and he opposed the new federal constitution as vice president of the Virginia ratification convention in 1788. Tyler was a justice on Virginia's High Court of Admiralty, 1785–88, after which he served on the state's General Court, 1788–1808. With TJ's strong endorsement, Tyler won appointment early in 1811 as judge of the federal court for the district of Virginia and served until his death. His son and namesake became the tenth president of the United States (*DAB*; TJ to James Madison, 25 May 1810).

TJ attended two banquets in his honor while in Richmond, one organized by the officers of the 19th Regiment, held at the Swan Tavern on 20 Oct. 1809, and the other given the next day at the EAGLE TAVERN, presided over by Tyler (Richmond *Enquirer*, 24 Oct. 1809; Malone, *Jefferson*, 6:14; *MB*, 2:1249).

# From Henry Banks

SIR Richmond 21. Oct. 1809

I have the honor, herewith to send you, a publication relating to the Manufactory of Arms. Upon perusal you will find a development of a greater tissue of fraud and folly than has ever been before exhibited in this country. Altho many of the guilty persons are unmasked yet there are others, and it is with regret that I speak it, who deserve to be equally exposed.

To you it must be obvious that no public consideration ought at this time to weigh more than that of arming the Militia with proper Weapons, and it will be equally a sourse of regret, when you perceive that altho half a Milion of dollars of the peoples Money have been dissipated, there are at this time but few muskets fit for use and still fewer which deserve confidence. The reasons for this public Calamity are fully disclosed in the book now sent

Were I not well assured of the deep Interest which you take in the welfare of your country, and particularly of this State I should not have called your Attention to a Subject which will afford nothing to amuse, and as little to satisfy you with the manner in which the best interests of this commonwealth have been managed

With the highest approbation of the manner in which you have conducted the helm of our public Vessel, and equal confidence and hope, that you will still cherish a fostering Care for its future prosperity as well as safety, I have presumed thus to call your attention to matters which deserve a stronger hand than I have been abl[e] to exert.

I am most respectfully Your fellow citizen HENRY BANKS

RC (DLC); frayed; endorsed by TJ as received 21 Oct. 1809 and so recorded in SJL. Enclosure: Banks, *A Compendious View of the Establishment & Operations of Manufactory of Arms, and of the Late Public Investigation from the Commencement to the Expulsion of the Officers in February, 1809* (Richmond, 1809).

Henry Banks (1761–1836) was a merchant, lawyer, and pamphleteer in Richmond whose extensive land speculations in Kentucky and western Virginia were ultimately unsuccessful. TJ sold him and Thomas A. Taylor his Elk Hill plantation in 1793, accepting as security a mortgage on a large tract of Banks's land in Greenbrier County which became an asset of TJ's when payment for Elk Hill was not forthcoming. On behalf of Hunter, Banks & Company, Banks sued TJ in 1795 for the value of several vessels impressed by Virginia during the British invasion of 1781. As the wartime governor, TJ was the defendant only nominally, and he had himself removed from the suit before its eventual dismissal. In 1806 Banks published a series of newspaper articles lauding Napoleon. By 1823 he had moved to Frankfort, Kentucky (*PTJ*, 24:22n, 28:245–6, 353n; Joseph I. Shulim, "Henry Banks: A Contemporary Napoleonic Apologist in the Old Dominion," *VMHB* 58 [1950]: 335–45; Sowerby, nos. 3400–1; Clay, *Papers*, 3:449–50n).

# From Alexander McRae

Dear Sir, Richmond, 21st Oct., 1809

IT IS but a poor return I make for the friendship you have shewn to me, when I put you on your guard against a scoundrel.

If your leisure had permitted, it was my intention this day, in the course of conversation, to have communicated the information I shall now give you, and I would yet prefer a verbal communication, because it might be more full and satisfactory, than it can now be, writing as I do in great haste, but that will be impossible, as, at day-break tomorrow morning I shall be obliged to go on my way to Petersburg.

I think it my duty to guard you against the insidiousness and perfidy of the Sycophant and Hypocrite *William W. Hening*, the brother in law of the noted *Henry Banks*. I think it the more my duty, because I observed to-day, the obsequiousness and apparent good will, with which he approached you on the Porticoe of the Swan-tavern: He was pale however, and he trembled, for he saw that I was present, and he knew that I could and *ought* to disclose what would sink him forever in your estimation.

During the summer 1808, speaking of your administration, W. W. Hening said to me in presence of John Heth of the Council, that some of your appointments were worse than those made by either of your Predecessors, and by way of example he mentioned *two*. The first was, the appointment of Mr. Trist to some office at Natchez, made as he said, "to get rid of a Hanger-on." The second was the appointment of Doctor Bache: Concerning this latter appointment he observed, "that Doctor Bache was insolvent, and that Mr. Randolph your son in law was bound as his security for £1000. or more, which he would have been obliged to pay without the possibility of being reimbursed, but that you found it convenient to give the Doctor a lucrative Office." He added, "that he cared not a damn who might know this to be his opinion, for he had proclaimed it at a tavern in Charlottesville, and he doubted not it had been immediately conveyed to you, (then at Monticello) and that consequently he had been put down on the *black-book*."

Let this man say what he may, his calumnies can never merit your attention, further than as they may serve to guard you against him. It is for that purpose only, that I have troubled you with this communication, for my contempt and execration of his character are such, as to deprive me of any other motive for making the communication.

Believe me, Sir, while I may not have been the foremost among those who have given praise, you have no fellow-citizen who more highly admires the general course of your administration than I do. I do indeed believe it to be the best with which God ever blessed the People of any Country, and for the great good you have done, you shall always have my best prayer for your health and happiness.

AL: McRAE

N. B. I stated the fact I have now communicated in the presence of four Republican members of the State Legislature, Messrs. Sebrell and Curry of the Senate, and Messrs. Yerby and Sherman of the House of Delegates, where John Heth also was present, and he affirmed the statement to be correct. A: McR.

Printed in *Jefferson Correspondence*, Bixby, 187–9; endorsement given as "*Recd. Oct. 21.*" and so recorded in SJL.

McRae abused HENRY BANKS in an earlier letter (McRae to TJ, 14 Feb. 1809 [DLC]). Hore Browse TRIST was the deceased son of TJ's friend Elizabeth Trist (note to Elizabeth Trist to TJ, 22 Mar. 1809).

In June 1802 TJ appointed William BACHE, a grandson of Benjamin Franklin, to establish a marine hospital in Spanish-controlled New Orleans. In October of the same year Bache mortgaged Thomas Mann RANDOLPH his Albemarle County property called Franklin, and he departed for New Orleans in April 1803. Despite the failure of his New Orleans mission, Bache secured an appointment from TJ as surveyor and inspector for the port of Philadelphia in 1804 (Jane Flaherty Wells, "Thomas Jefferson's Neighbors: Hore Browse Trist of 'Birdwood' and Dr. William Bache of 'Franklin,'" *MACH* 47 [1989]: 1–13; W. E. Rooney, "Thomas Jefferson and the New Orleans Marine Hospital," *Journal of Southern History* 22 [1956]: 167–82; *JEP*, 1:471, 473 [12, 20 Nov. 1804]; Albemarle County Deed Book, 14:389–91).

# From St. George Tucker

Richmond Octo: 21st 1809.

Will Mr Jefferson have the goodness to accept the enclosed Attempt, from the pen of one who has not for more than thirty years thought of a composition in Latin, as a small tribute of the most sincere respect, esteem; and as a Testimony of the best wishes of his friend.

ST: G: TUCKER

RC (DLC); dateline at foot of text; endorsed by TJ as received 21 Oct. 1809 and so recorded in SJL.

St. George Tucker (1752–1827), judge and poet, attended the College of William and Mary early in the 1770s and studied law under George Wythe. During the Revolutionary War, Tucker smuggled arms and ammunition to the colonists from his native Bermuda, and during service with the Virginia militia he witnessed the British surrender at Yorktown. He served as commonwealth's attorney for Chesterfield County, 1783–86, attended the Annapolis Convention the latter year, but later opposed the ratification of the United States Constitution. Tucker was elected to the Virginia General Court in 1788 and served as professor of law at William and Mary from 1790–1804. He served on the Virginia Court of Appeals, 1803–11, and was judge of the federal court for the district of Virginia from 1813 until he resigned due to poor health in 1825. A prolific writer throughout his career, Tucker composed numerous poems, edited William Blackstone's *Commentaries on the Laws of England* to suit American republican sensibilities, and wrote works supporting the gradual abolition of slavery and TJ's purchase of Louisiana (*ANB*; *DAB*; Charles T. Cullen, "St. George Tucker," in W. Hamilton Bryson, ed., *Legal Education in Virginia, 1799–1979: A Biographical Approach* [1982], 657–86; Phillip Hamilton, *The Making and Unmaking of a Revolutionary Family: The Tuckers of Virginia, 1752–1830* [2003]; William S. Prince, ed., *The Poems of St. George Tucker of Williamsburg, Virginia, 1752–1827* [1977]).

ENCLOSURE

## St. George Tucker's Ode to Thomas Jefferson

Ad Thomam Jefferson.

Inclyte Civis! primus inter pares;
patriae Sortis impigerque Custos,
Dudum, et Salutis nostræ præsidium,
Et dulce decus:

Dum Iovis Ira Terruit Europam,
Fulmina dum jam diruerunt urbes;
Dumque Bellona populos extinxit,[1]
pax nobis risit:

Te nec Ambitio (semper et iniqua,
Semperque fallax) maxima promittens,
Nec clamittantum Civium Caterva
Movit ad Bella:[2]

Te[3] neque ferox Gentium Tyrannus,
Nutu qui Reges tollitque, dimovet,
Nec qui Neptuni Regnum usurpavit,
pollet[4] tecum:[5]

Socium Belli sibi dum uterque
Iungere exoptat Minisque Insidiis,
Spectans utrumque, vultu non iniquo,
Abnegas Cædes.[6]

Te duce, nobis quicquid est Telluris
Fructus abundat, Laribus dilectis;
Iani bifrontis foribus occlusis,
Dexterâ tuâ.

Tu Libertatis dulcia Munera, et
Gaudia, nunquam peritura, monstras;
Commoda pacis, Fideique puræ,
premia doces.[7]

Patriae carae stes consulentibus[8]
Semper Exemplar, resonentque Laudes,
Inter faventis Libertatis plausus,
Dum volat Ætas.[9]

XX die Octobris. MDCCCIX

## EDITORS' TRANSLATION

To Thomas Jefferson.

Renowned Citizen! First among equals;
Energetic guardian of the country's destiny,
Long since, and the protector of our welfare,
And sweet glory:

While Jupiter's anger terrified Europe,
While lightning bolts have now destroyed cities;
And while Bellona extinguished peoples,
Peace has smiled upon us:

Neither ambition promising the greatest things,
(Always dangerous and always deceptive)
Nor a crowd of clamoring citizens
Moved you to war:

The warlike tyrant of nations,
Who with a nod deposes kings, does not influence you,
Nor does he who has possession of the kingdom of Neptune,
Have influence over you:

While each longs to join to himself a companion in war
Amid threats and treachery,
You, observing each with an unprejudiced look,
Reject bloodshed.

With you as our leader, fruits abound
In whatever land we own; the Lares are beloved;
The doors of two-faced Janus have been closed,
By your hand.

You reveal the sweet gifts of Liberty and the
Joys of freedom, which will never perish;
You teach the advantages of peace
And the rewards of true loyalty.

May you always stand as an example for those looking after
Our dear country, and may praises of you resound,
Amid the applause of Liberty showing her favor,
While time flies.

20 October 1809

MS (DLC); entirely in Tucker's hand. 2d Dft (ViW: TC); dated 11 Oct. 1809. 1st Dft (ViW: TC); undated. FC (ViW: TC); in Tucker's hand; dated 20 Oct. 1809; endorsed by Tucker: "Ode." FC (ViW: TC, St. George Tucker Poetry

Notebook, 1810–23); in Tucker's hand, with his notation at foot of text: "written at Cary's brook, Fluvanna County, on seeing a fine print of M[r] Jefferson in the Room in which I slept. Octo: 20[th] 1809." Translation by Dr. John F. Miller.

[1] In both Dfts this line reads, with slight variations: "Sæva et Bellona Gentes extinxit" ("And savage Bellona has extinguished the peoples").

[2] Tucker reworked this stanza in 1st Dft, including deletion in second line of "neq Gloria Falsa" ("nor false glory"), before rewriting the stanza in margin.

[3] Manuscript: "Ter."

[4] Manuscript: "pollicit."

[5] Tucker's footnotes to notebook FC indicate that Napoleon and George III are the persons successively alluded to in this stanza.

[6] In both Dfts, the final line of this stanza originally read: "Neutrum adjuvas" ("You encourage neither").

[7] Tucker reworked this stanza in 1st Dft, changing ending to "Curia præclara" ("good government") before rewriting the stanza in margin. Preceding two words interlined in place of "Curia præclara" in 2d Dft.

[8] 1st Dft gives two variations of this line: "Sis Reipublicæ consulentibus/ Semper Exemplar" ("May you always be an example to those looking after the Republic") and "pro Republicâ Consulentibus" ("those watching over the Republic"). 2d Dft reads: "publico Bono sis consulentibus/Semper Exemplar" ("May you always be an example for those looking after the public good").

[9] In 1st Dft Tucker deleted: "Nobis in mente" ("With us in mind") and otherwise reworked the stanza, then rewrote the revised stanza below it.

# From William W. Hening

Dear Sir, Richmond 22[nd] Oct[r] 1809.

I have now the pleasure of presenting to you the first volume of the Statutes at Large, which was published on yesterday, only. In the execution of this work I have had to encounter many difficulties; but I have spared no pains to render it as perfect as possible. The typography is the best that could be procured in this place, where I was compelled to publish it, for the purpose of revising the proof-sheets as they came from the press. The second volume, (which is now in the press,) is considerably advanced, & promises to be much better executed than the first.

The views which all our historians have taken of the early history of Virginia, (even Marshall & Burke) have been so grossly inaccurate, that I have felt it a duty incumbent on me to intersperse the volume with various notes, pointing those errors out. These you will particularly find in pages 429, 513, 526; to which I invite your attention.

In the preface, I fear I have been too prolix.—Believing that it would be important to give a concise summary of the rise and progress of the most remarkable of our laws, (especially in a work of so much antiquity, which few would be disposed to read, for the purpose of forming their own conclusions,) I attempted the task.—As far as it is executed, I believe it is done with tolerable [ac]curacy; but many other topics might have been introduced to advantage; which I was deterred from noticing, lest the preface itself should be so long that few would be disposed to read it.

To this volume is prefixed all the ancient Charters relating to Virginia, which have hitherto been printed, together with some others from MS copies; & to the whole, a complete set of marginal notes has been given.

Altho' I have been gratified by the patronage of many enlightened men of our country, yet I cannot say that the encouragement has been so extensive as the intrinsic merit of such a performance would induce me to expect;—laying out of view any pretensions of the editor.—It is from the approbation of such characters as yourself, that I can ever expect such a circulation of the work, as will remunerate me for my arduous labours.—I neither ask nor expect this approbation unless it be deserved; for, tho' I well know your disposition to encourage literature, of every kind, yet I equally well know your candor, & the importance of your own literary character to be such that you would not recommend any performance which did not deserve it.—If, from a perusal of this volume you should be of opinion that it merited public patronage, an expression of that sentiment would be very serviceable.—

I am respectf[ly] Yrs WM: W: HENING

RC (DLC); margin torn; addressed: "Thomas Jefferson Esq[r] Present"; endorsed by TJ as received 22 Oct. 1809 and so recorded in SJL. Enclosure: vol. 1 of Hening, ed., *The Statutes at Large: being A Collection of all the Laws of Virginia, from the First Session of the Legislature, in the year 1619*, 13 vols. (Richmond, 1809–23; Sowerby, no. 1863; Poor, *Jefferson's Library*, 10 [no. 573]).

The publication of Hening's *Statutes at Large* was a landmark in Virginia legal scholarship and the culmination for TJ of many years of collecting material and encouraging such an enterprise (TJ to George Wythe, 16 Jan. 1796, *PTJ*, 28:582–91). Hening inserted long footnotes at PAGES 429, 513, 526 faulting John Daly Burk for his failure to gain access to pertinent primary sources and also taking issue with statements in William Robertson's *History of America* (London, 1777; see Sowerby, no. 469).

# To the Citizens of Richmond

SIR

The expressions of esteem & approbation with which I am a[ddressed, by the] meeting of the citizens of Richmond, through yourself as their org[an, and] the testimonies of respect with which they have been pleased to [welcome] my visit to the metropolis of my native state, are highly flat[tering to me,] and I pray you to convey to them, & to accept for yourself, the [assurances] of my great thankfulness.

I am sensible of the indulgence with which they have [reviewed] the various acts of duty to our country which have been made incumb[ent on me,] in the course of it's long struggles to recover & to establish it's ri[ghts and] liberties. the object of these struggles was of a character to comm[and every] effort which the love of our country, or the sense of it's wrongs co[uld] inspire. I claim no other merit than that of having, with my bes[t en]deavors contributed, together with my fellow citizens at large, to th[e es]tablishment of those rights, without which man is a degraded being. and I am happy in meeting here those who have been fellow laborer[s] in the same holy cause, & who have marked their way, through all the trying scenes of our contest, by a steadfastness of purpose & of principle superior to all events.

should the injustice of nations still destine us to further trial, my own confidence in the well-proved spirit and virtue of my fellow citizens, in their readiness to make every sacrifice for the rights and honor of our country, confirms your assurances that they will, [wi]thout dismay, breast the storm which hovers over us & prove that [we ar]e able to maintain what we have been able to acquire.

Under circumstances like these it is indeed a great con[solation,] that the enlightened choice of our country has confided i[t's high]est trusts to a citizen so distinguished by his valuable se[rvices,] whose exact impartiality towards foreign nations, whose [dispo]sition to meet them on terms of reciprocity & friendship, & [firmness] in resenting their oppressions, are a pledge to his country[, that no] wrong will be offered, and no right surrendered, to any [power] whatever.

I am particularly thankful, Sir, for the interest [which my] fellow citizens are so good as to feel & to express, in the tranq[uility] & happiness of the remaining scenes of my life. nothing will [contri]bute more to this than the possession of their good will: and [to] those for their personal welfare, I add my sincere prayers for [a con]tinuance of that prosperity so visible in the growth and aspec[t] of the city of Richmond, and so confidently to be augured from the enterprize of it's citizens, and the advantages it has recie[v]ed from the hands of nature.

TH: JEFFERSON
Richmond Oct. 22. 1809.

SC (DLC); edges torn and frayed, with gaps supplied from version printed in Richmond *Enquirer*, 24 Oct. 1809. At foot of text in *Enquirer*: "Dr. WILLIAM FOUSHEE." Recorded in SJL as "Richmond citizens. Answer."

# From Alexander Burot

MONSIEUR Richmond 23 8$^{bre}$ 1809

Ce n'est point à M$^{r}$ Thomas Jefferson président des États unis, dont le nom Sera à Jamais Celebre dans les deux hémispheres, pour avoir su allier les qualités Sublimes de L'homme d'État, avec les vertus du Citoyen, que je m'adresse; c'est à M$^{r}$ Jefferson habitant, planteur de Virginie et pere de famille au quel j'ay L'honneur d'avoir recours dans L'infortune.

par Suitte des malheurs de S$^{t}$ Domingue, je me Suis refugié dans cet état dès L'année 1796 avec ma femme et deux enfans. à mon arrivée j'achettai une plantation dans la comté de Chesterfield, et mon épouse me fit pere de trois autres enfans nés en Virginie. j'amenai aussi avec moy neuf domestiques Negres et Mulâtres, que je choisis sur mes plantations de S$^{t}$ Domingue pour servir ma famille. lors de l'arrivée des francais, je retournai à S$^{t}$ Domingue. la rupture du traité d'Amiens, nous fit évacuer dans L'isle de Cuba, d'ou je suis parti en vertu des proclamations du Cap$^{e}$ général de Cette Isle Espagnole. à mon arrivée ici le 1$^{er}$ aoust de Cette année, j'ay trouvé tous mes negres libres, ma femme chassée de Sa plantation, n'ayant pu payer un Mortgage par le défaut de ses cultivateurs devenus libres, en un mot, ma famille et moi réduits à la mendicité.

1° Je déclare avec Verité que ni moy, ni aucuns francais refugiés ici, n'a connu cette Loy qui nous fait payer bien cher L'hospitalité.

2° Cette Loi faitte avant la révolution francaise, n'a pas pu prévoir le cas forcé de L'émigration des colons francais chéz leurs alliés, et les États unis ayant garanti à la france ses colonies des West-Indies, n'ont-ils pas garanti par conséquent les propriétés des colons? cette loy n'est donc pas applicable aux colons francais que des malheurs trop Connus ont jetté Sur Cette terre hospitaliere Sans avoir pu prévoir, qu'ils Seroient dépouillés des débris de leur fortune en y abordant[1]

3° Pourquoi ma femme et ses enfans privés de ma présence et qui alors étoient Censés la veuve et L'orphelin ont-ils été les Seuls dans l'état de Virginie soumis à Cette Loi Rigoureuse qui n'a jamais été appliquée à Norfolck, ni autres villes de cet état; ce dont j'ay des preuves matérielles.

Ce sont des questions que je Soumets à Votre humanité et à Votre generosité.

Pere d'une famille Nombreuse, partie créoles, partie Virginiens, réduit à L'indigence, à qui m'adresserai-je dans ma détresse? Es-ce à la cour de Justice, où à L'assemblée Législative de cet état? J'ose implorer le secours de Vos Lumieren. si mes foibles talents, fruits d'une éducation distinguée en france, pouvoient vous être de quelque utilité, Je consacrerois volontiers Le reste de mes Jours à Votre Service

J'ay L'honneur d'être avec le plus profond respect Monsieur Votre très humble et très obéïssant Serviteur

Alexander Burot

EDITORS' TRANSLATION

Sir Richmond 23 October 1809

It is not at all Mr. Thomas Jefferson, president of the United States, whose name will be forever famous in the two hemispheres for having been able to ally the sublime qualities of a statesman with the virtues of a citizen, whom I address; it is Mr. Jefferson, Virginia planter and father of a family, to whom I have the honor of appealing in my misfortune.

As a result of the calamities in Saint Domingue, I took refuge in this state beginning in the year 1796 with my wife and two children. Upon my arrival, I bought a plantation in the county of Chesterfield, and my wife made me the father of three more children born in Virginia. I also brought with me nine negro and mulatto domestics, whom I chose from my plantations in Saint Domingue to serve my family. When the French arrived at Saint Domingue, I returned there. The rupture of the Treaty of Amiens forced us to evacuate to the island of Cuba, which I left in accordance with the proclamations of the captain general of that Spanish island. Upon my arrival here the 1st of August of this year, I found all my negroes had been freed, my wife evicted from her plantation, having not been able to pay a mortgage in the absence of her laborers who had been freed, in a word, my family and myself reduced to beggary.

1st I declare truthfully that neither I nor any of the French refugees here knew about this law that makes us pay very dearly for your hospitality.

2d This law that was passed before the French Revolution, could not foresee the forced emigration of French colonists to the lands of their allies, and did not the United States, having guaranteed to France her colonies in the West Indies, consequently guarantee the property of its colonists? This law is therefore not applicable to French colonists who, thrown into this hospitable land by infamous misfortunes, were unable to foresee that they would be stripped of the remains of their fortunes upon landing.

3d Why was it that my wife and her children, deprived of my presence and therefore considered a widow and orphans, were the only ones in the state of Virginia to be subjected to this rigorous law that was never applied in Norfolk, nor in other cities in this state; of which I have material proof.

These are questions that I submit to your humanity and to your generosity.

To whom will I, the father of a large family that is part Creole and part Virginian, reduced to indigence, appeal in my distress? Is it to the courts of justice, or to the legislative assembly of this state? I dare to implore the aid of your wisdom. If my feeble talents, the fruits of a distinguished education in France, might be of some use to you, I would willingly devote the rest of my days to your service.

I have the honor of being with the deepest respect Sir your very humble and very obedient servant ALEXANDER BUROT

RC (MHi); endorsed by TJ as received 31 Oct. 1809 and so recorded in SJL. Translation by Dr. Amy Ogden.

Alexander Burot was listed in the 1810 census as a resident of Richmond with four slaves (DNA: RG 29, Census Schedules, Henrico County, 1810). He does not appear in the 1820 Virginia census.

CETTE LOY was presumably an 1806 Virginia statute prohibiting the bringing of slaves into the state, under penalty of a $400 fine and the sale of the slaves to benefit the overseers of the poor. The law replaced earlier versions in which contraband slaves were freed. In 1807 federal law prohibited the importation of slaves into the United States. The influx in the summer of 1809 of Saint Domingue refugees from Cuba, many with slaves, led to a statute permitting the president to exempt selected refugees from these restrictions (Robert McColley, *Slavery and Jeffersonian Virginia* [1973], 165–7; Madison, *Papers, Pres. Ser.*, 1:219–20).

[1] Burot's inadvertent question mark omitted.

# From William Eustis

DEAR SIR, Washington October 25. 1809.

Arriving at the seat of Government a few days since I find your very kind letter of the 6th instant. Be pleased to receive my grateful acknowlegement of the favorable terms in which you express your approbation of my appointment to an office, the arduous duties of which I wish it was in my power more satisfactorily to discharge. In my native state and in New Hampshire I derived great satisfaction in perceiving the great change which had taken place in the public opinion. The late[1] proceedings of the British Government and of the British merchants appear to have occasioned a different turn of thinking and (I am not without hopes) will produce a different course of conduct on the part of the citizens on the atlantic coast.

A revolution of sentiment has undoubtedly taken place. The friends of G. Britain are no longer able to justify her cause before the tribunal of the public. principles and sentiments more becoming Americans are taking place of the violence & prejudice which have too long prevailed: and it is to be apprehended that the intercourse (diplomatic), which will come before the public in its proper time, will not be calculated to abate those sentiments or to shake those principles.

I pray you to receive this hasty expression of my respect and regard, with my best wishes for your enjoyment of every blessing which the evening of life can shed over a meridian devoted to the service of your country. Every suggestion with which I may be favored from your retirement will be gratefully received:

The enclosed, made out by the clerk, is perhaps too general & too indefinite for the guidance of Mr Porter in regard to his claim. His answer is briefly this. His claim for compensation for services is barred by the statute of limitation. His claim for compensation on account of disability is at least doubtful. The statute provides for disability the result of known wounds received in the line of actual duty. But the Statute has in several instances been construed more liberally than its strict Letter would justify. Whether the case of Mr Porter would be so construed must depend on the[2] testimony produced before the commissioners appointed by the District Judge to whom his application is to be made in the first instance.

With the highest respect & regard I am Dr Sir, your obedt Servt

W. Eustis

RC (DLC); at foot of text: "Thomas Jefferson Esqr"; endorsed by TJ as received 31 Oct. 1809 and so recorded in SJL. Enclosure not found.

[1] Word interlined.

[2] Manuscript: "the the."

## From Samuel Greenhow

Sir. Richmond 25th Octr 1809.

You executed two declarations for assurance some time past, which were delivered at this Office by the S. Agent Mr Dawson; with verbal Instructions, that, they should not be recorded until you directed it.—As there were no written Instructions to hold them up, I did not wish to take them into my Keeping, since it is my duty to record every declaration on receipt of it, & to address a letter to the proprietor of the houses intended to be Assured informing of the præmium, unless I have written Orders, as to any delay—After recording the declaration, the præmium accruse & must be charged on the books.

Will you Sir, be good enough to direct, whether, I shall immediately record these declarations—whether I shall return them—or whether I shall continue to hold them subject to your future Orders.—

The præmiums of Assurance will be, as on the other side.—

I am Sir with great Respect Yrs &c Samuel Greenhow.

P.S. I should have called on you while you were in this City; but being much engaged, I delayed it until you had set off on your Return—which I had been informed would not be so soon; hence I am obliged to trouble you with this Letter. Saml Greenhow[1]

| | Value | $\frac{1}{5}$ | Insurable | | amount of prem[m] |
|---|---|---|---|---|---|
| Merchant Mill | $10,000 | $2000 | $8000 | @ $2\frac{1}{2}$p[r]C[t] | $200 |
| Dwell[g] house | 1 600 | 120 | 480 | " $1\frac{1}{2}$ " | 7.20 |
| Ditto | 200 | 40 | 160 | " $1\frac{1}{2}$ " | 2.40 |
| Grist mill | 900 | 180 | 720 | " $2\frac{1}{2}$ " | 18. |
| | | Sum to be Insured | $9,360 | Total præmium | $227.60 |

equal to an Average of $2$\frac{43}{100}$ p[r] hundred dollars, to be paid as the price of a right to future Assurance at the rate of about 35 Cents per annum on each $100.—

Rate of Præmiums—

| | | | |
|---|---|---|---|
| merchant mill. | Stone, wooden cover | $2. | p[r]C[t] |
| | over $5000. value | .50 | " " |
| | | 2.50 | |
| Dwell[g] house | Stone, Wooden cover | 1.50 | |
| Ditto | Stone, Wooden cover | 1.50 | |
| Grist-mill | Body Stone, wooden cover & Wing all wood. | 2.50 | |

RC (DLC); addressed: "M[r] Thomas Jefferson. Albermarle"; franked and postmarked; endorsed by TJ as received 5 Nov. 1809 and so recorded in SJL.

[1] Remainder on verso of address cover.

# To James Madison

Dear Sir Eppington Oct. 25. 09

I recieved at Richmond your favor covering a check on the bank of Norfolk for 743. Doll. 15. cents the balance in full of our accounts. I have learnt from P. Carr that under an idea that Rodney was about to resign, & on a desire expressed by mr R. Smith to him or some other person that Wirt should be sounded, it had been found that he would accept. I do not know whether it was communicated to me in expectation that I should write it to you, or whether it may have communicated to you more directly.

Altho' I repel all applications generally to recommend candidates for office yet there may be occasions where information of my own knolege of them may be useful & acceptable, & others where particular delicacies of situation may constrain me to say something. of the latter description is the application of John Monroe (cousin of the

Colonel) who in expectation that the Governor of Illinois means to resign, has sollicited my saying to you he would accept that office. I had formerly appointed him Atty of the West district of Virginia. he resided at Staunton & there lost the respect of many by some irregularities which his subsequent marriage has probably put an end to. his talents I believe are respectable, without being prominent: but I really believe you know as much of him as I do, having seen him my self once or twice only, & then for short intervals. particular circumstances oblige me to mention him, without feeling a single wish on the subject, other than that it should be given to the fittest subject, which you will do of your own motion. ever affectionately yours

Th: Jefferson

RC (DLC: Madison Papers); at foot of text: "The President of the US." SC (DLC); endorsed by TJ.

Madison's FAVOR of 13 Oct. 1809, not found, is recorded in SJL as received in Richmond from Washington on 20 Oct. 1809. Caesar RODNEY continued to serve as attorney general until his resignation in December 1811 after being passed over for a Supreme Court judgeship (*ANB*). JOHN MONROE had asked that TJ recommend him for the governorship of Indiana. TJ's conflation of the governorships of the Indiana and ILLINOIS territories probably resulted from the newness of Illinois, formed out of the western part of Indiana Territory by a congressional act of 3 Feb. 1809 (*U.S. Statutes at Large*, 2:514–6).

# From Lafayette

My dear friend — Paris 26[t] October 1809

I wish I might make use of the present Opportunity to tell You the Conditions of the peace Lately made with Austria—But Last Evening, the first members of Government knew no more of it than myself—I am Returning to La Grange—the Emperor is Expected this day at fontainebleau, and if the Vessel is Somewhat detained, G[al] Armstrong will Be able to write the particulars of the treaty.

inclosed You will find a Letter from m[de] de tessé: I Have Seen Her, m. de tessé, and m. de mun, a few days Ago, at Aulnay—m[r] warden Has taken Care to forward the Chest to dieppe—we Have Again Lamented, Your Aulnay friends and myself, the Sudden departure of m[r] Coles—it Has Been particularly fatal to me who might Have Given Him for You many Explanations which I wanted to Convey. How Happy I would Be to give them myself at monticelo!—But instead of the Joy to Embrace my friend, and of a Conversation in which I would delight, I Have not Even the full Ressource of Epistolary Correspondance.

No News from Louïsiana Have Reached me—The Last Letter of m$^{r}$ duplantier Expressed a Hope that the Remisness of the City of Orleans in Accepting the Gift of Congress might prove very Beneficial to me—But no documents or titles for what is unquestionably mine Have Been forwarded—in the mean while the mere increase of interest Has Augmented my debt and urged my danger to a degree most distressing—The Endeavours made for my Relief, altho' Great Scope Has Been Given By Your Opinion that Any interest was preferable to a present[1] Sale, Have Hitherto Been defeated By this Simple Query, what documents and titles Can You Give as a Security? there is an other affair in Contemplation for which we fear the Same fate—You Remember, my dear friend, the Letters where indulging a fanciful disposition of the precious Gift of Congress I was Saying that Exclusive of my debt to my Brother in law which might Be paid in Land Hundred thousand dollars were necessary to Clear my fortune—now without much more Expence, and only By the Means taken to Ajourn a Ruin which Your friendship and the Bounty of Congress Have many Years Ago provided Against one Half of the Sum more would Be Requisite—My Expences in the two Revolutions did not Lessen my Capital of more than a million and a Half francs[2]—there Remained for me, of my own fortune, about two millions of francs. But I found almost my all pillaged, and old Engagements to which must Be added the debts of Captivity to Be paid—the Afairs were So Circumstanced as to preclude my Accepting a Share in public Life,—Yet I ought to Stay—in this Situation Your first letter, after the Bountiful Vote of Congress, Had upon me the Effect of a providential delivery—the pleasure to Be for it indebted to Your friendship, to the Benevolence of An American Congress Was inexpressible—I Had then the Comfort to Enjoy it with the partner of my Life—I Cannot Refrain from mentionning Again the Grateful feelings which shall Animate[3] me to my Last Breath, and I Love to Remind You of the danger from which You Have Rescued me—But to finish Your work it is Highly important and urging that I may Have titles and documents indispensable to fix the Opinion Respecting the Location and value of the precious Grant—However Enormous my wants they are still[4] under your own idea of its worth—But if my fortune Could Be disincumbered, Little more than the Produce of my farm, which thrives well, would Suffice for my family and myself to Live in the frugal way we Have Adopted.

I wanted, my dear friend, to adress to Your kind Heart this Present Communication Relative to my actual Situation, and I am Sure I will find You indulgent, nor will You find me importunate.

it Had Lately Been my Expectation to Arrange the Sending over a few merinos—the minister of police, who managed, By interim, the Interior department, Had positively promised it to me, and to my Certain knowledge, very Readily Given proper orders in the Office—But He was informed there of a General defense from the Emperor, So positive, that He durst not do it of Himself, and now we are Return'd to uncertainties in which You may depend Your Name will not Be Committed.

My children and Grand children are well and Continue to inhabit La Grange in private life—present my Respects to M[rs] Randolph and think, with Your usual Sentiments, in Your Retirement, of Your Affectionate friend LAFAYETTE

RC (DLC); endorsed by TJ as received 27 Dec. 1809 and so recorded in SJL. Enclosure: Madame de Tessé to TJ, 9 Oct. 1809.

DEFENSE: prohibition.

[1] Word interlined.
[2] Word interlined.
[3] Manuscript: "Animated."
[4] Lafayette here canceled "much."

# From David Bailie Warden

SIR, Paris, 27 october, 1809.

I had the pleasure of writing to you by the Wasp sloop of war, and of sending you several brochures. I am instructed, by the Secretary of the agricultural Society, to send you the last volume of their transactions. I inclose a map which the author beg you to accept.

more than twenty American vessels, with rich[1] cargoes, have been lately carried to different ports of France, Holland, and Italy, and ordered for trial before the Council of Prizes, at Paris, some of which have not infringed the Imperial Decrees. The Lydia, a vessel of this description, was restored, a few days since, to the owners, by a decision, of the above-mentioned Tribunal. Whether the others, under like circumstances, will be restored, is yet unknown—a maritime Court has been lately established, in Holland, for the purpose of fixing the limits of the territorial sea, within which several of our vessels are said to have been arrested. at this moment, there appears to be but little hope of an amicable arrangement between france, and the united States. the emperor seems determined to adhere to his decrees. He is now at[2] Fontain bleau.

Messrs Humboldt, Lacepede, Thouin &c bid me present you their respects—I hope you received the copy of Callets Logarithms, dedicated to you, and of which I prepared the Introduction.—It will give me great pleasure to send you any Book or article you may wish to possess.[3]

I am, with great esteem and respect, Your ever obliged Servant

DAVID BAILIE WARDEN

RC (DLC); at foot of text: "Thomas Jefferson Esquire Monticello"; endorsed by TJ as received 8 Jan. 1810 but recorded as received 7 Jan. 1810 in SJL. Dupl (DLC); between dateline and salutation: "Duplicate"; endorsed by TJ as received 17 June 1810 and so recorded in SJL. FC (MdHi: Warden Letterbook). Enclosed in James Madison to TJ, 15 June 1810.

Augustin François Silvestre, the SECRETARY OF THE AGRICULTURAL SOCIETY, had requested Warden to send TJ the *Mémoires* of the Société d'agriculture du département de la Seine, vol. 11 (Paris, 1808; Sowerby, no. 776). The map's AUTHOR was Jan Chrzciciel Komarzewski (Warden to TJ, 17 Sept. 1809; TJ to Warden, 15 July 1810).

[1] Dupl and FC: "valuable."

[2] Dupl and FC substitute "returned to" for preceding two words.

[3] Sentence omitted in Dupl and FC.

# From Zadok Cramer

FRIEND JEFFERSON Pittsburgh, Oct$^{r}$ 30, 1809

I take the liberty, and the pleasure at the same, of transmitting a copy of a new spelling for thy inspection—It is totally of domestic materials of the western country, and will give thee an idea of our progress in the book manufactury, west of the mountains

With high respect for thy Services to the United States, and for the compliment thou paid me on a former occasion

I remain Thy friend ZADOK CRAMER

RC (MHi); endorsed by TJ as received 22 Nov. 1809 and so recorded in SJL.

Zadok Cramer (1773–1813) was a native of New Jersey who established a bookshop, printing press, bindery, and circulating library in Pittsburgh in 1800. His firm published the *Navigator* (1801–13), a guide to the Ohio River for boatmen, and *Cramer's Pittsburgh Magazine Almanack* from 1806 until well after his death. Cramer's edition of the journal of Patrick Gass was the first published memoir by a member of the Lewis and Clark Expedition (*Pittsburgh Gazette*, 30 Mar. 1800; Charles W. Dahlinger, *Pittsburgh: A Sketch of Its Early Social Life* [1916], 161–208; Gass, *A journal of the voyages and travels of a corps of discovery* [Pittsburgh, 1807; for a Philadelphia reprint owned by TJ see Sowerby, no. 4078]).

The enclosed NEW SPELLING was most likely *The United States spelling book* (Pittsburgh, 1809), published by Cramer, Spear, and Eichbaum. The COMPLIMENT was probably TJ to Cramer, 12 Mar. 1808 (DLC), acknowledging receipt of Cramer's edition of John Brown's *Dictionary of the Holy Bible* (Pittsburgh, 1807; Sowerby, no. 1506).

## From Thomas Lomax

Dear Sir Pt Tobago Oct. 30th 1809.

By the Carriage, which I now send up for my Daughter, you will receive some filbert Cions,[1] and Nuts, as well as the Juboli, and Acacia, the latter I have been obliged to lay in a flat Box, as the weight of those, out of which they were taken, I was afraid would be too heavy, and dangerous to be put into the Carriage. They will I hope reach you in safety, to be placed in other Boxes. The Nuts, if you chuse to plant any of them, it ought to be done immediatly; but I am doubtful, whether they will vegitate; as I always after they are put into Bags, expose them very much to the heat of the Sun; but you can try them, and should they come up in the Spring, they should, as well as the young trees, be watered whenever the weather becomes dry. The trees I think you had better set at 20 feet asunder; as mine are only fifteen, which I discover to be too near each other. I have also sent some of the Star-Jasmine, and a beautiful flowering Shrub, which I took from the Woods, and not[2] knowing its real name, have given it that, of modesty, from its handsome delicete appearance, a quality which will disgrace no Garden. If you have any of the Paccan nut, that you can conveniently spare, I will thank you for some by the return of the Carriage; as I expect they can now be moved with safety. It would have given me great pleasure to have visited the President, and met with[3] you there; but being informed, he was, at the time I was in his neighbourhood,[4] to set off in a few days to the City, was fearful that I might intrude upon that short time he had to remain at home. I beg you to present my affectionate Regard to Colo Randolph & his Lady, and to accept the same yourself from

Yor Sincere friend & Humbe Servt Tho. Lomax

T.L requests some of Mr Jeffersons fine Lima-Beans, if he has any to spare. The Silk-Tree is very flourishing. There is an Orange and Lime Tree sent, the Orange has the broadest Leaf.

RC (CSmH: JF-BA); dateline adjacent to signature; postscript on address cover; addressed: "Thomas Jefferson Esqr Montecello"; endorsed by TJ as received 5 Nov. 1809 and so recorded in SJL.

Thomas Lomax (1746–1811), an attorney and planter, served on the first Caroline County Committee during the American Revolution and represented Caroline and Hanover counties in the Senate of Virginia in 1776 and Caroline County in the House of Delegates, 1779 and 1781–82 (Edward L. Lomax, *Genealogy of the Virginia Family of Lomax* [1913], 19; Thomas E. Campbell, *Colonial Caroline: A History of Caroline County, Virginia* [1954], 234, 236, 343, 348, 467, 469; Leonard, *General Assembly*, 124, 133, 141).

On 6 Nov. 1809 TJ planted the items received from Lomax, including twenty-four *Corylus avellana* (filbert), five *Zizyphus jujuba* (juboli or jujubes), two

*Acacia farnesiana* (ACACIA), twenty-one *Jasminum officinale* (STAR-JASMINE), three MODESTY shrubs, a *Citrus aurantium* (ORANGE), and a *Citrus aurantifolia* (LIME). The acacia, orange, and lime were planted in boxes in the greenhouse (Betts, *Garden Book*, 387, 398–9).

[1] Variant spelling of "Scions."
[2] Word interlined.
[3] Word interlined.
[4] Manuscript: "neighourhood."

## From James Madison

DEAR SIR Washington Oc[r] 30. 1809

In the operation of removing from my former quarters, the Digest of the City Code & business, which you had been so good as to furnish me, has, by some unaccountable accident, been either lost, or possibly so thrown out of place, as not to be found. I have written to Capt: Coles, to take Monticello in his way, and ask the favor of you to permit him to take another copy, from your Original. As that letter however may not reach him, I must beg you to signify my wishes to him, in case he should call on you as he probably will.

The Works of Turgot, remain on hand for want of some person to take charge of them to Fred[g]. They fill a Box ab[t] 15 inch[s] by 12. & 8 inch[s] deep; too large therefore for the Mail. I shall avail myself of the 1[st] opp[y] for sending it on by the Stage. I was in hope, that the Race-field would have furnished some known person, returning by way of Fred[g]: but I was disappointed; there being very few Virginians there, & none from the Southern districts.

We just learn the melancholy fate of Gov[r] Lewis which possibly may not have travelled so quickly into your neighbourhood. He had, it seems betrayed latterly repeated symtoms of a disordered mind; and had set out under the care of a friend on a visit to Washington. His first intention was, to make the trip by water; but changing it, at the Chickasaw Bluffs, he struck across towards Nashville. As soon as he had passed the Tennissee, he took advantage of the neglect of his Companion, who had not secured his arms, to put an end to himself. He first fired a pistol, at his head, the ball of which glancing, was ineffectual. With the 2[d] he passed a Ball thro' his body, w[ch] being also without immediate effect, he had recourse to his Dirk with w[ch] he mangled himself considerably. After all he lived till the next morning, with the utmost impatience for death.

I inclose the latest acc[ts] from Europe. Onis has returned to Philad[a]. The reality or degree of his disapp[t] is not easily ascertained. His last conversation with M[r] Smith, did not manifest ill humour. How could he expect a different result, in the actual State of things? And what motive Can Spain or the Colonies have, in any State of things, to make enemies of the U.S.? I see nothing to change the view of Jackson, which I formerly hinted to you.

RC (DLC: Madison Papers, Rives Collection); closing and signature clipped; endorsed by TJ as received 5 Nov. 1809 and so recorded in SJL. Enclosures not found.

The DIGEST OF THE CITY CODE & BUSINESS was probably TJ to the Commissioners of the District of Columbia, 12 Oct. 1803 (DLC), in which TJ listed legislation pertaining to the capital while also defining the president's role and power in implementing the city plan after Congress had established a corporation for the city's government.

## To Louis H. Girardin

SIR Monticello Oct. 31. 09.

The bearer hereof, T. Jefferson Randolph, my grandson, proceeds to Richmond with a view to enter as a student in the academy at that place under your care. having been taught Latin & French (the former however not as perfectly as should be) he passed a year at Philadelphia, attending courses of lectures in Botany, Natural history, Anatomy & Surgery. our object in sending him to your academy is that he may go through a compleat course of Mathematics & Natural philosophy. in the former I comprehend Geometry, trigonometry plain & spherical, Conic sections & Algebra, not meaning however to push the latter to fluxions, which are little useful in ordinary life, [as?][1] may be said also indeed of the higher branches of Algebra generally. in the hope that he can be recieved, I recommend him to the attentions of yourself & the other professors, with the assurance that you will find his dispositions entirely amiable, and his capacity equal to the objects proposed: to which I may add that his conduct hitherto has been so correct as to strengthen our confidence that it will not be changed in his new situation. Mess^rs Gibson & Jefferson will make the advances necessary in the first instance, & will be enabled to meet others as they occur. the interest I feel in whatever concerns him will render me extremely thankful for every degree of attention to him consistent with your duties to others, and I pray you to be assured of my high respect & consideration. TH: JEFFERSON

RC (PPAmP: Thomas Jefferson Letters); addressed: "M^r L. H. Girardin Richmond by T. J. Randolph."

Louis Hue Girardin (1771–1825), educator, journalist, and historian, was a royalist born in Normandy who changed his name from Louis François Picot and fled to America to avoid his enemies during the French Revolution. Starting in 1803 Girardin taught modern languages, history, and geography at the College of William and Mary, and while in Williamsburg he published the short-lived, pioneering illustrated magazine *Amœnitatis Graphicæ* (1805). With partners and on his own he ran an academy in Richmond, 1807–10, and he later operated similar academies in Milton and Staunton before serving as head of the struggling Baltimore College from 1821 until his death. Girardin briefly edited two Richmond newspapers, the *Daily Compiler*, 1815–16, and the *Virginia Argus* in the latter year. He corresponded regularly with TJ, especially during the latter's retirement. Between 1813 and its publication in Petersburg in 1816, Girardin worked to complete the fourth volume of a *History of Virginia* (Sowerby, no. 464; Poor, *Jefferson's Library*, 4 [no. 127]) begun by John Daly Burk and Skelton Jones. TJ carefully advised Girardin on this project, seeing this concluding volume, dedicated to TJ and dealing with the American Revolution, as a means of defending his actions as governor of Virginia against criticisms in John Marshall's *Life of Washington* (Philadelphia, 1804–07; Sowerby, no. 496; Poor, *Jefferson's Library*, 4 [no. 133]) and Henry Lee's *Memoirs of the War in the Southern Department* (Philadelphia, 1812; Sowerby, no. 533) (Norfleet, *Saint-Mémin*, 166–7; Edith Philips, *Louis Hue Girardin and Nicholas Gouin Dufief and Their Relations with Thomas Jefferson: An Unknown Episode of the French Emigration in America* [1926]; Wayne Barrett, "Monsieur Girardin's Prescient Little Magazine," *Colonial Williamsburg* 14 [Winter 1991/92]: 24–8; Brigham, *American Newspapers*, 2:1137, 1142–3; *PTJ*, 4:256–68; Malone, *Jefferson*, 6:218–24; Baltimore *American & Commercial Daily Advertiser*, 17 Feb. 1825).

[1] Word, obscured by ink stain, interlined in place of "which."

# To George Jefferson

DEAR SIR Monticello. Oct. 31. 09

T. J. Randolph now proceeds to Richmond in order to enter at mr Girardin's academy. I have explained to mr Girardin our wish that he should go through a course of mathematics & Natural philosophy. the annual charges for these in the academy, according to their printed statement will be 67. D. to be paid quarterly in advance, say 16.75 D each quarter. this you will be so good as to pay on my account, & also for his board. I have mentioned to mr Randolph, that mrs Page will be willing to take him, but have desired him to decide where he would rather have him placed. should Jefferson bring nothing to the contrary from him, place him at mrs Page's or where you think best. mr Randolph & family being at present at Edgehill prevents my consulting with him verbally. I must pray you also to furnish Jefferson his other proper expences. he has been so correct in them heretofore as to give me strong confidence they will be reasonable with you. were any contrary indications to arise, I would sollicit your confidential communication of it to me that I may take such measures for his good as may in no wise commit you with him or any body. Affectionately yours Th: Jefferson

PoC (MHi); at foot of text: "Mr George Jefferson"; endorsed by TJ.

# From Gideon Fitz

Sir, Opelousas Church November 1st 1809.

My personal acquaintance with you and the kind attention you have been pleased to bestow on me in my outsetting in life is my apology for the freedom I take in offering you the following remarks.

This is the third letter I have ventured to trouble you with relative to the adjustment of the land claims in this country.—It is with diffidence I write it, though I have long been convinced, that it is proper to give you such information as is contained in some parts of it.

Since about the middle of September last the business of the Board of Commissioners has ceased altogether.—Mr Cocke is gone to his family on the sea shore near new Orleans, and told me he should probably resign his Office here, and either accept of an apointment that governor Claiborne had offered him, or return with his family to Kentucky. Colonel Tompson is attending the courts in the different districts of the territory, and Mr Garrat waiting his return. The clerk of the Board Coln. Tompsons Son,[1] is also clerk of the Court, and when the Court is sitting here, the Register, the clerk of the Board, and the translator are all engaged in Court and Completely puts a stop to the business in the land office.—And if the Register attends the Courts as they occur, he must inevitably neglect the land office nearly six months in the year. The inhabitants in this quarter so far as my acquaintance and observation extends are exceedingly desirous that the adjustment of the claims should progress with all possible speed. Some of them think hard of the Union of the offices of Judge and Register in the same person; it is evident to all that no one person can perform the duties of one of[2] those offices, without neglecting the other. It seems too to create an idea among the inhabitants, that the government is very easy about the landed property in the country which is so interesting to them. Many persons are desirous to improve land which they claim by settlement but are detered from it on account of their claims being undecided on.

It appears there are some who think the Commissioners have

power to take away their claims, and it is often reported that the Americans mean ultimately to deprive the french of their lands altogether. Such reports, though in themselves inconsistent, nevertheless serve in some degree to fan the flame of prejudices. I have been frequently told, that some of those who have not entered their claims, now rejoice at their good fortune in not having placed them out of their controul. Many are becoming solicitous for fear their title papers in the land office should get destroyed by fire or other accident, for they are kept where there is but little security for them.—The delay also opens a door for speculation. There is actually much inconvenience felt in making transfers while the titles remain undecided on, for the purchaser is seldom[3] satisfied without a warranty deed, which the seller is seldom willing to give. The Commissioners have also set out upon one principal which will certainly be productive of great delay and trouble both to themselves and the claimants, and which if not relinquished, will in the opinion of many here, render the adjustment of the claims impracticable in many cases, for they require of the claimant to prove all the different transfers, which may have taken place in the tract claimed. This in a Country where the people so generally are illeterate, and where hundreds of sales have taken place, perhaps, without the script of a pen, and where the seller has long ago left the country, renders it now impossible for the claimant to adduce such testimony. I have heard of several claims in this situation which the commissioners have laid over, though the title in it self appears to be good, and is sufficient to show that the land has been properly granted by the former government.

This scrupulous mode of investigating the titles of land here is already considered as a hardship by a people whose rights in this respect have been secured to them by treaty, in a part of the country too where fraud or speculation has been hardly known. Another consideration in favor of the claimants, and which might serve at once to establish the usages and customs of the spanish government, is the encouragement hel̄d out at all times by that government, for the settling of their public land.

It was also an established rule that no person should come into the country without a pasport, or permission; therefore it is evident that if a person got foot-hold in the country at all it must have been with the permission of the government, and if he made a settlement it must necessarily have been done with the Consent of the government in some shape or other, and under a belief that land would be granted in a formal manner whenever it might be found convenient to make formal application for it. I have heard it remarked that an application of this sort has scarcely ever been known to fail of success. It is certainly the interest and an object with the American government to forward the settling of this country, as well as to quiet the minds of the original inhabitants, by confirming them in their rightful & equitable claims as early and with as little inconvenience to them as possible, and thereby secure their confidence &[4] attachment to the Common interest & welfare of the country. In the adjustment of the claims it is no doubt the wish of government to keep down fraud & speculation, such as antedated titles &c. but where it seems so well understood as it is generally in this country, that little or nothing of this nature exist it seems unnecessary to put every individual to the great inconvenience of trying to prove all the transfers which may have taken place in the tract he claims, and that they were just and legal. It is thought sufficient on the part of the claimant to shew that the tract claimed has been fairly granted, that it has not been forfeited nor abandoned, and that the government can have no claim on it. From every consideration I would give it as my humble opinion that the government could not do better than to pass an act confirming every individual in his claim, for which a notice or title papers have been filed in the registers office, except such as may appear evidently fraudulent or unfounded, and such as are to be reported to Congress for their determination. The claimants should be required to point out the boundaries of their respective tracts, that the lines and corners may be established, and the vacant land ascertained. In clashing claims it should be the duty of the Board to examine the titles and give their opinion as to the best right:—If the parties should be dissatisfied with such opinion and could not be brought to a compromise, or settlement they could then have their choice to settle it in a Court of law, or otherwise.

In cases of very large tracts and those derived from Indians, and land claimed by indians & such like, might be reported to congress with a statement of the circumstances and testimony relative thereto, for their determination thereon. Thus I think the adjustment of the claims might speedily take place, with little trouble or expense. It would set the minds of the people at rest and satisfy them that the government wished nothing else than to keep down fraud. If by this summary mode of decision[5] a few claims should be allowed whose title did not appear very clear the evil would be far less than to pursue a close scrupulous mode of investigation in which years uppon years will elapse before the business be brought to a close. The tracts generally are small. For want of information relative to the situation of the claims, I believe some instances have happened in which the Board have unnecessarily spent time, and several claimants put to the inconvenience of proving the validity of their titles, whose tracts are parts of a large grant, the title of which has been long ago perfected. Thus for want of a knowledge of the relative situation of the tracts claimed, the commissioners and claimants are subjected to this kind of inconvenience. Another reason why the commissioners should have a knowledge of the shape & situation of[6] such tracts as they are to decide on, is that imposition may be avoided

I think I recollect an instance on the Tombigbee river, where a person claiming 640 acres by settlement laid out his tract seven miles in length on the river bank, though the low ground at that place was nearly wide enough to have got the quantity of acres in a tract but little longer than wide. In the Mississippi territory the law, I believe, did not authorise the Board to have surveys made for their information.

The Board east of Pearl river ardently wished for such authority; and to supply the defect as much as possible, got several surveyors there to lay the plats down in a connected form as well as the nature of the case would admit of, which was of much service to them; but those surveys were very inaccurate, which has since occasioned some inconvenience.

The Board west of Pearl river, I think consulted Mr Gallatin on the subject, and with the concurrence of his Opinion, they caused a great number of surveys to be made, especially where the claims did, or were likely to clash; but in this territory the Board have objected to have a single line run, though the claimants themselves, in some instances have solicited it, and the law has authorised it to be done.

It is the opinion of several persons of experience in this Country, that the government has set out on a wrong[7] plan for adjusting land claims; and indeed the practise of it in the Mississippi territory shews it to be the case: for the business has been uniformly begun where it should end. Both in the Mississippi territory, and in this, Commissioners have been appointed to investigate the titles[8] before the necessary information for that purpose could be obtained. In the Mississippi territory, the commissioners found it necessary in many cases to wait for such information as the surveys would afford; and in this territory the commissioners acknowledge that such information is so necessary that they cannot consistently decide without it. From what I have seen of the business I am clearly of opinion, that, if the country where land claims are to be adjusted was first laid out into regular Townships & Ranges, and an accurate map made of the claims in each seperate Township before the Commissioners were appointed, that the whole business of adjusting the claims might be done with much greater ease, and with half the expense which has, & will attend the mode now in practise.

If the surveys were first properly made and connected, it would enable the Commissioners to issue their certificates in conformity with such surveys, and thus any misunderstanding afterwards might be avoided; but where the Board issue their certificates and merely confirm the claim without specifying or knowing its shape or situation it must afterwards be left to the claimant to point it out, and the business then seems to be as indefinite & unsettled as it was at first. The law has provided that the Surveys shall be made "agreeable to the true intent and meaning of the Commissioners certificates," and therefore those certificates should be made out in a manner that would admit of no doubt as to their true meaning.—And where the expense of making the necessary surveys before the claims are decided on, cannot cost the government, or the claimant one cent more than it will afterwards, and so many advantages are to be derived from it, and not one objection against it, it seems unaccountable why the opposite course should be prefered, and the making the proper Surveys put off for the last thing to be done. Where the Commissioners are fully authorised as they are here, to decide on claims agreeable to the customs and usages of the spanish government, and where the general policy and customs of that government are so well established & understood as they are here, it seems astonishing that the Commissioners should yet be at a loss how to proceed, and to remain in fact, years nearly, without doing any thing. It appears almost impossible that the laws on this subject could be made more favorable either as respects the commissioners or claimants.—However, without further speculation on the subject, I will venture to say, that I have seen too much business of this nature transacted in the Mississippi territory, and by a person of talents and industry, not to know that the time actually employed by the Board here, in the land office is not sufficient to enable them to accomplish the business of their appointments in several years to come, even if there were nothing to do but to examine the title papers, and write certificates.—In this matter I surely cannot be mistaken.

I will further mention to you, that it has come to my knowledge that M^r^ M,Gruder has been applied to by a respectable farmer of this neighbourhood to draw up a statement, to be signed by the inhabitants generally, setting forth the many disadvantages and inconveniences flowing from the delay in the adjustment of the land claims.—That the great scrupulosity evinced by the Board in the investigation of transfers, is for good reasons, unnecessary, and exceedingly inconvenient, and that the inhabitants generally are becoming solicitous about the safety of their title papers, and that they are very desirous to know the fate of their respective claims, whether they can be confirmed or not. I have been asked to do the same thing, and from what I have heard from good authority, I feel no hesitation in saying to you, that I am of opinion, the inhabitants of this country will not rest silently on this subject a great while longer.

For my own part I think it best to give you this information, that it may privately find its way to a source from whence a remedy can come without further inconvenience.

It appears to be entirely the opinion of the Board, and is well understood here, that three years will be the shortest time in which their business will close—indeed a longer time is sometimes mentioned; and therefore I calculate, that the cases to be reported to congress for their determination, will take up another year; then eighteen months more will be necessary to complete the surveys south of red river, making in all five years and six months[9] yet to come before the public land can be offered for sale; which calculation, I think may be made to a complete certainty, unless a total change of circumstances takes place. That the principal persons concerned in the adjustment of the claims, should be so connected & highly interested in the number of suits in the courts of law, is in the opinion of some here a circumstance, which in the end, will be more unfortunate to this country than all the delay which it has or may occasion in the adjustment of the claims before the Board.

I am Sir, With great respect your Obedient Humb[l] Servant.

GIDEON FITZ

P.S. I will mention one species of speculation, or traffick in land here, a case of which has lately occured.—A person lately from the United States wanting to purchase land, met with a man who offered a tract which he claimed by settlement, and went to the Registers office, where he satisfied the purchaser that the proof in support of the claim was sufficient to establish it; and consequently the land was purchased.—My informant says it is known to him that the land is covered by two other claims, both of a superior nature. This sort of imposition purchasers will be liable to, and without any means of avoiding it so long as the surveys remain unconnected. The consequence will tend to involve innocent persons, and the inhabitants into vexatious & expensive litigation, which in any country is an unfortunate thing; but where the result is so extremely expensive & uncertain, and which must continue to be so in this country while the society is in its present state, it cannot be too much guarded against by the general government; and I think it much to be regreted that every proper means has not been resorted to, to prevent this great evil as much as possible.

To give you an idea of the general mode practised in laying out land under the spanish government in this country, I give the following representation which I take from the tract of land I live on, and some others adjoining.—

The tract A, is laid out by measureing[10] the dotted line BC, for the front,—at each extremity of which a post is set, and on the direction of the side lines two others are set, one on each side line about the width of a square arpent from the others towards the Bayaus, as at D & E, which in general is at the margin of the woods & prairie some distance from the Bayau.—The plot is then made out without any further measurement, and an imaginary representation made of the shape of the Bayau for the front of the tract.—The other tracts are laid out in the same manner on another Bayau, and when the lines come to be extended are found to intersect as above represented. Many instances of this kind have come to my knowledge, and I have no doubt but there are some hundreds of the same sort, yet totally unknown even to the owners of the lands. When an american purchases land, it is common for him to have a warranty deed made for so much land as is contained within such bounds as are mentioned, and are represented in the plot, and whenever a connected plot of the claims be completed and such purchaser shall find that a great portion of his claim is covered by a title of superior dignity, it may be expected that he will then call on the seller for indemnification, which if refused upon any grounds, will probably lay the foundation of a law suit—And indeed in all other cases of interferences where the parties may think there is any advantage to be had

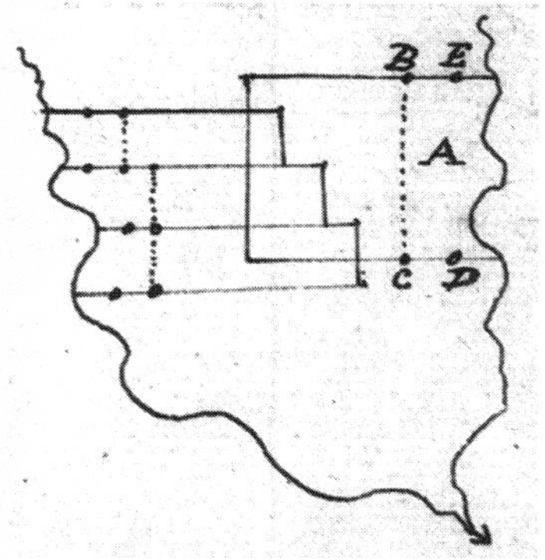

in law, it is to be expected that suits will be instituted. For these and many other reasons, it has long been my opinion that the claims in the whole country, should have been properly surveyed, & connected in a map as early as possible, and by all means before they were decided on by the Commissioners. Every days delay in the accomplishment of this business is giving opportunities for sowing the seeds of litigation. Land is every day augmenting in value, and with it every inducement for contention.— Deaths and removals among the inhabitants daily lessens the means of procuring proof for establishing the validity of claims, and therefore I think that every day the business is unnecessarily delayed is peculiarly injurious to the interest of the general government, and highly derogatory to the future peace and welfare of this invaluable country. G. F.

Tr (DNA: RG 49, Unbound Records of the General Land Office Relating to Private Land Claims in Louisiana, Letters Received from the Commissioners for the Western District of Orleans Territory); in Fitz's hand; between signature and postscript: "The Honourable, Thomas Jefferson late President of the United States"; docketed on separate sheet in part: "rec[d] in Th. H. Williams's letter to Sec[y] Treas[y] of Feb. 10. 1810" and "NB. He has been appointed Land Commiss. vice Richard Cocke at Opelousa."

TJ probably never received this letter, and while Fitz describes it as his THIRD LETTER on the subject, only one earlier, related letter has been identified (note to TJ to Albert Gallatin, 4 Nov. 1809).

In 1807 TJ appointed Richard COCKE to the Board of Commissioners responsible for determining land rights in the western district of Orleans Territory, based at Opelousas. Cocke did RESIGN HIS OFFICE in September 1809, and Fitz was appointed to replace him the following May. TJ appointed William Garrard (GARRAT) to the commission in 1808. John Thompson Jr., the SON of a territorial judge, was clerk of the territory's Superior Court for the Fifth District. In 1805 Allan B. Magruder (M,GRUDER) became federal agent for investigating land claims in the western district (TJ to Cocke, 3 May 1807 [DLC]; *Terr. Papers*, 9:468–9, 778, 805–6, 835, 882–3, 987–9).

Land claims in the western district of Orleans Territory were reportedly even more tangled than those in its eastern counterpart (*Terr. Papers*, 9:496–8; Harry L. Coles Jr., "Applicability of the Public Land System to Louisiana," *Mississippi Valley Historical Review* 43 [1956]: 39–58).

1 Preceding three words interlined.

2 Preceding two words interlined in place of "<*tho*> both."

3 Manuscript: "seldon."

4 Preceding two words interlined.

5 Fitz here canceled "the government."

6 Manuscript: "of of."

7 Manuscript: "rong."

8 Manuscript: "tilles."

9 Manuscript: "month."

10 Word interlined.

## From Elias Glover

D^R Sir, Cincinnati Nov^r 1^t 1809

Being desirous of repeling Certain Calumnies injurious to my reputation, which have been circulated by my inveterate & insatiable enemy John Smith—It is deemed necessary to procure if possible a copy of a certain letter addressed to you while President of the U States by Matthew Nimmo, Esquire, under date of the 28^th November 1806. Communicating certain information relative to Burrs late treasonable conspiracy—

I regret being under the necessity of troubling you on this occasion—Nor should I have done so, but that the evidence which that letter affords, is considered highly important as constituting a link in that Chain of evidence, for the protection of that reputation, which it has been the great object of my life to guard, and which my enemies, by the envenomed breath of slander, are seeking to destroy—

If the letter above mentioned is in your possession, you will confer on me a high obligation by forwarding to me a Copy of it, with as much expedition as your convenience will admit—If not, you will confer an equal obligation by informing me of the mode by which, a Copy may be obtained—

I have this day written the secretary of State on the same subject, but being uncertain whether it was in his possession, have taken the liberty also of addressing you—

Be pleased to accept my highest respect, for the many valuable & important services, rendered Your Country in public life, and my best wishes for your health & happiness in your retirement—

Respectfully Your Ob^t Hble Serv^t Elias Glover

RC (DLC); between dateline and salutation: "Th. Jefferson Esq^r"; endorsed by TJ as received 22 Nov. 1809 and so recorded in SJL.

Elias Glover was an attorney and secretary of Cincinnati's Republican party. Early in 1807 he sent TJ information concerning the possible participation of John Smith, United States senator from Ohio, in the alleged conspiracy of Aaron Burr. After TJ submitted Glover's affidavit to the Senate on 2 Dec. 1807, Glover feared reprisals (*JS*, 4:200, 220 [2 Dec. 1807, 18 Jan. 1808]; Glover to TJ, 30 Jan., 13 Apr. 1807, 3 Jan., 12 Mar. 1808 [DLC]).

In response to a request that he turn over a letter from matthew nimmo of 28^th november 1806, TJ informed the Senate on 8 Apr. 1808 that his records from 1 Nov. 1806–30 June 1807 gave no indication that he had received this letter (*JS*, 4:262–3).

## To William Miller

SIR Monticello Nov.[1] 1 09.

I shall be obliged to you if you will send me by post[2] a copy of Reuben Skelton's will duly authenticated from your office. it is dated May 18. 1752. but he did not die till Aug. 1759. which will guide you in your search for it. the ticket for the copy shall be paid to our sheriff if addressed to me, or to any other person to whom you may commit it. I am Sir

Your humble serv^t TH: JEFFERSON

PoC (MHi); at foot of text: "M^r Millar Clerk of Goochland"; endorsed by TJ.

William Miller (ca. 1767–1846) was clerk of Goochland County from 1791 to 1846 (Frederick Johnston, *Memorials of Old Virginia Clerks* [1888], 189; *Richmond Whig & Public Advertiser*, 9 June 1846).

[1] Word interlined in place of "Oct."
[2] Preceding two words interlined.

## To John Porter

SIR Monticello Nov.[1] 2. 09

On the reciept of your letter I inclosed it to the Secretary at War at Washington, with a request that the clerk, whose department it was, might inform you by letter what your right & remedy was. he has written the inclosed letter to you (forgetting however to sign it,) which the Secretary at war inclosed to me with explanations now also inclosed. you will percieve that you are to apply to Commissioners appointed by the District judge of Virginia, mr Griffin who lives in Williamsburg, and to satisfy them as to the wounds you have recieved. their report you had better deliver to m^r Dawson your representative in Congress, who by a few words of conversation at the War office may do what would require a long correspondence to effect. my occupations & desire to be unimplicated in any business will put it out of my power to be further useful to you in it. accept my salutations & best wishes. TH: JEFFERSON

PoC (DLC); at foot of text: "M^r John Porter Louisa"; mistakenly endorsed by TJ as a letter of 1 Nov. 1809 and so recorded in SJL. Enclosure not found.

John Porter (1759–1842), of Louisa County, claimed to have been confined at home for more than twenty years by rheumatism contracted during more than three years of Revolutionary War service as an enlisted man in the 2d and 11th Virginia regiments. In 1793 he unsuccessfully submitted a claim for arrears in pay during six months as a wagon master. Porter addressed similar claims to James Madison in 1802 and 1806, and in July 1809 he sought Madison's aid in obtaining a pension (Hamilton J. Eckenrode,

*Virginia Soldiers of the American Revolution*, 1:356, 2:244; *ASP, Claims*, 36:173, 178; Madison, *Papers, Sec. of State Ser.*, 3:476–7, and *Pres. Ser.*, 1:315; Porter to Madison, 1 Oct. 1806 [DLC: Madison Papers]).

YOUR LETTER is described in note to TJ to William Eustis, 6 Oct. 1809, in which it was enclosed. The EXPLANATIONS NOW ALSO INCLOSED, not found, were presumably extracted from Eustis's 25 Oct. 1809 reply to TJ.

[1] Word interlined in place of "Oct."

# To Dudley Richardson

SIR — Monticello Nov. 2. 09.

Your letter of Sep. 22. is just come to hand. on the 17th of that month I recieved one from your son Richard dated at the Parish of St Elizabeth's Cornwall county Jamaica July 27. 09. informing me he was well, that he was endeavoring to wind up his affairs on a small scale in order to return finally to the US. which however he supposed would require a year or more. he is desirous his brother George, <u>if not married</u>, should go to him. I have endeavored to find means of notifying this to George, but as yet have not been able to hear where to direct a letter to him. this being the sum of his letter to me I communicate it to you with pleasure and tender you my salutations & good wishes.

TH: JEFFERSON

PoC (MHi); at foot of text: "Mr Dudley Richardson"; endorsed by TJ.

On 15 July 1823 TJ sent Richard Richardson's letter of 27 JULY 1809, not found but recorded in SJL as received from Jamaica on 17 Sept. 1809, to his BROTHER GEORGE.

# From William Fontaine

DEAR SIR — Hanover Novr 3d 1809

Your letter gave me great relief—It reconciles me to my self—The friendly & flattering terms in which it is conceived, and the promptitude with which it was dispatched, afford the most decisive & consolatory[1] evidence, that you take an interest in my feelings; & that I have not lost your friendship. Far from any thing unpleasant having arisen at the hand of yourself or family, it was a conviction of the reverse that served to aggravate my suffering—as it appears that nothing particular, of the things apprehended, struck your observation, some explanation is rendered necessary—I have said enough upon the subject of that alarming situation in which I found myself, the day on which I left Montecello—Looking back upon the incidents of the preceding day & evening, in that indistinct form which my memory presented, I was struck with the recollection of a very abrupt & familiar address, made to that eminently respectable man, M$^{r}$ Galatine, upon the subject of his report upon the Canels, & the Dismal Swamp Country through which they pass, such an address as it appeared nothing but equality of rank and an intimate acquaintance could justify—another cause of disquietude was an apprehension that I had been indelicate in the matter or the manner of introducing the Story of our retreat through the mountains—and by the way, I have never been exempt from some emotion when that subject has been introduced, because I have so frequently heared & seen it made an occasion of the vilest & most execrable slander toward you—

But your goodness it appears is prepared to remedy or to overlook all the evils, whatever they may have been, of my indiscretion—

I thought, when my apprehensions seized Me, that every body must have heared, seen & felt—in truth I perceive that a sort of diseased sensibility increases upon me as I advance in years—that brings many a pang—In the present instance, you have happily effected my relief, and, as at first said, reconciled me to myself—

Should it happen that any thing carry me, at any time, near Montecello, I shall not forget your friendly invitation—I shall not neglect the opportunity of paying my respects to you—with the highest esteem & respect

I am, Yr. most obed$^{t}$ Serv$^{t}$ W. Fontaine

RC (MHi); endorsed by TJ as received 22 Nov. 1809 and so recorded in SJL.

In June 1781 a British raid on Charlottesville nearly captured TJ and obliged the Virginia General Assembly to RETREAT THROUGH THE MOUNTAINS to Staunton, bringing his service as governor of Virginia to an end (Malone, *Jefferson*, 1:355–66).

[1] Manuscript: "consolarty."

# From David K. Hopkins

Sir, Cynepuxent 09. nov. 3$^{d}$

Since I wrote you last year, I have not been Idle, I understand the Subject on which I wrote much better.—I observed[1] to you that all kinds of motion aught to be communicated by the Screw or, circularly inclined plane.—with water I wou'd (for to communicate motion to a Mill) inclose a circularly inclined plane, or Screw, nearly equal in length to the fall of water, erect it perpendicular & this wou'd be the

Spindle of the Mill; then we'll Suppose there's no opposition, the Screw wou'd yeald to the water, in consequence of which, the water wou'd fall perfectly perpendicular through[2] the inclos'd Screw.—by wasteing the Same quantity of water, that is wasted in any other way to communicate motion to a Mill, there's more power gain'd, but I cannot Say how much. we know in the overshot wheel, that nearly all the water is liberated by the time it falls half way down; much the greater part of water falls out of the buckets at that distance: but in this way not a drop escapes untill it descends to the bottom of the Screw, it runs in quietly & escapes quietly, having communicated the[3] whole of its motion to the Screw in falling: that is if the Screw is opposed by grinding, if there's no opposition it falls as rash through the Screw as tho, t'were not there.—I have never tried the experiment with a Screw longer than about a foot; you perceive that by carrying the Screw or thread round oftener, the motion will be increas'd, but the power lessen'd in a revolution & the contrary.—being at New-haven not long Since I was informed, I think by Col. Humphries, that a young man near there had communicated motion to a Mill by means of the archemedian Screw, (it was made about eighteen inches high & the water introduced below) with Success; this of Course was attended with more expence, & friction than the plan I propose the greatest difficulty with me is, whether or not there be the Same objection to the plan I propose that there is to Barkers Mill, that the water taking a centrifugal force looses its tendency downwards & causes the mill to run irregular. I cannot See how the water can either take, or, be inclined a centrifugal force in the method I propose; on this I wish your opinion most particularly as I Cannot ascertain without going to the expence of erecting one.—I remarked to you in my letter last year that the Sails of my wind-mill were on that principle. when the Mill was first put up the Sails were made in the usual Shape, I altered them a while before I wrote you last year, each Sail is a Section of a Screw, & I find about Eighty yards is as powerfull as a hundred & ten was. the Sails extend about eleven feet from the Shaft & I believe that a wind-Mill Can be built but twelve feet high to be better & Safer than when they are higher.—The observations on the action of the water on the Screw, may be applied to the action of the wind on the Sail of a wind-mill.—a Sail moveing in a horizontal direction Aught to be of the Same angle at top & bottom, but a Sail moveing in a circular direction, the Idea is foreign to what

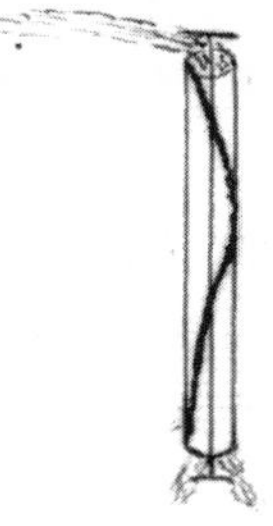

is correct to Suppose that the angle Augt to be the Same at any two distances from the Centre. The greater the distance of any pairt of the Sail from the Centre of motion, the greater is the motion of that part. a body of air rushes equally on all parts, the air cannot pass by as[4] rapid near the Centre as at a more remote distance. if the Sail be a Screw it's equally rapid & has the Same effect on a yard of Canvass near the Centre, that it has on one more remote, or, a yard of canvass does as much Service next the centre as one more remote.—I am affraid I Cannot easily communicate[5] the method Which I make use of to cause motion by application of wheels on the Screw I have applied it to a grind Stone & two hand-mills it Multiplies four time. you will See that it is a Concave Spindle with a thread passing round it, like a Screw or Circularly inclined plane: the perpendicularity of the thread increases as the Spindle decreases, & the contrary, So that the motion & power are equable, & the motion communicated by the wheels 1. 2. 3. & 4. being press'd down the inclin'd plane, each wheel causing a revolution in the Spindle. It required a great deal of time & attention to proportion So that the wheels might roll down perfectly free. but without a Model, its not easily described[6] but is extremely[7] Simple.—I hope you will Consider the Subject I have been writing on, & particularly relative to the operation of water on the Spindle before mentioned.

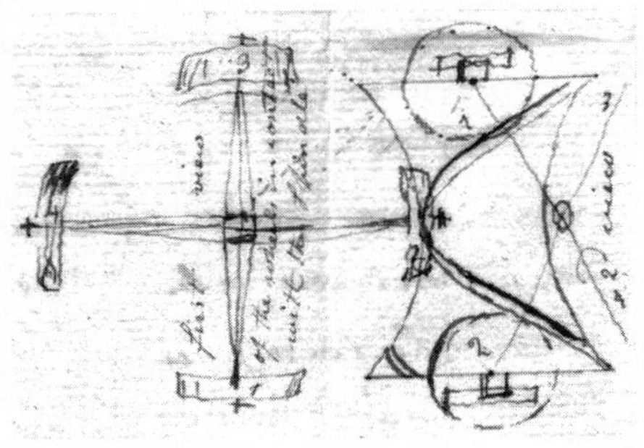

Take a cylinder of wood about 9 inches long & 2 in diameter lay it out with two threads each going half round, Cut away the Supperfluous wood, Stick a cupple of pins in the end, & Cover it with pasteboard, then place it in a perpendicular[8] possition,[9] & pour wa[ter] into it keeping it full, & I think I can venture [to say?] that you will be highly pleas'd; by doing this you can give a more Satisfactory opinion of it, you will be convince'd on trying it that the water has a more powerfull opperation than in any other way.—I have made[10] but few experiments as to the operation of Steem on the Circularly inclined plane, but from the experiments I have made & from reason, I believe it is the most perfect Steem engine.—it will give me great pleasure when you peruse this paper if you can tell me that you think my time has not been Spent totally in vain.[11]—its utility in pushing boats through the water must be very great, the operation will be

Silent & constant, & is exactly on the principle of Sculling only more perfect.—

Sir with the greatest respect I am your[12] most ob$^{t}$ & humble Serv$^{t}$

David K. Hopkins

NB if you will be So condescending as to give this Some considdeeration you will please[13] direct the result to the care of Matthew Hopkins Esqr. Snow Hill Maryland— David K Hopkins

RC (MHi); dateline between signature and postscript; torn at seal; addressed: "Tho$^{s}$ Jefferson Esqr Montcello Virginea"; franked and postmarked; endorsed by TJ as received 22 Nov. 1809 and so recorded in SJL.

David K. Hopkins (1781–1856) was a resident of Worcester County, Maryland, with a deep interest in the mechanics of motion. He visited TJ in Washington in 1806 and wrote him LAST YEAR seeking TJ's permission to lay his research before him, to which TJ responded encouragingly but noncommittally (Hopkins's tombstone at cemetery of Makemie Memorial Presbyterian Church, Snow Hill; Hopkins to TJ, 26 Sept. 1808, and TJ to Hopkins, 19 Oct. 1808 [DLC]).

1 Manuscript: "obseved."
2 Manuscript: "though."
3 Manuscript: "the the."
4 Manuscript: "a."
5 Manuscript: "commuicate."
6 Manuscript: "desribed."
7 Manuscript: "extemely."
8 Manuscript: "perpendicula."
9 Word interlined in place of "direction."
10 Manuscript: "mde."
11 Reworked from "been totally lost."
12 Manuscript: "you."
13 Manuscript: "pleas."

# To Clotworthy Stephenson

Sir Monticello Nov. 3. 09.

An absence from home has prevented my sooner acknoleging the reciept of your letter of Oct. 16. on looking into my papers I find nothing respecting you but your letter of Feb. 24. 09. requesting to be informed of the result of your documents & claims for services at the Marine barracks. the date of that letter will suggest the press of business which prevented an answer. with respect to your papers I can only say that according to the invariable course of business they must have been referred to mr Smith, the then Secretary of the Navy, first to be acted on & then to be filed in his office: and what confirms this is that I have examined my papers with that office as far back as the beginning of 1807. and do not find yours among them. indeed, if I can trust my memory, I think I recollect that I recieved mr Smith's explanations verbally in a conversation on your case. but for this I should rely more on his memory than my own, which is a very bad one. he will inform you on this head & probably enable such a search as may find your papers which I have no doubt are in the Navy office.

it is out of my power to give any other account of them than the present. I tender you my salutations with wishes that your search may be succesful Th: Jefferson

PoC (MoSHi: TJC-BC); at foot of text: "Mr Clotworthy Stephenson"; endorsed by TJ.

On 7 Nov. 1811 Benjamin Henry Latrobe sent documents relating to Stephenson's case, including this one, to Paul Hamilton, secretary of the navy (MdHi: Latrobe Letterbook).

# To Albert Gallatin

Dear Sir Monticello Nov. 4. 09

Not knowing whether the inclosed letter may give you information either new or useful, I hazard it on the bare possibility that it may. the writer both as to candor & understanding is worthy of entire credit. he is the son of a wheat-fan maker in my neighborhood, & living in the hollow of a mountain unknown to every body & with only a common education, he by some means got a copy of Gibson's surveying, an Euclid Etc and became, without aid from any one, master of their contents. hearing of him accidentally, I proposed to him to come to Monticello, gave him the use of my books his board, lodging, & moderate wages, with the liberty of dividing his time between reading & work as he pleased. he staid here about two years, & improved himself highly in Mathematics, & being desirous of going into the Western country, I gave him a recommendation to Briggs then Chief Surveyor South of Tennissee. Briggs soon discovered his value & made him his factotum, delivering the care of his office to him entirely, & left him in charge of it when he came away. since this I had heard nothing from him till the reciept of the inclosed letter. he is a man of the purest & most disinterested character, and harbors malice against no mortal. his views may be mistaken, but they are always clear of passion. I have gone thus far into his character that you may estimate properly his information if it contains any thing material. ever affectionately Yours Th: Jefferson

RC (NHi: Gallatin Papers); at foot of text: "Mr Gallatin." PoC (DLC); endorsed by TJ. Enclosure: Gideon Fitz to TJ, 12 Aug. 1809, not found, but recorded in SJL as received from Opelousas on 30 Oct. 1809.

# To Luis de Onís

Monticello Nov. 4. 1809.

Th: Jefferson presents his respectful compliments to his Excellency the Chevalier de Onis, & congratulates him on his safe arrival in the United States, & at a season so propitious to the preservation of health against the effects of a sensible & sudden change of climate. he hopes that his residence here will be made agreeable to him, and that it will be useful in cementing the friendship & intercourse of the two nations so advantageous to both. he would have been happy to have paid his respects to the Chevalier de Onis in person, & to have had the honor of forming his acquaintance: but the distance & bad roads deny him that pleasure. he learns with great satisfaction that his venerable & worthy friend, mr Yznardi, continues in life and health, and takes this occasion of bearing testimony to his loyal & honorable conduct while in the United States. he salutes the Chevalier de Onis with assurances of his high respect & consideration.

PoC (DLC); dateline at foot of text. Tr (TJ Editorial Files); 1955 typescript by an Onís descendant; at head of text: "His Excellency The Chevalier de Onis Ambassador of Spain at Washington."

# From Johann Severin Vater

SIR, Konigsberg in Pruss. the 4th Novbr. 1809.

Be pleased to accept the book, which I take the liberty to offer You as a mark of the high veneration, I have allways felt for the wise ruler of a great people,[1] and which I feel more particularly for the philosopher, who instituted and still pursues profound inquiries into the history of the native American tribes and their languages. I flatter myself, that, if You find my book deserving of some attention, You may perhaps be pleased to have it's principal contents published in Your language,[2] and I am confident, Sir, that You will promote the success of my passionat and perservering studies[3] of the languages of Your part of the world. The list of the Grammars and Dictionaries I had the opportunity to make use of, be pleased to see in my book pag 154ff. But nothing in this way would be more important to me, than texts of these languages, little narrations or dialogues, taken down from the conversation of the Indians, and explained by a litteral translation. I need not tell You, Sir, how important are extensive collections of the words of the American languages, but how little sufficient a collection of words, however extensive, can be for the purpose of obtaining an intimate knowledge of the structure and affinities of any language, how seldom it can be expected to gather information about the grammatical points, the terminations of nouns and of persons and tenses of the verbs; from such persons as may have an opportunity of collecting words, such, as Mr. Volney has given about the language of the Miamis, and that such specimens, as I desire to obtain, are the principal means of obtaining that knowledge what it is my wish to have.

I sollicit Your generous assistance not only for the interests of my own researches; it is not I believe too presumptuous to add, that it will be interesting to the general enlargement of historical information in Europe

Any communications, which You, Sir, may be disposed to send me, I beg You to direct to John Gibson Esq. to the care of Mst[s] Cox, Heisch and Compy at London or to the Consul of the United states at Petersbourgh

I am most respectfully
Sir Your most humble servant JOHN SEVERIN VATER
Professor.

RC (CSmH: JF-BA); dateline at foot of text; endorsed by TJ as received 16 Sept. 1810 and so recorded in SJL. Enclosure: Vater, *Untersuchungen über Amerika's Bevölkerung aus dem alten Kontinente* (Leipzig, 1810; Sowerby, no. 443). Enclosed in Levett Harris to TJ, 13 June 1810, and William Lee to TJ, 8 Aug. 1810.

Johann Severin Vater (1771–1826), philologist, was educated at the University of Jena and the University of Halle, where he received his doctoral degree in 1794. He became a full professor of theology and Oriental languages at the University of Jena in 1799 and was named to the same chair at the University of Königsberg in January 1809. Vater published grammars of numerous languages, including Polish and Russian, and completed Johann Christoph Adelung's *Mithridates: Oder Allgemeine Sprachenkunde* (Berlin, 1806–17) after Adelung's death in 1806 (Ernst Eichler and others, eds., *Johann Severin Vater—Ein Wegbereiter der Deutsch-Slawischen Wechselseitigkeit* [1984], 1–18; Greene, *American Science*, 382).

VOLNEY printed a four-page "Vocabulaire de la Langue des Miamis" at the end of the second volume of his *Tableau du Climat et du Sol des États-Unis d'Amérique* (Paris, 1803; Sowerby, no. 4032).

[1] Reworked from "country."
[2] Reworked from "tongue."
[3] Manuscript: "studis."

# From David Campbell

DEAR SIR. State of Tennessee Knox Ville Nov[r] 5[th] 1809—

Having a direct conveyance I cannot deny myself the pleasure of expressing the high consideration and Esteem I continue to entertain for you. I shall not name public or political matters to you. You know them all better than I do myself. The State of Tennessee increases in population and consequence remarkably indeed. The Cherokees will soon leave us their Country. They are daily emigrating to their new Settlements West of the Mississippi.

America is the fortunate Country, and the State of Tennessee is the fortunate spot in America. No invading enemy can ever reach our peaceful Country. No part of the Earth exceeds us in Soil, climate, and fine Streams of Water. We will be a farming and a manufacturing Country. When I consider that happiness is the endowment of the mind, I rejoice I have settled here, where my family can enjoy plenty, and ease.

My Son Thomas Jefferson Campbell is now eighteen years old, a fine constitution, and tolerable education. He hesitates whether he will study law or physic. Will you give me your opinion on this Subject, if not too troublesome. I have now another Son three years old. I have named him for another favourite, General Victor Moreau. I intend my Son Jefferson shall visit you at Monte Cello shortly that he may see the man for whom he was named, and who has allways been the Admiration of his father.

May every felicity attend you through the revolving Ages of time and Eternity DAVID CAMPBELL

RC (DLC); addressed: "The Honble Thomas Jefferson esqr Monte Cello State of Virginia Fav[d] by Lieu[t] Payton"; endorsed by TJ as received 3 Jan. 1810 and so recorded in SJL.

David Campbell (1750–1812) was born in Augusta County. Late in the 1770s he combined service as a Virginia militia officer, rising to major, with employment as clerk of Washington County. Campbell was admitted to the bar and moved to North Carolina, where he represented Greene County in the state legislature and served as a judge both for North Carolina and for the short-lived state of Franklin in what is now eastern Tennessee. In 1790 George Washington appointed Campbell a judge for the Southwest Territory, and after Tennessee won statehood he sat on its Superior Court of Law and Equity, 1797–1807. James Madison appointed Campbell a territorial judge in Mississippi in 1811 but poor health kept him from filling that position (*PTJ*, 16:478; Jackson, *Papers*, 1:122n; *JEP*, 1:50, 2:174, 175 [7, 8 June 1790, 2, 3 Mar. 1811]; Thomas Jefferson Campbell, *Records of Rhea: A Condensed County History* [1940], 118–20).

On 3 Nov. 1791 Campbell advised TJ of the naming of THOMAS JEFFERSON campbell (*PTJ*, 22:290, 27:805). The French revolutionary general Jean VICTOR MOREAU was accused of complicity with the Royalists, exiled from France in 1804, and soon settled near Trenton, New Jersey (Connelly, *Napoleonic France*, 344).

## From Thomas Eston Randolph

Dear Sir Milton 5th Novr 1809

I have taken advantage of Mrs Randolph's absence to employ the house servant at my buildings—who has had the care of the rabbits—and I observe they have suffer'd by a change of keepers—I therefore send you a pair which have been long reserv'd for you—and hope you may succeed with them better than I have done—They may be fed with Cabbage leaves—clover—indeed almost any kind of green food—when they will not require water—but if feed with wheat bran of which they are very fond—a little water will be necessary—

I salute you with Affectionate regards

Thos Eston Randolph

RC (MHi); dateline at foot of text; endorsed by TJ as received 5 Nov. 1809 and so recorded in SJL.

## From William Turpin

Most Respected Sir [received 5 Nov. 1809]

this will be handed you by my Neighbor Thos Mitchell, he intends calling on you as he passes through Albermarle, you will find him a Man of information and friendly to the present administration.

the high esteem which I have for you, has originated in the love and good will, which I have discovered in your writings as well as in almost every public act of your administration, the more perfect any Mans works are the more good may be hoped for, from opening and canvassing of them, if you should be disposed to admit of Such a Correspondence, with an humble unambitious Citizen, its possible that I may take Some Texts from Jeffersons Notes on Virginia if happily I might glance a Ray of Light that might be improved, Towards releaving the distress of any part of Creation, I doubt not it will be acceptable to your inlightened mind.

Several of my communications to you when in Office was without Signature that you might have the benefit of the information without Knowing from whence it Came, to avoid a surmise, that I wished to ingraciate myself into favor, as my only object was to defeat the designs of those who by a mistaken polecy might endanger the peace of our Country.

We are Sorry that your abode is so far from the Seat of Government, where your Councel might be of the utmost importance at this Trying time, altho we have full confidence in your successor, and hope that the experiments which he has ventured to make, of accepting the British deceptive propositions, and admitting their Ships of War into our Ports, will have a good effect to conciliate ourselves, which is a desirable object, for now their are but few amaricans that will openly dare to Espouse their Cause, unity among ourselves is of more Consiquince to us, than the Smiles or frowns, of any of the Powers at War, if they are to be Scourged let the hand of desolation destroy them alone, let us follow your policy and have as little as possible to do with them, if we are anywise Connected with either of them, and partake of their Crimes, we must partake of their Punnishment also, therefore its our safest way to Stand a far off, from any connection with either, until their destiney is determined, you See that Great Britain has ordered all her desposable force into foreign Service, if they should continue this Plan and they Should be intraped, may not the fall of their own Island be the natural Consiquince,

M[r] Mitchell is able to inform you of every thing in this part of the Country that you may wish to Know

Your Friend

WILL[M] TURPIN

RC (MHi); undated; endorsed by TJ as received 5 Nov. 1809 "(by mr Mitchill of S.C.)" and so recorded in SJL.

William Turpin (ca. 1755–1835), a prominent Charleston merchant, held a variety of local positions and represented St. Philip and St. Michael parishes in the South Carolina House of Representatives briefly in 1809. He owned property in South Carolina and in New York City, where he spent the last years of his life. Turpin later advocated the colonization of slaves and in 1825 sent TJ an abolitionist tract and urged him to follow Turpin's lead by freeing his slaves in his will and sending them to Haiti (*BDSCHR*, 4:574–5; Turpin to TJ, 29 Mar. 1825).

Thomas Rothmahler MITCHELL served with Turpin in the South Carolina House of Representatives in 1809 (*BDSCHR*, 4:404–5). Turpin wrote TJ WITHOUT SIGNATURE at least twice, on 30 May and 1 June 1808 (DLC).

# To George Jefferson

DEAR SIR Monticello Nov. 6. 09.

M[r] I. Coles was mentioning to me to day a sale of tobacco by mr Carter, his brother in law, the other day, under the hammer as he termed it for 39/6 tho the remnant & most indifferent of the crop, & that his brothers had sold in this way for high prices for two years past. the sale he says was by his agent there (perhaps of the name of Gwathney) getting some merchants together to bid against one another, himself taking care by a by-bidder not to let it go below a certain price. I barely mention this to you, assured that in this or such other way as you judge best, you will procure a sale of mine whenever you can obtain my minimum of 6.D. a sale before the meeting of Congress will be more probably advantageous than afterwards. Jackson's budget will then be known & will probably be a damper. I wish to begin the reduction of my note to mrs Tabb. always affectionately yours TH: JEFFERSON

PoC (MHi); at foot of text: "M[r] G. Jefferson"; endorsed by TJ.

The sister of Isaac A. COLES, Mary Elizabeth Coles, married Robert CARTER (William B. Coles, *The Coles Family of Virginia* [1931, repr. 1989], 52, 55). TJ had sold tobacco to the firm of R. & T. GWATHNEY through Gibson & Jefferson the previous year (*MB*, 2:1233; Gibson & Jefferson to TJ, 29 Oct. 1808 [MHi]). BUDGET: figuratively, a collection or stock of news or a letter containing it (*OED*), presumably here referring to information from British envoy Francis James Jackson on trade restrictions that could lower tobacco prices.

# From Jacob L. Kesteloot

MONSIEUR! La hayé le 6 Novembre 1809

J'ai l'honneur de vous offrir, par l'occasion de M[r] Troost, ún exemplaire du discours Sur les progrès des Sciences, lettres et arts depuis 1789, (Première partie); Ouvrage au qúel j'ai ajouté quelques notes. Je m'estimerais heureux, S'il vous plaisait, Monsieur, de considérer cet offre, comme úne faible marque [de] la haute considération avec la quelle [j'ai l'] honneur d'être.

Monsieur Votre Devoué Serviteur J. L. KESTELOOT

P.S. J'espère trouver une occasion favorable pour Envoyer le 2. Vol. dès qu'il sortira de la presse.

EDITORS' TRANSLATION

SIR! The Hague 6 November 1809

I have the honor of offering you, by means of an opportunity presented by Mr. Troost, a copy of Discours sur les progrès des sciences, lettres et arts depuis 1789 (Part One); a work to which I have added several notes. I would deem myself happy if it pleased you, Sir, to consider this offering as a feeble token [of] the high esteem with which [I have the] honor of being.

Sir your devoted servant J. L. KESTELOOT

P.S. I hope to find a favorable opportunity for sending the second volume as soon as it leaves the press.

RC (MWA); mutilated; at head of text: "à M[r] Jefferson"; endorsed by TJ. Recorded in SJL as received 1 Sept. 1818. Translation by Dr. Amy Ogden. Enclosure: Kesteloot, *Discours sur les progrès des sciences, lettres et arts, depuis MDCCLXXXIX jusqu'à ce jour*, vol. 1 (The Hague, 1809; Poor, *Jefferson's Library*, 13 [no. 831]). Enclosed in Gerard Troost to TJ, 21 July 1818.

Jacob Lodewijk Kesteloot (1778–1857) received an M.D. from the University of Leiden in 1800 and established himself at Rotterdam. Active in the European scientific and literary community, he had translated medical treatises on vaccination and yellow fever before publishing the enclosed overview of recent intellectual developments. Kesteloot was named professor of medicine at the University of Ghent in 1817 (Académie Royale des sciences, des lettres, et des beaux-arts de Belgique, *Biographie Nationale* [1866–1944], 10:696–705; Abraham J. van der Aa and others, *Biographisch Woordenboek der Nederlanden* [1852–78, repr. 1969], 4:43–4).

# To Thomas Lomax

DEAR SIR Monticello Nov. 6. 09.

Your carriage arrived here last night only, having been detained some days at Edgehill by the late rains & consequent rise of the river. all the donations which you have been so kind as to charge on it have arrived in perfect order; and being to set out tomorrow for Bedford, this day will be employed in setting out the plants. by the return of the carriage I shall send you three or four Paccans and some Lima beans.[1] I propose to make me a large orchard of Paccan & Roanoke & Missouri scaly barks which I possess, & of Gloucester & common scaly barks of which I shall plant the nuts. to these I shall add the sugar maple tree if I can procure it. I do not see why we may not have our sugar orchards as well as our cyder orchards. having nothing new to communicate I shall only add that I am at all times Affectionately Yours TH: JEFFERSON

PoC (CSmH: JF-BA); at foot of text: "Col° Lomax"; endorsed by TJ.

[1] Preceding four words interlined.

# To James Madison

DEAR SIR Monticello Nov. 6. 09.

Yours of Oct. 30. came to hand last night. Cap^t Coles passed this place on the 31^st to Washington. I gave a copy of the paper you desire to Thomas Monroe for his government; and, through him, another to Mayor Brent, that the city magistracy might understand what I considered as the limits separating our rights & duties. Cap^t Coles can borrow either of these probably for copying. should they be lost, on my return from Bedford, for which place I set out tomorrow, I will send you mine to be copied.

On the 3^d & 4^th we had a fall of 3. I. rain, more than had fallen in the 3. months following the 14th of July. this morning the thermometer is at 33½°. a few spiculae of white frost are visible here; but I expect it is severe in the neighborhood, & that there is ice. I recieved a note from the Chevalr de Onis which I answered. perhaps he may make this the occasion of expressing his mind inofficially to me. Affectionately yours TH: JEFFERSON

RC (DLC: Madison Papers). PoC (DLC); at foot of text: "President Madison"; endorsed by TJ.

THOMAS Munroe was superintendent of the District of Columbia, 1802–16.

# From James Madison

DEAR SIR Washington Novr 6. 1809

I recd your letter from Eppington. I had not heard that either the Attorney Genl or the Govr of Illinois meant to resign.

Inclosed are several letters for you recd from France by the return of the Wasp. You will see the propriety of my adding one to myself from Mr Short; to be returned after perusal. Our information from Paris, of the 19th of Sepr gives no countenance to the rumoured[1] renewal of hostilities in Austria. The delay of peace in form, alone keeps alive such rumours. But why should such an event flatter the hopes of G.B? According to all the lessons of experience, it would quickly be followed by a more compleat prostration of her Ally. Armstrong had forwarded to the French Court the measure taken here in consequence of the disavowal of Erskine's arrangement, but there had not been time for an answer. The answer to the previous communication, had been, let England annul her illegal blockade of France, & the Berlin decree will be revoked; let her then revoke her Orders of Novr & the Milan decree falls of course. This State of the question between the two Powers, would promise some good; if it were ascertained that by the Blockade of F. previous to the Berlin decree was meant that of May, extending from the Elb to Brest, or any other specific Act. It is to be feared, that there is an intentional obscurity, or that an express & general[2] renunciation of the British practice is made the Condition. From G.B. we have only Newspaper intelligence. The change in the Ministry seems likely to make bad worse; unless we are to look for some favorable change, in the extremity to which things must rapidly proceed under the quackeries & corruptions of an administration headed by such a Being as Percival. Jackson is proving himself a worthy instrument of his Patron Canning. We shall proceed with a circumspect attention to all[3] the circumstances mingled in our affairs; but with a confidence at the same time, in a just Sensibility of the Nation, to the respect due to it.

RC (DLC: Madison Papers, Rives Collection); closing and signature clipped; endorsed by TJ as received 24 Nov. 1809 and so recorded in SJL. Enclosures: (1) Count Nicolas de Romanzoff to William Short, Saint Petersburg, 12 June 1809, expressing his and Emperor Alexander I's regret that Short's nomination as minister has not been confirmed; reiterating Russia's friendship for the United States and intention to send Count Pahlen as minister plenipotentiary even if the United States does not reciprocate, provided only that assurances are made that he will be officially received; and stating that Alexander had been moved by Short's reference to the friendly allusion to him in TJ's letter of credence and would like to have that letter, now without official value, as a keepsake of someone so virtuous, talented, and devoted to the betterment of mankind as TJ (Tr in DLC; entirely in TJ's hand; in French; at head of text: "Copy of the letter of Count Romanzoff to W. Short in answer to one informing him of the end put to his mission by the negative of the Senate"; Dft in RuAVPR [microfilm at DLC], dated 7 [19] June 1809; English translation in Bashkina, *United States and Russia*, 564–5). (2) Short to TJ, Paris, 15 Sept. 1809, abstracted by Short: "inclose to P.—letter of Romanz. to be communicated to him—to recieve Taylors letters for me—Mle Bouti [i.e. Botidoux] & Mrs Rs letter—inclose one now for Taylor—p.s. as to the articles agaist [against] him—as to my coming by France" (FC DLC: Short Papers, 34:6184–5; abstract in Short's hand from a portion of his epistolary record containing entries from 6 June 1808 to 16 Oct. 1809, written on sheets folded to make narrow pages; recorded in SJL as received 24 Nov. 1809). (3) Short to Madison, Paris, 15 Sept. 1809, enclosing no. 1, stating that he had immediately replied to Romanzoff that Pahlen would be received, requesting that no. 1 be sent to TJ so that he could be aware of the emperor's favorable opinion, reporting that he had sent the letter of credence to Romanzoff as requested, and asking that he forward no. 2 to TJ (RC in DLC: Madison Papers; printed in Madison, *Papers, Pres. Ser.*, 1:379–80). (4) Lafayette to TJ, 16 Sept. 1809. (5) John Armstrong to TJ, 19 Sept. 1809.

The CHANGE in the British MINISTRY occurred on 2 Oct. 1809, when Spencer Perceval replaced the duke of Portland as prime minister (Denis Gray, *Spencer Perceval: The Evangelical Prime Minister, 1762–1812* [1963], 254–5).

[1] Madison here canceled "delay."
[2] Preceding two words interlined.
[3] Word interlined.

# To Samuel Greenhow

SIR Monticello Nov. 7. 09.

Your favor of Oct. 25. was recieved the day before yesterday. I had always intended to get my mills ensured against fire, but was deterred by information that the mutual insurance co. was in a state of bankruptcy. mr Dawson being here, proposed to have the mills valued, & to keep up the report until I should decide, & promised in the mean time to procure information for me. this you were so kind as to send me, and I have entire confidence in the candor of your statement. but in your letter you express apprehension that the institution will be attacked at the next session of the legislature, & not without danger of suppression. under these circumstances I have thought it best to wait & see the result. I will therefore ask the favor of you to keep up the report[1] till further instructions from me. I salute you with esteem and respect. TH: JEFFERSON

RC (PHC); addressed: "Mr Samuel Greenhow Richmond"; franked; postmarked: "Milton Va 17th Nov"; endorsed by Greenhow as received 20 Nov. 1809 and answered a day later. PoC (DLC); endorsed by TJ.

[1] In RC Greenhow keyed to this word with an asterisk his notation at foot of text that "'Report' means Declaration."

# From William Fleming

DEAR SIR, Richmond, 9th Novr 1809.

I send you by mail the rattle of a snake which capt Mann, who presented it to me, said was six feet and a half long; and, from the length of the rattle, I have no doubt but his information was correct: tho' I do not recollect ever to have seen one more than four feet.—

Inclosed you have a lily of the Allegheny mountain; but it is so much withered as to have lost its fragrance: and I much regret that the roots I brought down have been mislaid, or would have sent you a few of them also. If they should be found they shall be sent by a future opportunity.

Pray present me very respectfully to mr Randolph his lady & family; and accept the assurance of my highest respect and esteem.

WM FLEMING.

RC (MHi); endorsed by TJ as received 22 Nov. 1809 and so recorded in SJL.

# From Gabriel Richard

SIR Detroit the 9th of 9ber 1809

I arrived at Detroit the 24th of July last. I found then about a Dozen of Indian children already at the School of Spring Hill. They appear till This momment, very content with their new Condition. I have written several letters from New york and from Detroit to mr Galatin and mr Smith the first Clerk in the dept of war. The Governor Hull has done the Same thing. and we have not yet received any answer from the Govt. The Governor does not wish to act before to receive

Some Special Instructions relative to the Institution I have under my immediate direction. your Excellency knows very well that Such Institution as this requires great expences especially in the Biginning, for the house furniture cloths, food, horses, cows &c.

As I Think your humanity inclines much to ameliorate the condition of the Indians; I apply with confidence to your Excellency that you may assist me in my undertaking. One or two[1] lines from You adressed to m^r^ Eustis & m^r^ Madisson Should do more than Several letters from me. I have neither time nor means to go again to the City of washington.

my presence is absolutly necessary at Spring Hill. I have already expended great deal of money to buy an Electrical machine, an air-Pump, an optics, a Spinning Jennie of 24 Spindles Cotton, wool, Spinning wheels, Cards, cloths for children, Timber, Shingles, Boards nails Glass, for Some buildings to be erected for the Indian School, and many other articles.

There are three women to attend the Children that is to Say to instruct them, to prepare their food make their cloths, mind them, walk &c. there is a Schoolmaster for Boys, a weaver, a man to cut wood and take care of the horses & Cattles. I had a Gardener all the Summer and falls, I have a Carpenter, I want also a Good farmer. for want of means we have lost the Crop of the year 1809.

I have written to the Dep^t^ of war, that I understood that the wages and rations of the three workmen or tradesmen at the usual rate, Should be paid from the 24^th^ July when I arrived here, and really I cannot do without, because I am in debt to a very large Summ of money expended for the use of the Indian School.

The Governor of Michigan advised me to Send my accounts which he will Certify to be correct and to draw on the Gov^t^ (N.B. I desired that he Should do it himself, but he has declined.) he has not a Single blanket to Give to these poor children who came to our School almost quite naked. I most take on credit at Some Store, to cloth them to feed them, or I most Send them back to the woods.

I Expect that you will be So Good to writ to m^r^ Eustis that what I require is perfectly corresponding with what was agreed between Gov^t^ & me last January. remember[2] him that 400 dollars yearly were agreed besides the three workemen.

In order to make our Institution durable, you have wisely thought that it would be very Convenient that the property of the farm of Spring Hill Should be conveyed. pursuant to this your own Idea I have made the proposal to the Secretaries of the Treasury and of the war dep^ts^ to pay to the Gov^t^ the Same Summ of 2000 dollars, the

Same that it was Sold at the public auction, to be paid in 4 or five years, one 4th or 5th each year. I ernestly pray you to Suggest it to the new Secretary of war. the distance to washington city is So great and the oportunity So Seldom occurs to receive what we may want, the change of the Public officers of Governement, all these require that This Institution Should be Established on a Permanent[3] Basis to Save all uncertainties:

If your Excellency finds proper to Give me Some directions Relative to my Correspondence with the Government, I will Submit me to them exactly. few lines from you will honour me exceedingly and will be accepted as a great favor by your

Sir most obedt & humble Servt

GABRIEL RICHARD
Director of the Indian School of Spring Hill.

P.S. your Excellency will have perhaps Some pleasure to hear that I make use of The method of mr Lancaster it is an Amusement for These young Indians to write on Sand. I make use also of the manual Alphabet of mr Sicard with his deef & Dumb—it is my intention to make my Instructions a kind of Amusement & Recreation for children.

RC (DLC: Madison Papers); dateline adjacent to signature; addressed: "His Excellency Ths Jefferson Late Presidt of the U.S.—Monticello"; franked and postmarked; endorsed by TJ as received 3 Dec. 1809 and so recorded in SJL. Enclosed in TJ to James Madison, 7 Dec. 1809.

Gabriel Richard (1767–1832), a French Sulpician priest, immigrated in 1792 to Baltimore, where Bishop John Carroll assigned him the task of spreading Christianity among the traders, settlers, and Indians of Illinois Territory. After spending six years there, in 1798 Richard moved to Detroit, where he soon won recognition as a staunch supporter of public education. He founded schools for whites, Native Americans and, later, deaf-mutes. Having obtained a printing press from Baltimore in 1809, Richard published the territory's first newspaper, which was short-lived. During his long and varied career, he also assembled a large private library, helped found both the University of Michigan and the Michigan Historical Society, and served from 1823 to 1825 as Michigan's territorial delegate to the United States House of Representatives (*ANB*; *DAB*; Dolorita Mast, *Always the Priest: The Life of Gabriel Richard* [1965]; Leonard A. Coombs and Francis X. Blouin Jr., eds., *Intellectual Life on the Michigan Frontier: The Libraries of Gabriel Richard & John Monteith* [1985]).

Richard sent a similar letter to James Madison on 17 Nov. 1809 (*Terr. Papers*, 10:287–92). He used the METHOD of English educator Joseph LANCASTER, which relied on older pupils to teach younger students (*DNB*; Sowerby, no. 1113). Richard also evidently employed the work of Roch Ambroise Cucurron SICARD, an influential instructor of the deaf (Sicard, *Théorie des Signes . . . Indispensable pour l'Enseignement des Sourds-Muets* [Paris, 1808]).

1 Manuscript: "tow."
2 Manuscript: "remenber."
3 Manuscript: "Permanet."

## From Nathaniel Chapman

SIR, Philadelphia, Nov 10th 1809.

By the Linnean Society of this City, I have recently been appointed to deliver their next anniversary discourse. The subject which I have selected for the occasion, is, an inquiry into the causes, and changes of climate. In consequence of the almost total want of written documents, I find that I am exceedingly embarrassed to collect a sufficient number of facts to warrant any conclusion respecting the alterations of climate in the United States. This, indeed, is a point which can only be traced by the help of the observations of persons now living, or by those traditional accounts, or unpublished registers of weather, which may have been handed down to us.

Knowing how active is your curiosity, and how wide the scope of your intelligence on all questions of Natural history, and especially those relating to our own Country, I am persuaded that it is eminently in your power to aid my researches.

May I be permitted to ask of you such assistance, as it may be convenient to you to give me, in this interesting, but very difficult investigation? My only claim, I am sensible, to your attention, in the present instance, arises from our belonging, in common, to the family of Science; you certainly one of the most distinguished; I, the humblest of its members.

With the greatest respect, I am, Sir, &c

N. CHAPMAN, M. D.

RC (DLC); endorsed by TJ as received 29 Nov. 1809 and so recorded in SJL.

Nathaniel Chapman (1780–1853), physician, was a native Virginian who studied under Benjamin Rush, took his medical degree at the University of Pennsylvania in 1801, continued his studies in London and Edinburgh, and then settled in 1804 in Philadelphia, where he established a prosperous private practice. He visited TJ during his presidency and sent him the prospectus for his *Select Speeches, Forensick & Parliamentary, with Prefatory Remarks*, 2 vols. (Philadelphia, 1808). Chapman taught at his alma mater, 1810–50, holding the prestigious chair of theory and practice of medicine from 1816. A member of the American Philosophical Society starting in 1807 and its president, 1846–50, he also founded the Medical Institute of Philadelphia, the first American postgraduate medical school, edited a prominent medical journal, and in 1848 was elected the first president of the American Medical Association (*ANB*; *DAB*; Irwin Richman, *The Brightest Ornament: A Biography of Nathaniel Chapman, M.D.* [1967]; Chapman to TJ, 13 Jan. 1807 [DLC]; APS, Minutes, 17 Apr. 1807, 2 Jan. 1846 [MS in PPAmP]).

## From Albert Gallatin

Dear Sir Washington Nov^er^ 11^th^ 1809

I perused your affectionate letter of the 11th ult° with lively sensations of pleasure excited by that additional evidence[1] of your continued kindness and partiality. To have acquired and preserved your friendship and confidence is more than sufficient to console me for some late personal mortifications; tho' I will not affect to conceal that these coming from an unexpected quarter, and being, as I thought, unmerited, wounded my feelings more deeply than I had at first been aware of.[2] Yet I can assure you that[3] I will not listen to those feelings in forming a final determination on the subject on which I conversed with you at Monticello. The gratitude and duty I owe to the Country which has received me and honoured me beyond my deserts, the deep interest I feel in its future[4] welfare & prosperity, the confidence placed by Mr Madison in me, my personal and sincere attachment for him, the desire of honorably acquiring some share of reputation, every public and private motive would induce me not to abandon my post, if I am permitted to retain it, and if my remaining in office can be of public utility. But in both respects, I have strong apprehensions to which I alluded in our conversation. It has seemed to me, from various circumstances,[5] that those who sought they had injured[6] were disposed to destroy, and that they were sufficiently skilful & formidable to effect their object.[7] As I may not, however, perhaps[8] see their actions with an unprejudiced eye, nothing but irresistible evidence both of the intention & success will make me yield to that consideration. But if that ground which you have so forcibly presented to my view[9] is deserted; if those principles which we have uniformly asserted,[10] & which were successfully[11] supported during your administration are no longer adhered to, you will[12] agree with me that to[13] continue in the Treasury would be neither useful to the public or honorable to myself.

The reduction of the public debt was certainly the principal object in bringing me into office; and our success in that respect has been due both to the joint & continued efforts[14] of the several branches of Government and to the prosperous situation of the country. I am sensible that the work cannot progress under adverse circumstances. If the United States shall be[15] forced into a state of actual war, all the resources of the country must be called forth to make it efficient, and new loans will undoubtedly be wanted. But whilst peace is preserved, the revenue will at all events be sufficient to pay the interest & to defray necessary expences. I do not ask that in the present situation of our foreign relations, the debt be reduced, but only that it shall not be encreased so long as we are not at war. I do not pretend[16] to step out of my own sphere and to controul the internal management of other departments. But it seems to me that, as Secretary of the Treasury, I may ask that, whilst peace continues,[17] the aggregate of the expences of those departments be kept within bounds such as will preserve the equilibrium between the national revenue and expenditure without recurrence to loans. I cannot, my dear Sir, consent to act the part of a mere financier, to become[18] a contriver of taxes, a dealer of loans, a seeker of resources for the purpose of supporting useless baubles, of encreasing the number of[19] idle & dissipated members of the community, of fattening contractors, pursers and agents, and of introducing, in all its ramifications, that system of patronage, corruption & rotenness which you so justly execrate.

I thought I owed it to candour & friendship to communicate, as I did to M[r] Madison & to yourself, my fears of a tendency in that direction, arising from the quarter & causes which I pointed out, and the effect such a result must have on my conduct. I earnestly wish that my apprehensions may have been groundless: and it is a question which facts and particularly the approaching session of Congress will decide. No efforts shall be wanted on my part in support of our old principles. But whatever the result may be, I never can forget either your[20] eminent services to the United States, nor how much[21] I owe you for having[22] permitted me to take a subordinate share in your labours.

With sincere respect and attachment Your obed[t] Serv[t]

Albert Gallatin

Moussier's letter is returned with an answer endorsed. Fitz's communication enclosed in your's of 7[th] inst[t] just received will be duly attended to.

RC (DLC); at foot of first page: "M[r] Jefferson"; endorsed by TJ as received 22 Nov. 1809 and so recorded in SJL. Dft (NHi: Gallatin Papers); dated 8 Nov. 1809; lacking postscript; with numerous emendations. Enclosure: J. B. Moussier to TJ, 14 Sept. 1809.

[1] Preceding seven words interlined in Dft.

[2] In Dft Gallatin here canceled "Had I listened only to those feelings I would have resigned & probably taken this winter a seat in Congress, which, as a personal object, would have been much more pleasing than my present situation, & also better calculated to regain the ground which to my surprize I found I had lost at least in one of the branches of the Legislature. After mature consideration I relinquished the idea at least for that time, in a great degree on account of my personal attachment to M[r] Madison which is of old standing, I am sure reciprocal, and strengthened from greater intimacy; and also because I mistrusted my own judgment and doubted whether I was not more useful where I was than I could be

as a member of Congress. All this passed in my mind before the last session; and the communication which I made to you at Monticello arose from subsequent circumstances."

[3] In Dft Gallatin here canceled "that circumstance alone would not induce me to carry into effect the intention, although I neither have listened nor will."

[4] Word interlined in Dft in place of "permanent."

[5] Preceding three words interlined in Dft.

[6] Thus in RC and Dft: the intent was probably "who sought to injure me."

[7] In Dft Gallatin here canceled "Perhaps my mind is prepossessed, and I <*see common occurrences with*> will not yiel."

[8] Word interlined in Dft.

[9] Reworked in Dft from "It is therefore solely on that ground which you have so forcibly presented to my view that I wish to place."

[10] Preceding five words interlined in Dft in place of "heretofore avowed & supported by."

[11] Word interlined in Dft.

[12] Dft: "must."

[13] In Dft Gallatin first wrote "<*I cannot*> my vow to" and then canceled "my vow."

[14] Reworked in Dft from "due to the joint efforts."

[15] In Dft Gallatin here canceled "draw."

[16] Word interlined in Dft in place of "mean."

[17] Reworked in Dft from "But I cannot consent to be Secretary of the Treasury unless."

[18] Reworked in Dft from "be."

[19] Preceding four words interlined in Dft in place of "feeding the."

[20] Preceding two words interlined in Dft in place of "what I owe to you, that you enabled me to lend my feeble aid in the."

[21] Preceding two words interlined in Dft in place of "what."

[22] Remainder of sentence substituted in Dft for "enabled me to lend my feeble aid to your labours."

# From John Milledge

DEAR SIR, near Augusta, Georgia. 11th Nov. 1809.

I recieved your packet of the 11th of last month containing Twelve different kinds of rice, for which you have my thanks—I am no rice Planter, but will divide the rice among Planters of that grain, who I know will pay particular attention to its culture, and ascertain whether any or the whole of them, are preferable to the aquatic, which we have in common cultivation—Three parcels contain bearded rice, which is the first of the kind I ever saw—the result of the experiment shall be communicated to you—

When ever you wish the cotton seed sent, you have only to drop me a line—I expect in a few years the cultivation of the short staple, or green seed cotton, will be done away, and the Orleans introduced in its place, it is better in quality by 5 or 6 cents in the English market, and more productive—the seed is small, and very little fuz attached to it—I thank you for the Ice land ram, the wool from the breed of that animal, will answer for clothing our negroes—The climate of Georgia is well adapted for fine wool, I sent some time back to Colo Humphrey's woolen manufactory, in connecticut, about forty weight, from the common sheep of our country, raised at a place I have on a sea Island, near Savannah—in return I got two parcels of broad cloth—one a fine piece of bottle green—the other inferior, but a substantial good cloth—In travelling home the other day from the low country, near midway of Augusta and savannah, at a widow Ladies by the name of Bonnel, who was engaged in her family, in making home wear—I got the wool which I have inclosed, and from what I recollect of the texture of the merino wool, which I saw last winter in Washington, it appears to me little inferior, and equal I think to the wool of Smith's Island—Hardly a Planter in the middle and up country of Georgia but makes his cloth, for his white family and negroes, and many make their cotton baging—

The crops of corn and cotton in this quarter are abundant. I have made about Fifty barrels of bene seed—I set off tomorrow morning for the City of Washington—M^rs^ Milledge is still confined to her bed, but better than she has been for some months past. She unites with me in our respects to you M^r^ and M^rs^ Randolph—

I salute you with assurances, of my esteem, and regard.

Jn^o^ Milledge

RC (DLC); addressed: "Thomas Jefferson, Esq^r^ Monticello"; franked and postmarked; endorsed by TJ as received 14 Dec. 1809 and so recorded in SJL.

# From Isaac A. Coles

D^r^ Sir, Washington, Nov. 12^th^ 1809

M^r^ Madison has just given me a Box for you, containing some Books I believe, which shall be sent by the friday's Stage, addressed to the care of M^r^ Benson the Post Master at Fredericksburg—

he has also given me for you M^r^ Livingston's treatise on Sheep which shall be forwarded by the next Mail. I have read it with some interest, and regret more than ever that I was not permitted to bring from France some of M^r^ Parker's fine flock.

M^r^ Boudwie the Partner of M^r^ Dupont de Nemours of Wilmington has lately been here, and pronounces the Green Mountain Sheep to be very far superior to those of M^r^ Custis—he was surprised at the fineness of the wool, and declared they were worth ten Dollars a head—I mention this as I know they are very inferior to M^r^ Randolph's, who is probably not apprized of the high value he ought to set on his flock.—He agrees to bind himself to take from me, and to give me one dollar p^r^ pound, for all the wool I will send him from my

Sheep, provided I will give them a single cross with a $\frac{7}{8}$th's Marino Ram; and if I will still continue to improve the flock, he will gradually increase the price to two Dollars. he will make this contract for any number of years, & for any quantity of wool, considering it always as a Cash Article—.

There are several articles of your property, I believe, still remaining here, and which were probably overlooked or forgotten when you left this, there is a large skin of the grisly Bear, and three or four Pictures which I have seen, & which shall be forwarded to Monticello unless you should desire to dispose of them in some other way—.

Inclosed you will find the last National Intelligencer which I send as it contains an Article of an interesting character—it will best explain itself. I beg to be presented to M[rs] Randolph[1] & to add the assurances of my warm and respectful Attachment.

I. A. Coles

RC (DLC); endorsed by TJ as received 22 Nov. 1809 and so recorded in SJL. Enclosure: Washington *National Intelligencer*, 10 Nov. 1809.

The BOOKS were part of an edition of the works of Anne Robert Jacques Turgot (James Madison to TJ, 6 Oct. 1809), and the TREATISE was Robert R. Livingston, *Essay on Sheep* (New York, 1809; Sowerby, no. 796). BOUDWIE: Peter Bauduy. George Washington Parke CUSTIS, George Washington's stepgrandson and adopted son, resisted the merino craze, citing the patriotic duty to cultivate native sheep and the prohibitive cost of merino sheep to the average American farmer (Sara B. Bearss, "The Farmer of Arlington: George W. P. Custis and the Arlington Sheep Shearings," *Virginia Cavalcade* 38 [1989]: 124–33). Meriwether Lewis had sent TJ a grizzly BEAR skin from Fort Mandan (Lewis to TJ, 7 Apr. 1805 [DLC]).

[1] Manuscript: "Randolp."

## From C. & A. Conrad & Company

Sir Philad[a] November 13th 1809

When Captn Lewis was last in Philadelphia we contracted with him to publish his travels & then & since incurred considerable expences in preparing[1] for the publication. The accounts recieved here yesterday by the Nashville newspapers of his decease induce us to use the freedom[2] to advise you of the contract. That such a contract was made should be known to whoever has controul over his M.S. and not knowing who to apply to we have after some hesitation presumed to adress ourselves to you, as most likely & most willing to point out to us what we ought to do—

It is with much regret & some apprehension of incurring your Displeasure that we address you on this painfull subject so soon after the unfortunate circumstance that gives occasion for it. But the consideration that it is not alone our individual interests, but those of our country and of science, that are promoted by forwarding the publication, (already much too long delayed) we hope will be deemed some excuse for troubling you, and perhaps may induce you to take the further trouble to inform us where and to whom we are now to look for the copy. Govr[r] Lewis never furnished us with a line of the M.S. nor indeed could we ever hear any thing from him respecting it tho frequent applications to that effect were made to him

With the highest Respect Yours C & A CONRAD & CO

RC (DLC); at foot of text: "Thomas Jefferson Esq[r]"; endorsed by TJ as received 22 Nov. 1809 and so recorded in SJL.

In the spring of 1807 John Conrad contracted with Meriwether Lewis to PUBLISH the journals of the Lewis and Clark Expedition (Jackson, *Letters of Lewis and Clark*, 2:392–7).

[1] Manuscript: "prepaping."

[2] Conrad & Co. here canceled "of addressing."

# From George Jefferson

DEAR SIR Richmond 13[th] Nov[r] 1809

Immediately on the receipt of your favor of the 31[st] ultimo by T.J. Randolph, (with which however he did not call until Saturday) I waited on M[rs] Page, and to my surprise was informed, that she had not a spare room, having lately taken two young ladies to board with her during the winter: and that it was therefore out of her power to accommodate Jefferson, unless he could stay in the same room with young Burwell, whom I formerly mentioned to you.—M[rs] P. expressed a fear of offending M[rs] R., and said that she did not know when she offered to take Jefferson, whose son he was.

I soon discovered that Jefferson was anxious to remain at his Aunts, where he had been from the time of his arrival—and that she likewise wish'd him to board with her. He said after I had been to M[rs] Pages, (which he had before forgotten) that his Father wish'd him to board with his Aunt, provided she could furnish him with a room: but this it seems she cannot do, & can only give him a part[1] of one with a young Gentleman now boarding there.—He appeared to be so very anxious that I should not place him elsewhere until he could hear from home, that I could not have done it, even could I have found an eligible situation for him: which however I find to be much more difficult than I apprehended.

A M$^{rs}$ Starke will furnish him with a room after the Session of the legislature, but will ask 250$. M$^{rs}$ Nelson as you will observe from the inclosed will board him, but cannot give him a room to himself. I desired him to ask his aunt what her charge would be, and to call on me this morning, but he has not during the whole day: perhaps he has been told that I have no right to make such an enquiry, & am interfering between such connexions improperly.

I hope my dear Sir, it is not necessary for me to say, that it would afford me infinite pleasure to render any service in my power to M$^{r}$, & M$^{rs}$ Randolph's Son, even were he not your Grand Son.

If he cannot be more eligibly situated than to board elsewhere & to have a room with me, it will give me very great pleasure to accommodate him.

I am Dear Sir Your Very humble serv$^{t}$ GEO. JEFFERSON

RC (MHi); at foot of text: "Thomas Jefferson esq$^{r}$"; endorsed by TJ as received 22 Nov. 1809 and so recorded in SJL. Enclosure: Judith Nelson to George Jefferson, 13 Nov. 1809, stating that her house was constructed in such a way that no boarder could have a room to himself; that she was boarding "several young Gentlemen of the first rate Talents & respectability, who have all agreed to Take a Companion"; that each provided for his own bedding, fuel, washing, and candles; that the quarterly charge was fifty dollars paid in advance; and that Randolph would be welcomed on these terms (RC in MHi).

Elizabeth Burwell PAGE was the aunt of William Armistead Burwell, who had previously served as TJ's private secretary and was now a congressman from Virginia. YOUNG BURWELL was presumably one of his relations. Thomas Jefferson Randolph's AUNT Mary Randolph opened a boardinghouse in Richmond in 1808 (Richmond *Virginia Gazette*, 4 Mar. 1808; Sterling P. Anderson, "'Queen Molly' and *The Virginia Housewife*," *Virginia Cavalcade* 20 [Spring 1971]: 29–35).

About this time the younger Randolph wrote his mother from his aunt's house that he had "waited with impatience for nearly a month expecting to hear from some one of the family (yourself excepted) respecting my final arrangements for the winter; The house is very much crowded at present, but we experience no inconvenience from it, having a room in another, I never see or hear the company except at meals . . . I am perfectly satisfyed with my situation" (Thomas Jefferson Randolph to Martha Jefferson Randolph, [1809], ViU: Edgehill-Randolph Papers).

[1] Preceding seven words interlined in place of "unless he will partake."

# Notes on Ivy Creek Lands

1809. Nov. 14. lands on Ivy creek to wit Tullas's 374. a$^{s}$ & Stith's 100. a$^{s}$ Campbell James Martin who lives adjoining them, thinks, Stith's worth 15.D. p$^{r}$ acre & both together worth 10.D. p$^{r}$ acre. he says a mr Tinsley of Amherst wishes to buy them & said he would give 1200.£—510. £ down, and two annual paiments of 350£ each, and meant to come when he should know me to be in Bedford. I authorised James Martin to sell to him or any other person on these or any better terms, & engaged to allow him $\frac{1}{12}$ of the price obtained for his trouble.

W[m] Martin the Surveyor says these lands will sell readily at 10. D. they are of excellent quality, well timbered, & have 2. good mill seats on Ivy creek. they lie about 2. miles on the road to Trent's ferry, extending to within 3. miles of Lynchburg in a direct line, & 4. by the road.

Nov. 17. gave James Martin written authority to sell on the above terms

MS (MHi); entirely in TJ's hand.

On NOV. 17. TJ gave James Martin WRITTEN AUTHORITY to sell as indicated this land, which his wife, Martha Wayles Skelton Jefferson, had inherited from her father, John Wayles (TJ to Martin, 17 Nov. 1809; *MB*, 2:1254).

# From the Citizens of Lynchburg

Tuesday Morning—[14 Nov. 1809]

The Citizens of Lynchburg, with unaffected pleasure, behold the arrival of M[r] Jefferson among them. Desirous to offer him, in the plain and simple mode that the infancy of their Society permits, an evidence of their Cordiality and respect, they wish to invite him to partake of a public dinner with them, at M[rs] Ward's tavern, on Saturday next.

RC (MHi); partially dated at foot of text; endorsed by TJ as an undated "Lynchburg. invitation" received 14 Nov. 1809 and so recorded in SJL.

# From Anonymous

[15 Nov. 1809]

The nature & importance of the Object of this Prospectus is the only apology I can offer, for an intrusion, that may appear novel & singular. The Preamble as published in the Boston papers, is added, & may give some explanation for me, unnecessary to repeat here—but only add, that this is a proposal for a publication, in which I shall never have any other concern, than as a subscriber, & zealous well wisher, (if it should ever appear,) & will do all in my power to support it, and look for my reward, in the pleasing reflection, of at least good intentions & earnest desires, to do some public service, as far as my poor ability & small sphere give me opportunity. If this humble effort should have a tendency, tho' in the smallest degree to bring forward & hasten a Virginia Garden, I Shall have an abundant reward. If you should think it worthy a republication in Virginia, I beg it may have such pruning & improvement, as you may think proper, by any addition, omision, or alteration. It is implicitly submited to your disposal. As I abhor flattery, I will not here detain you to tell how much I admire your maxims of policy, espescially in what relates to Peace, War, Commerce, the Indian tribes &c—& the undiminished confidence I have always had in your administration & still hope for in its effects, I hope the object & plan of this Prospectus, will be found in full accordance with your System, and as such it is offered, as a hearty testimonial of the sincere & grateful respect, I feel for you

THE AUTHOR OF THE PROSPECTUS

A word on Louisiana.

It may perhaps be asked, why a Territory of such [extent and] importance as Louisiana, should be left out of any project of [. . .] description, that has, or pretends to have, a public & National Object [in] view. This enquiry would deserve a respectful answer, and I do n[ot] consider it sufficient to say, that so extensive a range was not contemplated. The subject is too copious, & would open too wide a field of argument, to give even in the most summary way the numerous reasons. In a few lines then, I can only briefly say, for myself, tha[t] I have from the first to the present day, been an ardent admirer of the whole business, concerning the acquisition of Louisiana, & as far as my narrow ability & means would go, in its defence—and if no mo[re] benefit should come from it, than we have yet received, that would alwa[ys][1] abundantly justify it, & the authors & Agents of it forever deserve the gratitude of the Nation, for the good it has already produced.

But I look forward for much more. I think we have as yet received only the first fruits, & that by good management, many harvests of good things are yet to be reaped. This however cannot be, if it should be suffered to be within the grasp of the insatiable avarice of Land Jobb[ers] & Speculators, who would under a variety of new forms & plausible pretences, renew their "Land Banks," Missisippi, & Yazoo Scheme's, & "South Sea bubbles"—equal to the evils of Pandora's box But let it suffice for the present to say—Upon the excellent principles & motives which procured Louisiana, let the same excellent pacific policy, now govern & dispose us, to alienate all that we acquired, in exchange for all the remaining British Provinces on the Continent—but[2] excluding Newfoundland, because of its distance, and we have m[ore] than enough[3] & do better without it. and it would[4] require Ships & an army to defend it. I am opposed to a Navy in any form or degree, or for any cause, for none has yet appeared, unless it should be in such a case as the possession of Nfoundland.

As I always said, & am still of the opinion, it would require a Volume to detail all the reasons & display all the advantages and policy of the acquisition of Louisiana, in short to do justice to the subject—so now for reasons equally strong,[5] it might require an equal volume to do justice to the subject of the exchange, on the same principles, motives, & the benefits it would procure for us, & the great and permanent good it would secure to Posterity. I always[6] heartily wished for such a Volume, in the former case & there is now the additional reason for it, that the arguments,[7] in support of the negociation for Louisiana, would apply with equal force for the exchange

I have only to lament that I want both the ability & health necessary to write such a book, as I am persuaded a man of moderate ability & sufficient reading & information, would make it all plain

These crude thots so clumsily put together, should be copied over & made more fit for your attention, if haste & indisposition would permit—but it would be indecorus to take up any more of your time in apology—Please to accept my respects, and wishes for your Health

RC (DLC: TJ Papers, 189:33562–3); undated; postscript on Louisiana on second and third pages of sheet folded to form four pages; margin torn; endorsed by TJ as "Anon. (prospectus Mass. garden) Boston Nov. 15" received 10 Jan. 1810 and so recorded in SJL. Enclosure: *Prospectus of a new monthly publication, upon the plan, and embracing the several subjects herein specified: The Massachusetts garden and the patriot's common place book* [1809?] (printed broadside in MWA).

PREAMBLE . . . BOSTON PAPERS: a version of the enclosed prospectus with a preface by "George Public Good" appeared in the Boston *Independent Chronicle*, 20 Nov. 1809. The prospectus may have been written by Thomas Wallcut, a clerk in the office of the secretary of state of Massachusetts. The journal was apparently never published.

[1] Word interlined in place of an illegible word.

[2] Preceding four words interlined.

[3] Preceding six words interlined.

[4] Preceding three words interlined in place of "I am opposed to."

[5] Reworked from "the same reasons."

[6] Word interlined.

[7] Word interlined in place of "reasoning."

# From Marc Antoine Jullien

MONSIEUR, paris, 15 novembre 1809.

j'ai connu dans ma premiére jeunesse votre estimable compatriote le Docteur Priestley, qui a bien voulu m'honorer de son amitié et correspondre quelquefois avec moi. j'ai depuis été lié en france avec plusieurs de ceux qui vous ont connu personnellement et qui vous ont apprécié. Dans le moment actuel, M. Dupont de nemours, membre de l'institut, que je vois habituellement à paris, me parle souvent de vous et se rappelle toujours avec reconnaissance l'accueil qu'il a reçu dans votre patrie.

Permettez aujourdhui, Monsieur, que je saisisse une occasion favorable pour vous adresser directement, par les mains de M. Porée, qui retourne aux Etats-unis, un faible témoignage des sentimens d'estime et de vénération, dont je suis depuis longtems pénétré pour vous. Veuillez agréer l'hommage d'un Essai général d'Education, que j'ai composé, il y a deux années, et dont la seconde partie contient un petit traité sur l'Emploi du tems, qui a été publié séparément. j'en prépare une Seconde édition, que je prendrai la liberté de vous offrir. j'ose espérer que vous accueillerez cet ouvrage avec bienveillance et indulgence; je m'estimerai heureux qu'il vous paraisse renfermer quelques idées bonnes et utiles, et que vous ne le jugiez pas indigne d'être désigné, sous ce rapport, soit aux sociétés Savantes et aux académies, soit aux individus qui s'occupent, dans les Etats-Unis, de vues théoriques ou de méthodes pratiques, relatives à l'éducation et à l'instruction de la jeunesse. M. Dupont de Nemours, qui a rédigé, sur le même sujet, un plan général adapté spécialement à votre pays, a bien voulu donner quelques éloges à mon travail.

je joins à l'Essai général d'Education plusieurs programmes qui en exposent le plan, et un numéro du Moniteur qui fait connaître les jugemens qu'en ont portés diverses personnes, dont l'opinion aura peut-être quelque poids à vos yeux. mais, je vous prie de croire, Monsieur, que votre suffrage, si je puis l'obtenir, est un de ceux auxquels j'attacherai le plus de prix, parcequ'il sera celui d'un homme connu dans toute l'Europe par la sincérité et la noblesse de ses sentimens, par la sagesse, l'élévation et l'énergie de ses discours publics, et par la magnanimité de sa conduite politique et privée.

agréez, je vous prie, Monsieur, l'expression bien Sincère de ma considération la plus distinguée et de mon profond respect

JULLIEN L'AINÉ

Inspecteur aux Revues,

chef de l'administration
de l'habillement des troupes
au ministére de
l'administration de la guerre,
Rue Varennes, à paris.

EDITORS' TRANSLATION

Sir,
Paris, 15 November 1809.

In my earliest youth I knew your esteemed compatriot Dr. Priestley, who kindly honored me with his friendship and corresponded with me a few times. In France, I have since made friends with several people who knew you personally and appreciated you. At the present time, Mr. Du Pont de Nemours, a member of the Institut, whom I see regularly in Paris, often speaks to me of you and remembers with gratitude the welcome he received in your fatherland.

Permit me today, Sir, to seize a favorable opportunity to send you directly, by means of Mr. Porée, who is returning to the United States, a feeble token of the sentiments of esteem and veneration for you which have filled me for so long. Please accept the tribute of an Essai général d'Education, which I composed two years ago, and of which the second part contains a little traité sur l'Emploi du tems, which was published separately. I am preparing a second edition of it, which I will take the liberty of offering to you. I dare to hope that you will welcome this work with goodwill and indulgence; I will deem myself happy if it should seem to you to contain a few good and useful ideas, and if you will consider it not unworthy of being pointed out, in this regard, either to scholarly societies and academies, or to individuals in the United States, who are concerned with theoretical views or practical methods relative to the education and the instruction of youth. Mr. Du Pont de Nemours, who composed a general plan on the same subject adapted especially for your country, has kindly given some praise to my work.

I am attaching to the Essai général d'Education several outlines that explain its plan, and an issue of the Moniteur which publishes the judgments diverse persons have expressed about it, whose opinions will perhaps carry some weight in your eyes. But, I beg you to believe, Sir, that your approval, if I can obtain it, is one of those to which I attach the highest worth, because it will be that of a man known throughout Europe for the sincerity and the nobility of his sentiments, for the wisdom, the elevation and the energy of his public speeches, and for the magnanimity of his political and private conduct.

Accept, I beg you, Sir, the truly sincere expression of my most distinguished esteem and of my deepest respect

Jullien the elder
Parade Inspector,
Quartermaster General
of the Ministry of War,
Rue Varennes, in Paris

RC (DLC); at head of text: "à Monsieur Jéfferson, membre associé de l'institut de france, ex-président des Etats-Unis"; endorsed by TJ as received 6 May 1810 and so recorded in SJL. Enclosures: (1) Jullien, *Essai Général d'Education physique, morale, et intellectuelle* (Paris, 1808; Sowerby, no. 1108). (2) *Gazette nationale, ou, Le Moniteur universel*, 18 Dec. 1808, containing favorable reviews of the preceding. Other enclosures not found. Enclosed in Jean B. Porée to TJ, 2 May 1810.

Marc Antoine Jullien (1775–1848), French revolutionary turned liberal, was a cosmopolitan and complex figure who participated in the Italian revolutionary movement in 1797 and supported Latin American revolutions against Spain but also served Napoleon as a military bureaucrat. Jullien corresponded sporadically with TJ, sent him his works on politics and educational theory, and edited the *Revue Encyclopédique*, 1819–35 (*DBF*; *Biographie universelle*, 21:324–6; Robert R. Palmer, ed., *From Jacobin to Liberal: Marc-Antoine Jullien, 1775–1848* [1993]; Poor, *Jefferson's Library*, 5, 11, 13 [nos. 211, 680, 835]).

Jullien's enclosed general discussion of education appeared as Napoleon sought to organize an imperial university, which Jullien's work supported (Palmer, *Jacobin to Liberal*, 111–3).

# Appendix

## Supplemental List of Documents Not Found

JEFFERSON'S epistolary record and other sources describe a number of documents for which no text is known to survive. The Editors generally account for such material at documents that mention them or at other relevant documents. Exceptions are accounted for below.

From Elisha Tracy, 5 Mar. 1809. Recorded in SJL as received from Norwich, Connecticut, on 16 Mar. 1809.

From the Editors of the Raleigh *Star*, 19 Mar. 1809. Recorded in SJL as received from Raleigh on 3 Apr. 1809.

From P. Deane, 2 July 1809. Recorded in SJL as received 5 July 1809.

From B. S. Bulfinch, 23 July 1809. Recorded in SJL as received from Providence, Rhode Island, on 6 Aug. 1809.

From William Tatham, 28 July 1809. Recorded in SJL as received from Norfolk on 23 Aug. 1809.

From Adriaan G. Camper, [ca. 31 July 1809]. Written (most likely from Franeker in the Netherlands) to TJ in his capacity as president of the American Philosophical Society. It was probably never received by him, being known only from Camper's letter of 10 Nov. 1809 to Caspar Wistar (PPAmP: Caspar Wistar Papers), in which Camper alludes to his earlier "letter to your President, containing my humble thanks for the Honour of being associated to that illustrious Society" and requesting a duplicate of his membership diploma, the original having been detained by the French government.

From Peter Lawur, 18 Aug. 1809. Recorded in SJL as received from New York on 23 Aug. 1809.

From John Muzzy, 23 Aug. 1809. Recorded in SJL as received from Monkton, Vermont, on 25 Sept. 1809.

From Maj. Zuthke, 19 Oct. 1809. Recorded in SJL as received from New Orleans on 22 Nov. 1809.

# INDEX


*Acacia farnesiana* (sweet acacia), 555, 631–2
Adams, George: *Geometrical and Graphical Essays*, 581; *Lectures on Natural and Experimental Philosophy*, 581
Adams, John: friendship with TJ, 185–6n; on retirement, 513
Adams, John Quincy: and charges against Waterhouse, 296; minister to Russia, 38, 328, 360, 537; rumored as secretary of state, 118
Addington, Henry, 507
*Address at the Opening of the Botanic Garden of Liverpool* (Roscoe), 164n
*Address to the People of the United States* (Robert Smith), 340n
Adelung, Johann Christoph: *Mithridates: Oder Allgemeine Sprachenkunde*, 265, 267n, 652n
Adlum, John: *Adlum on Making Wine*, 587n; identified, 587n; letter to, 586–7; *A Memoir on the Cultivation of the Vine in America, and the Best Mode of Making Wine*, 587n
*Adlum on Making Wine* (Adlum), 587n
*Aesculus hippocastanum* (horse chestnut), 593, 594n
*Aesop's Fables*: advocated for Indians, 110
agriculture: Agricultural Society of Albemarle, 53–4n; Agricultural Society of Philadelphia, 133; books on, 35, 36, 37, 508, 581–2; British Board of Agriculture, 252; Columbian Agricultural Society, 23n, 40n, 133, 134n; *Domestic encyclopædia*, 18, 19n, 252; Pennsylvania moldboard, 111, 252; Philadelphia Society for Promoting Agriculture, 477, 479–80n; TJ buys fruit trees, 40; TJ on, 110, 252, 559. *See also* dynamometer; ploughs; Société d'agriculture du département de la Seine
Ainsworth, Robert: *Latin and English Dictionary abridged*, 35
Akers, John, 415
Alabama River, 351
Albaflor wine, 345, 346
Albemarle Baptist Church of Christ. *See* Buckmountain Baptist Church (Albemarle Co.)
Albemarle County, Va.: Agricultural Society of, 53–4n; Buckmountain Baptist Church, 63–4, 126; inhabitants of, address TJ, 46–7, 74; inhabitants of, meet with TJ, 79; map of, xliii; schools in, 82n; TJ addresses inhabitants of, 102–3; Woods, Micajah (deputy sheriff), 590, 595
Albemarle County Court, Va., 415n
*Albizia Julibrissin* (mimosa tree; silk tree), 631
alcohol: beer, 299; cider, 581, 657; claret, 387, 397n; French brandy, 268, 368; gin distilling, 465; Madeira, 387, 397n; medicinal uses of, 483; rum, 299; whiskey, 31, 465. *See also* drunkenness; wine
Aleutian Islands, 447
Alexander, Eli: grinds wheat, 109, 353; identified, 137–8n; letter from, 353; letters to, 137–8, 353; rent due from, 353
Alexander I (emperor of Russia): diplomatic appointments, 537; and letters of credence, 328, 343–4, 359, 484, 485n; TJ's relationship with, 38, 433, 659n; and U.S., 115–6, 233, 328, 659n
*Alisma plantago-aquatica* (water plantain), 57–8n
Allegany County, Md.: letter to citizens of, 94
Allegheny lily (*Lilium Martagon*; Turk's-cap), 660
Allone, William B. W.: letter from, 101–2
allspice, 45
*American, and Commercial Daily Advertiser* (Baltimore): prints TJ's correspondence, 178n, 221n
*American Artillerist's Companion* (Tousard), 412
American Colonization Society, 30n, 39n
*American Magazine*, 106n
American Philosophical Society: foreign members of, 72n, 146n, 452, 453n, 471n; forwards publications to TJ, 452, 453n; librarian of, 452–3, 455, 482; and mastodon bones, 511; members of, 152n, 172n, 194n, 482, 571–2; officers of, 101n; and Philadelphia Museum, 46n; TJ as president of, 540; TJ forwards material to, 97–8,

American Philosophical Society (*cont.*) 100–1, 140, 152n, 482, 535, 571–2, 608–9; *Transactions*, 36; Wistar and, 100, 677
American Revolution: historiography of, 288–9, 334, 634n
*American State Papers and Public Documents*, 36
Amherst, Sir Jeffery, 290
Amiot, Mme, 450
ammonium chloride (sal ammoniac): for copper utensils, 467
*The Anabasis* (Xenophon; trans. Spelman), 580
Analysis of Green Tobacco (Vauquelin), 142–6, 482
Analysis of Prepared Tobacco (Vauquelin), 147–52, 482
anatomy: books on, 35, 307; study of, 101n
*Anatomy of the Human Body* (Bell), 35, 307
anchovies, 366
Anderson, Joseph, 119, 473
Anderson, Richard: and Henderson lands, 440, 454, 459, 460
Anderson, William, 444, 445n
Andrei, Giovanni: and carving for TJ, 474–5, 595; sculptor for U.S. Capitol, 78n
Anglo-Saxon laws, 383
Ann Smith Academy (Lexington), 367, 368n, 506, 507n
anonymous correspondents: letters from, 69–70, 291–2, 654, 655n, 671–3
Anthony, Benjamin, 257n
Antient Plymouth Society (New London), 58–9, 102
antimony, 189; used in casting type, 18, 19n, 283, 314, 315–6
antiquities: and government, 254n; *Husbandry of the Antients* (Dickson), 581; paintings of, 522, 523–4n; and vases, 452, 453n, 482; *Villas of the Ancients Illustrated* (Castell), 390, 397n
Antoinette, Marie, queen of France, 250n
apoplexy, 526
*Apuntes ligeros sobre la nueva constitución* (Foronda), 470–1, 577, 604, 606n
Archbald, James, 238–40
Archbald, Mary Ann Wodrow: identified, 240n; letter from, 238–40
architecture: TJ's opinion on Monticello as, 595–6. *See also* building materials
Arcueil, Société de, 264, 267n, 316
Arkansas (trading post): meteorological observations at, 97–8, 482, 608–9
Arkansas River, 97n
Arkwright, Sir Richard: spinning jenny of, 525
Armstrong, John: advocates war against France and Great Britain, 536–7; carries Short's letters to U.S., 115, 120; comments on Coles, 260; dispatches to and from, 65, 113, 117, 229–30, 370, 658, 659; and Du Pont de Nemours, 314; identified, 20n; letters from, 260, 536–8; letters to, 19–21, 412–3; rumored as secretary of war, 118, 140, 375; sends dynamometer to TJ, 20; sends Guillaume plow to TJ, 313; sends spinning wheel to TJ, 313; TJ's letters of introduction to, 402, 423; U.S. minister to France, 235n, 331, 374–5, 413, 528, 529, 627; and Warden, 141n
Army, U.S.: officers' commissions sought, 583
Artzt, Charles: designs spinning jenny, 524–5
Ashlin, John, 560
Asia: immigrants from, 253
Aspern-Essling, Battle of, 371–2, 377n, 436
Ast, William Frederick, 219n, 244n
astronomy: ancient Mexican, 521, 556; and Banneker, 588, 590n; books on, 24, 35, 576n, 581; and calculations of prime meridian, 54–5n, 275–6, 356–9, 489–98, 511–2, 534; computation of moon's motion, 540–54; study of, 535
*Astronomy explained upon Sir Isaac Newton's principles* (Ferguson), 576n, 581
Atlantic Ocean, 443
Auerstaedt, Duke of. *See* Davout, Louis Nicolas, Duc d'Auerstädt, Prince of Eckmühl
Augusta County, Va.: springs at, 191–2; Weyers Cave, 309
Auriol, M., 536
*Aurora* (Philadelphia): TJ's subscription to, 48, 49n
Austin, John: letter to, 608
Austria: defeated by Napoleon, 328, 370–1; invaded by Napoleon, 140–1; and Treaty of Tilsit, 516, 517n, 529, 627. *See also* Charles, archduke of Austria; Francis I, emperor of Austria; John, archduke of Austria; Schwarzenberg, Karl Philipp (Austrian ambassador)

autobiography: TJ on his, 383, 384n
avisos, 19, 21n, 117, 230

Bache, Benjamin Franklin, 49n
Bache, William: appointment, 615–6
Backer, T. H. (Amsterdam agent), 50n
Backus, Azel, 277, 278, 350n
Bacon, Edmund: delivers nails, 64; describes travels with TJ, 51–2; identified, 52n; Monticello overseer, 52n, 81n; paid by TJ, 41n, 81n; seeks cottonseed for TJ, 81, 159
Baird, Sir David: killed by French forces, 108
Baker, Harriet Weissenfels (John Martin Baker's wife): requests landscape view of Monticello, 345–6, 366, 434
Baker, Henry: *The Microscope made easy*, 581
Baker, Jerman, 363, 378
Baker, John Martin: identified, 346n; letters from, 345–6, 434; letter to, 365–6
Baker, William, 156n
Bakewell, Robert: *Observations on the influence of soil and climate upon wool*, 479, 480n
Balearic Islands, 345, 346n, 365
Ballendenies. *See* A free translation of the Preface to Bellendenus, containing animated strictures on the great political characters of the present time (Parr)
Balsam copaiba (*Copaiba Brasiliensis*), 56, 58n
Baltimore, Md.: *American, and Commercial Daily Advertiser*, 178n, 221n; Church of St. Mary, 450–1; merchants in, 50; St. Mary's Academy, 450–1
Baltimore Tammany Society: letter from, 176–9; letter to, 221
Bankhead, Ann (Anne) Cary Randolph (TJ's granddaughter; Charles Bankhead's wife): infant of, 387, 396n; and letter writing, 245
Bankhead, Charles Lewis: at family dinner, 387; marries Ann Randolph, 396n; studies law under TJ, 245, 389, 416
Bankhead, John, 590–1
Bank of Norfolk, 626
Bank of Pennsylvania: drafts on, 407, 421, 455; stock owned by Kosciuszko, 32n, 166, 217, 218n, 408
Bank of the United States: drafts on, by TJ, 41n, 45, 49, 455, 458; loan through Barnes and Madison, 212–3, 217–8, 246, 281, 285, 408
Bank of the United States, Second, 30n, 223n
Bank of Virginia, 302, 318, 344. *See also* Venable, Abraham
Bank of Washington (D.C.), 30n, 481, 535
Banks, Henry: attacked by McRae, 616n; *A Compendious View of the Establishment & Operations of Manufactory of Arms*, 614–5; identified, 615n; letter from, 614–5; mentioned, 615
Bankson, John: identified, 179n; letter from, 176–9
Banneker, Benjamin, 588–9, 590n
Banyalbufar wine, 366
barbecues, political, 515, 517n
Barbour, Mordecai, 25
Baring, Alexander, 1st Baron Ashburton: *An Inquiry into the Causes and Consequences of the Orders in Council*, 35
barley, 44, 268, 368
Barlow, Joel: *The Columbiad*, 35; identified, 589–90n; letter to, 588–90; *Letter to Henri Gregoire*, 588, 590n; *Oration delivered at Washington, July Fourth, 1809*, 588, 590n
Barlow, Ruth Baldwin: health of, 589
Barnes, John: cosigns loan to TJ with Madison, 212–3, 217–8, 246, 281, 285, 408; handles financial transactions, 458, 467; identified, 32n; injures arm, 166, 206, 218; letters from accounted for, 166n, 281n, 408n, 455n, 509n; letters to, 165–6, 217–8, 281, 408, 455, 467; paid by TJ, 41; ships goods to TJ, 44–5, 509; TJ's account with, 31–2, 166, 217
Barnett's Tavern (Fauquier Co.), 52n
Barney, Joshua, 515, 517n
Barry, Richard: painter at President's House, 200
Barthélemy, Jean Jacques: *Voyage du Jeune Anacharsis en Grèce*, 580, 582n
Barton, Benjamin Smith: and botanical lectures, 45, 46n, 191, 245, 308; *Elements of Botany*, 35, 581; Humboldt sends greetings to, 453n; identified, 521n; letter from, 520–2; letter to, 555–7; medical instruction by, 193; names plant after TJ, 57n; *New Views of the Origin of the Tribes and Nations of America*, 520–1

Baton Rouge, La., 442
Batture Sainte Marie: TJ receives books on, 37, 38n, 287
Bauduy, Peter, 199, 200n, 667–8
Baxter, John: *A New and Impartial History of England*, 580
beans: black-eyed pea (cowpea), 157; crowder, 157; lima, 631, 657
bear, grizzly: skin sent to TJ, 668
Beauharnais, Hortense de, 250n
beef: purchased for Monticello, 81n; received as pay, 419, 421n
beer, 299; *Theory and Practice of Brewing* (Combrune), 581
beets, 56, 157
Beggs, Charles: and Indiana Territory Legislative Council, 96
Belknap, Jeremy: *The History of New-Hampshire*, 581
Bell, John: *Anatomy of the Human Body*, 35, 307
Bellenden, William (Bellendenus), 35
Belsham, William: *History of Great Britain, from the Revolution to the Accession of the House of Hanover*, 580
Belvoir (Nelson's Albemarle Co. estate), 500n
benne (sesame; *Sesamum indicum*), 84, 211–2, 436–7n, 555, 667; Spafford requests from TJ, 105, 198
Bennet, George: *New Translation of the Morals of Seneca*, 576
benni. *See* benne (sesame; *Sesamum indicum*)
Benson, Egbert, 14n
Benson, John: Fredericksburg postmaster, 592, 667; identified, 14n; letter to, 14
Bentley, William, 191n
Beresford, William: *A Voyage Round The World*, 445–6, 449n
Berlin and Milan decrees, 19, 21n, 183, 313–4, 658
Berthollet, Claude Louis, 267n
Bible: dictionary of, 36; quoted, 291, 292n; quoted by TJ, 103, 154, 156n, 564, 565n, 596, 597n
*Bibliothecae Historicae Libri Quindecim de quadraginta* (Diodorus Siculus), 580
Billy (Couch's slave): and lost trunk, 346, 347, 348
Bingham, William, 56n
Binny, Archibald, 17, 18n
Binny & Ronaldson: letter from, 283; letter to, 314–5; as sheep raisers, 17; typefounding firm, 18n
biography: books of, 288–9, 580
Biot, Jean Baptiste, 267n
Birch, W. Y., & A. Small (Philadelphia publisher), 18, 19n, 172n
birds: mockingbird, 162; nightingale, 599; skylark, 599
bittersweet, American (*Celastrus scandens*; waxwork), 57, 58n
Blackden, Samuel: and Ky. land, 131n
black-eyed peas (cowpea), 157
blackmail letter, 425–8
blacksmiths: charges from, 3; at Monticello, 419n, 464n
Bladen, Martin, trans.: *Caius Julius Cæsar's Commentaries of his wars in Gaul, and civil war with Pompey*, 580
Blair, Hugh: *Lectures on Rhetoric and Belles Lettres*, 576
Blake, James Heighe: letter from accounted for, 12n
Bland, Richard, 403
blankets: Indian, 510
Bloodgood, Abraham: identified, 534n; letter from, 530–4; letter from accounted for, 533n; letter to, 568–9
Bloomfield, Samuel F.: and post road, 350, 352
Blue Ridge Mountains, 197–8
Blumenbach, Johann Friedrich: corresponds with TJ, 207, 208n
boats: transfer goods to and from Richmond, 44n, 81, 114–5, 153, 176, 246, 257, 319, 368, 457, 488n
Bonaparte, Caroline, 250n
Bonaparte, Joseph, king of Spain, 96, 108
Bonaparte, Josephine, 417n
Bonaparte, Louis, king of the Netherlands, 194
Bonaparte, Napoleon. *See* Napoleon I, emperor of France
Bonnel, Mrs., 667
Bonpland, Aimée Goujaud: *Voyage de Humboldt et Bonpland*, 24–5n, 455
books: bound for TJ, 35–8, 225, 286; carried by B. Hemmings, 321; school textbooks, 455–6; sent by Milligan, 332–3, 384; sent by Warden, 613n, 629–30; TJ purchases, 35; TJ recommends to Demaree, 576–7; TJ recommends to Wyche, 205–6, 508, 579–82
Bordley, John Beale: *Essays and Notes on Husbandry and Rural Affairs*, 581

Boston, Mass.: newspapers, 50n, 533, 569n, 671, 673n; pharmacopoeia of, 35
*Boston Patriot* (newspaper): prints TJ's correspondence, 533n, 569n
botany, 25n; books on, 436–7n; Bradbury's expedition, 435–7; Liverpool Botanic Garden, 163, 164n, 435; T. J. Randolph's enthusiasm for, 191; and T. M. Randolph, 436–7
*Botany Boards. See* Elements of Botany (Barton)
Botidoux, Marie Jacinthe de: correspondence with M. J. Randolph, 377, 659n
Boudet, Jean, comte, 371
Bouquet, Henri, 290
Bowdoin, James, 524
Boyle, John J., 14, 25
Bracton, Henry de: *Legibus et Consuetudinibus Angliæ*, 383
Bradbury, John: botanical expedition of, 163, 435–7; letter of introduction from Roscoe, 163; proposes garden at Saint Louis, 436–7n; visits Monticello, 164n, 435–6
Bradbury, John Leigh, 164n
Bradley, Abraham: identified, 480n; letters from, 480, 514; letter to, 505–6
Brahan, John: identified, 603–4n; letter from, 602–4
Bramham, James W.: and Henderson lands, 440, 460
Bramham, Nimrod, 47n
Brand, Joseph: and Henderson lands, 459
brandy, French, 268, 368
Brantz, Lewis: identified, 50n. *See also* Mayer & Brantz
Brazil: U.S. consul at, 26, 155
Bremo (Cocke's Fluvanna Co. estate), 136n
Brent, Daniel, 15n
Brent, Robert, 657; identified, 12n; letter from, 11–12; letter from accounted for, 12n; and merino sheep, 481
Brent, William Leigh: identified, 29n; letter from, 26–9
*A Brief History of the Influenza, Which prevailed in New-York in 1807* (Ricketson), 257, 294–5
brier, sun, 56
Briggs, Isaac: surveyor of federal lands, 215n, 650
Bright, Michael, 213–4n
briquet phosphorique, 376, 377n
briquet pneumatique, 376, 377n
Bristol County, R.I.: convention of, letter to, 88–9
*Britain Independent of Commerce; or, Proofs, Deducted from an Investigation into the True Causes of the Wealth of Nations* (Spence), 35
British Board of Agriculture, 252
*Britton* (Wingate, ed.), 383
Brodeau, Ann, 466, 479
Brodie, Francis, 75
Brodnax, William E., 66
Brooke, George, 503
Broome, John: identified, 80n; letter from, 79–80; letter from accounted for, 80n; letter to accounted for, 125n
brooms (stable), 3
Brougham, Henry Peter, Baron Brougham and Vaux: *The Speech of Henry Brougham, Esq. before the House of Commons*, 35
Brown, Benjamin: identified, 320n; letter from, 320; letter to, 333
Brown, Harriot: described, 74n; money for, 73; at Monticello, 210, 509
Brown, John: *Dictionary of the Holy Bible*, 36, 630n
Brown, William: absconds with public funds, 210n, 509n; assists Trist, 73, 74, 85; collector at New Orleans, 80, 81n, 510; described, 74n; identified, 210–1n; letters to, 210–1, 509; letter to mentioned, 408n
Bruin, Peter Bryan, 25
Brunswick County: Westwardmill Library Society, 66–7, 205–6, 508
Brunt, Jonathan: identified, 403n; letter from, 402–3; *The Little Medly: containing short remarks on the. . .New Testament*, 403; visits Monticello, 402
Buccarella, Antonio Maria: voyage to Northwest Coast, 446
Buccarella, Port of, 448
Buchan, David Steuart Erskine, 11th Earl of: and model of Swedish stove, 122n
Buchanan, George: *Rerum Scoticarum Historia*, 580
Buckmountain Baptist Church (Albemarle Co.): letter from, 63–4; letter to, 126
Bucks County, Pa., 69n
Buffon, Georges Louis Leclerc, comte de, 250n; *Histoire Naturelle des Oiseaux*, 581

building materials: carpentry tools, 135–6; paint, 55n, 97; pine planking, 192; stone, 626; stucco, 195–6
Bulfinch, B. S.: letter from accounted for, 677
Bullock, Eliza Henderson (Bennett Henderson's daughter; John H. Bullock's wife), 440, 459, 460–1
Bullock, John H.: and Henderson lands, 461
Bullus, John, 535
Burk, John Daly: *The History of Virginia*, 288–9, 331, 457, 581, 619, 620n, 634n; and TJ's laws of Va., 370n, 381; and TJ's newspaper collection, 381, 457, 469, 472–3
Burnley, Nathaniel, 505, 506; letter from accounted for, 506n
Burot, Mme, 622
Burot, Alexander: identified, 624n; letter from, 622–4
Burr, Aaron, 209n; conspiracy, 350, 643; treason trial of, 161n, 341n, 355n, 426, 427–8n; *Trial of Col. Aaron Burr*, 35; western expeditions of, 62, 63n
Burwell, Mr.: rooms with T. J. Randolph, 669, 670n
Burwell, William Armistead: mentioned, 199, 670n; trunk of, 186, 204
Butler, John West: identified, 304n; letter from, 303–4
Byrd, Mary Willing: and bounty land, 290, 335
Byrd, William (1728-1777): and bounty land, 290
Byrne, Patrick: letter from accounted for, 214n; *Report of the Whole Trial of Gen. Michael Bright and Others*, 214n

Cabanis, Charlotte Grouchy (Pierre Jean Georges Cabanis's wife), 261, 262n
Cabanis, Pierre Jean Georges: death of, 261, 262n
Cádiz: U.S. consul at, 87, 96, 113–4, 155, 156n; U.S. naval agent at, 155, 156n
Cadore, duc de, Jean Baptiste Nompère de Champagny, 370, 373, 377n, 528, 529n
Cadwalader, Thomas: identified, 583n; letter from, 583
Caesar, Julius: *Caius Julius Cæsar's Commentaries of his wars in Gaul, and civil war with Pompey* (trans. Bladen), 580; quoted, 6, 6n
*Caius Julius Cæsar's Commentaries of his wars in Gaul, and civil war with Pompey* (trans. Bladen), 580
Caldcleugh & Thomas (Philadelphia mercantile firm), 190, 191n
Callender, James Thomson, 499n; and sedition law, 278
Callet, Jean François: *Tables of Logarithms*, 316–7, 629–30
Calloway (black boatman): and lost trunk, 311
Calvert County, Md.: sheep breeding in, 478
camel: hair used for weaving, 16; introduced to U.S., 479, 480n, 599
Campan, Jeanne Louise Henriette, 250n
Campbell, David: identified, 653n; letter from, 652–3
Campbell, John Wilson: identified, 385n; letters from, 385, 538–9; letters to, 486–8, 569–70; proposes to publish TJ's public papers, 385, 486–8, 538–9, 569–70
Campbell, Thomas Jefferson, 653
Campbell, Victor Moreau, 653
Campbell County, Va.: TJ sells Stith tract in, 670–1
campeachy chairs, 80, 81n, 211n
Camper, Adriaan G.: letter from accounted for, 677
canals: books on, 36, 38n
candles, 31, 32
Canning, George: British foreign minister, 284, 518, 658; instructions to Erskine, 170n, 409, 438–9; TJ's opinion of, 442, 519
Canonsburg Academy and Library Company (Pa.), 6n
capers, 366
Capitol, U.S.: construction of, 65n, 473, 475, 595; corncob capitals for, 473, 475n, 595; Latrobe works on, 65, 92, 474n; longitude measurement, 356–9, 489–98, 534, 553; sculptors at, 78n
Caroline County Court (Va.), 519
Carpenter, Stephen Cullen: *Memoirs of the Hon. Thomas Jefferson*, 456, 457n
carpentry tools, 135–6
Carr, Dabney (TJ's nephew), 83n
Carr, Frank, 64
Carr, Peter (TJ's nephew), 505, 626; carries comforter to Monticello, 286, 310; and Moore estate, 204
Carr, Samuel (TJ's nephew), 75, 134–5
Carroll, John, 7
carrots, 56, 157

Carter, Elizabeth, trans.: *Stoici Philosophi Encheiridion item* (Epictetus), 576
Carter, Mary Elizabeth Coles (Robert Carter's wife), 656n
Carter, Robert: grinds wheat, 109; sells tobacco, 655, 656n
*Carte réduite de la Mer Méditerranée et de la mer Noire* (Zannoni and Lapie), 247–8
Caruthers, William: identified, 367n; letter from, 367–8; letter to, 506–7
*Carya laciniosa* (Gloucester-nut hickory), 657
*Castanea sativa* (European chestnut; sweet chestnut), 594n
Castell, Robert: *The Villas of the Ancients Illustrated*, 390, 397n
Castle-Hill (Rives's Albemarle Co. estate), 416n
Castlereagh, Robert Stewart, Viscount: British secretary of war, 284
*Catalogue of Plants in the Botanic Garden, at Liverpool* (Roscoe), 164n
Cathalan, Mme (Stephen Cathalan's mother), 312
Cathalan, Eulalie (Stephen Cathalan's daughter), 312
Cathalan, Stephen (Étienne): forwards TJ's correspondence, 207; identified, 313n; letter from, 312–3
cattle: in Pennsylvania, 69n; raised by Indians, 110
Caulainourt, Armand, 537
*Celastrus scandens* (waxwork; American bittersweet), 57, 58n
celery, 157
Census, Report on (Thomas Jefferson), 569–70
Central College (Charlottesville), 65n, 193n. *See also* Virginia, University of
Cervoni, Jean Baptiste, 372
Champagny, Jean Baptiste Nompère de, duc de Cadore. *See* Cadore, duc de, Jean Baptiste Nompère de Champagny
Chapman, Nathaniel: identified, 663n; letter from, 663
Chaptal, Jean Antoine Claude: *Elements of Chemistry*, 307
chariots, 41n
charity: requests to TJ for, 67, 68n, 402–3, 467–9; TJ comments on, 506
Charles, archduke of Austria, 371, 372
Charles II, king of England, 489
Charleston, S.C., 513–4
Charpentier de Cossigny, Joseph François: *Observations sur "L'art de faire le vin,"* 35; *Recherches physiques et chimiques sur la Fabrication de la Poudre à Canon*, 35
Chastellux, Marquis de: *Travels in North America in the Years 1780, 1781 and 1782*, 197, 198–9n
cheese: fine, 45, 368; ordinary, 45, 369
chemistry: books on, 36, 37, 307, 581; experiment with tobacco, 142–52
Cherokee Indians: lands of, 6–7; migration of, 653; TJ on government of, 110
Cherry, Robert, 516–7
*Chesapeake*, USS: incident, 409
Chester County, Pa., 69n
Chesterfield, Philip Dormer Stanhope, 4th Earl of. *See* Stanhope, Philip Dormer, 4th Earl of Chesterfield
chestnuts: European or sweet, 594n; horse, 593, 594n
Chew, Maj., 478
Chickasaw Indians: lands of, 6–7; U.S. Indian agent for, 26
children: books for, 35, 294, 332, 333
China, 253, 447
Chinese language: treatise on by A. Palmer, 518
chisels, 135–6
chocolate, 44
Christie, Gabriel, 586, 587n
Church, Angelica Schuyler, 174, 175n
Churro sheep, 18, 19n
Cicero: *De Officiis*, 576; *Letters to Friends*, 386; Middleton's life of, 35, 580
cider, 657; *Treatise on the Culture of the Apple & Pear, and on the Manufacture of Cider & Perry* (Knight), 581
cigars, 466
cinnamon, 31, 44, 368
*Citrus aurantifolia* (lime), 631–2
*Citrus aurantium* (orange), 631–2
*De Cive* (Hobbes): quoted by TJ, 507–8
Claiborne, William Charles Coles: governor of Orleans Territory, 635; identified, 179–80n; letters from, 179–80, 202–3, 287; letter to, 509–10
Claparède, Michel Marie, comte, 372
claret, 387, 397n
Clark, Julia Hancock (William Clark's wife), 511
Clark, Meriwether Lewis, 511n
Clark (Clarke), William: identified, 511n; letter to, 510–1; sends mammoth

Clark (Clarke), William (*cont.*)
bones to TJ, 509; sends sheepskin to TJ, 327, 328n, 510
Clarke, George Rogers, 511n
Clarke, John: and silk-manufacturing project, 341, 342n, 355, 412–3, 413, 414, 423–4, 472
Clarke, Mary Anne, 82–3n
Clavigero, Francesco Saverio: *Storia Antica del Messico*, 196, 198n
Claxton, Thomas (d. *1821*), 76; identified, 43n; letter from, 42–3
Claxton, Thomas (ca. *1794–1813*), 42, 43n
Clayton, John, 57n
Clement, James, 158, 159n
Clément de la Roncière, François Marie, baron, 372
Clener, Ange (engraver), 453n
Clinton, DeWitt, 106, 198
clocks: in President's House, 85, 96
cloth: home-based manufacture of, 561, 573–4, 591
clothing: homespun, 100n, 561, 591, 667; manufacture of, 15–6; slave, 420, 666–7; for T. J. Randolph in Philadelphia, 308; wool recommended for, 479n, 573
clover seed, 45n
cloves, 44
coal: at President's House, 155
Cocke, John Hartwell, 136n
Cocke, Richard, 635, 642n
cod: New England, 115n, 176, 279; TJ's report on fisheries, 487; tongues and sounds, 153, 154n, 369
Coe, Jesse, 66
coffee: Bourbon, 268; East India, 268, 368; green, 268, 368; served at Monticello, 389; smuggling of, 439; TJ purchases, 31, 318–9; at U.S. Marine Hospital, 299; West India, 268
coinage: TJ and, 487
coins: in Va., 334
Coke, Sir Edward: *Institutes of the Laws of England*, 382
Colbert, Melinda, 156n
Coles, Isaac A.: agent to Europe, 65, 232, 263, 269–70, 271–2, 331, 452, 528, 530n, 593, 627; Armstrong comments on, 260; carries TJ's correspondence to Europe, 19, 20, 173, 175n, 207, 229, 247; on European sheep, 479; identified, 53–4n; letters from, 53–4, 370–7, 667–8; Madison forwards letter from, 518; at Monticello, 536, 632, 655, 657; at Montpellier, 439, 441; observes Parker's plough, 233, 538; paid by TJ, 41; as secretary to TJ, 34n, 64
Colle (Albemarle Co.), 420n
colleges. *See* schools and colleges
Collier, Jeremy: *The Emperor Marcus Antoninus*, 576
Collin, Nicholas, 453n
Collins, Charles: identified, 89n
Collins's Marcus Antoninus. *See* Collier, Jeremy, *The Emperor Marcus Antoninus*
*The Columbiad* (Barlow), 35
Columbian Agricultural Society for the Promotion of Rural and Domestic Economy, 23n, 40n, 133, 134n
Columbian Institute for the Promotion of Arts and Sciences, 54–5n
Colvin, John B.: identified, 107n; letter to, 107
Combrune, Michael: *The Theory and Practice of Brewing*, 581
comforters, 28, 64, 76, 153, 310
*Commentary and Review of Montesquieu's Spirit of the Laws* (Destutt de Tracy), 260–1, 262–3n, 270
Commerce, Report on (Thomas Jefferson), 487
*Del Commercio de' Romani Dalla prima Guerra Punica* (Mengotti), 36
common law, 276, 278, 381
*A Compendious View of the Establishment & Operations of Manufactory of Arms* (Banks), 614–5
*A Complete Book of Husbandry* (Hale), 581
*A Complete Collection of all the Lavvs of Virginia now in force* (Purvis), 404
*A Complete History of England* (Kennett), 580
Condorcet, Marie Jean Antoine Nicolas de Caritat, marquis de, 261, 262–3n
confitures: Havana, 505
Congress, U.S., 224; approves Latrobe's capital design, 474n; Committee of Investigation, 361, 362n, 378; early session called, 21n; and Non-Intercourse Act, 21n, 314; resolution on prosecutions at common law, 276, 278
*Connaissance des Temps: ou, des Mouvements célestes à l'usage des astronomes et des navigateurs*, 35
Connecticut: Antient Plymouth Society, 58–9, 102; Federalists in, 39, 162; Hartford, spotted fever at, 95n; libel

prosecutions in, 276–8, 278n, 349–50; Republicans of, address TJ, 95; TJ addresses Republicans of, 126–7
Conrad, Andrew, 412
Conrad, C. & A., and Company: identified, 412n; letters from, 412, 668–9; to publish journals of Lewis and Clark, 668–9; publishes Shakespeare, 412
Conrad, Cornelius, 412
Conrad, John, 412n, 668n
Conrad, Michael, 412n
Conrad, Solomon White, 256n
*Considerations on the Executive Government of the United States of America* (Woodward), 164–5, 236, 253–4
*Constitution de la république Beninienne* (Ruelle), 219, 220n
*Conversations on Chemistry: in which the elements of that science are familiarly explained* (Marcet), 36, 37, 581
Cook, James: *A Voyage to the Pacific Ocean*, 445, 446, 449n
Cook, Orchard, 25
Cooper, Samuel: *The first lines of the practice of surgery*, 35
*Copaiba Brasiliensis* (Balsam copaiba), 56, 58n
Copeland, Charles, 288
Copeland, David: and *Gilliam v. Fleming*, 330, 331; letter from accounted for, 305n; letters to, 304–5, 362
Copeland, Susan Skelton (David Copeland's wife): mentioned, 304
Copenhagen, Denmark: British bombardment of, 442, 559
copper utensils, 467
Corcoran, Thomas, 23n
*coreopsis* (tickseed), 436–7n
*Corinne ou l'Italie* (Staël-Holstein), 35
corn: cob capitals for U.S. Capitol, 473, 475n, 595; crop at Monticello, 592; maize, 436–7n; purchased for Monticello, 81n; received as pay, 419, 421n
*Cornus florida* (dogwood), 272, 274n
Corny, Louis Dominique Ethis de, 175n
Corny, Marguérite Victoire de Palerne de, 377; identified, 175n; letter from, 173–5
Corse, Miss: marries Samuel House, 475
Cortés, Hernán: *Historia de Nueva-España*, 390, 396n
*Corylus avellana* (filbert), 631
Cosby, Minor M.: TJ recommends as Milton postmaster, 505–6
Cossigne. *See* Charpentier de Cossigny, Joseph François
*Du Cotonnier et de sa Culture* (Lasteyrie-Du Saillant), 37
cotton: black, 258, 259–60n; green seed (Sea Island), 82, 258, 259–60n, 666; grown at Tufton, 420; price of in Great Britain, 82; scarcity of seed, 81; spinning of, 525, 591; TJ orders seed, 115n, 154, 159, 176; TJ sends seed to Silvestre, 258, 596
Couch, James Bartlett: slaves of, 346–8
Couch, William, 44
*Coup-d'Oeil rapide sur les causes réelles de la Décadence de la Pologne* (Komarzewski), 535, 536n
*A Course of Lectures on Elocution* (Sheridan), 576
Covington, Leonard, 516
Coweta, 350, 351, 352
cowpeas (black-eyed pea), 157
Cox, Heisch and Company (London), 652
Cox, John: paid by TJ, 41
Coxe, Charles D.: U.S. consul at Tunis, 26
crackers, 45, 368
Craig, Ann Pasteur: identified, 68n; letter from, 67–8
Craig, Thomas, 68n
Cramer, Zadok: identified, 630n; letter from, 630; *The United States spelling book*, 630
Craven, John H., 136n, 419
Creasy, William: and lost trunk, 348
Creek Indians: TJ on government of, 110
criminal law, 382, 384n
*Crispi Opera Omnia* (Sallust; trans. Gordon), 580
*Critical Observations on the poem of Mr. Joel Barlow, The Columbiad* (Grégoire), 588, 590n
Crocket, Joseph, 78n
Crookes, John: letter from accounted for, 96n; letter to accounted for, 96n
Cross, Caleb: identified, 138n; letter from, 138
Cross, Stephen, 86n
crowder bean, 157
Crowninshield, Jacob: *Hortus Siccus*, 37, 189, 191n
*Crozophora tintoria* (turnsole plant), 142, 143, 146n
Cruger, Catherine "Kitty" Church, 174, 175n

Cuba: acquisition by U.S. likely, 154, 169–70, 224; refugees from, 203, 450, 510, 624n; TJ on U.S. acquisition of, 183–4
Culpeper Court House (Fairfax, Culpeper Co.), 51
Cumberland, Richard: *Memoirs written by himself*, 35
Cumberland Road: commissioners of, 26, 172–3
currency, Indian, 334, 369
Currie, Ellison, 616
Curtius Quintus: *Historia Alexandri Magni Regis* (trans. Digby), 580
Custis, George Washington Parke, 240n, 667, 668n
Cutts, Anna Payne (Richard Cutts's wife), 53, 54n
Cutts, Richard, 53, 54n, 434
Cuvier, Georges: analyzes bones for Institut de France, xlviii, 100–1, 103–4, 187; and Lacépède's *Histoire naturelle de l'homme*, 250n; *Recherches sur les Ossemens Fossiles*, 101n
*Cypripedium* (lady-slipper), 436–7n
*Cyrus's Expedition into Persia, and the Retreat of the Ten Thousand Greeks* (*The Anabasis*) (Xenophon; trans. Spelman), 580

Daingerfield, Mary Willis: identified, 48n; letter to, 47–8; paid by TJ, 41n; TJ hires slaves from, 48n
Daingerfield, Sarah, 41n, 48n
Daingerfield, William, 48n
dancing: TJ attends inaugural ball, 9, 10n
Darsonel. *See* Durosnel, Antoine Jean Auguste Henri, comte
Daschkoff, André: identified, 329n; and letter of credence to Madison, 484, 485n; letters from, 328–9, 484–5; letter to, 433; Russian consul general to U.S., 120, 329, 332, 360; visits Monticello, 120, 433, 484, 519
Dashwood. *See* Despencer, Sir Francis Dashwood, baron le
dates, 366
Daveny. *See* Rioult-Davenay, Archange Louis, baron
Davidson, Capt., 15, 217
Davis, Daniel: identified, 419n; letter from, 419
Davis, George: U.S. consul at Tripoli, 26
Davout, Louis Nicolas, Duc d'Auerstädt, Prince of Eckmühl, 372
Davy. *See* Hern, David (TJ's slave)
Davy, William, 16, 17; identified, 172n; letter from, 170–2
Dawson, John: U.S. Representative from Va., 644
Dawson, William: identified, 219n; letter from, 417; letters to Greenhow, 218–9, 240, 244n, 317–8; and Mutual Assurance Society, 218–9, 240, 244n, 333, 417, 472, 625, 659
Deane, P.: letter from accounted for, 677
Deane, Samuel: *The New-England farmer, or, Georgical dictionary*, 581
Dearborn, Dorcas Marble (Henry Dearborn's wife): mentioned, 301; TJ sends greetings to, 280
Dearborn, Henry, 574; and charges against Waterhouse, 295; consults with TJ on botany, 189; identified, 280n; letters from, 301, 301–2; letters to, 279–80, 572–3; as secretary of war, 6, 7, 48, 351; sends fish to TJ, 153, 279
Dearborn, Henry A. S.: military commission of, 78, 280, 301–2
debt, public, 62, 168–9, 177, 598, 610, 664
Debue, Monsieur, 372
DeButts, Samuel: identified, 75n; letter from, 75; letter to, 134–5
Decatur, Capt., 252
Decatur, Stephen, 111
Declaration of Independence, 11, 487, 610
Defoe, Daniel: *Essay upon Projects*, 572; *Robinson Crusoe*, 110
Deforge, Mr. *See* Desforgues, Mr.
Degen & Purviance (Leghorn mercantile firm), 361, 362n, 515
Delambre, Jean Baptiste Joseph, 100–1, 357
Delaware County, Pa., 69n
Delessert, Jules Paul Benjamin, & Cie, 235
Demaree, Samuel R.: identified, 457n; letter from, 455–7; letter to, 575–6; TJ recommends books, 576–7
*Democrat* (Boston newspaper), 50n
Demosthenes, 70
Desalination of Sea Water, Report on (Thomas Jefferson), 487
*Descripción histórica y cronológica de los piedras* (León y Gama), 521, 556
Desforgues, Mr. (French consul at New Orleans), 203

Deshay, Madame: letter from, 450–1
Despencer, Sir Francis Dashwood, baron le, 124
Destutt de Tracy, Antoine Louis Claude: *Commentary and Review of Montesquieu's Spirit of the Laws*, 260–1, 262–3n, 270; *Discours prononcés dans la séance publique tenue par la classe de la langue*, 262; identified, 262n; letter from, 260–3
Detroit, Mich. Territory, 7, 660–2
Dickson, Adam: *The Husbandry of the Antients*, 581
*Dictionary of Arts & Sciences* (Owen), 582
*Dictionary of the Holy Bible* (Brown), 36, 630n
*Dictionnaire Historique et Bibliographique Portatif* (Ladvocat), 580
Didot, Firmin, 316–7
Digby, John, trans.: *Historia Alexandri Magni Regis* (Curtius Quintus), 580
Digges, Frank, 516
Digges, Thomas Attwood: identified, 517n; letter from, 515–7
Dinsmore, James: accounts with TJ, 64, 65n; identified, 136n; list of carpenter's tools, 135–6; works at Montpellier, 155
Diodorus Siculus: *Bibliothecae Historicae Libri Quindecim de quadraginta*, 580; *Historiarum Libri Aliquot, qui extant, opera & studio Vincentii Obsopoei in lucem editi*, 580
Diomed (horse), 52n
Diomede (horse), 51
Dionysius Halicarnasseus: *Opera Omni Graece et Latine* (trans. Spelman), 580
*Discours prononcés dans la séance publique tenue par la classe de la langue* (Destutt de Tracy), 262
*Discours sur les progrès des sciences* (Kesteloot), 656
*Dissertations de Maxime de Tyr, philosophe platonicien*: (Maximus of Tyre), 35
distiller's syphon, 482–3
Divers, George: grinds wheat, 109; hosts Trist, 73; identified, 157–8n; letter from, 157–8; TJ visits, 80, 98n
Divers, Martha Walker (George Divers's wife), 157n; hostess to Trist, 73
Divers, Thomas Jefferson, 157n
*The Diversions of Sidney* (Margaret Bayard Smith), 10n
Dixon, George, ed.: *A Voyage Round The World* (Beresford), 445–6, 449n
Dobson, Mr., 308
Dobson, Thomas: *Encyclopaedia*, 576, 577n, 582
*The Doctrine of fluxions* (Emerson), 576
dogs: bill for taxing, 17, 68; breeding of, 3n; kill sheep, 476; shepherd, 376, 457, 469–70, 483
dogwood (*Cornus florida*), 272, 274n
*Dolphin of York* (ship), 53, 64
*Domestic encyclopædia* (Willich), 18, 19n, 252
Don Pedro (sheep), 16, 18, 19n
Dorsenne, Jean Marie Pierre François Lepaige, comte, 372
Dossie, Robert: *The Handmaid to the Arts*, 581
Doublehead: Cherokee leader, 7
Doublehead's Reserve, Tenn., 7
Dougherty, Joseph: account with TJ, 3–4; acquires sheep for TJ, 153, 464, 465–6, 467, 476–7, 486; acquires sheep from Thornton, 465–6, 476, 480–1; identified, 3–4n; letters from, 64, 153, 199–200, 286, 320–1, 480–1; letters to, 76, 224–5, 310, 464, 467; and merino sheep, 3n, 153, 199, 225, 286, 310, 320–1, 467; oversees transport of TJ's belongings, 53; paid by TJ, 41, 42n; travels to Monticello, 53
Dougherty, Mary (Joseph Dougherty's wife), 3n, 53
drawknives, 135–6
drayman. *See* Ned (Couch's slave)
drunkenness: of Fontaine, 526, 645–6; of Madison's maitre d'hotel, 53; of TJ's blacksmith, 419n
Duane, William, 278; identified, 49n; letter to, 48–9
Duane, William J., 49n
Duckett, Allen Bowie, 516
ducks: summer, 56
Dufief, Nicolas Gouin: *Nature Displayed, in her Mode of Teaching Language to Man*, 581
Dunbar, William, 97n, 498n
dunfish (New England cod), 115n, 176, 279
Dunn, William: letter from, 467–9; requests charity, 467–9
Duplantier, Gabriel Armand Allard, 529, 530n, 628
DuPonceau, Peter Stephen: and batture controversy, 287

du Pont de Nemours, Éleuthère Irénée, 667; gunpowder manufactory of, 200n; and merino sheep, 16, 18, 19n, 153

Du Pont de Nemours, Pierre Samuel: and Armstrong, 314; edits Turgot's *Oeuvres*, 263, 264n, 584–5; on education, 202n, 584–5; identified, 201–2n; letter from, 263–4; letters to, 201–2, 315–6, 385–6; letter to Madison, 584–5, 592; and merino sheep, 199, 584–5n; *Sur l'éducation nationale dans les États-Unis d'Amérique*, 592, 593n, 674; TJ praises, 402

Durosnel, Antoine Jean Auguste Henri, comte, 372

Duval, Benjamin, 288

Duvall, Gabriel: comptroller of the Treasury, 352

dynamometer, 20, 21n, 376; lost in transit, 180, 204, 205

dysentery, 483; among slaves, 354, 416

Eagle Tavern (Richmond), 611n, 613, 614n

Eaton, William: and broad-tailed sheep, 477

*An ecclesiastical history, ancient and modern, from the birth of Christ to the beginning of the eighteenth century* (Mosheim), 581

*Eclogues* (Virgil), 345n

École de Pharmacie, 146n

Écoles Normale. *See* Séances des Écoles Normales, recueillies par des Sténographes et revues par les Professeurs

*Edinburgh Review*, 348, 349n

education: Du Pont de Nemours on, 202n, 584–5; of Indian children, 7, 660–2; in Ky., 456; Samuel H. Smith on, 30n; TJ provides at Monticello, 181–2, 215n, 245, 389, 416, 650. *See also* schools and colleges

Edwards, Ninian: and sedition law, 278

"Elegy Written in a Country Churchyard" (Gray), 238, 240n

*Élemens de l'Histoire de France, depuis Clovis jusqu'à Louis XV* (Millot), 580

*Elemens d'hygiène* (Tourtelle), 597n

*Elements of Botany* (Barton), 35, 581

*Elements of Chemistry* (Chaptal), 307

*Elements of Criticism* (Kames), 576

*The Elements of Euclid* (Simson), 576, 650

*Elements of General History* (Millot), 580

*Elements of the Philosophy of the Human Mind* (Stewart), 576

Elizabeth I, queen of England, 382

Elk Hill (TJ's Goochland Co. estate), 305n, 615n

Elk Island (Fluvanna Co.), 305n

Ellicott, Andrew, 357, 453n, 588

Ellicott, Elias, 590n

Ellicott, George, 590n

Elliot, Samuel, 535

Ellzey, Arnold: purchases chariot from TJ, 41n

elm, witch, 192n

Elzey, Dr. *See* Ellzey, Arnold

Embargo Act (*1807*): American vessels seized under, 373; Gilpin's comments on, 418; opposition to, 86n, 138n; support for, 94n, 95, 100, 532; TJ accused of smuggling during, 426; TJ on, 19, 21n, 39, 85–6, 99–100; tracts on, 37, 38n

Emerson, William: *The Doctrine of fluxions*, 576

Emory, Robert: identified, 63n; letter from, 62–3

*The Emperor Marcus Antoninus* (Collier), 576

*Encyclopaedia* (Dobson), 576, 577n, 582

Enfield, William: *The History of Philosophy*, 576

Engano, Cape, 447

Enniscorthy (Coles's Albemarle Co. estate), 53n

*Enquirer* (Richmond newspaper): advertises TJ's lost trunk, 205; prints Margaret Bayard Smith's account of visit to Monticello, 396n; prints TJ's correspondence, 47n, 63n, 126n, 172n, 611n, 621n; TJ subscribes to, 214n

*Entretiens sur la Pluralité des Mondes* (Fontenelle), 581

Epictetus: *Stoici Philosophi Encheiridion item*, 576

Eppes, Elizabeth Wayles (TJ's sister-in-law; John Wayles Eppes's mother), 337, 338n, 363

Eppes, Francis (TJ's brother-in-law), 339n

Eppes, Francis Wayles (TJ's grandson), 488n; relations with TJ, 336–7

Eppes, John Wayles (TJ's son-in-law): and *Gilliam v. Fleming*, 206, 304,

305, 306, 307, 331, 339, 362, 365; identified, 337–8n; letter from, 336–8; letter from accounted for, 338n; letter to, 362–3; letter to accounted for, 338n; receives slaves from TJ, 156n; slaves of, 156n, 321; and TJ's newspapers, 457, 469
Eppes, Maria (Mary) Jefferson (TJ's daughter; John Wayles Eppes's wife): acquaintances in France, 174, 175n; receives slaves from TJ, 156n, 321n; travels to France, 450n
Eppington (Eppes's Chesterfield Co. estate): TJ plans to visit, 363, 364, 365, 626
Erskine, David M.: agreement with U.S., 271, 407, 409–10n, 438–9, 441, 504, 518, 658; dispatches for, 108, 113; instructions to, 170n, 284–5, 408, 409, 418, 438–9; negotiates with R. Smith, 168, 170n, 409
Erskine, David Steuart, 11th Earl of Buchan. *See* Buchan, David Steuart Erskine, 11th Earl of
Erving, George W.: and Cádiz consulate, 87, 96, 113–4
Espagne, Jean Louis Brigitte, comte d', 372
*Essai Général d'Education physique, morale, et intellectuelle* (Jullien), 674–5
*Essai politique sur le royaume de la Nouvelle-Espagne* (Humboldt), 24, 25n, 264, 267n
*Essai sur la géographie des plantes* (Humboldt), 265, 267n
*An Essay concerning Human Understanding* (Locke), 576
*An Essay on Government* (Lee), 123–4
*An Essay on Ophthalmia, or Inflammation of the Eyes* (Griffiths), 237n
*Essay on Sheep* (Livingston), 667, 668n
*An Essay on the principle of population* (Malthus), 35
*Essays and Notes on Husbandry and Rural Affairs* (Bordley), 581
*Essays on poetical and prosaic numbers, and elocution* (Mason), 576
*Essays on the Principles of Morality and Natural Religion* (Kames), 576
*Essay upon Projects* (Defoe), 572
Essex County, Mass.: TJ addresses Republicans of, 85–6
Essex Junto, 246–7, 298, 300n
Europe: and silk manufacturing, 341, 342n, 355, 412–3, 413, 424, 425n, 472
European chestnut (*Castanea sativa*; sweet chestnut), 594n
Eustis, William: identified, 584n; letter from, 624–5; letter to, 583–4; secretary of war, 583–4, 607, 644, 661
Everette, Charles, 47n, 499
Ewell's Mill (Fairfax Co.), 52n
*Examination of the Memorial of the Owners and Underwriters of the American Ship the New Jersey*, 36
"The Expedient" (McCoy), 322–7
*Exposition du Systême du Monde* (Laplace), 348, 349n, 357, 491

*Fabius* (ship), 312
fables: TJ receives books of, 37
Fagg, John, 420
Fairfax (Culpeper Co.), 51
Falkenstein, Konstantin Karl, 24n
fameflower *(Talinum)*, 436–7n
Farish, Hazlewood, 139n
*The Farmer's Guide in Hiring and Stocking Farms* (Young), 581
Farmington (Divers's Albemarle Co. estate), 98n, 157n
Faujas de Saint-Fond, Bartelémy: identified, 202n; letter to, 201–2
Fauquier Court House, Va., 466
Federalist party: and charges against Waterhouse, 298; in Conn., 39, 162; Madison on, 246–7; in Mass., 301; in Md., 515–6; in New England, 301, 583–4. *See also* Essex Junto
Feltre, Henri Jacques Guillaume Clarke, duc de, 538
Fenwick, Eliza: *Mary and Her Cat*, 294
Ferguson, James: *Astronomy explained upon Sir Isaac Newton's principles*, 576n, 581; *Lectures on Select Subjects in Mechanics, Hydrostatics, Pneumatics, and Optics*, 581
Ferrer, José J. de, 492, 498n
Ferrier, Louis, 522
*La Fête du Petit Blé; ou, L'Heroisme du Poucha-Houmma* (le Blanc de Villeneufve), 202, 203n, 509
Few, William, 198
Fielding, Henry: *A History of Tom Jones, a Foundling*, 174, 175n
Fielding, Sarah (trans.): *Xenophon's Memoirs of Socrates*, 576

figs: grown at Monticello, 395, 398n; Marseilles, 600; roots from Thornton, 479, 481, 600; TJ sends to Walker, 500
filberts (*Corylus avellana*), 631
Findley, William, 193, 194n; *History of the Insurrection, in the Four Western Counties of Pennsylvania*, 581
*The first lines of the practice of surgery* (Cooper), 35
first meridian. *See* prime meridian
fish: anchovies, 366; cod, 115n, 176, 279; herring, 77, 115, 176, 369; salted, 279; shad, white, 369; TJ's report on, 487; tongues and sounds, 153, 154n, 369
Fishback, James: identified, 255n; letter from, 254–5; letter to, 563–6; *A new and candid investigation of the question, is revelation true?*, 254–5, 563–4, 565–6
Fisheries, Report on the (Thomas Jefferson), 487
Fitch, Gideon. *See* Fitz, Gideon
Fitch, Jabez, 95n
Fitz, Gideon, 665; identified, 215n; letter from, 635–42; letter from accounted for, 650n; letter to, 215; surveying work of, 181, 650
Fitzhugh, Denis, 510
flax: grown at Tufton, 420; spinning of, 525, 591
Fleming, John, 363, 591
Fleming, William: and *Gilliam v. Fleming*, 304–5, 305, 306, 362, 363, 365, 378–9, 591; identified, 364n; letters from, 378–9, 660; letter to, 363–4
*Flora Antillarum* (Tussac), 100–1
*Flora Boreali-Americana* (Michaux), 436–7n
Florida: acquisition by U.S. likely, 154, 160, 169, 224; French citizens in, 203; TJ on U.S. acquisition of, 183–4, 442
flour: price of, 61, 407, 451; received as pay, 419, 421n
Flushing (Netherlands), 529, 530n, 593n
Fluvanna County, 305n; Bremo, 136n; Magruder's Mill, 109, 110n
fodder: purchased for Monticello, 81n
Fontaine, William: drunkenness, 526, 645–6; identified, 527n; letters from, 525–8, 645–6; letter to, 591–2; visits Monticello, 525–8, 645–6
Fontenelle, Bernard Le Bovier de: *Entretiens sur la Pluralité des Mondes*, 581
food: anchovies, 366; barley, 44, 268, 368; beef, 81n, 419, 421n; beets, 56, 157; black-eyed peas (cowpea), 157; black peaches, 483; capers, 366; carrots, 56, 157; celery, 157; cheese, 45, 368, 369; chestnuts, 594n; chocolate, 44; cod, 115n, 176, 279; cod tongues and sounds, 153, 154n, 369; confitures, 505; corn, 81n, 419, 421n, 436–7n, 592; crackers, 45, 368; crowder beans, 157; dates, 366; dunfish, 115n, 176, 279; figs, 395, 398n, 479, 481, 500, 600; filberts, 631; flour, 61, 407, 419, 421n, 451; grapes, 587n; herring, 77, 115, 176; hickory nuts, 111, 252, 657; lima beans, 631, 657; mustard, 45; mutton, 16, 477, 481; oats, 3; olive oil, 84n, 188, 257, 366; olives, 313n; parsnips, 157; pecans, 80, 81n, 211n, 631, 657; pork, 419, 421n, 451; potatoes, 157, 196–7; raisins, 366, 368; raspberries, 222; salad oil, 31, 161; salsify, 157; salt, 77; sesame oil, 84n, 212; spices, 31, 44, 45, 368; tarragon, 479, 481, 660; tea, 31, 32n, 44, 368; vanilla, 161, 188–9, 190; vinegar syrup, 161, 188–9, 190, 222, 257. *See also* alcohol; coffee; rice; sugar
Ford, Peter, 505
Foronda, Valentín de: *Apuntes ligeros sobre la nueva constitución*, 470–1, 577, 604, 606n; identified, 471n; letters from, 470–1, 604–6; letter to, 577–8
Forrest, Richard: letter from accounted for, 313n
Forsyth, William: *A Treatise on the Culture and Management of Fruit Trees; in which A New Method of Pruning and Training is Fully Described*, 17
Fort Massac, 511
Fort Stoddert, Ala., 350, 351, 352
Fort Warburton (later Fort Washington), 517
Fossett, Edith (Edy) Hern (TJ's slave): trained in French cooking, 162, 188, 189n
Foster, Augustus John: attends Madison's inauguration, 8, 10n
Fothergill, Anthony: *Remarks on the Smut and Mildew of Wheat*, 72
Fouché, Joseph, duc d'Otrante, 528, 529n, 538, 629
Fouler, Albert Louis Emmanuel de, comte de Relingue, 372

four-o'clock (marvel-of-Peru; *Mirabilis jalapa*), 57, 58n
Foushee, William: identified, 611n; letter from, 609–11; letter from accounted for, 611n; letter to, 620–1
Fowler, Mr., 129
Fox, Charles James, 507; *A History of the Early Part of the Reign of James the Second*, 36, 37, 580
Foxall, Henry: identified, 76–7n; iron castings for TJ, 157, 158n; letter from, 122; letter to, 76–7; and stew stove for TJ, 76–7, 122
Foxall Foundry, 76n
Francais, Port des, 445, 446
France: Berlin and Milan decrees, 19, 21n, 183, 313–4, 658; Council of Prizes, 629; imperial university for, 676n; Marie Antoinette, queen of, 250; marriage in, 121, 122n; sheep raising in, 375–6, 479, 537–8, 584–5n; ships quarantined in, 373, 374, 376; TJ's acquaintances in, 120–1; and Treaty of Tilsit, 516, 517n, 529, 627; and U.S., 162; Woodward on government of, 254n. *See also* Armstrong, John; Institut de France; Napoleon I, emperor of France
Francis I, emperor of Austria, 344; and treaty with Russia, 529
franking privilege, 82, 189–90, 191n, 278, 349, 455–6
Franklin, Benjamin: mentioned, 124; *Miscellaneous and philosophical pieces*, 581
Franzoni, Giuseppe Antonio: and carving for TJ, 473–4, 595; sculptor for U.S. Capitol, 78n; wages of, 87, 113
Frederic II, king of Prussia: *Oeuvres Complettes de Frederic II, Roi de Prusse*, 580
Frederick Augustus, Duke of York and Albany, 82–3n, 182
Fredericksburg, Va.: Benson, John (postmaster), 592, 667; citizens of, invite TJ, 14; Ker, David C. (bank president), 47, 48n; racefield at, 632; TJ's bank account at, 47
Freeman, John (dining room servant): and indenture with TJ, 155, 156
Freeman, John Holmes: letter from accounted for, 48n; Monticello overseer, 48n
Freeman, Richard, 357
*A free translation of the Preface to Bellendenus, containing animated strictures on the great political characters of the present time* (Parr), 35
French and Indian War, 290, 291n, 335
French brandy, 268, 368
French language, documents in, from: Burot, 622–4; Corny, 173–5; Daschkoff, 328–9, 484–5; Deshay, 450–1; Destutt de Tracy, 260–3; Du Pont de Nemours, 263–4; Humboldt, 264–7; Jullien, 674–6; Kesteloot, 656–7; Kosciuszko, 206–7; Lacépède, 248–50; Lemaire, 59–60, 71–2, 188–9, 222; Lormerie, 128–31, 131–4, 342–3; Moussier, 522–4; Ruelle, 219–21; Silvestre, 258–60, 611–3; Tardieu, 247–8; Tessé, 271–4, 593–4; Vrolik, 194–5
French Revolution, 622
French wine, 313n, 387
Freneau, Philip: identified, 113n; letters from, 112–3, 225–6; letter to, 211; "Poem on Thomas Jefferson's Retirement," 226–9; *Poems Written and Published during the American Revolutionary War*, 112, 113n
"A Friend to the Christian Religion," 292n
furniture: campeachy chairs, 80, 81n, 211n; and President's House, 42, 43n; seed press, 190, 191n, 245, 308, 309n, 380 (*illus.*), 390, 400n; TJ orders, 44; Windsor chairs, 44, 287, 319
fur trade: on Northwest Coast, 445–6, 447

Gale Hill (Albemarle Co.), 75
Gales, Joseph, Jr., 30n
Gallatin, Albert: and case of Moussier, 523n, 597–8, 665; and charges against Waterhouse, 295, 298; circular to customs collectors, 438, 439n; considers resigning, 598, 664–6; conversation with Turreau, 183; friendship with TJ, 598–9; and Giles, 598, 599n; identified, 599n; investigation of Degen & Purviance, 361, 362n; and land claims in Orleans Territory, 638; letter from, 664–6; letters to, 597–9, 650; and Madison, 664, 665–6n; *Report of the Secretary of the Treasury, on the subject of public roads and canals*, 646; and Robert Smith, 598, 599n; secretary of the treasury, 331, 409, 660, 661; in TJ's administration, 172; visits Monticello, 441,

Gallatin, Albert (*cont.*) 464, 466, 599n, 664; visits Montpellier, 439

Gallatin, Hannah Nicholson (Albert Gallatin's wife): visits Monticello, 441, 464, 466; visits Montpellier, 439

Gama, Antonio de León y. *See* León y Gama, Antonio de

Gannin, Mr. (barber), 41n

Gardenier, Barent, 438, 439n

gardens: and English landscape design, 191–2n; Jardin des Plantes, 202n; Jardin du Roi, 202n, 274n, 596; Liverpool Botanic Garden, 163, 164n, 435; in Mass., proposed publication on, 671–3; at Monticello, described, 388, 398n, 436–7n; at Monticello, locks for, 302; at Monticello, TJ's plans for, 400–1n, 410; at Saint Louis, proposed by Bradbury, 436–7n; at Shadwell Mills, 451–2; TJ spends time in his, 162, 166, 187; Washington botanic garden, 479; at Woodlands, 192, 479. *See also* McMahon, Bernard

Garnett, John, 572n; *Nautical Almanac and Astronomical Ephemeris*, 35, 225, 286, 492, 498n; *Tables Requisite to be used with the Nautical Ephemeris*, 492, 498n

Garrard, William, 635, 642n; letter from accounted for, 642n

Garrett, Alexander, 47n, 462–3n

Gass, Patrick, 630n

Gay-Lussac, Joseph Louis, 264, 267n, 317n

*Gazette nationale, ou, Le Moniteur universel* (Paris newspaper), 674–5

Gazzera, Jeane Antoine Henri Eugene: *Importance, et Avantages d'une Morale Publique et Privée*, 522, 523n; *Les Nuits de Ste Marie-Magdelaine pénitente*, 522, 523n; *Les Veilles de Saint-Augustin, Évêque d'Hippone*, 522, 523n

geese: at Tufton, 420; wild, 56, 153, 161, 167, 186, 199, 225, 466, 467, 469, 486

Gelston, David: identified, 282n; letter from, 294; letter to, 281–2; sends wine to TJ, 180, 247, 268, 281–2

Gelston, Maltby, 183, 374, 409

*A General Collection of the Best and Most Interesting Voyages* (Pinkerton), 256n

*General Geography, and Rudiments of Useful Knowledge* (Spafford), 105–6, 196–9

*The General History of Polybius* (trans. Hampton), 580

General Republican Committee of the City and Co. of N.Y.: letter from, 530–4; letter to, 568–9

*A general system of nature, through the three grand kingdoms of animals, vegetables, and minerals* (Linnaeus; trans. Turton), 581

Genet, Edmond Charles: correspondence with TJ, 487, 570

*The Gentleman Farmer* (Kames), 581

geography: books on, 105–6, 256n

geology: books on, 184; scholars of, 202n

*Geometrical and Graphical Essays* (Adams), 581

George (slave): murder of, 168n

George III, king of Great Britain: TJ on, 442; in Tucker's poem, 617, 619n

Georgetown, D.C.: bills drawn at, 458; Mason, John, ferry of, 52n; Republicans of, address TJ, 21–3; TJ addresses Republicans of, 34

geraniums: TJ gives to Margaret Bayard Smith, 29

Gerry, Elbridge: and charges against Waterhouse, 296–7, 299; identified, 573n; letter to, 572–3; mentioned, 574

Gholson, Thomas, Jr., 66

Giannini, Nicholas, 81n

Gibbon, Lieut. (ship's officer), 182

Gibbon, Edward: *History of the Decline and Fall of the Roman Empire*, 580

Gibbon, James: collector of customs for Richmond, 268

Gibson, John, 652

Gibson, Patrick, 44n, 186–7, 451. *See also* Gibson & Jefferson

Gibson, Robert: *A Treatise of Practical Surveying*, 576, 650

Gibson & Jefferson: agents for TJ, 281–2, 506, 596; arrange for T. J. Randolph's schooling, 633, 634–5; Bacon seeks cottonseed from, 81, 159; to deliver stew stove, 76; identified, 44n; letter from S. J. Harrison, 346–8; receives shipment for TJ, 55, 190, 246n, 307, 483. *See also* Gibson, Patrick; Jefferson, George (TJ's cousin)

gigs, 488

Giles, William Branch: correspondence with Monroe, 93n; and Gallatin, 598, 599n; rumored as secretary of state, 118; senator, 232

Gillet, Thomas: identified, 124n; letter from, 123–4
Gilliam, Robert, 305n
*Gilliam v. Fleming*: and settlement of accounts, 206, 304, 305, 306–7, 329–30, 331, 339, 362–5, 378–9, 591, 608, 644
Gillies, John: *The History of the World, from the reign of Alexander to that of Augustus*, 539
Gilpin, George: identified, 418–9n; letter from, 418–9; letter to, 507–8; on Non-Intercourse Act, 418
Gimbrede, Thomas: engraving of *Tho: Jefferson the Pride of America*, 23, 380 (*illus.*); identified, 23n; letter from, 23; letter to, 32
gimlets, 135–6
gin distilling, 465
gingko tree, 192n
Girard, Stephen, 209n
Girardin, Louis Hue: and *History of Virginia*, 289n, 634n; identified, 633–4n; letter to, 633–4; Richmond academy of, 520, 557, 633, 634–5
Gloucester-nut hickory *(Carya laciniosa)*, 657
Glover, Elias: identified, 643n; letter from, 643
Godon, Silvain: member of American Philosophical Society, 152n, 452; mineralogical lectures of, 104n, 187, 189, 193
Godwin, William, 254n
gold: found at Passamaquoddy Bay, Me., 330
goldenrain tree (*Paulinia aurea*; *Koelreuteria paniculata*), 272, 274n, 594n
Goldsborough, Charles W.: chief clerk of Navy Department, 445n, 601
Goochland County, Va.: Elk Hill, 305n, 615n
"Goodwill": letter from, 291–2
Gordon, Nathaniel, 52n
Gordon, Robert, 319n; identified, 369n
Gordon, Thomas, trans.: *Crispi Opera Omnia* (Sallust), 580; *The Works of Tacitus*, 580
Gordon, Trokes & Company: identified, 369n; letters from accounted for, 369n; letter to, 368–9; supplies groceries to TJ, 284, 318–9, 457, 483
Gordon, William: *History of the Rise, Progress, and Establishment of the Independence of the United States of America*, 581
Gordon's Tavern (Gordonsville), 52n, 562
gouges, 135–6
government: books on, 253–4
Graham, Henry R., 351, 352n
Graham, John: identified, 161n; letters from, 167, 186; letter to, 161
Graham, Robert: identified, 469n; letter from, 486; letter to, 469; and wild geese, 161, 167, 225, 469, 486
Grand & Cie, 43n
Grandmaison, Aubin Louis Millin de, 453n
Granger, Gideon: and Conn. libel prosecution of, 277, 278n, 349–50; postmaster general, 216, 350–2, 364, 407, 480
grapes: Catawba, 587n
grass: Egyptian, 555; oat, 585–6
Gray, Thomas: "Elegy Written in a Country Churchyard," 238, 240n
Great Britain: "algerine system," 137, 168; *An Inquiry into the Causes and Consequences of the Orders in Council* (Baring), 35; British Board of Agriculture, 252; commercial channels reopened, 160, 168–9, 170n; Gilpin criticizes policies of, 418; laws, 382, 424; manufacturing laws, 424; Non-Intercourse Act reimposed on, 421, 439n; Orders in Council, 21n, 137, 154, 156n, 170n, 271, 284, 285n, 409, 438, 439n, 658; political works on, 35, 38n; prices in, 82; Woodward on government of, 254n. *See also* Canning, George; Erskine, David M.; George III, king of Great Britain; Jefferson, Thomas, Opinions on; Pinkney, William
Greece: Woodward on government of, 254n
Greene, Mark, 66
Greenhow, Samuel: identified, 244n; letters from, 240–5, 625–6; letters from Dawson to, 218–9, 240, 244n, 317–8; letter to, 659–60
Greenwich Observatory, England: and prime meridian, 275–6, 356–8, 489–98, 534, 551
Grégoire, Henri: *Critical Observations on the poem of Mr. Joel Barlow, The Columbiad*, 588, 590n; *De la Littérature des Nègres*, 36, 588, 590n; on *Notes on the State of Virginia*, 588–9
Griffin, Burgess: letters from accounted for, 181n; letter to accounted for, 181n;

Griffin, Burgess (*cont.*)
Poplar Forest overseer, 157n, 180, 181n; and sale of Bedford Co. land, 318
Griffin, Cyrus: district judge, 625, 644
Griffiths, Elijah: *An Essay on Ophthalmia, or Inflammation of the Eyes*, 237n; identified, 237n; letter to, 236–7
Grinder, Mrs. Robert, 602–3, 606
Grinder, Robert, 603, 606
groceries: purchased by Shoemaker, 452; purchased by TJ, 31–2, 44–5, 77, 267–8, 346n; suppliers of, 284, 346n, 365–6, 483. *See also* food
Guadeloupe: books on, 184
Guiana: and potato, 196, 197
gun barrels, 419
gunboats, 203, 510
Gustine, Joel Trumbull, 427, 428n
Gwathney, R. & T., 655, 656n

Hackley, Harriet Randolph (Richard Hackley's wife), 114n
Hackley, Richard: dispute over vice-consulship at Cádiz, 113–4, 155, 156n
hair powder, 190, 245
Hale, Thomas: *A Complete Book of Husbandry*, 581
Hall, John (master of *Rebecca*), 44
Hamilton, Paul: secretary of the navy, 443, 475
Hamilton, William: gardens of, at Woodlands, 192, 479; identified, 192n; letter to, 191–2; and seeds of Lewis and Clark Expedition, 192n
Hammond, George: British minister plenipotentiary, 516, 517n; correspondence with TJ, 487
Hammond, Judah: identified, 534n; letter from, 530–4; letter from accounted for, 533n; letters to, 568–9
Hampton, James, trans.: *The General History of Polybius*, 580
Hand, Edward, 477
Hand, John (captain of *Sally*), 84
*The Handmaid to the Arts* (Dossie), 581
Hare, Robert, 453n
Hare, William B., 611n
Harper, Robert Goodloe, 516
Harper's Ferry, W.V., 197, 198–9n
Harrington, James, 254n
Harris, Cunningham: letter from, 84; letter to, 211–2
Harris, Levett: identified, 379–80n; letter to, 379–80; U.S. consul at Saint Petersburg, 652
Harrison, John (of Brunswick Co.), 66
Harrison, John (of Philadelphia): identified, 172n; letter from, 170–2
Harrison, Richard: auditor of the treasury, 43; identified, 43n; letter from, 43
Harrison, Samuel J.: delivers chairs to TJ, 287; identified, 348n; letter to Gibson & Jefferson, 346–8; and lost trunk, 311, 346–8
Harrison, William Henry: and appointment of territorial delegate, 96; governor of Indiana Territory, 405, 406n; identified, 575n; letter from, 574–5
Harry (boatman): carries goods from Richmond, 319n; and lost trunk, 186–7, 204–5, 257, 268, 311
Hartford, Conn.: spotted fever in, 95n
Harvard University: medical school, 51n, 300n; T. M. Randolph (*1792–1848*) attends, 524, 572–3, 574; Waterhouse's professorship at, 299, 300
Havana: cigars, 466; confitures, 505; goods lost at, 505, 510
Hawkins, Benjamin: and post road, 350, 351
Hawkins, John Isaac: and polygraph, 46n
Hay, Eliza Monroe (George Hay's wife), 93n
Hay, George, 93n, 288, 454
Hazard, William, 312
health: apoplexy, 526; dysentery, 354, 416, 483; gout, 191–2; insanity, 209n; *Means of Preserving Health, and Preventing Diseases* (Ricketson), 257, 294–5; pamphlets on, 257, 294–5; rheumatism, 192, 223, 644n; smallpox vaccination, 300n; spotted fever (typhus), 95n; and Tidewater Va., 306; of TJ's family, 387, 391, 392, 395, 410, 519, 536; and warm springs, 191–2, 451. *See also* medicine
Hearne, Samuel: *Journey from Fort Prince Wales in Hudson's Bay to the Northern Ocean*, 443, 444–5n
Hector, Cape, 448
Heleborine, 436–7n
*Hellenica* (Xenophon), 580
Hellings, John, 256
Helsham: *Lectures on Mechanics*, 581
Hemmings, Betsy (slave): carries books, 321
Hemmings, John (TJ's slave): and seed press, 380 (*illus.*), 397n

Hemmings, Peter (TJ's slave): as cook, 162n
hemp: grown at Tufton, 420; spinning of, 525
Henderson, Bennett: lands of, 415–6n, 439–41, 454, 459–63, 463, 470
Henderson, Bennett Hillsborough, 440, 454, 459, 460, 461, 462
Henderson, Charles, 440, 454, 459, 460
Henderson, Eliza. *See* Bullock, Eliza Henderson
Henderson, Elizabeth Lewis (Bennett Henderson's wife), 415n, 439–40, 454, 459, 461
Henderson, Frances, 440, 459, 460–1, 463
Henderson, Isham, 440, 454, 459, 462
Henderson, James L., 440, 459, 460
Henderson, John, 415–6n, 440, 454, 459
Henderson, Lucy, 440, 459, 460–1, 463
Henderson, Matthew, 440
Henderson, Nancy C., 440, 459, 460–1, 463
Henderson, Sarah. *See* Kerr, Sarah Henderson
Henderson, William, 459, 461
Henderson case, 415–6, 439–41, 453–4, 454, 459–63, 470
Hening, William Waller: criticized by McRae, 615–6; identified, 158–9n; letters from, 158–9, 333–4, 369–70, 403–4, 472–3, 488–9, 619–20; letter to, 570; *Reports of Cases Argued and Determined in the Supreme Court of Appeals of Virginia* (Hening & Munford), 334, 370, 404; *Statutes at Large*, 158–9n, 333–4, 489, 619–20; and TJ's collection of Va. laws, 158–9, 334, 381
Hern, David, Sr. (TJ's slave), 464n
Hern, David (TJ's slave), 464, 467, 480, 481, 486; identified, 464n
Hern, Fanny Gillette (TJ's slave; David Hern's wife), 162, 188, 189n
Hern, Isabel (TJ's slave; David Hern Sr.'s wife), 464n
Herodotus (trans. Littlebury), 580
herring, 77, 115, 176, 369
Heth, John, 615, 616
Hewat, Alexander: *An Historical Account of the Rise and Progress of the Colonies of South Carolina and Georgia*, 581
Hewson, Thomas Tickell: identified, 609n; letter from, 608–9
hickory nuts, 111n, 252, 657; Gloucester-nut, 657
Higginbotham, David: letter from accounted for, 139n; letter to accounted for, 139n; TJ's debt to, 137, 138–9, 353, 364, 407, 421
Highland (Monroe's Albemarle Co. estate), 93n
Hill, Henry, 26
Hinckley, Capt., 124
Hiort, Henry: identified, 196n; letter from, 195–6
*Histoire d'Angleterre* (Rapin Thoyras), 580
*Histoire de l'Anarchie de Pologne, et du Démembrement de Cette République* (Rulhière), 35
*Histoire de l'empire de Russie sous Pierre le Grand* (Voltaire), 580
*Histoire Naturelle de l'Homme* (Lacépède), 250n
*Histoire Naturelle des Oiseaux* (Buffon), 581
*Historia Alexandri Magni Regis* (trans. Digby), 580
*Historia de Nueva-España* (Cortés), 390, 396n
*Historiarum Libri Aliquot, qui extant, opera & studio Vincentii Obsopoei in lucem editi* (Diodorus Siculus), 580
*Historiarum Libri Qui Extant* (Livius), 580
*An Historical Account of the Rise and Progress of the Colonies of South Carolina and Georgia* (Hewat), 581
*An Historical Review of the State of Ireland* (Plowden), 580
historiography: of American Revolution, 288–9, 334, 634n; of Va., 619; of Va. statutes, 334, 381–4, 489
history: TJ recommends books on, 508, 580–1; works on, bound for TJ, 36
*History of America* (Robertson), 521, 581, 620n
*The History of Charles XII* (Voltaire), 580
*The History of England from the Accession of James I. to that of the Brunswick Line* (Macaulay), 580
*History of Great Britain, from the Revolution to the Accession of the House of Hanover* (Belsham), 580
*History of Modern Europe* (Russell), 580
*The History of New-Hampshire* (Belknap), 581

*The History of Pennsylvania in North America* (Proud), 581
*The History of Philosophy* (Enfield), 576
*The History of Philosophy* (Stanley), 580
*The History of Printing in America* (Thomas), 333, 334n
*The History of Scotland* (Robertson), 580
*History of the American Revolution* (Ramsay), 581
*The History of the Colony of Massachusetts-Bay* (Hutchinson), 581
*The History of the Colony of Nova Caesaria, or New-Jersey* (Smith), 581
*History of the Corruptions of Christianity* (Priestley), 581
*History of the Decline and Fall of the Roman Empire* (Gibbon), 580
*A History of the Early Part of the Reign of James the Second* (Fox), 36, 37, 580
*History of the Insurrection, in the Four Western Counties of Pennsylvania* (Findley), 581
*The History of the Insurrections* (Minot), 581
*History of the Life of Marcus Tullius Cicero* (Middleton), 35, 580
*The History of the Peloponnesian War, Translated from the Greek of Thucydides* (Smith), 580
*History of the Proceedings of the House of Commons, in the Inquiry into the Conduct of His Royal Highness the Duke of York*, 182
*The History of the Reign of Charles V* (Robertson), 580
*History of the Rise, Progress, and Establishment of the Independence of the United States of America* (Gordon), 581
*History of the Rise, Progress and Termination of the American Revolution* (Warren), 37, 581
*The History of the World, from the reign of Alexander to that of Augustus* (Gillies), 539
*A History of Tom Jones, a Foundling* (Fielding): characters in, 174, 175n
*The History of Virginia* (Burk and Jones), 581, 619, 620n; and Girardin, 289n, 634n; TJ's role in, 288–9, 331, 457, 634n
Hobbes, Thomas: *De Cive*: quoted by TJ, 507–8
Hobbs, Hubbard, 66
Hochie, James: letter from, 58–9; letter to, 102
Hog, David, 26
hogs: owned by J. Shoemaker, 451
Holcus sorghum, 436–7n
Holmes, David, 25
holm oak (*Quercus ilex*), 594
Hooe, Nathaniel H., 48n
Hopkins, David K.: identified, 649n; letter from, 646–9
Hopkins, Matthew (of Snow Hill, Md.), 649
Horace: quoted, 226, 228
horehound: as snakebite remedy, 57
*Horrors of Slavery: or, The American Tars in Tripoli* (Ray), 33, 77–8
horse chestnut (*Aesculus hippocastanum*), 593, 594n
*Horse-Hoeing Husbandry: or, An Essay on the Principles of Vegetation and Tillage* (Tull), 581
horses: owned by TJ, 51, 52n; Spanish, 478
*Hortus Siccus* (Crowninshield), 37, 189, 191n
Houdetot, Elisabeth Françoise Sophie de la Live Bellegarde, comtesse d': marital arrangement of, 121, 122n
Houmas Indians, 509
House, Mary, 475, 513
House, Samuel: death of, 475, 476n, 513
household articles: alabaster lamp, 190, 309; brooms, 3; candles, 31, 32; chariots, 41n; clocks, 85, 96; coal, 155; comforters, 28, 64, 76, 153, 310; distiller's syphon, 482–3; drawknives, 135–6; gig, 488; hair powder, 190, 245; lanterns, 303; linseed oil, 55n, 77, 97; looking glasses, 303; milkpans, 303; padlocks, 302–3; saddles, 3; sal ammoniac, 467; stoves, 122; tea chests, 44; tools, 135–6, 397n; turpentine, 82; varnish, 419; wagons, 3; white lead, 55n, 77. *See also* building materials; clothing; furniture
House of Representatives, U.S., 275, 512. *See also* Lambert, William
Howard, Benjamin: U.S. representative from Ky., 199, 200n, 224
Hudson Bay, 448
Hũlings, William E., 521
Hull, William, 660–1
Humboldt, Friedrich Wilhelm Heinrich

Alexander, Baron von: *Essai politique sur le royaume de la Nouvelle-Espagne*, 24, 25n, 264, 267n; *Essai sur la géographie des plantes*, 265, 267n; identified, 24–5n; letter from, 264–7; letter to, 24–5; likeness of, at Monticello, 593; *Nivellement barométrique*, 452, 453n, 455, 482; *Recueil d'observations astronomiques*, 24, 25n, 264, 267n, 455; sends books to TJ, 24, 25n; sends greetings to TJ, 141, 629; *Tableaux de la Nature*, 264, 267n, 482, 483n; TJ praises scientific writings of, 482; *Voyage aux régions équinoxiales du nouveau continent*, 25n, 37, 267n, 482; *Voyage de Humboldt et Bonpland*, 24–5n, 455
Hume, David, 254n
Humphreys, David: mentioned, 647; wool manufactory of, 16, 17, 18, 19n, 666
Huntingdon, Selina Hastings, countess of: address of, 110, 111n
Huntington, Samuel, 277, 278
*The Husbandry of the Antients* (Dickson), 581
Hutchinson, Thomas: *The History of the Colony of Massachusetts-Bay*, 581
Hutton, Charles: *Mathematical Tables*, 576
Hylton, Daniel, 25

icehouses: at President's house, 155
icognitum, American. *See* mammoth, Siberian
Illinois Territory: appointments in, 25, 627
*Importance, et Avantages d'une Morale Publique et Privée* (Gazzera), 522, 523n
impressment: of American seamen, 85–6; and Monroe-Pinkney Treaty, 170n
*Improvements in Education* (Lancaster), 662
inauguration: Madison's presidential, 8–9, 10n
indentures, 156
*Independent Chronicle* (Boston newspaper), 50n, 671, 673n
India, 449
Indiana Territory, 96, 405, 406n; Indian agent for, 574–5. *See also* Harrison, William Henry
Indian Camp (Short's Albemarle Co. estate), 234, 235n
Indians: artifacts of, at Monticello, 397n; blankets, 510; cattle raised by, 110; Cherokee, 6–7, 110, 653; Chickasaw, 6–7, 26; Creek, 110; currency of, 334, 369; dialects of, 205, 520–1, 555–6, 651–2; education of children, 7, 660–2; hair of, described, 478; Houmas, 509; Indiana Territory agent for, 574–5; land claims in Orleans Territory, 637; language, 205, 269, 520–1, 555–7, 599n, 651–2; Mandan, 520–1; Miami, 652; of Northwest Coast described, 446; Osage, 520; Pawnee, 521, 556; plans for civilizing, 110–1; and post road, 351; recommended readings for, 110; sculpture of, for TJ, 473–4, 475n; in Tenn., 653; TJ's vocabularies of dialects of, 269, 555–6; training school for, 7, 660–2, 662n; treaties of, 6–7
influenza, 257
Ingle, Henry, 41n, 42n
*An Inquiry into the Causes and Consequences of the Orders in Council* (Baring), 35
*An Inquiry into the Use of the Omentum* (Rush), 185, 558–9
Institut de France: fossils analyzed by, 100–1, 103–4, 187, 248–9, 250n; TJ and Wistar give fossil bones to, 100–1, 248, 510–1; and work on ancient vases, 452, 453n, 482
*Institutes of the Laws of England* (Coke), 382
Institut Roÿal des Sciences, de Littérature et des beaux Arts: admits TJ, 194–5
insurance. *See* Mutual Assurance Society
*An Introduction to Natural Philosophy* (Nicholson), 581
inventions: impenetrable stucco, 195–6; invisible ink, 111n; matches, 376, 377n; metallic pen, 106; refrigerator, 173n
Ireland: and introduction of potato to U.S., 197
iron. *See* naileries, nailrod and iron stock
Irujo, Carlos Fernando Martínez de. *See* Yrujo (Irujo), Carlos Fernando Martínez de
Irwin, James, 290, 335
Italian wine, 387

*Iustini Historae Phillipicae Cum integris Commentariis Iac* (Justinius), 580
Ivy Creek (Bedford Co.), 670–1
Iznardi, Josef. *See* Yznardy, Josef

Jackson, Benoni (master of the *Jane*), 55
Jackson, Francis James: British minister to U.S., 418, 513, 516, 517n, 518, 584, 592, 633, 656, 658; expected to make treaty with U.S., 169, 170n
Jackson, John G.: U.S. representative from Va., 232, 235n
James River: land on, in *Gilliam v. Fleming*, 305n; and lost trunk on, 269, 408. *See also* boats, transfer goods to and from Richmond
James River Company, 367n, 560, 579
*Jane* (schooner), 55
Japan, 447
Jardin du Roi, 202n, 274n, 596
Jarvis, William, 26, 114, 155
*Jasminum officinale* (star-jasmine), 631–2
Jay, Sir James: identified, 110–1n; letter to, 110–1
Jay, John, 110–1n
Jay Treaty: TJ criticizes, 169; and U.S. relations with France, 162
Jefferson, Field (TJ's uncle), 44n
Jefferson, George (TJ's cousin): account with TJ, 114, 595n; agent for TJ, 368, 404, 417, 488, 505; handles TJ's newspaper subscriptions, 214; identified, 44n; invoice from, 176; letters from, 84, 114–5, 157, 159, 186–7, 246, 268–9, 269, 284, 287, 302, 311, 344, 451, 469–70, 483, 557–8, 669–70; letters from accounted for, 176n, 246n, 319n, 348n, 595n; letters to, 44, 77, 81, 153–4, 180–1, 204–5, 257, 267–8, 318–9, 353–4, 457, 472, 520, 590–1, 595, 634–5, 655–6; offers reward for lost trunk, 205; paid by TJ, 41n; pays TJ's insurance premium, 219, 472; receipt from, 483; sends goods to TJ, 123; as U.S. consul at Cádiz, 155, 156n. *See also* Gibson & Jefferson
Jefferson, George, & Company: as TJ's agent in Richmond, 44n
Jefferson, Isham R., 462
Jefferson, Martha Wayles Skelton (TJ's wife): dower right of, 305n, 671n; family of, 338n
Jefferson, Peter (TJ's father), 420n; relations of, 67
Jefferson, Randolph (TJ's brother), 168n

JEFFERSON, THOMAS

*Addresses to*

Citizens of Richmond, 620–1; Convention of R.I., 88–9; Democratic Republicans of Washington Co., Pa., 99–100; N.Y. legislature, 125; Republican Mechanics of Leesburg, Va., 89–90; Republicans of Conn., 126–7; Republicans of Essex Co., Mass., 85–6; Republicans of Georgetown, 34; Republicans of New York City and County, 533n, 568–9; Republicans of Queen Annes Co., Md., 127–8; Republicans of Washington Co., Md., 98–9

*Books & Library*

and newspaper subscriptions, 48, 49, 50n, 85, 96, 107, 214; orders books, 35–7, 50; poetry subscriptions, 211, 225–6, 504n; receives books, 25n, 50–1, 72; recommends books, 205–6, 576–7, 579–82; TJ's personal, 35–8, 390, 400n

*Business & Financial Affairs*

account with Barnes, 31–2; account with Dinsmore, 64, 65n; account with Dougherty, 3–4; account with Leitch, 64–5; conveys indentured servant to Madison, 156; debt to Higginbotham, 137, 138–9, 353, 364, 407, 421; debt to Jones & Howell, 422–3, 435, 503; loans requested of, 33, 67–8, 101–2, 566–7; note cosigned by Madison and Barnes, 212–4, 217–8; notes on expenses, 41–2, 81n; orders furniture, 44; payments to Taggart, 111–2; pays taxes, 590, 595; renews bank note, 353–4; sells land, 213; terminates mill lease, 421–2, 422–3; witnesses land purchase by Lormerie, 129, 130, 131n. *See also* Mutual Assurance Society

*Correspondence*

anonymous letters to, 69–70, 291–2, 654, 655n, 671–3; franking privilege, 82, 189–90, 191n, 278, 349, 455–6; kept by daughter, 392n, 397n; letters of application and

Jefferson, Thomas (*cont.*)
recommendation from, 626–7; letters of application and recommendation to, 14–15, 91–2, 167–8, 193–4, 404–6, 464–5; letters of congratulation to, 4–6, 11–12, 26–9, 46–7, 54, 62–3, 63, 79–80; letters of introduction from, 191–2, 201–2, 215, 216, 283, 315–6, 360–1, 379–80, 385–6, 412–3, 414, 572–3, 633–4, 650; letters of introduction to, 163, 179–80, 329n, 410–1, 574–5, 601–2; with Monroe published, 93n; publication of papers, 385, 486–8, 538–9, 569–70; with Short to be destroyed, 182n; stylograph, 182n; threats against, 425–8. *See also* French language, documents in; Latin, document in; Spanish language, documents in

*Descriptions of*

appearance, 387, 395–6; conversation, 9, 397–8n; by Margaret Bayard Smith, 9; and toasts to, 358–9; by Trist, 98n

*Family & Friends*

dining, 387, 388–9, 397n, 399n; friendship with Gallatin, 598–9, 664; importance of family, 393–4, 396, 511; opinion of T. J. Randolph, 633; relations with daughter, 391–2, 401n; relations with grandchildren, 393, 401n

*Literary Quotes*

Bible, 103, 103n, 154, 156n, 564, 565n, 596, 597n; Hobbes, 507–8; Paine, 512

*Opinions on*

agricultural lifestyle, 559; architecture, 595–6; British government, 154, 279–80, 441–2, 507–8, 512; British Orders in Council, 137; charity at home, 506; circulating libraries, 205–6; civilizing the Indians, 110; congressional library, 592; Cuba, 169–70, 183–4; Declaration of Independence, 487; domestic manufacturing, 110; duplicity of Great Britain, 107; effect of British policy, 168–9, 279–80, 441–2; French Directory, 236; his presidential administration, 338–9; immoral laws, 472; importance of Union, 126–7; intellectual capacity of blacks, 588–9, 590n; Jesus, 564; landscape design, 190, 191; Marshall's *Life of George Washington*, 589, 590n; morality in government, 559; Napoleon, 20, 154–5, 169, 442; newspapers, 49; patronage, 30–1, 181; poetry, 504; possibility of war with Great Britain, 442, 510; public debt, 168–9, 598; and recommendations for office, 77; religion, 563–6; Republicans in Pennsylvania, 236–7; retirement, 20, 162, 187; study of mathematics, 633; treaties with Great Britain, 169; university in Va., 592; U.S. as free society, 13; U.S. Congress, 61; U.S. Constitution, 86; Walpole, 512; warm springs as a cure, 191–2; writing less, 166, 383

*Portraits*

cameo by Gimbrede, 23, 32, 380 (*illus.*)

*Public Service*

administration criticized, 138n; administration supported, 21–2, 26–9, 86n, 120, 176–9, 530–4; as governor of Va., 646; as member of Va. Assembly, 487, 502–3; as minister to France, 43, 610; and revision of Va. laws, 381–3, 384n; as secretary of state, 487, 569–70

*Travels*

notes on distances between Monticello and Montpellier, 562–3; to Richmond, Va., 608, 611n, 620–1, 625; visits Divers family, 98n; from Washington, D.C., 14, 51–2, 61

*Writings*

Act for establishing Religious Freedom, 384n, 487; Bill for Proportioning Crimes and Punishments, 382, 384n; Campbell's proposed edition of, 385; Craven and Jane Peyton's Conveyance of the Henderson Lands, 459–63; Declaration to Craven Peyton, 463; draught in *Gilliam v. Fleming* accounted for, 365n; "Libels" notebook, 400n; List of Recommended Books for Wyche, 580–2; *Manual of Parliamentary Practice*, 486–7; Memorandum Book, 380 (*illus.*);

Jefferson, Thomas (*cont.*)
*Messages to Congress*, 538–9, 569–70; Notes on Distances between Monticello and Montpellier, 562–3; Notes on Ivy Creek Lands, 670–1; *Notes on the State of Virginia*, 197, 265, 385, 486, 567–8, 587–8, 588–9, 600–1, 654; Report on Census, 569–70; Report on Commerce, 487; Report on Copper Coinage, 487; Report on Desalination of Sea Water, 487; Report on the Fisheries, 487; Report on Weights and Measures, 487; Summary Journal of Letters, 380 (*illus.*); *A Summary View of the Rights of British America*, 486, 487n, 539, 569–70; translates Destutt de Tracy's works, 260–2, 262n, 270

Jefferson, Thomas (TJ's nephew), 462
Jefferson College (Washington Co., Pa.): students address TJ, 4–6
*Jeffersonia Antivenena. See* Jeffersonia diphylla (twinleaf)
*Jeffersonia diphylla* (twinleaf): medicinal properties of, 56–7
Jenkings, William: identified, 319–20n; letter to, 319–20; and Natural Bridge land, 318, 319n, 506–7
Jervaux (Napoleon's aide-de-camp), 372
Jesus: TJ on, 564
Jewett, Leonard: identified, 380n; letter from, 380
John, archduke of Austria, 372
Johnson, Samuel: and edition of Shakespeare, 412n
Johnson, William: and benne seed, 211; identified, 555n; letter from, 555
Johnston, John: Indian agent at Indiana Territory, 574–5
Jones, Mr. (Richmond boardinghouse owner), 590
Jones, Levin, 522
Jones, Martha Burke, 338n
Jones, Mary Brown Trist (Philip L. Jones's wife), 74n, 509
Jones, Philip Livingston, 74n, 509
Jones, Skelton: and *Gilliam v. Fleming*, 304, 305n, 307, 329–30; *The History of Virginia*, 288–9, 289n, 331, 634n; identified, 289n; letters from, 288–9, 331; letters to, 305–6, 381–4
Jones, Stephen, 330
Jones, Thomas, 305n
Jones & Howell: account with TJ, 41, 422–3, 435, 503; identified, 423n; letter from, 435; letters from accounted for, 423n, 503n; letters to, 422–3, 503; letter to accounted for, 423n
Joseph, king of Spain. *See* Bonaparte, Joseph
*Journal of a Voyage in 1775* (Mourelle de la Rúa), 446, 449n
*Journey from Fort Prince Wales in Hudson's Bay to the Northern Ocean* (Hearne), 443, 444–5n
Joyce, Jeremiah: *Scientific dialogues, intended for the instruction of young people*, 36, 332, 333, 384, 482, 483n, 581
juboli (jujube; *Zizyphus jujuba*), 631
*Juglans squamosa* (Missouri scaly bark; scaly bark hickory), 657
jujube (juboli; *Zizyphus jujuba*), 631
Julien, Honoré: carries letter to TJ, 64; paid by TJ, 42n; trains chefs for TJ, 162; visits Monticello, 59, 76
Jullien, Marc Antoine: *Essai Général d'Education physique, morale, et intellectuelle*, 674–5; identified, 676n; letter from, 674–6
Justinius, Marcus Junianus: *Iustini Historae Phillipicae Cum integris Commentariis Iac*, 580

Kamchatka (Kamtschatka), 447
Kames, Henry Home, Lord: *Elements of Criticism*, 576; *Essays on the Principles of Morality and Natural Religion*, 576; *The Gentleman Farmer*, 581
Kennett, Basil: *Romae Antiquae Notitia: or, The Antiquities of Rome*, 580
Kennett, White: *A Complete History of England*, 580
Kentucky: education in, 456; judiciary, 405; land speculation in, 129, 131n; Lewis family at, 168n. *See also* Howard, Benjamin
Ker, David C.: letter from accounted for, 48n; letter to accounted for, 48n; president of Fredericksburg bank, 47, 48n
Kercheval, Samuel: identified, 567n; letter from, 566–7
Kerr, James: identified, 100n; letter to, 99–100
Kerr, John B.: and Henderson lands, 439–40, 460, 461
Kerr, Joseph: as commissioner of Cumberland Road, 26, 173n

Kerr, Sarah Henderson, 439–40, 459, 460, 461
Kersner (Kershner), Martin, 27
Kesteloot, Jacob Lodewijk: *Discours sur les progrès des sciences*, 656; identified, 657n; letter from, 656–7
Keteltas, William, 26
Kimber, Emmor, 256
Kimber & Conrad: identified, 256n; letter from, 256
Kimber & Sharpless, 256n
King, John Edwards, 25
King, Nicholas: identified, 12n; letter from, 11–12
Knight, Thomas Andrew: *A Treatise on the Culture of the Apple & Pear, and on the Manufacture of Cider & Perry*, 581
*Koelreuteria paniculata* (*Paulinia aurea*; goldenrain tree), 272, 274n, 594n
Komarzewski, Jan Chrzciciel: *Coup-d'Oeil rapide sur les causes réelles de la Décadence de la Pologne*, 535, 536n; *Memoir on a subterranean graphometer*, 535, 536n
Koontz, John: identified, 574n; letter from, 573–4
Kosciuszko, Tadeusz (Thaddeus) Andrzej Bonawentura: Bank of Pennsylvania stock, 32n, 166, 217, 218n, 408; financial arrangement with TJ, 207n, 281; identified, 207n; letter from, 206–7

Lacépède, Bernard Germain Étienne de La Ville-Sur-Illon, comte de, 158, 416; analyzes bones for Institut de France, 101n, 250n; *Histoire naturelle de l'homme*, 250n; identified, 250n; letter from, 248–50; sends greetings to TJ, 629; TJ forwards letter from, to Turreau, 249, 417
Ladd, Thomas: and *Gilliam v. Fleming*, 304, 305, 306–7, 329–30, 331, 362–3, 364–5, 591, 608; identified, 307n; letter from, 329–30; letter to, 306–7
Ladvocat, Jean Baptiste: *Dictionnaire Historique et Bibliographique Portatif*, 580
lady-slipper (*Cypripedium*), 436–7n
Lafayette, Marie Joseph Paul Yves Roch Gilbert du Motier, marquis de: debt of, 376, 628; family of, 629; identified, 270–1n; La. land of, 270n, 529, 628; letters from, 269–71, 528–30, 627–9; recommends Lormerie to TJ, 342; sends dogs, 376, 457; sends merino sheep, 529, 537–8, 629; and Tessé, 528, 593–4, 627
La Forest. *See* Mathurin, Antoine René Charles, comte de La Forest
La Grange: home of Lafayette, 270n, 529
La Grange et de Fourilles, Adélaïde Blaise François Le Lièvre, marquis de, 372
Lallemand, François Antoine, baron, 372
Lambert, William: calculates prime meridian, 356–9; clerk of the House of Representatives, 275, 359n, 512; on House of Representatives, 534–5; identified, 54–5n; letters from, 54–5, 274–6, 356–9, 489–98, 534–5, 539–40, 560–2; letters to, 237–8, 511–2; Table for Computing the Moon's Motion, with Explanations, 540–54, 571–2, 608–9
lamps, alabaster: brass chain for, 190, 309
Lancaster, Joseph: *Improvements in Education*, 662
Lane's Ordinary (Fairfax Co.), 52n
Langhorne, John, trans.: *Lives* (Plutarch), 580
Langhorne, William, trans.: *Lives* (Plutarch), 580
Langland, William: *The Vision of Pierce Plowman*, 390, 397n
language: Chinese, 518; French training of T. J. Randolph, 520, 557; Indian, 205, 269, 520–1, 555–7, 599n, 651–2; Russian, 556; sign, 662; TJ and Spanish, 556; translations by TJ, 260–2, 262n, 270; translations by Warden, 142–52, 316–7, 482, 608–9, 629–30. *See also* French, Latin, and Spanish languages
Lannes, Jean, Duc de Montebello, 371, 372
lanterns, 303
La Pérouse, Jean François de Galalup, comte de: *Voyage de La Pérouse autour du Monde*, 445–9
Lapie, Pierre: *Carte réduite de la Mer Méditerranée et de la mer Noire* (Zannoni and Lapie), 247–8
Laplace, Pierre Simon, marquis de: *Exposition du Systême du Monde*, 348, 349n, 357, 491
Lasteyrie-Du Saillant, Charles Philibert de: *Du Cotonnier et de sa Culture*, 37; sends greetings to TJ, 141

Latin, document in, from: Tucker, 617–9
*Latin and English Dictionary abridged* (Ainsworth), 35
Latrobe, Benjamin Henry: to find work for Dougherty, 199; furnishes President's House, 43n; identified, 474–5n; letter from, 473–5; letter to, 595–6; and model of corncob capitals, 473, 475n, 595; and payment for Italian sculptors, 78n, 113, 114n; proposed visit to Monticello, 366, 474, 595–6; works on Capitol, 65, 92, 474n
Latrobe, Henry, 65n
law: books on, 158, 416; common, 381; criminal, 382, 384n; of Great Britain, 382, 424; and judicial review, 380; martial, 571; TJ provides training in, 245, 389, 416. *See also* Virginia, laws of
Law, Jonathan: identified, 95n; letter from, 95; letter to, 126–7
Lawur, Peter: letter from accounted for, 677
lead, white, 55n, 77
*Leander* (British warship), 228n
le Blanc (Siblong) de Villeneufve, Paul Louis: *La Fête du Petit Blé; ou, L'Heroisme du Poucha-Houmma*, 202, 203n, 509
LeBourdais, Mr., 557
*Leçons d'Histoire* (Volney), 580
*Lectures on Mechanics* (Helsham), 581
*Lectures on Natural and Experimental Philosophy* (Adams), 581
*Lectures on Rhetoric and Belles Lettres* (Blair), 576
*Lectures on Select Subjects in Mechanics, Hydrostatics, Pneumatics, and Optics*, 581
Lee, Edmund Jennings, 516
Lee, Henry (*1756–1818*): as defense witness, 277, 278–9n
Lee, Rachel Fanny Antonina: *An Essay on Government*, 123–4
Lee, Thomas Ludwell, 381–3
Lee, William: consul at Bordeaux, 118, 121n
Leeds, Francis Godolphin Osborne, 5th Duke of, 516, 517n
Leesburg, Va.: Republican mechanics of, address TJ, 89–90
*Legibus et Consuetudinibus Angliæ* (Bracton), 383
Lego (TJ's estate): lease of, 488n; overseers at, 137–8n
Leib, Michael: and Gallatin, 598, 599n
Leitch, James: accounts with TJ, 64–5; identified, 65n; letters from, 64–5, 458; letter to, 302–3; trades nails for goods, 64, 303, 458
Lemaire, Etienne: identified, 56n; and kitchen inventory of President's House, 43n, 155, 156n; letters from, 59–60, 71–2, 188–9, 222; letters to, 55–6, 161–2; maître d'hôtel, 42; paid by TJ, 41, 294; sends oil and syrup to TJ, 188–9, 222, 245, 257
Le Maire, Jacques, 450
Lenox, Peter, 41
Lenthall, John, 65n, 92
León y Gama, Antonio de: *Descripción histórica y cronológica de los piedras*, 521, 556
Lescallier, Daniel: identified, 184n; letter from, 184; *Vocabulaire des Termes de Marine Anglais et Français*, 36, 184n
*Letters to Friends* (Cicero), 386
*Letters to the Inhabitants of Northumberland and its neighbourhood* (Priestley), 119, 121–2n
*Letter to Henri Gregoire* (Barlow), 588, 590n
Lewis, Mr. (captain of *Liberty*), 307
Lewis, Charles, Jr. (TJ's uncle), 168n
Lewis, Charles Lilburne (TJ's brother-in-law), 167, 168n, 415n
Lewis, Henry, 27
Lewis, Isham (TJ's nephew): identified, 168n; letter from, 167–8; letter of introduction for, 215, 216; letter to, 181–2; and murder of slave, 168n
Lewis, James: and Henderson lands, 440, 454, 459
Lewis, Lilburne (TJ's nephew): and murder of slave, 168n
Lewis, Lucy Jefferson (TJ's sister), 168n, 415n
Lewis, Meriwether: and artifact collection of Clark, 510; death of, 436n, 602–3, 606–8, 632, 668; identified, 436n; and Indian dialects, 520, 556; journal of expedition, 603, 607, 668–9; letter to, 435–7; prepares for expedition, 101n, 194n; and publication of journals, 249, 412n, 436, 443, 668–9; TJ sends greetings to, 511
Lewis, Randolph (TJ's nephew): moves to Ky., 168n
Lewis and Clark Expedition: journals of, 603, 607, 630n, 668–9; publication of journals, 249, 412n, 436, 443, 630n,

668–9; seeds from, 192n; stone block for TJ, 473, 475n
Lexington, Va.: Ann Smith Academy, 367, 368, 506, 507n; Washington Academy, 367, 368n
*Liberty* (ship), 307
Liberty Hall Academy. *See* Washington Academy (later Washington & Lee University)
Liblong, Col. *See* le Blanc de Villeneufve, Paul Louis
libraries: formed by Demaree in Ky., 455–7; TJ on, 205–6; TJ on congressional, 592; TJ's personal, 35–8, 390, 400n; Westwardmill Library Society, 66–7, 205–6, 508
*Life and Pontificate of Leo the Tenth* (Roscoe), 163, 164n, 435
*The Life of Catharine II, Empress of all the Russias* (Tooke), 580
*The Life of George Washington* (Marshall), 619, 634n; TJ on, 589, 590n
*The Life of George Washington* (Ramsay), 35
*Life of Lorenzo de' Medici, called the Magnificent* (Roscoe), 164n, 435
lilac, 61
*Lilium Martagon* (Allegheny lily; Turk's-cap), 660
lima beans, 631, 657
lime (*Citrus aurantifolia*), 631–2
Lincoln, Levi: identified, 49–50n; letter to, 49–50; paid by TJ, 41, 49
Lindsay, Reuben, 562–3
Lindsey's Hotel (Washington, D.C.), 359n
Lingan, James McCubbin, 75
Linnaeus, Carolus: *A general system of nature, through the three grand kingdoms of animals, vegetables, and minerals* (trans. Turton), 581
Linnean Society of London, 163, 164n, 521n
Linnean Society of Philadelphia, 663
linseed oil, 55n, 77, 97
lion's foot (*Prenanthes serpentaria*): as snakebite remedy, 58n
Lisbon: consulate at, 114
*List of Post Offices in the United States*, 514
*De La Littérature des Nègres* (Grégoire), 36, 588, 590n
Littlebury, trans.: Herodotus, 580
Littlejohn, John: and committee of Republican mechanics, 90n
*The Little Medly: containing short remarks on the . . . New Testament* (Brunt), 403
Lively, Charles, 234, 235n
Liverpool Botanic Garden, 163, 164n, 435
*Lives* (Plutarch; trans. W. & J. Langhorne), 580
livestock: for Monticello, 81n
Livingston, Brockholst, 195n
Livingston, Edward, 287n
Livingston, Robert R., 20n; *Essay on Sheep*, 667, 668n; merino sheep of, 529
Livingston, William, Jr., 195n
Livius, Titus: *Historiarum Libri Qui Extant*, 580
Lloyd, James, 473
Lloyd, Thomas, 214n
Locke, John, 254n; *An Essay concerning Human Understanding*, 576
Logan, George, 16
Lomax, Elizabeth, 305n
Lomax, Thomas: identified, 631n; letter from, 631–2; letter to, 657
Lombardy poplars, 192n
London: Linnean Society of, 163, 164n, 521
Long, Gabriel, 415, 416n
Long, James: letter from, 464–5
Long's Hotel (Washington D.C.), 10n
Long's Ordinary (Spotsylvania Co.), 416n
looking glasses, 303
Lormerie, Louis Philippe Gallot de: identified, 131n; and Ky. land, 342; letter from accounted for, 343n; letters from, 128–31, 342–3; letter to, 354–5; Memoir on American Forest Management, 131–4, 342, 354; seeks permission to ship goods to France, 128–9, 342, 354
Loudoun, John Campbell, earl of, 291
Loudoun County Superior Court, 417
Louisiana Territory: and botanical expedition, 164n; maps of, 247, 248n; purchase of, 448, 672–3; tracts on, 36, 37, 38n; vouchers for public money, 603, 607
Lowry, Andrew, 335
Lowry, Morrow, 335
Ludlow, Edmund: *Memoirs*, 37, 580
*Luzerne Federalist* (Wilkes-Barre, Pa.): prints poems on TJ, 429–33
*Lydia* (ship), 629
Lyman, William: identified, 182n; letter from, 182

Lynchburg, Va.: citizens of, address TJ, 671
Lyon, Oliver, 33n
Lyons, Mr., 338

Macaulay, Catherine: *The History of England from the Accession of James I. to that of the Brunswick Line*, 580
McCally, Hugh, 96
McCandless, William: identified, 91n; letter to, 90–1
McCoy, Joseph: broadside from accounted for, 504n; "The Expedient," 322–7; identified, 322n; letter from, 321–2; letter to, 504; "The Moment," 504n; sends poetry to TJ, 322–7
mace (spice), 368
McGehee, William, Sr., 420n
McGehee, William: agreement with TJ, 419–21; identified, 420n; Tufton overseer, 419–20
MacGowty, John: identified, 83n; letters from, 83, 162
machines: distiller's syphon, 482–3; dynamometer, 20, 21n, 180, 204, 205, 376; polygraph, 46n, 307; refrigerator, 173n; spinning jenny, 313, 524–5, 591, 661
Mackay, Andrew: *The theory and practice of finding the Longitude at Sea or Land*, 492, 498n
Mackenzie, Alexander: *Voyages from Montreal*, 443, 444–5n
McKinney, James: identified, 92n; letter from, 91–2; partnership with T. M. Randolph, 92n
McLean, James Sylvanus: identified, 209n; letter from, 209; visits Monticello, 209n
McMahon, Bernard: *McMahon's American Gardener's Calendar*, 35, 582; and seeds of Lewis and Clark Expedition, 192n
*McMahon's American Gardener's Calendar* (McMahon), 35, 582
Macomb, Alexander: identified, 571n; letter to, 571; *A Treatise on Martial Law, and Courts-Martial*, 571
Macon, Nathaniel, 191n, 349
McRae, Alexander: and Banks, 616n; considered for appointment by TJ, 25; identified, 355–6n; letters from, 355–6, 423–5, 615–6; letters to, 413, 472; and silk-manufacturing project, 341, 342n, 412–3, 413, 414, 423–4, 472
Madeira, 387, 397n
Madison, Dolley Payne Todd (James Madison's wife): arrives in Washington, 53; false pregnancy of, 200; furnishes President's House, 43n, 199; and Madison's inauguration, 8; TJ refers gardener to, 155; TJ sends greetings to, 593; and visit from TJ, 519; visits Monticello, 344, 360, 441, 466; writings on, 10n
Madison, George (clerk in Frankfort, Ky.), 129, 131n
Madison, James: administration supported, 29n, 405, 610–1; arrives in Washington, 53; Brunt requests assistance from, 402–3; and charges against Waterhouse, 297–8, 299, 300n; cosigns loan to TJ with Barnes, 212–3, 217–8, 246, 281, 285; on Erskine agreement, 409; on Federalists, 246–7; and Gallatin, 664, 665–6n; identified, 7n; and Indian training school, 661, 662n; letter from accounted for, 627n; letter from Du Pont de Nemours, 584–5, 592; letter from Freneau, 113n; and letter of credence from Daschkoff, 484, 485n; letters from, 65, 85, 87, 113–4, 160, 183–4, 246–7, 271, 292–3, 313–4, 327–8, 331–2, 359–60, 408–10, 437–9, 464, 518–9, 584–5, 632–3, 658–9; letters to, 60–2, 77–8, 92–3, 96, 154–6, 168–70, 212–4, 284–5, 343–4, 441–2, 519–20, 536, 592–3, 626–7, 657–8; memoranda to, 6–8; and pardon in *Olmstead* case, 213–4n; and Pinckney, 513–4; and Porter's voyage of discovery, 445n; presidential appointments of, 20n, 23n, 26n, 38, 44n; presidential inauguration, 8–9, 10n; presidential proclamations of, 170n, 436–7n, 439n, 441–2; purchases Freeman indenture, 156; purchases items from TJ, 41, 155; as secretary of state, 62n; seeks advice from TJ, 65; sends books to TJ, 667; sends sheepskin to TJ, 328; and Short's diplomatic expenses, 232, 233; visits Monticello, 344, 360, 441, 466; weather journal of, 518, 519n
Madison, James, Bishop, 497; identified, 251n; letter from, 251

Mager, John (captain of *Dolphin of York*), 64, 186–7
Magruder, Allan B., 639–40, 642n
Magruder, John Bowie: letter from accounted for, 110n
Magruder's Mill (Fluvanna Co.), 109, 110n
Maille, Antoine: vinegar syrup of, 188, 189n
Main (Maine), Thomas, 51, 170
Maine: gold found in, 330
Maisonneuve, Dubois, ed.: *Peintures des Vases Antiques*, 452, 453n, 482
maize (*Zea mays*): from Lewis and Clark Expedition, 436–7n. *See also* corn
Malthus, Thomas Robert: *An Essay on the principle of population*, 35
mammoth, Siberian: in hall at Monticello, 397n; Institut de France analyzes bones of, 100–1, 103–4, 187; lost in transit, 509, 510
Mandan Indians, 520–1
Mann, William, 660
*A Manual of Parliamentary Practice* (Thomas Jefferson), 486–7
manufacturing, domestic: books on, 37; cloth, 100n, 561, 573–4, 591, 667; ironworks, 210n; mills, 92n; Petersburg, Va. paper mill, 489; shot towers, 319–20n, 367n; silk manufacturing in Va., 341, 342n, 412–3, 413, 414, 425, 472; society for, 170–2; spinning jenny, 313, 524–5, 591, 661; TJ on, 94, 99, 315–6, 591
maps: of Albemarle Co., xliii; in hall at Monticello, 397n; Louisiana, 247, 248n; Mediterranean, 247–8; of TJ's Virginia, xliv–xlv; Upper Mississippi, 247; of the U.S., 37, 480n; of Va., 251n
marble: Pennsylvanian, 473
Marcet, Jane Haldimand: *Conversations on Chemistry: in which the elements of that science are familiarly explained*, 36, 37, 581
March, John, 37n
Marinot, Michael, 59, 60n, 71
Markham, Mary, 67, 68n
marriage: in France, 121, 122n
Marshall, John: *The Life of George Washington*, 589, 590n, 619, 634n; witnesses experiment, 195n
Martin, Benjamin: *The Philosophical Grammar: being a view of the Present State of Experimental Physiology, or Natural Philosophy*, 581
Martin, Francis Xavier, 25
Martin, James, 670–1
Martin, William, 671
marvel-of-Peru (four-o'clock; *Mirabilis jalapa*), 57, 58n
*Mary and Her Cat* (Fenwick), 294
Maryland: elections in, 515–6, 517n; Hagerstown, 26–9; legislature of, 361–2n; newspapers in, 28, 99n, 107, 303–4; sheep husbandry in, 478. *See also* Allegany County, Md.; Queen Annes County, Md.; Washington County, Md.
*Maryland Herald, and Hager's-Town Weekly Advertiser* (newspaper): prints TJ's correspondence, 28n, 99n
*Maryland Republican* (Annapolis newspaper), 303–4
Mason, George, 381–2
Mason, John, *Essays on poetical and prosaic numbers, and elocution*, 576
Mason, John (Georgetown): and address to TJ, 21–3, 107; commissioner of Cumberland Road, 173; Georgetown ferry of, 52n; identified, 23n
Massachusetts: legislature of, protests Embargo, 86n; Medical Society, 35, 51n; proposed publication on gardening in, 671–3; U.S. Marine Hospital, 295–300. *See also* Essex County, Mass.; newspapers
Masséna, André, Duc de Rivoli and Prince d'Essling, 371, 372
mastodon (mastodonte): bones analyzed by Institut de France, 100–1, 103–4, 187, 248–9; dinner held in skeleton, 104; excavated by Peale, 101n, 103–4; jawbone of, 380 (*illus.*); at Philadelphia Museum, 46n, 187
*Mathematical Tables* (Hutton), 576
mathematics: books on, 37; study of, 520, 535, 557, 576, 633
Mathurin, Antoine René Charles, comte de La Forest, 537
Maturin, Charles Robert: *The Wild Irish Boy*, 391, 397n
Maury, James, Sr., 82
Maury, James: identified, 82n; letter from, 82–3
Maury, Matthew, 82, 83n
Maury, Thomas W., 47n
Maximus of Tyre: *Dissertations de*

Maximus of Tyre (*cont.*)
*Maxime de Tyr, philosophe platonicien*, 35
Mayer, Christian: identified, 50n. *See also* Mayer & Brantz
Mayer & Brantz: identified, 50n; letter from accounted for, 50n; letter to, 50
Mazzei, Philip: seeks payment for sculptors, 78, 113, 114n; TJ's letter forwarded to, 207
Meade, Richard Worsam: U.S. naval agent at Cádiz, 155, 156n
*Means of Preserving Health, and Preventing Diseases* (Ricketson), 257, 294–5
Mease, James: edits *Domestic encyclopædia* (Willich), 18, 19n, 252; Humboldt sends greetings to, 453n; and merino wool, 16, 18, 19n
Mechanics Hall (New York City), 171
medicine: books on, 237, 257; plants used as, 56–7, 84; snakebite cures, 57–8n; works on, bound for TJ, 36. *See also* health
Meigs, Return Jonathan, 6
Meigs, Timothy, 26
Melvin, James, 41n, 42n
*Mémoires Agricoles de 1806*, 35
*Mémoires de la Société d'agriculture du département de la Seine*, 258, 259n, 611–2, 629, 630n; bound by Milligan, 35, 37
Memoir on American Forest Management (Lormerie), 131–4, 342, 354
*Memoir on a subterranean graphometer* (Komarzewski), 535, 536n
*A Memoir on the Cultivation of the Vine in America, and the Best Mode of Making Wine* (Adlum), 587n
*Memoirs* (Ludlow), 37, 580
*Memoirs of the Hon. Thomas Jefferson* (Carpenter), 456, 457n
*Memoirs of the Philadelphia Society for Promoting Agriculture*, 477, 479–80n
*Memoirs written by himself* (Cumberland), 35
Mengotti, Francesco: *Del Commercio de' Romani Dalla prima Guerra Punica*, 36
*Mentor* (ship): carries dispatches, 7, 169–70, 229, 314, 373, 374, 375; carries packets to TJ, 452, 522; to carry books for TJ, 50n; departs France, 536; shepherd dogs carried on, 457
*Mercantile Advertiser* (New York City newspaper), 96n
merino sheep: Bauduy breeds, 667–8; Custis breeds, 667–8; Dougherty breeds, 199, 225, 286, 310, 320–1, 467; in France, 375–6, 479, 537–8, 584–5n; Koontz requests, 573; Lafayette to send to TJ, 529, 537–8, 629; Mason breeds, 23n; in Pennsylvania, 69n; and R. Brent, 481; Thornton breeds, 477–8; wool of, 16, 17, 19n, 667
Meriwether, David, 350
Meriwether, Thomas, 483–4
Meriwether, William Douglas: chairs Albemarle Co. meeting, 46–7, 74; identified, 74n; letters from, 74, 483–4; letter to, 79
*A Message of the President of the United States to Congress Relative to France and Great-Britain* (George Washington), 487, 569–70
*Messages to Congress* (Thomas Jefferson), 569
meteorological observations: Chapman seeks, 663; by Madison, 518, 519n; by Treat, 97, 98n, 482, 608–9
*The Method of Fluxions* (Saunderson), 576
Mexico: astronomy of ancient, 521, 566; histories of, 521; Humboldt's work on, 24, 25n, 264, 267n; and potato, 196; TJ on, 20, 169; and U.S., 183–4n
Miami Indians, 652
Michaux, André: accounts of travel through U.S., 57n, 258; *Flora Boreali-Americana*, 436–7n
Michaux, François André: foreign member of American Philosophical Society, 452, 453n; ships goods to France, 128, 131n, 342
Michie, David, 415–6n
Michigan Territory: Indian training school in, 7, 660–2
*The Microscope made easy* (Baker), 581
Middleton, Conyers: *History of the Life of Marcus Tullius Cicero*, 35, 580; *Miscellaneous Works*, 580
military: Kosciuszko advocates school, 206, 207n; TJ receives books on, 36
milkpans, 303
Milledge, John: absence of, 286; and benne seed, 211–2, 596n; and cottonseed, 259n, 596; identified, 596–7n; letter from, 666–7; letter to, 596–7; and merino sheep, 225; sends wool samples to TJ, 667

Milledge, Martha Galphin (John Milledge's wife), 596, 667
Miller, William: identified, 644n; letter to, 644
Milligan, Joseph: account with TJ, 35–8; binds books for TJ, 35–8, 225, 286; identified, 37–8n; letter from, 384; letter to, 332–3; paid by TJ, 41; sends books to TJ, 332–3, 384
Millot, Claude François Xavier: *Élemens de l'Histoire de France, depuis Clovis jusqu'à Louis XV*, 580; *Elements of General History*, 580
mills: grist, 626; iron castings for, 158n; manufacturing, 92n; mechanics of, 646–9; paper, 489; at Pen Park, 136n; on Rivanna River, 74n, 108–10, 560, 579; wind, 647–8
Milton, John: *Paradise Lost*, 228–9n
Milton, Va.: manufacturing mill at, 92n; postmaster at, 505–6; post office at, 107, 139n, 310, 480, 514; T. E. Randolph's lands at, 488n. *See also* Henderson case
mimosa tree (*Albizia Julibrissin*; silk tree), 631
Miner, Charles, 428; identified, 431n; "Poem on Thomas Jefferson," 429–31
mineralogy: and the American Philosophical Society, 452; lectures on, 104, 187, 189, 193
Minor, Dabney, 47n
Minor, John, 200; identified, 204n; letters from, 204, 519; letters to, 338–9, 585
Minor, Peter, 47
Minot, George Richards: *The History of the Insurrections*, 581
Mint, U.S.: analyzes gold nugget, 330; TJ and, 487
*Mirabilis jalapa* (four-o'clock; marvel-of-Peru), 57, 58n
Miranda, Francisco de, 577–8, 604
mirrors, 303
*Miscellaneous and philosophical pieces* (Franklin), 581
*Miscellaneous Works* (Middleton), 580
Mississippi River, 448, 449
Mississippi Territory: appointments in, 25; land claims in, 638, 639
Missouri River, 473, 475n
Missouri scaly bark (*Juglans squamosa*; scaly bark hickory), 657
Mitchell, Thomas Rothmaler: visits Monticello, 555, 654, 655
Mitchill, Samuel Latham, 597
*Mithridates: Oder Allgemeine Sprachenkunde* (Adelung), 265, 267n, 652n
mockingbirds: TJ brings from Washington, 162
*Modern Geography* (Pinkerton), 576n, 581; recommended by Kimber & Conrad, 256
modesty shrub, 631–2
molasses, 77, 81, 114
moldboards: Pennsylvania, 111, 252. *See also* ploughs
Molitor, Gabriel Jean Joseph, comte, 372
"The Moment" (McCoy), 504n
*Monitor* (Washington, D.C. newspaper), 107
Monroe, James: correspondence with Giles, 93n; and diplomatic outfit, 118; identified, 349n; letters from, 348–9, 498–9; letter to, 500; and Monroe-Pinkney Treaty, 170n; and Pinckney, 514; and Richmond junto, 92–3; sends book to TJ, 348; and Walker's health, 498–9
Monroe, John, 626–7; identified, 406n; letter from, 404–6
Monroe, Thomas. *See* Munroe, Thomas
Monroe-Pinkney Treaty (*1806*), 169, 170n, 414n
Monteagle (Peyton's Albemarle Co. estate), 415n
Montebello, Duc de. *See* Lannes, Jean, Duc de Montebello
Monterey, Ca., 446, 447
Montesquieu, Charles Louis de Secondat, 262–3n, 270
Montgomery, John, 516
Montgomery County, Pa., 69n

MONTICELLO (TJ's estate): blacksmiths at, 419n, 464n; builders at, 136n, 192n, 215n; circuit roads, 388, 391, 398n; corn crop, 592; cuisine at, 162, 389; daily schedule of, 389; described, 386–7, 389–90, 398n, 399–400n; distance from Montpellier, 562–3; east front, 380 (*illus.*); education at, 181, 245, 389, 416; figs grown at, 395, 398n; freight charges to, 3; garden locks, 302; gardens, TJ's plans for, 400–1n, 410; gardens described, 388, 398n, 436–7n; hall described, 397n; landscape view of, 346, 366, 434, 596; longitude of, 54n; padlocks for buildings at, 302–3; plants grown at, 57n, 632n; portraits at, 46n, 593; slave

MONTICELLO (TJ's estate) (*cont.*) dwellings at, 388; slaves at, during meals, 399n; stables at, 317; stew stove at, 76–7, 122; TJ describes architecture of, 595–6; view from, 388, 389, 390–1, 399n. *See also* naileries

*Overseers at*

Bacon, Edmund, 52n, 81n; Freeman, John Holmes, 48n; Richardson, Richard, 558n

*Visitors to*

Bradbury, John, 164n, 435–6; Brown, Harriot, 210, 509; Brunt, Jonathan, 402; Coles, Isaac A., 536, 632, 655, 657; Daschkoff, André, 120, 433, 484, 519; Fontaine, William, 525–8, 645–6; Gallatin, Hannah and Albert, 441, 464, 466, 599n, 664; Julien, Honoré, 59, 76; Latrobe, Benjamin Henry, 366, 474, 595–6; Madison, Dolley and James, 344, 360, 441, 466; McLean, James S., 209n; Mitchell, Thomas R., 555, 654, 655; Smith, Margaret Bayard and Samuel H., 386–401, 410, 434–5; Trist, Elizabeth, 210, 396n, 509; Woodward, Augustus E. B., 165n

Montpellier (Montpelier; Madison's Orange Co. estate): distance from Monticello, 562–3; weather journals at, 518, 519n; work at, 136n, 155
moon: calculation of position of, 489–98, 540–54, 571–2
Moore, Bernard, 200, 204, 338, 585
Moore, Edward, 440, 561, 562n
Moore, Sir John, 108
Moore, Mildred Lewis, 562n
Moore, Thomas: identified, 173n; letter from accounted for, 173n; letter to, 172–3
Moors, Spanish, 478
More, Thomas, 254n
Moreau, Jean Victor, 653
Morgan, Rufus: identified, 210n; letter from, 209–10
Morneveck, Charles, 195–6; patent of, 196n
Mosheim, Johann Lorenz: *An ecclesiastical history, ancient and modern, from the birth of Christ to the beginning of the eighteenth century*, 581
mosquitoes, 478
Mount Crillon, 448
Mount St. Elie, 446–7
Mourelle de la Rúa, Francisco Antonio: *Journal of a Voyage in 1775*, 446, 449n
Moussier, J. B., 597–8, 665; letter from, 522–4; letterhead of, 380 (*illus.*)
Moussier, Jean Baptiste, 523n
Mouton, Georges, comte de Lobau, 372
mulberry: American, 40; English, 40
Mun, Alexandre François, comte de, 627
Munford, William, 25; identified, 611n; letter from, 609–11; *Reports of Cases Argued and Determined in the Supreme Court of Appeals of Virginia* (Hening & Munford), 334, 370, 404
Munroe (Monroe), Thomas, 349, 657, 658n
murder: of slave, 168n
muscatel raisins, 366
muscovado sugar, 31, 44
museum: Philadelphia Museum, 45, 46n, 104n, 187; plans for an American, 522
mustard: prepared, 45
mutton, 16, 477, 481
Mutual Assurance Society: economic health of, 240–4, 244–5n; premium collection, 241–2; and TJ's insurance, 218–9, 240, 317–8, 320, 333, 417, 472, 625–6, 659–60
Muzzy, John: letter from accounted for, 677

naileries, 64; at Monticello, 39n, 282, 422, 423n, 503; Morgan proposes establishing, 209; nailrod and iron stock, 246, 282, 319, 422, 423n, 435, 503
nails: traded with Leitch for goods, 64, 303, 458
Napoleon I, emperor of France, 528, 529; and Austria, 140–1, 328, 370–1; Battle of Aspern-Essling, 371–2, 377n, 436; Continental System, 331–2, 373, 442, 517n; diplomatic appointments, 537; family of, 250n; at Fontainebleau, 627, 629; intentions unclear, 160, 169, 224, 251n; and publication on ancient vases, 452n, 453n; and Spain, 160, 344; TJ on, 20, 154–5, 169, 442; in Tucker's poem, 617, 619n; and U.S., 154–5
*National Aegis* (Worcester, Mass. newspaper), 50n

*National Gazette* (Philadelphia newspaper), 113n
National Institute of France. *See* Institut de France
*National Intelligencer* (Washington, D.C. newspaper): on Conn. libel prosecutions, 349–50; as party newspaper, 30n, 65; prints TJ's correspondence, 12n, 14n, 23n, 34n, 569n
"A Native Virginian": accuses TJ of misuse of public funds, 43n
*The Natural and Civil History of Vermont* (Williams), 581
Natural Bridge, Va.: drawing of, by Baron de Turpin, 197, 198–9n; sale of TJ's lands at, 318, 319–20, 367, 368n, 506–7; saltpeter cave near, 367, 506; and shot manufactory, 319–20n, 367n
natural history: TJ receives books on, 36
natural philosophy: books on, 37, 38n, 508, 580
*Nature Displayed, in her Mode of Teaching Language to Man* (Dufief), 581
*Nautical Almanac and Astronomical Ephemeris* (Garnett), 35, 225, 286, 492, 498n
Navy Department, U.S.: chief clerk of, 445n, 601; congressional committee investigates, 361, 362n; gunboats, 203, 510; Marine Barracks, 601, 649; and Porter's voyage of discovery, 443, 445n. *See also* Hamilton, Paul
Ned (Couch's slave): and lost trunk, 186, 204, 257, 268; trial of, 311, 346–8, 483
Neelly, James, 602, 603; identified, 607n; letter from, 606–8
Neilson (Nelson), John: and lost box, 77, 84; and work at Montpellier, 136n, 155
Nelson, Mr. *See* Neilson (Nelson), John
Nelson, Hugh: identified, 500n; letter from, 500
Nelson, Judith, 670
Nelson, Thomas, 25
Nelson, William: identified, 291n; letter from, 290–1; letter to, 334–5
Nepos, Cornelius: *Vitae Excellentium Imperatorum*, 580
The Netherlands: battle at Flushing, 529, 530n, 593n; Bonaparte, Louis (king), 194; and British trade, 464; Royal Netherlands Academy of Arts and Sciences, 194–5
*A new and candid investigation of the question, is revelation true?* (Fishback), 254–5, 563–4, 565–6
*A New and Complete System of Arithmetic* (Pike), 576
*A New and Impartial History of England* (Baxter), 580
*The New and Universal Gazetteer: or, Modern Geographical Dictionary* (Scott), 581
Newburyport, N.H.: collector at, 25
*The New Cyclopædia* (Rees), 252, 456, 457n
New England: and criticism of TJ's administration, 138n; Federalist party in, 301, 583–4
*The New-England farmer, or, Georgical dictionary* (Deane), 581
*New Jersey* (ship), 36
New Orleans: commissioner, 179n; and French refugees, 203; goods shipped to, for TJ, 80, 81n, 211, 510; gunboats at, 203, 510. *See also* Batture Sainte Marie; Brown, William
newspapers: Annapolis *Maryland Republican*, 303–4; Boston *Democrat*, 50n; Boston *Independent Chronicle*, 50n, 671, 673n; *Boston Patriot*, 533n, 569n; bound for TJ, 37; British, 82; collection of Va., owned by TJ, 289n, 369, 370n, 381, 457, 469, 472–3; comments on, by TJ, 49; in Frederick, Md., 107; New York *Mercantile Advertiser*, 96n; New York *Public Advertiser*, 226–9; Philadelphia *Aurora*, 48, 49n; Philadelphia *National Gazette*, 113n; Philadelphia *Universal Gazette*, 30n; *Raleigh Star*, 125, 677; Richmond *Spirit of 'Seventy-Six*, 93; Richmond *Virginia Argus*, 290, 291n; *Salem Register* (Mass.), 50n; subscriptions to, of TJ, 48, 49, 50n, 85, 96, 107, 214; Trenton *True American*, 226–9; Virginia, 288–9, 369; Washington *Monitor*, 107; in Williamsburg, 370n; Worcester *National Aegis* (Mass.), 50n. *See also* Enquirer (Richmond newspaper); National Intelligencer (Washington, D.C. newspaper)
Newton, Sir Isaac, 357
Newton, John: and committee of Republican mechanics, 90n
Newton, Thomas, 596
*New Translation of the Morals of Seneca* (trans. Bennet), 576
*New Views of the Origin of the Tribes and Nations of America* (Barton), 520–1

New York (city): influenza in, 257, 294–5; Mechanics Hall, 171; *Mercantile Advertiser*, 96n; *Public Advertiser*, 226–9; Republicans in, address TJ, 530–4; Spanish consul at, 578, 604; TJ addresses Republicans in, 568–9
New York (state): elections in, 183; legislature of, addresses TJ, 79–80; TJ addresses legislature of, 125; U.S. Military Academy (West Point), 23n
Nicholas, Jane Hollins, 190n, 223n
Nicholas, John, 318, 462–3n
Nicholas, Philip Norborne, 611n
Nicholas, Wilson Cary: identified, 223n; letters from, 223, 349–50; letters to, 224, 276–9
Nicholson, William: *An Introduction to Natural Philosophy*, 581
*Nicotiania latifolia. See* tobacco
nicotine, 149–50
Niles, Hezekiah, 176–9
Nimmo, Matthew, 643
*Nivellement barométrique* (Humboldt), 452, 453n, 455, 482
Non-Intercourse Act, 21n, 154, 314; effect on commerce, 421; Gilpin's comments on, 418; Madison on, 409, 437–8, 518; N.Y. Republicans support, 532; and parlementaires, 128, 522; reimposed on Great Britain, 421, 439n; support for, 532; suspended, 170n; TJ on, 442
Nootka, 446
Norfolk, Bank of, 626
Northcut, Daniel: and lost trunk, 311, 347
Northwest Coast: exploration of, 443–9; fur trade, 445–6, 447; Indians of, described, 446
Norvell, John: identified, 15n; letter from, 14–5
*Notes on the State of Virginia* (Thomas Jefferson): description of Harper's Ferry, 197; Grégoire on, 588–9; Humboldt requests copy of, 265; Paris edition, 587–8, 600; revised edition proposed, 385, 486, 567–8, 587–8, 600–1, 654; Stockdale edition, 588; TJ on posthumous revised edition, 587
Nourse, Joseph, 23n, 585
*Les Nuits de Ste Marie-Magdelaine pénitente* (Gazzera), 522, 523n
nutmeg, 44, 368
nuts: chestnut, 593, 594n; filbert, 631; hickory, 111, 252, 657; pecan, 80, 81n, 211n, 631, 657

Oakley, Charles: secretary of British legation to U.S., 154, 156n, 418, 516
oats, 3
O'Brien, Richard, 479, 480n
*Observations on the influence of soil and climate upon wool* (Bakewell and Somerville), 479, 480n
*Observations sur "L'art de faire le vin"* (Charpentier de Cossigny), 35
"Ode to Thomas Jefferson" (Tucker), 617–9
*Oeuvres* (Turgot), 202n, 263, 264n, 584–5, 592, 632, 667, 668n
*Oeuvres Complettes de Frederic II, Roi de Prusse* (Frederick II), 580
*De Officiis* (Cicero), 576
Ogden, Samuel G., 578n
Ohio: senator from, 643n; state legislature, 380
oil: olive, 84n, 188, 257, 366; salad, 31, 161; sesame, 84n, 212; spermaceti, 31
Oliver, Julius, 312, 313n
olives, 313n; oil, 84n, 188, 257, 366
*Olmstead v. the Executrices of the late David Rittenhouse*, 213–4
Onís y González, Frederica de Merkleiny (Luis de, Vara, López y Gómez, Onís y González's wife), 410
Onís y González, Luis de, Vara, López y Gómez: identified, 602n; letter from, 601–2; letter to, 651; minister plenipotentiary of Spain, 410–1, 604, 632, 658
Opelousas District, Orleans Territory, 635–42
*Opera Omnia Quae Extant* (Suetonius), 580
*Opera Omni Graece et Latine* (trans. Spelman), 580
orange (*Citrus aurantium*), 631–2
Orange Court House (Orange Co.), 52n, 328, 359
*Oration delivered at Washington, July Fourth, 1809* (Barlow), 588, 590n
Orchidaceae, 436–7n
Orders in Council. *See* Great Britain, Orders in Council
Orleans Territory: clerk in, 635, 642n; French refugees in, 203; Lafayette's land in, 270n, 529, 628; land claims

in, 635–42. *See also* Claiborne, William Charles Coles
Osage Indians, 520
ostriches, 479
Otis, Samuel Allyne, 535
Oudinot, Nicolas Charles, Duc de Reggio, 371, 372
overseers: at Lego, 137–8n; at Monticello, 48n, 52n, 81n, 558n; at Poplar Forest, 157n, 180, 181n; at Shadwell, 137–8n; at Tufton, 419–20
Owen, W.: *Dictionary of Arts & Sciences*, 581

Pace, Edward, 462
*Pacific* (ship), 271, 284
Pacific Ocean, 443, 449
padlocks, 302–3
Page, Elizabeth Burwell, 557, 634, 669, 670n
Page, Francis: recommended for collector of Yorktown, 77, 78n, 87
Page, John, 25, 78n; and TJ's newspapers, 469
Pagowski, Jérome, 53n
Pahlen, Théodore, Count: Russian minister to U.S., 233, 329n, 537, 659n
Paine, Thomas: TJ quotes, 512
paint, 55n, 97
paintings, 522, 523–4n
paleontology: and Institut de France, xlviii, 100–1, 103–4, 187, 248–9, 250n, 511; mastodon jawbone, 380 (*illus.*)
Palm, John, 58n, 59
Palmer, Aaron H., 518
pans, milk, 303
paper. *See* stationery; trunk, lost in return from Washington, contents of
paper mills: at Petersburg, Va., 489
*Paradise Lost* (Milton), 228–9n
Paris: U.S. consul at, 26, 207, 208n, 317, 536
Parker, Mr.: considered for appointment by TJ, 26
Parker, Daniel: and design for plough, 233–4, 235n, 375, 538; and financial scheme for Lafayette, 376; merino sheep of, 479, 538, 667; sends dynamometer to TJ, 376
Parks, William, 370n
parlementaires, 128, 131n, 522
Parr, Samuel: *A free translation of the Preface to Bellendenus, containing animated strictures on the great political characters of the present time*, 35
Parrott, Richard, 23n
parsnips, 157
partridge, red-legged, 479, 599
Passamaquoddy Bay, Me.: gold found at, 330
Pasteur, William, 67, 68n
patents: of Morneveck, 196n; of Spafford, 106n
patronage: circular to office seekers, 30–1; letters of application and recommendation from TJ, 77–8, 626–7; letters of application and recommendation to TJ, 14–5, 91–2, 167–8, 405–7, 464–5; literary, 321–2
Patterson, Mr.: acquaintance of Nicholas, 276
Patterson, Robert: director of the Mint, 330; friendship with TJ, 201; Humboldt sends greetings to, 435n; identified, 193–4n; letters from, 193–4, 330–1; letters to, 482, 571–2; letter to accounted for, 201n; member of American Philosophical Society, 152n, 482, 571–2
Patterson, Robert Maskell, 193, 194n; letter of introduction from TJ, 201–2, 331
*Paulinia aurea* (*Koelreuteria paniculata*; goldenrain tree), 272, 274n, 594n
Pauw, Cornelius de: *Recherches philosophiques sur les américains*, 521
Pawnee Indians, 521, 556
Payerne, Francis, 222
peaches: black, 483
Peale, Charles Willson: and expenses for T. J. Randolph, 41, 45, 70–1, 307–10, 455, 458, 467; Humboldt sends greetings to, 435n; identified, 45–6n; letters from, 70–1, 103–4, 307–10; letters to, 45–6, 187, 458; lodges T. J. Randolph while in Philadelphia, 101n, 104; and mastodon, 101n, 103–4, 187; and meeting with Humboldt, 25n; portrait of T. J. Randolph, 45, 46n, 380 (*illus.*)
Peale, Hannah Moore (Charles Willson Peale's wife), 71; T. J. Randolph on, 458
Peale, Rembrandt: and portraits of Europeans, 71, 104, 187, 309
Pease, Seth, 181, 215; identified, 216n; letter to, 216
pecans: TJ orders via New Orleans, 80, 81n, 211n; TJ to plant, 631, 657

Pechin, William, 41n
*Peintures des Vases Antiques* (ed. Maisonneuve), 452, 453n, 482
*Pekin* (ship), 331
Pelham, William: identified, 217n; letter from, 216–7; *A System of Notation; Representing the Sounds of Alphabetical Characters*, 216–7
pen, metallic, 106
penal institutions, 383, 384n, 474n
Pendleton, Edmund, 339, 381–2; identified, 200n; letter from, 200
Pendleton, Edmund (*1721–1803*), 200n
penmanship: books on, 37
Pennsylvania: legislature of, purchases sheep, 18; legislature of, resolutions for, 90–1; moldboard of, 111, 252; *Olmstead v. the Executrices of the late David Rittenhouse*, 213–4; Pittsburgh Republicans address TJ, 90, 91n; Provincials in French and Indian War, 290; Republicans in, TJ comments on, 236–7; sheep in, 18, 69n; statute taxing dogs, 17, 68–9; Washington County Republicans, 4–6, 99–100. *See also* Bank of Pennsylvania
Pennsylvanian marble, 473
pepper, black, 31, 45, 368
Peray. *See* Piré, Hippolyte Marie Guillaume de Rosnyvinen, comte de
Perceval, Spencer, 285n, 658, 659n
Percivall, Joseph, 66
Pernier (Purney), John: Meriwether Lewis's servant, 602, 603, 606, 607, 608n
perry: *Treatise on the Culture of the Apple & Pear, and on the Manufacture of Cider & Perry* (Knight), 581
Perry, John M.: identified, 192–3n; letters from accounted for, 193n; letter to, 192–3
Persoon, Christiaan Hendrik, 436–7n
Peter (Couch's slave): and lost trunk, 346, 347, 348
Peters, Richard, 133, 134n, 477
Petersburg, Va.: paper produced in, 489
Peyton, Craven: conveys Henderson lands to TJ, 415n, 439–41, 453–4, 454, 459–63; declaration concerning Henderson lands by TJ, 463; grinds wheat, 109; and Henderson case, 415–6, 453–4; identified, 415n; letters from, 415–6, 454; letters to, 439–41, 453–4, 470
Peyton, H., 462
Peyton, Jane Jefferson Lewis (Craven Peyton's wife), 415n; conveys Henderson lands to TJ, 441, 459–63; identified, 463n
Peyton, John: Milton postmaster, 506n
*Pharmacopoeia of the Massachusetts Medical Society*, 35
Philadelphia: *Aurora*, 48, 49n; banks in, 458; Birch & Small (publishers), 18, 19n, 172n; Linnean Society of, 663; Museum, 45, 46n, 104n, 187; *National Gazette*, 113n; society for domestic manufacturing, 170–2; Society for Promoting Agriculture, 133, 477, 479–80n; tax on dogs in, 69n; *Universal Gazette*, 30n; Walnut Street prison, 383, 384n; yellow fever epidemic (*1793*), 185n. *See also* Randolph, Thomas Jefferson
*Philadelphia* (ship), 33n
Philadelphia Society for Promoting Agriculture, 133; *Memoirs*, 477, 479–80n
*The Philosophical Grammar; being a view of the Present State of Experimental Physiology, or Natural Philosophy* (Martin), 581
philosophy: study of, 502. *See also* natural philosophy
Physick, Philip Syng, 307
physics: pamphlets on, 36, 38n
Pickering, Timothy: opposes H. A. S. Dearborn's nomination, 78, 280, 301–2
Pictet, Marc Auguste, 452
Pierce, John, 227, 228n
Piers Plowman. *See* The Vision of Pierce Plowman
Pike, Nicholas: *A New and Complete System of Arithmetic*, 576
*Pilgrim* (ship), 294
Pinckney, Charles: identified, 476n; letter from, 513–4; letter to, 475–6; and Madison, 513–4
Pinckney, Frances Henrietta, 514
Pinckney, Mary Eleanor, 512
Pinckney, Thomas, 39n
Pindar, Peter [John Wolcott]: "A Similie," 538n
pine planking, 192
Pinkerton, John: *A General Collection of the Best and Most Interesting Voyages*, 256n; *Modern Geography*, 256, 576n, 581
Pinkney, William: forwards letter to TJ, 124; identified, 414n; letter to, 414; and Monroe, 514; and Monroe-

Pinkney Treaty, 169, 170n, 414n, 514; and Orders in Council, 271; TJ recommends McRae and Clarke to, 414; U.S. minister to Great Britain, 113, 118, 374, 409, 413, 423, 436–7n, 464, 518
Piré, Hippolyte Marie Guillaume de Rosnyvinen, comte de, 372
Pitt, William (the younger): TJ on, 507
Pittsburgh, Pa.: Republicans of, address TJ, 90, 91n
planes, 135–6
plantain. *See* water plantain
plant geography: *Essai sur la géographie des plantes* (Humboldt), 265, 267n; forests, 131–4, 354. *See also* botany
plants: medicinal properties of, 56–7, 84; nursery, TJ purchases from, 51. *See also specific plant names*
play: sent to TJ, 202, 203n, 509
Playfair, William, 265, 267n
ploughs: Guillaume, 20, 21n; moldboard designed by TJ, 252; Parker's double, 538; Pennsylvania moldboard, 111, 252
Plowden, Francis: *An Historical Review of the State of Ireland*, 580
Plutarch: *Lives* (trans. J. & W. Langhorne), 580
"Poem on Thomas Jefferson" (Miner), 429–31
"Poem on Thomas Jefferson" (Welles), 431–3
"Poem on Thomas Jefferson's Retirement" (Freneau), 226–9
*Poems Written and Published during the American Revolutionary War* (Freneau), 112, 113n
poetry: sent to TJ, 226–9, 322–7, 429–33, 617–9; subscriptions to, sent to TJ, 225–6, 504n; TJ comments on, 504, 509; works on, bound for TJ, 36
Poindexter, George, 25
Poland: history of, 35, 535
politics: works on, bound for TJ, 36
Polybius: *The General History of Polybius* (trans. Hampton), 580
polygraph, 46n, 307
poplar: Lombardy, 192n
Poplar Forest (TJ's Bedford Co. estate): annual income of, 213; builders at, 192n; furniture for, 44, 287, 319; overseers at, 157n, 180, 181n; TJ travels to, 519; tobacco grown at, 157n
Porée, Jean Baptiste, 674
pork: received as pay, 419, 421n; supply of, 451
Porter, David: identified, 444n; letter from, 443–5; Plan for a Voyage of Discovery to the Northwest Coast of America, 445–9
Porter, John: claim for compensation, 583–4, 625, 644; identified, 644–5n; letter from accounted for, 584n; letter to, 644–5
postmaster general, U.S. *See* Granger, Gideon, postmaster general
Post Office, U.S.: contracts with, 139–40, 350–2; funds of, 407, 421; *List of Post Offices in the United States, including all established before December 31st, 1807*, 514; and post road, 350–2; TJ requests local schedule, 506, 514
potatoes, 157, 196–7
Pouncey's tract (TJ's property), 488n
Poydras, Julien Lalande, 179, 180n
*Prenanthes serpentaria* (lion's foot): as snakebite remedy, 58n
*President* (ship), 509
President's House: description of, 199–200; inventory of, 42, 43n, 76, 155, 156n; Madisons alter, 53; sitting room clock at, 85, 96; stew stoves at, 76; during TJ's presidency, 29n, 55–6
Price, Joseph, 234, 235n
Priddy, John, 246n
Priestley, Joseph: *History of the Corruptions of Christianity*, 581; *Letters to the Inhabitants of Northumberland and its neighbourhood*, 119, 121–2n; mentioned, 674; on university courses, 592, 593n; *A view of the principles and conduct of the Protestant dissenters, with respect to the civil and ecclesiastical constitution of England*, 581
prime meridian, 54–5n, 275–6, 356–9, 489–98, 511–2, 534
*The Principles of Health: Elements of hygiene* (Williamson), 597n
print: and antimony, 18, 283, 315–6
Proclamation of *1763*, 335
*Prospectus of a new monthly publication: the Massachusetts Garden*, 671–3
Proud, Robert: *The History of Pennsylvania in North America*, 581
Provenchere, Peter, 612, 613n
*Public Advertiser* (N.Y. newspaper): publishes Freneau poem, 226–9
punch, syrup of, 268, 368
Purdie, Alexander, 381

Purney, John. *See* Pernier (Purney), John
Purviance, Samuel, 140, 362n, 515
Purvis, John: *A Complete Collection of all the Lavvs of Virginia now in force*, 404

Quarles, Robert: identified, 560n; letter from, 560; letter to, 579
Queen Annes County, Md.: Republicans of, address TJ, 62–3; TJ addresses Republicans of, 127–8
*Quercus ilex* (holm oak), 594

rabbet (rabbitt) plane, 135, 136n
rabbits and hares, 479, 654
raisins, 368; muscatel, 366
Raleigh, Sir Walter, 197
*Raleigh Star* (newspaper): letter from editors of, accounted for, 677; prints TJ's correspondence, 125n
Ramsay, David, 513; *History of the American Revolution*, 581; *The Life of George Washington*, 35
Randolph, Benjamin Franklin (TJ's grandson): illness of, 519, 520n, 536
Randolph, David Meade, 277, 278–9n
Randolph, Edmund, 67, 403
Randolph, Ellen Wayles (TJ's granddaughter): described, 387; and letter writing, 245; and Margaret Bayard Smith's visit, 389, 390, 391
Randolph, Jane Cary (TJ's granddaughter-in-law), 488n
Randolph, John (of Roanoke): heads congressional committee of investigation, 350, 361, 362n, 378; resolution on common law prosecution, 276, 278n; and Richmond junto, 93
Randolph, Martha Jefferson (TJ's daughter; Thomas Mann Randolph's wife): children of, 190n, 389, 390, 399n, 519, 536, 669–70; correspondence with Botidoux, 377, 659n; at Edgehill, 654; health of, 387, 391, 392, 395, 410; informs TJ of mill operations, 110n, 139n; marriage of, 420n; reads novels, 391, 397n; regards sent to, 53, 71, 73, 301, 629, 660, 667, 668; relations with J. W. Eppes, 337, 338n; TJ's correspondence with, 80
Randolph, Mary (TJ's aunt): runs Richmond boardinghouse, 669–70
Randolph, Mary Elizabeth Cleland, 488n
Randolph, Mary Isham (TJ's great-grandmother), 68n
Randolph, Mary Jefferson (TJ's granddaughter), 390, 393, 397n; book for, 294
Randolph, Peyton, 159n, 611n
Randolph, Thomas Eston (TJ's cousin): account with TJ, 470; boats of, transfer goods, 488n; identified, 488n; letters from, 488, 654; sends rabbits to TJ, 654; and TJ's gig, 488
Randolph, Thomas Jefferson (TJ's grandson): attends botanical lectures, 70–1, 100; attends mineralogical lectures, 104, 187; botany, enthusiasm for, 191; carries books to TJ, 321; carries package to Trist, 80–1; clothing, 308; education of, arranged by TJ, 101n, 458, 520, 557, 590–1, 633, 634–5, 669–70; expenses paid by TJ, 41–2, 45, 70–1, 307–10, 455, 458, 467, 557; at family dinner, 387; forwards trunk from Washington, 64; identified, 190–1n; letter from, 245; letter from accounted for, 191n; letters to, 189–91, 293–4; pays TJ's account in Philadelphia, 97, 111, 161–2, 188, 190, 245; Peale portrait of, 45, 46n, 380 (*illus.*); surveying, 389
Randolph, Thomas Mann (*1741–93*), 420n, 572
Randolph, Thomas Mann (*1768–1828*) (TJ's son-in-law; Martha Jefferson Randolph's husband): acquaintance with Fontaine, 525, 527; agreement with McGehee, 419–21; arrangements for T. J. Randolph's schooling, 189, 634; botanical skills of, 436–7n; buys land from Bache, 616; children of, 190n; correspondence with Reibelt, 504, 505; at family dinner, 387; family of, 420n; grinds wheat, 109; identified, 420n; manufacturing mill at Milton, 92n; and merino sheep, 199, 321, 667; regards sent to, 53, 301, 660, 667; relations with J. W. Eppes, 337, 338n
Randolph, Thomas Mann (*1792–1848*): attends Harvard University, 524, 572–3, 574; identified, 524n; letter from, 524; letter to, 574
Randolph, Virginia Jefferson (TJ's granddaughter), 390, 397n

Randolph, William (TJ's great-grandfather), 68n
Randolph, William (TJ's uncle), 488n
Randolph, William Eston, 488n
Raphael (Raphall), Solomon, 318n
Rapine, Daniel, 412
Rapin Thoyras, Paul de: *Histoire d'Angleterre*, 580
*Rapport sur les Travaux de la Société d'Agriculture du Département de la Seine* (Silvestre), 612, 613n
raspberries, 222
Ratisbon, Battle of, 371
rattlesnakes: TJ receives rattle of, 660
Ravensworth (Fairfax Co.), 52n
Ray, William: *Horrors of Slavery: or, The American Tars in Tripoli*, 33, 77–8; identified, 33n; letter from, 33; requests loan from TJ, 33
*Rebecca* (sloop): transports goods to Richmond, 44
*Recherches philosophiques sur les américains* (Pauw), 521
*Recherches physiques et chimiques sur la Fabrication de la Poudre à Canon* (Charpentier de Cossigny), 35
*Recherches sur les Ossemens Fossiles* (Cuvier), 101n
recipes: for vinegar syrup, 222
*Recueil d'observations astronomiques* (Humboldt), 24, 25n, 264, 267n, 455
Reed, Isaac: and edition of Shakespeare, 412n
Rees, Abraham: *The New Cyclopædia*, 252, 456, 457n
refrigerators, 173n
Reibelt, Mr. (J. Philippe Reibelt's son), 504–5
Reibelt, J. Philippe: identified, 505n; letter from, 504–5
Reintzel, Daniel: and address to TJ, 21–3; identified, 23n
religion: laws on, 382; TJ on, 563–6; Virginia Act for establishing Religious Freedom, 384n, 487; works on, bound for TJ, 36, 38n
*Remarks on Education* (S. H. Smith), 30n
*Remarks on the Smut and Mildew of Wheat* (Fothergill), 72
rent: due from Alexander, 353; due from Henderson lands, 470; due from Shoemaker, 353, 364, 407, 408, 421–2, 422, 451–2; from Natural Bridge lands, 506
*Reply to Mr. Duponceau* (Thierry), 287
*Report of the Secretary of the Treasury, on the subject of public roads and canals* (Gallatin), 646
*Report of the Whole Trial of Gen. Michael Bright and Others* (Byrne), 214n
*Reports of Cases Argued and Determined in the Supreme Court of Appeals of Virginia* (Hening & Munford), 334, 370, 404
Republicans: of Bristol Co., R.I., 88; of Conn., 95, 126–7; of Essex Co., Mass., 85–6; of Georgetown, D.C., 21–3, 34; of Leesburg, Va., 89–90; of New York City and County, 530–4, 568–9; of Pa., TJ comments on, 236–7; of Pittsburgh, Pa., 90, 91n; of Queen Annes County, Md., 62–3, 127–8; of Washington Co., Md., 26–9, 98–9; of Washington Co., Pa., 99–100
*Rerum Scoticarum Historia* (Buchanan), 580
rheumatism root. *See* Jeffersonia diphylla (twinleaf)
Rhine, Confederation of the, 141
Rhode Island: Bristol Co. convention, 88–9
Rhodes Hotel (Washington, D.C.), 357
rice: price of in Great Britain, 82; sent from Île de France, 208, 596, 666; TJ orders, 44, 268, 368
Richard, Gabriel: identified, 662n; and Indian training school, 7, 660–2; letter from, 660–2
Richardson, Dudley: identified, 558n; letter from, 558; letter to, 645
Richardson, George, 645
Richardson, Joseph, 558n
Richardson, Richard, 558, 645; letter from accounted for, 645n
Richmond, Va.: boardinghouses in, 520, 557, 590, 634, 669–70; boats transfer goods to and from, 44n, 81, 114–5, 153, 176, 246, 257, 319, 368, 457, 488n; chancery court at, 415n; citizens of, address TJ, 609–11; Eagle Tavern, 611, 613, 614n; flour prices at, 61; Girardin's academy at, 520, 557, 633, 634–5; junto (Old Republicans), 92–3; refugees in, 622, 624n; TJ addresses citizens of, 620–1; TJ orders groceries from, 77, 267–8, 284; TJ visits, 611n, 613–4; tobacco prices at, 157, 180, 302, 655–6. *See*

Richmond, Va. (*cont.*)
*also* Enquirer (Richmond newspaper); Gibbon, James; Gibson & Jefferson
Ricketson, Shadrach: *A Brief History of the Influenza, Which prevailed in New-York in 1807*, 257, 294–5; identified, 257n; letter from, 257; letter to, 294–5; *Means of Preserving Health, and Preventing Diseases*, 257, 294–5
Riley, Isaac: identified, 568n; letters from, 567–8, 600–1; letter to, 587–8; seeks to publish *Notes on the State of Virginia*, 567–8, 587–8, 600–1
Rind, William, 369, 370n
Ringold, Tench, 23n
Rioult-Davenay, Archange Louis, baron, 372
Ritchie, Thomas, 611n; identified, 214n; letter to, 214
Rittenhouse, David, 213–4n
Rivanna Company, 74n, 158n
Rivanna River: canals on, 415n; dams, 579; described, 386; milling operations on, 74n, 108–10, 560, 579. *See also* Henderson case
Rives, Robert, 251
Rives, William Cabell: expelled from College of William and Mary, 251; identified, 416n; letter to, 416; studies law under TJ, 416, 572
Rivoli, André Masséna Duc de, and Prince d'Essling. *See* Masséna, André, Duc de Rivoli and Prince d'Essling
roanoke (Indian currency), 334, 369
Robert (Madison's servant at the President's House), 53
Robertson, William: *History of America*, 521, 581, 620n; *The History of Scotland*, 580; *The History of the Reign of Charles V*, 580
Robertson, William (clerk of council of state), 611n
Robinson, John: estate of, 200, 338, 519
*Robinson Crusoe* (Defoe): advocated for Indians, 110
Robiquet, Pierre Jean, 142, 146n
Rochester, Nathaniel, 99n; identified, 28–9n; letter from, 26–9
Rodney, Caesar Augustus: attorney general, 335; rumor of resignation, 626, 627n, 658
Rogers, John: grinds wheat, 109
*Romae Antiquae Notitia: or, The Antiquities of Rome* (Kennett), 580
Romani, commercis de. *See* Del Commercio de' Romani Dalla prima Guerra Punica (Mengotti)
Romanzoff, Nicolas de: relations with Daschkoff, 329n; Russian foreign minister, 115–6, 116, 117, 120, 230, 231, 233, 537, 659n
Rome: Woodward on government of, 254n
Ronaldson, James: on breeding sheep, 15–18, 19n; on domestic manufacture, 170–2; identified, 18–9n; letters from, 15–9, 68–9, 170–2; on taxing dogs, 68; travels to Europe for antimony, 18, 283, 314, 315–6
Roscoe, William: *Address at the Opening of the Botanic Garden of Liverpool*, 164n; and Bradbury's botanical expedition, 163, 435, 436–7n; Bradbury's letter of introduction from, 163; *Catalogue of Plants in the Botanic Garden, at Liverpool*, 164n; identified, 164n; letter from, 163–4; *Life and Pontificate of Leo the Tenth*, 163, 164n, 435; *Life of Lorenzo de' Medici, called the Magnificent*, 164n, 435
Royal Netherlands Academy of Arts and Sciences, 194–5
Rozell, Stephen C., 244
Ruelle, Claude Alexandre: *Constitution de la république Beninienne*, 219, 220n; identified, 220–1n; letter from, 219–21
Rulhière, Claude Carloman de: *Histoire de l'Anarchie de Pologne, et du Démembrement de Cette République*, 35
rum, 299
Rumford, Benjamin Thompson, count, 106n
*Rural Oeconomy: or, Essays on the Practical Parts of Husbandry* (Young), 581
Rush, Benjamin: Humboldt sends greetings to, 435n; identified, 185–6n; letter from, 184–6; letter to, 558–9
Rush, James: *An Inquiry into the Use of the Omentum*, 185, 558–9
Russell, Gilbert C., 603, 607
Russell, Jonathan, 26, 207, 208–9n
Russell, William: *History of Modern Europe*, 580
Russia: and British trade, 464; emperor of (*See* Alexander I, emperor of Russia); language, 556; and Treaty of Tilsit, 516, 517n, 529; and U.S., 38, 39n, 329n, 360; and U.S. minister to, 38, 233, 328, 329n, 360, 537, 659n. *See also* Daschkoff, André, Russian

consul general to U.S.; Pahlen, Théodore, count, Russian minister to U.S.; Romanzoff, Nicolas de, Russian foreign minister

saddles, 3
Saint Domingue: blacks in, 589; refugees from, 450, 622, 624n; trade with U.S., 160, 517n
Sainte Marie, Batture. *See* Batture Sainte Marie
Saint Hilaire, Louis Vincent Joseph Le Blond, comte de, 371, 372
Saint-Lambert, Jean François de, 121, 122n
St. Mary, Church of (Baltimore), 450–1
St. Mary's, Ga., 509, 510
St. Mary's Academy (Baltimore), 450–1
Saint Petersburg: U.S. consul at, 38, 61n, 65
Saint-Sulpice, Raymond Gaspard de Bonardi, comte de, 372
salad oil, 31, 161
sal ammoniac (ammonium chloride): for copper utensils, 467
*Salem Register* (Mass. newspaper), 50n
Sallust (Caius Sallustius Crispus): *Crispi Opera Omnia* (trans. Gordon), 580
*Sally* (ship), 84
salsify (*Tragopogon porrifolius*), 157
salt: consumed by sheep, 478; TJ orders, 77
salted fish, 115n, 176, 268, 279
saltpeter, 367, 506
*Sampson* (ship), 80, 81n, 210
Sampson, William: letter from accounted for, 78n
Sanford, Capt., 509
San Francisco, 446
Sangster's (Songster's) ordinary (Fairfax Co.), 52n
Satterwhite, Rachel: letter from accounted for, 68n
Saunders, Joseph, 66
Saunderson, Nicholas: *The Method of Fluxions*, 576
scaly bark hickory (*Juglans squamosa*; Missouri scaly bark), 657
Schnebly, Jacob, 27
schools and colleges: in Albemarle Co., 82n; Ann Smith Academy (Lexington), 367, 368n, 506, 507n; Central College (Charlottesville), 65n, 193n; Girardin's academy (Richmond), 520, 557, 633, 634–5; Jefferson College (Pa.), 4–6; military, proposed by Kosciuszko, 206, 207n; Spring Hill School (Mich. Terr.), 7, 660–2; St. Mary's Academy (Baltimore), 450–1; Stephensburg Academy (Frederick Co.), 566–7; and TJ's plans for a university in Va., 592; United States Military Academy (West Point), 23n; University of Virginia (Charlottesville), 136n, 191n, 466n, 474; Washington Academy (Lexington), 367, 368n; for women, 367, 368n, 506, 507n
Schwarzenberg, Karl Philipp (Austrian ambassador), 117, 121n
*Scientific dialogues, intended for the instruction of young people* (Joyce), 36, 332, 333, 384, 482, 483n, 581
scientific instruments: in lost trunk, 153, 347
Scott, Alexander, 23n, 516
Scott, James, 269, 284
Scott, John, 320, 321n
Scott, John Washington, 504n
Scott, Joseph: *The New and Universal Gazetteer: or, Modern Geographical Dictionary*, 581
Seabrook, Richard, 440, 454, 459, 616
*Séances des Écoles Normales, recueillies par des Sténographes et revues par les Professeurs*, 37
Sebrell, Nicholas, 616
sedition law, 278
seed press, 380 (*illus.*); described, 390, 400n; vials for, 190, 191n, 245, 308, 309n
seeds: acacia, 555; benne (sesame), 84, 105, 198, 211–2, 436–7n, 555, 667; black cotton, 258, 259–60n; cotton, 666; Egyptian grass, 555; green cottonseed, 82, 258, 259–60n; parsnip, 157; sent by Warden, 141
Selden, Miles, 25
Senate, U.S.: clerk of, 535; construction of chamber, 473, 475n, 595; messages from TJ, 643n; rejects Short's nomination, 38; Samuel Smith's reelection to, 515–6
Seneca: *A New Translation of the Morals of Seneca* (trans. Bennet), 576
Serres, Olivier de: *Le Théâtre d'Agriculture et Mesnage des Champs*, 35, 581
sesame. *See* Sesamum indicum (benne; sesame)
sesame oil, 84n, 212

*Sesamum indicum* (benne; sesame), 84, 211–2, 436–7n, 555, 667; Spafford requests from TJ, 105, 198
Seybert, Adam: Humboldt sends regards to, 435n; identified, 172n; letter from, 170–2
Shackelford, Benjamin, 52n
shad, white, 368
Shadwell (TJ's estate): overseers at, 137–8n
Shadwell Mill: builders at, 192n; leased, 488n; mismanagement of, 108–10, 139n, 139–40, 282–3; rent for, 407, 408, 421–2, 451–2; TJ's insurance for, 218–9, 417, 625–6, 659–60
Shakespeare, William: plays of, 412
Sharpless, Blakey, 256n
Shattuck, George Cheyne: identified, 51n; letter to, 50–1; *Three Dissertations on Boylston Prize Questions for the Years 1806 and 1807*, 50–1
Shearman (Sherman), Martin, 616
sheep: broad-tailed, 465–6, 477; Cape, 477, 599; Churro, 18, 19n; Dougherty acquires for TJ, 153, 464, 465–6, 467, 476–7, 486; *Essay on Sheep* (Livingston), 667, 668n; Green Mountain, 667; Iceland ram, 320, 596, 666; in Pa., 18, 69n; raising in Va., 238–9, 240n; skin of Rocky Mountain, 327–8, 510; Spanish, 16, 320. *See also* merino sheep
Sheridan, Thomas: *A Course of Lectures on Elocution*, 576
Sherman, Mr. *See* Shearman (Sherman), Martin
Shoemaker, Isaac: identified, 139n; letter to, 138–9; and mismanagement of Shadwell Mill, 108–9, 110n, 138–9, 139–40, 282; and postal route, 353
Shoemaker, Jonathan: identified, 109–10n; letters from, 139–40, 256, 407, 451–2; letters to, 108–10, 282–3, 364, 421–2; to manage Shadwell Mill, 282–3; and mismanagement of Shadwell Mill, 108–9, 139–40, 282–3; rent due from, 353, 364, 408, 421–2, 422, 451–2; seeks abatement in rent, 407, 421–2; sells mill near Washington, D.C., 256
Short, William: advocates unrestricted commerce, 119–20, 359–60; Armstrong carries letters of, 115, 120; awaits instructions, 117, 331; conveys news to and from French acquaintances, 173, 537; correspondence with TJ, 182n; and diplomatic outfit, 61, 85, 118, 232–3, 235n; identified, 39n; Indian Camp, 234, 235n; investments of, 32n; letter from accounted for, 329n; letter of credence for, 328, 343–4, 359, 658, 659n; letters from, 115–22, 229–35; letter to, 38–9; mentioned, 433; nomination of, rejected, 38, 39n, 229–30, 231, 375, 659n; recess appointment to Saint Petersburg, 65
Shorter, Jack: accompanies TJ to Monticello, 59, 60n; delivers letters, 85, 153; as hosteler, 3, 60n; paid by TJ, 41–2n
Siberian mammoth. *See* mammoth, Siberian
Siblong, Col. *See* le Blanc de Villeneufve, Paul Louis
Sicard, Roch Ambroise Cucurron: *Théorie des Signes*, 662
*Le Siècle de Louis XIV* (Voltaire), 580
silk manufacturing: in Europe, 341, 342n, 355, 412–3, 424, 425n, 472
silk tree (*Albizia Julibrissin*; mimosa tree), 631
Silvestre, Augustin François, 629, 630n; cottonseed sent by TJ, 258, 596; identified, 259n; letterhead of, 380 (*illus.*); letters from, 258–60, 611–3; *Rapport sur les Travaux de la Société d'Agriculture du Département de la Seine*, 612, 613n
"A Simile" (Pindar), 538n
Simpson, Thomas: *A treatise of algebra*, 576
Simson, Robert: *The Elements of Euclid*, 576, 650
*Siren. See* Syren (sloop)
60th Royal American Regiment, 290
Skelton, Bathurst: estate of, 304–5, 362, 363, 591, 608
Skelton, John, 305n
Skelton, Lucy, 305n
Skelton, Meriwether, 304, 305n
Skelton, Reuben: and *Gilliam v. Fleming*, 305n, 644
Skelton, Sally, 305n
Skelton family, 305n, 364
Skipwith, Anne Wayles (TJ's sister-in-law; Henry Skipwith's wife), 339n
Skipwith, Fulwar, 26
Skipwith, Henry (TJ's brother-in-law): and *Gilliam v. Fleming*, 304, 305, 306, 331, 339, 362, 363, 364–5; identified, 339n; letter from, 339; letter to, 364–5

slavery: books on, 33
slaves: clothing of, 420, 666–7; Couch's, 346–8; dwellings of, 388; health of, 354, 416; hiring of, 48n; Humboldt on, 264, 267n; of J. W. Eppes, 156n, 321; law prohibiting importation of, 624n; at Monticello during meals, 399n; requested by Dougherty, 321; and skilled trades, 388; trained in French cooking, 162, 188, 189n; Va. statute regarding, 622, 624n
Small, Abraham: identified, 172n; letter from, 170–2; publishing firm, 18, 19n
smallpox: vaccination, 300n
Smilie (Smiley), John, 361
Smith, Mr. (of Richmond): considered for appointment by TJ, 25
Smith, Ann, 367, 368n. *See also* Ann Smith Academy (Lexington)
Smith, Gilbert H. (captain of *Sampson*), 210
Smith, James Edward, 164n, 437n
Smith, John (*1750–1836*): identified, 586n; letter to, 585–6
Smith, John (chief clerk of War Department), 78, 280, 301, 660; letter from accounted for, 571
Smith, John (senator from Ohio), 643n
Smith, John Rhea, 572n
Smith, John Spear: as secretary of Russian legation, 360–1, 378, 379, 385–6, 402
Smith, Jonathan: letter to accounted for, 408n
Smith, Julia Harrison, 390, 397n, 434
Smith, Larkin: identified, 88n; letters from, 87–8, 108; letter to, 136–7
Smith, Margaret (Robert Smith's wife), 340
Smith, Margaret Bayard (Samuel H. Smith's wife): comments on Dougherty, 3n; *The Diversions of Sidney*, 10n; identified, 10n; letter to, 29; on Madison's inauguration, 8–10; Monticello visit described, 386–401; receives geranium from TJ, 29; sends greetings to TJ, 435; TJ sends greetings to, 410; visits Monticello, 386–401, 410, 434–5; *A Winter in Washington: or, Memoirs of the Seymour Family*, 10n, 397n
Smith, Robert: *Address to the People of the United States*, 340n; congratulates TJ, 345; and Gallatin, 598, 599n; identified, 340n; investigated by congressional committee, 361, 362n; letter from, 345; letter to, 340; negotiates with Erskine, 168, 170n, 409; secretary of state, 20, 38, 113, 155, 232, 335, 402, 464, 518, 616, 632, 643; secretary of the navy, 340, 649–50; and Short's diplomatic expenses, 232–3
Smith, S., & Buchanan (mercantile firm), 362n
Smith, Samuel (historian): *The History of the Colony of Nova Caesaria, or New-Jersey*, 581
Smith, Samuel (of Maryland): identified, 361n; letter from, 360–2; and letter of introduction for son, 360–1, 377–8, 379, 385–6, 402; letters to, 377–8, 402; and reelection to Senate, 515–6; senator, 232
Smith, Samuel (of Pennsylvania): identified, 335n; letter from accounted for, 335n; letter to, 335–6; and Lowry pardon, 335, 340, 345
Smith, Samuel Harrison, 10n; editor of *National Intelligencer*, 349; identified, 30n; letter from accounted for, 12n; letters from, 72, 434–5; letters to, 30, 410; prints circular for TJ, 30; *Remarks on Education*, 30n; transmits Fothergill tract, 72; visits Monticello, 386–401, 410, 434–5
Smith, Susan Harrison, 390, 397n, 434
Smith, William: on conspiracy to kill TJ, 425–8
Smith, William (historian): *The History of the Peloponnesian War, Translated from the Greek of Thucydides*, 580; letter from, 425–8
Smith, William Stephens, 578
Smithers (Smuthers; Smythers), Michael: and lost trunk, 348
snakes: rattle, 660; remedy for bite, 57–8
snuff (prepared tobacco), 147–52
Snyder, Simon, 213–4n
Société d'agriculture du département de la Seine: approves TJ's moldboard, 252; books by, 35, 258, 259n; and cottonseed from TJ, 258, 259–60n, 596; *Mémoires*, 35, 37, 258, 259n, 611–2, 629, 630n; sends plough to TJ, 21n
Society of United Irishmen, 141n, 465n
Somerville, John Southey, Lord: *Observations on the influence of soil and climate upon wool* (Bakewell), 479, 480n
Songster's ordinary. *See* Sangster's (Songster's) ordinary (Fairfax Co.)
Sonthonax, Léger Félicité, 515, 517n

*Sorghum vulgare* (bicolor): grown by T. M. Randolph, 436–7n
South Carolina College: catalogue of, 112
Spafford, Horatio Gates: *General Geography, and Rudiments of Useful Knowledge*, 105–6, 196–9; identified, 106n; letter from, 105–6; letter to, 196–9
Spain: and British army against the French, 108; constitution of, 470–1, 577; exploration of Northwest Coast, 447, 448; and raising of horses and sheep, 478; resisting Napoleon, 160, 344; status of Florida and Cuba, 154; TJ on, 20; and U.S., 632–3; and U.S. land claims, 636, 639, 641. *See also* Bonaparte, Joseph, king of Spain; Onís y González, Luis de, Vara, López y Gómez; sheep, Spanish; Spanish language; Stoughton, Thomas, Spanish consul at N.Y.
Spanish language, documents in, from: Foronda, 470–1, 604–6; Yznardy, 410–1
*The Speech of Henry Brougham, Esq. before the House of Commons* (Brougham), 35
Spelman, Edward, trans.: *Cyrus's Expedition into Persia, and the Retreat of the Ten Thousand Greeks* (*The Anabasis*; Xenophon), 580; *Opera Omni Graece et Latine*, 580
Spence, William: *Britain Independent of Commerce: or, Proofs, Deducted from an Investigation into the True Causes of the Wealth of Nations*, 35
spermaceti oil, 31
spices: allspice, 45; black pepper, 31, 41, 368; cinnamon, 31, 45, 368; cloves, 44; mace, 368; nutmeg, 44, 368
spinning jenny, 313, 524–5, 591, 661
*Spirit of 'Seventy-Six* (Richmond newspaper), 93
Sprague, Joseph, Jr., 86n
Spring, Samuel: *Two Sermons, Addressed to the Second Congregational Society in Newburyport*, 138
Spring Hill School (Indian training school, Mich. Terr.), 7, 660–2
springs, warm, 191–2, 451
squash, 170
stable: brooms, 3; insurance for, 317–8; padlocks, 303
Staël-Holstein, Anne Louise Germaine de: *Corinne ou l'Italie*, 35
Stanhope, Philip Dormer, 4th Earl of Chesterfield: quoted by Rush, 184
Stanley, Thomas: *The History of Philosophy*, 580
star-jasmine (*Jasminum officinale*), 631–2
Starke, Mrs. (boardinghouse keeper in Richmond), 670
State Department, U.S.: letter of credence for Short, 328, 343–4, 359, 658, 659n; receives packet for TJ, 408. *See also* Smith, Robert
stationery: letter paper, 332, 347, 384, 489; of Moussier, 380 (*illus.*); of Silvestre, 380 (*illus.*)
*Statutes at Large* (Hening), 158–9n, 333–4, 489, 619–20
steam power, 648–9
Steevens, George: and edition of Shakespeare, 412n
Stephensburg Academy (Frederick Co.): request for donation to, 566–7
Stephenson, Clotworthy: identified, 601n; letter from, 601; letter to, 649–50
Stevenson, Mr., 79
Stevenson, Andrew, 611n
Stewart, Dugald: *Elements of the Philosophy of the Human Mind*, 576
Stewart, William: blacksmith at Monticello, 419
Stith, Elizabeth, 68n
Stith, Richard, 670–1
Stith tract (Bedford Co.), 670–1
Stockdale, John: publisher of *Notes on the State of Virginia*, 588
*Stoici Philosophi Encheiridion item* (Epictetus), 576
*Storia Antica del Messico* (Clavigero), 196, 198n
Stoughton, Thomas, Spanish consul at New York, 578, 604
Stout, Isaiah, 462, 572n
Stout, John, 462; identified, 572n; letter from, 572
stoves: stew, 122; Swedish, 122n
Strickland, William, 21n
Stuart, Archibald, 585
stucco, 195–6
stylograph, 182n
subscriptions: newspaper, 48, 49, 50n, 85, 96, 107, 214; poetry, 225–6, 504n
Suetonius (Gaius Suetonius Tranquillus): *Opera Omnia Quae Extant*, 580
sugar: brown, 268, 368; loaf, 31, 44,

222; maple, 657; muscovado, 31, 44; refined, 268, 368; smuggling of, 439
suicide: and Isham and Lilburne Lewis, 168n; and Meriwether Lewis, 436n, 602–3, 606–8, 632, 668
Sullivan, George: identified, 525n; letter from, 524–5; letter to, 591
Sullivan, John L., 524, 525
*A Summary View of the Rights of British America* (Thomas Jefferson), 486, 487n, 539, 569–70
sun: and astronomical calculations, 489–98
sun brier, 56
sundial: and corncob capital base, 473, 475n
Superior Court of Chancery for the Richmond District, 415n
Supreme Court, U.S.: appointments to, 49n; justices review invention, 195–6
*Sur l'éducation nationale dans les États-Unis d'Amérique* (Du Pont de Nemours), 592, 593n, 674
surveying: occupation of, 215, 216; TJ provides training in, 181–2, 215n, 650
Swan Tavern (Richmond): TJ lodges at, 591, 614n, 615
Swanwick, John: bankruptcy of, 129, 131n
sweet acacia (*Acacia farnesiana*), 555, 631–2
sweet chestnut (*Castanea sativa*; European chestnut), 594n
*Syren* (sloop): carries dispatches, 183, 452; quarantined in France, 373, 374, 376
syrup: of punch, 268, 368; of vinegar, 161, 188–9, 190, 222, 257
*A System of Notation: Representing the Sounds of Alphabetical Characters* (Pelham), 216–7

Tabb, Frances Peyton: loan from, 180, 181n, 302, 344, 656
Tabb, Philip: identified, 111n; letter from, 111; letter to, 252
*Tableau du Climat et du Sol des États-Unis d'Amérique* (Volney), 197, 198–9n, 652n
*Tableaux de la Nature* (Humboldt), 264, 267n, 482, 483n
Table for Computing the Moon's Motion, with Explanations (Lambert), 540–54, 571–2, 608–9
*Tables of Logarithms* (Callet; trans. Warden), 316–7, 629–30
*Tables Requisite to be used with the Nautical Ephemeris* (Garnett), 492, 498n
Tacitus, Cornelius: *The Works of Tacitus* (trans. Gordon), 580
Taggart, John: identified, 55n; letters from, 55, 111–2; letter to, 97; paid by TJ, 97, 111; sends oil and paint to TJ, 55, 77, 123
Taggart, Samuel, 39n
*Talinum* (fameflower), 436–7n
Tammany societies, 176–9, 358–9
Tammany Society of Washington, 358–9
tar: price of in Great Britain, 82
Tardieu, Antoine François: identified, 248n; letter from, 247–8
tarragon: from Thornton, 479, 481, 600
Tartary, coasts of, 447
Tatham, William: letter from accounted for, 677
taxes: on land, 470, 590, 595
Taylor, George Keith, 382–3, 384n
Taylor, William, 318n
tea: chest, 44; Hyson, 31, 32n, 44, 368; Imperial, 31; served at Monticello, 389; at U.S. Marine Hospital, 299
telescope: lost in transit, 180, 205
Tennessee: Doublehead's Reserve, 7; Indians in, 653; whiskey, 31
Tenon, Jacques, 100–1
Tessé, Adrienne Catherine de Noailles de: and Coles, 269, 593; exchanges seeds with TJ, 272, 274n, 593, 594; identified, 274n; and Lafayette, 528, 593–4, 627; letters from, 271–4, 593–4; mentioned, 265; sends engraving of Humboldt, 593
Tessé, René Mans Froulay, comte de, 274n, 528, 627
textiles: cotton cassimer, 308; homespun, 100n, 561, 591, 667; jean, 308; manufacturing, 524–5; Oznaburg, 303; silk manufacturing, 341, 342n, 355, 412–3, 413, 414, 423–4, 472; wool, 16, 479n
*Le Théâtre d'Agriculture et Mesnage des Champs* (Serres), 35, 581
Thebaud, Joseph, 522
Thénard, Louis Jacques, 264, 267n, 317n
*Théorie des Signes* (Sicard), 662
*The Theory and Practice of Brewing* (Combrune), 581

*The theory and practice of finding the Longitude at Sea or Land* (Mackay), 492, 498n
Thierry, Jean Baptiste Simon: *Reply to Mr. Duponceau*, 287
*Tho: Jefferson the Pride of America* (Gimbrede), 23, 380 (*illus.*)
Thomas, Isaiah: *The History of Printing in America*, 333, 334n
Thomas, Jesse B., 96
Thompson, Benjamin. *See* Rumford, Benjamin Thompson, count
Thompson (Tompson), John (clerk in Orleans Territory), 635, 642n
Thompson, John (judge in Orleans Territory), 635
Thornton, Anna Maria Brodeau: sends greetings to TJ, 479; TJ sends greetings to, 466
Thornton, William: Humboldt sends greetings to, 435n; identified, 466n; letter from, 476–80; letters to, 465–6, 599–600; and sheep, 199, 224–5, 286, 464, 467, 476–7, 480–1, 599–600; and shot manufactory, 367n; supports importation of merino sheep, 479
Thoüin, André: identified, 202n; letter to, 201–2; Patterson introduced to, by TJ, 201; sends greetings to TJ, 141, 629; sends rice to TJ, 208, 596
*Three Dissertations on Boylston Prize Questions for the Years 1806 and 1807* (Shattuck), 50–1
Threlkeld, Elizabeth (John Threlkeld's wife): mentioned, 40
Threlkeld, John: identified, 40n; letter from, 40; letter to, 40
Thruston, Buckner, 473
Thweatt, Archibald, 469
ticks, 478
tickseed (*coreopsis*), 436–7n
Tilsit, Treaty of, 516, 517n, 529
Tingey, Thomas: and lost trunk, 268, 294
Tinsley, Mr. (of Amherst Co.), 670–1
tobacco: chemical experiments with, 142–52; cigars (Havana), 466; and depletion of land, 561; effect of weather on, 285; grown at Poplar Forest, 157n; physical effect on user, 152; prices in Great Britain, 82; prices in Richmond, 157, 180, 302, 655–6; TJ's income from, 422; Vauquelin's Analysis of Green, 142–6, 482; Vauquelin's Analysis of Prepared, 147–52, 482
Tombigbee River, 351, 638
Tomlinson, Benjamin: identified, 94n; letter to, 94
Tompkins, Richard, 519, 585
Tompkins, William, 200
Tompson, John. *See* Thompson, John (clerk in Orleans Territory)
Tooke, William: *The Life of Catharine II, Empress of all the Russias*, 580
tools: at Monticello, 397n; woodworking, 135–6
topography: works on, bound for TJ, 36
Tories. *See* Federalist party
Tourtelle, Étienne: *Elemens d'hygiène*, 597n
Tousard, Anne Louis de: *American Artillerist's Companion*, 412
Tracy. *See* Destutt de Tracy, Antoine Louis Claude
Tracy, Elisha: letter from accounted for, 677
*Tragopogon porrifolius* (salsify), 157
*Travels During the Years 1787, 1788, and 1789* (Young), 581
*Travels in North America in the Years 1780, 1781 and 1782* (Chastellux), 197, 198–9n
Treasury, U.S.: comptroller (*see* Duvall, Gabriel); Furniture Fund, 43n; report on Degen & Purviance, 361, 362n; and TJ's salary as minister plenipotentiary, 43. *See also* Gallatin, Albert
Treat, John Breck: identified, 97–8n; journal of Arkansas meteorological observations, 97, 98n, 482, 608–9; letter from, 97–8
*A Treatise of Algebra* (Simpson), 576
*A Treatise of Practical Surveying* (Gibson), 576, 650
*A Treatise on Martial Law, and Courts-Martial* (Macomb), 571
*A Treatise on the Culture and Management of Fruit Trees: in which A New Method of Pruning and Training is Fully Described* (Forsyth), 17
*A Treatise on the Culture of the Apple & Pear, and on the Manufacture of Cider & Perry* (Knight), 581
trees: acacia, 555, 631–2; apricot, 40; ash, 398n; aspen, 398n; Balsam copaiba, 56, 58n; cedar, 478; chestnut, 272, 593; conservation of, 131–4, 561; dogwood, 272, 274n; fig, 479, 481; Gloucester-nut hickory, 657; golden-rain, 272, 274n, 594n; holm oak, 594;

lime, 631–2; Lombardy poplar, 192n; maple, red, 61; maple, sugar, 657; mimosa, 631; Missouri scaly bark, 657; mulberry, 40; oak, green, 272; olive, 313n; orange, 631–2; peach, 93; peach-apricot, 40; pecan, 657; pine, 478; Roanoke, 657; willow, weeping, 61
*Trial of Col. Aaron Burr* (Burr), 35
Tripoli: U.S. consul at, 26
Trist, Elizabeth House: and Brown, 73, 74, 80–1, 85, 98; family of, 475, 513; identified, 73–4n; letters from, 73–4, 98; letter to, 80–1; visits Monticello, 210, 396n, 509
Trist, Hore Browse (*1775–1804*): appointment of, 615, 616n; death, 73n, 74n, 210n
Trist, Hore Browse (*1800–1874*): provided for by Brown, 74n
Trist, Nicholas Philip: provided for by Brown, 74n
Trokes, Maxwell: identified, 369n
Troost, Gerard, 656
Troup, George, 278n
*True American* (Trenton, N.J. newspaper), 226–9
trunk, lost in return from Washington: account of, 346–8, 555–6; contents of, 153, 180–1, 205, 269, 284, 311; presumed lost, 159, 166, 180, 186–7, 257, 408; returned to TJ, 483
Tucker, St. George: identified, 617n; letter from, 617; letter from accounted for, 78n; "Ode to Thomas Jefferson," 617–9; seeks statutes from Hening, 333
Tufton (TJ's estate): Nicholas moves to, 223n; overseers at, 419–20; T. J. Randolph resides at, 190n
Tull, Jethro: *Horse-Hoeing Husbandry: or, An Essay on the Principles of Vegetation and Tillage*, 581
Tullos tract (Campbell Co.), 670
Tunis: U.S. consul at, 26
Tunnicliff, William: letter to accounted for, 31n
Turgot, Anne Robert Jacques: *Oeuvres*, 202n, 263, 264n, 584–5, 592, 632, 667, 668n
turkeys: kept at Tufton, 420
Turk's-cap (Allegheny lily; *Lilium Martagon*), 660
turnsole plant (*Crozophora tintoria*), 142, 143, 146n
turpentine: price of in Great Britain, 82
Turpin, Baron de: and drawing of Natural Bridge, 197, 198–9n
Turpin, Philip, 67
Turpin, William: identified, 655n; letter from, 654–6
Turreau, Louis Marie, de Garambouville: dispatches to France, 370; identified, 417n; letter to, 417; negotiations with U.S., 183–4; sends ship to France, 118, 224; TJ transmits letter to, 249, 417
Turton, William, trans.: *A general system of nature, through the three grand kingdoms of animals, vegetables, and minerals* (Linnaeus), 581
Tussac, François Richard de: *Flora Antillarum*, 100–1
Tuttle, Gershom: letter from accounted for, 78n
twinleaf (*Jeffersonia diphylla*), 56–7
*Two Sermons, Addressed to the Second Congregational Society in Newburyport* (Spring), 138
Twyman, George Buford: identified, 63–4n; letter from, 63–4; letter from accounted for, 64n
Tybout, Andrew, 15, 16, 19n
Tyler, John: identified, 614n; letter from, 613–4
Tyler, Trueman, 516
type foundries, 17

Ulmo, Anthony, 70n
*Union* (ship), 117, 129, 230; carries letters to TJ, 115, 118, 182, 231, 235n
Union Mills. *See* Magruder's Mill (Fluvanna Co.)
United States: and Alexander I, 115–6, 233, 328, 659n; and Napoleon, 154–5; House of Representatives, 257, 512, 534–5; Mint, 330, 487; political works on, bound for TJ, 36; and Russia, 38, 39n, 329n, 360; and Spain, 632–3; Supreme Court, 49n, 195–6; Treasury, 43, 361, 362n; War Department, 571; Woodward on government of, 164–5, 236, 253–4. *See also* Bank of the United States; Congress, U.S.; Navy, U.S.; Post Office, U.S.; State Department, U.S.
United States Marine Hospital (Charlestown, Mass.): and charges against Waterhouse, 295–300

United States Military Academy (West Point, N.Y.), 23n
*The United States spelling book* (Cramer), 630
*Universal Gazette* (Philadelphia newspaper), 30n
*Untersuchungen über Amerika's Bevölkerung aus dem alten Kontinente* (Vater), 651–2

vanilla: TJ orders, 161, 188–9, 190
varnish, 419
Varnum, Joseph B.: and Newburyport collectorship, 25
Vater, Johann Severin: identified, 652n; letter from, 651–2; *Untersuchungen über Amerika's Bevölkerung aus dem alten Kontinente*, 651–2
Vaughan, John: Humboldt sends greetings to, 453n; identified, 453n; letters from, 452–3, 455; letter to, 482–3; librarian of the American Philosophical Society, 452–3, 455, 482
Vauquelin, Louis Nicolas: Analysis of Green Tobacco, 142–6, 482; Analysis of Prepared Tobacco, 147–52, 482; identified, 146n; Warden translates experiments of, 142–52, 482, 668–9
*Les Veilles de Saint-Augustin, Évêque d'Hippone* (Gazzera), 522, 523n
Venable, Abraham, 181n, 302, 318, 344
Vest, Charles, 505–6
vicuña, 479, 599
*A view of the principles and conduct of the Protestant dissenters, with respect to the civil and ecclesiastical constitution of England* (Priestley), 581
*The Villas of the Ancients Illustrated* (Castell), 390, 397n
Villeneufve, Paul Louis le Blanc de. *See* le Blanc (Siblong) de Villeneufve, Paul Louis
Vince, Samuel, 357, 492
vinegar: syrup, 161, 188–9, 190, 222, 257
Virgil (Publius Vergilius Maro): Armstrong quotes, 538; *Eclogues*, 345n; McCoy alludes to, 326, 327
Virginia: Act for establishing Religious Freedom, 384n, 487; charters, early, 620; elections in, 168; General Assembly, 242, 245n; historiography of, 619; laws of, 334, 369–70, 381–3, 403–4, 404, 469, 472–3, 488–9, 570; Manufactory of Arms, 614–5; maps of, xliv–xlv, 251n; revision of laws, 381–3, 384n; seal of, 345n; State Penitentiary, 474n; statute prohibiting bringing slaves into, 622, 624n; statutes, historiography of, 334, 381–4, 489; TJ's collection of laws of, 158–9, 334, 381. *See also* Bank of Virginia; Central College; Mutual Assurance Society; The History of Virginia; Virginia, University of
Virginia, University of (Charlottesville), 191n, 466n, 474. *See also* Central College
*Virginia Argus* (Richmond newspaper), 290, 291n
Virginia Convention of *1774*: TJ as member of, 486
*The Vision of Pierce Plowman* (Langland), 390, 397n
*Vitae Excellentium Imperatorum* (Nepos), 580
viticulture, 586–7
"Vocabulaire de la Langue des Miamis" (Volney), 652
*Vocabulaire des Termes de Marine Anglais et Français* (Lescallier), 36, 184n
Volney, Constantin François Chasseboeuf, comte de: *Leçons d'Histoire*, 580; Spafford's proposed work on, 106n; *Tableau du Climat et du Sol des États-Unis d'Amérique*, 197, 198–9n, 652n; "Vocabulaire de la Langue des Miamis," 652
Voltaire, François Marie Arouet: *Histoire de l'empire de Russie sous Pierre le Grand*, 580; *The History of Charles XII*, 580; quoted by Rush, 185; *Le Siècle de Louis XIV*, 580
*Voyage aux régions équinoxiales du nouveau continent* (Humboldt), 25n, 37, 267n, 482
*Voyage de Humboldt et Bonpland*, 24–5n, 455
*Voyage de La Pérouse autour du Monde*, 445–9
*Voyage du Jeune Anacharsis en Grèce* (Barthélemy), 580, 582n
*A Voyage Round The World* (Beresford), 445–6, 449n
*Voyages from Montreal* (Mackenzie), 443, 444–5n
*A Voyage to the Pacific Ocean* (Cook), 445, 446, 449n
Vrolik, Gerardus: identified, 195; letter from, 194–5

Waddell, Mr. (of Philadelphia), 376, 457
Wafford's Settlement (Tellico Garrison): treaty of, 6–7
wagons: repair of, 3
Walcheren Island, battle of, 529, 530n, 592, 593n
Walker, Elizabeth Moore (John Walker's wife): health of, 500; relations with TJ, 279n, 499n
Walker, John: illness of, 498–9, 500; relations with TJ, 279n, 499n, 500
Walker, Thomas, 157n
Wallace, James Westwood: identified, 57n; letter from, 56–8; letter to, 466
Wallcut, Thomas, 673n
Walnut Street prison (Philadelphia), 383, 384n
Walpole, Sir Robert, 512
wampompeke (Indian currency), 334, 369
Ward, Mrs. (Lynchburg): tavern of, 671
Warden, David Bailie: and Armstrong, 141n; assists Vauquelin in tobacco experiments, 142; forwards chest to TJ, 627; identified, 141n; letters from, 140–1, 207–9, 316–7, 535–6, 629–30; letters of mentioned, 344, 359; sends books, 613n, 629–30; sends books to American Philosophical Society, 452; sends seeds to TJ, 141; translates Callet's work, 316–7, 629–30; translates Vauquelin's tobacco experiments, 142–52, 482, 608–9; and U.S. consulship at Paris, 26, 207, 208n, 317, 536
War Department, U.S: forwards publication to TJ, 571. *See also* Eustis, William; Smith, John (chief clerk of War Department)
Warren (Albemarle Co.), 223n
Warren, Mercy Otis: *History of the Rise, Progress and Termination of the American Revolution*, 37, 581
Washington, Bushrod, 195n
Washington, D.C.: bank of, 30n, 481, 535; calculation of prime meridian for, 275–6, 356–9, 489–98, 511–2, 534, 551; citizens of, address TJ, 11–2; digest of city code, 632, 633n; Lindsey's Hotel, 359n; Long's Hotel, 10n; newspapers in, 107; Rhodes Hotel, 357; TJ addresses citizens of, 13–4. *See also* National Intelligencer (Washington, D.C. newspaper)
Washington, George: appointments of, 43n; and donation to Liberty Hall Academy, 367–8n; Duane's pamphlet on, 49n; lauded as hero of Revolution, 12; *A Message of the President of the United States to Congress Relative to France and Great-Britain*, 487, 569–70; portraits of, by Peale, 45n; and raising of sheep, 286; and Seven Years' War, 290
Washington Academy (later Washington and Lee University), 367, 368n
Washington and Jefferson College (Washington, Pa.), 6n
Washington and Lee University (Lexington), 368n
Washington City Library, 30n
Washington County, Md.: Republicans of, address TJ, 26–9; TJ addresses Republicans of, 98–9
Washington County, Pa.: Jefferson College students address TJ, 4–6; TJ addresses Democratic Republicans of, 99–100
Washington Female Orphan Asylum, 10n
Washington National Monument Society, 30n
*Wasp* (American warship), 629, 658
Waterhouse, Benjamin: and Dearborn, 295; and Federalist party, 298; and Gallatin, 295, 298; and Gerry, 296–7, 299; identified, 300n; letter from, 295–300; and Madison, 297–8, 299
Waterhouse, Elizabeth Oliver (Benjamin Waterhouse's wife), 297
water plantain (*Alisma plantago-aquatica*), 57–8n
Watson, Dr., 190
Watts, Isaac, 468, 469n
waxwork (American bittersweet; *Celastrus scandens*), 57, 58n
Wayles, John (TJ's father-in-law): and Campbell Co. land, 671n; and *Gilliam v. Fleming*, 305n, 362, 365, 608
weather: Chapman seeks journals of, 663; drought, 213, 600, 657; effect on tobacco, 285; effect on wheat, 170, 285; journal of Madison, 518, 519n; journals of Treat, 97, 98n, 482, 608–9
Webster, Capt., 294
Weightman, Roger Chew: and newspaper account, 48; prints Senate proceedings, 49n
weights and measures: TJ's report on, 487
Welles, Charles Fisher: identified, 428n;

Welles, Charles Fisher (*cont.*)
letter from, 428; "Poem on Thomas Jefferson," 431–3
Wellesley, Sir Arthur, 593n
West, Benjamin, 45n
Western Road. *See* Cumberland Road
Westwardmill Library Society (Brunswick Co.): books for, 66–7, 205–6, 508
Weyers Cave, Va., 309
wheat: effect of weather on, 93, 285; from lost trunk, 347; price of in France, 373; price of in Great Britain, 82; *Remarks on the Smut and Mildew of Wheat* (Fothergill), 72; at Shadwell Mill, 108–9, 282, 421
Wheaton, Joseph: identified, 352n; letter from, 350–2
whiskey, 465; Tennessee, 31
Whitby, Henry, 228n
White, Mr. (of Tuckabatchee), 351
White, Solomon, 256
White House. *See* President's House
white lead, 55n, 77
Whitner, Benjamin Franklin: identified, 112n; letter from, 112
Whittle, Robert, 16
*The Wild Irish Boy* (Maturin), 391, 397n
Wilkin, James Whitney: identified, 80n; letter from, 79–80; letter from accounted for, 80n; letter to accounted for, 125n
Wilkinson, James: and Burr's treason trial, 426, 427–8n; as New Orleans commissioner, 179n
Willcox, Joseph: federal marshal, 278, 279n
Williams, Jonathan, 294
Williams, Robert, 25
Williams, Samuel: *The Natural and Civil History of Vermont*, 581
Williamsburg, Va.: newspapers in, 370n
Williamson, George: identified, 597n; letter from, 597; *The Principles of Health: Elements of hygiene*, 597n
Willich, Anthony F. M.: *Domestic encyclopædia* (ed. Mease), 18, 19n, 252
willow, weeping, 61
Wilson, Mr. (Maryland clothier), 16
Wilson, Henry, 515, 517n
windmills, 647–8
wine: Albaflor, 345, 366; Banyalbufar, 366; burgundy, 257, 586; cognac, 32; delivered to TJ, 281–2; French, 313n, 387; Italian, 387; Madeira, 155, 387, 397n; Noyau, 155, 156n; port, as treatment for dysentery, 483; at U.S. Marine Hospital, 299; viticulture, 586–7
Wingate, Edmund: ed. *Britton*, 383
*A Winter in Washington: or, Memoirs of the Seymour Family* (Margaret Bayard Smith), 10n, 397n
Wirt, William: drafts address to TJ, 611n; endorses silk-manufacturing project, 341–2, 355, 424; identified, 341–2n; letter from, 341–2; recommended as attorney general, 626
Wistar, Caspar: and American Philosophical Society, 100, 677; Humboldt sends greetings to, 453n; identified, 101n; letter to, 100–1; and mastodon bones, 100, 510–1; and T. J. Randolph, 309
Wistar, Elizabeth Mifflin (Caspar Wistar's wife), 309
Wolcott, John: "A Simile," 538n
women: schools for, 367, 368n, 506, 507n
women, documents by: Margaret Bayard Smith, 8–10, 386–401; Peyton, 459–63
women, letters from: Archbald, 238–40; Corny, 173–5; Deshay, 450–1; Tessé, 271–4, 593–4; Trist, 98
women, letters to: Daingerfield, 47–8; Margaret Bayard Smith, 29; Trist, 80–1
Wood, James: identified, 503n; letter from, 501–3
Wood, John, 520
Woodhouse, James, 307, 452, 453n
Woodlands (Hamilton's Pa. estate), 191, 192, 479
Woods, Micajah (deputy sheriff), 590, 595
Woodson, Tucker, 440, 460
Woodward, Augustus Elias Brevoort: *Considerations on the Executive Government of the United States of America*, 164–5, 236, 253–4; on foreign government, 254n; identified, 165n; letter from accounted for, 165n; letters from, 164–5, 253–4; letter to, 236; visits Monticello, 165n
woodworking: tools of, 135–6
wool: production of, 15–18, 478–9, 573–4; samples of, 16, 17, 19n, 667; sent by Dougherty, 320; spinning of, 525, 591
Worcester *National Aegis* (Mass. newspaper), 50n

*The Works of Tacitus* (trans. Gordon), 580
Wright, Robert, 361–2n; identified, 107n; letter to, 106–7
Wright, Thomas (Chickasaw agent), 26
Wright, Thomas (Queen Annes Co., Md.), 128n; identified, 63n; letter from, 62–3; letter from accounted for, 63n; letter to, 127–8
Wyche, James, 66
Wyche, John: books recommended to, by TJ, 205–6, 579–82; identified, 67n; letters from, 66–7, 508; letters to, 205–6, 579
Wythe, George: monument to, at Monticello, 391; and revision of Virginia laws, 381–3

Xenophon: *Cyrus's Expedition into Persia, and the Retreat of the Ten Thousand Greeks* (*The Anabasis*) (trans. Spelman), 580; *Hellenica*, 580; *Xenophon's Memoirs of Socrates* (trans. Fielding), 576
*Xenophon's Memoirs of Socrates* (trans. Fielding), 576

Yazoo land scheme, 672
yellow fever: tracts on, 36, 38n
Yerby, William, 616
York and Albany, Duke of. *See* Frederick Augustus, Duke of York and Albany
Young, Arthur: *The Farmer's Guide in Hiring and Stocking Farms*, 581; *Rural Oeconomy: or, Essays on the Practical Parts of Husbandry*, 581; *Travels During the Years 1787, 1788, and 1789*, 581
Yrujo (Irujo), Carlos Fernando Martínez de: Spanish minister to U.S., 87, 577, 578
Yznardy, Josef, 651; dispute over vice-consulship at Cádiz, 113–4, 155, 156n; identified, 411n; letter from, 410–1; letter of introduction for Onís, 410–1, 601–2

Zannoni, Giovanni Antonio Rizzi: *Carte réduite de la Mer Méditerranée et de la mer Noire*, 247–8
*Zea mays* (maize): from Lewis and Clark Expedition, 436–7n. *See also* corn
Zimmermann, Eberhard August Wilhelm von: *Zoologie Géographique*, 196, 198n
*Zizyphus jujuba* (juboli; jujube), 631
*Zoologie Géographique* (Zimmermann), 196, 198n
zoology: books on, 25n, 196, 198n. *See also* Lacépède, Bernard Germain Étienne de La Ville-Sur-Illon, comte de
Zuthke, Maj.: letter from accounted for, 677

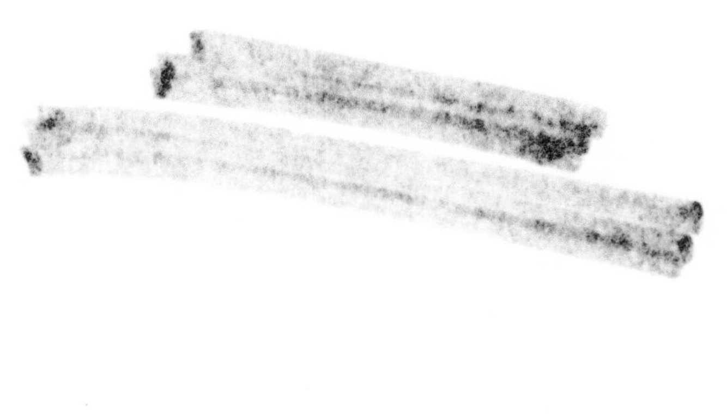